AF731507

What is

McGraw Hill edge COURSEWARE

McGraw Hill Edge Courseware is a versatile learning and assessment solution, that uses credible content and innovative pedagogies to make the readers' exam preparation journey holistic and adaptive to changing examination trends. By blending the strengths of authoritative McGraw Hill books with cutting-edge digital resources and latest updates, this Courseware offers a dynamic content solution for exam aspirants. It provides the students a thorough understanding of the subject matter, enhances learning and retention, and shares deep insights about their performance, ultimately boosting their confidence. This Courseware is at the forefront of innovation; revolutionising learning to guide learners on their path to success!

Unlock Your Potential with McGraw Hill Edge Courseware

Conceptual Videos
To transform complex ideas into engaging visual storytelling!

Study Aids
To simplify learning with visual summaries, mind maps, flash cards, infographics etc.

Knowledge Enrichment Content
To craft your path to success with exclusive reading materials

Previous Years' Questions
To practice from an extensive collection of PYQs with detailed explanations

Mock Tests
To simulate real exam conditions and boost confidence

Performance Analytics
To optimise exam preparation with data-driven insights

Live Interactive Sessions
To gain valuable insights from the author through interactive sessions

eBook Access
To conveniently access study materials anytime, anywhere

What do you get with Courseware on Logical Reasoning for CAT?

The **Courseware on Logical Reasoning for CAT** is an end-to-end learning solution meticulously designed for CAT and management entrance exam applicants:

- **Previous Years' Questions:** Access to CAT 2017–2025 LR questions with detailed solutions and analytics
- **Problem-solving Videos:** Over 170 assisted problem-solving videos to improve learning outcomes
- **Practice Questions:** 2500 + practice questions with detailed explanations
- **Mock Test Papers:** 2 CAT (full-length) and 30 LR solved mock tests for knowledge assessment and confidence building
- **Live Interactive Sessions:** Interactive author sessions on the right approach and preparation strategy for CAT 2026

SCAN NOW

Scan this QR code to know all about this Courseware

COUNTER THE COUNTERFEIT & BUILD A STRONG FOUNDATION FOR SUCCESS

Books are our best friends, is the adage we have grown up with. However, the pirates of piracy are continuously forging 'our best friends'. Our books and their supplementary online resources are copyrighted, and we don't lend any right-to-copy. Piracy is synonymous to stealing books.

Knowledge comes real, let's not encourage its counterfeit. Therefore, we appeal all our readers to discourage pirated books and **choose authentic ones**.

HOW TO IDENTIFY THE PIRATED BOOKS?

1 Transparency Code on the Book

Congratulations! The book you have purchased is protected by Transparency. Transparency by Amazon is a unit-level product serialization service that verifies a unit's authenticity and enables you to view rich information about the product you purchased. Please look for the Transparency logo and code on the book back cover (Transparency barcode is a square code that can be found next to the "T" symbol). You can scan the barcode with the Transparency app to verify the book's authenticity. Simply download the Transparency app from the App Store or Google Play. Scan the barcode with the app. The app will display a green checkmark when the book has been verified as authentic.

2 Cover and Spine

- Look and feel (new or used book)
- Blurred images on the cover
- Hologram pasted on front
- Defective spine (wrinkles) or air pocket at its bottom
- Unclear ISBN/bar codes
- Missing/non-operational Unique Coupon Code for exclusive access to McGraw Hill Edge

3 Text/Printing/Binding

- Uneven inking of pages
- Poor quality or blurred photographs/images/charts
- Substandard paper quality and opacity
- Misaligned pages
- Missing pages
- Inferior binding quality

You can further watch this video on How to identify a pirated book

For more information about identifying piracy, visit **https://www.mheducation.co.in/piracy**

To report a pirated book, send 'Hi' on WhatsApp code given on the back cover or write to us at **support.india@mheducation.com**.

Reported pirated books are examined to combat their piracy.

Let's fight the Pirates of Piracy and resolve to go for original!

9e

2026

McGraw Hill edge® COURSEWARE

LOGICAL REASONING

for

CAT

Common Admission Test & Other Management Examinations

Arun Sharma

McGraw Hill

McGraw Hill Education (India) Private Limited

Published by McGraw Hill Education (India) Private Limited,
Registered Office: Anjana Complex No: 5/90 A, Butt Road, St. Thomas Mount, Chennai - 600016

Courseware on Logical Reasoning for CAT 2026, 9e

Copyright © 2026, by McGraw Hill Education (India) Private Limited.

This book is protected under copyright law. Any unauthorized copying, reproduction, distribution, adaptation, conversion, transmission, storage or use of this publication or any part or extract of it, through any means or any medium, including electronic, mechanical, photocopied, recorded, or otherwise, whether for any direct/indirect commercial gain or not, and without the prior written consent of the publisher, is explicitly prohibited and will result in severe legal consequences. Such restrictions apply to social media channels/groups, YouTube videos, audiobooks, AI applications, and any other means of copying, reproducing, distributing, adapting, converting, transmitting, storing the content of this book, using current or future technologies.

This edition can be exported from India only by the publisher,
McGraw Hill Education (India) Private Limited.

Print Edition:
ISBN (13): 978-93-6444-613-6
ISBN (10): 93-6444-613-5

E-Book Edition:
ISBN (13): 978-93-6444-719-5
ISBN (10): 93-6444-719-0

1 2 3 4 5 6 7 8 9 7107374 30 29 28 27 26

Printed and bound in India

Information contained in this work has been obtained by McGraw Hill Education (India), from sources believed to be reliable. However, neither McGraw Hill Education (India) nor its authors guarantee the accuracy or completeness of any information published herein, and neither McGraw Hill Education (India) nor its authors shall be responsible for any errors, omissions, or damages arising out of use of this information. This work is published with the understanding that McGraw Hill Education (India) and its authors are supplying information but are not attempting to render engineering or other professional services. If such services are required, the assistance of an appropriate professional should be sought.

Typeset at MAP Systems, Bangalore -560004 and printed
at Rajkamal Electric Press, Kundli, Haryana-131 028.

Cover Designer: Yaman

Visit us at: www.mheducation.co.in
Write to us at: support.india@mheducation.com
CIN: U80302TN2010PTC111532
Toll Free Number: 1800 103 5875

Dedicated to my late father.

Mr. Mithilesh Kumar Sharma

whose ability to logically analyse varied situations
amazed me through a lifetime;
a small portion of that I have imbibed
and which has helped me become the person I am today

Preface to the Ninth Edition

Welcome to one of the most powerful resources for mastering Logical Reasoning (LR) for the CAT! This Courseware is a fully updated edition of a highly popular book, designed to prepare you for the crucial Logical Reasoning section of the CAT's DI & LR segment. With the introduction of QR codes throughout, this is no longer just a book–it's a complete, hands-on guide to help you excel in Logical Reasoning for the CAT and other management entrance or aptitude exams.

In the ever-evolving landscape of technology, we seize this opportunity to be your go-to resource for mastering your preparation journey. This book is more than just its contents–it's a comprehensive learning ecosystem enriched with QR codes that grant you access to 170+ exclusive video lessons and expert guidance. Inside this Courseware, you will find four distinct types of videos, each tailored to elevate your learning experience:

1. **Chapter Launchpad:** Introductory and descriptive videos at the start of each chapter to set the foundation
2. **Going Beyond the Book:** Assisted problem-solving videos that tackle examples and miscellaneous questions
3. **High Yield Questions:** Guided walkthroughs of select question sets from Level of Difficulty 2 and 3 exercises to sharpen your problem-solving skills
4. **Concept Explainer:** Deep-dive videos designed to enhance conceptual understanding and mastery

With over 170 + videos, some extending beyond 30 minutes, this is far more than just a book–it's a comprehensive learning experience.

This Courseware brings together expert guidance, structured learning, and immersive video content–ensuring you have everything needed to excel.

Reasoning has always been one of the critical components of the CAT. Since CAT moved back to the 3-section pattern from 2015 onwards and Logical Reasoning and Data Interpretation being section-2 of the examination, the importance of Reasoning has got enhanced drastically. The obvious reasons for the same are:

1. Every aspirant must qualify the DI-LR section with a minimum score, so you cannot depend only on the DI questions to crack this section.
2. Furthermore, if you are looking for a good performance in the DI and LR sections of the examination, you cannot depend only on the DI questions.

To add to this trend change, a glance at what the CAT examination was like for the past ten years will tell you that it is the Data Interpretation and Logical Reasoning section that has become extremely tough and difficult. Perhaps in the last four years, the questions in the Data Interpretation and Logical Reasoning section of the examination, were the most difficult in the history of CAT. In fact, every year, after the examination, the one section, the majority of the candidates report as tough or unsolvable is the DI & LR section of the CAT. The questions and quality of analysis required for the questions in this section have acquired a distinctive quality and theme.

The toughness of the examination is actually accentuated by the fact that when you solve a set of questions from this section–you are in an all or nothing situation. If you get through the logic of the set, you get through the whole set, else–you are left with no outcomes for all the efforts. This is what makes maximizing one's score in this section even more difficult. Because of the all or nothing situation one finds oneself in, the stakes while solving an LR set in the examination are 4 to 6 times the stakes that you are dealing with when you are solving the Quants section of the examination. Added to that the fact, that as time ticks, and you keep getting pulled into a heavy analytical/logical situation, your emotions (especially the negative ones) start interfering in your problem-solving experience. Once that starts happening your capacity to take even small logical steps correctly, gets severely impaired. **The only thing that can help you keep a stable mind at such a stage is your internal belief about your ability to get through the question**. Test takers routinely complain about the fact that question sets that they could have solved easily in practice, could not be solved by them under examination conditions.

If you are going to be smart about your preparations, you will make sure that you do not fall into this trap. How do you avoid it?

Well, the 3 Step strategy is:

Step 1: Learn the ropes and the tricks of how to solve LR (& DI) sets.

Step 2: Practice, Practice, Practice, till you reach the point of 'Supreme Belief' in your abilities to get through a LR set.

Step 3: Improve your efficiencies of solving till the point where you can solve the tough CAT level sets in around 10–12 minutes and the slightly easier ones in 6–8 minutes.

The Step 2 mentioned above is perhaps the most critical step of the process, which in my opinion, test takers forget to remember and execute during their preparations. Getting to the point of supreme belief is absolutely essential, if you are going to fight back against a question in the examination, once it has pinned you down.

In such a scenario, mastering the Reasoning questions will go a long way towards helping you stand on a strong footing in this all-important section of the examination. In fact, not only for the CAT, but Reasoning is also an important and omni-present question type in all management entrance and competitive aptitude examinations that you might be interested in preparing for. Hence, the preparation that you do for Reasoning when preparing for the CAT, will help you a lot in all other aptitude examinations you might take up. Moving forward, as you prepare for CAT and other parallel MBA entrance and aptitude examinations, you need to realise that most of these examinations contain a very high reasoning component. At various times in the examinations, you will come across reasoning questions that would be necessary to crack in the next 2-3-5-8-10-12 minutes. Therefore, it would be a good idea to equip yourself with the skills required to face such situations and come out with flying results.

Naturally, you must work extremely hard in a focused fashion, in order to develop your skills in Logical Reasoning. Ignore the Reasoning preparations at your own peril.

Thus, the logic underlying the reason why one should be good at Logical Reasoning is clear.

Besides, you may already know that LR has huge importance for the other parallel MBA and aptitude examinations like XAT, IIFT, SNAP, CET Maharashtra, CMAT, NMAT, Bank P.O., etc. The current edition of the book has a lot of features inbuilt into it to help you as a one-stop preparation resource for Reasoning. The key features you can look forward to in this edition are:

1. Part I Section 1 of the book contains the 11 most important question types for the CAT. These are Arrangements, Rankings, Team Formations, Quantitative Reasoning, Generic Puzzles, Set Theory and Venn Diagrams, Network Diagrams, Cubes and Dices, Games and Tournaments, Puzzles on Scheduling and Cryptarithmetic. Each of these chapters have graded exercises based on the level of difficulty of the questions. We have introduced Level of Difficulty (LoD) 2 and Level of Difficulty 3 exercises in these chapters, wherever it was felt necessary. These exercises will help you understand how the difficulty level of an individual question type increases.

Note: The level of difficulty will progressively rise from LoD 1 to 3.

2. In the examination, questions are always from a variety of concepts–with no announcement about which question type/chapter the question belongs to. A new section consisting of mock test papers based on the latest pattern of the CAT helping you to practice and understand what it takes to solve reasoning tests under time and examination pressure. The Mock tests in Section 2 of Part I of the book are an invaluable resource for you to practise and sharpen your reasoning skills. In this section, we have taken utmost care to ensure that you get an exact feel of the current CAT pattern. Also, for an improved learning experience, we have divided the tests into LoD 1 (1-12), LoD 2 (1-10) and LoD 3 (1-8) tests. As a student solving this book, you should keep in mind that you have to try to solve each test in a strict time limit of 40 minutes. Apart from simulating the actual test paper conditions, these tests will help you to sharpen your skills in a real world kind of situation, where you do not know which chapter/question type you are solving. These exercises would further accentuate your understanding about how the difficulty level of an LR set changes–and what it takes to recognise and solve tougher questions. I would advise you to track how your score changes as you go through with the tests - also how it changes as you move from one difficulty level to the next. Once you finish solving the test under a time limit, you should make sure that you try to solve those sets you could not solve within the time limit. Remember, that every set is a learning experience and self-problem solving is the best mode to learn and improve one's problem solving ability. Your endeavour through these tests and through the contents of this book has to be to finally reach 2 milestones: 1. Supreme belief 'I can solve any reasoning question'. 2. Improved time efficiencies, where you move from being a 15-minute solver of a reasoning set to a 10-12 minute solver of a reasoning set.

3. Given the increasing difficulty of Reasoning questions in recent CAT exams, the extensive collection of LoD II and LoD III questions across Part I Section 1 and Part I Section 2 of this book serves as a crucial resource for anyone preparing for the current CAT pattern.
4. New chapters and question types that have become a common feature of examinations, like the CAT had been introduced in the 8th edition of this highly successful book and have been retained in this edition. These include:
   (a) Puzzles on Scheduling
   (b) Crypt Arithmetic
5. Acting on the feedback of our readers, we also added a new section in the 8th edition and we have retained this section in Part II of this book - on Abstract/Visual Reasoning. While the CAT has not been known to test students on visual reasoning, almost all other Management entrance exams as well as other aptitude exams, have questions on visual reasoning. Since most students who use this book, also appear for these exams, we have retained this entire section in Part II of this book for the benefit of our readers - on visual reasoning, divided into 8 question types viz:
   (i) Analogy
   (ii) Odd Man Out
   (iii) Embedded Figures
   (iv) Counting of Figures
   (v) Completion of Figures
   (vi) Series
   (vii) Mirror Image and Water Image
   (viii) Paper Folding and Cutting
6. The book is fully solved, so that the aspirants finding an issue in solving any question, has the requisite guidance and hand holding needed wherever required.
7. The archives section of the book (Part III) contains the latest reasoning questions from CAT 2022 to CAT 2025 (however, you will also get exclusive access to CAT 2017-2025 solved papers on McGraw Hill Edge).
   These changes have been done keeping intact the original strengths of the book which include:
   (i) Coverage of each and every type of question that comes under the category of Reasoning—covering not just the question types of the CAT examination but the question types of all other aptitude examinations with a Reasoning component to them.
   (ii) Solutions to most exercises and questions written with the unique approach of the 'Reaction Tracker' which shows you exactly how to crack an LR question.
   (iii) The 'Reasoning Archives' part which gives you an immediate perspective of the kinds and the depth of questions that have been asked earlier in CAT.

   With so much to do, practice and learn, I would now ask you, dear reader, to move headlong into the Courseware.

Focus on learning from every question and scenario while leveraging the exclusive QR-coded video resources embedded throughout. Unlike theory-based subjects, reasoning is a skill—and skills are built through experience and practice. The best way to sharpen your reasoning ability is through a balanced mix of:

- Assisted Problem-solving - by reading solutions or watching expert-guided video explanations.
- Self Problem-solving - by tackling questions independently to refine your thought process.

CAT reasoning questions can be challenging, but this Courseware strategically prepares you for even the toughest problems. Our carefully selected question bank ensures comprehensive coverage, so no exam question will feel unfamiliar. Plus, expert-led solution videos for Level of Difficulty 2 and 3 questions will help you see how professionals approach the most complex challenges.

Use this Courseware the right way, and you'll gain the competitive edge needed to ace your exam with confidence!

Wishing you success—happy learning!

Arun Sharma

Contents

PART I

Reasoning for CAT

SECTION 1
Logical Reasoning

Scan this QR code to access a video on this section's chapters, their importance and weightage in the examination!

CHAPTER 1

Important Concepts in Logical Reasoning

Chapter Launchpad
Scan this QR code for an introductory video on Important Concepts in Logical Reasoning

Ever since the beginning of time, man has always been surrounded by logic (time and logic seem to have coexisted) –it exists all around us, and is all encompassing. There is implicit logic in all human and natural activities–right from the primary level of logic seen in our day-to-day lives to its very advanced form which operates the machines and tools we use for our day-to-day work. Every subject we study, every product we build, every activity we undertake etc., is guided by its own inherent logic.

For instance, when faced with the situation of starting a car, switching on an electric appliance like an electric bulb, etc., we use logic inherently. In fact, it would be difficult to imagine life today without even a thought on most of the logical structures that we use inherently.

LOGIC AND LANGUAGE

The ancient Greeks were the first to study logic as a subject in depth. The lack of any systematic notation for the process of logic during its initial development led the Greeks to rely extensively on the use of language to explain logic. Each one of us even today instinctively uses language to explain what we are doing. Thus, we use logical language in each of the following cases–

1. Where is my key?

Ans: It's on the blue table.

Or

It's in the second shelf from the bottom inside your cupboard.

2. Could you direct me to Mr Mehta's house?

Ans: Proceed straight from here and take the right turn from the second crossing. Move about 100 metres after the right turn and you will reach a 'Y' junction. Take the left leg of the 'Y' and this road leads to a dead end. Mr Mehta lives on the second floor of the second last house on the left of this road.

3. If I put water in a working refrigerator it will become cold.

4. To turn on the car, one needs to switch on the ignition.

Thus, each of us comes across millions of such everyday situations where we use logic inherently as part of our day-to-day language.

The study of logic by the Greeks was largely confined to the study and documentation of logical language. However, the problems of understanding logic through language are very intricate, since this approach becomes extremely complex and unwieldy the moment the logical string becomes longer. This complexity was the reason that when Aristotle summed up Greek logic in his *Treatise on Logic* in the 4th century BC, many of the greatest minds were at a loss to understand it.

Symbolic Logic

It was only in the late 19th century when Gottlob Frege brought about a revolution in the whole field of reasoning by inventing 'symbolic logic'– the use of symbols to represent ideas; that the next phase of development in logical thought started. With this improvement of notation, logical and mathematical ideas could be precisely written down perhaps for the first time. The inconsistencies and vagueness of language were overcome through the use of symbols to denote logical thoughts. The development of 'symbolic logic' further led to the development of 'logical thinking'.

Consider the statement: "If a car has poor air conditioning or low fuel efficiency then it is not a nice car, then the fact that a car is nice means that it will have neither poor air conditioning nor low fuel efficiency".

This long language string used to express the above logic can be condensed using the following symbols:

P (poor air conditioning) and L (low fuel efficiency) and N(C) (Nice car).

Thus, if P or L then not N(C) then N(C) means not P or L.

The words OR, NOT and AND all can have their own logical symbols.

Thus OR is 'v', NOT is ~ AND is +.

Thus, the above sentence can be condensed in its logical form as:

$$(P v L) \rightarrow (\sim N(C)) \rightarrow N(C) \rightarrow (\sim P) \text{ and } (\sim L).$$

In fact, to reduce ambiguity, tediousness and complexity of language based interpretation, solving logical problems involves as its first step the interpretation of the language of the question and conversion of the language of the question into symbolic form. Moreover, this also aids in cutting down the time required to solve complex reasoning questions.

Thus, when the language of logic is converted to symbolic form, the truth of such a sentence depends only on its logical form and not on its content.

Any similar sentence (using totally different language), which uses the same logical form will be true under the same circumstances. The process of mastering reasoning then has to take as its first step the understanding of the process of conversion of language into symbolic logic. In fact, the process of solving logical problems is greatly eased through the use of symbols to document the language.

Some Standard Symbols that You can Use for Logical Language

NOT	~
OR	v
AND	+
If and Only if	≡
Not, if	≠
If, Then	⊃

Besides, you would do well keeping in mind the following factors while creating a symbolic framework for your question:

→ Proper nouns should always be denoted by capitals.

→ In questions where the sex of the proper noun is crucial to solve the questions, you can denote the female by underlining the capital letter used.

→ As you start solving Reasoning questions, create your own set of symbols for standard relational sentence structures. (*See the highlighted box*):

(1) Is next to

Thus, A is next to B can be: AB v BA

(2) (a) Is to the immediate left of

Thus, A is to the immediate left of B can be: AB

(b) Is to the left of

Thus, A is to the left of B can be: A___B

(3) (a) Are at the ends

Thus A and B are at the ends means:

(A _________ B) v (B _________A)

(b) Is at the extreme left

Thus A is at the extreme left means:

(A_______________)

(4) Is more than/taller than/greater than

Thus A is greater than/ taller than/ more than B and C can be symbolically represented by:

A > (B + C) [Note here that we do not know the relationship between B and C]

(5) Is less than/shorter than/lower than

Thus A is less than/shorter than/lower than B and C can be symbolically represented by:

A < (B + C) [Again, note here that we do not know the relationship between B and C]

(6) Is between

Thus, A is between B and C means that A can be anywhere between B and C.

(B___A ___C) v (C___A ___B)

(7) Is the son of

Thus, A is the son of B → $\begin{array}{c}B\\A\end{array}$

(8) Is the daughter of

Thus, A is the daughter of B → $\begin{array}{c}B\\\underline{A}\end{array}$

(9) Is the Parent of

Thus, A is the parent of B → $\begin{array}{c}A\\B\end{array} \vee \begin{array}{c}\underline{A}\\B\end{array}$

(10) Is the spouse of

Thus, A is the spouse of B → $\underline{A}$–B v A–$\underline{B}$

(11) Is the wife of

Thus, A is the wife of B → $\underline{A}$–B

(12) Is the sibling of

Thus, A is the sibling of B → (A..B) v ($\underline{A}$..B) v (A..$\underline{B}$) v ($\underline{A}$..$\underline{B}$)

Some Important Logical Maneuvers:

(1) If, Then

The condition If A, then B leads to the following valid conclusions_

Valid Reasoning 1: A therefore B.

Valid Reasoning 2: Not B, therefore not A.

At the same time If A then B also throws up the following invalid conclusions.

Invalid Reasoning 1: B, therefore A.

Invalid Reasoning 2: Not A, therefore not B.

The above structures of logical thought can be illustrated through the following examples:

If A teaches, B will go to the movies.

Valid Reasoning 1: A teaches, therefore B will go to the movies.

Valid Reasoning 2: B has not gone to the movies, therefore A did not teach.

Invalid Reasoning 1: B went to the movies, therefore A must have taught. This is an invalid line of reasoning.

Invalid Reasoning 2: A did not teach, therefore B did not go to the movies. This too is invalid.

(2) If and Only If

The condition If and Only If A, then B leads to the following valid conclusions.

Valid Reasoning 1: A, therefore B.

Valid Reasoning 2: Not B, therefore not A.

Valid Reasoning 3: B therefore A.

Valid Reasoning 4: Not A therefore not B.

The above structures of logical thought can be illustrated through the following examples:
If and only if A teaches, B will go to the movies.
Valid Reasoning 1: A teaches, therefore B will go to the movies.
Valid Reasoning 2: B has not gone to the movies, therefore A did not teach.
Valid Reasoning 3: B went to the movies, therefore A must have taught.
Valid Reasoning 4: A did not teach, therefore B did not go to the movies.

(3) Either Or
Either A or B
Valid Reasoning 1: Not A then B
Valid Reasoning 2: Not B then A
Valid Reasoning 3: A then Not B
Valid Reasoning 4: B then Not A
The above structures of logical thought can be illustrated through the following examples:
Either A teaches or B goes to the movies.
Valid Reasoning 1: A does not teach, therefore B will go to the movies.
Valid Reasoning 2: B has not gone to the movies, therefore A must have taught.
Valid Reasoning 3: A taught, then B did not go to the movies.
Valid Reasoning 4: B went to the movies, then A did not teach.

(4) If, Then Not
If A then Not B:
Valid Reasoning 1: A then not B
Invalid Reasoning 1: Not B then A
Valid Reasoning 2: B then Not A
The above structures of logical thought can be illustrated through the following examples:
If A teaches, then B will not go to the movies.
Valid Reasoning 1: A teaches, therefore B will not go to the movies.
Invalid Reasoning 1: B has not gone to the movies, therefore A taught.
Valid Reasoning 2: B went to the movies, therefore A did not teach.

As a student it is important for you to follow a few standard steps while solving logical questions:

1. Take a complete 'preview of the situation' to clearly understand the context. Remember to accept the situation as it is given.
2. Read each and every part of the question carefully. You should concentrate hard and focus fully while reading the question. This is a very important prerequisite for solving questions on logic since very often in long sentences there will be individual single words which will transform the meaning of the sentences. If you fail to take into account these words, the end result will be errors in logic and deduction.

Let us now proceed to understand how all this applies to real life problem solving through examining questions which have been asked in different competitive exams and CAT.

Example 1: A party was held at the house of the Mehtas. There were five other couples present (besides Mr and Mrs Mehta), and many, but not all, pairs of people shook hands. Nobody shook hands with anyone twice, and nobody shook hands with his/her spouse. Both the host and hostess shook some hands.

At the end of the party, Mr Mehta polled each person present to see how many hands each person (other than himself) shook. Each person gave a different answer. Determine how many hands Mrs Mehta must have shaken.

Can we prove that it was not Mrs Mehta who shook 10 hands?

Solution: Let there be 5 couples:

A — *A*
B — *B*
C — *C*
D — *D*
E — *E*
and M — *M*

Deduction 1: From the condition that nobody shook hands with his/her spouse, it is clear that none of the twelve people in the party shook more than 10 hands.

(Since, nobody shakes hands with himself or his/her spouse, it leaves a maximum of 10 people to shake hands with).

Deduction 2: Mr Mehta has asked the question to eleven different people and each of them has given a different answer. Also, the highest answer anyone could have possibly given is 10. Hence, the only way to distribute different numbers of hand shakes amongst the 11 people is:

0, 1, 2, 3, 4, 5, 6, 7, 8, 9, 10. [*Note*: somebody shook 0 hands and somebody shook 10].

Deduction 3: Since the host and hostess have both shaken some hands, the person who shook '0' hands cannot be either M or M̲. It has to be one of the other 10 people in the party.

[At this point you need to realise that in the context of this problem A, A̲, B, B̲, C, C̲, D, D̲, E and E̲ are alike, i.e. there is no logical difference amongst these 10 and you have exactly the same information about each of these 10 people. However, Mrs Mehta is different because she stands out as the hostess as well as the wife of the person who has asked the question].

Since all ten guests are the same, assume 'A' shook no hands. This leads us to the following deduction.

Deduction 4: Take any one person apart from A and $\underline{A}$; say B. B will not shake hands with himself and his wife. Besides, B will also not shake hands with A (who has shaken no hands). Thus, B can shake a maximum of 9 hands and will thus not be the person to shake 10 hands.

What applies to B, applies to $\underline{B}$, C, $\underline{C}$, D, $\underline{D}$, E, $\underline{E}$ and $\underline{M}$.

Hence, $\underline{A}$ is the only person who could have shaken 10 hands. Hence, amongst the couple A and $\underline{A}$, if we suppose that A had shaken 0 hands, then $\underline{A}$ must have shaken 10 hands.

Note: The main result here is that, out of the people to whom M has asked the question, and amongst whom we have to distribute the numbers 0 to 10, there has to be a couple who has had 0 and 10 handshakes. It could be any of the five couples, but it cannot be M who has either 0 or 10 handshakes.

We now proceed, using the same line of reason as follows.

Deduction 5: Suppose B has 1 handshake – he must have shaken hands with $\underline{A}$ (who has shaken everybody's hands she can).

Then, B wouldn't have shaken hands with anyone out of A, $\underline{B}$, C, $\underline{C}$, D, $\underline{D}$, E, $\underline{E}$ and $\underline{M}$. At this point the following picture emerges:

A — 0	$\underline{A}$ — 10
B — 1	$\underline{B}$ —
C —	$\underline{C}$ —
D —	$\underline{D}$ —
E	$\underline{E}$
$\underline{M}$	

Numbers left to be allocated – 2, 3, 4, 5, 6, 7, 8, 9.

Considering C, as a general case, he cannot shake hands with $\underline{C}$, A (who shook no hands) and B (who shook hands only with $\underline{A}$. This is mandatory since $\underline{A}$ has shaken hands with 10 people).

Thus, C can shake hands with a maximum of 8 people and this deduction will be true for $\underline{C}$, D, $\underline{D}$, E, $\underline{E}$ and $\underline{M}$ too. Hence, the only person who could get 9 handshakes is $\underline{B}$.

Thus, we conclude that just like 0 and 10 handshakes were in one pair, similarly 1 and 9 handshakes too have to be part of one pair of husband and wife.

Similar deductions will lead to the realisation that 2 and 8, 3 and 7 and 4 and 6 handshakes will also occur for couples amongst the 11 people questioned.

Hence, $\underline{M}$ must have shaken 5 hands.

Let us consider another example:

Example 2: Consider the following grid:

L		P
M	O	Q
N		R

Each letter in the above grid represents a different digit from 0 to 9, such that

L × M × N = M × O × Q = P × Q × R. Find the value of 'O'.

Going Beyond the Book

Scan this QR code to access a video explanation of Example 2

Solution: In order to solve such a question, one needs to proceed systematically making one deduction at a time.

Deduction 1: There are 7 alphabets and 10 digits. We need to somehow eliminate 3 of these 10 to define the 7 digits required to be allocated.

It is obvious that '0' cannot be used because if we make any alphabet '0' we will end up with a product that is '0' in one or a maximum of two of the three cases.

Deduction 2: You need to find a product which can be made in three different ways.

Deduction 3: Two of these three ways have to be independent of each other with no matching digits and the third way has to be drawn out of one digit each from the first two ways and one independent digit that has not been used.

Also, at this point there are 9 digits and 2 more to be eliminated.

Now we move to the process of Trial and Error.

Notes on Interpretation

Trial and Error is one of the most useful processes for solving questions based on reasoning. Principally there are three ways for carrying out trial and error search.

(1) Complete trial and error.

(2) Directed trial and error.

(3) Blind trial and error.

The blind trial and error is what most students practice and hence, are unable to solve logical questions. Since they do not use their deductive logic to do a more focused search, they end up going round in circles while trying to solve such questions.

Instead, directed trial and error and comprehensive trial and error are superior problem solving processes and therefore, score above the complete trial and error method.

Application of Directed Trial and Error: The question above is a classical situation warranting a directed trial and error. Hence, this is best illustrated through the example.

At this stage, we are at a situation where we know: 1, 2, 3, 4, 5, 6, 7, 8 and 9 have to be allocated to L, M, N, O, P, Q and R.

At this point, take a call as to whether you want to use 9 or not? 9 and 1 are different from the other numbers primarily because they are the highest and lowest numbers respectively and also because 9 gives us "maximum room for manoeuvering" the question as compared to the other numbers, while 1 is a useful tool for a third multiplier if we do not want to change the value of the multiplication.

Note: The student should analogise the thinking process applied here to the thinking process used to unravel a ball of wool which has got entangled.

To disentangle an entangled ball of wool, we need to search the end of the ball. Once you identify either end, the remaining process of disentangling the ball requires very elementary logic coupled with patience and perseverance. The logic for picking up the end point of the ball of wool is that it is different from all other points in the ball.

Similarly, in reasoning questions, we need to identify things/objects/people which are different from other things/objects/people and start our solution from there.

After that, the whole process becomes one of the use of elementary logic for elementary deductions coupled with patience and perseverance.

In the question under consideration, if we take a call on using '9' and decide to do so, we can then deduce that the required product has to be a multiple of 9.

[Remember that at this point of time, we have ignored the line of thinking that neglects 9. We will have to consider it, if we do not get an answer by using 9].

Since the product has to be a multiple of 9, assume that the product is 36. But this product eliminates the use of 8, 7 and 5 and leaves only 6 digits. Going below 36 as a product for further trial and error will further reduce the number of possibilities. Hence, let us try to go to the higher extreme and try to experiment with the number 72.

We see that $72 = 3^2 \times 2^3$ and can be formed by $9 \times 8 \times 1$ or $6 \times 3 \times 4$ or $9 \times 4 \times 2$.

This satisfies our deduction that 72 gives three ways of solving the question. Also, the second requirement that there should be two ways which are independent of each other and a third way which uses one term each from the two independent ways and one unique term is also satisfied.

Hence, $6 \times 3 \times 4$ is independent of $9 \times 8 \times 1$ in all its digits. Also, $9 \times 4 \times 2$ uses the number 9 from $9 \times 8 \times 1$ and 4 from $6 \times 3 \times 4$.

Hence, the following possibility emerges:

L = 6	P = 8	
M = 4	O = 2	Q = 9
N = 3	R = 1	

You need to understand here that, the digit '2' is the only one which is fixed to its place in the grid. All the other digits can be changed. Thus, we can have alternative arrangements like:

L = 3		P = 1
M = 4	O = 2	Q = 9
N = 6		R = 8
OR		
L = 8		P = 6
M = 9	O = 2	Q = 4
N = 1		R = 3

The only thing that is fixed is the number 2 for O.

Example 3: Let us now consider another question, which is a classic case of complete or comprehensive trial and error method.

Going Beyond the Book

Scan this QR code to access a video explanation of Example 3

Two people A and B are playing a game. Both A and B are logical people. There are two boxes on the table. One of them contains 9 balls, the other contains 4 balls. In this game, the players are supposed to take alternate turns of picking up balls according to the following rules:

(a) Pick up as many balls as you want to from any box.

(b) Pick up an equal number of balls from both boxes. (if you pick from both boxes).

The person who picks up the last ball wins the game. In his/her turn, it is mandatory to pick up at least one ball. A has to play first. What should he do to ensure a win?

Solution:

Deduction 1: The rules of the game define that there are two legal moves:
Picking up an equal number from each box or picking up any number from either box (at least 1).

Deduction 2: A has 17 possible moves to make and since the question asks for one particular move that will ensure a win, one of these 17 must be the winning move. It is at this stage that you should realise that the question calls for a comprehensive trial and error which should result in the elimination of 16 possibilities.
The starting position is 9, 4.
A's options at the start of the game can be basically divided into three options:

I	II	III
Pick up balls from the first box.	Pick up balls from the second box.	Pick up balls from both the boxes.

The position after A plays his move can be documented as follows (in terms of the number of balls B has in front of him.):

[There are 9 moves in option I.] (Balls from first box are picked by A.) If

(a) A picks up 1 ball, B will be left with 8, 4.
(b) A picks up 2 balls, B will be left with 7, 4
(c) A picks up 3 balls, B will be left with 6, 4
(d) A picks up 4 balls, B will be left with 5, 4
(e) A picks up 5 balls, B will be left with 4, 4
(f) A picks up 6 balls, B will be left with 3, 4
(g) A picks up 7 balls, B will be left with 2, 4
(h) A picks up 8 balls, B will be left with 1, 4
(i) A picks up 9 balls, B will be left with 0, 4

Similarly, if he picks up balls from the second box (option II) he will have an end result of: If

(a) A picks up 1 ball, B will be left with 9, 3
(b) A picks up 2 balls, B will be left with 9, 2
(c) A picks up 3 balls, B will be left with 9, 1
(d) A picks up 4 balls, B will be left with 9, 0

And for option III, If:

(a) A picks up 1 ball each from both boxes, B is left with 8, 3
(b) A picks up 2 balls each from both boxes, B is left with 7, 2
(c) A picks up 3 balls each from both boxes, B is left with 6, 1
(d) A picks up 4 balls each from both boxes, B is left with 5, 0

Out of these 17 options, the options of leaving (0, 4), (9, 0) and (5, 0) are infeasible, since it will result in an immediate win for B who can clean up the board in one move. Similarly, leaving (4, 4) will also cause an immediate win for B. *This leaves A with 13 options which he needs to consider. These are:*

I	II	III
8, 4	9, 3	8, 3
7, 4	9, 2	7, 2
6, 4	9, 1	6, 1
5, 4		
3, 4		
2, 4		
1, 4		

From these 13, the easiest option to check is (1, 4). *If B gets (1, 4) he has the following options:*

I	II	III
0, 4	1, 3	0, 3
	1, 2	
	1, 1	
	1, 0	

Obviously, he cannot play (0, 4), (1, 0), (1, 1) or (0, 3). This means he can leave A with (1, 2) or (1, 3). These need to be further investigated.

If B leaves (1, 2), A has the following options to leave for B:

I	II	III
0, 2	1, 1	0, 1
	1, 0	

Obviously, if he plays any of this, A will lose. Hence, if B leaves A with (1, 2), A will definitely lose.

Deduction 3: A cannot leave B with a situation in which B can make into (1, 2) or (2, 1).

Evaluating the 13 options left for A, we get that (1, 4), (2, 4), (3, 4), (5, 4), (9, 1), (9, 2), (6, 1) and (7, 2) are situations from which B can reach (2, 1) or (1, 2) in one move. This means B will win if A leaves him with any of these eight situations.

Thus, A will eliminate these eight options from his list of 13 and come down to five options which need further checking. These are: (6, 4), (7, 4), (8, 4), (9, 3) and (8, 3). At this stage we further need to eliminate four of these five options to come to the correct answer.

Now let us start our investigation with (6, 4). *If B is left with (6, 4) he has the following options:*

I	II	III
5, 4	6, 3	5, 3
4, 4	6, 2	4, 2
3, 4	6, 1	3, 1
2, 4	6, 0	2, 0
1, 4		
0, 4		

Of this, B cannot play (0, 4), (1, 4), (2, 4), (3, 4), (4, 4), (5, 4), (6, 0), (6, 1), (6, 2), (2, 0), (3, 1) and (4, 2) [since these lead to a (2, 1) or a clean win in one move]. Thus, B can either leave (6, 3) or (5, 3).

If B leaves (5, 3) for A, A's options are:

I	II	III
4, 3	5, 2	4, 2
3, 3	5, 1	3, 1
2, 3	5, 0	2, 0
1, 3		
0, 3		

In each of these cases, B will either win in one move or get to (2, 1) in one move. Thus, A cannot do anything if B leaves (5, 3) in return for A leaving (6, 4).

Deduction 4: Just like being left with (2, 1) means a definite loss, so does being left with (5, 3).

Hence, A cannot allow a situation in which B can make it (5, 3) in one move.

Thus, A cannot leave B with (6, 4), (9, 3) or (8, 3) since, each of these will result in B giving back (5, 3) in one move.

Thus, A's option are down to (7, 4) or (8, 4). These need to be further investigated now:

Let us consider A leaving (7, 4) for B.

B's options are:

I	II	III
(6, 4)		
(5, 4)	(7, 3)	(6, 3)
(4, 4)	(7, 2)	(5, 2)
(4, 4)	(7, 1)	(4, 1)
(3, 4)	(7, 0)	(3, 0)
(2, 4)		
(1, 4)		
Or (0, 4)		

After closely evaluating each of these, all possible options will get eliminated because in one move they lead to either a straight win or a (2, 1) situation or a (5, 3) situation.

If A does any of this, then B cannot do anything to stop from losing the game.

The above question obviously is extremely long and complicated. However, what needs to be noticed is that even for this extremely long question, at no point of time is there any big logical jump, i.e., from one logic emerges the next one and so on.

Let's now tackle an original CAT question, taken from the 2004 exam paper. This set marked a shift in the DI-LR section, introducing more complex puzzles like those seen today. As we go through the solution together, you'll notice some ambiguities in the questions. However, we've chosen to include this set because it offers valuable learning opportunities.

Example 4: The year was 2006. All six teams in Pool A of World Cup Hockey plays with each other exactly once. Each win earns a team three points, a draw earns one point and a loss earns zero point. The two teams with the highest points qualify for the semifinals. In case of a tie, the team with the highest goal difference (goals for–goals against) qualifies. In the opening match, Spain lost to Germany. After the second round (after each team played two matches), the Pool A table looked as shown on the next page.

In the third round, Spain played against Pakistan, Argentina played against Germany and New Zealand played against South Africa. All the third round matches were drawn. The following are some results from the fourth and fifth round matches.

(a) Spain won both the fourth and fifth round matches.

(b) Both Argentina and Germany won their fifth round matches by 3 goals to 0.

(c) Pakistan won both the fourth and fifth round matches by 1 goal to 0.

Solution: For solving the above question, one requires tremendous alacrity, logical consistency and above all a cool head.

Also, the solution of the above question is dependent on your ability to interpret the table and find out the appropriate linkages (something that might not be as easily done as said).

Let us look at the table and create our interpretations:

Deduction 1: Germany and Argentina have both won their matches while New Zealand and South Africa have lost both theirs.

Let us start by making tables for the possible result of the first two rounds for each of the six teams.

Germany

Round	Result
1. Spain	Won 1–0/2–1
2. Pak/New Zealand/South Africa	Won 2–1/1–0
3. Argentina	Drawn

It is given that Germany has played against Spain in the opening match (and obviously won that game).

Looking at the goals for and goals against columns and the fact that Germany has won both the first and second round matches, we deduce that its two wins must have been in one of the following combinations:

(Pool A)

Team	Games Played	Won	Drawn	Lost	Goals For	Goals Aganist	Points
Germany	2	2	0	0	3	1	6
Argentina	2	2	0	0	2	0	6
Spain	2	1	0	1	5	2	3
Pakistan	2	1	0	1	2	1	3
New Zealand	2	0	0	2	1	6	0
South Africa	2	0	0	2	1	4	0

Won 1 – 0 and Won 2 – 1

Or

Won 2 – 1 and Won 1 – 0

Notes on Interpretation

Germany cannot win either match by 2-0 or 3-0 or 3-1 margins since it will not be able to win the other match and maintain 3-1 goals for goals against situation.

Deduction: If Germany had won the first game 2-1 against Spain, Spain would have won its second round match by 4-0, while if Germany won by 1-0, then Spain would have won its second round match 5-1 (since Spain has Goals For = 5 and Goals Against = 2).

Further, since only two teams – New Zealand and South Africa have conceded 4 or more goals, Spain must have played one of them. Looking into South Africa's Goals For/Goals Against columns, if South Africa had conceded 4 goals in the second round, then it should have won the first round (1, 0). But, South Africa has lost both rounds.

Hence, Spain played its second round against New Zealand. Further, if this is true, no other team can play against New Zealand in round two.

At this stage, the following possibilities emerge.

Team Germany

Round 1	vs.	Spain	Won	1–0 or 2–1
Round 2	vs.	Pak/S.A.	Won	2–1 or 1–0
Round 3	vs.	Argentina	Draw	

Team Spain

Round 1	vs.	Germany	Lost	0–1 or 1–2
Round 2	vs.	New Zealand	Won	5–1 or 4–0
Round 3	vs.	Pakistan	Draw	

Team New Zealand

Round 1	vs.	Arg/Pakistan	Lost	0–1 or 1–2
Round 2	vs.	Spain	Lost	1–5 or 0–4
Round 3	vs.	South Africa	Draw	

Deduction: Team Pakistan won one round and lost one and Goals For/Goals Against 2/1. Hence, Team Pakistan won 2-0 and lost 0-1.

Now, since New Zealand played its first round against Pakistan or Argentina, it could not have lost 1-2. This is because in the case of Pakistan, if Pakistan had won 2-1 against New Zealand in round 1, its round 2 would have been a draw.

Further, Argentina has conceded no goals. Hence, it could not have won 2-1 against New Zealand.

This means that New Zealand must have lost 0-1 in its first match against Argentina (that cannot happen against Pakistan, because Pakistan cannot win 1-0 in the first round, since it will result in a 1-1 draw in round 2).

Consequently, New Zealand lost 1-5 in its second match to Spain and hence, Spain must have lost 0-1 to Germany.

The following scenario emerges from these deductions:

Team Germany

Round 1	vs.	Spain	Won	1–0
Round 2	vs.	S.A.	Won	2–1

Note: Here Germany's round 2 has to be vs. S.A., since Pakistan cannot lose 2-1

Team Spain

Round 1	vs.	Germany	Lost	0–1
Round 2	vs.	N.Z.	Won	5–1

Team New Zealand

Round 1	vs.	Argentina	Lost	0–1
Round 2	vs.	Spain	Lost	1–5

Team Pakistan

Round 1	vs.	S.A.	Won	2–0
Round 2	vs.	Argentina	Lost	0–1

The first three rounds are as under:

Round 1 matches:

Germany	beat	Spain	1–0
Argentina	beat	N.Z.	1–0
Pakistan	beat	S.A.	2–0

Round 2 matches:

Spain	beat	N.Z.	5–1
Argentina	beat	Pak	1–0
Germany	beat	S.A.	2–1

Putting all the deductions into one table, the following picture emerges:

	Germany	Argentina	Spain	Pak	New Zealand	S. Africa
Germany	—	D#3	W (1–0)#1			W (2–1)#
Argentina	D#3	—		W (1–0)#2	W (1–0)#1	
Spain	L (0–1)#1		—	D#3	W (9–1)#2	
Pakistan		L (0–1)#2	D#3	—		W (2–0)#1
New Zealand		L (0–1)#1	L (1–5)#2	—	D#3	
South Africa	L (1–2)#2			L (0–2)#1	D#3	—

According to the information available about the fourth and fifth round of matches:

Germany	—	Pakistan, lost (0–1) and N.Z. won (3–0)
Argentina	—	Spain, lost by 'x' goals and S.A. won (3, 0)
Spain	—	Argentina won by 'x' goals and S.A. won by 'y' goals
Pakistan	—	Germany won (1–0) and N.Z. won 1–0
N.Z.	—	Germany lost (0–3) and Pakistan lost (0–1)
S.A.	—	Argentina lost (0–3) and Spain lost by 'y' goals

When analyzing the clues about the last two rounds, a discrepancy emerges. Four teams are shown to have won their fifth-round matches, which wouldn't normally be possible if only three matches were played in that round. However, if a team's fifth-round match also serves as another team's fourth-round match, the scenario becomes plausible. This is similar to tournament formats like the IPL, where one team might be playing its 14th match while another is only on its 12th or 13th.

Germany, Argentina, Spain and Pakistan have all scored 10 points. Hence, the pool toppers would be determined on the basics of goal difference.

And the goal differences for the six teams are:

Germany	$+1 + 1 + 0 - 1 + 3 = +4$
Argentina	$+1 + 1 + 0 - x + 3 = 5 - x =$ Max. 4 or less
Spain	$-1 + 4 + 0 + x + y = 3 + x + y =$ Min. 5 or more
Pakistan	$2 - 1 + 0 + 1 + 1 = +3$
New Zealand	$-1 - 4 + 0 - 3 - y = -8 - y$

Based on these deductions, the following questions can be answered.

1. Which one of the following statements is true about the matches played in the first two rounds?
   (a) Pakistan beat South Africa by 2 goals to 1.
   (b) Argentina beat Pakistan by 1 goal to 0.
   (c) Germany beat Pakistan by 2 goals to 1.
   (d) Germany beat Spain by 2 goals to 1.
2. Which one of the following statements is true about the matches played in the first two rounds?
   (a) Germany beat New Zealand by 1 goal to 0.
   (b) Spain beat New Zealand by 4 goals to 0.
   (c) Spain beat South Africa by 2 goals to 0.
   (d) Germany beat South Africa by 2 goals to 1.
3. Which team finished at the top of the pool after five rounds of matches?
   (a) Argentina (b) Germany
   (c) Spain (d) Cannot be determined
   Spain must be top of the pool since it has the best goal difference even in it's worst case scenario.
4. If Pakistan qualified as one of the two teams from Pool A, which was the other team that qualified?
   (a) Argentina (b) Germany
   (c) Spain (d) Cannot be determined
   Answers: 1. (b) 2. (d) 3. (c) 4. (d)

Notes on Interpretation

This question has an ambiguity. According to the deductions, Spain and Germany both should be above Pakistan in terms of goal difference and hence, Pakistan cannot qualify. However, if Pakistan qualifies, so do both Spain and Germany.

Example 5: Prof. Singh has been tracking the number of visitors to his homepage. His service provider has provided him with the following data on the country of origin of the visitors and the university they belong to:

Going Beyond the Book

Scan this QR code to access a video explanation of Example 5

Number of Visitors/Day

University	1	2	3
University 1	1	0	0
University 2	2	0	0
University 3	0	1	0

University	1	2	3
University 4	0	0	2
University 5	1	0	0
University 6	1	0	1
University 7	2	0	0
University 8	0	2	0

Number of Visitors/Day

Country	1	2	3
Canada	2	0	0
Netherlands	1	1	0
India	1	2	0
UK	2	0	2
USA	1	0	1

Deduction 1: Looking at Day 3, University 4 must belong to the UK and University 6 must belong to the USA.

Deduction 2: From Day 2 it is clear that University 8 has to be an Indian University while University 3 has to be from the Netherlands.

Deduction 3: From the analysis of Day 1 data, University 2 and University 7 should be distributed amongst the UK and Canada in either order, i.e. 2 belongs to the UK and 7 to Canada or 2 belongs to Canada and 7 to the UK. [Symbolically, (2 UK + 7 Canada) vs (2 Canada + 7 UK)]

Deduction 4: The visitor from USA on Day 1 must have come from University 6. Hence, University 1 and University 5 should be distributed between India and the Netherlands.

With this set of deductions, we get the following table. Using this table the answers to the following questions become quite elementary.

Number of Visitors/Day

University	1
University 1	I v N
University 2	UK v C
University 3	N
University 4	UK
University 5	N v I
University 6	USA
University 7	C v UK
University 8	I

1. To which country does University 5 belong?
   (a) India or the Netherlands but not the USA
   (b) India or the USA but not the Netherlands
   (c) The Netherlands or the USA but not India
   (d) India or the USA but not the UK
2. University 1 can belong to:
   (a) The UK (b) Canada
   (c) The Netherlands (d) The USA
3. Which among the listed countries can possibly host three of the eight listed universities?
   (a) None (b) Only the UK
   (c) Only India (d) Both India and the UK
4. Visitors from how many universities from the UK visited Prof. Singh's homepage in three days?
   (a) 1 (b) 2
   (c) 3 (d) 4

The answers are:
1. (a) 2. (c) 3. (a) 4. (b).

CHAPTER 2

Logical Reasoning based on Arrangements

Chapter Launchpad

Scan this QR code for an introductory video on Arrangements

Arrangement questions are one of the most common question types in logical reasoning. As the name suggests, questions on arrangements typically involve arranging people or objects in straight lines or around circles or squares or other geometrical shapes.

The key skills involved in solving questions on arrangements include but are not limited to:

(i) The ability to visualise the geometrical shape of the arrangement situation.

(ii) The ability to order the clues in the correct order of usage (as explained in the theory of logical reasoning).

(iii) The ability to perceive what indirect clues are talking about–and how to use them.

(iv) The ability to convert clues written in language form into visual cues so that you do not need to read the text again and again. Also, converting the language clues to visual cues is critical for the purpose of being able to 'see' all the clues at one go.

Illustrated below are the solutions to a few typical questions on arrangements. We would advise you to first have a look at the question and try to solve the same on your own before looking at the step by step process of solving the same–illustrated through the revolutionary "Reaction Tracker" mechanism which is an integral part of this section of the book.

> **Note:** The Reaction tracker is a blow-by-blow account of exactly what reaction should go on in your mind as you solve an individual question in reasoning.

Look at the following questions and try to solve them:

Example 1: ***Directions:*** *Study the following information to answer these questions.*

(i) Alex, Betsy, Chloe, Dennis, Edward, Fiona, Giles and Herbert are gamblers sitting around a round table facing the centre.

(ii) Dennis is the neighbour of Alex but not of Herbert.

(iii) Betsy is the neighbour of Fiona and 4th to the left of Dennis.

(iv) Edward is the neighbour of Herbert and 3rd to the right of Fiona.

(v) Chloe is neither the neighbour of Alex nor of Giles.

1. Which of the following is wrong?

(a) Betsy is to the immediate left of Herbert.
(b) Herbert is to the immediate left of Edward.
(c) Dennis is 4th to the right of Fiona.
(d) All are correct.

2. Which of the following is correct?

(a) Dennis is to the immediate left of Giles.
(b) Alex is between Chloe and Dennis.
(c) Fiona is 3rd to the right of Dennis.
(d) Edward is between Herbert and Betsy.

3. Which of the following groups has the 2nd person sitting between the 1st and the 3rd?

(a) Alex-Fiona-Chloe
(b) Giles-Alex-Dennis
(c) Betsy-Edward-Herbert
(d) Herbert-Fiona-Betsy

4. Which of the following pairs has the 1st person sitting to the immediate right of the second?

(a) Betsy-Herbert
(b) Fiona-Betsy
(c) Edwards-Giles
(d) Alex-Dennis

5. Which of the following pairs are fourth to one another?

(a) Chloe-Edwards (b) Fiona-Herbert
(c) Dennis-Chloe (d) Dennis-Betsy

6. If Chloe and Giles interchange their positions, which of the following will indicate Alex's position?

(a) To the immediate right of Giles
(b) 4th to the right of Chloe
(c) 2nd to the left of Giles
(d) To the immediate left of Chloe

Solution: From clues (i) and (iii), we get the following two possibilities:

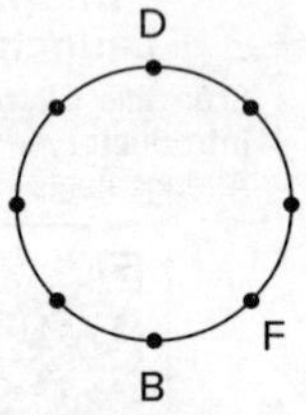

Case I

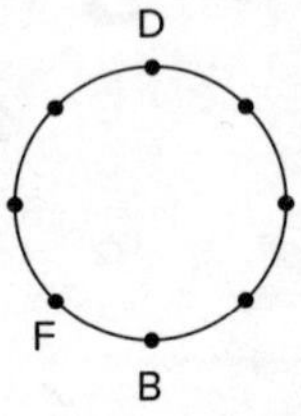

Case II

Now, read clue (iv): Edward is third to the right of Fiona. This information rejects Case I. Using clue (iv), we get the following two possibilities, i.e., Case II (a) and Case II (b).

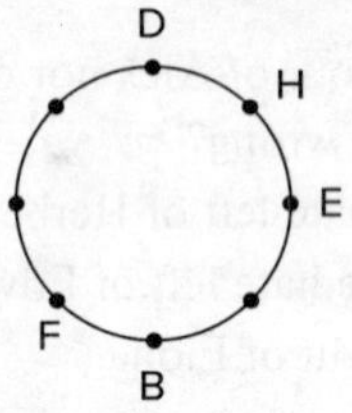

Case II (a)

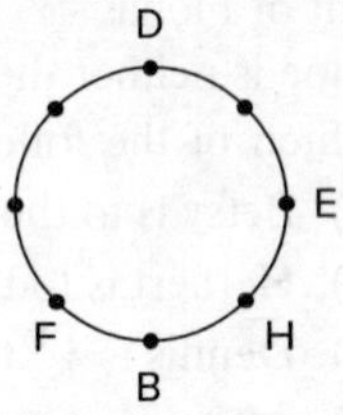

Case II (b)

Now, from clue (ii), we come to know that Dennis is not the neighbour of Herbert. Hence, reject Case II (a). From clue (ii), we get the following two possibilities:

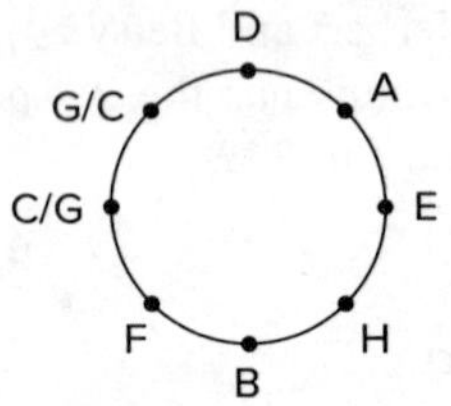

Case II (c)

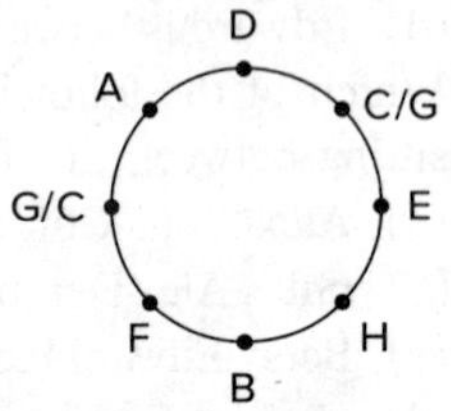

Case II (d)

Now, from clue (v), Chloe can't be the neighbour of Giles. Therefore, reject Case II (c).

Again, since Chloe can't be the neighbour of Alex, the final seating arrangement will be as follows:

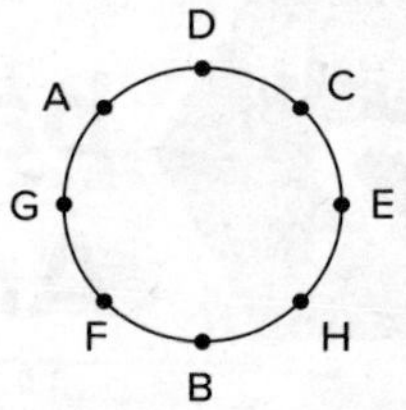

The answers then become pretty straight forward:

1. (c) **2.** (c) **3.** (b) **4.** (d) **5.** (d) **6.** (d)

Example 2: ***Directions:*** These questions are based on the information that follows:

In a row of soldiers facing North, (i) Lambert is 8th to the right of Khurusheva; (ii) Mickey is 16th from the left end; (iii) Lambert is 16th to the right of Jackson who is 27th from the right end of the row; (iv) Khurusheva is nearer than Mickey to the right end of the row; (v) there are 5 boys between Mickey and Khurusheva.

1. How many soldiers are there between Jackson and Mickey?
(a) One (b) Two
(c) Three (d) Data inadequate

2. How far away is Khurusheva from the right end of the row?
(a) 30th (b) 10th
(c) 19th (d) 18th

3. How many soldiers are there in the row?
(a) 50 (b) 40
(c) 36 (d) Data inadequate

4. How far away is Jackson from the right end of the row?
(a) Data inadequate (b) 24th
(c) 25th (d) 27th

Reaction Tracker

Let us arrange the whole information.
From clue (i), we get

Khurusheva	7 soldiers	Lambert

Now, using clue (iii), we get:

Jackson	7 soldiers	Khurusheva	7 soldiers	Lambert	10 soldiers

Now, using clue (iv) and clue (v), we get:

Jackson	1 soldier	Mickey	5 soldiers	Khurusheva	7 soldiers	Lambert	10 soldiers

Now, from clue (ii), we get the complete information as following:

13 soldiers	Jackson	1 soldier	Mickey	5 soldiers	Khurusheva	7 soldiers	Lambert	10 soldiers

Hence the answers are:

1. (a) Clearly from the above information, there is 1 soldier present between them
2. (c) From the above information it is obvious that Khurusheva occupies 19th position from the right end of the row.
3. (b) Total numbers of soldiers = 13 + 3 + 5 + 1 + 7 + 1 +10 = 40
4. (d) No of Soldiers from right hand side - 10 + 1 + 7 + 1 + 5 + 1 + 1 + 1(Jackson) = 27th position from the right end.

LEVEL OF DIFFICULTY (I)

Directions for Questions 1 to 5:

(i) Six balls with shapes of triangle, square, heptagon, pentagon, hexagon and octagon printed on them are coloured in six different colours - blue, red, green, grey, yellow and brown, and are arranged from left to right (not necessarily in the same order).

(ii) The balls are labelled as P, Q, R, S, T and U.

(iii) The ball with the picture of a pentagon is blue but it is not ball S or Ball P. Ball P has a picture of a heptagon, is brown and is placed at the extreme right.

(iv) The picture of the square is neither on ball S nor on ball T and is not in either the green or the yellow colour. Ball R has a picture of the triangle in a grey colour and it is fifth from the right and next to ball Q having the picture of the octagon.

1. If the square's ball is immediately between the balls of the pentagon and the octagon then at which number is the hexagon's ball placed from the left?
   (a) Fifth (b) Second
   (c) First (d) Data inadequate
2. Which is the correct combination of ball and color?
   (a) T-Yellow (b) U-Red
   (c) Q-Green (d) Data inadequate
3. The picture of the hexagon is in which color?
   (a) Yellow (b) Green
   (c) Blue (d) Data inadequate
4. The picture of the pentagon is printed on which ball?
   (a) S (b) T
   (c) U (d) None of these
5. If the color of the ball with the octagon picture and the ball with the hexagon picture is interchanged, then the color of the octagon is:
   (a) Green (b) Yellow
   (c) Blue (d) Data inadequate

Directions for Questions 6 to 8: *Six persons–Akshay, Bobby, Celina, Dimple, Esha and Faisal took up a job with XYZ Consultants in a week from Monday to Saturday. Each of them joined for different posts on different days. The posts were of Clerk, Officer, Technician, Manager, Supervisor and Sales Executive, though not in the same order.*

Faisal joined as a Manager on the first day. Bobby joined as a Supervisor but neither on Wednesday nor Friday. Dimple joined as a Technician on Thursday. The officer joined the firm on Wednesday. Esha joined as a clerk on Tuesday. Akshay joined as a Sales Executive.

6. Who joined the firm on Wednesday?
   (a) Bobby (b) Celina
   (c) Esha (d) Data inadequate
7. Who was the last to join the firm?
   (a) Esha (b) Faisal
   (c) Bobby (d) Akshay
8. On which of the following days did the Sales Executive join?
   (a) Thursday (b) Friday
   (c) Saturday (d) None of these

Directions for Questions 9 to 11:

(i) Six friends A, B, C, D, E and F are sitting along the sides of a hexagonal table for playing a game, though not necessarily in the same order.

(ii) F, who is sitting exactly opposite to A, is to the immediate right of B.

(iii) D is between A and B and is exactly opposite to C.

9. Who are the people sitting next to A?
   (a) D & E (b) D & F
   (c) C & E (d) B & D
10. Who is sitting opposite to B?
    (a) E (b) F
    (c) A (d) C
11. Three of the following are alike in a certain way on the basis of sitting positions and so form a group. Which is the one that does not belong to the group?
    (a) B, C (b) A, D
    (c) B, F (d) E, A

Directions for Questions 12 to 15: *A group of five boys–Abdul, Bony, Chandan, Devdas and Eram, and a group of five girls–Paro, Queen, Reena, Saifali and Tulika are standing in rows facing each other (not in the same order). The group of girls is facing north.*

Eram is not at any of the ends. Chandan is to the immediate right of Bony and Devdas is to the immediate left of Abdul who is facing Paro. There are as many girls between Paro and Queen as between Reena and Saifali. Abdul is second to the left of Bony. Saifali and Reena are not facing either Bony or Devdas.

12. Which pair of boys is standing at the ends of the row?
    (a) Chandan & Devdas
    (b) Chandan & Bony
    (c) Devdas & Bony
    (d) Data inadequate
13. Which of the following is definitely true?
    (a) Chandan is third to the right of Devdas
    (b) Devdas is facing Paro
    (c) Chandan is facing Saifali
    (d) None of these
14. Who is standing to the immediate right of Abdul?
    (a) Eram
    (b) Chandan
    (c) Devdas
    (d) Data inadequate
15. Who is facing Bony?
    (a) Reena (b) Saifali
    (c) Queen (d) Data inadequate

Directions for Questions 16 to 19:

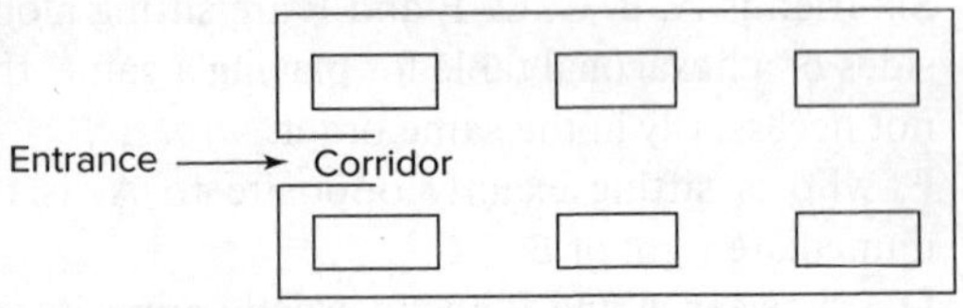

The plan above shows an office block for six officers–A, B, C, D, E and F. Both B and C occupy offices to the right of the corridor (as one enters the office block) and A occupies an office to the left of the corridor. E and F occupy offices on the opposite sides of the corridor but their offices do not face each other. The offices of C and D face each other. E does not have a corner office. F's office is further down the corridor than A's, on the same side.

16. If E sits in his office and faces the corridor, whose office is to his left?
    (a) A (b) B
    (c) C (d) D
17. Whose office faces A's office?
    (a) B (b) C
    (c) D (d) E
18. Who is/are F's neighbour(s)?
    (a) A only (b) A & D
    (c) C (d) B & C
19. D was heard telling someone to go further down the corridor to the last office on the right. To whose room was he trying to direct that person?
    (a) A (b) B
    (c) C (d) F

Directions for Questions 20 to 24: *Four families decided to go for a picnic to Jhumri Talaiya and agreed to meet at a place called Rani ka Talab before moving for the picnic. One family has no kid, while the others have at least one kid each. Amongst each family with kids, at least one kid goes to the picnic. Following is the information about the families.*

(i) The family with two kids came just before the family with no kids.
(ii) D who does not have any kids reached just before C's family.
(iii) P and his wife reached last with their only kid.
(iv) Q is not B's husband.
(v) Q and S are fathers.
(vi) Daughters of C and A go to the same school.
(vii) B came before D and met A when she reached the fixed place.
(viii) R stays farthest from the place and he is a good singer.
(ix) S explained that his son could not come because of exams.

20. Who amongst the females arrived third?
    (a) A (b) B
    (c) C (d) D
21. Which is the correct pair of husband and wife?
    (a) S and D (b) P and C
    (c) Q and C (d) S and A
22. Whose daughters go to the same school?
    (a) Q and R (b) P and R
    (c) P and Q (d) Q and S
23. Whose family has definitely more than one kid?
    (a) R's (b) S's
    (c) Q's (d) P's
24. Among the males, who arrived second?
    (a) P (b) Q
    (c) R (d) S

Directions for Questions 25 to 28: *Seven sports awardees–A, B, C, D, E, F and G are to be honoured at a special luncheon. The players will be seated on the dias in a row. A and G have to catch the flight for their One Day International Cricket Match and so must be seated at the extreme right. B, the Rajiv Gandhi Khel Ratna recipient must be in the centre. C and D are bitter rivals and therefore, must be seated as far apart as possible.*

25. Which of the following cannot be seated at either end?
    (a) C (b) D
    (c) F (d) Cannot be determined

26. Which of the following pairs cannot be seated together?
(a) B & D (b) C & F
(c) D & G (d) E & A

27. Which of the following pairs cannot occupy the seats on either side of B?
(a) F & D (b) E & G
(c) D & E (d) None of these

28. What can be the position of C from the right side?
(a) Third (b) Seventh
(c) Third or Seventh (d) Cannot be determined

Directions for Questions 29 to 33: *Study the following information carefully and answer the questions that follow:*

Six friends- Alok, Bheem, Chandar, Devdas, Earl and Ferguson are sitting on a bench facing North. Chandar is sitting between Alok and Earl. Devdas is not at the end. Bheem is sitting to the immediate right of Earl. Ferguson is not at the right end.

29. Who is to the immediate right of Ferguson?
(a) Devdas (b) Alok
(c) Either Devdas or Alok
(d) Cannot be determined

30. How many persons are there to the left of Chandar?
(a) One (b) Two
(c) Three (d) Four

31. Who is fourth from the left end?
(a) Alok (b) Chandar
(c) Bheem (d) Cannot be determined

32. Who is at the left end?
(a) Ferguson (b) Alok
(c) Bheem (d) Cannot be determined

33. Which of the following is sitting to one side of Devdas?
(a) Ferguson-Earl (b) Ferguson-Bheem
(c) Ferguson-Chandar (d) None of these

Directions for Questions 34 to 37: *Eight friends Ashok, Bikki, Chris, Dilawar, Eshwer, Farooq, Gebriel and Hetmayer have different professions among Cricketer, Footballer, Swimmer, Boxer, Wrestler, Racer, Kabaddi player and Tennis player, not necessarily in the same order. They are sitting around a circular table as per the following instructions:*

(i) Dilawar is sitting opposite to the Cricketer and to the left of the Wrestler.
(ii) Farooq is sitting opposite to the Racer and next to the Tennis player who is sitting to the left of Bikki.
(iii) The Footballer is sitting opposite to Ashok and Hetmayer is sitting adjacent to the Boxer.
(iv) Bikki who is sitting next to Gebriel and Chris, sits opposite to the Kabaddi player.
(v) Gebriel is a Footballer and sits between the Cricketer and the Racer, she sits opposite to the Wrestler.
(vi) Eshwer is a Boxer.

34. Who is the Racer?
(a) Dilawar (b) Ashok
(c) Hetmayer (d) None of these

35. What sport does the person who sits opposite to Eshwer play?
(a) Tennis player (b) Cricketer
(c) Racer (d) Swimmer

36. Which of the following combinations is incorrect?
(a) Bikki-Cricketer (b) Chris-Tennis player
(c) Hetmayer-Racer (d) None of these

37. If you are a Swimmer, who are you?
(a) Farooq (b) Dilawar
(c) Hetmayer (d) Ashok

Directions for Questions 38 to 40: *In an annual presentation ceremony of BCCI ten cricketers Rohit, Dhawan, Kohli, Rahane, Yuvraj, Raina, Dhoni, Ashwin, Jadeja and Shami–are to be seated in a row, all facing in the North direction. The following information is also known:*

(i) Exactly 5 players sit between Rahane and Yuvraj.
(ii) Exactly three players sit between Raina and Dhoni.
(iii) Rohit sits to the immediate left of Dhawan who sits to the immediate left of Raina.
(iv) Exactly six players sit between Rohit and Shami.
(v) Exactly six players sit between Dhawan and Kohli.

38. If Yuvraj sits to the immediate right of Raina, then how many players sit between Rahane and Rohit?

39. If there are only two players sitting between Kohli and Rahane, then who sits to the immediate right of Rahane?
(a) Dhoni (b) Yuvraj
(c) Ashwin (d) None of these.

40. Using information from the previous questions, find out how many players sit between Ashwin and Jadeja?

Directions for Questions 41 to 44: *Answer the questions on the basis of information given below.*

Seven friends A, B, C, D, E, F and G live on different floors in a 7-floor apartment. It is also known that:

(i) B lives on the 3rd floor.
(ii) The flat number of A cannot be expressed as the arithmetic mean of two flat numbers of any other friends.
(iii) There are exactly three people living between E and F.
(iv) D lives either on top or bottom floor.
(v) C lives either on 5th or 3rd floor.

41. Find the sum of all possible floor numbers of A.

42. If D lives on the top floor, what can be the maximum possible sum of floor numbers of A, E and F?

43. On which floor does G live?

44. What is the definite sum of floor numbers of A and D?

(a) 13 (b) 8
(c) 11 (d) 12

Directions for Question 45:

45. Abraham, Border, Charlie, Dennis and Elmer and their respective wives recently dined together and were seated at a circular table. The seats were so arranged that men and women alternated and each woman was three places distant from her husband. Mrs. Charlie sat to the left of Mr. Abraham. Mrs. Elmer sat two places to the right of Mrs. Border. Who sat to the right of Mr. Abraham?

(a) Mrs. Dennis
(b) Mrs. Elmer
(c) Mrs. Border
(d) Mrs. Border or Mrs. Dennis

Directions for Question 46:

46. At a village mela, the following six nautankis (plays) are scheduled as shown in the table below.

No.	Nautanki	Duration	Showtimes
A.	*Sati Savitri*	1 hour	9.00 a.m. and 2.00 p.m.
B.	*Joru ka Gulam*	1 hour	10.30 a.m. and 11.30 a.m.
C.	*Sunder Kand*	30 minutes	10.00 a.m. and 11.00 a.m.
D.	*Veer Abhimanyu*	1 hour	10.00 a.m. and 11.00 a.m.
E.	*Reshma aur Shera*	1 hour	9.30 a.m., 12.00 noon and 2.00 p.m.
F.	*Jhansi ki Rani*	30 minutes	11.00 a.m. and 1.30 p.m.

You wish to see all the six nautankis. Further you wish to ensure that you get a lunch break from 12:30 p.m. to 1.30 p.m.

Which of the following ways can you do this?

(a) Sati Savitri is viewed first; Sunder Kand is viewed third and Jhansi Ki Rani is viewed last
(b) Sati Savitri is viewed last; Veer Abhimanyu is viewed third and Reshma aur Shera is viewed first.
(c) Sati Savitri is viewed first; Sunder Kand is viewed third and Joru ka Gulam is viewed fourth
(d) Veer Abhimanyu is viewed third; Reshma aur Shera is viewed fourth and Jhansi Ki Rani is viewed fifth.

Directions for Question 47:

47. Six persons are playing a card game. Suresh is facing Raghubir who is to the left of Ajay and to the right of Pramod. Ajay is to the left of Dhiraj. Yogendra is to the left of Pramod. If Dhiraj exchanges his seat with Yogendra and Pramod exchanges with Raghubir, who will be sitting to the left of Dhiraj?

(a) Yogendra (b) Raghubir
(c) Suresh (d) Ajay

LEVEL OF DIFFICULTY (II)

Directions for Questions 1 to 4: *Refer to the data below and answer the questions that follow.*

A, B, C, D, E, F, G and H are the eight professors teaching in different departments of a University. They are seated across a rectangular table on chairs, such that each longer side of the table has four chairs each. One professor belongs to the Department of Accountancy.

High Yield Questions

Scan this QR code to access a video explanation of questions 1-4

The following points are known:

(i) The professor of Sociology is seated opposite to the professor of Law.
(ii) A is seated opposite to the professor of Political Science.
(iii) The professor of History is seated second to the left of the professor of Economics on the same side of the table. The professor of Economics sits opposite to D.
(iv) Exactly one professor is seated between the professors of Law and Humanities on the same side of the table.
(v) The professor of Taxation is seated third to the right of H on the same side of the table. H is seated opposite to the professor of Humanities.

1. If G is seated second to the right of C, which of the following departments can G belong to?

(a) Law (b) Economics
(c) History (d) Political Science

2. If B is the only professor who is seated between F and the professor of Accountancy, which department does B belong to?
   (a) Sociology (b) Taxation
   (c) Law (d) Cannot be determined
3. **Additional information:** H and the professor of History swap their seats.
   Which of the following statements cannot be correct?
   (a) Professors of Accountancy and Law are seated next to each other.
   (b) Professors of History and Accountancy are seated next to each other.
   (c) Professors of Political Science and Economics are seated next to each other.
   (d) Professors of History and Accountancy are seated farthest apart from each other.
4. **Additional information:** H and the professor of History swap their seats.
   Which of the following statements can be correct?
   (a) The professor of Accountancy is seated between the professors of History and Sociology on the same side of the table.
   (b) The professor of Sociology is seated between the professors of Taxation and History on the same side of the table.
   (c) The professor of Law is seated between the professors of Humanities and Economics on the same side of the table.
   (d) The professor of Accountancy is seated between the professors of Taxation and Economics on the same side of the table.

Directions for Questions 5 to 8: *Refer to the data below and answer the questions that follow.*

Hazratganj is a popular shopping destination in Lucknow. It has five cinema halls - Naya ghar(N), Chidiya ghar(C), West coast hall(W), Benett Hall(B) and Elvis Hall(E). Five different movies - DON, KICK, JAWAN, PATHAN and CHAVVA - were shown over five consecutive days on these cinema halls. Each movie was shown in a different cinema hall every day. Similarly, each cinema hall had shown a different movie every day. The following points are known:

(i) In all the cinema halls, except Chidiya ghar, KICK was shown before CHAVVA.
(ii) DON was the third movie to be shown on Benett Hall, and it was shown after PATHAN.
(iii) PATHAN was shown on two other cinema halls prior to West coast hall, and was shown on Naya ghar immediately after it was shown on West coast hall.

5. Which movie was shown on the first day on Chidiya ghar?
   (a) JAWAN (b) CHAVVA
   (c) PATHAN (d) Cannot be determined
6. On which cinema hall KICK shown on the fourth day?
   (a) Benett Hall (b) Naya ghar
   (c) Chidiya ghar (d) Cannot be determined
7. Which of the following is the correct order of cinema halls (from first day to fifth day) on which JAWAN was shown?
   (a) Benett Hall, Naya ghar, Chidiya ghar , West coast hall, Elvis Hall
   (b) West coast hall, Elvis Hall, Naya ghar, Chidiya ghar, Benett Hall
   (c) Elvis Hall, Benett Hall, Chidiya ghar, West coast hall, Naya ghar
   (d) Cannot be determined
8. On which cinema hall was CHAVVA shown immediately on the next day after it was shown on Naya ghar?
   (a) Benett hall
   (b) Elvis hall
   (c) Chidiya ghar
   (d) Cannot be determined

Directions for Questions 9 to 12: *Refer to the data below and answer the questions that follow: Eight friends A, B, C, D, E, F, G and H sit in a circular arrangement (equidistant from each other) facing the centre of the circular table wearing shoes of one of the three colors viz. Black, Brown or Blue. Following conditions about their seating arrangement are given:*

(i) A and B do not sit opposite or adjacent to each other.
(ii) C sits second to the left of H who in turn sits to the immediate right of D.
(iii) E and F have exactly two people between them but A is not one of them.
(iv) E sits next to H, but not next to G.
(v) No two adjacent people wear same coloured shoes.
(vi) The person opposite to G wears Black shoes.
(vii) A, F and B do not wear Brown shoes.
(viii) Exactly three people wear Brown shoes.
(ix) F does not sit opposite a person wearing Blue shoes.

9. Who sits opposite E?
   (a) D (b) A
   (c) G (d) C
10. At least how many people sit between G and D?
    (a) Three (b) Four
    (c) Two (d) One
11. If exactly two people wear Blue shoes and F is one of them then who is the other person?
    (a) E (b) H
    (c) B (d) Cannot be determined
12. At least how many people definitely wear Black shoes?
    (a) Two (b) One
    (c) Three (d) Four

Directions for Questions 13 to 16: *Refer to the data below and answer the questions that follow: Four couples, i.e., the Guptas, the Patels, the Khannas and the Shahs join a party. They sit on equally spaced chairs around a circular table facing the centre of the table. Following conditions have to be abided by:*

(i) No husband and wife sit next to each other.
(ii) No two husbands sit next to each other.
(iii) Mrs. Patel sits opposite to Mrs. Khanna.

13. In how many ways, can these four couples be seated?

14. If Mrs. Shah and Mr. Patel sit next to each other then who sits opposite to Mr. Shah?
(a) Mr. Khanna (b) Mrs. Patel
(c) Mr. Gupta (d) Cannot be determined

15. If Mr. Gupta and Mrs. Khanna are adjacent to each other then who among the following is to the right of Mr. Shah?
(a) Mrs. Gupta (b) Mrs. Patel
(c) Mrs. Khanna (d) Either a or b

16. If all the female members are made to face outside and all the male members face inside then which of the following is definitely false?
(a) Mrs. Khanna is third to the right of Mr. Khanna.
(b) Mr. Gupta is second to the left of Mr. Patel.
(c) Mrs. Shah is always to the right of Mr. Gupta.
(d) Mrs. Khanna is to the immediate left of Mr. Gupta.

Directions for Questions 17 to 20: *Beljamin is in love with his own name and does not do anything apart from chanting his own name. His mother wanted him to appear for CAT, and hence, wanted him to start enjoying solving puzzles. For this purpose she got a special game created for him. In this game, she got wooden letters carved for the letters of his name B, E, L, J, A, M, I, N. She then asked Beljamin to rearrange all these letters and make a new word subject to the following instructions:*

(i) No letter other than the two vowels 'E' and 'I' in the original word can occupy adjacent positions (immediately to the right or immediately to the left of its position in the original word) in the new word.
(ii) Exactly two letters in the word 'BELJAMIN' retain their original position in the new word.
(iii) The letter A must precede the letter M and there are exactly three letters between them.
(iv) The letters B, A and L must be together with B and L being adjacent to each other.
(v) The 'E' occupies the extreme left position and the letter 'I" occupies the extreme right position.

High Yield Questions
Scan this QR code to access a video explanation of questions 17-20

17. How many new words can be formed that satisfy all the conditions?

18. Which two letters retain their original position in the new word?
(a) Both L and A (b) Both L and M
(c) Both M and A (d) Cannot be determined

19. Letter 'B' in the new word is the only letter between which of the following two letters?
(a) L and N (b) L and M
(c) M and N (d) Cannot be determined

20. Which letter is third to the right of 'L' in the new word?
(a) M (b) E
(c) I (d) None of the above

Directions for Questions 21 to 24: *Answer the questions on the basis of the information given below.*

Six ladies, meeting at a reading retreat- Alice, Barbara, Claire, Donna, Estaire and Fiona having favourite colours as Grey, Maroon, Lilac, Lavender, Coral and Peach, not necessarily in the same order, are sitting around a circular reading table, all facing the center of the table.

(i) Ladies having Grey and Maroon as their favourite colours are sitting opposite to each other.
(ii) Ladies with names starting with a vowel are neither sitting opposite to each other nor adjacent to each other.
(iii) Barbara and Claire are best friends and always sit together. Neither of them has maroon as their favorite color.
(iv) Ladies having favourite colours as Peach and Coral are not sitting next to each other.
(v) Alice loves the colour Grey.
(vi) Estaire does not like Coral.

21. If Claire's favourite colour is Peach and Estaire does not like the colour Coral then who cannot be next to the person who likes Coral?
(a) Lady who loves the colour Lilac
(b) Estaire
(c) Lady who loves Lavender
(d) Lady who loves Maroon

22. If Barbara likes Coral and Estaire does not like Peach, then at most how many ladies can be seated between the ladies who like Peach and Maroon? (TITA)

23. If the lady who likes Maroon is on the immediate right side of Estaire then who is the lady on the immediate left of Estaire?
(a) Lady who likes the colour Lilac
(b) Lady who likes the colour Lavender
(c) Either Donna or Fiona
(d) Lady who likes either the colour Lilac or Lavender

24. Which of the following options is not possible?
   (a) Barbara likes Maroon and Estaire likes Coral
   (b) Barbara likes Lavender and Claire likes Lilac
   (c) Donna likes Maroon and Fiona likes Lavender
   (d) Claire likes Lavender and Fiona likes Coral

Directions for Questions 25 to 26: *Answer the questions on the basis of the information given below.*

I was expecting deliveries from 6 posts for my birthday from 6 different postal services named- Super late, Late, On-time, Quick, Quicker and Quickest. The Sent-in time is the time at which the person sending the post dispatches it and the Receiving time is the time at which I collect it. No two services have the same Sent-in and Receiving time. The following information is also known:

(i) The postal service which was sent-in first was received first and the one that was sent-in last was received last. Except for these 2, no other posts were sent-in and received in the same order number.
(ii) The Late postal service is always received by me just after Quick postal service delivery but always starts before it.
(iii) The On-Time postal service is always sent-in third and the Quickest postal service is always received by me the fifth.

25. If the Quickest postal service starts before On-time postal, then which of the following is necessarily true?
   (i) The Quickest postal delivery was received just after the Late postal service.
   (ii) The On-time postal service delivery was received just after the Quickest postal service.
   (iii) The Late postal service delivery was received third by me.
   (a) Only (i) and (iii) (b) Only (ii) and (iii)
   (c) Only (ii) (d) None of these
26. If Super Late postal service started first and Quicker delivery was received last, then in how many ways can different deliveries be made?

Directions for Questions 27 to 30: *Answer the questions on the basis of the information given below.*

Eight students, A, B, C, D, E, F, G and H are sitting in a circular arrangement with one of the 3 things in their hands- a pen, a pencil or a book. Following conditions about their seating arrangement is given:

(i) E and H do not sit opposite or adjacent to each other
(ii) D sits second to the left of B who in turn sits to the immediate right of C.
(iii) A and F have exactly two people between them but E is not one of them.
(iv) A sits next to B, but not next to G.
(v) No two adjacent people have the same item in their hands.
(vi) The person opposite to G has a pen.
(vii) E, F and H do not have a pencil in their hands
(viii) Exactly three people have a pencil.
(ix) F does not sit opposite to a person holding a book

27. Who sits opposite to A?
   (a) C (b) E
   (c) G (d) D
28. At least how many people sit between G and C?
29. If exactly two people have a book and F is one of them then who is the other person?
   (a) A (b) B
   (c) H (d) Cannot be determined
30. At least how many people definitely have a pen?

Directions for Questions 31 to 34: *There are 12 students, of which 6 are senior students: A, B, C, D, E, F and 6 are junior students: G, H, I, J, K and L. Each senior and junior student wears dresses of different colours among red, yellow, blue, white, orange and pink (i.e. one senior and one junior student wear a red dress, one of each wears a yellow dress and so on). The 12 students sit in a circle with the students wearing the same colour dress sharing the same seat. The students wearing red sit between yellow and blue dressed students. J wears a white dress. The white dressed students sit opposite L who is in blue colour. Students with the orange dress are adjacent to H. A and H share the same seat. I is adjacent to the students wearing blue and pink dresses. B is to the immediate right of E, who is opposite to K.*

31. Who among the following is definitely sitting opposite the students wearing pink?
   (a) G (b) C
   (c) D (d) J
32. If C sits opposite L, which of the following cannot be true?
   (a) F is wearing yellow
   (b) F is wearing orange
   (c) D is wearing yellow
   (d) None of these
33. Which of the following definitely represents people wearing the same color dress?
   (a) I, E (b) L, C
   (c) J, F (d) J, C
34. If C and F do not sit next to each other, then which of the following is definitely true?
   (a) D wears blue (b) D wears white
   (c) D wears yellow (d) D wears red

Directions for Questions 35 to 40: *Ankur has 14 first cousins. All of them gathered for his wedding. They were all* *sitting together for the reception dinner. Seven of them - Amit, Baldev, Charan, Devashish, Eeshwarya, Falguni and Gony- want to sit in Row-1 facing South, while Prince, Quindal, Ravi, Seeta, Tanuj and Urvashi want to sit in Row-2 facing North. However, each row on the table had only 6 chairs, so 1 cousin in each row did not find a place to sit and had to leave. Each sitting cousin was facing another sitting cousin from the other row. Their ages (in years) were among - 8, 9, 10, 11, 12, 14, 15, 16, 17, 18, 19, 22, 23 and 26 - in any order. It is also known that:*

Ravi is older than Amit but younger than Charan, and all of them are sitting. Only two cousins were sitting between Devashish and Charan, and Devashish is 4 years older than Tanuj. Baldev is the youngest and sits opposite to Quindal who is 18 years old. The ages of each of the persons sitting at the extreme ends of both the rows are prime numbers. Prince, whose age is a multiple of 7, was sitting second to the right of Seeta. The sum of the ages of the persons who were sitting at the extreme ends of Row- 2 is 36 with Tanuj being one of them. Urvashi was sitting at an equidistant position from both Ravi and Tanuj (Tanuj being to her right) and the sum of the ages of Urvashi and the one who was sitting to her immediate left is 23. The sum of the ages of Falguni and the one who was sitting opposite to her is 30. Eeshwarya who is an immediate neighbour of Devashish, is 2 years older than Prince. The oldest cousin and Amit who was not well, were given places to sit. Moreover, cousins with ages being a multiple of 5 managed to sit.

35. What were the sum of ages of the cousins who were not sitting at the dinner table?
(a) 32 (b) 34
(c) 31 (d) None of these

36. What was the position of the cousin aged 26 years with respect to the one aged 8 years ?
(a) Second to the left (b) Immediate right
(c) Second to the right (d) Third to the right

37. Which of the following options, does not contain any cousin who is sitting at the extreme ends of any of the rows? (All cousin names are denoted by the first alphabet of their respective names)
(a) B,C,Q and S (b) E,P,R and F
(c) A,C,P and U (d) D,F,S and T

38. The sum of the ages of two cousins sitting opposite to each other shows its highest value for which pair of cousins?
(a) C and R (b) C and U
(c) D and S (d) E and R

39. For pairs not sitting in the extreme positions in the rows, what is the least sum of ages for any pair of opposite cousins?

40. For any pair of two cousins sitting adjacent to each other, what is the maximum sum of their ages?

Directions for Questions 41 to 44: *Amar, Pankaj, Tanuj, Sameep, Ravi and Chetan each have an apartment on a different floor of Jagat Amravati apartments, a six floor building on Bailey Road, Patna. They all live in their own apartments. On a particular day, each of these six people left their apartments to their respective office at different times. The following information is further known about the order in which the six persons left for their office and the floor their apartment is on:*

(i) The person who was first to leave his apartment did not have his apartment either on the 4th floor or the 2nd floor, while the person who was last to leave his apartment did not live on the 5th floor.
(ii) The person who lived on the 2nd floor left for office immediately before the person who lived on the 5th floor.
(iii) Pankaj who did not live on the 4th floor, left for office immediately before Amar who was a resident of a first floor apartment.
(iv) Ravi who lives on the 6th floor, left for office immediately before the person who has an apartment on the 4th floor.
(v) Chetan whose apartment was not on the fifth floor, left for office immediately after Tanuj left for office but both of them left for their office before Ravi left for his office.

41. Who was the last person to leave for office?
(a) Amar (b) Sameep
(c) Chetan (d) Tanuj

42. How many persons left for office before Amar did?
(a) 0 (b) 1
(c) 2 (d) More than 2

43. What is the floor number of the person who left for office immediately before the person who lives on 6th floor?
(a) 2nd floor (b) 3rd floor
(c) 1st floor (d) None of the above

44. If the number 1 is assigned to the person who left for office first, number 2 to the person who left for office 2nd and so on, for which of the following person is the number assigned to them same as the floor number their of their apartment?
(a) Chetan
(b) Ravi
(c) Amar
(d) More than one of the above

Directions for Questions 45 to 48: *Answer the following questions on the basis of information given below.*

During the school Parade eight students A, B, C, D, E, F, G and H stand in four rows and each row has exactly two students. Each student is facing north. The following information is also known:

(i) C is standing on the right side in the 2nd row.
(ii) A and G are standing in the same row.
(iii) D and F are standing in the same row.
(iv) D and G are standing on the same side of the row.
(v) Either A or H (but not both) stands on the right side and neither of them is standing in the 4th row.
(vi) B and E are standing on the same side of the row.

45. Who amongst the following is on the right side of his respective row?
(a) A (b) G
(c) B (d) E

46. If G is in 1st row, what is the sum of row numbers of B and E.

47. Further information to question number 46 is given as: If B stands in 3rd row, who is in the same row as E?

48. Which of the following is correct?
(a) A stands in 3rd row and C stands in 4th row.
(b) G can only stand in 1st or 3rd row.
(c) If A stands in 3rd row and D may/may not stand in 1st row.
(d) Only if A stands in 3rd row, D can stand in 1st row.

Directions for Questions 49 to 53: *Answer the questions on the basis of the information given below.*

Five couples are sitting around a regular pentagonal table, with two persons along each edge. Among the five couples, Aman, Baman, Charan, Dhawan and Emaan are male members and Alisha, Binny, Chiranjeevi, Denny and Emmi are female members. It is also known that (i) Persons sitting along the same edge are neither of the same gender nor married to each other. (ii) Emaan is sitting three places to the left of his wife, Chiranjeevi. (iii) Baman is equidistant from Aman and Emmi, who are not married to each other. (iv) Members of none of the couples, except Alisha and Baman, are sitting next to each other. (v) Dhawan, who is married to neither Denny nor Emmi, is sitting five places to the right of Alisha. (vi) Charan is sitting three places to the right of Dhawan and four places to the left of Binny.

49. Who is Aman's wife?

50. Who is sitting three places to the right of Baman?
(a) Binny (b) Denny
(c) Emmi (d) Emaan

51. Who is sitting between Dhawan and Chiranjeevi?
(a) Emaan (b) Denny
(c) Charan (d) Cannot be determined

52. Which of the following pairs represents a pair sitting along one edge?
(a) Chiranjeevi- Charan (b) Dhawan - Denny
(c) Both (a) and (b) (d) None of these

53. Who is the wife of Dhawan?

Directions for Questions 54 to 58: *Twelve people Aaliya, Abraam, Fahim, Harish, Jack, Mark, Mohnish, Sadiq, Sahil, Shanti, Tariq and Vineet are sitting at a -rectangular table. The table has 12 chairs numbered from 1 to 12 (see figure) and each chair is occupied by one of the 12 people (not necessarily in the same order). Some additional information is given below:*

(i) Mark is diagonally opposite to Fahim who is sitting opposite to Harish.
(ii) Jack is sitting opposite to Sahil who is the only person sitting between Abraam and Vineet.
(iii) Aaliya is sitting opposite to Tariq who is the only person sitting between Fahim and Shanti.
(iv) Mark is sitting at chair number 1.

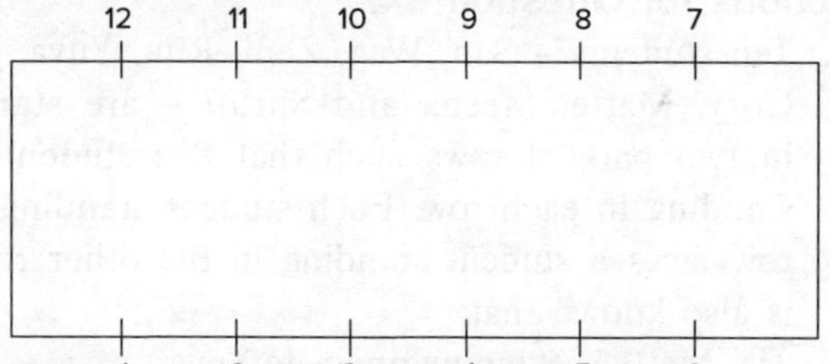

54. How many arrangements are possible?

55. What is the position of Tariq?

56. If Mark is sitting opposite to Sadiq and Shanti is sitting opposite to Vineet, then what is the seat number of Abraam?

57. If Shanti is not sitting opposite to Vineet, then who is sitting next to Mark?
(a) Abraam (b) Jack
(c) Vineet (d) Either Jack or Vineet

58. If Sadiq is sitting at one of the corner seats, then who is sitting opposite to him?
(a) Mark (b) Jack
(c) Harish (d) Aaliya

Directions for Questions 59 to 63: *Answer the questions on the basis of the information given below.*

Ten employees - Cheteshwar, Bantuklal, Dinesh, Gotya, Elangovan, Capoor, Janardan, Pankaj, Krish and Harender - work in a building that has six floors numbered 1 to 6 (lowest to highest). Each floor is occupied by at least one of the ten employees. If F(x) represents the number of employees living on floor x, then $F(1) = F(6) \neq F(3)$ and $F(2) = F(5)$. Also, $F(1) < F(2)$.

Also, $F(x) \neq F(x+1)$ for x = 1 to 5. It is also known that:

(i) Dinesh works on a higher floor as compared to Capoor, Janardan and Harender but on a lower floor as compared to Cheteshwar.
(ii) Both Cheteshwar and Bantuklal work on the floor that is immediately above the floor on which Krish works.
(iii) Gotya and Pankaj work on the same floor.
(iv) The number of employees who work on the floor on which Janardan works is equal to that on which Elangovan works.

59. On which floor does Dinesh Work?

60. Who works on floor-4?

61. What is the difference between the number of employees who work on floors 3 and 5?

62. Who among the following works on floor 6?
(a) Elangovan (b) Dinesh
(c) Cheteshwar (d) Gotya

63. How many employees work on a floor higher than on which Janardan works?

Directions for Question 64:

64. Ten students - San, Wag, Zeni, Rita, Yuva, Inna, Cory, Matte, Meena and Shruti - are standing in two parallel rows such that five students are standing in each row. Each student standing in a row faces a student standing in the other row. It is also known that:
(i) Matte is standing opposite Yuva.
(ii) Rita is standing to the immediate right of Meena and opposite Wag.
(iii) No student is standing to the left of both Zeni and Shruti.
(iv) The number of students standing between Inna and Matte is the same as the number of students standing between Meena and San.

Which of the following statements cannot be true?
(a) Inna is standing opposite Zeni.
(b) Shruti is standing opposite San.
(c) The number of students standing between Cory and Matte is the same as the number of students standing between Shruti and Meena.
(d) The number of students standing to the left of Cory is the same as the number of students standing to the left of Yuva.

Directions for Questions 65 to 69: IIM Timbuktu invited seven faculties from Mindworkzz, a CAT Prep academy led by Arun Sharma, to give a speech at the campus. Although the college had ample seating capacity, it had advised the faculties to arrive 15 mins before the event to avoid any inconvenience. However, the circular table on which the speakers were made to sit had only 6 seats. On enquiry the college mentioned that they had planned it that way, since they knew that there will be one speaker at any point of time on the dais and only 6 people would be seated. The faculties decided their order of speaking amongst themselves and also that, the current speaker would take the seat vacated by the next speaker, when he/she moves to the dais for the speech. The speaker would then come back to occupy the seat vacated by the person speaking next.

High Yield Questions
Scan this QR code to access a video explanation of questions 65-69

At the beginning of the event, Mrs. Meenakshi Upadhyay was sitting opposite to Mr. Virendra Mahajan, who occupied at most one seat during the whole event. These two also occupied the same seat at some point during the event. Mr. Arun Sharma was sitting next to Mr. Mahajan at the beginning. Mr. Saeed Khan, who was to the left of Mr. Sharma at the beginning, gave his speech immediately after the person who was sitting to his right. Mr. Anit Suri sat on 2 different seats during the event, neither of which were opposite to any seat in which Meenakshi was sitting. Mr. Vinay Singh only occupied seats which were opposite to each other during the whole conference.

65. Who was sitting opposite Mr. Suri while the third person gave his speech?
(a) Arun Chaturvedi (b) Arun Sharma
(c) Vinay Singh (d) Saeed Khan

66. Who among the following was not sitting opposite Mr. Sharma at any point during the conference?
(a) Vinay Singh
(b) Anit Suri
(c) Arun Chaturvedi
(d) Meenakshi Upadhyay

67. Who was sitting opposite Vinay when Mr. Chaturvedi was giving his speech?
(a) Arun Sharma
(b) Saeed Khan
(c) Virendra Mahajan
(d) Meenakshi Upadhyay

68. Who was sitting to the left of Meenakshi when the last person was giving his speech?
(a) Arun Sharma (b) Saeed Khan
(c) Arun Chaturvedi (d) Vinay Singh

69. Who among the seven faculties could have given the closing speech?
(a) Arun Sharma (b) Anit Suri
(c) Vinay Singh (d) Virendra Mahajan

Directions for Questions 70 to 74: Seven employees: Amit, Bharat, Chaitanya, Dhruv, Ebrahim, Farrokh and Gautam are travelling from Delhi to Mumbai in the new

D-M train specially running from Delhi to Mumbai. In the train, the seating is arranged in 15 rows, numbered 1 to 15, consisting of 6 seats marked by A to F, from left to right, respectively. The seats located on the left side of the aisle are labelled as A to C, while the seats on the right side are labelled as D to F. Window seats are positioned at A and F, while aisle seats are located at C and D. The seats in the middle are marked as B and E. Consecutive seats refer to seats with letters that appear one after the other, indicating that they are next to each other. A seat's identification is formed by the row number and the letter which shows its position in that row. For instance, 1B represents the left middle seat in the 1st row, and 12F represents the right window seat in the 12th row.

1. All of them were seated in 5 different rows.
2. DM Train charges 1000 extra for any seats in the rows 1, 6 and 7, as they have extra legroom and luggage space. For Rows 2-4, it charges 300 for window seats and 500 for aisle seats. For rows 5, 8-10, it charges ₹200 extra for window and ₹300 extra for aisle. All other seats are available at no extra charge.
3. Six of them had to pay extra amounts, totalling to ₹3600, for their choices of seat. One of them did not pay any additional amount for his/her choice of seat.
4. Amit, Chaitanya and Bharat were sitting in seats marked by the same letter, in consecutive rows in increasing order of row numbers; but all of them paid different amounts for their choices of seat. One of these amounts may be zero.
5. Dhruv was sitting next to Amit
6. Gautam was sitting next to Bharat
7. Farrokh and Ebrahim were sitting in seats marked by the same letter, in consecutive rows in increasing order of row numbers; but they paid different amounts for their choices of seat. One of these amounts may be zero.
8. Gautam sits in the same column as Dhruv and both of them sit on the left side of the plane.

70. In which row does A sit?
(a) 4 (b) 3
(c) 8 (d) 10

71. In which Row does F sit?
(a) 10 (b) 12
(c) 13 (d) 8

72. What is the amount paid by B and G together for their seats?
(a) 1500 (b) 2000
(c) 1800 (d) 800

73. In which seat does G sit?
(a) Aisle
(b) Middle
(c) Window
(d) Cannot be determined

74. Who is not paying any money?
(a) Dhruv (b) Gautam
(c) Farrokh (d) Ebrahim

ANSWER KEY

Level of Difficulty (I)

1. (c)	2. (b)	3. (d)	4. (b)
5. (d)	6. (b)	7. (c)	8. (b)
9. (a)	10. (a)	11. (a)	12. (a)
13. (d)	14. (a)	15. (c)	16. (c)
17. (d)	18. (a)	19. (b)	20. (d)
21. (b)	22. (c)	23. (b)	24. (d)
25. (c)	26. (d)	27. (b)	28. (c)
29. (a)	30. (c)	31. (b)	32. (a)
33. (d)	34. (c)	35. (a)	36. (d)
37. (a)	38. 8	39. (a)	40. 0
41. 8	42. 9	43. 4th floor	44. (b)
45. (d)	46. (c)	47. (c)	

Level of Difficulty (II)

1. (b)	2. (a)	3. (c)	4. (a)
5. (b)	6. (a)	7. (c)	8. (b)
9. (b)	10. (a)	11. (d)	12. (c)
13. 4	14. (c)	15. (d)	16. (c)
17. 1	18. (b)	19. (a)	20. (a)
21. (d)	22. 1	23. (c)	24. (b)
25. (d)	26. 2	27. (b)	28. 3
29. (d)	30. 3	31. (a)	32. (b)
33. (a)	34. (c)	35. (b)	36. (b)
37. (c)	38. (c)	39. 24	40. 39
41. (b)	42. (d)	43. (c)	44. (a)
45. (b)	46. 5	47. Student C	48. (b)
49. Denny	50. (d)	51. (b)	52. (c)
53. Binny	54. 8	55. 8	56. 2nd
57. (d)	58. (a)	59. 3	60. Krish
61. 1	62. (a)	63. 9	64. (c)
65. (b)	66. (d)	67. (a)	68. (d)
69. (d)	70. (a)	71. (a)	72. (b)
73. (a)	74. (d)		

SOLUTIONS AND SHORTCUTS

Level of Difficulty (I)

Solutions for Questions 1 to 5:

For this question, start by using the direct clues first.

We know that there are six balls P, Q, R, S, T, U; six colours-blue, red, green, grey, yellow and brown and, six pictures on the balls-Triangle, Square, Heptagon, Pentagon, Hexagon and Octagon.

The following set of deductions gives us the entire solution of the problem.

The second part of the third statement is the most directly usable → P-Brown-Heptagon-Extreme right. We also know that R-Triangle-Grey-Fifth from Right (iv statement).

Also, Q being next to R, the following arrangements are possible.

Possibility Table 1:

Q	R	--	--	--	P
	Triangle				Heptagon
	Grey				Brown

Possibility Table 2:

	R	Q	--	--	P
	Triangle				Heptagon
	Grey				Brown

From this point we start using the indirect clues.

From statement (iii), Pentagon-Blue-Not S → Hence T or U Further, from statement (iv), Square – Not S and not T, → Not Green or Yellow → Hence, Red and U. This further gives us Pentagon–T-Blue.

Hence, S must be the hexagon (only pair left). Also, green and yellow must be shared between Q and S.

Thus, the following pairings emerge:

P – Brown – Heptagon
Q – Green/Yellow – Octagon
R – Grey – Triangle
S – Yellow/Green –Hexagon
T – Blue –Pentagon
U – Red – Square

At this point we have used all the statements. Hence, go straight into the questions.

1. For the Square ball (U) to be placed immediately in between the Pentagon (T) and the Octagon (Q), Possibility Table 2 must emerge to be the correct one. In such a case, the arrangement of balls becomes: SRQUTP. Hence, the Hexagon's balls must be at the extreme left. Option (c) is correct. The remaining 4 questions can be directly answered from what is available.
2. U-Red is correct. Option (b) is correct.
3. Data inadequate since we don't know whether the Hexagon is Yellow or Green. Option (d) is correct.
4. The Pentagon is on Ball T. Option (b) is correct.
5. Data remains inadequate since we do not know which colour is for which ball. Option (d) is correct.

Solutions for Questions 6 to 8:

Basic information:

Six persons A, B, C, D, E and F on six days, Monday to Saturday; six posts – Clerk (C), Officer (O), Technician (T), Manager (M), Supervisor (S) and Sales Executive (SE).

The second paragraph gives the clues directly to fit in the following table:

A → Sales Executive	
B →	X Wednesday, X Friday
C →	Thursday
D → Technician	Tuesday
E → Clerk	Monday
F → Manager	

We also know that the officer joined on Wednesday. It can only be Celina (C). Thus, the table will look like:

A → Sales Executive	Friday
B → Supervisor	Saturday
C → Officer	Wednesday
D → Technician	Thursday
E → Clerk	Tuesday
F → Manager	Monday

Thus the answers are:

6. Celina (b)
7. Bobby (c)
8. Friday (b)

Solutions for Questions 9 to 11:

The arrangement is:

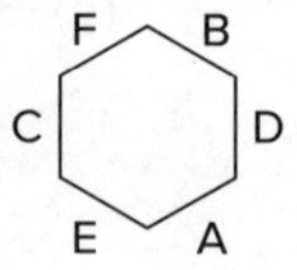

Hence,

9. (a) D & E
10. (a) E
11. (a) B & C

Solutions for Questions 12 to 15:

Since Chandan-Bony (C-B) and Abdul-Devdas (A-D) are definitely next to each other, in that order (Note: C is to the right of B will be represented by C-B when they are facing south), Eram (E) will definitely be in the centre place (as he is not at the end).

This gives us two possible arrangements for the men:

(1) <u>C B E A D</u>   or   (2) <u>A D E C B</u>

(2) is not possible since Abdul has to be second to Bony's left.

Thus the arrangement is:

C	B	E	A	D
R/S	Q	S/R	P	T

(Where Paro, Queen, Reena, Saifali and Tulika are represented by P, Q, R, S, T respectively)

The answers are:

12. Chandan and Devdas (a)
13. (d)
14. Eram (a)
15. Queen (c)

Solutions for Questions 16 to 19:

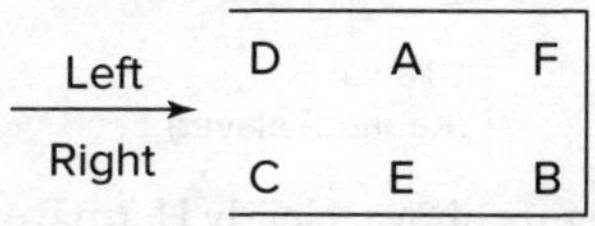

From the last sentence, we get that F is also on the left side, so E will be on the right side. D will be on the left side. E does not have a corner office, so he must be in the middle. E and F do not face each other and F's office is further down the corridor, so F occupies the last office on the left side. Office of C and D face each other, so C will have the first office on the right side and D will have the first office on the left side.

The answers are:

16. (c) C's office is on E's left.
17. (d) E's office faces A's office.
18. (a) Only A is F's neighbour.
19. (b) He was giving directions to reach B's office.

Solutions for Questions 20 to 24:

The following reaction tracker table would help you solve this question set.

Reaction Tracker Table

<table>
<tr><th>Opening Paragraph</th><th>4 families, one with no kid and others with at least one kid each</th></tr>
<tr><td>Statement (i)</td><td>(Family with 2 kids-Family with no kids)
At this point, we just make a visual representation of this clue. It is not directly usable as it gives many possibilities.
Further, it is also now known to us that we are trying to create a structure of the order in which the respective families come in. Mentally, we picture this as:<table><tr><td></td><td></td><td></td><td></td></tr></table></td></tr>
<tr><td>Statement (ii)</td><td>D reached just before C. Not usable at this point. Also D has no kids.</td></tr>
<tr><td>Statement (iii)</td><td>Usable at this point<table><tr><td></td><td></td><td></td><td>P & Wife</td></tr><tr><td></td><td></td><td></td><td>Only kid</td></tr></table></td></tr>
<tr><td>Statement (iv)</td><td>Q is not the husband of B (means B is female). Again, this clue is not directly usable.</td></tr>
<tr><td>Statement (v)</td><td>Q and S are fathers. Hence, males. Not usable at this point.</td></tr>
<tr><td>Statement (vi)</td><td>A and C have daughters. Not usable at this point.</td></tr>
<tr><td>Statement (vii)</td><td>A – B – D. Add the reaction of C coming after D (Statement ii) and we get the entire structure for the 4 women's arrival. The table now becomes.<table><tr><td>A</td><td>B</td><td>D</td><td>C</td></tr><tr><td></td><td></td><td>No kids</td><td>1 kid</td></tr></table>Add Statement (i)'s reaction and the table further evolves to:<table><tr><td>A</td><td>B</td><td>D</td><td>C</td></tr><tr><td>Daughter</td><td>2 kids</td><td>No kids</td><td>1 kid</td></tr></table>Now concentrate on the husbands (Q, R & S)</td></tr>
<tr><td>Statement (viii)</td><td>No information</td></tr>
</table>

Opening Paragraph	4 families, one with no kid and others with at least one kid each
Statement (ix)	S must have 2 kids. Since his son has not come and it is known that every family which has kids has at least 1 kid coming to the picnic. Thus the table now evolves to the following:

Q-A	S – B	R – D	P & C
Daughter	2 kids	No kids	1 kid

Note: Since Q is a father, he cannot be D's husband and R is D's only possible husband.

Hence, the answers are:

20. (d)
21. (b)
22. (c)
23. (b)
24. (d)

Solutions for Questions 25 to 28:

Reaction Tracker

Statement	Reaction
Statement 1	----, ----, ----, ----, ----, ----, ---- A, B, C, D, E, F and G
Statement 2 and 3	----, ----, ----, B, ---- A, G OR ----, ----, ----, B, --- G, A.
Statement 4	1st and 5th places must be occupied by C and D in any order.

Hence, the answers are:

25. The end seats have to be occupied by either A, G, C or D. F cannot occupy any end seat. Hence, option (c) is correct.
26. For E and A to be together, the only way is to put E on the 5th seat. But this is not possible since the 5th seat has to have either C or D. Hence, option (d) is the correct answer.
27. One of the seats adjacent to B has to be taken by either C or D. Hence, option (b) is the correct answer.
28. C can be third or seventh. Hence, option (c) is correct.

Solutions for Questions 29 to 33:

From the clues, it is evident that ACEB should be 4 people in that order and should be sitting together with no one in between. This means that they can be seated in one of the following 3 ways:

Possibility 1: A C E B _ _

Possibility 2: _ A C E B _

Possibility 3: _ _ A C E B

This leaves us to place two people–D and F. Since, Devdas is not at the end and Ferguson is not at the right end, we know that Possibility 1 and Possibility 2 get rejected. This leaves us with Possibility 3 and the final placement would be:

F D A C E B

The answers are:

29. (a)
30. (c)
31. (b)
32. (a)
33. (d)

Solutions for Questions 34 to 37:

We can represent the textual information diagrammatically in the following circular arrangement.

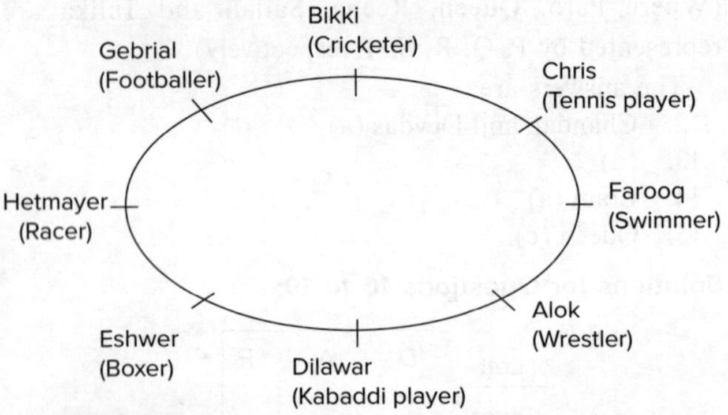

34. From the figure above, clearly Hetmayer is the Racer. Hence, option (c) is correct.
35. Opposite to Eshwer sits Chris who is a Tennis player. Hence, option (a) is correct.
36. All choices are correct, hence, the correct answer is (d) None is incorrect.
37. I am Farooq, the Swimmer. Hence, option (a) is correct.

Solutions for Questions 38 to 40:

Let's represent Rohit (P), Dhawan (Q), Kohli (R), Rahane (S), Yuvraj (T), Raina (U), Dhoni (V), Ashwin (W), Jadeja (X) and Shami (Y) by P, Q, R, S, T, U, V, W, X, Y, respectively. Let's mark the seats from 1 to 10 from left to right.

According to statement-(iii), P, Q, U sit together in the same order. Therefore, P cannot sit at 9 or 10. If P sits on seat 8 then Y sits on seat-1 (statement (iv)). Then R, Q, U sit on seat-2, 9, 10. According to statement-(i), there are 5 players between S (Rahane) and T (Yuvraj). But if 'P' sits on seat-8, this is not possible, therefore, this case is not possible.

Now, following cases are possible:

Case A: P occupies seat-1.

If 'P' occupies seat-1 then Q and U occupy seats 2 and 3 respectively and Y sits on seat-8 and R sits on seat-9 (statement-(v)).

From statement-(ii), it can be concluded that V (Dhoni) sits on seat-7. From statement-(i), it can be concluded that S and T can occupy seat 4, 10 in any order.

Therefore, we can conclude that the final arrangement should be like the diagram given below:

P	Q	U	T or S	W or X	X or W	V	Y	R	S or T

Case B: When P sits on seat-2

S or T	P	Q	U	W or X	X or W	T or S	V	Y	R

Case C: When P sits on seat-3

This case is not possible because if P sits on seat-3 then Q must occupy seat-4 then R must sit on seat 11 which is not possible.

38. If Yuvraj sits on the seat immediate right to Raina then according to case-A, Rahane must be at seat-10. Therefore, the required answer is 8.
39. If there are only two players sitting between Kohli and Rahane then Dhoni sits to the immediate right of Rahane (from case-B). Option (a) is correct.
40. There is no player in between Ashwin and Jadeja in both the cases. Hence, the answer is 0.

Solutions for Questions 41 to 44:

From the given information, we can prepare the following table:

Floor#	Name of Resident
7	A or D
6	E or F
5	C
4	G
3	B
2	F or E
1	D or A

41. Statement 2 states that floor number of A cannot be expressed as Arithmetic mean of any other 2 floor numbers. Only number 1 and 7 satisfy this condition. Therefore, A can be living on floor 1 or 7. Sum = 1 + 7 = 8.
42. If D lives on the top floor, A has to be living on 1st floor. E and F live on 2nd and 6th floor (not necessarily in that order). Therefore, sum = 6 + 2 + 1 = 9.
43. From the table above, G lives on 4th floor.
44. A and D live on 7th and 1st floors, not necessarily in that order, so required sum = 1 + 7 = 8. Hence, option (b) is the correct answer.

Solution for Question 45:

45. If you were to place Mr. Abraham and Mrs. Charlie next to each other on the circle (as stated) you would get two possible positions for Mrs. Abraham and Mr. Charlie. Using the other clue given in the question, it can be seen easily after that, that the place to the right of Mr. Abraham would have the option of placing either Mrs. Border or Mrs. Dennis in it.

Solution for Question 46:

46. The correct order would be:
Sati Savitri (9 to 10), Veer Abhimanyu (10 to 11), Sunder Kand (11 to 11:30), Joru Ka Ghulam (11:30 to 12:30), Jhansi Ki Rani (1:30 to 2) and Reshma and Shera (2 to 3).
Option (c) matches with this order.

Solution for Question 47:

47. The following figures would make the answer clear:
Initial arrangement:

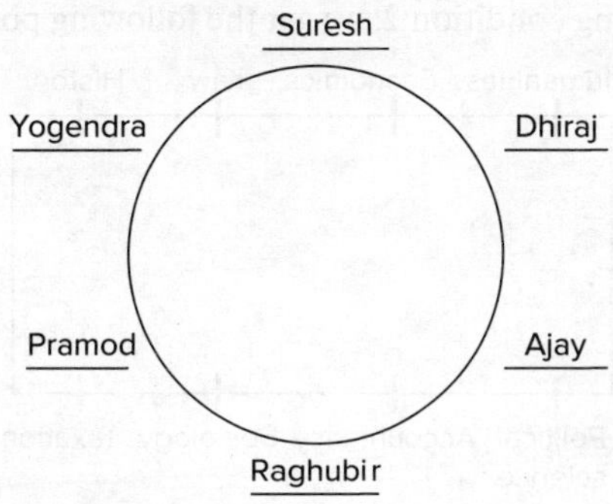

Final arrangement:

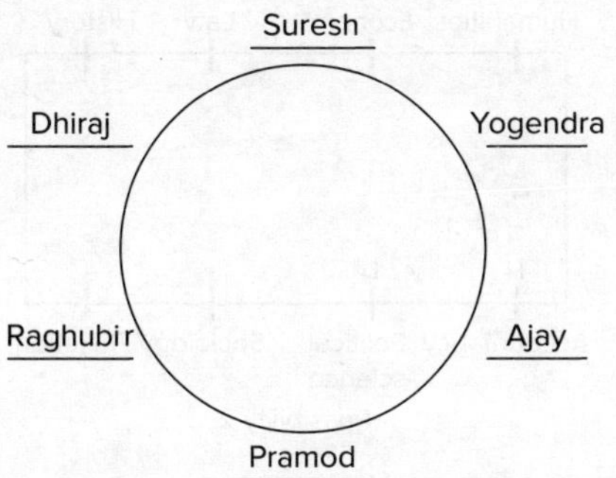

Hence, Suresh is sitting to the left of Dhiraj.

Level of Difficulty (II)

Solutions for Questions 1 to 4:

1. Using conditions 1, 4 and 5, we get the following:

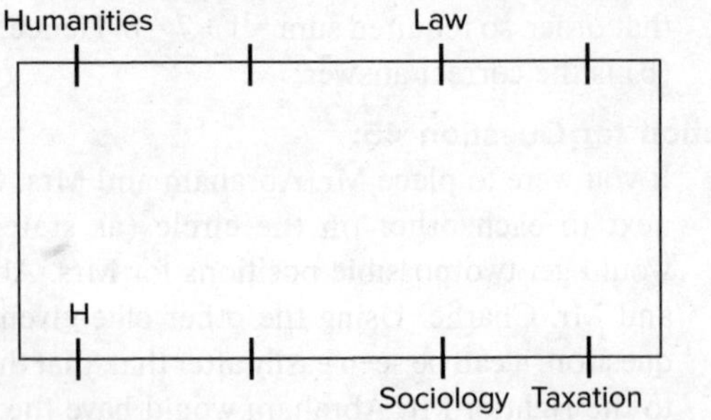

Using condition 3, we get the following:

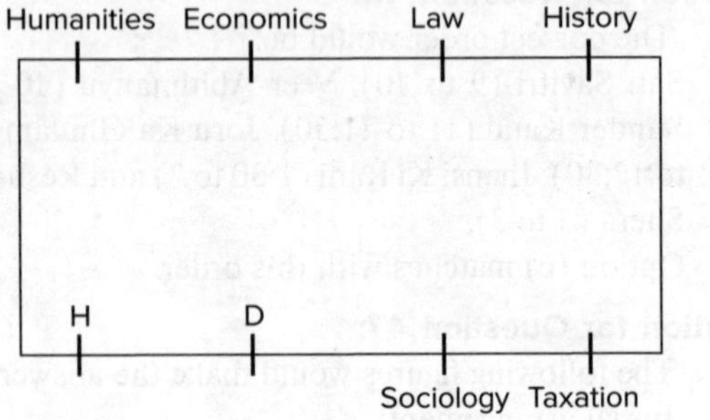

Using condition 2, we get the following possibilities:

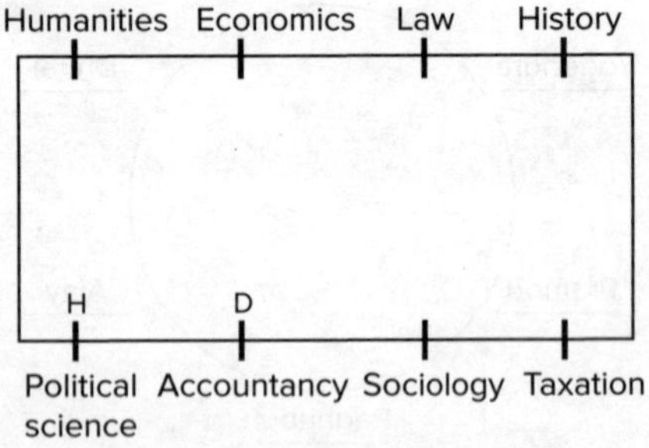

Possibility 1

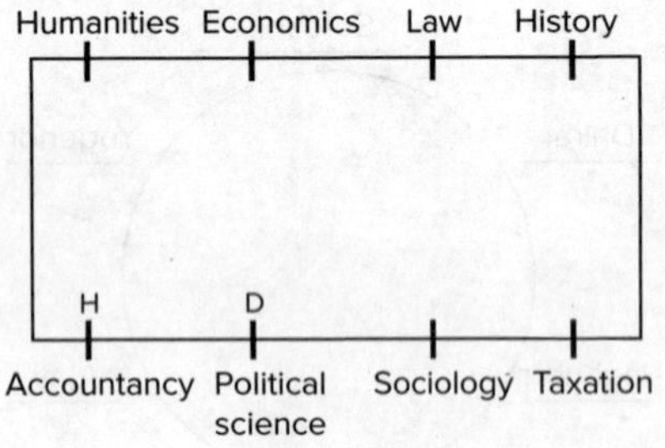

Possibility 2

Now all the questions can be answered.

If G is seated second to the right of C, we get the following:

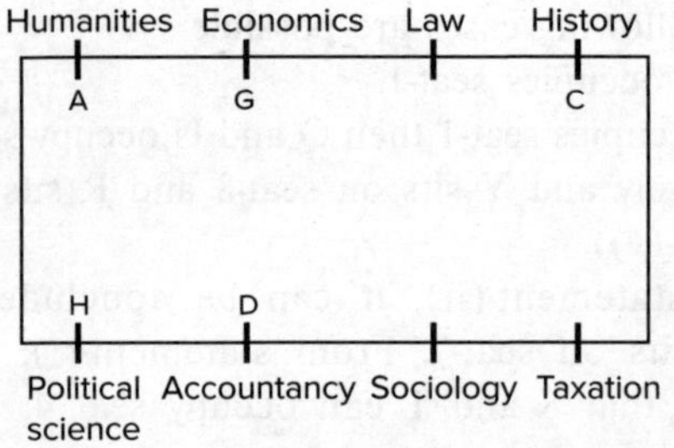

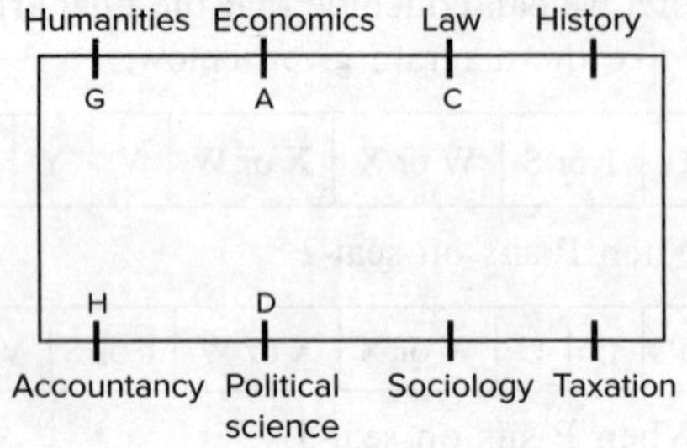

Thus, G can belong to either Economics or Humanities department. Hence, (b).

2. If B is the only professor seated between F and the professor of Accountancy, only possibility 1 is valid. We get the following:

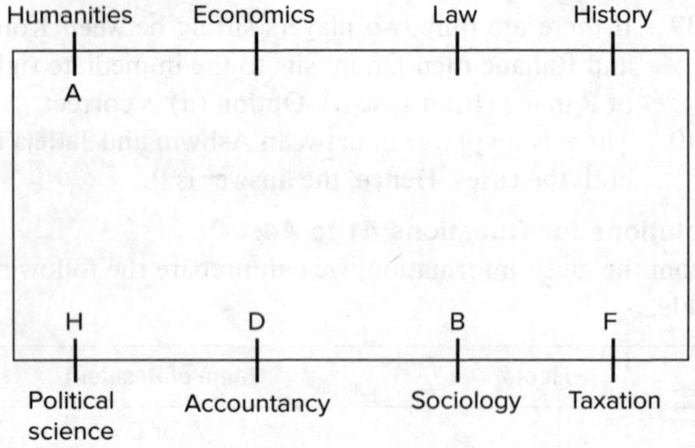

Therefore, B belongs to the Department of Sociology. Hence, option (a) is correct.

3. If H and the professor of History swap their seats, we get the following:

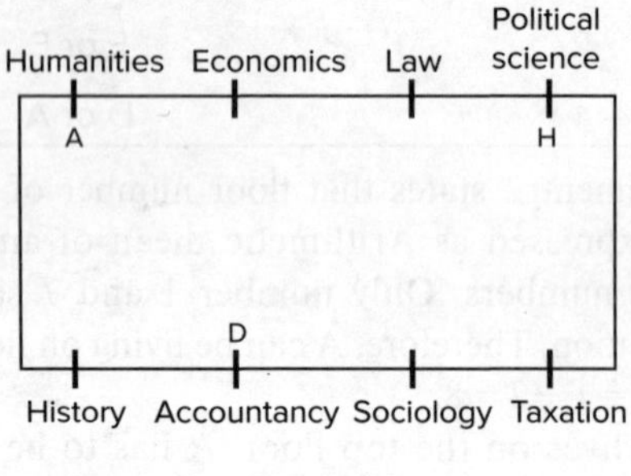

Possibility 1

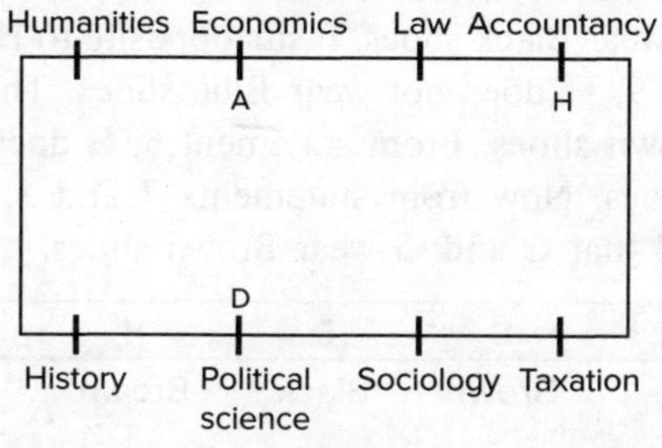

Possibility 2

It can be seen that the professors of Political Science and Economics cannot be seated next to each other. Hence, option (c) is correct.

4. If H and the professor of History swap their seats, we get the following:

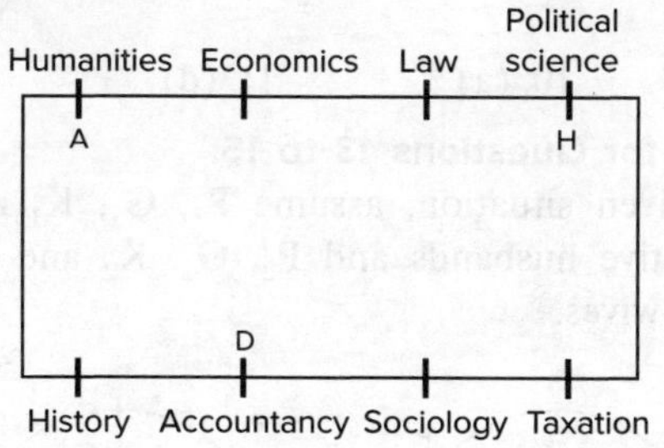

Possibility 1

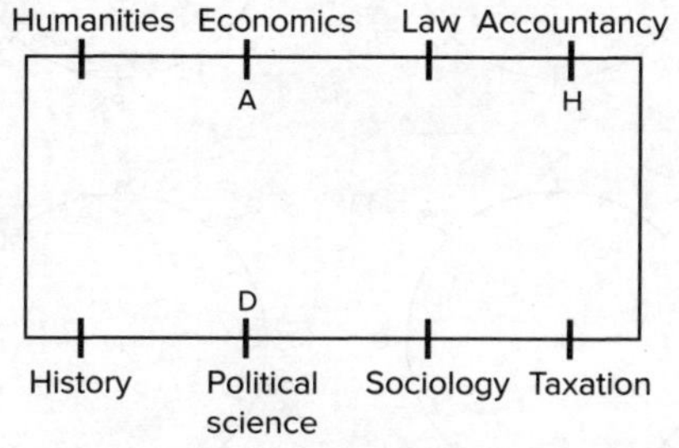

Possibility 2

It can be seen that only statement [1] can be correct. Hence, option (a) is correct.

Solutions for Questions 5 to 8:

Cinema hall	1st Day	2nd Day	3rd Day	4th Day	5th Day
N				PATHAN	
Chidiya ghar (C)					
West coast hall (W)			PATHAN		
Benett Hall (B)			DON		
E					

It is given that in all the cinema halls, except C, KICK was shown before CHAVVA. From this, we can say that on no other cinema hall except C, CHAVVA was shown on the first day and KICK was shown on the fifth day. But as every movie was shown on the five cinema halls on each day, it must be Chidiya ghar on which CHAVVA was shown on the first day and KICK on the fifth day. Now, on one among the remaining four cinema halls, CHAVVA was shown on the second day. As on all, except Chidiya ghar, KICK was shown before CHAVVA, the cinema hall on which CHAVVA was shown on the second day must have shown KICK on the first day. On another cinema hall, CHAVVA was shown on the third day and on this cinema hall KICK was shown on the second day. Similarly, we can say that on the cinema hall on which CHAVVA was shown on the fourth day, KICK must have been shown on the third day and in the cinema hall in which CHAVVA was shown on the fifth day, KICK must have shown on the fourth day. From the above, we can conclude that in all other cinema halls apart from C, KICK and CHAVVA must have been shown on consecutive days. Also, from (ii), as in Benett Hall, PATHAN was shown before DON, which was shown third, PATHAN must have been shown on the first two days. So, in Benett Hall, KICK and CHAVVA could not have been shown on the first two days. Therefore, on Benett Hall, KICK and CHAVVA were shown on the fourth and fifth days. Now, from the above conclusion regarding Benett Hall, we can say that in West coast hall, KICK was not shown on the fourth day. Also, KICK could not have been shown on the second day (according to (iii), PATHAN was shown on the third day). Therefore, in West coast hall, KICK must have been shown on the first day and therefore, CHAVVA was shown on the second day. Now, from the above conclusions and from (iii), we can say that in Naya ghar, KICK could not have been shown on the first day and third day. So, KICK must have been shown on the second day and CHAVVA on the third day and therefore, on Elvis Hall, KICK must have been shown on the third day and CHAVVA on the fourth day. Now, on the third day, JAWAN must have been shown in C. PATHAN must have been shown in C on the second day and DON on the fourth day. DON must have been shown in E on the second day. PATHAN on the fifth day and JAWAN on the first day. On Naya ghar, DON must have been shown on the first day and JAWAN on the fifth day. In West coast hall, JAWAN and DON have been shown on the fourth and the fifth days respectively. Finally, in Bennett Hall, PATHAN and JAWAN have been shown on the first two days in the given order.

Cinema hall	1st Day	2nd Day	3rd Day	4th Day	5th Day
N	DON	KICK	CHAVVA	PATHAN	JAWAN
C	CHAVVA	PATHAN	JAWAN	DON	KICK
W	KICK	CHAVVA	PATHAN	JAWAN	DON
B	PATHAN	JAWAN	DON	KICK	CHAVVA
E	JAWAN	DON	KICK	CHAVVA	PATHAN

Now all the questions can be answered.

5. (b) 6. (a) 7. (c) 8. (b)

Solutions for Questions 9 to 12:

Let the position at which C sits is position 1. Also assume that position 2 is on C's right and so on. Now from statement 2, D and H are at positions 2 and 3 respectively. From statement 4, E must be at position 4. Therefore, from statement 3, F must be at position 7 and A at position 8. From statement 4, G must be at position 6 and B at position 5.

From statement 6, D wears Black shoes. Therefore, H and C do not wear Black shoes. F sits opposite to H. So, from statement 9, H does not wear Blue shoes. Therefore, H wears Brown shoes. From statement 5, E does not wear Brown shoes. Now from statements 7 and 8, it can be concluded that C and G wear Brown shoes.

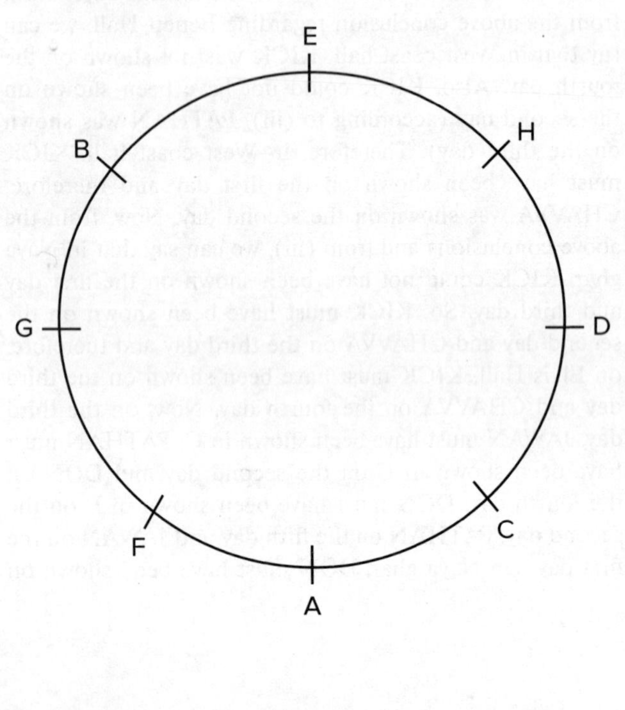

From statement 6, D wears Black shoes. Therefore, H and C do not wear Black shoes. F sits opposite to H. So, from statement 9, H does not wear Blue shoes. Therefore, H wears Brown shoes. From statement 5, E does not wear Brown shoes. Now from statements 7 and 8, it can be concluded that C and G wear Brown shoes.

Person	C	D	H	E
Shoe colour	Brown	Black	Brown	Black/ Blue
Position	1	2	3	4

Person	B	G	F	A
Shoe colour	Blue/ Black	Brown	Blue/ Black	Black/ Blue
Position	5	6	7	8

Answers:

9. (b) 10. (a) 11. (d) 12. (c)

Solutions for Questions 13 to 16:

For the given situation, assume P_1, G_1, K_1 and S_1 as the respective husbands and P_2, G_2, K_2 and S_2 as the respective wives.

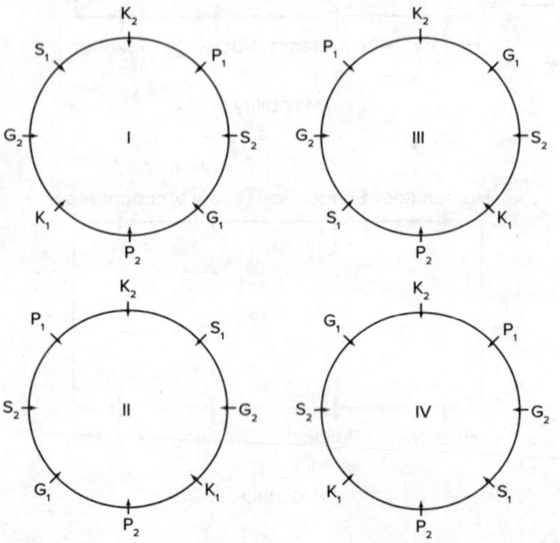

From statement 2, no two wives also sit next to each other. Hence, all men and women sit alternately on 8 chairs. Now, it's given that Mrs. Patel and Mrs. Khanna sit opposite to each other. That means Mrs. Shah and Mrs. Gupta will occupy the other two chairs which are alternately placed between Mrs. Khanna and Mrs. Patel. Also, only Mr. Shah or Mr. Patel or Mr. Gupta can sit next to Mrs. Khanna. Similarly, only Mr. Shah or Mr. Khanna or Mr. Gupta can sit next to Mrs. Patel. This is shown in the diagrams. P1 and P2 denote Mr. and Mrs. Patel respectively. Similar notations are used to denote other couples also. The four couples can be seated in 4 ways

13. There are 4 solutions.
14. If Mrs. Shah and Mr. Patel sit next to each other, then Mr. Gupta will sit opposite to Mr. Shah. Hence, option (c).
15. If Mr. Gupta and Mrs. Khanna are adjacent to each other, then either Mrs. Gupta or Mrs. Patel is to the right of Mr. Shah. Hence, option (d).
16. In this case, it can be seen that each of the options (a), (b) and (d) have at least one possibility. However, option (c) tells us that 'Mrs. Shah is always to the right of Mr. Gupta'. This means it is saying that this conclusion has to be always true. While this is a possibility in (I), yet this cannot be true always and hence, is false. Thus, option (c) is correct.

Solutions for Questions 17 to 20:

The word Beljamin has 8 letters.

Using the conditions given in 3 and 5, we get the following 2 cases:

Case	1	2	3	4	5	6	7	8
1	E	A				M		I
2	E		A				M	I

From condition 1, M cannot be in 7th position. Hence, case 2 is eliminated.

Now, further following 2 cases are possible.

Case	1	2	3	4	5	6	7	8
1a	E	A	B	L	N	M	J	I
1b	E	A	L	B	N	M	J	I

Case 1a is ruled out as it violates condition 1 because L is in position 3 in the original word and in position 4 in the new word.

Therefore, 1b is the only possibility.

17. 1 18. (b) 19. (a) 20. (a)

Solutions for Questions 21 to 24:

Based on the information in the question, we can make the following possibilities for the given situation:

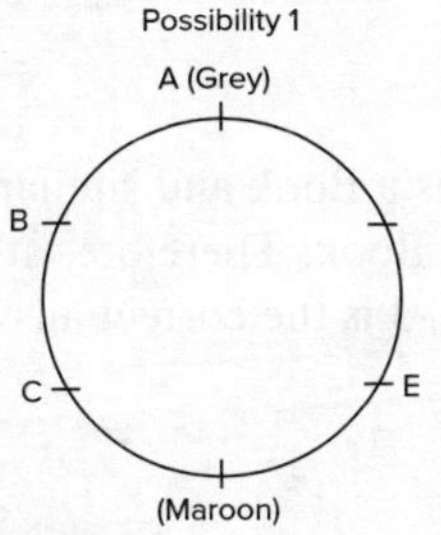

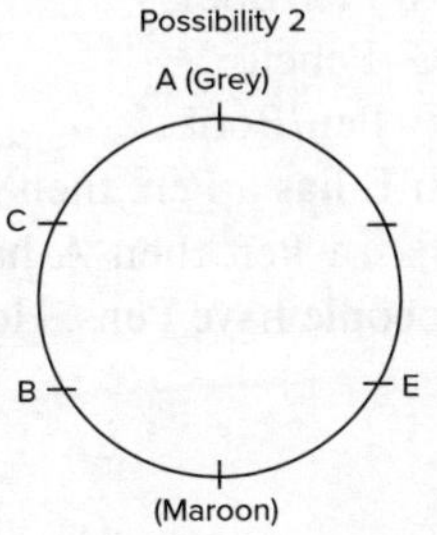

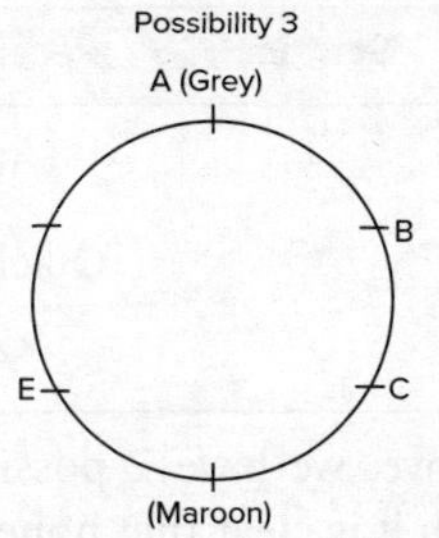

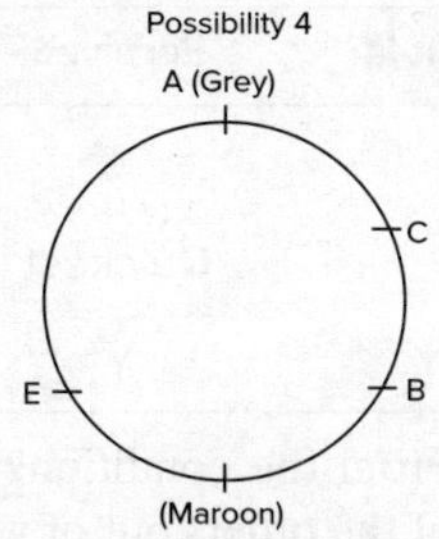

In each of the 4 possibilities, we are able to place A, B, C and E relative to each other and place the colours Grey (with A) and Maroon (Opposite A). Moving forward, we can solve the questions based on our understanding the above optional figures.

21. Keeping in mind all the conditions in the situation above, we can form 4 basic seating arrangements. Let all the ladies be represented by the first letter of their names i.e., A, B, C, D, E and F. From the conditions in the question, if C's favourite colour is Peach, then B cannot have Coral as her favourite colour. And also, E cannot have Coral as the favourite colour according to the question. So, the only position Coral can be in is between A and E where E can take any colours from Lilac and Lavender. And, since Coral lies between A and E, they are always the neighbours. So, only the lady who likes Maroon cannot be next to the lady who likes Coral. Hence, (d) is the correct answer.
22. Answer is 1. If Estaire does not like Peach, the lady who likes Peach must be seated between A and E. And only Estaire can be seated between the ladies who like Maroon and Peach. Hence, the answer is 1.
23. This question is referring to Possibilities 3 and 4. We cannot be sure of the colours that can sit to the left of E. Thus, either Donna or Fiona can be seated to the left of Estaire. Option (c) is correct.
24. From the cases we made above in question 21, the only case that is not possible is option (b) where if B likes Lavender and C likes Lilac, the only colours left to be placed together are Coral and Peach which violates the conditions in the question and hence, option (b) is the correct answer.

Solutions for Questions 25 to 26:

25.

Sent-in	Received	Sent-in	Received
X	X	X	X
	Quick		
On-time	Late	On-time	Quick

Sent-in	Received	Sent-in	Received
			Late
	Quickest		Quickest
Y	Y	Y	Y

From the conditions above, we have 2 possibilities of the orders out of which it is clear that none of the options is necessarily true since it depends upon which possibility we go with. All of the options are feasible but not necessarily true and hence, option (d) is the correct answer.

26. Let's first try to fill in all the constraints and see how many possibilities can exist.

Possibility# 1- Cannot exist because Sent in & Received number for Quickest cannot be the same.

Sent-in	Received
Super Late	Super Late
Late	Quick
On-time	Late
Quick	On-time
Quickest	Quickest
Quicker	Quicker

Possibility# 2- This is possible.

Sent-in	Received
Super Late	Super Late
Late	Quick
On-time	Late
Quickest	On-time
Quick	Quickest
Quicker	Quicker

Possibility# 3- Cannot exist because Sent in & Received number for Quickest cannot be the same

Sent-in	Received
Super Late	Super Late
Late	On-time
On-time	Quick
Quick	Late
Quickest	Quickest
Quicker	Quicker

Possibility# 4- This is possible.

Sent-in	Received
Super Late	Super Late
Late	On-time
On-time	Quick
Quickest	Late
Quick	Quickest
Quicker	Quicker

Therefore, there are 2 ways in which deliveries can be made.

Solutions for Questions 27 to 30:

27. The arrangement comes out as follows:

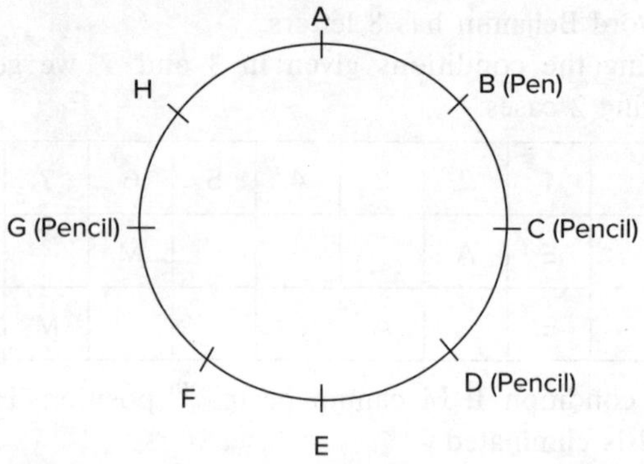

Hence, option (b) is the correct answer.

28. From the arrangement above, only 3 people are possible.

29. From the arrangement above, We can see that if F has a book, E cannot have a book. Therefore, 2 people, H and A can have the book. Hence, the exact person holding the other book cannot be determined. Correct answer is (d).

30. If we check the possibilities of people holding different items,

E- Pen/Book
H- Pen/Book
D- Pencil
B- Pencil
C- Pen
A- Pen/Book
G- Pencil
F- Pen/Book

If E has a Pen, then F has a Book and similarly if H has a Pen then A has a Book. Therefore, atleast 3 people have Pens. Hence, 3 is the correct answer.

Solutions for 31 to 34:

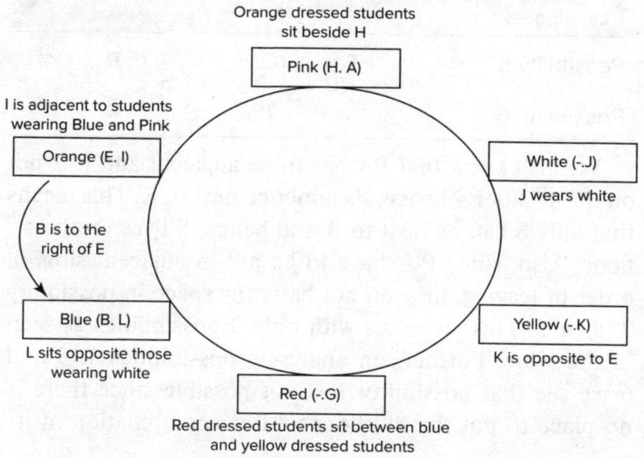

31. (a) 32. (b) 33. (a) 34. (c)

Solutions for Questions 35 to 40:

For the purpose of this solution, individuals are denoted with the first letters of their names from time to time.

From the direct information in the question, we get the following:

Baldev = 8 years old, Quindal = 18 years old. The people sitting on the extreme ends of the row 1 have ages of 11 and 23, while the people sitting on the extreme ends of row 2 have ages 17 and 19. Also, Prince has an age of 14 (that's the only multiple of 7 in the list) and Eeshwarya's age is 16 years.

Now, from this point, we start to analyse the multiple possibility clues:

(i) 'Urvashi was sitting at an equidistant position from both Ravi and Tanuj (Tanuj being to her right) and the sum of the ages of Urvashi and the one who was sitting to her immediate left is 23.' → Urvashi cannot be at the extremes of row 2. Also, since the sum of Urvashi and the person to her immediate left is 23, we get that the sum of 23 is only possible as 8 + 15; 9 + 14 or 11 + 12. But, we already know that the ages 8 and 11 are in row 1. Hence, the only possible combination is 9 and 14. Also, since we already know that Prince is 14 years old, it means that Urvashi is 9 years old. Also, we know 'Prince, whose age is a multiple of 7, was sitting second to the right of Seeta, which means that the order of sitting in the row 2 would be S,_ P, U. We also know that U is equidistant from R and T, with T being on her right. This means that the arrangement in row 2 can only be: SRPUQT with ages for P = 14, U = 9 and Q = 18.

If we think of Tanuj's and Devashish's age at this point, we get:

D = T + 4. Since, Tanuj, is in the extreme of Row 2, it means that his age can either be 17 or 19. But we cannot think of Tanuj as 17 years because then Devashish would have to be 21 years old - something which is not available in the list of ages in the question. Hence, T = 19 and D = 23 years old.

The next clue we have to use is: 'The sum of the ages of Falguni and the one who was sitting opposite to her is 30.' A sum of 30 can occur in 4 possible ways: 8 + 22; 11 + 19; 12 + 18 and 14 + 16. Out of these possibilities, we can eliminate 8–22 (since 8 is for B who is opposite to Q and 12–18 (since 18 is for Q who is opposite to B). 14–16 for F and opposite to her is also not possible, since P = 14 and E = 16. Thus, F and the one opposite to her have to be 11 + 19. We already know that T is 19 years old. Hence, F sits opposite to T and is 11 years old. Also, since D is 23 years old (already deduced), we can put D in the other extreme in row 1, E next to him and C next to F (since between C and D, there are two cousins sitting).

The final piece of the puzzle is to deduce the ages of A, C and R. Since, the age of A < R < C, it means that the three additional numbers that are to be used have to be used in increasing order. Also, it is given to us that the multiples of 5 were used. Hence, the 3 numbers to be used are 10, 15 and 26 respectively for A, R and C. The final table would be:

Row 1	D – 23	E – 16	A – 10	C – 26	B – 8	F – 11
Row 2	S – 17	R – 15	P – 14	U – 9	Q – 18	T – 19

35. The ages not used are: 12 and 22. Hence, the required sum is 34. Option (b) is correct.
36. Option (b) is correct.
37. Option (c) is correct.
38. Option (c) is correct.
39. 24 for A and P. The Correct answer is 24.
40. 39 is the sum of ages of D and E. This is the highest. The correct answer is 39.

Solutions for Questions 41 to 44:

We can make the following notations from the given information contained in the clues:

P (not 4th) $\xrightarrow{1}$ A

2nd floor $\xrightarrow{1}$ 5th floor

First to leave, not 2 not 4 T $\xrightarrow{1}$ C (not 5th)

Last to leave (not 5th) R $\xrightarrow{1}$ 4th

Note: In these images, 1 on top of the arrow shows immediate after or before. In these pictures, we also know that R → 4th is after T → C. Since, this is a multiple possibility situation, the best way to think is to draw out the various possibilities. Also, we know from the directly given information in the question, that Amar is on the 1st floor, and Ravi lives on the 6th floor.

We can use T-C-R-4th as a backbone to see how to place the 6 people.

Order of Leaving →	First	Second	Third	Fourth	Fifth	Sixth
Possibility 1	T	C	R	4th		
Possibility 2	T	C		R	4th	
Possibility 3	T	C			R	4th
Possibility 4		T	C	R	4th	

Order of Leaving →	First	Second	Third	Fourth	Fifth	Sixth
Possibility 5		T	C		R	4th
Possibility 6			T	C	R	4th

We also know that PA has to be adjacent and P is not on the 4th floor – hence, P cannot be next to R. This means that only S can be next to R and hence, S lives on the 4th floor. Also, since P-A have to be put in adjacent slots in order of leaving, they do not have any space in possibility 2, 4 or 5. This leaves us with only 3 possibilities as seen in the table. Further, on analysing possibilities 1, 3 and 6 we see that possibility 1 is not possible since there is no place to put the 2nd floor-5th floor combination in it.

Order of Leaving →	First	Second	Third	Fourth	Fifth	Sixth	Remarks	Final Remarks
Possibility 1	T	C	R (6)	S (4)	P	A (1)	Rejected as there is no place to fix the 25 combination.	REJECTED
Possibility 3	T (3)	C (2)	P (5)	A (1)	R (6)	S (4)	Note: 2-5 have been attributed to C-P because, the first person to leave is not from the 2nd floor.	POSSIBLE AS THERE IS NO CONTRADICTION
Possibility 6	P (3)	A (1)	T (2)	C (5)	R (6)	S (4)	In this case, after allotting 1st, 6th and 4th floors, to A,R,S respectively, we are forced to allot 25 to TC. But C cannot be 5.	REJECTED BECAUSE C IS NOT ON THE 5TH FLOOR.

The answers can be read off this table:

41. Option (b) is correct.
42. Option (d) is correct.
43. Option (c) is correct.
44. Option (a) is correct.

Solutions for Questions 45 to 48:

If we assume that A is standing on the right side of the row, then according to statement 5, H is on the left side of the row. From statement 2, 3, 4 and 6, D and G should be standing on the left side and F on the right side of the row. Now, there is no place in the left side for B and E. Hence, A cannot be on the right side.

Therefore, A must be on the left side of the row then H must be on the right side of the row. Also, D and G are on one side and B and E on another side of the row.

Now from statement 2, we can conclude that G is on the right side, from statement 4, D is on the right side and from statement 3, F is on the left side. Thus, B and E are on the same side of the row.

We now have the following data:

On the right side of the rows, we have students D, C, G and H standing.

On the left side of the rows we have students F, B, E and A standing.

From statement 3 and 5—Since H cannot stand in the 4th row and because A cannot, his right side counterpart G cannot stand in the 4th row either. We conclude that D and F are standing in the 4th row with D on the right side to concur with the fact that G and D stand on the same side.

Now, we can draw the following arrangement:

Left	Right	Row
		1
	C	2
		3
F	D	4

45. Since A is necessarily on the left side, G would be on the right side of the row. Hence, option (b) is correct.
46. Given, if G is in the 1st row, final arrangement would look like:

Left	Right	Row
A	G	1
B/E	C	2
E/B	H	3
F	D	4

Therefore, the required sum = 2 + 3 = 5.

47. If B stands in 3rd row, final arrangement would look like:

Left	Right	Row
A	G	1
E	C	2
B	H	3
F	D	4

Hence, C is in the same row as E.

48. From the table, only option (b) is correct.

Solutions for Questions 49 to 53:

In order to solve this question set, we should first focus on the husband wife pairings. From statement (iv), we know that Alisha and Baman are married to each other and from statement (ii), we know that Emaan and Chiranjeevi are married to each other. Once we know these two, we are left with three men and three women amongst whom we have to determine the husband wife pairs. Amongst the men, we are left with Aman, Charan and Dhawan, while amongst the women we are left with Binny, Denny and Emmi. At this point, clue (v) helps us identify that since Dhawan is not married to Denny or Emmi, he must be married to Binny. Next, clue (iii) tells us that Aman is not married to Emmi, so he must be married to Denny. The final husband wife pairings are identified as:

Husband	Wife
Aman	Denny
Baman	Alisha
Charan	Emmi
Dhawan	Binny
Emaan	Chiranjeevi

In order to solve the remaining part of the question, with respect to the seating places, we can start from clues (v) and (vi) and first place Alisha, Dhawan, Charan and Binny on the table.

Note: Since, initially all the ten seats are equal with respect to their placement, we can place them as we wish. We also need to take care of the fact that there is one male and one female sitting on each side of the table.

We get the following initial picture:

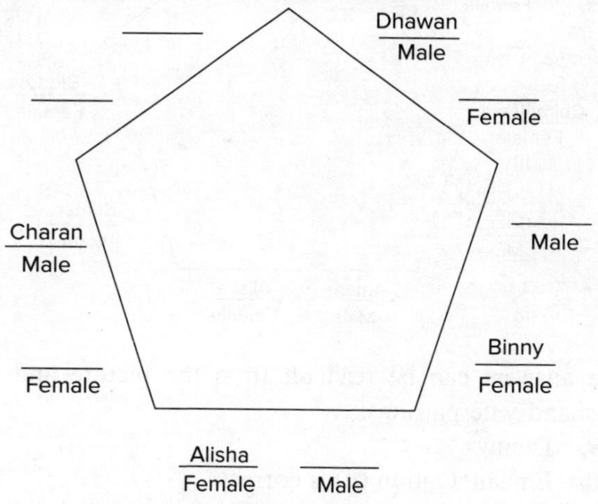

Now, since Baman and Alisha are sitting together according to clue (iv), Baman can only occupy the seat to the right of Alisha – since to the left of Alisha there is a female sitting. But this is a contradiction of a couple cannot sit on the same edge (clue i). So, we would need to recast the picture as follows – if we make Alisha sit on the right side of the edge, we will get to this point of the seating arrangement after placing Binny, Baman, Dhawan and Charan.

INTERMEDIATE PICTURE

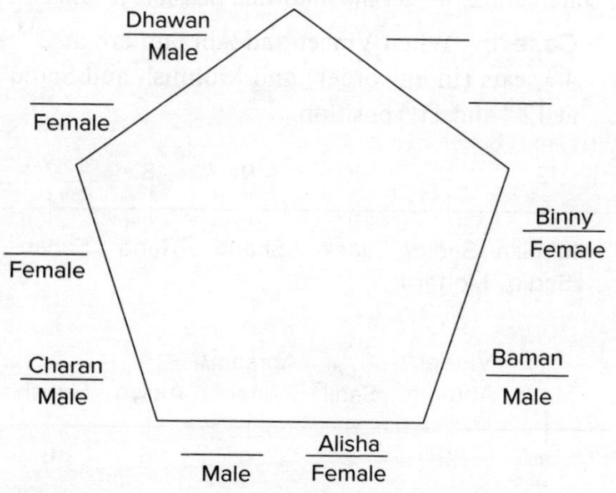

At this point, we realize that, since Aman and Emmi are equidistant to Baman, they must be two places away from him on either side. And after placing these two, there is only one place left for the remaining male - viz, Emaan. Using clue (ii) we can place Chiranjeevi and then Denny. The final seating arrangement is shown in the final arrangement picture.

FINAL PICTURE

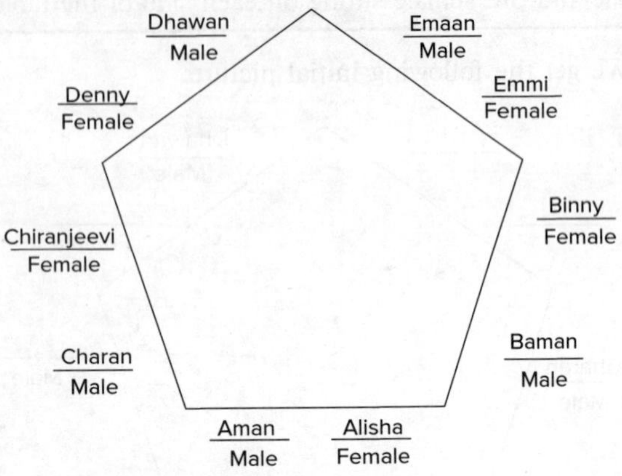

The answers can be read off from the picture and the Husband wife pairings:

49. Denny
50. Emaan. Option (d) is correct.
51. Denny is sitting between Dhawan and Chiranjeevi. Option (b) is correct.
52. Both the pairs given in option (a) and (b) are sitting along one edge. Hence, option (c) is correct.
53. Binny

Solutions for Questions 54 to 58:

From statement 4 and 1: If Mark is at number 1, Fahim and Harish are at seat number 7 and 6 respectively. From statement 1, 3 and 4: Aaliya, Tariq and Shanti must be at seat number 5, 8 and 9 respectively. Now, from the above analysis and statement 2, we get the following possible arrangements:

Case 1: When Vineet and Abraam are at 2nd and 4th seats (in any order) and Mohnish and Sadiq are at 12th and 11th position.

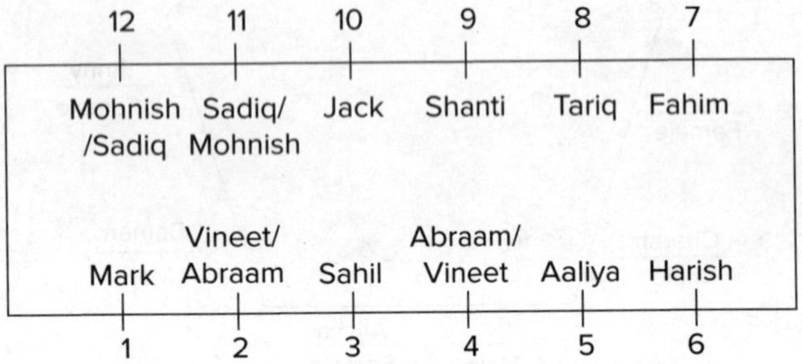

Case 2: When Vineet and Abraam are at 12th and 10th seats (in any order) and Mohnish and Sadiq are at 3rd and 4th position.

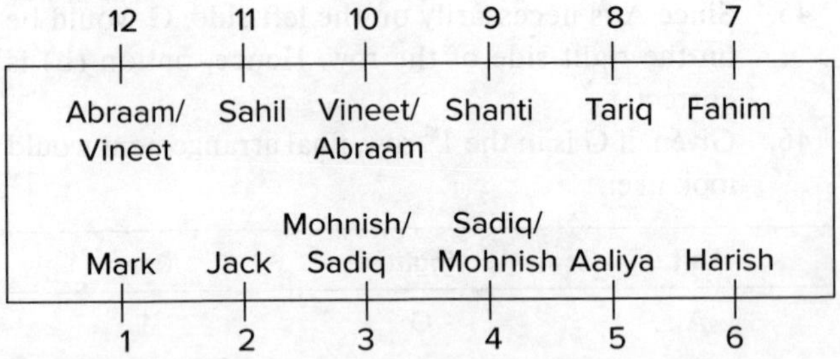

54. 4 arrangements are possible for case 1 and similarly four arrangements are possible in case 2 also. Hence, there are total 4 + 4 = 8 arrangements are possible.
55. 8
56.

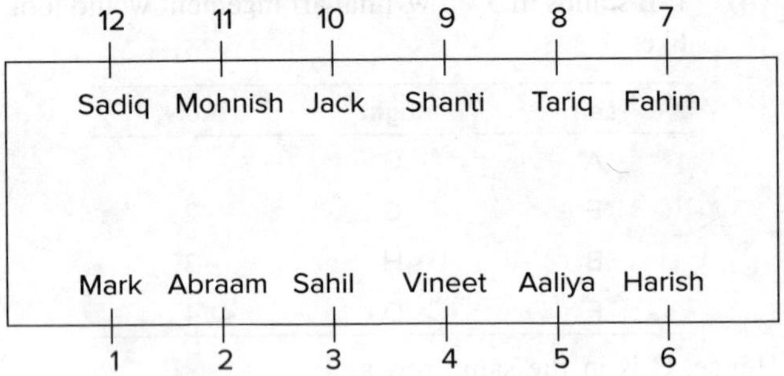

Hence, Abraam must be in 2nd position.

57. If Shanti is not sitting opposite to Vineet then either Vineet (case 1) or Jack (case 2) is sitting next to Mark. Hence, option (d) is correct.
58. If Sadiq occupies the corner seat (which is possible in case 1).

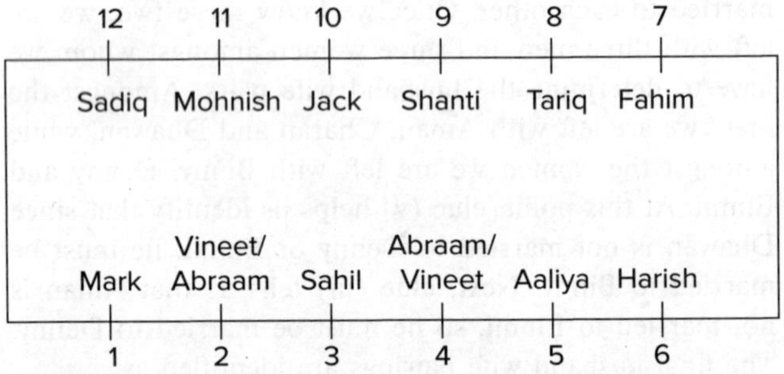

Hence, Sadiq can only sit opposite to Mark (case 1). Hence, option (a) is correct.

Solutions for Questions 59 to 63:

It is given to us that: F(1) = F(6), F(2) = F(5). Since the total number of employees is 10, we know that F(1) + F(2) + F(3) + F(4) + F(5) + F(6) = 10.

Hence, 2F(1) + 2F(2) + F(3) + F(4) = 10 → 2[F(1) + F(2)] + F(3) + F(4) = 10

The least possible value of 'F(1) + F(2)' is 3. This means that F(3) + F(4) can be a maximum of 4.

Hence, none of among F(1), F(2), F(3) and F(4) can be greater than or equal to 4. The only possible integer solution to the above equation is when F(1), F(2), F(3) and F(4) are equal 1, 2, 3 and 1 respectively. Then F(2) = F(5) gives us that F(5) = 2 and then F(6) = 1.
We can make the following table for greater clarity of the number of workers on each floor:

Floor	Number of Employees
Floor 6	1
Floor 5	2
Floor 4	1
Floor 3	3
Floor 2	2
Floor 1	1

From statement (i) and the above deduction it is evident that Cheteshwar's floor number is greater than 3 and hence, from statement (ii) and the above it can be concluded that Cheteshwar and Bantuklal work on floor 5. Krish and Dinesh work on floor 4 and floor 3 respectively. Capoor, Janardan and Harender must occupy floor 1 and floor 2 (in no particular order), as they work below Dinesh.

From statement (iii), it can be concluded that Gotya and Pankaj work on floor 3 with Dinesh. Finally, it can be concluded from statement (iv) that Janardan and Elangovan work on floor 1 and floor 6 respectively. The table can be completed as given below.

Floor No.	Number of Employees Living in the Floor	Name of the Employee
6	1	Elangovan
5	2	Cheteshwar, Bantuklal
4	1	Krish
3	3	Dinesh. Gotya, Pankaj
2	2	Capoor, Harender
1	1	Janardan

59. 3
60. Krish
61. Difference = 3 - 2 = 1
62. Elangovan works on floor 6. Hence, option (a) is correct.
63. Janardan works alone on floor 1. The rest of the 9 employees work on floors higher than his floor, hence answer is 9

Solution for Question 64

64. (c)

Let San, Wag, Zeni, Rita, Yuva, Inna, Cory, Matte, Meena and Shruti be represented by S, W, Z, R, Y, I, C, M, X and Sc respectively. The arrangement can be started by fixing the positions of Z and Sc at the extreme left of the two rows. X can be standing either to the immediate right of Z/Sc or in the middle of the row. If X is standing in the middle of the row, Statement (iv) is violated. Further analysis leads to the following table:

Row I	Inna	Cory	Wag	Matte	Shruti/Zeni
Row II	Zeni/Shruti	Meena	Rita	Yuva	San

Therefore, the number of students standing between Cory and Matte cannot be the same as the number of students standing between Shruti and Meena.

Solutions for Questions 65 to 69:

Before you start solving the problem, you need to have worked out the following:

Only the first and last speaker would occupy only 1 seat during the event. Everyone else, would occupy 2 seats during the event. For the purpose of this solution we have coded Arun Sharma (AS); Meenakshi Upadhyay (MU); Vinay Singh (VS); Virender Mahajan (VM); Anit Suri (Anit): Saeed Khan (SK); Arun Chaturvedi (AC)

We can make the following picture to start off the seating at the beginning, when the first speaker is speaking. Hence, the first speaker must be AC. For making this picture, we are directly given the relative positioning of AS, SK, MU, and VM. We also know that VS and Anit occupied 2 seats during the event and hence cannot be the first or last speakers. Thus, they must be occupying the other two seats at the beginning. Also, VS has to occupy a seat that is opposite his initial seat, which means that he must have spoken immediately before either AS or SK. As, we are given that SK spoke immediately after AS – it follows that VS is opposite AS at the start and must have spoken immediately before AS, so that he can occupy the opposite seat (AS's seat) when AS goes to the dais to speak.

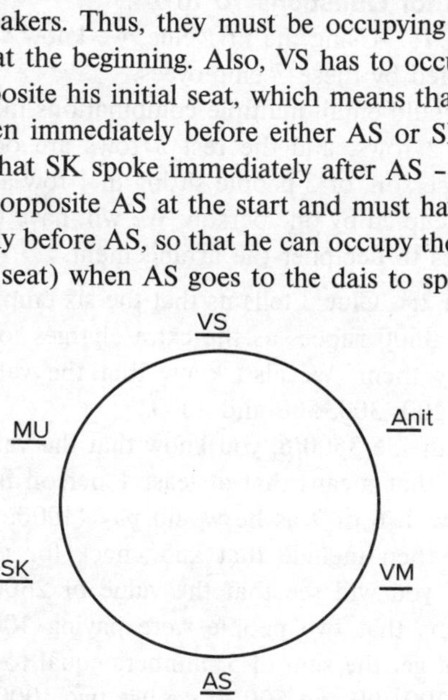

We also know that VM did not occupy any other seat during the event. Hence, he would be the last speaker. This leaves us to place the speaking order of MU and Anit. Since, MU and VM occupied the same seat at some time and since VM is the last speaker, it follows that MU must have spoken second last (just before VM). Since, VS-AS-SK speak in that order without a break, Anit would either be the second or 5th speaker. However, he cannot be the fifth speaker based on the clue: 'Mr. Anit Suri sat on 2 different seats during the event, neither of which were opposite to any seat in which Meenakshi was sitting.'

Note: If you do try to make him the 5th speaker, he would occupy MU's seat when MU goes to speak 6th – MU's original seat is opposite her final seat and this would contradict this clue.

Hence, the order of speakers is:

1. Arun Chaturvedi
2. Anit Suri
3. Vinay Singh
4. Arun Sharma
5. Saeed Khan
6. Meenakshi Upadhyay
7. Virendra Mahajan

We can answer the questions given:

65. Option (b) is the correct answer.
66. Option (d) is the correct answer.
67. Option (a) is the correct answer.
68. Option (d) is the correct answer.
69. Option (d) is the correct answer.

Solutions for Questions 70 to 74:

Deduction 1: Using the first clue, we know that 5 rows are occupied by these 7 employees.

So, it could entail multiple combinations like 2 people sitting in 2 rows, and the rest 3 rows are occupied by only one person, or 3 people sitting in 1 row and the rest 4 rows occupied by one person. We will have to consider other clues to decipher the arrangement.

Deduction 2: Clue 3 tells us that the six employees paid a total of 3600 rupees as the extra charges for the seats booked by them. We also know that the values of the seats are 200, 300, 500 and 1000.

If you divide 3600/6, you know that the value is more than 500, that means that at least 1 person is sitting on either Row 1, 6 or 7 as he would pay ₹1000.

If you then include that and check for the total of 5 people, you will see that the value of 2600/5 is 520. This means that two people were paying 1000 each as we cannot get the sum of 5 numbers equal to 2600 if we only use 200,300 and 500. If we use two 1000s, then the sum of the payments of the remaining 4 people must be 1600. This can only be done using 300 + 300 + 500 + 500.

Deduction 3: Clue 4 gives us the crux. If A, C and B are sitting in consecutive rows, in increasing order, and on the same seat, it would mean that they're either sitting in the aisle seat or the window seat. The row numbers definitely have to be 4, 5 and 6 as no other combination would lead each person sitting on the same seat alphabet paying a different amount. Also, if we think of whether they are sitting on the window or aisle seats, we can see that window of 4, 5, 6 means a total payment of 1000 + 200 + 300 =1500 for these 3 people. Of the other three people one pays 1000. So the other two have to pay 1100 jointly - which is not possible using any combination. Thus, we get that A, C and B are sitting in the aisle seats and paying 500, 300 and 1000 respectively.

Deduction 4: Gautam also sits in the same row as Bharat, which means that Gautam must be in row 6 and he must be paying 1000. At this stage, we still need to work out whether he is in the aisle or middle seat of row 6. In order to work that out, we need to see who of the remaining 3 (Dhruv, Ebrahim and Farrokh) are paying the balance 500 + 300 and who among them is not paying. Clue 7 and the current situation of the seating tells us that we cannot use rows 4-5-6 and because we have to use consecutive rows, both Ebrahim and Farrokh cannot be paying 500 and 300 (as the only instance of the same is on rows 4-5).Thus, Farrokh must be sitting on row 10 aisle (paying 300) and Ebrahim on row 11 aisle paying 0. (in either C or D). This also means that Dhruv must be paying 500, for which he has to be sitting in the aisle on the left side of the plane (left side from clue 8). Thus, the final seating is as shown here

X	A	B	C	D	E	F
1						
2						
3						
4			D (500)	A (500)		
5				C (300)		
6			G (1000)	B (1000)		
7						
8						
9						
10			F?	F? (300)		
11			E?	E? (0)		
12						
13						
14						
15	15A	15B	15C	15D	15E	15F

70. Option (a) is correct.
71. Option (a) is correct.
72. Option (b) is correct.
73. Option (a) is correct.
74. Option (d) is correct.

CHAPTER 3

Logical Reasoning based on Rankings

Chapter Launchpad
Scan this QR code for an introductory video on Logical Reasoning based on Rankings

Reasoning questions on Rankings involve an ordering of people/objects based on their heights/weights/performance in an exam, etc. As the name suggests, in questions on rankings you are supposed to place people/objects in a decreasing or increasing order based on the attribute being measured.

Following are the key skills required in solving Logical Reasoning questions based on rankings:

(i) The ability to visualise the structure in which the rankings have to be created.

(ii) The ability to order the clues in the correct order of usage (as explained in the theory of logical reasoning).

(iii) The ability to perceive what indirect clues are talking about and find the appropriate point in the solving process about how to use them.

(iv) The ability to convert clues written in language form into visual cues so that you do not need to read the text again and again, and also are able to 'see' all the clues at one go.

The following illustrated examples (with the reaction tracker used to explain the solutions) would help you get acquainted with questions based on rankings. For each of the following questions, first try to solve them on your own before looking at the reaction tracker process of solving the same.

Example 1:

(i) Six students A, B, C, D, E and F participated in a self-evaluation test of Quants and Data Interpretation (D.I.).

(ii) The total marks of A in Quants was just above C and in D.I., just above F.

(iii) B was just above C in D.I. but he scored less than D in Quants.

(iv) F got more marks than D and E in D.I. but did not perform as well in Quants as in D.I. as compared to D and E.

(v) No one is in between C and D in Quant and C and A in D.I.

1. Who got the highest marks in D.I.?
(a) A (b) B
(c) C (d) Data inadequate

2. Which of the following students has scored the least in D.I.?
(a) Only D (b) Only E
(c) Only D or E (d) None of these

3. Who was just below D in Quants?
(a) B (b) E
(c) C (d) Data inadequate

4. Which of the given statements is not necessary to answer the questions?
(a) (ii) (b) (iii)
(c) (iv) (d) All are necessary

Reaction Tracker

From the second statement, we have:

QUANTS	D.I.
A C	A F

From statement (iii) we have: B just above C in D.I. and B somewhere below D in Quants. At this point, our figure remains the same as we cannot put this information into the figure.

QUANTS	D.I.
A C	A F

From Statement (iv), we have:

QUANTS	D.I.
A C D & E above F	A F D & E below F

From Statement (v), we have:

QUANTS	D.I.
A	B
C	C
D	A
	F
	D & E below F

This leads us to the following table:

In Quants	In Data Interpretation
A	B
C	C
D	A
Also, B is less than D,	F
F is below D and E.	D and E are below F.
Note: E could be placed anywhere as we don't have any information about E.	Hence, B must be first.

The answers are:

1. B. Option (b).
2. Only D or E. Option (c).
3. Data inadequate. Option (d).
4. All are necessary. Option (d).

Example 2: Solve the following questions based on the information provided:

(i) A, B, C, D, E, F, G and H are eight friends. Three of them play cricket and table tennis each and two of them play football. Each one of them has a different height.

(ii) The tallest does not play football and the shortest does not play cricket.

(iii) F is taller than A and D but shorter than H and B.

(iv) E who does not play cricket, is taller than B and is second tallest.

(v) G is shorter than D but taller than A.

(vi) H, who is fourth from the top, plays table tennis with D.

(vii) G does not play either cricket or football. B does not play football.

1. Who is the tallest?
   (a) B (b) H
   (c) C (d) Data inadequate
2. Who is the shortest?
   (a) G (b) D
   (c) A (d) Data inadequate
3. Which of the following pairs of friends play football?
   (a) EA (b) EH
   (c) HF (d) Data inadequate
4. What is F's position from the top when they are arranged in descending order of their height?
   (a) Fifth (b) Fourth
   (c) Sixth (d) None of these

Reaction Tracker

The first direct clue in the question is clue (vi). Clue (vii) is the next clue to use as using the last 2 clues we get that H,G and D play table tennis (thus fixing our list of TT players). Hence, when we read that B does not play football, we can deduce that B plays cricket– as he cannot be playing table tennis since we already know the three people playing TT. The other direct clue that we can use for placing an individual in our starting figure based on height is clue (iv). According to this, E does not play cricket (hence, must be football) and he is second to the tallest. At this point, we also need to keep aside the information that E is taller than B outside the purview of the figure for later use. At this point, our figure would be as given below with the additional knowledge that H, G and D play TT and B plays cricket.

E	Football
H	Table tennis

From this point, we need to first focus on placing the other 6 people in the decreasing order of their heights inside the figure above.

Clue (iii) combined with clue (v) helps us understand that:

Between A, G and D, the order of heights from lower to higher would be A → G → D.

And, since F is taller than A and D, F must be taller than A → G → D. Also because F is shorter than H and B; and F cannot take the topmost or the third position from the top in the figure. Based on these deductions the figure changes to:

E	Football
H	Table tennis
F	
D	Table tennis
G	Table tennis
A	

Placing B in the above figure is easy because we had kept aside the information that "E is taller than B". Thus, B can only take the third place position and the highest place goes to C. Thus, the figure becomes:

C	
E	Football
B	Cricket
H	Table tennis
F	
D	Table tennis
G	Table tennis
A	

At this point, we can use the clues about who does not play what and identify the remaining 2 people for cricket and the remaining person for football as:

The tallest does not play football → deduction → the tallest plays cricket.

The shortest does not play cricke → deduction → the shortest plays football. The table can be completed at this point as below:

C	Cricket
E	Football
B	Cricket
H	Table tennis
F	Cricket
D	Table tennis
G	Table tennis
A	Football

The answers can be read off easily at this point from the table above:

1. C is the tallest. Option (c).
2. A is the shortest. Option (c).
3. E & A are the two football players. Option (a).
4. F is placed fifth from the top. Option (a).

LEVEL OF DIFFICULTY (I)

Directions for Questions 1 to 5: *Read the details below and answer the questions that follow.*

Six sisters Kristy, Kevin, Kiara, Kelly, Koshi and Kristine are living in Countryside in London.

(i) Kristy is not the tallest while Kelly is not the most qualified.
(ii) The shortest is the most qualified amongst them all.
(iii) Kristine is more qualified than Kevin who is more qualified than Kiara.
(iv) Kristy is less qualified than Kevin but is taller than Kevin.
(v) Kristine is shorter than Kiara but taller than Koshi.
(vi) Kiara is more qualified than Kristy while Kevin is taller than Kiara.
(vii) Kelly is the least qualified amongst the sisters.

1. Who is the third tallest starting in decreasing order of height?
(a) Kristy (b) Kevin
(c) Kiara (d) Koshi

2. Who is the most qualified?
(a) Kevin (b) Kiara
(c) Kelly (d) Koshi

3. What is the rank of Kiara in increasing order of qualification?
(a) 2 (b) 3
(c) 5 (d) 4

4. What is the rank of Kristy in increasing order of height?
(a) 3 (b) 5
(c) 4 (d) 2

5. Who is the tallest girl?
(a) Kevin (b) Kiara
(c) Kelly (d) Koshi

Directions for Questions 6 to 8: *Refer to the following information to answer the questions that follow.*

(i) Seven students A, B, C, D, E, F and G take a series of tests.
(ii) No two students get similar marks.
(iii) G always scores more than A.
(iv) A always scores more than B.
(v) Each time either C scores the highest and E gets the least, or alternatively, D scores the highest and F or B scores the least.

6. If G is ranked fifth, which of these must be true?
(a) D scores the highest.
(b) C is ranked second.
(c) E is ranked third.
(d) B is ranked fourth.

7. If D is ranked second, which of the following can be true?
(a) A gets more than C.
(b) G gets more than D.
(c) A gets more than G.
(d) F gets more than G.

8. If D is ranked sixth and B is ranked fifth, which of these can be true?
(a) G is ranked first or fourth.
(b) C is ranked second or third.
(c) A is ranked second or fifth.
(d) F is ranked third or fourth.

Directions for Questions 9 to 13: *Each of the following questions gives information about an individual attribute through statements (i), (ii) and (iii). For each question, if the first two statements are true, what conclusion can be drawn about the third statement?*

9.
(i) Karela is more bitter than Palak but neem is more bitter than Karela.
(ii) Palak is more bitter than Babool but Bhindi is more bitter than Palak.
(iii) Of the five kinds of vegetables, Babool is the least in terms of bitterness.
If the first two statements are true, the third statement is:
(a) True
(b) False
(c) Uncertain

10. On the day the triplets were born to Shyama, the cow,
(i) A weighs more than B.
(ii) B weighs less than C.
(iii) Among the three calves, C weighs the most.
If the first two statements are true, the third statement is:
(a) True
(b) False
(c) Uncertain

11. At a Tata car showroom,
(i) The price of Punch was lower than that of Altroz.
(ii) The price of Curvv was lower than that of Altroz.
(iii) The price of Punch was higher than that of Curvv.
If the first two statements are true, the third statement is:
(a) True
(b) False
(c) Uncertain

12. In India,
(i) KHO-KHO is bigger than GILLI-DANDA and smaller than UNO.
(ii) HIDE-SEEK is smaller than UNO and bigger than KHO-KHO.
(iii) GILLI-DANDA is bigger than HIDE-SEEK.
If the first two statements are true, the third statement is:
(a) True
(b) False
(c) Uncertain

13. Ramesh has 3 ball boxes.
(i) Red packet contains more balls than Blue packet.
(ii) Blue packet contains more balls than Green packet
(iii) Green packet contains more balls than Red packet
If the first two statements are true, the third statement is:
(a) True
(b) False
(c) Uncertain

Directions for Questions 14 to 17: *Five cities all got more rain than usual this year. The five cities are: Aurangabad, Ahmednagar, Pune, Mumbai and Nagpur. The cities are located in five different areas of the country: the mountains, the forest, the coast, the desert, and in a valley. The rainfall amounts were: 24 inches, 54 inches, 64 inches, 88 inches and 130 inches.*
(i) The city in the desert got the least rain; the city in the forest got the most rain.
(ii) Pune is in the mountains.
(iii) Aurangabad got more rain than Mumbai.
(iv) Ahmednagar got more rain than Nagpur, but less rain than Pune.
(v) Mumbai got 88 inches of rain.
(vi) The city in the mountains got 64 inches of rain; the city on the coast got 54 inches of rain.

14. Which city is in the desert?
(a) Aurangabad (b) Ahmednagar
(c) Pune (d) Nagpur

15. Which city got the most rain?
(a) Aurangabad (b) Ahmednagar
(c) Pune (d) Mumbai

16. How much rain did Ahmednagar get?
(a) 24 inches (b) 54 inches
(c) 64 inches (d) 88 inches

17. Where is Mumbai located?
(a) The mountains (b) The coast
(c) In a valley (d) The desert

Directions for Questions 18 to 22: *Six research associates of a research institute were to attend four lectures, each lasting for an hour, from 3:30 p.m. to 7:30 p.m. to discuss various aspects of business. Each of the four lectures was attended by exactly four of the six research associates. After each lecture, exactly one research associate left the group and exactly one research associate joined. It is also known that:*
(i) The Physics research associate joined the group at 4:30 p.m. and the Zoology research associate left at 6:30 p.m. These two research associates attended an equal number of lectures.
(ii) The Chemistry research associate rejoined the group at 6:30 p.m.
(iii) The Maths research associate joined the group for the first time when the Statistics research associate left.
(iv) One of the research associates was from Biology.
(v) The lectures were held back-to-back and nobody left/joined in between any lecture.

18. Which subject's research associate left after 3rd lecture?

19. Which subject's research associates joined the 4th lecture?

20. How many lectures were attended by the Biology research associate?

21. Which of the following is an incorrect combination of research associates who attended any of the lectures together?
(a) Biology, Zoology, Statistics, Chemistry
(b) Chemistry, Biology, Maths, Physics
(c) Zoology, Physics, Biology, Chemistry
(d) Physics, Maths, Biology, Zoology

22. Which research associate left the group after the first lecture?
(a) Statistics (b) Chemistry
(c) Biology (d) None of these

Directions for Questions 23 to 27: *Six athletes - Anil, Bumrah, Dhawan, Gautam, Kriti and Satnam - appeared in a race. They were ranked 1 to 6, in no particular order, based on their finishing time in the race. It is also known that:*

(i) Exactly two athletes were ranked between Dhawan and Anil.
(ii) Exactly one athlete was ranked between Satnam and Dhawan.
(iii) The rank of Kriti was worse than the ranks of both Anil and Dhawan.
(iv) The rank of Bumrah was better than that of Anil.

23. Whose rank can exactly be determined?
(a) Anil (b) Dhawan
(c) Kriti (d) None of these

24. What is the sum of all the possible ranks of Dhawan?

25. Which of the following could not be the rank of Gautam?
(a) 1 (b) 2
(c) 3 (d) 5

26. Gautam was disqualified from the race as he was found cheating. If the remaining five athletes were ranked 1 to 5, who got Rank 1?
(a) Dhawan (b) Anil
(c) Bumrah (d) Cannot be determined

27. In the previous question, if it is also known that Dhawan was ranked in top 3, then who scored Rank 4?

Directions for Question 28: *Each question is followed by two statements, A and B. Answer each question using the following instructions:*

Choose (a): If the question can be answered by using statement A alone but not by using B alone.

Choose (b): If the question can be answered by using statement B alone but not by using A alone.

Choose (c): If the question can be answered by using either statement alone.

Choose (d): If the question can be answered by using both the statements together but not by either Statement alone.

28. Four friends, A, B, C and D got the top four ranks in a competitive examination, but A did not get the first, B did not get the second, C did not get the third, and D did not get the fourth rank. Who secured which rank?
(a) Neither A nor D were among the first 2.
(b) Neither B nor C was third or fourth.

LEVEL OF DIFFICULTY (II)

Directions for Questions 1 to 5: *Study the following information carefully and answer the questions given below:*

High Yield Questions

Scan this QR code to access a video explanation of questions 1-5

Five geeks (enthusiasts) entered a comic book character costume contest, held during the comic con festival. The contestants were dressed up and were given two awards–one for being best in a particular category (i.e., strongest, smartest, most efficient, scariest and powerful) and one for being ranked (i.e., 1st, 2nd, 3rd, 4th and 5th). Determine who wore which costume and which two awards they received.

(i) The winner of the most efficient character's costume was ranked just above costume of Sacha's character (which wasn't the Superman).
(ii) The winner of the strongest category (which wasn't the Wonderwoman) was not worn by Billy.
(iii) The Joker's costume was ranked just above Sacha's costume (which wasn't the strongest costume winner).
(iv) The Wonderwoman costume ranked just above the scariest costume and just below Vladimir's costume.
(v) The Batman costume was placed just higher than the winner of the strongest costume and just lower than Catherine's costume.
(vi) The Lex Luthor costume ranked just above Jelena's (which wasn't the Superman) and just below the smartest.

1. Who among the following ranked fifth?
(a) Billy (b) Jelena
(c) Vladimir (d) Can't be determined

2. Who among the following got the award of the scariest costume?
(a) Billy (b) Catharine
(c) Sacha (d) Vladimir

3. Which of the following is the costume of Sacha?
(a) Joker (b) Batman
(c) Lex Luthor (d) Wonderwoman

4. Which of the following shows the correct order of ranks 1st, 2nd, 3rd, 4th and 5th respectively?
(a) Billy, Jelena, Vladimir, Sacha and Catherine
(b) Vladimir, Sacha, Catherine, Billy and Jelena
(c) Catherine, Sacha, Vladimir, Jelena and Billy
(d) Vladimir, Billy, Catherine, Sacha and Jelena

5. Which of the following are not correctly matched?

Costume	Category
I. Joker	Most Efficient
II. Batman	Smartest
III. Lex Luthor	Strongest
IV. Wonderwoman	Scariest
V. Superman	Powerful

(a) Only IV and V (b) Only III and IV
(c) Only II and III (d) Only I and II

Directions for Questions 6 to 10: *Sprinters in Olympics running on the track are carrying numbers from 1 to 7 at the back of their vests. They complete the race when their feet touches the finish line at 9.10, 9.20, 9.30 seconds till 9.7 seconds i.e., at an interval of one millisecond each. Each athlete is ranked from 1 (for the fastest) to 7 (for the slowest). The following additional information is known:*

High Yield Questions

Scan this QR code to access a video explanation of questions 6-10

(i) The square of the highest total of the vest number and rank is 169 which occurs only once.
(ii) The square of the lowest total of vest number and rank is 16 and occurs only once.
(iii) The square of the total of vest number and rank = 81, occurs thrice.
(iv) The winners' vest number exceeds that of the first runner-up.

6. The vest number of the sprinter coming first is:
(a) 3 (b) 6
(c) 1 (d) 5

7. The sprinter number finishing second is:
(a) 7 (b) 6
(c) 4 (d) 3

8. The sprinter number finishing third is:
(a) 6 (b) 3
(c) 1 (d) 2

9. The sprinter number finishing last is:
(a) 7 (b) 2
(c) 5 (d) 1

10. The sprinter number finishing last but one is:
(a) 7 (b) 2
(c) 5 (d) 1

Directions for Questions 11 to 15: *In a bike racing competition, ten selected bikers from a city were to compete in various stunts. The structure of the competition requires all bikers to compete in five events before the elimination round begins so as to choose the top five bikers who will participate from that city at the national level. The ranks attained by each biker in the five events from first to tenth are:*

Names	Event A	Event B	Event C	Event D	Event E
Alex	2	5	8	5	1
Ben	8	1	7	1	2
Charlie	5	6	1	4	9
Devon	1	10	2	10	3
Ethan	9	4	9	2	7
Frank	6	7	6	6	8
Garry	3	2	3	7	4
Harry	10	8	5	3	10
Ian	7	9	10	8	5
John	4	3	4	9	6

It is also stated that:
(i) The biker with the first rank in most events gets to eliminate the biker with the last rank in most of the events.
(ii) The first rank holder of event E is not to be eliminated.
(iii) A biker whose highest rank and the lowest rank difference is the second highest among all bikers is not to be eliminated.
(iv) A biker who does not rank in the top five positions in any of the five events gets eliminated.
(v) The biker with the same rank in most of the events gets to eliminate that biker with an immediately lower rank than his same ranks in all events.
(vi) A biker who got the second highest rank in event D gets to eliminate the biker who got the same rank in event B.
(vii) Any biker who gets the first rank in two or more events will not be eliminated.
(viii) Among the bikers who got the lowest rank in event B and the one who got the ninth rank in event D, the one who got a higher rank in the event E gets to eliminate the other.

(ix) The biker whose sum of all the ranks in the events is the highest and does not get eliminated by any other condition will not be eliminated.

It is also known that if more than 5 people are getting eliminated by one rule or the other, then it is allowed. However, if less than 5 people are getting eliminated, then there is a toss up between the remaining ones and the results are determined by the toss of a coin.

11. Who among the following is a biker who does not get a chance to eliminate another biker?
(a) Ben (b) Charlie
(c) Devon (d) Frank

12. Who among the following is a biker who does not rank in the top four positions in any of the five events but does not get eliminated?
(a) Ethan (b) Frank
(c) Harry (d) Ian

13. If a new condition is included in the problem stating that, 'any biker who gets second rank in any event will not be eliminated', then who among the following will not get eliminated?
(a) Garry (b) Harry
(c) Ian (d) John

14. Which of the following conditions, if not included in the problem does not change the final solution?
(a) ii (b) iv
(c) vi (d) viii

15. It is found that the results of event D are wrong and the last two ranks have been mistakenly interchanged, then who among the following bikers cannot be definitely eliminated in the elimination round?
(a) Ethan & Devon (b) Garry & John
(c) Harry & Devon (d) John & Devon

Directions for Questions 16 to 19: *Answer the following questions based on the given information:*

Eight boxers P, Q, R, S, T, U, V and W participated in an interstate boxing championship. These players were ranked from 1 to 8 (in any order) based on their rating before the tournament. In the tournament, each boxer had exactly two bouts against every other boxer. The bouts were scheduled on consecutive days. Any day, exactly three bouts were scheduled and these bouts involved six different boxers. 2 points were awarded for a win and 1 point for a tied bout and 0 point for a loss. At the end of the championship, the boxer who scored most points got the 1st rank and the boxer with the 2nd most points got the 2nd rank and so on. If two or more boxers scored the same number of points then the boxer with the best rank before the championship would get the best rank among other players with same points.

16. If the tournament started on Monday and there are no rest days, then it would be finished on which of the following day?
(a) Thursday (b) Friday
(c) Saturday (d) None of these

17. If P ranked 1 before the tournament and he got the 1st rank after the tournament then which of the following could be his minimum possible points?
(a) 13 (b) 12
(c) 14 (d) None of these

18. If P got the 1st rank in the tournament and Q got the last rank then minimum possible difference between the points of P and Q?
(a) 0 (b) 2
(c) 3 (d) None of these

19. If only two boxers R and S finished with the same number of points then find the maximum possible score obtained by the last ranked boxer in the championship?

Directions for Questions 20 to 23: *Answer the following questions based on the given information:*

Eight boxers P, Q, R, S, T, U, V and W participated in an international boxing championship. In the first round of the championship, these eight boxers were divided into two groups of four boxers each. In a group, each boxer had to box twice against each of the other boxers. Every bout had a decisive result, i.e., no bout ended in a tie. The boxer with the highest and the second highest number of wins in both the groups reached the semifinal. Q, U, W and V were the four boxers who qualified for the semifinal.

It is also known that in the first round:

(i) Each boxer of each group had a different number of wins.
(ii) R lost all of his bouts against all the other players except S, who won at least one bout against each of the other boxers except one.
(iii) V won both the bouts against U.
(iv) P and W won the same number of bouts.

20. Who won the least number of bouts after the 1st round?
(a) P (b) R
(c) S (d) T

21. What was the total number of wins of P after the first round?
(a) 1 (b) 2
(c) 3 (d) 4

22. Who won the most number of bouts after the 1st round?
(a) Q (b) U
(c) W (d) V

23. Which of the following player lost at least one bout against P in the 1st round?

(a) Q (b) S
(c) U (d) V

Directions for Questions 24 to 27: *Answer the following questions based on the given information:*

In ISI Kolkata, five students Aman, Baman, Chaman, Daman and Elvis take the final year exam. The exam has three subjects Probability, Statistical methods and Six Sigma, and the cutoff scores of these three subjects are–22, 25 and 20, respectively. Maximum possible score on each of these three subjects is 100. The student who scores the highest marks gets 1st rank and one who scores the 2nd highest marks gets 2nd rank and so on. The following information is given about the score of these five students:

(i) In a particular subject, the scores obtained by each student are different integers.
(ii) The lowest score in the subject was twice the cutoff score.
(iii) For any student, rank obtained in any two subjects was not same.
(iv) The total score of a student was the sum of scores obtained in all the three subjects.
(v) For any subject, the difference between the highest and the lowest score was 4.
(vi) An overall topper is a student whose overall score is greater than all other students.

24. Which of the following can be the maximum possible score of the overall topper?
(a) 134 (b) 142
(c) 144 (d) 143

25. Which of the following is the least possible score of a student?
(a) 131 (b) 137
(c) 128 (d) None of these

26. If total score of Aman is the least among all the students then what can be the maximum possible value of the total score of Aman?

27. What is the maximum possible difference of total scores of any two students?

Directions for Questions 28 to 31: *Answer the following questions based on the given information:*

Eight teams from different states participated in IPL 2015. The tournament comprises three stages–Group stage, Semifinals and Final. In the group stage, each team played exactly two games against each other– one at home and one away. Winning team of the group stage match is rewarded six points, losing team gets no point and in case of a tie each team is rewarded two points. If at the end of group stage rounds, 2 or more than 2 teams end up with the same number of points then their placing in the points table would be determined by their respective run rates. The top 4 teams of group stage round advanced to semifinals and winner of semifinals advanced to final and winner of final would be declared the champion of IPL-2015.

28. If Pune Warriors reached semifinals, difference between the minimum and maximum possible points obtained by them at the end of group stage round would be:
(a) 66 (b) 68
(c) 72 (d) None of these

29. What are the maximum possible points scored by the team who did not advance to semifinals?

30. If Mumbai Indians won IPL 2015, then difference between the maximum and minimum possible points scored by them (matches of semifinal and final did not end in tie and points distribution in matches of semifinal and final is same as group stage rounds) is
(a) 56 (b) 68
(c) 76 (d) None of these

31. What are the minimum possible points achieved by the team at 7th rank after the group stage round?

Directions for Questions 32 to 36: *Answer the questions on the basis of the information given below.*

Four students Raman, Sharan, David and Gabrial are ranked 1 to 4, based on their performance in a physics test.

The following information is also known:

(i) If Raman is ranked 1, then Sharan is not ranked 3.
(ii) If Sharan is not ranked 1, then Gabrial is ranked 4.
(iii) If David is ranked 3, then Gabrial is not ranked 2.
(iv) If David is not ranked 2, then Gabrial is ranked 2.
(v) If Gabrial is ranked 3, then Raman is not ranked 4.

32. What is the rank of Raman?

33. Who is ranked 1 among the four students?
(a) Sharan (b) David
(c) Raman (d) Cannot be determined

34. Who is ranked 4 among the four students?
(a) Sharan (b) Gabrial
(c) David (d) Cannot be determined

35. The ranks of how many of the four students can be determined?

36. What is the sum of all possible ranks of Gabrial and David?

Directions for Questions 37 to 39: *Answer the questions on the basis of the information given below.*

Eight players- Ashwin, Bumrah, Chahal, Dhoni, Eshant, Axar, Nehra and Srishant - participated in a match consisting of three rounds - I, II and III. Each player got a different rank in different rounds and no two friends got the same rank in any round. It is also given that:

(i) The sum of ranks in the three rounds together was equal for Chahal and Bumrah.

(ii) The rank of Srishant in round II was higher than that in round I but lower than that in round III.
(iii) In each round Bumrah, Nehra and Axar got three consecutive ranks from higher to lower, in that order.
(iv) Ashwin was ranked 1st and last in round II and round III, in any order.
(v) Eshant got rank 6 in round III and rank 4 in round I. Dhoni got rank 2 in round II and rank 1 in round I. Chahal got rank 3 in round II.

[**Note:** Rank 1 was the highest and rank 8 was the lowest among them.]

37. Which of the following pair of players must be on two consecutive positions in each round?
(a) Dhoni and Bumrah (b) Axar and Srishant
(c) Ashwin and Nehra (d) None of these

38. The lowest rank which Dhoni could get in round II was:
(a) 1 (b) 2
(c) 7 (d) 8

39. What was the difference between the highest and the lowest possible sum of the ranks obtained by Bumrah in the three rounds?
(a) 6 (b) 2
(c) 5 (d) 1

Directions for Questions 40 to 44: *Saeed Chaturvedi, a faculty at Mindworkzz, A CAT Prep institute led by Arun Sharma, conducted a mock test for five students, Manu, Rohan, Rahi, Roshan and Navya. Each student received a different rank in the test. Saeed wanted to test the students on their ability to judge themselves and their fellow classmates. So, he asked his students to predict the rank of everyone. From the response he got from the students, Saeed was able to deduce the following:*

1. Rohan predicted that Manu would be ranked better than Rahi, while Manu predicted Rahi would be ranked first.
2. Except for Navya and Rahi, none of the others predicted that Roshan would be ranked third, and Navya predicted Manu's rank to be four.
3. Roshan predicted the rank of the student whose actual rank was five to be one, and the rank of the student whose actual rank was three to be five.
4. No student was able to correctly estimate the rank of any student. Moreover, none of the students expected themselves to be in the bottom 2 of the class.
5. Except for Rohan, none of the students predicted their own rank to be one. Also, none of the students expected Manu to be amongst the top 2 performers.
6. Only Manu thought that Rahi would outperform Navya.
7. Except for Rohan, the rank of each student was predicted to be five by at least one student, while Roshan predicted the rank of Navya to be less than four.

40. Rohan predicted Rahi's rank to be
(a) 2 (b) 3
(c) 4 (d) 5

41. Which student was actually ranked first?
(a) Manu (b) Roshan
(c) Navya (d) Cannot be determined

42. What could be the rank of Navya according to Manu?

43. How many students expected Rohan to top the class?

44. For which of the following persons is it possible that none of the persons predicted their rank to be two?
(a) Rohan (b) Roshan
(c) Navya (d) None of the above

ANSWER KEY

Level of Difficulty (I)

1. (b)	2. (d)	3. (b)	4. (b)
5. (c)	6. (a)	7. (d)	8. (d)
9. (a)	10. (c)	11. (c)	12. (b)
13. (b)	14. (d)	15. (a)	16. (b)
17. (c)	18. Zoology	19. Chemistry	20. 4
21. (c)	22. (b)	23. (d)	24. 8
25. (b)	26. (d)	27. Anil	28. (c)

Level of Difficulty (II)

1. (a)	2. (a)	3. (b)	4. (c)
5. (a)	6. (b)	7. (d)	8. (c)
9. (b)	10. (a)	11. (b)	12. (d)
13. (a)	14. (a)	15. (d)	16. (b)
17. (c)	18. (a)	19. 11 points	20. (d)
21. (c)	22. (a)	23. (d)	24. (d)
25. (b)	26. 139	27. 6	28. (b)
29. 60	30. (b)	31. 4	32. 3
33. (a)	34. (d)	35. 2	36. 12
37. (d)	38. (b)	39. (b)	40. (c)
41. (b)	42. 5th	43. 3	44. (a)

SOLUTIONS AND SHORTCUTS

Level of Difficulty (I)

Solutions for Questions 1 to 5:

From the 1st statement we can conclude that Kristy is not the tallest, Kelly is not most qualified

From the 2nd statement we can conclude that shortest is most qualified

From the 3rd statement we can conclude that in terms of qualification Kristine > Kevin > Kiara

From the 4th statement we can conclude that in terms of qualification Kevin > Kristy. And in terms of Height: Kristy > Kevin

From the 5th statement we can conclude that in terms of height Kiara > Kristine > Koshi

From the 6th statement we can conclude that in terms of qualification Kiara > Kristy. And in terms of height Kevin > Kiara

From the 7th statement we can conclude that Kelly is least qualified

Now, Order of Height is :-

Kelly > Kristy > Kevin > Kiara > Kristine > Koshi

In Order of qualification:-

Koshi > Kristine > Kevin > Kiara > Kristy > Kelly

1. Kevin. Option (b) is correct.
2. Koshi. Option (d) is correct.
3. Kiara is 3rd if we place them in increasing order of qualification. Option (b) is correct.
4. Kristy is 5 if we place them in increasing order of height. Option (b) is correct.
5. From the order of height, we can see that it is Kelly. Hence, Option (c) is correct.

Solutions for Questions 6 to 8:

6. If G is fifth, then A and B must be ranked 6th and 7th respectively. This can only happen if D scores the highest (as, if C is the highest, then E must be 7th). Option (a).
7. The first three options are not feasible. Option (d) is the only thing that can be true.
8. Option (d) is possible.

Solutions for Questions 9 to 13:

9. The ordering in terms of bitterness would be Neem > Karela > Palak > Babool and Bhindi must be bitter than Babools. Thus, clearly the third statement is true. Thus, option (a) is correct.
10. Both A and C weigh more than B. However, it is not certain whether C weighs the most. Thus, we choose Option (c).
11. Uncertain. Option (c) is correct.
12. We will get from the first two statements U > H > K > G.
    Thus, Statement 3 is false if the first two statements are true. Thus, option (b) is correct.
13. False, as we get Red > Blue > Green and hence, Green > Red is definitely false. Option (b) is correct.

Solutions for Questions 14 to 17:

The solution table would be:

Rainfall (From Max to Min)	Location	City
130	Forest	Aurangabad
88	Valley	Mumbai
64	Mountains	Pune
54	Coast	Ahmednagar
24	Desert	Nagpur

Hence, the answers are:

14. Nagpur (Option d).
15. Aurangabad (Option a).
16. Ahmednagar ranked fourth and got 54 inches of rain. (Option b).
17. Mumbai is located in a valley (Option c).

Solutions for Questions 18 to 22:

From statements (i) and (iii) → research associates of Physics and Maths didn't attend the 1st lecture.

Since the Physics research associate joined before the 2nd lecture and the Chemistry research associate rejoined before the 4th lecture, from statement (iii), the Maths research associate must have joined before the 3rd lecture and the Statistics research associate must have left after the 2nd lecture. Now, since the Chemistry research associate rejoined in the 4th lecture, he must have left after the 1st lecture.

From statement (i), the number of lectures attended by the Zoology and Physics research associates must be 3 each. So the Zoology research associate attended the 1st, 2nd and 3rd lectures while the Physics research associate attended the 2nd, 3rd and 4th lectures.

The above analysis leads to the table given below.

Time Slot	Research Associates	Associates who joined	Associates who left
3:30	Chemistry, Zoology, Statistics, Biology		Chemistry
4:30	Physics, Zoology, Statistics, Biology	Physics	Statistics
5:30	Physics, Zoology, Maths, Biology	Maths	Zoology
6:30	Physics, Chemistry, Maths, Biology	Chemistry	

18. Zoology
19. Chemistry
20. 4
21. Zoology, Physics, Biology, Chemistry. Hence, option (c) is correct.
22. Chemistry. Hence, option (b) is correct.

Solutions for Questions 23 to 27:

From statement (iv), the rank of Bumrah was better than that of Anil and from statement (iii), the rank of Kriti was worse than the ranks of both Anil and Dhawan. Also, we know that there are exactly two athletes ranked between Anil and Dhawan- combining these information, we can see that Anil would not be ranked 1 or 6. Thus, they can only be ranked 2 and 5- in any order or 4 and 1 with Anil as 4 and Dhawan as 1. Now, there are three cases possible:

Case I: The ranks of Anil and Dhawan were 2 and 5 respectively. Then the ranks of Bumrah and Kriti would be 1 and 6 respectively. Satnam's rank would be 3. Hence, the rank of Gautam would be 4.

Case II: The ranks of Anil and Dhawan were 5 and 2 respectively. Then the rank of Kriti would be 6. Satnam's rank would be 4. Hence, the ranks of Bumrah and Gautam would be 1 and 3, in no particular order.

Case III: The ranks of Anil and Dhawan were 4 and 1 respectively. Then the rank of Kriti would be either 5 or 6. From statement (ii), Satnam's rank would be 3. Hence, the rank of Bumrah was 2 and the rank of Gautam was either 5 or 6.

The cases can be tabulated as shown below.

Rank	1	2	3	4	5	6
Case 1	Bumrah	Anil	Satnam	Gautam	Dhawan	Kriti
Case 2	Bumrah/ Gautam	Dhawan	Gautam/ Bumrah	Satnam	Anil	Kriti
Case 3	Dhawan	Bumrah	Satnam	Anil	Kriti/ Gautam	Gautam/ Kriti

23. None of these athletes' rank can exactly be determined. Hence, option (d) is correct.
24. 5 + 2 + 1 = 8.
25. Gautam could not have got Rank 2. Hence, option (b) is correct.
26. If Gautam was disqualified, it can be seen from the table below, that Bumrah or Dhawan would be ranked 1.

Rank	1	2	3	4	5
Case 1	Bumrah	Dhawan	Satnam	Anil	Kriti
Case 2	Dhawan	Bumrah	Satnam	Anil	Kriti

Hence, Dhawan or Bumrah must have got Rank 1. Hence, option (d) is correct.

27. Anil can be seen to be getting rank 4 in each case.

Solution for Question 28:

28. The basic information can be summarised as:

Rank	Ruled Out	Possible
First	A	B, C, D
Second	B	A, C, D
Third	C	A, B, D
Fourth	D	A, B, C

From statement A, we see that

Rank	Ruled Out	Possible
First	A	Deduction 2: B
Second	B	Deduction 1: C
Third	C	Deduction 4: D
Fourth	D	Deduction 3: A

We get the information about all the ranks and this statement alone is sufficient to answer the question.

From statement B, we see that

Rank	Ruled Out	Possible
First	A	Deduction 4: B
Second	B	Deduction 3: C
Third	C	Deduction 2: D
Fourth	D	Deduction 1: A

We get the information about all the ranks and this statement alone is sufficient to answer the question.

Level of Difficulty (II)

Solutions for Questions 1 to 5:

This question seems to be quite confusing due to the reason that all the clues seem to be the same/similar in nature. While that might be true on the surface, there are a few distinctions in the ways the clues can be used– especially when we look at the clues in the correct order.

On combining clues (i) and (iii), we would get the following Table 1:

Costume	Person	Category best
Joker		Most efficient
	Sacha	

Note: We combine clues (i) and (iii) because clue (ii) is not usable at this stage, as it is what can be described as "a checking" clue, i.e., once we have multiple final figure possibilities in place, we use clues of the nature of clue (ii) and also clue (i) (Sacha was not the Superman), to eliminate one of the possibilities.

Clue (iv) will give us Table 2:

Costume	Person	Category best
	Vladimir	
Wonderwoman		
		Scariest

Clue (v) would give us Table 3:

Costume	Person	Category best
	Catherine	
Batman		
		Strongest

Clue (vi) would give us Table 4:

Costume	Person	Category best
		Smartest
Lex Luthor		
	Jelena	

From this point we need to focus on Sacha's costume. We would realise that Sacha cannot wear Superman (given clue (i)); cannot wear Joker (as Joker is above Sacha according to Table 1) and cannot wear Lex Luthor because we cannot superimpose Table 4 on Table 1 by making Sacha correspond to Lex Luthor as it leads to the Joker being the smartest (but Table 1 has Joker as the most efficient).

This leaves us with 2 possibilities for Sacha's costume–Wonderwoman or Batman.

Let us take a look at how possibility 1 rolls out:

For Sacha to be **Wonderwoman**, we would need to merge Tables 1 and 2 to get Table 5 below:

Costume	Person	Category best
Joker	**Vladimir**	Most Efficient
Wonderwoman	Sacha	
		Scariest

To this, we need to merge Table 3, which would give us Table 6 below:

Costume	Person	Category best
Joker	Vladimir	Most Efficient
Wonderwoman	Sacha	
	Catherine	Scariest
Batman		
		Strongest

There is only one way from this point that Table 4 can get merged into Table 6. That would give us:

Costume	Person	Category best
Joker	Vladimir	Most Efficient
Wonderwoman	Sacha	**Smartest**
Lex Luthor	Catherine	Scariest
Batman	**Jelena**	
		Strongest

That leaves us with the final solution as below:

Costume	Person	Category best
Joker	Vladimir	Most Efficient
Wonderwoman	Sacha	Smartest
Lex Luthor	Catherine	Scariest
Batman	Jelena	Most powerful
Superman	Billy	Strongest

We can clearly see that this solution table contradicts clue (ii), i.e., Billy was not the strongest.

Thus, we reject Possibility 1 and move to a possibility which would give us that Sacha must be Batman. In this case the thinking pattern would go as follows:

Combining Table 3 with Table 1:

Costume	Person	Category best
Joker	**Catherine**	Most efficient
Batman	Sacha	
		Strongest

To this we merge Table 2 and get:

Costume	Person	Category best
Joker	Catherine	Most efficient
Batman	Sacha	
	Vladimir	Strongest
Wonderwoman		
		Scariest

To this, we merge Table 4 and get:

Costume	Person	Category best
Joker	Catherine	Most efficient
Batman	Sacha	**Smartest**
Lex Luthor	Vladimir	Strongest
Wonderwoman	**Jelena**	
		Scariest

This leaves us with the task of placing the remaining values in each column. When we do this, we get:

Costume	Person	Category best
Joker	Catherine	Most efficient
Batman	Sacha	Smartest
Lex Luthor	Vladimir	Strongest
Wonderwoman	Jelena	**Powerful**
Superman	**Billy**	Scariest

This solution does not contradict any of the basic clues, given in the question. Hence, the answers are:

1. Billy ranked fifth. Option (a) is correct.
2. Billy got the scariest costume. Option (a) is correct.
3. Sacha's costume is Batman. Option (b) is correct.
4. Option (c) is the correct order.
5. Only (iv) and (v) are not properly matched. Hence, option (a) is correct.

Solutions for Questions 6 to 10:

There are essentially two logical forks in this question: The first one comes from clue (i), according to which the highest total of vest number and time must be 13 (as the square is 169).

This could mean two scenarios:

Vest number 7 with time = 6; or vest number 6 with time = 7.

The two scenarios can be shown as:

Possibility 1		Possibility 2	
Vest Number	Rank	Vest Number	Rank
1		1	
2		2	
3		3	
4		4	
5		5	
6		6	7
7	6	7	

Inside these two scenarios we need to merge the other three way fork:

The square of the least total of vest number and rank is 16 and occurs only once. It gives us 3 scenarios on the surface:

However, in this scenario we can reject Vest 3 ranking 1 because then the second ranker's vest number would exceed the winner's vest number (clue (iv))–as we cannot put the 2nd rank for either 1 or 2 as the total of 4 is the least sum and occurs only once.

This leaves us with 4 principal situations 1A, 1B, 2A and 2B. Let us evaluate each of these separately:

Possibility 1A (starting thought)	
Vest number	Rank
1	3
2	4/5/7
3	2/4/5/7
4	1/2/4/5/7
5	1/2/4/5/7
6	1/2/4/5
7	6

In the above situation, the total of vest number + rank = 9 has to occur thrice. There are only 3 places where this can actually occur given the possibilities listed above. These are 2-7; 4-5 and 5-4. Hence, the following conclusions can be made:

Possibility 1A (starting thought)	
Vest number	Rank
1	3
2	7
3	2
4	5
5	4
6	1
7	6

3-2 and 6-1 get automatically selected. As for the vest number 3, only rank possibility left is 2nd rank and after that, rank 1 must go to vest number 6.

If we go for a similar analysis with the other possibilities you can see that they do not work out. For instance, in possibility 1B, if we put down what is possible to be placed against vest numbers 1 and 3 respectively, we get the following figure.

Possibility 1B	
Vest number	Rank
1	4/5/7
2	2
3	3/4/5/7
4	
5	
6	
7	6

From this point, we know that there have to be exactly 3 totals of 9, which can only be achieved by matching 4-5, 5-4 and 6-3. Then, the 3rd vest must be on 7th rank but that leaves us with no rank possibility for vest 1 and also rank 1 not getting allotted anywhere. Thus, this possibility does not exist.

Similarly, we can reject possibilities 2A and 2B:

Possibility 2A	
Vest number	Rank
1	3
2	4/5/6

Possibility 2A	
3	2/4/5/6
4	1/2/4/5/6
5	1/2/4/5/6
6	7
7	1/2/4/5/6

In the above table we need three 9s. There are 4 possibilities for the sum of vest number and rank to be 9. These are 3-6, 4-5, 5-4 and 7-2. Only 3 of these 4 have to make up 9, hence, we will have to leave out one of the 4. If we leave out 3-6, 4-5 or 5-4, then vest number 7 must take Position 2 (runner-up). This will contradict Clue (iv) as the winner's vest number > the runner-up's vest number. If we leave out 7-2 and place 3-6, 4-5 and 5-4, there will be no place to put rank 2. Thus, this possibility gets rejected.

Possibility 2B also gets rejected as follows:

Possibility 2B	
Vest number	Rank
1	4/5/6
2	2
3	3/4/5/6
4	1/3/4/5/6
5	1/3/4/5/6
6	7
7	1/3/4/5/6

In the table above, there are only 3 cases of total of vest number + rank = 9. Thus, the table should become:

Possibility 2B	
Vest number	Rank
1	4/5/6 no place for 3rd rank?
2	2
3	6
4	5
5	4
6	7
7	1

Thus, this possibility is also rejected.

The answers are:

6. Vest number 6. Option (b) is correct.
7. Vest number 3. Option (d) is correct.
8. Vest number 1. Option (c) is correct.
9. Vest number 2. Option (b) is correct.
10. Vest number 7. Option (a) is correct.

Solutions for Questions 11 to 15:

11. Ben gets a chance to eliminate (clue (i)); Frank gets a chance to eliminate (clue (v)); Devon gets a chance to eliminate (clue (viii)); Only Charlie does not get a chance to eliminate someone. Option (b) is correct.
12. Frank and Ian satisfy the condition of not being in the top four in any event. Between them Ian would not get eliminated (clue (ix)) and Frank would get eliminated (clue (iv)). Hence, option (d) is correct.
13. Garry who is getting eliminated by clue (vi), would not be eliminated due to this clue.
14. Clue (ii) does not have any usage in this question.
15. John is getting eliminated due to clue (viii), which pertains to 9th rank in the event D. Also, Devon is getting eliminated due to maximum number of last ranks, which would no longer be true. Thus, option (d) is correct.

Solutions for Questions 16 to 19:

16. There are total 56 bouts that have been fought in the tournament.
    Only three bouts were contested in a day. The tournament will take a total of 56/3 = 18.66 day or the tournament would get finished after 19 days. Therefore, the tournament would be finished on a Friday.
17. Each boxer has fought exactly 14 bouts. Since in each bout the total number of points available are 2, the total number of points available in the tournament is 56 × 2 = 112 points. For the top ranker to get the minimum possible number of points, each of the eight boxers should have scored the same number of points. This means that the total number of points for each boxer is 112/8 = 14. Hence, option (c) is correct.
18. In this case, it is possible again for P and Q both to get 14 points each (and their rankings to get decided on the basis of their rankings before the tournament). Hence, in this case, the required difference between the two is 0. Option (a) is correct.
19. If all the points are distributed equally among the 8 boxers, then each boxer would have got 14 points. Now, according to the question, since only R and S got the same number of points– let us keep them fixed on 14 points. In such a case, the other boxers would each get different points with a difference of 1 point– so, if we give 3 boxers points above 14, they would get 15, 16 and 17 points, while we give 3 boxers points below 14, they would get 13, 12 and 11 points, respectively. Hence, the maximum number of points that can be scored by the boxer ranked last would be 11 points.

Solutions for Questions 20 to 23:

It is given that Q, U, W, V reached the semis, therefore, P, R, S and T were eliminated in the first round.

From clue (iii):

	1st	2nd	3rd	4th
Group A	V or U	U or V		
Group B	W or Q	Q or W		

From clues (iv) and (i): P and W were not in the same group.
From clue (ii) and (iv): R and S are in the same group and they must be in Group B (as P and W cannot be in the same group – as they have won an equal number of bouts).

	1st	2nd	3rd	4th
Group A	V or U	U or V	P or T	T or P
Group B	W or Q	Q or W	R or S	S or R

As per the first clue, since each boxer won a different number of bouts and each fought exactly two bouts against all other boxers in the same group, it means that there are a total of 12 bouts in every group. Therefore, the following possibilities of number of wins are possible for the four players of each group:
(6, 4, 2, 0) or (6, 3, 2, 1) or (5, 4, 2, 1) or (5, 4, 3, 0)
According to the statement 4, P and W have the same number of wins. We also know that P has not qualified, while W has qualified. Therefore, the number of wins possible for boxers of group B = (6, 3, 2, 1) and number of wins possible for boxers of group A: (5, 4, 3, 0), with P and W at 3 wins each. Also, U cannot have 5 wins in Group A, since he has lost both his bouts to V. The respective boxers would get ranked as follows:

	1st	2nd	3rd	4th
Group A	V	U	P	T
Number of wins	5	4	3	0
Group B	Q	W	S	R
Number of wins	6	3	2	1

20. T won the least bouts after the 1st round. Option (d) is correct.
21. 3. Option (c) is correct.
22. Q won the most number of bouts after 1st round. Option (a) is correct.
23. From the clue (iii), V won both of his bouts against U and from the above table V won both his bouts against T. Therefore, he must have lost one bout against P. Therefore, option (d) is correct.

Solutions for Questions 24 to 27:

24. Cutoff of Probability = 22. From clue (i), (ii), (v): possible scores in Probability are 44, 45, 46, 47, 48. Cutoff of Statistical methods: 25. From clue (i), (ii), (v): possible scores in Statistical methods are 50, 51, 52, 53, 54 Cutoff of Six Sigma = 20. From clue (i), (ii), (v): possible scores of Six Sigma = 40, 41, 42, 43, 44.
The highest possible score of the topper = Total score of the student when he gets 1st, 2nd and 3rd rank in these 3 subjects because from statement 3, no student can have the same rank for any 2 subjects so he cannot have 1st rank in all. Also, please note that the order of these ranks in respective subjects is not important. We'll get the same result if we consider this highest scorer scoring 1st, 2nd or 3rd rank in any of the subjects. Take any case to find answer, say 48 + 53 + 42 = 143. Hence, option (d) is the answer.
25. Minimum possible marks would be obtained if the scorer scores 5th, 4th and 3rd ranks. From same logic as in the previous question, we calculate the least score as 46 + 51 + 40 = 137. Hence, option (b) is the answer.
26. A student gets the lowest marks, then his maximum possible marks are calculated by allotting him the least score in one subject, 2nd least in another and maximum in the 3rd, so we get 44 + 51 + 44 = 139 as the maximum marks obtained him. Also, you can try this by trial and error method. Try to allot marks to these students randomly, you'll learn that the maximum score which is the least amongst all in the group is indeed 139.
27. The difference between the two total scores will be maximum when these 2 scores are the highest and lowest scores. The highest score one can achieve is = 143 The lowest score one can achieve is = 137 Therefore, the required difference = 143 – 137 = 6 is the correct answer.

Solutions for Questions 28 to 31:

Every team gets to play 7 × 2 = 14 matches in the group stage. Total number of matches that'll be played in the group stage = (14 + 2) × 7/2 = 56 matches.

28. Team Pune Warriors scores maximum points if it wins all the matches it played, thus maximum 14 × 6 = 84.
Now, if team Pune Warriors reached the semifinals with least number of points, then it must be at 4th spot after group stage and top three must have won maximum games while the other five teams should draw all the games among themselves.
Number of matches played amongst the bottom five teams 5 × 4 = 20 matches.
Minimum number of total points of the bottom five teams = 20 × 4 = 80. Therefore, the minimum number of points scored by Pune Warriors = 80/5 = 16.
Required difference = 84 – 16 = 68.
Hence, (b) is the correct answer.
29. If top five teams score equal points then the team with least run rate would be eliminated.

In this case, points of top five teams would be maximum when they win all of their games against bottom three teams and win and lose exactly one game against each of their competitors in the top 5 spots.

Therefore, maximum possible points of the team who does not advance to the semifinals is 6 × 6 + 6 × 4 = 60.

30. Points obtained by team Mumbai Indians will be maximum when it wins all the matches in the group stage, Semifinal and Final. In this case, total points obtained by Mumbai Indians = 14 × 6 + 1 × 6 + 1 × 6 = 96.

From the previous question, minimum points obtained by Mumbai Indians = 16 + 6 + 6 = 28.

Required difference= 96 – 28 = 68. Hence, option (b) is the correct answer.

31. Points obtained by 7th spot team will be minimum when the last two teams only scored points in the matches among themselves, so team at 7th and 8th tied both their matches against each other, and their ranking was done on the basis of their run-rates. Therefore, minimum points obtained by the 7th spot team = 4.

Solutions for Questions 32 to 36:

From the 4th information, it can be deduced that either David or Gabrial would be ranked 2.

We will need to look at two cases from here:

Case 1: If David is ranked 2. If Raman is ranked 1 then Sharan is ranked 4 (by the 1st information). But it is contradicted (by the 2nd information). So Raman is not ranked 1. By the 2nd information, if Sharan is not ranked 1, then Gabrial is ranked 4, Sharan is ranked 3 and Raman is ranked 1, which is not possible. So, Sharan is ranked 1. Gabrial can be ranked 3 but then Raman is ranked 4, which contradicts the 5th information. So, Gabrial is ranked 4 and Raman is ranked 3.

Case 2: Gabrial is ranked 2. As seen before, Raman can't get rank 1. So, Sharan is ranked 1. From the 4th information, David can't be ranked 3 as in that case Gabrial can't be ranked 2. So, David is ranked 4 and Raman is ranked 3.

32. 3
33. Sharan. Hence, option (a) is correct.
34. Option (d) is correct.
35. 2
36. 4 + 2 + 2 + 4 = 12

Solutions for Questions 37 to 39:

37. From the statement (iii), Bumrah, Nehra And Axar can be ranked either 5,6,7 or 6,7,8 in round I. Suppose, Bumrah got rank 5 in round I, then Srishant got 8 in this round (statement (ii)) and Chahal got 2 and Ashwin got 3 in round I.

We have the following cases from statement (i):

	Round I	Round II	Round III	
Bumrah	5	4	1	Case I
Chahal	2	3	5	Case I
Bumrah	5	4	3	Case II
Chahal	2	3	7	Case II
Bumrah	5	6	1	Case III
Chahal	2	3	7	Case III
Bumrah	5	6	2	Case IV
Chahal	2	3	8	Case IV

Case I

Rank/Round	I	II	III
1	Dhoni	Ashwin	Bumrah
2	Chahal	Dhoni	Nehra
3	Ashwin	Chahal	Axar
4	Eshant	Bumrah	Srishant
5	Bumrah	Nehra	Chahal
6	Nehra	Axar	Eshant
7	Axar	Srishant	Dhoni
8	Srishant	Eshant	Ashwin

Case II

Rank/Round	I	II	III
1	Dhoni	Eshant	Ashwin
2	Chahal	Dhoni	Srishant
3	Ashwin	Chahal	Bumrah
4	Eshant	Bumrah	Nehra
5	Bumrah	Nehra	Axar
6	Nehra	Axar	Eshant
7	Axar	Srishant	Chahal
8	Srishant	Ashwin	Dhoni

2 cases are possible when Bumrah got rank 5. Now, suppose, Bumrah got rank 6 in round I, you will see, this is not possible due to statement (i) and (iv).

No one is on the consecutive positions in each round. Hence, option (d) is the correct answer.

38. From the tables above, it can be seen that in round II, Dhoni got rank 2 in both the cases. Hence, option (b) is the correct answer.
39. Bumrah's sum of ranks in case I is 10. And in that case, it was 12. Thus, the difference between is 2. Hence, option (b) is the correct answer.

Students↓/Guesses→	Manu	Rohan	Rahi	Roshan	Navya
Manu	3 (From clue 4 and 5)		1 (direct clue 1)		
Rohan	3/4/5 (direct clue 5)	1 (direct Clue 5)			
Rahi	3/4/5 (direct clue 5)		2 (Clues 2,4,5)	3 (direct clue 2)	
Roshan	3/4/5 (direct clue 5)			2/3 (Clue 4,5)	
Navya	4 (direct clue 2)	1	5 (clue 6)	3(direct clue 2)	2 (Clue 5 and 6)

Solutions for Questions 40 to 44:

For this set, we need to calculate 2 tables, 1 for the predicted rank and 1 for the actual rank. From the information given to us directly, we can form the table as given below:

From this point, the following set of deductions helps us get to complete the table and get to the answers:

Deduction 1: Since no one expected Rohan to come last and everyone was predicted to come last by atleast one of the students, and none of them was able to correctly predict the rank of any student, therefore the actual rank of Rohan would be 5. From Statement 3, Roshan predicted the rank of student who came 5th to be 1. So he must have predicted Rohan's rank as 1.

Deduction 2: From Clue 6, Navya's predicted rank should be better than Rahi for all cases other than for Manu's prediction. Hence, Rahi would also place Navya above himself and would have given her the first rank.

Deduction 2a: After placing these two in the table, Roshan would have two more ranks 5 and 4 to give between Rohan and Manu. But nobody gives Rohan 5th rank. Hence, Rahi would have guessed 4 for Rohan and 5 for Manu.

Deduction 3: Roshan's rank for himself was 2nd or 3rd as deduced in the first table. But, from Statement 2, except Navya & Rahi, none of the students predicted Roshan's rank to be 3. Hence, Roshan would have predicted the 2nd rank for himself. Also, from Statement 3, we know that Roshan has predicted the actual third ranker to be 5th. At this stage, we have to place Manu, Rahi and Navya as 3/4/5 in some order. Navya cannot be 4th or 5th as per clue 7. So, she is guessed as the 3rd ranker in Roshan's estimate. This puts us in a situation of distributing 4/5 amongst Manu and Rahi (in Roshan's guesses).

Deduction 3a: According to clue 3, if we place Manu as 5th in Roshan's guesses row, it would mean that Manu actually got the third rank. But Manu was guessed as the third ranker by Manu (we deduced that to get to the first table). Hence, Roshan could not have guessed Manu to be 5th. Thus, Roshan's guesses are completed as Rahi 5th and Manu 4th. This also means that Rahi would be the actual 3rd ranker).

Deduction 4: According to the the 7th clue, there has to be a 5th rank prediction for each student at least once (other than Rohan). If we look at Navya's column after the deductions upto 3a, we can see that she has been predicted to be 1st, 2nd and 3rd by Rahi, Navya herself and Roshan respectively. So, either Manu or Rohan has to predict 5th rank for Navya. Out of these, it has to be Manu (as per clue 6). So, Rohan and Roshan would have been gueseed as 2 or 4 by Manu.

Deduction 5: Again as per clue 7, there has to be a 5th rank prediction for each student at least once (other than Rohan). Hence, looking at Roshan's column, he must be guessed as 5th ranker by Rohan. This leaves us to distribute ranks 2,3,4 between Manu, Rahi and Navya for Rohan's guesses. Navya, has to be ranked above Rahi by Rohan. Hence, she cannot be 4th. Also, since we know from Roshan's row that Rahi is the third ranked student, Rahi cannot be placed 3rd by Rohan too. Thus Rahi is 4th, in Rohan's row of guesses.

Deduction 5a: Rohan must have predicted Manu to be 3rd and Navya to be 2nd. (As no one predicted Manu to be in the top 2).

Deduction 6: Based on the table position of guesses, we can deduce the actual ranks:

Rohan was 5th, Navya would be 4th, Roshan would be 1st, Manu 2nd and Rahi 3rd.

Final Table of guesses: (Deductions beyond the first table have been marked with a # to show the deduction number that helps us finalise the values in this final table:

Students↓/Guesses→	Manu – 2nd (#6)	Rohan – 5th (#1)	Rahi – 3rd (#3a)	Roshan – 1st (#6)	Navya -4th (#6)
Manu	3 (from 1st table)	2/4 (#4)	1 (from 1st table)	4/2 (#4)	5 (#4)
Rohan	3 (#5a)	1 (from 1st table)	4 (#5)	5 (#5)	2 (#5)
Rahi	5 (#2a)	4 (#2a)	2 (from 1st table)	3 (from 1st table)	1 (#2)
Roshan	4 (#3a)	1 (#1)	5 (#3a)	2 (#3)	3 (#3)
Navya	4 (from 1st table)	1 (from 1st table)	5(from 1st table)	3(from 1st table)	2(from 1st table)

The answers can be read off the solution table:

40. Option (c) is correct.

41. Option (b) is correct.

42. 5th

43. 3

44. Option (a) is correct as Rohan could have been predicted as 2 or 4 by Manu.

CHAPTER 4

Team Formations

Chapter Launchpad
Scan this QR code for an introductory video on Team Formations

Team formation questions are another question type which are commonly seen in most exams. The questions consist typically of a group of people/objects that have to be put together in teams–albeit with a set of constraints/conditions about certain people who need to be put together/cannot be put together in a team.

The key skills involved in solving team formation questions would involve the following:

(i) The ability to visualise the structure of the teams to be formed including the number of people/objects in each team.
(ii) The ability to order the clues in the correct order of usage (as explained in the theory of logical reasoning).
(iii) The ability to create symbolic representations of the various clues provided so that you can bring together each of the relevant clues while creating the teams.
(iv) The ability to wait for and reach the appropriate time in the problem solving situation from where the indirect clues provided in the question can be used.

Illustrated below are the solutions to a few typical questions on team formations. We would urge you to first have a look at the questions and try to solve the same on your own before looking at the solutions.

Example 1: Directions for Questions 1 to 2: *Read the information given below and answer the questions:*

A director is casting a movie about twins. Selection must be made from among nine people–Amartya, Bhupesh, Caruna, Divya, Elangovan, Farly, Girish, Harish and Isha. Amartya is Bhupesh's twin, Caruna is Divya's twin, and Elangovan is Farly's twin. Girish, Harish Farly and Isha may each be selected only as "extras." Caruna, Divya and Isha are the women, while the rest are men.

(i) At least two pairs of twins must be selected.
(ii) At least as many women as men must be selected.
(iii) Amartya and Bhupesh must both be selected if either is selected.
(iv) Caruna and Divya must both be selected if either is selected.
(v) Elangovan and Farly need not both be selected.
(vi) At least one "extra" must be selected.
(vii) Amartya, Bhupesh, Elangovan, Girish and Harish are men.

1. Which of the following is an acceptable cast for the movie?
   (a) Amartya, Bhupesh, Elangovan, Farly, Isha
   (b) Caruna, Divya, Farly, Girish, Harish, Isha
   (c) Bhupesh, Caruna, Divya, Elangovan, Harish, Isha
   (d) Caruna, Divya, Elangovan, Farly, Girish, Harish, Isha
2. Which of the following people must be included in the cast?
   (a) Divya (b) Isha
   (c) Farly (d) Harish

Solution: To solve this we will create a diagram where men will be denoted by the upper case letters and women with the lower case letters and we will list the extras separately to avoid confusion. Here given that Caruna and Divya must both be selected because if they were not selected then Amartya and Bhupesh or Elangovan and Farly (three of whom are men) would all be selected; as a result only two women Farly and Isha at most will be selected. However, according to the constraints at least as many women as men must be selected, thus, Caruna and Divya must both be selected.

[A B] [ⓒ ⓓ] [E / F]

G H i [≥ I]

women≥ MEN

1. Eliminate each options using the clues given in the information. Only option (d) suffices. Hence, option (d) is the correct answer.
2. Caruna and Divya must both be selected. Hence, option (a) is the correct answer.

Example 2: Directions for Questions 1 to 3: *Answer the questions based on the following information.*

Vijayshree wants to take four courses this trimester. There are only seven courses in which she is interested: three marketing courses–Distribution, Advertising and PR; and four finance courses–International Finance, Accounting, Corporate Finance and Financial Services. To meet college requirements, she must take two marketing courses. There are some scheduling problems: International Finance overlaps with both Advertising and Corporate Finance but she can choose Advertising and Corporate Finance as two different courses. Distribution is given at the same time as Accounting.

1. If Vijayshree decides she will take International Finance, what will her other three courses be?
   (a) Distribution, PR and Advertising
   (b) Distribution, PR and Financial Services
   (c) Distribution, PR and Accounting
   (d) PR, Advertising and Financial Services
2. If Vijayshree takes four courses this trimester, then which of the following statement is not possible?
   I. She takes Accounting and does not take Advertising.
   II. She takes Corporate Finance and does not take Advertising.
   III. She takes International Finance and does not take PR.
   (a) I only (b) II only
   (c) III only (d) I and III only
3. Which of the following must always be true?
   I. Vijayshree must take PR if she takes Corporate Finance.
   II. Vijayshree must take Advertising if she takes Accounting.
   III. Vijayshree must take Accounting if she takes Advertising.
   (a) I, II and III (b) II and III only
   (c) I and II only (d) II only

Solution:

1. It can be seen that if she takes International Finance, she would not be able to take the Advertising and Corporate Finance course. This means that she has to choose Distribution and PR as her two marketing courses and because Distribution overlaps with Accounting, her second finance course must be Financial Services. Option (b) is correct.
2. Statement I is definitely not possible because if she takes Accounting, she cannot take Distribution and she must have to take Advertising.
   Statement II is possible, while statement III can be seen not to be possible as, if she takes International Finance, she has to take PR, as Advertising would not be available to her.
   Option (d) is correct.
3. Statement I is not necessarily true as, if she takes Corporate Finance, she can take up Distribution and Advertising and skip PR, i.e., PR is not necessary if she has taken Corporate Finance.
   Statement II is mandatorily true because if she takes Accounting, she cannot take Distribution and hence, she would be forced to take up Advertising as one of her two compulsory marketing courses. Statement III is not necessarily true. Thus, option (d) is correct.

Example 3: Directions for Questions 1 to 3: *Answer the questions based on the following information.*

At Semco, Ricardo Semlar has perfected the art of employee motivation. Due to this, his staff works 7 days a week. However, he has given them the leeway that in every week, they are allowed to work for the company on any 4 days and for the remaining 3 days of the week, every employee is allowed to work on their own entrepreneurial project. On a particular day, Mr. Semlar was looking closely at the functioning of 3 of his most trusted executives and found out a few facts about their weekly schedule:

(i) Each of them works for the company only 4 days a week and works on their own projects for 3 days every week.
(ii) All the three executives work together (for the company) only once in a week.
(iii) None of them works for the company for 3 consecutive days.
(iv) Amit works on his project on Tuesdays, Thursdays and Sundays.
(v) Bimlesh works on his own project on Saturday.
(vi) Chetan does not work for the company on Fridays and Sundays.
(vii) No two executives have an own project work day on the same day more than once a week.
(viii) At least 1 person works for the company everyday of the week.

1. On which day of the week do all the three executives work together for the company?
   (a) Monday (b) Wednesday
   (c) Friday (d) Cannot be determined
2. Which of the following days does Chetan work on his own project?
   (a) Monday (b) Tuesday
   (c) Wednesday (d) Thursday
3. Which of the following days is surely a company working day for Bimlesh?
   (a) Wednesday (b) Friday
   (c) Sunday (d) Cannot be determined

Solution: The following table emerges from the given conditions: (P denotes working on own project)

	Amit	Bimlesh	Chetan
Monday			
Tuesday	P		
Wednesday			P
Thursday	P		
Friday			P

Saturday		P	
Sunday	P		P

Note: Chetan's third P is on Wednesday because it cannot be on Tuesday or Thursday (as in that case, Chetan and Amit would be working on their projects together on two days of the week.) Also, Chetan's third P cannot be on Monday, in which case, Chetan would be working continuously for the company for 3 days.

Thus, the answers are:

1. Monday. Option (a) is correct.
2. Wednesday. Option (c) is correct.
3. Sunday is necessarily a company working day for Bimlesh. Option (c) is correct. if we try to put Bimlesh's Sunday as a personal working day for him, there would be no person working for the company on that day. Hence, option (c) is correct.

Example 4: Directions for Questions 1 to 3: *Study the following information carefully and answer the questions given below:*

7 friends A, B, C, D, L, M and Z are going to a new year's party on bikes in Goa. Since it is late at night, they do not anticipate any police presence and hence, have taken only 3 bikes–an Enfield, a Honda and a TVS, with at least 2 of them sitting on each bike (hence, there is triple riding on at least 1 bike). There is exactly one male on each bike. Amongst the group, there are two executives, two designers and three psychologists among them.

(i) C is a lady designer and she does not travel with the pair of sisters, A and M.
(ii) B, a male executive, travels with only Z, a psychologist on an Enfield bike.
(iii) D is a male designer.
(iv) Two persons belonging to the same profession do not travel on the same bike.
(v) A is not an executive and travels on the Honda.

1. What is M's profession?
(a) Executive (b) Psychologist
(c) Designer (d) Data inadequate

2. On which bike does C travel?
(a) Enfield (b) Honda
(c) TVS (d) Either Honda or TVS

3. Which of the following represents the three psychologists?
(a) ZLM (b) ZLA
(c) ZLM or ZLA (d) None of these

Solution: We start from clue (ii) and get the following table:

Enfield	Honda	TVS
B <u>Z</u>		
Executive Psychologist		

Note: We can conclude that Z is a female because there is exactly 1 male on each bike. We denote females in our figures with an underline.

We further know that A and M are sisters and C is a lady designer. Since 2 persons with the same profession cannot travel together, D and C must be travelling on different bikes. Thus, D should be clubbed with A and M. Also, since A is on a Honda, the Honda should have 3 people A, M and D.

Enfield	Honda	TVS
B <u>Z</u>	<u>A</u> <u>M</u> D	<u>C</u> L
Executive Psychologist	?, ?, Designer	Designer, ?

From this point in the solution, we need to concentrate only on the professions of A, M and L. We also know that we are yet to identify 1 executive and 2 psycholoigsts. Further, according to the constraint of clue (iv), both A and M cannot be psychologists. Thus, L must be a psychologist. Also, since, we know that A is not an executive we can conclude that A must be a psychologist and the final table emerges as follows:

Enfield	Honda	TVS
B <u>Z</u>	<u>A</u> <u>M</u> D	<u>C</u> L
Executive, Psychologist	Psychologist, Executive, Designer	Designer, Psychologist,

The answers are:

1. Executive. Option (a) is correct.
2. On the TVS. Option (c) is correct.
3. Z, L and A represent the three psychologists. Option (b) is correct.

Example 5: Directions for Questions 1 to 3: *Study the following information carefully to answer the questions given below:*

Examinations of eight papers were conducted in a week, from Monday to Saturday. The papers were: Advertising, Biology, Chemistry, Distribution, Quantitative Techniques, Finance, Marketing and Heuristics. Not more than two papers were organised in a day. Only one of the days, during Monday to Saturday, was the rest day. The paper on Distribution was held just before the Finance paper, but immediately after the Heuristics paper. It is also known that there was no rest day between any two of these three papers. The tests were split equally between the days before the rest day and the days after the rest day, i.e., tests of four papers were held before the rest day, whereas four papers were held after the rest day. Thursday was not the rest day. Quantitative Techniques and Finance were held on the same day. The paper on Heuristics was not held either on Thursday or on Friday. The papers on Marketing and Biology were held just before Advertising and Chemistry respectively. The paper on Advertising was held just before the paper on Biology.

1. Examinations of which papers were held on Monday?
   (a) Heuristics and Distribution
   (b) Distribution and Finance
   (c) Marketing and Advertising
   (d) Can't be determined
2. Which of the following days was the rest day?
   (a) Tuesday (b) Wednesday
   (c) Thursday (d) Can't be determined
3. Examination(s) of which of the following papers was /were held on Friday?
   I. Marketing II. Advertising
   III. Biology IV. Chemistry
   (a) Only II (b) Only III
   (c) Either II or III or both II and III
   (d) Both II and III

Solution: The thinking in this question would go as follows:

From the statements "Examinations of eight papers were conducted in a week, from Monday to Saturday. Not more than two papers were organised in a day and only one of the days, during Monday to Saturday, was the rest day." We realise:

8 papers are conducted in 5 days with not more than 2 papers on any single day. This means that there must be exactly 3 days when 2 papers each are conducted.

Further, when we read "Tests of four papers were held before the rest day whereas four papers were held after the rest day", we realise that there must be at least 2 days before the rest day and 2 days after the rest day. This obviously means that the rest day must be either on Wednesday or on Thursday.

Also, as we go further down the problem we realise: "Thursday was not the rest day." We realise that the rest day must be on Wednesday. Thus, both Monday and Tuesday must have had 2 exams each.

From the statements: "The papers on Marketing and Biology were held just before Advertising and Chemistry respectively. The paper on Advertising was held just before the paper on Biology." We get that **Marketing-Advertising-Biology-Chemistry** must be the order for these 4 subjects and also that there must not be any other paper between these 4 papers.

At this point, we know the following structure of the respective days and the papers on each day:

Monday	Tuesday	Wednesday	Thursday	Friday	Saturday
2 Papers	2 Papers	REST DAY			

In the above figure, we also know that between Thursday to Saturday exactly one day has 2 papers. Thus, there could be 2 papers on any one of the days viz.: Thursday, Friday or Saturday.

Further using the statements "The paper on Distribution was held just before the Finance paper, but immediately after the Heuristics paper. It is also known that there was no rest day between any two of these three papers and Quantitative Techniques and Finance were held on the same day. The paper on Heuristics was not held either on Thursday or on Friday." We get:

Heuristics-Distribution-Finance-Quantitative Techniques as one order of papers which can either be placed before the rest day or after. However, if we try to place these 4 papers after the rest day, we would need to put Heuristics on Thursday which contradicts the conditions of the problem. Thus, these 4 papers can only be assigned to Monday and Tuesday (2 papers each). This also means that: **Marketing-Advertising-Biology-Chemistry** must be after the rest day.

Based on these conclusions, there are 3 possible ways in which the exams can be structured (depending on which day, we use for putting 2 papers after Wednesday). These are:

Possibility 1:

Monday	Heuristics	Distribution
Tuesday	Finance	QT
Wednesday	REST DAY	
Thursday	Marketing	
Friday	Advertising	Biology
Saturday	Chemistry	

Possibility 2:

Monday	Heuristics	Distribution
Tuesday	Finance	QT
Wednesday	REST DAY	
Thursday	Marketing	
Friday	Advertising	
Saturday	Biology	Chemistry

Possibility 3:

Monday	Heuristics	Distribution
Tuesday	Finance	QT
Wednesday	REST DAY	
Thursday	Marketing	Advertising
Friday	Biology	
Saturday	Chemistry	

The answers can be read off from the tables (based on what is correct for each of these possibilities):

1. Heuristics and Distribution are always on Monday. Option (a) is correct.
2. Wednesday is the rest day in all possibilities. Option (b) is correct.
3. It could be either Biology (possibility 3) or Advertising (possibility 2) or both (possibility 1). Option (c) is correct.

LEVEL OF DIFFICULTY (I)

Directions for Questions 1 to 3:

(i) A guest house has 6 rooms A, B, C, D, E and F. Among these, A and C can accommodate two persons each; the rest can accommodate only one each.

(ii) Eight guests P, Q, R, S, T, U, W and X are to be kept in these rooms. Q, T and X are females while the rest are males. The two sexes can't be put together in the same room. No man is willing to stay in room C or F.

(iii) P wants to be alone but does not want to stay in rooms B or D. S needs a partner but is not ready to stay with U or W. X does not want to share her room.

1. Who among the following will stay in room E?
(a) U (b) W
(c) P (d) Data inadequate

2. In which of the following rooms will U stay?
(a) B (b) D
(c) A (d) B or D

3. X will stay in which of the following rooms?
(a) C (b) F
(c) B (d) Data inadequate

Directions for Questions 4 to 8:

(i) M, N, P, Q, S and T are six members of a group in which there are three female members. Females work in three departments–Accounts, Administration and Personnel and sit on three different floors–Ist, IInd, IIIrd. Persons working in the same department are not on the same floor. Two persons work on each floor.

(ii) No two females work in the same department or on the same floor. N and S work in the same department but not in Personnel. Q works in Administration. S and M are on the Ist and IIIrd floors respectively and work in the same department. Q, a female, does not work on the IInd floor, P, a male, works on Ist floor.

4. Which of the following groups of persons are females?
(a) SQT (b) QMT
(c) QPT (d) Data inadequate

5. Which of the following pairs of persons work in Administration?
(a) QP (b) QN
(c) SP (d) Data inadequate

6. In which department does T work?
(a) Accounts
(b) Administration
(c) Personnel
(d) Accounts or Personnel

7. Which of the following pairs work on the IInd floor?
(a) PT (b) SM
(c) QN (d) NT

8. If T is transferred to Accounts and S is transferred to Administration, who is to be transferred to Personnel to maintain the original distribution of females on each floor?
(a) P (b) N
(c) Q (d) Data inadequate

Directions for Questions 9 to 13: *A, B, C, D, E, F and G are travelling in three different vehicles. There are at least two passengers in each vehicle–Maruti, Santro, Opel, and only one of them is a male. There are two engineers, two doctors and three teachers among them.*

(i) C is a lady doctor and she does not travel with the pair of sisters A and F.

(ii) B, a male engineer, travels with only G, a teacher in a Maruti.

(iii) D is a male doctor.

(iv) Two persons belonging to the same profession do not travel in the same vehicle.

(v) A is not an engineer and travels in a Santro.

9. What is F's profession?
(a) Engineer (b) Doctor
(c) Teacher (d) Data inadequate

10. In which vehicle does C travel?
(a) Maruti (b) Santro
(c) Opel (d) Data inadequate

11. Which of the following represents the three teachers?
(a) GEF (b) GEA
(c) GBF (d) Data inadequate

12. How many lady members are there among them?
(a) Three (b) Four
(c) Three or four (d) Data inadequate

13. Which of the following is not correct?
(a) E-Male-Teacher (b) B-Male-Engineer
(c) A-Female-Teacher (d) All are correct

Directions for Questions 14 to 19: *Ten students–A, B, C, D, E, F, G, H, I and J are chosen to represent their college in four sports–tennis, badminton, table tennis and snooker. The badminton team has one student less than the tennis team. A, B and C are not tennis players, individually or as a group. D, E and F are not in badminton team individually or as a group. G, H and I are not in the table tennis team, individually or as a group. J is a table tennis player. None of the students is a snooker player.*

14. Which of the following students could be table tennis players?
(a) J, B and G (b) J, C and F
(c) J, D, E and F (d) J, B, C and D

15. Of those listed, what is the largest possible number of students who could be table tennis players?
(a) 6 (b) 7
(c) 9 (d) None of these

16. If no other student except I is in the badminton team, which of the following students could be tennis players?
(a) D and H (b) F and E
(c) E and G (d) G and H

17. If the table tennis team has one member, who of the following must be a tennis player?
(a) A (b) B
(c) D (d) G

18. If G, H and C are the only students in the badminton team, which three must be the only students who are table tennis players?
(a) A, B and J (b) A, D and J
(c) B, E and J (d) B, F and J

19. If A and G are the only badminton players, how many students must be in the table tennis team?
(a) 2 (b) 3
(c) 5 (d) 6

Directions for Questions 20 to 21: *Study the information given below and answer the questions that follow.*

If Mayank goes to Singapore he makes Neha or Omar (but not both of them) also to go to Singapore. Ravi goes to Singapore only if Omar goes. Pawan goes to Singapore if Neha or Omar goes. Shawn goes to Singapore only if Neha goes. Varun goes to Singapore only if Ravi or Shawn goes. If Pawan goes to Singapore, he makes Tanvi or Unni or both to accompany him. Tanvi goes to Singapore only if Shawn goes. Unni goes to Singapore only if Ravi goes.

20. If Mayank has gone to Singapore, who of the following may have also gone to Singapore?
A. Ravi and Unni B. Shawn and Tanvi
C. Pawan
(a) A, B and C
(b) A and C *or* B and C but not both
(c) A only
(d) B only

21. If Varun has gone to Singapore, who of the following must have also gone?
(a) Both Ravi and Shawn
(b) Both Neha and Omar
(c) Either Omar or Neha
(d) Ravi

Directions for Questions 22 to 23: *Read the following information carefully and answer the questions given as follows:*

Amir, Bikram, Charlie, David, Emraan, Fahim and Gaurav are seven students in a class. They are sitting on three benches–Mahogany, Oak and Maple, in such a way that there is at least two of them on each bench and there is at least one girl on each bench. Charlie, a girl student, does not sit with Amir, Emraan and David. Fahim, a boy student, sits only with Bikram. Amir sits with his best friend on bench Mahogany. Gaurav sits on bench Maple. Emraan is the brother of Charlie.

22. How many girl students are there?
(a) 3 (b) 4
(c) 3 or 4 (d) None of these

23. Which of the following is a group of girls?
(a) Bikram, Amir and Charlie
(b) Bikram, Fahim and Charlie
(c) Charlie, David and Fahim
(d) Bikram, Charlie and David

Directions for Questions 24 to 26: *Study the following information carefully and answer the questions given below:*

Geetika, Deep, Niharika, Shwetabh, Akansha, Aishwarya and Aparajita are travelling in three vehicles. There are at least two passengers in each vehicle–Maruti, Santro and Octavia and only one of them is a male. There are two engineers, two doctors and three teachers among them.

(i) Niharika is a lady doctor and she does not travel with the pair of sisters, Geetika and Aishwarya.
(ii) Deep, a male engineer, travels with only Aparajita, a teacher in a Maruti.
(iii) Shwetabh is a male doctor.

(iv) Two persons belonging to the same profession do not travel in the same vehicle.
(v) Geetika is not an engineer and travels in vehicle Santro.

24. What is Aishwarya's profession?
(a) Engineer (b) Teacher
(c) Doctor (d) Data inadequate

25. In which vehicle does Niharika travel?
(a) Maruti (b) Santro
(c) Octavia (d) Santro or Octavia

26. Which of the following represents the three teachers?
(a) Aparajita, Akansha and Aishwarya
(b) Aparajita, Akansha and Geetika
(c) Aparajita, Akansha and Aishwarya or Aparajita, Akansha and Geetika
(d) Data inadequate

Directions for Questions 27 to 28: *Study the following information carefully and answer the questions given below:*

(i) G, H, I, J, K, L, M and N are eight students in a class. Three of them play cricket and badminton each and two of them play hockey. Each one of them has a different height.
(ii) The tallest does not play hockey and the shortest does not play cricket.
(iii) L is taller than G and J but shorter than N and H. K, who does not play cricket, is taller than H and is second to the tallest. M is shorter than J but taller than G.
(iv) N, who is the fourth from the top, plays badminton with J.
(v) M does not play either cricket or hockey. H does not play hockey.

27. Which of the following pair of students plays hockey?
(a) K and L (b) N and K
(c) N and L (d) None of these

28. What is L's position from the top when they are arranged in the descending order of their height?
(a) Third (b) Fifth
(c) Fourth (d) None of these

Directions for Questions 29 to 30: *Study the following information carefully and answer the questions given below:*

Bali, Chinkara, Dabang, Fateh, Giri, Himesh and Jeev are seven students studying in three colleges IIM A, IIM B and IIM R. There are three boys and four girls. There are at least one boy and one girl in each college. Three of them are in HR discipline and two each in Finance and Marketing. Bali and her sister Giri are in Marketing but in different colleges. Fateh studies Finance in college IIM B and he does not study with either Jeev or Chinkara. Dabang is not in HR and he studies in college IIM R only with Bali. All the three from HR do not study in the same college. Himesh studies in the same college with her friend Giri.

29. In which college do only HR students study?
(a) None (b) IIM B
(c) IIM R (d) IIM A

30. If Chinkara and Bali interchange their colleges satisfying all the other conditions, which of the following will definitely represent the girls?
(a) Bali, Chinkara, Himesh and Dabang
(b) Bali, Chinkara, Himesh and Giri
(c) Bali, Fateh, Himesh and Giri
(d) Dabang, Chinkara, Himesh and Fateh

Directions for Questions 31 to 32: *Study the following information carefully and answer the questions given below:*

Seven specialist persons Bebe, Meme, Keke, Pepe, Dede, Fefe and Hehe visit an office on four days– Tuesday, Wednesday, Friday and Saturday in a week. At least one person but not more than two persons visit the office on each of these days. Each of them is a specialist in different fields–Paramedic, Business, Engineering, Genetics, Biometrics, Defence and Biotech.

(i) Pepe visits on Friday with a specialist in Defence.
(ii) The engineer does not visit on Saturday and not with Dede and Hehe.
(iii) The Biotech specialist Fefe visits alone on Tuesday.
(iv) Meme visits on Wednesday and he is not engineer.
(v) Keke visits on Wednesday. Hehe is not a specialist in Defence.
(vi) The engineer visits with the Paramedic specialist.
(vii) The Genetics specialist visits on Friday.
(viii) Bebe is neither a Business specialist nor a specialist in Defence.

31. What is the speciality of Bebe?
(a) Biometrics (b) Paramedics
(c) Engineer (d) Data inadequate

32. On which day of the week does Dede visit?
(a) Wednesday
(b) Saturday
(c) Wednesday or Saturday
(d) Friday

Directions for Question 33:

33. A King has unflinching loyalty from eight of his ministers M1 to M8, but he has to select only four to make a cabinet committee. He decides to choose these four such that each selected person shares a liking with at least one of the other three selected. The selected persons must also hate at least one of the likings of any of the other three persons selected.

M1 likes fishing and smoking, but hates gambling.
M2 likes smoking and drinking, but hates fishing.
M3 likes gambling, but hates smoking.
M4 likes mountaineering, but hates drinking.
M5 likes drinking, but hates smoking and mountaineering.
M6 likes fishing, but hates smoking and mountaineering.
M7 likes gambling and mountaineering, but hates fishing, and
M8 likes smoking and gambling, but hates mountaineering.
Who are the four people selected by the king?
(a) M1, M2, M5, M6
(b) M3, M4, M5, M6
(c) M4, M5, M6, M8
(d) M1, M2, M4, M7

Directions for Questions 34 to 35: *Answer the questions on the basis of the information given below.*

The Head of a newly formed government desires to appoint five of the six elected members A, B, C, D, E and F the portfolios of Home, Power, Defence, Telecom and Finance. F does not want any portfolio if D gets one of the five. C wants either Home or Finance or no portfolio. B says that if D gets either Power or Telecom then she must get the other one. E insists on a portfolio if A gets one.

34. Which is a valid assignment?
(a) A-Home, B-Power, C-Defence, D-Telecom, E-Finance.
(b) C-Home, D-Power, A-Defence, B-Telecom, E-Finance.
(c) A-Home, B-Power, E-Defence, D-Telecom, F-Finance.
(d) B-Home, F-Power, E-Defence, C-Telecom, A-Finance.

35. If A gets Home and C gets Finance, then which is NOT a valid assignment for Defence and Telecom?
(a) D-Defence, B-Telecom.
(b) F-Defence, B-Telecom.
(c) B-Defence, E-Telecom.
(d) B-Defence, D-Telecom.

LEVEL OF DIFFICULTY (II)

Directions for Questions 1 to 3: *Answer each of the questions independent of each other.*

1. There are ten animals–two each of lions, panthers, bisons, bears and deer in a zoo. The enclosures in the zoo are named X, Y, Z, P and Q and each enclosure is allotted to one of the following attendants: Jack, Mohan, Shalini, Suman and Rita. Two animals of different species are housed in each enclosure. A lion and a deer cannot be together. A panther cannot be with either a deer or a bison. Suman attends to animals from among bison, deer, bear and panther only. Mohan attends to a lion and a panther. Jack does not attend to deer, lion or bison. X, Y and Z are allotted to Mohan, Jack and Rita, respectively. X and Q enclosures have one animal of the same species. Z and P have the same pair of animals.
The animals attended by Shalini are:
(a) Bear and Bison (b) Bison and Deer
(c) Bear and Lion (d) Bear and Panther

High Yield Questions
Scan this QR code to access a video explanation of question 1

2. Eight people carrying food baskets are going for a picnic on motorcycles. Their names are A, B, C, D, E, F, G and H. They have four motorcycles Ml, M2, M3 and M4 among them. They also have four food baskets O, P, Q and R of different sizes and shapes and each can be carried only on motorcycles Ml, M2, M3, or M4, respectively. No more than two persons can travel on a motorcycle and no more than one basket can be carried on a motorcycle. There are two husband–wife pairs in this group of eight people and each pair will ride on a motorcycle together. C cannot travel with A or B. E cannot travel with B or F. G cannot travel with F, H or D. The husband–wife pairs must carry baskets O and P. Q is with A and P is with D. F travels on Ml and E travels on M2 motorcycles. G is with Q, and B cannot go with R.
Who is travelling with H?
(a) A (b) B
(c) C (d) D

3. In a "keep-fit" gymnasium class there are fifteen females enrolled in a weight-loss programme. They all have been grouped in any one of the five weight-groups–Wl, W2, W3, W4 or W5. One instructor is assigned to one weight-group only. Sonali, Shalini, Shubhra and Shahira belong to the same weight-group. Sonali and Rupa are in one weight-group. Rupali and Renuka are also in one weight-group. Rupa, Radha, Renuka, Ruchika and Ritu belong to different weight-groups. Somya cannot be with Ritu, and Tara cannot be with Radha. Komal cannot be with Radha, Somya or Ritu. Shahira is in W1 and Somya is in W4 with Ruchika. Sweta and Jyotika cannot be with Rupali, but are in a weight-group with total membership of four. No weight-group can have more than five or less than one member. Amita, Babita, Chandrika, Deepika and Elina are instructors of weight-groups with membership sizes 5, 4, 3, 2 and 1, respectively. Who is the instructor of Radha?

(a) Babita (b) Elina
(c) Chandrika (d) Deepika

Directions for Questions 4 to 6: *A group of three or four has to be selected from seven persons. Among the seven there are two women–Fiza and Kavita, and five men–Ram, Shyam, David, Peter and Rahim. Ram would not like to be in the group if Shyam is also selected. Shyam and Rahim want to be selected together in the group. Kavita would like to be in the group only if David is also there. David, if selected, would not like Peter in the group. Ram would like to be in the group only if Peter is also there. David insists that Fiza must be selected in case he is there in the group.*

4. Which of the following is a feasible group of three?
(a) David, Ram, Rahim
(b) Peter, Shyam, Rahim
(c) Kavita, David, Shyam
(d) Fiza, David, Ram

5. Which of the following is a feasible group of four?
(a) Ram, Peter, Fiza, Rahim
(b) Shyam, Rahim, Kavita, David
(c) Shyam, Rahim, Fiza, David
(d) Fiza, David, Ram, Peter

6. Which of the following statements is true?
(a) Kavita and Ram can be part of a group of four.
(b) A group of four can have two women.
(c) A group of four can have all four men.
(d) None of the above.

Directions for Questions 7 to 8: *Read the information given below and answer the questions that follow.*

At a secret location in Nevada, a science lab exists where four research projects ROC-I, ROC-II, ROC-III and ROC-IV are underway. The projects are assigned difficulty level L_1 or L_2 or L_3. A total of six researchers who are given code names in order to protect their identity are–Ax, Bx, Cx, Dx, Ex and Fx–are chosen for working on the projects with the provision that for the project of difficulty level L_1, only one research associate will be engaged while for the other projects, two researchers will be engaged. There are, however, some constraints to be overcome before allotting the work.

(i) Ax, Bx and Dx do not work with each other.
(ii) Projects ROC-II and ROC-III are respectively of difficulty level L_2/L_3. Remaining projects are of L_1 level.
(iii) Ex cannot work with anyone else.
(iv) Cx and Dx cannot work together.
(v) Fx can work either with Dx or Cx only.
(vi) Fx cannot be engaged in L_3 level projects.
(vii) Ax and Cx cannot work together.

7. Researcher Ax can be allotted which of the following projects?
(a) ROC-I or ROC-II but not ROC-III
(b) ROC-II or ROC-III but not ROC-IV
(c) ROC-III or ROC-IV but not ROC-I
(d) ROC-IV or ROC-I but not ROC-II

8. If researcher Fx is engaged neither for ROC-I nor for ROC-II, and it is also known that Bx works in Project III, then assignments for how many of the six researchers can be decided?
(a) 2 (b) 4
(c) 3 (d) All

Directions for Question 9: *Study the information and answer the question:*

Alexis, Benny, Carena and Davis–four executives are to be sent to four countries–Afghanistan, Pakistan, Japan and China to head the company's operations there, not necessarily in that order. Four assistants–Dave, Catty, Billy and Arnold, are also to be sent, one to each country. Following facts are known:

(i) Alexis does not like Billy and Dave.
(ii) Dave and Arnold are not to be considered for Pakistan.
(iii) Billy and Catty are not to be considered for Afghanistan.
(iv) Benny would not go to Pakistan or Japan.
(v) Davis loves to work with Catty.
(vi) China operations would not be headed by someone whose name ends in 's'.
(vii) Arnold and Catty would not go to China.
(viii) Benny has excelled in working with Dave earlier and hence, would like him as his assistant.
(ix) Davis has built up good contacts in Japan and is considered a specialist for that country. (sure posting is expected.)

9. Which of the following postings is possible?
(a) Afghanistan-Davis-Catty
(b) Pakistan-Carena-Billy
(c) China-Benny-Billy
(d) Pakistan-Alexis-Catty

Directions for Questions 10 to 13: *At an apartment in Lucknow, 6 security guards Aman, Bimal, Charan, Deepak, Ehsaan and Famid guard the apartment for at least 1 of the 3 time-shifts- Morning, Noon and Evening. It is also known that:*

(i) Only 1 guard guards the apartment in any particular shift.
(ii) Aman can work only in the morning shift.
(iii) Each of Bimal and Charan can work only in the morning and the noon shifts but not in the evening shift.
(iv) Ehsaan can work in the morning and evening shifts but not in the noon shift.
(v) Deepak can work in the noon and the evening shifts but not in the morning shift.
(vi) Famid can work only in the evening shift.

Mr. Dubey, the Secretary of the Apartment Council schedules the duty of these 6 guards satisfying the following conditions:

A. In a week, any guard does not guard the building for more than 2 times in the same shift and not more than 3 times in total.
B. Any guard can guard the apartment at most 1 time in a single day.

If all the above conditions cannot be met for any day of the week, then no guard will come on that day.

10. For a given week, what is the maximum number of shifts all guards can do?

11. For a given week, what is the minimum number of days the apartment will be left unguarded?
(a) 0 (b) 1
(c) 2 (d) 3

12. Of the following, which group of 3 guards cannot be formed to guard the apartment on any day of the week?
(a) Aman, Bimal, Famid
(b) Aman, Ehsaan, Famid
(c) Bimal, Charan, Famid
(d) None of these

13. In a particular week,
(I) Guarding shifts are arranged for maximum number of days; and
(II) Ehsaan takes two morning shifts.
Which of the following options represent the correct combination of "Guard Name–Number of noon shifts done by him in this week"?
(a) Bimal-1 (b) Charan-1
(c) Deepak-2 (d) None of these

Directions for Questions 14 to 17: *During ENCORE-2016, four students of IIT Kanpur namely A, B, C and D participated in four events: Robotics, Singing, Dancing and Painting. The following additional information is also known:*

(i) The number of students who participated in Singing was one more than that of those who participated in Dancing.
(ii) The number of students who participated in Robotics, was twice that of those who participated in Painting.
(iii) Each student participated in at least one event.
(iv) At least one student participated in each event.
(v) 'A' participated in Singing but not in Painting while C participated in Dancing but not Robotics.
(vi) None of these four students participated in both Dancing and Painting.
(vii) D participated in exactly three events.
(viii) Between Singing and Robotics, B participated in exactly one event.
(ix) Number of students who participated in Dancing is same as number of students who participated in Robotics.

14. What is the sum of number of the students, who participated in Robotics and Dancing?

15. If A participated in Robotics, then which of the following is definitely true?
(a) A also participated in Dancing.
(b) B participated in Singing.
(c) C participated in Singing.
(d) None of the above.

16. If A participated in exactly three events, then which of the following statements is definitely true?
(a) B participated in Painting.
(b) D participated in Dancing.
(c) B participated in exactly three events.
(d) C participated in exactly one event.

17. If A participated in exactly three events and B participated in exactly 1 event, then which of the following statements is definitely true?
(a) B participated in Dancing.
(b) C participated in Painting.
(c) D did not participate in Painting.
(d) None of these.

Directions for Questions 18 to 23: *There are 5 students–Andrew, Ben, Chris, Dom and Ervin. Each belongs to exactly one school among Ryan, Bal Bharti, Modern, Kidzee and Presidium, not necessarily in that order. Each school has its unique physical fitness test that a student needs to qualify in, to move to the next class. It is given that the maximum achievable marks of such tests in these schools are different and are: 24, 28, 16, 18, 20 in no particular order. Each student scored at least 4 marks and at most 9 marks in his test. Ratio of maximum marks to marks obtained for each student is an integer and is less than or equal to 4.*

High Yield Questions
Scan this QR code to access a video explanation of questions 18-23

Also, some additional information is given below regarding these fitness tests:

(i) Maximum achievable marks in Modern school are 6 marks, more than that in Chris's school.
(ii) Numerical difference between maximum achievable marks in Bal Bharti and Ryan school is half the

numerical difference between the maximum marks in Dom's school and that of Ervin's school.

(iii) The ratio of maximum marks to marks obtained for each student is not less than that for the student who studies in a school in which the maximum marks were 4 less than the maximum marks in Kidzee school.

(iv) Ervin is not from Modern School.

(v) Ben scored least. Also, it is given that, maximum achievable marks in Ben's school are 2 more than that of a school which is not Bal Bharti.

18. Chris is a student of which school?

(a) Ryan (b) Bal Bharti
(c) Kidzee (d) Presidium

19. Who is a student of Bal Bharti school?

(a) Andrew (b) Ben
(c) Chris (d) Dom

20. What is the maximum possible sum of the scores of Chris and Dom?

21. What is the sum of the maximum achievable marks in Kidzee and Ryan?

22. Which of the following statements is true about Andrew?

(a) He studies in Presidium school and obtained 5 marks in his physical test.
(b) He studies in Bal Bharti and obtained 5 marks in his physical test.
(c) He studies in Bal Bharti and obtained 8 marks in his physical test.
(d) None of these.

23. Which of the following combination of students represents correctly the decreasing order of the maximum marks in their respective schools?

(a) Ervin, Dom, Ben, Andrew, Chris
(b) Ervin, Ben, Dom, Andrew, Chris
(c) Ervin, Dom, Ben, Chris, Andrew
(d) None of these

Directions for Questions 24 to 27: *Answer the following questions based on the given information:*

During campus recruitment at four colleges–A, B, C and D, Mindworkzz selected some students for the different posts– Manager, Developer, Counsellor and Typist.

High Yield Questions
Scan this QR code to access a video explanation of questions 24-27

The following additional information is given about the recruited students:

(i) From each college, at least 1 student and at most, 4 students were recruited for each of the four posts.

(ii) The number of Typists was equal to the number of Developers.

(iii) The number of Counselors was 1/3rd of the number of Developers.

(iv) 2 Developers were recruited from College C.

(v) The number of Counsellors was 3 less than the number of Managers.

(vi) The number of students recruited from each of the Colleges A, C and D is twice the number of students recruited from College B.

24. The number of Developers recruited from College D is:

25. The number of Managers recruited from college A is:

26. If 3 typists were recruited from College D, which of the following statements must be true? (this additional information is limited to this question only)

(a) Two Managers were recruited from college A.
(b) Two Managers were recruited from college C.
(c) Two Typists were recruited from college A.
(d) Four Typists were recruited from college- C.

27. Which of the following can definitely be determined from the provided information?

(a) Number of Managers from college C.
(b) Number of Typists from college A.
(c) Number of Typists from college C.
(d) None of these.

Directions for Questions 28 to 31: Adriana, Bandita, Chitra, and Daisy are four female students, and Amit, Barun, Chetan, and Deb are four male students. Each of them studies in one of three institutes - X, Y, and Z. Each student majors in one subject among Marketing, Operations, and Finance, and minors in a different one among these three subjects. The following facts are known about the eight students:

(i) Three students are from X, Three are from Y, and the remaining two students, both female, are from Z.

(ii) Both the male students from Y minor in Finance, while the female student from Y majors in Operations.

(iii) Only one male student majors in Operations, while three female students minor in marketing.

(iv) One female and two male students major in Finance.

(v) Adriana and Deb are from the same institute. Daisy and Amit are from the same institute.

(vi) Barun is from Y and majors in Operations. Chetan is from X and majors in finance.

(vii) Daisy minors in Operations.

28. Who are the students from the institute Z?

(a) Adriana and Bandita
(b) Bandita and Chitra
(c) Chitra and Daisy
(d) Adriana and Daisy

29. Which subject does Deb minor in?
(a) Finance
(b) Marketing
(c) Operations
(d) Can't be determined uniquely from the given information

30. Which subject does Amit major in?
(a) Finance
(b) Marketing
(c) Operations
(d) Can't be determined uniquely from the given information

31. If Chitra majors in Finance, which subject does Bandita major in?
(a) Finance
(b) Marketing
(c) Operations
(d) Can't be determined uniquely from the given information

ANSWER KEY

Level of Difficulty (I)

1. (c)	2. (d)	3. (b)	4. (a)
5. (d)	6. (c)	7. (d)	8. (c)
9. (a)	10. (c)	11. (b)	12. (b)
13. (d)	14. (b)	15. (b)	16. (d)
17. (c)	18. (a)	19. (c)	20. (b)
21. (c)	22. (c)	23. (d)	24. (a)
25. (c)	26. (b)	27. (d)	28. (b)
29. (d)	30. (b)	31. (a)	32. (d)
33. (d)	34. (b)	35. (d)	

Level of Difficulty (II)

1. (c)	2. (c)	3. (b)	4. (b)
5. (c)	6. (d)	7. (d)	8. (c)
9. (b)	10. 16	11. (b)	12. (b)
13. (d)	14. 4	15. (b)	16. (d)
17. (d)	18. (a)	19. (a)	20. 17
21. 38	22. (c)	23. (c)	24. 4
25. Either 1 or 2	26. (d)		27. (d)
28. (b)	29. (a)	30. (a)	31. (c)

SOLUTIONS AND SHORTCUTS

Level of Difficulty (I)

Solutions for Questions 1 to 3:

Initial information:
A (2)
B (1)
C (2)
D (1)
E (1)
F (1)

Also, P^+, Q^-, R^+, S^+, T^-, U^+, W^+, X^-. From clue (ii), Room C (2 people) and Room F (1 person) should be women's rooms as men cannot be placed there. From clue (iii)–P must be in E, S must be in A (where U and W cannot be). Thus, S must be sharing his room with R. Also, U and W must be in some random order in Rooms B or D. Also, X must be in Room F as she is a female and wants a single room.

Collating all this, we get:
A (2) S, R
B (1)
C (2) Q, T
D (1)
E (1) P
F (1) X

Hence, the answers are:
1. P (c)
2. B or D (d)
3. F (b)

Solutions for Questions 4 to 8:

From the first clue, we know that:

Six people M, N, P, Q, S and T

3 departments for females: Accounts, Admin and Personnel.

3 floors (2 people each)

		III
		II
		I

Using the direct information in clue (ii), we get:

M	Q–	III
		II
S	P+	I

Note: (– Denotes Female and + denotes male)

Since P is a male (denoted by '+' in the figure), S must be a female (since no two females work in the same department or on the same floor).

If S is female, M must be male (since they are in the same department).

Also, since N and S are in the same department, N is also a male. This gives us the final figures as:

M+	Q–	III
N+	T–	II
S–	P+	I

Also, S, M and N work in either Accounts or Administration. Q–Administration. At this stage, we can answer the questions:

4. S,Q and T. Option (a) is correct.
5. Data is inadequate since we just know that Q works in Admin, but we do not know who else works in Admin (and whether someone works in Admin or not). Hence, option (d) is correct.
6. Since Q is in Admin, S must be in Accounts (as she cannot be in Personnel). Thus, T is in Personnel. Hence, option (c) is correct.
7. N, T (d).
8. Q needs to move to Personnel to have the three women in three different departments.

Solutions for Questions 9 to 13:

The following table will emerge out of the given clues:

Vehicle	Profession	Profession
Maruti	B(+)	Engineer
	G–	Teacher
Santro	A–	Teacher
	F–	Engineer
	D+	Doctor
Opel	C–	Doctor
	E+	Teacher

Since C and D are doctors and A is not an engineer, hence, A is a teacher.

Since A travels in a Santro, C will travel in an Opel. Also, A and F will be together. Given A and F are pair of sisters, both are females.

In a Maruti, only two persons B and G travel, so G is a female. Two persons belonging to the same profession do not travel in the same vehicle, so D travels in a Santro. There are two doctors, two engineers and three teachers and persons of the same profession do not travel in the same vehicle, so F is an engineer. E is a male teacher.

The answers are:

9. (a)
10. (c)
11. (b)
12. (b)
13. (d)

Solutions for Questions 14 to 19:

The following table will emerge out of the given clues:

	Tennis	Badminton	Table tennis
A	×	.	.
B	×	.	.
C	×	.	.
D	.	×	.
E	.	×	.
F	.	×	.
G	.	.	×
H	.	.	×
I	.	.	×
J	×	×	
Total	N	N–1	

14. (b) Looking at the options, the only possible solution is option (b) (as Table Tennis should be an odd number of people as Tennis + Badminton is 2n – 1)
15. (b) If Table Tennis players are 7 in number then,
    $n + n - 1 = 3.$
    $2n = 4.$
    $n = 2.$ This is possible.
16. (d) Going through options, we find that the only possibility is G and H as we would need 7 people to be Table Tennis players in such a case.
17. (c) If the Table-Tennis team has just one member J, then the Tennis team will surely have D, E and F as players.
18. (a) A, B and J would then be definitely Table Tennis players.
19. (c) If the Badminton team has 2 players, then the Tennis team will have 3 players. The remaining players will be in the Table-Tennis team.

Solutions for Questions 20 to 21:

For this question, let us form a tree since there are separate events related to going of Neha and Omar with Mayank. There will be two scenarios that we need to analyse which is graspable from the very first line of the information given, i.e., if Mayank goes to Singapore he takes with him either Neha or Omar.

(i) If Neha goes then Pawan goes. Shawn will go with Neha only. Tanvi will go, if Pawan goes and same condition goes for Varun who goes to Singapore, if Shawn accompanies him.

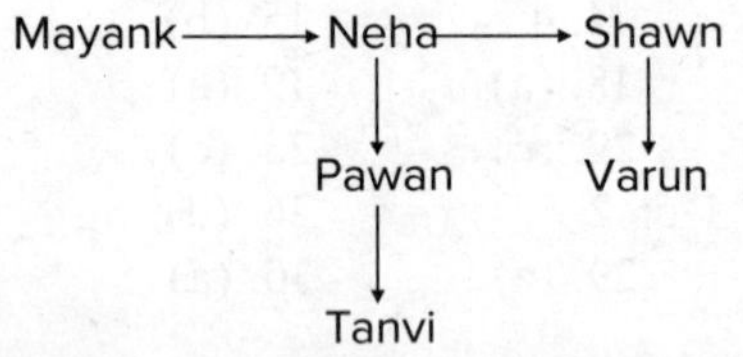

(ii) If Omar goes then Ravi goes with him, and Pawan also will go with Omar. Varun will accompany Ravi and Unni will accompany Pawan.

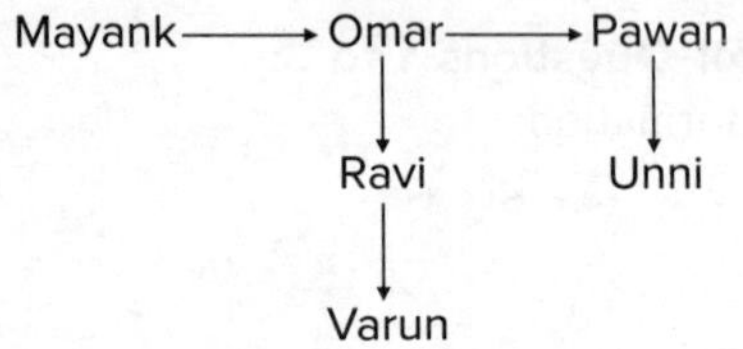

20. Hence, option (b) is the correct answer.
21. Look at the trees, Varun goes due to either Neha and Omar who go with either Shawn or Ravi.
Hence, option (c) is the correct answer.

Solutions for Questions 22 to 23:

We have been given that Amir and Gaurav sit on benches Mahogany and Maple. Now, since Fahim is a boy and sits with only Bikram, this implies that Bikram is a female. (This conclusion was made on the grounds that there is at least one girl on each bench). Fahim and Bikram sit on the Oak bench.

On the basis of the above information we get:

Mahogany:	**Amir**	**—**
Oak:	**Fahim (boy)**	**Bikram (female)**
Maple:	**Gaurav**	**—**

Now, since Charlie is a girl student and she does not sit with Amir, Emraan and David, it implies that Charlie sits on Maple bench because on Oak bench only two persons can be seated. By elimination of clues, Emraan and David sit on Mahogany bench. Now see the clue, "Amir sits with his friend", this means that Amir is male. Again, Emraan is the brother of Charlie implies that Emraan is a male. By elimination, David is a female. But sex of Gaurav is still unknown.

Thus, the information obtained above can be summarised as follows:

Mahogany:	**Amir (boy)**	**David (female)**	**Emraan (boy)**
Oak:	**Fahim (boy)**	**Bikram (female)**	
Maple:	**Gaurav**	**Charlie (female)**	

22. David, Bikram and Charlie are girls. Possibility of fourth girl still exists because sex of Gaurav is unknown. Hence, option (c) is the correct answer.
23. Option (d) is the correct answer.

Solutions for Questions 24 to 26:

If there are at least two passengers in each vehicle and one of them is a male then, in the group there are at least three males. Among them, Niharika is a female and she is a doctor. Geetika and Aishwarya are also females. From the second clue, we get Aparajita is a teacher. Deep is a male and he is an engineer. He travels with only Aparajita, which means Aparajita is a female. And both of them travel in Maruti. From the third clue, Shwetabh is a male and he is a doctor. From fifth clue, Geetika is not an engineer and she cannot be a doctor because there can be only two doctors (Niharika and Shwetabh). Hence, Geetika is a teacher and she travels in Santro. So, there are four females Niharika, Geetika, Aishwarya and Aparajita. Hence, the remaining persons will be male because in each vehicle there has to be at least one male. Hence, Akansha is a male and Shwetabh and Akansha will occupy seats in two different cars (Santro and Octavia) because in Maruti, Deep travels only with Aparajita. Again, Niharika can travel neither with Shwetabh nor with Geetika and Aishwarya. Thus, we have the final arrangement as follows:

Person	Profession	Vehicle	Sex
Deep	Engineer	Maruti	M
Aparajita	Teacher	Maruti	F
Geetika	Teacher	Santro	F
Shwetabh	Doctor	Santro	M
Aishwarya	Engineer	Santro	F
Akansha	Teacher	Octavia	M
Niharika	Doctor	Octavia	F

Now, we can answer the questions as follows:
24. Option (a) is the correct answer.
25. Option (c) is the correct answer.
26. Option (b) is the correct answer.

Solutions for Questions 27 to 28:

From the clues given, we can directly arrange the persons according to their heights.

I > K > H > N > L > J > M > G

Now, let us arrange the persons to their games that they play.

Persons	Cricket	Badminton	Hockey
G	X	X	√
H	√	X	X
I	√	X	X
J	X	√	X
K	X	X	√
L	√	X	X
M	X	√	X
N	X	√	X

Now, we can answer the questions.
27. Option (d) is the correct answer.
28. Option (b) is the correct answer.

Solutions for Questions 29 to 30:

Let us decode the clues to clear the picture and sequence all the events that are given in the information. We have been given that Bali and Giri are in Marketing, Fateh in Finance and Dabang is not in HR. This means that Dabang is in Finance. By the process of elimination, remaining Chinkara, Jeev and Himesh are in HR.

Discipline	Students
Marketing	Bali and Giri
Finance	Fateh and Dabang
HR	Chinkara, Jeev and Himesh

Now, to arrange students with their respective colleges is the next task. We have been given Dabang who is a male student studies in IIM R only with Bali. This means that in IIM R only two students study and Bali is a female, since at least one boy and one girl study in a college. Now, we have been given Fateh who is a male student studies in IIM B but not with either Jeev or Chinkara. This means that Jeev and Chinkara study at IIM A. Also, we have been given that Bali's sister Giri and Himesh, who is a female, study in the same college. This college cannot be IIM A because then there will be only a single student in IIM B. Hence, Himesh and Giri study at IIM B. Still, we do not know about the sex of Jeev and Chinkara.

College	Students
IIM A	Jeev and Chinkara
IIM B	Fateh (Male), Himesh (Female) and Giri (Female)
IIM R	Dabang (Male) and B (Female)

Now, we can answer the questions.

29. The students who study HR are Chinkara, Jeev and Himesh. Among the three, Chinkara and Jeev study at IIM A. Hence, option (d) is the correct answer.
30. If Chinkara and Bali interchange their colleges, satisfying all other conditions, it implies that Chinkara is a female and Jeev is a male. Thus, the group consists of Chinkara, Bali, Giri and Himesh. Hence, option (b) is the correct answer.

Solutions for Questions 31 to 32:

This question is a classic example of primary and secondary clues being provided in the information. To solve this set, one must be able to analyse all the possibilities given in the clues to derive conclusive data arranged in an appropriate manner, according to the given conditions.

Let us solve the problem. From clue (i) we get that the two persons who visit on Friday are Pepe and the person who visits with Pepe is a Defence specialist. Now, from clue (iii) Fefe is a Biotech specialist and he visits alone on Tuesday. Also, from clue (vii), we get that the specialist in Genetics visits on Friday. This means that Pepe is a specialist in Genetics.

Moving onto clues (iv) and (v), we get that Meme and Keke visit on Wednesday and from clue (vi), the engineer visits with Paramedics. Thus, they visit either on a Wednesday or on a Saturday. Again, from clue (ii), the engineer does not visit on Saturday. Thus, engineer and paramedics visit on Wednesday. Now using clue (iv), we get that Meme is Paramedics and Keke is the engineer. Again, from clue (v), we get that Hehe is not a Defence specialist and Hehe does not visit on Friday. Hence, Hehe visits on Saturdays. Similarly, from clue (viii), we get that Bebe also visits on Saturday.

The only person left to analyse is Dede who is the specialist in Defence. Also, since Bebe is not a businessman, Hehe is a businessman and Bebe is a specialist in Biometrics.

Now, we can summarise our analysis in a table:

Tuesday	Fefe (Biotech)
Wednesday	Meme (Paramedic), Keke (Engineer)
Friday	Pepe (Genetics), Dede (Defence)
Saturday	Hehe (Business), Bebe (Biometrics)

Now, we can answer the questions:

31. Option (a) is the correct answer.
32. Option (d) is the correct answer.

Solution for Question 33:

33. Solve this question through options.

Check option (a) through the following process:

Note: Since all likes and dislikes start with different letters we can just use the first letter to denote the likes and dislikes.

Minister	Likes	Dislikes
M1	F, S	G
M2	S, D	F
M5	D	S, M
M6	F	S, M

It can be observed that M1 does not hate any of the likings of the other three and hence this option is wrong.

For option (d) it can be seen that each of the 4 selected ministers likes one of the likes of at least one of the other three and the hate criteria is also fulfilled.

Minister	Likes	Dislikes
M1	F, S	G
M2	S, D	F

Minister	Likes	Dislikes
M4	M	D
M7	G, M	F

Hence, Option (d) is correct.

Solutions for Questions 34 to 35:

The following constraints operate in the question-

(i) We have to take only one of D and F. This also consequently means that each of A, B, C and E should be selected for a portfolio.

(ii) C has to be given Home or Finance.

(iii) B's condition is more open than C's and is dependent on what (and whether D gets anything.) So if D is power or telecom- then B is the other of these two portfolios. i.e if D get telecom, B must be given Power and vice versa. However, if D is not getting either of these two portfolios then B has no constraint.

(iv) A and E must be part of the ministry.

34. In order to find the correct answer, we need to see each of the options for any rules they might be violating.
   (a) Is rejected because C has to be given Home or Finance only - but in this case C is getting defence. So that condition is violated here.
   (b) Does not contravene any condition.
   (c) D and F are selected together. Hence, the option is not valid.
   (d) C is not getting Home or finance.
   Thus Option (b) is correct as it meets all conditions.
35. Option (d) is clearly not valid as D is given telecom but B is not getting Power.

Level of Difficulty (II)

Solutions for Questions 1 to 6:

1. (c)
2. The following table would get formed based on the deductions:
   Starting table–based on the initial direct information, viz:
   'Four food baskets O, P, Q and R of different size and shapes and each can be carried only on motorcycles M1, M2, M3 or M4 respectively.'
   'Q is with A and P is with D.'
   'F travels on M1 and E travels on M2 motorcycles.'
   'G is with Q'.

Motorcycle	M1	M2	M3	M4
Basket	O	P	Q	R
Person 1	F	E	A	
Person 2		D	G	

Now at this point, if we use the fact that B cannot go with R, it means that B must be placed with Basket O on M1. Consequently, on M4 with basket R, C and H would travel together. Thus, option (c) is correct.

3. The conditions given can be summarised as follows:
   Sonali, Shalini, Shubhra, Shahira, Rupa together.
   Rupali, Renuka together.
   In separate groups are:
   Rupa,
   Radha, (not with Tara) (not with Komal)
   Renuka, Rupali
   Ruchika,
   Ritu (not with Sowmya)
   Komal (not with Radha, Somya or Ritu)
   Shweta, Jyotika, __, __ (not with Rupali and Renuka)

		Who cannot be there
W1 (5)	Sonali, Shalini, Shubhra, Shahira, Rupa	
Group of (4)	Shweta, Jyotika, _, _	
Group of (3) or (2)	Rupali, Renuka	
W4 Group of (2) or (3)	Somya, Ruchika	Komal, Ritu
Group of (1)		

At this point it is clear that:
Ritu and Somya are separate and hence Komal must also be separate.
Also the three groups from the second to the fourth row in the table above must be of 2, 3 or 4 members.
This leaves us with only Tara, Komal, Radha, Ritu to place.
Thus, Radha and Ritu must be in group of 4 or 1 (since Renuka and Ruchika must be in the groups of 2 and 3 in some order and Rupa has already been placed in a group of 5.)
If you were to place Ritu in the group of 1, then Radha must go to the group of 4. In such a case, either Komal or Tara would have to be placed in Radha's group. This contravenes the basic conditions. Hence, Ritu cannot be alone and must be in the group of 4.
Consequently, Radha must belong to the group of 1–which means that she must be instructed by Elina.

4. First of all summarise the basic information as follows:
   Women: Fiza, Kavita
   Men: Ram, Shyam, David, Peter and Rahim.
   Ram not Shyam.
   Shyam + Rahim
   Kavita only if David
   David does not want Peter
   Ram only if Peter

David only if Fiza.
After this go through each question through options meeting all the conditions:
Option (a) is rejected as it selects David without Fiza.
Option (c) is rejected for the same reason.
Option (d) is rejected as it selects Ram without Peter.
Only Option (b) obeys all conditions.

5. Only the third group can be seen to be feasible.
6. Option (a) cannot be true since if Kavita and Ram are selected, David and Peter must also be selected and David wants Fiza as a part of his group. Thus we would not be able to create a group of 4.
Option (b): If Fiza and Kavita are selected, then David has to be part of the group. The fourth person has to be selected from amongst the four men left. However, Ram, Shyam and Rahim have to be selected with at least one more of the 4 males. Also since David is selected, Peter cannot be. Thus there is no way to select exactly 4 people in the group.
Option (c): This is also not possible as David wants Fiza so he cannot be selected amongst a selection of 4 males. This means that we must take all the other 4, but Ram does not want to be in a group with Shyam.
Hence, None of these is true.

Solutions for Questions 7 to 8:

Refer to the clues given to us in the information, the best way to solve this question is to tabulate as well as comprehend the direct and indirect clues given to us. The first clue given to us is that L_1 difficulty projects will have single researchers and other difficulty level will have two researchers. Now it is given that ROC II and ROC III are L_2 and L_3 respectively. Thus, ROC I and ROC IV are L_1 level. Direct clues given to us point that Ex can be assigned only L_1 projects which are ROC I and ROC IV. Next set of clues given to us says that Ax cannot work with Bx, Cx, Dx and Fx. Thus, Ax will also be assigned to project requiring a single researcher, hence, either ROC I or ROC IV. Now, since Fx cannot be assigned to L_3 level so he must have been assigned to ROC II and he can work with either Dx or Cx, but Fx will work with Dx since Cx cannot work with Dx. Now, Bx will be assigned to the remaining L_3 project i.e., ROC III and Bx has the option of working with Cx.

	L_1	L_2	L_3	L_1
	ROC I	ROC II	ROC III	ROC IV
Ax	X/√	X	X	√/X
Bx	X	X	√	X
Cx	X	X	√	X
Dx	X	√	X	X
Ex	√/X	X	X	X/√
Fx	X	√	X	X

7. Hence, option (d) is the correct answer.
8. If Fx can neither work in ROC I and ROC II then we become uncertain about the project assignment for each of Ax, Ex and Fx.
Hence, option (c) is the correct answer.

Solution for Question 9:

9. To solve the question lets look into the clues given and try to pair assistants with bosses and respective countries. For this, one must start reacting to the clue that gives a clear picture of the relationship such as the clue of Davis and Catty working together. China operations would not be headed by a person whose name ends in 's'. Let us tabulate the information in the clues and draw a clear picture of the scenario.

	Alexis	Benny	Carena	Davis
	Arnold	Dave	Billy	Catty
Afghanistan	√	X	X	X
Pakistan	X	X	√	X
Japan	X	X	X	√
China	X	√	X	X

Hence, option (b) is the correct answer.

Solutions for Questions 10 to 13:

From the information given, we can deduce and prepare the following table:

	Aman	Bimal	Charan	Deepak	Ehsaan	Famid
Morning	Y	Y	Y	N	Y	N
Noon	N	Y	Y	Y	N	N
Evening	N	N	N	Y	Y	Y

10. From statements A and B: Aman and Famid can guard the apartment at most 2 times and others can guard at most 3 times. Therefore, the total number of shifts in a week in which at least 1 guard is guarding the apartment $4 \times 3 + 2 \times 2 = 16$.
11. Maximum number of days the apartment can be guarded = $16/3 = 5.33$ or 6.
Therefore, the minimum number of days the apartment is left unguarded = $7 - 6 = 1$.
12. We can solve this problem through the options. Analysing (b), we find that Aman and Famid can work in morning and evening shifts respectively but Ehsaan also necessarily works in morning and evening shifts only → Hence, no guard will be available for noon shift. Therefore (b) cannot be formed.
13. As Ehsaan works in the morning shift twice, he can work in the evening shift once. To maximise the number of days on which a guard is available in all shifts, Deepak has to work in evening shift twice and in noon shift once.

Bimal and Charan have to work in noon shift twice and Famid in evening shift twice. Therefore, none of the given options is a possible combination.

Solutions for Questions 14 to 17:

From statement (i), (ii) and (ix) we get the number of students participated in Robotics, Singing, Dancing, Painting are 2, 3, 2, 1, respectively.

From statements (v) and (vii):

	Robotics	Singing	Dancing	Painting	Total number of events
A		Y		N	
B					
C	N		Y		
D					3
Total number of students	2	3	2	1	

From statements (vi) and (vii), we find that D participated in both Robotics and Singing and C did not participate in Painting.

	Robotics	Singing	Dancing	Painting	Total number of events
A		Y		N	
B					
C	N		Y	N	
D	Y	Y			3
Total number of students	2	3	2	1	

14. From the tables above,
Number of students who participated in Robotics = 2
Number of students who participated in Dancing = 2
Sum = 2 + 2 = 4
15. If A participated in Robotics then the table changes to

	Robotics	Singing	Dancing	Painting	Total number of events
A	Y	Y		N	
B	N	Y			
C	N	N	Y	N	
D	Y	Y			3
Total number of students	2	3	2	1	

From the table above, it is clear that if A participated in Robotics then B must have participated in Singing. Thus, (b) is true.

16. If A participated in three sports then he would have participated in Robotics and Dancing. In this case, we deduce the following table:

	Robotics	Singing	Dancing	Painting	Total number of events
A	Y	Y	Y	N	3
B	N	Y	N	N	1
C	N	N	Y	N	1
D	Y	Y	N	Y	3
Total number of students	2	3	2	1	

Only option (d) is correct.

17. If A participated in three events and B participated in one event, then the given information can be tabulated in the following table:

	Robotics	Singing	Dancing	Painting	Total number of events
A	Y	Y	Y	N	3
B	N	Y	N	N	1
C	N	N	Y	N	1
D	Y	Y	N	Y	3
Total number of students	2	3	2	1	

From the table above, we can conclude that none of the given options is true. Hence, option (d) is correct.

Solutions for Questions 18 to 23:

From the information given, we can deduce the following table:

Student	School	Maximum Marks	Obtained marks
		24	6 or 8
		28	7
		16	4 or 8
		18	6 or 9
		20	5

From statement (i) it is clear that maximum marks of M.D. school are 24 and that of Chris's Physical test are 18.

Student	School	Maximum Marks	Obtained marks
	Modern	24	6 or 8
		28	7
		16	4 or 8
Chris		18	6 or 9
		20	5

From statement (v), Ben either scored 4 or 5 marks. If he scored 4 marks, then maximum possible marks of his test must be 16. But according to statement (v), maximum marks of Ben's test are 2 more than that of the student of the student who is referred to be not from the Bal Bharti school. In that case, the maximum marks of that student must be 14 (2 less than 16), which is not possible. Hence, Ben obtained 5 marks and the maximum marks of the other student referred to here must be 18. Therefore, that student must be Chris and he was not from Bal Bharti school. Ben scored the least marks, then all other students obtained 6 or more marks. Therefore, the student whose test had 16 as its' maximum possible marks scored 8 marks. After incorporating these changes, the table now becomes:

Student	School	Maximum Marks	Obtained marks
	Modern	24	6 or 8
		28	7
		16	8
Chris	Not Bal Bharti	18	6 or 9
Ben		20	5

From statement (iii) and the above table, it is clear that maximum marks of Kidzee School is 20.

Student	School	Maximum Marks	Obtained marks
	Modern	24	6 or 8
		28	7
		16	8
Chris	Not Bal Bharti	18	6 or 9
Ben	Kidzee	20	5

From condition (ii) it is clear that maximum marks of Bal Bharti and Ryan is 16, 18 in any order and the maximum marks in the schools of Dom and Ervin are 24 and 28 in any order.

From statement (iv), Ervin is not from Modern School. Therefore, Ervin's maximum marks must be 28 and Dom's maximum marks must be 24. Ervin must be from Presidium. As Chris is not from Bal Bharti, he must be from Ryan.

Student	School	Maximum Marks	Obtained marks
Dom	Modern	24	6 or 8
Ervin	Presidium	28	7
Andrew	Bal Bharti	16	8
Chris	Ryan	18	6 or 9
Ben	Kidzee	20	5

18. Chris is from Ryan.
19. Andrew is from Bal Bharti School.
20. Maximum possible sum of scores of Chris and Dom = 8 + 9 = 17.
21. Sum of maximum marks in Physical tests of schools-Kidzee and Ryan = 18 + 20 = 38.
22. Andrew studies in Bal Bharti College and obtained 8 marks in his physical test. Option (c) is correct.
23. Ervin > Dom > Ben > Chris > Andrew. Option (c) is correct.

Solutions for Questions 24 to 27:

From clue (vi): Number of students selected from A, B, C, D could be any of the following combinations: 10,5,10,10; 12,6,12,12; 14,7,14,14; 16,8,16,16.

Note: This list is created since there are a maximum of 62 students and a minimum of 16 students selected from the four colleges. The upper limit is actually 16 × 4 = 64, but since one of the college-post selection combinations is given as 2, the upper limit is 62.

In the above cases, the total number of recruitments is 35,42,49 and 56 respectively. From the clues about the number of developers, managers, counselors and typists we also know the following:

If total number of developers is 'a', then from statement (iii): Total number of counselors = a/3

From statement (ii): Total number of typists = a

From statement (v): Total number of managers = a/3 + 3

The total number of recruitments is a + a + a/3 + a/3 + 3 = (8a/3) + 3.

If we try to match the values of the number of recruitments in each of the four combinations for number of recruitments of A,B,C and D to the number of recruitments in terms of 'a', we get the following four situations:

(8a/3) + 3 = 35; (8a/3) + 3= 42; (8a/3) + 3 = 49; (8a/3) + 3 = 56

Solving for 'a' in these four cases, we see that 'a' is an integer only if we take (8a/3) + 3 = 35. In this case, we have: a = 12 and the number of recruitments from the four colleges would be 10, 5, 10 and 10, respectively for A, B, C and D.

Also, since the number of counselors is a/3 = 4, each college must be having 1 counselor selected from it. The table becomes:

	A	B	C	D	Total
Manager					7
Developer			2		12
Counselor	1	1	1	1	4
Typist					12
Total	10	5	10	10	

Looking at the column for College B, the numbers possible for Manager, Developer and Typist include three 1's and one 2. Further, if we put 1 developer from College B, we would not be able to recruit a total of 12 developers (as we can maximum take 4 people for every post from any college). Thus, we can conclude that: The number of developers from colleges A, B, C and D:are 4, 2, 2 and 4, respectively.

	A	B	C	D	Total
Manager		1			7
Developer	4	2	2	4	12
Typist		1			12
Counselors	1	1	1	1	4
Total	10	5	10	10	

Number of typists selected from college A, B, C, D can be (4, 1, 4, 3) or (4, 1, 3, 4) or (3, 1, 4, 4).

Case A: When number of typists selected from college A = 3.

	A	B	C	D	Total
Manager	2	1	3	1	7
Developer	4	2	2	4	12
Typist	3	1	4	4	12
Counselor	1	1	1	1	4
Total	10	5	10	10	

Case B: When number of typists selected from college C = 3:

	A	B	C	D	Total
Manager	1	1	4	1	7
Developer	4	2	2	4	12
Typist	4	1	3	4	12
Counselor	1	1	1	1	4
Total	10	5	10	10	

Case C: When number of typists selected from college D = 3:

	A	B	C	D	Total
Manager	1	1	3	2	7
Developer	4	2	2	4	12
Typist	4	1	4	3	12
Counselor	1	1	1	1	4
Total	10	5	10	10	

24. 4.
25. From the above, it is clear that number of managers from College A was either 1 or 2.
26. (d)
27. (d)

Solutions for Questions 28 to 31:

In order to solve questions of this sort, getting the data structure in a pictorial form is of the utmost importance. Let the girls be denoted by a, b, c, d and the boys as A, B, C and D respectively. From the direct clues in the question set, we can make the following structure of people, their institutes and their majors and minors:

X	Y	Z
Female	Female (Operations, ____)	Bandita, Female
Chetan, Male (Finance, ____)	Barun, Male (Operations, Finance)	Chitra, Female
Male	Male (____, Finance)	

Deduction 1: The other information in the question set is based on the fact that amongst the men there are two finance majors and one operations major (given in clues (ii) and (iii)). This means that the remaining male must be majoring in Marketing. If we try to make sense of this information with respect to the current status of the table, we can see that the Male majoring in Marketing has to be from institute Y. Then, the remaining male from institute X must be majoring in Finance.

Deduction 2: We also know that Adriana and Deb belong to the same institute, while Daisy and Amit too belong to the same institute. Thus, between Institute X and Y, we have to distribute these two pairs. For this, we need to understand that since there are three females who minor in Marketing and Daisy minors in Operations (Clue (vii)), Daisy can only be fit into the female position for institute X. [As the female in institute Y is majoring in Operations, she cannot be Daisy.] Thus, Daisy- Amit should be from institute X and Adriana-Deb must be from Institute Y.

Deduction 3: At this point it is a good idea to take a count of the majors and minors amongst the women and the men.

For the women: We know that three women minor in marketing, and one minors in operations. We also know that exactly 1 woman majors in finance, while another one majors in operations (she has to be Adriana as she is from Y). The other two majors are indeterminate - and can be shared as (operations and operations) or (Marketing and operations), depending on which majors and minors you attribute to the people from X, Y and Z.

For the men: We know that exactly two men major in Finance, exactly one majors in Operations and hence one majors in Marketing. Amongst the minors there are two finance and the other two are either marketing or operations. Once we have this, then we can move onto filling the remaining majors and minors for the people for whom we know the same.

X	Y	Z
Daisy Female (______, Operations)	Adriana, Female (Operations, Marketing)	Bandita, Female (______, Marketing)

X	Y	Z
Chetan, Male (Finance, _____)	Barun, Male (Operations, Finance)	Chitra, Female (______, Marketing)
Amit Male (Finance, ______)	Deb, Male (Marketing, Finance)	

The answers can be read off this table:

28. Bandita and Chitra are from institute Z. Option (b) is correct.
29. Deb minors in Finance. Option (a) is correct.
30. Amit majors in Finance. Option (a) is correct.
31. If you put Chitra as the only Finance woman, then Bandita cannot have Marketing as her major and neither can she have finance as her major. This leaves only 1 option for Bandita's major –i.e. Operations. Hence, option (c) is correct.

CHAPTER 5

Quantitative Reasoning

Chapter Launchpad
Scan this QR code for an introductory video on Quantitative Reasoning

Quantitative reasoning, as the name itself suggests, is reasoning involving numbers and numerical logic. Quantitative reasoning questions are common in all kinds of aptitude exams and require the student to work out numerical relationships as defined by the parameters in the problem.

The key skills involved in solving quantitative reasoning questions are the following:

(i) The ability to understand the specific quantitative logic being utilised inside the questions

(ii) The ability to order the clues in the correct order of usage (as explained in the theory of logical reasoning)

(iii) The ability to understand basic mathematical concepts like, percentages, averages, ratios, multiplications, etc.

(iv) The ability to create symbolic representations of the various clues provided so that you can bring together each of the relevant clues while creating the teams.

(v) The ability to wait for and reach the appropriate time in the problem solving situation from where the indirect clues provided in the question can be used.

Illustrated below are the solutions to a few typical questions on quantitative reasoning. We would urge you to first have a look at the questions and try to solve the same on your own before looking at the solutions.

Example 1: A man would like to take a new health insurance. An officer taking care of these matters says to the man, "Please tell me how many children you have." The man answers, "I have three of them." The officer, "What are the ages of your children?" The man answers, "The product of the ages is equal to 36." The officer replies, "This is not enough information, Sir!"; the man replied, "Sorry that I was a little bit unclear, but the sum of the ages is equal to the number of shops in front of your office." The officer: "This still isn't enough information, Sir!"; The man replies, "My oldest child loves chocolate." The officer: "Thanks for your cooperation, I now know the ages." Are you as smart as the officer? Then, give the sum of the ages of the children.

(a) 13 (b) 22
(c) 36 (d) 38

Solution: The product of the ages is 36*. Using this, one can make the following combination of ages:

1, 36, sum = 38
1, 18, 2 sum = 21
1, 12, 3 sum = 16
1, 9, 4 sum = 14
1, 6, 6 sum = 13
2, 9, 2 sum = 13
2, 6, 3 sum = 11
3, 3, 4 sum = 10

After the man had said that the product of the ages is equal to 36, the officer didn't have enough information. Then he was told that the sum is equal to number of shops in front of the office. He replied by saying that this still isn't enough information. So the sum of the ages should be 13, because otherwise he would have known the ages immediately. The last statement is that the oldest child loves chocolate. So there is an oldest child. Hence the officer concludes that the ages of the children are 2, 2 and 9 years.

Hence, option (a) is the correct answer.

Example 2: Early one Monday morning, four snails—Aman, Bubbly, Charu and Devi set off together down the garden path. Aman and Bubbly kept the same steady pace, slithering only 8 meters by the time Charu and Devi had already reached the azalea.

Charu was winded and had to stop for an hour to rest. Although Devi was tired, too, she pressed on, but reduced her pace to be the same as Aman's and Bubbly's.

Charu started off again just as Aman and Bubbly got even with her. She raced off at her original pace. Aman promptly sped up to the same speed as Charu and kept even with her. Bubbly just kept going at her original pace.

When Aman reached the end of the path, she was 1 meter ahead of Bubbly, but she was half an hour later than Devi was.

How many meters long was the path?

(a) 10 (b) 15
(c) 8 (d) None of these

Solution: A few things are evident from the current situation:

Deduction 1: Since Charu rests for 1 hour before Aman and Bubbly reach the azalea, it is clear that Devi would be exactly 1 hour ahead of Bubbly when she reaches the end point.

Deduction 2: As Devi has already reached half an hour ago when Aman and Charu reach, Bubbly must be only

half an hour away from her destination. As, Bubbly is 1 meter away from the destination, she would cover this 1 meter in 30 minutes. Thus, Bubbly's speed must be 2 m/hr. This would be the slower of the two speeds.
This would also be the speed of Bubbly and Aman for the first 8 meters.

Deduction 3: As, Bubbly and Aman take 4 hours to reach 8 meters, in 1 hour more (when Charu rests), they will cover 2 meters more. Thus, the azalea is at a distance of 10 meters from the starting point.

Deduction 4: The 10 meter distance to the azalea is covered in 4 hours by Charu and Devi. Thus, the faster speed would be 2.5 m/hr.

Deduction 5: After the azalea, when Aman and Charu start moving at 2.5 m/hr, Bubbly would be moving at 2 m/hr. When Aman and Charu reach the end, Bubbly is 1 meter behind. This gap can only be created in a 2 hour journey.

Thus, the distance from the azalea to the end point is 5 meter. Total distance is 10 + 5 = 15 meters. Option (b) is correct.

Example 3: Dhiman was admiring the output of her new program to generate random numbers. She had printed out the first ten numbers of the results. She soon noticed something interesting. Each of the 10 numbers had exactly one digit, in the proper placement, of the 5 digit code she used to open her car door without a key.

Going Beyond the Book

Scan this QR code for a video explanation of Example 3

In the first number 14073, for example, Dhiman's car code could not be 34170 (two digits correctly placed) or 92365 (none).

Find Dhiman's car entry code from these first 10 randomly generated numbers: 14073, 79588, 05892, 84771, 63136, 42936, 37145, 50811, 98174 and 29402.

(a) 05892 (b) 63136
(c) 42936 (d) None of these

Solution: In the given grid of 10 five digit numbers, since every number has exactly 1 digit matched correctly with the correct code, there must be exactly 10 instances of correct code matches amongst the 50 possible instances (10 × 5).

If we were to look at the first digit it is clear that the first digit has 10 different values in the ten numbers. Thus, only 1 number can be correctly matched for the first digit's value.

The other 4 places in the 5 digit number must match 9 more times for the above grid to be correct. This can be principally done in 2 ways:

First way: 3 + 3 + 2 + 1 or Second way: 2 + 2 + 2 + 3

If we were to observe the numbers, the following deductions would come up:

First place	Second place	Third place	Fourth place	Fifth place
Each digit (from 0 to 9) happens only once	4 & 9 occur twice	1 occurs thrice & 8 occurs twice	7 occurs thrice & 3 occurs twice	1, 2 & 6 occur twice each
	5, 3, 2, 7, 0 & 8 occur once each	0, 5, 7, 9, 4 occur once	8, 9, 4, 1 & 0 occur once each	5, 4, 3 & 8 occur once each

Looking at the number 98174, it is clear that both 1 and 7 cannot occur in the third and fourth place digits, as then the number 98174 would have 2 numbers matched with the code.

Thus, the structure 1 + 2 + 3 + 3 + 1 or indeed 1 + 1 + 3 + 3 + 2 is ruled out (i.e., the use of two triplicate matches is ruled out).

Thus, the 10 matches between the code and the 10 random numbers must be in one of the following structures:

	First place	Second place	Third place	Fourth place	Fifth place
Number of digits matched with the code	1	2	3	2	2
Number of digits matched with the code	1	2	2	3	2

Thus, the number would be either xx13x or xx87x. The first possibility is rejected because 63136 contains both 1 and 3 in the third and fourth places of the number. Thus, the number must be of the form xx87x. From this point, thinking about the second place digit, gives us that the second place has to be occupied by 9 (as only 4 and 9 give us 2 matches with the code and amongst this 4 cannot be taken for the second place because if the number is x487x then the number 84771 contradicts the basic condition of the problem).

Thus, the number must be x987x.

Thinking of the last digit–this digit must be either 1, 2 or 6. It cannot be 1 because of the presence of 84771 in the ten number. It cannot be 2 because the number 29402 would have 2 digits in the correct place. Hence, it must be 6. Thus, the number becomes x9876.

Thinking of the first digit, it has to be 3, because it is only the number 37145 which lacks a single digit matching with the 2nd to 5th digit of the code x9876. Thus, the code is 39876. Option (d) is correct.

Example 4: Abe, Buddy, Carmen, Dennis and Earl, all live on Pine Street which has house numbers from 10 to 111, both inclusive. Two of them live in the same house. The others all live in different houses. They all have made remarks about where they live, but not all the remarks are true.

Abe said, "My house number is a factor of Buddy's house number. Earl's house number is 10 greater than Dennis."

Buddy said, "My house number is greater than 70. Abe's house number is greater than 30."

Carmen said, "My house number is both a cube and a square. Dennis's house number is greater than 50."

Dennis said, "My house number is a square. Buddy's house number is a cube."

Earl said, "My house number is twice Buddy's."

But who's telling the truth? It turns out that all statements made by people living in houses with numbers greater than 50 were false. All the other statements were true.

Can you tell the house number of Earl?

(a) 49 (b) 16
(c) 59 (d) None of these

Solution: In order to solve this question, you need to look at the options for Earl's house number. Option 1 cannot be true since if Earl's house number is 49, he must be speaking the truth–but his statement cannot be true. If we take Earl's house number as 16 (option 2), then Buddy must be 8 which is against the problem's basic condition that all house numbers are between 10 to 111.

If we go with option 3–59, then if Abe is true, then Dennis must be 49. Hence, Dennis's statements must be true. So Buddy's house number would be a cube. There are only 2 perfect cubes between 10 and 111–viz 27 and 64. If Buddy's house number is 27, then he must be speaking the truth–which is not true if we look at the statement of the problem. Thus, Buddy must be 64 and Abe's house number must be less than 30–only factor of 64 less than 30 and greater than 10 is 16.

At this time we have the grid as:

Abe	16
Buddy	64
Earl	59
Dennis	49

We just need to place Carmen in this grid. Looking at Carmen's statement and looking at the numbers available below 50, the two numbers (16 and 49) do not satisfy the condition that the room number is both a square and a cube. Hence, Carmen must be lying and the possible values of Carmen is 59 and 64. If we were to place Carmen at 64, then Carmen's first statement becomes true– an internal contradiction. Thus, Carmen must be at 59. The final arrangements of the house numbers are:

Abe	16
Buddy	64
Carmen and Earl	59
Dennis	49

Example 5: During a game of five card draw poker, played with a standard deck, you are dealt a hand with the following characteristics:

(i) It contains no aces or face cards.
(ii) No two cards have the same value.
(iii) All four suits are present.
(iv) The total value of the odd cards equals the total value of the even cards.
(v) There are no three card straights.
(vi) The total value of the black cards is 10.
(vii) The total value of the hearts is 14.
(viii) The card with the lowest value is a spade.

Exactly what are the five cards in your hand?

(a) 2 of spades, 5 and 9 of diamonds, 4 of spades and 8 of clubs.
(b) 2 of diamonds, 5 and 9 of spades, 4 of hearts and 8 of clubs.
(c) 2 of clubs, 5 and 9 of hearts, 4 of diamonds and 8 of spades.
(d) 2 of spades, 5 and 9 of hearts, 4 of diamonds, 8 of clubs.

Solution: Deduction 1: Since there are no aces or face cards, we only have 2, 3, 4, 5, 6, 7, 8, 9 or 10 as the value of the cards.

Deduction 2: Since total of odd = total of evens and the minimum even total is 12 (2 + 4 + 6), there must be 2 odds and 3 evens. Only then can the two odds add up to an even total and be equal to the total of 3 even cards.

Deduction 3: There are 2 cards of 1 suit and 1 card each of the other 3 suits. The two cards belonging to 1 suit must be hearts because there is no other way for the hearts to total up to 14.

Deduction 4: There are 3 cases:

a) If the sum of the evens is 12, the odds would be 5 and 7 and the evens would be 2, 4, 6. This cannot happen because in such a case 2 cards would not add up to 14–which is the requirement for the 2 hearts.

b) If the sum of the evens is 14, the odds would be 5 and 9 and the evens would be 2, 4, 8. This can happen if we put the hearts as 5 and 9 and 2 goes to spades and since the total of the blacks is 10, clubs must be the 8 of clubs and 4 would be the 4 of diamonds.

c) If the sum of the evens is 16, the evens should be 2, 4 and 10; the odds must be 7 and 9. But this is not possible because if we take the two hearts to total 14, it is not possible.

Thus, the solution is: 2 of spades, 5 and 9 of hearts, 4 of diamonds, 8 of clubs
Option (d) is correct.

LEVEL OF DIFFICULTY (I)

Directions for Questions 1 to 5: *A quiz competition was organised in a school and the performance of students was recorded on piece of paper with ink. But somehow, some water fell on the paper and the information remained incomplete.*

However, the scorer has some clues which are:

	Average	Good	Excellent	Total
Male			12	
Female				36
Total		33		

(i) Half the students were either excellent or good.
(ii) 40% of the students were females.
(iii) One-third of the male students were average.

1. How many students are both female and excellent?
(a) 0 (b) 8
(c) 16 (d) None of these

2. What proportion of good students are male?
(a) 0.73 (b) 0
(c) 0.4 (d) None of these

3. What proportion of female students are good?
(a) 0.25 (b) 0
(c) 0.5 (d) None of these

4. How many students are both male and good?
(a) 16 (b) 24
(c) 27 (d) None of these

5. Among average students, what is the ratio of males to females?
(a) 1:3 (b) 2:3
(c) 3:2 (d) None of these

Directions for Questions 6 to 10: *A, B, C and D are four friends living together in a flat and they have an agreement that whatever edible comes they will share equally among themselves. One day A's uncle came to him and gave him a box of laddoos. Since no one was around, A divided the laddoos in four equal parts and ate his share after which he put the rest in the box. As he was closing the box, B walked in, took the Box from A and divided the ladoos in 4 equal parts and A and B took one part each and ate it. Suddenly, C appeared and snatched the box. He again divided the laddoos in four equal parts, the three of them ate one part each and kept the remaining laddoos in the box. Later when D came, he again divided the laddoos in four equal parts and all four ate their respective share. In total D ate 3 laddoos.*

6. How many laddoos in total did C eat?
(a) 12 (b) 15
(c) 39 (d) None of these

7. How many laddoos in total did B eat?
(a) 24 (b) 15
(c) 39 (d) None of these

8. How many laddoos in total did A eat?
(a) 56 (b) 68
(c) 71 (d) None of these

9. How many laddoos were given to A by his Uncle?
(a) 128 (b) 125
(c) 113 (d) None of these

10. How many laddoos did A eat the first time?
(a) 32 (b) 24
(c) 15 (d) None of these

Directions for Questions 11 to 14: *Rajeev planted some plants in his lawn but in a certain fixed pattern:*

(i) In most of the rows there are neither Roses nor Marigolds.
(ii) There are two more rows of Orchids than Tulips and two more rows of Roses than Orchids.
(iii) There are four more rows of Roses than Tulips.
(iv) There aren't as many rows of Lilly as Fireball.
(v) There is one less Marigold row than Rose.
(vi) There is just one row of Tulips.
(vii) The maximum number of rows he planted is six.

11. How many rows of rose did he plant?
(a) Two (b) Five
(c) Four
(d) Cannot be determined

12. Which of the above information is redundant and can be dispensed with?
(a) (i) (b) (iii)
(c) (i) and (iii) both (d) All are necessary

13. What is the sum of the rows of Orchids and Marigold he planted?
(a) Three (b) Nine
(c) Seven
(d) Cannot be determined

14. How many rows of fireball did he plant?
(a) Two (b) Six
(c) Two or Six (d) Data inadequate

Directions for Questions 15 to 20: *In a class of 540 students, for every 9 girls there are 11 boys. The weight of students varies from 40 to 50 kg. There are as many 44 kg girls as there are 46 kg boys and as many 40 kg boys as 50 kg girls. The number of 50 kg boys is 35 more than that of 44 kg girls while there are as many 44 kg boys as 46 kg girls. The ratio of 40 kg boys and girls is 4:3 while that of 50 kg girls and boys is 1:3.*

15. How many boys weigh 40 kg?
(a) 22 (b) 24
(c) 28 (d) None of these

16. How many girls weigh 44 kg?
(a) 37 (b) 36
(c) 39 (d) None of these

17. How many girls weigh 46 kg?
(a) 165 (b) 164
(c) 146 (d) None of these

18. The number of boys weighing 50 kg is:
(a) 72 (b) 74
(c) 76 (d) None of these

19. The number of girls weighing 40 kg is:
(a) 16 (b) 18
(c) 22 (d) None of these

20. The number of students weighing 50 kg is:
(a) 96 (b) 42
(c) 201 (d) None of these

Directions for Questions 21 to 26: *A, B, C, D and E are five different integers. When written in the ascending order of values, the difference between any two adjacent integers is 4. D is the greatest and A the least. B is greater than E but less than C. The sum of the integers is equal to E.*

21. The value of A is:
(a) -7 (b) -9
(c) -5 (d) None of these

22. The sum of A and B is:
(a) -10 (b) -15
(c) 10 (d) None of these

23. The greatest number has the value:
(a) 9 (b) -5
(c) 3 (d) 7

24. The sum of the integers is:
(a) 25 (b) -6
(c) -15 (d) None of these

25. The product of the integers is:
(a) -945 (b) 945
(c) 315 (d) None of these

26. What is the positive difference between the lowest and the highest integers?
(a) 8 (b) 6
(c) 16 (d) None of these

Directions for Questions 27 to 30: *Three classmates–X, Y and Z live on the AN Jha Marg, yet they do not know the house number of each other. The houses are numbered from 1 to 99. Since Z is a regular student and attends every class sincerely, his notes are very good and updated. X and Y are not so regular, therefore, they desire to meet Z at his house individually.*

One day X asks Z, "The number of your house in which you reside is a perfect square or not?" Z replies. Then X asks, "Is it greater than 50?" He again replies. X thinks that he has got the address and decides to visit Z. When X reaches at the address, he realises that he is wrong. He then thinks over it again and is not surprised as Z answered only the second question honestly.

Y not aware of X's conversation, asks Z two questions of his own. Y asks "Is your house number a perfect cube?" Z replies. Then Y asks "Is it greater than 25?"

He answers again. Y thinks that he has got the address but upon reaching there he finds the address incorrect and realises that Z answered only the second question honestly.

If Z's house number is less than the house number of X and Y and the sum of all three of their house numbers is twice the perfect square of some number then answer the following question:

27. What is X's house number?
(a) 64 (b) 81
(c) 49
(d) Cannot be determined

28. What is Y's house number?
(a) 64 (b) 81
(c) 36
(d) Cannot be determined

29. What is Z's house number?
(a) 55 (b) 65
(c) 25 (d) 85

30. What is the sum of house numbers of all the three X, Y and Z?
(a) 100 (b) 200
(c) 128
(d) Cannot be determined

Directions for Questions 31 to 34: *Some friends went to Netram Sweets. Following is the information about the number of rosogollas they ate:*

(i) Gimmy ate 8 less than Akshit.
(ii) Dileep and Raj together ate 37.
(iii) Jugal ate 8 more than Dileep.
(iv) Akshit ate 5 more than Dileep.
(v) Akshit and Gimmy together ate 40.

31. How many rosogollas did Raj eat?
(a) 18 (b) 24
(c) 16 (d) 27

32. Jugal and Dileep ate how many rosogollas in total?
(a) 46 (b) 36
(c) 40 (d) None of these

33. What is the difference between number of rosogollas eaten by Dileep and Raj?
(a) 1 (b) 2
(c) 3 (d) Data inadequate

34. If the cost of each rosogolla is ₹ 2, what was the total amount they had to pay?
(a) ₹ 208 (b) ₹ 200
(c) ₹ 198 (d) None of these

Directions for Questions 35 to 37: *Five women decided to go shopping to M.G. Road, Bangalore. They arrived at the designated meeting place in the following order: 1. Archana, 2. Chellama, 3. Dhenuka, 4. Helen and 5. Sahnaz.*

Each woman spent at least ₹ 1000. Below are some additional facts about how much they spent during their shopping spree.

(i) The woman who spent ₹ 2234 arrive before the lady who spent ₹ 1193.
(ii) One woman spent₹ 1340 and she was not Dhenuka.
(iii) One woman spent ₹ 1378 more than Chellama.
(iv) One woman spent ₹ 2517 and she was not Archana.
(v) Helen spent more than Dhenuka.
(vi) Shahnaz spent the largest amount and Chellama the smallest.

35. The woman who spent ₹ 1193 is:
(a) Archana (b) Chellama
(c) Dhenuka (d) Helen

36. What was the amount spent by Helen?
(a) ₹ 1193 (b) ₹ 1340
(c) ₹ 2234 (d) ₹ 2517

37. Which of the following amounts was spent by one of them?
(a) ₹ 1139 (b) ₹ 1378
(c) ₹ 2571 (d) ₹ 2718

Directions for Questions 38 to 39: *Elle is three times older than Yogesh; Zaheer is half the age of Wahida. Yogesh is older than Zaheer.*

38. Which of the following can be inferred?
(a) Yogesh is older than Wahida.
(b) Elle is older than Wahida.
(c) Elle may be younger than Wahida.
(d) None of these.

39. Which of the following information will be sufficient to estimate Elle's age?
(a) Zaheer is 10 years old.
(b) Both Yogesh and Wahida are older than Zaheer by the same number of years.
(c) Both 1 and 2 above.
(d) None of these.

Directions for Questions 40 to 43: *Read the information given below and answer the questions that follow:*

Casey, Ben, Alexander, Fred, Brian, Kian and Antony were standing in a queue (not necessarily in the same order) in a dance event and they have different points that they have received from the judge. The number of points that each person received is a distinct positive integer less than eight. The following information is known about the number of points with each of them and their positions in the queue.

(i) Alexander, who was standing immediately behind Kian, received three points more than Kian.
(ii) There were at least four persons standing in front of Antony and none of them received a lower number of points than him.
(iii) There is only one person between the person who received the least number of points and Brian.
(iv) Fred, who was not standing at either end, was standing in front of Brian.
(v) The person standing immediately in front Casey received two points less than Antony.

40. Who had the highest number of points among the seven persons?
(a) Alexander (b) Brian
(c) Fred (d) Casey

41. How many persons had a higher number of points than Casey?
(a) 4 (b) 5
(c) 6 (d) 7

42. Who was standing immediately in front of the person with the second highest number of points?
(a) Brian (b) Fred
(c) Alexander
(d) Cannot be determined

43. How many persons are there in between Kian and Fred ?
(a) 0 (b) 1
(c) 2
(d) Cannot be determined

Directions for Questions 44 to 46: *These questions are based on the situation given below:*

A young girl Roopa leaves home with x flowers, and goes to the bank of a nearby river. On the bank of the river, there are four places of worship, standing in a row. She dips all the x flowers into the river. The number of flowers doubles. Then, she enters the first place of worship, offers y flowers to the deity. She dips the remaining flowers into the river, and again the number of flowers doubles. She goes to the second place of worship, offers y flowers to the deity. She dips the remaining flowers into the river, and again the number of flowers doubles. She goes to the third place of worship, offers y flowers to the deity. She dips the remaining flowers into the river, and again the number of flowers doubles. She goes to the fourth place of worship, offers y flowers to the deity. Now, she is left with no flower in hand.

44. If Roopa leaves home with 30 flowers, the number of flowers she offers to each deity is
(a) 30 (b) 31
(c) 32 (d) 33

45. The minimum number of flowers that could be offered to each deity is
(a) 0 (b) 15
(c) 16 (d) Can't be determined

46. The minimum number of flowers with which Roopa leaves home is
(a) 16 (b) 15
(c) 0 (d) Can't be determined

Directions for Questions 47 to 49: *Each question is followed by two statements A and B. Answer each question using the following instructions.*

Choose (a) if the question can be answered by using one of the statements alone, but cannot be answered using the other statement alone.

Choose (b) if the question can be answered by using either statement alone.

Choose (c) if the question can be answered by using both statements together, but cannot be answered using either statement alone.

Choose (d) if the question cannot be answered even by using both statements together.

47. Three professors A, B and C are separately given three sets of numbers to add. They were expected to find the answers to 1 + 1, 1 + 1 + 2, and 1 + 1 respectively. Their respective answers were 3, 3 and 2. How many of the professors are mathematicians?
(a) A mathematician can never add two numbers correctly, but can always add three numbers correctly.
(b) When a mathematician makes a mistake in a sum, the error is + 1 or – 1.

48. How many among the four students A, B, C and D have passed the exam?
(a) The following is a true statement: A and B passed the exam.
(b) The following is a false statement: at least one among C and D has passed the exam.

49. Mr. Mendel grew one hundred flowering plants from black seeds and white seeds, each seed giving rise to one plant. A plant gives flowers of only one colour. From a black seed comes a plant giving red or blue flowers. From a white seed comes a plant giving red or white flowers. How many black seeds were used by Mr. Mendel?
(a) The number of plants with white flowers was 10.
(b) The number of plants with red flowers was 70.

Directions for Questions 50 to 51: *There are three bottles of water, A, B, C, whose capacities are 5 litres, 3 litres, and 2 litres, respectively. For transferring water from one bottle to another and to drain out the bottles, there exists a piping system. The flow through these pipes is computer controlled. The computer that controls the flow through these pipes can be fed with three types of instructions, as explained below:*

Instruction Type	Explanation of the Instruction
FILL (X,Y)	Fill bottle labelled X from the water in bottle labelled Y, where the remaining capacity of X is less than or equal to the amount of water in Y
EMPTY (X,Y)	Empty out the water in bottle labelled X into bottle labelled Y, where the amount of water in X is less than or equal to the remaining capacity of Y.
DRAIN (X)	Drain out all the water contained in bottle labelled X.

Initially, A is full with water, and B and C are empty.

50. After executing a sequence of three instructions, bottle A contains one litre of water. The first and the third of these instructions are shown below:
First instruction FILL (C, A)
Third instruction FILL (C, A)
(a) The second instruction is FILL (B, A).
(b) The second instruction is EMPTY (C, B).
(c) The second instruction transfers water from B to C.
(d) The second instruction involves using the water in bottle A.

51. Consider the same sequence of three instructions and the same initial state mentioned above. Three more instructions are added at the end of the above sequence to have A contain 4 litres of water. In this total sequence of six instructions, the fourth one is DRAIN (A). This is the only DRAIN instruction in the entire sequence. At the end of the execution of the above sequence, how much water (in litres) is contained in C?

(a) One (b) Two
(c) Zero (d) None of these

Directions for Question 52:

52. A shipping clerk has five boxes of different but unknown weights each weighing less than 100 kg. The clerk weighs the boxes in pairs. The weights obtained are 110, 112, 113, 114, 115, 116, 117, 118, 120 and 121 kgs. What is the weight, in kgs, of the heaviest box?

(a) 60 (b) 62
(c) 64 (d) Can't be determined

Directions for Questions 53 to 54: *Read each of the two problems given below and choose the answer from among the four given choices.*

53. My bag can carry no more than ten books. I must carry at least one book each of management, mathematics, physics and fiction. Also, for every management book I carry I must carry two or more fiction books, and for every mathematics book I carry I must carry two or more physics books. I earn 4, 3, 2 and 1 points for each management, mathematics, physics and fiction book, respectively, I carry in my bag. I want to maximise the points I can earn by carrying the most appropriate combination of books in my bag. The maximum points that I can earn are

(a) 20 (b) 21
(c) 22 (d) 23

54. Eighty kilograms (kg) of store material is to be transported to a location 10 km away. Any number of couriers can be used to transport the material which can be packed in any number of units of 10, 20 or 40 kg. Courier charges are ₹ 10 per hour. Couriers travel at the speed of 10 km/hr if they are not carrying any load, at 5 km/hr if carrying 10 kg, at 2 km/hr if carrying 20 kg and at 1 km/hr if carrying 40 kg. A courier cannot carry more than 40 kg of load. The minimum cost at which 80 kg of store material can be transported will be

(a) ₹ 180
(b) ₹ 160
(c) ₹ 140
(d) ₹ 120

Directions for Questions 55 to 57: *Each question is followed by two statements A and B. Answer each question using the following instructions.*

Choose (a) if the question can be answered by using one of the statements alone but cannot be answered by using the other statement alone.

Choose (b) if the question can be answered by using either statement alone.

Choose (c) if the question can be answered by using both the statements together but cannot be answered by using either statement alone.

Choose (d) if the question cannot be answered even by using both the statements together.

55. How many people are watching TV programme P?

(a) Number of people watching TV programme Q is 1000 and number of people watching both the programmes P and Q is 100.
(b) Number of people watching either P or Q or both is 1500.

56. Ghosh Babu has decided to take a non-stop flight from Mumbai to No Mans Land in South America. He is scheduled to leave Mumbai at 5 am Indian Standard Time on December 10, 2000. What is the local time at No Mans Land when he reaches there?

(a) The average speed of the plane is 700 km/hr.
(b) The flight distance is 10,500 km.

57. What are the ages of two individuals *x* & *y*?

(a) The age difference between them is 6 years.
(b) The product of their ages is divisible by 6.

Directions for Questions 58 to 61: *Answer each of the questions independent of each other.*

58. Three friends, returning from a movie, stopped to eat at a restaurant. After dinner, they paid their bill and noticed a bowl of mints at the front counter. Sita took 1/3rd of the mint, but returned four because she had a momentary pang of guilt. Fatima then took 1/4th of what was left but returned three for similar reasons. Eswari then took half of the remainder but threw two back into the bowl. The bowl had only 17 mints left when the raid was over. How many mints were originally in the bowl?

(a) 38 (b) 31
(c) 41 (d) None of these

59. Shyama and Vyom walk up an escalator (moving stairway). The escalator moves at a constant speed. Shyama takes three steps for every two of Vyom's steps. Shyama gets to the top of the escalator after having taken 25 steps, while Vyom (because her slower pace lets the escalator do a little more of the work) takes only 20 steps to reach the top. If the escalator were turned off, how many steps would they have to take to walk up?

(a) 40 (b) 50
(c) 60 (d) 80

60. Ashish is given ₹ 158 in one rupee denominations. He has been asked to allocate them into a number of bags such that any amount required between ₹ 1 and ₹ 158 can be given by handing out a certain number of bags without opening them. What is the minimum number of bags required?

(a) 11 (b) 12
(c) 13 (d) None of these

61. December 9, 2001 is Sunday. What was the day on December 9, 1971?

(a) Thursday (b) Wednesday
(c) Saturday (d) Sunday

Directions for Questions 62 to 64: *Answer each of the questions independent of each other.*

62. Four friends Ashok, Bashir, Chirag and Deepak are out shopping. Ashok has less money than three times the amount that Bashir has. Chirag has more money than Bashir. Deepak has an amount equal to the difference of amounts with Bashir and Chirag. Ashok has three times the money with Deepak. They each have to buy at least one shirt, or one shawl, or one sweater, or one jacket, that are priced ₹ 200, ₹ 400, ₹ 600 and ₹ 1000 a piece, respectively. Chirag borrows ₹ 300 from Ashok and buys a jacket. Bashir buys a sweater after borrowing ₹ 100 from Ashok and is left with no money. Ashok buys three shirts. What is the costliest item that Deepak could buy with his own money?

(a) A shirt (b) A shawl
(c) A sweater (d) A jacket

63. I have a total of ₹ 1000. Item A costs ₹ 110, item B costs ₹ 90, item C costs ₹ 70, item D costs ₹ 40 and item E costs ₹ 45. For every item D that I purchase, I must also buy two of item B. For every item A, I must buy one of item C. For every item E, I must also buy two of item D and one of item B. For every item purchased I earn 1000 points and for every rupee not spent I earn a penalty of 1500 points. My objective is to maximise the points I can earn. What is the number of items that I must purchase to maximise my points?

(a) 13 (b) 14
(c) 15 (d) 16

64. On her walk through the park, Sheetal collected 50 coloured leaves, all either maple or oak. She sorted them by category when she got home, and found the following:

(a) The number of red oak leaves with spots is even and positive.
(b) The number of red oak leaves without any spot equals the number of red maple leaves without spots.
(c) All non-red oak leaves have spots, and there are five times as many of them as there are red spotted oak leaves.
(d) There are no spotted maple leaves that are not red.
5. There are exactly 6 red spotted maple leaves.
6. There are exactly 22 maple leaves that are neither spotted nor red.

How many oak leaves did she collect?

(a) 22 (b) 17
(c) 25 (d) 18

Directions for Questions 65 to 66: *Answer the following questions based on the information given below:*

Elle is three times older than Yogesh, Zaheer is half the age of Wahida. Yogesh is older than Zaheer.

65. Which of the following information will be sufficient to estimate Elle's age?

(a) Zaheer is 10 years old.
(b) Both Yogesh and Wahida are older than Zaheer by the same number of years.
(c) Both (a)and (b) above
(d) None of the above.

66. Which of the following can be inferred?

(a) Yogesh is older than Wahida.
(b) Elle is older than Wahida.
(c) Elle may be younger than Wahida.
(d) None of the above.

Directions for Questions 67 to 69: *Each item is followed by two statements, A and B. Answer each questions using the following instructions.*

Choose A: if the question can be answered by one of the statements alone but not by the other.

Choose B: if the question can be answered by using either statement alone.

Choose C: if the question can be answered by using both the statements together, but cannot be answered by using either statement alone.

Choose D: if the question cannot be answered by either of the statements.

67. In a hockey match, the Indian team was behind by 2 goals with 5 minutes remaining. Did they win the match?

A. Deepak Thakur, the Indian striker, scored 3 goals in the last five minutes of the match.
B. Korea scored a total of 3 goals in the match.

68. Four students were added to a dance class. Would the teacher be able to divide her students evenly into a dance team (or teams) of 8?

A. If 12 students were added, the teacher could put everyone in teams of 8 without any leftovers.

B. The number of students in the class is currently not divisible by 8.

69. A sum of ₹ 38,500 was divided among Jagdish, Punit and Girish. Who received the minimum amount?

A. Jagdish received 2/9 of what Punit and Girish together received.

B. Punit received 3/11 of what Jagdish and Girish together received.

Directions for Questions 70 to 72: *Answer the questions independent of each other.*

70. Five boys went to a store to buy sweets. One boy had ₹ 40. Another boy had ₹ 30. Two other boys had ₹ 20 each. The remaining boy had ₹ 10. Below are some more facts about the initial and final cash positions.

(i) Alam started with more money than Jugraj.

(ii) Sandeep spent ₹ 1.50 more than Daljeet.

(iii) Ganesh started with more money than only one other person.

(iv) Daljeet started with 2/3 of what Sandeep started with.

(v) Alam spent the most, but did not end with the least.

(vi) Jugraj spent the least and ended with more than Alam or Daljeet.

(vii) Alam spent 10 times more than what Ganesh did.

In the choices given below, all statements except one are false. Which one of the following statements can be true?

(a) Alam started with ₹ 40 and ended with ₹ 9.50.

(b) Sandeep started with ₹ 30 and ended with ₹ 1.00.

(c) Ganesh started with ₹ 20 and ended with ₹ 4.00.

(d) Jugraj started with ₹ 10 and ended with ₹ 7.00.

71. Two boys are playing on a ground. Both the boys are less than 10 years old. Age of the younger boy is equal to the cube root of the product of the age of the two boys. If we place the digit representing the age of the younger boy to the left of the digit representing the age of the elder boy, we get the age of the father of the younger boy. Similarly, if we place the digit representing the age of the elder boy to the left of the digit representing the age of the younger boy and divide the figure by 2, we get the age of the mother of the younger boy. The mother of the younger boy is younger than his father by 3 years. Then what is the age of the younger boy?

(a) 3 (b) 4

(c) 2 (d) None of these.

72. Flights A and B are scheduled from an airport within the next one hour. All the booked passengers of the two flights are waiting in the boarding hall after check-in. The hall has a seating capacity of 200 out of which 10% remained vacant. 40% of the waiting passengers are ladies. When boarding announcements came, passengers of flights A left the hall and boarded the flight. Seating capacity of each flight is two third of the passengers who waited in the waiting hall for both the flights put together. Half the passengers who boarded flight A are women. After boarding for flight A, 60% of the waiting hall seats became empty. For every twenty of those who are still waiting in the hall for flight B, there is one airhostess in flight A. Then, what is the ratio of empty seats in flight B to the number of airhostesses in flight A?

(a) 10:1 (b) 5:1

(c) 20:1 (d) 1:1

Directions for Questions 73 to 76: *Answer these questions based on the table given below.*

The table below gives information about four different crops, their different quality categories and the regions where they are cultivated. Based on the information given in the table below, answer the questions that follow:

Type of Crop	Quality	Region
Crop 1	High	R1, R2, R3, R4, R5
	Medium	R6, R7, R8
	Low	R9, R10, R11
Crop 2	High	R5, R8, R12
	Medium	R9, R13
	Low	R6
Crop 3	High	R2, R6, R7, R13
	Medium	R3, R9, R11
	Low	R1, R4
Crop 4	High	R3, R10, R11
	Medium	R1, R2, R4
	Low	R5, R9

73. How many regions produce medium qualities of Crop-1 or Crop-2 and also produce low quality of Crop-3 or Crop-4?

(a) Zero (b) One

(c) Two (d) Three

74. Which of the following statements is true?
(a) All medium quality Crop-2 producing regions are also high quality Crop-3 producing regions.
(b) All high quality Crop-1 producing regions are also medium and low Crop-4 producing regions.
(c) There are exactly four Crop-3 producing regions, which also produce Crop-4 but not Crop-2.
(d) Some Crop-3 producing regions produce Crop-1, but not high quality Crop-2.

75. How many low quality Crop-1 producing regions are either high quality Crop-4 producing regions or medium quality Crop-3 producing regions?
(a) One (b) Two
(c) Three (d) Zero

76. 10 straight lines, no two of which are parallel and no three of which pass through any common point, are drawn on a plane. The total number of regions (including finite and infinite regions) into which the plane would be divided by the lines is
(a) 56 (b) 255
(c) 1024 (d) Not unique

Directions for Questions 77 to 78: *Answer these questions based on the information given below.*

A boy is asked to put in a basket one mango when ordered 'One', one orange when ordered 'Two', one apple when ordered 'Three' and is asked to take out from the basket one mango and an orange when ordered 'Four'. A sequence of orders is given as:

1 2 3 3 2 1 4 2 3 1 4 2 2 3 3 1 4 1 1 3 2 3 4

77. How many total oranges were in the basket at the end of the above sequence?
(a) 1 (b) 4
(c) 3 (d) 2

78. How many total fruits will be in the basket at the end of the above order sequence?
(a) 9 (b) 8
(c) 11 (d) 10

79. Davji Shop sells samosas in boxes of different sizes. The samosas are priced at ₹ 2 per samosa up to 200 samosas. For every additional 20 samosas, the price of the whole lot goes down by 10 paise per samosa. What should be the maximum size of the box that would maximise the revenue?
(a) 240 (b) 300
(c) 400 (d) none of these

80. The owner of a local jewellery store hired 3 watchmen to guard his diamonds, but a thief still got in and stole some diamonds. On the way out, the thief met each watchman, one at a time. To each he gave ½ of the diamonds he had then, and 2 more besides. He escaped with one diamond. How many did he steal originally?
(a) 40 (b) 36
(c) 25 (d) None of these

81. A test has 50 questions. A student scores 1 mark for a correct answer, $-1/3$ for a wrong answer, and $-1/6$ for not attempting a question. If the net score of a student is 32, the number of questions answered wrongly by that student cannot be less than:
(a) 6 (b) 12
(c) 3 (d) 9

82. A leather factory produces two kinds of bags, standard and deluxe bags. The profit margin is ₹ 20 on a standard bag and ₹ 30 on a deluxe bag. Every bag must be processed on machine A and on machine B. The processing time per bag on the two machines are as follows:

Time required (Hours/bags)

	Machine A	Machine B
Standard Bag	4	6
Deluxe Bag	5	10

The total time available on machine A is 700 hours and on machine B is 1250 hours. Among the following production plans, which one meets the machine availability constraints and maximises the profit?
(a) Standard 75 bags, Deluxe 80 bags
(b) Standard 100 bags, Deluxe 60 bags
(c) Standard 50 bags, Deluxe 100 bags
(d) Standard 60 bags, Deluxe 90 bags

Directions for Questions 83 to 84: *Answer the questions on the basis of the information given below.*

A certain perfume is available at a duty-free shop at the Bangkok international airport. It is priced in the Thai currency Baht but other currencies are also acceptable. In particular, the shop accepts Euro and US Dollar at the following rates of exchange:

US Dollar 1 = 41 Bahts; Euro 1 = 46 Bahts

The perfume is priced at 520 Bahts per bottle. After one bottle is purchased, subsequent bottles are available at a discount of 30%. Three friends S, R and M together purchase three bottles of the perfume, agreeing to share the cost equally. R pays 2 Euros. M pays 4 Euros and 27 Thai Bahts and S pays the remaining amount in US Dollars.

83. How much does R owe to S in Thai Baht?
(a) 428 (b) 416
(c) 334 (d) 324

84. How much does M owe to S in US Dollars?

(a) 3 (b) 4

(c) 5 (d) 6

Directions for Questions 85 to 86: *In each question there are two statements A and B.*

Choose (a) if the question can be answered by one of the statements alone but not by the other.

Choose (b) if the question can be answered by using either statement alone.

Choose (c) if the question can be answered by using both the statements together but cannot be answered using either statement alone.

Choose (d) if the question cannot be answered even by using both the statements A and B.

85. A game consists of tossing a coin successively. There is an entry fee of ₹ 10 and an additional fee of ₹ 1 for each toss of the coin. The game is considered to have ended normally when the coin turns heads on two consecutive throws. In this case the player is paid ₹ 100. Alternatively, the player can choose to terminate the game prematurely after any of the tosses. Ram has incurred a loss of ` 50 by playing this game. How many times did he toss the coin?

(a) The game ended normally.

(b) The total number of tails obtained in the game was 138.

86. Each packet of soap costs ` 10. Inside each packet is a gift coupon labelled with one of the letters S, O, A and P. If a customer submits four such coupons that make up the word Soap, the customer gets a free Soap packet. Ms. X kept buying packet after packet of Soap till she could get one set of coupons that formed the world Soap. How many coupons with label P did she get in the above process?

(a) The last label obtained by her was S and the total amount spent was ₹ 210.

(b) The total number of vowels obtained was 18.

Directions for Questions 87 to 88: *Answer the questions on the basis of the information given below.*

Some children were taking free throws at the basketball court in school during lunch break. Below are some facts about how many baskets these children shot.

(i) Ganesh shot 8 baskets less than Ashish.

(ii) Dhanraj and Ramesh together shot 37 baskets.

(iii) Jugraj shot 8 baskets more than Dhanraj.

(iv) Ashish and Ganesh together shot 40 baskets.

(v) Ashish shot 5 baskets more than Dhanraj.

87. Which of the following statements is true?

(a) Ramesh shot 18 baskets and Dhanraj shot 19 baskets.

(b) Ganesh shot 24 baskets and Ashish shot 16 baskets.

(c) Jugraj shot 19 baskets and Dhanraj shot 27 baskets.

(d) Dhanraj shot 11 baskets and Ashish shot 16 baskets.

88. Which of the following statements is true?

(a) Dhanraj and Jugraj shot 46 baskets.

(b) Ganesh shot 18 baskets and Ramesh shot 21 baskets.

(c) Dhanraj shot 3 more baskets than Ramesh.

(d) Ramesh and Jugraj together shot 29 baskets.

LEVEL OF DIFFICULTY (II)

Directions for Questions 1 to 5: *In November the answers of a prestigious test held nationwide were leaked to a group of unscrupulous people. The CBI has arrested the Don, the mastermind behind it and nine other people–P, Q, R, S, T, U, V, W and X in this matter. On interrogation, certain facts came into light:*

High Yield Questions

Scan this QR code to access a video explanation of questions 1-5

Their *modus operandi* consisted of the Don initially obtaining the answer key, then the other nine persons created their answer keys in the following manner:

They obtained the answer key from one or two sources, then he/she compares the answer keys to a question from both sources. If the key to a question from both sources is identical, it is copied, otherwise it is left blank. If the person has only one source, he/she copies the source's answer into his/her copy. Finally, each person compulsorily replaces one of the answers (not a blank one) with a wrong answer in his/her answer key.

The paper contained 150 questions. So the CBI has ruled out the possibility of two or more of them introducing wrong answer to the same question. The CBI has a copy of correct answer key and tabulated the following data. The data represents question numbers.

Name	Wrong Answer (s)	Blank Answer (s)
P	46	----------
Q	96	46, 90, 25
R	27, 56	17, 46, 90

S	17	------------
T	46, 90	------------
U	14, 46	92, 90
V	25	
W	46, 92	------------
X	27	17, 46, 90

1. Who among the following must have two sources?
(a) P (b) Q
(c) R (d) S

2. How many people (excluding the Don) needed to make answer keys before R could make his answer key?
(a) 3 (b) 4
(c) 6 (d) None of these

3. Both T and W were sources to:
(a) U (b) X
(c) Q (d) None of these

4. Which of the following is definitely true?
(a) R introduced the wrong answer to question 27.
(b) T introduced the wrong answer to question 46.
(c) U introduced the wrong answer to question 14.
(d) W introduced the wrong answer to question 46.

5. Which of the group has the same sources?
(i) P, S and V (ii) T and W
(a) Only (i) (b) Only (ii)
(c) Both (i) and (ii) (d) None of these

Directions for Questions 6 to 9: *Coach John sat with the score cards of Indian players from the 3 games in a one-day cricket tournament where the same set of players played for India and all the major batsmen go out. John summarised the batting performance through three figures, one for each game. In each figure, the three outer triangles communicate the number of runs scored by the three top scorers from India. K, R, S, V and Y represent Kaif, Rahul, Saurav, Virender and Yuvraj, respectively. The middle triangle in each diagram denotes the percentage of total score that was scored by the top three Indian scorers in that game. No two players score the same number of runs in the same game. John also calculated two batting indices for each players based on his scores in the tournament; the R-index of a batsman is the difference between his highest and lowest scores in the 3 games while the M-index is the middle number, if his scores are arranged in a non-increasing order.*

High Yield Questions
Scan this QR code to access a video explanation of questions 6-9

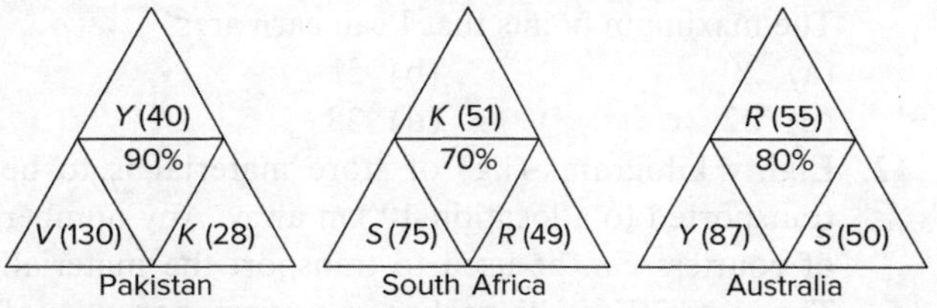

Batting performance of five Indian batsmen in three games of One-day International Cricket Tournament.

6. For how many Indian players, is it possible to calculate the exact M-Index?
(a) 0 (b) 1
(c) 2 (d) More than 2

7. Among the players mentioned, who can have the lowest R-index from the tournament?
(a) Only Kaif, Rahul or Yuvraj
(b) Only Kaif or Rahul
(c) Only Kaif or Yuvraj
(d) Only Kaif

8. How many players among those listed definitely scored less than Yuvraj in the tournament?
(a) 0 (b) 1
(c) 2 (d) More than 2

9. Which of the players had the best M-index from the tournament?
(a) Rahul (b) Saurav
(c) Virendra (d) Yuvraj

10. Three travellers are sitting around a fire, and are about to eat a meal. One of them has five small loaves of bread, the second has three small loaves of bread. The third has no food, but has eight coins. He offers to pay for some bread. They agree to share the eight loaves equally among the three travellers, and the third traveller will pay eight coins for his share of the eight loaves. All loaves were of the same size. The second traveller (who had three loaves) suggests that he be paid three coins, and that the first traveller be paid five coins. The first traveller says that he should get more than five coins. How much the first traveler should get?
(a) 5 (b) 7
(c) 1 (d) None of these

11. My bag can carry no more than ten books. I must carry at least one book each of management, mathematics, physics and fiction. Also, for every management book I carry, I must carry two or more fiction books, and for every mathematics book I carry I must carry two or more physics books. I earn 4, 3, 2, and 1 points for each management, mathematics, physics and fiction book, respectively, I carry in my bag. I want to maximise the points I can earn by carrying the most appropriate combination of books in my bag.

The maximum points that I can earn are:
(a) 20 (b) 21
(c) 22 (d) 23

12. Eighty kilograms (kg) of store material is to be transported to a location 10 km away. Any number of couriers can be used to transport the material. The material can be packed in any number units of 10, 20 or 40 kg. Courier charges are ₹ 10 per hour. Couriers travel at the speed of 10 km/hr, if they are not carrying any load, at 5 km/hr if carrying 10 kg, at 2 km/hr if carrying 20 kg and at 1 km/hr if carrying 40 kg. A courier cannot carry more than 40 kg of load.
The minimum cost at which 80 kg of store material can be transported to its destination will be:
(a) ₹ 180 (b) ₹ 160
(c) ₹ 140 (d) ₹ 120

13. On the walk through the park, Hamsa collected 50 coloured leaves, all either maple or oak. She sorted them by category when she got home, and found the following:
(i) The number of red oak leaves with spots is even and positive.
(ii) The number of red oak leaves without any spot equals the number of red maple leaves without spots.
(iii) All non-red oak leaves have spots, and there are five times as many of them as there are red spotted oak leaves.
(iv) There are no spotted maple leaves that are not red.
(v) There are exactly 6 red spotted maple leaves.
(vi) There are exactly 22 maple leaves that are neither spotted nor red.
How many oak leaves did she collect?
(a) 22 (b) 17
(c) 25 (d) 18

14. I have a total of ₹ 1000. Item A costs ₹ 110, item B costs ₹ 90, item C costs ₹ 70, item D costs ₹ 40 and item E costs ₹ 55. For every item D that I purchase, I must also buy only two items of B. For every item A, I must buy one item of C. For every item E, I must also buy two of item D and one of item B. For every item purchased, I earn 1000 points and for every rupee not spent, I earn a penalty of 1500 points. My objective is to maximise the points earned. What is the number of items that I must purchase to maximise my points?
(a) 13 (b) 14
(c) 15 (d) 16

15. Four friends Ashok, Bashir, Chirag and Deepak are out for shopping. Ashok has less money than three times the amount that Bashir has. Chirag has more money than Bashir. Deepak has an amount equal to the difference of amounts with Bashir and Chirag. Ashok has three times the money with Deepak. Each of them have to buy at least one shirt, or one shawl, or one sweater, or one jacket that are priced ₹ 200, ₹ 400, ₹ 600, and ₹ 1000 a piece, respectively. Chirag borrows ₹ 300 from Ashok and buys a jacket. Bashir buys a sweater after borrowing ₹ 100 from Ashok and is left with no money. Ashok buys three shirts.
What is the costliest item that Deepak could buy with his own money?
(a) A shirt (b) A shawl
(c) A sweater (d) A jacket

16. A professor thinks of 2 consecutive numbers between 1 and 10 (both inclusive). Student "A" knows 1 number and "B" knows another.
A: I do not know your number.
B: Neither do I know your number.
A: Now I know your number.
There are 4 solutions possible, what are they?

17. Armaan has two sons both born in the 1st week of October in different years. The Date of Birth (DOB) of his sons are two consecutive numbers. Now he tells the DOB of his first son to his friend Sumit and DOB of his second son to his friend Sunil.
Sumit to Sunil: I don't know your number.
Sunil to Sumit: Neither do I know your number.
Sumit to Sunil: Now, I know the DOB of both the sons.
Find the maximum value of the sum of date of births of Armaan's two sons?

18. 100 criminals are sitting around a table in a circular arrangement with chair numbers marked from 1 to 100. The criminal sitting in Chair# 1 has a gun with 100 bullets. He shoots dead the criminal sitting next to him in Chair# 2 and passes on the pistol to the criminal in Chair# 3. This criminal shoots the criminal in Chair# 4 and passes on the pistol to the criminal in Chair# 5 and so on. This activity is carried out until one criminal survives. Find the chair number of this criminal.

Directions for Questions 19 to 22: *There are 10 packets of candies numbered #1 to #10, each containing 'x' candies. Each candy in 9 of these 10 packets weighs 10 grams, whereas each candy in one packet weighs 20 grams. Now a logician, Mr. Bhavuk Pujara, is invited. The task was assigned to him to find out the packet that contained 20 grams candies in it. He is given a weighing machine that measures the exact value of the weight of objects in grams.*

19. If $x = 9$, what is the minimum possible number of times for which the weighing machine is to be used?

(a) 1 (b) 2
(c) 3 (d) None of these

20. If $x = 7$, what is the minimum possible number of times for which the weighing machine is to be used?
(a) 1 (b) 2
(c) 3 (d) None of these

21. If $x = 3$, what is the minimum possible number of times for which the weighing machine is to be used?
(a) 1 (b) 2
(c) 3 (d) None of these

22. If $x = 2$, what is the minimum possible number of times for which the weighing machine is to be used?
(a) 1 (b) 2
(c) 3 (d) None of these

Directions for Questions 23 to 24: *Three faces of a cube are painted Black, Yellow and Pink with each face being painted in a different color. Two colors are randomly chosen among Black, Yellow and Pink, and are painted on any two of the three uncoloured faces of the cube. The cube is now cut into 720 identical pieces using minimum possible cuts.*

23. What is the maximum possible number of smaller pieces with exactly two colours on them?

24. What is the minimum possible number of pieces which have Black colour but not Pink colour on them?

25. Habibul is an orange trader who wants to transport 3000 oranges to the market, located 1000 km away from his farm. For transportation, he owned a notorious horse. This horse can carry a maximum of 1000 oranges at a time and eats one orange for every 1 kilometer it travels. If Habibul sells one orange at ₹ 1 in the market, find the maximum amount he can earn?
(a) 1000 (b) 532
(c) 533 (d) 998

26. A courier company XYZ has a fleet of 50 cars each with a full fuel tank. The company wants to deliver a courier for the maximum possible distance. If they can transfer the courier from car to car and can also transfer fuel from car to car and each car can go 100 kms with tank full fuel, then what is the maximum distance (in km) upto which the courier can be delivered (rounded off to the nearest integer)?
(a) 350 km (b) 5000 km
(c) 2500 km (d) 450 km

Directions for Questions 27 to 32: *Answer the following questions based on the given information:*

In a class there were 5 students–P, Q, R, S and T. Once, they all participated in the Mathematics Olympiad. Six teachers A, B, C, D, E and F announced the results in a unique way. Each of these six teachers announced the sum of scores of exactly four students. So A, B, C, D, E, F announced their sums as 660, 780, 690, 720, 630 and 750 respectively. One of the teachers is very bad with calculation, so he committed a mistake in adding the scores. Score of each contestant is an integer value.

High Yield Questions
Scan this QR code to access a video explanation of questions 27-32

27. What is the maximum possible marks any student can score?
(a) 225 (b) 255
(c) 270 (d) None of these

28. In the above question, who made the mistake in adding the sum of marks obtained by the students?
(a) C (b) F
(c) E
(d) Cannot be determined

29. Which of the following teachers could not make a mistake while adding the scores of the students?
(a) E (b) F
(c) C (d) D

30. If the sum of scores obtained by two students was 480, then which of the following teachers could have made a mistake?
(a) F (b) C
(c) E (d) Not possible

31. If the sum of scores obtained by two students was 495, then which of the following teachers could have made a mistake?
(a) F (b) C
(c) E (d) Not possible

32. What is the least possible sum of scores of 3 students?
(a) 375 (b) 420
(c) 405 (d) 450

Directions for Questions 33 to 36: *Answer the following questions based on the given information:*

Mr. Rajendra Prasad, who retired from his job at the end of 2019, was reminiscing about his career. His career spanned thirty-five years and he worked exactly once in each of seven different cities - Hong Kong, Prague, Berlin, Istanbul, Paris, Vienna and Dublin. It is known that he started working in each city at the start of a year, and the number of years for which he worked in any city was a distinct integer. The following information is known about the cities that he worked in and the duration for which he worked in each city:

(i) Mr. Prasad worked in Hong Kong for five years immediately before he worked in Paris.
(ii) No city did he work for more than eight years and he worked in Vienna for a lesser duration than in Paris.
(iii) He started working in Vienna in 2012 and he worked in Vienna immediately after Prague.
(iv) Istanbul was not the first city that he worked in but he worked in Istanbul before he worked in Paris.

(v) He was working in the first city of his career in 1990 and he worked in Berlin for a lesser duration than in Hong Kong.

33. For how many years did Mr. Prasad work in Berlin? (TITA)

34. Which was the first city he worked in?
(a) Dublin
(b) Hong Kong
(c) Berlin
(d) Cannot be determined

35. For how many years did he work in Dublin?
(a) 8 (b) 7
(c) 6
(d) Cannot be determined

36. For how many years combined did he work in Prague and Istanbul?

Directions for Questions 37 to 40: *Answer the questions on the basis of information given below.*

TABLE 1 Number of goals scored by six strikers in three weeks of the English Premier League: Week 1, Week 2 and Week 3

Name	Week 1	Week 2	Week 3
Alan	4	4	1
Bergkamp	2	1	2
Cryuff	2	1	4
Di Stefano	1	1	1
Eusebio	2	1	1
Facchetti	2	2	1

TABLE 2 Number of goals scored against six teams in 3 weeks of the EPL

Topic	Week 1	Week 2	Week 3
Chelsea	2	0	0
Seville	2	2	0
Bromwich	4	4	1
Palmeiras	2	2	1
AC Milan	1	1	1
Everton	2	1	7

The following conditions are true:

(i) In any given week, each one of them scored goals against only one team.
(ii) From amongst Alan, Di Stefano and Facchetti, exactly two scored goals in Weeks 2 and 3 against the same team, as they scored against in Week 1.
(iii) The striker who scored exactly one goal against Everton in Week 3, had also scored goals against Everton, in each of the first two weeks.
(iv) Di Stefano did not score a goal against Seville in Week 2.

37. Who scored against Everton in all three weeks?
(a) Di Stefano
(b) Eusebio
(c) Eusebio or Facchetti
(d) Cannot be detrmined

38. For how many strikers can we conclusively determine the number of goals against each club in each week?

39. What can be the maximum number of goals against Palmeiras that Facchetti scored in the 3 weeks taken together?

40. What is the number of goals scored by DI Stefano against AC Milan?
(a) 1 (b) 2
(c) 3
(d) Cannot be determined

Directions for Questions 41 to 44: *Read the information given below and answer the questions that follow:*

A child is making a house using six Lego pieces, LP-1, LP-2, LP-3, LP-4, LP-5 and LP-6, which has three floors. The ground floor consists of three pieces which are fitted on the ground; the first floor consists of two pieces which are fitted on the three pieces at the ground floor; the second floor consists of one piece which is fitted on the two pieces on the first floor. Further, on each floor, every piece supports an equal weight and all the pieces on a particular floor together support the total weight of all the pieces on all the floors above. The weights of the six pieces are 5g, 6g, 7g, 8g, 9g and 10g, not necessarily in the same order. The following information is known about the pieces on each floor of the pyramid:

(i) LP-1 supports the same weight as LP-2, which is not the same as the weight supported by LP-3.
(ii) No piece is fitted on LP-5 but it does not weigh the least.
(iii) LP-4, which weighs the most, is not on the same floor as LP-3, while LP-2 weighs more than each of LP-5 and LP-6.
(iv) LP-3 weighs less than LP-6 and the weight of LP-6 is the average of the weights of LP-1 and LP-2.
(v) Every piece on the ground floor supports a weight of 7 g.

41. Which among the following is fitted on the first floor?
(a) LP-1 (b) LP-4
(c) LP-5 (d) LP-6

42. What is the weight of LP-5?
(a) 6 g (b) 7 g
(c) 8 g
(d) Cannot be determined

43. Which among the following weighs the least?
(a) LP-1 (b) LP-2
(c) LP-3 (d) LP-6

44. What is the weight supported by each LP3 and LP6 individually?
(a) 4 (b) 8
(c) 5 (d) 6

Directions for Questions 45 to 48: *Read the information given below and answer the questions that follow:*

Five bright students studying in Mount Carmel School- Falgun, Garima, Hemant, Ishaan and Jaya appeared in class 10th board exam. The examination paper consisted of 200 questions with 40 questions in each of the five subjects History, Political Science, Geography, Economics and Hindi. For any of these 200 questions, a right answer fetches (+1) mark while a wrong answer fetches (−0.2) marks. Each of them attempted all the 200 questions. The following table shows the sum of the number of right answers given by each of the friends for five different combinations of two subjects.

Student → Subjects ↓	Falgun	Garima	Hemant	Ishaan	Jaya
History and Political Science	14	37	33	46	36
Geography and Economics	37	23	38	44	32
Hindi and History	25	32	34	26	51
Political Science and Geography	34	28	36	47	33
Economics and Hindi	32	16	31	47	36

45. How many questions did Falgun attempt correctly in the exam?
(a) 74 (b) 71
(c) 75
(d) Cannot be determined

46. Out of the questions attempted by Hemant, how many of them were wrong?
(a) 114 (b) 120
(c) 130 (d) None of these

47. Who among the five students had the highest score in the exam?
(a) Ishaan (b) Garima
(c) Hemant (d) Jaya

48. The total number of wrong answers given by these five students altogether was same in which of the two subjects?
(a) Political Science and Geography.
(b) History and Hindi.
(c) Economics and Hindi.
(d) Economics and History.

Directions for Questions 49 to 52: *Read the information given below and answer the questions that follow:*

An old man had the following assets: (a) ₹ 70 lakh in bank deposits; (b) 1 house worth ₹ 50 lakh; (c) 3 flats, each worth ₹ 30 lakh; (d) Certain number of gold coins, each worth ₹ 1 lakh. He has the final wish to distribute his assets among his three children- Aman, Arun and Ganpati. The house, any of the flats or any of the coins were not to be split. That is, the house went entirely to one child; a flat went to one child and similarly, a gold coin went to one child. Among the three, Aman received the least amount in bank deposits, while Ganpati received the highest. The value of the assets was distributed equally among the children, as were the gold coins.

49. Among the three, Aman received the least amount in bank deposits, while Ganpati received the highest. The value of the assets was distributed equally among the children, as were the gold coins. How much did Ganpati receive in bank deposits (in lakhs of rupees)?

50. Among the three, Aman received the least amount in bank deposits, while Ganpati received the highest. The value of the assets was distributed equally among the children, as were the gold coins. How many flats did Arun receive?

51. The value of the assets distributed among Aman, Arun and Ganpati was in the ratio of 1 : 2 : 3, while the gold coins were distributed among them in the ratio of 2 : 3 : 4. One child got all three flats and did not get the house. One child, other than Ganpati, got ₹ 30 lakh in bank deposits. How many gold coins did the old man have?

52. The value of the assets distributed among Aman, Arun and Ganpati was in the ratio of 1 : 2 : 3, while the gold coins were distributed among them in the ratio of 2 : 3 : 4. One child got all three flats and did not get the house. One child, other than Ganpati, got ₹ 30 lakh in bank deposits. How much did Ganpati get in bank deposits (in lakhs of rupees)?

Directions for Questions 53 to 57: *Read the information given below and answer the questions that follow:*

In an MBA entrance exam, there are four different sections, LR, DI, VARC and QA. Each section comprised 35 questions. The QA section comprised questions from four different areas - Arithmetic, Algebra, Geometry and Modern Maths. All the questions in the exam could be classified based on their level of difficulty as LOD 1 (Easy), LOD 2 (Medium), LOD 3 (Difficult) and HOTS (Very difficult). Further, the following information is known regarding the questions in the QA section:

(i) The number of questions from each of Arithmetic, Algebra and Modern Maths is twice the number of questions from Geometry.
(ii) Each of the four areas within the QA section had at least one and at most four questions of each of the four the levels of difficulty.
(iii) The number of LOD 2 questions is the same as the number of LOD 1 questions, which, in turn, is thrice the number of HOTS questions.
(iv) If there had been three less LOD 3 questions, the number of LOD 3 questions would have been the same as the total number of HOTS questions.
(v) The number of LOD 1 questions from Algebra is two.

All the questions in this set pertain only to the questions in the QA ability section of the exam.

53. Which of the following combinations of questions is not possible?
(a) The number of LOD2 questions from each of Arithmetic and Algebra is four.
(b) Three LOD 2 questions from Arithmetic and four LOD 3 questions from Algebra.
(c) The number of LOD 3 questions from Algebra and Modern Math are three and one respectively.
(d) There are three LOD 3 questions from Algebra and four LOD2 questions from Arithmetic.

54. Which of the following is true of the number of LOD 3 questions from Arithmetic?
(a) It is at least two and at most three.
(b) It is at least one and at most three.
(c) It is at least two and at most four.
(d) It is at least one and at most two.

55. Which of the following details cannot be uniquely determined?
(a) Number of HOTS questions from Algebra.
(b) Number of LOD 1 questions from Arithmetic.
(c) Number of LOD 2 questions from Modern Math.
(d) Number of LOD 3 questions from Geometry.

56. If the number of LOD 2 questions from Arithmetic are not equal to 4, then which of the following is/are true?
(i) LOD 3 Algebra is 3;
(ii) LOD 3 Modern Maths is 2 and
(iii) LOD 3 Arithmetic is 2.
(a) Only (i) is true.
(b) All three are true.
(c) Only (i) and (ii) are true.
(d) Only (i) and (iii) are true.

57. If there are two LOD 3 questions from Modern Math in the section, which of the following is definitely false?
(a) There is one LOD 3 question from Arithmetic.
(b) There are four LOD 2 questions from Algebra.
(c) There are four LOD 2 questions from Modern Math.
(d) More than one of the above.

Directions for Questions 58 to 62: *Kaushik went to the market and bought a wallet, a badminton racket and a radio for a total amount of ₹ 1019. He had money in coins of only three denominations - ₹ 10, ₹ 2 and ₹ 1 - and had a total of 180 coins with him. He used all his money in purchasing these items. It is known that the wallet is the least expensive, whereas the radio is the most expensive item.*

It is also known that:

(i) In purchasing each item, he used at least two and at most 35 coins of each denomination.
(ii) The total number of ₹ 2 coins used in purchasing the badminton racket and the wallet put together is 54.
(iii) Worth of the badminton racket and the wallet put together is ₹ 635.
(iv) The number of ₹ 10 coins used in purchasing the radio is 35 and that of ₹ 1 coins used in purchasing the badminton racket is 15.
(v) Number of ₹ 10 coins and the number of ₹ 2 coins used in purchasing the wallet are prime numbers but the number of ₹ 10 coins and the number of ₹ 2 coins used in purchasing the badminton racket are not prime numbers.

58. If it is known that the number of ₹ 2 coins used in purchasing the wallet is 19, then what is the difference in the cost of badminton racket and wallet? (TITA)

59. How many ₹ 10 coins did the person use to purchase the badminton racket?
(a) 35 (b) 19
(c) 25
(d) Cannot be determined

60. What is the cost of the wallet?
(a) 290 (b) 230
(c) 280
(d) Cannot be determined

61. What is the number of ₹ 1 coins that he used in purchasing the wallet?
(a) 2
(b) 12
(c) 22
(d) Cannot be determined

62. What is the number of ₹ 2 coins used to purchase the radio?

Directions for Questions 63 to 65: *These questions are based on the situation given below:*

Ten coins are distributed among four people P, Q, R, S such that one of them gets one coin, another gets two coins, the third gets three coins and the fourth gets four coins. It is known that Q gets more coins than P and S gets fewer coins than R.

63. If the number of coins distributed to Q is twice the number distributed to P then which one of the following is necessarily true?
(a) R gets an even number of coins.
(b) R gets an odd number of coins.
(c) S gets an even number of coins.
(d) S gets an odd number of coins.

64. If R gets at least two more coins than S, then which one of the following is necessarily true?
(a) Q gets at least two more coins than S.
(b) Q gets more coins than P.
(c) P gets more coins than S.
(d) P and Q together get at least five coins.

65. If Q gets fewer coins than R, then which one of the following is not necessarily true?
(a) P and Q together get at least four coins.
(b) Q and S together get at least four coins.
(c) R and S together get at least five coins.
(d) P and R together get at least five coins.

Directions for Questions 66 to 67: *The following table presents the sweetness of different forms relative to sucrose, whose sweetness is taken to be 1.00.*

Lactose	0.16
Maltose	0.32
Glucose	0.74
Sucrose	1.00
Fructose	1.70
Saccharin	675.00

66. What is the minimum amount of sucrose (to the nearest gram) that must be added to one-gram of saccharin to make a mixture that will be less than 100 times as sweet as glucose?
(a) 7 (b) 8
(c) 9 (d) 100

67. Approximately how many times sweeter than sucrose is a mixture consisting of glucose, sucrose and fructose in the ratio of 1: 2: 3?
(a) 1.3 (b) 1
(c) 0.6 (d) 2.3

Directions for Questions 68 to 70: *These questions are based on the situation given below.*

There are fifty integers a_1, a_2, ..., a_{50}, not all of them necessarily different. Let the greatest integer of these fifty integers be referred to as G and smallest integer be referred to as L. The integers a_1, through a_{24} form sequence S_1, and the rest form sequence S_2. Each member of S_1 is less than or equal to each member of S_2.

68. All values in S_1 are changed in sign, while those in S_2 remain unchanged. Which of the following statements is true?
(a) Every member of S_1 is greater than or equal to every member of S_2.
(b) G is in S_1
(c) If all numbers originally in S_1 and S_2 had the same sign, then after the change of sign, the largest number of S_1 and S_2 is in S_1.
(d) None of these

69. Elements of S_1 are in ascending order, and those of S_2 are in descending order, a_{24} and a_{25} are interchanged. Then which of the following statements is true?
(a) S_1 continues to be in ascending order.
(b) S_2 continues to be in descending order.
(c) S_1 continues to be in ascending order and S_2 in descending order.
(d) None of these

70. Every element of S_1 is made greater than or equal to every element of S_2 by adding to each element of S_1 an integer x. Then x cannot be less than
(a) 210
(b) The smallest value of S_2
(c) The largest value of S_2
(d) $(G - L)$

Directions for Questions 71 to 72: *These questions are based on the situation given below.*

A robot moves on a graph sheet with x and y-axes. The robot is moved by feeding it with a sequence of instructions. The different instructions that can be used in moving it, and their meaning are

Instruction	Meaning
GOTO (x, y)	Move to point with coordinates (x, y) no matter where you are currently
WALK X (p)	Move parallel to the x-axis through a distance of p, in the positive direction if p is positive, and in the negative direction if p is negative
WALK Y (p)	Move parallel to the y-axis through a distance of p, in the positive direction if p is positive, and in the negative direction if p is negative

71. The robot reaches point (6, 6) when a sequence of three instructions is executed, the first of which is a GOTO(x, y) instruction, the second is WALK X(2) and the third is WALK Y(4). What are the values of x and y?

(a) 2, 4 (b) 0, 0
(c) 4, 2 (d) 2, 2

72. The robot is initially at (x, y), $x > 0$ and $y < 0$. The minimum number of instructions needed to be executed to bring it to the origin (0, 0) if you are prohibited from using the GOTO instruction is:

(a) 2 (b) 1
(c) x + y (d) 0

Directions for Question 73:

73. Shyam visited Ram on vacation. In the mornings, they both would go for yoga. In the evenings they would play tennis. To have more fun, they indulged only in one activity per day, i.e., either they went for yoga or played tennis each day. There were days when they were lazy and stayed home all day long. There were 24 mornings when they did nothing, 14 evenings when they stayed at home, and a total of 22 days when they did yoga or played tennis. For how many days did Shyam stay with Ram?

(a) 32
(b) 24
(c) 30
(d) None of these

Directions for Question 74:

74. Three travellers are sitting around a fire, and are about to eat a meal. One of them has five small loaves of bread; the second has three small loaves of bread. The third has no food, but has eight coins. He offers to pay for some bread. They agree to share the eight loaves equally among the three travellers, and the third traveller will pay eight coins for his share of the eight loaves. All loaves were the same size. The second traveller (who had three loaves) suggests that he be paid three coins and that the first traveller be paid five coins. The first traveller says that he should get more than five coins. How much should the first traveler get?

(a) 5
(b) 7
(c) 1
(d) None of these

Directions for Questions 75 to 77: *Answer the questions on the basis of the information given below.*

Table A below provides data about ages of children in a school. For the age given in the first column, the second column gives the number of children not exceeding that age. For example, first entry indicates that there are 9 children aged 4 years or less. Tables B and C provide data on the heights and weights respectively of the same group of children in a similar format. Assuming that an older child is always taller and weighs more than a younger child, answer the following questions.

Table A		Table B		Table C	
Age (Years)	**Number**	**Height (Cm)**	**Number**	**Weight (Kg)**	**Number**
4	9	115	6	30	8
5	12	120	11	32	13
6	22	125	24	34	17
7	35	130	36	36	28
8	42	135	45	38	33
9	48	140	53	40	46
10	60	145	62	42	54
11	69	150	75	44	67
12	77	155	81	46	79
13	86	160	93	48	91
14	100	165	100	50	100

75. What is the number of children of age 9 years or less whose height does not exceed 135 cm?

(a) 48 (b) 45
(c) 3 (d) Can't be determined.

76. How many children of age more than 10 years are taller than 150 cm and do not weigh more than 48 kg?

(a) 16 (b) 40
(c) 9 (d) Can't be Determined.

77. Among the children older than 6 years but not exceeding 12 years, how many weigh more than 38 kg?

(a) 34 (b) 52
(c) 44 (d) Can't be Determined

Directions for Question 78:

78. An intelligence agency forms a code of two distinct digits selected from 0, 1, 2,......9, such that the first digit of the code is non-zero. The code, handwritten on a slip, can however potentially create confusion when read upside down. For example, the code 91 may appear as 16. How many codes are there for which no such confusion can arise?

(a) 80 (b) 78
(c) 71 (d) 69

Directions for Questions 79 to 88:

79. Early one morning, four snails, A, B, C and D, set off together down the garden path. A and B kept the same steady pace, slithering only 8 metres by the time C and D had already reached the azalea.

C was wounded and had to stop for an hour to rest. Although D was tired, too, she pressed on, but reduced her pace to be at the same speed as A's and B's.

C started off again just as A and B got even with her. She raced off at her original pace. A promptly sped up to the same speed as C and kept even with her. B just kept going at her original pace.

When A reached the end of the path, she was 1 metre ahead of B, but she was a half hour later than D was. How many meters long was the path?

(a) 10 (b) 15
(c) 8 (d) None of these

80. Coach Pathak has one tennis scholarship left. He's just heard of a family with four boys who are all great tennis players. He's never seen them play, but his scouts assure him that all four play equally well. With no more knowledge available to him, he decides that he wants to give the scholarship to the tallest boy. But their parents do not want to show any favouritism.

The parents agree to have the boys exit the house, one at a time and let Coach Pathak pick the one he wants. He has to make an immediate decision on whether or not to offer the scholarship to that boy. If the coach uses his best strategy, what is the probability of him offering the scholarship to the tallest boy? Assume he can tell whether the boy is taller or shorter than the other boys he's seen.

(a) 0 (b) 1/3
(c) 11/24 (d) None of these

81. Fanny, Gopal and Harish play a challenge tennis tournament where two of them play a set, then the winner stays in the court to play the one who sat out.

During the tournament, Fanny played 15 sets, Gopal played 14 and Harish played 9.

Who played in set 13?

(a) Fanny and Harish (b) Gopal and Harish
(c) Fanny and Gopal (d) None of these

82. In chess, a knight moves two squares in one direction and one square in another direction, ending up on the diagonally opposite corner of a 2 × 3 grid. Intervening squares can be occupied. Find the maximum number of knights which can be placed on an 8 × 8 chess board so that so that no knight threatens another knight (can move into a square occupied by one of the other knights).

(a) 34 (b) 32
(c) 30 (d) None of these

83. Three brothers, Armani, Birianni and Chutanmi are all different ages. They each do strange things with numbers, that is, instead of saying the actual number, they change it in a certain way first.

One brother divides the number in half.

Another brother squares the number.

The third brother reverses the digits. (21 becomes 12, 50 and also 5 become 5)

When they were asked their ages, the oldest whispered his "age" to the thinnest, who whispered it to Chutanmi, who whispered it to the youngest, who answered: 6.

Then the youngest whispered his "age" to the tallest, who whispered it to Birianni, who whispered it to the shortest, who answered: 23

Lastly, the youngest whispered his "age" to the shortest, who whispered it to the thinnest, who whispered it to Armani, who answered: 16.

What are the ages of the three brothers?

(a) 12, 16 and 8 (b) 21, 8 and 16
(c) 5, 21 and 50 (d) 16, 21 and 50

84. Deepika was admiring the output of her new program to generate random numbers. She had printed out the first ten numbers of the results. She soon noticed something interesting. Each of the 10 numbers had exactly one digit, in the proper placement, of the 5 digit code she used to open her car door without a key.

In the first number 14073, for example, Deepika's car code could not be 34170 (two digits correctly placed) or 92365 (none).

Find Deepika's car entry code from these first 10 randomly generated numbers: 14073, 79588, 05892, 84771, 63136, 42936, 37145, 50811, 98174 and 29402?

(a) 05892 (b) 63136
(c) 42936 (d) None of these

85. A, B, C, D and E all live on Pine Street which has house numbers from 10 to 111, inclusive. Two of them live in the same house. The others all live in different houses. They all have made remarks about where they live, but not all the remarks are true.

A said, "My house number is a factor of B's house number. E's house number is 10 greater than D'."

B said, "My house number is greater than 70. A's house number is greater than 30."

C said, "My house number is both a cube and a square. D's house number is greater than 50."

D said, "My house number is a square. B's house number is a cube."

E said, "My house number is twice B's"

But who's telling the truth? It turns out that all statements made by people living in houses with numbers greater than 50 were false. All the other statements were true.

Can you find out the house number of E?

(a) 49 (b) 16
(c) 59 (d) None of these

86. During a game of five card draw poker, played with a standard deck, you are dealt a hand with the following characteristics:

(i) It contains no aces or face cards.
(ii) No two cards have the same value.
(iii) All four suits are present.
(iv) The total value of the odd cards equals the total value of the even cards.
(v) There are no three card straights.
(vi) The total value of the black cards is 10.
(vii) The total value of the hearts is 1(d)
(viii) The card with the lowest value is a spade.

Exactly what are the five cards in your hand?

(a) 2 of spades, 5 and 9 of diamonds, 4 of spades and 8 of clubs
(b) 2 of diamonds, 5 and 9 of spades, 4 of hearts and 8 of clubs
(c) 2 of clubs, 5 and 9 of hearts, 4 of diamonds and 8 of spades
(d) None of these

87. A man would like to take a new health insurance. An officer taking care of these matters says to the man: "Please tell me how many children you have." The man answers: "I have three of them." The officer: "What are the ages of your children?" The man answers: "The product of the ages is equal to 36." The officer replies: "This is not enough information Sir!"; the man replied "Sorry that I was a little bit unclear, but the sum of the ages is equal to the number of shops in front of your office," says the man. The officer: "This still isn't enough information Sir!"; The man replies: "My oldest child loves chocolate." The officer: "Thanks for your cooperation, Now I know the ages."

Are you as smart as the officer? Then give the sum of the ages of the children.

(a) 13 (b) 21
(c) 16 (d) 38

88. There are fifteen boxes and each box contains seven gemstones. Each gemstone in one of the boxes weighs 22 grams and each gemstone in the rest of the fourteen boxes weighs 20 grams each. What is the minimum number of weighings required to identify the box containing 22-gram gemstones using an electronic weighing machine?

(a) 1 (b) 5
(c) 7 (d) 3

Directions for Questions 89 to 92: *Read the information provided and answer the questions which follow.*

A new game show on TV has 100 boxes numbered 1, 2, . . . , 100 in a row, each containing a mystery prize. The prizes are items of different types, a, b, c, . . . , in decreasing order of value. The most expensive item is of type a, a diamond ring and there is exactly one of these. You are told that the number of items, at least doubles as you move to the next type. For example, there would be at least twice as many items of type b as of type a, at least twice as many items of type c as of type b and so on. There is no particular order in which the prizes are placed in the boxes.

89. What is the minimum possible number of different types of prizes?

90. What is the maximum possible number of different types of prizes?

91. Which of the following is not possible?

(a) There are exactly 45 items of type c.
(b) There are exactly 30 items of type b.
(c) There are exactly 75 items of type e.
(d) There are exactly 60 items of type d.

92. You ask for the type of item in box 45. Instead of being given a direct answer, you are told that there are 31 items of the same type as box 45 in boxes 1 to 44 and 43 items of the same type as box 45 in boxes 46 to 100. What is the maximum possible number of different types of items?

(a) 5 (b) 4
(c) 3 (d) 6

Directions for Questions 93 to 96: *Read the information provided and answer the questions which follow.*

The first year students in a business school are split into six sections. In 2019, the Business Statistics course was taught in these six sections by Annie, Beti, Chetan, Dave, Esha and Fakir. All six sections had a common midterm (MT) and a common end term (ET), worth 100 marks each. ET contained more questions than MT. Questions for MT and ET were prepared collectively by the six faculty members. Considering MT and ET together, each faculty member prepared the same number of questions.

Each of MT and ET had at least four questions that were worth 5 marks, at least three questions that were worth 10 marks, and at least two questions that were worth 15 marks. In both MT and ET, all the 5-mark questions preceded the 10-mark questions, and all the 15- mark questions followed the 10-mark questions.

The following additional facts are known.

(i) Annie prepared the fifth question for both MT and ET. For MT, this question carried 5 marks.
(ii) Annie prepared one question for MT. Every other faculty member prepared more than one question for MT.

(iii) All questions prepared by a faculty member appeared consecutively in MT as well as ET.
(iv) Chetan prepared the third question in both MT and ET; and Esha prepared the eighth question in both.
(v) Fakir prepared the first question of MT and the last one in ET. Dave prepared the last question of MT and the first one in ET.

93. Who prepared the second question in ET?
(a) Chetan (b) Esha
(c) Beti (d) Dave

94. How many 5-mark questions were there in MT and ET combined?
(a) 13 (b) 10
(c) 12
(d) Cannot be determined

95. Who prepared 15-mark questions for MT and ET?
(a) Only Dave, Esha and Fakir
(b) Only Beti, Dave, Esha and Fakir
(c) Only Esha and Fakir
(d) Only Dave and Fakir

96. Which of the following questions did Beti prepare in ET?
(a) Tenth question (b) Ninth question
(c) Fourth question (d) Seventh question

Directions for Questions 97 to 100: You are given an n × n square matrix to be filled with numerals so that no two adjacent cells have the same numeral. Two cells are called adjacent if they touch each other horizontally, vertically or diagonally. So a cell in one of the four corners has three adjacent to it, and a cell in the first or last row or column which is not in the corner has five cells adjacent to it. Any other cell has eight cells adjacent to it.

97. What is the minimum number of different numerals needed to fill a 3 × 3 square matrix?

98. What is the minimum number of different numerals needed to fill a 5 × 5 square matrix?

99. Suppose you are allowed to make one mistake, that is, one pair of adjacent cells can have the same numeral. What is the minimum number of different numerals required to fill a 5 × 5 matrix?
(a) 9 (b) 16
(c) 25 (d) 4

100. Suppose that all the cells adjacent to any particular cell must have different numerals. What is the minimum number of different numerals needed to fill a 5 × 5 square matrix?
(a) 25 (b) 16
(c) 9 (d) 4

Directions for Questions 101 to 104: According to a coding scheme the sentence

Peacock is designated as the national bird of India is coded as

5688999 35 1135556678 56 458 13666689 1334 79 13366

This coding scheme has the following rules:
(i) The scheme is case-insensitive (does not distinguish between upper case and lower case letters).
(ii) Each letter has a unique code which is a single digit from among 1, 2, 3, ..., 9.
(iii) The digit 9 codes two letters, and every other digit codes three letters.
(iv) The code for a word is constructed by arranging the digits corresponding to its letters in a non-decreasing sequence.

Answer these questions on the basis of this information.

101. What best can be concluded about the code for the letter L?
(a) 1 (b) 6
(c) 8 (d) 1 or 8

102. What best can be concluded about the code for the letter B?
(a) 1 (b) 3
(c) 3 or 4 (d) 1, 3 or 4

103. For how many digits can the complete list of letters associated with that digit be identified?
(a) 0 (b) 1
(c) 2 (d) 3

104. Which set of letters CANNOT be coded with the same digit?
(a) X, Y, Z (b) S, U, V
(c) I, B, M (d) S, E, Z

Directions for Questions 105 to 108: In a square layout of size 5m × 5m, 25 equal-sized square platforms of different heights are built.

The heights (in metres) of individual platforms are as shown below:

6	1	2	4	3
9	5	3	2	8
7	8	4	6	5
3	9	5	1	2
1	7	6	3	9

Individuals (all of same heights) are seated on these platforms. We say an individual A can reach an individual B if all the three following conditions are met:
(i) A and B are in the same row or column.
(ii) A is at a lower height than B
(iii) If there is/are any individual(s) between A and B, such individual(s) must be at a height lower than that of A.

Thus in the table given above, consider the individual seated at height 8 on 3rd row and 2nd column. He can be reached by four individuals. He can be reached by the individual on his left at height 7, by the two individuals on his right at heights of 4 and 6 and by the individual above at height 5.

Rows in the layout are numbered from top to bottom and columns are numbered from left to right.

105. How many individuals in this layout can be reached by just one individual?
(a) 3 (b) 5
(c) 7 (d) 8

106. Which of the following is true for any individual at a platform of height 1 m in this layout?
(a) They can be reached by all the individuals in their own row and column.
(b) They can be reached by at least 4 individuals.
(c) They can be reached by at least one individual.
(d) They cannot be reached by anyone.

107. We can find two individuals who cannot be reached by anyone in
(a) The last row (b) The fourth row
(c) The fourth column (d) The middle column

108. Which of the following statements is true about this layout?
(a) Each row has an individual who can be reached by 5 or more individuals.
(b) Each row has an individual who cannot be reached by anyone.
(c) Each row has at least two individuals who can be reached by an equal number of individuals.
(d) All individuals at the height of 9 m can be reached by the least 5 individuals.

Directions for Questions 109 to 112: Eight friends: Ajit, Byomkesh, Gargi, Jayanta, Kikira, Manik, Prodosh and Tapesh are going to Delhi from Kolkata by a flight operated by Chear Air. In the flight, sitting is arranged in 30 rows, numbered 1 to 30, each consisting of 6 seats, marked by letters A to F from left to right, respectively. Seats A to C are to the left of the aisle (the passage running from the front of the aircraft to the back), and seats D to F are to the right of the aisle. Seats A and F are by the windows and referred to as window seats, C and D are by the aisle and are referred to as Aisle seats while B and E are referred to as Middle seats. Seats marked by consecutive letters are called consecutive seats (or seats next to each other). A seat number is a combination of the row number, followed by the letter indicating the position in the row, e.g., 1A is the left widow seat in the first row, while 12E is the right middle seat in the 12th row.

Cheap Air charges Rs. 1000 extra for any seats in Rows 1, 12 and 13 as those have extra legroom. For rows 2-10, it charges Rs. 300 extra for window seats and Rs. 500 extra for Aisle seats. For rows 11 and 14 to 20, it charges Rs. 200 extra for window seats and Rs. 400 extra for Aisle seats. All other seats are available at no extra charge.

The following are known:
(i) The eight friends were seated in six different rows.
(ii) They occupied 3 window seats, 4 Aisle seats and 1 Middle seat.
(iii) Seven of them had to pay extra amounts, totaling to Rs. 4600, for their choices of seat. One of them did not pay any additional amount for his/her choice of seat.
(vi) Jayanta, Ajit and Byomkesh were sitting in seats marked by the same letter, in consecutive rows in increasing order of row numbers; but all of them paid different amounts for their choice of seat. One of these amounts may be zero.
(v) Gargi was sitting next to Kikira, and Manik was sitting next to Jayanta.
(vi) Prodosh and Tapesh were sitting in seats marked by the same letter, in consecutive rows in increasing order of row numbers; but they paid different amounts for their choices of seat. One of these amounts may be zero.

109. In which row was Manik sitting?
(a) 10 (b) 11
(c) 12 (d) 13

110. How much extra did Jayanta pay for his choice of seat?
(a) ₹300 (b) ₹400
(c) ₹500 (d) ₹1000

111. How much extra did Gargi pay for her choice of seat?
(a) 0 (b) ₹300
(c) ₹400 (d) ₹1000

112. Who among the following did not pay any extra amount for his/her choice of seat?
(a) Kikira (b) Manik
(c) Gargi (d) Tapesh

ANSWER KEY

Level of Difficulty (I)

1. (a)	2. (a)	3. (a)	4. (b)
5. (b)	6. (b)	7. (c)	8. (c)
9. (a)	10. (a)	11. (b)	12. (b)
13. (c)	14. (b)	15. (b)	16. (a)
17. (b)	18. (a)	19. (b)	20. (a)
21. (b)	22. (a)	23. (d)	24. (d)
25. (a)	26. (c)	27. (b)	28. (a)
29. (a)	30. (b)	31. (a)	32. (a)
33. (a)	34. (a)	35. (c)	36. (b)
37. (a)	38. (b)	39. (c)	40. (a)

41. (b)	42. (d)	43. (b)	44. (c)
45. (c)	46. (b)	47. (d)	48. (c)
49. (d)	50. (b)	51. (c)	52. (b)
53. (c)	54. (b)	55. (c)	56. (d)
57. (d)	58. (d)	59. (b)	60. (d)
61. (a)	62. (a)	63. (b)	64. (b)
65. (c)	66. (b)	67. (d)	68. (a)
69. (c)	70. (d)	71. (c)	72. (a)
73. (b)	74. (d)	75. (c)	76. (d)
77. (d)	78. (c)	79. (b)	80. (b)
81. (c)	82. (a)	83. (d)	84. (c)
85. (a)	86. (c)	87. (a)	88. (a)

Level of Difficulty (II)

1. (b)	2. (b)	3. (a)	4. (c)
5. (c)	6. (c)	7. (a)	8. (b)
9. (b)	10. (b)	11. (c)	12. (b)
13. (b)	14. (b)	15. (b)	
16. 2,3; 3,4; 8,7; 9,8		17. 11	18. 73
19. (a)	20. (b)	21. (b)	22. (c)
23. 62	24. 54	25. (c)	26. (d)
27. (b)	28. (a)	29. (d)	30. (b)
31. (d)	32. (c)	33. 2	34. (a)
35. (d)	36. 7	37. (b)	38. 3
39. 3	40. (c)	41. (d)	42. (c)
43. (a)	44. (a)	45. (b)	46. (a)
47. (a)	48. (b)	49. 40	50. 0
51. 90	52. 20	53. (b)	54. (d)
55. (c)	56. (d)	57. (c)	58. 95
59. (d)	60. (d)	61. (a)	62. 11
63. (d)	64. (b)	65. (a)	66. (c)
67. (a)	68. (d)	69. (a)	70. (d)
71. (c)	72. (a)	73. (c)	74. (b)
75. (b)	76. (a)	77. (c)	78. (b)
79. (b)	80. (c)	81. (c)	82. (b)
83. (b)	84. (d)	85. (c)	86. (d)
87. (a)	88. (a)	89. 2	90. 6
91. (a)	92. (a)	93. (d)	94. (a)
95. (a)	96. (a)	97. (4)	98. (4)
99. (d)	100. (c)	101. (a)	102. (c)
103. (c)	104. (b)	105. (c)	106. (d)
107. (c)	108. (c)	109. (a)	110. (c)
111. (d)	112. (d)		

SOLUTIONS AND SHORTCUTS

Level of Difficulty (I)

Solutions for Questions 1 to 5:

From clue no. (iii),

40% of the total students are female

40% = 36

100% = 90

Total students = 90

	Average	Good	Excellent	Total
Male	18	24	12	54
Female	27	9	0	36
Total	45	33	12	90

Half of the students are either good or excellent means that total of (good + excellent) students = 45

∴ Number of excellent = 12

1/3 of male = average male students = 18

Solutions for Questions 6 to 10:

The following structure would work:

	A	B	C	D	Total left
Last	3	3	3	3	0
Second last	12	12	12		12
Third last	24	24			48
First	32				96
Start					128

Hence, the answers are:

6. 3 + 12 = 15. Option (b) is correct.
7. 3 + 12 + 24 = 39. Option (c) is correct.
8. 3 + 12 + 28 + 32 = 71. Option (c) is correct.
9. 128. Option (a) is correct.
10. 32. Option (a) is correct.

Solutions for Questions 11 to 14:

From clues (i), (ii), (iii), (iv) and (v), we get:

Orchids = Tulips + 2, Rose = Tulips + 4 Marigold = Tulips + 3 and since Lily < Fireball.

If Tulips is 1 (clue (vi)), we get,

Tulip = 1, Orchids = 3, Marigold = 4, Rose = 5

Hence, Lily = 2 and Fireball = 6.

The answer are:

11. Five. Option (b) is correct.
12. Statement (iii) is redundant. Hence, (b).
13. 3 + 4 = 7. Option (c) is correct.
14. Six. Option (b) is correct.

Solutions for Questions 15 to 20:

Weight	Boys	Girls
40	(a + 35)/3	(a + 35)/4
44	b	a
46	a	b
50	a + 35	(a + 35)/3
Total	297	243

Start from the fourth line and take 'a' as the number of girls of 44 kgs.

Solutions for Questions 21 to 26:

Reaction Tracker

First Statement	A, B, C, D and E
Second Statement	The numbers are in A.P. with common difference 4. D _ _ _ A (descending order from left to right)
Third Statement	D C B E A
Fourth Statement	For the sum to be equal to E, the sum of A, B, C and D shall be zero. (using options in Q21 the value of A should be –9.) Then the series becomes: D C B E A 7 3 –1 –5 –9

Hence, the answers are:

21. Option (b) is correct.
22. -10. Option (a) is correct.
23. D is '7'. Hence, option (d) is correct.
24. The value of E is -5. Hence, option (d) is correct.
25. $7 \times 3 \times -1 \times -5 \times -9 = -945$. Option (a) is correct.
26. $7-(-9) = 16$. Hence, option (c) is correct.

Solutions for Questions 27 to 30:

Paragraph 2	Since X has thought that he has the answer to the house number of Z, he must have got 'yes' as an answer to both questions he asked. In such a case, he would think that Z's number is one of 64 or 81 (the two 2 digit perfect squares which are greater than 50). Also, we can deduce that since he thinks that he knows the answer he must be living in one of the two houses. Hence, X's house number is either 64 or 81.
Paragraph 3	By a similar logic, Y's house number is either 27 or 64.
Paragraph 4	We know Z's house number is greater than 50 but less than Y's and X's house numbers. Hence, Y's number must be 64 and X's number is 81. Also, from options of Q. No. 30, we get that Z's number must be 55, since (81 + 64 + 55) is the only addition that satisfies the condition of the sum of the three numbers to be double of a perfect square.

Hence, the answers are:

27. (b).
28. (a).
29. (a).
30. (b).

Solutions for Questions 31 to 34:

You will get the following equations:

A + G = 40 __________ (1)

A - D = 5 __________ (2)

J - D = 8 __________ (3)

This means that A is 3 less than J.

D + R = 37________ (4)

A - G = 8 ________ (5)

Using (1) and (5), we get A = 24 and G = 16,

Hence, D = 19, J = 27 and R = 18.

Thus, the answers are:

31. R = 18. Option (a) is correct.
32. 27 + 19 = 46. Option (a) is correct.
33. 19 - 18 = 1. Option (a) is correct.
34. $24 + 16 + 19 + 27 + 18 \rightarrow 104 \times 2 = 208$. Option (a) is correct.

Solutions for Questions 35 to 37:

From the given information, it is clear that four numbers which must have been the values of money spent, would be: 2517 (clue (iv)), 2234 (clue (i)), 1340 (clue (ii)) and 1193 (clue (i) again).

We need to work out the fifth value.

Also, since Chellamma spent the least and Shahnaz the maximum and since one woman spent ₹ 1378 more than Chellamma, a little bit of introspection will give you the following possibilities for the five numbers:

Possibility 1: If 1193 is the least value,

The five numbers are:

1193, 1340, 2234, 2517 and 2571 (since 2571 = 1193 + 1378).

Possibility 2: If 2517 is the maximum value, the five numbers are:

1139 (since 1139 = 2517 - 1378), 1193, 1340, 2234 and 2517.

Accordingly, we have the following possible arrangements for the five women and the amount they spent:

	Possibility 1	Possibility 2
A (x 2517)	2234	
C (least)	1193	
D (x 1340)	2517	
H	1340	
S (max)	2571	

Note: The thought structure for placing the 5 values with 5 women in the case of possibility 1, goes as follows:

Step 1:

A
C 1193
D
H
S 2571

After placing the least and maximum.

Step 2: 2234 should be before 1193 and Dhenuka cannot have spent ₹ 1340.

A 2234
C 1193
D 2517
H 1340
G 2571

A close look at the above table shows that clue 5 (H > D) is not obeyed by this arrangement. Hence, this solution is wrong.

We, thus, move into possibility 2, i.e.:

1139, 1193, 1340, 2234 and 2517 are the five values. The thought structure for placing the five numbers for the five women goes as:

Step 1: Place the maximum and least values for G and C respectively.

A (x 2517)	
C (least)	1139
D (x 1340)	
H	
G (maximum)	2517

This leaves us with 1340, 1193 and 2234 to place.

Step 2: We need to keep 2 constraints in mind while doing this.

(a) 2234 has to come before 1193 (remember not immediately before). At the same time, H > D. (clue 5)

We can arrange 2234 before 1193 in 3 ways as shown below and then 1340 automatically falls into the vacant space.

A 2234	
C 1139	
D 1193	(1)
H 1340	
G 2517	

(Not possible since Dhenuka cannot be 1340)	
A 2234	
C 1139	
D 1340	(2)
H 1193	
G 2517	

(Not possible since H should be greater than D)	
A 1340	
C 1139	(3)
D 2234	
H 1193	
G 2517	

Hence, the only possible arrangement is as in (1) above. Hence, the answers are:

35. (c) Dhenuka
36. (b) 1340
37. (a) 1139

Solutions for Questions 38 to 39:

Elle	3y	
Yogesh	y	Wahida 2z
Zaheer	z	

38. (b). From the above table we can infer that Elle must be older than Wahida (as she is thrice a higher value (y) while Wahida's age is twice a lower value (z)).
39. (c). Using both pieces of information we get that if Zaheer = 10, then Wahida and Yogesh = 20 and hence, Elle = 60 years.
Thus, option (c) is correct.

Solutions for Questions 40 to 43:

Given that, at least four persons were standing in front of Antony and all these persons have higher number of points than Antony. Hence, Antony can have at the most 3 points and at least 1 point (since no one can have more than 7 points). From (5), the person in front of Casey had two points less than what Antony had. Hence, Antony must have at least 3 points.

Therefore, Antony has exactly 3 points and the person in front of Casey has 1 point. This person must be the one with the least number of points. Further, this person cannot be in front of Antony (since he has lesser number of points). Hence, Antony must be in the 5th position, the person with the lowest number of points in the 6th position and Casey must be in the last position.

From (3), there is only one person between the person who received the least number of points and Brian. Hence, Brian must be in the 4th position. Further, the four persons in front of Antony must have 4, 5, 6 and 7 points in any order. Alexander and Kian are in front of Antony, and from (1), Alexander must have 7 points and Kian 4 points. Also, Casey must have 2 points.

Fred cannot be in the first place (from (4)). He cannot be in the second place because then, Kian and Alexander cannot be next to each other. Hence, he has to be in the third place, Kian must be in the first place and Alexander in the second place. Brian and Fred must have 5 and 6 points in any order.

The following table presents the order and the number of points that each person had.

Order	1	2	3	4	5	6	7
Person	Kian	Alexander	Fred	Brian	Antony	Ben	Casey
No. of points	4	7	6/5	5/6	3	1	2

40. Alexander had the highest number of points. Option (a) is the answer.

41. Except for Ben, all the other persons have higher number of points than Casey. Option (b) is the answer.
42. The person with the second highest number of points can be Brian or Fred. Hence, the answer cannot be determined. Option (d) is the answer.
43. Positions of Kian and Fred are fixed, there is only one people between them. Option (b) is the answer.

Solutions for Questions 44 to 46:

44. If she leaves with 30 flowers she has to offer at least more than 30 in order to be left with 0 flowers after 4 iterations of doubling and offering a certain number of flowers. Hence, the options we need to look at are 31, 32 and 33. Looking at the middle value of 32 makes most sense because of two principal reasons-
    1. In case we are left with some flowers at the end, it would mean that we would need to increase the number of flowers offered to each deity- thus in that case the number of flowers offered would need to be increased.
    2. In case the flowers left at the end of the fourth deity end up as negative, then we can reduce the value of the number of flowers offered to the deity.

    The other reason why we should look at only 32 is even more compelling. The logic can be called as the even number logic. Since, the flowers are doubled just before being offered to the deity, and when Rupa offers flowers to the last deity she is left with none- it must follow that the number of flowers she offers is an even number. In case you see this logic, you need to solve no further and can mark 32 as the correct answer to this question.

    In case, you do not see this logic, you can still work out the numbers as follows:

    30 → doubled to 60 → after offering 32 flowers to the first deity left with 28 → doubled to 56 → after offering 32 flowers to the second deity left with 24 → doubled to 48 → after offering 32 flowers to the third deity left with 16 → doubled to 32 → after offering 32 flowers to the fourth deity left with 0.
45. The solution to this question depends on the solution for Question 46. The answer is 16.
46. If she starts with 15 flowers and gives 16 flowers, she would be left with 0 flowers after 4 iterations. This is the minimum number of flowers she would have to take from her home.

Solutions for Questions 47 to 49:

47. Using statement A, we know that B is not a mathematician, and neither is C. But we cannot make a judgment about A–he may or may not be a mathematician. Thus we cannot say how many of A, B and C are mathematicians.

    Using Statement B, we cannot again say how many of A, B and C are mathematicians because, A might be a mathematician, B too might be a mathematician and C could also be a mathematician.

    Even if we use both the statements we still would not be able to make a judgment about A–he could or could not be a mathematician.

    Thus, we mark option (d).
48. From A alone we know that A and B definitely passed the exam, while from B alone we definitely know that neither C nor D has passed the exam. Thus, if we use both A and B, we know definitely that 2 among the four students has passed the exam.
49. Data is insufficient even if we were to use both statements together as we would not know, how many of the 70 plants with red flowers were coming out of white seeds and how many of them were coming out of black seeds.

Solutions for Questions 50 to 51:

The instructions are self explanatory here. Perhaps the only thing you need to notice is that the first two instruction types would work only if there is enough capacity in the receiving vessel.

50. After the first FILL(C,A) instruction, the water situation would be:

    A = 3, B = 0 and C = 2.

    Since, the third instruction is again FILL (C,A) we first need to make space in C by emptying it. From the options, Option (b) fits the requirements.
51. There is a total of 5 liters in the three vessels at the start. Drain A, would result in the draining off of 1 liter of water from this. This leaves 4 liters of water in the system. If after 6 instructions, A contains 4 liters (as mentioned in the question) it is obvious that neither B nor C can contain any water. Thus the amount of water in C would be 0. Option (c) is correct.

Solution for Question 52:

52. For solving this question, we can take the weight of the heaviest box from the options. There are 3 options which we are given in this regard–64, 62 and 60. Since the highest weight total for any two boxes is given as 121 kgs, it is not possible for the heaviest box to be only 60 kgs in weight. Thus we can eliminate option (a).

    Trying option 2 the following thought structure would follow:

Total 121 kgs–If the heaviest box is 62 kgs, the second heaviest would be 59.

Total 120 kgs–62 + 58 = 120 → one box of 58 kgs → 117 kgs total gets explained by (59 + 58).

Total 118 kgs–(62 + 56) → one box of 56 kgs → 115 kgs gets explained by (59 + 56) and 114 kgs gets explained by the combination (58 + 56)

Total 116 kgs–(62 + 54) → one box of 54 kgs → 113 kgs gets explained by (59 + 54), 112 kgs gets explained by the combination (58 + 54) and 110 kgs gets explained by the combination (56 + 54).

Thus, 5 boxes of weights 62, 59, 58 56 and 54 kgs explains each of the 10 weight values which are given in the problem. Hence, the heaviest box is 62 kgs.

Solution for Question 53:

53. Use the following thought process to solve this question:

First the minimum requirements need to be met–Every subject should have at least 1 book.

	Management (4 points)	Mathematics (3 points)	Physics (2 points)	Fiction (1 point)	Total (Books/points)
First Step—Minimum requirements	1	1	2	2	6 books
Second Step		+1	+2		+3 books
Third Step			+1		+1 book
Total numbers of each category	1	2	5	2	10 books
Points earned	4	6	10	2	22 points

After the mandatory first step you should realise that you have a slack of 4 books to be put into the bag. We have two options: 1 management + 2 fiction books (6 points using 3 books)

OR 1 Mathematics + 2 Physics Books (7 points using 3 books)

Obviously, the use of 1 mathematics + 2 Physics books is a better point generator than 1 management and 2 fiction books. Thus, the second step in the table gets explained by this logic.

After this, we still have to put 1 more book. We need to ensure that we get maximum points added when we add the last book, at the same time we should not break any of the rules while doing so. It is obvious that we cannot add a management or a mathematics book by itself since it has other constraints attached to it. Thus, we should add a physics book as it gives 1 point more than a fiction book.

Thus the third step in the table above gets explained; and we have a total of 22 points.

Solution for Question 54:

54. If we are to give the courier 10 kg packs, we need to send 8 such packs–a total transportation time of 16 hours @ 5kmph. One courier would require 2 hours to reach the destination.

If we are to use 20 kg packs, we need to send 4 such packs and each pack would require 5 hours (@ 2kmph). The total time required would be 20 hours.

Similarly, for 40 kg packs, 2 packs would require a total transportation time of 20 hours (since the courier would travel @ 1kmph). Each pack would require 10 hours.

Thus, the minimum courier cost is for 10 kg packs–16 hours × ₹ 10/hour = ₹ 160.

Solutions for Questions 55 to 57:

55. This is a conventional Venn diagram (set theory) problem. Only from statement 1 or only from statement 2 we cannot answer the question about how many people are watching P. But if we use both, we have all the information we need to solve this question.

56. We have no information, in either of the two statements about the time difference between Mumbai and No mans land. Thus, option (d) is correct.

57. There could be multiple answers satisfying the two conditions, thus we cannot find the ages of x and y based on the information provided. Option (d) is correct.

Solutions for Questions 58 to 62:

58. Such questions have to be solved using reverse thinking. So start thinking about the last person, Eswari must have seen 30 mints (only in such a

case would you get 17 mints left after taking half and then returning 2 to the bowl.) For Eswari to see 30 mints, it must be the case that after Fatima took 1/4th of what she saw, there must have been 27 mints left and when she put 3 back, Eswari would have seen 30 mints.

Further, for Fatima to see 36 mints, Sita must have seen 48 chips to start with - as to leave 36 after taking 1/3rd of the chips she sees and then giving back 4 the only starting point possible is 48.

59. This question has to be seen from the perspective of the work done by the escalator. Since the ratio of speeds of walking of Shyama and Vyom is 3:2, when Shyama takes 25 steps, Vyom would take 16.66 steps. Let us say that the escalator would do x steps of work in this time. The value of x would be such that 25 + x would be equal to the number of steps. We also know that when Vyom walks up the escalator he does 20 steps. Hence, in the time Vyom does 20 steps, the escalator should do 1.2x steps. So 20 + 1.2x should also give us the same value for the number of steps. This means that the work done by the escalator should be 20% higher when Vyom reaches the top than the work that was done when Shyama reached the top. From this point you can go in two ways:
   (i) By equating $25 + x = 20 + 1.2x \rightarrow x = 25$. Hence, the escalator has 50 steps.
   (ii) By going through options, we can easily see that if the escalator had 50 steps, then there would be a coverage of 25 steps for Shyama and 30 for Vyom–which represents the required increase of 20%.
60. In order to do this he should allocate an independent power of 2 in every bag. Thus, the first bag should contain 1 ₹, the second 2 ₹, the third 4 ₹, 8, 16, 32, 64 . Using these he can form any value from 1 to 127. The last bag should contain the remaining ₹ 31 as we can add any combination of the above to 31 to get all values between 128 to 158.
61. In a normal year for the same date the day of the week is advanced by 1, while for leap years the same is advanced by 2 days. Calculating backwards, we get +30 + 8 = 38. Gives 38/7 = +3 giving us a Thursday.
62. From the given conditions we can make the following table:

Chirag (c)	700 (since he takes 300 from Ashok to buy a jacket)
Bashir (b)	500 (Since he has to borrow ₹ 100 from Ashok to buy a Shawl)
Deepak (d) = c – b	200
Ashok = 3d	600

It is clear from the numbers, that the costliest item Deepak can buy is a shirt.

Solutions for Questions 63 to 64:

63. In order to solve this question, you need to understand that the requirement is to buy the maximum number of items. The least cost per item would occur if we buy 1E, 2D's and 4B's. In this case 7 items cost ₹ 485 and hence 14 would cost ₹ 970. Hence, option (b) is correct.
64. We can construct the following table based on the information given:

Species	Color	Spotted/ Non Spotted	Number
Oak	Red	Spotted	y (even and positive)
Oak	Red	Non-Spotted	X
Oak	Non-Red	Spotted	$5y$
Oak	Non-Red	Non-Spotted	0
Maple	Red	Spotted	6
Maple	Red	Non-Spotted	X
Maple	Non-Red	Spotted	0
Maple	Non-Red	Non-Spotted	22
		TOTAL	50

Solving we get: $6y + 2x = 22$. Since, y is even and positive it can only be 2 and x would then be 5. Hence the number of oak leaves would be $6y + x = 17$.

Solutions for Questions 65 to 66:

65. If we know both 1 and 2 we can easily find that if Zaheer is 10, Yogesh and Wahida are 20 and hence Elle is 60.
66. Option (b) is the clear answer since Elle is three times older than Yogesh, who is elder than Zaheer. Also, Wahida is only double Zaheer's age. Hence Option (b) is correct.

Solutions for Questions 67 to 69:

Theory Point: The beauty of DS questions is that you do not need to solve to get an answer. All you need to see is whether you are getting a unique answer to the question asked or not. The standard process of solving a DS question involves checking individual data sets to see whether you have a unique answer to the question asked.

In a typical DS question, you would need to check three separate data sets–

Data Set 1: Includes the information given in the question statement Plus the information in the first Statement.

Data Set 2: Includes the information given in the question statement Plus the information in the second Statement.

Data Set 3: Includes the information given in the question statement Plus the information in both Statements.

Whenever you are checking for any data set and it's sufficiency, look at whether the information you are checking for is sufficient to answer the question asked, i.e., whether it gives a unique answer to the question asked. A unique answer here means that as far as we are considering the same set of data, we should get only 1 answer to the question asked.

67. From the first statement we cannot determine the answer as we do not know whether Korea scored any goals. From the second statement alone, the data is again insufficient. Even if we use both A and B we get that there could be two scenarios. If Korea was leading 2-0 the match would be a draw. If Korea was leading 3-1 India would win. Hence, we cannot say for sure whether India won the match or not.
68. A alone is sufficient to answer the question asked– as if adding 12 gives a number divisible by 8, then adding 4 should also do so. B alone is not sufficient to answer the question because the number you get could be or could not be divisible by 8.
69. Using both the statements we have three unknowns and three unique equations as:
$J + P + G = 38500$, $J = 2/9\ (P + G)$ and $P = 3/11\ (J + G)$. Solving you can get all the three values.

Solutions for Questions 70 to 72:

70. From the given clues (third and fourth) we can clearly see that Ganesh and Daljeet have ₹ 20 each and Sandeep had ₹ 30. Also, since Jugraj has less than Alam, we get the following table:

Alam	Sandeep	Daljeet	Ganesh	Jugraj
40	30	20	20	10

Now, the first three statements are not possible and must be false because:
(i) If Alam ended with 9.5, he must have spent 30.5. Given that he has spent ten times more than Ganesh, he must have spent 11 times what Ganesh Spent–which is an impossible decimal value.
(ii) If Sandeep spends ₹ 29, then Daljeet must have spent ₹ 27.5 which is not possible.
(iii) If Ganesh Spent ₹ 16, Alam would spend more than he had to start off with.
Only Option (d) is possible.

71. The only two pairs of single digit numbers that give their product as a perfect cube are the:
9×3 and 4×2. 9 and 3 are not in the options, so we start off our trials based on 2 and 4. Then according to the given situation, the father's age would be 24 and the mother's age would be half of 42 → 21. The difference between their ages would be 3 years as required by the problem. Thus, we see that the younger boy's age must be 2 years.
72. The following series of deductions would give us the answer:
(a) Number of passengers waiting initially → 90% of 200 = 180, with 72 women.
(b) Seating capacity of people in each flight = 2/3rd of 180 = 120.
(c) After boarding flight A, number of people in the hall = 80 (as 60% of the seats are vacant) → Thus, 100 people must have boarded flight A out of which there must have been 50 women (as half the passengers who boarded flight A were women).
(d) Thus, there are 80 people waiting in the hall for flight B–thus the number of air hostesses in flight A = 4.
(e) Vacant Seats in Flight B = 40.
Required ratio 40:4 = 10:1. Option (a) is correct.

Solutions for Questions 73 to 76:

73. Of R6, R7, R8, R9 and R13 (the regions which produce medium quality of Crop 1 or 2), only R9 produces low quality Crop 3 or 4. Hence, there is only 1 region.
74. Some crop-3 producing regions like R1, R2 etc, produce Crop-1 too but not high quality crop-2.
75. All the three low quality crop-1 producing regions produce either high quality crop-4 or medium quality crop-3.
76. There can be many possibilities and this can be tested by drawing 4 lines on a plane and seeing how many areas are made–you can easily see that the number of distinct areas into which the plane is divided can differ and is not unique.

Solutions for Questions 77 to 78:

77. There are six 2's and four 4's is sequence. Thus, these would be 2 oranges in the basket.
78. $19 \times 1 - 4 \times 2 = 11$. Option (c) is correct.
79. It can be easily seen that the revenues at different values would be:
200×2, 220×1.9, 240×1.8, 260×1.7, 280×1.6, 300×1.5 and 320×1.4. The value goes up till 300×1.5 and then reduces. Hence, option (b) is correct.

80. Since he is left with 1 diamond at the end, to the third watchman he must have reached with 6 diamonds, given him half (3) and two more (total 5) and be left with 1 diamond. With the same thought pattern you can solve the remaining part of the question.

    The thought process would go as this:

    $1 \rightarrow 6 \rightarrow 16 \rightarrow 36$.

Solutions for Questions 81 to 82:

81. It is possible to score 32 marks net with 35 corrects, 3 wrongs and 12 not attempted questions. Since, all other options are above 3, only option (c) can be the correct answer.
82. Checking the options, it is not possible to produce the number of bags in options (c) and (d) in the given time. Between options (a) and (b), option (a) is more profitable and hence is the correct answer.

Solutions for Questions 83 to 84:

The total cost of the three bottles would be 520 + 364 + 364 = 1248. Hence, the cost per person would be 416 bahts.

83. Since R has paid only 2 Euros (an equivalent of 92 bahts), he would have to further pay 324 bahts more. Option (d) is correct.
84. M has paid 4 Euros + 27 bahts which adds up to 211 bahts. So he has to pay 205 bahts to S. This would convert to 5 US Dollars.

Solutions for Questions 85 to 86:

85. A loss of ₹ 50 could mean two things: 1) If the game ended normally or if the game was terminated by the player. In both cases the number of coin tosses would be different. Since statement 1 defines how the game ended, we can define the number of tosses the player must have made uniquely.

    From the second statement alone we cannot decipher how many heads must have occurred. Thus, only statement 1 is sufficient to answer the question asked.
86. We do not get enough information from statement 1 alone or statement 2 alone. If we try to use statement 1 alone, we get that she bought 21 packets, out of which the last packet contained the first S. The remaining 20 packets must have had Os, As and Ps. There is no way to tell how many Ps these 20 contained. Thus, Statement 1 alone is not sufficient to answer the question.

    If we use statement 2 alone we just know that there were 18 Os and A's combined. We do not know the total number of packets she bought and also how many S's she got.

    Using both statements 1 and 2 together, we get that there was 1 S, and 18 Os and As combined. Thus there must have been 2 P's exactly.

Solutions for Questions 87 to 88:

We know the following equations:

$$G = A - 8 \quad (1)$$
$$D + R = 37 \quad (2)$$
$$J = D + 8 \quad (3)$$
$$A + G = 40 \quad (4)$$
$$A = D + 5 \quad (5)$$

From 1 and 4, we get A = 24 and G = 16.

So, D =19, J = 27 and R = 18

87. Option (a) is correct.
88. D + J = 46. Thus, Option (a) is correct.

Level of Difficulty (II)

Solutions for Questions 1 to 5:

Paragraph 1	Ten people P, Q, R, S, T, U, V, W, X and the Mastermind 3.
Paragraph 2 and 3	Two ways of creating an answer key: ONE SOURCE: Copy entire answer key and introduce 1 wrong answer. Deduction: If you have one source, then you introduce only 1 wrong answer and carry over any wrong answers as well as any blanks from the answer key of the source. TWO SOURCES: Introduce blank if the two answer keys differ on one particular question. [This means that if one answer key has the answer correct and the other answer key has it wrong, then we introduce a blank]. Note: If both answer keys are correct or if both answer keys are incorrect on a particular question, then they will give us the same answer and hence, will not differ. Consequently, their answer will be copied into the answer key ‘under construction’.
Paragraph 4	Note also that since it is given that two or more people have not introduced a wrong answer to the same question, we can deduce that if two answer keys have the same answer wrong, they will be showing the same incorrect answer to that question. Consequently, if someone has two sources who have the wrong answer to the same question, both of them will show the same

	incorrect answer to that particular question and that answer will get replicated as it is, into the answer key which is constructed using them both. With this understanding, we move to the information contained in the table.
Deductions from the table	The first thing we see when we see the table is that P, S and V have only 1 incorrect answer and no blanks. A little thought will give you that this can happen, only if there is a single all-correct answer key as the source. Hence, P, S and V must have had the Don as their source and further that, P must have introduced the wrong answer to Q 46. S must have introduced the wrong answer to Q 17 and V must have introduced the wrong answer to Q 25. At this point, we also know that— In case of 1 source, there will be the introduction of only 1 extra wrong answer and that blanks can only be introduced, if there are two sources. From this point on, move ahead in the question using two main objectives— (a) Decoding the answer key patterns of the remaining six people (Q, R, T, U, W and X) and (b) trying to decode the introduction of the remaining wrong answers and the blanks.
	From the table, T and W are pretty easy to decode. P must have been the source for both of them and T must have introduced the wrong answer to Q 90, while W must have introduced the wrong answer to Q 92.
	At this point, the table would look like:

Source	Wrong Answers	Blank Answers
Don	P 46	--
	Q 96	46, 90, 25
	R 27, 56	17, 46, 90
Don	S 17	--
P	T 46, 90	
	U 14, 46	92, 90
Don	V 25	--
P	W 46, 92	--
	X 27	17, 46, 90

	Q's Answer Key: He must have had T and V as his sources. In such a case, his answer to Questions 25, 46 and 90 would remain blank and he would introduce the wrong answer to Q. 96.
	We are now left with R, U and X and need to think how these answer keys could have been created. It is evident that X must have been R's only source (since the blanks are just carried forward by R and he has introduced the wrong answer to Q. 56). Further, X's answer key could have been formed if he had his sources as S and T. U's answer key could have been created only if his sources were T and W. In that case he would introduce the blank answers 90 and 92, copy the incorrect answer 46 as it is (since there would be no mismatch in that answer) and introduce the wrong answer to Q. 14. Thus, the final table would look like:

Source		Wrong Answers	Blank Answers
Don	P	46	--
T and V	Q	96	46, 90, 25
X	R	27, 56	17, 46, 90
Don	S	17	--
P	T	46, 90	
T and W	U	14, 46	92, 90
Don	V	25	--
P	W	46, 92	--
S and T	X	27	17, 46, 90

Thus, the answers to the questions are:

1. Option (b) is correct.
2. P, T, S, X. Hence, 4. Option (b) is correct.
3. U. Option (a) is correct.
4. Option (c) is correct.
5. Option (c) is correct.

Solutions for Questions 6 to 9:

Runs scored by the top three batsmen against Pakistan

= 40 + 130 + 28

= 198

90% = 198

100% = 220 runs

The rest of the players made only 22 runs.

Runs scored by the top three batsmen against South Africa

= 51 + 75 + 49

= 175

70% = 175

100% = 250

The rest of the players made only 75 runs.

Runs scored by the top three batsmen against Australia
= 55 + 87 + 50
= 192
80% = 192
100 = 240
The rest of the players made only 48 runs.
Y → 40 + South Africa + 87 = 127 + runs scored against South Africa.
V → 130 + South Africa + Australia =130. + runs scored against South Africa + Australia.
K → 28 + 51 + Australia = 79 + Runs scored against Australia.
S → Pakistan + 75 + 50 = 125 + Runs scored against Pakistan.
R → Pakistan + 49 + 55 = 104 + Runs scored against Pakistan.

6. Option (c) is correct. For Yuvraj, middle index cannot be determined as we don't know the exact runs scored by him against South Africa.
   Same is the case with Virendra and Kaif.
   For Saurav, the middle index will be 50 because whatever runs he scores against Pakistan, they could be maximum 22 or minimum zero. This will not affect the middle number 50.

For Rahul, middle index will be 49. (same logic)

7. The R Index ranges would be:
   Yuvraj: 47 to 87
   Kaif: 23 to 51
   Virender: 82 to 130
   Rahul: 33 to 55
   Saurav: 53 to 75. Hence, any of Yuvraj, Rahul or Kaif can have the lowest R Index. Option (a) is correct.
8. Option (b) is correct. Number of players who definitely scored less than Yuvraj is 1.
   In the worst case, if we suppose that Yuvraj scored zero against South Africa, so we have to find how many players definitely scored less than 127.
   This could be only Rahul who can score maximum 22 runs against Pakistan and will be able to get a score of 126, which is less than 127.
9. Option (b) is correct. Saurav's middle index is the best.
10. Option (b) is correct. Each loaf of bread is divided into 3 parts. So we have 24 parts and each traveller gets 8 parts.
    Ist traveller has 15 parts. He ate 8 parts and gave his 7 parts to the IIIrd traveller.
    IInd traveller has 9 parts. He ate 8 parts and gave his Ist part to the IIIrd traveller.
    So, 8 coins should be divided in the ratio 7: 1.
    First traveller gets 7 coins.
11. (c) Maximum points of 22 can be achieved by taking (1 Management + 2 Fiction + 2 Maths + 5 Physics) books.
    4 + 2 + 6 + 10 = 22.
12. Option (b) is correct.
13. Option (b) is correct.
14. Option (b) is correct.
15. Option (b) is correct.

Solutions for Questions 16 to 18:

16. The 4 solutions are:

A's number	B's number
2	3
3	4
8	7
9	8

Sample cases are:
(1,2); (2,3); (3,4); (4,5); (5,6); (6,7); (7,8); (8,9); (9,10); (2,1); (3,2); (4,3); (5,4); (6,5); (7,6); (8,7); (9,8); (10,9).

- **Step 1:** Starting with extreme numbers, suppose A had number 1 or 10, then he would have known B's number which would be 2 or 9 respectively, however, according to the question A did not know B's number. Hence, these 2 cases are not possible.
- **Step 2:** If A had the number 2, B can have 1 or 3, so A answered that he didn't know B's number. Now further, if B had 1, he could have answered that he knows A's number, viz. 2 but he says he doesn't know either which is only possible if B had the number 3 and he knew that A could have either 2 or 4 which also justifies A's response.
  Understanding this, A then answered that he now knew B's number viz. the number 3.
  Hence, a solution is obtained–(2, 3). With the same logic, we get–(9, 8) for (A, B).
- **Step 3:** If A had the number 3, B could have numbers 2 or 4, so A answered that he didn't know B's number. Now further, if B had 2 and A couldn't answer, that'd mean A did not have number 1 but number 3, so B could have answered easily, but he said he didn't know either, thus, B did not have 2. Now, if B had 4, A could have 3 or 5 and B could not have answered what A's number was, this is what happened, therefore, B had 4. Now understanding this logic, A answers that he now knows B's number viz. 4.
  Hence, a solution is obtained–(3, 4). With the same logic, we get–(8, 7) for (A, B).

- **Step 4:** If A had the number 4, B could have the numbers 3 or 5, so A answered that he didn't know. Now further, if B had 3, he could have deduced that A would have either the number 2 or 4, so he answered he didn't know A's number. And, if B had 5, he could have deduced that A could have either number 4 or 6, so he answered he didn't know. As we can see A cannot conclude from such information what the number of B is, so he cannot tell, but the question says that A could tell now what the number with B is. Hence, A cannot have the number 4 with him.

  With same logic, A cannot have number 5 or 6 or 7 with him.

  Therefore, only 4 cases possible of (A,B) are: (2,3); (3,4); (8,7); (9,8)

17. 1st week of any month has the below dates:

    1, 2, 3, 4, 5, 6, 7

    Sumit knows one date and Sunil knows another.

    Case 1: If Sumit had information about the DOB as 1st or 7th of October:

    In this case he'd have known the date with Sunil which would be either 2nd or 6th, but he says he doesn't know. Hence, he doesn't have these 2 dates.

    Case 2: If Sumit has information about the DOB as 2nd or 6th of October:

    Suppose, he has 2nd October as the DOB of one of the sons. Then, Sunil can have 1st or 3rd of October, so Sumit says, he doesn't know. Now if Sunil had 1st, he'd have known that Sumit has 2nd, but he says, he doesn't know either, hence, he had DOB 3rd with him, for which Sumit could have 2nd or 4th and Sunil wasn't sure which one. From this information, Sumit could easily tell that Sunil had DOB 3rd with him. Hence, solution is (2,3). With the same logic, we can deduce (6,5) as another solution.

    Case 3: If Sumit has DOB 3rd or 5th of October.

    Suppose, he has 3rd October as the DOB of one of the sons. Then, Sunil can have 2nd or 4th of October, so Sumit says, he doesn't know. Now, if Sunil had 2nd, he could not tell exact DOB with Sumit because Sumit can have 1st or 3rd, likewise if he has 4th, Sumit can have 3rd or 5th so he says, he doesn't know. Now, with this information Sumit cannot conclude what DOB Sunil has, but according to question he now tells the date. Therefore, this solution is not possible.

    Likewise if Sumit has 4th or 5th October, the conclusion won't exist.

    Therefore, the only 2 solutions are: (2,3) and (6,5) for (Sumit, Sunil).

    Maximum sum is 6 + 5 = 11.

18. **Round# 1:** ends with #99 killing #100 and passing on the pistol to #1

    Round# 2: ends with #97 killing #99 and passing on the pistol to #1

    Roudnd# 3: ends with #89 killing #93 and passing on the pistol to #97

    Round# 4: ends with #89 killing #97 and passing on the pistol to #9

    Round# 5: ends with #73 killing #89 and passing on the pistol to #9

    Round# 6: ends with #9 killing #41 and passing on the pistol to #73

    Round# 7: ends with #73 killing #9 and #73 survives the stand-off

Solutions for Questions 19 to 22:

This question is based on a standard logic that should be part of your knowledge. Once, you understand the first question, you would be able to solve all these questions quite easily.

19. According to the question, there are 10 packets and the number of candies in each packet is 9. One must think of coming up with a way to minimise the number of times the weighing machine should be used for measurement. Think about it like this: You take 45 candies in total in a way that you take 1 candy from packet# 1, 2 from packet# 2, 3 from packet# 3 and so on till 9 from packet# 9. You put them together on the weighing machine. Following scenarios appear:

Scenario#	Reading on weighing machine (in grams)	Conclusion— Which packet contains candies weighing 20 grams each?
1	450	Packet# 10
2	460	Packet# 1
3	470	Packet# 2
4	480	Packet# 3
5	490	Packet# 4
6	500	Packet# 5
7	510	Packet# 6
8	520	Packet# 7
9	530	Packet# 8
10	540	Packet# 9

Clearly, you had to use the weighing machine only once. Hence, (a) is the answer.

20. Here you take a total of 28 candies in a way that you take 1 candy from packet#1, 2 from packet# 2 and so on till 7 from packet# 7. Now you put them all on weighing machine, 2 scenarios appear:

    Scenario 1: The weighing machine reads 280 grams—then all these 7 packets have candies weighing

10 grams each, and candies weighing 20 grams are in packets #8 or #9 or #10. Now you take 1 candy from packet# 8, 2 from packet# 9, 3 from packet# 10 and put them all on weighing machine. If the machine reads 70 grams, then packet# 8 has candies weighing 20 grams; else if the machine reads 80 grams, then packet# 9 has candies weighing 20 grams; else if 90 grams, then packet# 10 is the answer.

Scenario 2: The weighing machine does not read 280 grams, then one of the following cases appear:

Case#	Reading on weighing machine (in grams)	Conclusion— Which packet contains candies weighing 20 grams each?
1	290	Packet# 1
2	300	Packet# 2
3	310	Packet# 3
4	320	Packet# 4
5	330	Packet# 5
6	340	Packet# 6
7	350	Packet# 7

In such a case, you get the answer in only one weighing. However, this is dependent on luck. In such problems, you have to think of the worst case scenario. Scenario 1 is the worst case scenario. The weighing machine will have to be used minimum 2 times to confirm the correct packet#. Hence, correct answer would be option (b).

21. Take 1 candy each from 1st 3 packets, 2 each from next 3 packets and 3 each from the next 3 packets. Put them together on weighing machine. Following 4 scenarios appear:

Scenario# 1: If the total weight is 180 grams, then 20 gm candies are in packet# 10.

Scenario# 2: If the reading of total weight is 190 grams, packet we are looking for is in the 1st group (amongst packet #1, #2, #3). Next, you take 1 from packet# 1, 2 from packet# 2, 3 from packet# 3 and weigh them. If the reading is 70 grams, answer is packet# 1; if the reading is 80 grams, answer is packet# 2 and if the reading is 90 grams, answer is packet# 3.

Scenario# 3: If the reading of the total weight is 200 grams, packet we are looking for is in the 2nd group (amongst packet# 4, #5, #6). Follow the same steps as above to find the correct packet.

Scenario# 4: If the reading of the total weight is 210 grams, packet we are looking for is in the 3rd group (amongst packet #7, #8, #9). Follow the same steps as above to find the correct packet.

Thus, we need to use weighing machine minimum 2 times to find the correct packet. Hence, correct answer is option (b).

22. In this case, take 1 candy each from first 5 packets and 2 each from next 5 packets. (A total of 15.) Weigh them 2 possible scenarios appear:

Scenario 1: Weight reads 160 grams. The packet we are looking for is in the 1st group of 5 packets. Now, take 1 candy each from packet 1 and packet 2, and take 2 candies each from packets 3 and 4. You will have a total of 6 candies. Weigh them. Three new outcomes emerge:

Outcome 1: Weight = 70 grams. The 20-gram candies are coming from packet 1 or 2. Take 1 from packet 1 and 2 from packet 2 and weigh once more and you will know the correct packet.

Outcome 2: Weight = 80 grams. The 20-gram candies are coming from packet 3 or 4. Take 1 from packet 3 and 2 from packet 4 and weigh once more and you will know the correct packet.

Outcome 3: Weight = 60 grams. The 20-gram candies are in packet 5.

Scenario 2: Weight reads 170 grams, packet we are looking for is in 2nd group of 5 packets. Now, follow the same steps as above to find the correct packet.

Thus, we need to use the weighing machine minimum 3 times to find the correct packet (taking the worst case scenario). Hence, correct answer is option (c).

Solutions for Questions 23 to 24:

23.

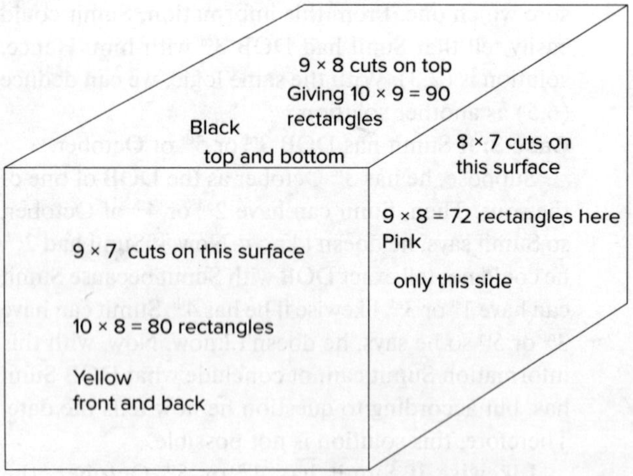

To maximise the number of cubes with exactly two colours we need to paint the same colours on opposite sides. Since this cube has only 5 sides painted, one side would be unpainted. Suppose, you cut the cube with 9 cuts and 8 cuts on the top surface (giving

10 × 9 = 90 small rectangles on the top) and 7 cuts to the lateral surfaces (giving 10 × 8 = 80 rectangles on one pair of lateral surfaces and 9 × 8 = 72 cuts on the other pair of lateral surfaces). The situation for the maximum number of pieces that would be in two colours would occur when the opposite sides are painted in the same colour. So, if we do Black on top and bottom, Yellow on front and back lateral surfaces and Pink on one side lateral surface. We will get a total of 9 (Black and Yellow) + 9 (Black and Yellow) + 7 (Black and Pink) pieces on the top surface's edges. We will get a similar number of pieces on the bottom surface with similar colouring pattern. On the lateral surface, we will have and 6 + 6 pieces (with Yellow and Pink).

Thus, the total would be 25 + 25 + 12 = 62 pieces.

24. To minimize the number of pieces having Black colour (and without Pink colour) we need to colour only one surface in Black colour and that surface should have the least number of cuts. So, we paint the side with 9 × 8 = 72 rectangles Black (and we do not paint the other side). The Pinks then need to be painted in such a way that there are a maximum number of reductions from the Black pieces (due to Black and Pink). In the situation shown in the diagram, there would be 9 pieces at the top having Black and Pink and 9 pieces at the bottom having Black and Pink. Thus, the required answer would be 9 × 8 − 18 = 54.

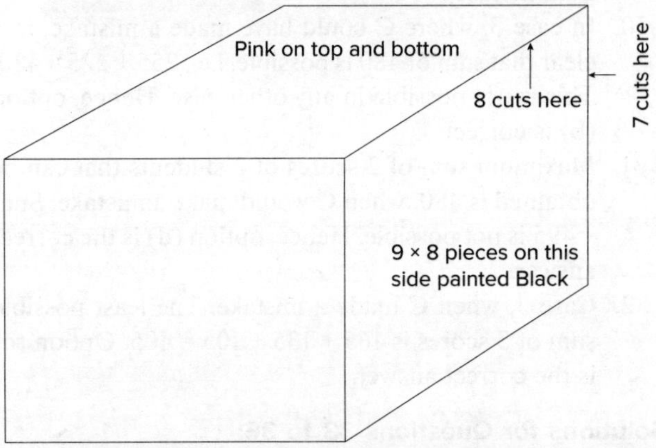

25. One could argue that Habibul fed the horse 2000 oranges at a time (for 1000 kms = 1000 Oranges each way) and sold the remaining 1000 oranges in the market and returned easily. As reasonable as a solution it may sound, it's incorrect. We understand from the question that the horse needs to be fed an orange for every 1 km it travels, so Habibul needs to feed it after every 1 km or during the journey of 1 km.

For this, you take up maximum load that this horse can carry (viz. 1000 oranges), travel 1 km, feed it with 1 orange and keep one for the way back. So you started from #0 km mark with 1000 oranges loaded on to the horse. You reach #1 km spot, unload 998 oranges and return. In this 1 trip #1 km spot has 998 oranges and the horse has been fed 2 oranges for 1 km to and fro. Now, you load another 1000 oranges, move to #1 km, unload another 998 oranges and return to #0 km spot. #1 km spot now has 998 + 998 = 1996 oranges. Now, you load the last lot of 1000 oranges and reach #1 km spot with 999 oranges (feeding 1 orange to the horse in the way). Total number of oranges now at #0 km spot = 0; Total number of oranges at #1 km spot = 2995 oranges; Total number of oranges consumed by horse to move all available oranges to #1 km spot ahead = 5 oranges. We observe that the horse had to make 3 trips. This will continue until we have 2000 oranges or just less oranges left with us.

We can move our horse like this from 0 to 200 kms. By this time, the horse would have consumed 5 × 200 = 1000 oranges and he would be left with 3000 − 1000 = 2000 oranges.

At #200 km spot with 2000 oranges left, we now start the similar trip, but now I would have to move to and fro just thrice i.e., to move further 1 km, I'd load my horse with 1000 oranges, unload 998 oranges at #201 km spot and return, pick another 1000 oranges and move them to #201 km spot. My horse would consume a total of 3 oranges in this process. We can continue this process until we have 1000 or just less oranges left with us (because for oranges less than or equal to 1000 oranges, the horse would have to make just a single trip forward, not to and fro. Hence, this is done until we are left with 2000 − 3 × 333 = 1001 oranges left. This means, we now have moved 333 kms ahead of #200 km spot viz. now #533 km spot.

We are at #533 spot with 1000 oranges loaded on the horse (1 orange would be left behind, since there is no point going back and forth for one orange). We now take a single trip towards the market, feeding the horse 1 orange per km on the way. Finally, we reach the market with 1000 − (1000 − 533) = 1000 − 467 = 533 oranges remaining. This is the maximum number of oranges Habibul could move from farms to market.

Now, if he sold these oranges at ₹ 1/orange, he'd make amount = ₹ 533. Hence, option (c) is the correct answer.

26. We want to use as little fuel as possible, so we can travel the maximum distance and try to minimise the number of cars we use, as we go along. Let's say we start with all 50 cars with full fuel (50 × 100 = 5000 km range in total). For each km, we lose 50 km in range. After two kms, we lose 100 kms leaving us with 4900 kms. This can be supported by 49 cars, so we drop one car

and distribute its fuel to the remaining 49 cars.As you can see for every 100 kms we lose in range, we drop a car.

Distance travelled:

50 cars = 100/50

49 cars = 100/49

48 cars = 100/48

..... and so on till 1 car is left.

Total distance = 100/50 + 100/49 + 100/48 + ... + 100/2 + 100/1 (Harmonic Progression) = 449.920533833 km

Nearest integer value = 450 km. Hence, option (d) is the correct answer.

Solutions for Questions 27 to 32:

For different scores of 5 students taken 4 at a time, we have 5 possible different values. These would be sums of (P, Q, R, S); (P, Q, R, T); (P, Q, S, T); (P, R, S, T) and (Q, R, S, T). However, in this case, we are given 6 different values. One of them must be surely incorrect (as given in the question too). Now, the sum of these values = 4P + 4Q + 4R + 4S + 4T = 4(P + Q + R + S + T). Hence, the logic of this question is based on the requirement that the sum of the five correct numbers must be a multiple of 4.

We are given 6 values of 6 people. Let us add all of these values.

= 660 + 780 + 690 + 720 + 630 + 750 = 4230.

Case 1: Assume, A made the mistake. In this case, the sum of 660 would need to be removed to get the sum of the 5 correct answers.

So 4230 – 660 = 3570.

This value should be a multiple of 4 since it represents the sum of 4P + 4Q + 4R + 4S + 4T.

However, the sum of the scores of 5 students in this case is not a multiple of 4 (3570/4 = 892.5). Hence, we can conclude that A did not make a calculation mistake.

Case 2: Assume, B made the mistake

4230 – 780 = 3450.

Then, sum of scores of 5 students = 3450/4 = 862.5 which is not possible, hence, B did not make a calculation mistake.

Case 3: Assume, C made the mistake

4230 – 690 = 3540

Then, sum of scores of 5 students = 3540/4 = 885 which is possible, hence, C could have made this mistake.

Possible individual scores are: 885 – 630 = 255;

885 – 660 = 225;

885 – 720 = 165;

885 – 750 = 135 and

885 – 780 = 105.

Case 4: Assume, D made the mistake

4230 – 720 = 3510.

Then, sum of scores of 5 students = 3510/4 = 877.5 which is not possible, hence, D did not make a calculation mistake.

Case 5: Assume, E made the mistake

4230 – 630 = 3600.

Then, sum of scores of 5 students = 3600/4 = 900 which is possible, hence, E could have made this mistake.

Possible individual scores are: 900 – 660 = 240,

900 – 690 = 210;

900 – 720 = 180;

900 – 750 = 150 and

900 – 780 = 120.

Case 6: Assume, F made the mistake

4230 – 750 = 3480.

Then, sum of scores of 5 students = 3480/4 = 870 which is possible, hence, F could have made this mistake.

Possible individual scores are: 870 – 630 = 240

870 – 660 = 210;

870 – 690 = 180;

870 – 720 = 150 and

870 – 780 = 90.

27. Maximum possible marks appear in Case 3. Where C could have made a mistake.
Here, maximum marks scored are = 255. Hence, option (b) is correct.
28. In the above question, C made a mistake. Hence, option (a) is correct.
29. Analysing the probable cases, it can be concluded that C, E or F could have made a calculation. Hence, option (d) is correct, i.e., D could not have made that mistake.
30. In case 3, where C could have made a mistake, it is clear that sum of 480 is possible, i.e., 255 + 225 = 480. This is not possible in any other case. Hence, option (b) is correct.
31. Maximum sum of 2 scores of 2 students that can be obtained is 480, when C would make a mistake. Sum = 495 is not possible. Hence, option (d) is the correct answer.
32. Case 3, when C made a mistake. The least possible sum of 3 scores is 165 + 135 + 105 = 405. Option (c) is the correct answer.

Solutions for Questions 33 to 36:

From the given clues, the following deductions emerge: Since each of the cities has a distinct integer for the number of years he has worked in them, it means that the number of years for the seven cities would be 2, 3, 4, 5, 6, 7 and 8 (in any order). This is because, with a sum of 35 and 7 distinct integers < 8, this is the only set of distinct numbers that can add up to 35.

His career would span from 1985 to 2019 and since he is working in his first city at least till 1990, it means that he worked for at least 6 years in his first city. Since Berlin < Hong Kong (5), the first city cannot be Berlin and has to be Dublin. Thus, Berlin becomes the last city.

We further see that Prague, Vienna have to be his fifth and sixth cities and then there is only one way to rationalize Istanbul before Paris and Paris immediately after Hong Kong.

Deducing about the number of years in each city, Vienna + Berlin (sixth and seventh city) has to be 8 years, since he started working in Vienna in 2012. This can only be done using Vienna as 6 and Berlin as 2. Consequently, Paris and Dublin have to share 7 or 8 years between themselves and Istanbul and Prague would share 3 and 4 years amongst themselves.

The correct order of locations where he worked can be seen in the following table:

City #	First	Second	Third	Fourth	Fifth	Sixth	Seventh
City Name	Dublin	Istanbul	Hong Kong	Paris	Prague	Vienna	Berlin
Number of years	7 or 8	3 or 4	5	8 or 7	4 or 3	6	2

The answers can be read off the table:

33. 2 years.
34. Option (a) is correct.
35. Option (d) is correct.
36. The correct answer is 7 years.

Solutions for Questions 37 to 40:

Based on the number of goals scored (and since, it is given that in any week, an individual player can score a goal only against one team), we can have a starting map for who scored against whom. For example, it is evident that Alan scored 4 goals against Bromwich in weeks 1 and 2, while the 7 goals against Everton in week 3 can only be scored, if Cryuff's 4 goals and Bergkamps 2 goals are included inside it. However, in this case, the 1 goal to complete the 7 goals against Everton in week 3, can only be scored by one of Alan, Di Stefano, Eusebio or Facchetti – we cannot determine the exact person who scored that goal. Also, we cannot determine against which team amongst Bromwich, Palmeiras or AC Milan, did the other three people score in week 3.

Thinking further, according to clue 2: 'From amongst Alan, Di Stefano and Facchetti, exactly two scored goals in weeks 2 and 3 against the same team, as they scored against in week 1.' There are three possibilities of who could be these two players.

Possibility 1: Alan and Di Stefano scored against the same team in all three weeks and Facchetti did not;

Or, Possibility 2: Alan and Facchetti scored against the same team in all three weeks and Di Stefano did not;

Or, Possibility 3: Di Stefano and Facchetti scored against the same team in all three weeks and Alan did not.

Checking for the first possibility (Alan and Di Stefano scored against the same team in all three weeks and Facchetti did not), we get the combination of tables as follows:

Tables under Possibility 1:

Name	Week 1	Week 2	Week 3
Alan (a)	4 (B)	4 (B)	1 (B)
Bergkamp (b)	2	1	2 (E)
Cryuff (c)	2	1	4 (E)
Di Stefano (d)	1 (AC)	1 (AC)	1 (AC)
Eusebio (e)	2 (E)	1 (E)	1 (E)
Facchetti (f)	2	2	1 (P)

Topic	Week 1	Week 2	Week 3
Chelsea (C)	2	0	0
Seville (S)	2	2	0
Bromwich (B)	4 (a)	4 (a)	1 (a)
Palmeiras (P)	2	2	1 (f)
AC Milan (AC)	1 (d)	1 (d)	1 (d)
Everton (E)	2 (e)	1 (e)	7 (b,c,e)

In this case, we cannot make out whether Seville conceded 2 goals against Facchetti in Week 2 or it conceded 1 goal each to Bergkamp and Cryuff in week 2. Likewise, the three 2's in table 1 week 1 cannot be clearly allocated to table 2 week 1. So, there are multiple possibilities for these allocations.

Under possibility 2, (Alan and Facchetti scored against the same team in all three weeks and Di Stefano did not), we can see that there is a clash amongst the clues, since if we continue placing the scorers logically against each of the clubs, we see that Di Stefano scored in all three weeks against the same team (AC Milan) too, which contradicts clue 2. The tables shown are what will emerge if you use all clues correctly, starting with possibility 2.

Tables under Possibility 2:

Name	Week 1	Week 2	Week 3
Alan (a)	4 (B)	4 (B)	1 (B)
Bergkamp (b)	2	1	2 (E)
Cryuff (c)	2	1	4 (E)
Di Stefano (d)	1 (AC)	1 (AC)	1 (AC)
Eusebio (e)	2 (E)	1(E)	1 (E)
Facchetti (f)	2 (P)	2 (P)	1 (P)

Topic	Week 1	Week 2	Week 3
Chelsea (C)	2	0	0
Seville (S)	2	2	0
Bromwich (B)	4 (a)	4 (a)	1 (a)

Palmeiras (P)	2 (f)	2 (f)	1 (f)
AC Milan (AC)	1 (d)	1 (d)	1 (d)
Everton (E)	2 (e)	1 (e)	7 (b,c,e)

Similarly, under possibility 3, there is again a clash as we want Di Stefano and Facchetti to have the same clubs in all three weeks. While we can put Di Stefano scoring against Palmeiras in all three weeks, we will not be able to allocate the same club for all three weeks to Facchetti. Hence, only possibility 1 exists in this situation.

The answers can be read off the tables under possibility 1:

37. Option (b) is correct.
38. We can determine the exact goals for Alan, Di Stefano and Eusebio. The correct answer is 3.
39. Facchetti would not score all his goals in each week against the same team. It is also clear that he has to score his single goal in week 3 against Palmeiras. Hence, he must have scored a maximum of 3 goals against Palmeiras, in all weeks considered together. The correct answer is 3.
40. DI Stefano scored 3 goals against AC Milan. Hence, option (c) is correct.

Solutions for Questions 41 to 44:

It is given that LP-1 and LP-2 are on the same floor. They can be on the ground or the first floor. Also, they are not on the same floor as LP-3. LP-4 is also not on the same floor as LP-3. Since LP-5 is fitted on the top (from statement (ii)), LP-4, LP-1 and LP-2 must be on the ground floor and LP-3 and LP-6 must be on the first floor.

From statement (iii), the weight of LP-4 is 10g. From statement (v), the total weight of LP-3, LP-6 and LP-5 must be 21g. This is possible in two ways. They can weigh 5g, 7g and 9g, or 6g, 7g and 8g. If they weigh 5g, 7g and 9g, then one among LP-5 and LP-6 must weigh 9g (since LP-3 has a lower weight than LP-6). In this case, LP-2 cannot have a weight greater than LP-5 and LP-6. Hence, the weights of LP-3, LP-6 and LP-5 must be 6g, 7g and 8g in any order. From statement (iii), LP-2 must weigh 9g. Hence, LP-1 must weigh 5g. Therefore, LP-6's weight must be 7g. LP-3 must weigh 6g and LP-5 must weigh 8g.

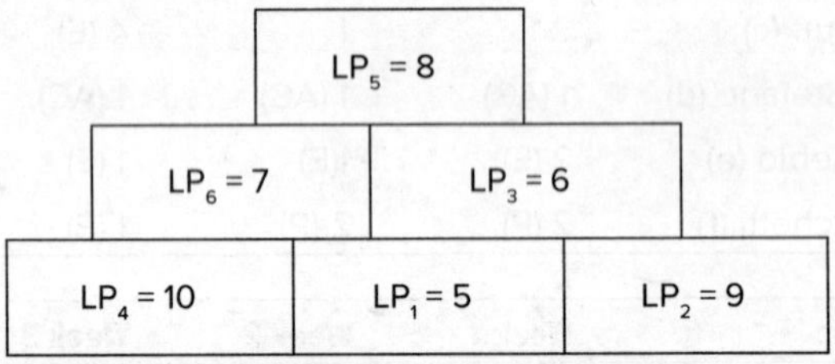

41. LP6 and LP3 are fitted on the first floor. From the options, (d) is correct.
42. Weight of LP5 is 8g, thus, option (c) is correct.
43. LP1 weighs the least, that is 5g. Option (a) is correct.
44. LP3 and LP6 carry on them LP5 which is 8g, thus, LP3 and LP6 both carry 4g each. Option (a) is correct.

Solutions for Questions 45 to 48:

Looking at the table, we realise that the number of questions correct for each subject is appearing twice for each student. Thus, if H,P,G,E and HI represent the number of correct questions in History, Political Science, Geography, Economics and Hindi respectively, it means that for Falgun:

$2 \times (H + P + G + E + HI) = 14 + 37 + 25 + 34 + 32 = 142$. Hence, the sum of number of correct answers for Falgn would be: $142/2 = 71$. Also since $H + P + G + E = 51$, we can find HI (the number of correct answers in Hindi for Falgun) as $= 71 - 51 = 20$. Then, we know $H + Hi = 25$, so, $H = 5$. Consequently, $P = 14 - 5 = 9$; $E = 32 - 20 = 12$ and $G = 37 - E = 25$.

Thinking the same way for all the five students, we can form a complete table of number of correct answers in each subject. The table will look as shown here:

Solution table for Questions 45 to 48:

Student → Subjects	Falgun	Garima	Hemant	Ishaan	Jaya
History	5	24	19	11	25
Political Science	9	13	14	35	11
Geography	25	15	22	12	22
Economics	12	8	16	32	10
Hindi	20	8	15	15	26

The answers can be directly read off the table.

45. Option (b) is correct.
46. Option (a) is correct.
47. Falgun has 71 correct answers, Garima has 68, Hemant has 86, Ishaan has 105, while Jaya has 95 correct answers. Hence, Ishaan had the highest score in the exam overall. Option (a) is correct.
48. There are 84 correct answers in History, 82 in Political Science, 96 in Geography, 78 in Economics and 84 in Hindi. Thus, Hindi and History are the two subjects with the same number of correct answers – and hence, the same number of wrong answers. Option (b) is correct.

Solutions for Questions 49 to 52:

49. Given value of the assets was distributed equally ∴ Aman, Arun & Ganpati received 70 lakh each. Since, Aman received the least amount and Ganpati received the highest amount in bank deposits ∴ The only possibility is Aman: 2 flats i.e., 30 × 2 = 60 lakhs and 70 – 60 = 10 lakhs in Bank deposits. Arun: 1 house i.e., 50 lakhs and 70 – 50 = 20 lakhs in Bank deposits. Ganpati: 1 flat i.e., 30 lakhs and 70 – 10 – 20 = 40 lakh in bank deposits. Thus, 40 is the answer.

50. Given value of the assets was distributed equally. ∴ Aman, Arun & Ganpati received 70 lakh each. Since, Aman received the least amount and Ganpati received the highest amount in bank deposits, ∴ The only possibility is Aman: 2 flats i.e., $30 \times 2 = 60$ lakhs and $70 - 60 = 10$ lakhs in bank deposits. Arun: 1 house i.e., 50 lakhs and $70 - 50 = 20$ lakhs in bank deposits. Ganpati: 1 flat i.e. 30 lakhs and $70 - 10 - 20 = 40$ lakh. As we see, Arun did not receive any flat. Thus, 0 is the answer.

51. Total amount distributed by the old man = ₹ 70 lakh (bank deposits) + ₹ 50 lakh (House) + ₹ 90 lakhs (3 flats) i.e. ₹ 210 lakhs + Gold coins worth ₹ 1 lakh each.

Ratio of total assets distributed = 1:2:3 and

Ratio of distributed gold coins = 2 : 3 : 4.

From these ratios, we see that

Arun received a third of the total property and a third of the gold coins. This means that his share is 1/3 (bank deposits + house + flats) = ₹ 70 lakhs.

Also, one child got all the three flats but not the house. One child other than Ganpati got ₹ 30 lakhs in bank deposits. From this, we can conclude that Arun cannot get all the three flats as his share is ₹ 70 lakhs + 1/3 of gold coins.

So, Arun should receive one house and bank deposits of ₹ 20 lakhs. This suggests that Aman should get ₹ 30 lakhs in bank deposits.

Therefore, Ganpati should get ₹ 20 lakhs in bank deposits. From this, all the three flats should be received by Ganpati. Let the number of gold coins received by Aman, Arun and Ganpati be 2x, 3x and 4x respectively.

From these we have, $(30 + 2x)/(70 + 3x) = 1/2 \Rightarrow x = 10$

So, total number of gold coins is 90. Thus, the answer is 90.

52. Same as above. Thus, the answer is 20.

Solutions for Questions 53 to 57:

The following set of deductions and filling the required table, leads us to the solution in this set of questions:

Deduction 1: We can start with a starting value of 'n' questions for Geometry and '2n' questions for each of Arithmetic, Algebra and Modern Maths. Hence, there are a total of 7n questions. Also, the lower limit for n is 4, while the higher limit for 2n is 16. However, since LOD 1 Algebra has only 2 questions, it means that 2n can at maximum be 14. This gives us 4 possible cases for the values of 'n' and '2n':

Case 1: 4,8 (total questions required $4 + 8 + 8 + 8 = 28$);

Case 2: 5,10 (total questions required $5 + 10 + 10 + 10 = 35$);

Case 3: 6,12 (total questions required $6 + 12 + 12 + 12 = 42$) and

Case 4: 7,14 (total questions required $7 + 14 + 14 + 14 = 49$).

Deduction 2: From clues (iii) and (iv), we can see that if we take the total number of questions in HOTS as 'm', then LOD 1 and LOD 2 would each have '3m' questions and LOD 3 would have 'm + 3' questions. The minimum value of m is 4, then $m + 3 = 7$ and $3m = 12$. This situation would require a total of $4 + 7 + 12 + 12 = 35$ questions. If we take $m = 5$, $m + 3 = 8$ and $3m = 15$. The total questions required would be $5 + 8 + 15 + 15 = 43$. The value of 3m cannot be more than 16 and hence, these are the only two situations to consider in this case. Of these, if we match them to the cases in deduction 1, we realise that the only situation possible is case 2 from there and $m = 4$, $3m = 12$ and $m + 3 = 7$ from here.

Deduction 3: The number of questions under HOTS will be 1 each for each of the subjects (since $m = 1$). Also, since LOD 1 Algebra is given as 2 questions, the only way in which we can reach $3m = 12$ for LOD 1 questions is to use 4 (for Arithmetic LOD 1), 4 (for Modern Maths LOD 1) & 2 (for Geometry LOD 1). Consequently, the LOD 2 and LOD 3 questions in Geometry have to be 1 each. Based on these three deductions, we can form table 1 for the solution of this question (with 6 unknowns marked as a, b, c, d, e and f.

Initial table will be as follows:

SUBJECT	ARITHMETIC (10)				ALGEBRA (10)				GEOMETRY (5)				MODERN MATHS (10)			
LOD	1	2	3	HOTS	1	2	3	HOTS	1	2	3	HOTS	1	2	3	HOTS
No of Questions	4	a	b	1	2	c	d	1	2	1	1	1	4	e	f	1

Further, we know the following: $a + c + e + 1 = 12 \rightarrow a + c + e = 11$. Hence, a/c/e would share the values of 4/4/3 in one of 3 possible ways.

Final table will be as follows:

SUBJECT	ARITHMETIC (10)				ALGEBRA (10)				GEOMETRY (5)				MODERN MATHS (10)			
LOD	1	2	3	HOTS	1	2	3	HOTS	1	2	3	HOTS	1	2	3	HOTS
No of Questions	4	a	b	1	2	c	d	1	2	1	1	1	4	e	f	1

SUBJECT	ARITHMETIC (10)				ALGEBRA (10)				GEOMETRY (5)				MODERN MATHS (10)			
Possibility 1 (using a = 4, c = 4, e = 3)	4	4	1	1	2	4	3	1	2	1	1	1	4	3	2	1
Possibility 2 (using a = 4, c = 3, e = 4)	4	4	1	1	2	3	4	1	2	1	1	1	4	4	1	1
Possibility 3 (using a = 3, c = 4, e = 4)	4	3	2	1	2	4	3	1	2	1	1	1	4	4	1	1

This question leaves us with a multiple possibility situation and the answers would have to be interpreted from the above table.

53. Each of options (a), (c) and (d) are possible. Only option (b) is not possible, since we do not get a situation, where we have 3 LOD 2 questions from Arithmetic and 4 LOD 3 from Algebra. Hence, option (b) is correct.
54. Under possibilities 1 and 2, the number of LOD 3 questions from Arithmetic are 1, while under possibility 3, the number of LOD 3 questions from Arithmetic are 2. Hence, option (d) is correct.
55. The number of LOD 2 questions from Modern Maths can be 3 or 4. Hence, option (c) is correct.
56. This question is referring to Possibility 3 in the solution table. In such a case, statements (i) and (iii) can be seen to be true. Hence, option (d) is correct.
57. This question is referring to Possibility 1 in the solution table. Option (c) is definitely false. Hence, option (c) is the correct answer.

Solutions for Questions 58 to 62:

We can solve this question by making a table for the various variables in the given question:

	Wallet	Racket	Radio
₹ 10 coins	(Prime number) 'W'	(not prime) 'R'	35
₹ 2 coins	Possibility 1: 19 Possibility 2: 29	Possibility 1: 35 Possibility 2: 25	C
₹ 1 coins	'N'	15	D
Total Price	x (such that x < y and x, y < 384)	y (such that y > x and y < 384)	384

In the table, x + y = 635 and the values of each of x and y have to be below 384, with x < y also to be obeyed. The other thing we need to remember is that all the numbers in the table have to be between 2 and 35. Also, W + R + N + C + D = 76, since the total number of coins is 180.

In the table, we have worked the values of the number of 2 rupee coins used to buy the wallet (say a) and the number of 2 rupee coins used to buy the racket (say 54-a), based on the condition, that the first number has to be prime and the second has to be non-prime. One should realise that one is in a multiple possibility situation in this case. First of all, we can start thinking of possible values of 'a' and (54-a) given that 'a' is prime and (54-a) is non-prime. There are possible values of these: Possibility 1: 19,35 or Possibility 2: 29,25. Coin: We derive these possibilities by thinking of 'a' as a prime starting from 19,23,29,31. The two instances, when we get (54-a) as non-prime is when a = 19 and when a = 29. Also, coin that values of a below 19 will not work as (54-a) would become greater than 35, which is not possible.

Next, we need to think of the fact that the total of x + y = 635 and the total payment made using two rupee coins is 54 × 2 = 108. Thus, the value of 10 × (W + R) + n = 512. The other constraints we are operating under in this situation are: 2C + D = 34 & W + R + N + C + D = 76 (since the total number of coins used is given to us as 180).

This leads us to another multiple possibility situation for the values of W, R, N, C and D. The way to think about this multiple possibility situation is that, N has possible values of 2, 12, 22 and 32.

CASE 1: If we take N = 2 & W + R = 51 (since 10 × (W + R) = 510): In the case of n = 2, we will be able to see that the only values that fit the given situation are: W = 23, R = 28, C = 11, D = 12. In this case, price of wallet is:

23 × 10 + 2 × 1 + 19 × 2 = 270 Or 23 × 10 + 2 × 1 + 29 × 2 = 290; Price of Racket = 28 × 10 + 15 × 1 + 35 × 2 = 365. Other possible price of racket = 28 × 10 + 15 × 1 + 25 × 2 = 345. Thus, in this case, the price of the wallet is 270/290, radio is 365/345. Also, the 384 for the radio is comprised of 35 × 10 + 11 × 2 + 12 × 1 = 384.

Other values that you might consider starting with W as a prime number will all get rejected. I have explained some cases of rejection here:

Cases rejected: N = 2, W = 17, R = 34, C = 9, D = 15. Rejected since the price of the racket is 34 × 10 + 15 × 1 + 25 × 2 = 400 (minimum) or 34 × 10 + 15 × 1 + 35 × 2 = 420. In either case, the price of the racket exceeds the price of the Radio. Similarly other cases rejected include W = 19, R = 32 (price of racket exceeds 385); W = 29, R = 22 (price of wallet exceeds price of racket).

CASE 2: If we take N = 12 & W + R = 50 (since 10 × (W + R) = 500): In the case of N = 12, Prime - Non-Prime values for W and R to be checked would be: W = 17, R = 33 (rejected as price of racket exceeds 384); W = 19, R = 31 (rejected since R is a prime). There are other cases that you would need to check if you follow this thought line, but you do not need to go into this thinking due to the reason explained below.

If N = 12 and W + R = 50; from W + R + N + C + D = 76, we have C + D = 14. But this is not possible, since 2C + D = 34 is not possible to achieve with C + D = 14. (given, of course that both C and D are positive integers greater than 2). Hence, we can reject the entire N = 12 case.

For N = 22, the situation becomes even more difficult to manage the values of C and D. Consider this thought: N = 22, W + R = 49 (since 10 × (W + R) = 490). Then, W + R + N = 71, so C + D = 5 and 2C + D = 34, not possible. Likewise, N = 32 is rejected and we reach the final solution in this situation, with only 1 possibility for N as 2, and within that possibility, we have two possible options for 'a' and (54-a).

Final Solution Table for 58 to 62:

	Wallet	Racket	Radio
₹ 10 coins	23	28	35
₹ 2 coins	Possibility 1: 19 Possibility 2: 29	Possibility 1: 35 Possibility 2: 25	11
₹ 1 coins	2	15	12
Total Price	Possibility 1: 270 Possibility 2: 290	Possibility 1: 365 Possibility 2: 345	384

58. The required difference is got from possibility 1, in the final solution table. 365 − 270 = 95.
59. It could be either 25 or 35. Hence, option (d) is correct.
60. There are 2 possible values for the cost of the wallet. Hence, we cannot determine this answer. Hence, option (d) is correct.
61. Option (a) is correct.
62. The correct answer is 11.

Solutions for Questions 63 to 65:

From the basic information given in the question, we know that either Q or R have to be given 4 coins and either P or S have to be given 1 coin. Also we need to keep in mind: Q > P and R > S in order to solve the question.

63. There could be two cases:

Case 1: Q = 4 and P = 2, then R = 3 and S = 1.

Case 2: Q = 2 and P = 1, then R = 4 and S = 3.

Of the four options, the only consistent solution is that S is always odd.

64. There could be the following three cases:

Case 1: R = 4 and S = 1, then Q = 3 and P = 2

Case 2: R = 4 and S = 2, then Q = 3 and P = 1

Case 3: R = 3 and S = 1, then Q = 4 and P = 2

In each of the three cases Q > P (which is in fact a basic condition in the question).

65. Q getting fewer coins than R, could mean one of the following cases:

Case 1: R = 4 and Q = 3, then

(a) S = 2 and P = 1 or (b) S = 1 and P = 2

Case 2: R = 4 and Q = 2 then S = 3 and P = 1.

In each of the above cases, the statements in options (b), (c) and (d) are necessarily true. Only the statement in the first option is not necessarily true as it fails in Case 2 above.

Solutions for Questions 66 to 67:

66. If we mix 8 grams of sucrose to 1 gram of saccharine, we would have 9 grams with a sweetness quotient of 683. The average sweetness would be 683/9 = 75.88 which is greater than 100 times the sweetness of sucrose. If we mix 9 grams of sucrose to 1 gram of saccharine, the average would be below 74; and hence, this is the required answer.
67. The average sweetness of the mixture as defined would be:

$(1 \times 0.74 + 2 \times 1 + 3 \times 1.7)/6 = 7.84/6 = 1.306$.

Thus, option (a) is correct.

Solutions for Questions 68 to 70:

68. In order to get to the correct option in this question, you need to try to disprove each of the options by thinking of possible values for the elements in S_1 and S_2.

Option (a), (b) and (c) would not be true in case we were to take the elements in S_1 to be 1 to 24, while the elements in S_2 as 25 to 50. Then if we change the signs of each element of S_1 we will get these values as -1,-2,...-24. It can be seen that neither of the first three option statements would be true, i.e., we would not have every member of S_1 greater than every member of S_2 [as stated in option (a)], we would not have *G* in S_1 [as stated in option (b)] and we would not have the largest number between S_1 and S_2 in S_1 [as stated in Option (c)].

69. Let the elements in S_1 be 1, 2, 3...24 and the elements in S_2 be 50, 49, 48...27, 26, 25. Then after interchanging a_{24} and a_{25}, S_1 would have (1, 2, 3, 4....22, 23 and 50) while S_2 would have (24, 49, 48, 47...28, 27, 26, 25). It is obvious that S_1 would continue to be in ascending order, while S_2 would

not continue to be in the descending order. Thus, option (a) is correct.

70. It is obvious that since every element of S_1 has to be made equal to or greater than every element of S_2, L would have to be made greater than or equal to G. For this the value of x cannot be less than G-L. Thus option (d) is correct.

Solutions for Questions 71 to 72:

71. After the GOTO instruction, the robot is given an instruction of WALK X(2) and WALK Y(4), after which it reaches (6,6). This means that x must be 4 and y must be 2. Thus, option (c) is correct.
72. If we are prohibited from using the GOTO instruction, we would need one WALK X and one WALK Y instruction. Thus we need 2 instructions to get to the origin.

Solutions for Questions 73 to 74:

73. Solve this question using options. If you try option (c) i.e. 30 days, you would get that they did yoga for six mornings and played tennis for 16 evenings. Thus on 8 days they did neither yoga nor played tennis. Hence, option (c) is correct.
74. The price per piece of bread would be 3 coins as the third traveller is paying 8 coins for his 2.66 loaves. Also the contribution of the first traveller is 2.33 loaves, while that of the second is only 0.33 loaves. Hence, the first traveller should get 2.33 × 3 = 7.

Solutions for Questions 75 to 77:

In order to solve this set of questions, you need to understand what the data in the tables mean. The basic interpretation of the table is that there are 6 children of height 115 cms or less and 11 children of height 120 cms or less. This also gives us that there are 5 children who have a height of above 115 cms but below 120 cms. Similarly there are 13 children having a height between 120 cms to 125 cms.

The other thing you need to understand about this situation is that since an older child is always taller and weighs more than a younger child, you would first fit all the least heights and weights with the youngest children.

Based on this understanding of the data in the table, we can move into the questions:

75. There are a total of 48 children aged below 9 years. Also there are a total of 45 children having a height less than 135 cms. Thus, all these 45 children would have been below 9 years of age. Hence 45 is the correct answer.
76. There are 40 children above 10 years of age. But there are only 25 children having a height greater than 150 cms. Thus, there would be 25 children who would have a height of over 150 cms and an age of over 10 years. We now need to see how many of these 25 also satisfy the criteria of less than 48 kg of weight. There are 9 children above 48 kg of weight. These should also be amongst the 25 we have earmarked above 10 years and 150 cms. Thus, there would be 16 children left in the category defined. Thus, option (a) is correct.
77. There are 55 students who are aged between 6 and 12. Also, there are 23 children who are above 12 years of age. Naturally these 23 would be in the highest weight categories from the top. So looking down the weights column, there are 33 children who are below 38 kgs and do not come under this category. So out of 67 children who are above 38 kgs, 23 would not be between 6 to 12 years. Thus, there would be 44 children in the category being defined.

Solution for Question 78:

78. The codes which will create a confusion would be: 16 and 91, 18 and 81, 19 and 61, 66 and 99, 68 and 89, 86 and 98: A total of 12 codes which will have confusion. Hence out of 90 two digit codes 78 would have no confusion.

Solutions for Questions 79 to 81:

79. The garden path is 15 metre long.
    In the second part of the journey, once they passed the azalea, A and C beat B by 1 metre. They are a half hour behind D, but remember that C rested for an hour. C would have beaten D by half an hour if she had not rested.
    Therefore, the slower speed is 1 metre in .5 hour, or 2 m/hr.
    That makes the first part of the journey 8 + 2 = 10 metre. The second part must be half as long, or 5 metre.
80. The best strategy is to not pick the first boy, then choose the next boy who is taller than the first. The probability is then 11/24 that he will pick the tallest boy.
    Let's call the boys: A, B, C and D, tallest to shortest. If any of them are the first to leave the house, then the probability of picking the tallest boy is 0, 1, 1/2 or 1/3, respectively.
    That results in a combined probability of P = (0 + 1 + 1/2 + 1/3) / 4 = 11/24.
81. Fanny and Gopal played in the 13th set.
    The total number of sets played = (15 + 14 + 9)/2 = 19.
    Harish played 9 sets and must have sat out 10 sets. Since no one sat out two sets in a row, he must have played and lost in all the even numbered sets and sat out all the odd numbered sets.

Solutions for Questions 82 to 88:

82. If you place a knight in every (black or white) square, then you can place the maximum number of knights with no knights threatening each other. There are a total of 64 squares in which, there are 32 squares each in black and white. So, the answer is 32.

83. Armani is 21 He is the tallest and squares numbers.
Birianni is 8. He is the thinnest and reverses numbers.
Chutanmi is 16. He is the shortest and divides numbers in half.

84. Deepika's car entry code is 39876.
Concentrate on the digits which have multiple potential matches per position because there are 10 numbers listed, but the access code is only 5 digits long. That means 5 of the random numbers in the list must be duplicates or triplicates so they can be ignored.
The first digit in random number list does not have any duplicates... It must be left to the end to solve.
The second digit has 4s and 9s duplicated.
The third digit has 1s triplicated and 8s duplicated.
The fourth digit has 3s duplicated and 7s triplicated.
The last digit has 1s and 6s duplicated.
Because the first digit has no duplicates, one or more triplicates must be used.
Because the 9th random number, 98174 uses both triplicates digits, we know that the answer cannot contain xx17x, but must be either xx13x or xx87x because we know that the other digit positions must all be duplicates. In other words, the solution will contain 1 unduplicated row (the first row), 3 duplicated rows, and 1 triplicated row.
The 5th random row, 63136 contains both the 1 and 3, leaving us with xx87x as the only possible solution.
By keeping track of which rows have been used, and which columns contain duplicates that must be used, the two duplicates are quickly found: x9876.
This leaves the 7th row which has not been used, which results in the final answer: **39876.**

85.

A	16
B	64
C and E	59
D	49

86. Your poker hand consists of
- 2 of spades
- 5 and 9 of hearts
- 4 of diamonds
- 8 of clubs

Since all suits are present, there must be at least two red cards and two black cards. And there is only one suit with two cards.
Since the hearts total 14 and there are no aces or face cards and all cards have a different value, the heart combination can only be (4, 10), (5, 9) or (6, 8).
The sum of the odd cards equals the sum of the even cards, therefore, there must be two odd and three even cards. The maximum of the odd cards is 7 + 9 = 16. The minimum of the even cards is 2 + 4 + 6 = 1(2). Therefore, the sums must be 12, 14, or 16.
The only combination of cards that meets all these criteria is the one shown above.

87. The factors of 18 being 36, 18, 12, 9, 6, 4, 3, 2 and 1 we can clearly visualize that the possible products for the three numbers to get a multiple of 36 are:
18, 2, 1 (sum of ages = 21); 12, 3, 1 (sum of ages = 16); 6, 3, 2 (sum of ages = 11); 4, 3, 3 (sum of ages = 10); 9, 4, 1 (sum of ages = 14); 9, 2, 2 (sum of ages = 13); 36, 1, 1 (sum of ages = 38); 6, 6, 1 (sum of ages = 13).
We further know that the sum of the ages is not enough information to identify the ages. This can only mean that the sum of the ages must be 13 - since that is the only sum of ages that still leaves confusion, once the sum of the ages is known (the confusion only gets resolved when it is known that there is an oldest child.

88. (a) Only one weighing is required as you can take 1 coin from the first box, 2 from the second, 3 from the third and so on till 15 from the 15th. One weighing will identify the box with 22 gram gemstones.

Solutions for Questions 89 to 92:

This is a puzzle based on quantitative reasoning- where you have to visualize the number of prizes of each kind kept in the boxes. Note: The two constraints we have to obey are:

(i) Total number of prizes is 100.

(ii) The number of type 'a' prizes is 1. Type 'b' is at least two times (can be more) - this can be interpreted as: Type 'b' can be anywhere between 2 to 33 prizes or 99 prizes. This is because, we can have a situation of 1 + 99 for a and b respectively to complete the 100 prizes. However, if we do not use 99 'b' prizes, then we would need to use 'c' prizes too, with the constraint that type 'c' would need to be at least twice the number of 'b' prizes. This, would not allow us to have: 1 + 34 + 65 for a,b,c respectively. However, distributions like 1 + 33 + 66, 1 + 32 + 67 etc. would be possible for a,b,c.

Hence, b can be between 2 to 33 or it can be exactly 99.

Based on this initial understanding, we can move to the questions:

89. We can have only 2 kinds of prizes with a + b being 1 + 99. Hence, the correct answer for this is 2.
90. The maximum prizes would be for the following distribution (such that, we use a multiplier of exactly 2, as long as possible):

Number of prizes	1	2	4	8	16	69
Type	a	b	c	d	e	f

Hence, maximum 6 prizes are allowed.
91. It can be seen that with 45 items of type 'c', there is no possibility of having a total of 100. For instance, 1 + 22 + 45 = 68. We cannot introduce 'd' in this, since 'd' requires to be at least 90 (given that 'c' is 45). Hence, option (a) is the correct answer.
We can, of course, check the other options to see that they are all possible. Thus: 1 + 30 + 69 allows option (b); 1 + 2 + 4 + 18 + 75 = 100 allows option (c); 1 + 12 + 27 + 60 = 100 allows option (d). Hence, option (a) is the only one, not possible and is hence, the correct answer.
92. From the information given in the question, it can be seen that there are 75 items of the type that are there in box 45. For the maximum possible types of items to be kept in the boxes, we will need to delay the use of 75 items to the latest possible, since obviously the type of item that is in 75 boxes, would be the last type. The maximum delay possible is for 1 + 2 + 4 + 18 + 75 = 100, where 'e' has 75 items. This means that there are a maximum of 5 types of items. Hence, option (a) is the correct answer.

Solutions for Questions 93 to 12:

Deduction 1 from the last line of the first paragraph: The total number of questions in the two papers combined should be a multiple of 6.

Deduction 2 from the second paragraph: Compulsory questions to be included–4 questions of 5 marks each, 3 questions of 10 marks each and 2 questions of 15 marks each. This would add up to 4 × 5 + 10 × 3 + 15 × 2 = 80 marks. That leaves us with a slack of 20 marks in each paper. There can be three ways of adding up to 20 marks using 5, 10 and 15 mark questions. These would be:

Possibility	20 additional marks created using	Break up of questions in the test (5 mark, 10 mark, 15 marks)	Total questions in the test
Possibility 1	5 + 5 + 5 + 5	8, 3, 2	13
Possibility 2	10 + 10	4, 5, 2	11
Possibility 3	5 + 15	5, 3, 3	11

Deduction 3: Both these deductions tell us that the total number of questions in MT + ET can be only 24. Hence, each faculty member created exactly 4 questions. We also know that ET has more questions than MT. Hence, MT = 11 questions and ET = 13 questions. This means that ET has 8 questions of 5 marks each, 3 questions of 10 marks each and 2 questions of 15 marks each.

Armed with these deductions, we can move into the clues 1 to 5. After using the direct information in the clues, we can make the table reach the following point:

Question #	MT (marks)	ET
1	F (5)	D (5)
2	F (5)	(5)
3	C (5)	C (5)
4	C (5)	(5)
5	A (5)	A(5)
6		(5)
7		(5)
8	E	E (5)
9		(10)
10		(10)
11	D (15)	(10)
12		(15)
13		F (15)

Note: We have inferred from clue 2 that F and C must have two questions each in the MT.

Next set of deductions:

Deduction 1: The only way to reach 11 questions for MT, given that A ends with her single question (the fifth one), is to take 2 questions each for B, E and D. Also, they would have to be the 6th and 7th questions for B, 8th and 9th for E and 10th and 11th for D.

Deduction 2: Since each faculty member has created a total of 4 questions each, we can conclude that: For ET, the number of questions of each are: A (3); B to F (2 each). The final table that emerges is shown.

Question #	MT (marks)	ET
1	F (5)	D (5)
2	F (5)	D (5)
3	C (5)	C (5)
4	C (5)	C (5)
5	A (5)	A (5)
6	B (10)	A (5)
7	B (10)	A (5)

8	E (10)	E (5)
9	E (15)	E (10)
10	D (15)	B (10)
11	D (15)	B (10)
12	Blank	F (15)
13	Blank	F (15)

The answers would be:

93. (d)
94. (a)
95. (a)
96. (a)

Solutions for Questions 97 to 100:

97. A sample matrix of 3 × 3 is shown in the figure. As can be seen it is possible to fill the matrix with only 4 numerals. Hence, the correct answer is 4.

1	2	1
3	4	3
1	2	1

98. A 5 × 5 matrix can also be filled using only 4 numerals. Please refer to the figure for the same.

1	2	1	2	1
3	4	3	4	3
1	2	1	2	1
3	4	3	4	3
1	2	1	2	1

99. One mistake does not improve the situation by reducing the number of numerals used – as each numeral is used in multiple places. Hence, the answer would continue to be 4 numerals. Hence, option (d) is correct.

100. In order to think about this, the first condition we realize is that since all the cells around a cell should have different numerals and we know that there are cells having 8 cells around them, the minimum number we can aspire for is 9. So, if we try to fit in the numbers in the cells so that we use only 9 numerals we get something like this. In order to do this, first fill any of the middle cells with 1 and put the numerals from 2 to 9 around it as follows.

Initial Figure

	2	3	4	
	6	1	5	
	7	8	9	

Then, try to fill in the remaining cells without using any new numerals. An intermediate arrangement is shown in the intermediate figure:

Intermediate Arrangement

5	2	3	4	2
4	6	1	5	6
9	7	8	9	7

Continuing the process, we get the final arrangement using only 9 numerals.

Final Arrangement

5	2	3	4	2
4	6	1	5	6
9	7	8	9	7
1	2	3	4	2
4	5	6	1	5

Hence, option (c) is correct.

Solutions for Questions 101 to 104:

Before embarking into the solution of this question set, there are a few things that you need to set inside your mind as the parameters on which you would be solving this set of questions:

(i) Each of the digits from 1 to 8 are used as the codes of 3 letters each.

(ii) 9 is used for the code of 2 letters. Thus, we can see that 8 × 3 + 1 × 2 = 26 means all the 26 letters of the alphabet are coded with the nine digits from 1 to 9.

(iii) The number codes are written in a non-decreasing order for each word.

Armed with this understanding, when you move to the words and the codes, you can move ahead with the following set of deductions:

PEACOCK	IS	DESIGNATED	AS	THE	NATIONAL	BIRD	OF	INDIA
5688999	35	1135556678	56	458	13666689	1334	79	13366

Deduction 1: From IS = 35; AS = 56, it is evident that S = 5. Hence, I = 3 and A = 6.

Deduction 2: From NATIONAL = 13666689 and OF = 79; we can conclude that O = 9 and F = 7;

Deduction 3: From Designated = 1135556678 and The = 458, we can see that H = 4 and T/E share 5 and 8. If we now look at National = 13666689, it is evident that since National does not have an E and it's code does not have a 5, hence E = 5 and T = 8.

At this point it might be a good decision to put our deductions simultaneously into the table above: S, I, A, O, F, E, T.

	PEACOCK = 5688999	IS = 35	DESIGNATED = 1135556678	AS = 56	THE = 458	NATIONAL = 13666689	BIRD = 1334	OF = 79	INDIA = 13366
Resolved	E = 5, A = 6, O = 9	I = 3 S = 5	E = 5, S = 5, I = 3, A = 6,T = 8	A = 6 S = 5	T = 8 E = 5 H = 4	A = 6, T = 8, I = 3, O = 9	I = 3	O = 9 F = 7	I = 3, A = 6
Unresolved	P, C, C, K 8, 8, 9, 9	NIL	D, D, G, N 1, 1, 6, 7	NIL	NIL	N, N, L 1, 6, 6	B, R, D 1, 3, 4	NIL	N, D 1, 6

The next set of deductions can be made based on the unresolved letters.

From the unresolved list for Designated, we get D = 1. From the unresolved of National we know that N = 6. Then coming back to Designated, we would know that G = 7. Also, from National we get L = 1. Then from the unresolved lists of Peacock and that of Bird, we would get that P, C, C, K would share the 8's and the 9's amongst themselves. However, there is another logic that would help us identify between 8's and 9's for P, C, C, K. That is based on the information in clue (iii), that the digit 9 codes only 2 letters, while each of the other digits code 3 letters each.

Also, from the unresolved list of Bird, we can see that B and R would share 3 and 4 amongst themselves. The final list after all these deductions would look as follows.

	PEACOCK = 5688999	IS = 35	DESIGNATED = 1135556678	AS = 56	THE = 458	NATIONAL = 13666689	BIRD = 1334	OF = 79	INDIA = 13366
Resolved	E = 5, A = 6, O = 9, C = 9, P = 8, K = 8	I = 3 S = 5	E = 5, S = 5, I = 3, A = 6, T = 8, D = 1, G = 7 and N = 6	A = 6 S = 5	T = 8 E = 5 H = 4	A = 6, T = 8, I = 3, O = 9, N = 6, L = 1	I = 3, D = 1	O = 9 F = 7	I = 3, A = 6, N = 6 and D = 1
Unresolved	NIL	NIL	NIL	NIL	NIL	NIL	B = 3 and R = 4 OR B = 4 and R = 3	NIL	NIL

The answers can then be read off the table:

101. L = 1. Option (a) is correct.
102. From the unresolved list of Bird, we know that B can be either 3 or 4. Option (c) is correct.
103. We know the two letters 9 codes (O and C) and the three letters 8 codes (P, K and T). Our information for the digits 1 to 7 is partial - 1 (D, L, one unknown letter); 2 (No letter known); 3 (I, 2 letters unknown); 4 (H, one of B/R and one other letter unknown); 5(E, S and one letter unknown); 6 (A, N and one letter unknown); 7(G, F and one letter unknown). Thus, the correct answer to this question would be 2. Option (c) is correct.
104. The letters in option (a) can be all coded as 2.

Hence X, Y, Z = 2 is a possibility. Checking the option (b), we see that S = 5 and E = 5. So, we cannot code both U and V as 5. Hence, option (b) is correct.

Solutions for Questions 105 to 108:

In order to solve this question, it is best to make a figure detailing how many people can reach each of the 25 individuals in the figure.

3	0	1	3	0
3	2	2	0	5
1	4	1	6	1
1	4	3	0	1
0	2	2	1	6

The solutions can be read off the given figure:

105. There are seven individuals who can be reached by only 1 individual. Option (c) is correct.
106. Clearly option (d) is correct, since an individual with height 1 would not have anybody having a height less than 1.
107. There are two zeroes in column 4. Hence, option (c) is correct.
108. Option (a) gets rejected due to the first and third rows; Option (b) can be rejected due to the third row; Option (c) is clearly correct since all the five rows have at least one pair of individuals who can be reached by the same number of individuals. Hence, option (c) is the correct answer.

Solutions for Questions 109 to 112:

Note: We will be using the acronyms A, B, G, J, K, M, P and T to denote the 7 friends

The following would be the diagram of the plane with the seat prices mentioned on various seats:

	Window		Aisle	Aisle		Window
ROW #	A	B	C	D	E	F
1	1000	1000	1000	1000	1000	1000
2	300	0	500	500	0	300
3	300	0	500	500	0	300
4	300	0	500	500	0	300
5	300	0	500	500	0	300
6	300	0	500	500	0	300
7	300	0	500	500	0	300
8	300	0	500	500	0	300
9	300	0	500	500	0	300
10	300	0	500	500	0	300
11	200	0	400	400	0	200
12	1000	1000	1000	1000	1000	1000
13	1000	1000	1000	1000	1000	1000
14	200	0	400	400	0	200
15	200	0	400	400	0	200
16	200	0	400	400	0	200
17	200	0	400	400	0	200
18	200	0	400	400	0	200
19	200	0	400	400	0	200
20	200	0	400	400	0	200
21	0	0	0	0	0	0
22	0	0	0	0	0	0
23	0	0	0	0	0	0
24	0	0	0	0	0	0
25	0	0	0	0	0	0
26	0	0	0	0	0	0
27	0	0	0	0	0	0
28	0	0	0	0	0	0
29	0	0	0	0	0	0
30	0	0	0	0	0	0

Once we have the structure of cost of the seats, we can start to make the following deductions:

Deduction 1: Exactly 3 friends must be sitting in the rows 1, 12 and 13. This is so because, if 7 friends have to pay 4600 in all, it cannot be achieved with only two people paying 1000 each – since if we use only two 1000 values, the other 5 would need to add up to 2600, which isn't possible since the highest priced seat outside the ₹ 1000 seat is the ₹ 500 seat. Even if all 5 friends paid ₹ 500 each, the total of their expense would only add up to 2500. Thus, we conclude that there are exactly 3 friends sitting in rows 1, 12 and 13 combined. The possible scenarios for paying 4600 for 7 people can be the following:

Friend #	1	2	3	4	5	6	7
Possibility 1	1000	1000	1000	400	400	400	400
Possibility 2	1000	1000	1000	500	400	400	300
Possibility 3	1000	1000	1000	500	500	400	200
Possibility 4	1000	1000	1000	500	500	300	300

Deduction 2: Since J, A and B are sitting in consecutive seats and paid different amounts, this can only occur if they are in the rows 10, 11 and 12 respectively (and in the aisle or the window seats). Further, from our list of 4 possibilities in the table, we can make out that they could not have been sitting in the window seats - since if we make them sit on the window seats, the extra charges J and A would pay would be 300 and 200 respectively - which is not part of any possibility of how 7 of them could pay 4600. Hence, J, A and B are sitting in the aisle seats of rows, 10, 11 and 12 respectively and must be paying 500,400 and 1000 respectively. This rules out possibilities 1 and 4 for the payments made by the 7 people, since possibility 1 has no friend paying 500, while possibility 4 has no friend paying 400.

Deduction 3: Since M was sitting next to J, M could be sitting in the aisle of row 10 or the middle seat of row 10. In the first case he would be paying 500, in the second he would not be paying any amount. Also, at this time we should know that we have placed J, A, B and their values being 500, 400 and 1000, we have exactly identified 3 values. At this point we still need to identify who were the two people who also paid 1000 each. Also, if possibility 2 is true, then we would also need to allocate a 400 and a 300. On the other hand if possibility 3 is true, we would need to allocate a 500 and 200. Note that in case M sits in the aisle - he would be paying 500 and hence we would be moving to possibility 3.

Deduction 4: At this point we are left with identifying the rows for G, K, P and T. We also know from clue 5 that G and K were sitting in the same row. Since P and T sit in different rows and the same lettered seats, at least one of them should be paying. Also, the row possibilities for them are 1-2; 10-11; 11-12; 13-14 or 20-21. Of these, we can rule out 1-2; 11-12 and 13-14, since in each of these cases one of them is paying 1000 - and if we use one of them as 1000, we would not be able to use 1000 for either of G or K and hence there would be no third person paying 1000. This in turn would then mean that we would not be able to create a payment structure of either possibility 2 or 3, leaving us with no valid cases to create a sum of 4600 paid by 7 of the 8 friends. So, P and T are sitting in either rows 10-11 (and both paying - in which case M in row 10 would not be paying) Or 20-21 (in which case T is not paying- and then M would be paying) Also, in all cases G, K sit in the same row and next to each other - means that they must be paying 1000 each (and hence sitting in either of the rows 1, 12 or 13).

At this stage, the payment values for the people whose payments we definitely know are: 1000, 1000, 1000 (for B, G, K); J = 500; A = 400. We are left with the task of allocating the values of the remaining two payments and the one person who did not pay - amongst P, T and M. Also, the remaining two payments are either 500 and 200 or 400 and 300. A quick look at the plane seat costing, shows us that we cannot allocate either 500 and 200 or 400 and 300 to P and T (if we need to make them sit in consecutive rows). Hence, T must be on row 21 and traveling free and P must be on row 20 and paying 200. In such a scenario, 500 is getting paid by M - and hence he must be in the aisle seat of row 10. All the deductions can then be encapsulated in order to solve the questions asked:

Person	Row	Seat Description	Payment
J	10	Aisle	500
A	11	Aisle	400
B	12	Aisle	1000
M	10	Aisle	500
G–K	1 or 12 or 13	One of them on Window, one on middle seat	1000 each
P	20	Window	200
T	21	Window	0

The answers can be read off from the above deductions:

109. Manik was sitting in row 10. Option (a) is correct.
110. Jayanta paid 500. Option (c) is correct.
111. Gargi paid 1000 for her seat. Option (d) is correct.
112. Tapesh did not pay for his choice of seat. Option (d) is correct.

CHAPTER 6

Generic Puzzles

Chapter Launchpad
Scan this QR code for an introductory video on Generic Puzzles

Reasoning puzzles are a favourite question type in all aptitude examinations. In the scheme of chapters on reasoning contained in this book, we have created separate chapters for specific kinds of puzzles which are often asked (like, arrangements, rankings, etc., which constitute the chapters prior to this one).

All other categories of puzzles–which cannot be specifically categorised as any of the foregoing chapters–you will get to see and practice in this chapter.

As the name suggests, questions on puzzles challenge you to match multiple factors (like name, colour of shirt, place of living, car model driven, etc.). The key skills involved in solving questions on puzzles include but are not limited to:

(i) The ability to make a relevant tabular structure for using the clues seamlessly: For example, suppose you have 5 people A, B, C, D and E wearing shirts of five colours- red, yellow, green, blue and white and drinking 5 kinds of soft drinks- Coke, Pepsi, Mirinda, Thums Up and Seven Up. The solution table structure would look like this:

	Red	Yellow	Green	Blue	White	Coke	Pepsi	Mirinda	Thums Up	Seven Up
A										
B										
C										
D										
E										
Coke										
Pepsi										
Mirinda										
Thums Up										
Seven Up										

In the table, you can see clearly that there is a direct correlation structure between each of the three 'variables' in the problem. More of this, you would get to see and experience as you move through the solved illustrations and the exercises that follow it.

(ii) The ability to order the clues in the correct order of usage (as explained in the theory of logical reasoning): This includes the ability to perceive the direct clues and use them first to set up the 'framework' of problem solving.

(iii) The ability to perceive what indirect clues are talking about – and how to use them;

(iv) The ability to convert clues written in language form into visual cues so that you do not need to read the text again and again. Also, converting the language clues to visual clues is critical for the purpose of being able to 'see' all the clues at one go.

Illustrated below are the solutions to a few typical questions on puzzles. We would advise you to first have a look at the questions and try to solve the same on your own before looking at the step-by-step process of solving the same.

WORKED-OUT PROBLEMS

Illustration 1 At a fancy dress party, people were asked to dress as an object, that represented their professions.

Mr. Abhijit, Mrs. Banerjee, Mrs. Chatterjee, Mr. Dipanjan De and Mr. Elangovan were among the guests. The costumes included a leaf, a pen, a fork, a camera reel, and a stethoscope.

The professions included a photographer, a gardener, a compounder, a teacher and a cook.

(i) Mr. Abhijit is a teacher.
(ii) Neither Mrs. Banerjee nor Mrs. Chatterjee was dressed as a fork.
(iii) None of the men is a compounder.
(iv) Mr. Dipanjan De is dressed as a camera reel.
(v) Mrs. Chatterjee is a gardener.
(vi) Each person wore the costume relevant to his profession only. E,g, the Pen was worn by the teacher, the camera reel by the photographer etc

1. Which person is dressed as a stethoscope?
   (a) Mr. Abhijit (b) Mrs. Banerjee
   (c) Mrs. Chatterjee (d) Mr. Dipanjan
2. What is Mr. Elangovan's profession?
   (a) Cook (b) Gardener
   (c) Compounder (d) Teacher

Solution: Putting the direct clues (i) and (iv) in the table, we get:

Male	Female	Female	Male	Male
Abhijit	Banerjee	Chatterjee	Dipanjan De	Elangovan
Pen			Camera reel	
Teacher			Photographer	
From clue (i)			From clue (iv)	

At this point, if we use clue (ii), it is evident that it must be Mr. Elangovan who is dressed as a fork. Also, using clue (v) (Mrs. Chatterjee is a gardener) completes the solution.

Male	Female	Female	Male	Male
Abhijit	Banerjee	Chatterjee	Dipanjan De	Elangovan
Pen		Leaf	Camera reel	Cook
Teacher		Gardener	Photographer	Fork
		From clue (v)		From clue (ii) once we know the details of Dipanjan and Abhijit.

Obviously, Mrs. Banerjee would be the compounder. The solutions are: 1. Mrs. Banerjee. Option (b) is correct. 2. Elangovan is the cook. Option (a) is correct.

Illustration 2 **Directions for Questions 1 to 4:** *Answer the following questions based on the information below:*

For admission into vacant seats of higher secondary classes, most schools prescribe an admission test. There is no uniformity in the nature of these tests, however, Anuja Sinha, Amit Agnihotri, Himesh Reshammiya, Mahima Sharma and Sonit Kala, whose parents had been transferred to Lucknow this summer and who were all seeking admission into Class IX, appeared in entrance tests of different schools. The number of questions in all these tests, happened to be different. Amit wrote an entrance test containing exactly twice as many questions as the test that Himesh wrote, Sonit wrote a test that contained 160 questions, but it was neither for admission into City Montessori School nor for Scindia School. Delhi Public School's (DPS) test contained 200 questions, but neither Himesh nor Mahima wrote this test. City Montessori School test had 120 questions, but it was not written by Himesh. The test that Mahima Sharma wrote had 25% less questions than the test Amit Agnihotri wrote, but it was not for City Montessori School and Scindia School.

Going Beyond the Book
Scan this QR code for a video explanation of Illustration 2

Anuja did not write Millennium School's or St. Mary's Convent's test. When all the tests are compared with regard to number of questions in them, St. Mary's Convent falls exactly in the middle of the list. Each of the five students wrote exactly one of the tests – the longest one of which contained 200 questions. There is no penalty for wrong answers.

1. Anuja Sinha wrote the test for admission in which school?
   (a) Scindia School
   (b) Sanskar Valley
   (c) City Montessori School
   (d) Delhi Public School
2. If Amit Agnihotri secured only 50 per cent marks in the test, each question carrying one mark, how many marks did he secure in this test?
   (a) 50 (b) 60
   (c) 100 (d) None of these
3. If both Sonit and Amit secured equal marks in their respective tests and the test, Sonit wrote carried 5 marks per question, how many marks did each

question in Amit's test carry? It is given that both Amit and Sonit answered 75% questions of their respective tests correctly. Wrong answers did not fetch any marks.

(a) 1 (b) 2.5
(c) 3 (d) 4

4. Which of the following combinations is true?

(a) Anuja Sinha - City Montessori School - 180 questions.
(b) Amit Agnihotri - Millennium School - 160 questions.
(c) Himesh Reshammiya - Scindia School - 150 questions.
(d) Mahima Sharma - Scindia School - 150 questions.

Solution: Reaction Tracker

With respect to the number of questions, in each test, it can be inferred that the number of questions are 200, 120 and 160. Two values are unknown and to compensate for them we have been given that the number of questions in the tests of Amit Agnihotri would be (2x), Himesh Reshammiya (x) and Mahima Sharma (1.5x). The starting table for this situation would be:

	Anuja Sinha	Amit Agnihotri (2x)	Himesh R (x)	Mahima Sharma (1.5 x)	Sonit Kala	CMS	Scindia	Millenium	St. Mary's	DPS
200			NO	NO	NO	NO	NO	NO	NO	YES
160	NO	NO	NO	NO	YES	NO	NO			NO
120			NO	NO	NO	YES	NO	NO	NO	NO
??					NO	NO				NO
??					NO	NO				NO
CMS			NO	NO	NO					
Scindia				NO	NO					
Millennium	NO									
St. Mary's	NO									
DPS			NO	NO	NO					

From the table it is clear that, DPS (200) and CMS (120) are shared between Anuja and Amit. This means two possibilities – Anuja 120 and Amit 200 or Amit 120 and Anuja 200. If we take the second possibility into account things would not work out because:

If Amit is 120, the missing numbers are 90 (25% less for Mahima) and 60 (Amit's test had twice Himesh's test). Then the number of questions placed in ascending order would be: 60, 90, 120 (CMS), 160 and 200 (DPS). This situation contradicts the condition that when all the tests are compared as to number of questions in them, St. Mary's Convent falls exactly in the middle of the list.

Thus, we must consider the other option, i.e., Amit had 200 questions and Anuja 120. Then the number of questions is 200, 160, 150 (Mahima), 120, 100. The table would now look as follows:

	Anuja Sinha	Amit Agnihotri (2x)	Himesh R (x)	Mahima Sharma (1.5 x)	Sonit Kapoor	CMS	Scindia	Millenium	St. Mary's	DPS
200	NO	YES	NO	NO	NO	NO	NO	NO	NO	YES
160	NO	NO	NO	NO	YES	NO	NO	YES	NO	NO
120	YES	NO	NO	NO	NO	YES	NO	NO	NO	NO
150	NO	NO	NO	YES	NO	NO	NO	NO	YES	NO
100	NO	NO	YES	NO	NO	NO	YES	NO	NO	NO
CMS	YES	NO	NO	NO	NO					
Scindia	NO	NO	YES	NO	NO					
Millennium	NO	NO	NO	NO	YES					
St. Mary's	NO	NO	NO	YES	NO					
DPS	NO	YES	NO	NO	NO					

The solutions are:

1. CMS. Option (c) is correct.
2. He would score 100 marks. Option (c) is correct.
3. Sonit and Amit would score 600 marks out of 800 (the total marks would be 800 because Sonit's test has 160 questions of 5 marks each totaling 800). Hence, Amit's score would also be out of 800 marks–4 marks per question. Option (d) is correct.
4. Option (c) is correct.

Illustration 3 Four engineers, designated as CE, SE, EE and AE, read a certain number of newspapers early in the morning. One of them reads four newspapers, another reads three newspapers, the third reads two newspapers while the fourth one reads one newspaper. Below are some additional facts regarding the names of these officers:

(i) Nahiri is not the EE.
(ii) Hari is the AE.
(iii) Nahiri is not the CE and he reads more number of newspapers than Lahiri.
(iv) The one who is the CE, reads more number of newspapers than Lahiri.
(v) The person, who is the SE reads the maximum number of newspapers.
(vi) Bahiri does not read two newspapers.

1. Which of the following statements is necessarily true?
   (a) Hari is the AE and reads two newspapers.
   (b) Lahiri is the EE and reads one newspaper.
   (c) Bahiri is the CE and reads three newspapers.
   (d) Nahiri is the EE and reads four newspapers.

Solution: From statement (ii), Hari is AE. From Statements (i) and (iii), Nahiri is not the CE or the EE. Hence Nahiri is the SE and reads 4 newspapers as from Statement (v). From statement (iv), Lahiri is not the CE; this obviously means that Lahiri is the EE and Bahiri is the CE. From statement (iv) and (vi), Bahiri reads three newspapers. As he reads more than at least one person, we cannot allocate one newspaper to him. Hence, Bahiri must read three newspapers. Hence, the final distribution is as follows:

Engineer	Name	No. of Newspapers
AE	Hari	2/1
CE	Bahiri	3
SE	Nahiri	4
EE	Lahiri	1/2

Hence, option (c) is the correct answer.

Illustration 4 Four brothers Rohan, Sohan, Mohan and Ganesh are at their annual family property fight sitting across a circular table. Their occupations are– author, biologist, chemist and doctor, but not necessarily in that order. Ganesh starts by setting the agenda of the meeting and after him the doctor gives a long discourse of what is right and what is wrong. Rohan is sitting across the doctor and next to the chemist. Mohan is silent throughout the meeting and the chemist speaks only at the very end.

1. The profession of Rohan is:
   (a) Author (b) Biologist
   (c) Doctor
   (d) Cannot be determined
2. Who among the following is the chemist?
   (a) Sohan (b) Mohan
   (c) Ganesh
   (d) Cannot be determined

Solution: The solution of the above question can be seen in the figure below. (note the interpretation of the last statement – Mohan was silent throughout the meeting is that Mohan spoke only at the end.)

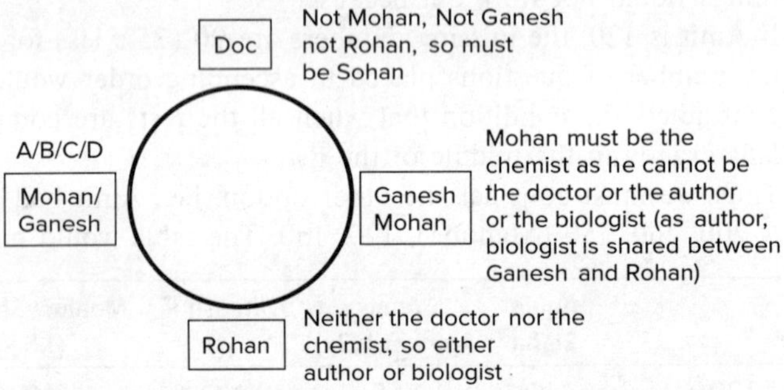

Based on the interpretations of the figure above, we can answer the questions as:

1. Rohan could be the author or the biologist. Hence, we cannot determine his profession. Option (d) is correct.
2. Mohan was the chemist. Option (b) is correct.

LEVEL OF DIFFICULTY (I)

Directions for Questions 1 to 5: *Six friends Pawan, Qureshi, Raman, Shyam, Tarun and Unnat study for CAT in Mindworkzz and work in different brands namely– Adobe, Bennett, Clarks, Deloitte, Evergrande and Falguni, and each wears a different coloured, company-sponsored shirt, viz., blue, green, pink, yellow, purple and red, though not necessarily in the same order.*

(i) The one wearing the blue shirt works in Deloitte and the one wearing a green shirt works in Adobe.
(ii) Unnat does not work in Clarks or Evergrande.

(iii) Pawan wears pink shirt and works in Bennett.
(iv) Shyam does not work in Evergrande and the purple coloured shirt is not sponsored by Clarks.
(v) Tarun works in Falguni and neither Shyam nor Qureshi work in Deloitte.
(vi) Evergrande does not sponsor purple or yellow coloured shirts and Raman works in Adobe.

1. Which colour shirt is sponsored by Clarks?
(a) Yellow (b) Blue
(c) Pink (d) Cannot be determined
2. Which pair is correctly matched?
(a) Red-Clarks -Pawan
(b) Red-Evergrande- Qureshi
(c) Green-Clarks-Raman
(d) None of these
3. Which of the following is true?
(a) Falguni sponsors green shirts.
(b) Shyam is working in Bennett
(c) Tarun wears red shirt.
(d) Red shirt is sponsored by Evergrande.
4. What is the sequence of companies representing Pawan, Qureshi , Raman, Shyam, Tarun and Unnat?
(a) Bennett, Deloitte, Adobe, Clarks, Evergrande, Falguni
(b) Bennett, Evergrande, Adobe, Clarks, Falguni, Deloitte
(c) Bennett, Adobe, Deloitte, Clarks, Evergrande, Falguni
(d) None of these
5. If Clarks and Deloitte decide to interchange the colours of the sponsored shirts, then which two persons will have to interchange their shirts?
(a) Shyam and Unnat (b) Pawan and Raman
(c) Tarun and Pawan (d) Qureshi and Shyam

Directions for Questions 6 to 8:
Five friends Praveen, Bhuvan, Charlie, Dhawan and Elangovan go hiking together every weekend.
(i) Each of them wear T-shirts of different colours–red, yellow, blue, white and green (not necessarily in this order).
(ii) Each one of them like to play different sports, *viz.*, Cricket, Tennis, Soccer, Pickleball and Padel.
(iii) Bhuvan, who likes to play Pickleball does not wear a yellow shirt. Charlie wears a red T-Shirt and does not like to play Cricket or Padel. Elangovan likes to play Tennis and does not wear a blue or yellow T-Shirt. Praveen likes to play Padel and Dhawan does not wear a yellow or green T-shirt.

6. What is the colour of Bhuvan's T-Shirt?
(a) White (b) Blue
(c) Green (d) Data inadequate
7. What sports does Charlie like to play?
(a) Padel (b) Soccer
(c) Cricket (d) Data inadequate
8. Which of the following combinations of person-colour-liking is correct?
(a) Dhawan-Blue-Cricket
(b) Elangovan-White-Tennis
(c) Praveen-Yellow-Padel
(d) None of these

Directions for Questions 9 to 14:
(i) Five MBA students–Arun, Bhavya, Cauvery, Dhritiman and Evaan have total five books on subjects–Organisational Behaviour, Business Mathematics, Accounting, Communication and Corporate Finance, which are written by authors Verma, Damodaran, Aswath, Sharma and Sinha. Each student has only one book on one of the five subjects.
(ii) Verma is the author of the Organisational Behaviour book which is not owned by Evaan or Arun. Dhritiman owns the book written by Sinha.
(iii) Cauvery owns the Accounting book. Evaan has the Corporate Finance book, which is not written by Damodaran. The book on Communication is written by Sharma.

9. Which of the following is the correct combination of subject-student and author?
(a) Accounting-Cauvery-Aswath
(b) Organisational Behaviour-Dhritiman-Verma
(c) Corporate Finance-Evaan-Sinha
(d) Communication-Arun-Sharma
10. The Business Mathematics book has been penned by whom?
(a) Verma (b) Sinha
(c) Aswath (d) Data inadequate
11. Who is the owner of the book written by Aswath?
(a) Bhavya (b) Evaan
(c) Arun (d) Dhritiman
12. Persons X, Y, Z and Q live in red, green, yellow or blue coloured houses which are in a sequence on a street. Z lives in a yellow house. The green house is adjacent to the blue house. X does not live adjacent to Z. The yellow house is in between the green and red house.
The colour of the house, X lives in is:
(a) Blue
(b) Green
(c) Red
(d) Not possible to determine
13. Five persons with names P, M, U, T and X live separately in any one of the following: in a palace, a hut, a fort, a house or a hotel. Each one likes

two different colours from among the following: blue, black, red, yellow and green. U likes red and blue. T likes black. The person living in a palace does not like black or blue. P likes blue and red. M likes yellow. X lives in a hotel. M lives in a:

(a) Hut (b) Palace
(c) Fort (d) House

14. The Banerjees, the Sharmas, and the Pattabhiramans each have a tradition of eating Sunday lunch as a family. Each family serves a special meal at a certain time of day. Each family has a particular set of chinaware used for this meal. Use the clues below to answer the following questions:

(i) The Sharma family eats at noon.
(ii) The family that serves fried brinjal uses blue chinaware.
(iii) The Banerjee family eats at 2 o'clock.
(iv) The family that serves sambar does not use red chinaware.
(v) The family that eats at 1 o'clock serves fried brinjal.
(vi) The Pattabhiraman family does not use white chinaware.
(vii) The family that eats last likes makki-ki-roti.

Which one of the following statement is true?

(a) The Banerjees eat makki-ki-roti at 2 o'clock, the Sharmas eat fried brinjal at 12 o' clock and the Pattabhiramans eat sambar from red chinaware.
(b) The Sharmas eat sambar served in white chinaware, the Pattabhiramans eat fried brinjal at 1 o'clock and the Banerjees eat makki-ki-roti served in blue chinaware.
(c) The Sharmas eat sambar at noon, the Pattabhiramans eat fried brinjal served in blue chinaware and the Banerjees eat makki-ki-roti served in red chinaware.
(d) The Banerjees eat makki-ki-roti served in white chinaware, the Sharmas eat fried brinjal at 12 o'clock and the Pattabhiramans eat sambar from red chinaware.

Directions for Questions 15 to 16: *Read the information and answer the questions.*

Amitabh, Bhagyashree, Chunky, Dharmendra, Ekta, Farhan and Govinda are students of a class. Each of them has a different favourite subject, *viz.*, Economics, Commerce, Zoology, Sociology, Statistics, Urdu and Computers, but not necessarily in the same order. There are two such students whose one sister each is there in the group. There is no other relation among the students. No boy likes Commerce or Urdu. Dharmendra, who does not like Sociology and Statistics, is the brother of that student who likes Computers. The student who likes Sociology is the sister of that boy student who likes Economics. F is a boy student, B is sister of A.

15. Which of the following is a pair of brother-sister other than Amitabh and Bhagyashree?

(a) Dharmendra and Govinda
(b) Dharmendra and Chunky
(c) Dharmendra and Ekta
(d) Data Inadequate

16. Which of the following is true?

(a) Dharmendra likes Commerce.
(b) Chunky, Bhagyashree and Dharmendra are girl students.
(c) The number of girls is more than that of the number of boys in the group.
(d) None of these.

Directions for Questions 17 to 19: *Read the information and answer the questions that follow.*

Five friends–Ramesh, Suresh, Tanveer, Umesh and Vikram–each present one paper to their class on Mathematics, History, Biology, Chemistry or Dermatology–one day a week, Monday through Friday.

(i) Vikram does not do Chemistry and does not give his presentation on Tuesday.
(ii) Suresh makes the Dermatology presentation and does not do it on Monday or Friday.
(iii) The Mathematics presentation is made on Thursday.
(iv) Tanveer presents his presentation, which is not on Chemistry, on Wednesday.
(v) The Biology presentation is on Friday, and not by Umesh.
(vi) Ramesh makes his presentation on Monday.

17. What day is the Chemistry presentation made?

(a) Friday (b) Monday
(c) Tuesday (d) Wednesday

18. What presentation does Vikram do?

(a) Chemistry (b) Dermatology
(c) Mathematics (d) Biology

19. What day does Umesh make his presentation on?

(a) Monday (b) Tuesday
(c) Wednesday (d) Thursday

Directions for Questions 20 to 24: *Eight students A, B, C, D, E, F, G and H study in eight different colleges namely–Motilal College, Nagarjuna College, Oregon International, Presidium, Queen's College, Ramjas College, Sriniwasan College and Thapar College not necessarily in the same order. They live in eight different cities Delhi, Mumbai, Chandigarh, Patna, Lucknow, Kanpur, Chennai and Pune, not necessarily in the same order. It is also known that:*

(i) G studies in Thapar College.
(ii) D who lives in Mumbai is not a student of Presidium.
(iii) C lives in Patna and studies in Queen's College.

(iv) H lives in Chandigarh and studies in Nagarjuna College.
(v) The student who studies in Motilal College lives in Pune.
(vi) E is not from Pune.
(vii) B lives neither in Delhi nor in Chennai and he studies in Sriniwasan College.
(viii) Neither E nor F studies in Oregon International and the student who studies in Oregon International lives in Lucknow.

20. Who lives in Delhi?
(a) A (b) E
(c) F (d) Can't be determined

21. Who studies in Ramjas College?
(a) A (b) D
(c) E (d) F

22. Which of the following is a correct combination of student- college- city?
(a) E- Motilal college -Pune
(b) H- Thapar college- Delhi
(c) E- Presidium - Delhi
(d) D- Ramjas- Mumbai

23. Which of the following combinations is not possible?
(a) E- Presidium- Chennai
(b) G- Thapar college- Delhi
(c) H- Nagarjuna- Patna
(d) E- Presidium- Delhi

24. If additional information is given that Thapar College is in Delhi, which of the following is definitely false?
(a) E lives in Chennai.
(b) Presidium is in Chennai.
(c) G lives in Delhi.
(d) G lives in Chennai.

Directions for Questions 25 to 28: *Five software engineers: Alan, Ben, Chris, Danny and Ervin participated in the International Tech Summit-2015 in Silicon Valley, California. They work in companies: Google, Microsoft, Facebook, Apple and Samsung, not necessarily in that order. They flew to California on different days of the week Monday, Tuesday, Wednesday, Thursday and Friday, not necessarily in that order. Their monthly salaries (in thousand dollars) are 11, 9, 58, 20 and 38, not necessarily in that order. It is also known that:*

(i) Danny's salary is second least in the group and he attended the summit on Thursday.
(ii) Chris does not work in Google and his salary package is 20,000 dollars per annum.
(iii) Engineers who attended the summit on Monday and Friday are from Samsung and Facebook respectively.
(iv) Ervin did not attend the summit on Monday.
(v) Ervin's salary was equal to the sum of salaries of the engineers who reached on Tuesday and Wednesday.
(vi) Ben neither worked in Google nor is his salary the least amongst all engineers.

25. Who works in Microsoft?
(a) Alan (b) Ben
(c) Danny (d) Cannot be determined

26. Which amongst the following is the possible sum of salaries of engineers working in Google and Apple? (figures are in dollars per annum)
(a) 49,000 (b) 47,000
(c) 58,000 (d) 69,000

27. How much does Ervin make (in dollars per annum)?

28. When did the engineer working in Samsung attend the summit?
(a) Monday (b) Tuesday
(c) Wednesday (d) Friday

Directions for Questions 29 to 33: *Five students namely– A, B, C, D and E got placed as entry level engineers in Microsoft, Yahoo, Google, Samsung and Facebook not necessarily in that order. They all have different heights, in the decreasing order of the person placed at Facebook, Samsung, Google, Microsoft and Yahoo. It is also known that:*

(i) The Monthly salaries offered by Google, Microsoft and Yahoo to their entry-level engineers are 23970, 23790 and 12130 INR.
(ii) One of the remaining two companies offered 11230 INR per month and other offered a sum between 12010 and 22880 INR per month.
(iii) The sum of the monthly salaries of A and C is same as the sum of monthly salaries of B and E.
(iv) E was taller than B and A was taller than C.

29. Who could be placed at Samsung?

30. Who could be placed at Facebook?

31. Who could be placed at Google?

32. What was D's monthly salary?

33. What was the value of the 5th (unknown) salary package (per month)?

Directions for Questions 34 to 38: *Answer the questions on the basis of the information given below.*

Five employees - Amritesh, Bhanu, Chirag, Dhiraj and Edwin - work in five different companies - A, B, C, D and E - not necessarily in the same order. During their last company trip, they visited five different places- Hyderabad, Rio, Japan, Karachi and Guyana, not necessarily in the same order. Each of the five places was hosted by five different persons among Pawan, Ishan, Dipen, Bhupendra and Tarun. It is also known that:

(i) Amritesh who works in E, visited Guyana.
(ii) Dhiraj went to Rio, hosted by Dipen.
(iii) Bhanu visited the place where he was hosted by Tarun.
(iv) Chirag went to Karachi where he was hosted by Bhupendra.

(v) The employee who works in B visited the place where he was hosted by Ishan.

(vi) The employee who works in C visited, Hyderabad.

34. Chirag works in which company?
(a) A (b) B
(c) E (d) Cannot be determined

35. Who hosted Amritesh?

36. Who works in B?
(a) Amritesh (b) Bhanu
(c) Edwin (d) Cannot be determined

37. Tarun hosted his guest in which of the following place?
(a) Guyana (b) Hyderabad
(c) Rio (d) Japan

38. Which of the following is a correct combination of Person – Company of Work – Place Visited – Host For?
(a) Bhanu - C - Hyderabad - Tarun
(b) Dhiraj - D - Rio - Dipen
(c) Chirag - A - Karachi - Bhupendra
(d) Edwin - E - Guyana - Ishan

Directions for Questions 39 to 40: *These questions are based on the situation given below:*

A, B, C, D, E and F are a group of friends from a club. There are two housewives, one lecturer, one architect, one accountant and one lawyer in the group. There are two married couples in the group. The lawyer is married to D who is a housewife. No lady in the group is either an architect or an accountant. C, the accountant, is married to F who is a lecturer. A is married to D and E is not a housewife.

39. What is E?
(a) Lawyer (b) Architect
(c) Lecturer (d) Accountant

40. How many members of the group are male?
(a) 2 (b) 3
(c) 4 (d) None of these

Directions for Questions 41 to 42: There are five machines A, B, C, D and E situated on a straight line at distances of 10 metres, 20 metres, 30 metres, 40 metres and 50 metres respectively from the origin of the line. A robot is stationed at the origin of the line. The robot serves the machines with raw material whenever a machine becomes idle. All the raw material is located at the origin. The robot is in an idle state at the origin at the beginning of a day. As soon as one or more machines become idle, they send messages to the robot-station and the robot starts and serves all the machines from which it received messages. If a message is received at the station while the robot is away from it, the robot takes notice of message only when it returns to the station. While moving, it serves the machines in the sequence in which they are encountered, and then returns to the origin, If any messages are pending at the station when it returns, it repeats the process again. Otherwise, it remains idle at the origin till the next message(s) is (are) received.

41. Suppose on a certain day, machines A and D have sent the first two messages to the origin at the beginning of the first second, and C has sent a message at the beginning of the 5th second and B at the beginning of the 6th second, and E at the beginning of the 10th second. How much distance in metres has the robot travelled since the beginning of the day, when it notices the message of E? Assume that the speed of movement of the robot is 10 metres per second.
(a) 140 (b) 80
(c) 340 (d) 360

42. Suppose there is a second station with raw material for the robot at the other extreme of the line which is 60 metres from the origin, that is, 10 metres from E. After finishing the services in a trip, the robot returns to the nearest station. If both stations are equidistant, it chooses the origin as the station to return to. Assuming that both stations receive the messages sent by the machines and that all the other data remains the same, what would be the answer to the above question?
(a) 120 (b) 140
(c) 340 (d) 70

Directions for Question 43:

43. There is a vertical stack of books marked 1, 2, and 3 on Table-A, with 1 at the bottom and 3 on top. These are to be placed vertically on Table-B with 1 at the bottom and 2 on the top, by making a series of moves from one table to the other. During a move, the topmost book, or the topmost two books, or all the three, can be moved from one of the tables to the other. If there are any books on the other table, the stack being transferred should be placed on top of the existing books, without changing the order of books in the stack that is being moved in that move. If there are no books on the other table, the stack is simply placed on the other table without disturbing the order of books in it. What is the minimum number of moves in which the above task can be accomplished?
(a) One (b) Two
(c) Three (d) Four

Directions for Questions 44 to 46: *Read the three problems given below and choose the answer from among the four given choices.*

44. Persons X, Y, Z and Q live in red, green, yellow or blue coloured houses placed in a sequence on a street. Z lives in a yellow house. The green house is adjacent to the blue house. X does not live adjacent to Z. The yellow house is in between the green and red houses. The colour of the house X lives in is

(a) blue
(b) green
(c) red
(d) not possible to determine

45. Five persons with names P, M, U, T and X live separately in any one of the following: A palace, a hut, a fort, a house or a hotel. Each one likes two different colours from among the following blue, black, red, yellow and green. U likes red and blue. T likes black. The person living in a palace does not like black or blue. P likes blue and red. M likes yellow. X lives in a hotel. M lives in a

(a) hut (b) palace
(c) fort (d) house

46. There are ten animals–two each of lion, panther, bison, bear, and deer, in a zoo. The enclosures in the zoo are named X, Y, Z, P and Q and each enclosure is allotted to one of the following attendants Jack, Mohan, Shalini, Suman and Rita. Two animals of different species are housed in each enclosure. A lion and a deer cannot be together. A panther cannot be with either a deer or a bison. Suman attends to animals from among bison, deer, bear and panther only. Mohan attends to a lion and a panther. Jack does not attend to deer, lion or bison. X, Y and Z are allotted to Mohan, Jack and Rita respectively. X and Q enclosures have one animal of the same species. Z and P have the same pair of animals. The animals attended by Shalini are

(a) Bear and bison (b) Bison and deer
(c) Bear and lion (d) Bear and panther

Directions for Question 47:

47. In a family gathering there are two males who are grandfathers and four males who are fathers. In the same gathering there are two females who are grandmothers and four females who are mothers. There is at least one grandson or a granddaughter present in this gathering. There are two husband wife pairs in this group. These can either be a grandfather and a grandmother, or a father and a mother. The single grandfather (whose wife is not present) has two grandsons and a son present. The single grandmother (whose husband is not present) has two grand daughters and a daughter present. A grandfather or a grandmother present with their spouses does not have any grandson or granddaughter present. What is the minimum number of people present in this gathering?

(a) 10 (b) 12
(c) 14 (d) 16

Directions for Questions 48 to 49: *Answer the questions independent of each other.*

48. While Balbir had his back turned, a dog ran into his butcher shop, snatched a piece of meat off the counter and ran out. Balbir was mad when he realised what had happened. He asked three other shopkeepers, who had seen the dog, to describe it. The shopkeepers really didn't want to help Balbir. So each of them made a statement which contained one truth and one lie.

A. Shopkeeper Number 1 said: "The dog had black hair and a long tail."
B. Shopkeeper Number 2 said: "The dog had a short tail and wore a collar."
C. Shopkeeper Number 3 said: "The dog had white hair and no collar."

Based on the above statements, which of the following could be a correct description?

(a) The dog had white hair, short tail and no collar.
(b) The dog had white hair, long tail and a collar.
(c) The dog had black hair, long tail and a collar.
(d) The dog had black hair, long tail and no collar.

49. Mrs. Ranga has three children and has difficulty remembering their ages and the months of their birth. The clues below may help her remember.

A. The boy, who was born in June, is 7 years old.
B. One of the children is 4 years old, but is not Anshuman.
C. Vaibhav is older than Supriya.
D. One of the children was born in September but it was not Vaibhav.
E. Supriya's birthday is in April.
F. The youngest child is only 2 years old.

Based on the above clues, which one of the following statements is true?

(a) Vaibhav is the oldest, followed by Anshuman who was born in September, and the youngest is Supriya who was born in April.
(b) Anshuman is the oldest being born in June, followed by Supriya who is 4 years old, and the youngest is Vaibhav who is 2 years old.
(c) Vaibhav is the oldest being 7 years old, followed by Supriya who was born in April, and the youngest is Anshuman who was born in September.
(d) Supriya is the oldest, who was born in April, followed by Vaibhav who was born in June, and Anshuman who was born in September.

Directions for Question 50: *In each question there are two statements A and B.*

Choose (a): if the question can be answered by one of the statements alone but not by the other.

Choose (b): if the question can be answered by using either statement alone.

Choose (c): if the question can be answered by using both the statements together but cannot be answered using either statement alone.

Choose (d): if the question cannot be answered even by using both the statements A and B.

50. F and M are father and mother of S, respectively. S has four uncles and three aunts. F has two siblings. The siblings of F and M are unmarried. How many brothers does M have?
(a) F has two brothers.
(b) M has five siblings.

Directions for Questions 51 to 53: *Answer the questions on the basis of the information given below.*

A, B, C, D, E and F are a group of friends. There are two housewives, one professor, one engineer, one accountant and one lawyer in the group. There are only two married couples in the group. The lawyer is married to D, who is a housewife. No woman in the group is either an engineer or an accountant. C, the accountant, is married to F, who is a professor. A is married to a housewife. E is not a housewife.

51. Which of the following is one of the married couples?
(a) A and B (b) B and E
(c) D and E (d) A and D

52. What is E's profession?
(a) Engineer (b) Lawyer
(c) Professor (d) Accountant

53. How many members of the group are males?
(a) 2 (b) 2
(c) 3 (d) Can't be determined

Directions for Question 54: *The question given below is followed by two statements, A and B. Answer the question using the following instructions:*

Choose (a): if the question can be answered by using statement A alone but not by using B alone.

Choose (b): if the question can be answered by using statement B alone but not by using A alone.

Choose (c): if the question can be answered by using either statement alone.

Choose (d): if the question can be answered by using both the statements together but not by either Statement alone.

54. In a cricket match, the 'man of the match' award is given to the player scoring the highest number of runs. In case of a tie, the player (out of those locked in the tie) who has taken the higher number of catches is chosen. Even thereafter if there is a tie, the player (out of those locked in the tie) who has dropped fewer catches is selected. Aakash, Biplab and Chirag, who were contenders for the award dropped at least one catch each. Biplab dropped 2 catches more than Aakash did, scored 50, and took 2 catches. Chirag got two chances to catch and dropped both. Who was the 'man of the match'?
(a) Chirag made 15 runs less than both Aakash and Biplab.
(b) The catches dropped by Biplab are 1 more than the catches taken by Aakash.

Directions for Question 55:

55. Divayabh gave an application for a new passport to the clerk on Monday afternoon. Next day was a holiday. So the clerk cleared the papers on the next working day on resumption of duty. The senior clerk checked it on the same day but forwarded it to the head clerk on the next day. The head clerk decided to dispose the case on the subsequent day. On which of the following days was the case put up to the head clerk by the senior clerk?
(a) Wednesday (b) Thursday
(c) Friday (d) None of these

LEVEL OF DIFFICULTY (II)

Directions for Questions 1 to 4: Seven friends P, Q, R, S, T, U and V have come to Connaught Place to enquire for CAT classes at Mindworkzz. Five of them have to go back to their homes via the Rajiv Chowk metro station. The friends who have to go back, their houses are in five different localities–Karol Bagh, Hauz Khas, Khan Market, Dwarka and Janakpuri.

(i) Five of them are Athletes and each of them specialises in one of the following sports: Long Jump, Javelin Throw, High Jump, Pole Vault and Shot Put.

(ii) T, an Athlete who is going to Khan Market, specialises in neither Shot Put nor High Jump. V is a specialist in Pole Vault and is leaving for Karol Bagh. U is an athlete but is not going to one of the five places.
(iii) Q is an athlete who specialises in Javelin Throw but has come to the metro station to see off his friends. P is an athlete but does not specialise in High Jump and is travelling to one of the destinations but not to Dwarka or Janakpuri.

1. The one who is going to travel to Khan Market is:
   (a) Not an Athlete
   (b) Specialises in Long Jump
   (c) Specialises in Pole Vault
   (d) Specialises in Shot Put
2. Who among the following specialises in High Jump?
   (a) S (b) P
   (c) U (d) V
3. R is an athlete in which Sport?
   (a) Shot Put
   (b) High Jump
   (c) Either Shot Put or High Jump
   (d) He is not an athlete
4. Who is travelling to Dwarka?
   (a) P (b) R
   (c) S (d) Data inadequate

Directions for Questions 5 to 9: Arnav, Bhavna, Chanda, Devesh, Enakshi, Faisal and Govind are seven persons who travel to office everyday in a particular train which stops at five stations–Depot Station, GNIDA Office, Delta 1, Alpha 1 and Pari Chowk respectively, after it leaves the base station.

(i) Three among them get in the train at the base station.
(ii) Devesh gets down at the station next to the station at which Faisal gets down.
(iii) Bhavna does not get down either with Arnav or Enakshi.
(iv) Govind alone gets in at Delta - 1 and gets down with Chanda after having passed one station.
(v) Arnav travels between only two consecutive stations and gets down at Pari Chowk.
(vi) None of them gets in at GNIDA office
(vii) Chanda gets in with Faisal but does not get in with either Bhavna or Devesh.
(viii) Enakshi gets in with two others and gets down alone after Devesh
(ix) Bhavna and Devesh work in the same office and they get down together at Delta -1.
(x) None of them gets down at Depot Station.

5. At which station does Enakshi get down?
   (a) GNIDA Office (b) Delta - 1
   (c) Alpha - 1 (d) Data inadequate
6. At which station do Chanda and Faisal get in?
   (a) Depot Station (b) GNIDA
   (c) Delta -1 (d) Data inadequate
7. At which station do Bhavna and Devesh get in?
   (a) Depot Station (b) Base station
   (c) Delta- 1 (d) Data inadequate
8. After how many stations does Enakshi get down?
   (a) One (b) Two
   (c) Four (d) None of these
9. Enakshi gets down how many stations after Faisal gets down?
   (a) Next station (b) One
   (c) Two (d) None of these

Directions for Questions 10 to 13: *Five friends went to an exhibition. At a shooting stall there are three things to be shot at– balloons, coins and needles. The number of balloons shot are 1, 4, 5, 6 and 8, while the number of coins shot are 0, 1, 2, 4 and 6.*

(i) The number of coins shot by A is three times the number of coins shot by the person who shot 4 balloons.
(ii) Three persons, including the one who shot four coins, did not shoot any needle.
(iii) B did not shoot any needle.
(iv) The one who shot one balloon did not shoot any needle or coin. Further, he was not C.
(v) D shot balloons and coins but no needle.
(v) C who did not shoot any needle, shot half as many coins as the person who shot twice as many balloons as he did.
(vii) E shot two more balloons than A, but A shot two more coins than E.

10. Which of the following is true?
    (a) C shot 8 balloons and 4 coins but no needles.
    (b) The person who shot 5 balloons and one coin shot some needles.
    (c) The person who shot an equal number of balloons and coins also shot needles.
    (d) The person who shot 4 balloons and 2 coins also shot needles.
11. Which of these is correct?
    (a) D shot 5 balloons (b) A shot 8 balloons
    (c) E shot 1 balloon (d) E shot 6 balloons
12. Which of the following is true?
    (a) B shot 2 coins (b) C shot 4 coins
    (c) A shot 6 coins (d) D shot 4 coins
13. The person who shot an equal number of coins and balloons is:
    (a) A (b) B
    (c) C (d) D

Directions for Questions 14 to 15: *The jailor of XYZ jail had 6 fruits–3 oranges, 2 apples and 1 pineapple. Four* *prisoners–101, 102, 103 and 104 are lined up one behind the other; the jailor helps them put the fruit on their head so that they cannot see the fruit kept on their head. Prisoner number 101 can see the fruit kept on the heads of 102, 103 and 104. Prisoner number 102 can see the fruit kept on 103's and 104's head. 103 can see the fruit kept on 104's head. 104 cannot see any of the fruits, since he is at the front of the line.*

Now, the jailor asks the prisoners 101, 102 and 103 to tell the name of the fruit kept on their head. Neither of them could reply.

14. What was the fruit on prisoner number 104's head?
(a) Orange (b) Apple
(c) Pineapple (d) Cannot be determined

15. Which of the following is definitely false?
(a) Prisoner number 101 did not see two apples and one pineapple.
(b) Prisoner number 102 did not see one apple and one pineapple or two apples.
(c) Prisoner number 103 did not see pineapple or apple on prisoner number 104's head.
(d) All are true.

Directions for Questions 16 to 20: *Four couples decided to play Holi. Each couple used three different colours. No two couples used the same combination of colours.*

Asha, Bhavna, Chanchal and Divya are females whereas Pradeep, Qartar, Rajeev and Sanjay are males.

The colours they use are red, green, yellow and black.

High Yield Questions

Scan this QR code to access a video explanation for questions 16-20

(i) Chanchal, who is not the wife of Sanjay, used red colour.
(ii) Pradeep's wife used yellow and black colours but Qartar's wife used only one of these colours.
(iii) Asha is not the wife of Pradeep or Sanjay.
(iv) Bhavna and Sanjay's wife both used red and yellow colours.

16. Who among the following is Asha's husband?
(a) Pradeep (b) Qartar
(c) Rajeev (d) Data inadequate

17. Who is Qartar's wife?
(a) Asha (b) Chanchal
(c) Divya (d) Data inadequate

18. Which of the following is not correctly paired?

	Person	Colours
(a)	Qartar	Green, Yellow, and Black
(b)	Pradeep	Red, Yellow and Black
(c)	Rajeev	Green, Yellow and Black
(d)	All of these	

19. Which of the following couples are incorrectly matched?
i. Asha and Rajeev
ii. Bhavna and Pradeep
iii. Chanchal and Sanjay
iv. Divya and Qartar
(a) Both (i) and (ii)
(b) All (i), (ii) and (iii)
(c) Both (iii) and (iv)
(d) All (ii), (iii) and (iv)

20. Which of the following is correctly matched?

	Person	Colours
(a)	Asha	Red, Yellow and Black
(b)	Bhavna	Green, Yellow and Black
(c)	Chanchal	Red, Green and Black
(d)	Divya	Yellow, Red and Black

Directions for Questions 21 to 25: *Abhay, Balbir, Chandan, Dinesh and Eklakh are alumni of the IAS Academy in Mussoorie. They are in Mussoorie to attend an alumni meet along with their wives Priya, Quindal, Riya, Shailja and Tulsi (not necessarily in the given order). They stay in the guest room of the academy in rooms numbered from 101 to 105. One interesting thing is that each couple's wedding anniversary is on the coming Friday.*

High Yield Questions

Scan this QR code to access a video explanation for questions 21-25

(i) No two married couples were married in the same year.
(ii) Balbir whose wife is not Shailja was married three-fourths of as many years ago as Dinesh.
(iii) Eklakh is staying in room number 103.
(iv) Priya was married five years before Abhay and three years before Eklakh.
(v) Only Shailja's room is in-between Abhay's and Eklakh's room.
(vi) Abhay, who was married before Shailja, was married five years after Chandan got married.
(vii) The couple staying in room number 101 got married 10 years before the couple staying in room 104.
(viii) Quindal is staying in room number 102.
(ix) Tulsi was married before Riya and she was married 12 years before Quindal got married.

Based on the above information, answer questions 21 to 25:

21. Who is the husband of Riya?
(a) Chandan (b) Abhay
(c) Balbir (d) Data inadequate

22. Who is celebrating the silver jubilee of his marriage anniversary?
(a) Chandan (b) Abhay
(c) Balbir (d) Data inadequate

23. Who is the wife of Balbir?
(a) Riya (b) Quindal
(c) Shailja (d) Data inadequate

24. If rooms are allotted on the basis of their married years, then which room number does not need shifting of its occupants? (105 is allotted to couples of maximum married years and 101 is allotted to couples of least married years).
(a) 101 (b) 103
(c) 104 (d) All rooms need a shift

25. For how many years has Eklakh enjoyed his married life?
(a) 30
(b) 27
(c) 25
(d) Data inadequate

Directions for Questions 26 to 27: *Answer the questions by studying the information given below.*

Five colleagues met at the party. While chatting that night they discovered that each of them has a favourite TV show that airs one night during the week. By coincidence, each of them loves a different show, each of which airs on a different night and channel. Given below are a few clues about the full name of each colleague, the genre their favourite show is in, the night each show airs and the channel the show airs on (one of the channel is Channel 6).

(a) Manmohan didn't watch a show on Friday night. Mr. Obama watched his favourite show on Channel 21, the highest numbered channel. The favourite shows airing on Tuesday and Thursday night were on channels one number apart.
(b) The man who watched the western show on Channel 7 didn't watch TV on Wednesday night. Mark watched a channel one digit lower than the man who watched the sports show.
(c) Mr. Singh watched the show on Channel 5, the lowest-numbered channel. The science fiction show aired on Channel 12.
(d) Barack didn't watch TV on Monday night. Mr. Twain didn't watch the action show. Manmohan didn't watch the sports show.
(e) Gordon's favourite show aired on a channel higher than the Tuesday night show but lower than the show that Charles watched.
(f) The five colleagues watched their favourite shows during the week in the following order: Mark, the man who watched Channel 7, the man who watched the mystery, Mr. Brown and Mr. Babbage.

26. What is the full name of Barack?
(a) Barack Babbage (b) Barack Singh
(c) Barack Brown (d) Barack Obama

27. Channel 5 is viewed by whom, on which day and which is his favourite program genre?
(a) Mark Twain, Monday and Western
(b) Charles Singh, Monday and Action
(c) Barack Babbage, Thursday and Sports
(d) Mark Singh, Monday and Action

Directions for Questions 28 to 29: *Read the following information and answer the questions that follow.*

Houses numbered 1A to 4D, situated east to west in that order, are each occupied by College of Commerce professors. They all teach different subjects, possess different makes and different models (years) of bikes:

(i) Anurag Kesarwani does not own a Suzuki (owner of which is professor of Gujrati language).
(ii) Anshul has a Honda bike.
(iii) Mr. Khanduja lives in house no. 3.
(iv) Mr. Singh is the professor of Sanskrit language.
(v) 2001 model of bike owned by the Urdu language professor is not of BMW make.
(vi) Vivek is the professor of Bengali language.
(vii) Mr. Saxena is not the owner of 2004 model bike, owner of which lives next to in a house westward of one owning 2002 model bike.
(viii) Siddhartha's is house no. 4.

28. Prof. Singh owns which make and model (year) of bike?
(a) Suzuki of 2001 (b) BMW of 2004
(c) Honda of 2002 (d) BMW of 2003

29. If Urdu and Sanskrit language professors exchange their bikes, who could be the owner of the latest model?
(a) Anurag only (b) Siddhartha only
(c) Vivek only (d) Siddhartha or Vivek only

Directions for Questions 30 to 32: *Study the following information carefully and answer the questions given below:*

Five friends Michael, Mark, Lewis, Karan and Jenson are students of five different disciplines–medical, engineering, architecture, arts, management and each plays a different musical instrument–sitar, tabla, sarod, guitar and violin.

(i) Lewis, a medical student, does not play sarod or sitar nor guitar.
(ii) Jenson is neither a student of Engineering nor Management.
(iii) Karan, who plays tabla, is an Arts student.
(iv) Neither Jenson nor Michael plays sarod.

30. Who among the following plays Sarod?
(a) Michael (b) Mark
(c) Jenson (d) Data inadequate

31. The guitarist is a student of which of the following disciplines?
(a) Engineering
(b) Either Engineering or Management
(c) Architecture
(d) Data inadequate

32. Who among the following plays Sitar?
(a) Michael (b) Mark
(c) Jenson (d) Data inadequate

Directions for Questions 33 to 37: *Four students– Alex, Boromir, Chris and Daniel have four different books: B1, B2, B3 and B4, of four different writers: Wren, Xavi, Yoko Han and Zara, respectively, necessarily in that order. Now each of the four students likes exactly one of the four books and has exactly one as his favorite writer. He may/may not own the book of his favourite writer. Each of the mentioned books and writers is liked by exactly one of the four students.*

High Yield Questions
Scan this QR code to access a video explanation for questions 33-37

It is also known that:
(i) Alex likes the book, owned by the student who likes Wren and book- B4.
(ii) The person who likes book- B3 is the only person who has his favorite writer's book and he is not Chris.

33. Which of the following writers is Chris's favourite?
(a) Wren (b) Xavi
(c) Yoko han (d) Zara

34. Which of the following statement is true about Alex?
(a) He likes B2 and Yoko Han.
(b) He likes B3 and Yoko Han.
(c) He likes B3 and Zara.
(d) None of these.

35. Which of the following books is liked by Daniel?
(a) B1 (b) B2
(c) B3 (d) B4

36. Person who likes B4, also likes which author?
(a) Yoko han (b) Wren
(c) Xavi (d) Zara

37. Chris does not like which book or author amongst the following?
(a) B1 (b) Xavi
(c) Both
(d) None. He likes both (a) and (b)

Directions for Questions 38 to 42: *Five employees- Arun, Barun, Carun, Darun and Earoon work in different companies- Parcos, Qarcos, Racos, Sarcos and Tarcos- not necessarily in the same order. The salary package of each of them is a different amount among 70, 80, 90, 110, 130 thousand dirhams. The following points are also known:*

(i) Barun works in Parcos.
(ii) The salary (in thousand dirhams) of Darun who does not work in Qarcos, is a prime multiple of 10.
(iii) The salary of the person who works in Sarcos is 10,000 k^2 (where k is a natural number).
(iv) The average salary of Arun and Darun is 10,000 dirhams less than the salary of Carun.

38. What is the possible sum of the salaries of Arun and Earoon?
(a) 150000 (b) 240000
(c) 160000 (d) None of these

39. Who works in Sarcos?

40. Which of the following could be an employee of Qarcos?
(a) Carun (b) Barun
(c) Darun (d) Earoon

41. Earoon works in:

42. What is the average salary package of the person who works for Parcos and the person who works in Sarcos?

Directions for Questions 43 to 47: *A group of 12 people - 8 men and 4 women employees are selected for an important project of the company.*

8 men: Amritesh, Chirag, Vijay, Varun, Munish, Shaurya, Vinay and Sudhir.

4 women: Rachna, Richa, Nidhi and Roma.

The employee group had three married couples and they went to the USA for the project in three private jets, belonging one to each Amritesh, Varun and Rachna.

The jets left from the same airport between 11:00 to 11:30 AM. But the airport has only one runway, so no two jets can take off at the same time.

The following information is also known:
(i) The maximum capacity of the jet is 5.
(ii) No two jets have same number of passengers.
(iii) No two jets have same number of couples.
(iv) The owner of each jet uses his/her own jet.
(v) The couples always travel together.
(vi) Vijay and Nidhi did not go in the same jet.
(vii) Chirag did not use those jets which had any couple in it.
(viii) Roma went in the jet which carried four employees in it.
(ix) Sudhir and Richa, who went in the same jet did not go with Munish and Vijay who went in two different jets.
(x) Amritesh was a bachelor.
(xi) Amritesh did not go in the jet which was the last to take off.
(xii) At least one of the couple went in Rachna's jet.
(xiii) Nidhi was married.

(xiv) Richa was the wife of Shaurya.

(xv) Nidhi's husband went in his own jet and went in the jet that was first to take off.

(xvi) Richa went in the jet that left the place immediately after the jet that had Vijay in it.

(xvii) No unmarried woman travelled in a jet alone with only unmarried men in it.

43. How many passengers were there in the jet which was 2nd to leave?

44. How many passengers there were in the jet which was last to leave?

45. How many couples were there in the plane which was 2nd to leave?

46. Which of the following could be the husband of Roma?

(a) Munish (b) Sudhir
(c) Vinay (d) None of these

47. Which of the following could be the husband of Rachna?

(a) Munish (b) Sudhir
(c) Amritesh (d) None of these

Directions for Questions 48 to 52: *Answer the questions on the basis of the information given below.*

Three teams - India, Bangladesh and Sri Lanka, participated in the Asia Cup football tournament in which the teams play with one another exactly once. A win fetches a team 2 points and a draw 1 point. A team gets no points for a loss. Each team scored exactly 1 goal in the tournament. India, Bangladesh and Sri Lanka scored 3, 2 and 1 points respectively.

48. What was the result of the match- India v/s Bangladesh?

(a) India won.
(b) Bangladesh won.
(c) India drew with Bangladesh.
(d) Cannot be determined.

49. How many goals were scored by Sri Lanka against Bangladesh?

(a) 1 (b) 2
(c) 0 (d) Cannot be determined

50. If India defeats Sri Lanka, then what is the result of India vs Bangladesh?

(a) Win (b) Loss
(c) Draw (d) Can't be determined

51. What is the total number goals scored by India against Sri Lanka?

52. What is the total number goals scored by Bangladesh against Sri Lanka?

Directions for Questions 53 to 57: *Read the information given below and answer the questions that follow:*

Five job candidates, all specialists in IT- Amrita, Manyata, Rishita, Sanya and Vanika, interviewed in five different companies- HCL, HP, KPMG, Google and Microsoft (not necessarily in the same order). They have been selected to work for one of the five different cities- Ohio, San Francisco, North Carolina, New York and Manhattan. All of them like to watch movies, but like different genres- Action, Romance, Comedy, Science Fiction and Biography (not necessarily in the same order). Further, the following additional information are provided:

(i) Vanika got selected in HCL.

(ii) Amrita did not get selected in KPMG.

(iii) Manyata's job location is not San Francisco and she does not like movies of Sci-Fi genre.

(iv) Sanya got selected for North Carolina office and Vanika is not selected for New York office.

(v) Amrita likes movies of Comedy genre and is selected either for San Francisco or Manhattan office and the candidate who got selected in Google does not like Sci-Fi movie genre and her job office is in the city amongst San Francisco or Manhattan.

(vi) The candidate who got selected in Microsoft likes watching Biographies and is not placed at New York office.

(vii) The candidate who likes watching romance movies is placed in Ohio office.

53. Rishita got selected in which company?

(a) HP (b) KPMG
(c) Google (d) Microsoft

54. Who likes watching movies of Science Fiction genre?

(a) Manyata (b) Rishita
(c) Sanya (d) Vanika

55. What genre does the candidate placed in New York office likes watching?

(a) Action (b) Comedy
(c) Sci-Fi (d) Biography

56. If Sanya is placed to Rishita's city and Rishita is placed to Sanya's city, then in which city the candidate who likes watching Sci-Fi movies will be placed?

(a) San Francisco (b) North Carolina
(c) New york (d) Manhattan

57. Who is posted in Manhattan?

(a) Manyata (b) Rishita
(c) Amrita (d) Cannot be determined

Directions for Questions 58 to 62: *Read the information given below and answer the questions that follow:*

Seven employees of a company, Anamika, Bheem, Chandni, Dev, Ekta, Farhan and Gaurav, live on different floors of a seven-storey building, but not necessarily in the same order. Ground floor of the building is named as floor 1, floor above the ground floor is named as floor 2 and so on. Each person likes a different fruit: Mango, Litchi, Banana, Kiwi, Grapes, Apple and Watermelon.

They went to the market to buy fruit of their choice and each one purchased fruit of different weight ranging from 2 kg to 8 kg but not in the fraction of a kilogram.

(i) Weight of fruit, purchased by Ekta and Dev together is the same as the weight of fruit, purchased by Chandni and Gaurav together.
(ii) Anamika lives on an odd numbered floor below the floor of the one who likes Kiwi.
(iii) Person who likes Kiwi lives on the floor numbered 4.
(iv) Only one person lives between the floors of Bheem and Farhan. Farhan lives on an even numbered floor.
(v) Only two persons live between the floors of Anamika and the one who likes Watermelon.
(vi) One who likes grapes lives on the floor which is immediately above the floor of the one who likes Apple.
(vii) Farhan does not live on the floor which is immediately next to the floor of the one who likes Mango.
(viii) Weight of Mango is square of the weight of the fruit which Anamika purchased. Weight of Watermelon bought is double the weight of Kiwi.
(ix) Farhan does not like Grapes. The weight of Apple and Grapes together is 10 kg.
(x) One who likes Mango lives just above the floor of Bheem but not on the topmost floor.
(xi) Gaurav lives on an even numbered floor but neither immediately above nor immediately below the floor of Anamika.
(xii) There is only one floor between the floors of Dev and the one who likes Litchi.
(xiii) Weight of Bananas purchased is less than the weight of Watermelon.
(xiv) Anamika does not live on the lowermost floor.

58. Which fruit does the person living on the top floor like?
(a) Apple (b) Litchi
(c) Watermelon (d) Banana

59. Who among the following lives on the floor immediately above the floor of Dev?
(a) Farhan (b) Chandni
(c) Ekta (d) Gaurav

60. Who among the following likes Bananas?
(a) Bheem (b) Anamika
(c) Gaurav (d) Chandni

61. What is the square of the weight purchased by Gaurav?
(a) 25 kg (b) 16 kg
(c) 64 kg (d) 36 kg

62. Amongst the given clues (i) to (xiv), which clue is redundant (i.e., not necessary to solve the question)?
(a) Clue (xii) (b) Clue (ix)
(c) Clue (xiv)
(d) All clues are necessary and there is no redundant clue.

Directions for Question 63:

63. Three labelled boxes containing red and white cricket balls are all mislabelled. It is known that one of the boxes contains only white balls and one only red balls. The third contains a mixture of red and white balls. You are required to correctly label the boxes with the labels red, white and red and white by picking a sample of one ball from only one box. What is the label on the box you should sample?
(a) White (b) Red
(c) Red and White
(d) Not possible to determine from a sample of one ball

Directions for Questions 64 to 65: *Answer the questions independent of each other.*

64. Four students (Ashish, Dhanraj, Felix and Sameer) sat for the Common Entrance Exam for Management (CEEM).
One student got admission offers from three National Institutes of Management (NIM), another in two NIMs, the third in one NIM, while the fourth got none. Below are some of the facts about who got admission offers from how many NIMs and what is their educational background.
(i) The one who is an engineer didn't get as many admissions as Ashish.
(ii) The one who got offer for admissions in two NIMs isn't Dhanraj nor is he a chartered accountant.
(iii) Sameer is an economist.
(iv) Dhanraj isn't an engineer and received more admission offers than Ashish.
(v) The medical doctor got the most number of admission offers.
Which one of the following statements is necessarily true?
(a) Ashish is a chartered accountant and got offer for admission in three NIMs.
(b) Dhanraj is a medical doctor and got admission offer in one NIM.
(c) Sameer is an economist who got admission offers in two NIMs.
(d) Felix who is not an engineer did not get any offer for admission.

65. Three children won the prizes in the Bournvita Quiz contest. They are from the schools: Loyola, Convent, Little Flowers, which are located in different cities. Below are some of the facts about the schools, the children and the city they are from.
(i) One of the children is Bipin.
(ii) Loyola School's contestant did not come first.
(iii) Little Flower's contestant was named Riaz.
(iv) Convent School is not in Hyderabad.
(v) The contestant from Pune took third place.

(vi) The contestant from Pune is not from Loyola School.
(vii) The contestant from Bangalore did not come first.
(viii) Convent School's contestant's name is not Balbir.

Which of the following statements is true?

(a) 1st prize: Riaz (Little Flowers), 2nd prize: Bipin (Convent), 3rd prize: Balbir (Loyola).
(b) 1st prize: Bipin (Convent), 2nd prize: Riaz (Little Flowers), 3rd prize: Balbir (Loyola).
(c) 1st prize: Riaz (Little Flowers), 2nd prize: Balbir (Loyola), 3rd prize: Bipin (Convent).
(d) 1st prize: Bipin (Convent), 2nd prize: Balbir (Loyola), 3rd prize: Riaz (Little Flowers).

Directions for Questions 66 to 68: *Answer the questions on the basis of the information given below.*

Five women decided to go shopping to M.G. Road, Bangalore.

They arrived at the designated meeting place in the following order:

1. Archana, 2. Chellamma, 3. Dhenuka, 4. Helen, and 5. Shahnaz.

Each woman spent at least ₹ 1000. Below are some additional facts about how much they spent during their shopping spree.

The woman who spent ₹ 2234 arrived before the lady who spent ₹ 1193.

One woman spent ₹ 1340 and she was not Dhenuka.

One woman spent ₹ 1378 more than Chellamma.

One woman spent ₹ 2517 and she was not Archana.

Helen spent more than Dhenuka.

Shahnaz spent the largest amount and Chellamma the smallest.

66. The woman who spent ₹ 1193 is

(a) Archana (b) Chellamma
(c) Dhenuka (d) Helen

67. What was the amount spent by Helen?

(a) ₹ 1193 (b) ₹ 1340
(c) ₹ 2234 (d) ₹ 2517

68. Which of the following amounts was spent by one of them?

(a) ₹ 1139 (b) ₹ 1378
(c) ₹ 2571 (d) ₹ 2718

Directions for Questions 69 to 71: *Answer the questions on the basis of the information given below.*

Five friends meet every morning at Sree Sagar restaurant for an idli-vada breakfast. Each consumes a different number of idlis and vadas. The number of idlis consumed are 1, 4, 5, 6 and 8, while the number of vadas consumed are 0, 1, 2, 4, and 6. Below are some more facts about who eats what and how much.

(i) The number of vadas eaten by Ignesh is three times the number of vadas consumed by the person who eats four idlis.
(ii) Three persons, including the one who eats four vadas, eat without chutney.
(iii) Sandeep does not take any chutney.
(iv) The one who eats one idli a day does not eat any vadas or chutney. Further, he is not Mukesh.
(v) Daljit eats idli with chutney and also eats vada.
(vi) Mukesh, who does not take chutney, eats half as many vadas as the person who eats twice as many idlis as he does.
(vii) Bimal eats two more idlis than Ignesh, but Ignesh eats two more vadas than Bimal.

69. Which of the following statements is true?

(a) Sandeep eats 2 vadas.
(b) Mukesh eats 4 vadas.
(c) Ignesh eats 6 vadas.
(d) Bimal eats 4 vadas.

70. Which one of the following statements is true?

(a) Daljit eats 5 idlis. (b) Ignesh eats 8 idlis.
(c) Bimal eats 1 idli. (d) Bimal eats 6 idlis.

71. Which of the following statements is true?

(a) Mukesh eats 8 idlis and 4 vadas but no chutney.
(b) The person who eats 5 idlis and 1 vada does not take chutney.
(c) The person who eats equal number of vadas and idlis also takes chutney.
(d) The person who eats 4 idlis and 2 vadas also takes chutney.

Directions for Questions 72 to 74: *Answer the questions on the basis of the information given below.*

A string of three English letters is formed as per the following rules:

(i) The first letter is any vowel.
(ii) The second letter is *m*, *n* or *p*.
(iii) If the second letter is *m* then the third letter is any vowel which is different from the first letter.
(iv) If the second letter is *n* then the third letter is *e* or *u*.
(v) If the second letter is *p* then the third letter is the same as the first letter.

72. How many strings of letters can possibly be formed using the above rules?

(a) 40 (b) 45 (c) 30 (d) 35

73. How many strings of letters can possibly be formed using the above rules such that the third letter of the string is *e*?

(a) 8 (b) 9 (c) 10 (d) 11

74. Using only 2, 5, 10, 25 and 50 paise coins, what will be the minimum number of coins required to pay exactly 78 paise, 69 paise, and Re. 1.01 to three different persons?

(a) 19 (b) 20 (c) 17 (d) 18

Directions for Questions 75 to 78: *Answer the questions on the basis of the following information.*

Four families decided to attend the marriage ceremony of one of their colleagues. One family has no kids, while the others have at least one kid each. Each family with kids has at least one kid attending the marriage. Given below is some information about the families, and who reached when to attend the marriage.

(i) The family with 2 kids came just before the family with no kids.
(ii) Shanthi who does not have any kids reached just before Sridevi's family.
(iii) Sunil and his wife reached last with their only kid.
(iv) Anil is not the husband of Joya.
(v) Anil and Raj are fathers.
(vi) Sridevi's and Anita's daughters go to the same school.
(vii) Joya came before Shanthi and met Anita when she reached the venue.
(viii) Raman stays the farthest from the venue.
(ix) Raj said his son could not come because of his exams.

75. Which woman arrived third?
(a) Shanthi (b) Sridevi
(c) Anita (d) Joya

76. Name the correct pair of husband and wife?
(a) Raj and Shanthi (b) Sunil and Sridevi
(c) Anil and Sridevi (d) Raj and Anita

77. Of the following pairs, whose daughters go to the same school?
(a) Anil and Raman (b) Sunil and Raman
(c) Sunil and Anil (d) Raj and Anil

78. Whose family is known to have more than one kid for certain?
(a) Raman's (b) Raj's
(c) Anil's (d) Sunil's

Directions for Question 79:

79. (i) Four friends, Mr. Barber, Mr. Carpenter, Mr. Stockbroker and Mr. Tanner all have different occupations, barber, carpenter, stock broker and tanner. But none of them has an occupation which matches his name.
(ii) Each man always wears the same colour shirt, black, crimson, silver or topaz. But the colour shirt he wears does not start with the same letter as his name or his occupation.
(iii) Mr. Stockbroker and the tanner dine together regularly.
(iv) The Stockbroker wears a black shirt.
(v) Mr. Carpenter is the barber.

What is the Stockbroker's occupation?
(a) Barbar (b) Tanner
(c) Carpenter (d) None of these

Directions for Questions 80 to 82: *Steffi, her brother, her daughter, and her son are tennis players. One day while playing tennis at home, a visitor noticed some facts.*

(i) Steffi's brother was directly across the net from her daughter.
(ii) Her son is diagonally across the net from the worst player's sibling.
(iii) The best player and the worst player are on the same side of the net.

High Yield Questions
Scan this QR code to access a video explanation for questions 80-82

80. Who is the worst player?
(a) Steffi (b) Daughter
(c) Son (d) Data inadequate

81. Who is the best player?
(a) Brother (b) Daughter
(c) Son (d) Steffi

82. Which of the following pair is on either of the sides?
(a) Steffi and her brother
(b) Brother and son
(c) Daughter and Steffi
(d) Data inadequate

Directions for Questions 83 to 84: *A game of Kattam-Kat is played between two players as shown below:*

Each player in his/her turn put his mark 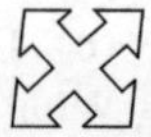 or.

 A player who first gets three or  in a horizontal, vertical or diagonal line wins.

High Yield Questions
Scan this QR code to access a video explanation for questions 83-84

 A player will always place his/her mark in a line that already contains (a) two of his /her own marks or (d) two of his.

Her opponent's marks–giving priority to (a) over (b). Only the last mark to be placed in the game shown is not given.

83. The player who started the game uses:

(a)  (b) 

(c) 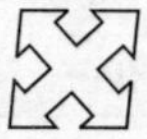 or  (d) Data inadequate

84. The player who won the game uses

(a)  (b) 

(c)  or  (d) Data inadequate

Directions for Question 85:

85. Each of the four friends – Amitesh, Bani, Chayaa and Devesh – got admission in different engineering colleges of Lucknow among Bansal, BBD, Ram Swaroop and BIT, not necessarily in the same order. Also, the four had different surnames among Joshi, Rao, Arora and Trivedi, in no particular order. Each of them was good at exactly one subject area among Maths, Physics and Chemistry. The one who got admission at BBD was named Arora and he/she was not good at Chemistry. Devesh got admission at Ram Swaroop, and he was not Joshi. Amitesh Rao who got admission at BIT, was good at Maths. Chayaa was good at Chemistry.
Which of the following is the correct combination of Bani's college and surname?

(a) BIT and Joshi
(b) BBD and Arora
(c) Ram Swaroop and Arora
(d) Can't be determined

Directions for Questions 86 to 90: *In a house there are seven rooms, labeled A through G. Each room has a painting, sculpture and a book on one among Sachin, Virat, Rohit, Messi, Ronaldo, Chettri and ShahRukh.*
Further, for any room, the painting in the room, the sculpture and the book are all distinct.
It is also known that:

1. The room which has a book on Virat is not A but has a painting of Messi and does not have a sculpture of Chettri.
2. The room which has a sculpture of Messi does not have Virat's painting but has a book on ShahRukh.
3. E has Rohit's sculpture and Ronaldo's painting, while the sculpture in D is not the same as the painting in F.
4. In the room which has a book on Chettri, the painting is neither of Ronaldo nor of Sachin, while the sculpture is not of Sachin.
5. D has a painting of Rohit but does not have books on either Chettri or ShahRukh, while the painting in A is the same as the sculpture in G.
6. C has a book on Ronaldo, while B has a painting of Sachin and a sculpture of Ronaldo.

86. Which of the following rooms has Sachin's Sculpture?
(a) A (b) F (c) G (d) D

87. E has a book on
(a) Sachin (b) Messi
(c) Chettri (d) Virat

88. The painting in G is the same as the
(a) Sculpture in A (b) Book in B
(c) Sculpture in C (d) Book in D

89. Which of the following rooms has a sculpture of Virat?
(a) A (b) D
(c) F (d) None of the above

90. Which room has a painting of Chettri?

ANSWER KEY

Level of Difficulty (I)

1. (a)	2. (b)	3. (d)	4. (b)
5. (a)	6. (d)	7. (b)	8. (c)
9. (d)	10. (b)	11. (b)	12. (a)
13. (b)	14. (c)	15. (d)	16. (c)
17. (b)	18. (d)	19. (d)	20. (d)
21. (b)	22. (d)	23. (c)	24. (d)
25. (d)	26. (a)	27. 58000	28. (a)
29. A, D or E	30. A, D or E	31. A or E	32. 11230
33. 12310	34. (d)	35. Pawan	36. (c)
37. (b)	38. (a)	39. (b)	40. (b)
41. (a)	42. (a)	43. (d)	44. (a)
45. (b)	46. (c)	47. (b)	48. (b)
49. (c)	50. (a)	51. (d)	52. (a)
53. (c)	54. (d)	55. (b)	

Level of Difficulty (II)

1. (c)	2. (c)	3. (b)	4. (b)
5. (c)	6. (d)	7. (d)	8. (c)
9. (b)	10. 16	11. (b)	12. (b)
13. (d)	14. 4	15. (b)	16. (d)
17. (d)	18. (a)	19. (a)	20. 17
21. 38	22. (c)	23. (c)	24. 4
25. Either 1 or 2		26. (d)	27. (d)
28. (b)	29. (a)	30. (a)	31. (c)
32. (d)	33. (b)	34. (a)	35. (c)
36. (b)	37. (d)	38. (c)	
39. Earoon	40. (a)	41. Sarcos	
42. 85000 dirhams		43. 3	44. 5
45. 0	46. (a)	47. (b)	48. (c)
49. (a)	50. (c)	51. 1	52. 1
53. (b)	54. (b)	55. (c)	56. (b)
57. (a)	58. (b)	59. (d)	60. (d)
61. (d)	62. (c)	63. (c)	64. (c)
65. (c)	66. (c)	67. (b)	68. (a)
69. (c)	70. (a)	71. (c)	72. (d)
73. (c)	74. (a)	75. (a)	76. (b)

77. (c)	78. (b)	79. (c)	80. (d)
81. (a)	82. (d)	83. (b)	84. (b)
85. (b)	86. (d)	87. (a)	88. (d)
89. (a)	90. F		

SOLUTIONS AND SHORTCUTS

Level of Difficulty (I)

Solutions for Questions 1 to 5:

Deduction 1: The direct clues give you the following linkages–Green - Adobe, Blue- Deloitte. Pawan - Pink - Bennett, Tarun- Falguni, Raman- Adobe. Combining these clues will give you the following table

Pawan	Qureshi	Raman	Shyam	Tarun	Unnat
Bennett		Adobe		Falguni	
Pink		Green			

Deduction 2: At this point, use clue no. (ii) [about Unnat]. This will give you that the correct pairing for Deloitte is with Unnat. Also, use clue (iv) at this stage. The table would evolve to:

Pawan	Qureshi	Raman	Shyam	Tarun	Unnat
Bennett	Evergrande **#2**	Adobe	Clarks **#2**	Falguni	Deloitte **#2**
Pink		Green			Blue **#2**

Deduction 3: Now using clue (vi), you will get that Evergrande is red and since, purple is not with Clarks, the final table will be:

Pawan	Qureshi	Raman	Shyam	Tarun	Unnat
Bennett	Evergrande	Adobe	Clarks	Falguni	Deloitte #2
Pink	Red **#3**	Green	Yellow **#3**	Purple **#3**	Blue

The answers are:

1. Yellow. Option (a) is correct.
2. Option (b) is correct.
3. Option (d) is correct.
4. Option (b) is correct.
5. Option (a) is correct.

Solutions for Questions 6 to 8:

Reaction Tracker

	Reaction
Clue (i)	5 People and 5 T-Shirts
Clue (ii)	They like to play 5 different Sports
Clue (iii) Statement (i)	Bhuvan - Pickleball -not yellow
Statement (iii)	Elangovan - Tennis – not blue or yellow
Statement (iv)	Praveen likes to play Padel Dhawan does not wear a yellow or T-shirt.

At this stage, combining statements (i), (ii), (iii) and (iv) of clue (iii) you will get the following table:

Name	Praveen	Bhuvan	Charlie	Dhawan	Elangovan
Sport	padel	Pickleball	Soccer*	Cricket*	Tennis
T-Shirt	Yellow#	Blue/white/ green	Red	Blue/ white	White/ green

* Since Charlie does not play Cricket, Dhawan must like playing cricket and Charlie must like playing Soccer.

\# Praveen must be yellow, since Bhuvan, Dhawan and Elangovan are not yellow.

Further we are not able to define the exact colours of Bhuvan (who can be blue/white or green), Dhawan (blue or white) or Elangovan (white/ green). Hence, the above table is the final one.

Thus, Bhuvan's T-shirt's colour cannot be answered (question 6), Charlie likes to play soccer (question 7) and Praveen-yellow-Padel is the correct combination.

The answers are:

6. Option (d) is correct.
7. Option (b) is correct.
8. Option (c) is correct.

Solutions for Questions 9 to 11:

Reaction Tracker

Firstly, to make the picture simpler, it is recommended to use acronyms wherever possible. So, for this set, we will be assigning acronyms to the names of the subjects:

Organisational Behaviour - OB, Business Mathematics - BM, Accounting - AC, Communication - CO, Corporate Finance - CF

	Reaction
Clue (i)	5 students, 5 books and 5 authors
Clue (ii) Statement (i)	Verma - OB - not Evaan or Arun
Statement (ii)	Sinha-Dhritiman
Clue (iii) Statement (i)	AC -Cauvery
Statement (ii)	CF – Evaan -not Damodaran
Statement (iii)	Sharma - CO

Based on the reaction to clue (ii) and (iii) as shown above, you should realise that the maximum numbers of direct links are between the author and the subject. Hence, your solution table should first give a structural placement of authors and subjects. When you do so, the following table shall emerge.

Author	Sharma	Sinha	Verma		
Subject	CO		OB	AC	CO
Student		Dhritiman		Cauvery	Evaan

Reacting to the above the table, you will immediately see that Sinha must be the author of the book Business Mathematics (BM) . Further using sentence (ii) of clue (iii), you will get that since Evaan is not using a book authored by Damodaran, he must be using the book authored by Aswath and consequently Damodaran must have authored Accounting (AC).

We also know from clue (ii) sentence 1 that Verma and Organisational Behaviour (OB) is not owned by Evaan or Arun. Hence, Arun must be owing the book on Communication (CO) and Bhavya must be owning the book on Organisational Behaviour (OB). The final table then becomes:

Author	Sharma	Sinha	Verma	Damodaran	Aswath
Subject	CO	BM	OB	AC	CO
Student	Arun	Dhritiman	Bhavya	Cauvery	Evaan

Consequently, the correct answers are:

9. Sharma – CO- Arun (d)
10. Sinha (b)
11. Evaan (b)
12. We have two possible combinations.

	Z		X
red	yellow	green	blue

X		Z	
blue	green	yellow	red

But from both combinations, we get that X lives in the blue house. Option (a) is correct.

13. M would live in a palace as U, T and P like either black or blue and X lives in a hotel. Option (b) is correct.
14. The grid would be:

12	1	2
Sharma's	Pattabhiraman	Banerjee
White	Blue	Red
Sambar	Fried Brinjal	Makkai-ki-roti

Option (c) is correct.

Solutions for Questions 15 to 16:

Let us tabulate the given information to get a clear picture of the scenario.

The first piece of information that fills the blanks is that no boy likes Commerce or Urdu. Then next information that is useful is that Dharmendra does not prefer Sociology and Statistics and is a boy, hence, he does not like Urdu and Commerce also. He is also brother of the person who opts for Computers. (Thus, the person opting for computers must be a girl). So, he must be having either Economics or Zoology. Now, we are given that Amitabh and Bhagyashree are brother and sister and, hence, Amitabh and Bhagyashree both will not have computers. Also, Farhan is given as a boy student hence, by default from previous information, he does not like Urdu and Commerce, and also, since he is a boy, he cannot be Dharmendra's sister and thus, cannot have computers. Thus, we have covered all the possibilities for boys except for the pair of brother and sister having Economics and Sociology. Clearly, since Amitabh and Bhagyashree are the only brother and sister mentioned in the information, they must be the ones, having those subjects. Consequently, Dharmendra must be having Zoology and Farhan would have Statistics. Commerce, Urdu and Computers would be shared between Chunky, Ekta and Govinda in some random order. Hence, they must be girls. The resultant table can be drawn as follows:

	Brother of Bhagyashree	**Sister of Amitabh**	**Girl**	**Boy**	**Girl**	**Boy**	**Girl**
	Amitabh	**Bhagyashree**	**Chunky**	**Dharmendra**	**Ekta**	**Farhan**	**Govinda**
Economics	√	X	X	X	X	X	X
Commerce	X	X	????	X	????	X	????
Zoology	X	X	X	√	X	X	X
Sociology	X	√	X	X	X	X	X
Statistics	X	X	X	X	X	√	X
Urdu	X	X	????	X	????	X	????
Computers	X	X	????	X	????	X	????

The answers are:

15. Option (d) is the correct answer, as we do not know who Dharmendra's sister is.
16. Option (c) is the correct answer, as there are 4 girls in the group.

Solutions for Questions 17 to 19:

The following solution table would emerge out of these clues.

Day	Monday	Tuesday	Wednesday	Thursday	Friday
Person	Ramesh	Suresh	Tanveer	Umesh	Vikram
Presentation topic	Chemistry	Dermatology	History	Mathematics	Biology

Hence, the answers are:

17. Monday. Option (b) is correct.
18. Biology. Option (d) is correct.
19. Thursday. Option (d) is correct.

Solutions for Questions 20 to 24:

From the information given, we can deduce the following table:

Student	School	City
A		
B	Sriniwasan	(x Delhi, x Chennai)
C	Queen's	Patna
D	(x Presidium)	Mumbai
E	(x Oregon International)	(x Pune)
F	(x Oregon International)	
G	Thapar	
H	Nagarjuna	Chandigarh

It is clear from the table that A lives in Lucknow and studies in Oregon International. From statement (v), we can say that F studies in Motilal College and lives in Pune. From statement (ii), D studies in Ramjas and E studies in Presidium. B lives in Kanpur. The final table evolves to:

Student	College	City
A	Oregon International	Lucknow
B	Sriniwasan	Kanpur
C	Queen's	Patna
D	Ramjas	Mumbai
E	Presidium	Delhi or Chennai
F	Motilal	Pune
G	Thapar	Chennai or Delhi
H	Nagarjuna	Chandigarh

20. Either E or G lives in Delhi. Hence, option (d) is correct.
21. From the table, D studies in Ramjas College. Option (b) is correct.
22. From the table, D- Ramjas- Mumbai is the correct combination. Hence, (d) is correct.
23. From the table, option (c) is incorrect. Correct combination is H- Nagarjuna- Chandigarh. Hence, option (c) is the correct answer.
24. This information brings about 2 new combinations- E- Presidium- Chennai; and G- Thapar college- Delhi. Hence, option (d) is the correct answer.

Solutions for Questions 25 to 28:

Name of person	Company	Day of arrival	Salary
Alan			
Ben	(x Google)		(x 9)
Chris	(x Google)		20
Danny		Thursday	11
Ervin		(x Monday)	

From statement (i) and (v), we can obtain Ervin's salary package as 58,000 dollars per annum. From statement (vi), Ben's salary package was 38,000 dollars per annum.

Name of person	Company	Day of arrival	Salary
Alan			9
Ben	(x Google)		38
Chris	(x Google)		20
Danny		Thursday	11
Ervin		(x Monday)	58

From statement (v), Ben and Chris attended the event on Tuesday and Wednesday in any order. Therefore, Ervin attended the event on Friday and Alan attended the event on Monday.

Name of person	Company	Day of arrival	Salary
Alan	Samsung	Monday	9
Ben	(x Google)	Tuesday/ Wednesday	38
Chris	(x Google)	Wednesday/ Tuesday	20

Name of person	Company	Day of arrival	Salary
Danny		Thursday	11
Ervin	Facebook	Friday	58

From statement (iii), Alan is from Samsung and Ervin is from Facebook and Danny is from Google (as Ben and Chris were not from Google, therefore, Danny is from Google.)

Name of person	Company	Day of arrival	Salary
Alan	Samsung	Monday	9
Ben	Microsoft/ Apple	Tuesday/ Wednesday	38
Chris	Microsoft/ Apple	Wednesday/ Tuesday	20
Danny	Google	Thursday	11
Ervin	Facebook	Friday	58

The answers can be read off the table:

25. From the table above, either Ben or Chris works in Microsoft. Hence, option (d) is correct.
26. From the table above, Google offers salary = 11,000 dollars per annum, and Microsoft and Apple offer 38,000 and 20,000 dollars per annum (correct combination cannot be determined). Therefore, possible sums are either 11 + 20 = 31 or 11 + 38 = 49 (in '000 dollars per annum). Therefore, option (a) is correct.
27. From the table above, Ervin's salary is 58,000 dollars per annum. Hence, the answer is 58000.
28. From the table above, the answer is Monday. Option (a) is correct.

Solutions for Questions 29 to 33:

From the information provided in the statements, we can make the following starting table:

Tallest to shortest →	Facebook 11230 / 12010 to 22880	Samsung 12010 to 22880/ 11230	Google 23970	Microsoft 23790	Yahoo 12130
A					Not possible
B	Not possible				
C	Not Possible				
D					
E					Not possible

From the condition that A + C = B + E and the fact that the one missing value is between 12010 to 22880, we can create the following thinking:

Deduction 1: The values of A + C and B + D cannot be distributed amongst the four known values of salaries – 11230, 23970, 23790 and 12130, simply because we cannot have any distribution of these four numbers amongst A, B, C and D making A + C = B + E. This means that the missing number has to be one of the values amongst A, B, C and E. This also means that we would use only three of the four known values for the values of A, B, C and E and then try to work out the fourth value.

Now, there are 4 possibilities to do this.

Case 1: If we leave out 11230 (by allocating it to D) and distribute 23970, 23790 and 12130 amongst A, B, C and E. By iterating the values amongst them, we can see that 23790 + x = 23970 + 12130. This gives us 12310 as a possible salary for one of the five. You should be able to check that none of the other combinations of numbers gives a value between 12010 and 22880 (as required by the question). For instance, if you were to try: 23790 + 12130 = 23970 + x, you would get the value of x as 11950 (which is outside the required range.)

Cases 2, 3, 4: Leaving out 23970, 23790 and 12130, one after the other. It can be checked that the value of the missing number goes out of range in each of the possible combinations.

Thus, we can deduce that the missing number is necessarily 12310. Thus, the salaries of the Facebook and the Samsung engineers would be shared between 12310 and 11230.

We would next need to work out the possible distributions of the numbers 23970, 23790, 12130 and 12310 amongst A, C, B and D such that A + C = B + E.

There are four possibilities for the same:

	Facebook 11230	Samsung 12310	Google 23970	Microsoft 23790	Yahoo 12130
Possibility 1	D	A	E	C	B
Possibility 2	D	E	A	B	C
	Facebook 12310	Samsung 11230	Google 23970	Microsoft 23790	Yahoo 12130
Possibility 3	A	D	E	C	B
Possibility 4	E	D	A	B	C

The answers would be:

29. A, D or E.
30. A, D or E.
31. A or E.
32. INR 11230.
33. INR 12310.

Solutions for Questions 34 to 38:

From statements (i), (v) and (vi), we can draw a following table:

Company Name	Name of employees	Place	Host
A			
B			Ishan
C		Hyderabad	
D			
E	Amritesh	Guyana	

From statements (ii) and (iv), we can deduce Danial and Chirag work in A and D, not necessarily in the same order.

From statement (ii), it can be concluded that Bhanu works in C. Further, analysis leads to the following table.

Company Name	Name of employees	Place	Popular for
A/D	Chirag	Karachi	Bhupendra
B	Edwin	Japan	Ishan
C	Bhanu	Hyderabad	Tarun
D/A	Dhiraj	Rio	Dipen
E	Amritesh	Guyana	Pawan

34. Option (d) is correct.
35. Pawan.
36. Option (c) is correct.
37. Option (b) is correct.
38. Option (a) is a correct combination, as options (b) and (c) are probable combinations, not necessarily correct.

Solutions for Questions 39 to 40:

Basic information summary: 2 housewives, 1 lecturer, 1 architect (male), 1 accountant (male), 1 lawyer.

Also, since A is married to D and the lawyer is married to D, A is the lawyer. Using the direct clues given in the question, we can reach the following conclusions:

A (lawyer—male)	Married to D (housewife—female)
B	
C (accountant—male)	Married to F (lecturer—female)
E	

At this point, we are left with one architect (male) and 1 housewife to place between B and E. Since, it is given that E is not a housewife, we may complete the above table as shown below:

A (lawyer—male)	Married to D (housewife—female)
B (housewife—female)	
C (accountant—male)	Married to F
E (architect—male)	

The answers can be read off this table:

39. E is an architect.
40. A, C and E are males. Thus, there are 3 males in the group.

Solutions for Questions 41 to 42:

Origin	A	B	C	D	E
Distance from origin	10	20	30	40	50

41. The robot would begin its travels at the start of the first second when he starts from the origin. At this time it would have requests from A and D and would hence go to D and come back to the origin after meeting both these requests. A distance of 80 meters traveled in 8 seconds. When it reaches the origin it would see the message from C and B and move immediately to cater to these. By the time it comes back after catering to C, it would have travelled an additional 60 meters, and would see the message from E after travelling a total of 140 meters.
42. The robot's travels would be A to D to second raw material station (as that would be closer) a distance of 60 meters covered by the end of the sixth second. It would see the messages from C and B when it reaches the second station and move towards C and then B and then go on to the origin. A total of 120 meters would be traversed before it sees the message from E.

Solution for Question 43:

43. It would require four moves to get the desired result. First shift the entire stack from the first table to the second; then shift the top two books (2 and 3) from Table B to Table A. Next, Shift the top Book (Book 3) from Table A to Table B. The fourth and final move is to shift Book 2 from Table A to Table B. Thus the number of moves required would be 4.

Solutions for Questions 44 to 46:

44. There are two possible placements for the 4 houses as illustrated below:

Possibility 1	Red	Yellow	Green	Blue
		Z		X
Possibility 2	Blue	Green	Yellow	Red
	X		Z	

In both the cases, X can be seen to be living in the blue house. Thus we get a definite answer for where X lives.

45. The use of all the clues will yield the following table:

Person	P	M	U	T	X
Colors liked	Red and Blue	Yellow + ___	Red and Blue	Black + ___	___ + ___
Stays At	Hut/Fort/House		Hut/Fort/House	Hut/Fort/House	Hotel

From the above table, it is clear that the hut, fort and house would be shared in any order between P, U and T. Thus, M must be living in a palace.

46. On putting the basic information in a tabular format we would reach the following position:

Enclosures	X	Y	Z	P	Q
Attendants	Mohan	Jack	Rita	Suman	Shalini
Animals	Lion, Panther	Bear, Panther	Deer, Bison	Deer, Bison	Lion, Bear

From the table, we can see that option (c) is correct.

Note: While solving this question, you have to keep track of the number of each animal since we are given that each animal is used exactly twice. That X and Q share 1 animal in common is a key point to be used in the solution. Since, the two panthers have already been used in X and Y–the only possible animal which can be common between X and Q is the Lion. Also, another key point is the information that the animal pairs in Z and P are the same. At this stage of the solution we just have deers and bisons which have 2 animals left. Panthers and Lions have been used fully, while 1 bear has also been used.

Solution for Question 47:

47. The distribution of males and females that would give us the minimum number of people in the family would be as follows.

Note: In the table M# represents a Male and F# represents a female.

					Explanation
Generation 1	M1 (single grand-father whose wife is not present)	M2-F1 (Couple)	F2 (Single grandmother whose husband is not present)		We have 2 grandfathers and 2 grandmothers out of which we are constrained to have at least 1 single grandfather and one single grandmother
Generation 2	M3-F3 (Couple)		F4	M4	There are a total of 4 fathers and 4 mothers which means that after the two grandfathers and 2 grandmothers there must be another two fathers and two mothers. Thus we have to introduce M3, M4 and F3 and F4.
Generation 3	M5, M6		F5, F6		The single grandmother has two granddaughters and the single grandfather has two grandsons- thus we need to introduce F5, F6 and M5, M6 respectively. Also note that the son of the single grandfather is M3 and the daughter of the single grandmother is F4

From the logic of the above table, we see that we can do the required conditional match by using 6 men and 6 women. Thus, we require a total of 12 people–the minimum number that can be present in the gathering.

Solutions for Questions 48 to 49:

48. Create the following truth table we can get 2 cases:
Case 1: If we take the second statement of the first shopkeeper to be true we get case 1 as follows:

Shopkeeper Number	First Statement	Second Statement
1	F	T
2	F	T
3	T	F

This means that the dog had white hair, a long tail and wore a collar. Option (b) matches this as a possibility.

Note: This is just a possibility and not a definite truth–as there could be another case if we take the first statement of the first shopkeeper as true. However, we do not need to solve any further as the question is just asking us to identify a possibility. Hence, we do not need to make a table for case 2.

49. From the information we can create the following starting table:

Age	Month	Name
7	June (boy)	Vaibhav/Ashuman
4	April/September	Supriya/Vaibhav
2	September/April	Supriya/Vaibhav/ Anshuman

Also from the information about birth months it is clear that:
Since Supriya is in April and Vaibhav is not in September, he must be in June and Anshuman should be in September.
The table would evolve to:

Age	Month	Name
7	June (boy)	Vaibhav
4	April	Supriya
2	September	Anshuman

Option (c) can be seen to be correct.

Solution for Question 50:

50. From the first statement alone, we can answer the question asked as once we know that F has 2 brothers, we can deduce that M must also have 2 brothers.
From the second statement we cannot answer the question asked. Thus we should mark option (a).

Solutions for Questions 51 to 53:

First of all collate the information of all the clues together.

D–Housewife married to lawyer

Engineer and Accountant are men. C–Accountant (man) married to F (Professor–woman)

A (man) married to a housewife.

Deduction 1: Since, there are 2 housewives and F the professor is also a woman; there are at least 3 women in the group.

Deduction 2: Engineers and Accountant being men and also the lawyer must be a man.

Combining the two deductions, we know that there are 3 men and 3 women in the group.

Men	Women
A (married to housewife)	D (Housewife—married to the Lawyer)
C Accountant	F (Professor)
E (since E is not a housewife, and there is only 1 slot left in the women—that of a housewife, E must be a man.)	Since E is a man, B is a housewife.

At this point we also know that there are only 2 married couples in the group. One of these couples is C-F, and the other couple is the lawyer and D. Since A is married to a housewife, A must be the lawyer.

The table now becomes much more clearer:

Men	
A (Lawyer) – D Housewife	Couple 1
C Accountant – F professor	Couple 2
E man Engineer	
B woman Housewife—but her husband does not belong to the group	

51. A and D are a married couple.
52. E is an engineer.
53. There are 3 males, as already deduced.

Solution for Question 54:

54. In order to solve this question, we are first bothered about the number of runs scored by each. From the basic information in the question, we know that Aakash scored 50 runs.
We can make a mental table of each player's performance based on the available information:

	Aakash	Biplab	Chirag
Runs scored	50	?	?
Catches taken	2		0
Catches dropped	n	$n + 2$	2

Minimum value of $n = 1$.
The above table is the summary of the basic information provided in the question.
Checking for sufficiency of information based on Statement A:
We get that Chirag and Biplab scored 35 and 50 runs respectively. Since Aakash also has the same number of runs as Biplab one of them should be the man of the match and this has to be decided on the basis of who amongst them took the higher number of catches. This information is not available for us;

hence statement A is not sufficient to answer the question asked.

From Statement B alone we again do not have enough information to answer the question asked because we do not know the runs scored by each if we are to consider only this statement.

From Both statements we first know the number of runs scored by each and we also know that Biplab drops 3 catches, and Aakash drops 1 catch. However we still do not know how many Biplab has taken. Thus, the question cannot be answered.

Solution for Question 55:

55. During the first reading of the questions one needs to react to the chain of events taking place in the questions:

Divayabh submitted the application form on Monday. Tuesday was a holiday. Clearance from clerk on Wednesday and consecutive clearance from senior clerk on Wednesday itself. Finally the application reached to the head clerk on Thursday.

Hence option (b) is the correct answer.

Level of Difficulty (II)

Solutions for Questions 1 to 4:

From clues (i), (ii), and (iii):

7 people– P, Q, R, S, T, U and V

5 localities – Karol Bagh, Hauz Khas, Khan Market, Dwarka and Janakpuri.

5 Athletic Sports– Long Jump, Javelin , High Jump, Pole Vault and Shot Put.

From clues (iii) and (iv), we have

S –	
T –Khan Market	X Shot Put , High Jump
V –Karol Bagh	Pole Vault
U – No Place	?
Q - No Place	Javelin
P - X Dwarka , X Janakpuri	X High Jump
R	

Refining the above table, the following deduction can be made: T must be an athlete specialising in Long Jump and P must be travelling to Hauz Khas. This further leads to the deductions that U must be an athlete specialising in High Jump and P must be an athlete specialising in Shot Put. The table evolves to:

S –	
T –Khan Market	Long Jump
V –Karol Bagh	Pole Vault
U – No Place	High Jump
Q - No Place	Javelin
P - Hauz Khas	Shot Put
R	

Hence, the answers are:

1. Option (b) is correct.
2. Option (c) is correct.
3. Option (d) is correct.
4. Option (d) is correct

Solutions for Questions 5 to 9:

The following table will emerge out of the given clues:

Station	Gets in	Gets down
Base Station	Enakshi, (Chanda + Faisal) / (Bhavna + Devesh)	
Depot Station	(Bhavna+ Devesh) / (Chanda+ Faisal)	NOBODY
GNIDA Office	NOBODY	Faisal
Delta - 1	Govind	(Bhavna+ Devesh)
Alpha - 1	Arnav	Enakshi
Pari Chowk		Govind + Chanda + Arnav

Start from the statement (iv).

Then go through statement (v): Arnav travels only two stations and gets down at Pari Chowk which means that he must have boarded at Alpha -1

Then go to statement (ix), proceed through (viii) to statement (ii) and proceed, as said in the remaining statements.

The answers are:

5. Alpha - 1 . Option (c) is correct.
6. Data inadequate as we do not know whether it is the base station or Depot Station. Option (d) is correct.
7. Data inadequate, as we do not know whether it is the base station or Depot Station. Option (d) is correct.
8. Enakshi gets down after 4 stations. Option (c) is correct.
9. Option (c) is correct.

Solutions for Questions 10 to 13:

Reaction Tracker

Opening Paragraph	5 friends A, B, C, D and E Balloons 1, 4, 5, 6 and 8
Clue (i) Clue (ii) Clue (iii) Clue (iv) Clue (v)	Coins 0, 1, 2, 4 and 6 needles, means A must have shot 6 coins and somebody must have shot 4 balloons and 2 coins.

	Balloons	Coins	Needles
A		6	
B			0
C			
D	√	√	0
E			
Someone	4	2	
Someone Not C	1	0	0

Clue (vi)	C shot no needle. Further, someone shot twice as many coins and balloons as C. This means that C must have shot 4 balloons and someone else must have shot 8 balloons. But, we also know that the person who shot 4 balloons shot 2 coins. Hence, someone else shot 8 balloons and 4 coins.
Clue (vii)	A shot 2 more coins than E, means that E must have shot 4 coins (and hence, 8 balloons). Hence, A must have shot six balloons. The table now evolves to:

	Balloons	Coins	Needles
A	6	6	
B	1	0	0
C	4	2	0
D	5	1	0
E	8	4	

Hence, the answers are:

10. Option (c) is true for A. Hence, option (c) is correct.
11. D shot 5 balloons is true. Hence, option (a) is correct.
12. Option (c) is again correct from the table.
13. A. Hence, option (a) is correct.

Solutions for Questions 14 to 15:

The following 19 possibilities emerge for what 101 could have seen. (Note: Be systematic while making this table.)

Possibility #	104	103	102
1	O	O	O
2	O	O	A
3	O	O	P
4	O	A	O
5	O	P	O
6	A	O	O
7	P	O	O
8	A	A	O
9	A	O	A
10	O	A	A
11	O	A	P
12	O	P	A
13	P	O	A
14	A	O	P
15	P	A	O
16	A	P	O
17	A	A	P
18	A	P	A
19	P	A	A

From the table above, it is clear that if 101 had seen 2 apples and 1 pineapple, he would have answered immediately. But, since he doesn't answer, possibilities 17, 18 or 19 can be ruled out.

102 also realises that 101 is not answering and hence, rules out possibilities 17, 18 and 19. He considers what he sees on 103 and 104 in the context of possibilities 1–16. It can be seen from the table that if he had seen 2 apples, he would know that there was only possibility 8 to consider. In such a case, he would know that there was definitely an orange on his head. However, he does not answer. Thus, we can conclude that possibility 8 is not possible. Also, if 102 sees an apple and a pineapple on 103 and 104, he could conclude from cases 15 and 16, that he had an orange on his head. So, cases 15 and 16 are also rejected. 103 realises that 102 is not answering and considers only possibilities 1-7 and 9-14.

Of these, we can realise that if he had seen an apple or a pineapple on 104, he would know that he had an orange on his head. But, since he doesn't answer, we can eliminate possibilities 6, 7, 9, 13 and 14. This leaves us with only possibilities 1–5, 10–12 and 15–16. Hence,

14. (a) 104 must have an orange on his head.
15. (d) All statements are true.

Solutions for Questions 16 to 20:

The starting grid in random order would be:

Wives	Husbands	Colour Combinations
Asha (A)	Pradeep (P)	(1) Red, Green, Yellow
Bhavna (B)	Qartar (Q)	(2) Red, Green, Black
Chanchal (C)	Rajeev (R)	(3) Red, Yellow, Black
Divya (D)	Sanjay (S)	(4) Green, Yellow, Black

Using clue (i) and clue (iii), we can make some conclusions about Asha and Chanchal.

Asha– Q/R	Pradeep (P)	(1) Red, Green, Yellow
Bhavna-	Qartar (Q)	(2) Red, Green, Black
Chanchal–P/ Q/R 1/2/3	Rajeev (R)	(3) Red, Yellow, Black
Divya	Sanjay (S)	(4) Green, Yellow, Black

Using clues (ii) and (iv), we get some conclusions about the men and the colour combination they used. (Note: We know Bhavna is not Sanjay's wife because clue (iv) mentions them as separate individuals).

Asha– Q/R	Pradeep 3/4	(1) Red, Green, Yellow
Bhavna– P,Q,R 1/3	Qartar 1/2	(2) Red, Green, Black
Chanchal– P/Q/R 1/2/3	Rajeev	(3) Red, Yellow, Black
Divya	Sanjay 1/3	(4) Green, Yellow, Black

From the above table (the wives column), it is clear that P, Q and R have to be shared amongst A, B and C in random order. Hence, Divya must be Sanjay's wife.

The table evolves to:

Asha– Q/R	Pradeep 3/4	(1) Red, Green, Yellow
Bhavna– P/Q/R 1/3	Qartar 1/2	(2) Red, Green, Black
Chanchal– P/Q/R 1/2/3	Rajeev	(3) Red, Yellow, Black
Divya– S 1/3	Sanjay 1/3	(4) Green, Yellow, Black

From the above table, it is evident that colour combination 4 belongs to Asha (as colour combinations 1/2/3 are shared between Bhavna, Chanchal and Divya). Also, Chanchal would get colour combination 2, as it cannot go to any other woman.

The table now becomes:

Asha– Q/R 4	Pradeep 3/4	(1) Red, Green, Yellow
Bhavna– P/Q/R 1/3	Qartar 1/2	(2) Red, Green, Black
Chanchal– P/Q/R 2	Rajeev	(3) Red, Yellow, Black
Divya– S 1/3	Sanjay 1/3	(4) Green, Yellow, Black

At this stage clue (ii) gives us that Qartar's wife used only one colour out of yellow and black.

Hence, Asha (colour combination 4) cannot be Qartar's wife and thus, must be Rajeev's wife.

This means that P and Q must be shared between B and C. Since, we know that Pradeep's wife used yellow and black colours, Chanchal cannot be married to Pradeep (Chanchal's colour combination does not use both the colours yellow and black). Thus Pradeep must be married to Bhavana. Thus, the table evolves to:

A – R – (4)
B – P – (3)
C – Q – (2)
D – S – (1)

Accordingly, the answers are:

16. Rajeev. Option (c) is correct.
17. Chanchal. Option (b) is correct.
18. Option (a) is correct.
19. Option (c) is correct.
20. Option (c) is correct.

Solutions for Questions 21 to 25:

The initial grid to start off would be something like:

	P	Q	R	S	T	101	102	103	104	105
A										
B										
C										
D										
E										

The following deductions would follow:

From clues (ii), (iii), (iv) and (v), the grid would evolve to:

	P	Q	R	S	T	101	102	103	104	105
A	×			×				×		
B				×				×		
C								×		
D								×		
E	×			×		×	×	√	×	×

Besides, from these 4 clues, we could also realise the following additional deductions:

(a) Order of marriage $P \xrightarrow{+3} E \xrightarrow{+2} A$ (from clue iv)
(b) Shailja must be in either 102 or 104.
(c) Abhay's room must be either 101 or 105.

Using clue (vi), we get that Shailja is not Abhay's wife and neither is she Chandan's wife. (since Chandan was married before Abhay and Shailja was married after Abhay). Hence, she must be Dinesh's wife.

Also, Clue (viii) gives us that Quindal is in Room 102, hence from deduction (b) above Shailja must be in Room 104 and consequently Abhay must be in Room 105. The table would evolve to:

	P	Q (102)	R	S(104)	T	101	102	103	104	105
A	×	×		×		×	×	×	×	√
B				×				×	×	×
C				×				×	×	×
D	×	×	×	√	×	×	×	×	√	×
E	×	×		×		×	×	√	×	×

> **Note:** One additional deduction we have drawn in the above table is that Quindal (being in Room 102) cannot be the wife of either Abhay (105) or Eklakh (103). Hence, R and T would be the wives of A and E (in random order), as they have to be shared between A and E.

This also means that P and Q must be shared between B and C. Thus the grid evolves to:

	P	Q	R	S	T	101	102	103	104	105
A	×	×		×		×	×	×	×	√
B			×	×	×			×	×	×
C			×	×	×			×	×	×
D	×	×	×	√	×	×	×	×	√	×
E	×	×		×		×	×	√	×	×

At this point use clue (ix), along with the deduction $P \xrightarrow{+3} E \xrightarrow{+2} A$.

Since Tulsi and Riya have to be shared between Abhay and Eklakh and Eklakh has got married before Abhay, he must be married to Tulsi and Abhay to Riya. The grid would evolve to:

	P	Q	R	S	T	101	102	103	104	105
A	×	×	√	×	×	×	×	×	×	√
B			×	×	×			×	×	×
C			×	×	×			×	×	×
D	×	×	×	√	×	×	×	×	√	×
E	×	×	×	×	√	×	×	√	×	×

At this stage, if you try to draw **a time line for their marriages,** you would get the following figure:

Existing figure: Priya $\xrightarrow{+3}$ Eklakh $\xrightarrow{+2}$ Abhay

If we use the logic contained in clue (vi), we get that Abhay got married 5 years after Chandan. Hence, Chandan and Priya must be married. Consequently Quindal and Balbir must be married. Also, since Balbir got married 3/4th the number of years ago as Dinesh, we can conclude that Balbir got married 15 years ago. Based on these deductions, the timeline looks like:

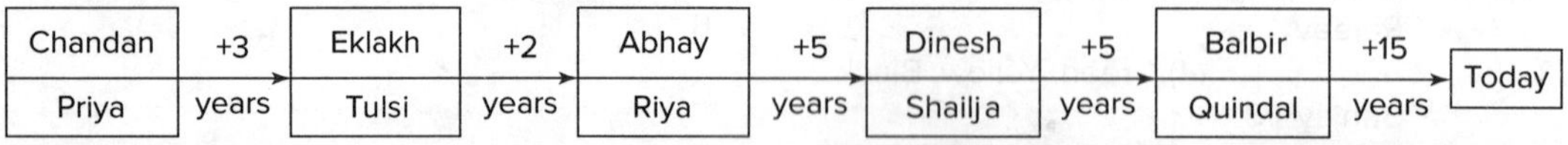

The final table is:

	P	Q	R	S	T	101	102	103	104	105
A	×	×	√	×	×	×	×	×	×	√
B	×	√	×	×	×	×	√	×	×	×
C	√	×	×	×	×	√	×	×	×	×
D	×	×	×	√	×	×	×	×	√	×
E	×	×	×	×	√	×	×	√	×	×

The answers are:

21. Abhay. Option (b) is correct.
22. Abhay has been married for 25 years. Option (b) is correct.
23. Quindal. Option (b) is correct.
24. All the rooms would need to shift. Option (d) is correct.
25. 27 years. Option (b) is correct.

Solutions for Questions 26 to 27:

From the given information, a table can be formed which will give a clear picture of the scenario.

First Name	Last Name	Program	Day	Channel
Barack	Brown	Sports	Thursday	6
Gordon	Babbage	Science Fiction	Friday	12
Manmohan	Twain	Western	Tuesday	7
Mark	Singh	Action	Monday	5
Charles	Obama	Mystery	Wednesday	21

26. Option (c) is the correct answer.
27. Option (d) is the correct answer.

Solutions for Questions 28 to 29:

To solve the question, we have to decode the information step by step and hence interpret the information.

Anshul owns the Honda and Vivek teaches Bengali => Gujrati teacher owning Suzuki – who isn't Anurag Kesarwani – is Siddhartha in house no. 4D (clues (ii), (vi), (i), (viii)).

Prof. Singh who teaches Sanskrit is Anshul (clue (iv)). Anurag Kesarwani, who teaches Urdu owns 2001 model bike which is not BMW (clue (v)), it is neither Suzuki nor Honda- an unknown make.

So, Vivek Khanduja owns BMW in house no. 3C and Siddhartha's surname is Saxena (clue (iii)).

Since Siddhartha's vehicle is not a 2002 or 2004 model (clue (vii)) and neither a 2001 model– it is model of an unknown year (which could be 2005 or an earlier year).

Now, 2002 model belongs to house no. 2 and 2004 model to house no. 4.

Anshul Singh's is 2002 model and Vivek Khanduja's is 2003 model.

Remaining house no. 1A is Anurag Kesarwani's.

The summary is as under:

Anurag - Kesarwani - Urdu -???? - 2001
Anshul - Singh - Sanskrit - Honda - 2002
Vivek - Khanduja - Bengali - BMW - 2004
Siddhartha - Saxena - Gujrati - Suzuki - ????

28. Option (c) is the correct answer.
29. Option (d) is the correct answer.

Solutions for Questions 30 to 32:

To understand the arrangement we need to tabulate all the clues and facts given in the question.

	DISCIPLINE					MUSICAL INSTRUMENTS				
NAME	MEDICAL	ENGG.	ARCH.	ART	MGMT	SITAR	TABLA	SAROD	GUITAR	VIOLIN
MARK	X	????	X	X	????	X	X	√	X	X
MICHAEL	X	????	X	X	????	????	X	X	????	X
LEWIS	√	X	X	X	X	X	X	X	X	√
KARAN	X	X	X	√	X	X	√	X	X	X
JENSON	X	X	√	X	X	????	X	X	????	X

30. Hence, option (b) is the correct answer.
31. There is a choice of Engineering, Architecture and Management. Hence, option (d) is the correct answer.
32. No clear clue provided, hence, option (d) is the correct answer.

Solutions for Questions 33 to 37:

Deduction 1: From statement (i), it is clear that the person who likes book- B4 also likes writer Wren (and he is someone other than Alex).

Deduction 2: From statement (ii), it is clear that Chris neither likes book- B3 nor likes writer Yoko Han.

Now, two cases are possible:

Case A: Daniel likes book-B3 and writer- Zara or Case B:Boromir likes B3 and Xavi.

Let us first explore Case A:

Book- B4 and author Wren combination cannot be liked by Chris, as putting B4-Wren combination with Chris creates a contradiction of Alex liking B3 (as Alex likes the book owned by the student who likes B4-Wren from the first clue). This has already been allocated to Daniel in this case. So, the B4-Wren combination has to go to Boromir. We get the following table:

Books owned with author names	Person	Favourite book	Favourite writer
B1- Wren	Alex		
B2- Xavi	Boromir	B4	Wren
B3- Yoko Han	Chris		
B4- Zara	Daniel	B3	Zara

Now, in this situation, we cannot put Yoko Han as Chris's favorite writer, since that would lead to a contradiction of the clue (ii) (the person who likes B3 is the only person who has his favorite writer's book). Thus, Xavi goes to Chris and Yoko Han to Alex. Also, B1 would be Chris's favourite book and B2 would be Alex's favourite book (as again if you try to do the opposite, it is a contradiction of the fact mentioned in clue (ii)).

In this case, the given information can be tabulated in the following form.

Books owned with author names	Person	Favourite book	Favourite writer
B1- Wren	Alex	B2	Yoko han
B2- Xavi	Boromir	B4	Wren
B3- Yoko Han	Chris	B1	Xavi
B4- Zara	Daniel	B3	Zara

Let us now move to consider case B:

Case B: Boromir likes book- B3 and writer- Xavi. Again we cannot put B4-Wren as Chris's liked combination (as we would then need to make Alex like the B3 – which is a contradiction of the starting premise here). Thus, B4-Wren combination of likes can only go to Daniel.

Books owned with author names	Person	Favourite book	Favourite writer
B1- Wren	Alex		
B2- Xavi	Boromir	B3	Xavi

Books owned with author names	Person	Favourite book	Favourite writer
B3- Yoko Han	Chris		
B4- Zara	Daniel	B4	Wren

But from the clue (i), the book owned by the person who likes B4-Wren is liked by Alex. Thus, Alex should like book B4 - which is again an internal contradiction. Hence, this case is rejected as a possibility.

33. From the table above, Chris likes writer Xavi. Option (b) is the correct answer.
34. From the table above, option (a) is the correct answer.
35. From the table above, option (c) is the correct answer.
36. From the table above, option (b)- Wren is the correct answer.
37. He likes both B1 and Xavi. From the table above, option (d) is the correct answer.

Solutions for Questions 38 to 42:

From the statement (iv), the average salary of Arun and Darun is 10,000 dollars, less than the salary of Carun.

We can deduce that the salary of Carun is 110 thousand and salaries of Arun and Darun are 70 and 130 thousand, respectively.

The salary package of the person who works in Sarcos is 90,000 ($10000(3)^2$).

From statement (i): Barun works in Parcos. Hence, the salary of Barun must be 80,000.

From the above analysis, we can get the following table:

Employee	Company	Salary Package (in $)
Arun	Qarcos or Racos or Tarcos	130,000 or 70,000
Barun	Parcos	80,000
Carun	Qarcos or Racos or Tarcos	110,000
Darun	Racos or Tarcos	70,000 or 130,000
Earoon	Sarcos	90,000

38. Possible sum of salaries of A and E = 130000 + 90000 = 220000 or 70000 + 90000 = 16,0000$. Hence, option (c) is correct.
39. Earoon.
40. Carun. Hence, option (a) is correct.
41. Sarcos.
42. Required average = $\dfrac{80,000+90,000}{2} = 85,000.$

Solutions for Questions 43 to 47:

From the statement (i), (ii) and (iii) we can deduce that number of employees in three Jets were 3, 4 and 5 and number of couple must be 0, 1 and 2 (in any order).

From the statement (ix), (xiii) and (xv), it is clear that Sudhir, Richa and Shaurya went on the same Jet.

From statement (vi) and (ix), we can deduce that Nidhi went with Munish.

From statements (x), (xi) and (xii), it is clear that Amritesh, Vijay and Chirag went in the same Jet.

By analyzing the rest of the statements, three combinations are possible:

Case 1:

First Jet	Second Jet	Third Jet
Nidhi- Varun	Amritesh	Richa- Shaurya
Munish	Vijay	Rachna- Sudhir
Roma	Chirag	Vinay

Case 2:

First Jet	Second Jet	Third Jet
Nidhi- Varun	Amritesh	Richa- Shaurya
Munish	Vijay	Rachna- Vinay
Roma	Chirag	Sudhir

Case 3:

First Jet	Second Jet	Third Jet
Nidhi- Varun	Amritesh	Richa- Shaurya
Munish- Roma	Vijay	Rachna
	Chirag	Vinay
		Sudhir

43. 3
44. 5
45. 0
46. Option (a) is correct.
47. Option (b) is correct.

Solutions for Questions 48 to 52:

India scores 3 points which is possible with a Win and a Draw only and Sri Lanka scores 1 point which means a Draw and a Loss. There are two possible cases that might match the number of points scored by each of the three teams:

Case 1: India defeats Sri Lanka:

	India	Bangladesh	Sri Lanka
India	-	Draw	Win
Bangladesh	Draw	-	Draw

	India	Bangladesh	Sri Lanka
Sri Lanka	Loss	Draw	-

Case 2: India defeats Bangladesh:

	India	Bangladesh	Sri Lanka
India	-	Win	Draw
Bangladesh	Loss	-	Win
Sri Lanka	Draw	Loss	-

Since, India has won a match and India scores exactly one goal, it means that this goal should have been scored by India in the match in which India wins. So, India wins by 1-0 and the other match of India gets drawn 0-0.

In the second case, if match between India and Sri Lanka is a draw with score 0-0, then it means that Sri Lanka scores a goal against Bangladesh in the match that Sri Lanka loses, which implies that Bangladesh has to score at least 2 goals to win against Sri Lanka, which is not possible because Bangladesh scores exactly one goal in the tournament. Hence, only the first case is feasible and the results are:

Result of the match – India v/s Sri Lanka: 1-0. Result of the match – India v/s Bangladesh: 0-0. Result of the Match – Bangladesh v/s Sri Lanka: 1-1.

48. Option (c) is correct.
49. Option (a) is correct.
50. Option (c) is correct.
51. 1
52. 1

Solutions for Questions 53 to 57:

We will need to create a 4-level tabular structure for this situation. In my solution, I am keeping Person, Company, Location and Movie genre from top to bottom, in that order. After putting in all the direct clues the table looks as shown:

Person	Amrita	Manyata	Rishita	Sanya	Vanika
Company (HP/KP/G/M)	Not KP				HCL
Location (SF/M/O/NY)	SF/M	Not SF		NC	Not NY
Movie Genre (A/R/SciFi/B)	Comedy	Not SciFi			

We also know the following additional clues:

Side Clue 1: From statement (v): Someone other than Amrita has the structure:

??
G
M/SF
Not SciFi

Side Clue 2: From statement (vii):

??
??
O
R

Side Clue 3: From statement (vi):

??
M
Not NY
B

If we consider, the side clue (i) and see where it can be fit into our current table, we realise that there are two cases:

Possibility 1: Google -M/SF – Not Sci-Fi can be aligned into Rishita's column.

Possibility 2: Google -M/SF – Not Sci-Fi can be aligned into Manyata's column.

Under possibility 1, New York has to go to Manyata and side clue (ii) has to get aligned with Vanika's column. This leads to side clue (iii), being aligned with Sanya's column. At this, stage we see that in the movie genres, we are left with Sci-Fi, but there is no column for it, since both Rishita and Sanya cannot be Sci-Fi (refer the table for possibility 2 shown). Hence, we can reject this possibility and move onto possibility 2.

Table for Possibility 1

Person	Amrita	Manyata	Rishita	Sanya	Vanika
Company (HP/KP/G/M)	Not KP		Google	M	HCL
Location (O/NY)	SF/M	NY	M/SF	NC	O
Movie Genre (A/R/SciFi/B)	Comedy	Not Sci-Fi	Not Sci-Fi	B	R

Thought Process for Possibility 2:

In this case, if we fit side clue 1, in Manyata's column, we see that side clue 2 can only go to Vanika (since NY has to go to Rishita in this case). Then side clue 3 can go only to Sanya's column. The residual variables can be easily inserted into this situation to complete the solution table.

Table for Possibility 2 = Solution table for the set of questions

Person	Amrita	Manyata	Rishita	Sanya	Vanika
Company (HP/KP/G/M)	HP	Google	KPMG	Microsoft	HCL

Table for Possibility 2 = Solution table for the set of questions					
Person	**Amrita**	**Manyata**	**Rishita**	**Sanya**	**Vanika**
Location (O/NY)	San Francisco	Manhattan	New York	North Carolina	Ohio
Movie Genre (A/R/SciFi/B)	Comedy	Action	Sci-Fi	Biography	Romance

The answers can be read off from the solution table:

53. Option (b) is correct.
54. Option (b) is correct.
55. Option (c) is correct.
56. Option (b) is correct.
57. Option (a) is correct.

Solutions for Questions 58 to 62:

In order to solve such questions with so many indirect clues, one of the key issues is to keep the clues organised in a clear usable form.

As we start looking at the clues, we can start noting down the information that is given readily to us.

Reaction to Clue (i): E + D = C + G.

Reaction to Clues (ii) and (iii): Anamika lives on floor 1 or 3; The person who likes Kiwi lives on floor 4.

Reaction to Clue (iv): Bheem and Farhan live on even number floors with 1 floor between them.

Reaction to Clue (v): Anamika cannot live on floor 1, since the person who likes Watermelons cannot live on floor 4. Hence, Anamika lives on floor 3 and the person who likes Watermelons lives on floor 6. (at this point you should start drawing the picture in your solving sheet).

Table after reaction to Clue (v)			
Floor	**Person**	**Favorite Fruit**	**Weight of Fruit**
Floors 1 to 7	B/C/D/E/F/G	M/L/B/G/A	2/3/4/5/6/7/8
7			
6		Watermelon	
5			
4		Kiwi	
3	Anamika		
2			
1			

Reaction to Clue (vi): Grapes to be placed just above Apples.

Reaction to Clue (viii) (Note: Clue (vii) isn't usable at this time): Weight of Mango = 4 kg; Kiwi and Watermelon can then only take 3 kg and 6 kgs respectively.

Reaction to Clue (ix): Farhan does not like grapes; Apple + Grapes = 10 kgs, means that they share the weights of 8 kg and 2 kg in some order. This also means that Anamika must like either Apple or Grapes.

Reaction to Clue (x): Mango has to be put just above Bheem. Checking where this can be put, we see that we cannot put them on floors 1 and 2 (Bheem is on an even floor); 2-3 is not possible, since floor 3 has Anamika and we know that she likes either Grapes of Apples and hence, she cannot like Mangoes. Checking further we see that the only place where Bheem and Mango can be adjusted is floors 4 and 5.

Reaction to Clue (xi): Gaurav has to live on floor 6 and that means that Farhan would be on floor 2.

Reaction to Clue (xii): Dev and the person who like Litchi can only be placed on floors 5 and 7.

Reaction to Clue (xiii): Bananas must be 5 kgs in weight. Clue (xiv) is redundant, as it does not give us any new information that we already don't know. For the remaining fitting of the variables, go back to clues (i) and (ix), which we have not used. From E + D = C + G, we can work out here that we need to equate E + 4 = C + 6 → E − C = 2. This can only be done using 5 and 7 as the weights. But we already know from clue (xiii), that Bananas weigh 5 kgs and now we know that they have to be the liking of Chandni. These can be fit into the table and finally, since Farhan does not like Grapes, it is Anamika who likes grapes and Farhan likes Apples. Thus, Grapes would be 2 kgs (since Anamika's liked fruit is 2 kgs) and Apples would be 8 kgs.

Final solution table for 58 to 62			
Floor	**Person**	**Favorite Fruit**	**Weight of Fruit**
7	Ekta	Litchi	7
6	Gaurav	Watermelon	6
5	Dev	Mango	4
4	Bheem	Kiwi	3
3	Anamika	Grapes	2
2	Farhan	Apples	8
1	Chandni	Bananas	5

The answers can be read off the solution table:

58. Option (b) is correct.
59. Option (d) is correct.
60. Option (d) is correct.
61. Option (d) is correct.
62. Option (c) is correct.

Solution for Question 63:

63. If you were to sample one ball from the box marked Red and White, you would get one of two situations:
    (a) You pick up a red ball. This would mean that the box marked red and white actually contains only red balls. We are now required to determine what the other two boxes contain–one of these

would be marked red and the other white. Since all three boxes are mislabelled, the box marked white would not actually contain only white balls–and hence must contain red and white balls; while the box marked red must be containing white balls. We are thus able to determine the color of the balls in each of the three boxes correctly by just picking out one ball from the box marked **Red and White.**

(b) If we were to pick up a white ball from the box marked red and white also, by a similar logic we would be able to answer the question asked.

Solutions for Questions 64 to 65:

64. Make the following table to analyse this:

Name	Background	Number of offers
Ashish	Engineer/CA/Economist/Doctor	0/1/2/3
Dhanraj	Engineer/CA/Economist/Doctor	0/1/2/3
Felix	Engineer/CA/Economist/Doctor	0/1/2/3
Sameer	Engineer/CA/Economist/Doctor	0/1/2/3

Using the clues given to eliminate possibilities the following table can be easily arrived at:

Name	Background	Number of offers
Ashish	CA	1
Dhanraj	Doctor	3
Felix	Engineer	0
Sameer	Economist	2

At this point we can see that the answer is (c).

65. The following tabular structure would help you in getting the best possible route to solve this question. The initial table would look like this:

Position	City	Name	School
1			
2			
3	Pune		

The sequence of deductions is as follows:

(i) Loyola not first, Pune third place and Pune not Loyola → Loyola second place.

(ii) Bangalore not first → Bangalore Second.

(iii) Convent School not in Hyderabad → Convent school in Pune and Hyderabad first place → Also gives us that Riaz and Little Flower both belong to Hyderabad and must come in the first position row.

(iv) Convent School not Balbir → Balbir from Bangalore and Loyola School and Bipin from Pune.

The final table after these deductions would look like:

Position	City	Name	School
1	Hyderabad	Riaz	Little flower
2	Bangalore	Balbir	Loyola School
3	Pune	Bipin	Convent School

Option (c) is correct.

Solutions for Questions 66 to 68:

From the clues we can make the following deductions:

(i) Somebody spent 2234 and someone else spent 1193. (Also, 2234 arrived before 1193).

(ii) Someone spent 1340 (not Dhenuka).

(iii) Someone spent 2517 (not Archana).

(iv) Chellamma + 1378 was another spending amount.

(v) Shahnaz spent the largest amount and Chellamma the least.

From the foregoing, it is clear that we know 4 amounts precisely–

2517
2234
1340
1193

This gives rise to two possibilities, considering the fact that there is a difference of 1378 between Chellamma and someone else. Also, before we look at those possibilities, we should also realise that the span between the highest and the lowest numbers in the table above is less than 1378; hence this difference of 1378 must be between the least and the highest numbers. Thus, Chellamma + 1378 = Shahnaz.

Possibility 1:

If 1193 is the least spending:

2571 (got by 1193 + 1378)	Shahnaz	Fixed
2517	A/D/H	Default possibility before using any clues
2234	A/D/H	
1340	A/D/H	
1193	Chellamma	Fixed

Using 1340 is not Dhenuka and 2517 is not Archana. Also using the information that 2234 came before 1193 (which means that 2234 must be Archana as Chellamma has spent 1193) in this case, we get

2571 (got by 1193 + 1378)	Shahnaz
2517	D
2234	A

1340	H
1193	Chellamma

But this contradicts the clue that Helen spent more than Dhenuka as in this case Helen (1340) < Dhenuka (2517).

Thus we reject this possibility and go to the second possibility.

Possibility 2:

If 2517 is the highest spending then we get the following table:

2517	Shahnaz	Fixed
2234	A/D/H	Default possibility before using any clues
1340	A/D/H	
1193	A/D/H	
1139 (got by 2517-1378)	Chellamma	Fixed

Using 1340 is not Dhenuka and 2517 is not Archana:

2517	Shahnaz
2234	A/D/H
1340	A/H
1193	A/D/H
1139 (got by 2517-1378)	Chellamma

Further, since Helen spent more than Dhenuka, Dhenuka cannot be put at 2234. At this point we realise that A and H are shared between 2234 and 1340. Thus, D becomes equal to 1193 and since 2234 comes before 1193, it must be the case that 2234 is Archana.

2517	Shahnaz
2234	Archana
1340	Helen
1193	Dhenuka
1139 (got by 2517-1378)	Chellamma

In this situation we can see that there is no contradiction. We can then mark the answers to the questions asked.

66. Dhenuka
67. 1340. Hence option (b) is correct.
68. 1139

Solutions for Questions 69 to 71:

In order to solve this set of questions, first of all use the basic information in order to get the following starting table where nothing is matched with each other:

Person	Vadas	Idlis
Sandeep (S)	1	0
Ignesh (I)	4	1
Mukesh (M)	5	2
Daljit (D)	6	4
Bimal (B)	8	6

Looking at the clues we can make the following deductions:

(i) From the first clue → Ignesh = 6 **Vadas and someone ate 2 Vadas and 4 idlis.**

(ii) From the third clue → Somebody ate 0 **Vadas and 1 idli and no** chutney.

(iii) From clue 7 → Bimal eats 4 Vadas.

Putting these deductions into the table we get:

	Vadas	Idlis	
Not Mukesh, also cannot be Ignesh or Bimal; so is either Sandeep or Daljit. From the fifth clue it also cannot be Daljit. Hence this has to be Sandeep.	0	1	Idlis and Vadas matched
Default options I/D/M/B. But cannot be Ignesh and Bimal as the number of Vadas do not tally. So this has to be either D/M.	2	4	Idlis and Vadas matched
	1	?	
Bimal	4	?	
Ignesh	6	?	
	?	5	
	?	6	
	?	8	

At this point if you use the 7th clue you would realise that the only way this can be fit into the current table is to use 4-8 for Bimal and 6-6 for Ignesh. Also, using the 6th clue we would get that 2-4 would be possible only for Mukesh.

The table would then become:

	Vadas	Idlis
Sandeep (no chutney)	0	1
Mukesh (no chutney)	2	4
Daljit	1	5
Bimal (no chutney)	4	8
Ignesh	6	6

The answers can be read off the table now:

69. Option (c) is correct.
70. Option (a) is correct.
71. Option (c) is correct.

Solutions for Questions 72 to 74:

First of all make a structure of what are the possible combinations:

With *m* as the middle letter–(vowel) *m* (another vowel)

With *n* as the middle letter–(vowel) *n* (*e* or *u*)

With *p* as the middle letter–(vowel) *p* (same vowel)

72. The number of possible letter strings are–

With *m*: $5 \times 4 = 20$, with $n = 5 \times 2 = 10$

With *p*: $5 \times 1 = 5$

Thus a total of 35 possible strings.

73. With *m*: 4, *n*: 5, *p*: 1. Thus a total of 10 strings.

74. $78 = 50 + 10 + 10 + 2 + 2 + 2 + 2 \rightarrow$ 7 coins

$69 = 50 + 10 + 5 + 2 + 2 \rightarrow$ 5 coins

Re $1.01 = 50 + 25 + 10 + 10 + 2 + 2 + 2 \rightarrow$ 7 coins

Thus a total 19 coins would be required.

Solutions for Questions 75 to 78:

The basic information may be summarised as:

Order of coming	1st	2nd	3rd	Last
Husband name				Sunil
Wife name				
Children details				1 kid

This is about the only direct clue in the question. Thus, we need to focus on the indirect clues to move further.

The first thing we should do perhaps is to collate the 4 names of men and women.

The four men are: Anil, Raj, Sunil and Raman.

The four women are: Shanthi, Sridevi, Joya and Anita.

From the (ii) and the (vii) clues together we get the information of the order of arrival of the women.

Shanthi who does not have any kids reached just before Sridevi AND Joya came before Shanthi and met Anita when she reached the venue.

Anita-Joya-Shanthi-Sridevi.

The table now becomes:

Order of coming	1st	2nd	3rd	Last
Husband name				Sunil
Wife name	Anita	Joya	Shanthi	Sridevi
Children details			No kids	1 kid

After this we start looking at the other clues to see which of those fit directly into the given situation.

Using the first and the sixth clues:

The table now becomes:

Order of coming	1st	2nd	3rd	Last
Husband name				Sunil
Wife name	Anita	Joya	Shanthi	Sridevi
Children details	At least 1 daughter	2 kids	No kids	1 kid (daughter)

Also given that Anil and Raj are fathers, and Anil is not the husband of Joya we further transform the table:

Order of coming	1st	2nd	3rd	Last
Husband name	Anil	Raj	Raman	Sunil
Wife name	Anita	Joya	Shanthi	Sridevi
Children details	At least 1 daughter	2 kids	No kids	1 kid (daughter)

The answers can be read off the table:

75. Shanthi. Option (a)
76. Sunil and Sridevi. Option (b)
77. Sunil and Anil. Option (c)
78. Raj's. Option (b)

Solution for Question 79:

79. In this question, the following would be the starting grid:

	Profession (Barber, Carpenter, Stockbroker, Tanner)	Shirt colour (Black, Crimson, Salmon, Topaz)
Mr. Barber		
Mr. Carpenter		
Mr. Stockbroker		
Mr. Tanner		

After using the clues, we get: The clues are used in the following manner to reveal the stockbroker's profession:

Since Mr. Carpenter is the barber and the stockbroker is friends with the tanner – the stockbroker must be neither the baker nor the tanner. Also, since we know that no person has a profession which equals his name. Hence, Mr. Stockbroker must be the Carpenter:

	Profession (Barber, Carpenter, Stockbroker, Tanner)	Shirt colour (Black, Crimson, Salmon, Topaz)
Mr. Barber	Tanner	
Mr. Carpenter	Barber	

	Profession (Barber, Carpenter, Stockbroker, Tanner)	Shirt colour (Black, Crimson, Salmon, Topaz)
Mr. Stockbroker	Carpenter	Black
Mr. Tanner	Stockbroker	

Option (c) is correct.

Solutions for Questions 80 to 82:

If we see clue (i) we get that the brother and daughter of Steffi are directly across the net from each other. Once we place these two we have two ways of placing Steffi and her son. The following figures illustrate this:

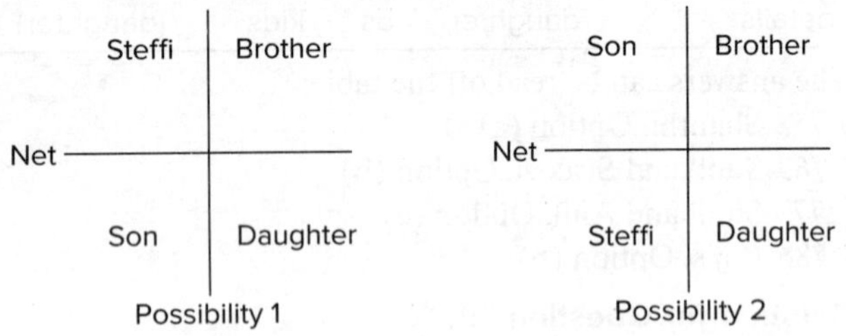

The following deductions can then be made:

Possibility 1	Possibility 2
Using Clue (ii)	Using Clue (ii)
Worst player's sibling → Brother	Worst player's sibling → daughter.
Hence, worst player → Steffi	Hence, worst player → Son
Also using clue (iii) (Best and worst player are on the same side of the net) We get.	Also using clue (iii) (Best and worst player are on the same side of the net) We get.
Best player → Brother	∴ Best player → Brother

The answers are:

80. (d) Since we do not know about the worst player (as it changes from possibility 1 to possibility 2).
81. (a) The brother emerges as the best player in both possibilities.
82. Data inadequate again as the answer would change based on which possibility we consider. Since both possibilities are possible, hence (d).

Solutions for Questions 83 and 84:

For convenience the squares can be numbered as:

1	2	3
4	5	6
7	8	9

It is obvious that the person who plays next will win by putting his mark in square 5. We need to hence find who will make the next move.

Obviously the 7th move (winning one in this case) would be placed by the person who has not played the previous move. Hence, we need to see as to which of the 6 moves in the grid could possibly be the sixth and last one.

A little bit of introspection will give you that the cross in the ninth square is the only possible 6th move. Hence, the next move (7th) will be that of a face.

Thus the answers are:

83. (b)
84. (b)

Solution for Question 85:

85. (b)

Solutions for Questions 86 to 90:

From the information given to us, We can derive the following table:

Clue	Room	Book	Painting	Sculpture
1	not(A)	Virat	Messi	not (Chettri)
2		ShahRukh	not (Virat)	Messi
3		Chettri	not (Ronaldo, Sachin)	not (Sachin)

Room	Book	Painting	Sculpture
A		Y	
B		Sachin	Ronaldo
C	Ronaldo		
D	Not (Chettri,ShahRukh)	Rohit	X
E		Ronaldo	Rohit
F		not(X)	
G			Y

Clue 1 can only be fit into F or G.

Possibility 1: Virat - Messi - Not Chettri combination of Clue 1 in F:

Room	Book	Painting	Sculpture
A		Y	
B		Sachin	Ronaldo
C	Ronaldo		
D	Not (Chettri,ShahRukh)	Rohit	not (Messi)
E		Ronaldo	Rohit

Room	Book	Painting	Sculpture
F	Virat	Messi	Not (Chettri)
G			Y

On using Clue 1-3, we can determine that this possibility will not be feasible, because, if we place Virat - Messi - not Chettri combination of Clue 1 in F, then the person denoted by Y cannot be Messi any longer - and we would have to place the Shahrukh-Not Virat -Messi combination necessarily in A (it cannot be placed anywhere else including G). Consequently, we are forced to put Chettri -not Ronaldo, Sachin - not Sachin of Clue 3 in G. The possibility fails at this point when we consider who could be Y? Since, Sachin, Rohit, Ronaldo and Messi already have their paintings identified it could only be Virat, Chettri or ShahRukh. But Y cannot be Virat (as we have placed the combination of Clue 2 in A); Y cannot be Chettri, since that would lead to G having Chettri's book and sculpture; Y cannot be ShahRukh too as that would lead entail ShahRukh's book and painting in the same room A. Thus, we have no possibility left to fit in all the clues into this structure and we reject this possibility. We should now move to possibility 2 of placing the Virat-Messi- not Chettri combination in G.

Possibility 2: Virat - Messi - Not Chettri combination of Clue 1 in G:

Room	Book	Painting	Sculpture
A	Chettri (#2)	ShahRukh (#1)	Virat (#2)
B	Rohit (#3)	Sachin	Ronaldo
C	Ronaldo	Virat (#1)	Chettri (#2)
D	Not (Chettri, ShahRukh) Messi (#3)	Rohit	Sachin (#2)
E	Sachin (#3)	Ronaldo	Rohit
F	ShahRukh (#1)	Chettri (#1)	Messi (#1)
G	Virat	Messi	ShahRukh (#1)

The table can be completed as shown using deductions 1 to 3. These deductions have been marked in the table with the # sign - to help you understand the logic of how a particular cell of the table is filled.

Deduction 1: In this case, Y in the position of the sculpture for G, cannot be Chettri or Virat. Here, Y can take only ShahRukh.

So, Clue 2's combination of ShahRukh- Not Virat - Messi will only fit in F. Therefore, Virat's painting would only find place in room C. So, painting in F would be of Chettri. This completes the placement of all the 7 paintings.

Deduction 2: Therefore, D cannot have a sculpture of Chettri. Using Clue 3, We can place Chettri's book in A (the only room possible). Therefore Chettri's sculpture would be in C only. From Clue 3, we can also determine that the sculpture of Sachin would be in Room D. Hence, Virat's sculpture would be room A.

Deduction 3: From this point of the table we can see that Rohit's book can only be placed in Room B and Sachin's book can only be placed in room E. Consequently, Messi's book would go into room D, completing our solution.

Using the above table, we can answer the questions given to us.

86. Option (d) is correct.
87. Option (a) is correct.
88. Option (d) is correct.
89. Option (a) is correct.
90. F

CHAPTER 7

Routes and Network Diagrams

Chapter Launchpad

Scan this QR code for an introductory video on Routes and Network Diagrams

A look at the past trends of various MBA entrance and aptitude exams shows that questions based on routes and network diagrams are asked very frequently these days. Hence, there is a clear need to understand these question types and how to think inside them. The typical question on routes and network diagrams is built around a travel/transport situation between two nodes, with several nodes in between them.

Let us look at the logic involved with respect to the number of routes diagram. Consider the given figure where you need to travel from A to G, along the given routes and you have to find how many routes there are.

Concept Explainer

Scan this QR code to access a conceptual video on routes and network diagrams

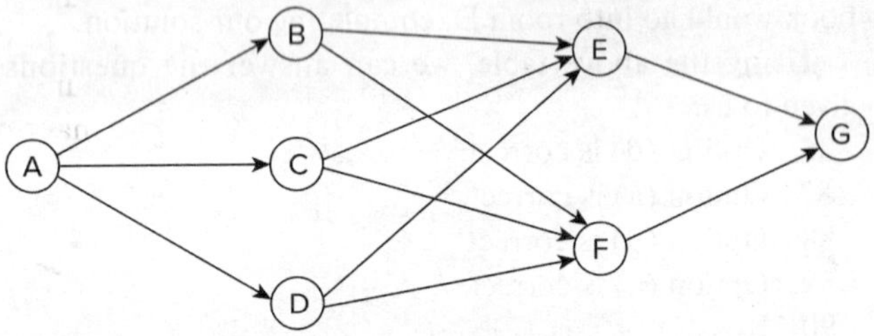

Can you count 6? ABEG, ABFG, ACEG, ACFG, ADEG and ADFG! What is the best way to think of the number of routes? How about 3 × 2 = 6? What's the thought process of that, you will ask me. Well, think of it as follows. Imagine: Node A as Stage 0; Nodes B, C and D as Stage 1 (since they are symmetrical to each other) and Nodes E and F as stage 2 and Node G as stage 3.

Going from stage 0 to stage 1 (A to any of B/C/D) has 3 routes.

Further, going from stage 1 to stage 2 has 2 routes (not 6!), since if you have reached stage 1, it means that you are already at either of the three nodes of stage 1 (Viz: B/C or D). In such a case, for the movement from stage 1 to stage 2, there will be 2 routes available for you to move. i.e., if you are moving from B, you can either take BE or BF. Similarly, if you are at Node C, you can only move in two ways. Hence, there are 2 routes to go from stage 1 to stage 2.

Similarly, going from stage 2 to stage 3, you have 1 route only. This is again because, if you are at E, you would have 1 way to move forward to G. Likewise, if you are at F, you will have only 1 way to move forward to G.

Thus, your journey consists of:

Stage 0 – Stage 1 – Stage 2 – Stage 3 = 3 × 2 = 6 ways.

So, how do you handle an asymmetrical situation? Suppose, they say that the route from B to E is closed for repairs. How do we deal with that situation?

Well, the answer is to divide stage 1 into stage 1A (symmetrical nodes C/D) and stage 1B (asymmetrical node B). Your journeys from A (stage 0) to G (stage 3) can go through:

Stage 0 – Stage 1A – Stage 2 – Stage 3 = 2 × 2 = 4 ways

OR Stage 0 – Stage 1B – Stage 2 – Stage 3 = 1 × 1 = 1 way. (stage 0 to stage 1B is necessarily A to B; & stage 1B to stage 2 is necessarily B to F, since B to E is closed).

Thus, there are a total of 5 ways in which you can go from A to G in this case.

Once you understand this logic, you can handle high degree of asymmetry in your route networks too. Take a look at the next figure in this discussion. In this, I have made B and E as asymmetrical nodes.

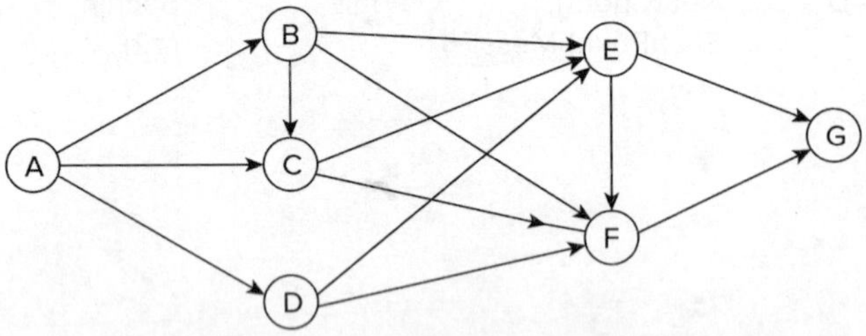

In the given figure, C and D are symmetrical since both of them provide the same number of routes going forward. Hence, you do not want to disturb your symmetrical thinking through A-C or A-D. B, however, is clearly asymmetrical as well as E. Hence, in this case, divide the stages into:

Stage #	Nodes
0	A – only 1 node
1A	C,D – 2 nodes
1B	B – only 1 node

Stage #	Nodes
2A	E
2B	F
3	G

Alternate route structures are:

0-1A-2A-3; 0-1A-2B-3; 0-1B-2A-3; 0-1B-2B-3.

The following table will clarify the thinking required to count these.

Route Structure	Number of routes	Remarks
0-1A-2A-3	$2 \times 1 \times 2 = 4$	0 to 1A is A to C or D, hence 2 routes. 1A to 2A leads you to E – hence, 1 route from either C or D. 2A to 3 is 2 routes, since you can go EG or EFG. (Note: You could also think of this route structure as 0-1A-2A-2B-3. But, that would be only required in case there are a lot of further complications in the routes. In this case, you do not need to do it, since it is obvious that if you are at E, you can move to G directly or through F.)
0-1A-2B-3	$2 \times 1 \times 1 = 2$	0 to 1A is A to C or D, hence, 2 routes. 1A to 2B leads you to F – hence, 1 route from either C or D. 2B to 3 is 1 route.
0-1B-2A-3	$1 \times 2 \times 2 = 4$	0 to 1B is A to B, hence, 1 route. 1B to 2A, means going from the node B to E. It can be seen from the figure that there are 2 ways of doing it- BE or BCE. 2A to 3 is 2 routes, since you can go EG or EFG.
0-1B-2B-3	$1 \times 2 \times 1 = 2$	0 to 1B is A to B, hence, 1 route. 1B to 2B, means going from the node B to F. It can be seen from the figure that there are 2 ways of doing it- BF or BCF. 2B to 3 is 1 route only, since you have to go from F (if you are at 2B).
Total routes	12	For the total routes, you have to add the number of routes for each route structure.

As, I have already mentioned in the table, there could be a need of sub dividing the route structures as follows: 0-1A-2A-3; 0-1A-2A-2B-3; 0-1A-2B-3; 0-1B-2A-3; 0-1B-2A-2B-3; 0-1B-1A-2A-3 and 0-1B-1A-2A-2B-3. However, you can avoid the need to use so many route structures by thinking about it in aggregations as shown in the table, where we have seen that to go from E to G, you can go EFG or EG directly. The thing you need to understand about this, is that you use the sub-structures only if they are required to sort out the confusions. Hence, use this logic of breaking the routes into sub-structures judiciously.

Sometimes, in questions on routes and diagrams, there is additional data about time taken, capacity of the routes and cost for the routes. However, even in such questions, the ability to count the number of routes is critical to solving questions on routes and network diagrams.

Let us now move into a few solved examples, in order to have a look at various patterns of questions. Once you finish looking at these solved examples, please go into the exercise where you will find a complete question bank to practice network diagram questions. Also, make sure to complete your knowledge of these questions, and go into the past year question papers of CAT (given at the end of the book) to see other examples of questions on network diagrams.

Illustration 1 The following sketch shows the pipelines carrying material from one location to another. Each location has a demand for material. The demand at Vaishali is 400, at Mathura is 400, at Jhampur is 700 and at Vidisha is 200. Each arrow indicates the direction of material flow through the pipeline. The flow from Vaishali to Mathura is 300. The quantity of material flow is such that the demands at all these locations are exactly met. The capacity of each pipeline is 1000.

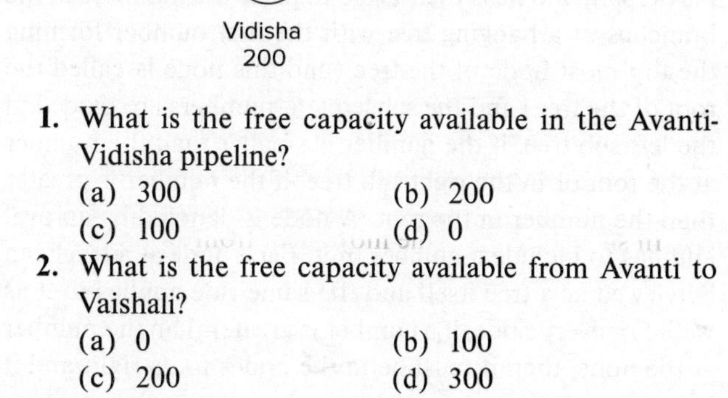

1. What is the free capacity available in the Avanti-Vidisha pipeline?
   (a) 300 (b) 200
   (c) 100 (d) 0
2. What is the free capacity available from Avanti to Vaishali?
   (a) 0 (b) 100
   (c) 200 (d) 300

3. The quantity moved from Avanti to Vidisha is:
(a) 200 (b) 800
(c) 700 (d) 1000

Solution: Since 700 is required at Jhampur, the requirement at Mathura must be 1100, which has to be supplied from the two pipelines coming into Mathura.

It is clear that since Vaishali to Mathura is only 300, the Vidisha-Mathura pipeline should carry 800. Hence, Avanti-Vidisha should have 1000.

1. There is no free capacity in the Avanti Vidisha pipeline. Option (d) is correct.
2. Avanti-Vaishali flow should be 700 and hence, the free capacity is 300. Option (d) is correct.
3. 1000. Option (d) is correct.

Illustration 2

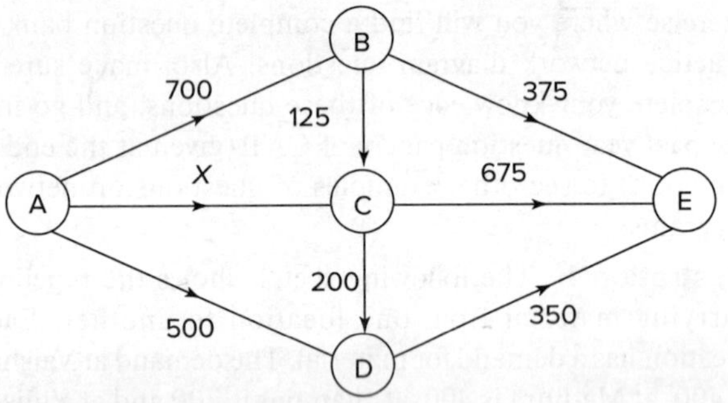

In the network diagram above, the figure represents the flow of natural gas through pipelines between major cities A, B, C, D & E (in suitable units). Assume that supply equals demand in the network (although not on individual nodes).

1. What is the number of units demanded at B?
(a) 175 (b) 200
(c) 225 (d) 250
2. If the number of units demanded in C is 225, what is the value of x?
(a) 975 (b) 875
(c) 775 (d) 950
3. What is the demand in D?
(a) 300 (b) 350
(c) 375 (d) 450

Solution: Refer to the following figure for the solution:

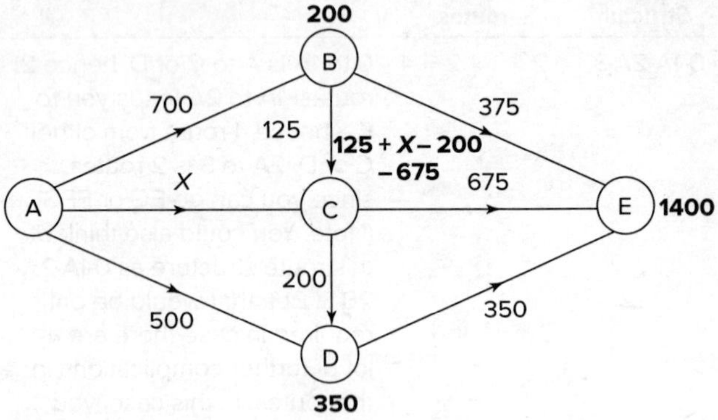

1. From the figure, it would be 700 – (375 + 125) = 200. Option (b) is correct.
2. 125 + X – 200 – 675 = 225 × X = 975. Option (a) is correct.
3. 500 + 200 – 350 = 350. Option (b) is correct.

EXERCISE

Directions for Questions 1 to 3: *Answer these questions based on the details below:*

In the ancient game of "placing the numbers on a tree branch", a sequence of numbers is provided to an individual participant and he is then asked to place the numbers in the branches of a hanging tree with the first number forming the top most node of the tree (and this node is called the root of the tree) and the subsequent numbers are placed in the left sub tree, if the number is smaller than the number at the root or in the right sub tree, if the number is greater than the number in the root. A node is denoted by an oval and has to include a number in it. Each node at a level can be viewed as a tree itself and the same rule applies to it as well. For every node, if a number is greater than the number at the node, then it must be in the nodes to its right and if the number be smaller than the number at the node, then it must be in the nodes to its left. New numbers must obey the rule of all nodes above itself.

Numbers shall not repeat themselves in the nodes and in case a number appears which has already appeared earlier in the tree it has to be placed on the right most of its possible positions.

E.g, 36, 28, 60, 92, 8, 44

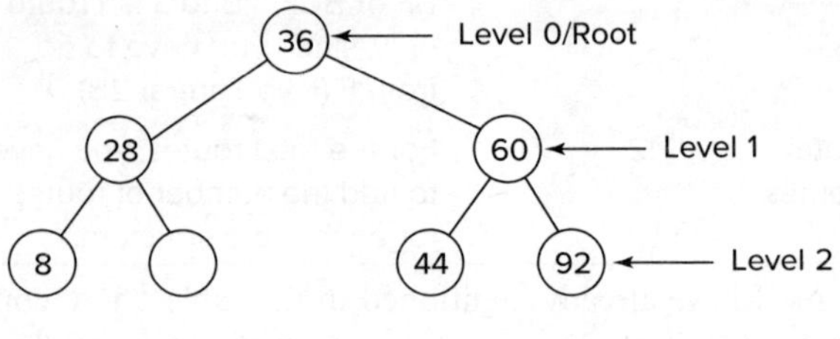

Given is a sequence of numbers and an empty tree. Fill the numbers in the appropriate nodes. The sequence is given in order and starts from 56:

56, 60, 16, 36, 28, 72, 12, 20, 64, 16, 80, 68, 36, 56, 20

1. What are the numbers at level 2?
(a) 12, 20, 28 (b) 12, 36, 72
(c) 12, 36, 56, 72 (d) 16, 36, 64, 80

2. What is the sum of the numbers at the level 3?
(a) 172 (b) 128
(c) 76 (d) 208

3. How many nodes are at the 4th level?
(a) 7 (b) 3
(c) 9 (d) 2

Directions for Questions 4 to 8: *Answer these questions based on the details below:*

High Yield Questions

Scan this QR code to access a video explanation of questions 4-8

A significant amount of traffic flows from point S to point T in the one-way street network shown below points A, B, C, and D are junctions in the network, and the arrows mark the direction of traffic flow. The fuel cost in rupees for travelling along a street is indicated by the number adjacent to the arrow representing the street, Motorists travelling from point S to point T would obviously take the route for which the total cost of travelling is the minimum. If two or more routes have the same least travel cost, then motorists are indifferent between them. Hence, the traffic gets evenly distributed among all the least cost routes. The government can control the flow of traffic only by levying appropriate toll at each junction. For example, if a motorist takes the route S-A-T (using junction A alone), then the total cost of travel would be ₹ 14 (i.e., ₹ 9 + ₹ 5) plus the toll charged at junction A.

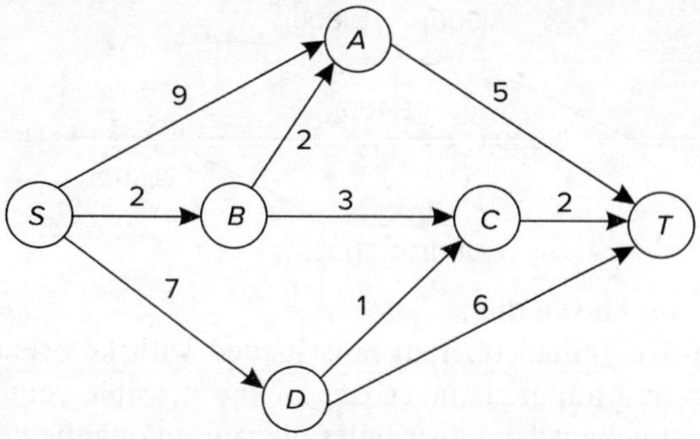

4. If the government wants to ensure that all motorists travelling from S to T pay the same amount (fuel costs and toll combined), regardless of the route they choose and the street from B to C is under repairs (and hence unusable), then a feasible set of toll charged (in rupees) at junctions A, B, C, and D respectively to achieve this goal at the minimum cost would be:
(a) 2, 5, 3, 2 (b) 0, 5, 3, 1
(c) 1, 5, 3, 2 (d) 2, 3, 5, 1
(e) 1, 3, 5, 1

5. If the government wants to ensure that no traffic flows on the street from D to T, while equal amount of traffic flows through junctions A and C, then a feasible set of toll charged (in rupees) at junctions A, B, C, and D respectively to achieve this goal is:
(a) 1, 5, 3, 3 (b) 1, 4, 4, 3
(c) 1, 5, 4, 2 (d) 0, 5, 2, 3
(e) 0, 5, 2, 2

6. If the government wants to ensure that all routes from S to T get the same amount of traffic, then a feasible set of toll charged (in rupees) at junctions A, B, C and D respectively to achieve this goal is:
(a) 0, 5, 2, 2 (b) 0, 5, 4, 1
(c) 1, 5, 3, 3 (d) 1, 5, 3, 2
(e) 1, 5, 4, 2

7. If the government wants to ensure that the traffic at S gets evenly distributed along streets from S to A, from S to B, and from S to D, then a feasible set of toll charged (in rupees) at junctions A, B, C, and D respectively to achieve this goal is:
(a) 0, 5, 4, 1 (b) 0, 5, 2, 2
(c) 1, 5, 3, 3 (d) 1, 5, 3, 2
(e) 0, 4, 3, 2

8. The government wants to devise a toll policy such that the total cost to the commuters per trip is minimized. The policy should also ensure that not more than 70 per cent of the total traffic passes through junction B. The cost incurred by the commuter travelling from point S to point T under this policy will be:
(a) ₹ 7 (b) ₹ 9
(c) ₹ 10 (d) ₹ 13
(e) ₹ 14

Directions for Questions 9 to 10: *Answer the questions on the basis of the following information.*

High Yield Questions

Scan this QR code to access a video explanation of questions 9 & 10

Shown below is the layout of major streets in a city. Two days (Thursday and Friday) are left for campaigning before a major election, and the city administration has received requests from five political parties for taking out their processions along the following routes.

Congress: A-C-D-E
BJP: A-B-D-E SP: A-B-C-E
BSP: B-C-E CPM: A-C-D

Street B-D cannot be used for a political procession on Thursday due to a religious procession. The district administration has a policy of not allowing more than one precession to pass along the same street on the same day. However, the administration must allow all parties to take out their processions during these two days.

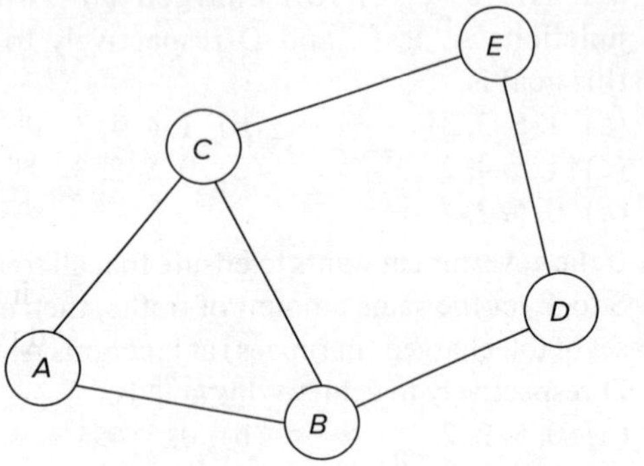

9. Congress procession can be allowed:
   (a) Only on Thursday
   (b) Only on Friday
   (c) On either day
   (d) Only if the religious procession is cancelled.
10. Which of the following is not true?
   (a) Congress and SP can take out their processions on the same day.
   (b) The CPM procession cannot be allowed on Thursday.
   (c) The BJP procession can only take place on Friday.
   (d) Congress and BSP can take out their processions on the same day.

Directions for Questions 11 to 14: *Answer the following questions on the basis of the information given below.*

The figure given below shows an oil distribution system consisting of tanks, pumps and the connecting pipelines. It supplies oil to five cities A, B, C, D and E. The oil can flow only in one direction in a pipeline. The oil stored (in million gallons) initially in the tanks 1, 2, 3 and 4 was 2000, 3000, 1000 and 5000 (million gallons) respectively. The system starts when the oil starts flowing out of each tank and is distributed equally among all the pipelines connected to a tank. The pumps do not consume any oil and the volume of the oil coming in and going out of a pump is the same. The consumption of oil (in million gallons) in A, D and E are 2500, 2000 and 1500 million gallons respectively. The consumption of oil in B and C is in the ratio 3 : 2. The oil which is left after consumption in a city flows out of it through a pipeline.

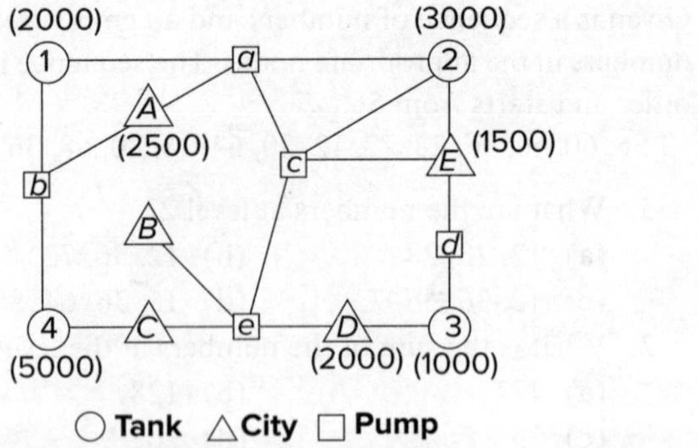

11. What is the ratio of the volume of the oil coming in to the oil going out of city C?
   (a) 5 : 1 (b) 4 : 1
   (c) 5 : 2 (d) 7 : 2
12. What is the consumption (in million gallons) of oil in city C?
   (a) 2000 (b) 2500
   (c) 3000 (d) 3500
13. What is the volume of the oil that flows through the pipeline joining pump c with city E?
   (a) 500 (b) 1000
   (c) 1500 (d) None of these
14. What is the ratio of the volume of the oil that flows through pump 'a' to the oil that flows through pump 'd'?
   (a) 5 : 2 (b) 3 : 2
   (c) 5 : 1 (d) 2 : 3

Directions for Questions 15 to 17: *Answer the questions on the basis of the information given below.*

In the diagram given below, all the routes of going from Kanpur to Lucknow are shown by the help of arrows. Each route passes through some of the seven villages called A, B, C, D, E, F and G. The number given in brackets along with the name of a village represents the number of people staying in that village.

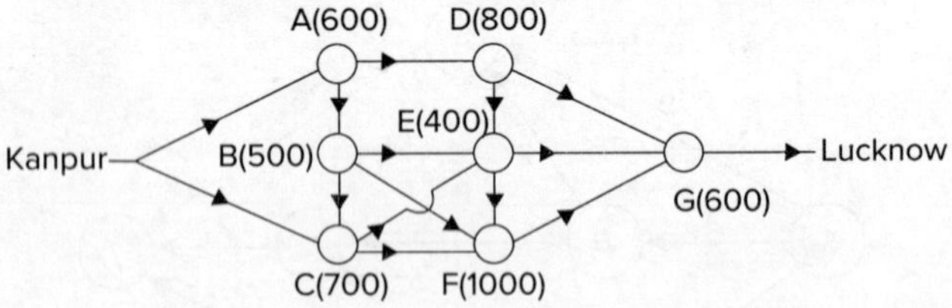

It is also known that:

(i) An Indian oil tanker is loaded with kerosene oil in Kanpur. It takes one of the possible routes to Lucknow and distributes oil cans among the people staying in all the villages along its route.

(ii) Each person staying in a village is given an oil can of 3 litres. A tanker is allowed to pass through a village on its route only after each person staying in the village gets the oil can.

15. How many different routes can a tanker, loaded with 8400 liters of oil, take from Kanpur to Lucknow, such that, it can give oil cans to all the people staying in villages along that route?

(a) 4 (b) 6
(c) 10 (d) 8

16. A tanker loaded with 8400 liters of oil is barely able to give oil cans to all the people staying in villages along its route and is left with no oil when it reaches Lucknow. How many villages fall in the route taken by the tanker?

(a) 5 (b) 4
(c) 3 (d) Can't be determined

17. A pair of two routes on which the quantity of oil that needs to be distributed by a tanker is exactly the same is called a "balanced-pair". How many balanced-pairs are there among the different routes from Kanpur to Lucknow?

(a) 0 (b) 1
(c) 2 (d) 3

Directions for Questions 18 to 22: *Answer the questions on the basis of the information given below.*

The network below gives the flow of supply of goods from dairy Q to its retailer factories: A, B, C, D, E, F and G. The arrows represent the direction in which milk is moved and the values alongside the arrows represent the distance between these points. The capacity (in tonnes) of each retailer factory is also given alongside the factory. Goods are moved in such way that only if the capacity of a retailer is completely used up, the goods are moved to the next retailer in the supply line. Milk is moved by tankers that have a maximum capacity of 40 tonnes per tanker and the running cost of moving a milk tanker is INR 8 per km. There are no other costs involved in the movement of goods (no cost for loading and unloading of milk canisters at the factory or the retailers).

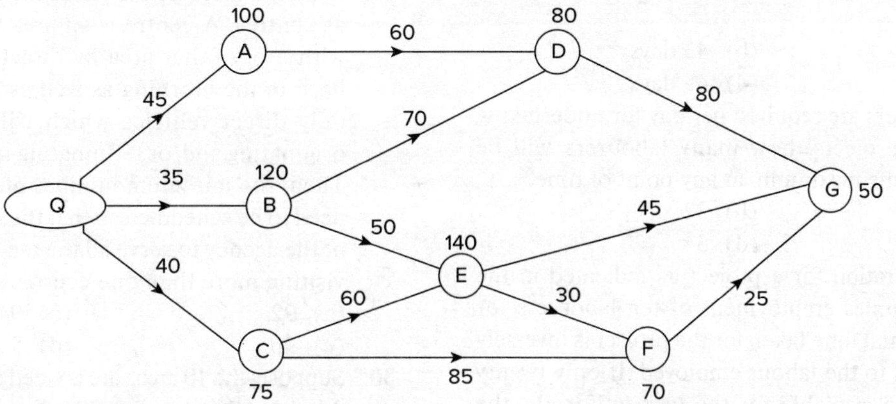

18. Assuming that all the retail factories are empty, what is the minimum cost of transporting milk canisters from the dairy to completely fill the factory E?

(a) 3680 (b) 3240
(c) 3790 (d) 3560

19. What is the minimum quantity (in tonnes) of goods transported by the company, if retailer factory G is to be filled to capacity and all retailer factories were empty when the dairy started transporting goods to G? (also, it is required to fill all the retailer factories along the path used)

(a) 192 (b) 190
(c) 195 (d) 210

20. If all retail factories are empty, then what is the maximum quantity (in tonnes) of material that can be taken to factory D with expenses not exceeding ₹1750?

(a) 25 (b) 60
(c) 40 (d) 35

21. The number of canister trucks of milk that has to be sent from the dairy to completely fill all the retailer factories which are empty is at least:

(a) 20 (b) 16
(c) 15 (d) 10

22. If dairy G received its full capacity of milk, then what is the least cost incurred in transporting the milk canisters, assuming that all retail factories were empty when the dairy started transporting milk to G? (assume that you will have to fully meet the requirements of all the intermediate stations for whichever route you choose)

(a) ₹ 3900 (b) ₹ 4040
(c) ₹ 4240 (d) ₹ 4020

Directions for Questions 23 to 27: *Answer these questions on the basis of the following information:*

The network diagram below depicts a task comprising of projects A, B, C, D, etc., represented in the diagram by arrows. Nodes 1, 2, etc., up to 11 represent notional start and end of activities.

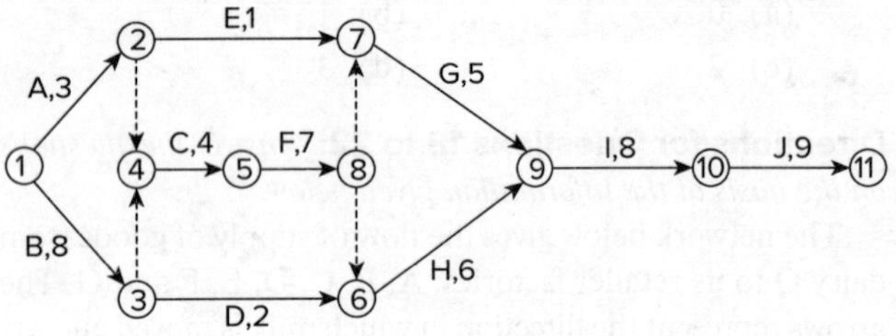

The task starts at node 1, proceeds in the direction of arrows - figures alongside arrows indicate time taken (in days) to complete the concerned activity - and ends at node 11. A project starts if and only if all projects preceding it are completed. Unless otherwise mentioned, there is no time lag between completion of last activity terminating at a node and start of all activities emanating from that node. No time and labour is consumed by the activities indicated by broken arrows.

23. How much time duration is required for the completion of the task?
(a) 42 days (b) 43 days
(c) 42 days (d) 45 days

24. If ten labourers are required per day for undertaking any of the projects, how many labourers will be required, at the maximum, at any point of time?
(a) 31 (b) 32
(c) 30 (d) 34

25. The time duration for a project as indicated in the diagram assumes employment of ten labourers for that project and time taken for the project is inversely proportional to the labour employed. If only twenty labourers are available for the task uniformly, the duration of the task can be reduced at most by approx. ? (the labour can be shifted at the end of the day only)
(a) 35% (b) 34%
(c) 37% (d) 36%

26. Activities C and F are outsourced; so, any labour problem in the firm undertaking the task does not affect the task duration. If the labourers in the firm are on strike from 9th to 18th day (days are counted from the start of the project), what is the approximate percentage change in the task duration?
(a) 0% (b) 2.4%
(c) 11% (d) 19%

27. If projects 2-4 and 8-7 each take 5 days to complete, what will be the new time duration required for task completion ?
(a) 38 days (b) 42 days
(c) 46 days (d) 63 days

Directions for Questions 28 to 31: *Answer the questions on the basis of the information given below.*

A new transport agency is planning to start operations in Belgium. The agency has identified ten different areas which they plan to connect through their network to start with. The travel duration between any two areas will be less than one hour. To start the operations, the agency has to decide on a daily schedule. The underlying principle that they are working on is the following:

Any person staying in any of these 10 areas should be able to make a trip to any other area in the morning and should be able to return by the evening of the same day.

28. If the underlying principle is to be satisfied in such a way that the journey between any two areas can be performed using only direct (non-stop) road transports, then the minimum number of direct vehicles to be scheduled is:
(a) 155 (b) 120
(c) 180 (d) 170

29. Suppose three of the ten areas are to be developed as centres. A centre is an area which is connected with every other area by direct vehicles each way, both in the morning as well as in the evening. The only direct vehicles which will be scheduled are originating and/or terminating in one of the centres. Then, the minimum number of direct vehicles that need to be scheduled so that the underlying principle of the agency to serve all the ten areas is met without visiting more than one centre during one trip is:
(a) 92 (b) 94
(c) 96 (d) 95

30. Suppose, the 10 areas are divided into 4 distinct groups A1, A2, A3, A4 having 3, 3, 2 and 2 areas respectively and that A1 consists of areas named P, Q and R. Further, suppose that direct vehicles are allowed only between two areas satisfying one of the following:
1. Both areas are in A1
2. Between P and any area in A2
3. Between Q and any area in A3
4. Between R and any area in A4

Then the minimum number of direct vehicles that satisfies the underlying principle of the agency is:

31. Suppose, the 10 areas are divided into 4 distinct groups Al, A2, A3 and A4 having 3, 3, 2 and 2 areas respectively and that A1 consists of cities named P, Q and R. Further, suppose that direct vehicles are allowed only between two areas satisfying one of the following:
1. Both areas are in A1
2. Between P and any area in A2
3. Between Q and any area in A3
4. Between R and any area in A4

However, due to operational difficulties at P, it was later decided that the only vehicles that would operate at P would be those to and from Q. Also, areas in A2 would have to be assigned to A3 or A4.
What would be the maximum reduction in the number of direct vehicles as compared to the situation before the operational difficulties arose?

Directions for Questions 32 to 34: *Answer the questions on the basis of the information given below.*

The following network gives the flow of water supplied from the storage tank A to the tanks B, C, D, E and F through pipelines. The supply of water is such that at each of the tanks B, C, D and E, only after the tank is full, the water is passed on to the next tank connected to it. The capacity of each pipeline is 1000 liters. The values alongside each tank gives the requirement (in liters) at each tank. The direction of flow of water is indicated by arrows. The slack in a pipeline is the additional flow required to bring it to full capacity.

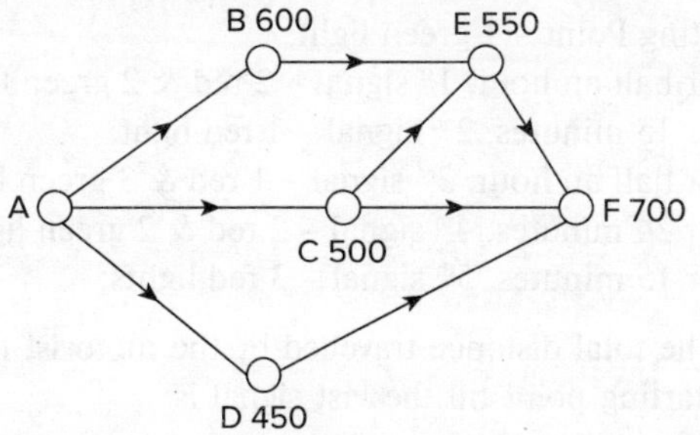

32. What is the maximum slack (in liters) in the pipeline connecting tanks A and C?

33. What is the minimum flow (in liters) in the pipeline connecting tanks B and E?

34. If the pipeline connecting C and F is under repair, what is the minimum volume of water (in liters) that needs to be sent through it such that the requirement at all the tanks are met?

Directions for Questions 35 to 37: *Answer the questions on the basis of the information given below.*

The figure below depicts the distribution network of Gowardhan Milk. Milk is transported from the dairy D to the company-owned outlets M, N, O, P, Q and R through a series of pipelines. The arrows show the direction of flow in the pipeline and the number above each outlet denotes the requirement (in litres) of milk at that outlet.

Milk is pumped to an outlet only when the requirement is met at the preceding outlet. The maximum capacity (in litres) of the pipeline connecting the dairy with any outlet is 1,200 litres and that of the pipelines connecting any two outlets is 600 litres. The slack in a pipeline is defined as the extra flow required to bring the pipeline to full capacity. The dairy pumps sufficient milk to fulfil the requirement at all the outlets.

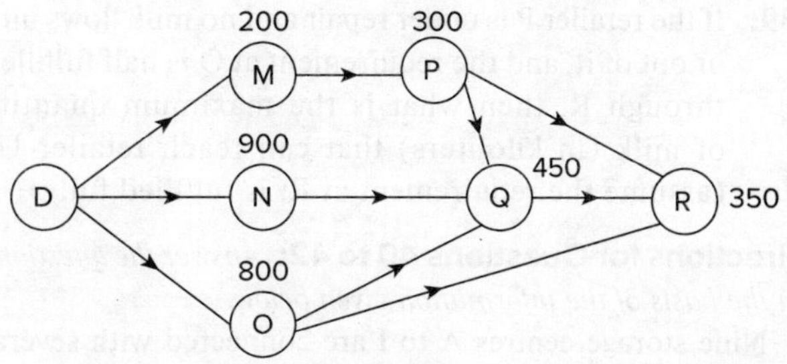

35. Due to a technical problem, if the pipeline connecting N and Q cannot be used, then what will be the flow at Q and R put together?

(a) 300 liters (b) 700 liters
(c) 100 liters (d) Zero liters

36. If the pipeline connecting N and Q is carrying only half its capacity, the pipeline connecting which other two points can also have a 50% slack?

(a) D and O (b) M and P
(c) D and M (d) D and N

37. If it is known that outlet P pumps exactly 100 litres of milk to an outlet connected to it, what is the range of the quantity of milk, that O pumps to R?

(a) 0 – 100 liters (b) 0 – 180 liters
(c) 0 – 250 liters (d) 0 – 350 liters

Directions for Questions 38 to 39: *Answer the questions on the basis of the information given below.*

The following pipeline diagram gives the milk flow from a dairy X to various retailers – P, Q, R, S, T and U located in six cities. At each retailer milk is stocked up and when the capacity is met milk is passed on to the next retailer connected to it. The figure also gives the capacity of each retailer. The flow in the network is such, that the requirement at all the retailers is exactly met. The arrows give the direction of flow of milk. The capacity of each pipeline connected to the dairy is 1500 kiloliters and that of pipelines connecting the retailers is 1000 kiloliters. The slack in a pipeline is defined as the excess flow required to bring the pipeline to full capacity.

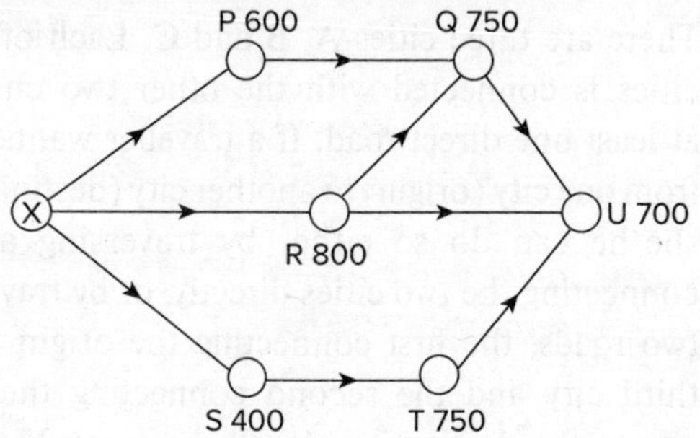

38. What is the minimum flow (in kiloliters) in the pipeline connecting the dairy with retailer R?

39. If the retailer P is under repair and no milk flows into or out of it, and the requirement at Q is half fulfilled through R, then what is the maximum quantity of milk (in kiloliters) that can reach retailer U? (assume the requirement at R, is fulfilled fully)

Directions for Questions 40 to 42: *Answer the questions on the basis of the information given below.*

Nine storage centres A to I are connected with several one-way routes and two-way routes as shown below.

The number beside each line in the diagram represents the distance between two centres.

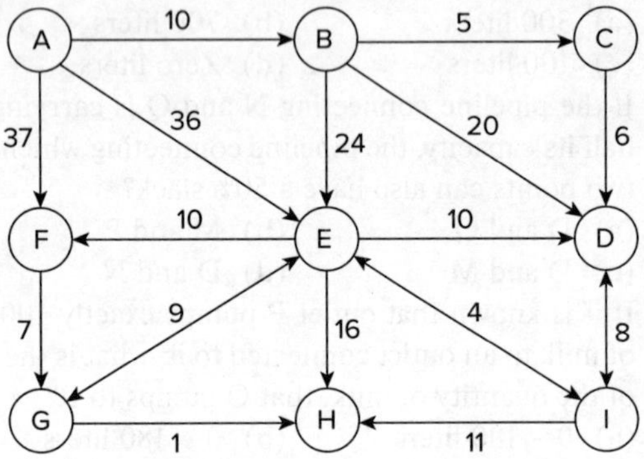

40. What is the minimum distance required to travel from A to H?

(a) 45 (b) 40
(c) 35 (d) 30

41. What is the maximum distance required to travel by a person starting from centre B and going to centre G without passing through any centre more than once?

(a) 45 (b) 46
(c) 47 (d) 49

42. In how many ways can one travel from centre A to I without passing through any centre more than once?

(a) 5 (b) 6
(c) 7 (d) 8

Directions for Question 43:

43. There are three cities A, B and C. Each of these cities is connected with the other two cities by at least one direct road. If a traveller wants to go from one city (origin) to another city (destination), she/he can do so either by traversing a road connecting the two cities directly, or by traversing two roads, the first connecting the origin to the third city and the second connecting the third city to the destination. In all there are 33 routes from A to B (including those via C). Similarly there are 23 routes from B to C (including those via A). How many roads are there from A to C directly?

(a) 6 (b) 3
(c) 5 (d) 10

Directions for Questions 44 to 47: *Answer these questions based on the information given below.*

A country has the following types of traffic signals.
3 red lights = stop;
2 red lights = turn left;
1 red light = turn right;
3 green lights = go at 100 kmph speed;
2 green lights = go at 40 kmph speed;
1 green light = go at 20 kmph speed.

A motorist starts at a point on a road and follows all traffic signals literally. His car is heading towards the north. He encounters the following signals (the time mentioned in each case below is applicable after crossing the previous signal).

Starting Point – 1 green light;
After half an hour, 1st signal – 2 red & 2 green lights;
After 15 minutes, 2nd signal – 1 red light;
After half an hour, 3rd signal – 1 red & 3 green lights;
After 24 minutes, 4th signal – 2 red & 2 green lights;
After 15 minutes, 5th signal – 3 red lights;

44. The total distance travelled by the motorist from the starting point till the last signal is:

(a) 90 km
(b) 100 km
(c) 120 km
(d) None of these

45. What is the position (radial distance) of the motorist when he reaches the last signal?

(a) 45 km directly north of the Starting Point.
(b) 30 km directly to the east of the Starting Point.
(c) 50 km away to the northeast of the Starting Point.
(d) 45 km away to the northwest of the Starting Point.

46. After the starting point if the 1st signal were 1 red and 2 green lights, what would be the final position of the motorist?

(a) 30 km to the west and 20 km to the south.
(b) 30 km to the west and 40 km to the north.
(c) 50 km to the east and 40 km to the north.
(d) Directly 30 km to the east.

47. If at the starting point, the car was heading towards south, what would be the final position of the motorist?

(a) 30 km to the east and 40 km to the south.
(b) 50 km to the east and 40 km to the south.

(c) 30 km to the west and 40 km to the south.
(d) 50 km to the west and 20 km to the north.

Directions for Questions 48 to 51: *During the shoot of Mission ImProbable 7, Tom Cruise and his team were required to perform stunts involving walking on tightropes between different high-rise buildings. Four buildings, A, B, C and D, are connected by ropes as shown in the figure below. Each rope can bear the weight of only one crew member at any time and if anyone wants to use any rope on which there is already a person attempting the stunt, he will wait in the building he is in until the person on the rope gets off. The length of each rope (in '00m) is also provided in the figure. For the purpose of these set of questions, all crew members are initially on building A and have to traverse towards building D (using any of the routes possible).*

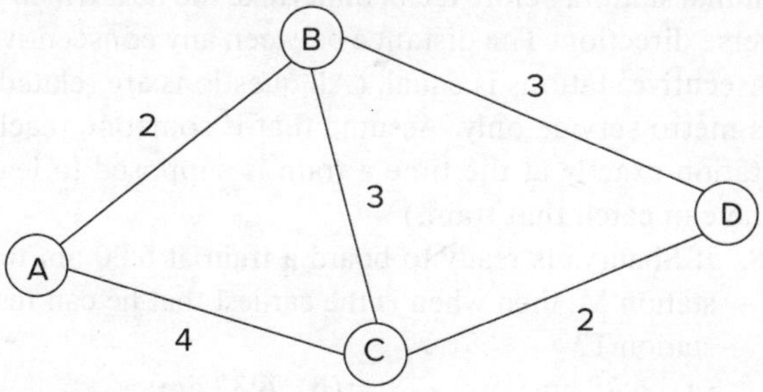

i. The time that any crew member takes to reach the destination includes the time spent waiting (if any) in the towers.
ii. Anyone who wants to go from one building to another will always try to minimize the time that they take to reach their destination and will decide the route that they want to take based on the crew members present on all the ropes at the time they start.
iii. Any person, after deciding the route that he wants to take, will always stick to the same route even if it involves additional waiting time at any of the buildings.
iv. Although the normal pace of any member is 16m/min but while walking on the rope, it comes down to 25% because of the fear of falling.

48. What is the minimum time taken for 3 crew members to reach from A to D?

49. A team of four members planned to go from A to D. What is the minimum time (in minutes) taken by the team to reach D?

50. What is the minimum time a 6 member team takes as a whole while moving from A to D?

51. At the last moment, there was an inclusion of Tom Cruise himself as the 7th member. Then what would be the minimum time in which the all the 7 persons can reach D from A?

Directions for Questions 52 to 57: *Shaurya, an Investment Banker, regularly travels between seven cities, C1 through C7, which are connected among themselves by roads. However, when traveling between any two cities, Shaurya always chooses the route which passes through the minimum Probable number of cities. If two or more routes pass through the minimum number of cities, he will choose the route for which the distance is also the least. It is known that the lengths of the roads directly connecting any two cities are distinct integers. For any pair of cities, the length of a route connecting the two cities and passing through the minimum Probable number of cities is called a Probable Distance between the two cities. The least among all the Probable Distances between two cities is called the Least Probable Distance (LPD) between the two cities. There is a road connecting C1 with C2 and C3. C2 and C3 are further connected to C4 which is further connected with C7. C7 & C2 are connected with C5 and C3 & C7 are further connected with C6. There is a road connecting C5 and C6 directly. There are no further connections between any of the other cities mentioned here.*

High Yield Questions
Scan this QR code to access a video explanation of questions 52-57

The following information is known about the distances between the cities:

i. The LPD between C4 and C6 is 9 km, while the LPD between C2 and C6 is 3 km.
ii. The Highest Probable Distance between C1 and C7 is 36 km.
iii. The LPD between C4 and C7 is 3 km.
iv. The sum of the lengths of the road directly connecting C5 to C6 and that directly connecting C5 and C7 is 10 km.
v. The LPD between C7 and C2 is 7 km, while the LPD between C3 and C7 is 11 km.
vi. The length of the road directly connecting C3 and C6 is greater than 11 km.
vii. The LPD between C1 and C4 is 11 km, while the highest Probable Distance between C2 and C3 is 24 km.
viii. All the roads are 2- way roads.

52. If Shaurya traveled from C1 to C7, the distance (in km) that Shaurya would have covered is

53. The LPD between which of the following pairs of cities is the least?
(a) C2 and C5
(b) C5 and C6
(c) C4 and C7
(d) C1 and C3

54. What is the highest Probable Distance (in km) between C3 and C7?

55. Shaurya's friend, Pallav, always travels along the shortest route (irrespective of the number of cities that he passes through), when traveling from one city to another. On a particular day, both Shaurya and Pallav started from C1 and reached X, which is one of the other six cities. If the length of the route that Shaurya took is greater than that of the route that Pallav took, how many of the six cities can X be?

(a) 0 (b) 1
(c) 2 (d) 3

56. What is the length of the road directly connecting C3 and C6?

(a) 12 km (b) 15 km
(c) 13 km (d) 14 km

57. The LPD between C3 and C5 is

(a) 18 km (b) 14 km
(c) 15 km (d) 12 km

Directions for Questions 58 to 61:

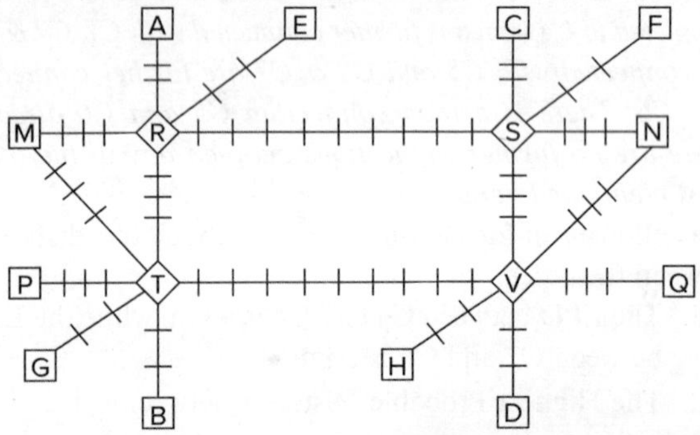

Given above is the schematic map of the metro lines in a city with rectangles denoting terminal stations (e.g. A), diamonds denoting junction stations (e.g. R) and all other markings (lines) denote other stations. Each train runs either in east-west or north-south direction, but not both.

High Yield Questions

Scan this QR code to access a video explanation of questions 58-61

There are special trains leaving stations M & N for T & V respectively. These trains leave every 20 mins after the third regular train leaves M&N respectively and travel at half the speed of the regular trains in that direction. It leaves simultaneously with the third train for the first time. The special trains do not travel to any other Junction/ Terminal Station apart from the ones mentioned. However, the trains traveling in the north-south direction do not use these routes (MT and VM). Also, for the North South trains, every second train diverts to the South West or the North East direction. Thus, trains leaving from A would have destinations to B&G alternatively in that order. For trains leaving from B, alternate trains would have A and E as their destinations. A similar pattern would be noted for Trains leaving from C and D. These trains maintain their speeds even when they change direction from North-South to move to the alternate destinations.

All trains stop for 2 minutes at each of the junction stations on the way and for 1 minute at each of the other stations. It takes 2 minutes to reach the next station for trains going in east-west direction and 3 minutes to reach the next station for trains going in north-south direction. Thus, a train starting from A will take a total of 3 + 1 + 3 + 1 + 3 = 11 minutes to reach R in it's north-south journey.

From each terminal station, the first train starts at 6 am; the last trains leave the terminal stations at midnight. Otherwise, during the service hours, there is a metro service every 15 minutes in the north-south lines and every 10 minutes in the east-west lines. A train must rest for at least 15 minutes after completing a trip at the terminal station, before it can undertake the next trip in the reverse direction. The distance between any consecutive 2 consecutive stations is equal. (All questions are related to this metro service only. Assume that if someone reaches a station exactly at the time a train is supposed to leave, (s)he can catch that train.)

58. If Shaurya is ready to board a train at 6:00 am from station M, then when is the earliest that he can reach station T?

(a) 6:28 am (b) 6:32 am
(c) 6:39 am (d) 6:49 am

59. If Pallav is to reach G by 7:00 am, then when should he be ready to board at station M?

(a) 6:24 am (b) 6:19 am
(c) 6:20 am (d) 6:18 am

60. Akash wants to go from D to E. He is ready to board at 6:55 am. What is the total minimum wait time at all the intermediate stations if the number of stations he travels to is minimum?

(a) 23 minutes (b) 18 minutes
(c) 11 minutes (d) 6 minutes

61. What is the minimum number of trains that are required to provide the service on the AB line (considering both north and south directions and if all trains only travel north south - i.e. they are not diverted to stations G and E)?

Directions for Questions 62 to 65:

Every day an iPhone supplier supplies iPhones from the newly opened Apple Store(AS) in Saket to four locations - Vasant Kunj (VK), Vasant Vihar (VV), Chanakyapuri (CK), and Mehrauli (M). The daily demand for iPhones in each location is uncertain and independent of each other. Vasant Kunj (VK), Vasant Vihar (VV), Chanakyapuri (CK) and Mehrauli (M) are 10 km, 20 kms, 24 kms and 4 kms away from the Apple Store respectively. The distance between VK and VV is 12 kms, VV and CK are 8 Kms apart. Besides, VK-VV; VK-M; CK-M and VV-CK are also connected through direct routes. All routes are two- way with the same distance both ways. The distance between CK and M is equal to the second highest distance between the two localities and the distance between M and VK is twice of localities which are closest to each other. There is a 40% chance that the demand at Vasant Kunj will be of 50 units and 60% chance that the demand would be of 70 units. For Vasant Vihar, demand of 40 units has a probability of 30% and for 60 units this figure is 70%. At Chanakyapuri, the probability that the demand would be of 70 units is 30% and that for 100 units is 70%. At Mehrauli, the demand for 30 units has a probability of 40% and that for 50 units is 60%.

Every day the supplier gets the information about the demand values of the four locations and creates the travel route that starts from the Apple Store and ends at a location after visiting all the locations exactly once. While making the route plan, the supplier goes to the locations in decreasing order of demand. If there is a tie for the choice of the next location, the supplier will go to the location closest to the current location. Also, while creating the route, the supplier can either follow the direct path (if available) from one location to another or can take the path via the Apple Store. If both paths are available (direct and via Apple Store), the supplier will choose the path with minimum distance.

62. If the total number of iPhones delivered in a day is 250 units, then what is the total distance covered in the route (in km)?

63. What is the chance that the total number of iPhones delivered in a day is 260 units and the route ends at Vasant Vihar?

(a) 10.80% (b) 33.33%
(c) 7.56% (d) 17.64%

64. If the first location visited from the Apple Store is Vasant Kunj, then what is the chance that the total distance covered in the route is 80 km?

(a) 3.24% (b) 30%
(c) 5.4% (d) 18%

65. If Vasant Kunj is not the first location to be visited in a route and the total route distance is 58 km, then which of the following is a possible number of iPhones delivered on that day?

(a) 210 (b) 200
(c) 250 (d) 220

Directions for Questions 66 to 69: *Read the information provided and answer the questions which follow.*

The figure below shows the street map for a certain region with the street intersections marked from a through l. A person standing at an intersection can see along the straight lines to the other intersections that are in her line of sight and all other people standing at these intersections. For example, a person standing at intersection g can see all people standing at intersections b, c, e, f, h and k. In particular, the person standing at intersection g can see the person standing at intersection e irrespective of whether there is a person standing at intersection f.

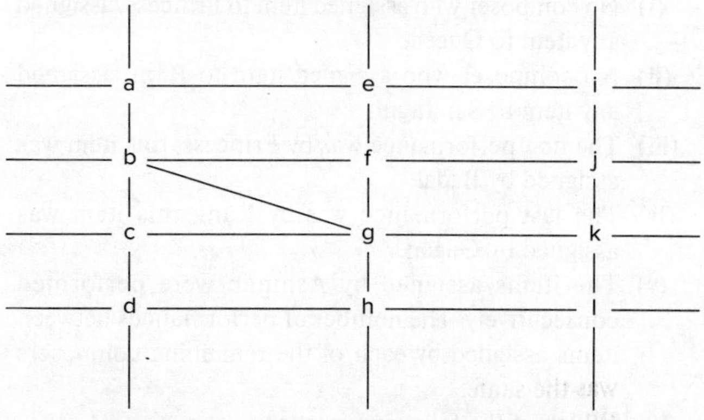

Six people U, V, W, X, Y and Z are standing at different intersections. No two people are standing at the same intersection.

The following additional facts are known.

(i) X, U and Z are standing at the three corners of a triangle formed by three street segments.
(ii) X can see only U and Z.
(iii) Y can see only U and W.
(iv) U sees V standing in the next intersection behind Z.
(v) W cannot see V or Z.
(vi) No one among the six is standing at intersection d.

66. Who is standing at intersection a?

(a) V (b) W
(c) No one (d) Y

67. Who can V see?

(a) U and Z only (b) Z only
(c) U only (d) U, W and Z only

68. What is the minimum number of street segments that X must cross to reach Y?

(a) 1 (b) 2
(c) 3 (d) 4

69. If a new person stands at intersection d, who among the six would she see?

(a) W and X only (b) U and W only
(c) V and X only (d) U and Z only

Directions for Question 70: *Read the information provided and answer the question which follow.*

Princess, Queen, Rani and Samragni were the four finalists in a dance competition. Ashman, Badal, Gagan and Dyu were the four music composers who individually assigned items to the dancers. Each dancer had to individually perform in two dance items, assigned by the different composers. The first items performed by the four dancers were all assigned by the different music composers. No dancer performed her second item before the performance of the first item by any other dancers. The dancers performed their second items in the same sequence of their performance of their first items.

The following additional facts are known.

(i) No composer who assigned item to Princess, assigned any item to Queen.

(ii) No composer who assigned item to Rani, assigned any item to Samragni.

(iii) The first performance was by Princess; this item was assigned by Badal.

(iv) The last performance was by Rani; this item was assigned by Gagan.

(v) The items assigned by Ashman were performed consecutively. The number of performances between items assigned by each of the remaining composers was the same.

70. Which of the following is true?

(a) The third performance was composed by Ashman.
(b) The second performance was composed by Gagan.
(c) The third performance was composed by Dyu.
(d) The second performance was composed by Dyu.

Directions for Questions 71 to 74: A new airlines company is planning to start operations in a country. The company has identified ten different cities which they plan to connect through their network to start with. The flight duration between any pair of cities will be less than one hour. To start operations, the company has to decide on a daily schedule.

The underlying principle that they are working on is the following.

Any person staying in any of these 10 cities should be able to make a trip to any other city in the morning and should be able to return by the evening of the same day.

71. If the underlying principle is to be satisfied in such a way that the journey between any two cities can be performed using only direct (non-stop) flights, then the minimum number of direct flights to be scheduled is:

(a) 45 (b) 90
(c) 180 (d) 135

72. Suppose three of the ten cities are to be developed as hubs. A hub is a city which is connected with every other city by direct flights each way, both in the morning as well as in the evening. The only direct flights which will be scheduled are originating and/or terminating in one of the hubs. Then the minimum number of direct flights that need to be scheduled so that the underlying principle of the airline to serve all the ten cities is met without visiting more than one hub during one trip is:

(a) 54 (b) 120
(c) 96 (d) 60

73. Suppose the 10 cities are divided into 4 distinct groups G1, G2, G3, G4 having 3, 3, 2 and 2 cities respectively and that G1 consists of cities named A, B and C. further, suppose that direct flights are allowed only between two cities satisfying one of the following:

(a) Both cities are in G1
(b) Between A and any city in G2
(c) Between B and any city in G3
(d) Between C and any city in G4

Then the minimum number of direct flights that satisfies the underlying principle of the airline is:

74. Suppose the 10 cities are divided into 4 distinct groups G1, G2, G3, G4 having 3, 3, 2 and 2 cities respectively and that G1 consists of cities named A, B and C. Further, suppose that direct flights are allowed only between two cities satisfying one of the following:

(a) Both cities are in G1
(b) Between A and any city in G2
(c) Between B and any city in G3
(d) Between C and any city in G4

However, due to operational difficulties at A, it was later decided that the only flight that would operate at A would be those to and from B. Cities in G2 would have to be assigned to B or to C.

What would be the maximum reduction in the number of direct flights as compared to the situation befire the operational difficulties arose?

Directions for Questions 75 to 78: Four cars need to travel from Akala (A) to Bakala (B). two routes are available, one via Mamur (M) and the other via Nanur (N). the road from A to M, and from N to B, are both short and narrow. In each case, one car takes 6 minutes to cover the distance, and each additional car increases the travel time per car by 3 minutes because of congestion. (For example, if only two cars drive from A to M, each car takes 9 minutes.) On the road from A to N, one car takes 20 minutes, and each additional car increases the travel time per car by 1 minute. On the road from M to B, one car takes 20 minutes, and each additional car increases the travel time per car by 0.9 minute.

The police department orders each car to take a particular route in such a manner that it is not possible for any car to reduce its travel time by not following the order, while the other cars are following the order.

75. How many cars would be asked to take the route A–N–B, that is Akala–Nanur–Bakala route, by the police department?

76. If all the cars follow the police order, what is the difference in travel time (in minutes) between a car which takes the route A–N–B and a car that takes the route A–M–B?

(a) 1 (b) 0.1

(c) 0.2 (d) 0.9

77. A new one-way road is built from M to N. Each car now has three possible routes to travel from A to B: A–M–B, A–N–B and A–M–N–B. On the road from M to N, one car takes 7 minutes and each additional car increases the travel time per car by 1 minute. Assume that any car taking the A–M–N–B route travels the A–M portion at the same time as other cars taking the A–M–B route, and the N–B portion at the same time as other cars taking the A–N–B route.

How many cars would the police department order to take the A–M–N–B route so that it is not possible for any car to reduce its travel time by not following the order while the other cars follow the order? (assume that the police department would never order all the cars to take the same route.)

78. A new one-way road is built from M to N. Each car now has three possible routes to travel from A to B: A–M–B, A–N–B and A–M–N–B. On the road from M to N, one car takes 7 minutes and each additional car increases the travel time per car by 1 minute. Assume that any car taking the A–M–N–B route travels the A–M portion at the same time as other cars taking the A–M–B route, and the N–B portion at the same time as other cars taking the A–N–B route.

If all the cars follow the police order, what is the minimum travel time (in minutes) from A to B? (Assume that the police department would never order all the cars to take the same route.)

(a) 26 (b) 32

(c) 29.9 (d) 30

ANSWER KEY

1. (c)	2. (d)	3. (d)	4. (b)
5. (e)	6. (d)	7. (a)	8. (c)
9. (a)	10. (d)	11. (a)	12. (a)
13. (d)	14. (d)	15. (d)	16. (a)
17. (c)	18. (d)	19. (c)	20. (c)
21. (b)	22. (b)	23. (c)	24. (c)
25. (c)	26. (b)	27. (c)	28. (c)
29. (c)	30. 40	31. 4	32. 200
33. 200	34. 0	35. 700	36. (c)
37. (d)	38. 1100	39. 625	40. (b)
41. (d)	42. (d)	43. (a)	44. (a)
45. (c)	46. (a)	47. (c)	48. 200
49. 225	50. 300	51. 325	52. 14
53. (b)	54. 19	55. (b)	56. (c)
57. (b)	58. (a)	59. (c)	60. (a)
61. 8	62. 76	63. (c)	64. (d)
65. (a)	66. (c)	67. (a)	68. (b)
69. (a)	70. (d)	71. (c)	72. (c)
73. 40	74. 4	75. 2	76. (b)
77. 2	78. (b)		

SOLUTIONS AND SHORTCUTS

Solutions for Questions 1 to 3:

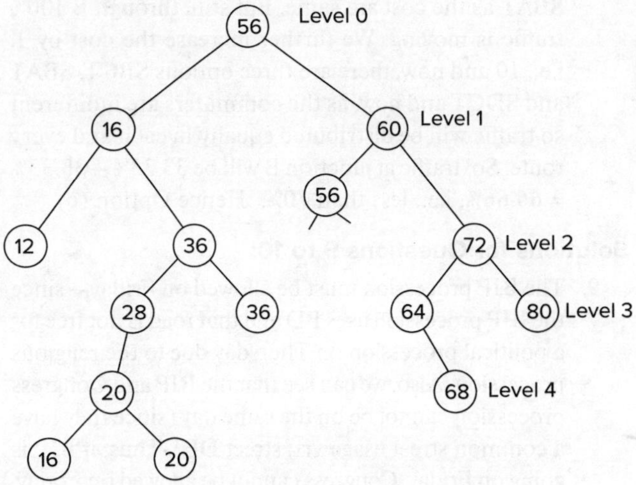

The answers can be read off the above grid:

1. Option (c) is correct.
2. The sum is 208 = 80 + 64 + 36 + 28. Option (d) is correct.
3. There are 2 nodes at the 4th level. Option (d) is correct.

Solutions for Questions 4 to 8:

4. Let the total toll tax at A, B, C and D be a, b, c and d respectively. For the given condition to be met, we have to equalize the cost on each road except SBCT (which is closed).
   So, 14 + a = 9 + a + b = 10 + d + c = 13 + d, from this equation we will get b = 5 and c = 3. Now a + 14 = d + 13. From this, we will set d - a = 1. Both option (b) and option (c) satisfy the given condition but toll value at option (b) is less than option (c). Hence, correct answer is option (b).
5. For the given condition to be met, we have to equalize the cost on each road except SDT. So, 14 + a = 9 + a + b = 7 + b + c = 10 + d + c. From this equation, we will get b = 5. Now, a + 4 = c + 12 = 10 + d + c. From this, we will get d = 2 and c – a = 2. Only option (e) satisfies the given conditions. Hence, the correct answer is option (e).

6. This question is same as the above two. Hence, option (d).
7. Option (a) is the answer.
8. We have to look for the routes which minimise the total cost of the commuters per trip. The minimum cost considering toll tax on any of the given four junctions as zero, then the total traffic will be attracted towards SBCT as it is the cheapest, i.e., 7 and now if we increase the cost to 8, the condition remains the same. Further, if we increase the cost by 1, then there will be two options for the commuters, i.e., SBCT and SBAT as the cost are same. But still, through B 100% traffic is moving. We further increase the cost by 1, i.e., 10 and now, there are three options SBCT, SBAT and SDCT and now, as the commuters are indifferent so traffic will be distributed equally in each and every route. So, traffic at junction B will be 33.33% + 33.33% = 66.66%. i.e., less than 70%. Hence Option (c).

Solutions for Questions 9 to 10:

9. The BJP procession must be allowed on Friday – since the BJP procession uses BD and that road is not free for a political procession on Thursday due to the religious procession. Also, we can see that the BJP and Congress procession cannot be on the same day (since they have a common street usage viz: street DE). Thus, if BJP is going on Friday, Congress cannot be allowed on Friday. Thus, the Congress procession would only be allowed on Thursday. Option (a) is correct.
10. From the previous question, we know that BJP is Friday and Congress is Thursday. Since street AD is used by both BJP and SP, SP must also be on Thursday. The BSP and SP use the same street CE. So, they should be on different days and hence, the BSP is on Friday. Also, the CPM should be on Friday as it cannot be on the same day as the Congress procession. Looking through the options, we have to spot the option that is false. Option (a), (b) and (c) can be seen to be true. Only option (d) is not true as we can see that the Congress and BSP procession cannot be on the same day. Hence, option (d) is correct.

Solutions for Questions 11 to 14:

The figure can be completed on the basis of the given information. The key to complete the figure is the thought that there is a total outflow of 11000 million gallons from the tanks - so there must be a total consumption of 11000 million gallons in the five cities-A, B, C, D and E. We have that, A, D and E consume 6000 million gallons. So, B and C must be consuming 11000 - 6000 = 5000 million gallons. In the ratio 3:2, it would mean 3000 to B and 2000 to E. The oil flow figure would look like this:

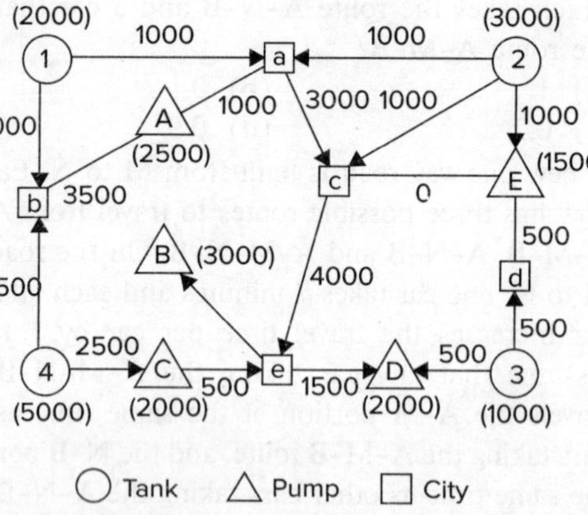

11. The oil flowing into city C is 2500 and the oil flowing out is 500. Thus, option (a) is correct.
12. City C has a consumption of 2000 million gallons. Option (a) is correct.
13. The flow in the pipeline, referred to is 0. Option (d) is correct.
14. Pump 'a' has a flow of 3000, while Pump 'e' has a flow of 4500. The required ratio is 2:3. Option (d) is correct.

Solutions for Questions 15 to 17:

The table given below lists all the possible routes, the number of villages covered in a route and the total number of people staying across all the villages covered in a route.

S. No.	Route	The number of villages covered	The total number of people
1	Kanpur-A-D-G-Lucknow	3	2000
2	Kanpur- A-D-E-G-Lucknow	4	2400
3	KANPUR-A-D-E-F-G-LUCKNOW	5	3400
4	KANPUR-A-B-E-G-LUCKNOW	4	2100
5	KANPUR-A-B-E-F-G-LUCKNOW	5	3100
6	KANPUR-A-B-F-G-LUCKNOW	4	2700
7	KANPUR-A-B-C-E-G-LUCKNOW	5	2800
8	KANPUR-A-B-C-E-F-G-LUCKNOW	6	3800
9	KANPUR-A-B-C-F-G-LUCKNOW	5	3400

S. No.	Route	The number of villages covered	The total number of people
10	KANPUR-C-E-G-LUCKNOW	3	1700
11	KANPUR-C-E-F-G-LUCKNOW	4	2700
12	KANPUR-C-F-G-LUCKNOW	3	2300

15. As the tanker contains 8400 liters of oil supply and everybody is given an oil can of 3 L, the tanker can deliver oil to at the most 8400/3 = 2800 people in a trip. There are eight routes on which the total number of people are either less than or equal to 2800. Option (d) is correct.
16. The only route along which exactly 2800 people stay in the villages is Kanpur-A-B-C-E-G-Lucknow. The number of villages covered is 5. Option (a) is correct.
17. The two balanced-pairs are:
    (i) 2700 people – Kanpur-C-E-F-G-Lucknow and Kanpur-A-B-F-G-Lucknow.
    (ii) 3400 people – Kanpur-A-D-E-F-G-Lucknow and Kanpur-A-B-C-F-G-Lucknow.

    Option (c) is correct.

Solutions for Questions 18 to 22:

18. For minimum cost of transportation, we have to make sure that the milk transported along the path where the cost is minimum.

    Cost for transporting along QBE
    $= 35 \times 8 \times 7 + 50 \times 8 \times 4$
    $= 1960 + 1600 = 3560$
    Cost for transporting along QCE
    $= 40 \times 8 \times 6 + 60 \times 8 \times 4$
    $= 1920 + 1920 = 3840$
    The minimum cost is ₹ 3560. Hence, option (d) is correct.
19. We have to transport milk along the route when the capacities of the intermediate factories is the least, i.e., along Q-C-F-G.

    Therefore, at least 75 + 70 + 50 = 195 tonnes is transported. Hence, option (c) is correct.
20. Assume through Q-A-D, 20 tonnes reaches D (as three trucks can carry 120 tonnes and 100 tonnes would be stored at factory A and through Q-B-D, 160 tonnes are transported and 40 tonnes reaches D.

    The costs involved in both the cases are:
    Q-A-D $= 45 \times 8 \times 3 + 60 \times 8 \times 1 = 1080 + 480 = 1560$
    Q-B-D $= 4 \times 35 \times 8 + 1 \times 70 \times 8 = 1120 + 560 = 1680$
    For any more milk to be transported to D, one truck has to be used which would take the cost above ₹ 1750. Therefore, maximum quantity transported will be 40 tonnes. Hence, option (c) is correct.
21. The milk requirement at all the factories = 635 tonnes Therefore, 635/40 = 16 trucks of material has to be sent to completely fill all the retailer factories. Hence, option (b) is correct.
22. For having the least cost of moving, we should change the route when the distance is not high and the capacities of the intermediate factories are also not high, so that only lower quantity need to be sent. Cost along route Q-C-F-G $= 5 \times 8 \times 40 + 3 \times 8 \times 85 + 2 \times 8 \times 25 = 1600 + 2040 + 400 = 4040$. Cost along route Q-A-D-G $= 45 \times 6 \times 8 + 60 \times 4 \times 8 + 2 \times 80 \times 8 = 5360$.

    Therefore, for 50 tonnes of material to reach G, the minimum cost is ₹ 4040. Hence, option (b) is correct.

Solutions for Questions 23 to 27:

23. The time duration of the longest path will be the time duration of the project, as it will cover all concurrent paths with shorter times. Hence, option (c) is correct. The longest path is 1-3-4-5-8-6-9-10-11. The time duration is 8 + 4 + 7 + 6 + 8 + 9 = 42 days.
24. On the 9th day, C, D and G are done simultaneously. Hence, option (c) is correct.
25. The project will be completed at the earliest if 20 number of labours are at work without stop. Since sum total of time duration of all activities is 53 days => 530 man-days are required to complete the project => 20 labourers will take 530/20 = 26.5 days which is 63% of original time duration of 42 days, thus, 37% less than original. Hence, option (c) is correct.
26. New duration for D = 12 days instead of original 2 days and for G = 15 days instead of original 5 days. Hence, the longest path becomes 1-3-6-9-10-11 and time taken would be 8 + 12 + 6 + 8 + 9 = 43 days. Original time taken = 42 days, thus percentage change $= 1/42 \times 100 = 2.4\%$. Hence, option (b) is correct.
27. The new longest path is 1-3-4-5-8-7-9-10-11 and project duration is 8 + 4 + 7 + 5 + 5 + 8 + 9 = 46 days. Hence, option (c) is correct.

Solutions for Questions 28 to 31:

28. There are ten areas. We need to find the minimum number of vehicles required to travel from any area to any area. Any two areas can be selected in ${}^{10}C_2$ ways. Now for these two areas, a person will need minimum 4 vehicles. (1 to go from A to B, 1 to go from B to A. Similarly, 1 to return to A and 1 to return to B). Thus, minimum number of required vehicles $= 45 \times 4 = 180$. Hence, option (c) is correct.

29. From each centre, there will be vehicles to 7 areas. So, total number of vehicles originating or terminating at each centre = 7 × 4 = 28. For all three centres, it would be 28 × 3 = 84. There are three centres in total. Each centre must also be interconnected. The total number of vehicles between any two centres will be 4. For three centres, it will be 12.
Hence, the required number will be 84 + 12 = 96. Hence, option (c) is correct.
30. In A1, we have three areas namely P, Q, R. A person living in any of these three areas should be able to travel to the other area once in the morning and once in the night (and both ways). Therefore, a total of 4 direct vehicles are required between a pair of areas.
P –> Q (morning vehicle)
P –> Q (evening vehicle)
Q –> P (morning vehicle)
Q –> P (evening vehicle)
Number of vehicles between the areas of A1 = $^3C_2 \times 4 = 12$
Between areas in P and any area in A2 = 3 × 4 = 12
Between Q and any area in A3 = 2 × 4 = 8
Between R and any area in A4 = 2 × 4 = 8
Total = 12 × 2 + 8 × 2 = 40. Hence, 40 vehicles are required.
31. The areas those were a part of A2 will be shifted to either A3 or A4, but that will not have any impact on the number of the total vehicles from A1. The only reduction which will take place due to the number of vehicles stopping from P to R.
Hence, the maximum reduction in the number of direct vehicles as compared to the situation before the operational difficulties arose = 4.

Solutions for Questions 32 to 34:

32. The total requirement at all the tanks = 600 + 500 + 450 + 550 + 700 = 2800.
As the capacity of each pipeline is 1000 liters, at least 800 liters has to flow through the pipeline connecting A and C as the pipeline connecting A and B and the pipeline connecting A and D can carry 1000 liters each. If minimum 800 liters has to flow, the maximum slack could be 200. (1000 – 800 = 200). The correct answer is 200.
33. The minimum flow in the pipeline connecting A and B is 800 liters. 600 liters would be stored at B and only 200 liters would flow from B to E. Hence, 200 is the correct answer.
34. A minimum of 800 liters must be sent through pipeline AC. After 500 liters water is consumed at C, the remaining can be sent through CE and no water need to flow through CF. Hence, 0 is the correct answer.

Solutions for Questions 35 to 37:

35. D sends 1200L (max from dairy to pipeline) to O. O keeps 800L and has 400L more to pump out to Q and R. D also sends 1200L to M. M keeps 200 & has 1000L to pump out, however, due to pipeline capacity constraint of 600L between any 2 pipelines, M can only pump out 600L to P. P keeps 300L and is left with 300L to pump out to Q and R.
Thus, the flow at Q and R together is = 400L + 300L = 700 liters. The correct answer is 700.
36. D needs to pump at least 800 to O, so 50% slack is not possible. Similarly, D needs to pump at least 900 to N, so D-N is also ruled out. M-P can't have a 50% slack as P needs to pump at least 100L to either Q and R (Hence, N can pump at most 300 and O can pump at most 400, but demand at Q + R = 800). Hence, option (c) is correct.
37. When P and N pump to Q, O can pump 350 liters to R. When P and Q pump to R, O can pump only to Q and nothing to R.
Max = 350 liters
Min = 0 liters. Hence, option (d) is correct.

Solutions for Questions 38 to 39:

38. The requirement at all the places = 600 + 800 + 400 + 750 + 750 + 700 = 4000 kiloliters.
Maximum of 1500 kiloliters can flow through the pipeline connecting X and P, and a maximum of 1400 kiloliters can flow through the pipeline connecting X and S (the requirement at S is 400 and as the capacity of the pipeline connecting S and T is 1000 kiloliters, only 1400 and not 1500 kiloliters can flow through X-S).
∴ 1100 kiloliters has to flow through X-R. The correct answer is 1100.
39. Q will receive 375 kiloliters from R. Also, of the 1500 kiloliters going from X to R (maximum possible), 800 is consumed at R and 375 flows to Q. So, U will receive a total of 375 kiloliters from R. Besides, U will receive, 250 kiloliters from T. Thus, U can receive a maximum of 625 kiloliters. The correct answer is 625.

Solutions for Questions 40 to 42:

40. The path for minimum distance is ABCDIH which adds upto 40 units. Hence, option (b) is correct.
41. BDIEFG is one such path which would satisfy the conditions and hence, the distance equals 49 units. Hence, option (d) is correct.
42. There are 8 possible ways, as below:
ABCDI, ABDI, ABEDI, ABEI, AEDI, AEI, AFGEDI, AFGEI. Hence, option (d) is correct.

Solution for Question 43:

43. We need to go through the options and use the MNP rule tool relating to Permutations and Combinations.

If the first option is true, i.e., there are 6 routes between A to C:

We can draw up the following possibilities table for the number of routes between each of the three towns.

A–C	Possibilities for C–B	Possibilities for total routes A–C–B (Say X)	Possibilities for Total routes A–B (Y)
6	5, 4, 3, 2, 1	30, 24, 18, 12, 6	3, 9, 15, 21, 27
			Note: these values are derived based on the logic that X + Y = 33

We further know that there are 23 routes between B to C.

From the above combinations the possibilities for the routes between B to C are:

B–A (X in the table above)	A–C	B–A–C	B–C	Total
3	6	18	5	23
9	6	54 not possible	4	
15	6	90 not possible	3	
21	6	126 not possible	2	
27	6	162 not possible	1	

It is obvious that the first possibility in the table above satisfies all conditions of the given situation.

Solutions for Questions 44 to 47:

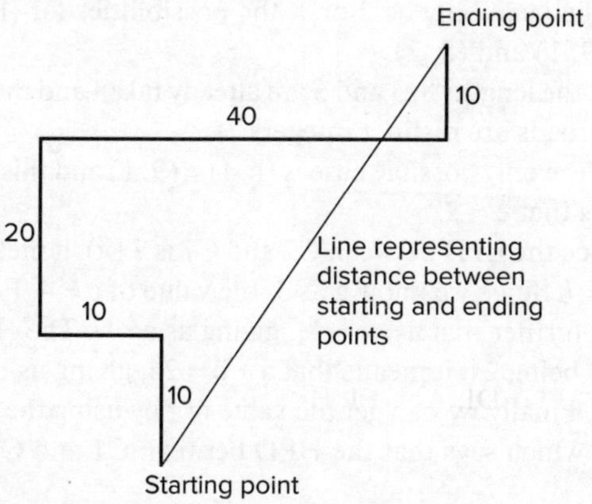

44. 90 kms

45. The end point makes a pythagoras triplet with the starting point, with two legs equal to 30 and 40. So the hypotenuse gives the required distance as 50 km and the direction is north east (as is evident from the figure).

46.

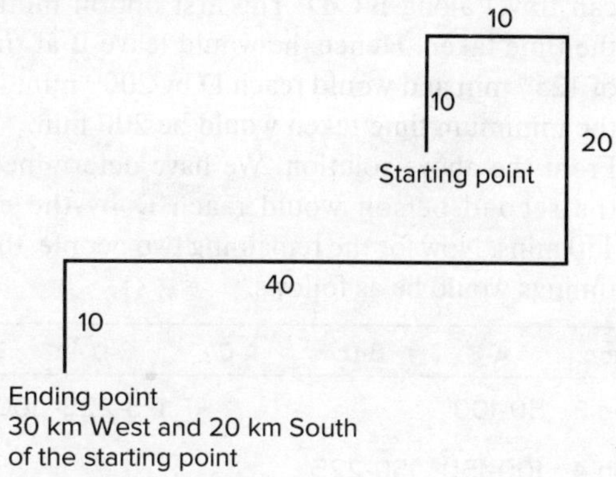

The revised figure would look as above and hence the answer would be 1 (30 west and 20 south).

47.

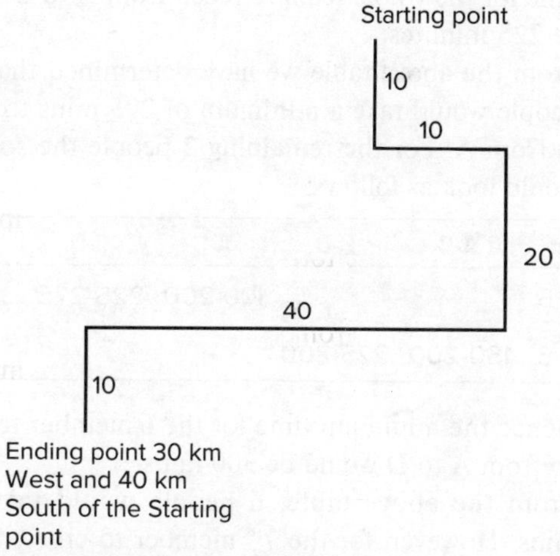

From the figure it is clear that he would be 40 south and 30 west.

Solutions for Questions 48 to 51:

From Statement 4, Speed of each member = 25% of 16 = 4m/min.

To go from A to D, we have the following routes available

A-B-D = 500 m

A-C-D = 600 m

A-B-C-D = 700 m

A-C-B-D = 1000 m

48. Now, the first person would take the shortest A-B-D and would take 125 mins. The second person has two options, he can either wait for the first person to reach B and then he would use that path or He can take the route A-C-D. The second option would

be a faster way. Hence he would take 150 mins to traverse that path. Now, the third person can start his journey at the end of the 50th min because the rope connecting A to B would be free by then. Hence he would reach B by the end of the 100th min. From here, he can either wait till the first person reaches D or he can travel along B-C-D. The first option minimizes the time taken. Hence, he would leave B at the end of 125th min and would reach D by 200th min. Hence the minimum time taken would be 200 min.

49. From the above solution, We have determined that the second person would reach D by the end of 150 mins. Now for the remaining two people, the best timings would be as follows.

Person	A-B	B-D	A-C	C-D	B-C
Person 3	50-100			175-225	100-175
Person 4	100-150	150-225			

From the above table it is clear that the minimum time for the whole team to reach from A to D would be 225 minutes.

50. From the above table we have determined that four people would take a minimum of 225 mins to reach D from A. For the remaining 2 people the solution would look as follows:

Person	A-B	B-D	A-C	C-D	B-C
Person 5			100-200	225-275	
Person 6	150-200	225-300			

Hence the minimum time for the 6-member team to go from A to D would be 300 mins.

51. From the above table, 6 people would take 300 mins. However, for the 7th member to cross, the 6th person need not take the shortest route. Although the individual time might not be the shortest, the time for the whole team would be minimized.

Person	A-B	B-D	A-C	C-D	B-C
Person 1	0-50	50-125			
Person 2			0-100	100-150	
Person 3	50-100			175-225	100-175
Person 4	100-150	150-225			
Person 5			100-200	225-275	
Person 6	150-200			275-325	200-275
Person 7	200-250	250-325			

Hence, the 7th person would reach D at the end of 325th minute.

Solutions for Questions 52 to 57:

From the information provided, we can form the following diagram.

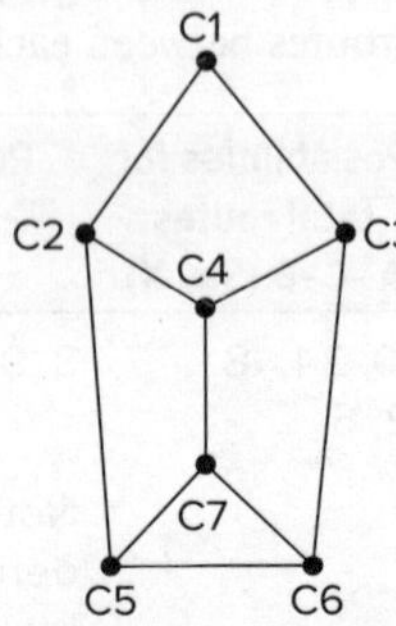

Let the distance of the following routes be as follows:

C1-C2 = a; C1-C3 = b; C2-C4 = c; C3-C4=d; C2-C5 = e C3-C6 = f; C4-C7 = g; C5-C7 = h; C6-C7=I; C5-C6 = j

We now proceed to use the clues to get to the values of the 10 unknown distances.

The third clue (iii), gives us the value of g directly as 3. and from (vi), we have f > 11 and from (i), we have the LPD between C4-C6 is 9. There are two routes between C4-C6: C4 - C7 -C6 and C4 - C3 - C6. The LPD (9 as given in i) would be when we use the route C4-C7-C6, since the other route involves the distance f as part of it, and we already know that it is more than 11. Thus, from C4-C7-C6 = 9, we get g + i = 9 → i = 6.

From (i). C2 - C6 = 3

Shortest route is C2 - C5 - C6

i.e., e + j=3

→ (e, j) = (1, 2) or (2, 1)

From (v), C3 - C7 = 11

The possible routes are C3 - C4 - C7 and C3 - C6 - C7, and the only way in which the LPD could be 11, is if we ignore the C3-C6 route that has a distance of f (>11).

For the route C3 - C4 - C7

d + g = 11 → d = 8

From (iv). C5 - C6 + C5 - C7 = 10 i.e., h + j = 10

Since j can only be 2 or 1, the possibilities for (h, j) are only (9, 1) and (8, 2).

But the lengths 8, 3 and 6 are already taken and the length of the roads are distinct integers.

So, the only possible case is (h, J) = (9, 1) and this further implies that e = 2.

Since the LPD between C2 and C7 is 7 (v), it means that g + c = 7. Since we know g as 3, the value of c = 4. From vii, we get further that a + c = 11, giving us a = 7. The HPD for C2-C3 being 24, it means that a + b = 24, giving us b = 24 - 7 = 17. Finally we can get the value of f by using the second clue - which says that the HPD between C1 and CY = 36.

The HPD between these cities would be got by the value of b + f + j = 17 + 6 + f = 36 → f = 13.

Using the above solution, we can answer the questions given:

52. He would travel C1-C2-C7 a distance of 7 + 4 + 3 = 14.
53. Option (b) is the correct answer
54. F + I = 13 + 6 = 19.
55. Let City X be the cities as follows, for each case we can check the distance traveled by Shaurya and Pallav according to their strategies:
    City 2: Pallav-7, Shaurya-7
    City 3: Pallav-17, Shaurya-17
    City 4: Pallav-11, Shaurya-11
    City 5: Pallav- 9, Shaurya-9
    City 6: Pallav-10, Shaurya-30
    City 7: Pallav- 14, Shaurya-14
    From the given condition given in the question X can only have 6 as its value. We only have 1 possibility for X. Hence, Option (b) is the correct answer.
56. Option (c) is the correct answer
57. Option (b) is the correct answer

Solutions for Questions 58 to 61:

From the information given, We deduce that A, B, C, D, E,F, G, H, M, N, P and Q are terminal stations and R, S, T and V are junction stations. Also, each train runs either in east-west or north-south direction, but not both. All trains stop for 2 minutes at each of the junction stations on the way and for 1 minute at each of the other stations. It takes 2 minutes to reach the next station for trains going in east-west direction and 3 minutes to reach the next station for trains going in north-south direction. From each terminal station, the first train starts at 6 am; the last trains leave the terminal stations at midnight. Otherwise, during the service hours, there are metro services every 15 minutes in the north-south lines and every 10 minutes in the east-west lines. A train must rest for at least 15 minutes after completing a trip at the terminal station, before it can undertake the next trip in the reverse direction.

Let's look at each question individually:

58. There are two possible ways to reach T from M, M-R-T and M-T. Shaurya is ready at 6:00 am. Although there is a direct route from M to T, The first train on that route will leave at 6:20 am and he would reach by 6:39 am. If he takes the route via R he would reach R by 6:11 am and would be able to catch the train coming from A. That train would leave R at 6:13 and reach T by 6:28 am. Hence Option (a) is the correct answer.
59. If Pallav wants to be at G by 7 am, then he should be ready at T at 6:49 am. The train for G would leave T at 6:45 and the next train for G would be at 7:15. So Pallav needs to be at T by 6:45 am. He would take 19mins to reach T directly from M. To reach T by 6:45, Pallav needs to catch the 6:20 train leaving for T. Hence, he should be there at the station by 6:20 am. Option (c) is correct.
60. To go from D to E, there are 2 possible routes for Akash, D-V-T-R-E and D-V-S-R-E. If he takes the first route, then his wait time at the stations would be 5 mins (at D) + 5 mins (at S) + 13 mins(at R) = 23 mins. However, If he takes the second route, his wait time is 5 mins (at D) 2 mins (at V) + 16 mins (at T) = 23 Mins. Hence the answer is Option (a).
61. Commuting time from A to B = 41 mins(Includes wait time & travel time)
    Wait time at Terminals = Minimum 15 mins
    Total time = 56 mins
    So a train coming from A at 6 am would be ready to leave B at 6:56 am. A train leaves station B every 15 mins. So from 6 am to 6:45 am we would have 4 new trains and then at 7 am the train which arrived from A would be ready for departure from B. Similarly 4 trains would be required from A. Hence the answer is 8.

Solutions for Questions 62 to 65:

Based on the information given in the initial paragraph, the distance between the localities would be as shown. The figures given alongside the locality blocks are the demands at these locations and their probabilities.

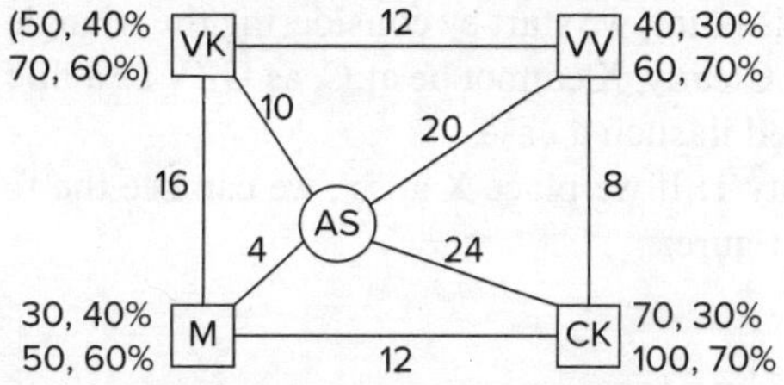

Now, let's analyze each question individually:

62. We can have a maximum of 280 iPhones and a minimum of 190 iPhones. The only possible way to achieve 250 iPhones is if Vasant Kunj had a demand of 70 iPhones, Vasant Vihar had 60, Chanakyapuri had 70 and Mehrauli had 50. According to the conditions given to use, the route we would follow is AS-VK-AS-CK-VV-AS-M. Hence, the total distance traveled is 76 kms.
63. If we end at Vasant Vihar, then the demand at that location is 40 (least demand). Hence the demand at Vasant Kunj, Chanakyapuri and Mehrauli would be 70, 100 and 50 respectively. Chance of this happening would be 0.6 × 0.3 × 0.7 × 0.6 = 7.56%. Hence, Option (c) is the correct answer.
64. From the question we can deduce that Vasant Kunj had a demand of 70 iPhones and Chanakyapuri had

a demand of 70 iPhones. The route for the above scenario would be AS-VK-AS-CK. This completes 44 kms. We have 36 kms left and that could be possible only if we got to Mehrauli from Chanakyapuri and then to Vasant Vihar. For this to be possible, Mehrauli has to have a demand of 50 iPhones and Vasant Vihar would have 40 iPhones. Hence, the chance for this to happen would be $0.6 \times 0.3 = 18\%$. Hence, Option (d) is the correct answer.

65. If Vasant Kunj is not the first location where we are starting from, then the starting location is definitely Chanakyapuri hence traveling 24 kms and Vasant Kunj had a demand of 50 iPhones. The only possibility where we can achieve the remaining 34 kms is if we follow the following route: CK-VV-VK-AS-M. Taking this route would mean that Vasant Vihar had demand for 60 iPhones. Chanakyapuri and Mehrauli can have any demand. The possible values for demand would be 210, 230, 240 or 260. Hence, Option (a) is the correct answer.

Solutions for Questions 66 to 69:

There are two constraints that we need to keep in mind, as we start the question.

(i) Since X, U, Z are standing on three corners of a triangle, they can only be standing on the triangle bcg or the triangle fbg.

(ii) U, Z and V have to be in the same horizontal or vertical line, with Z in the middle of U and V.

From this point, we start by considering the triangle bcg for X, U, Z. Clearly, X cannot be at C, as UZV as a line cannot be created in such a case.

Possibility 1: If we place X at 'b', we can see the following starting figure:

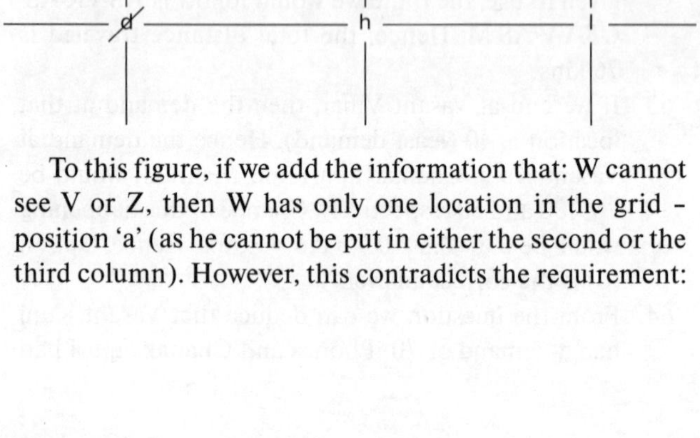

To this figure, if we add the information that: W cannot see V or Z, then W has only one location in the grid - position 'a' (as he cannot be put in either the second or the third column). However, this contradicts the requirement: X can see only U and Z. So, we reject this possibility of placing X.

Possibility 2: If we place X at G.

We will get the figure as shown for possibility 2. In this case, there is no place to put 'Y' in, so that he can see only U and W. Hence, we reject this possible position of X. We also reject the triangle bcg as a possibility to place X, U, Z.

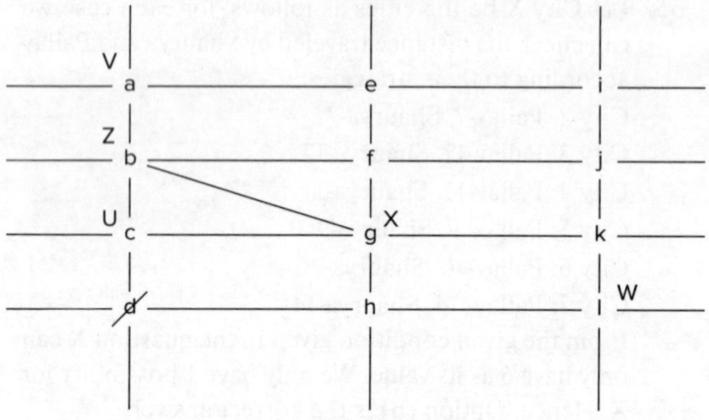

We then move to triangle bfg and can try to fit the six people in the following ways:

Possibility 1: No position for Y, such that he can only see U and W. Hence, rejected.

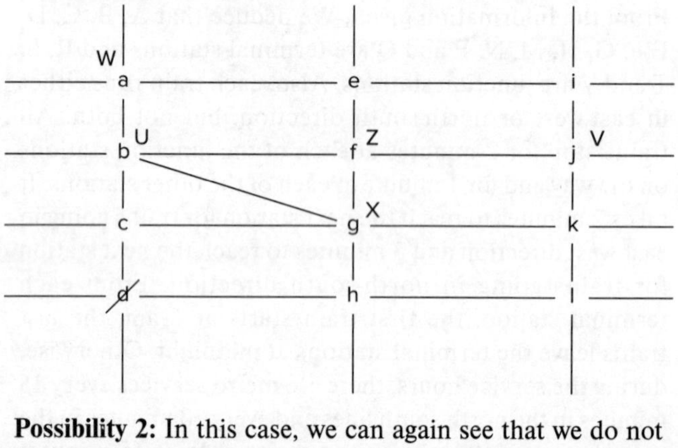

Possibility 2: In this case, we can again see that we do not have a position for Y, such that he can only see U and W.

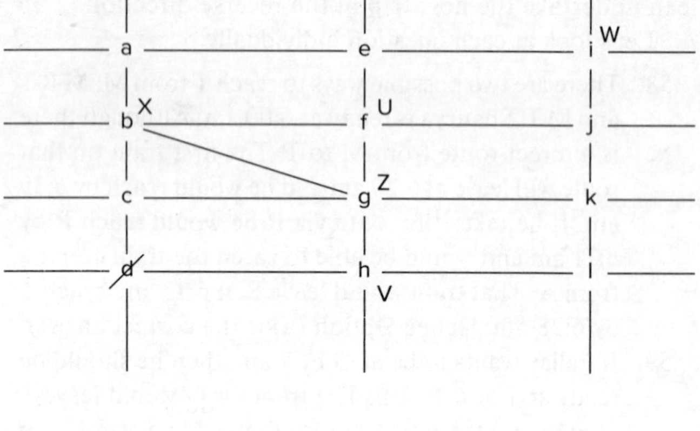

We move onto the last possible arrangement:

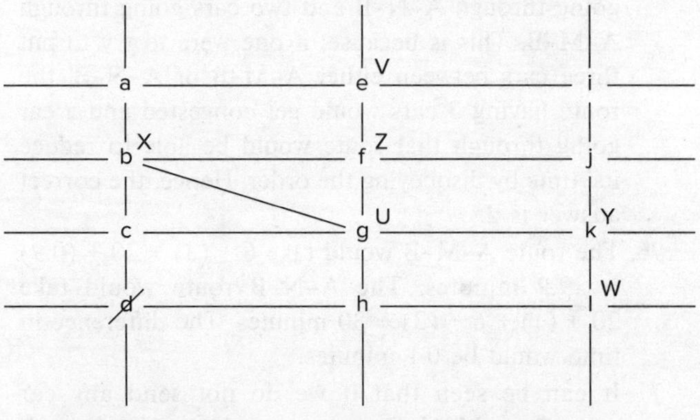

In this arrangement, we see that all the requirements are met. The answers can then be read off this placement.

Note: It might be possible that while solving, you might get luckier and chance upon this particular arrangement earlier, which would essentially depend on your luck- as there is no way in this question to decide on which triangle to start with. Hence, you should be ready to systematically check each arrangement, if required.

In case you can find this particular arrangement earlier, a quick look at the questions suggests that there is only one arrangement (since all the questions are asking for definite answers). In such a case, you can abort looking at the other arrangements and read the answers from here confidently.

The answers are:

66. No one. Option (c) is correct.
67. V can see Z and U only. Option (a) is correct.
68. X, standing at 'b', can go through g to k, using a minimum of 2 street segments. Option (b) is correct.
69. A person, standing at 'd', would see only X and W. Option (a) is correct.

Solution for Question 70:

For this solution, assume, 'Princess = P'; 'Queen = Q'; 'Rani = R' and 'Samragni = S'. Also, Ashman = A; Badal = B; Gagan = G and Dyu = D.

From the basic information in the question, we can make out the following:

There are eight dance performances overall, with each dancer giving two performances - and each music composer assigning two items. Also, from the statements *'No dancer performed her second item before the performance of the first item by any other dancers.'* and *'The dancers performed their second items in the same sequence of their performance of their first items.'*, we can deduce that performances 1 to 4 would be done by P, Q, R, S in same order and performances 5 to 8 would be done by them in the same order. Also, from the statement *'The first items performed by the four dancers were all assigned by different music composers'*, we can see that A, B, G and D would be assigning the first four dances in some order. Hence, dances 5 to 8 would also be assigned one each by the composers A, B, G, D (although their order might change from the order followed for 1 to 4).

Based on these deductions and the direct clues in 3, 4 and 5, we can make the following table to start with (Note: We can deduce that A has assigned items 4 and 5, as it is given to us in clue 5 that *'The items assigned by Ashman were performed consecutively'*. Also, from the second part of clue 5, *'The number of performances between items assigned by each of the remaining composers was the same.'* can only mean that B would have assigned performances 1 and 6; D can assign 2 and 7 and G can assign performances 3 and 8):

Performance #	1	2	3	4
Dancer	P			R
Composer	B	D	G	A
	5	6	7	8
Dancer	P			R
Composer	A	B	D	G

From clue 1, we can see that Q cannot be assigned an item by B or A (since clue 1 says *'No composer who assigned item to Princess, assigned any item to Queen'*). This means that Q must be assigned the 7th performance. She must also be assigned the 3rd performance then - as the order of performances of P, Q, R, S is the same for 5 to 8, as it is for 1 to 4. This also means that S should get the 2nd and 6th performances. The table completes as follows:

Performance #	1	2	3	4
Dancer	P	S	Q	R
Composer	B	D	G	A
	5	6	7	8
Dancer	P	S	Q	R
Composer	A	B	D	G

The answers can be read:

70. Option (d) is correct.

Solutions for Questions 71 to 74:

71. Each pair of cities would need to be connected with 4 flights and this can be understood as follows:

 Suppose, we are talking about cities A and B:

 A → B Morning Flight; B → A Evening Flight; B → A Morning Flight; A → B Evening Flight.

Since, there are 10 cities, there would be 10C2 = 45 pairs of cities. Thus, the number of flights required = 45 × 4 = 180. Option (c) is correct.

72. The three hubs would have 3C2 = 3 pairs of cities. These would be connected with 3 × 4 = 12 flights. The other seven cities need to be connected to each of the hubs. This would mean that for each of the seven non hub cities, there would be 3 pairs of cities created. [For example, if the hubs are A,B and C & the non hubs are D, E, F, G, H, I, J. Then for D, we would need connections D-A; D-B and D-C]. This means that there would be a total of 7 × 3 = 21 pairs of cities. Total flights required to connect the non hub cities with the hub cities = 21 × 4 = 84.

Thus, the total number of flights = 84 + 12 = 96. Option (c) is correct.

73. In this case, there would be 3 pairs of cities that would need to be connected amongst G1 (i.e. between A,B and C). Further, since A is connected to every city in G2 - A would be connected to 3 more cities. Likewise, B and C would be connected to 2 more cities. Thus, there would be a total of 10 pairs of cities that would need catering under the underlying principle of the airline. This would need 10 × 4 = 40 flights. The correct answer is 40.

74. The only reduction would be because of the connection A-C not being there. Though, the connections between A and the cities of G1 are also getting removed, but these connections would be replaced by connections between B and C with those cities that were earlier in G1. Hence, the number of flights gets reduced by 4. The correct answer is 4.

Solutions for Questions 75 to 78:

The road diagram is as shown in the figure:

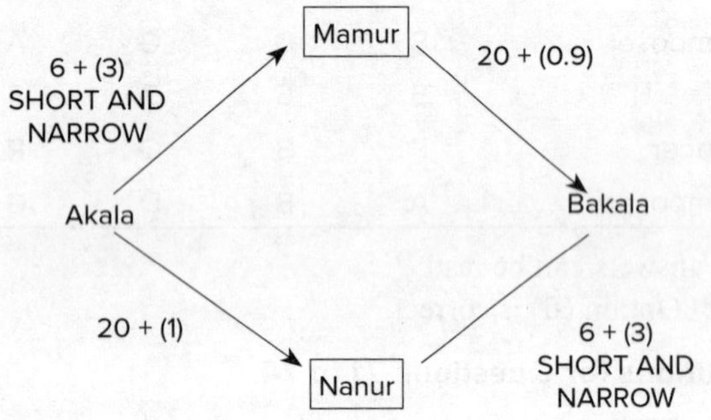

75. It is quite obvious that there should be two cars going through A-N-B and two cars going through A-M-B. This is because, if one were to try to put three cars between either A-M-B or A-N-B, the route having 3 cars would get congested and a car going through that route would be able to reduce its' time by disobeying the order. Hence, the correct answer is 2.

76. The route A-M-B would take 6 + (3) + 20 + (0.9) = 29.9 minutes. The A-N-B route would take 20 + (1) + 6 + (3) = 30 minutes. The difference in time would be 0.1 minutes.

77. It can be seen that if we do not send any car through A-M-N-B, cars ordered to move through A-M-B would disobey and save time - this is against the condition. Hence, 0 cars through A-M-N-B is not a possibility. Checking for 1 car through A-M-N-B, we would need to send 2 cars through either A-M-B or A-N-B. Any car ordered to go with 2 cars along a route would be able to save time by disobeying the order and traveling A-M-N-B. If we sent two cars through A-M-N-B, all cars would follow the order - as there would be no time saving as seen from the following table:

Route	Number of cars	Time taken
A–M–B	1	6 + (3) + (3) + 20 = 32
A–M–N–B	2	6 + (3) + (3) + 7 + (1) 6 + (3) + (3) = 32
A–N–B	1	20 + 6 + (3) + (3) = 32

Hence, the correct answer is 2.

78. As can be seen from the solution of the question above, the minimum travel time would be 32 minutes. Option (b) is correct.

CHAPTER 8

Set Theory and Venn Diagrams

Chapter Launchpad

Scan this QR code for an introductory video on Set Theory and Venn Diagrams

Questions on Set theory/Venn Diagrams are one of the most commonly asked questions in CAT. Besides, they are also very critical for all other aptitude exams - like XAT, IIFT, SNAP, NMAT, UPSC-CSAT, IPMAT, Banking etc.

Let us first take a look at some standard theoretical inputs related to set theory.

SET THEORY

Look at the following diagrams:

Figure 1: Refers to the situation where there are two attributes A and B. (Let's say A refers to people who passed in Physics and B refers to people who passed in Chemistry) Then, the shaded area shows the people who passed both Physics and Chemistry.

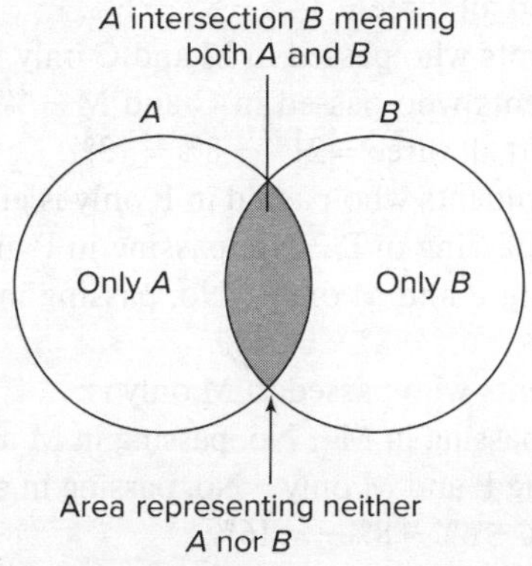

In mathematical terms, the situation is represented as:
Total number of people who passed at least 1 subject = A + B – A ∩ B

Figure 2: Refers to the situation where there are three attributes being measured. In the figure below, we are talking about people who passed Physics, Chemistry and/or Mathematics.

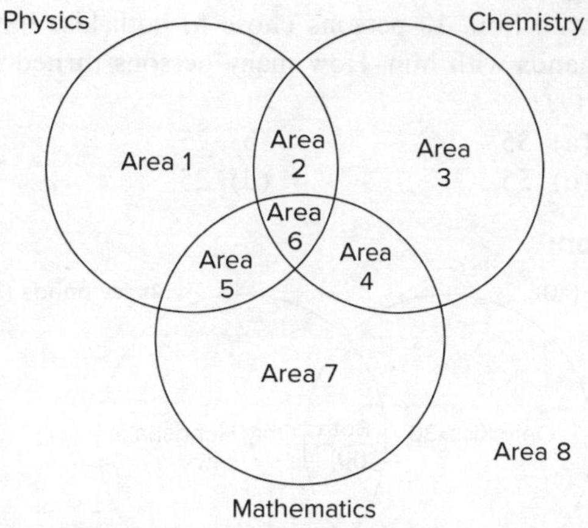

In the above figure, the following explain the respective areas:

Area 1: People who passed in Physics only.

Area 2: People who passed in Physics and Chemistry only (in other words–people who passed Physics and Chemistry but not Mathematics).

Area 3: People who passed Chemistry only.

Area 4: People who passed Chemistry and Mathematics only (also, can be described as people who passed Chemistry and Mathematics but not Physics).

Area 5: People who passed Physics and Mathematics only (also, can be described as people who passed Physics and Mathematics but not Chemistry).

Area 6: People who passed Physics, Chemistry and Mathematics.

Area 7: People who passed Mathematics only.

Area 8: People who passed in no subjects.

Also, take note of the following language which there is normally confusion about:

People passing Physics and Chemistry–represented by the sum of areas 2 and 6.

People passing Physics and Maths–represented by the sum of areas 5 and 6.

People passing Chemistry and Maths–represented by the sum of areas 4 and 6.

People passing Physics–represented by the sum of the areas 1, 2, 5 and 6.

In mathematical terms, this means:

Total number of people who passed at least 1 subject = $P + C + M - P \cap C - P \cap M - C \cap M + P \cap C \cap M$

Let us consider the following questions and see how these figures work in terms of real time problem solving:

WORKED-OUT PROBLEMS

Illustration 1 At the birthday party of Sherry, a baby boy, 40 persons chose to kiss him and 25 chose to shake hands with him. 10 persons chose to both kiss him and shake hands with him. How many persons turned out at the party?

(a) 35 (b) 75
(c) 55 (d) 25

Solution:

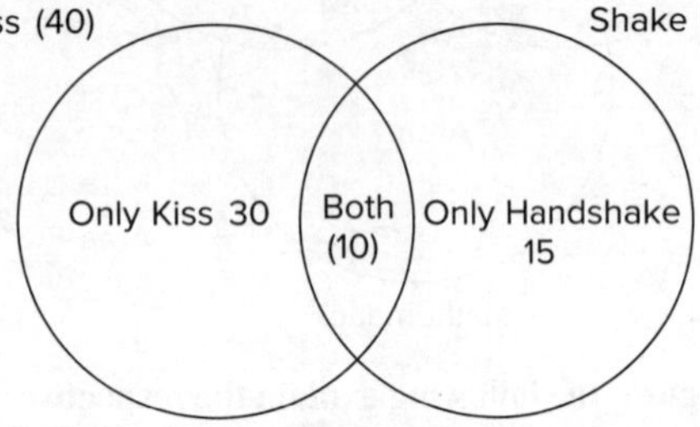

From the figure, it is clear that the number of people at the party were 30 + 10 + 15 = 55.

We can, of course, solve this mathematically as below:
Let n(A) = No. of persons who kissed Sherry = 40
n(B) = No. of persons who shake hands with Sherry = 25
and $n(A \cap B)$ = No. of persons who shook hands with Sherry and kissed him both = 10
Then using the formula, $n(A \cup B) = n(A) + n(B) - n(A \cap B)$
$n(A \cup B) = 40 + 25 - 10 = 55$. Option (c) is the correct answer.

Illustration 2 Directions for Questions 1 to 4: *Refer to the data below and answer the questions that follow:*
In an examination 43% passed in Math, 52% passed in Physics and 52% passed in Chemistry. Only 8% students passed in all the three. 14% passed in Math and Physics, 21% passed in Math and Chemistry, and 20% passed in Physics and Chemistry. Number of students who took the exam is 200.

Let set P, set C and set M denote the students who passed in Physics, Chemistry and Math respectively.

1. How many students passed in Math only?
   (a) 16 (b) 32
   (c) 48 (d) 80
2. Find the ratio of students passing in Math only to the students passing in Chemistry only.
   (a) 16:37 (b) 29:32
   (c) 16:19 (d) 31:49
3. What is the ratio of the number of students passing in Physics only to the students passing in either Physics or Chemistry or both?
   (a) 34/46 (b) 26/84
   (c) 49/32 (d) None of these
4. A student is declared passed in the exam only if he/she clears at least two subjects. The number of students who were declared passed in this exam is:
   (a) 33 (b) 66
   (c) 39 (d) 78

Solution: Let P denote Physics, C denote Chemistry and M denote Maths.

% of students who passed in P and C only is given by % of students who passed in P and C – % of students who passed all three = 20% – 8% = 12%.

% of students who passed in P and M only is given by % of students who passed in P and M – % of students who passed all three = 14% – 8% = 6%.

% of students who passed in M and C only is:
% of students who passed in C and M – % of students who passed all three = 21% – 8% = 13%.

So, % of students who passed in P only is given by:
Total no. passing in P – No. passing in P and C only – No. passing P and M only – No. passing in all three→ 52% – 12% – 6% – 8%– = 26%.

% of students who passed in M only is:
Total no. passing in M – No. passing in M and C only – No. passing P and M only – No. passing in all three → 43% – 13% – 6% – 8% – = 16%.

% of students who passed in Chemistry only is:
Total no. passing in C – No. passing in P and C only – No. passing C and M only – No. passing in all three → 52% – 12% – 13% – 8% – = 19%.

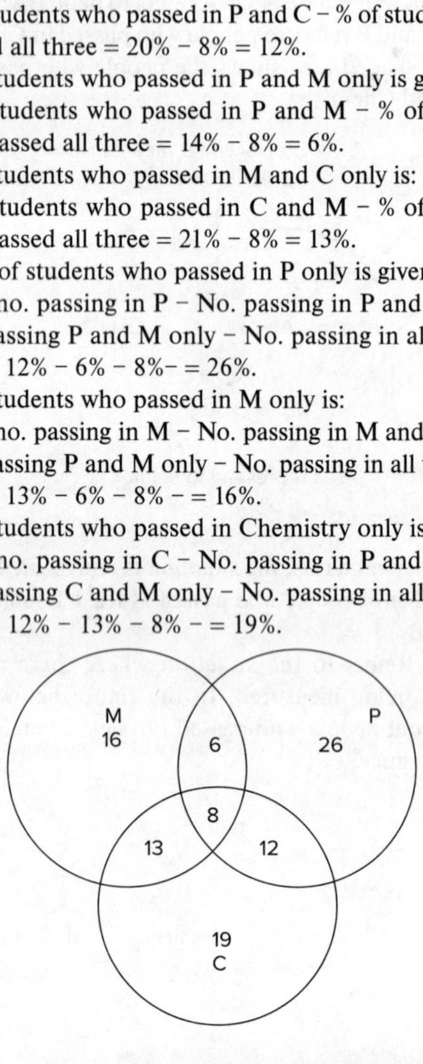

The answers are:
1. Only Math = 16% = 32 people. Option (b) is correct.
2. Ratio of Only Math to Only Chemistry = 16:19. Option (c) is correct.
3. 26:84 is the required ratio. Option (b) is correct.
4. 39% or 78 people. Option (d) is correct.

Illustration 3 In the Mindworkzz club, all the members participate either in the Tambola or the Fete. 320 participate in the Fete, 350 participate in the Tambola and 220 participate in both. How many members does the club have?

(a) 410 (b) 550
(c) 440 (d) None of these

Solution:

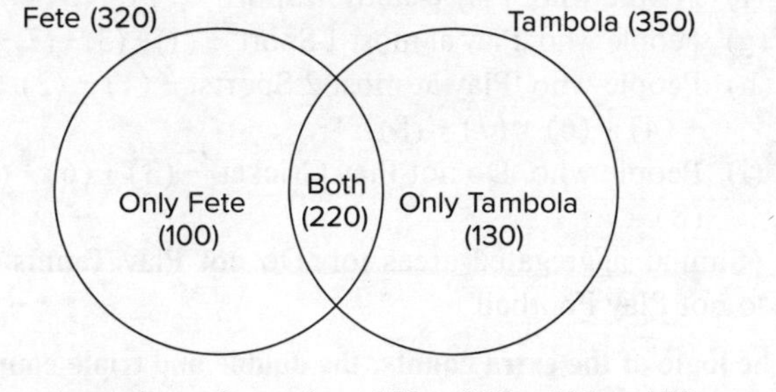

The total number of people = $100 + 220 + 130 = 450$. Option (d) is correct.

Illustration 4 There are 20000 people living in Defence Colony, Gurgaon. Out of them 9000 subscribe to Star TV Network and 12000 to Zee TV Network. If 4000 subscribe to both, how many do not subscribe to any of the two?

(a) 3000 (b) 2000
(c) 1000 (d) 4000

Solution:

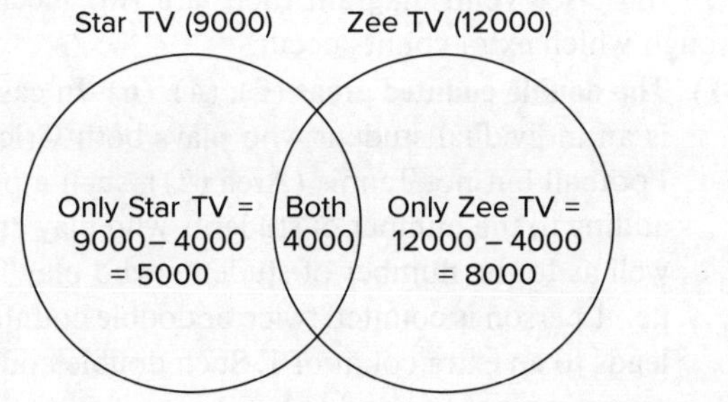

The required answer would be 20000 – 5000 – 4000 – 8000 = 3000. Option (a) is the correct answer.

Illustration 5 Last year, there were 3 sections in the Catalyst, a mock CAT paper. Out of them 33 students cleared the cut-off in Section 1, 34 students cleared the cut-off in Section 2 and 32 cleared the cut-off in Section 3. 10 students cleared the cut-off in Section 1 and Section 2, 9 cleared the cut-off in Section 2 and Section 3, 8 cleared the cut-off in Section 1 and Section 3. The number of people who cleared each section alone was equal and was 21 for each section.

1. How many cleared all the three sections?
   (a) 3 (b) 6
   (c) 5 (d) 7
2. How many cleared only one of the three sections?
   (a) 21 (b) 63
   (c) 42 (d) 52
3. The ratio of the number of students clearing the cut-off in one or more of the sections to the number of students clearing the cutoff in Section 1 alone is?
   (a) 78/21 (b) 3
   (c) 73/21 (d) None of these

Solution:

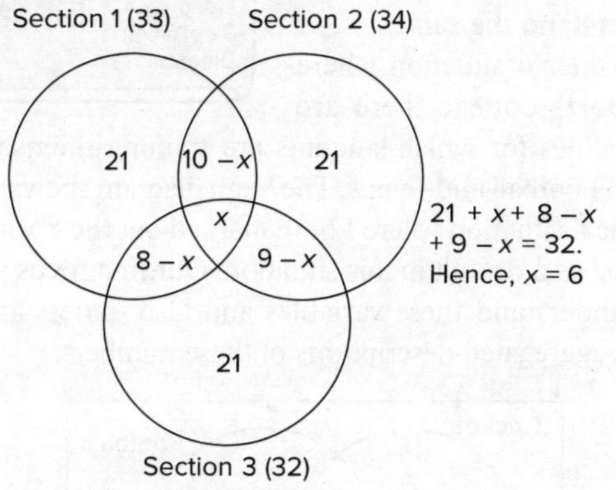

Since, $x = 6$, the figure becomes:

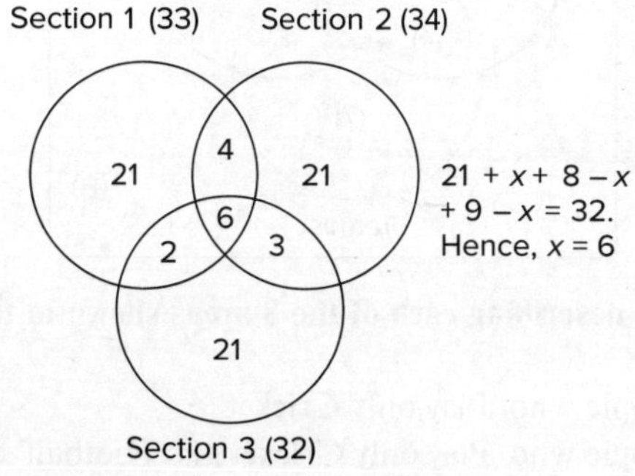

The answers would be:
1. 6. Option (b) is correct.
2. 21 + 21 + 21 = 63. Option (b) is correct.
3. (21 + 21 + 21 + 6 + 4 + 3 + 2)/21 = 78/21. Option (a) is correct.

SPECIAL NOTE ON VENN DIAGRAMS

It is important for you to understand that the Venn diagram is the most critical of all the question types in the Data Interpretation and Logical Reasoning for the CAT. Every year for the past decade, there is invariably at least one set on Venn diagrams in the CAT exam. The reason for the same is not difficult to understand. The 3 set Venn diagram and the 4 set Venn diagrams provide ample opportunity to the question setter to play with variables since they are an interaction of various variables with one another.

THE 3-SET VENN DIAGRAM

Let us take the example of the 3 set Venn diagram, which provides an interesting analytical situation. This diagram gives rise to 8 independent numbers, that are accessed through different languages. It also gives rise to a few aggregated descriptions of these numbers. Let's take a look to understand the same.

Concept Explainer

Scan this QR code to access a conceptual video on a 3-set Venn Diagram

Consider a situation where in a sports college there are 3 disciplines for which students are training themselves – Cricket, Football and Tennis. The Venn diagram shown shows the typical situation where I have marked out the 8 variables that exist as a default in this situation. Our first focus should be to understand these variables and also understand the various aggregated descriptions of these numbers.

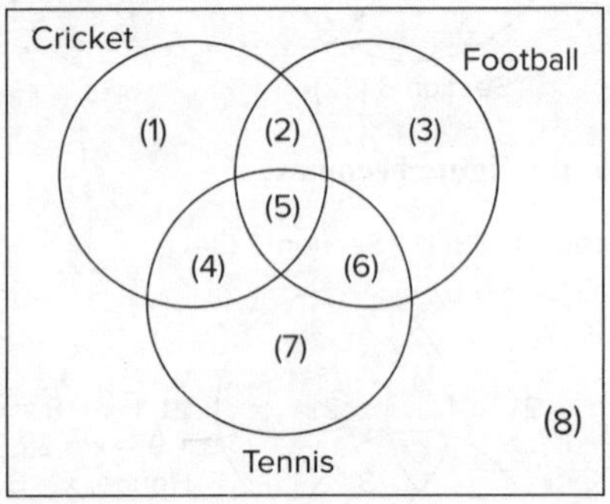

Language describing each of the 8 areas shown in the Venn diagram.

(1) People who 'Play only Cricket'.
(2) People who 'Play only Cricket and Football' can also be described by the language 'People who play Cricket and Football but not Tennis'.
(3) People who 'Play only Football'.
(4) People who 'Play only Cricket and Tennis' can also be described by the language 'People who play Cricket and Tennis but not Football'.
(5) People who 'Play all three sports'.
(6) People who 'Play only Tennis and Football' can also be described by the language 'People who play Tennis and Football but not Cricket'.
(7) People who 'Play only Tennis'.
(8) People who 'Play none of the games'.

Language normally used for the aggregated areas:

(a) People who 'Play Cricket' (1) + (2) + (4) + (5) – (not to be confused with 'Play only Cricket'). Similar for 'Play Tennis and Play Football'.
(b) People who 'Play Cricket and Football' (2) + (5) (not to be confused with 'Play only Cricket and Football' or with 'Play Cricket and Football but not Tennis'). Similar language and area aggregations for 'Play Cricket and Tennis' and 'Play Football and Tennis'.
(c) People who 'Play exactly 2 Sports' – (2) + (4) + (6).
(d) People who 'Play at least 2 Sports' – (2) + (4) + (5) + (6).
(e) People who 'Play at least 1 Sport' – (1) + (2) + (3) + (4) + (5) + (6) + (7).
(f) People who 'Play exactly 1 Sport' – (1) + (3) + (7).
(g) People who 'Play at most 1 Sport' – (1) + (3) + (7) + (8).
(h) People who 'Play at most 2 Sports' – (1) + (2) + (3) + (4) + (6) + (7) + (8).
(i) People who 'Do not Play Cricket' – (3) + (6) + (7) + (8).

Similar aggregated areas for 'Do not Play Tennis' and 'Do not Play Football'.

The logic of the extra counts, the double and triple counts.
Imagine the following situation:

In a school, with 100 students, where everyone plays at least 1 of the three sports of Cricket, Tennis or Football, it was found that 70 play Cricket, 50 play Tennis and 60 play Football.

Interpretation: In this situation, we have only 100 students, yet the sum of the three numbers given to us – viz: Cricket, Tennis and Football is 70 + 50 + 60 = 180. So, how do 100 people get counted 180 times? How does an extra count of 80 (i.e., 180 – 100) get generated?

In the 3-set Venn diagram there are two mechanisms through which extra counts occur.

(1) The double counted areas (2), (4), (6)–In case, there is an individual student who plays both Cricket and Football but not Tennis (Area (2)), such a person is adding to the number of students who play cricket as well as to the number of students who play football. i.e., 1 person is counted twice or double counted. This leads to an extra count of 1. Such double counts also occur in areas (6) and (4).

(2) The triple counted area–When a student falls under the area (5), i.e., plays all three sports, it is a case of 1 person getting counted thrice or triple counted. A triple count means an extra count of 2.

In the numerical situation we have, there is an extra count of 80. This has to get justified by: Number of double counts × 1 + Number of triple counts × 2 = 80.

This is what creates a highly interesting situation in such questions →i.e., there are 4 variables you have to play with in a multiple possibility situation, where you can move numbers from one part to another to see how various maxima/minima situations develop. These things are amply brought about in the problems, we have set for you in LOD 2 and LOD 3 exercise of this chapter. I suggest that for each of the question sets provided in LOD 2 and 3, you should go through closely and familiarize yourself with the situations created inside logical Venn diagram questions.

Concept Explainer

Scan this QR code to access a conceptual video on a 4-set Venn Diagram

Let us now look at the 4-set situation. Imagine a situation, where students are tested in 4 exams namely: Physics, Chemistry, Biology and Mathematics. And students can pass or fail in each exam, independent of each other. Just like the previous situation gave rise to 7 different areas inside the circles and 1 outside, the 4 set situation gives rise to 15 different areas inside the circles and 1 outside. Hence, the picture you need to draw in such a case has to have 15 areas represented inside. These include:

Passed all 4 subjects (PCMB) – 1 area; Passed exactly 3 subjects [PCM, PCB, PMB, CMB] – 4 areas; Passed exactly 2 subjects [PC, PM, PB, CM, CB, MB] – 6 areas; Passed exactly 1 subject [P, C, M, B] – 4 areas. Passed none of the subjects – 1 area. The best way to represent these 15 areas, that fall inside the sets is shown here:

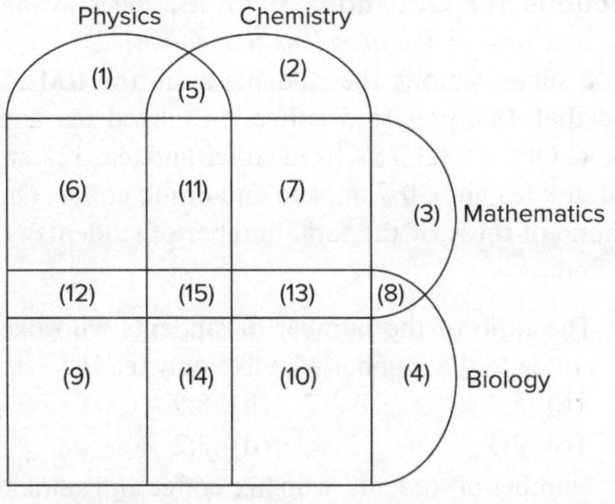

The table shows the various combinations represented in the figure.

Exactly 1 Subject	Area Number	Remarks
Physics Only	1	
Chemistry Only	2	
Mathematics Only	3	
Biology Only	4	
Exactly 2 Subjects		
P & C Only	5	
P & M Only	6	
C & M Only	7	
B & M Only	8	
P & B Only	9	
C & B Only	10	
Exactly 3 Subjects		
Only PCM	11	Also referred to as PCM but not B.
Only PMB	12	Also referred to as PMB but not C.
Only CMB	13	Also referred to as CMB but not P.
Only PCB	14	Also referred to as PCB but not M.
All 4 Subjects		
PCMB	15	
None of the 4 Subjects	16 (not shown in the figure)	

Various aggregations that would be referred to in problems include:

Aggregations	Areas	Similar aggregations
Passed Physics	1, 5, 6, 11, 12, 15, 9, 14	Passed Chemistry, Passed Mathematics, Passed Biology
Passed Physics and Chemistry (PC)	5, 11, 15, 14	PM (6, 11, 12, 15); CM (7, 11, 13, 15); BM (8, 12, 13, 15); PB (9, 12, 14, 15); CB (10, 13, 14, 15)
Passed Physics, Chemistry and Mathematics	11, 15	Not to be confused with Passed only PCM. Similar, definitions for Passed PCB (14, 15); Passed PMB (12, 15) ; Passed CMB (13, 15)
Did not Pass Physics	2, 7, 13, 10, 3, 4, 8, 16 (Note: 16 is not shown, but you can imagine it as the area outside the figure)	Similar areas for Did not pass Chemistry, Did Not Pass Mathematics; Did not Pass Biology.

Aggregations	Areas	Similar aggregations
Passed at least 3 subjects	11, 12, 13, 14, 15	
Passed at least 2 subjects	5, 6, 7, 8, 9, 10, 11, 12, 13, 14, 15	
Passed at most 2 subjects	16, 1, 2, 3, 4, 5, 6, 7, 8, 9, 10	
Passed at most 1 subject	16, 1, 2, 3, 4	
Did not pass either Physics or Chemistry	3, 4, 8, 16	Similar area aggregations for Did not pass any combination of 2 subjects

LEVEL OF DIFFICULTY (I)

Directions for Questions 1 to 2: *Refer to the data below and answer the questions that follow:*

In the Indian athletic squad that went to the Olympics, 21 athletes were in the triathlon team; 26 were in the pentathlon team; and 29 were in the marathon team. 14 athletes can take part in triathlon and pentathlon; 12 can take part in marathon and triathlon; 15 can take part in pentathlon and marathon; and 8 can take part in all the three games.

1. How many players are there in all?
   (a) 35 (b) 43
   (c) 49 (d) None of these
2. How many were in the marathon team only?
   (a) 10 (b) 14
   (c) 18 (d) 15

Directions for Questions 3 to 4: *Refer to the data below and answer the questions that follow:*

In a test in which 120 students appeared, 90 passed in History, 65 passed in Sociology and 75 passed in Political Science. 30 students passed in only one subject and 55 students in only two. 5 students passed no subjects.

3. How many students passed in all the three subjects?
   (a) 25 (b) 30
   (c) 35 (d) Data insufficient
4. Find the number of students who passed in at least two subjects.
   (a) 85 (b) 95
   (c) 90 (d) Data insufficient

Directions for Questions 5 to 8: *Refer to the data below and answer the questions that follow:*

5% of the passengers who boarded Guwahati-New Delhi Rajdhani Express on 20th February, 2025 do not like coffee, tea and ice cream and 10% like all the three. 20% like coffee and tea, 25% like ice cream and coffee and 25% like ice cream and tea. 55% like coffee, 50% like tea and 50 % like ice cream.

5. The number of passengers who like only coffee is greater than the passengers who like only ice cream by:
   (a) 50% (b) 100%
   (c) 25% (d) 0
6. The percentage of passengers who like both tea and ice cream but not coffee is:
   (a) 15 (b) 5
   (c) 10 (d) 25
7. The percentage of passengers who like at least 2 of the 3 products is:
   (a) 40 (b) 45
   (c) 50 (d) 60
8. If the number of passengers is 180, then the number of passengers who like ice cream only is:
   (a) 10 (b) 18
   (c) 27 (d) 36

Directions for Questions 9 to 16: *Refer to the data below and answer the questions that follow:*

In a survey among the students at all the IIMs, it was found that 48% preferred coffee, 54% liked tea and 64% smoked. Of the total, 28% liked coffee and tea, 32% smoked and drank tea and 30% smoked and drank coffee. Only 6% did none of these. If the total number of students is 2000 then find:

9. The ratio of the number of students who like only coffee to the number who like only tea is:
   (a) 5:3 (b) 8:9
   (c) 2:3 (d) 3:2
10. Number of students who like coffee and smoking but not tea is:
    (a) 600 (b) 240
    (c) 280 (d) 360
11. The percentage of those who like coffee or tea but not smoking among those who like at least one of these is:
    (a) More than 30 (b) Less than 30
    (c) Less than 25 (d) None of these

12. The percentage of those who like at least one of these is:
(a) 100 (b) 90
(c) Nil (d) 94

13. The two items having the ratio 1:2 are:
(a) Tea only and tea and smoking only.
(b) Coffee and smoking only and tea only.
(c) Coffee and tea but not smoking and smoking but not coffee and tea.
(d) None of these.

14. The number of persons who like coffee and smoking only and the number who like tea only bear a ratio:
(a) 1:2 (b) 1:1
(c) 5:1 (d) 2:1

15. Percentage of those who like tea and smoking but not coffee is:
(a) 14 (b) 14.9
(c) Less than 14 (d) More than 15

16. 30 monkeys went to a picnic. 25 monkeys chose to irritate cows while 20 chose to irritate buffaloes. How many chose to irritate both buffaloes and cows?
(a) 10 (b) 15
(c) 5 (d) 20

Directions for Questions 17 to 20: *Refer to the data below and answer the questions that follow:*

In the CBSE Board Exams last year, 53% passed in Biology, 61% passed in English, 60% in Social Studies, 24% in Biology and English, 35% in English and Social Studies, 27% in Biology and Social Studies and 5% in none.

17. Percentage of passes in all subjects is:
(a) Nil (b) 12
(c) 7 (d) 10

18. If the number of students in the class is 200, how many passed in only one subject?
(a) 48 (b) 46
(c) More than 50 (d) Less than 40

19. If the number of students in the class is 300, what will be the % change in the number of passes in only two subjects, if the original number of students is 200?
(a) More than 50% (b) Less than 50%
(c) 50% (d) None of these

20. What is the ratio of percentage of passes in Biology and Social Studies but not English in relation to the percentage of passes in Social Studies and English but not Biology?
(a) 5:7 (b) 7:5
(c) 4:5 (d) None of these

Directions for Questions 21 to 25: *Refer to the data below and answer the questions that follow:*

In the McGraw Hill Mindworkzz Quiz held last year, participants were free to choose their respective areas from which they were asked questions. Out of 880 participants, 224 chose Mythology, 240 chose Science and 336 chose Sports, 64 chose both Sports and Science, 80 chose Mythology and Sports, 40 chose Mythology and Science and 24 chose all the three areas.

21. The percentage of participants who did not choose any area is:
(a) 23.59% (b) 30.25%
(c) 37.46% (d) 27.27%

22. Of those participating, the percentage who choose only one area is:
(a) 60% (b) More than 60%
(c) Less than 60% (d) More than 75%

23. Number of participants who chose at least two areas is:
(a) 112 (b) 24
(c) 136 (d) None of these

24. Which of the following areas shows a ratio of 1:8?
(a) Mythology and Science but not Sports: Mythology only.
(b) Mythology and Sports but not Science: Science only.
(c) Science: Sports.
(d) None of these.

25. The ratio of students choosing Sports and Science but not Mythology to Science but not Mythology and Sports is:
(a) 2:5 (b) 1:4
(c) 1:5 (d) 1:2

Directions for Questions 26 to 30: *Refer to the data below and answer the questions that follow:*

The table here gives the distribution of students according to professional courses.

Courses	Students			
	English		Math	
	Males	Females	Males	Females
Part-time MBA	30	10	50	10
Full-time MBA only	150	8	16	6
CA only	90	10	37	3
Full time MBA and CA	70	2	7	1

26. What is the percentage of Math students over English students?
(a) 50.4 (b) 61.4
(c) 49.4 (d) None of these

27. The average number of females in all the courses is (count people doing full-time MBA and CA as a separate course):
(a) Less than 12 (b) Greater than 12
(c) 12 (d) None of these

28. The ratio of the number of girls to the number of boys is:
(a) 5:36 (b) 1:9
(c) 1:7.2 (d) None of these

29. The percentage increase in students of full-time MBA only over CA only is:
(a) Less than 20 (b) Less than 25
(c) Less than 30 (d) More than 30

30. The number of students doing full-time MBA or CA is:
(a) 320 (b) 80
(c) 160 (d) None of these

Directions for Questions 31 to 34: *Refer to the data below and answer the questions that follow:*

A newspaper agent sells The TOI, The HT and The IN in equal numbers to 302 persons. Seven get HT and IN, twelve get The TOI and IN, nine get The TOI and HT and three get all the three newspapers. The details are given in the Venn diagram:

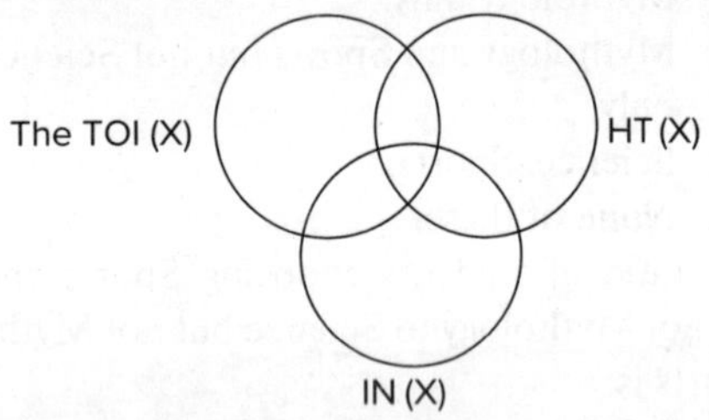

31. How many get only one paper?
(a) 280 (b) 327
(c) 109 (d) None of these

32. What percent get The TOI and/or The HT but not The IN?
(a) More than 65% (b) Less than 60%
(c) ≅ 64% (d) None of these

33. The number of persons buying The TOI and The HT only, The TOI and The IN only and The HT and The IN only are in the ratio of:
(a) 6:4:9 (b) 6:9:4
(c) 4:9:6 (d) None of these

34. The difference between the number reading The HT and The IN only and The HT only is:
(a) 77 (b) 78
(c) 83 (d) None of these

35. A group of 78 people watch Zee TV, Star Plus or Sony. Of these, 36 watch Zee TV, 48 watch Star Plus and 32 watch Sony. If 14 people watch both Zee TV and Star Plus, 20 people watch both Star Plus and Sony, and 12 people watch both Sony and Zee TV, find the ratio of the number of people who watch only Zee TV to the number of people who watch only Sony.
(a) 9:4 (b) 3:2
(c) 5:3 (d) 7:4

Directions for Questions 36 to 37: *Answer these questions based on the following information:*

The following data was observed from a study of car complaints received from 180 respondents at Colonel Verma's car care workshop, viz., engine problem, transmission problem or mileage problem. Of those surveyed, there was no one who faced exactly two of these problems. There were 90 respondents who faced engine problems, 120 who faced transmission problems and 150 who faced mileage problems. 30 of them faced no problems.

36. How many of them faced all the three problems?
(a) 45 (b) 60
(c) 90 (d) 20

37. How many of them faced either transmission problems or engine problems, but not mileage problems?
(a) 30 (b) 60
(c) 90 (d) 40

Directions for Questions 38 to 42: *Answer these questions based on the details below:*

Given below are five diagrams one of which describes the relationship among the three classes given in each of the five questions that follow. You have to decide which of the diagrams is the most suitable for a particular set of classes. The number of the diagram is your answer.

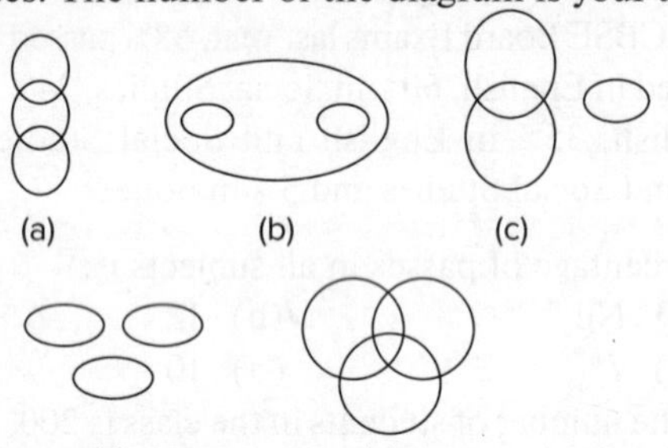

38. Elephants, Tigers, Animals
39. Administrators, Doctors, Authors
40. Platinum, Copper, Gold
41. Gold, Platinum, Ornaments
42. Television, Radio, Mediums of Entertainment

Directions for Questions 43 to 45: A and B are two sets (e.g., A = mothers, B = women). The elements that could belong to both sets (e.g., women who are mothers) is given by set C = A.B. The elements which could belong to either A or B, or both, is indicated by set D = A ∪ B. A set that does not contain any elements is known as a null set, represented by @ (for example, if none of the women in set B is a mother, then C = A.B. is a null set, or C = @). Let 'V' signify the set of all vertebrates; 'M' the set of all mammals; 'D' dogs; 'F' fish; 'A' Alsatian and 'P' a dog named Pluto.

43. If P.A. = @ and P ∪ A = D, then which of the following is true?
(a) Pluto and Alsatians are dogs
(b) Pluto is an Alsatian
(c) Pluto is not a Alsatian
(d) D is a null set.

44. If y = F ∪ (D.V) is not a null set, it implies that
(a) All fish are vertebrates
(b) All dogs are vertebrates.
(c) Some fish are dogs.
(d) None of the above.

45. If Z = (P.D) ∪ M, then
(a) The elements of Z consist of Pluto the dog or any other mammal.
(b) Z implies any dog or mammal.
(c) Z implies Pluto or any dog that is a mammal.
(d) Z is a null set.

Directions for Question 46: *Each item is followed by two statements, A and B. Answer each questions using the following instructions.*

Choose A: if the question can be answered by one of the statements alone but not by the other.

Choose B: if the question can be answered by using either statement alone.

Choose C: if the question can be answered by using both the statements together, but cannot be answered by using either statement alone.

Choose D: if the question cannot be answered by either of the statements.

46. People in a club either speak French or Russian or both. Find the number of people in the club who speak only French.
A. There are 300 people in the club and the number of people who speak both French and Russian is 196.
B. The number of people who speak only Russian is 58.

Directions for Question 47:

47. In a hospital there were 200 Diabetes, 150 Hyperglycemia and 150 Gastroenteritis patients. Of these, 80 patients were treated for both Diabetic and Hyperglycemia. Sixty patients were treated for Gastroenteritis and Hyperglycemia, while 70 were treated for Diabetes and Gastroenteritis. Some of these patients have all the three diseases. Doctor Dennis treats patients with only Diabetes. Doctor Hormis treats patients with only Hyperglycemia and Doctor Gerard treats patients with only Gastroenteritis. Doctor Paul is a generalist. Therefore, he can treat patients with multiple diseases. Patients always prefer a specialist for their disease. If Dr. Dennis had 80 patients, the other three doctors can be arranged in terms of the number of patients treated as:
(a) Paul > Gerard > Hormis
(b) Paul > Hormis > Gerard
(c) Gerard > Paul > Hormis
(d) None of these

Directions for Questions 48 to 49: *Answer the questions on the basis of the information given below.*

New Age Consultants have three consultants Gyani, Medha and Buddhi. The sum of the number of projects handled by Gyani and Buddhi individually is equal to the number of projects in which Medha is involved. All three consultants are involved together in 6 projects. Gyani works with Medha in 14 projects. Buddhi has 2 projects with Medha but without Gyani, and 3 projects with Gyani but without Medha. The total number of projects for New Age Consultants is one less than twice the number of projects in which more than one consultant is involved.

48. What is the number of projects in which Gyani alone is involved?
(a) Uniquely equal to zero
(b) Uniquely equal to 1
(c) Uniquely equal to 4
(d) Can't be determined uniquely

49. What is the number of projects in which Medha alone is involved?
(a) Uniquely equal to zero
(b) Uniquely equal to 1
(c) Uniquely equal to 4
(d) Can't be determined

Directions for Question 50:

50. A survey on a sample of 25 new cars being sold at a local auto dealer was conducted to see which of the three popular options (air-conditioning, radio and power windows) were already installed. The survey found:
15 had air-conditioning;
2 had air-conditioning and power windows but no radios;
12 had radio;
6 had air-conditioning and radio but no power windows;
11 had power windows;
4 had radio and power windows;
3 had all three options.
What is the number of cars that had none of the options?
(a) 4 (b) 3
(c) 1 (d) 2

LEVEL OF DIFFICULTY (II)

1. 60% of the people like to read TOI, 50% of the people like to read HT then at least what % of people like both?
2. 60% of the people like red colour, 90% of the people like yellow colour, 80% of the people like green colour; then at most what percentage of people like all three colours?

Directions for Questions 3 to 4: *Answer these questions based on the details below:*

Eighty-five friends went to a party where they were offered three drinks: Vodka, Whisky, and Rum. It was known that 20 of them took all the 3 drinks and 55 of them took at least 2 of the 3 drinks. Each drink cost ₹ 1000 and the total receipt of the party was ₹ 145000.

3. How many friends did not try any of the drinks?
4. How many friends took exactly one drink?

Directions for Questions 5 to 8: *Answer these questions based on the details below:*

In a school, the students are fans of none or of one or more of the four actors- Shahrukh, Salman, Aamir, Hritik. 20% of the students do not like any of these four actors. The four actors given in the above order are liked by 230, 180, 180 and 220 students respectively. The number of students who like exactly 2 actors for any two actors is 20. There are 30 students who like all the four actors but there is nobody who likes exactly three out of four actors.

5. How many students like exactly two actors?
6. How many students like at least two actors?
7. How many students are there in the school?
8. What is the percentage of the total students who like Hritik also like at least one other actor?

Directions for Questions 9 to 10: *Answer these questions based on the details below:*

In a college, where every student follows at least one of the three teams CSK, RCB or KKR, 60% follow CSK, 82% follow RCB and 66% follow KKR.

9. What can be the maximum percentage of students who follow exactly three teams?
10. What can be the minimum percentage of students who follow exactly three teams?

Directions for Questions 11 to 14: *Answer these questions based on the details below:*

150 students in a class were tested for QA, DI and VA. Pass marks were kept at 30% net marks for each subject. 56 passed in QA, 63 passed in only one subject, 11 passed in only QA and 17 passed in only DI & VA.

11. How many students are there who didn't pass in any subjects?
    (a) 28 (b) 25
    (c) 20 (d) Cannot be determined
12. Number of students who passed in all the three subjects:
    (a) 5 (b) 3
    (c) 6 (d) Cannot be determined
13. How many students are there who passed in at least two subjects?
    (a) 62 (b) 57
    (c) 61 (d) Cannot be determined
14. How many students are there who passed in VA?
    (a) 58 (b) 53
    (c) 5 (d) None of these

Directions for Questions 15 to 18: *Answer these questions on the basis of following information:*

2000 patients, currently suffering from lung fibrosis were selected to study the effectiveness of treatment of four types of medicines–P, Q, R and S. These patients were first randomly assigned into two groups of equal size, called the treatment group (T) and the control group (C). The patients in the group C were not treated with any of these medicines; instead they were given a dummy medicine, called placebo, containing only sugar and starch. The following information is known about the patients in the treatment group.

High Yield Questions
Scan this QR code to access a video explanation of questions 15-18

(i) A total of 500 patients were treated with type P medicine and a total of 420 patients were treated with type R medicine.
(ii) 50 patients were treated with type P medicine only. 40 patients were treated with type R medicine only. 20 patients were treated with type S medicine only.
(iii) 70 patients were treated with type P and type S medicines only. 40 patients were treated with type P and type Q medicines only. 30 patients were treated with type P and type R medicines only. 20 patients were treated with type R and type S medicines only.
(iv) 250 patients were treated with exactly three types of medicines.
(v) 40 patients were treated with medicines of types P, Q and R but not with medicines of type S. 20 patients were treated with medicines of types P, R and S, but not with medicines of type Q.

(vi) 100 patients were given all the four types of medicines. 150 patients were treated with exactly one type of medicine.

15. How many patients were treated with medicine type Q?

16. The number of patients who were treated with medicine types Q, R and S, but not type P was:

17. How many patients were treated with medicine types Q and S only?

18. The number of patients who were treated with medicine type S was:

Directions for Questions 19 to 22: *Answer these questions on the basis of following information:*

A survey of 1200 employees at Mindworkzz was conducted to gather information about their work from home processes. The following four facilities were studied.

P1: Own software for work from home.

P2: Dedicated office room for work from home.

P3: Training materials for work from home.

P4: Availability of laptop for work from home.

The following observations were summarized from the survey.

(i) 60 employees did not have any of the four facilities –P1, P2, P3 and P4.

(ii) 80 employees had all four facilities.

(iii) The number of employees with only P1, only P2, only P3 and only P4 was 50, 60, 52 and 40 respectively.

(iv) The number of employees with exactly three of the facilities was the same irrespective of which three were considered.

(v) 626 employees had P2.

(vi) 52 employees had only P2 and P3 (but neither P1 nor P4).

(vii) Among the employees having P4, 48 had only P3, and 90 had only P2.

(viii) 324 employees had both P1 and P2.

(ix) The number of employees having P1 was the same as the number of employees having P4.

19. What was the total number of employees having exactly two of the four facilities?

(a) 522 (b) 314

(c) 458 (d) None of these

20. What was the number of employees having facilities P2 and P4?

(a) 370 (b) 95

(c) 145 (d) 80

21. What was the number of employees having three or more facilities?

22. What was the number of employees having only facilities P1 and P4?

Directions for Questions 23 to 28: *Answer these questions on the basis of following information:*

The Venn diagram given below shows the estimated readership of three daily newspapers Hindustan Times (HT), Times of India (TOI) and Indian Express (IE) in a city (all figures are given in lakhs of readers). Newspaper advertising is a costly affair for advertisers and they need to carefully consider advertising options with readership estimates to come up with the most effective combination of mediums in which to advertise for the maximum value for money. The pricing of newspaper advertising is on the basis of per square centimetre of print space and is given to you in the table for three prominent newspapers of the city.

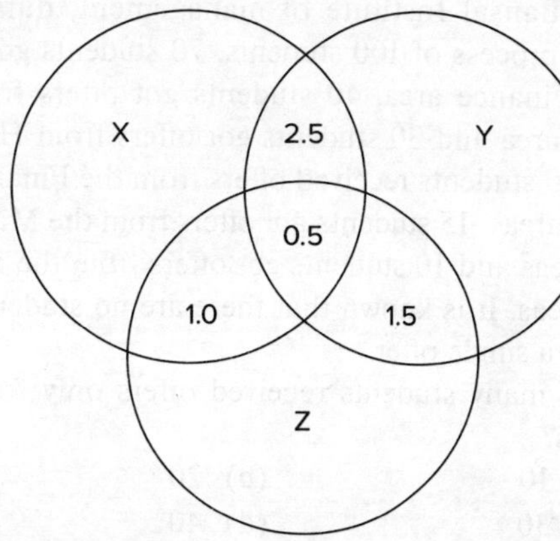

The total readership and advertising cost per square centimetre of print space for each of these newspapers is as follows:

Newspaper	Readership (lakhs)	Advertising Cost (₹ per sq. cm.)
Hindustan Times (X)	8.7	12000
Times of India (Y)	9.1	13000
Indian Express (Z)	5.6	10000

23. The number of people (in lakhs) who read at least one newspaper is:

(a) 4.7 (b) 11.9

(c) 17.4 (d) 23.4

24. The number of people (in lakhs) who read only one newspaper is:

(a) 4.7 (b) 11.9

(c) 17.4 (d) 23.4

25. The approximate percentage of population reading at least two newspapers is:

(a) 2.9 (b) 3.5

(c) 13.9 (d) None of the above

26. The ratio of readers reading only one newspaper to those reading only two newspapers is:

(a) 2.38: 1 (b) 3.65: 1

(c) 4.57: 1 (d) None of the above

27. The combination of two newspapers that gives the minimum advertising cost (in ₹ per sq. cm.) per 1000 readers is:

(a) HT and TOI (b) HT and IE
(c) TOI and IE (d) Cannot be determined

28. The minimum expenditure (in ₹ per sq. cm.) on advertising required to reach at least 12 lakhs readers is:

(a) 22000 (b) 23000
(c) 25000 (d) None of the above

Directions for Questions 29 to 32: *Answer these questions on the basis of following information:*

At the Bansal Institute of management, during the placement process of 100 students, 70 students got offers from the Finance area, 40 students got offers from the Marketing area and 30 students got offers from HR area. Of these, 20 students received offers from the Finance and Marketing areas, 15 students got offers from the Marketing and HR areas and 10 students got offers from the HR and Finance areas. It is known that there are no students who did not get a single offer.

29. How many students received offers only from two areas?

(a) 10 (b) 20
(c) 30 (d) 40

30. How many students received offers from the Finance area but not from any other area?

(a) 45 (b) 25
(c) 35 (d) 15

31. What percentage of students received offers both from Finance and Marketing but not from HR?

(a) 5% (b) 10%
(c) 15% (d) 20%

32. What is the percentage of people with offers from only one area?

(a) 65% (b) 70%
(c) 55% (d) None of these

Directions for Questions 33 to 36: *Answer these questions on the basis of following information:*

In the ancient training school of Dronacharya, The Kauravas, the Pandavas and some of their friends, a total of 220 trainees are getting trained in Archery, Horse Riding and Sword fighting. Each trainee is undergoing training for at least one out of the three skills. Some are undergoing training for more than one of the three skills.

High Yield Questions
Scan this QR code to access a video explanation of questions 33-36

Additionally, the following information is known:

(i) In all 113 trainees are not undergoing training for Archery.
(ii) In all 111 trainees are not undergoing training for Horse Riding.
(iii) In all 128 are not undergoing training for Sword Fighting.
(iv) In all 45 trainees are undergoing training in Sword Fighting and at least one more discipline.
(v) In all 52 trainees are undergoing training in Horse Riding and at least one more discipline.
(vi) In all 68 trainees are undergoing training in Archery and at least one more discipline.

33. How many trainees are undergoing training for all the three skills?

(a) 11 (b) 12
(c) 15 (d) Cannot be determined

34. How many trainees are undergoing training for at least 2 skills?

35. How many trainees are undergoing Horse Riding and at least one more skill?

36. How many trainees are undergoing training in Archery and Sword Fighting only?

Directions for Questions 37 to 39: *Answer these questions on the basis of following information:*

Out of 600 students who got interview calls from IIM-Bangalore, 320 students got distinction in their X standard and 251 students got distinction in their XII standard. It is also known that 113 students who got calls didn't get distinction in their X and XII standards.

37. How many students got distinction in either X or XII standards but not both?

38. What is the difference between the number of students who got distinction in both X and XII standards to that of the students who didn't get distinction in both X and XII standards?

39. What percentage of the students who got calls, got distinction in both the classes?

Directions for Questions 40 to 42: *Answer the questions on the basis of the information given below:*

Each person, out of the 400 people in a certain community, reads at least one newspaper among TOI, HT and Hindu. 37% of the people read at least two of the three newspapers, while 15% of the people read only HT. It was also known that 23% of the people read TOI and Hindu, while 20% read TOI and HT and 12% read all the three newspapers.

40. If the number of people who read TOI is less than that of those who read Hindu, at least what number of people do not read TOI?

(a) 185 (b) 166
(c) 215 (d) None of these

41. If the number of people who read HT is less than that of those who read TOI, then at most what percentage of the people read Hindu but not HT?

(a) 48% (b) 48.5%
(c) 48.75% (d) None of these

42. If the total number of people who read TOI is twice that of those who read Hindu, what percentage of the people read TOI or HT?

(a) 82% (b) 84%
(c) 87% (d) 93%

Directions for Questions 43 to 48: *Answer the questions on the basis of the information given below:*

At the Indian Hockey team selection trials, the selection committee called for new players. It had called 150 candidates for the purpose of recruiting some of them. They were looking for ideal players with a combination of three attributes which were Endurance, Stick Skills and High Speed. The breakup of the players with different attributes in that group of 150 was:

High Yield Questions

Scan this QR code to access a video explanation of questions 43-48

(i) Endurance and High Speed but not Stick Skills = 9.
(ii) Stick Skills and High Speed but not Endurance = 12.
(iii) Endurance or Stick Skills but not High Speed = 107.

Each player called for the trials had at least one of the three attributes that the selectors were looking for.

There was only 1 player who fit the bill with respect to having all the three attributes. It was also found that, for any attribute, the number of players who had that attribute alone did not exceed 32% of the total number of players called.

43. What is the minimum number of players who had at least two of the three attributes?

(a) 21 (b) 22
(c) 29 (d) 33

44. If 61 players had stick skills but did not have High Speed, then at most what percentage of the players had more than one attribute?

(a) 23.33% (b) 48%
(c) 52.33% (d) 55.33%

45. If the number of players who had stick skills is less than those who had endurance, then at least how many players had endurance as well as stick skills?

(a) 12 (b) 16
(c) 15 (d) None of these

46. If exactly half of the players who had endurance also had stick skills and exactly half of the players who had Stick Skills also had endurance, then how many players only had stick skills?

(a) 31 (b) 33
(c) 34 (d) 38

47. If the number of players who had endurance is twice that of those who had at least two attributes, then at least how many players only had Stick Skills?

(a) 37 (b) 45
(c) 43 (d) 47

48. For the above question, how many different scenarios for the players who had only Endurance, players who had only Stick Skills and players who had Endurance and Stick Skills but not High Speed are possible?

(a) 1 (b) 2
(c) 3 (d) More than 3

Directions for Questions 49 to 52: *Answer the following questions based on the above information:*

At Mindworkzz, in a particular batch, there are 100 students. A survey was conducted among these students to know about their likings for the 3 sections – Verbal Ability (VA), DI-LR (DL) and QA – and the 3 much loved teachers – Arun Sharma (AS), Meenakshi Upadhyay (MU) and Vinay Singh (VS).

Each student likes at least one of the three teachers and at least one of the 3 sections. Also, it is known that 65 students like AS, 50 students like MU and 40 students like VS. Also, 65 students like VA, 50 students like DL and 35 students like QA.

49. If there were total 10 students who like exactly two sections, then how many students like all the 3 sections?

50. What can be the maximum number of students who like AS and MU both as teachers, and also like VA and QA sections?

(a) 35 (b) 25
(c) 30 (d) None of these

51. If the students who like all the 3 sections is the maximum possible and all the students who like only QA also like AS, then what can be the maximum number of students who like both AS as well as VA?

(a) 65 (b) 25
(c) 55 (d) None of these

52. What can be the maximum number of students who like all the 3 sections and also all the 3 teachers?

(a) 50 (b) 25
(c) 27 (d) 30

Directions for Question 53: *Answer the question on the basis of the following information.*

53. Seventy per cent of the employees in a multinational corporation have VCD players, 75 per cent have microwave ovens, 80 per cent have ACs and 85 per cent have washing machines. At least what percentage of employees have all four gadgets?

(a) 15 (b) 5
(c) 10 (d) Can't be determined

LEVEL OF DIFFICULTY (III)

Directions for Questions 1 to 4: *Answer the following questions based on the above information:*

Applicants for the management programmes of IIM L and IIM B have to appear for a Common Admission Test (CAT). The test has three sections: QA, DI, and VA. Among those appearing for CAT, those at or above the 80th percentile in at least two sections, and at or above the 90th percentile overall, are selected for Advanced Admission Test (AAT) conducted by IIM L. AAT is used by IIM L for final selection. For the 400 candidates who are at or above the 90th percentile overall based on CAT, the following are known about their performance in CAT:

High Yield Questions

Scan this QR code to access a video explanation of questions 1-4

(i) No one is below the 80th percentile in all 3 sections.

(ii) 300 are at or above the 80th percentile in exactly two sections.

(iii) The number of candidates at or above the 80th percentile only in QA is the same as the number of candidates at or above the 80th percentile only in DI. The same is the number of candidates at or above the 80th percentile only in VA.

(iv) Number of candidates below 80th percentile in QA: Number of candidates below 80th percentile in DI: Number of candidates below 80th percentile in VA = 4:2:1. IIM B uses a different process for selection. If any candidate is appearing in the AAT by IIM L, IIM B consider their AAT score for final selection provided the candidate is at or above the 80th percentile in QA. Any other candidate at or above the 80th percentile in QA in CAT, but who is not eligible for the AAT, is required to appear in a separate test to be conducted by IIM B for being considered for final selection. Altogether, there are 800 candidates this year who are at or above the 80th percentile in QA.

(v) Number of people who scored 80 percentile only in QA section is less than 20.

1. What best can be concluded about the number of candidates sitting for the separate test for IIM B who were at or above the 90th percentile overall in CAT?
   (a) 6 or 13 (b) 19
   (c) 10 (d) 14 or 18

2. If the number of candidates who are at or above the 90th percentile overall and also at or above the 80th percentile in all three sections in CAT is actually a multiple of 2, what is the number of candidates who are at or above the 90th percentile overall and at or above the 80th percentile in both QA and VA in CAT?

3. If the number of candidates who are at or above the 90th percentile overall and also at or above the 80th percentile in all three sections in CAT is actually a multiple of 2, then how many candidates were shortlisted for the AAT for IIM L?

4. If the number of candidates who are at or above the 90th percentile overall and also are at or above the 80th percentile in QA in CAT, is more than 200, how many candidates had to sit for the separate test for IIM B?

Directions for Questions 5 to 7: *Answer these questions on the basis of following information:*

Mindworkzz provides training in three subjects - QA, DI-LR and VA. Currently, it has an enrollment of 78 students, each of whom is enrolled in at least one of the three subjects. The following details are known:

(i) The number of students enrolled only in VA is double the number of students enrolled in all the three subjects.

(ii) There are a total of 34 students enrolled in QA.

(iii) The number of students enrolled only in QA is two less than the number of students enrolled only in VA.

(iv) The number of students enrolled only in DI-LR is equal to the number of students who are enrolled in both DI-LR and VA.

(v) The maximum student enrollment is in VA.

(vi) Twenty students enrolled in QA are also enrolled in at least one more subject.

5. What is the minimum number of students enrolled in both QA and VA but not in DI-LR?

6. What is the number of people who enrolled only for DI- LR?

7. If the numbers of students enrolled in DI-LR and VA are in the ratio 19:24, then what is the number of students enrolled in VA?

Directions for Questions 8 to 12: *Answer these questions on the basis of following information:*

The following table represents the details regarding the number of persons who attended a film festival, where four movies – 'Terminator', 'Crossroads', 'GI Joe' and 'The Bridesmaid' were screened. Each person who attended the festival watched at least one of the four movies.

	Terminator	Crossroads	GI Joe	The Bridesmaid
Number of people of age more than 60 years, who watched the movie	50	30	40	30

Number of people of age more than 30 years, but not more than 60 years, who watched the movie.	110	60	60	70
Number of people of age not more than 30 years, who watched the movie.	90	110	60	70
Number of people who watched only that movie.	100	40	30	20

8. What is the minimum possible number of persons who attended the festival?
(a) 300 (b) 370
(c) 350 (d) 410

9. What is the maximum possible number of persons of age more than 60 years, who attended the festival?
(a) 200 (b) 170
(c) 130 (d) 140

10. The number of persons of age not more than 60 years, who attended the festival is at least:
(a) 150 (b) 200
(c) 210 (d) 220

11. The number of persons who watched all the four movies is at most:
(a) 150 (b) 130
(c) 140 (d) 120

12. The number of persons who watched exactly two of the four movies is at most:
(a) 280 (b) 290
(c) 295 (d) 385

Directions for Questions 13 to 18: *Answer these questions on the basis of following information:*

The company XYZ Ltd. recruited 80 trainees, of which it was observed that every trainee had:

I. Exactly one qualification among (a) B.E (b) M.Sc
II. At least one feature among the following two:
(a) He is from a reputed college.
(b) He had good academic record.
III. Experience in exactly one of the following two domains.
(a) Programming
(b) Testing

High Yield Questions
Scan this QR code to access a video explanation of questions 13-18

Further it is also known that:

(i) 20 trainees who are B.E had a good academic record as well as experience in Testing. These trainees form 50% of those with experience in Testing.
(ii) No trainee with experience in Programming had both the features mentioned in (ii), i.e., being from a good college and having a good academic record.
(iii) 30 trainees were M.Sc of which 15 had experience in Programming.
(iv) Of the trainees with experience in Testing, 15 were from a reputed college and they had good academic record.
(v) In total, 45 trainees had a good academic record, of which two-thirds were B.Es and one-third had experience in Programming.

13. How many of the trainees with experience in Programming are B.E candidates and also had a good academic record?
(a) 8 (b) 10
(c) 12 (d) 14

14. How many of the trainees with experience in Programming are B.E candidates and also came from a reputed college?

15. How many trainees with experience in Testing had a good academic record and also are B.E candidates and are from a reputed college?
(a) 5 (b) 7
(c) 12 (d) Cannot be determined

16. How many M.Scs are from a reputed college but had neither a good academic record nor any experience in programming?

17. If 19 B.Es had a good academic record but are not from a reputed college, how many M.Scs are from a reputed college and with good academic record?
(a) 3 (b) 4
(c) 5 (d) 6

18. How many B.Es are there having experience in testing and not having a good academic record?

Directions for Questions 19 to 22: *Answer these questions on the basis of following information:*

Mindworkzz Education Services (Institute) trains students for admission to country's top management colleges. It conducts CAT Scans, every fortnight, tests in Verbal, DI/LR and QA with a clear passing marks percentage at 35% net score. Results of one of the tests conducted among 163 students of the undergraduate batch of the institute are given below.

(i) The number of students who passed only in Verbal was equal to number of students who passed in only DI/R which in turn was equal to number of students who passed in only QA.

(ii) Number of students who passed in only Verbal and DI/LR or in only DI/LR and QA or in only QA and Verbal are all equal.
(iii) 57 students passed in Verbal.
(iv) The no. of students who could not pass in any of the three subjects was equal to no. of those who passed in QA.

19. If number of students who passed in Verbal and DI/LR is double the number of students who passed in Verbal and QA only, then what is the number of students who passed in DI/LR, but did not pass all three subjects?
(a) 44 (b) 31
(c) 49 (d) 39

20. Determine the minimum difference between number of students who passed in QA only and number of those who passed in QA and Verbal but not in DI/LR.
(a) 0 (b) 1
(c) 2 (d) 4

21. Determine the maximum difference between number of students who passed in QA only and number of those who passed in QA and Verbal but not in DI/LR.

22. It is given that the number of students who passed QA only was the maximum possible. Determine number of such students.
(a) 78 (b) 20
(c) 22 (d) 24

Directions for Questions 23 to 28: *Answer these questions on the basis of following information:*

At IIM Bangalore, Vishal Awal, the mess secretary, is trying to work out the preferences of the people who live in the hostel. While observing the same, he observes the following facts about Friday night diners:

Food categories of only three types are served: Italian, Portuguese and Chinese. Not all the hostel mates ate, but those who did, they ate at least one of the three types of cuisine. Also, everyone who came to the hostel that night ate at least one of the three food categories.

Further, some of his observations during last Friday's dinner are as follows:

(i) For every 1 hosteler who ate only Chinese and Portuguese, there were 3 hostelers who ate only Italian.
(ii) For every 1 hosteler who ate Portuguese and Chinese, there were 3 hostelers who ate Chinese and for every 3 hostelers who ate Portuguese, there was 1 who ate Italian and Portuguese.
(iii) The number of hostelers who ate only Chinese was twice the number of hostelers who ate only Portuguese.
(iv) The number of hostelers who ate both Chinese and Portuguese was 24 more than twice the number of guests who ate only Italian and Portuguese.
(v) The number of hostelers who ate only Italian and Chinese was 28.

23. What can be the minimum number of hostelers?

24. If the total number of hostelers who visited the mess was 250, then what could be the minimum number of guests who did not eat any of the 3 food items?

25. Which of the following could be a possible number of hostelers who ate exactly 2 of the 3 types of food items?
(a) 40 (b) 50
(c) 60 (d) 70

26. What is the difference between the number of hostelers who ate only Italian and the number who ate only Chinese?
(a) 18 (b) 16
(c) 24 (d) Cannot be determined

27. Which of the following is not a possible value for the number of hostelers who ate exactly 2 of the 3 types of food items?
(a) 99 (b) 100
(c) 106 (d) 113

28. If Vishal observed that there were a total of 71 people who ate exactly two kinds of food items, then what is the number of people who ate only Italian?

Directions for Questions 29 to 32: *Answer these questions on the basis of following information:*

At the USMF B School in Paris, the 300 students were required to choose one or more specialisations during their second year of the MBA course. It is compulsory for each student to take part in at least one specialisation, as part of his course work.

For the purpose of a particular study, the students in their 1980 batch were divided the in 3 groups of 100 students each and a varied set of specialisations was offered to each group.

For group 1, the available specialisations were Marketing, Finance and HR.

For group 2, the available specialisations were Consulting, Operations, Advertising and Corporate Strategy.

For group 3, the available specialisations were Systems, International Business and Entrepreneurship.

In group 1, some of the employees who chose Marketing also chose Finance. Also, some of those who chose Finance, also chose HR. No one specialised in both Marketing and HR. The Number of students who did Marketing was equal to those who did HR. The Number of students who did Marketing and Finance were five less than that of those who did Finance and HR. The Number of students who did only Marketing was 20 more than that of those who did Marketing with one more specialisation. 20 students did only Finance.

In group 2, some of the students who specialised in Consulting also did so in Operations. Some who specialised in Operations also specialised in at most one of Consulting or Advertising. In addition to that, some students who specialised in Advertising also specialised in at most one out of Operations or Corporate

Strategy. Further, no other combinations of specialisations other than the mentioned, were done by the students of group 2. The number of students who specialised in Consulting were twice the number of those who specialised in Corporate Strategy. 60 students specialised in Operations. The number of students who specialised in both Operations and Advertising is same as those who specialised in both Advertising and Corporate Strategy.

That number is equal to zero. 15 people specialised in Advertising and 35 people specialised in more than one subject.

In group 3, every student participated in at least two activities and equal number of students participated in every combination of exactly two activities. Further 10 people participated in all the three activities.

29. How many employees participated in exactly two activities, in their respective group?

(a) 60 (b) 90
(c) 150 (d) 160

30. Find the number of students who specialised in HR but not in Finance.

(a) 30 (b) 20
(c) 40 (d) 25

31. Find the number of students who specialised in Consulting but not in Operations, Advertising or Corporate Strategy.

(a) 30 (b) 35
(c) 40 (d) 5

32. If each specialisation means an attendance of exactly 200 hours of classroom contact, then find the total classroom hours spent by the group who was required to spend, the minimum amount of time in the classroom.

(a) 37000 (b) 25000
(c) 42000 (d) None of these

Directions for Questions 33 to 37: *Answer these questions based on the details below:*

In Karol Bagh, Delhi, the Shrivastav brothers run two bakery shops next to each other. They are Cherry Bakers and Strawberry Bakers. The children of the area are their major source of sales. While they are fierce competitiors, they also help each other out with data about their sales at the end of the month. When comparing notes about their sales in the month of February, they realised that in all 1050 children went to either bakery. The children bought either Cherry Tart only or Strawberry Cheesecake only or both Cherry Tart and Strawberry Cheesecake or a dessert other than Cherry Tart and Strawberry Cheesecake.

The following additional information is known:

(i) 450 children bought from Cherry Bakers.

(ii) The number of children who bought Cherry Tart was 600. Similarly, the number of children who bought Strawberry Cheesecake was also 600.

(iii) The number of children who bought only Strawberry Cheesecake from Strawberry bakers was 10% of the number of children who bought either Strawberry Cheesecake or Cherry Tart (but not both) from the two bakers taken together.

(iv) The number of children who bought both their desserts Strawberry Cheesecake and Cherry Tart from Strawberry Bakers was 400% more than bought from Cherry Bakers.

(v) The children who bought a dessert other than Cherry Tart or Strawberry Cheesecake bought only from Strawberry Bakers.

(vi) The number of children who bought only Cherry Tart was equal to the number of children who bought both Cherry Tart and Strawberry Cheesecake.

33. How many orders from Cherry Bakers were for Cherry Tart and Strawberry Cheesecake both?

(a) 50 (b) 150
(c) 125 (d) 75

34. How many children did not buy either Cherry Tart or Strawberry Cheesecake and bought some other kind of dessert?

35. Among the children who bought from Cherry Bakers, how many more children bought only trawberry Cheesecake than only Cherry Tart?

(a) 0 (b) 80
(c) 110 (d) 190

36. If it is known that all the children buying some other kind of dessert (apart from Cherry Tart and Strawberry Cheesecakes) bought only 1 dessert each, what was the total number of desserts sold to children by the two shops taken together?

37. If Strawberry Cheesecakes sold for ` 50 each, while Cherry Tarts sold for ` 100 each, how much revenue did Cherry Bakers earn from the sale of these two desserts to children in the month of February?

Directions for Questions 38 to 43: *Answer these questions based on the details below:*

At the Dronacharya sports club, each of the trainees has to play at least one sport amongst hockey, football and cricket. The number of people who play cricket is 100, the number of people who play football is 50 and the number of people who play hockey is 60. It is also known that the number of people who play cricket and football is 30, the number of people who play football and hockey is 35, while the number of people who play hockey and cricket is 45.

High Yield Questions
Scan this QR code to access a video explanation of questions 38-43

38. What is the maximum number of people who play all the 3 games?

39. What is the minimum number of people who play all the 3 games?

40. What is the maximum number of people who play exactly 2 games?

41. What is the minimum number of people who play exactly 2 games?

42. What is the maximum number of people who play all exactly 1 game?

43. What is the minimum number of people who play all exactly 1 game?

Directions for Questions 44 to 48: *Answer these questions based on the details below:*

ANI Marg organised a survey of farming families in rural areas of 5 states. The following table gives the number of families who had each of the given characteristic across these five states (amongst those families who were part of the surveys).

State	Number of families with min 0.1 acre land	Number of educated families	Number of families with highest education level above class 10	Number of families with more than 5 members	Number of families where the head of the family was a working member	Number of people surveyed
UP	12	16	15	22	18	30
AP	15	22	23	21	14	35
Karnataka	7	18	16	25	15	28
Maharashtra	10	19	15	22	28	36
Haryana	15	25	21	29	16	40

44. In AP, the number of families who had at least two of the five characteristics, is at least:
(a) 12 (b) 15
(c) 18 (d) 16

45. The number of families in Haryana who have exactly 3 characteristics is at most:
(a) 32 (b) 34
(c) 35 (d) 33

46. If a special central grant is awarded to all the families who have all the 5 characteristics, then the number of families that would be awarded the grant is at most:
(a) 120 (b) 104
(c) 62 (d) 58

47. In UP, what is the maximum number of families who could have shown at most 2 characteristics?
(a) 19 (b) 21
(c) 22 (d) 26

48. Find the minimum number of families in Haryana, who exhibit exactly 2 characteristics.
(a) 12 (b) 8
(c) 10 (d) 0

Directions for Questions 49 to 54: *Answer these questions based on the details below:*

At a sports college a group of 300 trainees students appeared for trials conducted in 4 different sports-Cricket, Hockey, Tennis and Badminton. For every 2 trainees who passed in the trial of all the 4 sports, there is 1 trainee in each combination of exactly 3 passed trials by the trainees, and for every 2 trainees who passed the trials in (Cricket, Hockey and Tennis) only, there is 1 trainee in each of the possibilities of exactly 1 trial passed test by the trainees. The number of trainees who passed in (Hockey and Badminton) is twice the number of trainees who passed in (Cricket and Tennis), and the number of trainees who passed the trial in (Cricket and Badminton) is twice the number of trainees who passed the trial in (Hockey and Tennis). The number of trainees who passed in only (Cricket and Hockey) is equal to the number of trainees who passed in only (Tennis and Badminton), which is 75. The total number of trainees who passed the trials in Cricket is 150 and the number of trainees who passed the trial in only cricket is an even number. The number of trainees who passed in Cricket is more than the number of trainees who passed in Hockey.

49. Find the minimum number of trainees who passed in none of the four mentioned trials.

50. How many trainees passed the trials in Tennis and Badminton?

51. How many trainees failed in at most 1 trial?

52. In which sport did the minimum number of trainees pass?
(a) Cricket (b) Hockey
(c) Tennis (d) Badminton

53. If it is known that the number of students who passed in Tennis is 117, what is the number of students who passed in Hockey?

54. If it is known that the number of trainees who did not pass a single trial is the maximum possible, then find the number of trainees who passed in exactly two trials?

Directions for Questions 55 to 59: *MINDWORKZZ, A CAT Prep academy led by Arun Sharma, conducted a total of 100 scholarship events during the year 2022. Four students,*

Pallav, Shaurya, Anshuman and Ritika, participated in some of these events. For any event, the rules dictated that students can participate either solo or in groups of 3/4.

It is also known that:

A. Although the 4 people were very good friends, they decided to break apart from their group of 4 from the 9th event.

B. Pallav went solo in thrice the number of events in which Anshuman went solo, which, in turn, is twice the number of events in which only Ritika participated.

C. The number of events in which both Shaurya and Anshuman participated is 22 more than that in which only Anshuman and Pallav participated.

D. The number of events in which Pallav and Shaurya participated is the same as that in which Ritika and Anshuman participated, which, in turn, is the same as that in which Ritika and Pallav participated.

E. The number of events in which only Shaurya participated is the same as that in which only Pallav, Anshuman and Ritika participated.

55. If the number of events in which only Pallav participated is at least 30 more than that in which only Shaurya participated, in how many events did Ritika participate?

(a) 42 (b) 36
(c) 32 (d) Cannot be determined

56. What is the maximum number of events in which only Anshuman participated?

(a) 10 (b) 14
(c) 12 (d) 16

57. What is the number of events in which both Pallav and Shaurya participated?

(a) 10 (b) 14
(c) 22 (d) Cannot be determined

58. In each of the 100 events, one of the four players was the winner of the event and Pallav was the winner of the event in exactly 38 events.

What is the minimum number of events in which Anshuman would have been the winner?

59. In each of the 100 events, one of the four players was the winner of the event and Pallav was the winner of the event in exactly 38 events.

If Ritika was the winner in at least 20 events, what is the maximum number of events in which Shaurya would have been the winner?

Directions for Questions 60 to 64: *A survey was conducted at Prateek Stylome, a housing society in Noida, regarding the type of vehicle each family owns. Total of 20 families participated in the survey. Among these families, it was found that they had only four types of vehicles- Sedans, SUV, Hatchbacks and Sports. Each person owns at least two vehicles and at most five vehicles. Further, it is known that the total number of vehicles in the colony is 69. In the Venn diagram given below, there are twenty markers, comprising four different shapes - circle, triangle, square and diamond - each marker representing one of the twenty families surveyed. The shape of each marker denotes the number of vehicles that the respective family owns. The number of vehicles denoted by each shape is distinct. Also, the location of the marker in the Venn diagram indicates the different types of vehicles that the family owns.*

High Yield Questions

Scan this QR code to access a video explanation of questions 60-64

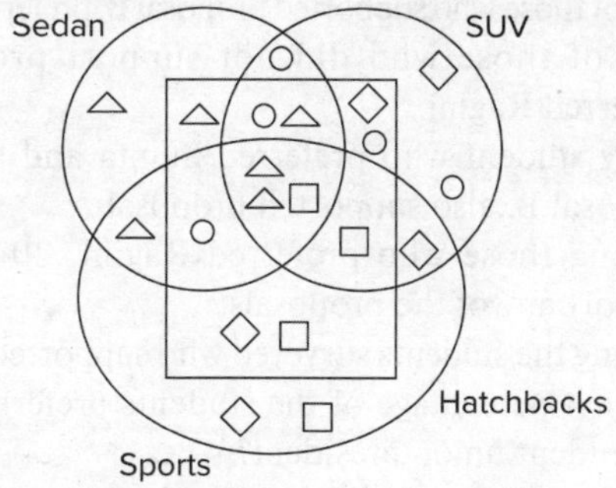

60. How many vehicles have owners who own all four types of vehicles?

(a) 13 (b) 14
(c) 15 (d) Cannot be determined

61. If the number of Sedans is the minimum possible, how many people definitely own more than one SUV?

(a) 2 (b) 3
(c) 4 (d) 5

62. If the total number of Sports Vehicles is 24, what is the maximum total number of Hatchbacks owned by the twenty persons?

63. If the total number of Sports Vehicles is 24, what is the minimum number of families who own at most one Sedan?

64. The number of SUVs in the colony is three more than the number of Sedans and the number of Hatchbacks is the same as the number of Sports Vehicles.

If the number of SUVs cannot be more than 16, what is the difference between the number of Sedans and the number of Hatchbacks?

(a) 4 (b) 3
(c) 7 (d) Cannot be determined

Directions for Questions 65 to 68: *Read the information provided and answer the questions which follow.*

Students in a college are discussing two proposals –

(i) A proposal by the authorities to introduce dress code on campus and

(ii) A proposal by the students to allow multinational food franchises to set up outlets on college campus.

A student does not necessarily support either of the two proposals. In an upcoming election for student union president, there are two candidates in fray: Sunita and Ragini. Every student prefers one of the two candidates. A survey was conducted among the students by picking a sample of 500 students. The following information was noted from this survey.

(i) 250 students supported proposal A and 250 students supported proposal B.
(ii) Among the 200 students who preferred Sunita as student union president, 80% supported proposal A.
(iii) Among those who preferred Ragini, 30% supported proposal A.
(iv) 20% of those who supported proposal B, preferred Sunita.
(v) 40% of those who did not support proposal B, preferred Ragini.
(vi) Every student who preferred Sunita and supported proposal B, also supported proposal A.
(vii) Among those who preferred Ragini, 20% did not support any of the proposals.

65. Among the students surveyed who supported proposal A, what percentage of the students preferred Sunita for student union president?

66. What percentage of the students surveyed who did not support proposal A, preferred Ragini as student union president?

67. What percentage of the students surveyed who supported both proposals A and B, preferred Sunita as student union president?
(a) 25 (b) 40
(c) 20 (d) 50

68. How many of the students surveyed, supported proposal B, did not support proposal A and preferred Ragini as student union president?
(a) 150 (b) 40
(c) 200 (d) 210

Directions for Questions 69 to 72: 1600 satellites were sent up by a country for several purposes. The purposes are classified as broadcasting (B), communication (C), surveillance (S) and others (O). A satellite can serve multiple purposes; however a satellite serving either B, or C, or S does not serve O.

The following facts are known about the satellites:

(i) The numbers of satellites serving B, C, and S (though may be not exclusively) are in the ratio 2:1:1.
(ii) The numbers of satellites serving all three of B, C, and S is 100.
(iii) The numbers of satellites exclusively serving C is the same as the number of satellites exclusively serving S. This number is 30% of the number of satellites exclusively serving B.
(iv) The numbers of satellites serving O is the same as the number of satellites serving both C and S but not B.

69. What best can be said about the number of satellites serving C?
(a) Can't be more than 800
(b) Must be at least 100
(c) Must be between 450 and 725
(d) Must be between 400 and 800

70. What is the minimum possible number of satellites serving B exclusively?
(a) 100 (b) 200
(c) 250 (d) 500

71. If at least 100 of the 1600 satellites were serving O, what can be said about the number of satellites serving S?
(a) Exactly 475
(b) At most 475
(c) At least 475
(d) No conclusion is possible based on the given information

72. If the number of satellites serving at least two among B, C, and S 1200, which of the following MUST be FALSE?
(a) All 1600 satellites serve B or C or S
(b) The number of satellites serving B is more than 1000
(c) The number of satellites serving C cannot be uniquely determined
(d) The number of satellites serving B exclusively is exactly 250

Directions for Questions 73 to 76: Fun Sports (FS) provides training in three sports - Gilli - danda (G), Kho-Kho (K), and Ludo (L). Currently it has an enrollment of 39 students each of whom is enrolled in at least one of the three sports. The following details are known:

(i) The number of students enrolled only in L is double the number of students enrolled in all the three sports.
(ii) There are a total of 17 students enrolled in G.
(iii) The number of students enrolled only in G is one less than the number of students enrolled only in L.
(iv) The number of students enrolled only in K is equal to the number of students who are enrolled in both K and L.
(v) The maximum student enrollment is in L.
(vi) Ten students enrolled in G are also enrolled in at least one more sport.

73. What is the minimum number of students enrolled in both G and L but not in K?

74. If the numbers of students enrolled in K and L are in the ratio 19:22, then what is the number of students enrolled in L?
(a) 17 (b) 19
(c) 22 (d) 18

75. Due to academic pressure, students who were enrolled in all three sports were asked to withdraw from one of the three sports. After the withdrawal,

the number of students enrolled in G was six less than the number of students enrolled in L, while the number of students enrolled in K went down by one. After the withdrawal, how many students were enrolled in both G and K?

76. Due to academic pressure, students who were enrolled in all three sports were asked to withdraw from one of the three sports. After the withdrawal, the number of students enrolled in G was six less than the number of students enrolled in L, while the number of students enrolled in K went down by one. After the withdrawal, how many students were enrolled in both G and L?

(a) 7 (b) 5
(c) 8 (d) 6

ANSWER KEY

Level of Difficulty I

1. (b)	2. (a)	3. (b)	4. (a)
5. (b)	6. (a)	7. (c)	8. (b)
9. (c)	10. (b)	11. (a)	12. (d)
13. (c)	14. (b)	15. (a)	16. (b)
17. (c)	18. (b)	19. (c)	20. (a)
21. (d)	22. (c)	23. (c)	24. (a)
25. (b)	26. (d)	27. (b)	28. (b)
29. (c)	30. (a)	31. (a)	32. (c)
33. (b)	34. (d)	35. (a)	36. (c)
37. (a)	38. (b)	39. (e)	40. (d)
41. (a)	42. (b)	43. (c)	44. (c)
45. (a)	46. (c)	47. (a)	48. (d)
49. (b)	50. (d)		

Level of Difficulty II

1. 10%	2. 60%	3. 15	4. 15
5. 120	6. 150	7. 750	8. 40.9%
9. 54%	10. 0%	11. (b)	12. (d)
13. (a)	14. (d)	15. 750	16. 40
17. 210	18. 630	19. (c)	20. (a)
21. 480	22. 140	23. (c)	24. (b)
25. (d)	26. (a)	27. (a)	28. (a)
29. (c)	30. (a)	31. (c)	32. (a)
33. (a)	34. 77	35. 52	36. 25
37. 403	38. 29	39. 14%	40. (a)
41. (c)	42. (d)	43. (d)	44. (d)
45. (b)	46. (a)	47. (b)	48. (b)
49. 20	50. (a)	51. (c)	52. (b)
53. (c)			

Level of Difficulty III

1. (a)	2. 166	3. 382	4. 598
5. 8	6. 18	7. 44	8. (c)
9. (d)	10. (d)	11. (b)	12. (c)
13. (b)	14. 15	15. (d)	16. 5
17. (b)	18. 5	19. (a)	20. (c)
21. 23	22. (d)	23. 133	24. 0
25. (b)	26. (a)	27. (b)	28. 90
29. (c)	30. (d)	31. (d)	32. (b)
33. (a)	34. 150	35. (b)	36. 1350
37. 35500	38. 30	39. 20	40. 50
41. 20	42. 80	43. 50	44. (d)
45. (d)	46. (d)	47. (c)	48. (d)
49. 14	50. 91	51. 24	52. (c)
53. 136	54. 239	55. (a)	56. (b)
57. (c)	58. 12	59. 30	60. (a)
61. (b)	62. 16	63. 16	64. (c)
65. 64	66. 84	67. (d)	68. (a)
69. (c)	70. (c)	71. (b)	72. (c)
73. 4	74. (c)	75. 2	76. (d)

SOLUTIONS AND SHORTCUTS

Level of Difficulty (I)

Solutions for Questions 1 to 2:

Since there are 14 who are in triathlon and pentathlon, and there are 8 who take part in all three games, there will be 6 who take part in only triathlon and pentathlon. Similarly,

Only triathlon and marathon = 12 − 8 = 4 and Only pentathlon and marathon = 15 − 8 = 7.

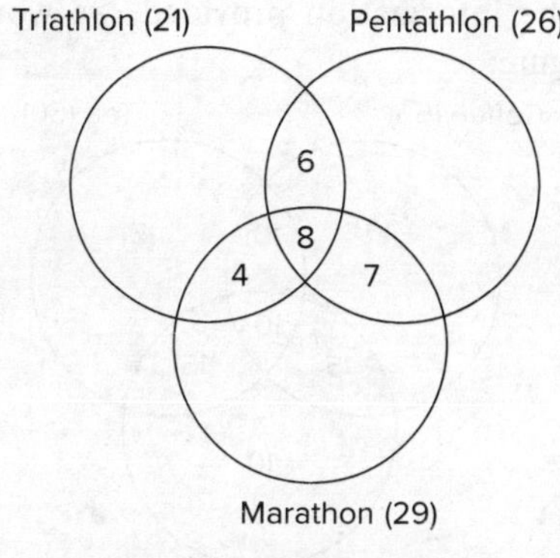

The figure above can be completed with values for each sport (only) plugged in:

The answers would be:

1. 3 + 6 + 8 + 4 + 5 + 7 + 10 = 43. Option (b) is correct.
2. Option (a) is correct.

Solutions for Questions 3 to 4:

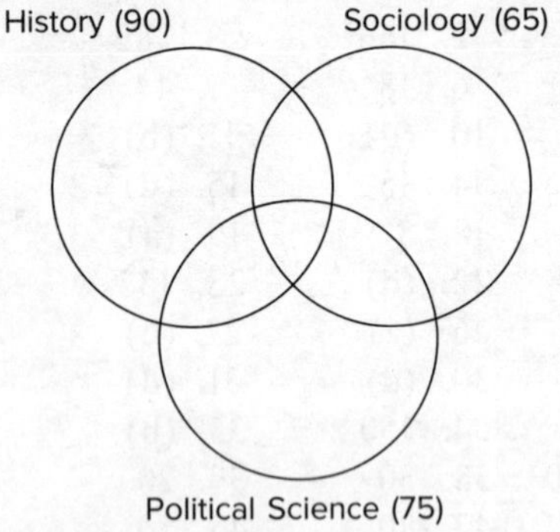

The given situation can be read as follows:

115 students are being counted 75 + 65 + 90 = 230 times.

This means that there is an extra count of 115. This extra count of 115 can be created in 2 ways:

A. By putting people in the 'passed exactly two subjects' category. In such a case each person would get counted 2 times (double counted), i.e., an extra count of 1.
B. By putting people in the 'all three' category, each person, put there would be triple counted. 1 person counted 3 times–meaning an extra count of 2 per person.

The problem tells us that there are 55 students who passed exactly two subjects. This means an extra count of 55 would be accounted for. This would leave an extra count of 115 – 55 = 60 more to be accounted for by 'passed all three' category. This can be done by using 30 people in the 'all 3' category.

Hence, the answers are:

3. Option (b).
4. Option (a).

Solutions for Questions 5 to 8:

Based on the information provided, we would get the following figure:

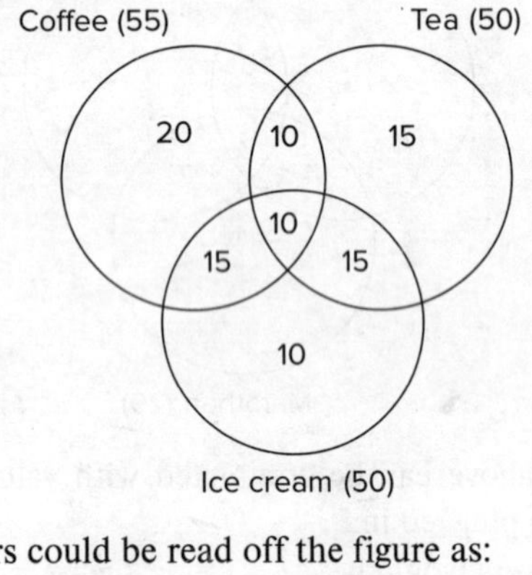

The answers could be read off the figure as:

5. [(20 – 10)/10] × 100 = 100%. Option (b) is correct.
6. 15% (from the figure). Option (a) is correct.
7. 10 + 10 + 15 + 15 = 50%. Option (c) is correct.
8. Only ice cream is 10% of the total. Hence, 10% of 180 = 18. Option (b) is correct.

Solutions for Questions 9 to 15:

If you try to draw a figure for this question, the figure would be something like:

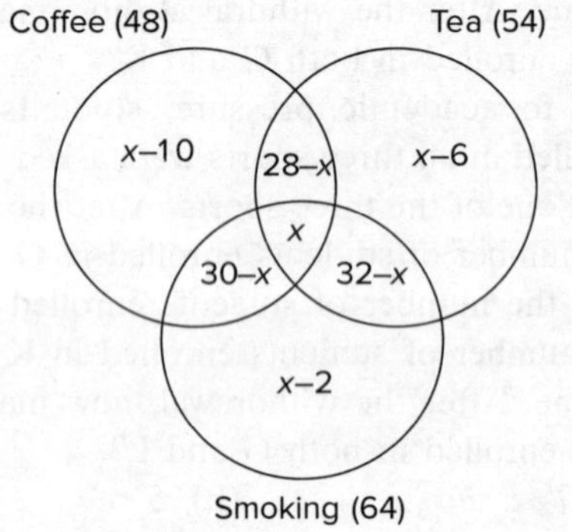

We can then solve this as:

$x - 10 + 28 - x + x + 30 - x + x + 2 + 32 - x + x - 6 = 94 \rightarrow x + 76 = 94 \rightarrow x = 18$.

Note: In this question, since all the values for the use of the set theory formula are given, we can find the missing value of students who liked all three as follows:

94 = 48 + 54 + 64 – 28 – 32 – 30 + All three → All three = 18.

As you can see, this is a much more convenient way of solving this question, and the learning you take away for the 3 circle situation is that whenever you have all the values known and the only unknown value is the center value-it is wiser and more efficient to solve for the unknown using the formula rather than trying to solve through a venn diagram.

Based on this value of x, we get the diagram completed as:

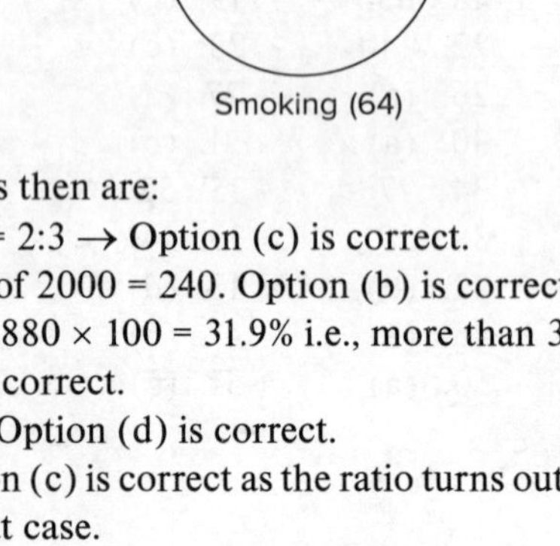

The answers then are:

9. 8:12 = 2:3 → Option (c) is correct.
10. 12 % of 2000 = 240. Option (b) is correct.
11. 600/1880 × 100 = 31.9% i.e., more than 30%. Option (a) is correct.
12. 94%. Option (d) is correct.
13. Option (c) is correct as the ratio turns out to be 10:20 in that case.

14. 12:12 = 1:1. Option (b) is correct.
15. 14%. Option (a) is correct.
16. $30 = 25 + 20 - x \rightarrow x = 15$. Option (b) is correct.

Solutions for Questions 17 to 20:

Let people who passed all three be x. Then:

$53 + 61 + 60 - 24 - 35 - 27 + x = 95 \rightarrow x = 7$.

The Venn diagram in this case would become:

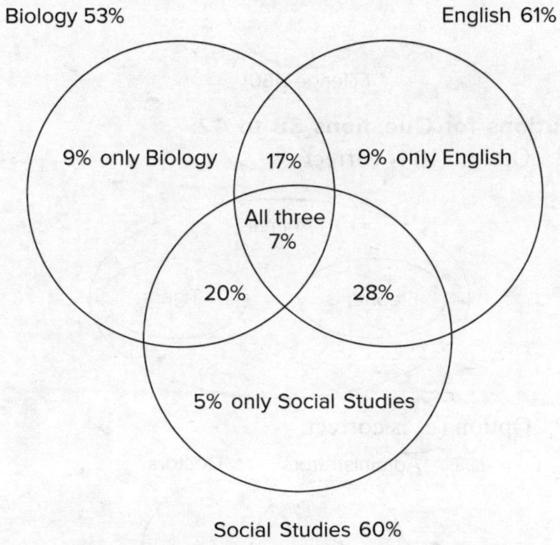

17. Option (c) is correct.
18. 23% of 200 = 46. Option (b) is correct.
19. If the number of students is increased by 50%, the number of students in each category would also be increased by 50%. Option (c) is correct.
20. 20:28 = 5:7. Option (a) is correct.

Solutions for Questions 21 to 25:

The following figure would emerge on using all the information in the question:

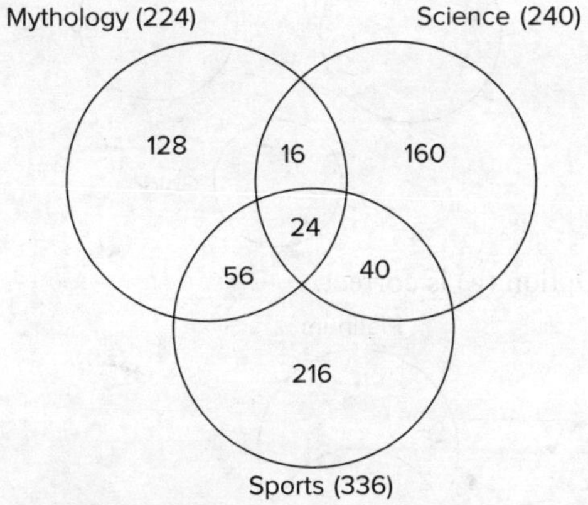

The answers would then be:

21. 240/880 = 27.27%. Option (d) is correct.
22. 504/880 = 57.27%. Hence, less than 60. Option (c) is correct.
23. 40 + 16 + 56 + 24 = 136. Option (c) is correct.
24. Option (a) gives us 16:128 = 1:8. Option (a) is hence, correct.
25. 40:160 → 1:4. Option (b) is correct.

Solutions for Questions 26 to 30:

The following Venn diagrams would emerge:

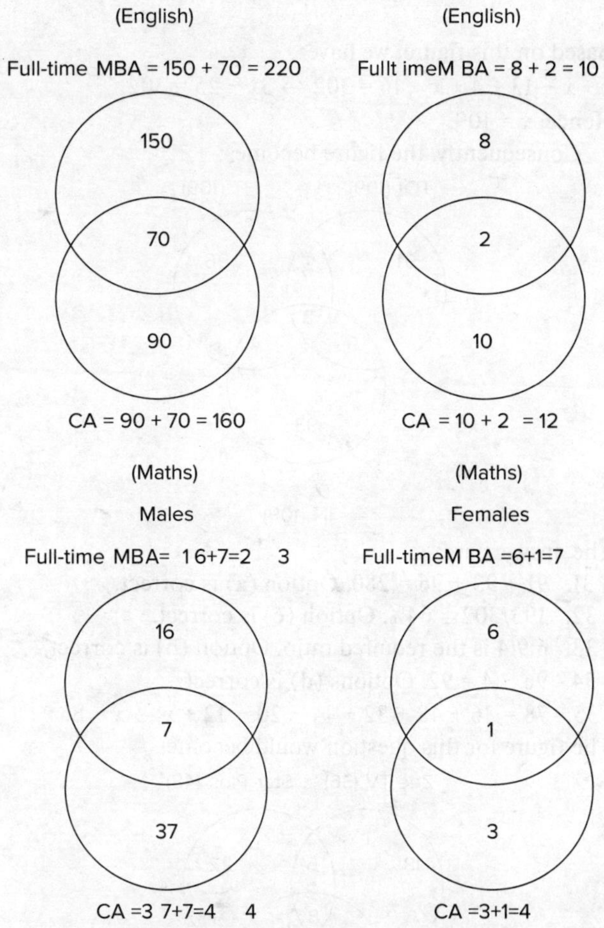

26. Math students = 130. English students = 370
130/370 = 35.14%. Option (d) is correct.
27. Number of female students = 10 + 8 + 10 + 2 + 10 + 6 + 3 + 1 = 50. Average number of females per course = 50/4 = 12.5. Option (b) is correct.
28. 50:450 = 1:9. Option (b) is correct.
29. 40/140 → 28.57%. Option (c) is correct.
30. From the figures, this value would be 150 + 8 + 90 + 10 + 16 + 6 + 37 + 3 = 320. Option (a) is correct.

Solutions for Questions 31 to 37:

The following figure would emerge:

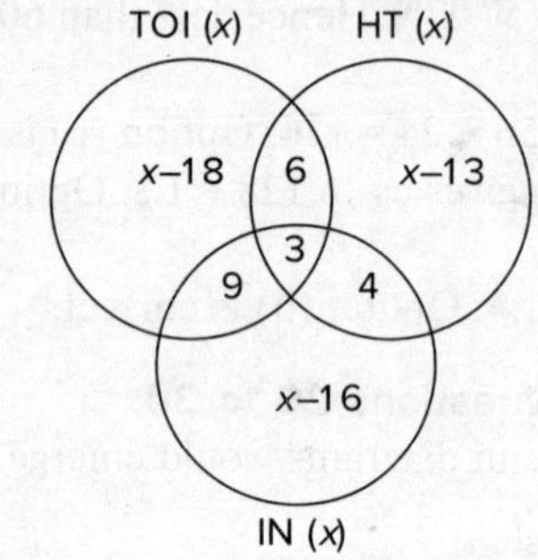

Based on this figure, we have:
$x + x - 13 + 4 + x - 16 = 302 \rightarrow 3x - 25 = 302.$
Hence, $x = 109$.

Consequently, the figure becomes:

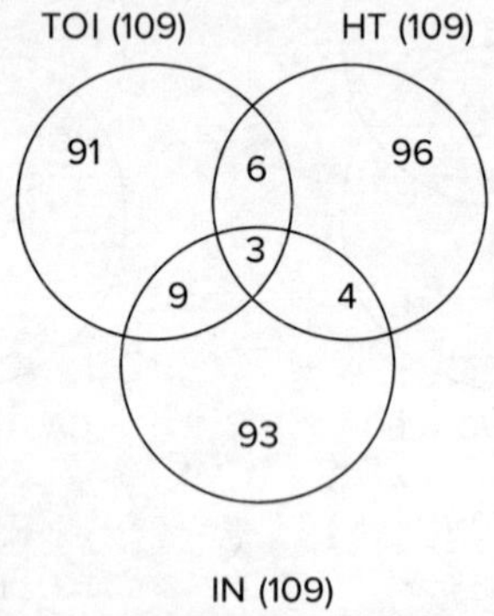

The answers are:

31. 91 + 93 + 96 = 280. Option (a) is correct.
32. 193/302 ≅ 64%. Option (c) is correct.
33. 6:9:4 is the required ratio. Option (b) is correct.
34. 96 − 4 = 92. Options (d) is correct.
35. $78 = 36 + 48 + 32 - 14 - 20 - 12 + x \rightarrow x = 8$.

The figure for this question would become:

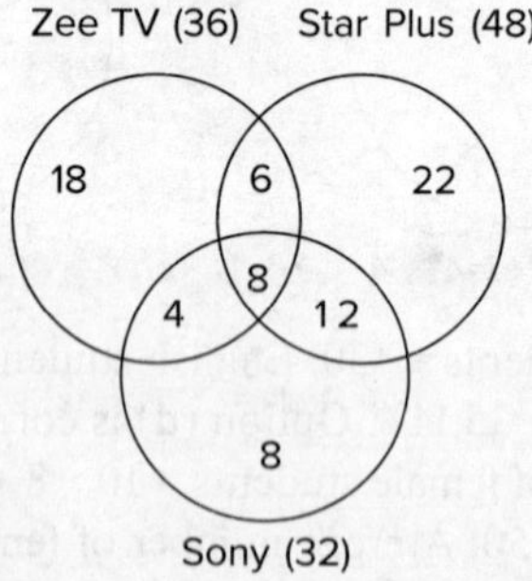

Required ratio is 18:8 → 9:4. Option (a) is correct.

36. Option (c) is correct.

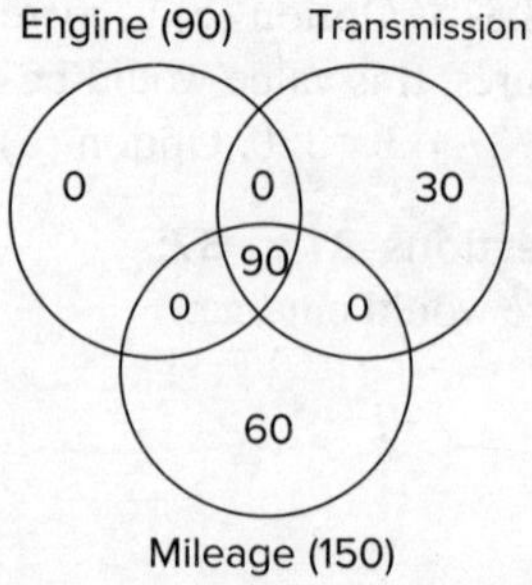

37. There are 30 such people. Option (a) is correct.

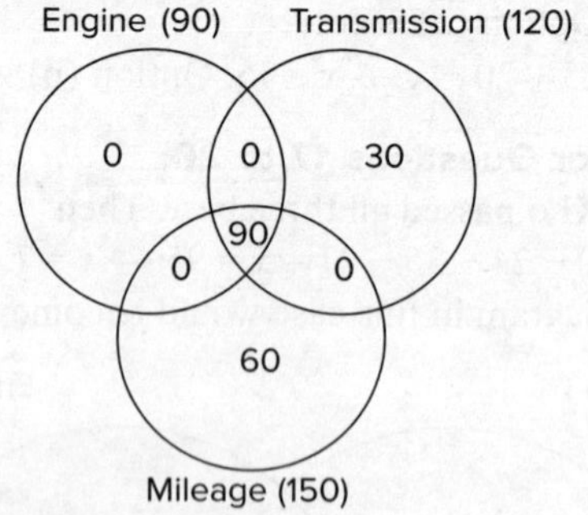

Solutions for Questions 38 to 42:

38. Option (b) is correct.

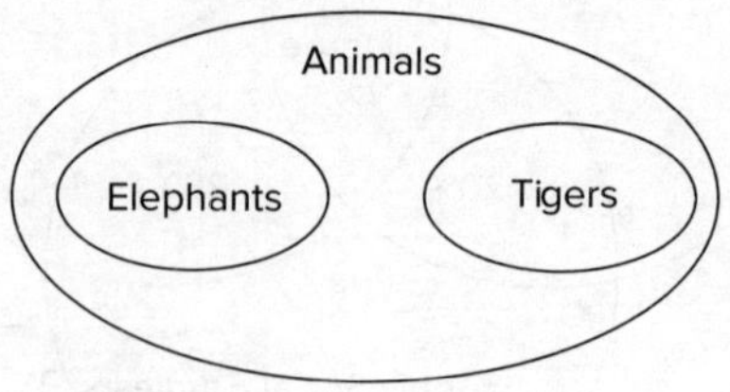

39. Option (e) is correct.

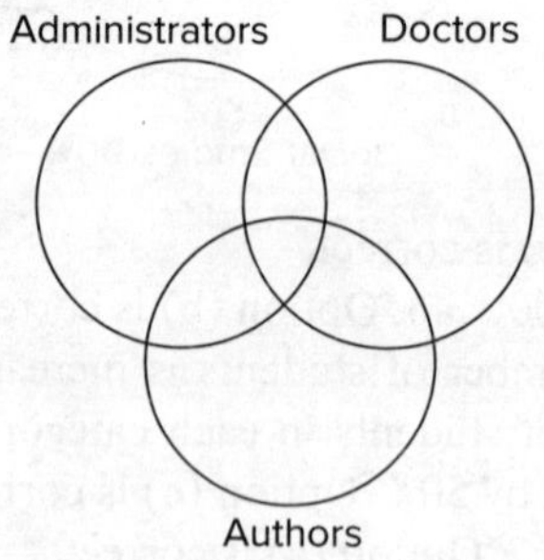

40. Option (d) is correct.

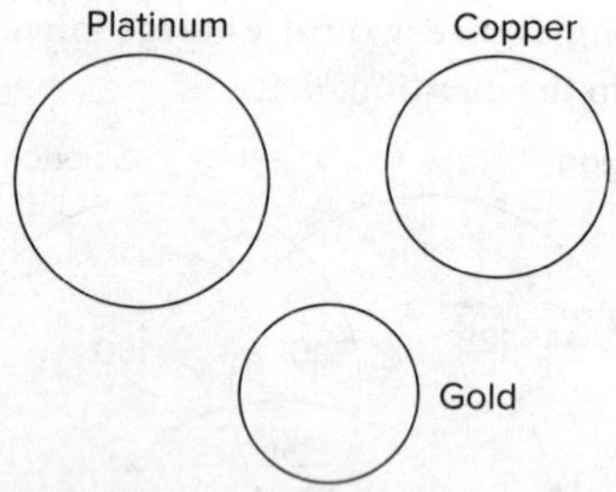

41. Option (a) is correct.

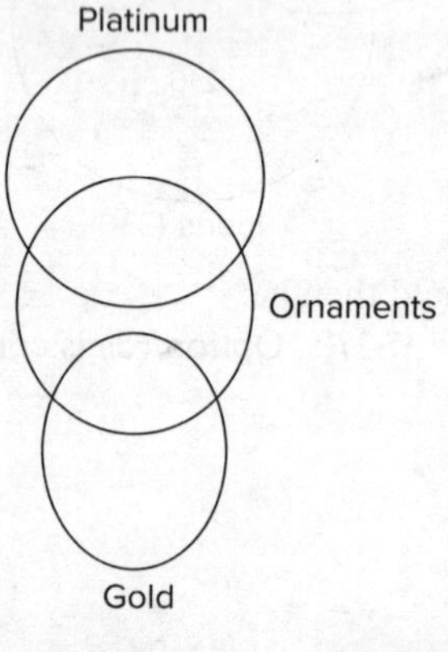

42. Option (b) is correct.

Solutions for Questions 43 to 45:

43. Since P.A is a null set, Pluto must not be an Alsation
44. F U (D.V) not being a null set means that some fish are dogs.
45. Since Z is the union of Pluto who is a dog and mammals, option (a) is correct.

Solutions for Questions 46 to 47:

46. Using both the statements we would get that there are 46 people who speak only French. (Refer to figure below)

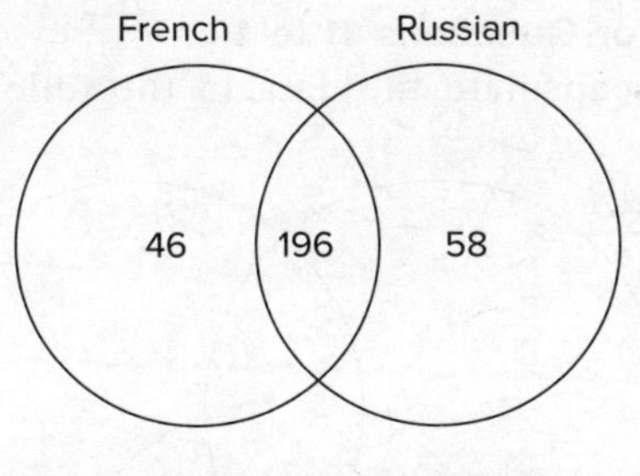

47. From the figure it is clear that Paul would have 150, Gerard 50 and Hornis 40 patients. Hence, option (a) is correct.

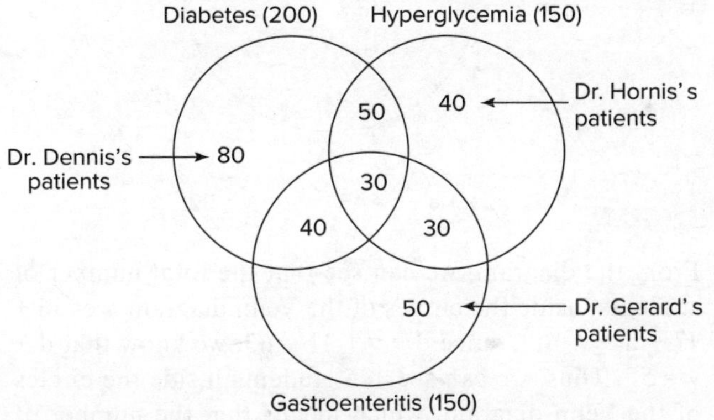

Solutions for Questions 48 to 49:

The following figure can be drawn based on the information provided in the question.

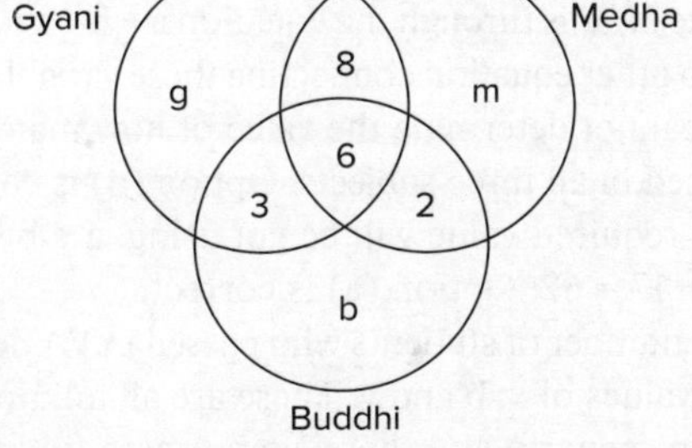

From the figure and the information given in the problem we know that total number of projects = 37. Hence, $g + m + b = 18$ and $g + b = 16 + m$.

48. Gyani alone is defined by b and m, which cannot be determined uniquely.
49. Solving the above two expressions for m, we get $18 - m = 16 + m \rightarrow m = 1$

Solution for Question 50:

50.

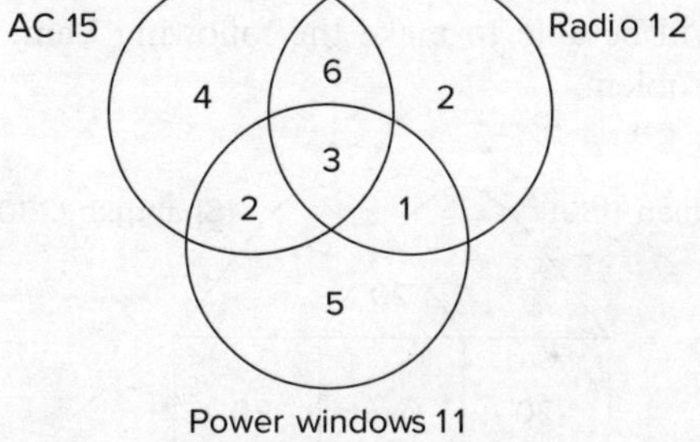

From the figure it is clear that there would be a total of 23 cars which had one or more of AC/Radio/ Power Steering. Hence, 2 cars had none of the three. Option (d) is correct.

Level of Difficulty (II)

Solutions for Questions 1 to 2:

1. 60 + 50 − 100 = 10 %.
2. Since there are only 100 (100% taken as 100) people in the surveyed people, and the addition of 60 + 90 + 80 is 230, it is clear that there is an extra count of 130. In such cases, the extra count can be justified using triple counts (one person is counted three times if he likes red, yellow and green) and double counts (one person is counted twice when a person likes exactly two colours). You should also know that triple counts account for 2 extra counts, while double counts account for 1 extra count in the Venn diagram you would make. Since, in this question, there is an extra count of 130, we can see that the maximum triple count would be 130/2 = 65. However, there is another constraint we need to look at while using this logic – and that is that the value of each of the three colours should be at least 65. However, in this case, since only 60% of the people like red colour, the number of people liking all three cannot be more than 60. Hence, the correct answer would be 60%.

Solutions for Questions 3 to 4:

3. The friends took a total number of 145000/1000 = 145 drinks. 20 of them took 3 drinks, which in effect, means a total of 60 drinks were taken by these 20 friends.
   55 of them took at least two out of three drinks; this means that 55 people took, two or three drinks. Since we already know that 20 people took three drinks, it means that 55 − 20 = 35 people took exactly two drinks. The total drinks taken by these 35 friends = 35 × 2 = 70.
   Now, we are left with 145 − (70+60) = 15 drinks.

These 15 drinks were taken by 15 different friends (who were each having one drink).

Total number of friends who did not take any of the three drinks = 85 − (20 + 35 + 15) = 15.

4. 15 friends took exactly one drink.

Solutions for Questions 5 to 8:

We will be able to make the following Venn diagram for the problem:

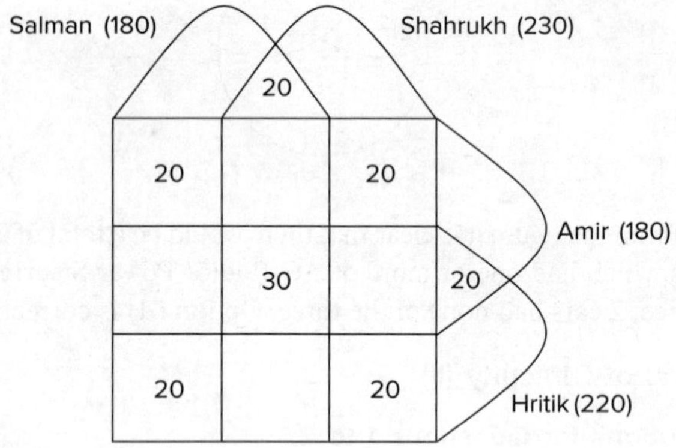

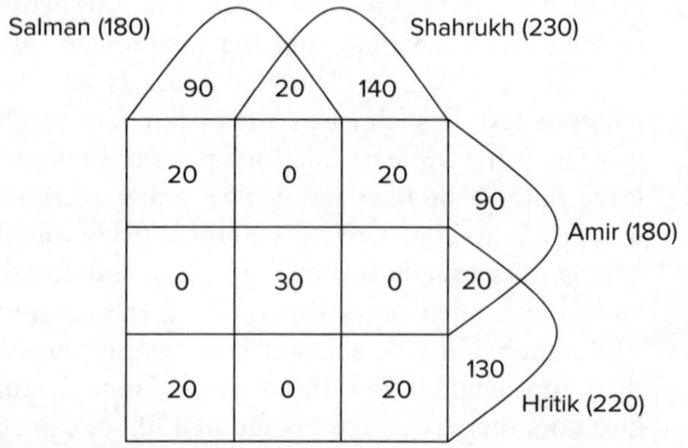

5. Students who like exactly two actors = 20 + 20 + 20 + 20 + 20 + 20 = 120.
6. Students who like at least two actors = 120 + 30 = 150.
7. Total students who like one or more actors = 90 + 20 + 140 + 90 + 20 + 130 + 20 + 20 + 20 + 20 + 30 = 600. 80% of the total students = 600 → So, 20% of total students = 600/4 =150. So, total number of students = 600 + 150 = 750.
8. Total students who like Hritik = 220.

   Total number of the students like Hritik and also like at least one other actor = 30 + 20 + 20 + 20 = 90. So, the required percentage = $\frac{90}{220} \times 100$ = 40.9%.

Solutions for Questions 9 to 10:

9. This question is again to be solved, using the logic used for question 62. In this case, 100% is counted as 60 + 82 + 66 = 208% → An extra count of 108%. The maximum number of people who follow all three teams would be given by 108/2 = 54. Since, each of CSK, RCB and KKR have more than 54% followers, it means that the correct answer to this question would be 54%.
10. Minimum percentage of students who like all three would occur, if we take care of the 'extra counts' using double counting. We can easily see a scenario where the double counting is: 42% (follow CSK and RCB); 18% (follow CSK and KKR) while 48% (follow RCB and KKR). Thus, we will get a total of 108% extra counts using this structure. In such a case, the percentage of people who follow all three teams = 0%.

Solutions for Questions 11 to 14:

We can encapsulate the data in the following Venn diagram:

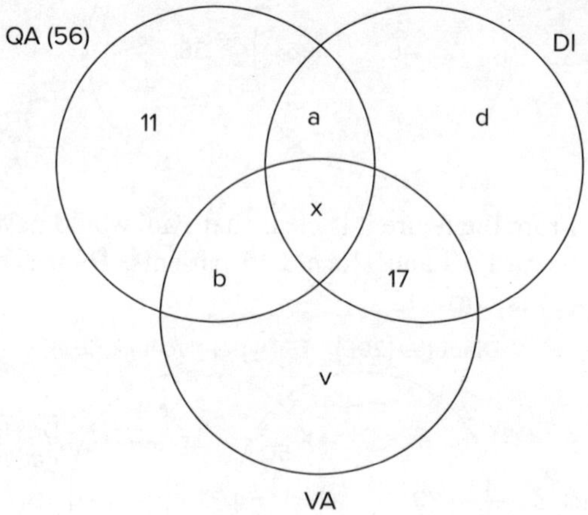

x + a + b = 45; d + v = 52

From the diagram, we can see that the total number of students inside the circles of the Venn diagram are: 56 + 17 + d + v. But, since d + v + 11 = 63, we know that d + v = 52. Thus, we can see 125 students inside the circles of the Venn diagram, which means that the number of students who did not pass any of the three subjects is 150 - 125 = 25.

11. Option (b) is correct.
12. This question is asking us to find the value of 'x' in our Venn diagram. The only information, we have about the value of 'x' is through the equation a + b + x = 45. There is no other equation connecting these variables. Hence, we cannot determine the value of how many students passed in all three subjects. Option (d) is correct.
13. The required value will be got using: a + b + x + 17 = 45 + 17 = 62. Option (a) is correct.
14. The number of students who passed in VA depends on the values of x, b and v. These are all unknown in the given scenario and there is no way to find them out. Hence, option (d) is correct. The absolutely correct

answer would have been cannot be determined, but, since that option isn't given, we will choose option (d) as the correct answer.

Solutions for Questions 15 to 18:

Once we insert all the information into the 4- set Venn diagram, we get the following picture:

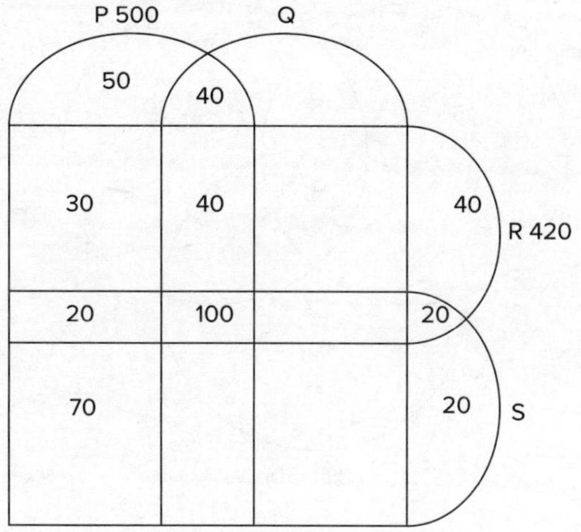

At this stage, we can see the following:

(i) P, Q & S but not R = 500 − (50 + 40 + 30 + 40 + 20 +100 + 70) = 150.

(ii) R, Q, S but not P = 250 − (40 + 20 + 150) = 40 (since, 250 patients were treated with exactly three types of medicines).

(iii) R & Q only = 420 − (30 + 20 + 40 + 100 + 40 + 40 +20) = 130.

(iv) Q only = 150 − (50 + 40 + 20) = 40 (150 patients were treated with exactly one type of medicine).

(v) Q & S only = 1000 − (500 + 40 + 130 + 40 + 40 +20 + 20) = 210.

The final figure shows all the numbers:

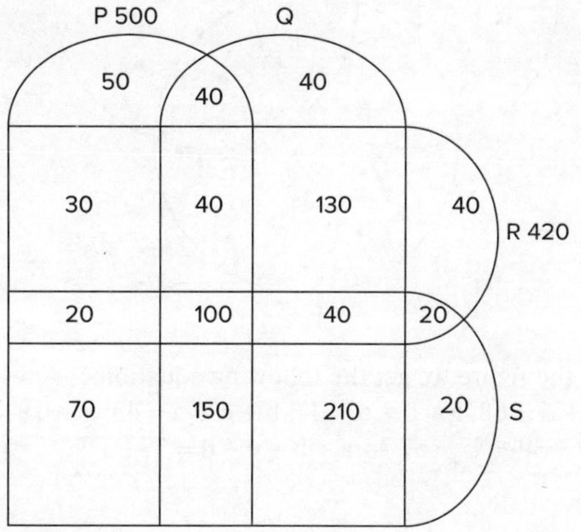

The answers are:

15. 750.
16. 40.
17. 210.
18. 630.

Solutions for Questions 19 to 22:

Based on the information in the problem, we can make the following starting figure.

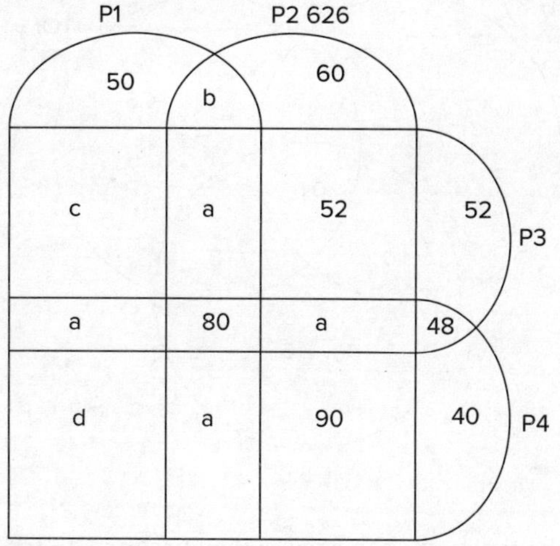

Looking at P2, we can see that: (60 + 52 + 90 + 80 + 3a + b) = 626 → 3a + b = 344.

Also, we are given that: "324 employees had both P1 and P2", which means that (80 + 2a + b) = 324 → 2a + b = 244. Solving these two equations, we get, a = 100 and b = 44.

Also, from clue (ix), we have P1= P4. Hence, 40 + 48 + 90 + 80 + 300 + d = 50 + 44 + c + 300 + 80 + d → c = 84.

Also, since there are 60 employees out of 1200, who have none of these, the total number of people in the figure is 1200 − 60 = 1140. From the given figure, if we replace a = 100, b = 44 and c = 84 in it, we can see that d = 1140 − (626 + 52 + 48 + 40 + 84 + 50 + 100) = 140.

The final figure gives us all the answers required:

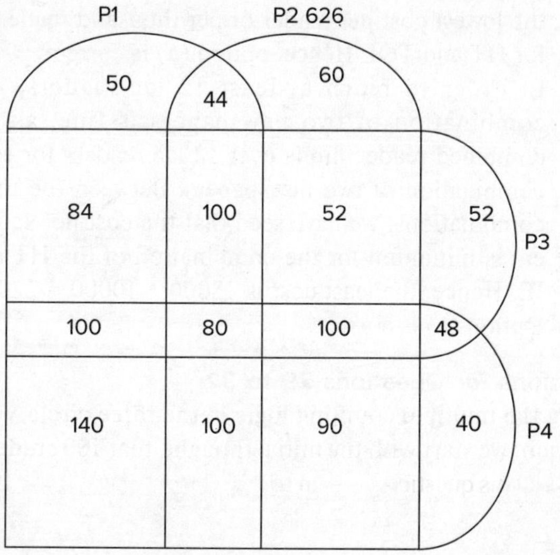

The answers are:

19. Option (c) is correct.
20. Option (c) is correct.
21. 480
22. 140

Solutions for Questions 23 to 28:

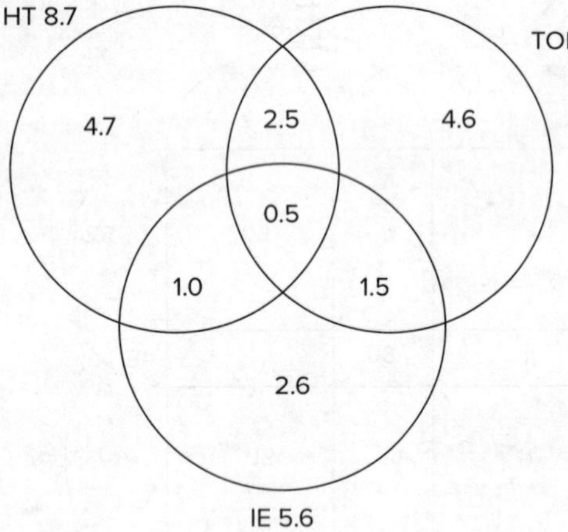

From the figure, we can answer the questions 23 to 28:

23. 8.7 (HT) + 4.6 + 1.5 + 2.6 = 17.4. Option (c) is correct.
24. 4.7 + 4.6 + 2.6 = 11.9. Option (b) is correct.
25. 5.5/17.4 = 31.6%. Option (d) is correct.
26. 11.9:5 = 2.38:1. Option (a) is correct.
27. To place an advertisement in HT and TOI, the total cost would be 12000 + 13000 = 25000 per sq.cm. This would cover a readership of: 8.7 + 4.6 + 1.5 = 14.8 lac readers.

    HT and IE, would cost 22000 to cover 8.7 + 2.6 + 1.5 = 12.8 lac readers.

    TOI & IE would cost 23000 to cover 9.1 + 2.6 + 1 = 12.7 lac readers. Comparing the three ratios of: 25000/14.8; 22000/12.8 and 23000/12.7, we see that the lowest cost per reader or per thousand readers is for HT and TOI. Hence, option (a) is correct.
28. In order to reach at least 12 lac readers, any combination of two newspapers is fine, as the combined readership is over 12 lac readers for each combination of two newspapers. Between the three combinations, we have seen that the cost per square cm is minimum for the combination of the HT and IE. Hence, the least cost is 12000 + 10000 = 22000. Option (a) is correct.

Solutions for Questions 29 to 32:

Using the multiple counting logic in the three circle Venn diagram, we start with the initial thought, that 100 students are being counted 70 + 40 + 30 = 140 times. Thus, there is an extra count of 40. With the given numbers of 20 (Finance and Marketing); 15 (Marketing and HR) and 10 (Finance and HR), we can make out that the number of people having offers from all areas would be 5. The Venn diagram, that encapsulates this is shown here, for your reference.

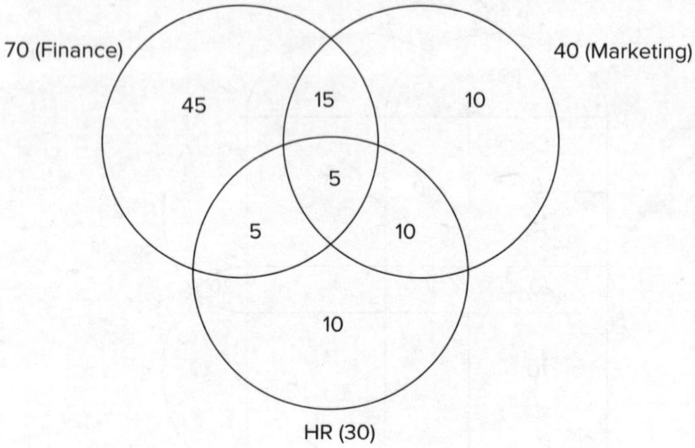

The answers can be read off from the above diagram:

29. 10 + 15 + 5 = 30. Option (c) is correct.
30. 45 students had offers from only Finance area. Option (a) is correct.
31. 15 out of 100 = 15%. Option (c) is correct.
32. 65 out of 100 have offers from only one area. Hence, 65%. Option (a) is correct.

Solutions for Questions 33 to 36:

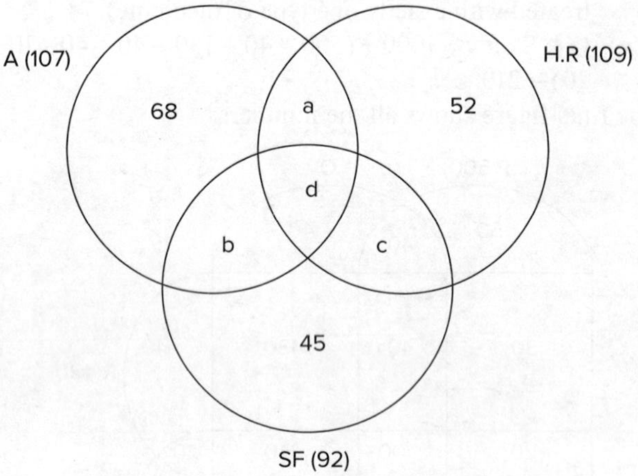

From the figure we get the following equations:

$a + b + d = 68$; $a + c + d = 52$; $b + c + d = 45$; $a + b + c + d = 220 - 39 - 47 - 57 \rightarrow a + b + c + d = 77$.

Adding the first three equations, we get:
$2a + 2b + 2c + 3d = 165$. Also, since $a + b + c + d = 77 \rightarrow 2a + 2b + 2c \; 2d = 154 \rightarrow d = 11$. Solving for a, b and c, we get: $a = 32$, $b = 25$ and $c = 9$. The final Venn diagram looks as shown:

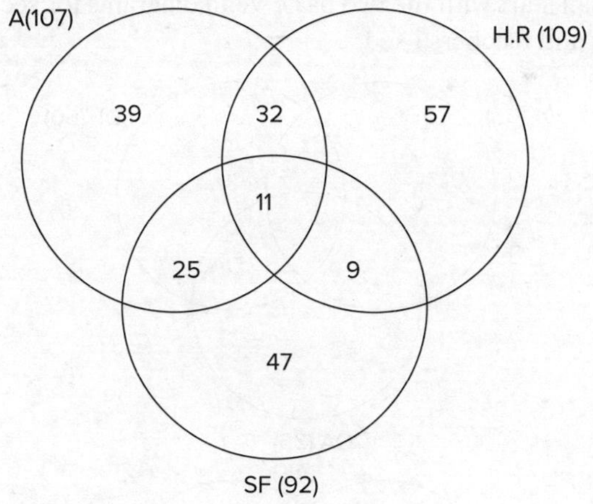

33. 11, So, option (a) is correct.
34. 77
35. 52
36. 25

Solutions for Questions 37 to 39:
The Venn diagram for this question looks as shown.

> **Note:** The key thought here is that since a total of 600 students have got calls and out of them 113 students do not have distinction in either 10th or 12th class, it means that there are a total of 600 − 113 = 487 students who would have a distinction in at least one subject. The central 84 can then be thought off as: 487 people are counted 320 + 251 = 571 times, which means that the double counted area has to be 84.

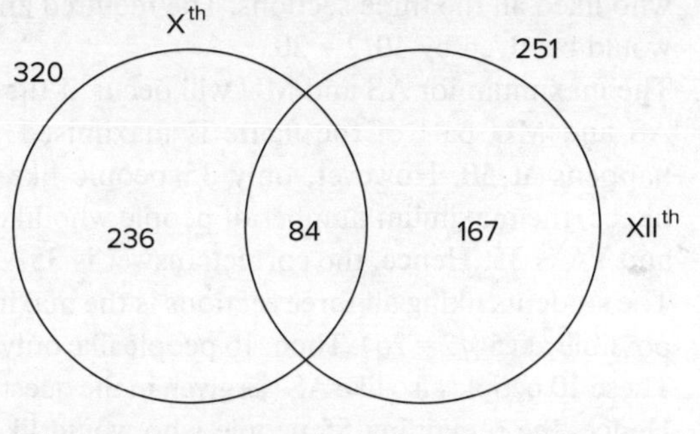

37. The required answer is 236 + 167 = 403.
38. 113 − 84 = 29
39. 84/600 = 14%

Solutions for Questions 40 to 42:
The basic Venn diagram that gets formed here is as follows:

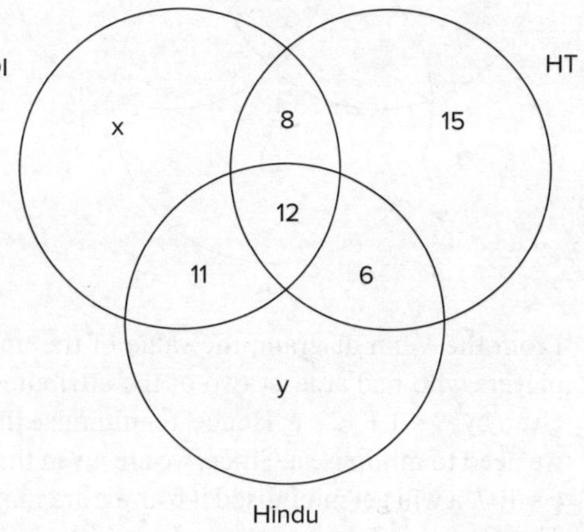

Since, everyone reads at least one newspaper, it follows that $x + y$ must be 48%. Also, since there are a total of 400 people, percentages can be allocated between x and y in increments of 0.25 only. In other words, x or y cannot be numbers like 10.1 or 10.4, but can be numbers ending with a decimal value of .25, .50 or .75 only.

40. TOI = 31 + x. Hindu = 29 + y. The two become equal at x = 23 and y = 25. However, since TOI < Hindu, it follows that the maximum value of x = 22.75 and hence, y = 25.25. In such a case, the total percentage of people who read TOI = 53.75 = 215 people. The maximum number who do not read TOI in such a case = 46.25% = 185 people. Hence, option (a) is correct.
41. People reading Hindu but not HT = 11 + y. If, HT (41%) < TOI, means x = 10.25% minimum. In such a case, y = 37.75, is the maximum value of y. The maximum percentage of people reading Hindu but not HT = 11 + 37.75 = 48.75. Option (c) is correct.
42. For TOI = twice Hindu, we have: $31 + x = 2(29 + y)$. With $x + y = 48 \rightarrow y = 7$ and $x = 41$. With y = 7, the percentage of people who read TOI or HT = 93. Option (d) is correct.

Solutions for Questions for 43 to 48:
The basic information can be encapsulated in a Venn diagram as shown:

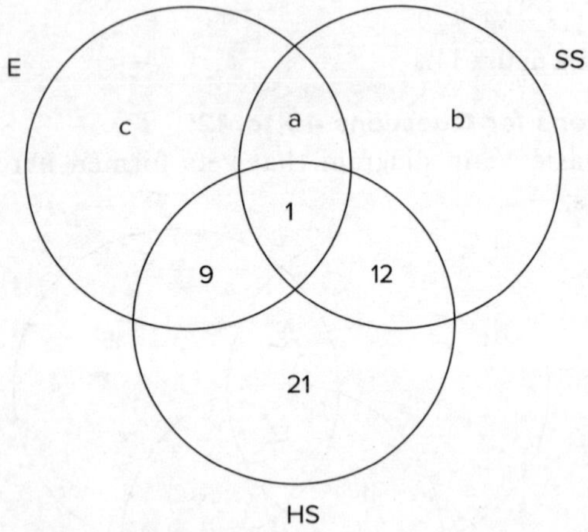

43. From the Venn diagram, the value of the number of players who had at least two of the attributes will be given by: 9 + 1 + 12 + a. Hence, to minimise this value, we need to minimise a. Since, we are given that a + b + c = 107, a will get minimised if b and c are maximised. The upper contstraint for b and c = 48 each (does not exceed 32% of 150). Hence, minimum value of a = 11. Hence, required minimum for the answer = 9 + 1 + 12 + 11 = 33. Option (d) is correct.
44. In this question, we are given that a + b = 61. The maximisation of players with more than one attribute would occur if a is maximised. In the given situation, there is no upper constraint for 'a' other than 61. Hence, if we put a = 61, we get 83 players having more than one attribute (out of 150). This is equal to 55.33%. Hence, option (d) is correct.
45. According to the question and the Venn diagram, $(13 + a + b) < (10 + a + c) \rightarrow (13 + b) < (10 + c) \rightarrow (c - b) > 3$. In this scenario, we are asked to work out the minimum value of a + 1. To minimise (a + 1), we should minimise 'a'. With the constraint that a + b + c = 107, b and c are maximum 48 each and the additional constraint that c − b > 3, the minimisation of 'a' occurs when we take c = 48, b = 44 and a = 15. Hence, minimum value of (a + 1) = 16. Option (b) is correct.
46. According to this question and the Venn diagram, we have: $(10 + a + c) = 2 \times (a + 1) \rightarrow a - c = 8$. Also, we are given that: $(13 + a + b) = 2 \times (a + 1) \rightarrow a - b = 11$. We also have a + b + c = 107 (basic condition of the question). Solving the three equations, we get: a = 42, c = 34 and b = 31. The required answer for only stick skills is the value of 'b'. Option (a) is correct.
47. $(10 + a + c) = 2 \times (22 + a) \rightarrow c - a = 34$. We are asked to find the minimum value of b. In this situation 'b' is minimised when c and a are maximised. Hence, c = 48, a = 14 and b = 45 will be the minimisation of b. Option (b) is correct.
48. Since, values of b and c can be maximum 48, the solutions are:
c = 48, a = 14 and b = 45; c = 47, a = 13 and b = 47. There are only two solutions, since if we try to put c = 46, b's value becomes 49, which is not possible. Hence, the correct answer is option (b).

Solutions for Questions 49 to 52:

We can start with the two basic Venn diagrams for sections liked and teachers liked.

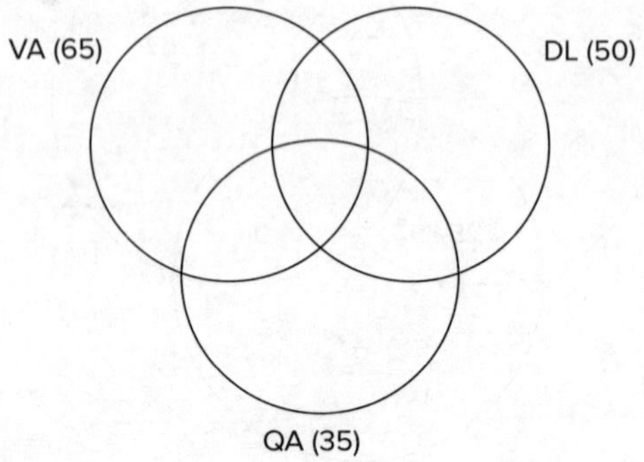

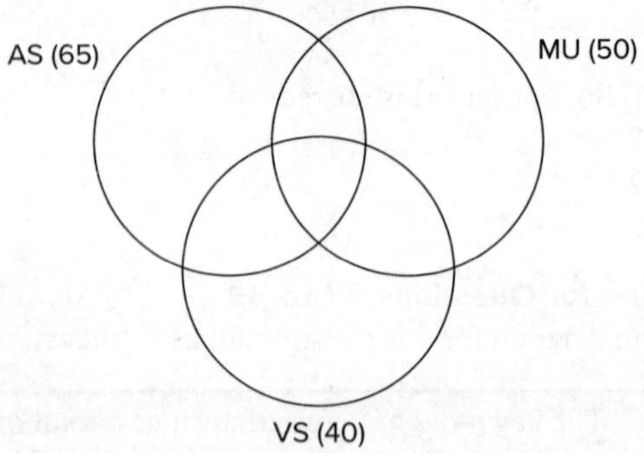

49. Since, every student liked at least one section, it means that in the Venn diagram for the sections, 100 students are being represented 150 times (65 + 50 + 35). This means an extra count of 50. If the number of students who like exactly 2 sections is 10, it means that they will account for 10 extra counts. The remaining 40 extra counts have to be managed using the students who liked all the three sections. The required answer would be given by 40/2 = 20.
50. The maximum for AS and MU will occur, if the only AS and MU part of the figure is maximised. This happens at 50. However, only 35 people like QA, hence, the maximum number of people who like QA and VA is 35. Hence, the correct answer is 35.
51. The students liking all three sections is the maximum possible at (50/2 = 25). Then, 10 people like only QA. These 10 people also like AS (as given in the question). Hence, the remaining 55 people who would like AS could also all like QA (and be part of the 65 students who like VA overall). Option (c) is correct.
52. The maximum for all the three sections is constrained at 25 (upper limit), while for all the three teachers it is 27. Hence, the correct answer is 25. Option (b) is correct.

Solution for Question 53:

53. The least percentage of people with all 4 gadgets would happen if all the employees who are not having any one of the four objects is mutually exclusive. Thus, 100 - 30 - 25 - 20 - 15 = 10

Level of Difficulty (III)

Solutions for Questions 1 to 4:

It is given that 400 candidates scored above 90th percentile overall in CAT. Let the following Venn diagram represent the number of persons who scored above 80 percentile in CAT in each of the three sections:

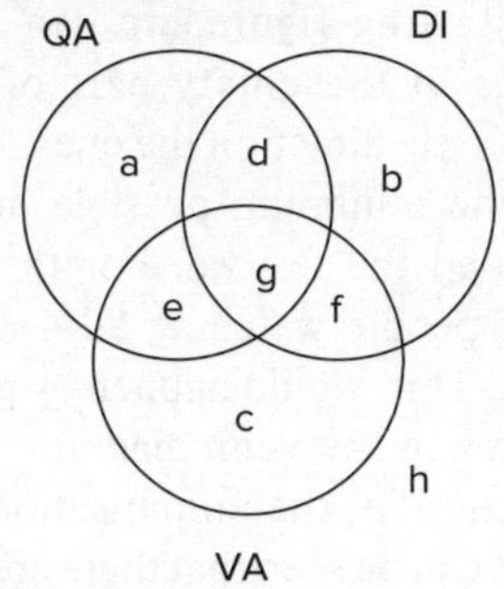

According to the statement 1, h = 0.

According to the statement 2, d + e + f = 300.

According to the statement 3, a = b = c.

a + b + c + g = 3a + g = 400 - 300 = 100.

According to the statement 4: (2a + f): (2a + e) : (2a + d) = 4 : 2 : 1.

Therefore, 6a + (d + e + f) is divisible by 4 + 2 + 1 = 7.

Since, d + e + f = 300, 6a + 300 is divisible by 7.

Possible values of a are 6, 13, 20, 27, . . .

Further, since 3a + g = 100, a must be less than 34. Therefore, only four cases are possible for the value of a, i.e., 6, 13, 20, 27.

From statement 5: a = 6 or 13.

Possible values of 6a + (d + e + f) are 336, 378.

2a + f = 192 or f = 180, 2a + e = 96 or e = 84, 2a + d = 48 or d = 36, 2a + f = 216 or f = 180, 2a + e = 108 or e = 82, 2a + d = 54 or d = 28. We can calculate the values of the other variables for the two cases. a = 6 or 13, d = 36 or 28, e = 84 or 82, f = 180 or 190 g = 82 or 61.

Candidates represented by d, e, f and g are selected for AAT. According to the question, IIM B will consider the candidates who are appearing for AAT and scored above 80th percentile in QA. Hence, IIM B will consider the candidates represented by d, e and g. Hence, the number of candidates considered by IIM can be 208 or 184. There are 800 candidates who scored above 80th percentile in QA, and since there are 208 or 184 candidates at or above 80th percentile in QA and are at or above 90th percentile overall, there must be 592 (800 - 208) or 616 (800 – 184) candidates at or above 80th percentile in QA who scored less than 90th percentile overall.

1. a = 6 or 13. Hence, option (a) is correct.
2. g is a multiple of 2. Hence, g = 82. In this case e = 84. Required number of candidates = e + g = 166.
3. g = 82. Required number of candidates shortlisted for AAT = d + e + f + g = 36 + 84 + 180 + 82 = 382.
4. If the number of candidates who are at or above the 90th percentile overall and also are at or above the 80th percentile in QA in CAT, is more than 200, then the number of candidates at or above 90th percentile overall and at or above 80th percentile in QA = 6 + 36 + 82 + 84 = 208.

   Hence, the required number of candidates who have to sit for the separate test = 800 - 208 + 6 = 598.

Solutions for Questions 5 to 7:

We can make the following Venn diagram based on the information provided:

> **Note:** The following deductions have been made in order to get to this point in the diagram. If we initially assume all three to be 'x', then only VA = 2x.

QA = 34 and only QA = 14, so people with QA and at least one more subject = 20. This area is represented by the three regions in the Venn diagram.

A, B and the area common to all three parts of the Venn diagram.

So, Only VA = 2x = 16 → x = 8. Then, we know that A + B = 12.

At this point, from the determined part of the diagram, we know about 34 + 16 = 50 people out of the 78 people. The remaining 28 should be shared in such a way that only DI and LR and DI and LR and VA should be equal. If we assume DI and LR + VA only as 'C' then only DI and LR would be C + 8. (from clue (iv)). Thus, 2C + 8 = 28 → C = 10 and C + 8 = 18.

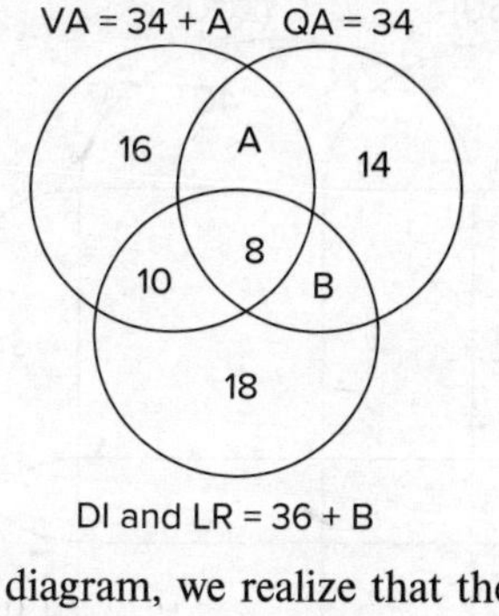

In this Venn diagram, we realize that there are multiple possibilities for the values of A and B, given two conditions: A + B =12 and VA has the maximum enrollments. So, 34 + A > 36 + B.

The following table of possible outcomes can be made out:

Possibility #	1	2	3	4	5	6	7		
	A = 12, B = 0	A = 11, B = 1	A = 10, B = 2	A = 9, B = 3	A = 8, B = 4	A = 7, B = 5	A = 6, B = 6	A = 5, B = 7	A < 5; B > 7
VA: 34 + A	46	45	44	43	42	41	40	39	
DI and LR: 36 + B	36	37	38	39	40	41	42	43	
Possible?	Yes	Yes	Yes	Yes	Yes	Not possible	Not possible	Not possible	Not possible

The answers can then be read off from the Venn diagram and the table:

5. This question is asking us for the minimum value of A in the above situation. A's minimum value is: 8.
6. Number of students enrolled for only DI and LR = 18.
7. For the given ratio to be 19:22, we are looking at possibility 3 in the table. For that possibility, the number of students in VA = 44.

Solutions for Questions 8 to 12:

We can make the following starting figure for the question. Please note that since there are 50 people above 60 who watched Terminator, 110 people between 30 to 60 who watched it and 90 people below 30 who watched it, it means that there are a total of 50 + 110 + 90 = 250 people who watched Terminator. Other totals for Crossroads, GI Joe and The Bridesmaid have been derived as 200, 160 and 170 in a similar fashion. It is also given to us in the table, as to how many people watched only that movie. So, to start off there are 150 people more who watched Terminator (T) and at least one more movie, 160 people more who watched Crossroads (C) and at least one more movie, 130 for GI Joe (GI) and at least one more movie and 150 for The Bridesmaid (TB).

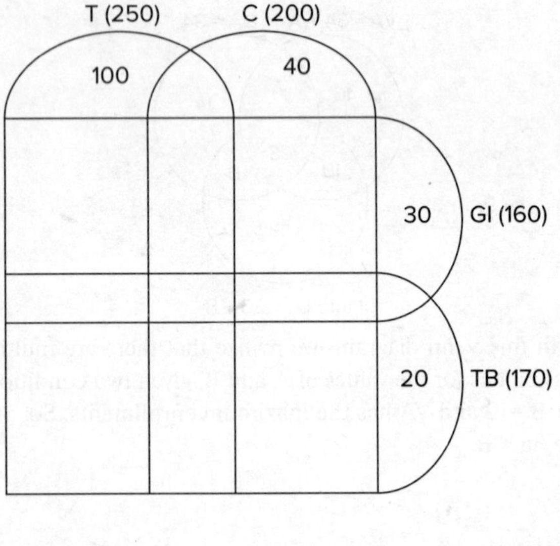

Based on this starting figure, we can try to fit in the remaining values in the empty part of the 4 set Venn diagram, based on the direction the question is taking us to.

8. We want the minimum possible number of people who attended the festival. For this to happen, the number of people watching all 4 movies should be maximised. This, would happen by placing 130 inside the all 4 area of the Venn diagram. The figure shows us the solution for the minimisation required in this question. It can be seen that there are 350 people used for this particular situation and that would be the least number of people. Hence, option (c) is correct.

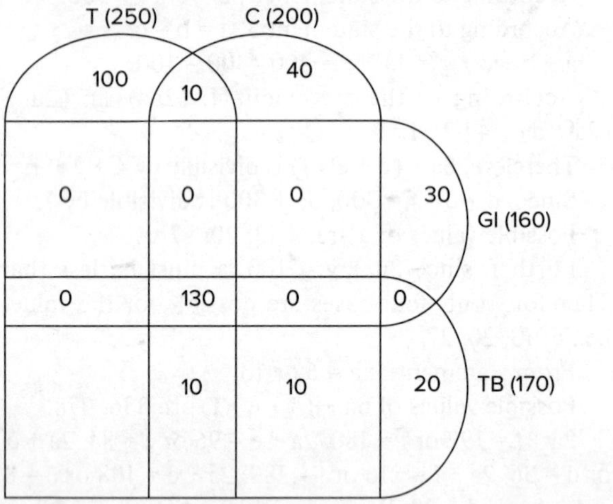

Figure for minimum people

9. There are a total of 50 people above 60, who watched Terminator, 30 who watched Crossroads, 40 watched GI Joe and 30 watched The Bridesmaid. The maximisation of the number of persons above 60, who attended the festival would occur when these people are kept separate from each other. So the answer should have been 50 + 30 + 40 + 30 = 150. However, there is another constraint in the data. This constraint is that there are only 30 persons who watched only GI Joe and 20 persons who watched only The Bridesmaid. Hence, we cannot have 40 persons above 60 years who watched only GI Joe. That number is maximised at 30

and likewise there can only be 20 new persons above 60, who watched The Bridesmaid separately. Hence, the number of unique above 60 viewers would be 50 + 30 + 30 + 20 = 130. To this, we would need to assume that 10 people more watch GI Joe and The Bridesmaid. Hence, the correct answer is 130 + 10 = 140.

Note: This can also be thought off as follows: Assume, P_1 to P_{50}, be 50 people above 60, who watch Terminator. P51 to P80 be 30 persons above 60 who watched Crossroads, P81 to P110 be 30 people above 60, who watch GI Joe. But since there are a total of 40 persons above 60, who watch GI Joe, we will have to have 10 people amongst GI Joe (& of course above 60), who would be common to other movies too. Note that, we cannot put 81 to 120 as GI Joe since only 30 people watched only GI Joe. Similarly, we can only allocate, unique people P111 to P130 who watched only The Bridesmaid. This leaves us with 10 more persons to add to TB and 10 more persons to add to GI Joe. So, we can imagine that P131 to P140 are persons who watched both GI Joe and The Bridesmaid. Hence, option (d) is correct.

10. For this question, we need to minimise the number of people below 60 years.

The total number of people below 60 for each movie are:

	Terminator	Crossroads	GI Joe	The Bridesmaid
30–60	110	60	60	70
Below 30	90	110	60	70

Between 30 to 60, there are a minimum of 110 people who need to be allocated for Terminator. Let's call these people P1 to P110. The 60 for Crossroads, 60 for GI Joe and 70 for The Bridesmaid can be accommodated inside this 110 only. So, for the 30–60 category, there are at least 110 persons. Likewise, for the below 30 category, to rationalise the numbers given in the table, we would need to use at least 110 more people. Thus, the minimum number of people in the below 60 category is 110 + 110 = 220. Option (d) is correct.

11. The solution for this can be thought through our discussion for question no. 8. There are at most 130 persons who watched all the four movies. Hence, option (b) is correct.

12. The value will be maximum, when people watch exactly 1 or exactly 2 movies. The maximum for exactly two movies, would be given as: (250 + 200 + 160 + 170 - 190)/2 = 295, Hence, option (c) is correct.

Solutions for Questions 13 to 18:

The first thing to do in this set is to understand that there is a Venn diagram only between Reputed College and Good Academic Record. The other two features - viz: qualification and domain experience is only in exactly one area.

So, the break up of the data would be as seen in the table:

B.E & only reputed college	A	M.Sc & only reputed college	D	Programming & only reputed college	G	Testing & only reputed college	J
B.E & only good academic record	B	M.Sc & only good academic record	E	Programming & only good academic record	H	Testing & only good academic record	K
B.E & both reputed college and good academic record	C	M.Sc & both reputed college and good academic record	F	Programming & both reputed college and good academic record	I	Testing & both reputed college and good academic record	L

In this initial structure, we know that: A + B + C + D + E + F = 80 & G + H + I + J + K + L = 80.

Then from clue (i), we know that: J + K + L = 40. Also, G + H + I = 40. From clue (ii), we see that I = 0. From (iii), we see that: D + E + F = 30, so A + B + C = 50. In clue (iii), there is also a cross referenced value, telling us that 15 people amongst M.Sc trainees 30 people had experience in Programming. From clue (iv), we have L =15

B.E & only reputed college	A	M.Sc & only reputed college	D	Programming & only reputed college	G	Testing & only reputed college	J
B.E & only good academic record	B	M.Sc & only good academic record	E	Programming & only good academic record	H	Testing & only good academic record	K
B.E & both reputed college and good academic record	20	M.Sc & both reputed college and good academic record	F	Programming & both reputed college and good academic record	0	Testing & both reputed college and good academic record	15

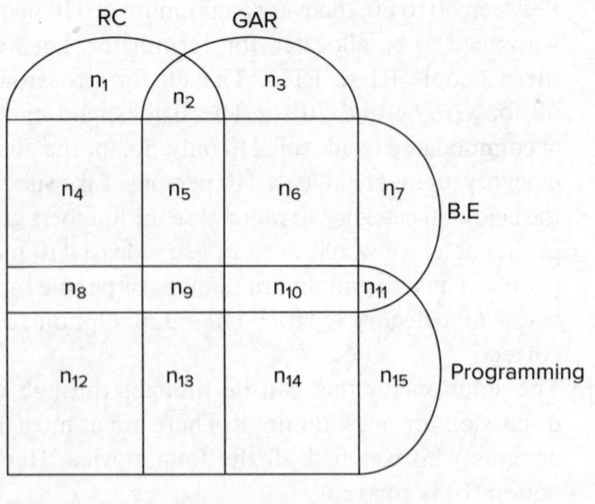

Interpreting the above picture: n_1 represents people who had Reputed college, M.Sc and Testing. Similarly, n_2 represents RC & GAR, M.Sc and testing and so on. n_{12} for instance, means M.Sc, Programming and Reputed College; n_{13} represents: (RC and GAR, Programming and M.Sc). It can also be deduced that $n_7 = 0$, $n_{11} = 0$ and $n_{15} = 0$, since all the people belong to either RC or GAR or both.

Now from statement (a): n5 + n6 = 20; Testing = 40 (n1, 2, 3, 4, 5, 6) → Programming = 40 (n8, 9, 10, 12, 13, 14). Also, from statement (b), we have n9 = n13 = 0. From (c) we get: MSc = 30, so BE = 50. Also, n12 + n14 = 15. So, n8 + n10 = 25 (since programming is only n8, n10, n12 and n14). At this stage, the picture transforms to:

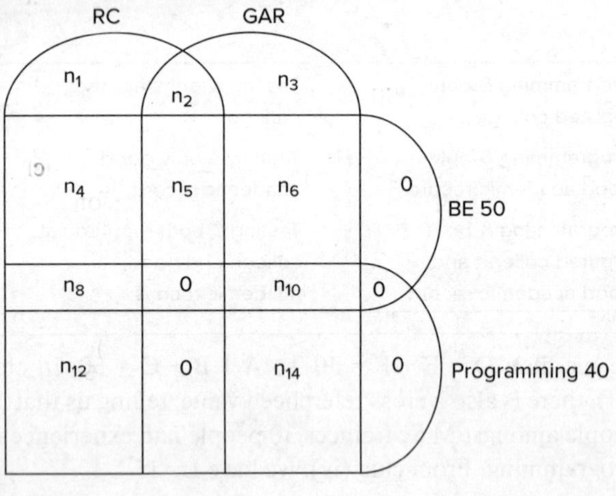

We also know that n1, n2, n3, n12 and n14 would add up to the MSc number of 30. Also, since n8, n10 add up to 25, n4, n5, n6 also add up to 25 (since together they have to account for the 50 of B.E). From statement (d) we know that n2 + n5 = 15.

From statement (e) we have: n5, n6, n10 adds up to 30 and n10 + n14 = 15. But, we also know that n5 + n6 = 20. So, n10 = 10 and n14 = 5. So, n12 = 10 (since n12 + n14 = 15) and n8 = 15 (since n8 + n10 = 25).

From the B.E (50), we know n5 + n6 = 20. So, n4 = 5. With these values, slotted into our diagram, we can make out from GAR (45), that n2 + n3 = 10. So, n1 = 80 – (n2 + n3) – (n5 + n6) – 5 – 15 – 10 – 10 – 5 = 80 – 10 – 20 – 5 - 15 – 10 – 10 – 5 = 5.

The final venn diagram looks as follows:

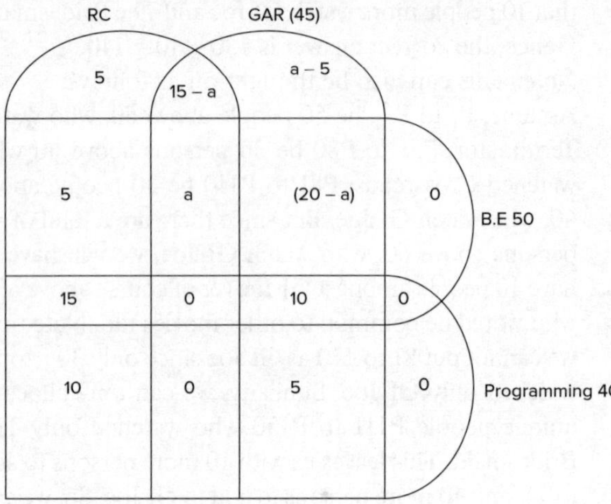

The answers can be read off as follows:

13. 10. Option (b) is correct.
14. 15.
15. We are looking for the value of n_5 here. n_5 was indeterminate in this question. Hence, option (d) is correct.
16. There are 5 such persons.
17. This question is giving us the value of 20 – a + 10 = 19. So, a = 11. We are being asked for the value of 15 – a = 15 – 11 = 4. Option (b) is correct.
18. 5.

Solutions for Questions 19 to 22:

The basic Venn diagram is given in the picture below:

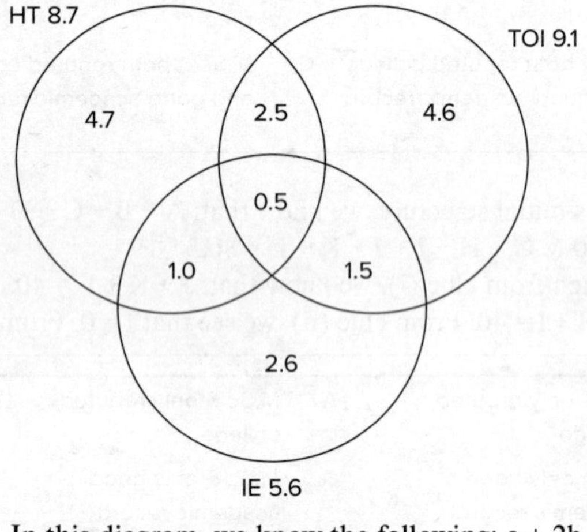

In this diagram, we know the following: a + 2b + c = 57. 3a + 3b + c = 106 and 2a + b = 49.

19. For the number of students, who passed in Verbal and DI/LR to be double of the number of students who passed in Verbal and QA only, we would need b + c = 2b → b = c. The equations become: a + 3b = 57 and

2a + b = 49. Solving simultaneously, we get b = 13 and a = 18. This question is asking us the value of a + 2b = 18 + 26 = 44. Option (a) is correct.

For questions 20 & 21 we are looking for the minimum and maximum values of |b – a|. The following table shows the multiple possibilities that exist in this context. The values for c can be such, that 3a + 3b should be a multiple of 3. Hence, possible values of c are 1, 4, 7, 10 and so on.

Value of c	Value of 3a + 3b	Value of a	Value of b	Value of lb – al
1	105	14	21	7
4	102	15	19	4
7	99	16	17	1
10	96	17	15	2
13	93	18	13	5
16	90	19	11	8
19	87	20	9	11
22	84	21	7	14
25	81	22	5	17
28	78	23	3	20
29	75	24	1	23

Value of c cannot be 30, as b will come out negative.

20. The minimum difference between a and b = 1. Option (b) is correct.
21. The maximum difference between a and b = 23.
22. For this question, we are being asked the maximum possible value of a. From the multiple possibilities, we can see that it is 24. Option (d) is correct.

Solutions for Questions 23 to 28:

The basic picture for the situation will be as seen below.

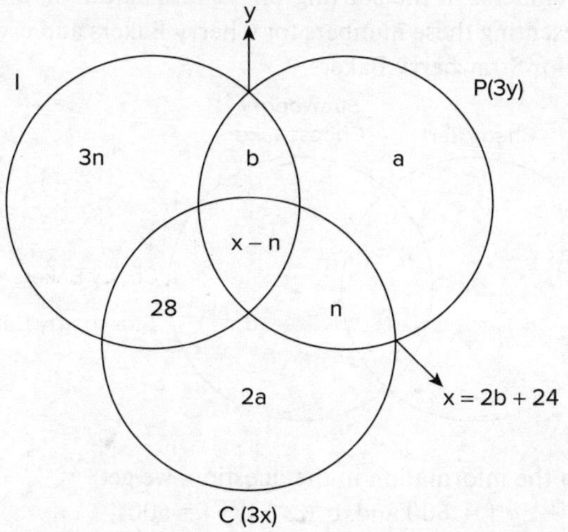

23. In order to solve question 23, you need to minimise the total number of people inside the diagram. The minimisation starts with b = 1, giving x = 26 and 3x as 78. This automatically means that 2a (only Chinese) would be 78 - 28 - 26 = 24. Consequently, we get a = 12, 3y then becomes 26 + 1 + 12 = 39. Also, since b = 1, b + x - n = 13, gives us x - n = 12 and n = 26 - 12 = 14. Thus, 3n = 42. The figure that solves this question would be as shown. In this case, the minimum number of people is 78 + 12 + 1 + 42 = 133.

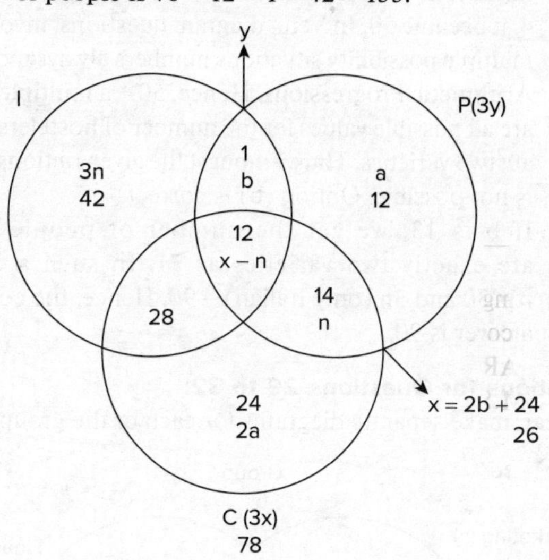

24. There is always a possibility of 0 people not eating anything. i.e., everyone eats. Hence, the correct answer to this question is 0.
25. If, you were to take the value of b as 2, you can see that x becomes 28, 3x becomes 84, 2a becomes 28, a becomes 14. In such a case, the value of 3y becomes 44, which is not possible (since it has to be a multiple of 3). Checking with b as 3, you can see that x becomes 30, 3x becomes 90, 2a becomes 32 and a becomes 16. In such a case, the value of 3y becomes 49, which is again not possible for 3y. The first value for b, that works is at b = 4. It gives the figure shown:

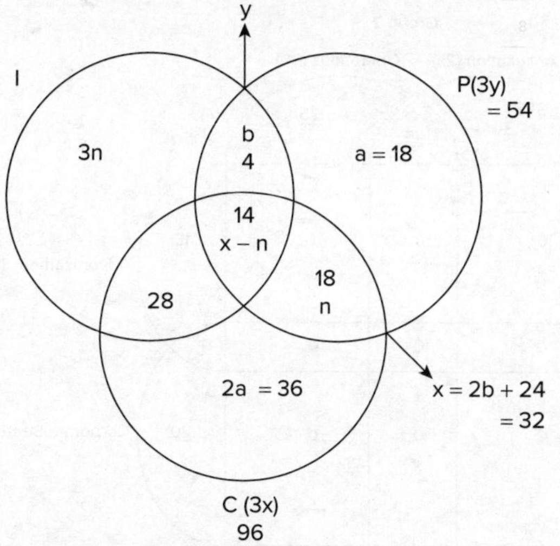

The required answer is: 18 + 28 + 4 = 50. Option (b) is correct.

26. This value is the difference between 3n and 2a. It can be seen that in all possible cases, this is always 18. Hence, option (a) is correct.
27. It can be seen that when we took 'b' as 1, we got the number of people eating two varieties was 43, at b = 4, it became 50. In Venn diagram questions, involving multiple possibility situations numbers always move in Arithmetic Progressions. Hence, 50 + a multiple of 7, are all possible values for the number of hostelers who ate two varieties. Thus, amongst the given options, 100 is not possible. Option (b) is correct.
28. If b is 13, we get the number of people who ate exactly two varieties as 71. In such a case, n = 30 and 3n (only Italian) = 90. Hence, the correct answer is 90.

Solutions for Questions 29 to 32:

We can make separate diagrams for each of the groups.

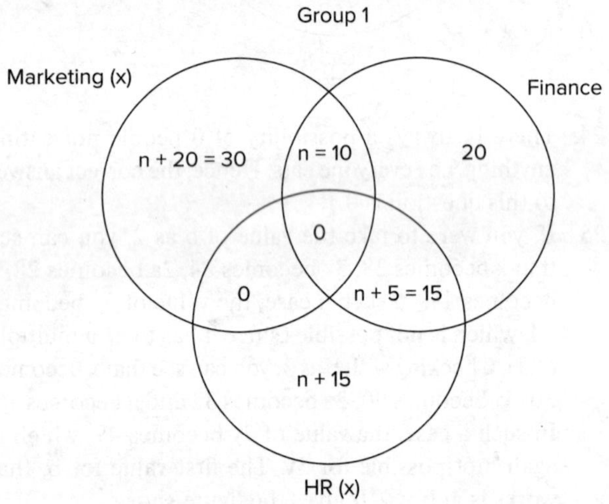

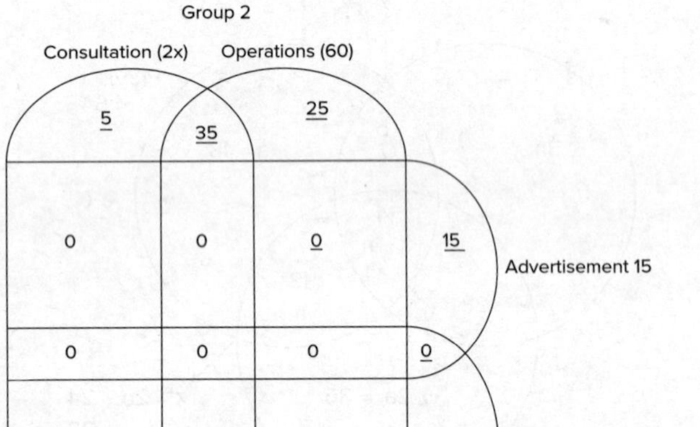

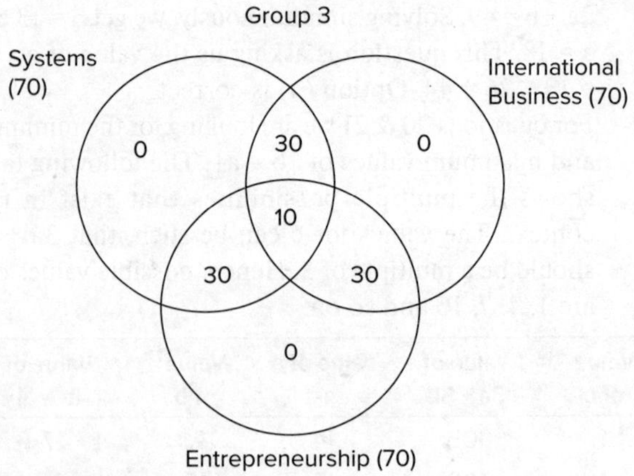

Based on the three Venn diagrams, we can answer the questions.

29. Group 1 = 10 + 15 = 25; Group 2 = 35 and Group 3 = 90. Total = 150. Option (c) is correct.
30. 25 students specialised in HR but not in Finance. Option (d) is correct.
31. The total number of students who specialised in only Consulting is 5. Option (d) is correct.
32. Group 1 has the minimum classroom hours required as it will be 125 ¥ 200 = 25000. Option (b) is correct.

Solutions for Questions 33 to 37:

You need to understand in this question, that there are basically 6 numbers that are being used.

These are: Number of children who bought only Cherry Tarts; Number of children who bought only Strawberry Cheesecakes; Number of children who bought both Cherry Tarts and Strawberry Cheesecakes. Each of these numbers would have one instance each for each baker. The obvious thing to do here is to build a Venn diagram showing these six numbers. In the starting off Venn diagram, a, b, e are representing these numbers for Cherry Bakers and c, d and f are for Strawberry Bakers.

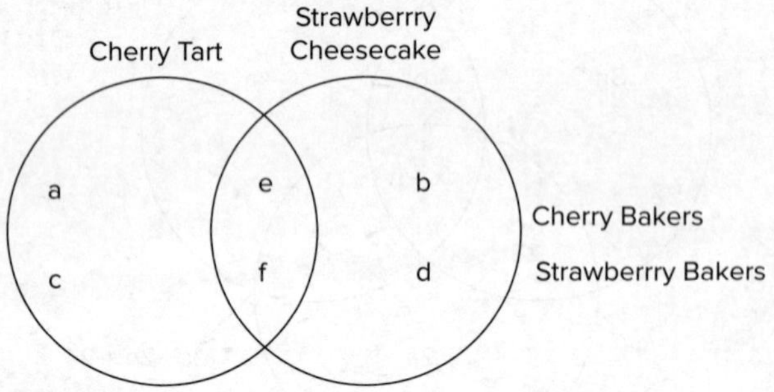

From the information in the question, we get:

a + e + c + f = 600 and, b + e + d + f = 600.

Therefore, a + c = b + d.

From clue (iii), a + b + c = 9d.

Also, f = 5e (clue (iv)).

From clue (vi), we get: a + c = e + f.
Therefore, a + c = e + f = 300 = b + d.
d = 10% of a + b + c + d = 10% of twice of a + c. 10% of 600 = 60. Hence, b = 300 - 60 = 240.
And, f = 5e gives us e + f = 300 → 6e = 300 → e = 50 and f = 250.

The Venn diagram gets completed using c = 140 and a = 160.

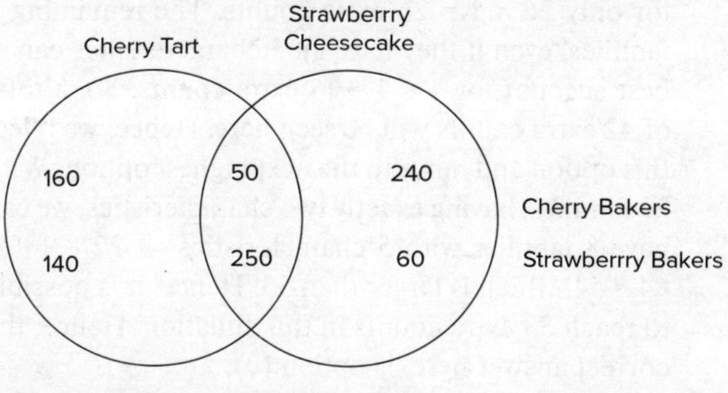

The answers can be read off from the diagram.

33. 50. Option (a) is correct.
34. 150.

600 children have bought from Strawberry Bakers, out of which 450 are seen in the Venn diagram. That leaves 150 children who must have bought some other kind of dessert. The correct answer is 150.

35. The required difference is 80. Option (b) is correct.
36. 1350.

We know that 150 children have bought some other kind of dessert. In the Venn diagram, the total number of desserts sold would have been (160 + 140 + 240 + 60) ¥ 1 + (50 + 250) ¥ 2 = 600 + 600 = 1200. So, the total number of desserts sold would be 1200 + 150 = 1350.

37. The revenue would be: 160 × 100 + 50 × 150 + 240 ¥ 50 = 35500.

Solutions for Questions 38 to 43:

The starting Venn diagram looks as follows:

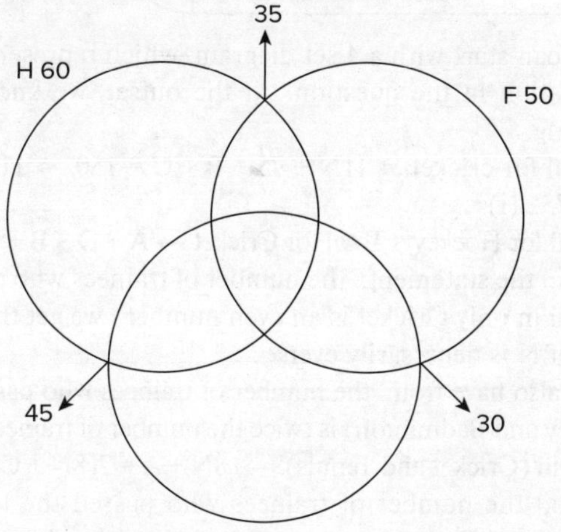

38. Since Cricket and Football, is 30, we start our trial for maximum for all 3 as 30. In the given figure, we can see that there is no problem in putting 30 in the middle, as all numbers match together. The correct answer is 30.

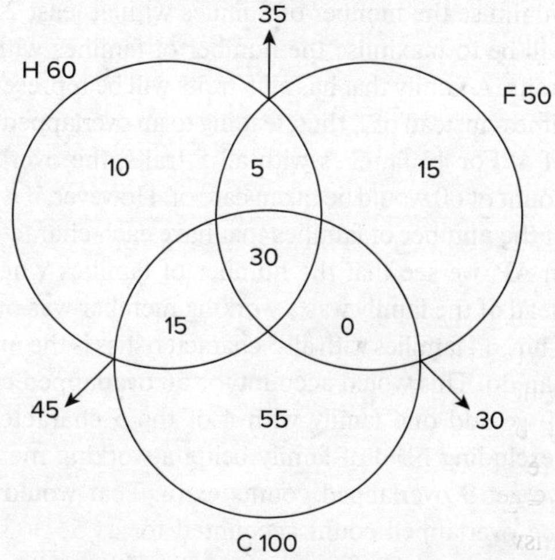

39. The natural minimum for the middle is 0. If we try to do this using 0 in the middle, it is evident, that the situation does not resolve itself as the 50 for Football is exceeded using 30 + 35. Also, the 60 for Hockey is also exceeded, since 45 + 35 = 80. This tells us that to resolve the Hockey situation, we should put 20 in the middle at least. Checking with 20, we see that all other numbers fall into place. The correct answer is 20.

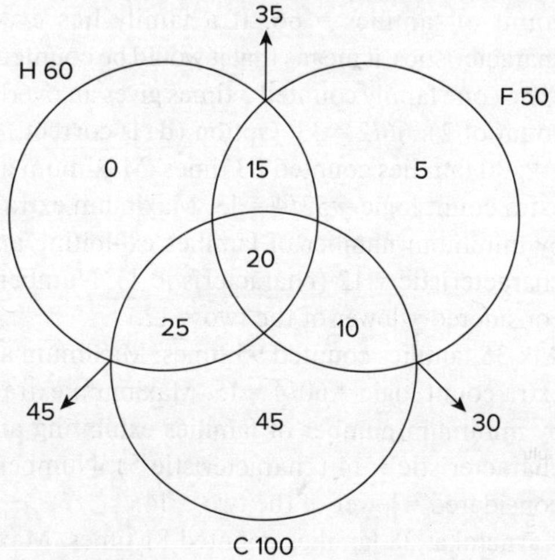

40. From the solution figure for question 39, we can see that this number is 50.
41. From the solution figure for question 38, we can see that exactly two games can be played by a minimum of 20 people.
42. For 1 game, the maximum is got from the figure for question 38. 55 + 15 + 10 = 80.
43. For 1 game, the minimum is got from the figure for question 39. 45 + 5 = 50.

Solutions for Questions 44 to 48:

44. In AP, the sum of the five columns is 95, while there are only 35 families. This means that 35 families are

represented 95 times amongst the 5 characteristics. That means an overlapped count of 60. The logic to minimise the number of families with at least 2 traits, will be to maximise the number of families with all 5 traits. A family that has all 5 traits will be represented 5 times - instead of 1, thus, leading to an overlapped count of 4. For 15 families with all 5 traits, the overlapped count of 60 would be taken care of. However, if we look at the number of families that have each characteristic in AP, we see that the number of families where the head of the family was a working member was only 14. Thus, 14 families with all 5 characteristics is the most we can do. This would account for 56 overlapped counts. If we add one family with 4 of the 5 characteristics (excluding head of family being a working member), we get 3 overlapped counts extra. That would make the overlapped count accounted for as 56 + 3 = 59. But we need 60. So, we can achieve that if one more family has exactly 2 characteristics - and there is ample opportunity to do that. Hence, the minimum number of families who had at least 2 of the five characteristics is 16. Option (d) is correct.

45. The maximum number of families in Haryana who have exactly 3 characteristics can be thought of as follows: Number of families = 40 and number of represented families = 15 + 25 + 21 + 29 + 16 = 106. Overlapped count of families = 66. If a family has exactly 3 characteristics, it means that it would be counted twice extra (one family counted 3 times gives an overlapped count of 2). 66/2 = 33. Option (d) is correct.

46. UP: 30 families counted 83 times. Maximum all 5 by extra count logic = 53/4 = 13. Maximum extra count by minimum number of families exhibiting any one characteristic = 12 (characteristic 1). Number to be considered = lower of the two = 12.

AP: 35 families counted 95 times. Maximum all 5 by extra count logic = 60/4 = 15. Maximum extra count by minimum number of families exhibiting any one characteristic = 14 (characteristic 5). Number to be considered = lower of the two = 14.

Karnataka: 28 families counted 81 times. Maximum all 5 by extra count logic = 53/4 = 13. Maximum extra count by minimum number of families exhibiting any one characteristic = 7 (characteristic 1). Number to be considered = lower of the two = 7.

Maharashtra: 36 families counted 94 times. Maximum all 5 by extra count logic = 58/4 = 14. Maximum extra count by minimum number of families exhibiting any one characteristic = 10 (characteristic 1). Number to be considered = lower of the two = 10.

Haryana: 40 families counted 106 times. Maximum all 5 by extra count logic = 66/4 = 16. Maximum extra count by minimum number of families exhibiting any one characteristic = 15 (characteristic 1). Number to be considered = lower of the two = 15.

Hence, the correct answer = 12 + 14 + 7 + 10 + 15 = 58.

47. In UP, the overlapped count is 53. With only 30 families, if we try to make 26 families (from option (d) have exactly 2 characteristics, we will be able to account for only 26 × 1 = 26 extra counts. The remaining 4 families, even if they have all 5 characteristics can at best account for 4 × 4 = 16 extra counts. So, a total of 42 extra counts will be seen here. Hence, we reject this option and move to the next highest option. With 22 families, having exactly two characteristics, we can have 8 families with 5 characteristics → 22 × 1 + 8 ×4 = 54, which is larger than 53. Hence, it is possible to reach 53 extra counts in this situation. Hence, the correct answer here, is option (c).

48. Haryana has an extra count of 66 in 40 families. This can be catered to by avoiding putting families with exactly 2 characteristics altogether. Hence, the correct answer here, would be 0.

Solutions for Questions 49 to 54:

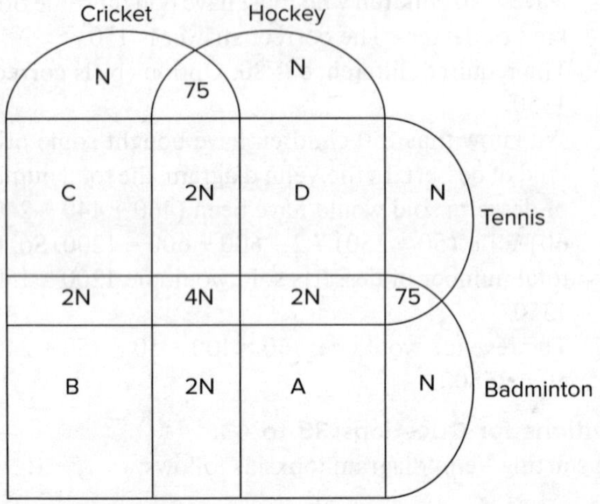

We can start with a 4 set diagram, which represents the information in the question. At the outset, we know the following:

Total for cricket = 11N + 75 + B + C = 150 → 11N + B + C = 75...(i)

Total for Hockey < Total for Cricket → A + D < B + C...(ii)

From the statement: 'the number of trainees who passed the trial in only Cricket is an even number', we get that the value of N is necessarily even.

We also have from 'the number of trainees who passed in (Hockey and Badminton) is twice the number of trainees who passed in (Cricket and Tennis)' → 8N + A = 2(8N + C)...(iii)

Also, 'the number of trainees who passed the trial in (Cricket and Badminton) is twice the number of trainees who passed the trial in (Hockey and Tennis)' gives us: 8N + B = 2(8N + D)...(iv)

Since, N is even, the starting out possibilities for the value of N are 2, 4, 6 (Note: This is constrained by equation (i) above).

We can then try to make a table of alternate possible values of A, B, C and D in order to see the various possible outcomes in the situation.

Value of N, B + C	Possibilities	D	B	C	A	Remarks	A + B + C + D
2, Value of B + C = 53	1	1	18	35	86	Not possible since A + D is more than B + C	
	2	13	42	11	38	Possible as A + D < B + C	104
	3	14	44	9	34	Possible	101
	4	15	46	7	30	Possible	98
	5	16	48	5	26	Possible	95
	6	17	50	3	22	Possible	92
	7	18	52	1	18	Possible	89
4, Value of B + C = 31	No possibility where B + C = 31						
6, Value of B + C = 9	No possibility where B + C = 9						

From the table of possibilities above, we can answer the questions.

49. We have from the diagram 16N + (A + B + C + D) + 150 + Number of trainees who passed none of the trials = 300. Since, N is 2, we get (A + B + C + D) + Number of trainees who passed none of the trials = 118. The value of the number of trainees who passed none of the trials will be minimised when (A + B + C + D) is maximised. From the table of possibilities, the maximum value of (A + B + C + D) = 104. Hence, the required minimum value is 14.
50. Tennis + Badminton = 8N + 75 = 91.
51. The count for this would be the sum of the trainees who passed all 4 and the trainees who passed exactly 3 trials. In other words, we are being asked the value of 12N. Since N = 2, is the only possible value of N, the value of 12N = 24.
52. Cricket = 75 + 11N + B + C; Hockey = 75 + 11N + A + D; Tennis = 75 + 11N + C + D; Badminton = 75 + 11N + A + B. From the table, we can see that the value of C + D is the smallest amongst all these combinations in all possible cases. Hence, Tennis would be the answer. Option (c) is correct.
53. Tennis = 75 + 11N + C + D. If Tennis is 117, it means that C + D = 20. In such a case, Hockey = 75 + 11N + 22 + 17 = 136.
54. The maximum number of people will not pass any of the four trials when (A + B + C + D) is minimised. From the table, we can see from the possibility number 7, that the minimum value of (A + B + C + D) = 89. The correct answer would be 89 + 75 + 75 = 239.

Solutions for Questions 55 to 59:

From the information given, we can form the following diagram:

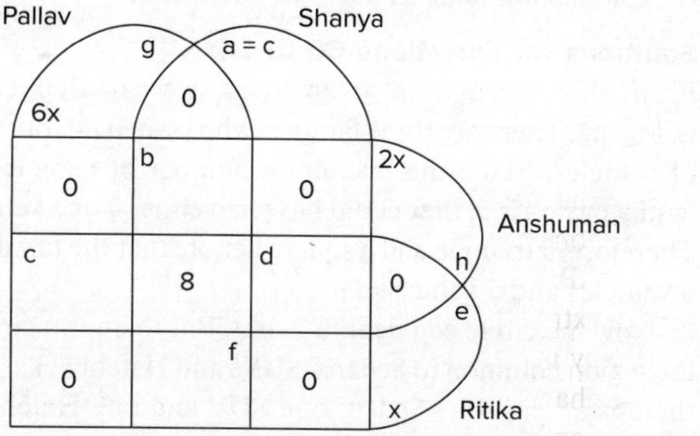

From statement C, b + d = 14

From statement D, b + f + 8 = c + d + 8 = c + f + 8, which means d = f and b = c = a. Hence, f + c = 14

Now, a + b + c + d + e + f + g + h = 92.

c + x + 6x + 2x = 64

c + 9x = 64.

Now, c should be less than or equal to 14. For this to be possible c can either be 1 or 10.

Therefore, x will be either 7 or 6. Hence we get two possibilities for the given set.

After putting the above values, we get the following diagram:

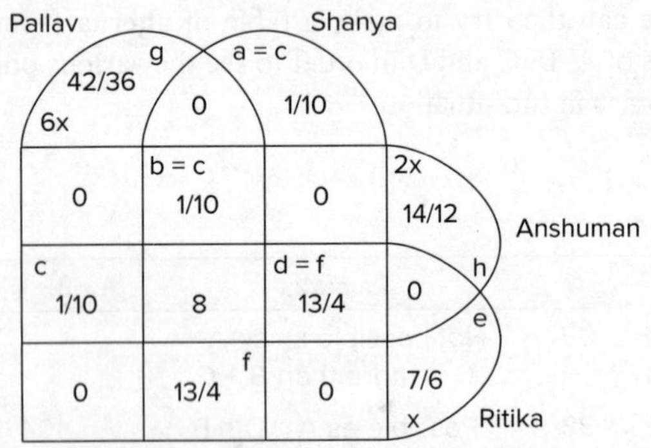

Using the above diagram we can answer the questions given:

55. Option (a) is the correct answer.
56. Option (b) is the correct answer.
57. Option (c) is the correct answer.
58. Anshuman would have to be necessarily the winner in all the events in which he was the only participant. Hence, the answer is 12.
59. Consider the case when x = 6. In that case, to get Ritika 20 wins, she will have 6(x) + 10 (c), plus at least 4 from the common events she has participated with Shaurya. Thus, amongst the 4 + 4 + 8 = 16 events Ritika and Shaurya has participated, Shaurya can win maximum 12. Further, to adhere to Pallav's 38 wins in this case, he wins all 36 events in which he participated alone plus 2 events in which he participates with Shaurya and Anshuman (b). Thus, Shaurya can win a maximum of 12 + 8 + 10 = 30 events.

Solutions for Questions 60 to 64:

From the information given to us, we can deduce the following. There are three families who owned all four types of vehicles. Since the maximum number of vehicles any family owned is 5, they could have had either 4 or 5 vehicles. Therefore, a triangle and a square denote that the family has 4 vehicles and 5 vehicles.

Now the circle can denote 2 or 3. But there is a circle in the region common to Sedans, SUVs and Hatchbacks. Since there is at least one Sedan, one SUV and one Hatchback, the circle cannot denote 2. Therefore, the circle denotes that the family has 3 vehicles. The diamond cannot denote 4 or 5 because 4 and 5 are the numbers denoted by the square and the triangle, not necessarily in that order. Therefore, the diamond denotes that the family has 2 vehicles.

It is given that the total number of vehicles in the colony is 69.

In the figure, there are 6 triangles, 5 circles, 5 diamonds and 4 squares.

If a triangle denotes that the family has 5 vehicles and a square denotes that the family has 4 vehicles, then the total number of vehicles in the colony = 6 × 5 + 5 × 3 + 5 × 2 + 4 × 4 = 71. This is not valid because the total number of vehicles in the colony is 69.

Therefore, a triangle denotes that the family has 4 vehicles and a square denotes that the family has 5 vehicles.

From the figure, we can say that the number of vehicles owned by families owning only Sedans, only SUVs, only Hatchbacks and only Sports Vehicles is 4, 5, 0 and 7 respectively.

For any region, there is at least one type of each vehicle that is represented by the region. For example, the family owning only Sedans and SUVs have 3 vehicles (circle) and hence, would have either 1 sedan and 2 SUVs or 2 Sedans and 1 SUV. We can work out similar logic for each of the 20 families represented in the diagram.

Minimum number of Sedans: There are 10 families represented in the Sedans circle. Out of these, the family that has only sedans, has 4 sedans (triangle). Each of the other 9 families would have at least 1 sedan each. Hence, there will be a minimum of 13 sedans in the society. Likewise: Minimum number of SUVs = 15; Minimum number of Hatchbacks = 12; Minimum number of Sports Vehicles = 16.

Using the above information we can answer the questions given:

60. The area representing families having all four vehicles shows 3 families and 2 triangles and one square. Thus, the total number of vehicles with these families would be 4 + 4 + 5 = 13. Option (a) is the correct answer.
61. If there are minimum number of sedans, it means that the family that owns only sedans and SUVs has 2 SUVs and 1 sedan. Also, the two families who own only SUVs have multiple SUVs with them. Hence, the number of families required is 3. Option (b) is the correct answer.
62. 24 is the maximum possible number of Sports Vehicles, and this number occurs, only when we increase the possibilities of sports vehicles wherever possible. In that case, the maximum number of hatchbacks would be 7 + 3 (if the Sedan + hatchback family has 3 hatchbacks) + 1 (the SUV, Sedan and Hatchback family represented by the circle would have only 1 hatchback at maximum) + 2 (the SUV, Sedan and Hatchback family represented by the triangle would have 2 hatchbacks at the maximum) +1 (the SUV and Hatchback family represented by the diamond would have only 1 hatchback at maximum) + 2 (the SUV and Hatchback family represented by the circle would have 2 hatchbacks at the maximum) = 16
63. Since 24 is the maximum possible number of Sports Vehicles, this number occurs, only when we increase the possibilities of sports vehicles wherever possible. In that case, We can be sure of 1 family with atleast 2 sedans (family with only sedans). For three of the other families we are unsure of whether they have at

least 2 sedans which include families in the region including only SUV and Sedan, families having only sedan and Hatchback, Families having only sedan, SUV and Hatchback. Hence minimum number of families with at most one sedan is 20 - 4 = 16.

64. We are given that SUVs = Sedan + 3 and Hatchbacks = Sports. Now, we know that number of SUVs is at least 15. Hence, let SUV be 15 + x. Similarly, Sedan = 13 + y, Hatchback = 12 + z and Sports = 16 + w. Now, we are given that 15 + x = 13 + y + 3 and 12 + z = 16 + w. So from the above equations, we get x = y + 1 and z = w + 4.

Now, we know that the total number of vehicles is 69. Hence, x + y + z + w = 13. Substituting the values of the above equations we get y + w = 4. Hence x + z = 9. Now, we are given that there are at most 16 SUVs. Hence, x can values 0 or 1. Hence z would take 9 or 8. But for x = 0, we get y as negative which is not possible. Hence, x = 1, y = 0, z = 8 and w = 4.

Therefore number of sedans = 13 and number of Hatchbacks = 20. Therefore the difference = 7. Hence Option (c) is the correct answer

Solutions for Questions 65 to 68:

The first thing you need to recognize in this set is the variables involved. From the first two paragraphs, it is amply clear that we need to make a Venn diagram between people who support proposal A and those who support proposal B. Also, there is a two way split of every area of the Venn diagram, between people who prefer Sunita (S) and those who prefer Ragini (R). It might help to point out here that there are two things to note in the starting instructions-

(i) There may be people who prefer both proposals A and B, people who prefer only A, people who prefer only B and also those who prefer neither A nor B. (hence, the Venn diagram between A and B).

(ii) Amongst the 500 people surveyed, everyone prefers either S or R for president (hence, the division of the 500 amongst those who prefer S or R would be tabular and not a Venn diagram).

The initial figure with the visualization of the variables involved would look as follows:

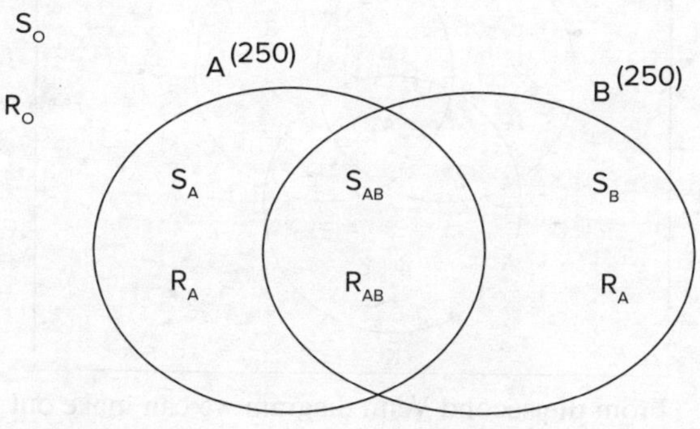

At this point, you should be aware from clues 2 and 3, that:

$S_A + S_B + S_{AB} + S_O = 200$ (1)

$R_A + R_B + R_{AB} + R_O = 300$ (2)

$S_A + S_{AB} = 80\%$ of $200 = 160$ (3)

$R_A + R_{AB} = 30\%$ of $300 = 90$ (4)

From the clue 4, '20% of those who supported Proposal B, preferred Sunita', we get $S_B + S_{AB} = 50$.

This also means that there are 200 people amongst those who support B, who prefer Ragini. At this point, the clues seem to be taking us in circles. But clue 6, is what helps us to move out of the puzzle as it says, "Every student who preferred Sunita and supported proposal B also supported proposal A.", which essentially should be interpreted as: $S_B = 0$. Using the equations, we have created above and starting with $S_B = 0$, we get the following chain → $S_{AB} = 50$ (from equation 5) → $S_A = 110$ (from equation 3) → $S_O = 40$ (from equation 1).

Also, from the clue 7 we have that: $R_O = 60$. Hence, from equations 2 and 4, we get $R_A = 300 - 60 - 90 = 150$. Subsequently, from the B circle in the figure, we can deduce that $R_{AB} = 50$ and then from equation 2, we get $R_B = 40$. The final picture looks as follows:

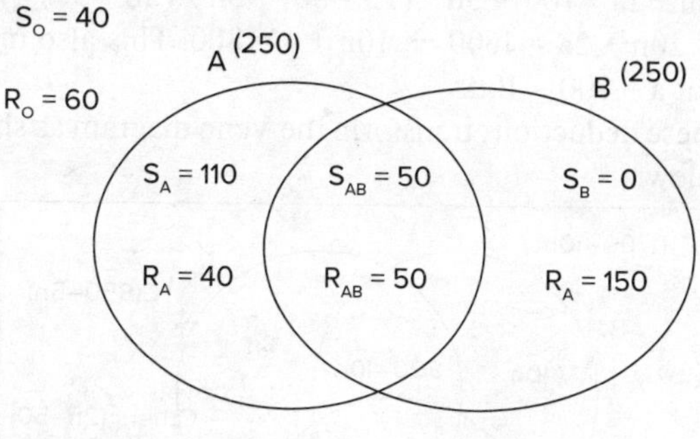

The answers can be read off from here.

65. A total of 250 students support proposal A. Out of these, 160 prefer Sunita. 160 out of 250 = 64%.

66. A total of 250 people did not support proposal A. Out of these 210 preferred Ragini. Hence, the required percentage is 210/250 = 84%.

67. 100 people support both proposals. Out of these, 50 prefer Sunita. 50 out of 100 = 50%. Hence, option (d).

68. There are 150 students who support only B and prefer Ragini. Hence, option (a) is correct.

Solutions for Questions 69 to 72:

The question set is based on Venn diagrams of B, C and S. O is the outside area. Based on the clues in the question, we can make the following starting Venn diagram for the situation.

> **Note:** The number of satellites for B and C but Not S should be equal to the number of satellites for B and S but Not C, because that is the only way the number of satellites for C and the number of satellites for S would be equal.

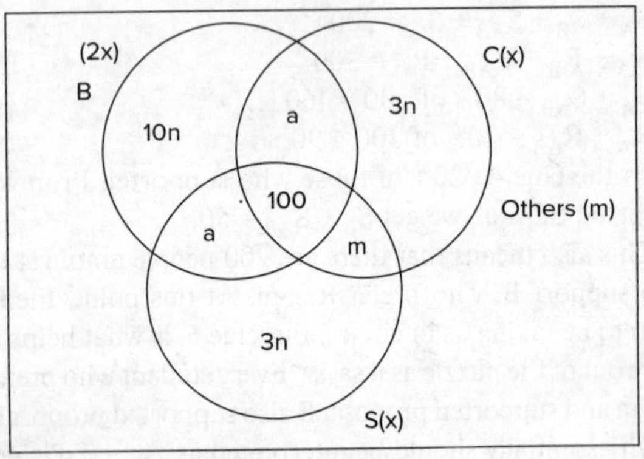

From the above diagram we get:

2x = 10n + 2a + 100 ......(a)

x = 3n + a + m + 100 ......(b)

From (a) and (b) we get: 10n + 2a + 100 = 2 × (3n + a + m + 100) →

10n + 2a + 100 = 6n + 2a + 2m + 200 → 4n = 2m + 100 → m = 2n – 50.

Then the sum of all the areas being 1600, we will get: 10n + 2a + 100 + 3n + (2n – 50) + 3n + (2n – 50) = 1600 → 20n + 2a = 1600 → 10n + a = 800. This also means that a = 800 – 10n.

These deductions transform the Venn diagram as shown below:

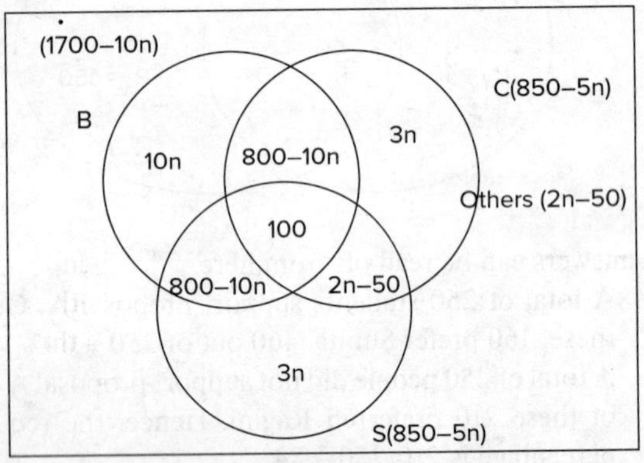

In the above figure the value of 2n – 50 ≥ 0 → n ≥ 25. Thus, 25 is the minimum value of n. Also, since 10n + a = 800 → n has a maximum value of 80. We can start to answer the questions asked at this point:

69. The number of satellites serving C = 850 – 5n. We know that the minimum value of n is 25 and the maximum value is 80. Hence, the value of C has to lie between 850 – 5 × 80 to 850 – 5 × 25 Or 450 to 725. Option (c) is correct.
70. The number of satellites serving B exclusively is 10n. The minimum value of n being 25, the minimum value of 10n = 250. Option (c) is correct.
71. This question tells us the value of Others is at least 100. This means that 2n – 50 ≥ 100 → n ≥ 75. With this, the value of the satellites serving S would be at most 850 – 5n = 850 – 5 × 75 = 475. Option (b) is correct.
72. The number of satellites serving at least two among B,C and S is given by: (800 – 10n) + (800 – 10n) + (2n – 50) + 100. The question tells us that this value is equal to 1200. Equating the expression to 1200 we get: (800 – 10n) + (800 – 10n) + (2n – 50) + 100 = 1200 → 1650 – 18n = 1200 → 18n = 450 → n = 25. With n as 25, we can see that each of options (a), (b) and (d) are true. Since, we have to look for the statement that is false, we can see that the statement in option (c) is indeed false, since with n = 25, we can exactly determine the number of satellites serving C. Hence, option (c) is correct.

Solutions for Questions 73 to 76:

Based on the starting information, the following Venn diagram can be made:

Venn diagram 1

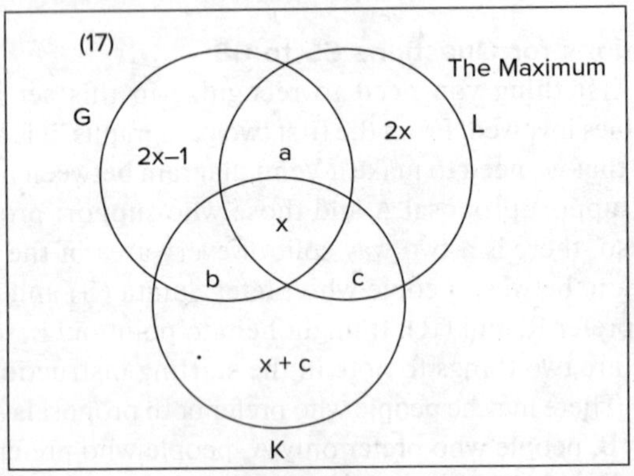

At this point, if we use the information in clue (vi), we will get that: a + x + b = 10. Hence, since (2x – 1) + x + a + b = 17, we get that (2x – 1) = 7 → x = 4. This changes the Venn diagram as follows:

Venn diagram 2

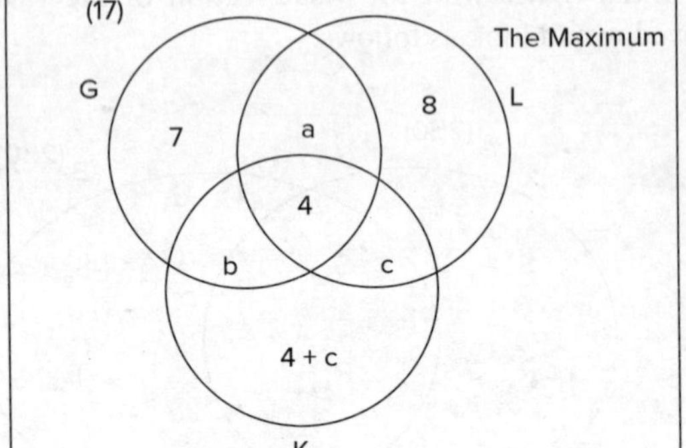

From the second Venn diagram we can make out the following:

a + b = 6; 4 + c + c = 14 → c = 5. The final diagram looks as the Venn diagram 3 shown in the figure:

Venn diagram 3

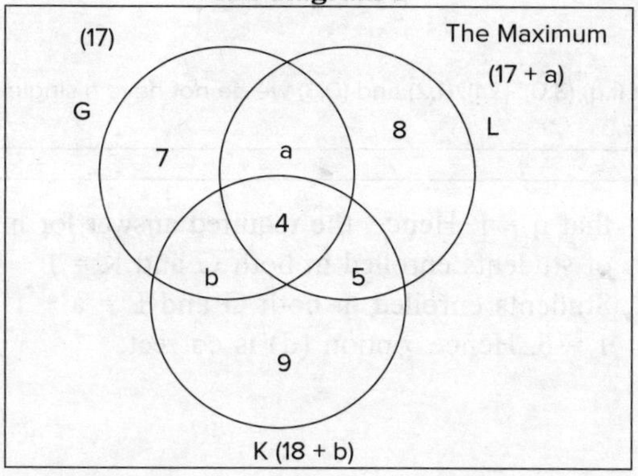

Since, the total number is the greatest for L, (17 + a) > (18 + b). Also, since we know that a + b = 6, the minimum value of a, should be 4 in which case the maximum for b would be 2. Overall, there are three possibilities for the values of (a,b). These are → (4,2); (5,1); (6,0).

The first two questions can be answered at this point as follows:

73. This question is asking for the minimum value of 'a'. We have already seen in our analysis that this number is 4. Hence, the correct answer would be 4.
74. For K:L to be 19:22, b should be 1 and a should be 5. Obviously, the total for L would be 22. Hence, option (c) is correct.
    For questions 49 to 50, the following Venn diagram modification would need to get done before you can anlayse the clues given in the question.

Venn diagram 4

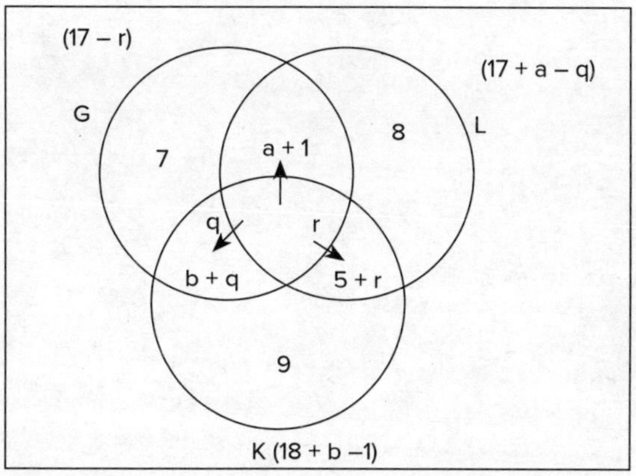

To understand the Venn Diagram 4, given in the figure, you need to understand first how it is made. The question says that of the 4 people who were enrolled in all three sports, each one of them was asked to withdraw from 1 sport. People who withdraw from Kho-Kho (K), would then be participating only in Gilli-Danda(G) and Ludo (L). These people would also have the effect of reducing the value of the K circle. Since, it is mentioned in the question, that the number of students who were enrolled in K, went down by 1, it means that 1 person must have left K and moved to G & L. That is the reason, why the area for G and L but not K increases from what it was earlier (a), to a + 1 now.

Once this change is done, the other three people need to leave the all three area of the diagram. Some of these people would leave L, others would leave G. We have denoted these as 'q' and 'r' respectively. This results in the following changes to the diagram:

(i) The number of people for K and G but not L becomes equal to (b + q);

(ii) The number of people for K and L but not G becomes equal to (5 + r)

(iii) The total number of people for G becomes equal to: (17 – r) [Since, r people have withdrawn from G]

(iv) The total number of people for L becomes equal to: (17 + a – q) [Since, q people have withdrawn from G]

(v) Also, we know that q + r = 3. This gives us the possible values for q and r as: (3,0); (2,1); (1,2) and (0,3).
The question also tells us that after this the number of people enrolled in G was six less than the number of people enrolled in L.
Thus, (17 + a – q) – (17 – r) = 6 → a – q + r = 6. From our earlier analysis in the question, we know that a = 4, 5 or 6. If we now check which value/s of a, q and r fit this situation, the following table would give us the analysis we need to do now:

Value of a	Value of r – q	Possible values of r,q	
4	2	Not possible	In each of the pairs of (r,q) (3,0); (2,1); (1,2) and (0,3) we do not have a single situation where r – q = 2.
5	1	Possible	q = 1, r = 2
6	0	Not possible	In each of the pairs of (r,q) (3,0); (2,1); (1,2) and (0,3) we do not have a single situation where r – q = 0.

Since, there is only one possible solution as reflected in the table, we can see that the values of a = 5, q = 1 and r = 2. We can now answer questions 3 and 4.

75. The value required is reflected by (b + q) in our Venn diagram 4. Since, a = 5, b = 1. Also, we know that q = 1. Hence, the required answer for number of students enrolled in both G and K = 1 + 1 = 2.

76. Students enrolled in both G and L = a + 1 = 5 + 1 = 6. Hence, option (d) is correct.

CHAPTER 9

Cubes and Dices

Chapter Launchpad
Scan this QR code for an introductory video on Cubes and Dices

Questions based on visualisation of cubes and dices are regularly asked in various management entrance exams and also in many other aptitude exams. The key skills required in order to solve these questions easily involve the ability to visualize the various shapes, their 3 - dimensional visualization, as well as where the faces of the cube/dice would go, in case the object is cut open. Also, simultaneously you need to understand the thought process that would help you visualise how the faces of an open cube would appear when they are folded into a cube. The following visualisations should be known as a part of the theory of this chapter.

I. Visualising Opening and Closing of Cubes

For each of the figures given below of an open cube, the text accompanying the same describes which faces would be opposite each other when the cube is closed into a box.

Case 1:

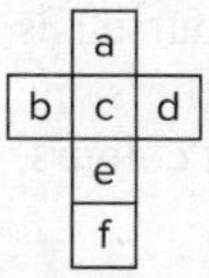

a lies opposite e
b lies opposite d
c lies opposite f

Case 2:

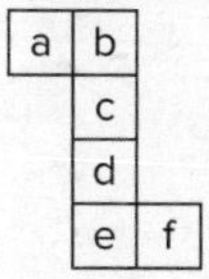

a lies opposite f
b lies opposite d
c lies opposite e

Case 3:

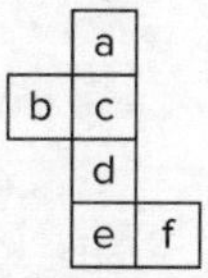

a lies opposite d
b lies opposite f
c lies opposite e

Case 4:

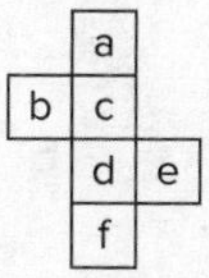

a lies opposite d
b lies opposite e
c lies opposite f

Case 5:

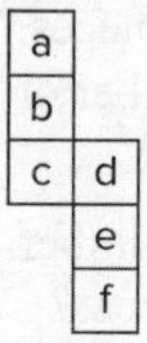

a lies opposite c
b lies opposite e
d lies opposite f

II. Cutting a Cube

A cube has 6 faces, 12 edges and 8 vertices.

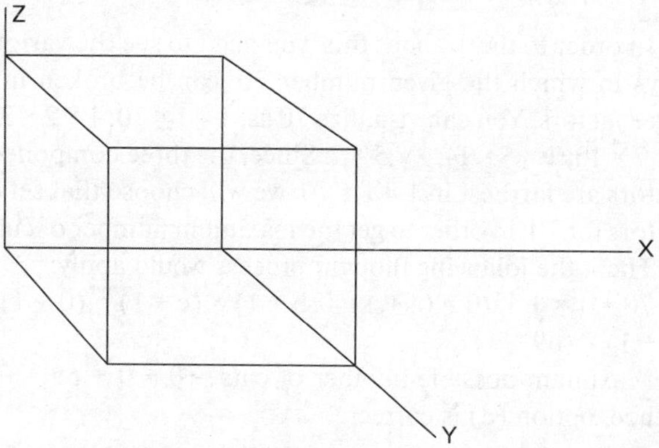

- When we make 'a' mutually parallel cuts along x - axis, 'b' mutually parallel cuts along y - axis and 'c' mutually parallel cuts along z axis, we get (a + 1) × (b + 1) × (c + 1) pieces of the original cube. These pieces may or may not be cubes and that essentially depends on whether the cuts are equidistant or not, and also on whether a, b and c are equal. The following cases occur:
  Case 1: All the pieces are cubes when a = b = c and all the cuts are equidistant.
  Case 2: All the pieces are not cubes when a = b = c and all the cuts are not equidistant.
  Case 3: All the pieces are not cubes when a ≠ b ≠ c.

Learning Point: To maximize the total number of pieces, with the minimum number of cuts, we need to minimize the difference between the number of cuts in any two axes.

Example 1: What is the least possible number of cuts required to cut a cube into 70 identical pieces?

(a) 35 (b) 15
(c) 17 (d) 11

In order to think about this, you need to see the various ways in which the given number 70, can be broken into three factors. You can visualize 70 as: $1 \times 1 \times 70$; $1 \times 2 \times 35$; $1 \times 7 \times 10$; $1 \times 5 \times 14$; $2 \times 5 \times 7$. Since, the three component factors are closest in $2 \times 5 \times 7$, we will choose that set of factors for 70, in order to get the minimum number of cuts.

Then, the following thought process would apply:

$70 = 2 \times 5 \times 7 = (a + 1) \times (b + 1) \times (c + 1) = (1 + 1) \times (4 + 1) \times (6 + 1)$.

Least possible number of cuts = 1 + 4 + 6 = 11. Hence, option (d) is correct.

Learning Point: To minimize the total number of pieces, we need to maximize the difference between the number of cuts in any two axis.

Example 2: What is the maximum possible number of cuts required to cut a cube into 70 identical pieces?

(a) 55
(b) 45
(c) 77
(d) 69

In order to think about this, you need to see the various ways in which the given number 70, can be broken into three factors. You can visualize 70 as: $1 \times 1 \times 70$; $1 \times 2 \times 35$; $1 \times 7 \times 10$; $1 \times 5 \times 14$; $2 \times 5 \times 7$. Since, the three component factors are farthest in $1 \times 1 \times 70$, we will choose that set of factors for 70, in order to get the maximum number of cuts.

Then, the following thought process would apply:

$70 = 1 \times 1 \times 70 = (a + 1) \times (b + 1) \times (c + 1) = (0 + 1) \times (0 + 1) \times (69 + 1)$.

Maximum possible number of cuts = 0 + 0 + 69 = 69. Hence, option (d) is correct.

III. Painting and Cutting a Cube

When we paint a cube and then make cuts along the axes of the cube, you are often asked to visualize the number of smaller cubes that have three faces painted, two faces painted, single face painted or no faces painted. The best way to work out such problems is through the formulae listed below. However, while I would want you to actually remember these formulae, I would also want you to visualize these outcomes for an actual problem.

A: Cutting equidistant along each axis with an equal number of cuts.

Let us say, the cube is painted black. If we make n - cuts in each axis then:

Number of cubes with 3 faces painted black = 8 (all corners painted cubes).

Number of cubes with 2 faces painted black = $(n - 1) \times 12$.

Number of cubes with 1 face painted black = $(n - 1)^2 \times 6$.

Number of cubes with no face painted black = $(n - 1)^3$.

Thus, if we make 2 equidistant cuts on each edge of the cube, we would get 27 smaller cubes. Out of these 27 smaller cubes, 8 cubes would be painted black on three sides; $(n - 1) \times 12 = (2 - 1) \times 12 = 12$ cubes painted black on 2 sides; $(n - 1)^2 \times 6 = (2 - 1)^2 \times 6 = 6$ cubes painted on 1 side and $(n - 1)^3 = (2 - 1)^3 = 1$ cube having no sides painted.

For n = 3, there would be 64 smaller cubes formed. In such a case, the number of cubes having:

3 sides painted = 8;

2 sides painted = $(n - 1) \times 12 = (3 - 1) \times 12 = 24$;

1 side painted = $(n - 1)^2 \times 6 = 24$ and

No side painted = $(n - 1)^3 = (3 - 1)^3 = 8$.

Please try to do your visualization for these cases too, so that you get a better understanding and grip on the problem.

B: Cutting equidistant along each axis with an unequal number of cuts.

If the number of cuts are not equal, let's say we have made 'a' cuts on the X - axis, 'b' cuts on the Y - axis, and 'c' cuts on the Z - axis, then, first of all, the smaller pieces formed would not be cubes - they will be cuboids. In such a case, the questions can be framed asking us to determine the number of cuboids that have 3 faces painted, 2 faces painted, 1 faces painted and no face painted.

Number of cuboids with 3 faces painted black = All the corner cubes, which is equal to 8 cubes.

Number of cuboids with exactly 2 faces painted = $(a - 2) \times 4 + (b - 2) \times 4 + (c - 2) \times 4$.

Number of cuboids with exactly 1 face painted = $2 \times [(a - 2)(b - 2) + (b - 2)(c - 2) + (a - 2)(c - 2)]$.

Number of cuboids with 0 face painted black = the inner cuboid = $(a - 2) \times (b - 2) \times (c - 2)$.

One more thing you need to visualize for yourself is if the faces of the cubes are not painted with the same colour - i.e., if the faces are painted with different colours, such that each colour is used to paint 2 faces:

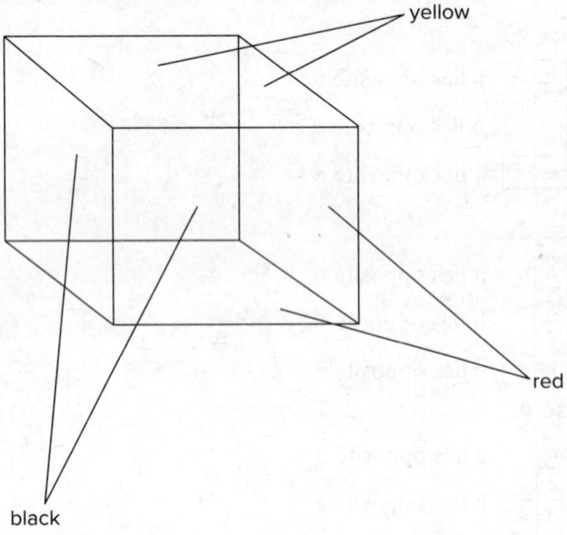

We make the following observations:

1. Number of cubes with all the three - colour faces = 2 cubes diagonally opposite to each other.
2. Number of cubes with only same colour on two faces = three edges without corner cubes = 3 × (n – 1).
3. Total cubes on the edges = 4 × (n + 1) + 8 × (n – 1).
4. Number of cubes with only 2 colour faces = total cubes on edges – same colour on two faces cubes – all three colour face cubes.
5. Number of cubes with exactly one face red = cubes on the two faces of the painted red surface = $2 \times (n - 1)^2$.
6. Number of cubes with faces only red = $(n - 1) + 2 \times (n - 1)^2$.
7. Number of cubes with exactly one face painted = $6 \times (n - 1)^2$.
8. Number of cubes with exactly two surfaces painted with different colours = 9 × (n – 1).

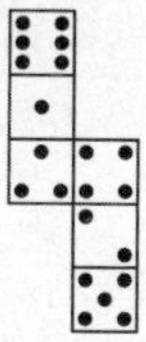

EXERCISE

Directions for Questions 1 to 20: *Answer these questions independent of each other.*

High Yield Questions

Scan this QR code to access video explanations of questions 3, 7, 8, 12, 15 and 16

The sheet of paper shown in the figure (X) given on the left hand side, in each problem, is folded to form a box. Choose from amongst the alternatives (1), (2), (3) and (4), the boxes that are similar to the box that will be formed.

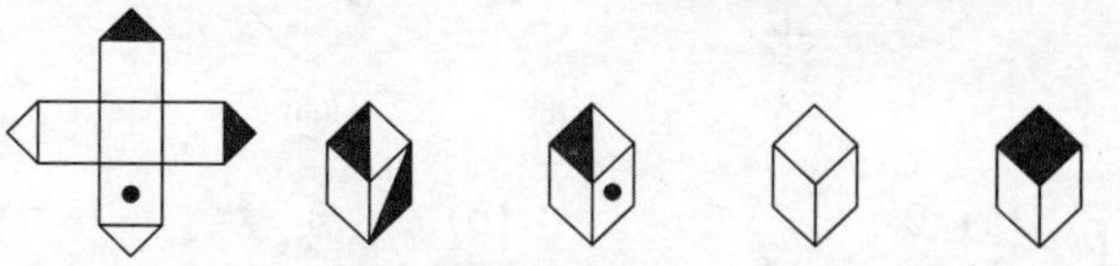

(X) (1) (2) (3) (4)

1. Choose the box that is similar to the box formed from the given sheet of paper (X).
   (a) Only 1 and 2 (b) Only 2 and 4
   (c) Only 2 and 3 (d) Only 1 and 4
2. Choose the box that is similar to the box formed from the given sheet of paper (X).

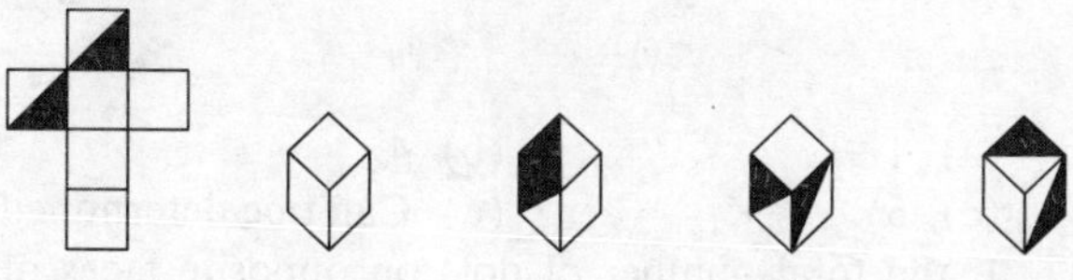

(X) (1) (2) (3) (4)

   (a) Only 1 and 4 (b) Only 3 and 4
   (c) Only 1 and 2 (d) Only 2 and 3
3. How many dots lie opposite to the face having three dots, when the given figure is folded to form a cube?
   (a) 2 (b) 4
   (c) 5 (d) 6
4. Choose the box that is similar to the box formed from the given sheet of paper (X).

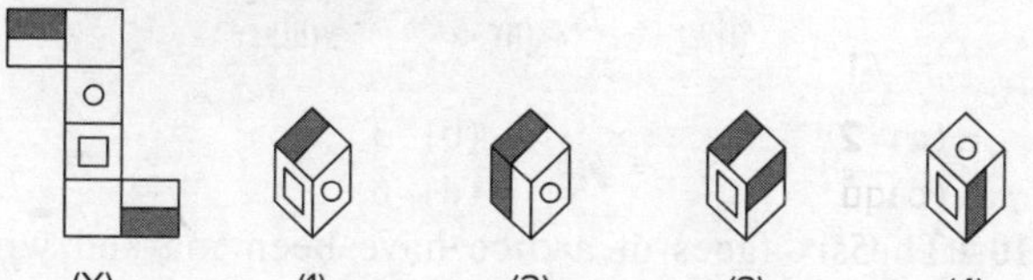

(X) (1) (2) (3) (4)

   (a) Only 1 (b) Only 2
   (c) Only 3 (d) Only 4
5. Which of the following finished patterns can be obtained from the piece of cardboard (X) shown below?

(X) (1) (2) . (3) (4)

   (a) 1 (b) 2
   (c) 3 (d) 4
6. Choose the box that is similar to the box formed from the given sheet of paper (X).

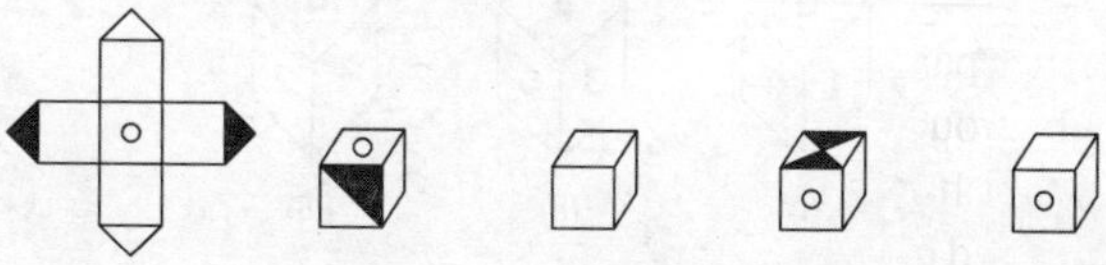

(X) (1) (2) (3) (4)

   (a) Only 1 (b) Only 2
   (c) Only 3 (d) Only 4
7. When the following figure is folded to form a cube, how many dots lie opposite the face bearing five dots?

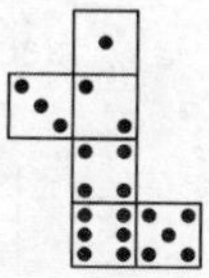

   (a) 1 (b) 2
   (c) 3 (d) 4
8. Observe the dots on a dice (one to six dots) in the following figures. How many dots are contained on the face opposite to that containing four dots?

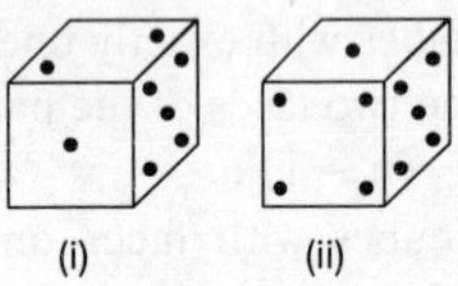

(i) (ii)

(a) 2 (b) 3
(c) 6 (d) Can't be determined

9. Three different positions of a dice are shown below. How many dots lie opposite 2 dots?

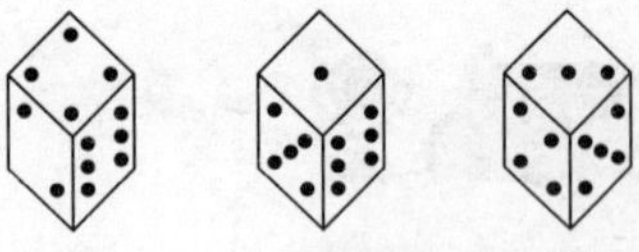

(i) (ii) (iii)

(a) 1 (b) 3
(c) 5 (d) 6

10. The six faces of a dice have been marked with alphabets A, B, C, D, E and F respectively. This dice is rolled down three times. The three positions are shown as:

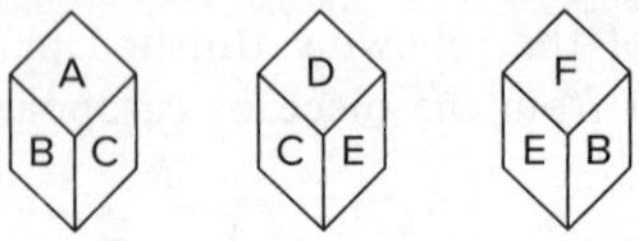

(i) (ii) (iii)

Find the alphabet opposite A.

(a) C (b) D
(c) E (d) F

11. Three positions of a dice are given. Based on them find out which number is found opposite the number 2 in the given cube.

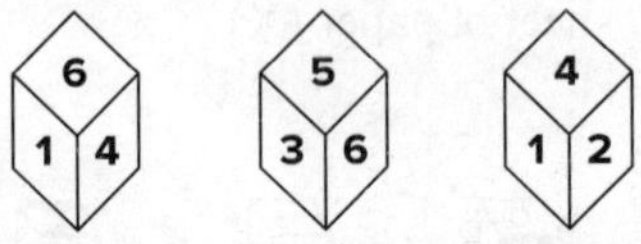

(i) (ii) (iii)

(a) 6 (b) 5
(c) 3 (d) 1

12. A dice is thrown four times and its four different positions are shown below. Find the number on the face opposite the face showing 2.

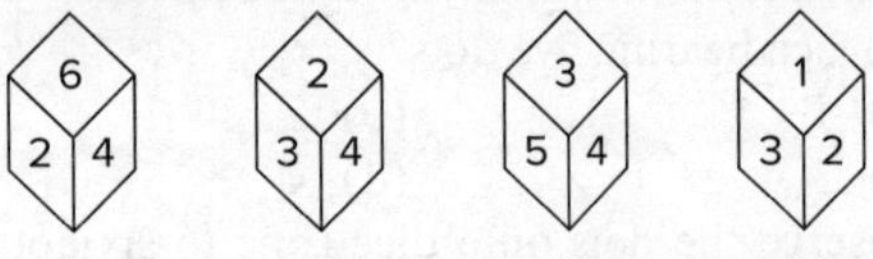

(i) (ii) (iii) (iv)

(a) 3 (b) 4
(c) 5 (d) 6

13. Two positions of a dice are shown. When 4 is at the bottom, what number will be on the top?

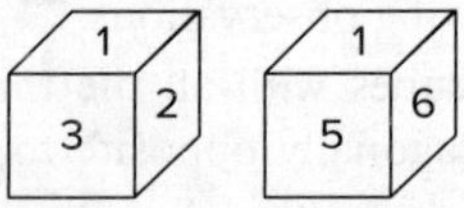

(i) (ii)

(a) 1 (b) 2
(c) 5 (d) 6

14. A dice is rolled twice and the two positions are shown in the figure below. What is the number of dots at the bottom face when the dice is in position (i)?

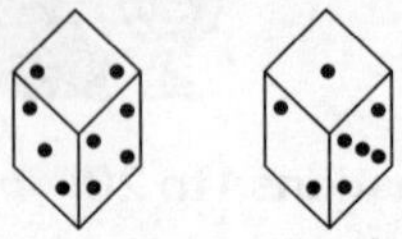

(i) (ii)

(a) 1 (b) 5
(c) 6 (d) Can't be determined

15. Below are depicted the three different positions of a dice. Find the number of dots on the face opposite to the face with one dot.

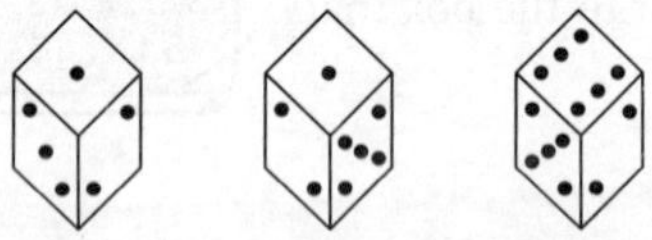

(i) (ii) (iii)

(a) 2 (b) 3
(c) 4 (d) 6

16. Two positions of a parallelepiped are shown below. When the number 3 will be on the top side, then which number will be at the bottom?

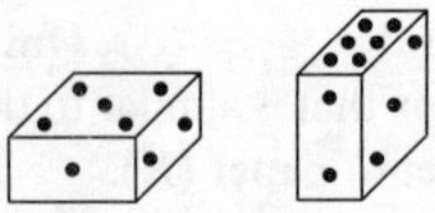

(i) (ii)

(a) 1 (b) 4
(c) 5 (d) Can't be determined

17. If the total number of dots on opposite faces of a cubical block is always 7, find the figure which is correct.

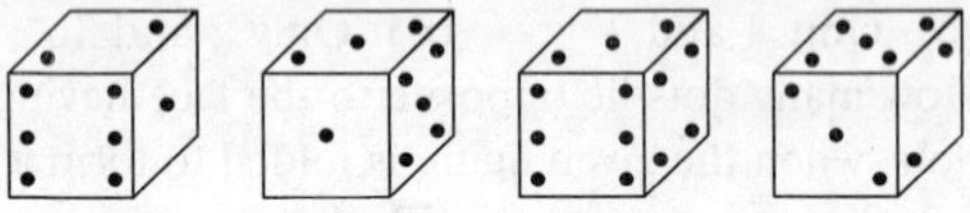

(1) (2) (3) (4)

(a) Figure 1 (b) Figure 2
(c) Figure 3 (d) Figure 4

18. Three different positions X, Y and Z of a dice are shown in the figures given below. Which number lies at the bottom face in position X?

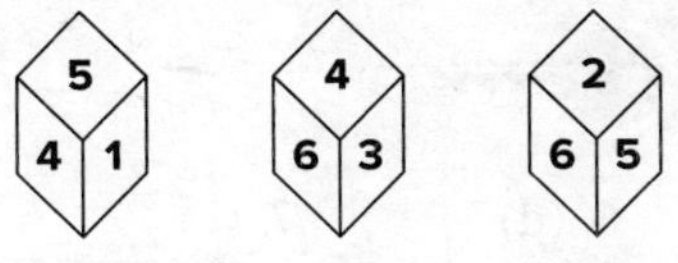

(a) 2 (b) 3
(c) 6 (d) Can't be determined

19. Two positions of a cube are shown below. When the number 4 will be at the bottom, then which number will be at the top?

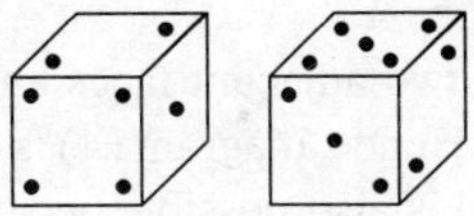

(a) 3 (b) 5
(c) 6 (d) Can't be determined

20. What is the least possible number of cuts required to cut a cube into 150 identical pieces?
(a) 27 (b) 13
(c) 16 (d) 34

Directions for Questions 21 to 22: *2 adjacent faces of a cube are painted with red colour. The cube is cut into 64 smaller cubes of equal dimensions.*

21. How many cubes have 2 faces coloured red?

22. How many cubes have only 1 face coloured red?

Directions for Questions 23 to 26: *A cube is painted red, yellow & blue with opposite sides painted in same color. It is then cut into 343 smaller blocks of size (1 ×1 × 1).*

23. What are the dimensions of the bigger cube?
(a) $3 \times 3 \times 3$
(b) $7 \times 7 \times 7$
(c) $9 \times 9 \times 9$
(d) $11 \times 11 \times 11$

24. Find the number of blocks that will have 3 sides painted with 3 different colours?

25. Find the number of blocks that will have 0 side painted?

26. Find the number of blocks that will have 2 sides painted in a way that 1 is painted yellow and the other is painted either red or blue?

Directions for Questions 27 to 29: *A standard Rubik's cube (of size 3 × 3 × 3) is perfectly solved. 6 colours on 6 faces are: orange, yellow, blue, green, black & white. This cube is dismantled into smaller unit cubes.*

27. Find the total number of cubes with only 1 side painted + 2 sides painted + 3 sides painted.

28. Find the total number of cubes with no side painted in any color?

29. If face painted blue is opposite to face painted white, find total no. of blocks with only 2 sides painted in a way that 1 is yellow & the other is blue.

Directions for Questions 30 to 35:
Akash has three different types of cubes:
- 1-unit cubes which are cubes of side 1 unit
- 2-unit cubes which are cubes of side 2 units
- 3-unit cubes which are cubes of side 3 units

All the 1-unit cubes are painted orange on all sides; all the 2-unit cubes are painted black on all sides; all the 3-unit cubes are painted blue on all sides.

He uses these cubes to form cubes of larger sizes. Any cube that he forms does not have any hollow spaces inside the cube.

30. If Akash made a cube of side 5 units using exactly two different types of cubes, What is the maximum number of 1 Unit cubes that he used?
(a) 98 (b) 125
(c) 61 (d) 0

31. For the above question, what is the minimum number of 1 unit cubes that he used?

32. If Akash made a cube of side n units using exactly one 3-unit cube, such that all the visible faces of the cube of side n units are completely Black, what is the minimum number of cubes that he would have used?
(a) 27 (b) 75
(c) 128 (d) 94

33. If Akash made a cube of side x units, where $x<10$ using exactly one 1-unit cube, such that all the visible faces of the cube thus formed are of the same color, what is the maximum number of 3-unit cubes that he would have used?
(a) 0
(b) 9
(c) 26
(d) Such a cube cannot be made.

34. Akash formed a cube of side n units such that all the visible faces of the cube of side n units are completely orange. If he used less than 200 cubes in total to form the cube of side n units, what is the maximum possible value of n?

35. Akash formed a cube of side n units such that one of its visible faces is completely black and another one of its faces is completely blue. What is the minimum number of cubes that he could have used to form the cube of side n units?

ANSWER KEY

1. (c)	2. (a)	3. (d)	4. (a)	5. (a)	6. (d)	7. (c)	8. (a)
9. (c)	10. (c)	11. (a)	12. (c)	13. (a)	14. (c)	15. (d)	16. (d)
17. (b)	18. (b)	19. (a)	20. (b)	21. 4	22. 24	23. (b)	24. 8
25. 125	26. 40	27. 26	28. 1	29. 1	30. (a)	31. 61	32. (d)
33. (d)	34. 6	35. 49					

SOLUTIONS AND SHORTCUTS

Hint for solving questions based on open and closed cubes: Always try to mark each of the faces with alphabets, symbols to be able to visualize the appropriate markings going to the appropriate faces. This approach will be evident in the following questions:

1. The original figure can be visualized as:

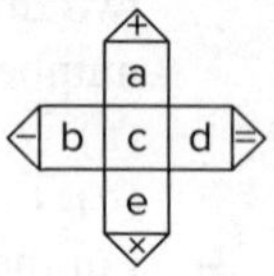

When we close the faces of the above to form a box,  will be the one of the faces of the cube and it lies opposite c; b lies opposite d and a lies opposite e.

\+ and = are shaded portions, e is a dot and the rest are plain. Hence, diagram 2 is definitely correct. Similarly, diagram (3) is also correct. Because, diagram (3) is the mirror image of diagram (2). Hence, option (c) is correct.

2. The original figure can be visualized as:

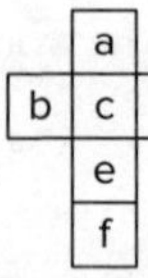

a lies opposite e

b lies opposite d

c lies opposite f

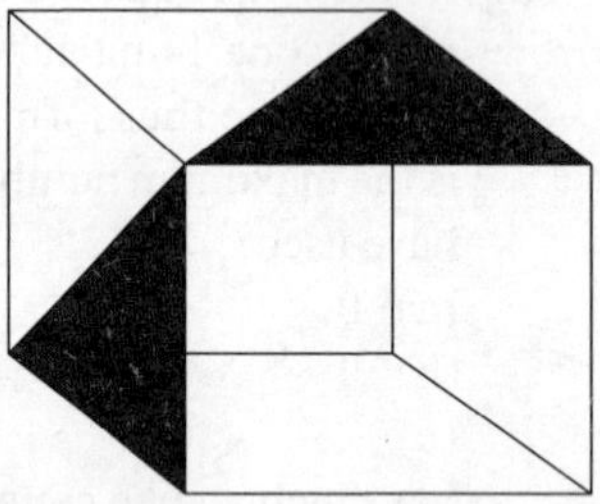

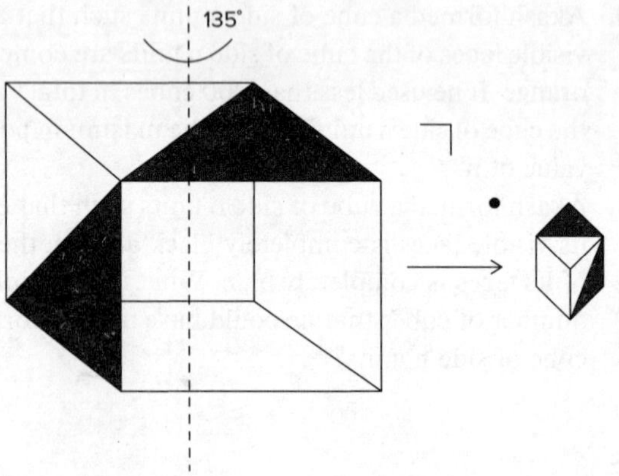

a and b are two adjacent faces and c, d, e and f are blank faces. Hence, diagram (4) is definitely possible. Diagram (1) is also possible because in diagram (1) the two shaded surfaces are hiding. Hence, option (a) is correct.

3. The original figure can be visualized as:

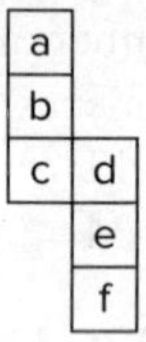

a lies opposite c

b lies opposite e

c lies opposite f

c has three dots and a has six dots. Hence, option (d) is correct.

4. The original figure can be visualized as:

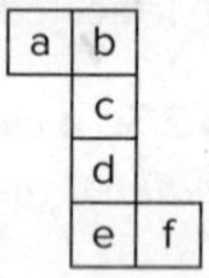

a lies opposite f

b lies opposite d

c lies opposite e

The half shaded portion must be opposite to each other. So, diagrams 2 and 3 are not correct. The diagram 4 is wrong because if we fix the position of ○ and □ then the 3rd face is as shown in the figure.

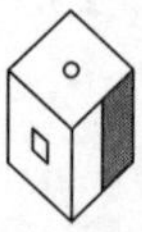

Hence, option (a) is correct.

5. The 3rd and 4th diagram cannot be the correct answer because the black dot is on a face for which the length is more than the breadth. Now, for the 2nd diagram, if the dot point is placed as shown in the 2nd diagram then, the 2nd diagram would look like this: . So, the diagram (2) is also incorrect. Hence, option (a) is correct.

6. From the diagram, the shaded portions won't be adjacent. It means that they are on the same face but opposite to each other. So (1) is rejected as a possible figure. That shaded portion would be opposite to the face with 'o', so (3) is also rejected as a possible figure.

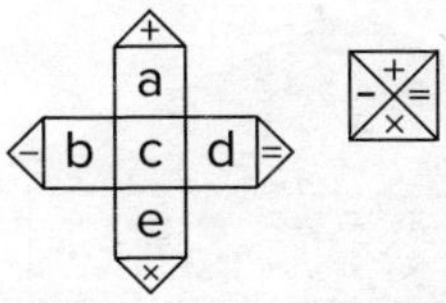

will be one of the faces of the cube and it lies opposite c, b lies opposite d and a lines opposite e.

Only diagram (4) is correct. Hence, option (d) is correct.

7. The original figure can be visualized as:

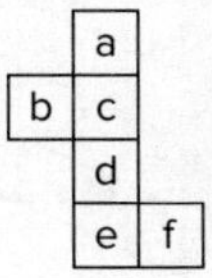

a lies opposite d

b lies opposite f

c lies opposite e

As b lies opposite f, f has five dots and b has three dots.
Hence, option (c) is correct.

8. Diagram (ii) can be found by rotating diagram (i) by 90 degrees clockwise through horizontal axis.
Hence, the face opposite to four dots face has two dots. Hence, option (a) is correct.

9. Diagram (ii) is found by rotating diagram (i) upside down.
From diagram (i) and (ii) we can get the following points:
   1. One dot face is opposite to four dots face.
   2. Two dots face is opposite to five dots face.

Hence, option (c) is correct.

10. From diagram (ii) and (iii) we get that C, D, B, F are the adjacent faces of E. Hence, the opposite face of A must be E. Hence, option (c) is correct.

11. From diagram (i) and (ii), it is clear that 1, 4, 5 and 3 are the adjacent faces of 6. Hence, 6 must be opposite to 2. Hence, option (a) is correct.

12. From (ii) and (iv), it is clear that there are four faces 1, 4, 3 and 6 adjacent to face with number 2. Now, we are left only with face with the number 2, which must be opposite to the number 5 face. Hence, option (c) is correct.

13. There are four faces adjacent to each face. Faces with numbers 2, 3, 5 and 6 are adjacent to number - 1 face. We are left with a face with number 4. That face must be opposite to number - 1 face. Hence, option (a) is correct.

14. 1, 3, 4 and 5 are adjacent to face 2. So, 6 is the face opposite face 2. Hence, option (c) is correct.

15. From diagrams (i), (ii) and (iii), we conclude 1, 3, 5 and 6 are the adjacent faces of 2. So, 4 is opposite to 2. From diagrams (i) and (ii), 2, 3 and 5 are adjacent to 1. Also, since 4 is opposite to 2. Hence, 2, 3, 5 and 4 are adjacent to 1. Hence, 6 is opposite to 1. Hence, option (d) is correct.

16. Here, it may be seen from both of the diagrams that 1, 3, 5 and 6 are adjacent to 2. So, 4 is definitely opposite to 2. Hence, either 1 or 5 might be opposite to 3. Thus, we cannot determine the answer to this question.

17. **Figure 1:** 1 can never be opposite to 6. Hence, this case is not possible.
Figure 2: Total number of dots on opposite faces of a cubical block is always 7 when 6 is opposite to 1, 3 is opposite to 4 and 2 is opposite to 5. All these possibilities exist in this picture. Hence, this option is correct.
Figure 3: 4 is next to 3 in this figure. This is not a possible scenario for all opposite faces to have a sum of 7. Hence, this option is wrong.
Figure 4: 2 is next to 5 in this figure. This is not a possible scenario for all opposite faces to have a sum of 7. Hence, this option is wrong.
Hence, option (b) is correct.

18. From diagram x and z, we get that 1, 4, 6 and 2 are adjacent to 5. Hence, 3 must be opposite of 5. Hence, option (b) is correct.

19. 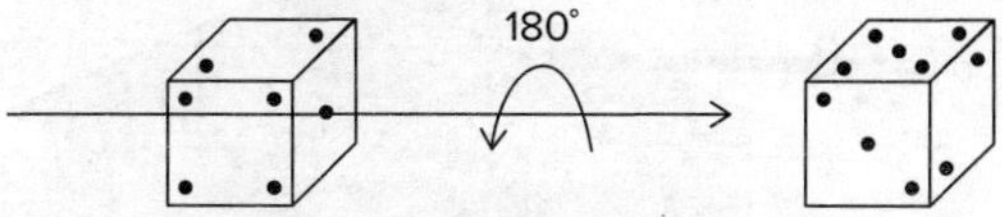

From the above figure, it is clear that 2 is opposite to 6 and 3 is opposite to 4. Hence, when 4 is at bottom then 3 must be at the top. Hence, option (a) is correct.

20. Total number of pieces obtained with X cuts in x-axis, Y cuts in y-axis and Z cuts in z-axis = $(X + 1) \times (Y + 1) \times (Z + 1)$. This would be least when the number 150 is broken into three factors as close to each other as possible. Thus,
total number of cuts = $150 = 5 \times 5 \times 6 = (X + 1) \times (Y + 1) \times (Z + 1) = (4 + 1) \times (4 + 1) \times (5 + 1)$.
Least possible number of cuts = 4 + 4 + 5 = 13. Hence, option (b) is correct.

Solutions for Questions 21 to 22:

21. $4^3 = 64$ unit blocks of equal size (i.e. $1 \times 1 \times 1$), thus n = 4.
This is a question of $(4 \times 4 \times 4)$ cube.
From the figure,
4 blocks with 2 faces painted red

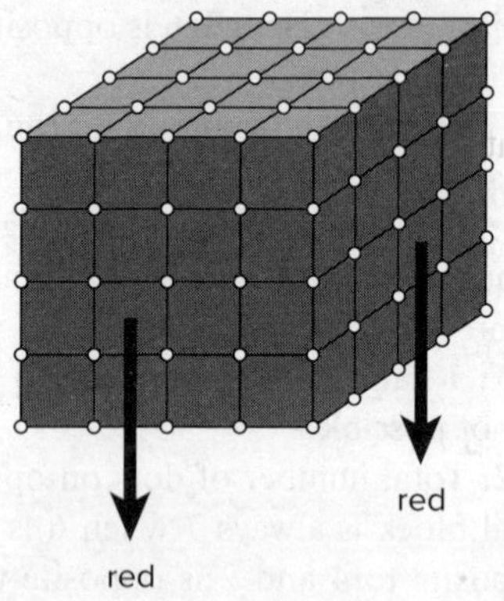

22. From the figure of the previous question, we can see that there are a total of 12 (front side) and 12 (lateral side) = 24 blocks with one face colored red.

Solutions for Questions 23 to 26:

23. Using total no. of blocks of size (1 × 1 × 1) that can be taken out from a bigger cube of size (n × n × n)
    = n^3 blocks.
    = 7^3 blocks
    = 343 blocks
    → Bigger cube is of size (7 × 7 × 7)

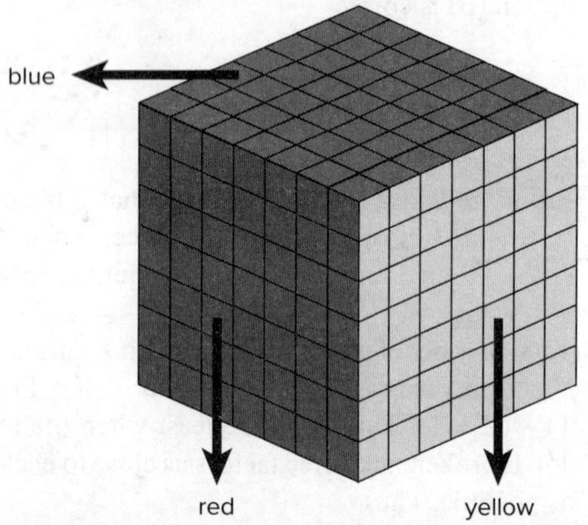

24. 3 faces painted in different colours will be at the vertices.
    There are 8 vertices in a cube
    → 8 blocks.
25. No. of blocks with 0 sides painted
    = $(n - 2)^3$ blocks
    = $(7 - 2)^3$ blocks
    = $(5)^3$ blocks
    = 125 blocks.
26. In order to think of this answer, check the faces that are painted yellow. There are two faces like that.
    Check edges:
    i. On one face = (5 × 4) = 20 blocks
    ii. On opposite face = (5 × 4) = 20 blocks
    Total such blocks = 20 + 20 = 40 blocks

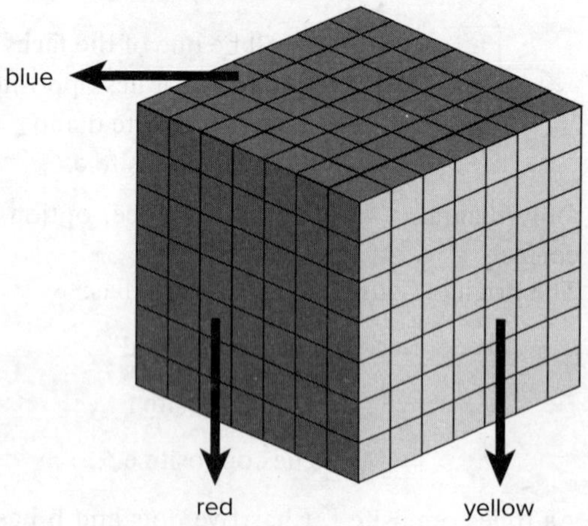

Solutions for Questions 27 to 29:

27. Using total number of cubes of size (1 × 1 × 1) that can be taken out from a bigger cube of size (n × n × n)
    = n^3 blocks
    = 3^3 blocks = 27 cubes.
    3 sides painted = 8 cubes.
    2 sides painted = 12(n - 2) cubes = 12 cubes.
    1 side painted = $6(n - 2)^2$ cubes = 6 cubes.
    → There are 26 such cubes.
28. Using, the total number of cubes of size (1 × 1 × 1) that can be taken out from a bigger cube of size (n × n × n)
    = n^3 cubes
    = 3^3 = 27 cubes.
    0 side painted = $(n - 2)^3$ cubes
    = 1 cube.
29. Yellow and Blue would be on adjacent surfaces. There will be one cube that would be painted Yellow and Blue.

Solutions for Questions 30 to 35:

General understanding of the situation: Before you move to the questions, you have to understand that a 5-unit cube would have a volume of 5^3 =125 units, a 3-unit cube would have a volume of 3^3 =27 units and a 1-unit cube would have a volume of 1^3 = 1 unit.

30. A 5 unit cube would require a volume of 5 × 5 × 5 = 125. He can make a length of 5 units on the edge by using either a 3 + 1 + 1 structure or a 2 + 2 + 1 structure (if he is using only two kinds of cubes such that he is using a 1 unit cube compulsorily (since we want to maximise the number of 1 unit cubes, we will have to use them).
    For the 3 + 1 + 1 case, the 3-unit cube would occupy a space of 27 units (volume wise), leaving 98 units to be made using unit cubes. Unit cubes have a volume of 1 unit per cube and hence, in this case there will be 98 cubes required.

For the 2 + 2 + 1 structure, there will be eight 2-unit cubes used so as to make the length of the 2-unit cubes as 4 on each of the 6 edges of the cube. This would entail a total volume of $8 \times 8 = 64$ units. The remaining $125 - 64 = 61$ units will be filled using 1-unit cubes and we would require 61 of those.

Since, this question asks us for the maximum value of the number of 1-unit cubes, the answer would be 98. Option (a) is correct.

31. In this case, since we have to minimise the number of 1 unit cubes, we can think of making an edge of 5 using a combination of 3 + 2. In such a case, we will not be using a single 1-unit cube. However, if we consider that a 3-unit cube has a volume of 27 and a 2-unit cube has a volume of 8, we see that we will not be able to achieve a perfect cube of 5 units using only 3-unit and 2-unit cubes - this is because if we use a single 3-unit cube, it's volume would be 27. The remaining volume of $125 - 27 = 98$, would be filled with volume 8 cubes which is not possible, since 98/8 is not an integer. Likewise, using two 3-unit cubes, leaves us $125 - 54 = 81$ volume to be filled with 2-unit cubes, which is not possible. Likewise, it is not possible to use three 3-unit cubes or four 3-unit cubes. Hence, in this case, we will have to go back to the 2 + 2 + 1 structure we used for question 1 and realise that the minimum number of 1 unit cubes would be 61. Hence, the correct answer is 61.

32. Since the side n unit cubes are all black from outside, it means that the outer core of the larger cube is made only using 2-unit cubes. Also, the problem tells us that there is at least one 3-unit cube in the mix. If we place a 3-unit cube in the center and try to cover it with 2-unit cubes on all sides, the minimum length of the edges would be 7. Also, since the outer core is to be formed only using 2-unit cubes, the minimum length of the edges would be 8.

    The next possible size is a cube of side 8 units. If the outer layer of this cube is formed using 2-unit cubes, then the available space inside this cube is $4 \times 4 \times 4$. In this space, we can place the 3-unit cube and fill the remaining space with 1-unit cubes.

    The number of 1-unit cubes required = $64 - 27 = 37$

    The number of 2-unit cubes required = $8 \times 8 \times 8 - 4 \times 4 \times 4 = 448$. Number of 2-unit cubes in this would be $448/8 = 56$ (where 8 is the volume of the $2 \times 2 \times 2$ - the 2-unit cube)

    Number of 3-unit cubes used = 1

    Total number of cubes = $37 + 56 + 1 = 94$

    Hence, the answer is 94. Option (d) is correct.

33. For $x = 9$ units

    If all the cubes which are on the outside are 3-unit cubes, then there will be a gap of $3 \times 3 \times 3$ in the middle of the cube. This cannot be filled using only 1-unit cubes and other 2-unit or 3-unit cubes as no combination of 27, 8 and a single 1 would fill in a volume of 27.

    All the cubes which are on the outside cannot be 2-unit cubes because using 2-unit cubes we cannot form a cube having an odd number (9) as its side if we are forming the outer faces using only 2-unit cubes.

    For $x = 8$ units

    All the cubes which are on the outside cannot be 3-unit cubes (since n is even).

    If all the cubes which are on the outside are 2-unit cubes, then there will be a gap of $4 \times 4 \times 4$ in the middle of the cube. This gap cannot be filled with one 1-unit cube and other 2-unit or 3-unit cubes as no combination of 27, 8 and a single 1 would fill in a volume of 64.

    For $x = 7$ units

    The cubes on the outside cannot be 3-unit cubes alone or 2-unit cubes alone.

    For $x = 6$ units

    If all the cubes on the outside are 3-unit cubes, then there will be no gap in the inside of this cube.

    If all the cubes on the outside are 2-unit cubes, then there will be a gap of $2 \times 2 \times 2$ on the inside. However, this cannot be filled using exactly one 1-unit cube and any combination of 3-unit and 2-unit cubes.

    Similarly, for $x = 5$, 4, 3 and 2 we wouldn't be able to form any desired cube. Hence Option (d) is the correct answer.

34. Since, the created cube is completely orange, the outer layer of the cube would have to be made using only 1-unit cubes. In order to maximise the value of n, we can start with the value of n as 6 since Akash can easily form a 5-unit cube with 125 unit cubes.

    For $n = 6$, he needs at least $216 - 64 = 152$ unit cubes to form the outer layer of the cube.

    This leaves a $4 \times 4 \times 4$ gap in the middle. This can be filled with 8 2-unit cubes. Hence, a total of $152 + 8 = 160$ cubes are needed and this number is below 200.

    For $n = 7$, he needs at least $343 - 125 = 218$ unit cubes to form the outer layer. Hence, it is not possible to form this cube with at most 200 cubes.

    Therefore, the maximum possible value of n is 6.

35. For one of the faces to be made from 3-unit cubes (to be Blue) and another face to be made from 2-unit cubes (to be Black), the value of n must be a multiple of 6. For $n = 6$, the surface area of each face would be 36. The 3-unit cubes have a surface area of 9 units each, the 2-unit cubes have a surface area of 4 units each. Hence, we can make one face of the cube completely blue by using 4 3-unit cubes. Another face

(the opposite face) can be made from nine 2-unit cubes. We will have to add a layer of 1-unit cubes on the lateral dimensions, in order to make the lateral edges of 6 units. To do this, we will need to add 36 1-unit cubes. The total number of cubes used in this case, would be 4 + 9 + 36 = 49.

The next possible value of n is 12, where the surface area of each side would be 144. A minimum of 16 3-unit cubes on one side and a minimum of 36 2-unit cubes for the other face would already cross the number 49, we achieved for n = 6. So the number of cubes required would cross 49.

CHAPTER 10

Games and Tournaments

Chapter Launchpad

Scan this QR code for an introductory video on Games and Tournaments

Reasoning situations based on games and tournaments have become one of the common occurrences in Aptitude exams, and are a special favourite of management entrance exams like the CAT, XAT and other top exams. While the solving of such questions is based on complete common sense based understanding of the situations involved, it might be a good idea to work on extracting certain standard analysis that goes into solving the various kinds of questions that can be classified under the games and tournaments chapter.

1. Analysis Tools for a Tennis/Badminton or a Knockout Tournament

A tennis/badminton tournament is played under the knockout format. In such cases matches between players have the format that the loser gets eliminated and the winner moves into the next round. The following structures apply in such cases:

The number of rounds in the tournament is decided on the basis of the number of players entered. Typically, in a Grand Slam tournament in tennis there are 128 players and the tournament consists of 7 rounds. This can be visualized as:

Round	1	2	3	4 –Pre Quarter Finals	5 Quarter Finals	6 Semi Finals	7 Finals
Number of Players	128	64	32	16	8	4	2
Number of Matches = Number of Winners	64	32	16	8	4	2	1
Cumulative Eliminated Players	64	64 + 32 = 96	96 + 16 = 112	112 + 8 = 120	120 + 4 = 124	124 + 2 = 126	127

Notice the following:

(i) The tournament as shown in the table, consists of a total of 127 matches (sum of 64 + 32 + 16 + 8 + 4 + 2 + 1).

(ii) In each round, half of the remaining players are eliminated, moving the other half (the winners) into the next round.

(iii) The winner of the final is determined at the end of the 127th match in the tournament.

As you can well imagine for a 64 player tournament, there would be 6 rounds and 63 matches and for a 32 player tournament there would be 5 rounds and 31 matches required to determine the winner.

An interesting thing to note is the system of byes in such tournaments and how it affects the numbers. Byes are necessitated when the number of players is not even in any round. Let us consider a tournament of 121 players. In such a case, the following structure would apply:

Round 1: 60 matches and 1 bye - so a total of 61 players progress to the second round;

Round 2: 30 matches and 1 bye - so a total of 31 players progress to the third round;

Round 3: 15 matches and 1 bye - so, a total of 16 players progress to the fourth round.

Beyond this, the tournament would play out normally without any more byes.

What would be the total number of matches in such a tournament?

Let's count: 60 + 30 + 15 + 8 + 4 + 2 + 1 = 120. It is still one less than the number of players.

In general, you can make out that: Number of matches in a knockout tournament of n players would always be (n - 1). This can also be thought of as: To determine the winner in a 123 players tournament, we need to identify 122 losers. Since every match determines one loser, to determine 122 losers for a 123 players tournament, we need to play 122 matches.

So, for a knockout tournament consisting of 13 players, there would be a total of 12 matches played. I would encourage you to create the tournament structures for various number of players and try to work out the rounds for the tournament.

You would notice another interesting thing when you do so. That is with respect to the number of rounds. We have already seen that the number of rounds for a 128 player tournament is 7, for a 64 player tournament is 6, for a 32 player tournament is 5 and so on. If we investigate how many rounds would be required in order to determine a 65 player tournament, we will notice the following:

Round 1: 32 matches and 1 bye - 33 players progress to round 2;

Round 2: 16 matches and 1 bye - 17 players progress to round 3;

Round 3: 8 matches and 1 bye - 9 players progress to round 4;

Round 4: 4 matches and 1 bye - 5 players progress to round 5;

Round 5: 2 matches and 1 bye - 3 players progress to round 6;

Round 6: 1 match and 1 bye - 2 players progress to round 7;

Round 7: 1 match - decides the winner of the tournament.

Thus, you can notice an important logic about the number of rounds. For a tournament with 65 to 128 players, the number of rounds would always be 7. For 33 players till 64 players, 6 rounds would be required to determine the winner and so on. In terms of powers of the number 2, you can think as follows: If the number of players crosses 2^6, the number of rounds is 7. If it crosses 2^5, there would be 6 rounds in the tournament and so forth.

SEEDING AND LOGIC AROUND SEEDING

Often, in knockout tournaments like tennis and badminton, seedings are given to the top players - based on who is favoured to win the tournament. In such cases, seed number 1 is often referred to as the top seed. Such tournaments, have their draws based on these seedings only. For instance, suppose, there is a tournament, having 32 players and a seeding is given for players from 1 to 32. In such a tournament, the first round consists of 16 matches and who plays who in the matches are defined by the seed numbers. The following table would make this clear to you:

Round 1	Round 2	Round 3 Quarter Finals	Semi Finals	Finals
Match 1: 1 vs 32	Match 1: 1 vs 16	Match 1: 1 vs 8	Match 1: 1 vs 4	1 vs 2
Match 2: 2 vs 31	Match 2: 2 vs 15	Match 2: 2 vs 7	Match 2: 2 vs 3	
Match 3: 3 vs 30	Match 3: 3 vs 14	Match 3: 3 vs 6		
		Match 4: 4 vs 5		
Match 15: 15 vs 18	Match 7: 7 vs 10			
Match 16: 16 vs 17	Match 8: 8 vs 9			

The following points need to be understood with respect to the above table:

1. Every match has a higher seed playing a lower seed. The higher seed is expected to win the match and proceed to the next round. The pairings of who plays whom in the next rounds is based on the assumption that the higher seed wins. Thus, match 1 of round 2, is expected to be between seed 1 (expected winner of match 1 of round 1) and seed 16 (expected winner of match 16 of round 1). However, this match would be disturbed in terms of the players playing this match in the event of an upset in round 1.

Note: Whenever a lower seed beats the higher seed, it is called an upset- as the result is against the expected result.

You should be able to visualize that match 1 of round 2 can have four possible match ups. 1 vs 16 is the expected match, but it could be 1 vs 17 also. Likewise, the match could also be 32 vs 16 or 32 vs 17 (depending on who wins the first round's match 1 and 16 respectively).

Similarly, match 1 of round 3 could have multiple match ups possible. These can be visualized as follows: Match 1 of round 3 is decided by the winners of matches 1 and 8 of round 2. Match 1 of round 2, as we have already seen, could be won by players 1,16,17 or 32. Similarly, match 8 of round 1 could be between: 8 vs 9 (expected match); 8 vs 24; 25 vs 9 or 25 vs 24. Thus, for match 1 of round 3, there could be 16 different match ups possible: viz, anyone of 1, 16, 17 or 32 vs anyone of 8, 9, 24 or 25.

Consider the following question that appeared in CAT 2005 on this structure:

Example 1: In the following table is the listing of players, seeded from the highest (#1) to the lowest (#32), who are due to play in an Association of Tennis Players (ATP) tournament for women. This tournament has four knockout rounds before the final, i.e., first round, second round, quarterfinals and semi-finals. In the first round, the highest seeded player plays the lowest seeded player (seed #32) which is designated match no. 1 of the first round; the 2nd seeded player plays the 31st seeded player which is designated match no. 2 of the first round and so on. Thus, for instance, match no. 16 of the first round is to be played between 16th seeded player and the 17th seeded player. In the second round, the winner of match no. 1 of the first round plays the winner of match no. 16 of first round and is designated match no. 1 of the second round. Similarly, the winner of match no. 2 of first round plays the winner of match no. 15 of first round and is designated match no. 2 of second round. Thus, for instance, match no. 8 of the second round is to be played between the winner of match no. 8 of the first round and the winner of match no. 9 of the first round. The same pattern is followed for later rounds as well.

Seed #	Name of Player	Seed #	Name of Player	Seed #	Name of Player
1.	Maria Sharapova	12.	Mary Pierce	23.	Silver Farina Elia
2.	Lindsay Davenport	13.	Anastasia Myskina	24.	Tatiana Golovin
3.	Amelie Mauresmo	14.	Alicia Molik	25.	Shinobu Asagoe
4.	Kim Clijsters	15.	Nathalie Dechy	26.	Francesca Schiavone
5.	Svetiana Kuznetsova	16.	Elena Bovina	27.	Nicole Vaidisova
6.	Elena Dementieva	17.	Jelena Jankovic	28.	Gisela Dulko
7.	Justine Henin	18.	Ana Ivanovic	29.	Flavia Pennetta
8.	Serena Williams	19.	Vera Zvonareva	30.	Anna Chakvetadze
9.	Nadia Petrova	20.	Elena Likhovtseva	31.	Ai Sugiyama
10.	Venus Williams	21.	Daniela Hantuchova	32.	Anna-lena Groenefeld
11.	Patty schnyder	22.	Dianara Safina		

1. If Elena Dementieva and Serena Williams lose in the second round, while Justine Henin and Nadia Petrova make it to the semi-finals, then who would play Maria Sharapova in the quarterfinals, in the event Sharapova reaches quarterfinals?
   (a) Dinara Safina (b) Justine Henin
   (c) Nadia Petrova (d) Patty Schnyder
2. If the top eight seeds make it to the quarterfinals, then who, amongst the players listed below would definitely not play against Maria Sharapova in the final, in case Sharapova reaches the final?
   (a) Amelie Mauresmo
   (b) Elena Dementieva
   (c) Kim Clijsters
   (d) Lindsay Davenport
3. If there are no upsets (a lower seeded player beating a higher seeded player) in the first round, and only match numbers 6, 7 and 8 of the second round result in upsets, then who would meet Lindsay Davenport in quarterfinals, in case Davenport reaches quarter finals?
   (a) Justine Henin
   (b) Nadia Petrova
   (c) Patty Schnyder
   (d) Venus Williams
4. If, in the first round, all even numbered matches (and none of the odd numbered ones) result in upsets, and there are no upsets in the second round, then who could be the lowest seeded player facing Maria Sharapova in semi-finals?
   (a) Anastasia Myskina
   (b) Flavia Pennetta
   (c) Nadia Petrova
   (d) Svetlana Kuznetsova

Solution:

Visualise the rounds as:

First Round	Second Round	Quarters	Semis	Final
1–32	1–16	1–8	1–4	1–2
2–31	2–15	2–7	2–3	
3–30	3–14	3–6		
4–29	4–13	4–5		
5–28	5–12			
6–27	6–11			
7–26	7–10			
8–25	8–9			
9–29				
10–23				
11–22				
15–18				
16–17				

1. In the quarters, Maria Sharapova is seeded to play the 8th seed (Serena Williams). But Serena Williams loses in the second round (where she must have played either the 9th or the 24th seed). But, it can be seen that the 9th seed Nadia Petrova reaches the semis. Hence, Maria Sharapova must play Nadia Petrova in the quarterfinals. Option (c) is correct.
2. Maria Sharapova is seeded to meet the 8th seed in the quarters and the 4th/5th seed in the semis. Neither of them can play her in the final, since they have to meet in the earlier rounds. Amongst these, only Kim Clijsters' name figures in the options. Hence, option (c) is correct.
3. Davenport being the 2nd seed is scheduled to play the winner of the match 7 of the second round in the quarters. As per the question, match 7 has resulted in an upset in the second round. This means that Venus Williams won the match 7 and will play Davenport in the quarters. Hence, Option (d) is correct.
4. According to this question, seeds 1, 3, 5, 7, 9, 11, 13, 15, 17, 19, 21, 23, 25, 27, 29 and 31 will reach the second round. In such a case, 4th seed is replaced by 29th seed. In the second round Seed 29 will play seed 13 and 13 will win, because there is no upset in the second round. In the third round the winner of 5 and 13 play each other. The result of round 3 is not known. Hence, the lowest seeded player who could play Sharapova in the Semis would be seed 13 - Anastasia Myskina. Hence, option (a) is correct.

2. Analysis Tools for a Hockey/Football Tournament (Round Robin)

Hockey and Football tournaments that are played in a round robin format are also interesting cases for building reasoning questions. A typical table of standings for a hockey/football tournament after two round robin rounds with the following results in the matches played: A vs F 5-0; A vs E 6-2; B vs C 2-1;B vs D 1-1; C vs D 4-1; E vs F 0-0, would look as follows:

Note: Wins are awarded 3 points and draws 1 point.

Team	Played	Won	Lost	Drawn	Goals For	Goals Against	Goal Difference	Points
A	2	2	0	0	11	2	+9	6
B	2	1	0	1	3	2	+1	4
C	2	1	1	0	5	3	+2	3
D	2	0	1	1	2	5	−3	1
E	2	0	1	1	2	6	−4	1
F	2	0	1	1	0	5	−5	1

Often in such tables, the individual match results are removed and you are asked to deduce the match results based on the information in the table.

In such cases, the following observations and overall rules would always hold:

(i) **Total matches played:** Total Number of matches played would be equal to the half of the total number of matches in the played column. This occurs since every time a match is played between two teams, the played column is incremented by +1 at two places - +1 for each of the two teams that played the match. Thus, in this table, since the sum of all the matches played is 12, it means that there have been 6 matches played in this tournament till date.

(ii) **Number of wins:** In the wins column = Number of losses in the loss column. This has to hold since every time a match is decisive, there would be an increment of one match in the wins column and one match in the losses column.

(iii) Number of decisive matches: Also, the number of decisive matches in such a case would be equal to the sum in either the wins or the losses column. Thus, in this case, since the total number of wins = 4, it means that 4 matches were decisive out of the 6 matches played.

(iv) Number of draws: The sum of the number of matches in the drawn column, needs to be divided by 2, in order to find out the number of matches, that were drawn. Thus, in the table above, the number of matches drawn would be equal to sum of the numbers in the drawn column divided by 2 = 4/2 = 2.

(v) Goals for – Goals Against = Goal difference: The 'goals for' column represents the number of goals scored by the team, the 'goals against' column represents the number of goals scored against the team (by the opponents of the team).

(vi) Sum of the goal difference column would always be zero.

(vii) The sum of goals for column = Sum of goals against column. This is so because, whenever a team scores a goal in its match against another team, there is an increment of +1 in the 'goals for' of the team scoring the goal and at the same time, there is an increment of +1 in the 'goals against' for the opponent team. Thus, every time there is a goal scored, both the goals for and goals against columns' totals would increase by 1.

Besides, these certain score specific deductions are also possible. Some of these (indicative list) are as follows:

(a) If a team has played 2 matches and won two matches, and it has a goals for 2 and goals against 0, it would mean that it has won both its matches by 1-0.

(b) If a team has played 2 matches and won two matches, and it has a goals for 3 and goals against 1, it would mean that it has won one match by 1-0 and another by 2-1.

(c) If a team has played 2 matches and won one match, and drawn another, and it has a goals for 2 and goals against 0, it would mean that it has won its match 2-0 and drawn 0-0.

(d) If a team has played 2 matches and won one match, and drawn another, and it has a goals for 3 and goals against 1, it could mean two possible cases: (i) It has won 2-0 and drawn 1-1 or, (ii) won 3-1 and drawn 0-0.

(e) If a team has played 2 matches and won one match, and lost another, and it has a goals for 3 and goals against 1, it would mean it has won 3-0 and lost 0-1.

These are just an indicative list and I would expect you to make sense of other such cases, that you would see regularly in such tables.

The following example would be a great way, to see how to analyse and work back given a table of a hockey or football tournament:

Example 2: The Men's Group A of the Hockey Championship in the recent New York Olympics was keenly fought out. Six teams comprised the group, and each played the other over five rounds of matches. A win secured 3 points, a draw secured 1 point for each team, while a loss meant that, the team got no points from that match.

Mr. Khushwinder Singh, who was representing the IOA and was keenly following the tournament, made a few documentations in his diary about the results. Unfortunately, in his enthusiasm for roaming around the city of New York, Mr. Singh forgot to note down the results of all matches. After his return to India, he was asked to reproduce the observations, he had made about the tournament. He is now in a fix, since the results have been wiped off the internet, due to a software mal function and the only way he has to trace back the results, is to look into the notings he had done in his little red diary. Can you help him retrace the tournament and answer the five questions he has to answer?

Extracts from his diary are reproduced for your benefit.

Table after 2 rounds:

Group A - men (13th Aug)							
	P	W	D	L	F	A	Pts
Spain	2	2	0	0	5	2	6
Germany	2	1	1	0	5	2	4
South Korea	2	1	0	1	6	5	3
New Zealand	2	1	0	1	3	2	3
Belgium	2	0	1	1	3	5	1
China	2	0	0	2	3	9	0

Table after 4 rounds (17th August)

	P	W	D	L	F	A	Pts
Spain	4	3	0	1	7	4	9
Germany	4	2	2	0	9	5	8
South Korea	4	2	1	1	12	9	7
New Zealand	4	2	1	1	9	6	7
Belgium	4	0	1	3	6	12	1
China	4	0	1	3	6	13	1

One of the matches in the second round ended in a 1-1 deadlock. China and New Zealand played a draw in the fourth round. South Korea scored less than 4 goals in the fourth round. In the fifth round, Germany played against New Zealand, South Korea played against Spain and China played against Belgium.

The following is the final group table at the end of the group stage of the tournament.

Group A - Men (19th August)	P	W	D	L	F	A	Pts
Spain	5	4	0	1	9	5	12
Germany	5	3	2	0	12	6	11
South Korea	5	2	1	2	13	11	7
New Zealand	5	2	1	2	10	9	7
Belgium	5	1	1	3	9	13	4
China	5	0	1	4	7	16	1

Questions

1. What was the result of the match between China and Spain?
   (a) 1-1 draw (b) China lost 1-2
   (c) China lost 0-1 (d) China lost 2-3
   (e) Can't be determined
2. In which round did South Korea play against China and what was the result?
   (a) 2nd round South Korea, won by 5-2.
   (b) 1st round South Korea, won by 5-2.
   (c) 2nd round South Korea, won by 4-1.
   (d) 1st round South Korea, won by 4-1.
   (e) Can't be determined.
3. Which country was the second in the group standing table after the third round of matches?
   (a) Germany (b) South Korea
   (c) New Zealand (d) Belgium
   (e) Can't be determined
4. What was the result of the New Zealand vs Belgium match?
   (a) New Zealand won 4-2.
   (b) New Zealand won 3-1.
   (c) New Zealand won 2-0.
   (d) New Zealand won 4-1.
   (e) Can't be determined.
5. Who did Spain lose to and by what margin?
   (a) South Korea 1-2. (b) Germany 2-3.
   (c) Germany 1-2. (d) Germany 0-1.
   (e) Can't be determined.

Solution: Look at the following solution closely to understand how to think in such situations:

Given table after 2 rounds:

Group A - Men (13th Aug)	P	W	D	L	F	A	Pts
Spain	2	2	0	0	5	2	6
Germany	2	1	1	0	5	2	4
South Korea	2	1	0	1	6	5	3
New Zealand	2	1	0	1	3	2	3
Belgium	2	0	1	1	3	5	1
China	2	0	0	2	3	9	0

One of the matches in the second round ended in a 1-1 deadlock.

China and New Zealand played a draw in the fourth round.

South Korea scored less than 4 goals in the fourth round.

In the fifth round Germany played against New Zealand, South Korea played against Spain and China played against Belgium.

First set of deductions:

The 1-1 draw of the second round must be the Germany Belgium match.

So, Germany won its first round match 4-1 and Belgium must have lost its first round match by 2-4. This means that some team must have lost its first round by 1-4 and another team would have won its first round match by 4-2. From this point move into a table formation and try to build a feasible table through trial and error.

At this point, we realize that there are only two teams (South Korea and China apart from Belgium) who have conceded 4 goals or more in the tournament. Hence, the 1-4 loss has two possibilities: either South Korea or China –

Possibility 1: S.Korea loses 1-4.

Suppose, we were to construct a table with South Korea being the 1-4 loser in the first round. We will get the following chain of deductions (with the deduction numbers written in brackets):

	Round 1	Round 2	Round 3	Round 4	Round 5
Spain	4-2 (3)	1-0 (4)			
Germany	4-1	1-1 vs Belgium			
South Korea	1-4 (1)	5-1 (2)			
New Zealand	4-2 (8)	0-1 (5)			
Belgium	2-4	1-1 vs Germany			
China	2-4(7)	1-5 (6)			

Note: When, we put 1-4 for S. Korea, 4-2 can only go to Spain, since New Zealand is the only other winner in the first round and New Zealand has scored only 3 goals.

So, the problem with this possibility is that when we complete the chain of deductions, the end result is that the number of goals for New Zealand does not match the given data. Hence, we can reject this possibility. Hence, China must have lost 1-4 in the first round. So, we try to rebuild the above table with this possibility as the starting point:

	Round 1	Round 2	Round 3	Round 4	Round 5
Spain	4-2 (5) Belgium	1-0 (6) New Zealand			South Korea
Germany	4-1 China	1-1 vs Belgium			New Zealand
South Korea	1-3 (4) New Zealand	5-2 (3) China			Spain
New Zealand	3-1(7) South Korea	0-1 (8) Spain			Germany
Belgium	2-4 Spain	1-1 vs Germany			China
China	1-4(1) Germany	2-5 (2)			Belgium

From, the above table it can be verified that, all the values of goals for and goals against as well as the number of wins and losses for each team have matched the initial table, hence, we can see that there is no contradiction.

So, at this stage we have the result of the first two rounds for all the teams.

From this point, we need to move to the next table which gives us the table after 4 rounds.

Table after 4 rounds (17th August)

		W	D	L	F	A	Pts
Spain	4	3	0	1	7	4	9
Germany	4	2	2	0	9	5	8
South Korea	4	2	1	1	12	9	7
New Zealand	4	2	1	1	9	6	7
Belgium	4	0	1	3	6	12	1
China	4	0	1	3	6	13	1

Table for net results of 3rd and 4th rounds matches:

The following table can be made by looking at the table after 2 rounds and by looking at the table after 4 rounds. This table shows the net results of each team in rounds 3 and 4:

	P	W	D	L	F	A
Spain	2	1	0	1	2	2
Germany	2	1	1	0	4	3
South Korea	2	1	1	0	6	4
New Zealand	2	1	1	0	6	4
Belgium	2	0	0	2	3	7
China	2	0	1	1	3	4

We also have the table of results and fifth round matches with us:

	Round 1	Round 2	Round 3	Round 4	Round 5
Spain	4-2 (5) Belgium	1-0 (6) New Zealand			South Korea
Germany	4-1 China	1-1 vs Belgium			New Zealand
South Korea	1-3 (4) New Zealand	5-2 (3) China			Spain
New Zealand	3-1 (7) South Korea	0-2 (8) Spain			Germany
Belgium	2-4 Spain	1-1 vs Germany	Loss	Loss	China
China	1-4 (1) Germany	2-5 (2)			Belgium

The following deductions can be made from the above two tables:

Spain is left with China and Germany as its two opponents. Hence, Spain must have lost to Germany and won against China.

Germany is left with South Korea and Spain as its two opponents. Since, Germany must beat Spain, the Germany vs South Korea match must be a draw.

Since, South Korea has drawn with Germany, South Korea must have won its other match against Belgium.

New Zealand has two opponents viz, Belgium and China left. Obviously, New Zealand and China must be a draw and New Zealand must have beaten Belgium.

We also have the following additional pieces of information about the third and fourth rounds:

China and New Zealand played a draw in the fourth round.

South Korea scored less than 4 goals in the fourth round.

Using these informations the table would evolve to:

We also have the table of results and fifth round matches with us:

	Round 1	Round 2	Round 3 (Opponent and Result)	Round 4 (Opponent and Result)	Round 5
Spain	4-2 (5) Belgium	1-0 (6) New Zealand	China Win	Germany Loss	South Korea
Germany	4-1 China	1-1 vs Belgium	South Korea Draw	Spain Win	New Zealand
South Korea	1-3 (4) New Zealand	5-2 (3) China	Germany Draw	Belgium Win	Spain
New Zealand	3-1 (7) South Korea	0-3 (8) Spain	Belgium Win	China Draw	Germany
Belgium	2-4 Spain	1-1 vs Germany	New Zealand Loss	South Korea Loss	China
China	1-4 (1) Germany	2-5 (2) South Korea	Spain Loss	New Zealand Draw	Belgium

From this point onwards, we need to just fix up the scores of each of these matches:

Looking at the net values for Spain, we get three possibilities for its results:

Possibility 1	2-0	0-2
Possibility 2	2-1	0-1
Possibility 3	1-0	1-2

We now need to check each of the three possibilities to see which one fits the situation and creates no contradictions.

Possibility 1: Spain wins 2-0 against China.

	Round 1	Round 2	Round 3 (Opponent & Result)	Round 4 (Opponent and Result)	Round 5
Spain	4-2 (5) Belgium	1-0 (6) New Zealand	China Win 2-0 (1)	Germany Loss 0-2 (2)	South Korea
Germany	4-1 China	1-1 vs Belgium	South Korea Draw 4-4 (11) Contradiction since Germany has only conceded 3 goals.	Spain Win	New Zealand
South Korea	1-3 (4) New Zealand	5-2 (3) China	South Korea Draw 4-4 (10)	Belgium Win 2-0 (9)	Spain
New Zealand	3-1 (7) South Korea	0-4 (8) Spain	Belgium Win 5-3 (6)	China Draw 1-1 (5)	Germany
Belgium	2-4 Spain	1-1 vs Germany	New Zealand Loss 3-5 (7)	South Korea Loss 0-2 (8)	China
China	1-4 (1) Germany	2-5 (2) South Korea	Spain Loss 0-2 (3)	New Zealand Draw 1-1 (4)	Belgium

Thus possibility 1 is rejected.

Possibility 2: Spain wins 2-1 against China.

	Round 1	Round 2	Round 3 (Opponent and Result)	Round 4 (Opponent and Result)	Round 5
Spain	4-2 (5) Belgium	1-0 (6) New Zealand	China Win 2-1 (1)	Germany Loss 0-1 (2)	South Korea
Germany	4-1 China	1-1 vs Belgium	South Korea Draw 3-3 (5)	Spain Win 1-0 (4)	New Zealand
South Korea	1-3 (4) New Zealand	5-2 (3) China	South Korea Draw 3-3 (6)	Belgium Win 3-1(7)	Spain
New Zealand	3-1(7) South Korea	0-5 (8) Spain	Belgium Win 4-2 (10)	China Draw 2-2 (11)	Germany
Belgium	2-4 Spain	1-1 vs Germany	New Zealand Loss 2-4 (9)	South Korea Loss 1-3 (8)	China
China	1-4 (1) Germany	2-5 (2) South Korea	Spain Loss 1-2 (3)	New Zealand Draw 2-2 (12)	Belgium

It can be seen that there is no contradiction in this whole process. Hence, this has to be the correct table.

We can reject possibility 3 on similar logic, you can work it out yourself and see that there will be a clash of values under possibility 3.

So we can consider the above to be the table of results for the 3rd and 4th rounds. The fifth round results can be easily seen from the difference between the points table of the fourth round and the points table of the fifth round.

Table after 4 rounds (17th August)

	P	W	D	L	F	A	Pts
Spain	4	3	0	1	7	4	9
Germany	4	2	2	0	9	5	8
South Korea	4	2	1	1	12	9	7
New Zealand	4	2	1	1	9	6	7
Belgium	4	0	1	3	6	12	1
China	4	0	1	3	6	13	1

The following is the final group table at the end of the group stage of the tournament.

Group A - Men (19th August)							
	P	W	D	L	F	A	Pts
Spain	5	4	0	1	9	5	12
Germany	5	3	2	0	12	6	11
South Korea	5	2	1	2	13	11	7
New Zealand	5	2	1	2	10	9	7
Belgium	5	1	1	3	9	13	4
China	5	0	1	4	7	16	1

Results table for all rounds:

	Round 1	Round 2	Round 3 (Opponent and Result)	Round 4 (Opponent and Result)	Round 5
Spain	4-2 (5) Belgium	1-0 (6) New Zealand	China Win 2-1 (1)	Germany Loss 0-1 (2)	South Korea Win 2-1
Germany	4-1 China	1-1 vs Belgium	South Korea Draw 3-3 (5)	Spain Win 1-0 (4)	New Zealand Win 3-1
South Korea	1-3 (4) New Zealand	5-2 (3) China	South Korea Draw 3-3 (6)	Belgium Win 3-1(7)	Spain Loss 1-2
New Zealand	3-1 (7) South Korea	0-6 (8) Spain	Belgium Win 4-2 (10)	China Draw 2-2 (11)	Germany Loss 1-3
Belgium	2-4 Spain	1-1 vs Germany	New Zealand Loss 2-4 (9)	South Korea Loss 1-3 (8)	China Win 3-1
China	1-4 (1) Germany	2-5 (2) South Korea	Spain Loss 1-2 (3)	New Zealand Draw 2-2 (12)	Belgium Loss 1-3

3. Analysis Tools for a Cricket Score Card

A typical cricket batting score card consists of the names of the players, with their runs scored, given individually and the overall team score.

1. At any point of time during the innings, two batsmen would be batting at the crease, each such pair is referred to as a partnership. The runs scored by a pair of batsmen, while they are batting together, is seen as the runs for that partnership. The first batsman to take strike during an innings is called batsman 1, the batsman who accompanies him is batsman 2, the batsman who comes in at the fall of the first wicket is batsman 3 and so on till batsman 11 who is the last batsman to walk in to bat during an innings.
   The first wicket partnership is the one that is between the two opening batsmen. Once, one of the opening batsmen gets out, the number 3 batsman of the team comes into bat, with the not out batsman. This partnership is referred to as the second wicket partnership. Once one of them gets out, the number 4 batsman comes out to bat with the batsman who is not out. This partnership is referred to as the third wicket partnership and so on. Note that, the third wicket partnership has 3 possibilities with respect to the batsmen number batting during the time - Possibility 1: batsman 1 and batsman 4; possibility 2: batsman 2 and batsman 4 and possibility 3: batsman 3 and batsman 4. The trend continues in the same way till the 10th wicket partnership, which is the last partnership of the innings. Notice that, batsman 4 would be a necessary constant for the 3rd wicket partnership. Similarly, for the 2nd wicket partnership, batsman 3 is necessary and can pair with either batsman 1 or 2, depending on who got out and who remains not out. Thus, we can visualize the following table of possible partnerships:

#	Possible Second Batsman	Compulsory Batsman	Number of Wickets Fallen
1st wicket	NA	1 and 2	0
2nd wicket	1 or 2	3	1
3rd wicket	1 or 2 or 3	4	2
4th wicket	1 or 2 or 3 or 4	5	3
5th wicket	1/2/3/4/5	6	4
6th wicket	1/2/3/4/5/6	7	5
7th wicket	1/2/3/4/5/6/7	8	6
8th wicket	1/2/3/4/5/6/7/8	9	7
9th wicket	1/2/3/4/5/6/7/8/9	10	8
10th wicket	1/2/3/4/5/6/7/8/9/10	11	9

   The innings is terminated at the fall of the 10th wicket.
2. It is sometimes possible to trace which particular batsmen would be batting at the fall of a particular wicket. For instance, if the batsman number 1 has scored 100 runs and the fall of the first 4 wickets were at 22,38,47 and 73 runs, then batsman 1 must be a part of the fifth wicket partnership (apart from of course being a part of the first, second, third and fourth wicket partnerships too).
3. Strike rate for a batsman: A batsman's strike rate is considered to be the number of runs he has scored per 100 balls faced. Thus, for a batsman who had a strike rate of 50, and faced 40 balls before getting out, we can deduce that he must have scored 20 runs.
4. Run rate is defined as the number of runs scored per over. Thus, a team scoring at 5 runs per over in a 50 over match, would have scored a total of 250 runs - if it played all the 50 overs.
5. The bowling score card shows the performance of the bowlers for the bowling side. Typical information you would be able to derive from the bowling scorecard would be: Overs bowled (the total number of overs bowled by a particular bowler); maidens (the number of overs in which there was no run scored); runs (The runs conceded by the particular bowler); wickets (the wickets taken by the particular bowler).
6. Extras: During a batting innings, some runs are given to the batting team, that were not scored by the batsman off his own bat. These runs are called as extras - and are of 4 kinds: Wides, no balls, byes and leg byes. These runs are added to the team score. Thus, the total score of an innings for a batting team = runs scored by all the batsman of the team + the runs in extras awarded to the team.

4. General Analysis Tools for a Round Robin Tournament or for a Round Robin Cum Knock out Tournament

For a round robin tournament of n teams, where each team plays against the other once, the total number of matches in the tournament would be: ${}^{N}C_2$. Thus, for a 6 team round robin tournament with each team playing against the other once, there would be a total of ${}^{6}C_2$= 15 matches.

Note: Here, we are using the formula for combinations where: NCR = $\dfrac{N!}{R!\times(N-R)!}$.

Sometimes, the tournaments are held on a round robin cum knockout basis. In such tournaments, the initial rounds are played in multiple groups on a round robin format - where teams within a group play each other once, and the top teams advance to the next round- which is held on a knock out basis, starting with either the semi final or quarter final or pre-quarter final. The world cup football is a classic example of this. 8 groups of 4 team each participate in the group stages, followed by the top two teams of each group qualifying to play the pre- quarterfinals, which is played in a knock out format.

LEVEL OF DIFFICULTY (I)

Directions for Questions 1 to 4: *Answer the following questions based on the given information:*

Eight boxers P, Q, R, S, T, U, V and W participated in an international boxing championship. In the first round of the championship, these eight players were divided into two groups of four players each. In a group, each player had to play two matches against each of the other players in its group. No match ended in a tie and the players with the highest and the second highest number of wins in both the groups reached the semifinal. Q, U, W, V reached the semifinal.

It is also known that in the first round:

(i) Each player of each group won different number of matches.

(ii) R lost all of his matches against all the other players except S, who won at least one match against each of the other player except one.

(iii) V won both the matches against U.

(iv) P and W won the same number of matches.

1. Who won the least number of matches after 1st round?
   (a) P (b) R
   (c) S (d) T
2. What was the total number of wins of P after the first round?
   (a) 1 (b) 2
   (c) 3 (d) 4
3. Who won the most number of matches after 1st round?
   (a) Q (b) U
   (c) W (d) V
4. Which of the following player lost at least one match against P in the 1st round?
   (a) Q (b) S
   (c) U (d) V

Directions for Questions 5 to 8: *Answer the following questions based on the information given below:*

In a sports event, six teams (A, B, C, D, E and F) are competing against each other. Matches are scheduled in two stages. Each team plays three matches in stage 1 and two matches in stage 2. No team plays against the same team more than once in the event. No ties are permitted in any of the matches. The observations after the completion of stage 1 and stage 2 are as given below.

Stage 1:

- One team won all the three matches.
- Two teams lost all the matches.
- D lost to A but won against C and F.
- E lost to B but won against C and F.
- B lost at least one match.
- F did not play against the top team of stage 1.

Stage 2:

- The leader of stage 1 lost the next two matches.
- Of the two teams at the bottom after stage 1, one team won both the matches, while the other lost both the matches.
- One more team lost both the matches in stage 2.

5. The only team(s) that won both the matches in stage 2 is/are:
   (a) B (b) E and F
   (c) A, E and F (d) B, E and F
6. The teams that won exactly two matches in the event are:
   (a) A, D and F (b) D and E
   (c) E and F (d) D and F
7. The team(s) with the most wins in the event is/are:
   (a) A (b) A and C
   (c) F (d) B and E
8. The two teams that defeated the leader of stage 1 are:
   (a) F and D (b) E and F
   (c) B and D (d) E and D

Directions for Questions 9 to 12: *Answer the questions on the basis of the information given below:*

The following tables show the batting performance of the Indian Cricket Team in the final match of Asia Cup 2014. Table 1 indicates the score of the team at the fall of each wicket (from 1 to 10). Table 2 gives the runs scored by the 11 batsmen and the order in which they appeared in the batting line up.

Table 1:

Fall of Wicket	Total Score
1	25
2	34
3	42

Fall of Wicket	Total Score
4	57
5	62
6	75
7	82
8	86
9	99
10	110

Table 2:

Sl. No.	Batsman	Runs Scored
1	Sachin	28
2	Sehwag	7
3	Gautam	8
4	Yuvraj	4
5	Kohli	20
6	Dhoni	3
7	Raina	18
8	Harbhajan	5
9	Ashwin	0
10	Bhuvi	11
11	Zaheer	6

Additional Information:

(i) At any point, there are two batsmen on the field, till the fall of the 10th wicket. Whenever the team loses a wicket, the new batsman comes as per the batting order. E.g., if one of the openers gets out, the no. 3 batsman takes the field.

(ii) A partnership between any two batsmen is the number of runs scored while both of them are batting.

9. How many batsmen lost their wicket between Sachin's and Dhoni's dismissal?

(a) 0 (b) 1
(c) 2 (d) More than 2

10. How many runs were scored by the batsman who was the 7th to be dismissed?

(a) 11 (b) 18
(c) 0 (d) 5

11. What was the percentage contribution to the second highest partnership of the batsman, to be dismissed first in that partnership?

(a) 33.33% (b) 61.53%
(c) 71.43% (d) None of these

12. If India's total comprised only 'Singles' and 'Fours'. The number of Fours scored cannot exceed:

(a) 27 (b) 24
(c) 21 (d) 20

Directions for Questions 13 to 15: *Answer these questions on the basis of the information given below.*

Rajesh and Kanhaiya are playing a game of coins. There are N coins on the table to start with. Each player, in his turn, picks up at least one coin and at most eight coins. The two players take turns alternately. They continue playing till the last coin is picked up off the table. The player who picks up the last coin loses. Assume that each player plays intelligently with an objective of winning. Rajesh has the first move. No player is allowed to pass his turn without picking up any coins.

13. If there are 88 coins in the game then how many coins should Rajesh pick in his first turn to ensure his win?

(a) 6
(b) 7
(c) 2
(d) He can't win in this game.

14. If, for some N, it is known that the number of coins picked up by Rajesh, in his first four moves were 6, 5, 5 and 6 respectively, then how many coins would Kanhaiya have picked up in his third move? Assume that both have played intelligently and Rajesh wins the game.

(a) 3 (b) 5
(c) 6 (d) Insufficient data

15. If it is known that the game was completed in 12 moves, what is the maximum possible value for N?

(a) 51 (b) 53
(c) 54 (d) None of these

Directions for Questions 16 to 17: *Assume that the player who picks the last coin wins the game.*

16. If it is known that N is greater than 11 but less than 55, for how many values of N will Rajesh certainly lose the game, irrespective of how he plays?

(a) 4 (b) 5
(c) 6 (d) 8

17. If it is known that N is greater than 88 but less than 98 and that Rajesh picked up 6 coins in his first move, then what is the value of N?

(a) 91 (b) 94
(c) 95 (d) 96

Directions for Questions 18 to 21: *These questions are based on the following information.*

128 players taking part in a knockout tennis tournament, are seeded from 1 to 128 with seed 1 being the top seed, seed 2 the second seed and so on. In the first round, seed 1 plays seed 128 which is termed match 1 of round 1, seed 2 plays seed 127, which is termed match 2 of round 1 and so on till match 64 of round 1, where seed 64 plays seed 65. In the next round, the winner of match 1 of round 1 plays the winner of the last match (match 64) of round 1, the winner

of match 2 of round 1 plays the winner of the second last match (match 63) of round 1 and so on. This continues till only one player is left undefeated. If, in any match a lower seeded player defeats a higher seeded player, it is called an upset.

18. How many matches are played in the tournament?
19. If the player seeded 37 reaches the third round, who would he play against, assuming there are no upsets in the first two rounds, apart from the upsets required to make the seed number 37 reach the third round?
20. If the number of upsets in the tournament is only three, then who is the lowest seeded player, who could have won the tournament?
21. Which of the seeded player could have faced the player seeded 76 in the second round?

Directions for Questions 22 to 25: *Read the information and answer the questions that follow:*

In a Formula 1 race, drivers from 4 teams Ferrari, McLaren, Suzuki and Nippon were participating. This particular year, the bookies were having a field day during the races. The official odds provided for winning, for each of these drivers by Mr. Varun, were 3:2, 8:5, 3:1 and 2:1 respectively. The odds of 3:2 mean that for a bet of 2, you get a profit of 3, if the bet proves correct - i.e., the team you put your bet wins. In other words, you get back ₹ 5 for a bet of ₹ 2, if you place a bet on team Ferrari, where ₹ 2 is the return of your bet amount and ₹ 3 is the profit you gained.

It is also known that if your team finished second, you would gain only 20% of the profit, while getting the entire bet amount back. However, if your team finishes third or fourth in the race, you would lose the entire bet amount and get nothing back.

There are a total of 4 races held, with all the 4 teams and their drivers participating in each race. Sameer Contractor placed equal bets of ₹40,000, on all the four teams and their drivers in all the 4 races. For the purpose of this question, assume that: [Return = Amount of profit + Amount of bet]

22. If Sameer Contractor received a return of ₹184,000 in a race, then which team finished first in that race?
    (a) Ferrari (b) McLaren
    (c) Suzuki (d) Nippon
23. If return received is of ₹176,000 in all the four races from his bets placed on Nippon, then how many times did Nippon finish in the top two? (TITA)
24. If return received is of ₹172,000, ₹216,000 and ₹152,800 in three of the four races, then what was the minimum return in the fourth race, given that each team won only 1 race? (TITA)
25. For the above question, if it is known that there is no repetition for the second place finish too, then which team finished second in the fourth race?
    (a) Ferrari (b) McLaren
    (c) Suzuki (d) Nippon

Directions for Questions 26 to 29: *Read the information below and answer the questions that follow:*

The Little Players Football coaching school organized a tournament, among the students and divided them into 7 teams- A, B, C, D, E, F and G. Each team played exactly once against each other in the tournament. The teams got 3 points for winning and no points for losing the match. If a match was a draw, each team got one point.

Further, the following points are known:

(i) Each team won at least one match.
(ii) Team B won four matches.
(iii) Team A drew a match against D, B and E.
(iv) E won the match against D and F and lost the match against B and C.
(v) B did not lose any match.

26. If the match between D and B was a draw, then for how many matches the result is definitely known? (TITA)
27. What could be the minimum difference between the total points scored by A and C?
28. If team B drew with team D, what was the result of the match between team A and C?
    (a) Team A won.
    (b) Team C won.
    (c) The match was a draw.
    (d) Cannot be determined.
29. If F got the maximum possible points for the remaining matches and G won only one match, which was against D and lost all other matches.
    Which teams got the lowest points among the combination of teams?
    (a) Team G (b) Team A
    (c) Team C (d) Cannot be determined

Directions for Questions 30 to 33: *Read the details and then answer the questions that follow:*

In a tennis tournament, players are seeded from 1 to 32, played in a knockout. Knockout means that the winner of a match, advances to the next round and the team losing the match, is eliminated from the competition. The loser is eliminated and the winners of the respective matches qualify for the next round. When the last 8 players are left, they play each other in the quarter finals, the last 4 stage is called the semi final and the final is between the last 2 players standing. In the first round, there are 32 players, and 16 matches are held between the players such that: Player seeded 1 plays against the player seeded 32 in match 1 of round 1; match 2 of round 1 is played between seed 2 and 31; match 3 between seeds 3 and 30 and so on. In the second round, match 1 is played between the winners of match 1 and match 16 of round 1; match 2 is played between the winners of match 2 and match 15 of round 1; match 3 between the winners of match 3 and match 14 of round 1 and so on. Subsequent rounds are held in the same way. An upset is said to have taken place, if in any match, in any round, a lower seeded player beats a higher seeded player. For a particular tournament, with 32 players, answer the following questions.

30. If during the course of tournament, there are only 2 upsets, then what can be the lowest seed who could be the winner of the tournament?

31. If in round 1 and round 2, all even numbered matches result in upsets, odd numbered matches do not result in upset and no upset happens in the further round, then what is the rank of the player who plays against the 27th seed in the quarter finals (the round before semi final)?

32. If there are 11 upsets in the 1st round and no upsets in the other rounds, then which seed could be the lowest possible seed who can win the tournament?

33. If there are 11 upsets in the 1st round and no upsets in the other rounds, then which seed could be the highest possible seed who can win the tournament?

Directions for Questions 34 to 38: *Read the information and answer the questions that follow:*

International team tennis is undergoing rapid changes these days. A new format tournament called the Davis Cup, was launched recently, in which India played with Australia in the quarter final and with France in semi final. The match between 2 teams is held in 3 days: day 1: 2 singles matches; day 2: one doubles match and Day 3: 2 reverse singles matches. In the reverse singles matches, the singles opponents of the first day are switched.

4 players played for each team and an individual player can play either in singles or in doubles. The Indian players were: Vijay Amritraj (VA); Ramanathan Krishnan (RK); Leander Paes (LP); Mahesh Bhupathi (MB).

The Australian players were: Rod Laver (RL); Roy Emerson (RE); Pat Cash (PC) and Mark Woodforde (MW).

The French players were: Cedric Pioline (CP); Gael Monfils (GM); Yannick Noah (YN) and Jo-Wilfred Tsonga (JWT).

India beat Australia by 3 – 2 in the quarter finals and France by 4 – 1 in the semi-finals.

Note: The players who played in single and reverse single matches in a particular round did not play the doubles match in that particular round. Except these matches, there were no extra matches played.

The following diagram provides the data of matches played and wins of all the players of India, France and Australia in Davis cup.

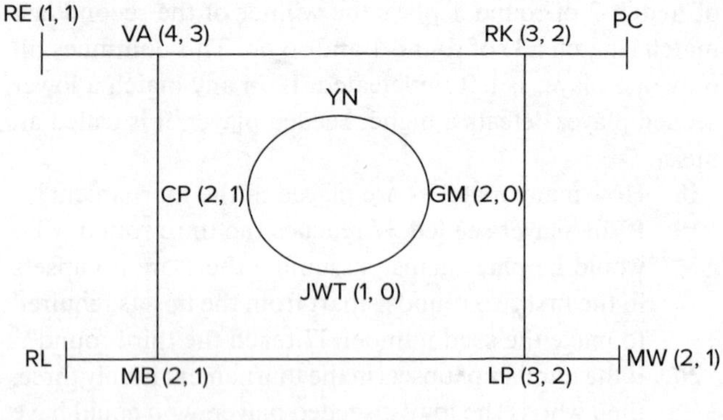

Note (in the diagram): VA (4, 3) means that VA (Vijay Amritraj) played 4 matches and won 3 out of those.

A player can play a maximum of 2 matches in a round.

34. India's doubles players in their match against Australia were:
(a) Mahesh Bhupathi & Leander Paes
(b) Mahesh Bhupathi & Ramanathan Krishnan
(c) Leander Paes & Ramanathan Krishnan
(d) Either (a) or (b)

35. How many matches did Rod Laver play in the tournament?
(a) 2 (b) 1
(c) Either 1 or 2 (d) Cannot be determined

36. Who were the players against whom Vijay Amritraj played in the semi finals?
(a) Cedric Pioline and Gael Monfils
(b) Gael Monfils and Yannick Noah
(c) Cedric Pioline and Yannick Noah
(d) Cannot be determined

37. The players who did not play in any of the doubles match definitely is/are:
(a) Vijay Amritraj
(b) Leander Paes
(c) Cedric Pioline
(d) Both Vijay Amritraj and Cedric Pioline

38. Which of the following statement/s are not definitely true:
1. India lost it's doubles match in the quarter finals.
2. Vijay Amritraj beat Cedric Pioline.
3. Leander Paes beat Mark Woodforde.
(a) All 3.
(b) 2 only.
(c) Both 2 and 3.
(d) All are not definitely true.

Directions for Questions 39 to 41: *These questions are based on the situation given below:*

Recently, Ghosh Babu spent his winter vacation on Kyakya Island. During the vacation, he visited the local casino where he came across a new card game. Two players, using a normal deck of 52 playing cards, play this game. One player is called the Dealer and the other is called the Player. First, the player picks a card at random from the deck. This is called the base card. The amount in rupees equal to the face value of the base card is called the base amount. The face values of Ace, King, Queen and Jack are ten. For other cards, the face value is the number on the card. Once, the Player picks a card from the deck, the Dealer pays him the base amount.

Then the Dealer picks a card from the deck and this card is called the top card. If the top card is of the same suit as the base card, the Player pays twice the base amount to the Dealer. If the top card is of the same colour as the base card (but not the same suit) then the Player pays the base amount to the Dealer. If the top card happens to be of a different colour than the base card, the Dealer pays the base amount to the Player. Ghosh Babu played the game 4 times. First time he picked eight of clubs and the Dealer picked queen of clubs. Second time, he picked ten of hearts and the dealer picked two of spades. Next time, Ghosh Babu picked six of diamonds and the dealer picked ace of hearts. Lastly, he picked eight of spades and the dealer picked jack of spades. Answer the following questions based on these four games.

39. If Ghosh Babu stopped playing the game when his gain would have been maximum, the gain in ₹ would have been

(a) 12 (b) 20
(c) 16 (d) 4

40. The initial money Ghosh Babu had (before the beginning of the game sessions) was ₹ X. At no point did he have to borrow any money. What is the minimum possible value of X?

(a) 16 (b) 8
(c) 100 (d) 24

41. If the amount of money that Ghosh Babu had with him at the end was ₹ 100, what was the initial amount he had with him?

(a) 120 (b) 8
(c) 4 (d) 96

LEVEL OF DIFFICULTY (II)

Directions for Questions 1 to 4: *Answer the questions on the basis of the information given below.*

Four teams – Sri Lanka, India, Bangladesh and Pakistan participated in ICC Asia Cup 2019. ICC decided to organize this tournament in T20 format. The tournament had two stages- league round and final. All these teams played against each other once in the league stage of the tournament. The table below shows the number of runs scored by the batting side against the fielding side in each of the matches. The value in the brackets just below the number of runs represents the number of over consumed by the batting side to score those runs. E.g., India scored 159 runs in 19.4 overs (118 balls) against Sri Lanka. In any of the six matches, the team which scored more runs is said to have secured a win over its opponent in that match. For instance, Sri Lanka won against India as Sri Lanka scored 162 runs while in the same match India scored only 159 runs. Top two teams with the highest number of wins qualified for the final. In case two teams had equal number of wins, the qualifier team with higher Run Rate (RR) qualified for the final.

Fielding side / Batting side	Sri Lanka	India	Bangladesh	Pakistan
Sri Lanka	—	162 (20)	179 (19)	132 (s)
India	159 (19.4)	—	180 (r)	210 (18)
Bangladesh	164 (16)	140 (q)	—	144 (18.2)
Pakistan	133 (p)	165 (20)	154 (19.1)	—

RR = RRa–RRb, where RRa for any team number of runs scored per ball by that team in all the matches played by it and RRb for a team is the number of runs scored per ball by the opponents in all the matches played against that particular team. Some values (p, q, r and s) are missing in the table, but it is known that each of them is neither less than 15 nor more than 20.

1. Which team cannot qualify for the final?

(a) India (b) Bangladesh
(c) Pakistan (d) Sri Lanka

2. How many teams definitely had a positive value of RR at the end of the first round?

(a) 0 (b) 1
(c) 2 (d) More than 2

3. If p = 15 and s = 20, which two teams did not qualify for the final?
   (a) Sri Lanka and Bangladesh
   (b) Bangladesh and Pakistan
   (c) India and Bangladesh
   (d) Cannot be determined
4. If p = q = r = s = 15, then which team was at the 2nd position at the end of the round?
   (a) Sri Lanka (b) India
   (c) Bangladesh (d) Pakistan

Directions for Questions 5 to 8: *Answer the questions on the basis of the information given below.*

Five players Sachin, Rahul, Mohit, Saurav and Aarav are awarded points by each of the five selectors A, B, C, D and E. Numbers mentioned in any parentheses are the points awarded to that particular player by the selector mentioned in the corresponding row.

'X' is the sum of the points earned by three players mentioned in any particular row of the table as a percentage of total points, awarded by the selector mentioned in the same row. Each selector awards distinct points to all the 5 players and points awarded by the selectors are non negative integers. For example, the aggregate points given to Sachin, Mohit and Rahul by the selector A is 80% of the total points given by selector A to all the five players.

Selector		Players		X
A	Sachin (9)	Mohit (6)	Rahul (5)	80
B	Saurav (8)	Aarav (6)	Sachin (4)	90
C	Mohit (11)	Aarav (7)	Saurav (6)	80
D	Saurav (8)	Sachin (7)	Aarav (2)	85
E	Rahul (8)	Mohit (5)	Sachin (3)	80

5. How much are minimum possible aggregate number of points earned by Saurav?
6. If the points given to Mohit by selectors B and D are the same and if the selector C gave 4 points to Sachin, then how much are the total points earned by Rahul?
7. How many players definitely would not earn more aggregate points than Saurav?
8. If Mohit scored the maximum possible points then what would be the maximum possible points earned by Rahul?

Directions for Questions 9 to 13: *Read the information and answer the questions that follow:*

5 players of a team participated in a tournament and played four matches (1 to 4). The following table gives partial information about their individual scores and the total runs scored by the team in each match.

Some values are missing in each of the given columns. The missing values are the runs scored by the two lowest scorers in that match. None of the two missing values is more than 10% of the total runs scored in that match.

High Yield Questions

Scan this QR code to access a video explanation of questions 9-13

Player	Match 1	Match 2	Match 3	Match 4
A		100		53
B	88	65		52
C			110	
D	72	75	20	56
E	60	78		
Total	270	300	240	200

9. What is the maximum possible runs scored by A in four matches?
   (a) 199 (b) 220
   (c) 175 (d) 232
10. What is the maximum possible percentage contribution of E in the total runs scored in the four matches?
   (a) 18% (b) 19.9%
   (c) 18.6% (d) 20.2%
11. If the absolute difference between the total runs scored by A and C in the four matches is minimum possible, then what is the sum of total runs scored by A and C in the four matches.
   (a) 284 (b) 376
   (c) 363 (d) 472
12. If the absolute difference between the total runs scored by A and C in the four matches is minimum possible, then what is the absolute difference between total runs scored by B and E in the four matches?
   (a) 32 (b) 37
   (c) 35 (d) 27
13. The players are ranked 1 to 5 on the basis of the total runs scored by them in the four matches, with the highest scorer getting rank 1. If it is known that no two players scored the same number of total runs, how

many players are there whose ranks can be exactly determined?

(a) 0 (b) 1
(c) 3 (d) Cannot be determined

Directions for Questions 14 to 18: *Read the information and answer the questions that follow:*

In a horse racing championship, six people A, B, C, D, E and F placed bets on seven horses as per the following table. Further, the following information is available:

(i) Every horse was bet upon correctly by at least 1 person.
(ii) No two persons had the same number of correct bets.
(iii) No person got all seven bets correct.

High Yield Questions
Scan this QR code to access a video explanation of questions 14-18

	A	B	C	D	E	F
1 -	H1	H7	H5	H6	H5	H6
2 -	H2	H3	H6	H2	H6	H7
3 -	H3	H4	H7	H3	H3	H1
4 -	H4	H6	H1	H1	H1	H3
5 -	H5	H1	H3	H7	H2	H4
6 -	H6	H2	H4	H4	H4	H5
7 -	H7	H5	H2	H5	H7	H2

Based on the table above, answer the questions which follow:

14. Which horse won the race?
(a) H1 (b) H5
(c) H6 (d) H7

15. Which horse came second?
(a) H2 (b) H7
(c) H6 (d) H3

16. Which horse finished fifth?
(a) H2 (b) H5
(c) H7 (d) H4

17. Which horse finished last?
(a) H2 (b) H5
(c) H7 (d) H6

18. Which horse finished third?
(a) H3 (b) H4
(c) H7 (d) H1

Directions for Questions 19 to 22: *Answer the questions on the basis of the information given below.*

Coach John sat with the score cards of Indian players from the 3 games in a one-day cricket tournament where the same set of players played for India and all the major batsmen got out. John summarized the batting performance through three diagrams, one for each game. In each diagram, the three outer triangles communicate the number of runs scored by the three top scorers from India, where K, R, S, V and Y represent Kaif, Rahul, Saurav, Virender, and Yuvraj respectively. The middle triangle in each diagram denotes the percentage of total score, that was scored by the top three Indian scorers in that game. No two players score the same number of runs in the same game. John also calculated two batting indices for each player, based on his scores in the tournament; the R-index of a batsman is the difference between his highest and lowest scores in the 3 games while the M-index is the middle number, if his scores are arranged in a non-increasing order.`

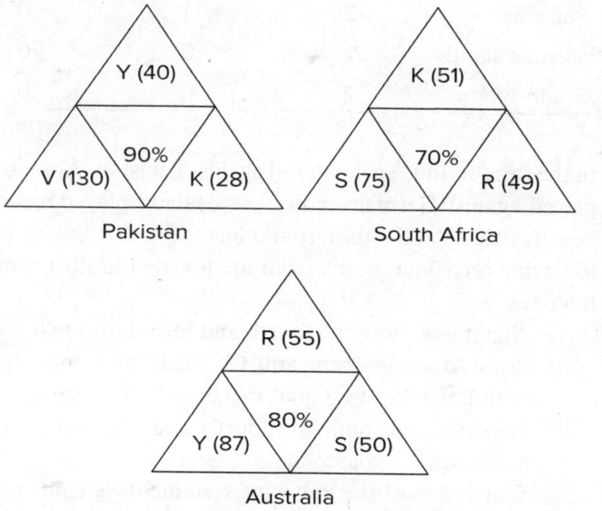

19. Among the players mentioned, who can have the lowest R-index from the tournament?
(a) Only Kaif, Rahul or Yuvraj
(b) Only Kaif or Rahul
(c) Only Kaif or Yuvraj
(d) Only Kaif

20. How many players among those listed definitely scored less than Yuvraj in the tournament?
(a) 0 (b) 1
(c) 2 (d) More than 2

21. Which of the players had the best M-index from the tournament?
(a) Rahul (b) Saurav
(c) Virender (d) Yuvraj

22. For how many Indian players is it possible to calculate the exact M-index?
(a) 0 (b) 1
(c) 2 (d) More than 2

Directions for Questions 23 to 26: *Answer the questions on the basis of the information given below.*

The year was 2006. All six teams in Pool A of World Cup hockey, play each other exactly once. Each win earns a team three points, a draw earns one point and a loss earns zero points. The two teams with the highest points, qualify for the semifinals. In case of a tie, the team with the highest goal difference (Goal For - Goals Against) qualifies.

In the opening match, Spain lost to Germany. After the second round (after each team played two matches), the pool table looked as shown below.

Pool A							
Teams	Games Played	Won	Drawn	Lost	Goals For	Goals Against	Points
Germany	2	2	0	0	3	1	6
Argentina	2	2	0	0	2	0	6
Spain	2	1	0	1	5	2	3
Pakistan	2	1	0	1	2	1	3
New Zealand	2	0	0	2	1	6	0
South Africa	2	0	0	2	1	4	0

In the third round, Spain played against Pakistan, Argentina played against Germany, and New Zealand played against South Africa. All the third round matches were drawn. The following are some results from the fourth and fifth round matches:

(i) Spain won both the fourth and fifth round matches.

(ii) Both Argentina beat and Germany won their fifth round matches by 3 goal to 0.

(iii) Pakistan won both the fourth and fifth round the matches by 1 goal to 0.

23. Which one of the following statements is true about the matches played in the first two rounds?
(a) Pakistan beat South Africa by 2 goals to 1.
(b) Argentina beat Pakistan by 1 goal to 0.
(c) Germany beat Pakistan by 2 goals to 1.
(d) Germany beat Spain by 2 goals to 1.

24. Which one of the following statements is true about matches played in the first two rounds?
(a) Germany beat New Zealand by 1 goal to 0.
(b) Spain beat New Zealand by 4 goals to 0.
(c) Spain beat South Africa by 2 goals to 0.
(d) Germany beat South Africa by 2 goals to 1.

25. Which team finished at the top of the pool after five rounds of matches?
(a) Argentina (b) Germany
(c) Spain (d) Cannot be determined

26. If Pakistan qualified as one of the two teams from Pool A, which was the other team that qualified?
(a) Argentina (b) Germany
(c) Spain (d) Cannot be determined

Directions for Questions 27 to 29: *Read the information and answer the questions that follow:*

Six teams are playing in a hockey tournament, where each team is playing against every other team **exactly once**. At an intermediate stage, the status is as follows:

Teams	No. of Matches Played	No. of Matches Won	No. of Matches Lost	No. of Matches Drawn	Goals Scored by the Team	Goals Conceded by the Team
Team A	2	2	0	0	5	1
Team B	2	1	0	1	5	1
Team C	2	1	0	1	2	0
Team D	2	0	0	2	1	1
Team E	2	0	2	0	1	4
Team F	2	0	2	0	0	7

Note: The team that scores more goals than it concedes wins the match, while, if both the teams score the same no. of goals, the match is declared drawn.
In a match played between Team X and Team Y, if team X scores 1 and concedes none, then the score line would read: Team X - Team Y (1-0).

27. Which of the following matches are yet to be played?
(a) Team A - Team B and Team C - Team D
(b) Team C - Team D and Team E - Team F
(c) Team E - Team F and Team B - Team D
(d) Team C - Team D and Team A - Team E
(e) Team A - Team B and Team E - Team F

28. Which of the following score line is a possible outcome in the tournament?
(a) Team A - Team D (1-0)
(b) Team A - Team E (2-1)
(c) Team B - Team D (1-0)
(d) Team C - Team F (2-0)
(e) None of the above

29. Which of the following score line is not a possible outcome in the tournament?
(a) Team A - Team F (4-0)
(b) Team B - Team F (4-0)
(c) Team C - Team D (0-0)
(d) Team C - Team E (2-0)
(e) All of the above options are possible.

Directions for Questions 30 to 33: *Read the information and answer the questions that follow:*

Data on an ongoing football league of a country is given here. 20 teams are playing in the league. The rules of the league are as follows:

(i) Each team plays against all the other teams twice, once in its home ground, and once in the opponent's home ground. These matches are known as the "Home" match and the "Away" match respectively.

High Yield Questions
Scan this QR code to access a video explanation of questions 30-33

(ii) A win results in 3 points, a draw in 1 point and a loss in 0 point for team.

(iii) The number of goals a team scores is termed as "Goals For" and the number of goals it concedes is termed as "Goals Against". We get the "Goal Difference" by subtracting "Goals Against" from "Goals For".
The ranking of the teams is decided on the total points. If two teams are tied on their total points, the team which has higher Goal Difference gets the higher rank. If the tie cannot be resolved on Goal Difference, Goals For is checked, followed by Goals Against. If the tie persists, the teams are ranked in the ascending order of their names.
Table 1 provides data on the current top 13 teams, based on the overall situation, i.e., by taking into account both Home matches and Away matches of each team.
Table 2 provides data on the current top 13 teams based on Home matches only.
Chart 1 provides a plot of the goal difference of each of the 13 teams based on the overall situation.

Table 1

Overall				
Team	**M**	**W**	**D**	**GF**
CH	3	3	0	8
SW	3	2	1	10
WB	3	2	1	6
MC	3	2	1	8
MU	3	2	0	6
WH	3	2	0	4
EV	3	2	0	4
AS	3	1	2	2
WG	3	1	1	4
NC	3	1	1	3
FU	3	1	0	7
ST	3	0	3	3
SU	2	0	2	2

Table 2

Home					
Team	**M**	**W**	**D**	**GF**	**GA**
WB	2	2	0	5	0
WH	2	2	0	4	0
CH	2	2	0	6	2
MC	2	2	0	6	3
SW	2	1	1	5	2
NC	2	1	1	3	2
FU	1	1	0	5	0
EV	1	1	0	1	0
MU	1	1	0	3	2
TOT	2	0	2	2	2
NW	1	0	1	1	1
AS	1	0	1	0	0
ST	1	0	1	0	0

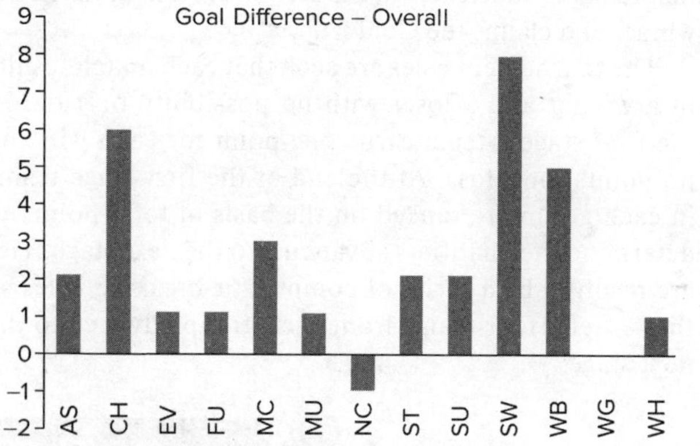

30. Considering away matches only, which of the following teams is the second ranking team?
(a) AS
(b) CH
(c) WG
(d) SW
(e) WB

31. Considering Away matches only, the least number of teams with either 0 or 1 point is:
(a) 2 (b) 3
(c) 4 (d) 5
(e) 6

32. Let us define a term *pos* as the difference between "Home rank" and "Away rank". Which of the following has the maximum value of *pos*?
(a) AS (b) WB
(c) WH (d) MC
(e) SW

33. How many unique values of goal difference are there for Away matches?
(a) 5
(b) 6
(c) ≥ 6
(d) ≥ 6 and ≤ 13
(e) ≥ 6 and ≤ 14

Directions for Questions 34 to 38: Sixteen teams have been invited to participate in the ABC Gold Cup Cricket tournament. The tournament is conducted in two stages. In the first stage, the teams are divided into two groups. Each group consists of eight teams, with each team playing every other team in its group exactly once. At the end of the first stage, the top four teams from each group advance to the second stage while the rest are eliminated. The second stage comprises of several rounds. A round involves one match for each team. The winner of a match in a round advances to the next round, while the loser is eliminated. The team that remains undefeated in the second stage is declared the winner and claims the Gold Cup.

The tournament rules are such that each match results in a winner and a loser with no possibility of a tie. In the first stage a team earns one point for each win and no points for a loss. At the end of the first stage teams in each group are ranked on the basis of total points to determine the qualifiers advancing to the next stage. Ties are resolved by a series of complex tie-breaking rules so that exactly four teams from each group advance to the next stage.

34. What is the total number of matches played in the tournament?
(a) 28 (b) 55
(c) 63 (d) 35

35. The minimum number of wins needed for a team in the first stage to guarantee its advancement to the next stage is:
(a) 5 (b) 6
(c) 7 (d) 4

36. What is the highest number of wins for a team in the first stage in spite of which it would be eliminated at the end of first stage?
(a) 1 (b) 2
(c) 3 (d) 4

37. What is the number of rounds in the second stage of the tournament?
(a) 1 (b) 2
(c) 3 (d) 4

38. Which of the following statements is true?
(a) The winner will have more wins than any other team in the tournament.
(b) At the end of the first stage, no team eliminated from the tournament will have more wins than any of the teams qualifying for the second stage.
(c) It is possible that the winner will have the same number of wins in the entire tournament as a team eliminated at the end of the first stage.
(d) The number of teams with exactly one win in the second stage of the tournament is 4.

LEVEL OF DIFFICULTY (III)

Directions for Questions 1 to 4: *Read the information and answer the questions that follow:*

High Yield Questions
Scan this QR code to access a video explanation of questions 1-4

In an international hockey tournament, a strange process is followed for the scheduling of matches. 10 teams are selected first through rigorous trials at the regional and world levels, to qualify to play the tournament. The teams who qualified for the tournament in 2042, were Argentina, Bangladesh, China, Denmark, England, Finland, Germany, Hungary, India and Japan. They were first divided in two groups of 5 teams each, Argentina to England formed Group Napolean and Finland to Japan formed Group Ashoka. Then matches were scheduled amongst each other - not within the group - but with each team playing one match each with the members of the other group. The winner of a match is awarded 3 points, the loser is awarded 0 points, while in case of a draw, both teams get 1 point each. The following table gives information about the points scored by each team, after each team had played their 5 scheduled matches.

Group Napolean		Group Ashoka	
Team Name	**Points Scored**	**Team Name**	**Points Scored**
Argentina	10	Finland	6
Bangladesh	5	Germany	7
China	9	Hungary	8
Denmark	12	India	6
England	3	Japan	6

Further, it is known that
China lost two matches.
Argentina lost to Japan, while Denmark lost against Finland.
Each team won at least one match.

1. What was the result of the match between China and Germany?
   (a) China won (b) Germany won
   (c) Drawn (d) Cannot be determined
2. England won against which of the following teams?
   (a) Finland (b) Japan
   (c) India (d) Either Finland or Japan
3. Which of the following statements is definitely true?
   (a) Hungary won the match against China.
   (b) Germany Won the match against Argentina.
   (c) India won the match against Denmark.
   (d) More than one of the above.
4. What were the total number of matches won by teams in both groups combined?
   (a) 12 (b) 10
   (c) 22 (d) 19

Directions for Questions 5 to 9: *Read the information and answer the questions that follow:*

In the kingdom of Raja Bhoj, who was a chess enthusiast, kingdom wide chess tournaments were the order of the day. The king used to conduct a series of Taluka level, province level and kingdom level tournaments every year in order to select players for the grand finale. The five Pandava brothers: Arjun, Bheem, Yudhistir, Nakul and Sahdev were all avid chess players and participated in these tournaments to get selected for the grand finale. Each player was supposed to play 100 matches each at the Taluka, province and kingdom levels. In order to qualify for the grand finale tournament, the minimum number of matches that each of these players have to win in their last 100 matches in each of these levels is 30, 25 and 35 respectively,

The five brothers were sitting together at the end of the three levels of tournaments and considering their relative performances. They came up with the following observations:

(i) The number of matches won by each brother is a distinct integer. They also have a seeding system between the five of them where for each level of tournament, they define the player with the highest number of wins as the seed 1, the one with the second-highest number of wins as seed 2 and so on.

(ii) The difference between the highest number of matches won and the lowest number of matches won at any of the three levels of tournaments is 6.

(iii) Each of the brothers was easily able to meet the qualifying criteria. In fact, the lowest number of matches won in any of the three levels is twice the minimum number of matches to be won, in order to qualify.

Additionally,

(iv) The seeding obtained in any two levels is not the same, for any of the five brothers.

(v) The total number of matches won is the sum of the number of matches won in all the three levels.

5. Assuming the total matches won by Bheem is more than any other player, what is the maximum possible total matches he won?
6. The maximum possible difference in the total number of matches won by any two players can be?
7. If it is known that the total number of matches won by Sahdev is less than that of any other player, the total number of matches won by him is at most.
8. What is the minimum possible number of total matches won by any player?
9. What is the maximum possible sum of the seed numbering of the person who has the least sum of seedings in any particular distribution of seed numbers amongst the brothers?

Directions for Questions 10 to 14: *Read the information and answer the questions that follow:*

The fastest rats were to be chosen in the Bannerghatta Road rat kingdom. After a series of complex competitions, the finals were down to three rats: R1, R2 and R3, who were made to participate in 96 races of various lengths (one every hour over 3 consecutive days).

The following was observed about the results of the races:

(i) There was no 3-way tie observed in any of the 96 races.

(ii) Two-way ties were observed in some of the races. In case the two way tie was for the first place, the third rat was placed in 2nd position. In case, the two way tie was for the second place these rats were placed in 2nd position.

Further, the following is observed:

(i) R3 never finished first, R1 never finished 2nd and R2 never finished 3rd.

(ii) In 22 rounds, R3 finished ahead of R1.

(iii) The number of rounds in which R2 finished 1st and ahead of R3, is half the number of rounds in which R1 finished 1st and ahead of R2.

At the end of the set of races, the ranks of each of the rats were added and whoever had the lowest total amongst the three rats was declared the winner, the rat with the second lowest total was declared the first runner up and the rat with the third lowest total was declared the second runner up.

10. In how many rounds, two of them finished together?
    (a) 22 (b) 32
    (c) 44 (d) Cannot be determined
11. Who was the first runner up of the competition?
    (a) R1 (b) R2
    (c) R3 (d) R1 or R2
12. If R2 finished ahead of R3 in 62 rounds exactly, then what is the final score of R3?
    (a) 222 (b) 248
    (c) 216 (d) None of these
13. For the above question, what is the total number of rounds that have two rats tied for any of the places?

14. In how many rounds did R1 finish first?
(a) 22 (b) 32
(c) 64 (d) 74

Directions for Questions 15 to 20: *Read the information and answer the questions that follow:*

Six teams, India, Spain, China, Denmark, France and Germany participated in a round robin hockey tournament. Each team played each of the other teams only once. The tournament started on Sunday with 3 matches between the 6 teams. Other days on which matches were held were Tuesday, Thursday, Friday and Saturday. On each day, 3 matches were held with each team participating in exactly one match each day. Each match ended as a win or a loss or a draw. The table below provides information on the results of the matches played by each team. The results for each team are given from left to right in the order in which the team played its matches. W indicates a win, L indicates a loss and D indicates a draw.

Team	Results
India	WDWLD
Spain	LLLWW
China	LWDDD
Denmark	WDDLL
France	LWWDD
Germany	WLLWD

15. Which of the following teams did Denmark play against on Sunday?
(a) Spain
(b) China
(c) France
(d) Cannot be determined exactly.

16. How many matches did Germany lose before it played its match against India?

17. Which of the following is/are result(s) that did not happen in the tournament?
1. India beat Germany on Thursday.
2. Spain lost to China on Tuesday.
3. Germany won against India on Friday.

(a) Only 1 (b) 1 and 3
(c) 1, 2 and 3 (d) Only 3

18. How many teams did not lose any match before they played against India?
(a) 0 (b) 1
(c) 2 (d) 3

19. On which day was the Germany vs France match held?
(a) Sunday (b) Tuesday
(c) Thursday (d) Saturday

20. Which of the following correctly represents the list of teams that Germany beat?
(a) Spain and India
(b) China and India
(c) China and Denmark
(d) Spain and Denmark

Directions for Questions 21 to 25: *Read the information and answer the questions that follow:*

Six teams Chelsea, Manchester United, Barcelona, Real Madrid, Leicester Square and Liverpool participated in La Liga in which each team played against each other team exactly once. The winning team got 2 points while the losing team did not get any points. For a draw, each team got half a point. The total points scored by five teams is given in the below table:

Team	Points
Chelsea	5
Manchester United	6
Barcelona	5
Real Madrid	4
Liverpool	6

21. For how many matches the result cannot be uniquely determined? (TITA)

22. If Liverpool lost against Manchester United and Real Madrid, then what was the result of the match between Manchester United and Chelsea?
(a) Manchester United won.
(b) Chelsea won.
(c) The match was a draw.
(d) Cannot be determined.

23. If Manchester United won against Chelsea and Barcelona, then who won the match between Real Madrid and Liverpool?
(a) Liverpool (b) Drawn match
(c) Real Madrid (d) Cannot be determined

24. If Real Madrid is the only team that won against Barcelona, then the results of how many matches cannot be uniquely determined (TITA)?

25. For the above question what was the result of the Manchester United - Liverpool match?
(a) Manchester United won.
(b) Liverpool won.
(c) The match was a draw.
(d) The result of the match cannot be determined.

Directions for Questions 26 to 30: *Read the information and answer the questions that follow:*

The ATP is a highly competitive tennis circuit comprising of some of the best players in the world. Due to the pandemic in 2020, most of the grand slams had changed their format to include 64 players instead of 128. Also,

High Yield Questions
Scan this QR code to access a video explanation of questions 26-30

in a departure from tradition, each of the players in the tournament were seeded for the Wimbledon Tennis Tournament that year.

64 players, seeded from 1 to 64, took part in Wimbledon. The matches in the tournament are conducted in six knockout rounds- First Round, Second Round, Pre-quarterfinals, Quarterfinals, Semi Finals and Finals. In any match in any round, the winner of the match advances to the next round while the looser gets eliminated from the tournament. Knockout means that the winner of a match advances to the next round and the team losing the match is eliminated from the competition. The loser is eliminated and the winners of the respective matches qualify for the next round. When the last 8 players are left, they play each other in the quarter finals, the last 4 stage is called the semi final and the final is between the last 2 players standing. In the first round there are 64 players, and 32 matches are held between the players such that: Player seeded 1 plays against the player seeded 64 in match 1 of round 1; match 2 of round 1 is played between seed 2 and 63; match 3 between seeds 3 and 62 and so on. In the second round, match 1 is played between the winners of match 1 and match 32 of round 1; match 2 is played between the winners of match 2 and match 31 of round 1; match 3 between the winners of match 3 and match 30 of round 1 and so on. Subsequent rounds are held in the same way.

An upset is said to have taken place, if in any match, in any round a lower seeded player beats a higher seeded player.

26. If the players seeded 6th, 9th, 12th, 23rd, 36th, 49th, 50th, and 62nd entered the quarter finals, then which of the following pairs of players could have played the finals?
(a) Seed 50 and seed 62
(b) Seed 9 and seed 36
(c) Seed 49 and seed 12
(d) Seed 9 and seed 62

27. If seed 2 was the winner of the tournament then who among the following could be the runner up?
(a) Seed 58 (b) Seed 10
(c) Seed 43 (d) Seed 49

28. If seed 47 reached the pre-quarter final round, then with which of the following seeded player could he have played in that round?
(a) Seed 27 (b) Seed 30
(c) Seed 43 (d) Seed 34

29. If each player causes at most one upset, then the lowest seeded player who could have won the tournament is:
(a) Seed 25 (b) Seed 32
(c) Seed 48 (d) Seed 33

30. If there are only four upsets in the tournament, and no player caused more than 3 upsets, then who could have been the lowest seeded player, who won the tournament?

Directions for Questions 31 to 35: *At the Sasta Auction organized by Laxmi Chit Fund, ten people - Avinash, Balram, Chitra, Dinesh, Ekanshi, Fatima, Gurnoor, Himesh, Ishan, Jasmeet - participated, in which exactly eight items - Dhoni's World Cup Bat, Messi's Golden Boot, Federer's Racquet, CSK's Trophy, RCB's Jersey, Kohli's Miniature, Arun Sharma's Book and an Antique Pen - were up for auction. Each of the ten people bid a certain amount for each of the eight items. The amount that each person bid for any object was a positive integral multiple of 5 and no person bid more than ₹ 70 for any item. Each item was sold to the person who bid the highest amount for it. Further, for any item, the highest amount was bid by exactly one person.*

	Bid Submitted by each Person							
	Bat	Boot	Racquet	Trophy	Jersey	Replica	Book	Pen
Avinash		35						
Balram								
Chitra								
Dinesh								
Ekanshi	40							
Fatima								
Gurnoor		70						
Himesh	10	50	25	40	30	15	70	
Ishan								
Jasmeet								

Further, it is also known that:

A. The amount that Balram bid for the eight items taken in that order, were in an Arithmetic Progression and he won the trophy.

B. The bids made by each of Avinash, Dinesh, Gurnoor, Ishan and Jasmeet comprised exactly three distinct numbers, while the bids made by each of Ekanshi and Chitra comprised exactly two distinct numbers.

C. For the Jersey, except for Avinash and one other person, the bids of every other person were of the same amount. Avinash's bid was exactly ₹10 more than that of exactly one other person for the Jersey.

D. Gurnoor, who did not win the Bat , bid less than ₹ 50 for every item except the boot, while for exactly five items, Ekanshi was among the persons who bid the lowest amount.

E. Avinash bid ₹ 20 for at least three items; Chitra bid ₹ 50 for at least five items; Ishan bid ₹ 55 for at least one item.

F. The bid that Jasmeet made for each item was a multiple of 10 and was the average of the bids made by Dinesh and Fatima for that item, while, for at least four items, the bid made by Ishan for that item was more than that made by Chitra.

G. For each item, the amount that Ekanshi bid was the same as that bid by Fatima, while for Jersey, Replica, Book and Pen, the sum of the bids made by Avinash and Ishan was constant.

H. Gurnoor won the auction for two items, everyone else won at most one item in the auction.

31. Who won the Pen?

(a) Dinesh (b) Chitra
(c) Gurnoor (d) Ishan

32. How much was Avinash willing to spend on the Trophy?

(a) Either ₹ 20 or ₹ 35
(b) ₹ 35
(c) ₹ 20
(d) Either ₹ 35 or ₹ 60

33. What is the maximum number of bids above 40 in the list of bids for all people combined?

34. How much was the Bat worth according to Dinesh?

(a) ₹ 20
(b) ₹ 40
(c) Either ₹ 20 or ₹ 40
(d) Either ₹ 30 or ₹ 40

35. How many people outbid Balram for the Racquet?

(a) 1 (b) 2
(c) 3 (d) More than 3

Directions for Questions 36 to 40: During XPL 2023, Five Bookies Akshat, Brij, Charu, Dharam and Eshwar decided to come out of retirement. They decided to bet amongst each other on the final match of the tournament. Each person placed at most one bet with every other person and none of these ended as a draw. The total money won by any person in all the bets he won is called his gain and the total money lost by any person in all the bets that he lost is called his loss. The following information is also known:

A. No two persons won the same number of bets and no two persons lost the same number of bets.

B. The stake of any bet is an integer amount and is neither less than ₹ 8 nor more than ₹ 42.

C. The gain of any person who won at least one bet and the loss of any person who lost at least one bet lies in the range of ₹ 40 and ₹ 80 (both figures included).

D. Eshwar won ₹ 34 against Akshat and Charu bet Dharam ₹ 8 that his team would win the Tournament. The amount that Akshat won was equal to the amount that Dharam lost.

E. The sums of the stakes of all the bets placed by each of Akshat, Brij, Charu, Dharam and Eshwar are 110, 74, 80, 110 and 106 respectively.

F. The number of bets won by Dharam is equal to the number of bets lost by Akshat. The number of bets lost by Charu is more than the number of bets lost by Dharam.

G. For any person, the stakes of any two bets are different.

H. All bets are even numbers

36. Which bookie had the most successful return after retirement in terms of the number of bets?

(a) Akshat (b) Brij
(c) Charu (d) Eshwar

37. How much was the risk taken by Brij against Charu?

38. How much did Akshat lose?

39. How much did Akshat lose to Dharam?

40. Who was definitely supporting the team that won the finals?

Directions for Questions 41 to 45: Exactly 128 players participated in a tennis knockout tournament in which each player was seeded from 1 to 128. The player seeded 1 is referred to as the highest seeded player, while the player seeded 128 is referred to as the lowest seeded player.

The tournament has a unique format such that, in any match in the tournament, if a higher seeded player wins against a lower seeded player, the lower seeded player is eliminated and the higher seeded player goes through to the next round. However, in any match, if a lower seeded player wins against a higher seeded player, the match is played one more time. The winner of this second match goes through to the next round. i.e. if the lower seeded player wins this match he goes through and the higher seeded player is eliminated. Likewise, in this second match, if the higher seeded player wins, he goes through to the next round and the lower seeded player is eliminated. This continues until the winner of the tournament is decided. Also, the outcome of any match for a player of that match is either a win or a loss i.e. there can be no draws.

41. If, in the finals of the tournament, the player seeded 35 and the player seeded 125 played against each other, what is the minimum number of matches in the tournament?

(a) 134 (b) 135
(c) 138 (d) 127

42. If a total of 134 matches were played in the tournament, what is the furthest round to which the player seeded 2 would have progressed?

(a) Second Round
(b) Third round
(c) Fifth round
(d) Winner of the tournament

43. If the player seeded six won the tournament, what is the maximum number of matches in which a lower seeded player won against a higher seeded player?

44. If the winner of the tournament played exactly one match in each round of the tournament, what is the lowest possible seed of this player?

45. If the player seeded 60 won the tournament, what is the minimum number of matches in the tournament?

(a) 133 (b) 134
(c) 135 (d) 131

Directions for Questions 46 to 49: TKR, a cricket team comprising five players, Palash (P), Pallav (P), Shaurya (S), Shashank(S) and Akash (A), participated in the Caribbean Premier League comprising four matches, Match 1 through Match 4.

The following table provides, for each match, the maximum number of runs scored by any player in the team, along with the initials of the player who scored the maximum number of runs, the minimum number of runs scored by any player in the team, along with the initials of the player who scored the minimum number of runs, the median of the number of runs scored by the five players and the average number of runs scored by the five players.

	Match 1	Match 2	Match 3	Match 4
Maximum runs	25(P)	35(A)	28(P)	37(S)
Minimum runs	12(S)	4(S)	3(P)	5(A)
	18	23	10	25.4
	17.4	22	15.4	30

It is also known that:

A. The person who scored the maximum runs in Match 1 and 3 was the same and also the lowest scorer of the first match became the highest scorer in the last match.

B. No one scored the least number of runs in consecutive matches

C. In each of Match 1 and Match 4, exactly two players scored the same number of runs. In all the other matches, no two players scored the same number of runs.

D. The number of runs scored by Shaurya in Match 4 is twice that scored by Shashank in one of the other matches.

E. In an even numbered match, the median runs were less than the average runs.

F. The number of runs scored by Shaurya in Match 1 is twice that scored by Akash in one of the other matches.

G. Pallav, who did not score the highest in any of the matches, scored more than Shashank in only one match, while Palash scored less than Shashank in exactly one match.

H. The total number of runs scored by Shashank in the tournament was ten more than that scored by Shaurya.

46. What is the difference between the second highest number of runs scored by any player of the team and the fourth highest number of runs scored by any player of the team in Match 3?

47. What best can be said about the runs that Palash scored in Match 4?

(a) Exactly 30 (b) Exactly 37
(c) Either 30 or 28 (d) Either 30 or 37

48. Who scored the second highest number of runs in the tournament?

(a) Either Palash or Shashank
(b) Either Pallav or Shashank
(c) Shaurya
(d) Either Palash or Shaurya

49. If the total number of runs scored by exactly one player in the tournament is a multiple of 17, what best can be said about the total number of runs scored by Palash in the tournament?

(a) It is a multiple of 29 but not a multiple of 4.
(b) It is a multiple of 21 but not a multiple of 2.
(c) It is a multiple of 21 but not a multiple of 5.
(d) It is a multiple of 29 but not a multiple of 5.

ANSWER KEY

Level of Difficulty (I)

1. (d)	2. (c)	3. (a)	4. (d)
5. (d)	6. (d)	7. (d)	8. (b)
9. (a)	10. (d)	11. (a)	12. (c)
13. (a)	14. (a)	15. (c)	16. (b)
17. (d)	18. 127	19. Seed 5	
20. Seed 8	21. Seed 12 or 117		22. (d)
23. 2	24. 156000	25. (c)	26. 11
27. 0	28. (d)	29. (a)	30. 4
31. 3	32. 12	33. 1	34. (d)
35. (c)	36. (a)	37. (d)	38. (c)
39. (a)	40. (b)	41. (d)	

Level of Difficulty (II)

1. (b)	2. (b)	3. (a)	4. (a)
5. 23	6. 20	7. 2	8. 18
9. (a)	10. (c)	11. (b)	12. (b)
13. (c)	14. (d)	15. (c)	16. (a)
17. (b)	18. (a)	19. (a)	20. (b)
21. (b)	22. (c)	23. (b)	24. (d)
25. (c)	26. (d)	27. (e)	28. (b)
29. (a)	30. (d)	31. (d)	32. (a)
33. (e)	34. (c)	35. (b)	36. (a)
37. (c)	38. (c)		

Level of Difficulty (III)

1. (b)	2. (d)	3. (a)	4. (c)
5. 195	6. 12	7. 189	8. 183
9. 8	10. (d)	11. (b)	12. (a)
13. 44	14. (d)	15. (c)	16. 1
17. (d)	18. (c)	19. (b)	20. (d)
21. 9	22. (b)	23. (a)	24. 3
25. (d)	26. (d)	27. (d)	28. (d)
29. (d)	30. 16	31. (a)	32. (b)
33. 26	34. (b)	35. (a)	36. (b)
37. 10	38. 70	39. 20	
40. Dharam	41. (c)	42. (d)	43. 240
44. 64	45. (a)	46. 18	47. (a)
48. (b)	49. (d)		

SOLUTIONS AND SHORTCUTS

Level of Difficulty (I)

Solutions for Questions 1 to 4:

It is given that Q, U, W and V reached in semis. Therefore P, R, S and T were eliminated in the group round.

From statement (iii):

	1st	2nd	3rd	4th
Group A	V	U		
Group B	W or Q	Q or W		

From statement (iv) and (i): P and W were not in the same group.

From statement (ii): R and S are in same group.

	1st	2nd	3rd	4th
Group A	V	U	P or T	T or P
Group B	W or Q	Q or W	R or S	S or R

As per the condition 1, each player won different number of matches and each player played exactly two matches against all other players in the same group. Therefore, the following possibilities of number of wins are possible for each player: (6, 4, 2, 0) or (6, 3, 2, 1) or (5, 4, 2, 1) or (5, 4, 3, 0) According to the statement (iv): P and W have same number of wins therefore: Number of wins possible for players group B: (6, 3, 2, 1) & number of wins possible for players of group A: (5, 4, 3, 0).

Again from statement (ii), (iii) and (iv):

	1st	2nd	3rd	4th
Group A	V	U	P	T
Number of wins	5	4	3	0
Group B	Q	W	S	R
Number of wins	6	3	2	1

1. T won least games after 1st round. Option (d) is correct.
2. Option (c) is correct.
3. Q won the most number of games after 1st round. Option (a) is correct.
4. From the statement (iii), V won both of his games against U and from the above table, V won both games against T, therefore, he must lost one game against P. Therefore, option (d) is correct.

Solutions for Questions 5 to 8:

The thought flowchart for this question set would go as follows:

Stage 1: From the first five clues:

Initial possibility	Team	Team name	Match 1 Results	Match 2 Results	Match 3 Results
ABCDEF	1	Not D, Not E, Not C, Not F & Not B Hence, A	Win	Win	Win
ABCDEF	2	D	Lost A	Win C	Win F
ABCDEF	3	E	Lost B	Win C	Win F
ABCDEF	4	—	—		—
ABCDEF	5	Not A, D, B, E Hence, C	Lost D	Lost E	Loss
ABCDEF	6	Not A, D, B, E Hence, F	Lost D	Lost E	Loss

Note: We have to allocate C and F to teams 5 and 6 in any order, as both those:

(a) Once we determine that Team 1 is A, we can eliminate A from the possibility list for team 2 to team 6.

(b) We also know that there would be a total of 9 matches in the first stage (18 entries in the table divided by 2).

Consequently, there would be 9 wins and 9 losses.

Out of the 9 wins A (3 wins) + D (2 wins) + E (2 wins) accounts for 7 wins. Thus, team 4 (Team B) would also win 2 and lose 1.

At this stage, the table would transform to matches (result and opponent).

Team	1	2	3
A	Won D	Won	Won
D	Lost A	Won C	Won F
E	Lost B	Won C	Won F
B	Lost	Won E	Won
C	Lost D	Lost E	Lost
F	Lost D	Lost E	Lost

At this stage, we still need to fix three wins and three losses. Since, two of these wins were for A and A has not won against F, it is natural that A's wins would have been against B and C. Thus, B's win would be against F. The final table would look like:

Team	Match 1 Result	Match 2 Result	Match 3 Result	To play
A	Won D	Won B	Won C	F and E
D	Lost A	Won C	Won F	B and E
E	Lost B	Won C	Won F	A and D
B	Lost A	Won E	Won F	C and D
C	Lost D	Lost E	Lost A	B and F
F	Lost D	Lost E	Lost B	A and C

We are now ready to work out the stage two results.

From the first two clues of the second stage, we know that A loses to E and F. So, C must have lost both its matches and F must have won both its matches.

Team	Stage 1			Stage 2	
	1	2	3	4	5
A	Won D	Won B	Won C	Lost E	Lost F
D	Lost A	Won C	Won F	E ?	B ?
E	Lost B	Won C	Won F	Won A	D ?
B	Lost A	Won E	Won F	Won C	D ?
C	Lost D	Lost E	Lost A	Lost B	Lost F
F	Lost D	Lost E	Lost B	Won A	Won C

To this table, we add the information that one more team lost both matches and get:

	Team	Stage 1			Stage 2	
		1	2	3	4	5
3	A	Won D	Won B	Won C	Lost E	Lost F
2	D	Lost A	Won C	Won F	Lost E	Lost B
4	E	Lost B	Won C	Won F	Won A	Won D
4	B	Lost A	Won E	Won F	Won C	Won D
0	C	Lost D	Lost E	Lost A	Lost B	Lost F
2	F	Lost D	Lost E	Lost B	Won A	Won C

The answers can be now read off from the table:

5. B, E and F. Hence, option (d) is correct.
6. D and F won two matches. Hence, option (d) is correct.
7. B and E with four wins the maximum number of matches. Hence, option (d) is correct.
8. E and F defeated A. Hence, option (b) is correct.

Solutions for Questions 9 to 12:

The first batsman, to get out can be either Sachin or Sehwag. Table 1 states that, the first wicket falls at score 25. As Sachin himself scored 28, which is greater than 25, we can conclude that Sehwag was the first to get out. At that time Sachin must have scored 25 - 7 = 18 runs. Similar analysis leads to the following table:

Fall of wicket	Total score	Runs scored by the batsman to get out (runs scored)	Runs scored by the batsman who is not out/batting	Partnership
1	25	Sehwag (7)	Sachin (18)	25
2	34	Gautam (8)	Sachin (19)	9
3	42	Yuvraj (4)	Sachin (23)	8
4	57	Sachin (28)	Kohli (10)	15
5	62	Dhoni (3)	Kohli (12)	5
6	75	Kohli (20)	Raina (5)	13
7	82	Harbhajan (5)	Raina (7)	7
8	86	Ashwin (0)	Raina(11)	4
9	99	Bhuvi (11)/Raina (18)	Raina (13) / Bhuvi (6)	13
10	110	Raina (18)/Zaheer (6) or Bhuvi (11)/ Zaheer (6)	Zaheer (6)/Raina (18) or Zaheer (6)/ Bhuvi (11)	11

9. Option (a) is the correct answer.
10. Option (d) is the correct answer.
11. The second highest partnership was for the fourth wicket between Sachin and Kohli for 15 runs. Option (a) is the correct answer.

    Percentage contribution of Sachin $\frac{5}{15} \times 100 = 33.33\%$.
    Hence, option (a) is correct.
12. The maximum number of fours that could have been scored between the fall of any two wickets:
    0 to 1st: 5 fours
    1st - 2nd: 2 fours
    2nd - 3rd: 2 fours
    3rd - 4th: 3 fours
    4th - 5th: 0 four
    5th - 6th: 3 fours
    6th - 7th: 1 four
    7th - 8th: 1 four
    8th - 9th: 2 fours
    9th - 10th: 2 fours
    So, in all 21 fours could have been scored. Hence, option (c) is correct.

Solutions for Questions 13 to 17:

In order to win the game, Rajesh who plays first, knows that he would have to force Kanhaiya to pick up the last coin. In order to do so, he needs to force Kanhaiya to leave him with between 2 to 9 coins when Kanhaiya plays his second last move. This is because, if Rajesh gets any number of coins between 2 to 9, he would have the option of picking up between 1 to 8 coins to leave 1 coin for Kanhaiya to pick up in his last move. However, Kanhaiya also knows this and he would not leave between 2 to 9 coins for Rajesh, unless he is forced to do so. To force Kanhaiya, Rajesh would need to leave 10 coins and so on. This can be tabulated as follows:

Move By	Kanhaiya	Rajesh	Kanhaiya	Rajesh	Kanhaiya	Rajesh	Kanhaiya
Coins left before the move	28	20 to 27	19	11 to 18	10	2 to 9	1
Coins Picked up	1 to 8	1 to 8	1 to 8	1 to 8	1 to 8	1 to 8	1
Coins left after the move	27 to 20	19	18 to 11	10	9 to 2	1	0

As you can see from this table, the winning points for Rajesh would be achieved whenever he leaves 1 or 10 or 19 or 28 or 37 or 9n + 1 coins. Once he reaches a 9n + 1 number after his move, Rajesh would always win.

13. From 88 coins, the nearest 9n + 1 point is 82. Hence, he should pick up 6 coins to leave 82 coins on the table and win the game. Option (a) is correct.
14. In this case, since Rajesh wins the game, it means that he must be hitting the 9n + 1 number with his first move of 6 coins. After that he would pick up coins in such a way that once Kanhaiya picks up his coins, he would make sure that he leaves 9n + 1 coins on the table. In order to do this, the net sum of any pair of moves by Rajesh and Kanhaiya should be 9. So, if Rajesh has picked up 5, 5 and 6 in his second to fourth moves, it means that Kanhaiya must have picked up 4, 4 and 3 coins in his first three moves. Thus, Kanhaiya must have picked 3 coins in his third move. Option (a) is correct.
15. Twelve moves means that Kanhaiya and Rajesh both completed 6 moves each. The maximisation of the number of coins on the table to start with - would occur if Rajesh picks up 8 coins in his first move to get to 9n + 1. In the next set of 5 moves each for Rajesh and Kanhaiya they would pick up a total of 9 × 5 = 45 coins. In the last move, Kanhaiya should pick up the remaining 1 coin. Thus, the total coins picked up would be: 45 + 8 + 1 = 54. This would represent the maximum number of coins on the table. Option (c) is correct.
16. When the question's logic moves to last person picking a coin, wins the game, it means that the objective of Rajesh becomes to get to 0 coin, instead of 1. The winning point and the winning cycle would shift from 9n + 1 to 9n. Hence, if the starting number of coins is a multiple of 9, the person starting this game cannot win. Between 11 and 55, there are 5 multiples of 9 (viz: 18, 27, 36, 45 and 54). Rajesh would not be able to win any of the games starting with N, having any of these values. Hence, option (b) is correct.
17. The only winning point in this game would be the only 9n value between 88 and 98 - i.e., 90. If Rajesh has picked 6 coins, there must have been 96 coins on the table. Hence, the correct answer would be option (d).

Solutions for Questions 18 to 21:

18. As we have seen in the theory of this chapter, the number of matches played in a knock out tournament with n players would always be (n - 1). Hence, the number of matches played in this tournament would be 127.
19. Seed number 37, would play 92 in round 1 (the sum of the pairs seedings for the first round opponents should be 129). Likewise, in the second round he would play seed 28 and win against him to reach the third round.

Note: This is because in round 2, the sum of the seeding of the opponents needs to be 64 + 1 = 65.

In round three, the originally expected match for seed 28 would be against seed 5 (since the sum of seeding in round 3 would be 32 + 1 = 33). However, seed 28 has lost to seed 37 in round 2. Hence, seed 37 would play seed 5 in round 3.

Note: Seed 5 would reach round 3, because there are no other upsets in the tournament.

20. You can think of this as follows: If there is only 1 upset, the lowest seed to win the tournament would be seed number 2. This would occur either by seed number 2, winning the final against seed number 1 or alternately seed number 1, losing his match somewhere down the line in the only upset of the tournament and then, seed 2 beats everyone else who comes in his path. Likewise, if there are only two upsets in the tournament, then the lowest seeded player who could win would be seed 4 - one of the ways this could happen would be: Seeds 1 to 4 reach the semi final, where 1 plays 4 and 2 plays 3. Seed 1 loses to 4 (and this would be first upset of the tournament). Seed 4 then moves into the final and beats seed 2, which is the second upset of the tournament. Of course, this could also occur if seed 1 loses earlier and then seed 4 faces seed 2 in the final and beats him. In the same way, if there were 3 upsets in the tournament, the lowest seed who could win would be seed number 8. If there were only four upsets in the tournament then the lowest seed would be seed number 16 and so on. Since there are only 3 upsets, the lowest seed winning the tournament would be Seed 8.
21. 76 plays 53 in the first round. If 76 reached the second round, he would be replacing 53 in that round. 53 would be supposed to play 12 in the second round. However, whether 12 reaches the second round depends on the result of 12 versus 117 in round 1. Thus, in round 2, 76 could play either 12 or 117.

Solutions for Questions 22 to 25:

As per the information given in the question, you get 100% of profit if the team wins and only 20% of the profit for finishing second. If your team finishes third or fourth, you win nothing.

It might be a good idea to make a table of 'Returns' to solve the questions conveniently.

Team →	Ferrari	McLaren	Suzuki	Nippon
Return if team comes first	100000	104000	160000	120000

Team →	Ferrari	McLaren	Suzuki	Nippon
Return if team comes second	52000	52800	64000	56000
Return if team comes third	0	0	0	0
Return if team comes fourth	0	0	0	0

The answers can be interpreted off the table above.

22. A return of 184000 is possible only through the addition of 120000 + 64000. Hence, Nippon must have finished first. Option (d) is correct.
23. For a return of 176000 on Nippon, Nippon has to finish first once and second once. Thus, the correct answer is 2.
24. For 172000, Nippon finishes first and Ferrari second, for 216000, Suzuki finished first and Nippon second; for 152800, Ferrari finished first and McLaren second. In the fourth race McLaren would finish first necessarily. Minimum return would happen if Ferrari finishes second. The value of the minimum return would be 104000 + 52000 = 156000. Thus, the correct answer is 156000.
25. From the previous question's explanation, we know that Suzuki hasn't finished second yet. Hence, option (c) is correct.

Solutions for Questions 26 to 29:

26. From the given information about a 7 team league, we can make out that there are a total of 21 matches played. Some of these results are directly given to us and we can tabulate a results table for the same. Based on this table, we realise that we already know the results of 7 matches and do not know the results of 14 matches.

Team	A	B	C	D	E	F	G
A	-------	Draw		Draw	Draw		
B	Draw	-------			Win		
C			-------		Win		
D	Draw			-------	Loss		
E	Draw	Loss	Loss	Win	-------	Win	
F					Loss	-------	
G							-------

If the match between B and D was a draw, it would mean that B would win against C, F and G. We would not be able to know the exact results of any other match. Hence, a total of 11 matches would be known and 10 would be unknown.

27. Team A can score anywhere between 3 to 9 points, while Team E can score anywhere between 7 to 10 point. A possible scenario for equality of points could be: A wins against C and draws against F and G to get to 8 points, while E draws against G, giving E also 8 points in total. Hence, the correct answer is 0.
28. From the solution to the first question of the set, we realise that the match in question is one of the ten matches, we do not know the results of. Hence, Option (d) is correct.
29. At the basic situation of the question, we know that A is at 3 points + 3 unknowns; B is at 14 points; C is at 3 points and 5 unknowns; D is at 1 point and 4 unknowns; E is at 7 points + 1 unknown match; F is at 0 and G is at 0 points. Also, since each team has at least 1 win, it means that each of F and G will have minimum 3 points, while D has at least 4 points. Also, A will get minimum 6 points, since it wins at least 1 match.

To this situation, if we add the information contained in this question, we can make out that F has 15 points, while G has only 3 points. Also, C will win against G, so C will also have a minimum of 6 points. Thus, G has the least points in the tournament. Option (a) is correct.

Solutions for Questions 30 to 33:

30. If there are 2 upsets in the tournament, any of players 1 to 4 can win the tournament. A particular way in which seed 4 wins the tournament, would be if the semi-finals are held between 1 vs 4 and 2 vs 3. 4 beats 1 in the first upset of the tournament. Then in the final, 4 beats 2 and wins. For any player ranked 5 or lower, there would be a minimum requirement of 3 upsets for the player to win. Hence, the correct answer is 4.
31. After round 1, only the odd seeds will be left in the tournament. Round 2 pairings will be 1 vs 17; 31 vs 15; 3 vs 19; 29 vs 13; 5 vs 21; 27 vs 11; 7 vs 23 and 25 vs 9. The winners will be 1, 31, 3, 29, 5, 27, 7 and 25. The quarter finals will be 1 vs 25; 31 vs 7; 3 vs 27 and 29 vs 25. The correct answer is 3.
32. For the lowest possible ranked team to win the tournament with 11 upsets in 1st round, we consider that the 11 upsets are with the top 11 seeds, i.e. seed numbers 1 to 11 will all lose. Hence, without any further upset, the player with rank 12 will win the tournament.
33. It could so happen that seed 1 is not one of the seeds who gets upset in the first round. Also, if there are no more upsets, then seed 1 will win the tournament. Hence, the correct answer is 1.

Solutions for Questions 34 to 38:

The data in the question can be encapsulated in the following table:

INDIA	AUSTRALIA	FRANCE
VA (4,3)	RL?	CP (2,1)
RK (3,2)	RE (1,1)	GM (2,0)

INDIA	AUSTRALIA	FRANCE
LP (3,2)	PC?	YN?
MB (2,1)	MW (2,1)	JWT (1,0)

Deductions from India's players:

VA played in 4 matches, hence, he must have played 2 singles matches in each of the rounds. Also, he won 3 out of them.

RK and LP played 3 matches each, while MB played 2 matches. This means, that one of RK or LP played two singles matches in the quarter finals and the doubles match in the semi-finals, while the other played the doubles match in the quarter finals and two singles matches in the semi-finals. MB must have played the two doubles matches, one with RK and another with LP in any order, depending on how we allocate LP and RK's singles and doubles matches.

Deductions from Australia's players (Australia was India's opponent in the quarter final):

MW, must have played 2 singles (won one of them and lost the other). One of RL or PC must have played the other two singles matches, while RE must have played doubles, with the other one. This leads to two broad cases for the India vs Australia quarter finals:

Case 1: Singles Matches: VA vs MW; RK vs (RL/PC); VA vs (RL/PC); RK vs MW.

Doubles match: (MB + LP) vs (RE + PC/RL)

Case 2: Singles Matches: VA vs MW; LP vs (RL/PC); VA vs (RL/PC); LP vs MW.

Doubles match: (MB + RK) vs (RE + PC/RL)

Deductions about France's players:

Cedric Pioline played 2 matches, hence, he must have been one of France's singles player. Also, he won one match, and since France lost 4-1, which means that Cedric Pioline won one of his singles matches. The other singles player for France has to be Gael Monfils (losing both his matches). Also, the doubles team of France must have been Jo-Wilfred Tsonga and Yannick Noah, and France must have lost it's doubles match against India.

Deductions around Wins and losses:

India lost one doubles and 1 singles match against Australia in the quarter finals, while they lost one singles match in the semi finals against France. So, the player who played doubles for India in the quarter finals (either LP or RK), must have lost his match in the doubles match. Hence, that player would have won both his singles matches in the semi finals. Thus, Vijay Amritraj must have lost one of his singles matches in the semi finals. That loss must have been against Cedric Pioline.

Amongst LP and RK, the player who played the singles in the quarter finals and the doubles in the semi finals, must have lost one of their singles matches in the quarter finals. This loss must have been against MW.

The answers can be read off from the above deductions:

34. Option (d) is correct.
35. Rod Laver must have played either in 1 or 2 matches. Option (c) is correct.
36. Option (a) is correct.
37. Option (d) is correct.
38. We are asked to identify what is not definitely true. This means, we are looking for what is definitely false or probably true. Testing the statements individually against our deductions, we can see that statement (1) is definitely true, while statement (2) is definitely false and statement (3) is probably true. Hence, the correct answer is option (c).

Solutions for Questions 39 to 41:

	Base Amount (after Player picks his card)	Top card characteristic	Resultant	Ghosh Babu's Total for the round	Ghosh Babu's net total for all rounds combined
Round 1	8	Same suit	Ghosh babu pays ₹ 16 to the dealer	–8	–8
Round 2	10	Opposite color	Dealer pays ₹ 10 more to Ghosh Babu	+20	+12
Round 3	6	Same color	Ghosh Babu pays ₹ 6 to the dealer	0	+12
Round 4	8	Same Suit	Ghosh babu pays the dealer ₹ 16	–8	+4

From the table we can answer the questions which follow.

39. His maximum gain is ₹ 12 after the second as well as the third round.
40. Since, he is not borrowing any money he should be able to cover his maximum loss which is ₹ 8 after the end of the first round. Thus, he should have had at least ₹ 8 at the beginning of the game sessions.
41. Since, Ghosh Babu ends with a profit of ₹ 4 after his 4 rounds of game sessions, he must have had ₹ 96 initially.

Level of Difficulty (II)

Solutions for Questions 1 to 4:

For Sri Lanka, RRa is maximum if s = 15, RRa (max) = $\left(\frac{473}{243+90}\right) = 1.46$

RRa is minimum if s = 20, RRb(min) = $\frac{473}{243+120} = 1.34$

Similarly, we can find the minimum and the maximum values of RRa, RRb and RR for other teams as well.

The values can be tabulated as follows:

Teams	Wins	Loses	RRa		RRb		RR	
			Min	Max	Min	Max	Min	Max
Sri Lanka	2	1	1.34	1.46	1.37	1.50	–0.16	+0.09
India	2	1	1.59	1.74	1.30	1.42	+0.17	+0.44
Bangladesh	0	3	1.37	1.51	1.47	1.61	–0.24	+0.04
Pakistan	2	1	1.27	1.39	1.44	1.58	–0.31	–0.05

1. Bangladesh cannot qualify as it lost all of its matches. Option (b) is correct.
2. Only India always has a positive run rate. Option (b) is correct.
3. India will definitely qualify because of its minimum run rate is higher than that of the maximum run rate of Sri Lanka and Pakistan (as Bangladesh cannot qualify for the finals).
   For p = 15 and s = 20, then:
   RR for Sri Lanka = 1.34 – 1.5 = –0.16
   RR for Pakistan= 1.39 – 1.44 = –0.05
   Hence, Pakistan will qualify for the final. Option (a) is correct.
4. If p = q = r = s = 15, then:
   RR for Sri Lanka = 1.46 – 1.5 = –0.04
   RR for India = 1.74 – 1.42 = 0.32
   RR for Pakistan = 1.39 – 1.58 = –0.19
   Hence, Sri Lanka will be at 2nd place at the end of the initial stage. Option (a) is correct.

Solutions for Questions 5 to 8:

The total points given by the selectors A, B, C, D and E is 25, 20, 30, 20 and 20 respectively. Selectors awarded distinct point to the candidates. The range of the possible points earned by the five players is given in the following table.

SELECTOR	SACHIN	MOHIT	RAHUL	SAURAV	AARAV
A	9	6	5	1 or 2 or 3 or 4	1 or 2 or 3 or 4
B	4	0 or 2	0 or 2	8	6
C	1 or 2 or 4 or 5	11	1 or 2 or 4 or 5	6	7
D	7	0 or 3	0 or 3	8	2
E	3	5	8	0 or 4	0 or 4

5. Minimum possible points earned by Saurav = 1 + 8 + 6 + 8 + 0 = 23.
6. According to the question: Selector B and D gave the same points to Mohit.
   This case is possible only if both the selectors gave 0 points to Mohit because, if Mohit got 1 point from the selector B, then Rahul will also get 1 point from the selector B and this is not possible.
   Given that, Sachin got 4 points from selector C, which means that Rahul got 6 – 4 = 2 points from selector C.
   The total points earned by Rahul = 5 + 2 + 2 + 3 + 8 = 20.
7. The range of the total points earned by all the five players is given below.
   Sachin: 24 – 28
   Mohit: 22 – 27
   Rahul: 14 – 23
   Saurav: 23 – 30
   Aarav: 16 – 23
   Therefore, both Rahul and Aarav will definitely not earn more points than Saurav. Hence, the required answer is 2.
8. Mohit's score would be maximum when B gives him 2 and D gives him 3 points respectively. In this case Both B and D would give 0 points to Rahul. To maximize Rahul's points, C gives him 5 points and in this case, his maximum possible points = 5 + 0 + 5 + 0 + 8 = 18.

Solutions for Questions 9 to 13:

9. Runs scored by A would be maximum when runs scored by A in matches 1 and 3 was maximum possible.
Maximum possible runs scored by A in **match-1** = 27
Maximum possible runs scored by A in **match-3** = 19
Maximum possible runs scored by A = 27 + 100 + 19 + 53 = 199.
Hence, option (a) is correct.

10. Maximum possible runs scored by E in **match-2** = 30
Maximum possible runs scored by E in **match-4** = 20
Maximum possible runs scored by E in four matches = 60 + 30 + 78 + 20 = 188.

$$\text{Required percentage} = \frac{188}{270+300+240+200}\times 100\%$$

$$= \frac{188}{1010}\times 100 = 18.6\%.$$

Hence, option (c) is correct.

11. Individual ranges for total score:
$A \rightarrow$ 189–199
$B \rightarrow$ 218–224
$C \rightarrow$ 182–187
$D \rightarrow$ 223
$E \rightarrow$ 187–188
The absolute difference between the total runs scored by A and C in the four matches is minimum if C scored 187 runs and A scored 189 runs.
Required sum = 187 + 189 = 376.
Hence, option (b) is correct.

12. If the absolute difference between the total runs scored by A and C in the four matches is minimum then runs scored by A = 189. This is possible when A scored 23 runs in the first match and 13 runs in the 3rd match. Runs scored by C = 187. This is possible when C scored 27 runs in the first match and 30 runs in the 2nd match and 20 runs in the 4th match.

Player	Match 1	Match 2	Match 3	Match 4	Total runs scored
A	23	100	13	53	189
B	88	65	19	52	224
C	27	30	110	20	187
D	72	75	20	56	
E	60	30	78	19	187
Total	270	300	240	200	

Absolute difference = 224 – 187 = 37.
Hence, option (b) is correct.

13. Individual ranges for total score:
$A \rightarrow$ 189–199 (3rd rank)
$B \rightarrow$ 218–224
$C \rightarrow$ 182–187 (5th rank)
$D \rightarrow$ 223
$E \rightarrow$ 187–188 (4th rank)
It is not possible to determine the exact rank of B and D. Hence, option (c) is correct.

Solutions for Questions 14 to 18:

From the first condition:
Every horse was bet upon correctly by at least 1 person:

Deduction 1:

We can deduce that each of the seven positions must be occupied by horses which have been bet upon for that position. Thus, the following table of possibilities emerges:

Position	Possibilities
1	H1/H5/H6/H7
2	H2/H3/H6/H7
3	H1/H3/H4/H7
4	H1/H3/H4/H6
5	H1/H2/H3/H4/H5/H7
6	H2/H4/H5/H6
7	H2/H5H7

From the second and third conditions:

(2) No two persons had the same number of correct bets.
(3) No person got all seven bets correct.

Deduction 2:

We should be able to realize that the maximum number of correct bets that any person would have got would be 5. (since no one has 7 correct bets, nobody can have 6 correct bets too- as anyone who gets 6 correct would automatically get the seventh bet correct too).

Deduction 3:

Also, since each person has to get a different number of ets correct the only way to do so with 5 bets maximum is if the number of correct bets are distributed as 0, 1, 2, 3, 4 and 5.

This also means that there would be a total of 15 correct bets in the given table and 27 incorrect bets.

With this information, we can look for how many bets would be correct for each of the horses in each position in the possibility table above:

Position	Possibilities	Minimum- Maximum correct bets
1	H1(1)/H5(2)/H6(2)/H7 (1)	1-2
2	H2(2)/H3(1)/H6(2)/H7(1)	1-2
3	H1(1)/H3(3)/H4(1)/H7(1)	1-3
4	H1(3)/H3(1)/H4(1)/H6(1)	1-3
5	H1(1)/H2(1)/H3(1)/H4(1)/ H5(1)/H7(1)	1-1
6	H2(1)/H4(3)/H5(1)/H6(1)	1-3
7	H2(2)/H5(2)/H7(2)	2-2
	Total Number of Correct Bets	8(minimum)-16 (maximum)

- We, thus, realise that for every position, if we were to assume the maximum number of correct bets, we would get a total of 16 correct bets. But, we already know that there have to be exactly 15 correct bets.
- We also notice that in the three places viz., 3rd, 4th and 6th places, if the horse which had three bets on it for that position, had not finished in that specific position, then the maximum number of correct bets in the table would drop by 2 to 14, which is not possible.

This logic can be explained better through an example: For instance, for the third position, if H3 were not to finish in that position then the third position would go to H1, H4 or H7. In each case, the number of correct bets for that position would be 1 instead of 3. This would result in the maximum number of correct bets being only 14. But, as we already know that that is not possible, since we definitely need 15 correct bets in the table. Thus, we can conclude that:

(i) H3 would have finished in the 3rd position.
(ii) H1 would have finished in the 4th position.
(iii) H4 would have finished in the 6th position.

- Armed with this conclusion, we could move forward to the table and make the possible deletions from the table to get a new refreshed table as below:

Position	A	B	C	D	E	F	Possibility table	Number of correct bets possible
1		H7	H5	H6	H5	H6	H5(2)/H6(2)/H7(1)	1 or 2
2	H2		H6	H2	H6	H7	H2(2)/H6(2)/H7(1)	1 or 2
3	H3			H3	H3		H3(3)	3
4			H1	H1	H1		H1(3)	3
5	H5			H7	H2		H2(1)/H5(1)/H7(1)	1
6			H4	H4	H4		H4(3)	3
7	H7	H5	H2	H5	H7	H2	H2(2)/H5(2)/H7(2)	2

An analysis of this table at this point of time clearly gives us that there are only two ways of going from 16 correct bets to 15- i.e., if we go from 2 correct bets to 1 in either the first or the second position (notice that there is no slack in terms of the number of bets for any other position).

Also, notice that the only way to go to 1 correct bet in either the first or the second position is by using H7 in either place. Hence, H7 must be used in either the first or the second position, which in turn means that H7 as a possibility in the 5th or the 7th position does not exist.

Thus, H2 and H5 must be shared between the 5th and 7th place.

This also means that both H2 and H5 would disappear from the first and second places. The above table would evolve to the following table.

Also, from this point we need to reconsider the question from a different angle, i.e., the number of correct bets that each person had:

Position	A	B	C	D	E	F	Possibility table	Number of correct bets possible
1		H7		H6		H6	H6(2)/H7(1)	1 or 2
2			H6		H6	H7	H6(2)/H7(1)	1 or 2

Position	A	B	C	D	E	F	Possibility table	Number of correct bets possible
3	H3			H3	H3		H3(3)	3
4			H1	H1	H1		H1(3)	3
5	H5				H2		H2(1)/H5(1)	1
6			H4	H4	H4		H4(3)	3
7		H5	H2	H5		H2	H2(2)/H5(2)	2
Definite corrects	1	0	1	3	3	0		
Non evaluated bets	1	2	3	2	2	3		
Range of possibilities	1 to 2	0 to 2	1 to 4	3 to 5	3 to 5	0 to 3		

Note: In the above table, the range of possibilities shows the minimum number of bets that must be correct to the maximum possible number of bets that could be correct. So, the interpretation is that for the person B the number of bets that are definitely correct at this point of time are 0 and the maximum possible number of corrects is 2.

We are now in a position where we need to fix the numbers 0 to 5 (for the number of correct bets) between A to F.

It can be easily seen at this point that 0 correct bets could go to either B or F.

This creates a dual possibility situation for us:

Try to put in B as the person with 0 correct bets and you would get the following table:

Position	A	B	C	D	E	F	Horses which finished in this position
1				H6		H6	H6
2						H7	H7
3	H3			H3	H3		H3
4			H1	H1	H1		H1
5	H5						H5
6			H4	H4	H4		H4
7			H2			H2	H2
Definite corrects	2	0	3	4	3	3	

It can be clearly seen that B as 0 correct bets does not satisfy the condition of everybody, having different number of correct bets.

Hence, we need to move to the other possibility, i.e., F is the person with 0 correct bets.

Position	A	B	C	D	E	F	Horses which finished in this position
1		H7					H7
2			H6		H6		H6
3	H3			H3	H3		H3
4			H1	H1	H1		H1
5					H2		H2
6			H4	H4	H4		H4
7		H5		H5			H5
Definite corrects	1	2	3	4	5	0	

This is the actual truth table showing the correct bets, since we have got a different number of correct bets for each of the six persons.

Hence, the answers are:

14. Option (d) is correct.
15. Option (c) is correct.
16. Option (a) is correct.
17. Option (b) is correct.
18. Option (a) is correct.

Solutions for Questions 19 to 22:

Construct the following table:

	Game 1	Game 2	Game 3
K	28	51	
V	130		
Y	40		87
R		49	55
S		75	50

	Game 1	Game 2	Game 3
Total	220	250	240
Other scores	22	75	48
Score range for remaining batsmen	(0-22)	(0-48)	(0-48)

Based on the table above, the answers can be formulated as under:

19. The R -index ranges will be the following:
    K - 23 to 51.
    V - 82 to 130.
    Y - 39 to 87.
    R - 33 to 55.
    S - 53 to 75.
    Based on this, the least R - index will be for least K, R or Y. Hence, option (a) is correct.
20. Yuvraj has scored a minimum of 127 runs. (we need to see the extreme case since, we are looking for an extreme condition.)
    Rahul is the only batsman who must have scored less than Yuvraj. Virender, Saurav, Kaif could have scored lower equal or higher than Yuvraj. Hence, option (b) is correct.
21. Saurav with an M - index of 50 will have the highest M - index in the tournament. Hence, option (b) is correct.
22. It is possible only for Rahul and Saurav. Hence, option (c) is correct.

Solutions for Questions 23 to 26:

The table of matches in the first two rounds will look like:

Round 1:

Germany beat Spain 1-0.
Argentina beat New Zealand 1-0.
Pakistan beat South Africa 2-0.

Round 2:

Germany beat SA 2-1.
Spain beat New Zealand 5-1.
Argentina beat Pakistan 1-0.

Round 3:

Germany drew with Argentina.
Spain drew with Pakistan.
New Zealand drew with South Africa.

23. Argentina beat Pakistan 1-0 is true. Hence, option (b) is correct.
24. Germany beat SA 2-1 is true. Hence, option (d) is correct.
25. Spain will finish on top after 5 rounds. Hence, option (c) is correct.
26. This cannot happen, since at least Spain and Germany will have a higher goal difference than Pakistan. Besides, all the teams except South Africa and New Zealand will score 10 points. Hence, option (d) is correct.

Solutions for Questions 27 to 29:

From the numbers in the table the following set of deductions can be made:

Deduction string 1: Team A won matches against teams E and F, since E and F are the only teams who have lost matches. Further, team A must have won it's match against team E by 2-1 or 3-1, since it is clear from the goals conceded column, that team A conceded 1 goal in it's two matches, while at the same time, team F has not scored a goal. Thus, team A has two possibilities for it's two matches against E and F: possibility 1: won 2-1 against E, won 3-0 against F; possibility 2: won 3-1 against E and won 2-0 against F.

Deduction string 2: Based on these possibilities if we look at team B's results, we realize that possibility 2 is not possible, since if team A won 2-0 against F, and since F has conceded 7 goals and scored none, team B should have won 5-0 against F. But, if team B wins 5-0, then it would have to lose it's second match 0-1 to match the numbers in its goals scored and goals conceded columns. This is not possible. Hence, we come up with the following conclusions:

Deduction string 3: Team A wins 2-1 against E, wins 3-0 against F, while team B wins 4-0 against F and draws 1-1 against D.

Deduction string 4: Team C must win it's game 2-0 against E and draw 0-0 against team D. At this point, we realize that we know the results of all the six matches played.

The answers can be read off from the information derived through the three deductions above:

27. Only option (e) is correct, since the matches between C and D & B and D have been played and each of the first 4 options contains one of these matches as a not played yet match. For option (e), we can see that A-B and E-F, both these matches haven't happened. Hence, option (e) is correct.
28. We can see from the results that we have derived, that option (b) is the correct answer.
29. Team A cannot beat team F by 4-0. Hence, option (a) is the correct answer.

Solutions for Questions 30 to 33:

The first thing you should do (once you look through the questions 30 and 31) is to make a table for the away matches based on the overall performance of each team and its home performance.

The following table gets formed:

TEAM	M	W	D	GF	GA	GD	Points	Rank
CH	1	1	0	2	0	2	3	3+
SW	1	1	0	5	0	5	3	2
WB	1	0	1	1	1	0	1	8+
MC	1	0	1	2	2	0	1	7+
MU	2	1	0	3	3	0	3	5+
WH	1	0	0	0	3	–3	0	10+
EV	2	1	0	3	3	0	3	4+
AS	2	1	1	2	0	2	4	1
WG	Data not available							
NC	1	0	0	0	2	–2	0	9+
FU	2	0	0	2	6	–4	0	11+
ST	2	0	2	3	3	0	2	6+
SU	Data not available							

Looking at the information in both the tables, we can synthesise the above information for the away matches for some of the top teams. Of course, there would be other teams who could have more than 0 point in Away matches, but most of these cannot have more than 2 points in Away matches (except WG) because, there are only 12 teams in table 1 which have 3 or more points overall. (A team cannot have 3 points in Away matches if it does not have 3 points overall in the tournament).

The case for WG is a little bit different. WG must have won its match in an Away tie, because WG is not in the top 13 in home matches. Thus, for WG, of its three matches the win must have definitely occurred in an Away match, the draw and loss could happen in either an Away or a home tie. In case, WG has 1 win and 1 draw in Away ties, it would have 4 points is its Away matches. However, that would place it at a possible best position of 3rd in the table above, since WG cannot be placed above SW since the maximum possible positive Goal Difference for WG would be 4. Thus, for the teams ranked 3rd onwards in the table above (team CH and all teams ranked below it), there might be a possibility of a shifting down of their ranks - which is why we have mentioned CH's rank in away matches as 3+ and not 3.

30. We can conclude that the team SW definitely ranks second. Option (d) is correct.
31. There are at least 5 teams that have scored 0 or 1 point (as can be seen from the above table). These are WB, MC, WH, NC and FU. There can, of course, be more than these 5, but these five are definite. Hence, option (d) is correct.
32. Clearly, AS has the maximum value of *'pos'* as its *'pos'* value is 12 - 1 = 11. Option (a) is correct.
33. There are six distinct values for the Goal Difference in Away matches. This can be seen in the table above. These are 0, 2, 5, –2, –3 and –4. Also, these Goal Differences account for 11 of the 20 teams in the tournament. Of the remaining 9 teams, by default, any team can have any value for the Goal Difference and if all these teams have a different value for their Goal Difference, it pegs the maximum value as 15 different values for the Goal Difference.

However, if we take a closer look at SU, we see that SU has played 2 drawn matches. Its Goal Difference is 0 and it has scored 2 goals. Hence, it must have conceded two goals. This leads to two scenarios: Scenario 1: SU drew one match 2-2 and one match 0-0.

Scenario 2: SU drew both its matches 1-1.

In both scenarios, SU cannot have played both its matches at home - since SU is not in the top 13 teams on a Home basis. Thus, it must have played at least one of its matches away and the result of this match would necessarily be a draw. Hence, SU's Goal Difference in Away matches cannot be anything but 0. This means that the number of possible distinct values of Goal Difference that can be possible is at least 6 and at most 14. i.e. ≥ 6 and ≤ 14. Option (e) is the correct answer.

Solutions for Questions 34 to 38:

34. The number of matches would be $8C_2$ (group 1) + $8C_2$ (group 2) + 4 (quarter finals) + 2 (semi finals) + 1 (final) = 63
35. Given that there are 8 teams in a group and a total of 28 matches. Since every match has a winner, it follows that there would be 28 wins and 28 losses in the group stage. Further 4 teams advance from every group—even if a team wins 5 matches it can still be eliminated, as it is possible that 5 teams win 5 matches each and a team winning 5 matches cannot be sure of advancement. However, if a team wins 6 of it's matches in the first round, it is not possible for more than 4 teams in the group to win 6 matches; and hence the team would be assured of advancement.
36. For this question we are looking for the highest number of wins for a team to get definitely eliminated in the tournament. It is possible for a team to advance even if it has only 2 wins. The scenario that would lead to this would be– 7 wins for 1 team, 6 wins for 2nd team, 5 wins for third team and 2 wins each for each of the other 5 teams. In such a case, a team with even 2 wins can move to the second round. Thus, the highest number of wins for definite elimination is 1.

37. The quarter finals, the semi finals and finals would be the three rounds in the second stage of the tournament.
38. Option (a) can be eliminated, as it is not necessary that the winner would have more wins than all other teams in the tournament. For example, as seen above, a team with 2 wins in the group stage + 3 wins in the second stage of the tournament would have a total of 5 wins in the tournament (and would also be the winner of the tournament). On the other hand, a team with 7 wins in the first stage could be eliminated in the first round of the second stage and would not be the winner of the tournament.

    Option (b) is also eliminated because it might be possible that in one group a team with just two wins qualifies (wins are distributed as 7, 6, 5, 2, 2, 2, 2, 2) while in the other group wins are distributed as 5, 5, 5, 5, 5, 1, 1, 1—and a team with 5 wins does not qualify.

    Option (c) is correct in the scenario—a team with 2 wins in the group stage ends up winning the tournament (so a total of 5 wins for this team), while a team in the other group gets eliminated with 5 wins in the first stage.

    Option (d) is also eliminated as the number of teams with exactly 1 win in the second stage would be the 2 losing semi finalists.

Level of Difficulty (III)

Solutions for Questions 1 to 4:

Based on the deductions about points scored by each team, we can make the following deductions:

Group Napolean					Group Ashoka				
Team Name	**Won**	**Loss**	**Draw**	**Points**	**Team Name**	**Won**	**Loss**	**Draw**	**Points**
Argentina	3	1	1	10	Finland	2	3	0	6
Bangladesh	1	2	2	5	Germany	2	2	1	7
China	3	2	0	9	Hungary	2	1	2	8
Denmark	4	1	0	12	India	2	3	0	6
England	1	4	0	3	Japan	2	3	0	6

Also, a results table can be drawn as shown (note: In the table, we can see that Argentina beat Finland and Finland would have lost to Argentina and so on):

Team	Vs Finland	Vs Germany	Vs Hungary	Vs India	Vs Japan
Argentina	Won	Won	Drawn	Won	Lost
Bangladesh	Won/Lost	Draw	Draw	Lost	Lost/Won
China	Won	Lost	Lost	Won	Won
Denmark	Lost	Won	Won	Won	Won
England	Lost/Won	Lost	Lost	Lost	Won/Lost

The answers can be read off the two tables:
1. Option (b) is correct.
2. Option (d) is correct.
3. Option (a) is correct.
4. Option (c) is correct.

Solutions for Questions 5 to 9:

5. The minimum matches won by any brother is 60 at Taluka level, 50 at province level and 70 at kingdom level. Bheem will get the maximum wins, if he gets seed 1, seed 2 and seed 3 amongst the brothers in the three levels of tournaments. Also, for each case he needs to win the maximum possible number of matches. If we assume, he was seed 1 at Taluka level, his maximum matches won would be 60 + 6 = 66; seed 2 at Province level, his maximum possible number of matches would be 50 + 5 = 55 (since seed 1 would be at 56); seed 3 at kingdom level, his maximum possible number of matches would be 70 + 4 = 74. Thus, the maximum total possible is: 66 + 55 + 74 = 195. The correct answer is 195.

Note: Even if we try seedings the other way round: 64 + 55 + 76 = 195, the answer would still be same.

6. We have already seen that the maximum number of matches won by any one of the five brothers is 195. For minimum number of matches, the seedings of one particular brother should be 5, 4 and 3. His minimum

matches in such a case would be 60 + 51 + 72 = 183. The required difference is 12.

7. There are a total of three seed 1's, 3 seed 2's, 3 seed 3's, 3 seed 4's and 3 seed 5's in the given situation. It is possible that Sahdev's sum of seed numbers is 5 + 4 + 1 = 10 and yet he wins the least number of matches. In such a case, we can make the others seeded as 5, 3, 1; 5, 2, 1; 4, 3, 2 and 4, 3, 2. In such a case, the maximum matches he wins would be: (assume seed 5 in Taluka level, Seed 4 in province level and seed 1 in kingdom level) 60 + 53 + 76 = 189. The correct answer is 189.
8. We have already worked this out in the question prior to the last one. The correct answer would be 60 + 51 + 72 = 183.
9. We have already seen in question 7, a possible situation where seed numbers allotted are: (5, 4, 1); (5, 3, 1); (5, 2, 1); (4, 3, 2); (4, 3, 2). The maximum possible sum for the brother whose sum of seedings is the minimum is seen in this case as 5 + 2 + 1 = 8. Hence, the correct answer is 8.

Solutions for Questions 10 to 14:

There are three kinds of race outcomes possible, according to the conditions:

1. 3 rats finish 1st, 2nd and 3rd respectively; 2. Two rats finish first and one rat finishes second; 3. One rat finishes first and two rats finish second.

Based on the information of who cannot finish in which position, we will get the following table for the outcomes of the races:

	Case 1	Case 2	Case 3	Case 4
NUMBER OF INSTANCES	N	22	10	64-N
1st (Not R3)	R1	R2	R1,R2	R1
2nd (Not R1)	R2	R3	R3	R2,R3
3rd (Not R2)	R3	R1		

Now, from the clue: 'In 22 rounds, R3 finished ahead of R1' we can see that case 2 happened 22 times.

Again, from clue (iii), we have: 'The number of rounds in which R2 finished 1st and ahead of R3, is half the number of rounds in which R1 finished 1st and ahead of R2.' This means that the instances of case 2 and case 3 = 32 and the instances of case 1 and case 4 is 64. Thus, case 3 happened 32 - 22 = 10 times.

10. Two of them finished together in 10 + 64 − N rounds, which cannot be determined.
11. In order to identify the first runner up of the competition, we can calculate the sum of the ranks for each rat.
$R1 = 22 \times 3 + N + 64 - N + 10 = 140$
$R2 = 22 \times 1 + 2N + 2 \times (64 - N) + 10 = 160$
$R3 = 22 \times 2 + 3 \times N + 2 \times (64 - N) + 20 = 192 + N$
Clearly R1 finished first and R2 finished second.
12. According to the condition of the question, N + 22 + 10 = 62. So, N = 30. Score of R3 = 222.
13. There is a tie for a position in cases 3 and 4. Since, we know the value of N = 30, The required answer would be 10 + 64 − 30 = 44.
14. R1 has finished first in cases 1, 3 and 4. The required total = N + 10 + 64 − N = 74.

Solutions for Questions 15 to 20:

We can start with making the following table of the teams that won, lost or drew on each day. From this table, we can start deductions about who played whom on which day, with what result.

	Won	Loss	Drawn
Sunday	India, Denmark, Germany	Spain, China, France	
Tuesday	China, France	Spain, Germany	India, Denmark
Thursday	India, France	Spain, Germany	China, Denmark
Friday	Spain, Germany	India, Denmark	China, France
Saturday	Spain	Denmark	India, China, France, Germany

Results table: Please note, that the table has been drawn through a series of 15 deductions, starting from the Tuesday result of the India vs Denmark game being a draw. The deduction numbers are indicated in the appropriate cells in the table.

	Sunday	Tuesday	Thursday	Friday	Saturday
India	Vs China (Won) 10	Vs Denmark (drawn) 1	Vs Germany (Won) 8	Vs Spain (Lost) 6	Vs France (Drawn) 12
Spain	Vs Germany (Lost) 11	Vs China (Lost) 14	Vs France (lost) 9	Vs India (Won) 6	Vs Denmark (Won) 4
China	Vs India (Lost) 10	Vs Spain (Won) 14	Vs Denmark (drawn) 3	Vs France (drawn) 2	Vs Germany (Drawn) 13

	Sunday	Tuesday	Thursday	Friday	Saturday
Denmark	Vs France (Won) 7	Vs India (Drawn) 1	Vs China (drawn) 3	Vs Germany (Lost) 5	Vs Spain (Lost) 4
France	Vs Denmark (Lost) 7	Vs Germany (Won) 15	Vs Spain (Won) 9	Vs China (drawn) 2	Vs India (Drawn) 12
Germany	Vs Spain (Won) 11	Vs France (Lost) 15	Vs India (Lost) 8	Vs Denmark (Won) 5	Vs China (Drawn) 13

The answers can be all read from the table.

15. Denmark played against France on Sunday. Option (c) is correct.
16. Germany lost 1 match to France before it played against India on Thursday. The correct answer is 1.
17. Only the third result has not occurred, since we can see that Germany won against Denmark on Friday and not against India. Hence, option (d) is correct.
18. There are 2 such teams - China and Denmark. Option (c) is correct.
19. Option (b) is correct.
20. Option (d) is correct.

Solutions for Questions 21 to 25:

Based upon the given table, we can deduce the following.

Deduction 1: There must have been a total of 15 matches played. (6 teams playing each other in a round robin format once each, gives us $^6C_2$ = 15 matches.)

Deduction 2: Chelsea and Barcelona each must have 2 wins, 2 draws and 1 loss.

Deduction 3: Manchester United and Liverpool, each must have 3 wins and 2 losses as that's the only way to get to 6 points.

Deduction 4: Real Madrid could get to 4 points in 2 ways. 1 win and 4 draws or 2 wins and 0 draw. However, since Manchester United and Liverpool do not have any draws, it is not possible for a team to play out 4 draws. Hence, we can conclude that Real Madrid had 2 wins, 0 draw and 3 losses.

Deduction 5: If you draw the table to this point, you realise that, Leicester Square is still to be accounted for:

(a) The total number of wins in the wins column is 12, while the losses in the losses column is adding up to only 9. Since, every decisive match has a winner and a loser, there have to be a minimum of 3 losses for Leicester square in order to equal up the number of wins and losses. Thus, Leicester Square has either: 3 losses and 2 draws or 4 losses and 1 win.

(b) For Leicester Square you can deduce that it is 3 losses and 2 draws only. This is because, if we try to insert 4 losses and 1 win for Leicester Square, it means that the draw column shows only 2 draws for Chelsea and 2 for Barcelona - i.e., no other team would have drawn. This is not possible, since Chelsea and Barcelona could not have drawn with each other twice. Hence, we can complete the table as shown:

Team	Won	Draw	Loss	Points
Chelsea	2	2	1	5
Manchester United	3	0	2	6
Barcelona	2	2	1	5
Real Madrid	2	0	3	4
Liverpool	3	0	2	6
Leicester Square	0	2	3	2

For the results of the matches, only a few of them can be determined with certainty

1. Chelsea-Barcelona was a tie.
2. Chelsea-Leicester square was a tie.
3. Barcelona-Leicester square was a tie.
4. Since, the rest of the matches for Leicester square resulted in losses, the 3 matches of Leicester square with Manchester United, Real Madrid and Liverpool were losses.

We can make the following table for the known and unknown results:

Team	Chelsea	Manchester United	Barcelona	Real Madrid	Liverpool	Leicester Square
Chelsea	--------------	?	Draw	?	?	Draw
Manchester United	?	-------------	?	?	?	Win
Barcelona	Draw	?	--------------	?	?	Draw
Real Madrid	?	?	?	-------------	?	Win
Liverpool	?	Loss	?	Loss	---------------	Win
Leicester Square	Draw	Loss	Draw	Loss	Loss	---------------

21. Hence, 6 can be determined with certainty and 9 of them cannot be determined.
22. If Liverpool lost to Manchester United and Real Madrid, we can create a chain of thoughts as follows:
Liverpool will win its remaining 3 matches meaning that they would beat Chelsea, Barcelona and Leicester Square, which would mean that Chelsea would have to be the winner against Manchester United and Real Madrid. Option (b) is correct.
23. Liverpool would be the winner of this match. Again, thinking from the point in the results table showing 6 known results and adding the information contained in this question i.e., Manchester United won against Chelsea and Barcelona. Option (a) is correct.
24. If Real Madrid won against Barcelona, then Barcelona would have won against Manchester United and Liverpool. This would mean, we know Real Madrid's 2 wins. Hence, we know their losses come against Chelsea, Manchester United and Liverpool. We still cannot make out the result of the matches between Chelsea - Manchester United; Chelsea - Liverpool and Manchester United - Liverpool. Hence, we know a total of 12 matches, but cannot determine the results of 3 matches.
25. The result of this match cannot be determined as explained in the previous question's solution.

Solutions for Questions 26 to 30:

The track of the tournament is as follows (if all matches go according to seedings):

Match no:	Round 1	Round 2	Round 3	Round 4	Round 5 (semi final)	Round 6
1	1 vs 64	1 vs 32	1 vs 16	1 vs 8	1 vs 4	1 vs 2
2	2 vs 63	2 vs 31	2 vs 15	2 vs 7	2 vs 3	
3	3 vs 62	3 vs 30	3 vs 14	3 vs 6		
4	4 vs 61	4 vs 29	4 vs 13	4 vs 5		
5	5 vs 60	5 vs 28	5 vs 12			
6	6 vs 59	6 vs 27	6 vs 11			
7	7 vs 58	7 vs 26	7 vs 10			
8	8 vs 57	8 vs 25	8 vs 9			
and so on	and so on	and so on				
	31 vs 34	15 vs 18				
	32 vs 33	16 vs 17				

26. The question tells us that the seeds 6th, 9th, 12th, 23rd, 36th, 49th, 50th and 62nd entered the quarter finals. This means that in the quarter finals, seed 6 takes his appointed place; 9 will take the place of 8; 12 would take the place of 5; 23 will take the place 10 (and hence, 7); 36th would take the place 4; 49th would take the place of 16 and hence, 1; 50 would take the place of 15 and hence, 2 and 62 will take the place of 3. Thus, the quarter final line up would be:49 vs 9; 50 vs 23; 62 vs 6 and 36 vs 12. The winner of the 49 vs 9 and 36 vs 12 matches would play one semi final, while the winner of the other two matches would place the other semi final. Hence, among the given options, the final can only be played between 9 and 62. Option (d) is correct.
27. If seed 2 was the winner of the tournament, the players in the half of seed 2, would not have played against him in the finals. 2 plays 63 in the first round, the winner of 31 vs 34 in the second round; in the third round, 2 is supposed to play 15, which means that he can play any of 50, 18 or 47 in the third round. Also, in the fourth round, 2 is supposed to play 7, which means that he can play any of 7/58/26/39/10/55/23/42 in this round. From the given options, it is clear that 2 can possibly play in the finals against 49. Option (d) is correct.
28. 47 is playing 18 in the first round. If 47 reaches the pre-quarter final, he must win his first 2 rounds. So, he must beat 18 in round 1. In round 2, he replaces 18 against 15 (or 50, depending upon who won the first round match between 15 and 50). 47 has to win this match too. So, he replaces 15, in the designated 15 versus 2 match of round 3 (the pre-quarter final). In order to trace, who he could play against, we need to see the track of how 2 is supposed to reach the pre-quarter final. 2 is supposed to play 31 in round 2. 31 was supposed to play against 34 and 2 was supposed to play against 63 in round 1. Thus, 47's opponent in the pre-quarter final can be 2, 63, 31 or 34. Option (d) is correct.

29. We need to check the options for whether an individual seed number could win the tournament and we will need to start from the lowest available seeds in the options. Checking for seed 48: For 48 to win the tournament, he has to first win the first round. He should beat 17 in round 1 (and that has to be his only upset). In round 2, he is supposed to play 16, but if 16 is upset in round 1 by 49, 48 will play 49 in round 2 and win without an upset. He would thus reach round 3, where he takes the place against 1 (as per seedings). If we see, who all can replace 1, in this match, we see that if 1 loses to 64 in round 1, 64 will necessarily lose to either 32 or 33 in round 2. Thus, 1 will be at best replaced by 32 or 33. In such a case, 48 needs a second upset to go ahead in the tournament. This isn't possible and hence 48 cannot win the tournament under the given conditions. Checking for 33 we can see that 33 can win the tournament while the constraint is met. Option (d) is correct.
30. The basic logic of these knock out tournaments is that with only 1 upset, seed number 2 could be the lowest player who could win; with only 2 upsets seed 4 can be the lowest seeded player; with only 3 upsets seed 8 could be the lowest seed who could win and with only 4 upsets, seed 16 could be the lowest seed who could win. You can verify it in this way: Assume, there were no upsets in the first round and only 1 upset in match 1 of the second round, where 32 beats 1. In such a case, 16 will play 32 in round 3. He does not need an upset to win this match. Subsequently, he upsets 8, 4 and 2 in the quarter finals, semi-finals and finals to win the tournament. Hence, the correct answer is 16.

Solutions for Questions 31 to 35:

Deduction 1: From clue H, Gurnoor won two items and everyone else won at most one item. Also, from the table, he won the Boot and Himesh won the Book. As Ekanshi and Fatima bid equal amounts and the winning Bid was distinct for each item, they both did not win any items in the auction. Also, from statement F, Jasmeet's bid is the average of the bids of Dinesh and Fatima. As one of these bids will always be higher than Jasmeet's bids, he could not have won any item in the auction. Hence, the remaining people must have won exactly one item in the auction. Thus, the list of number of items won would be: Avinash 1; Balram 1; Chitra 1; Dinesh 1; Ekanshi 0; Fatima 0; Gurnoor 2, Himesh 1; Ishan 1; Jasmeet 0.

Deduction 2: Next, we focus on Balram's row of bids - since that is the most meaty clue at this point. His bids from left to right on the table have to be in an Arithmetic Progression (as given in clue A). Also, since he wins the trophy, his bid for the trophy has to be above 40 (Himesh's bid). Since all bids are in multiples of 5, we can easily understand that the AP must have either a common difference of +5 or –5 (we cannot fit in a common difference of 10 and keep all the numbers below 70). Using these conditions, we can see that if we fix the trophy bid for Balram as 45, there would be two possibilities: 30, 35, 40, 45, 50, 55, 60, 65 or 60, 55, 50, 45, 40, 35, 30, 25 from Bat to Pen. Also, there is a possibility that the winning trophy bid was 50, in which case the numbers would be 65, 60, 55, 50, 45, 40, 35, 30.

These possibilities can be tabulated as:

	Bat	Boot	Racquet	Trophy	Jersey	Replica	Book	Pen
Balram Possibility 1	30	35	40	45	50	55	60	65
Possibility 2	60	55	50	45	40	35	30	25
Possibility 3	65	60	55	50	45	40	35	30

Hence, for the Trophy, his bid can be 45/50, which must be the winning bid. For Jersey, his bid can be 40/45/50. For the jersey, we know that Himesh has bid 30. In order to satisfy the condition stated in Clue C, we need to work out who amongst Himesh and Balram is the person who is referred to in the clue and who is the other one, who has the same bid as everyone else.

If Himesh, is the person referred to as 'one other person' in the clue, it follows that Avinash would have bid either 20 or 40 and Balram's bid for the jersey would get replicated by all the others. This is not possible as in both the cases, the highest bid would be by multiple people, which goes against the conditions of the question.

Hence, the other person referred to in the clue is Balram and it follows that Avinash would have necessarily bid 10 more than Balram and Himesh's bid for the jersey would get replicated by all the others. Hence, Avinash got the jersey with a bid of 50, 55, or 60.

Deduction 3: Once, we insert this information into our table and add the clue from statement B that Ekanshi bid exactly two distinct amounts, we now know here amounts to be exactly ₹ 40 and ₹ 30. Also, she was among the least bidders for at least 5 items. Since Himesh bid ₹ 10, ₹ 25 and ₹ 15 for Bat, Racquet and Replica respectively, Ekanshi must have been the lowest bidder for all the remaining items. This means we have to make her the lowest bidder for the boot, the trophy, the book and the pen.

For the Boot, Ekanshi must have bid ₹ 30 since Avinash bid ₹ 35. Ekanshi must have bid ₹ 30/₹ 40 for the Trophy, the Book and the Pen and must have been among the lowest bidders.

Deduction 4: From statement E, Avinash bid ₹ 20 for at least three items. He cannot bid ₹ 20 for the Trophy, Book and Pen since Ekanshi is the lowest bidder. Avinash cannot bid ₹ 20 for Boot since he bid ₹ 35 and for Jersey since he bid 50/55/60. Hence, he must have bid ₹ 20 for the Bat, Racquet and Replica.

Deduction 5: From the clue in Statement G, the sum of bids made by Avinash and Ishan were constant for Jersey, Replica, Book and Pen. This sum can be 80/85/90 as can be seen from their bids for Jersey, 80/85/90.

For the Replica, since Avinash bid ₹ 20, Ishan must have bid 60/65/70. The three distinct bids that Ishan made must be 30, 55 and 60/65/70.

Deduction 6: Let us move our focus now to Gurnoor. We know that he has won the boot and must have won one more item other than the bat with a bid below 50 (as per clue D). The possibilities are: Racquet, Replica, Book or Pen. He cannot win the bid for the Replica and the Book with a bid less than ₹ 50 (as we already know of bids above 60 for both these items. He also cannot win the pen, since if he won with a bid below 50, Avinash would have to have bid 35 for the same. If he won the bid for the Pen, then Avinash must have bid 35 for the same. In this case, Ishan must have bid 45/50/55 (in order to complete the constant total of 80/85/90 as discussed in deduction 5). In this case, the pen would be won by Ishan. Hence, Gurnoor would not have won the pen and must have won the Racquet (only possibility left). He must have won the bid for the Racquet with a bid less than ₹ 50. Hence, Balram's bid for the Racquet must also be less than ₹ 50 and can only be 40 from the 3 possibilities discussed in deduction 2. Gurnoor must have bid more than Balram to win the racquet and hence he bid 45 for the same and won.

We can fill the values deduced in the table and the solution table would look as shown:

Table After Deduction 6:

	Bid Submitted by each Person							
	Bat	Boot	Racquet	Trophy	Jersey	Replica	Book	Pen
Avinash	20	35	20		60	20		
Balram	30	35	40	45	50	55	60	65
Chitra					30			
Dinesh					30			
Ekanshi	40	30	30/40	30/40	30	30/40	30/40	30/40
Fatima					30			
Gurnoor		70 (W)			30			
Himesh	10	50	25	40	30	15	70 (W)	
Ishan					30	60/65/70		
Jasmeet					30			

Deduction 7: We can deduce from the table that the constant sum of Avinash and Ishan (mentioned in Clue G) would be 60 + 30 = 90. Hence, for replica Ishan would have bet 70 (20 + 70 = 90). He would also be the winner of the replica.

Deduction 8: Since the distinct bids of Chitra are 50 (from statement E) and 30, for the Racquet, she must have bid 30. For the Trophy also, Chitra must have bid 30 (less than the winning bid). From statement E, for the Bat, Boot, Replica, Book and Pen, Chitra must have bid 50.

The only item that Chitra can win is the Bat since Balram bid 65 for the Pen. Hence, Dinesh must have won the bid for the Pen. Since Balram's bid for the Pen is 65, Dinesh's bid must be 70. At this stage we know the winners of each of the items.

Deduction 9: Ishan's 3 bid values are 30,55 and 70. He cannot bid 70 more than once (Replica) since he has only won one item. Thus, his remaining bids are 30 or 55. For the bat, racquet and trophy his bid has to be less than the winning bid - and hence his bids for these items have to be 30 each. Also, from the statement F, for at least four items, Ishan's bid was greater than that of Chitra. For Bat, Racquet, Trophy and Jersey, Ishan's bid is not greater than Chitra's bid. Hence, for the Boot, Replica, Book and Pen, Ishan's bid must be greater than Chitra's bid. Hence, Ishan must have bid 55 for the Boot, Book and Pen. This also means that

Avinash must have bid 35 for the Book and Pen (since the sum of bids of Avinash and Ishan is constant).

Deduction 10: Since Avinash's bid is 35 for the Book and Pen, Ekanshi's bid and Fatima's Bid must be 30 for the above objects (since it must be the lowest). Also Ekanshi has to be the lowest bidder for boot, trophy, jersey , book and pen. For her to be the lowest bidder for the trophy her bid should be 30 for the same (as also for Fatima)

Deduction 11: From statement F, Jasmeet's bid for the Pen must be 50 (from Dinesh's bid and Fatima's bid).

For the Bat, Fatima's bid is 40. For Jasmeet's bid to be a multiple of 10, Dinesh's bid must be an even multiple of 10. Hence, Dinesh's bid can only be 20 or 40 for the Bat(it cannot be higher because of the winning bid). The three distinct bids of Dinesh must be 20/40, 30 and 70. Since Fatima's bid is 30 (odd multiple of 10) for the Boot, Trophy and Book, Dinesh's bid must also be 30 for the above objects, so that Jasmeet has a multiple of 10 while being the average of Dinesh and Fatima, for each of these objects

> **Note:** We cannot use 70 for Dinesh in any of the blanks as that would become the winning bid.

Deduction 12: At this point, we have to only fit in Dinesh's and Jasmeet's bids for Bat, Racquet and Replica. For the bat, Dinesh's bid needs to be an even multiple of 10- which can only be 20 or 40 (as per deduction 11). If Dinesh's bid for the Bat is 20, then Jasmeet's bid will be 30 for the Bat. In this case, the distinct bids for Dinesh will be 20, 30, 70.

For every item that Fatima bid 40 (except the Pen which Dinesh won), Dinesh must bid 20 and for every item that Fatima bid 30, Dinesh must bid 30. Hence, for every item, Jasmeet's bids can only be two distinct integers - 50 and 30, which violates Statement B, that Jasmeet has 3 distinct values in his bids. Hence, Dinesh's bid for the Bat cannot be 20. Hence, Dinesh's bid for the Bat must be 40. We can draw up the final bids table based on these deductions.

Final Bids Table:

	Bid Submitted by each Person							
	Bat	**Boot**	**Racquet**	**Trophy**	**Jersey**	**Replica**	**Book**	**Pen**
Avinash	20	35	20	35	60	20	35	35
Balram	30	35	40	45	50	55	60	65
Chitra	50	50	30	30	30	50	50	50
Dinesh	40	30	30/40	30	30	30/40	30	70
Ekanshi	40	30	30/40	30	30	30/40	30	30
Fatima	40	30	30/40	30	30	30/40	30	30
Gurnoor	30/45	70	45	30	30	30/45	30/45	30/45
Himesh	10	50	25	40	30	15	70	
Ishan	30	55	30	30	30	70	55	55
Jasmeet	40	30	30/40	30	30	30/40	30	50

Using the above table we can answer the questions given:

31. Option (a) is the correct answer
32. Option (b) is the correct answer
33. There are a maximum possible 26 values above 40 (including the unknown bid of Himesh for the pen).
34. Option (b) is the correct answer
35. Option (a) is the correct answer

Solutions for Questions 36 to 40:

Since the number of wins is different for each person, the values for the same would be 0,1,2,3 and 4. This means that for one of these five people, the win loss combination is 0-4. For the others this combination is 1-3; 2-2; 3-1;4-0. So there would be a total of 10 bets taking place. Let's denote the people in the group as A, B, C, D, E.

We need to focus on trying to find which person had which win-loss combination first.

Deduction 1: Akshat has lost to Eshwar, so Akshat cannot be 4-0 and Eshwar cannot be 0-4. Also, from clue F, we see that Dharam must have won at least 1 bet. Also, since Akshat lost as many bets as Dharam won and we cannot place the 4-0 & 0-4 combinations for them, they necessarily take the 1-3, 3-1 combination in some order. Hence, Dharam has lost either 1 or 3 bets. Consequently from clue F, Charu would have lost at least 2 bets and hence cannot have the 4-0 combination. With these deductions our win-loss combination possibilities look as shown.

Table showing Win-Loss combinations after deduction 1: (figures in brackets show the total bet stakes for each person as detailed in Clue E.)

Win-Loss combination	A (110)	B (74)	C (80)	D (110)	E (106)
4-0	Not possible		Not possible		
3-1		Not possible	Not possible		Not possible
2-2	Not possible			Not possible	
1-3		Not possible	Not possible		Not possible
0-4	Not possible			Not possible	Not possible

Deduction 2: At this stage we still need to work out who amongst B,D and E won all 4 bets i.e. had the 4-0 combination. According to clue C, it has to be B (since D and E if they won all their bets their stakes won would go over 80, which is not allowed. Consequently, the only person who could have lost all the bets is C and the 2-2 combination would go to E. We only have to finalise who amongst A and D will have the 3-1 and the 1-3 combination. In that context, we know that Akshat has lost to Eshwar and everyone loses their bets to Brij. Hence, Akshat has at least 2 losses and would take the 1-3 combination.

Final Table showing Win-Loss combinations after deduction 2:

Win-Loss combination	A (110)	B (74)	C (80)	D (110)	E (106)
4-0	Not possible	Yes	Not possible	No	No
3-1	No	Not possible	Not possible	Yes	Not possible
2-2	Not possible	No	No	Not possible	Yes
1-3	Yes	Not possible	Not possible	No	Not possible
0-4	Not possible	No	Yes	Not possible	Not possible

The bet matrix would be:

Bet #	Bet Between	Winner?	Stake
Bet 1	A vs B	B	
Bet 2	A vs C	A	
Bet 3	A vs D	D	
Bet 4	A vs E	E	34
Bet 5	B vs C	B	
Bet 6	B vs D	B	
Bet 7	B vs E	B	
Bet 8	C vs D	D	8
Bet 9	C vs E	E	
Bet 10	D vs E	D	

Deduction 3: We now need to focus on the bet amounts. Since the total stakes of all the people combined is 480, it means that the sum of all stakes won and sum of all stakes lost would be 240 each. B having won all bets would have won 74 and lost 0. C having lost all his bets would have won 0 and lost 80. Clue, D tells us that that the amount won by Akshat and amount lost by Dharam were equal.

Therefore, Amount won by Akshat + Amount lost by Akshat = 110 = Amount won by Dharam + Amount lost be Dharam.

So, Amount lost by Dharam + Amount lost by Akshat = 110

Hence, Amount Gain of Akshat + Amount gain of Dharam = 110

Now, total gain=240.

Therefore amount won by Eshwar = 240 – 110 – 74 = 56

Eshwar wins 34 against Akshat (given), so Eshwar would win 22 against Charu.

Deduction 4: Akshat has won against Charu and his minimum win has to be 40 (as per clue C). It cannot be 41 (odd numbers not allowed or 42 – as if Akshat wins 42 against Charu, it would mean that Charu's other loss would be 8, which is not possible as Charu is already betting 8 against Dharam and that will be a contradiction of Clue G). Thus, Akshat would have necessarily won 40 against Charu. Consequently, Charu lost 10 against Brij.

Now, in the bet between Akshat and Charu, Akshat would have won ₹ 40 because if Akshat won more than that then we would be contradicting statements B & C. D's loss has to be 40 also, so the stake between D and B would be 40. Consequently, A vs D, the stake would be 20. So the stake of A vs B would be 110 - 40 - 34 - 20 = 16.

B would win 8 against E and Dharam against Eshwar would be a ₹ 42 stake.

Final bet matrix:

Bet #	Bet Between	Winner?	Stake
Bet 1	A vs B	B	16
Bet 2	A vs C	A	40
Bet 3	A vs D	D	20
Bet 4	A vs E	E	34
Bet 5	B vs C	B	10
Bet 6	B vs D	B	40
Bet 7	B vs E	B	8
Bet 8	C vs D	D	8
Bet 9	C vs E	E	22
Bet 10	D vs E	D	42

The total won and lost amount would be: Akshat: won 40, lost 70; Brij: Won 74 lost 0; Charu: won 0 lost 80; Dharam Won 70, lost 40 & Eshwar Won 56, lost 50.

We can now answer the questions given:

36. Option B is the correct answer
37. 10
38. 70
39. 20
40. In statement D, it is given that Charu bet Dharam that his team would win the finals and lost the bet. Hence Dharam was definitely supporting the team that won the finals.

Solutions for Questions 41 to 45:

41. For the player seeded 35 to reach the finals, He would have to cause upsets in Rounds 2-6. Hence 1 extra game would be played in each of these rounds +5. For seed 125 to reach the finals, he would have to cause upsets in each of the first 6 rounds +6. It doesn't matter who won the tournament. Hence the total minimum number of matches would be 127(usual) + 5 + 6 = 138. Hence Option (c) is the correct answer.
42. Since there were 134 matches played in total, there were 7 extra matches played. This happened because of the 7 upsets that took place. Hence we could use 1 upset in the finals and adjust the remaining 6 in any of the other rounds. Hence Seed 2 beats Seed 1 in the finals. Hence Option (d) is the correct answer.
43. Seed 6 will be a higher seed up till round 4. Hence except the matches involving Seed 6, We can have upsets in every match.
    Upsets in Round 1: 63
    Upsets in Round 2: 31
    Upsets in Round 3: 15
    Upsets in Round 4: 7
    Now, because of these upsets, seed 6 becomes a higher seed in other rounds as well as seeds 1 to 5 get eliminated at the start only. Hence there could be 3 upsets in round 5 and 1 upset in round 6. Hence there would be a total of 120 upsets. Now, after each first upset, the two players would play for the second time to determine who would actually get eliminated. Hence, the maximum number of matches in which a lower seeded player beat a higher seeded player would be 120 × 2 = 240.
44. Consider the seed number 64. If he wins his first match in the first round against seed 65, he will win in 1 match itself. Also assume, that there are upsets in each of the other matches - i.e. 1 loses to 128, 2 loses to 127 ...63 loses to 66. For the remainder of the tournament, the highest seed left in the draw would be seed number 64. Hence, he would face lower seeds and keep beating them in 1 match itself (without the need for a second match) and win the tournament. Hence, the correct answer is 64.
45. For player seeded 60 to win the tournament and if we want the minimum number of matches in the tournament for this to happen, we would have to minimise the number of upsets in the tournament:
    Upsets in Round 1: 0; Upsets in Round 2: 1 (to make sure that seed 60 progresses)
    Further, we can see that in each of rounds 3 to 7, seed 60 would be playing a higher seed and would need to upset him to win the tournament. Hence minimum upsets in Round 3 to 7 = 5.
    Total Upsets = 6. Hence, we would have 6 extra matches. Hence the total number of matches is 127 + 6 = 133. Hence, Option (a) is the correct answer.

Solutions for Questions 46 to 49:

Since the number of runs can only be integers The median would also be an integer. From Clue E, we can deduce that for match 2, the average was 23 and median was 22.

From the information given to us, we can deduce the following table:

	Match 1	Match 2	Match 3	Match 4
Top Scorer	25 (Palash)	35 (Akash)	28 (Palash)	37 (Shashank)
2nd highest				
Median	18	22	10	30
4th highest				
Bottom Scorer	12 (Shashank)	4 (Shaurya)	3 (Pallav)	5 (Akash)
Total Runs	87	115	77	127

Match 1:

Remaining Runs = 32

The ways in which we achieve this is 14 + 18 or 12 + 20 considering the given constraints in clue C.

Match 2:

Remaining Runs = 54

One number would lie in the range 5 - 21 and the second one would lie in 23 - 34

The possibilities for this are 20 + 34 and 21 + 33.

Match 3:

Remaining Runs = 36

One number would lie in the range 4 - 9 and the second one would lie in the range 11 - 27. The only possible way to achieve a sum of 36 with the above values is 9 + 27.

Match 4:

Remaining Runs = 55

The ways in which we can achieve this are 37 + 18 or 30 + 25 considering the given constraints in clue C.

Now we are given that runs by Shaurya in Match 4 is twice that of Shashank in one of the other matches. This is only possible if Shaurya scores 18 in Match 4. Then Shashank would score 9 runs in Match 3. Now, the number of runs scored by Shaurya in Match 1 is twice that scored by Akash in one of the other matches. This would only be possible if Shaurya scores 20 runs in Match 1 and Akash scores 10 runs in Match 3. Now, Shaurya scored 69 run in 4 matches. Hence from Clue H, Shashank scored 79 Runs. We've already accounted for 58 runs for Shashank in 3 matches. Hence, in Match 2 Shashank scored 21 runs.

Now, Pallav scored more than Shashank in only 1 match and this would definitely be Match 2. Hence in match 1 Pallav scored 12 runs. Also, Palash scored less than Shashank in only 1 match and this would only be possible in Match 4, if he scores 30. Hence, Pallav scores 37 in Match 4.

Match 1	Match 2	Match 3	Match 4
25 (Palash)	35 (Akash)	28 (Palash)	37 (Shashank)
20 (Shaurya)	33 (Pallav/Palash)	27 (Shaurya)	37 (Pallav)
18 (Akash)	22 (Pallav/Palash)	10 (Akash)	30 (Palash)
12 (Pallav)	21 (Shashank)	9 (Shashank)	18 (Shaurya)
12 (Shashank)	4 (Shaurya)	3 (Pallav)	5 (Akash)
87	115	77	127

Using the above table we can answer the questions given:

46. The difference is 27 - 9 = 18
47. Option (a) is the correct answer.
48. We can calculate the runs scored by each: Palash =25 + 22/33 + 28 + 30 = 105/116; Shaurya 69; Akash =68; Pallav = 12 + 33/22 + 3 + 37 = 85/74; Shashank = 79. Hence, either Shashank or Pallav scored the second highest number of runs.

    Option (b) is the correct answer.
49. In the case of the condition mentioned, Pallav cannot score a total of 85, hence he scored a total of 74, which means that in Match 2 Pallav scored 22 runs and Palash scored 33 runs. The total runs scored by Palash would be 116 in this case. 116 satisfies the condition expressed in option (d). Hence, Option (d) is the correct answer.

CHAPTER 11

Puzzles on Scheduling

Chapter Launchpad
Scan this QR code to access an introductory video on Puzzles on Scheduling

Sets based on scheduling are common as Logical Reasoning Puzzles in all types of exams. The key factor in these sets is the time dimension–every scheduling set inherently involves an element of chronology. Hence, in such sets, while drawing up the solution picture/chart, it is best to use the chronology dimension as the backbone for the solution. The following examples will help you understand Logical Reasoning sets involving a time element.

Example 1: Question at an easy level of difficulty:
Directions: *Study the following information to answer these questions.*

(i) Arnold's fitness schedule consists of cycling, rowing, gymnasium, jogging and boxing from Monday to Saturday, each workout is for one day, one day being a rest day.
(ii) Gymnasium workout is done neither on the first nor on the last day but is done earlier than rowing.
(iii) Jogging is done on the immediate next day of the rowing day.
(iv) Cycling is done on the immediate previous day of the rest day.
(v) Jogging and boxing are done with a two-day gap between them.
(vi) Boxing is done on the following day of the rest day.

1. Which of the following is a rest day?
   (a) Wednesday (b) Tuesday
   (c) Friday (d) Thursday
2. How many days of gap are there in between cyling and jogging?
   (a) Nil (b) Two
   (c) Three (d) Four
3. On which day is boxing done?
   (a) Thursday (b) Friday
   (c) Monday (d) Wednesday
4. Which of the following is the wrong statement?
   (a) Gymnasium workout is done on the immediate previous day of rowing.
   (b) Jogging is done three days after the day on which boxing was done.
   (c) There is a gap of three days between the days on which cycling and rowing are done.
   (d) There is a two days' gap between the rest day and the day on which gymnasium workout is done.
5. Which of the following is the correct statement?
   (a) Jogging competition is done after rowing.
   (b) Cycling is done on Thursday.
   (c) No workout is done on Wednesday.
   (d) Rowing is done earlier than cycling.

Reaction Tracker

The starting figure we begin with when we read the first statement is:

Monday	Tuesday	Wednesday	Thursday	Friday	Saturday

Workouts are cycling, rowing, gymnasium, jogging and boxing.

From the second and third clues (gymnasium workout is done neither on the first nor on the last day but was done earlier than rowing and jogging, was done on the day immediately following the rowing day), we know that rowing and jogging should be together and also that gymnasium has to be somewhere before this.

Visually, this can be represented as:

G ⇨ RJ

From the fourth and sixth clues we have:

C-Rest day-B

Note: Putting it in a box signifies that there is no break between the items in the box.

Once we have these two visual representations, we can go back to our original figure and think as follows:

Monday	Tuesday	Wednesday	Thursday	Friday	Saturday

Since gymnasium has to precede rowing and jogging, and gymnasium is not on the first day, we can have 3 possibilities for placing gymnasium–viz.: Tuesday, Wednesday or Thursday.

Possibility 1:

Monday	
Tuesday	Gymnasium
Wednesday	
Thursday	
Friday	
Saturday	

This case is rejected because, once we place gymnasium we would need to place rowing and jogging in either, **Wednesday-Thursday** or **Thursday-Friday** or **Friday-Saturday**. In each of these cases, we would also need to place a 3 day period having **Cycling-Rest day-Boxing.** It can be easily seen that in any of these 3 situations under Possibility 1, we do not have a completely free 3 day period anywhere in the week. Thus, we can reject Possibility 1.

Possibility 2:

Monday	
Tuesday	
Wednesday	Gymnasium
Thursday	
Friday	
Saturday	

Rejected on the same logic as Possibility 1. There is no availability of a 3 day window to place **Cycling-Rest day-Boxing.**

Possibility 3:

Monday	
Tuesday	
Wednesday	
Thursday	Gymnasium
Friday	
Saturday	

This is the only possibility that would work as in this case, the respective work outs ordering would be:

Monday	Cycling
Tuesday	Rest Day
Wednesday	Boxing
Thursday	Gymnasium
Friday	Rowing
Saturday	Jogging

Thus, the answers are:

1. (b) Tuesday is the rest day.
2. (d) 4 days
3. (d) Boxing is done on Wednesday.
4. (d) The statement in option (d) is incorrect.
5. (a) Only the statement in option (a) is correct.

Example 2: Directions: *Study the following information and answer the questions that follow:*

A company is planning to organise 8 lectures–A, B, C, D, E, F, G and H for 3 subjects–Quants, D.I. and English. The lectures are spread over three days.

Quants is to be covered first in 3 lectures followed by English and then D.I. in 2 lectures. Lectures A, C and D have to be on different days. (Lectures B and F have to be on the same day), but lecture B cannot be clubbed with A or G or D. Lecture G and H should come on the same day. Lecture A is a lecture on Quants and Lecture C cannot be on the last day. It is also known that there are at least 3 lectures on day 1.

1. Which of the following pairs of lectures can go along with lecture 'A' on Quants?
(a) B, C (b) G, H
(c) D, E (d) Data inadequate

2. Which combination of lectures was arranged on the second day of the series?
(a) D, E, F (b) B, C, E
(c) C, G, H (d) Data inadequate

3. Which of the following lectures were for D.I.?
(a) D, F (b) B, C
(c) G, H (d) Data inadequate

Solution: Given that A, C and D have to be separate and that A is Quants, and C cannot be on the last day. Also that there are 3 lectures (at least) on day 1, the order of A, C and D must be:

Day 1	Day 2	Day 3
A	C	D

Further, B cannot be clubbed with A or D, hence, must be on the second day. Thus, F must also be on the same day. This gives us the following table.

Day 1	Day 2	Day 3
A	C B F	D

This leaves us with G, H and E. Since, day 1 has to have at least 3 lectures, G and H must be on day 1. This leaves us with E, which can be placed on day 1 or 2 or 3.

Thus, the final table is:

Day 1	Day 2	Day 3
A, G, H, E?	C, B, F, E?	D, E?

Hence, the answers are:

1. G, H. Option (b) is correct.
2. The data is inadequate, since we do not know whether E was on Day 2 or not. Option (d) is correct.
3. Again, the data is inadequate since we do not know for sure, which the last 2 lectures were. Option (d) is correct.

Example 3: Directions: *Read the information provided and answer the questions which follow.*

A supermarket has to place 12 items (coded A to L) in shelves numbered 1 to 16. Five of these items are types of biscuits, three are types of candies and the rest are types of savouries. Only one item can be kept in a shelf. Items are to be placed such that all items of same type are clustered together with no empty shelf between items of the same type and at least one empty shelf between two different types of items. At most, two empty shelves can have consecutive numbers.

The following additional facts are known.

(i) A and B are to be placed in consecutively numbered shelves in increasing order.

(ii) I and J are to be placed in consecutively numbered shelves both higher numbered than the shelves in which A and B are kept.

(iii) D, E and F are savouries and are to be placed in consecutively numbered shelves in increasing order after all the biscuits and candies.

(iv) K is to be placed in shelf number 16.

(v) L and J are items of the same type, while H is an item of a different type.

(vi) C is a candy and is to be placed in a shelf preceded by two empty shelves.

(vii) L is to be placed in a shelf preceded by exactly one empty shelf.

1. In how many different ways can the items be arranged on the shelves?
   (a) 4 (b) 2
   (c) 8 (d) 1
2. Which of the following items is not a type of biscuit?
   (a) A (b) L
   (c) B (d) G
3. Which of the following can represent the numbers of the empty shelves in a possible arrangement?
   (a) 1,7,11,12 (b) 1,5,6,12
   (c) 1,2,6,12 (d) 1,2,8,12
4. Which of the following statements is necessarily true?
   (a) There are two empty shelves between the biscuits and the candies.
   (b) All candies are kept before biscuits.
   (c) All biscuits are kept before candies.
   (d) There are at least four shelves between items B and C.

Solution: First, collect all the starting information to start off with an initial framework on which you would solve the set:

Global lists: 12 items- A, B, C, D, E, F, G, H, I, J, K, L in 16 shelves; 5 biscuit items (B), 3 candies (C) and 4 savouries (S).

All items to be placed such that each kind of item is together. Thus, there would be six ways of putting the B, C and S groups on the shelves to start with. Also, since there are 12 items and 16 shelves, it is evident that 4 shelves would be empty.

The following set of deductions follows:

Deduction 1: A and B are one kind of item. Also placed together only in the increasing order AB.

Deduction 2: I and J are one kind of item, placed together in any order, i.e., IJ or JI– and after AB.

Deduction 3: From 3 and 4: D, E, F, K are savouries and placed in 13 to 16. At this point, we can start to make our figure.

Shelf #	1	2	3	4	5	6	7	8	9	10	11	12	13	14	15	16
Item													D	E	F	K
Category													S	S	S	S

At this stage, the items left are: A, B, C, G, H, I, J, L.

Deduction 4: I, J, L are of one type, while H is of another type. That leaves us with AB and H. Also, C is a candy. In such a situation, to accommodate 5 biscuit items and 3 candy items, the only way to do it, is to have C and H both as candies (as IJL cannot be candies – since there are only 3 candies and C is one of them). Consequently, we get that CHG are the candies and ABIJL are the biscuits.

The next step is to think about how we want to place these, considering the requirements of two blanks before C and one blank before L. The following possibilities emerge:

Possibility 1:

Shelf #	1	2	3	4	5	6	7	8	9	10	11	12	13	14	15	16
Item	–	–	C	H/G	G/H	–	L	A	B	I/J	J/I	–	D	E	F	K
Category	–	–	C	C	C	–	B	B	B	B	B	–	S	S	S	S

Possibility 2:

Shelf #	1	2	3	4	5	6	7	8	9	10	11	12	13	14	15	16
Item	–	L	A	B	I/J	J/I	–	–	C	H/G	G/H	–	D	E	F	K
Category	–	B	B	B	B	B	–	–	C	C	C	–	S	S	S	S

The answers can be read off the possibilities:

1. As can be seen that, in each possibility, there are 4 ways depending on how you place H/G and I/J respectively. Thus, there are a total of 8 possibilities. Hence, option (c) is correct.
2. In both scenarios, G is a type of candy. Hence, option (d) is correct.
3. 1, 2, 6, 12 are the banks in possibility 1. Option (c) is correct.
4. Necessarily, true would be a statement that would be true in each of the two possibilities. We can see that only the statement in option (d) is necessarily true. Hence, option (d) is correct.

Example 4: Directions: Study the following information carefully and answer the questions given below:

Four people were being interviewed for the same job. They were all interviewed on the same day, but in different rooms (Dharti, Prithvi, Akash and Agni), at different times and by different persons. Determine the name of each candidate, which room they were interviewed in and their appointment time and answer the questions.

(i) Aishwarya's appointment was just after Mr. Sharma's, which was just after that of the person in room Prithvi.

(ii) Mr Narurkar's appointment was at least two hours later in the day than Bhagat's.

(iii) Mr Joshi's appointment was just after the person who had an interview in room Agni, who had an appointment just after Chiranjeev.

(iv) Three of the four interviewees were: Dhanush, the one with the interview in room Dharti, and the person who had an appointment at 1 pm.

(v) The four people were interviewed at 11 am, 12 noon, 1 pm and 2 pm.

(vi) Joshi, Narurkar, Zaidi and Sharma were the interviewers whereas Aishwarya, Bhagat, Chiranjeev and Dhanush were the interviewees.

1. Sharma's appointment was with:

(a) Aishwarya (b) Bhagat
(c) Chiranjeev (d) Can't be determined

2. Dhanush's appointment was in the room:

(a) Dharti (b) Prithvi
(c) Akash (d) Agni
(e) Can't be determined

3. Zaidi's appointment was in the room:

(a) Dharti (b) Prithvi
(c) Akash (d) Agni
(e) Can't be determined

Solution: In order to solve this question the starting table should be like this:

			A/B/C/D	A/B/C/D	A/B/C/D	A/B/C/D
			J/N/Z/S	J/N/Z/S	J/N/Z/S	J/N/Z/S
			11 am	12 noon	1 pm	2 pm
A/B/C/D	J/N/Z/S	Dharti				
A/B/C/D	J/N/Z/S	Prithvi				
A/B/C/D	J/N/Z/S	Akash				
A/B/C/D	J/N/Z/S	Agni				

The first clue gives us: Prithvi–Sharma–Aishwarya. This means that these three can only be at 11 am, 12 noon and 1 pm or 12 noon, 1 pm or 2 pm.

The table evolves to:

			B/C/D	B/C/D	A/B/C/D	A/B/C/D
			J/N/Z	J/N/Z/S	J/N/Z/S	J/N/Z
			11 am	12 noon	1 pm	2 pm
A/B/C/D	J/N/Z/S	Dharti				

			B/C/D	B/C/D	A/B/C/D	A/B/C/D
			J/N/Z	J/N/Z/S	J/N/Z/S	J/N/Z
			11 am	12 noon	1 pm	2 pm
A/B/C/D	J/N/Z/S	Prithvi			X	x
A/B/C/D	J/N/Z/S	Akash				
A/B/C/D	J/N/Z/S	Agni				

The second clue tells us that Narurkar's appointment is at least 2 hours after Bhagat's appointment. This could only mean that Bhagat is at either 11 am or 12 noon and Narurkar could only be at 1 or 2 pm. The table evolves to:

			B/C/D	B/C/D	A/C/D	A/C/D
			J/Z	J/Z/S	J/N/Z/S	J/N/Z
			11 am	12 noon	1 pm	2 pm
A/B/C/D	J/N/Z/S	Dharti				
A/B/C/D	J/N/Z/S	Prithvi			X	X
A/B/C/D	J/N/Z/S	Akash				
A/B/C/D	J/N/Z/S	Agni				

Clue (iii) gives us that the sequence Chiranjeev - Agni - Joshi. This again means that this sequence could only be at 11, 12 and 1 pm or 12, 1 and 2 pm. Thus, Chiranjeev can only be at 11 or 12, Agni only at 12 or 1 and Joshi only at 1 or 2 pm. Introducing these deductions into the existing table we get:

			B/C/D	B/C/D	A/D	A/D
			Z	Z/S	J/N/Z/S	J/N/Z
			11 am	12 noon	1 pm	2 pm
A/B/C/D	J/N/Z/S	Dharti				
A/B/C/D	J/N/Z/S	Prithvi			x	X
A/B/C/D	J/N/Z/S	Akash				
A/B/C/D	J/N/Z/S	Agni	x			X

Note: In the above table, we are now sure about Zaidi's position at 11 am. Then Sharma fits in at 12 noon. This means that Prithvi, Sharma and Aishwarya fit in at 11-12-1. The table then becomes:

			B/C	B/C	A	D
			Z	S	J/N	J/N
			11 am	12 noon	1 pm	2 pm
A/B/C/D	J/N/Z/S	Dharti	x			
A/B/C/D	J/N/Z/S	Prithvi	Definite	x	x	x
A/B/C/D	J/N/Z/S	Akash	x			
A/B/C/D	J/N/Z/S	Agni	x			x

Clue (iv) tells us that: Dhanush, the person in Dharti and the 1 pm person are different people. So, Dhanush is not in Dharti and Dharti is also not at 1 pm.

The table changes to:

			B/C	B/C	A	D
			Z	S	N	J
			11 am	12 noon	1 pm	2 pm
B/C	S	Dharti	x	Definite	x	X
B/C	Z	Prithvi	Definite	x	x	X
D	J	Akash	x	x	x	definite
A	N	Agni	x	x	definite	X

From this point, if we go back to clue (iii), we get: Joshi would be at 2 pm (as he is just after the person who had an interview in Agni– which is fixed at 1 pm). Also, Chiranjeev must be at 12 noon, as he is just before Agni.

			B	C	A	D
			Z	S	N	J
			11 am	12 noon	1 pm	2 pm
C	S	Dharti	x	Definite	X	x
B	Z	Prithvi	Definite	x	X	x
D	J	Akash	X	x	X	Definite
A	N	Agni	X	x	Definite	x

The answers are:

1. Sharma's appointment was with Chiranjeev. Option (c) is correct.
2. Akash. Option (c) is correct.
3. Prithvi. Option (b) is correct.

EXERCISE

Directions for Questions 1 to 3: *Five courses–A, B, C, D and E, each of one month duration are to be taught from January to May, one after the other, though not necessarily in the same order by lecturers P, Q, R, S and T. P teaches course 'B' but not in the month of April or May. Q teaches course 'A' in the month of March. R teaches in the month of January but does not teach course 'C' or 'D'.*

1. Which course is taught by S?
   (a) C (b) E
   (c) Either C or D (d) D
2. Which lecturer's course immediately follows course B?
   (a) Q (b) P
   (c) S (d) T
3. Which course is taught in the month of January?
   (a) C (b) D
   (c) E (d) Data inadequate

Directions for Questions 4 to 7: *The annual gathering of a college was organised on a day. Six different programmes–drama, singing, mimicry, speech, story-telling and dance are to be performed by six students A, B, C, D, E and F, not necessarily in the same order. The programme begins with a song not sung by B and ends with a dance. C performs mimicry immediately after the speech. E performs drama just before the dance. D or F are not available for the last performance. The speech is not given by A. An interval of 30 minutes is given immediately after mimicry with three more items remaining to be performed. D performs immediately after the interval.*

4. Which item is performed by F?
   (a) Song (b) Dance
   (c) Speech (d) Data inadequate
5. Who performed the dance?
   (a) A (b) B
   (c) Either A or B (d) F
6. Who was the first performer?
   (a) D (b) E
   (c) A (d) Data inadequate
7. Who was the last performer?
   (a) A (b) B
   (c) F (d) Data inadequate

Directions for Questions 8 to 11: *In a bar, there are seven frequent visitors who visit the bar daily. On being asked about their visit to the bar the preceding Sunday, the following were the answers:*

Jai Chand: I came in first and the next two persons to enter were Sohan Singh and Shail Munshi. When I left the bar, Jai Prakash and Vinod Rai were present in the bar. Deepak Garg left with me.

Jai Prakash: When I entered the bar with Vinod Rai, Jai Chand was sitting there. There was someone else also, but I was not in a position to recognise him.

Shail Munshi: I went to the bar for a short while last Sunday and met Jai Chand, Sohan Singh and Deepak Garg there.

Sohan Singh: I left immediately after Shail Munshi left.

Deepak Garg: I met Jai Chand, Sohan Singh, Shail Munshi, Jai Prakash and Vinod Rai during my first visit to the bar. But I got an urgent call and came out of the bar with Jai Chand. When I went to the bar for the second time, Jai Prakash and Vinod Rai were there.

Pradeep Kumar: I had some urgent work, so I did not sit in the bar for a long time. Jai Prakash and Deepak Garg were the only people in the bar when I was there.

Vinod Rai: I was drunk and I don't remember anything.

8. Who among Jai Prakash and Deepak Garg, entered the bar first?
   (a) Jai Prakash (b) Deepak Garg
   (c) Both entered (d) Cannot be determined
9. Who was sitting with Jai Chand when Jai Prakash entered the bar?
   (a) Sohan Singh (b) Shail Munshi
   (c) Deepak Garg (d) Pradeep Kumar
10. How many of the seven members did Vinod Rai meet on Sunday in the bar?
   (a) 2 (b) 3
   (c) 4 (d) 5
11. Who were the last two persons to leave the bar?
   (a) Jai Chand & Deepak Garg
   (b) Pradeep Kumar & Deepak Garg
   (c) Jai Prakash & Pradeep Kumar
   (d) Jai Prakash & Deepak Garg

Directions for Questions 12 to 15: Three lawyers, Binod, Kriti and Wasim visit the chambers in the Saket court from Monday to Saturday to meet their clients. Binod discusses the matter with each client for 10 minutes and charges ₹1000/-. Kriti discusses the matter with each client for 15 minutes and charges ₹2000/-, while Wasim discusses the matter with each client for 25 minutes and charges ₹3000/-. The court has three rooms numbered 1, 2 and 3 which are assigned to the three lawyers as per the following table.

High Yield Questions
Scan this QR code to access a video explanation of questions 12-15

Room No.	Monday & Tuesday	Wednesday & Thursday	Friday & Saturday
1	Binod	Wasim	Kriti
2	Kriti	Binod	Wasim

Room No.	Monday & Tuesday	Wednesday & Thursday	Friday & Saturday
3	Wasim	Kriti	Binod

The court is open from 2 p.m. to 4.30 p.m. every Monday to Saturday. On arrival each client is handed a numbered token indicating their position in the queue, starting with token number 1 every day. As soon as any lawyer becomes free, the next client in the queue enters that emptied room for consultation. If at any time, more than one room is free then the waiting client enters the room with the smallest number. For example, if the next two clients in the queue have token numbers 7 and 8 and if rooms numbered 1 and 3 are free, then client with token number 7 enters room number 1 and client with token number 8 enters room number 3. For these questions (unless explicitly mentioned), assume that the court house had enough visitors that day, so that no lawyer had any free time.

12. What is the maximum number of clients who can visit the court to meet the lawyers on any single day?

13. The queue is never empty on one particular Saturday. Which of the three lawyers would earn the maximum amount in consultation charges on that day?
(a) Wasim (b) Kriti
(c) Binod (d) Can't be determined

14. Sachin visited the court on Monday, Wednesday, and Friday of a particular week, arriving at 2:50 p.m. on each of the three days. His token number was 13 on all three days. On which day was his matter discussed with Wasim?
(a) Monday (b) Wednesday
(c) Friday (d) Can't be determined.

15. On a slow Thursday, only two clients are waiting at 2 p.m. After that two clients keep arriving at exact 15 minute intervals starting at 2:15 p.m. – i.e. at 2:15 p.m., 2:30 p.m., 2:45 p.m. etc. Then the total duration in minutes when Kriti and Binod were simultaneously engaged (in minutes) is:

Directions for Questions 16 to 19:

Technocrat is a printing shop which provides three types of service: typing, scanning and printing. It has two employees Anil and Binod who prepare the items ordered by the clients. Completion time is 10 minutes for 1 page of typing and 2 minutes for an order of printing of 1 page. An employee can work only on one of these items at a time. The scanning is done in an automatic scanner which can do up to 3 pages of scanning at a time, and take 5 minutes irrespective of the number of pages (1, 2 or 3). The scanner does not need an employee to constantly attend to it, and we can ignore time taken by an employee to start and stop the scanner; thus, an employee can be engaged in working on other services while the scanner is on.

Technocrat wishes to complete the orders as early as possible. The individual items in any orders are delivered as and when ready; however, the order is considered to be completed only when all the tasks of that order are completed

The table below gives the orders of three clients and the times at which they placed their orders:

Customer no.	Time	Order
1	11:00	1 page typing, 3 page of scanning, 1 page of printing
2	11:05	2 page of scanning, 1 page of printing
3	11:17	1 page typing, 1 page of scanning

16. Assume that only one client's order can be processed at any given point of time. So, Anil or Binod cannot start working on a new order while working on the previous order At what time is the order placed by client 1 completed?
(a) 11:10 (b) 11:05
(c) 11:07 (d) None of these

17. Assume that only one client's order can be processed at any given point of time. So, Anil or Binod cannot start working on a new order while previous order is being prepared. At what time is the order placed by client 3 completed?
(a) 11:30 (b) 11:25
(c) 11:27 (d) None of these

18. Suppose the employees are allowed to work on multiple orders at a time, but the preference would be to finish orders of clients who placed their orders earlier. At what time is the order placed by client 2 completed?
(a) 11:07 (b) 11:10
(c) 11:12 (d) None of these

19. Suppose the employees are allowed to process multiple orders at a time, but the preference would be to finish orders of clients who placed their orders earlier. Also assume that the fourth client came in only at 11:35. Between 11:00 and 11:30, for how many minutes is exactly one of the employees idle (in minutes) ?

Directions for Questions 20 to 23: *Answer the questions based on the information given below.*

Ajeet went for holidays in different country every year from 2014 to 2018. His holidays lasted for a different number of day(s) among 1, 2, 3, 4 and 5 on each occasion, in no order. It is also known that:

(i) His holidays in 2017 lasted a day longer as compared to the year when he went to Manali.

(ii) He went to Guwahati in the year next to the one in which he went to the Nainital.

(iii) He went to Ooty in the year next to the one in which his holidays lasted for just 1 day.

(iv) He didn't go to Guwahati in 2018. His holidays in Guwahati lasted for less than 5 days.

(v) His holidays in 2016 lasted a day longer as compared to the year when he went to Chakrata.

(vi) He went to Ooty in 2015 and his holidays lasted for less than 5 days.

20. Which of the following combinations of the destination and the year of holidays is not correct?

(a) Chakrata - 2018 (b) Guwahati - 2017
(c) Manali - 2014 (d) None of these

21. How many days did Ajeet spend on his holidays in Guwahati?

22. Which of the following statement(s) is/are true?

I. He spent 1 day on his holidays in Chakrata.
II. He spent 4 days on his holidays in the Nainital.

(a) Only I (b) Only II
(c) Both I and II (d) Neither I nor II

23. Find the sum of number of days Ajeet spent on his holidays in Manali and Nainital.

Directions for Questions 24 to 27:

In Sahu theatre in Lucknow there was only 1 screen in which movies can be played for 6 hours a day from 12 pm to 3 pm and from 3:30 pm to 6:30 pm, every day from Monday to Saturday. Three movies- A, B and C were played for 2 hours each day and each movie is 1 hour long. The following information is also known:

(i) There were total 6- slots for movies and each slot has a length of 1 hour. Slot starts from 12 pm and each movie was allotted two slots according to the comfort of distributer of the movie.

(ii) Movie C's shows are never played consecutively during the week.

(iii) Movie 'A' which did not take the last slot on any day, took its playing slots continuously without a break.

(iv) Movie 'A' took the 1st and 2nd slots on Wednesday and Friday.

(v) Movie 'C' took 3rd slot on four days and 1st slot on 3 days of the week.

(vi) The slot-schedule allotted to any movie was not identical for more than 2 days.

(vii) Movie 'B' took the 4th slot from Wednesday to Saturday. It was allotted the last slot only on three days- Monday, Wednesday and Friday.

(viii) Movie A's slots allocation are identical on Thursday and Saturday.

24. On how many days both shows of Movie 'B' were played after 3:00 pm?

25. Which movie was played on 12 – 1 pm slot on Monday?

26. In the week on how many days did both the shows of the movie 'B' were played before both the shows of movie 'C'?

27. Which movie was played on 4:30 – 5:50 pm slot on Thursday?

Directions for Questions 28 to 31: *Read the information provided and answer the questions which follow.*

Three doctors, Dr. Ben, Dr. Kane and Dr. Wayne visit a particular clinic from Monday to Saturday to see patients. Dr. Ben sees each patient for 10 minutes and charges ₹ 100/-. Dr. Kane sees each patient for 15 minutes and charges ₹ 200/-, while Dr. Wayne sees each patient for 25 minutes and charges ₹ 300/-.

The clinic has three rooms numbered 1, 2 and 3 which are assigned to the three doctors as per the following table.

Room No.	Monday & Tuesday	Wednesday & Thursday	Friday & Saturday
1	Ben	Wayne	Kane
2	Kane	Ben	Wayne
3	Wayne	Kane	Ben

The clinic is open from 9 a.m. to 11.30 a.m. every Monday to Saturday.

On arrival each patient is handed a numbered token, indicating their position in the queue, starting with token number 1 every day. As soon as any doctor becomes free, the next patient in the queue enters that emptied room for consultation. If at any time, more than one room is free then the waiting patient enters the room with the smallest number. For example, if the next two patients in the queue have token numbers 7 and 8 and if rooms numbered 1 and 3 are free, then patient with token number 7 enters room number 1 and patient with token number 8 enters room number 3.

28. What is the maximum number of patients that the clinic can cater to on any single day?

(a) 12 (b) 30
(c) 15 (d) 31

29. The queue is never empty on one particular Saturday. Which of the three doctors would earn the maximum amount in consultation charges on that day?

(a) Dr. Ben
(b) Dr. Kane
(c) Both Dr. Wayne and Dr. Kane
(d) Dr. Wayne

30. Mr. Singh visited the clinic on Monday, Wednesday, and Friday of a particular week, arriving at 8:50 a.m. on each of the three days. His token number was 13 on all three days. On which day was he at the clinic for the maximum duration?

(a) Friday
(b) Same duration on all three days.
(c) Wednesday
(d) Monday

31. On a slow Thursday, only two patients are waiting at 9 a.m. After that, two patients keep arriving at exact 15 minute intervals, starting at 9:15 a.m.– i.e., at 9:15 a.m., 9:30 a.m., 9:45 a.m. etc. Then, what is the total duration in minutes when all three doctors are simultaneously free?

(a) 30 (b) 10
(c) 0 (d) 15

Directions for Questions 32 to 35: Seven candidates, Akil, Balaram, Chitra, Divya, Erina, Fatima, and Ganeshan, were invited to interview for a position. Candidates were required to reach the venue before 8 am. Immediately upon arrival, they were sent to one of three interview rooms: 101, 102, and 103. The following venue log shows the arrival times for these candidates. Some of the names have not been recorded in the log and have been marked as '?'.

High Yield Questions

Scan this QR code to access a video explanation of questions 32-35

Time	7:10 am	7:15 am	7:25 am	7:30 am	7:40 am	7:45 am
Person	Akil,?	?	?	Chitra	Fatima	?

Additionally here are some statements from the candidates:

Balaram: I was the third person to enter Room 101.

Chitra: I was the last person to enter the room I was allotted to.

Erina: I was the only person in the room I was allotted to.

Fatima: Three people including Akil were already in the room that I was allotted to when entered it.

Ganeshan: I was one among the two candidates allotted to Room 102.

32. What best can be said about the room to which Divya was allotted?

(a) Definitely Room 101
(b) Definitely Room 102
(c) Definitely Room 103
(d) Either Room 101 or Room 102

33. Who else was in Room 102 when Ganeshan entered?

(a) Akil (b) Divya
(c) Chitra (d) None of these

34. When did Erina reach the venue?

(a) 7:10 am (b) 7:15 am
(c) 7:25 am (d) 7:45 am

35. If Ganeshan entered the venue before Divya, when did Balaram enter the venue?

(a) 7:10 am (b) 7:15 am
(c) 7:25 am (d) 7:45 am

Directions for Questions 36 to 39: There are 21 employees working in a division, out of whom 10 are special-skilled employees (SE) and the remaining are regular-skilled employees (RE). During the next five months, the division has to complete five projects every month. Out of the 25 projects, 5 projects are "challenging", while the remaining ones are "standard". Each of thechallenging projects has to be completed in different months. Every months, five teams - T1, T2, T3, T4 and T5, work on one projects each. T1, T2, T3, T4 and T5 are allotted the challenging project in the first, second, third, fourth and fifth month, respectively. The team assigned the challenging project has one more employee than the rest.

In the first month, T1 has one more SE than T2, T2 has one more SE than T3, T3 has one more SE than T4, and T4 has one more SE than T5. Between two successive months, the composition of the teams changes as follows:

(i) The team allotted the challenging project, gets two SE from the team which was allotted the challenging project in the previous month. In exchange, one RE is shifted from the former team to the latter team.

(ii) After the above exchange, if T1 has any SE and T5 has any RE, then one SE is shifted from T1 to T5, and one RE is shifted from T5 to T1. Also, if T2 has any SE and T4 has any RE, then one SE is shifted from T2 to T4, and one RE is shifted from T4 to T2.

Each standard project has a total of 100 credit points, while each challenging project has 200 credit points. The credit points are equally shared between the employees included in that team.

36. The number of times in which the composition of team T2 and the number of times in which composition of team T4 remained unchanged in two successive months are:

(a) (2, 1) (b) (1, 0)
(c) (0, 0) (d) (1, 1)

37. The number of SE in T1 and T5 for the projects in the third month are, respectively:

(a) (0, 2) (b) (0, 3)
(c) (1, 2) (d) (1, 3)

38. Which of the following CANNOT be the total credit points earned by any employee from the projects?

(a) 140 (b) 150
(c) 170 (d) 200

39. One of the employees named Aneek scored 185 points. Which of the following CANNOT be true?

(a) Aneek worked only in teams T1, T2, T3, and T4.
(b) Aneek worked only in teams T1, T2, T4, and T5.
(c) Aneek worked only in teams T2, T3, T4, and T5.
(d) Aneek worked only in teams T1, T3, T4, and T5.

ANSWER KEY

1. (c)	2. (a)	3. (c)	4. (d)
5. (c)	6. (d)	7. (d)	8. (b)
9. (c)	10. (b)	11. (d)	12. 31
13. (b)	14. (a)	15. 50	16. (a)
17. (c)	18. (b)	19. 16	20. (d)
21. 2	22. (d)	23. 6	24. 3
25. Movie C	26. 1	27. Movie B	28. (d)
29. (a)	30. (d)	31. (c)	32. (a)
33. (d)	34. (d)	35. (c)	36. (b)
37. (a)	38. (b)	39. (d)	

SOLUTIONS AND SHORTCUTS

Solutions for Questions 1 to 3:

Using the three clues we get the following pairings:

P – B – Not April or May
Q – A – March
R–Not C or D – January

Put them together to get the following table.

A	B	C	D	E
Q March	P February			R January

This leaves S and T to be teaching either C or D and either in April or May.

1. We do not know who teaches C or D (between S and T). Hence, Option (c) is correct.
2. Course B occurs in February. Hence, we need to look for who is teaching in March. The answer to the question is Lecturer Q. Option (a) is correct.
3. In January, Course E is taught. Option (c) is correct.

Solutions for Questions 4 to 7:

The first two statements are just introductions to the situation. Going ahead from third statement onwards, the following chain of thoughts should arise.

REACTION TRACKER

Statement	Reaction
3	Song _ _ _ _ _ Dance Song Not B → To be used later
4	To be used later
5	Song _ _ _ Drama/E Dance
6	
7	D or F not dance. To be used later (since it is an indirect clue)
8	To be used later
9	Song – Mimicry/C – Drama/E Dance Song – Mimicry (C) _ (D) Drama (E) Dance

At this stage, use Statement 4 to get the following figure. Since speech comes before mimicry, storytelling comes after mimicry.

Song	Speech	Mimicry	Storytelling	Drama	Dance
		C	D	E	

The unused clues at this stage are (B not song), (F not last) and (A not speech).

Using them does not give a definite placement for any of A, B or F.

Hence,

4. Data inadequate, since F can be either song or speech. Option (d) is correct.
5. Either A or B. Option (c) is correct.
6. Can be either A or F. Hence, data inadequate. Option (d) is correct.
7. Again, could be A or B. Hence, data inadequate. Option (d) is correct.

Solutions for Questions 8 to 11:

This question looks extremely complicated due to the multiple statements, but the main issue required to be resolved while solving this question is the structure of the diagram. While solving this question, concentrate mainly on who is present in the bar at different times of the day and correlate this information to the statements. Also try to number the events so as to give order to the various going-ins and coming-outs of the people. The following reaction tracker table gives the step by step reactions to the clues in the question.

REACTION TRACKER TABLE

Statement of	Reaction
Jai Chand (JC)	Event 1: JC comes in Event 2: Sohan Singh (SS) comes in. Event 3: Shail Munshi (SM) comes in. Constraint: JC leaves with Deepak Garg (DG) leaving Jai Prakash (JP) and Vinod Rai (VR) in the bar.
Jai Prakash (JP)	Event (Number not known): JP and VR enter. Constraint: JC and someone else was there.
Shail Munshi (SM)	Event: SM enters Constraint: Meets JC, SS and DG
Sohan Singh (SS)	Event x: SM leaves Event (x + 1): SS leaves
Deepak Garg (DG)	Event: DG enters. Constraint: Meets JC, SS, SM, JP and VR during his first visit. Event: DG and JC leave. Event: DG enters for second time. Constraint: JP and VR are there when DG enters again. (no one else is present)

Statement of	Reaction
Pradeep Kumar (PK)	Event: PK enters. Constraint: Only JP and DG are present at this time.
Vinod Rai (VR)	No info. Deductions: When JP and VR enter only 2 people are there. We also know the first 3 events—JC enters, SS enters and SM enters. Also, DG meets SC, SS, SM, JR and VR in his first visit. This gives us that: Event 4: DG enters. Event 5: SM leaves. Event 6: SS leaves. Event 7: JP and VR enter (at this time only JC and DG are there). Event 8: JC and DG leave (Now only JP and VR are present). Event 9: DG comes back again (now JP, VR and DG are inside). Event 10: VR leaves (Since when PK enters only JP and DG are there). Event 11: PK enters. Event 12: PK leaves.

Hence, the answers are:

8. DG enters before JP. Hence, (b).
9. DG was sitting there (Event 7). Hence, (c).
10. VR meets JC, DG and JP. He comes in after SM and SS have left and leaves before PK enters. Hence, he meets only 3 people. Hence, (b).
11. JP and DG must be leaving last since they are there when PK leaves. Hence, (d).

Solutions for Questions 12 to 15:

Binod, Kriti and Wasim discuss the matter for 10 minutes, 15 minutes and 25 minutes respectively.

12. All the three lawyers work for 150 minutes daily.
    To maximize the number of clients visit we need to maximize the engagement duration of the lawyers, it means none of the lawyers was free (or totally engaged) from 2:00 pm to 4:30 pm in any of the given days.
    Binod meets 150/10 = 15 clients daily.
    Kriti meets 150/15 = 10 clients daily.
    Wasim meets 150/25 = 6 clients daily.
    Daily they together meet 15 + 10 + 6 = 31 clients.
    Hence, correct answer must be 31.
13. It is given that queue was never empty on a particular Saturday, it means all the lawyers are completely engaged for the entire duration on that day. So, each lawyer worked for exactly 150 minutes.
    Per minute consultation fee for Binod = 1000/10 = ₹100 per minute.
    Per minute consultation fee for Kriti = 2000/15 = ₹133.33 per minute.
    Per minute consultation fee for Wasim = 3000/25 = ₹120 per minute.
    Per minute consultation fee is maximum for Kriti, so Kriti earned the maximum amount = 133.33 × 150 = ₹20,000
14. The distribution of visitor no. 1 to 13 (On Monday, Wednesday and Friday) can be done as shown below.

Monday			Wednesday			Friday		
1	2	3	1	2	3	1	2	3
Binod	Kriti	Wasim	Wasim	Binod	Kriti	Kriti	Wasim	Binod
2:00 (1)	2:00 (2)	2:00 (3)	2:00 (1)	2:00 (2)	2:00 (3)	2:00 (1)	2:00 (2)	2:00 (3)
2:10 (4)	2:15 (5)	2:25 (7)	2:25 (7)	2:10 (4)	2:15 (5)	2:15 (5)	2:25 (7)	2:10 (4)
2:20 (6)	2:30 (9)	**2:50 (13)**	2:50 (12)	2:20 (6)	2:30 (9)	2:30 (8)	2:50 (12)	2:20 (6)
2:30 (8)	2:45 (11)	3:15	3:15	2:30 (8)	2:45 (11)	2:45 (11)	3:15	2:30 (9)
2:40 (10)	3:00	3:40	.....	2:40 (10)	3:00	3:00	.....	2:40 (10)
2:50 (12)				**2:50 (13)**	3:15			**2:50 (13)**

So, he discussed his matter with Wasim on Monday.

15.

Time	Thursday			
	1	2	3	
	Wasim	Binod	Kriti	Binod and Kriti simultaneous engagement (in minutes)
2:00 pm	1	2	-	

Time	Thursday			
	1	2	3	
	Wasim	Binod	Kriti	Binod and Kriti simultaneous engagement (in minutes)
2:15 pm	---	3	4	10
2:30 pm	5	6	--	
2:45 pm	--	7	8	10
3:00 pm	9	10	--	
3:15 pm	--	11	12	10
3:30 pm	13	14	--	
3:45 pm	--	15	16	10
4:00 pm	17	18	--	
4:15 pm	--	19	20	10
Total				50

Kriti and Binod were simultaneously engaged (in minutes) for 50 minutes.

Solutions for Questions 16 to 19:

We can first create a table for when orders are not allowed to be processed parallelly. The following work chart would help us answer questions 16 and 17.

Customer no.	Time	Order	Working
1	11:00	1 page typing, 3 page of scanning, 1 page of printing	10 minutes of typing by one worker and 2 minutes for printing of another page. [Scanning work would take 5 minutes for these three pages but it does not require engagement of any worker] So, the work would be delivered at 11:10.
2	11:05	2 page of scanning, 1 page of printing	Work would start at 11:10. 1 Page of printing would take 2 minutes, and scanning could be done in parallel in 5 minutes so the order would be delivered at 11:15
3	11:17	1 page typing, 1 page of scanning	Typing would take 10 minutes and will be done at 11:27.

16. The order for client 1 would get delivered at 11:10. Hence, option (a) is correct.
17. The order for client 1 would get delivered at 11:27. Hence, option (c) is correct.

For Questions 18 and 19, the following table can be made – and the answers can be read off this table.

Customer no.	Time	Order	Working	Idle time
1	11:00	1 page typing, 3 page of scanning, 1 page of printing	10 minutes of typing by Binod and 2 minutes for printing by Anil. [Scanning work would take 5 minutes for these three pages but it does not require engagement of any worker] So, Anil would be free at 11:02. At 11:10 the order would be delivered.	Binod: 0 Anil: 11:02 to 11:05 Exactly one of the employees idle for 3 minutes.
2	11:05	2 page of scanning, 1 page of printing	1 Page of printing would take 2minutes, and scanning could be done in parallel in 5 minutes so Anil can start printing at 11:05 and finish it by 11:07, simultaneously scanning would take 5 minutes and at 11:10 the order would be delivered.	Binod: 0 Anil: 11:07 to 11:10 [Then, Binod and Anil both are free from 11:10 to 11:17] Exactly one of the employees idle for 3 minutes.

3	11:17	1 page typing, 1 page of scanning	1 Page of typing would take 10 minutes, and scanning could be done in parallel in 5 minutes so Binod could start typing at 11:17 and finish it by 11:27,	Binod: 0 Anil: 11:17 to 11:27 [Then, Binod and Anil both are free from 11:27 to 11:30] Exactly one of the employees idle for 10 minutes.

18. The order of client 2 is completed at 11:10. Hence, option (b) is correct.
19. Exactly one employee is free for 3 + 3 + 10 = 16 minutes between 11:00 and 11:30. Hence, the correct answer is 16.

Solutions for Questions 20 to 23:

Ajeet visited Ooty in 2015, he must have gone to the Nainital and Guwahati respectively in either 2016 and 2017 or 2017 and 2018. But from statement (iv) we are given that he has not gone to Guwahati in 2018. Hence, he visited Nainital in 2016 and Guwahati in 2017. Also, given directly to us is that In the year 2014 he spent only 1 day .

Let the number of days spent on holidays in Manali and Chakrata be M and C respectively. Therefore, he spent 'M +' and 'C + 1' days in Guwahati and the Nainital respectively. Let the number of days he spent in Ooty be z. At this point we know that he has not spent 5 days in Ooty (given), Guwahati (given), Chakrata or Manali (Since he spent more days than there in Guwahati and Nainital respectively. Hence, he must have spent 5 days in Nainital and 4 days in Chakrata. We get the following table depicting his holiday destinations and days at each destination.

Year	Destination	Number of days
2014	Manali	1
2015	Ooty	3
2016	Nainital	5
2017	Guwahati	2
2018	Chakrata	4

20. (d) None of these
21. 2
22. (d) Neither I nor II
23. 6

Solutions for Questions 24 to 27:

From statements 2, 4, 5 and 7 we can form the following table:

Slot Timing	Monday	Tuesday	Wednesday	Thursday	Friday	Saturday
12:00–1:00			A		A	
1:00–2:00			A		A	
2:00–3:00			C		C	
3:30–4:30			B	B	B	B
4:30–5:30			C		C	
5:30–6:30	B		B		B	

From statement 3, movie 'A' did not play on the last slot on any day, hence on the last slot on Tuesday, Thursday and Saturday, movie C must be played. Next, if we look at the Thursday and Saturday schedules, we can see that movie A can only go to the second and third slots (since it has to be used for consecutive slots). This means that on these days movie C would have to take the first slot (as it cannot go to the 5th slot – since it is never played consecutively, during the week – clue 2).

From statement 5, we can say that the 2:00 PM – 3:00 PM slot (3rd slot) on Monday and Tuesday movie 'C' was played. 4th and 5th slot on Monday and Tuesday movie A was played.

From the above analysis we can fill the following table:

Slot Timing	Monday	Tuesday	Wednesday	Thursday	Friday	Saturday
12:00–1:00	C	B	A	C	A	C
1:00–2:00	B	B	A	A	A	A
2:00–3:00	C	C	C	A	C	A
3:30–4:30	A	A	B	B	B	B
4:30–5:30	A	A	C	B	C	B
5:30–6:30	B	C	B	C	B	C

24. 3
25. C
26. 1
27. B

Solutions for Questions 28 to 31:

We should start the question with the following table:

	Monday	Tuesday	Wednesday	Thursday	Friday	Saturday
Room 1	Ben	Ben	Wayne	Wayne	Kane	Kane
Room 2	Kane	Kane	Ben	Ben	Wayne	Wayne
Room 3	Wayne	Wayne	Kane	Kane	Ben	Ben

We also know that the time slots would be fixed for each doctor daily, irrespective of the room he consults in. Henceforth, in the solution, we will be using B for Ben, K for Kane and W for Wayne. Thus, the time slots are:

	P1	P2	P3	P4	P5	P6	P7	P8	P9	P10	P11	P12	P13	P14	P15
B	9	9:10	9:20	9:30	9:40	9:50	10	10:10	10:20	10:30	10:40	10:50	11	11:10	11:20
K	9	9:15	9:30	9:45	10	10:15	10:30	10:45	11:00	11:15					
W	9	9:25	9:50	10:15	10:40	11:05									

Clearly, B sees 15 patients, K sees 10 and W sees 6. Also, take a note of the order in which patients are allotted rooms when more than one room is free.

28. The clinic can cater to a maximum of 15 + 10 + 6 = 31 patients, if all the doctors are occupied all the time. Hence, option (d) is correct.
29. From the queue is never empty on one particular Saturday, we get that all the doctors would treat the maximum number of patients. If this were to occur the incomes would be: A = 15 × 100 = 1500, B = 10 × 200 = 2000 and C = 6 × 300 = 1800. It is clear that B earns the maximum. Option (a) is correct.
30. From the timings table, it can be seen that the 12th and 13th patient on each day will enter the doctor's rooms at the same time viz, 9:50 am Also, these two patients go to the doctors B and W respectively. For the patient with token 13 to be in the clinic for the maximum duration, he should go to Dr. W, since he sees the patient for a longer time. 13 will get allocated to W, only on Monday. On Wednesday and Friday, since the room number of W is less than the room number of B, patient 13 would go to B and get to leave the clinic in 10 minutes. Hence, the correct answer is (d).
31. At 9 am, the two patients on Thursday would go to the rooms of W and B. B will get free in 10 minutes at 9:10 am Hence, at 9:15, both B and K would be free, while W would still be occupied with his first patient. W and B would get free at 9:25 am, but K would be occupied till 9:30. Hence, between 9 and 9:30 am there would be '0' minutes when all the three doctors would be free. At 9:30 AM, all the three doctors would be free, and the situation would be exactly similar to the 9 am situation, as the two patients walk in at 9:30 am They will again go to W and B respectively, and so on. You can easily see that for each half an hour time period, there is not a single minute when all the three doctors are free together. Hence, till 11:30 am, the required time would be zero minutes. Option (c) is correct.

Solutions for Questions 32 to 35:

From the clues of the statements of Balaram and Fatima, it is clear that room 101 had 4 people. These must have been Akil, Divya, Balaram and Fatima, with Fatima coming last amongst them. So, Balaram and Divya must have entered at any two times of 7:10; 7:15 or 7:25. Also, from Ganeshan's statement we know that there were only 2 people in Room 102. If we add the information of Chitra's statement to this, we get that Ganeshan and Chitra must have been allotted Room 102. That leaves Erina alone in Room 103. Further, with respect to the timing of Ganeshan, the only thing we know is that he must have come before Chitra - means he came in either at 7:10, 7:15 or 7:25. Thus, the three timings of Balaram, Divya and Ganeshan must be shared between 7:10, 7:15 and 7:25. However, Balaram being the third person to enter the room (deduced as 101) cannot come in at 7:10. Hence, 7:10 is shared between D and G, while 7:15 can go to any of B,D and G. Also, 7:25 cannot go to D, since Balaram has to come after Divya. However, we are not able to resolve the timings any further than that, since we would run out of clues at this point. What we know can be encapsulated in a table as follows:

7:10	7:15	7:25	7:30	7:40	7:45
A, D/G	B/G/D	B/G	Chitra	Fatima	Erina

The room numbers can be allotted as follows:

Room Number	101	102	103
	Akil, Balaram, Divya, Fatima	Ganeshan, Chitra	Erina

We can now move onto the questions:

32. Divya is definitely in Room 101. Option (a) is correct.
33. Ganeshan was the first of two people to enter Room 102. Hence, there was no one in the room when Ganeshan entered. Option (d) is correct.
34. Erina reached the venue at 7:45 am Option (d) is correct.
35. We know that G/D have to share 7:10 and B/G/D have to share 7:15 and 7:25 has to be shared between B and G as their entry times. If Ganeshan enters before Divya, it means that Ganeshan must necessarily come in at 7:10. Then, Divya comes in at 7:15 and Balaram would come in at 7:25. Hence, option (c) is correct.

Solutions for Questions 36 to 39:

The given diagram shows the number of special, number of regular and the total number of employees working in each team T1 to T5 during the five months. The team for the month that is doing the challenging project - is put in a box - thus, we can see the box on T1 in month 1, T2 in month 2, T3 in month 3, T4 in month 4 and T5 in month 5. Also, in the first month the number of Special employees in each team is given by the sentence 'In the first month, T1 has one more SE than T2....than T5'. For the second month, the following transfers will occur: The Challenging project moves to T2, so 2 Special Employees move from T1 to T2, while 1 RE moves from T2 to T1. At this stage T1 has (2) + 2, while T2 has (5) + 0. Next, one SE will shift from T1 to T5 and 1 RE will shift from T5 to T1. Thus, T1 ends with (1) + 3 while T5 ends with (1) + 3 also. Then, one SE moves from T2 to T4 and one RE moves from T4 to T2 - so T2 ends with (4) + 1, while T4 ends with (2) + 2. The further months are completed on the same logic.

	T_1	T_2	T_3	T_4	T_5
(i)	$\boxed{(4) + 1}_5$	$\underline{(3) + 1}_4$	$\underline{(2) + 2}_4$	$\underline{(1) + 3}_4$	$\underline{(0) + 4}_4$
(ii)	$\underline{(1) + 3}_4$	$\boxed{(4) + 1}_5$	$\underline{(2) + 2}_4$	$\underline{(2) + 2}_4$	$\underline{(1) + 3}_4$
(iii)	$\underline{(0) + 4}_4$	$\underline{(1) + 3}_4$	$\boxed{(4) + 1}_5$	$\underline{(3) + 1}_4$	$\underline{(2) + 2}_4$
(iv)	$\underline{(0) + 4}_4$	$\underline{(1) + 3}_4$	$\underline{(2) + 2}_4$	$\boxed{(5) + 0}_5$	$\underline{(2) + 2}_4$
(v)	$\underline{(0) + 4}_4$	$\underline{(0) + 4}_4$	$\underline{(2) + 2}_4$	$\underline{(4) + 0}_4$	$\boxed{(4) + 1}_5$

The answers would be read from the above figure and would be:

36. Looking through the T2 column for the figure, we can see that between months 3 and 4, T2 has the same composition. T4 on the other hand does not show any months with the same composition. Hence, the correct answer is (1,0). Option (b) is correct.
37. The number of SE in T1 and T5 in month 3 are 0 and 2 respectively. Option (a) is correct.
38. When an employee works on a challenging project, he earns 200/5 = 40 points. When an employee works on a standard project, he earns 100/4 = 25 points. Thus, points that can be made using 5 values combining 40s and 25s are possible, while anything that cannot be made from 25s and 40s are not possible. It can be seen that we can make 40 + 25 + 25 + 25 + 25 = 140; 40 + 40 + 40 + 25 + 25 = 170; 40 + 40 + 40 + 40 + 40 = 200, but we cannot make 150 through a combination of 40 and 25. Hence option (b) is correct.
39. To score 185 points, Ashok should work in 4 challenging projects and 1 standard project. Each of options (a), (b) and (c) are possible and a sample thought to check that possibility is illustrated for option (b):
He works in T1 in month 1, T2 in month 2; T4 in months 3 and 4 & T5 in month 5. In such a case he would earn: 40 + 40 + 25 + 40 + 40 = 185 points.

CHAPTER 12

Cryptarithmetic

Chapter Launchpad

Scan this QR code to access an introductory video on Cryptarithmetic

WHAT IS CRYPTARITHMETIC?

Cryptarithmetic is a popular question type in all aptitude exams. It is a type of mathematical puzzle in which the digits in an arithmetic equation are replaced by letters or symbols. The goal is to determine the unique digits that correspond to each letter while ensuring that the mathematical operation remains valid.

In a cryptarithmetic puzzle, every letter/symbol represents a unique digit from 0 to 9. For the entire problem, the same letter/symbol will represent the same digit - hence, once you can determine the value of a letter/symbol, the value gets frozen for the rest of the problem. Also, the value of every letter/symbol is unique - which means that each digit can only represent a single letter/symbol. In other words, no two different letters can have the same digit.

Further, the number/s in the problem cannot start with leading zeroes, i.e., a number cannot be like 0124 (where it starts with a 0).

In order to take you through a few solving logics and rules, let us look at a few solved examples:

Example 1:

Let us start from a simple example:

```
    E G G
  + E G G
  -------
= P A G E
```

Deduction 1: In this addition based cryptarithmetic puzzle, we should first notice that two three digit numbers are adding upto a 4 digit number. This can only happen for a final outcome between 1000-1999. Hence, the value of P must be 1.

Deduction 2: The addition in the right most column gives us G + G = E, while the addition in the second column gives us G + G = G. Thus, G + G is adding up to two different values. This can only occur in case, of a carry-over of + 1 from the first column to the second. In this case, G + G = E gives us that E must be even and G + G + 1 = G gives us that G must be odd. Thus, we realise that the value of G must be > 5. Also, since it must be odd, the only possible values of G are 5, 7 or 9. Using these possibilities to check the second column's addition of G + G + 1 = G, we can see that this only works for 9 + 9 + 1 = 9. Hence, G = 9 and consequently G + G = E → E = 8. Hence, EGG = 899 and the addition is 899 + 899 = 1798.

Example 2:

In the given problem, each letter represents a different digit from 0 to 9. Based on standard addition principles, try to identify the numerical code for the word LATER.

```
      S A T U R N
  +   U R A N U S
  ---------------
  = P L A N E T S
```

Deduction 1: The value of P has to be 1, since the addition is two six digit numbers add upto a 7 digit number. Also, from the first column, we have N + S = S. A column like this can only be seen in two conditions - N = 0 or the column is getting a carry-over of 1 from a previous column and in that case 1 + N + S = S → N has to be 9. In the current problem, since this is the right most column of the addition, we cannot use N as 9 (as there can be no carry-over being received in this column). Hence, the value of N = 0.

Deduction 2: Also, since 0 + S = S, it means that the second column has no carry-over from the first column of the addition. Further we see that in the third column, we have U + 0 = E. This can only occur, if there is a carry-over into the third column from the second one (else it would have been U + 0 = U). Hence, E = U + 1.

Deduction 3: We also see from the 5th column, that A + R = A. Now, R cannot be 0. Hence, this is only possible if R = 9 and the actual column addition is happening because there is a carry-over of 1 from the previous column. Further, there will also be a carry-over of 1 to the 6th column of S + U = L. We can also infer that the third column of U + N = E would have no carry-over (since N = 0 and E cannot be 0). Thus, there is no carry-over into the 4th column. Our addition looks as follows, once these deductions are placed into the image:

```
      1   1   0   1   0
  S   A   T   U   R   0
+     U   9   A   0   U   S
  1   L   A   0   E   T   S
```

Deduction 4: Looking at the second column now, we see that R + U = T. But we already know that R = 9 and also that there is no carry-over into this column. Hence, this could be values like 9 + 3 = **12**; 9 + 4 = **13**; 9 + 5 = **14**; 9 + 6 = **15**; 9 + 7 = **16**; 9 + 8 = **17**. Thus, T + 1 = U.

We also have E = U + 1. Hence, T, U (U + 1) and E (T + 2) are three consecutive digits.

Possibilities for T, U and V are: 2, 3, 4; 3, 4, 5; 4, 5, 6; 5, 6, 7; 6, 7, 8.

We will have to go through a trial and error from this point to check which of these values fit the given situation. The following structures will be visible if we try these one by one:

Using 2, 3, 4 for T, U, V we can reject this case, since the last column has to have a carry over hane S = U should be 10 or greater, while L cannot be 0. So we reject this case as shown in the figure 1.

1 1 0 1 0

S A_8 T_2 U_3 9 0

\+ U_3 9 A_8 0 U_3 S

1 L A_8 0 E_4 T_2 S

0 N, 1 P, 2 T, 3 U, 4 E, 8 A, 9 S

S 5/6/7 not possible

Checking for 3, 4, 5 for T, U, V. This case is again rejected as shown in the figure 2:

1 1 0 1 0

S A_7 T_3 U_4 9 0

\+ U_4 9 A_7 0 U_4 S

1 L A_7 0 E_5 T_3 S

0 N, 1 P, 2, 3 T, 4 U, 5 E, 6, 7 A, 8, 9 R

S = 2/6/8

@ S = 6 L = 1 not possible

@ S = 8 L = 3 not possible

Checking for 4, 5, 6 for T, U, V. This case is again rejected as shown in the figure 3:

1 1 0 1 0

S A T_4 U_5 9 0

\+ 5 9 A 0 U_5 S

1 L A 0 E_6 T_4 S

0 N, 1 P, 2, 3, 4 T, 5 U, 6 E, 7, 8, 9 R

Rejected since A cannot be 6

Checking for T, U, V as 5, 6, 7. This case is again rejected as shown in the figure 4:

1 1 0 1 0

S A T_5 U_6 9 0

\+ 6 9 A 0 U_6 S

1 L A 0 E_7 T_5 S

0 N, 1 P, 2, 3, 4, 5 T, 6 U, 7 E, 8, 9 R

Rejected since A cannot be 5

We get the final solution at T = 6, U = 7 and E = 8.

1 1 0 1 0

S_5 A_4 T_6 U_7 9 0

\+ U_7 9 A_4 0 U_7 S_5

1 L_3 A_4 0 E_8 T_6 S_5

0 N, 1 P, 2, 3, 4 A, 5, 6 T, 7 U, 8 E, 9 R

S = 5 L = 3

Hence, the code for LATER would be 34689.

Let us now look at a question based on multiplication:

Example 3:

```
      A P D
    ×   A D
    -------
    R P A D
  D D C D
  ---------
  D P C E D
```

The following set of deductions help us get to the answer.

Deduction 1: APD*D = RAPD. The first thing we realise is that a 3-digit number APD is multiplied by a single digit number 'D' to give us a 4-digit number RAPD. Also, from the units digit of the multiplication, we see that D × D = D. This can only occur for values of D as 1,5 or 6. However, if D is 1, APD × D cannot be a 4 digit value. Hence, D is either 5 or 6.

Deduction 2: From the third column of the addition we have P + C = C. This can only occur, if P is 0 or 9. If P = 0, then in the next column, R + D = P can only occur if R + D = 10 (with or without carry-over). This would mean a carry over of +1 to the left most column, where we have D = D. However, the outcome of the left-most column would then have been a different letter (other than D, representing D + 1). As this is not the case, we can conclude that P cannot be 0. Hence, P is 9. We now shift our attention to D.

Deduction 3: We have already observed that D is either 5 or 6. If D = 6, we have a multiplication A96 × 6 = R9A6, where R represents the thousands place of R9A6. However, a trial and error with A as 1, 2, 3, 4, 5, 7 or 8 gives us that we have no such multiplication possible, which will satisfy this expression. For instance if we use A = 1, we have 196 × 6 = 1176 ≠ R9A6. For instance again at A = 4, we have 496 × 6 = 2976, but with A as 4, this should have been

R946. Hence, we can reject the value of A as 4. Similarly values of A = 2, 3, 5, 7 or 8 do not fit the situation. Thus, we realise that at D = 6, A has no possible value fitting the given multiplication. Hence, we conclude that D ≠ 6 and D = 5 necessarily. At this stage the multiplications we have are: A95 × 5 = R9A5. Checking for values of A from 1, 2, 3, 4, 6, 7 or 8, we see that only A = 7 fits this situation as we get 795 × 5 = 3975. Hence, A = 7. Hence, our multiplication is: 795 × 75 = 3975 + 55650 = 59625.

Basis our deductions and observations in the previous questions, we can formulate some standard rules for cryptarithmetic problems:

Rule 1: If A + B = A, it means that B is either 0 or 9. In case I, A + 0 = A; Case II, A + 9 + 1(carry) = 1A.

Rule 2: If you are adding 2 single digit numbers and getting a 2 digit number, this 2 digit number has to start with 1. If you are adding two 2-digit numbers and getting a 3-digit number, the 3 digit number has to start with 1. This applies generally, to all situations where one is adding two 'n' digit numbers and getting a 'n + 1' digit number – such a number would start with 1.

Rule 3: In an addition of two digits in a column, the sum can either be a single digit value or in case, it has a two digit value, the value has to be between 10 to 18. In case, the column had a carry-over of 1 it received, then the maximum sum of two digits can be 19 in the case of addition of 9 + 9 + 1.

Rule 4: In case, of multiplication if A × A = A, then the possible scenarios for the digit A could be 0, 1, 5 or 6 only. In these cases, we would get 0 × 0 = 0; 1 × 1 = 1; 5 × 5 = _5 & 6 × 6 = _6.

Rule 5: If A × B = _A then possible values of A and B:

Case I: When A = 5, B = 3, 7 or 9. These would give us the scenarios:

5 × 3 = 15; 5 × 7 = 35; 5 × 9 = 45.

In each of these cases, we will consider only the last digit and carry over the previous digit to the next column.

Case II: When A = 2, 4, 8. B = 6 necessarily. These would give us the scenarios:

2 × 6 = 12; 4 × 6 = 24; 8 × 6 = 48.

In each of these cases, we will consider only the last digit and carry over the previous digit to the next column.

You are now equipped to move to the chapter exercise and solve level 1 and 2 difficulty exercises.

LEVEL OF DIFFICULTY (I)

Directions for Questions 1 to 18: *In the following problems, each letter represents a unique digit. No digit is represented by more than one letter. Also, none of the numbers start with a leading 0. Using standard principles of calculations and mathematics, try to identify the value of each letter in the puzzle and answer the questions that follow*

Directions for Questions 1 to 3:

```
    F A T
  + C A B
  -------
  S C B T
```

1. What is the value of A^2?
2. What is the sum of the values of C,B and T?
   (a) 12
   (b) 11
   (c) 9
   (d) Cannot be determined
3. How many values can T take?

Directions for Questions 4 to 5:

```
    T O T
  + T O P
  -------
    O P T
```

4. What is the value of O = ?
5. TOT × TOP = ?

Directions for Questions 6 to 7:

```
     L O
   + G O
   -----
   O W L
```

LO + GO = OWL

6. What is the value of W?
7. What is the value of LO + OWL?

Directions for Questions 8 and 9:

```
    F A T
  + F A A
  -------
    3 F F
```

8. What is the value of T?
9. What is the sum of T × A + A × T?

Directions for Questions 10 to 13:

NOON + MOON + SOON = JUNE

10. Which of the following could be a possible value of M?
    (a) 2 (b) 3
    (c) 4 (d) 5
11. Which of the following could be a possible value of S?
    (a) 1 (b) 3
    (c) 4 (d) 7

12. What is the value of J?
13. The value of J + U+ E is equal to?

Directions for Questions 14 to 16:

```
      B O B × B O B
      M E O Y
    M I L O
  M E O Y
  M A R L E Y
```

14. What is the value of E?
15. YAR = ?
16. BOB + MARLEY = ?

Directions for Questions 17 to 18:

```
    T O
  + G O
  O U T
```

17. What is the value of G?
18. What is the value of T + G + O + U + T = ?

LEVEL OF DIFFICULTY (II)

Directions for Questions 1 to 20: *In the following problems, each letter represents a unique digit. No digit is represented by more than one letter. Also, none of the numbers start with a leading 0. Using standard principles of calculations and mathematics, try to identify the value of each letter in the puzzle and answer the questions that follow*

1. Find the sum of the values of X + Y + Z, if XYZ = X! + Y! + Z!, where XYZ is a 3-digit number.
   (a) 8
   (b) 9
   (c) 11
   (d) 10

Directions for Questions 2 to 4:

```
    O N E
  + O N E
  + O N E
  + O N E
    T E N
```

High Yield Questions

Scan this QR code to access a video explanation of questions 2-4

2. Value of O = ?
3. What is the value of E?
4. What is the value of the product T × E × N = ?

Directions for Questions 5 to 6:

```
    D E F
  – F E D
    2 9 7
```

5. Which of the following is a possible value of F?
   (a) 7 (b) 8
   (c) 9 (d) 4
6. How many values can E take?
   (a) 7 (b) 8
   (c) 9 (d) 10

Directions for Questions 7 to 9:

```
      S E N D
    + M O R E
    M O N E Y
```

High Yield Questions

Scan this QR code to access a video explanation of questions 7-9

7. Find value of Y.
8. What is the number represented by the code YON?
9. What is the value of O + N + E = ?

Directions for Questions 10 to 12:

```
        H E
      × E H
        H E
    H H A
    H N M E
```

10. What is the value of E?
11. HEH is divisible by which of the following number.
    (a) 17 (b) 13
    (c) 11 (d) 19
12. What is the sum of the letters N + A + M + E

Directions for Questions 13 to 16:

```
          E Y E
          M A T
        S Y I A
      G M T A
    A I R Y
    A A S M A A
```

13. What is the value of A?
14. ET is divisible by which of the following number?
    (a) 12 (b) 7
    (c) 2 (d) ET is a prime number
15. What is the value of R?
16. What are the numbers representing the code YMT

Directions for Questions 17 to 20:

$$\begin{array}{r} A\ B\ C\ D \\ +\ E\ B\ C\ B \\ \hline A\ F\ G\ A\ G \end{array}$$

17. What is the value of E?
18. What is the sum of A + G + D?
19. What is the product of B × G × C?
20. What is the value of B?

High Yield Questions

Scan this QR code to access a video explanation of questions 17 & 18

ANSWER KEY

Level of Difficulty (I)

1. 25	2. (d)	3. 6	4. 5
5. 63000	6. 0	7. 123	8. 6
9. 60	10. (d)	11. (a)	12. 9
13. 18	14. 0	15. 924	
16. 124962	17. 8	18. 13	

Level of Difficulty (II)

1 (d)	2. 1	3. 2	4. 112
5. (d)	6. (d)	7. 2	8. 206
9. 11	10. 7	11. (d)	12. 18
13. 2	14. (d)	15. 5	16. 837
17. 8	18. 11	19. 90	20. 6

SOLUTIONS AND SHORTCUTS

Level of Difficulty (I)

Solutions for Questions 1 to 3:

FAT + CAB = SCBT

As two 3 digit numbers are adding upto a 4 digit number, the value of S must be 1.

From the first column we have T + B = T, so B = 0.

In the second column we have A + A gives B as units digit so, A + A must be 10, giving us A = 5, and a carry-over of 1 to the last column.

In the last column, we then have 1 + F + C = C. [1 carry from the previous step F + C]

So, F must be 9.

1. $A^2 = 5^2 = 25$
2. As we have no information about the values of C and T so we cannot determine the values of C + B + T. Hence, option (d) is correct.
3. T cannot take 0, 5, 1, 9 as these values have already been taken by B, A, S and T respectively. So T can take 2, 3, 4, 6, 7, 8 (total 6 values).

Solutions for Questions 4 to 5:

From the first column we have T + P = T, so P = 0.

From the second column we have: O + O = P, giving us 5 + 5 = 10 – thus O is 5.

In the third column, we will have a carry-over of 1. Hence, we get 1 + T + T = O = 5, so T = 2.

4. O = 5.
5. TOT = 252, TOP = 250
   252 × 250 = 63000.

Solutions for Questions 6 to 7:

O must be 1, since two 2-digit numbers are added to give a 3 digit number – which must start with 1.

Then from the first column, we can find the value of L = 1 + 1 = 2.

In the second column, L + G = 1W or 2 + G = 1W

G must be either 8 or 9.

If G = 8, then 2 + 8 = 10, W = 0 in this case.

If G = 9, then 2 + 9 = 11, W = 1 in this case (which is not possible as O = 1)

So, G = 8 & W = 0.

6. W = 0.
7. LO + OWL = 21 + 102 = 123.

Solutions for Questions 8 to 9:

FAT + FAA = 3FF

In the last column of the addition we have F + F = 3, which means 1 carry from the previous step and F must be 1. So the value of 3FF = 311.

In the second column, we have A + A = 1F = 11, A must be 5. (1 carry from the previous summation T + A = F)

T + A = 1 (as F = 1) is not possible.

So, T + A = 11 or T + 5 = 11 or T = 6.

8. T = 6
9. TA + AT = 6 × 5 + 5 × 6 = 60.

Solutions for Questions 10 to 13:

NOON + MOON + SOON = JUNE

The value of N cannot be 3 as then the first column gives us E = 9, and the second column gives is O + O + O = 3, giving us O as 1, then the third column cannot give us a different value of O + O + O. If N = 0, E = 0 which is not possible. Likewise, values of N as 7, 8, 9 can also be easily rejected (as the last column addition has to be a single digit J), which cannot be achieved with N as either 7 or 8 or 9. Likewise, N as 4, 5 and 6 are also not possible. This leaves us only 2 values for N (1 or 2) which we need to check one by one.

At N = 1: If N = 1, E = 3 (from the first column).

From the second column we see that we would have O + O + O = 1 which is possible only for O = 7.

If O = 7, O + O + O = 21. (carry to the next column is 2).

Column 3 then gives us: 2 + O + O + O = U

2 + 7 + 7 + 7 = 23

U = 3 (not possible as E = 3). Hence, we reject the case of N as 1.

Now check for N = 2.

At N = 2, the first column gives us 2 + 2 + 2 = E = 6.

The second column then is: O + O + O = N = 2. This can only occur at O = 4 and we would get 4 + 4 + 4 = 12, thus carrying over 1 to the next column.

Then, in the third column, we can see that we would have 1 + O + O + O = 1 + 4 + 4 + 4 = 13

Giving us U = 3 and a carry over of 1.

For the last column we have N + M + S + 1 = 2 + M + S + 1= 3 + M + S = J (which has to be a single digit outcome). However, M and S are leading digits and hence cannot be 0. As we have already used 2, 6, 4, 3 so we are left with 1, 5, 7, 8, 9. Out of these five values M and S can only share the values of 1 and 5 - in some order. In both cases, J = 3 + 1 + 5 = 9

10. (d)
11. (a)
12. 9
13. J + U + E = 9 + 3+ 6 = 18

Solutions for Questions 14 to 16:

O × B gives O as unit digit.

Values of (O,B) would come from amongst: (2, 6), (4, 6), (8, 6), (5, 3), (5, 7), (5, 9) & (5, 1) are possibilities. We also see that B × B = Y, which is not possible for B = 6. Hence, we can reject the first three possibilities in the list. Also, (5, 1) is not possible because if B = 1, then multiplying B with any number will give you the same number, which is not a case in the question.

B × B also gives Y as units digit so B can be 3/7/9 consequently Y would be 9/1/7 respectively.

Now by using trial and error we get that B = 3 is the only possible value.

BOB = 353

Y = 9, E = 0, M = 1, L = 6, I = 7, A = 2, R = 4.

14. E = 0
15. YAR = 924
16. BOB + MARLEY = 353 + 124609 = 124962.

Solutions for Questions 17 to 18:

It is clear that O = 1.

If O = 1, then T = 2.

If T =2, then G must be 8 or 9 but if G = 9 then T + G = 2 + 9 = 11. U = 1.

As, O =1, so U = 1 is not possible. So, G = 8, T + G = 2 + 8 = 10.

U = 0.

17. Value of G = 8
18. T + G + O + U + T = 2 + 8 + 1 + 0 + 2 = 13.

Level of Difficulty (II)

Solution for Question 1:

1. XYZ = X! + Y! + Z!

   100X + 10Y + Z = X! + Y! + Z!

   None of X, Y or Z can be greater than 6 otherwise the factorial value would become greater than 1000, which is not possible as XYZ is a 3-digit number. Using trial and error we get: 5! + 4! + 1! = 145

   So, XYZ = 145. X + Y + Z = 1 + 4 + 5 = 10. Option (d) is correct.

Solutions for Questions 2 to 4:

Value of 'O' is either 1 or 2 (as there is no carry).

If E = 1, N = 4 and 4N = 16 , so E = 6, which is not possible.

Let's try this for E = 2:

4E = 4*2 = 8.

So, N = 8

4N = 32 or E = 2.

So, E = 2 is a possible solution. If E = 2, then N = 8.

4O = 32, 3 is carry now. If. O = 2, 4O = 8, 4O + 3 = 8 + 3 = 11. (which is a 2-digit number)

So, O = 2 is not possible.

So, O = 1 and T = 4O + 3 = 4 + 3 = 7

2. 1
3. 2
4. T × E × N = 7 × 2 × 8 = 112.

Solutions for Questions 5 to 6:

5. FED is the reverse of DEF.

   FED = 100F + 10E + D

   DEF = 100D + 10E + F

   DEF - FED = 99(D - F) = 297 OR D - F = 3

Hence, F cannot take 7 or 8 or 9.

So, F = 4 is correct. Option (d) is correct.

6. E can take any value from 0 to 9. Hence, 10 values are possible. Option (d) is correct.

Solutions for Questions 7 to 9:

Deduction 1: In the question of SEND + MORE = MONEY, we have two 4 digit numbers adding up to become a five digit number. Hence, deduction 1 is that M = 1.

Deduction 2: From the thousands column, we have S + M = 10. With M = 1, we have S + 1 = 10 S + M can only be 10 as O = 1 is not possible. Hence, S can be either 8 or 9 (8 if there is a carryover from the hundreds column, 9 if there is none). If we look at the hundreds column by inserting O = 0, we have E + 0 = N, which is only possible if there is a carryover being received by the hundreds column. Hence, E + 1 = N (i.e. N is 1 more than E). This also means that there can be no carryover from the hundreds to the thousands column. Thus, we can conclude that S = 9.

Note: I would encourage you to actively keep a pen paper handy to note down these deductions so that you can follow the next deductions.

Deduction 3: We know that N is one more than E (deduction 2). From the tens column, we can see that N + R = E. This can only occur if R = 9 (not possible), or if R = 8 and the tens column is receiving a carryover of 1 from the units column. Hence we can conclude that R = 8. At this stage the puzzle looks as shown in the figure after replacing the values of S, M, O and R.

```
       1
   9 E N D
+  1 0 8 E
----------
 1 0 N E Y
```

We now move our attention to the values of E and N & consequently D and Y.

The possible values of E, N are 2–3; 3–4; 4–5; 5–6; 6–7 (7-8 and 8-9 are not possible as 8 and 9 have already been allocated).

E = 2, N = 3	E = 3, N = 4	E = 4, N = 5	E = 5, N = 6	E = 6, N = 7
D + E = Y column needs to have a carry over	D + E = Y column needs to have a carry over	D + E = Y column needs to have a carry over	D + E = Y column needs to have a carry over	D + E = Y column needs to have a carry over
No possible values for D as 8, 9 are not available.	No possible values for D as 8, 9 not available and D = 7 gives Y = 0, which is not possible	Values for D cannot be 6, 7, 8, 9 – D at 6, makes Y = 0, D as 7 makes Y = 1, (both 0 and 1 are not available) D as as 8, 9 not available	Values for D can only be 7, which makes Y = 2.	No possible value of D.
Case rejected	Case rejected	Case rejected	Case possible	Case rejected

Since, there is only one case possible we conclude that the addition represents:

```
   9 5 6 7
+  1 0 8 5
----------
 1 0 6 5 2
```

7. Value of Y = 2
8. YON = 206
9. O + N + E = 0 + 6 + 5 = 11.

Solutions for Questions 10 to 12:

According to the question:

HE × H = HE. So, H = 1.

H + A = M or 1 + A = M

If 1 + A is a single digit number then and 1 + A = M and H = N (Next step). But H cannot be equal to N. Hence, 1 + A won't give a single digit number. So A= 9, M = 0, N = 2.

HE × E = HHA = 119. This can only occur at E = 7. And HE × EH represents 17 × 71 = 1207.

10. Value of E = 7.
11. HEH = 171, which is divisible by 19. Hence, option (d) is correct.
12. N + A + M + E = 2 + 9 + 0 + 7 = 18.

Solutions for Questions 13 to 16:

E × T gives A, A × E gives A & M × E gives Y.

E cannot be 1 and A cannot be 1.

10's place addition: I + A = A. So, I = 0.

G + 0 = A (possible only if 1 carry is coming from previous addition).

So, G + 1 = A. So possible values of A = 2, 3, 4, 5, 6, 7, 8, 9 with G as 1, 2, 3, 4, 5, 6, 7, 8.

A is not 1 and A is such that , A × E gives A as units digit & E × T gives A as units digit. A bit of trial and error will tell us that A can only be 2 and hence G is 1 - as A = 2, E = 6 and T = 7 are the only set of values of A, E, T that work in this situation.
Now moving to the product of Y × T, we can see that since E × T = 6 × 7 = 42. So, 4 is the carryover from A to I. From Y × T + 4 = 0, we can see that the value of Y can only be 8.
In the addition of the hundreds place digits, we see that: 2Y + T = M → 2 × 8 + 7 = 23, so M = 3. We now know the full value of EYE. Hence, using EYE × T = SYIA, we can see that this corresponds to 686 × 7 = 4802. Hence, the value of S = 4. Also from, EYE × M = AIRY → 686 × 3 = 2058 → R = 5. Hence, the puzzle represents the multiplication EYE × MAT = 686 × 327 = 224322.

13. 2
14. 67 is a prime number. Hence, option (d) is correct.
15. 5
16. YMT = 837.

Solutions for Questions 17 to 20:

A must be 1.
C + C gives 1 as units digit. So C = 5 and D + B must produce carry 1.
B + B + 1 gives G, as units digit and **D + B = 1G** (since there is a carryover in D + B). However, we do not know whether the B + B + 1 = G or B + B + 1 = 1G.
In the case of B + B + 1 = G (equation 1) and having D + B = 1G (equation 2) → Subtracting equation 1 from equation 2, we get: D-B = 11, which is not possible for single digit values of D and B. Hence B + B + 1 = 1G has to be true.
If **B + B + 1 = G** then D - B = 1.

So, D and B are consecutive numbers with sum more than 10. These can only be Case 1: 7, 6; Case 2: 8, 7 or Case 3: 9, 8 respectively. However, cases 2 and 3 lead to contradictions in the sum and hence D = 7 and B = 6 are the only values possible. G = 3. In the thousands column, we would now get 1 + 1 + E = 1F (a two digit number). This is only possible for E = 8 or 9. However, E = 9, makes F = 1, which is again a contradiction. Hence, E = 8. The addition puzzle sorts out 1657 + 8656 = 10313.

17. The value of E = 8
18. A + G + D = 1 + 3+ 7 = 11.
19. B × G × C = 6 × 3 × 5 = 90
20. The value of B is 6.

PART I

Reasoning for CAT

SECTION 2

Logical Reasoning Tests based on the Latest CAT Pattern

LEVEL OF DIFFICULTY I

Mock Test Paper 1
Mock Test Paper 2
Mock Test Paper 3
Mock Test Paper 4
Mock Test Paper 5
Mock Test Paper 6
Mock Test Paper 7
Mock Test Paper 8
Mock Test Paper 9
Mock Test Paper 10
Mock Test Paper 11
Mock Test Paper 12

LEVEL OF DIFFICULTY II

Mock Test Paper 1
Mock Test Paper 2
Mock Test Paper 3
Mock Test Paper 4
Mock Test Paper 5
Mock Test Paper 6
Mock Test Paper 7
Mock Test Paper 8
Mock Test Paper 9
Mock Test Paper 10

LEVEL OF DIFFICULTY III

Mock Test Paper 1
Mock Test Paper 2
Mock Test Paper 3
Mock Test Paper 4
Mock Test Paper 5
Mock Test Paper 6
Mock Test Paper 7
Mock Test Paper 8

Scan this QR code to access a video on this section's mock tests and the approach to solve them!

1 Mock Test Paper

LEVEL OF DIFFICULTY (I)

Directions for Questions 1 to 5:
Eight teams-Kolkata, Mumbai, Pune, Chennai, Delhi, Indore, Bangalore and Hyderabad participated in Gali cricket Premier league 2015. The tournament was played in three different rounds- Group stage, semifinal, final.

In the Group stage, two groups of four teams each were made and in each group each team played exactly one game against every other team. The top two teams (in terms of number of matches won) of each group advanced to the semifinals and winner of semifinals moved to the final. In one group two teams won two games each and two teams won one game each. In the other group each team won different number of games. In the Group stage Indore and Bangalore were in the same group and Indore won more games than Bangalore. Hyderabad and Delhi were in the same group and Hyderabad won more games than Delhi in the group round. The following information is also given:

(i) None of the team won all the games played by it.
(ii) Kolkata qualified for the final and lost exactly two games in the tournament.
(iii) The two finalist teams were from different groups.
(iv) Hyderabad, Pune and Chennai won the same number of games in the group stage.

1. Which team won the most number of games?
   (a) Bangalore (b) Kolkata
   (c) Indore (d) None of these
2. Which team won the least number of games?
   (a) Hyderabad (b) Delhi
   (c) Pune (d) None of these
3. Find the difference between the number of games won by the winner and the loser of the final match.
4. Which of the following team could play semifinal against Kolkata?
   (a) Indore (b) Hyderabad
   (c) Bangalore (d) None of these
5. Who was the runner up of the tournament?

Directions for Questions 6 to 7: *Read the following information and answer the questions:*

There are five teams–Paraguay, Qatar, Russia, Spain and Turkey playing In a tournament where each team plays against every other team only once. These are the following possibilities: each match can result in a draw where each team scores two points; or a team can win where it scores three points, while the losing team scores one point.

6. If Paraguay has won all the matches and Turkey has lost all the matches and all the remaining three teams score equal points, how many points have each of the three remaining teams scored?
   (a) 5 (b) 7
   (c) 8 (d) 6
7. If all the five teams have an equal score, what is the number of points scored by each team ?
   (a) 5 (b) 6
   (c) 7 (d) 8

Additional Directions for Questions 8 to 10: If it is known that Paraguay and Qatar topped the group with Equal Points, Russia came third, Spain was fourth (Spain and Russia drew the match with each other and they had equal points), and Turkey lost all the matches:

8. What is the maximum sum of the number of points of Paraguay and Qatar?
   (a) 22 (b) 24
   (c) 20 (d) 18
9. What is the maximum possible points gained by Russia, if the condition for the previous question is adhered to?
   (a) 6 (b) 7
   (c) 8 (d) 9
10. What is the number of points of Turkey?
    (a) 4 (b) 5
    (c) 6 (d) 7

Directions for Questions 11 to 15: *Answer the questions based on the following information.*

Indian athlete association organized a 100 meters race at five consecutive levels - Level 1 through Level 5. Five players participated at every level. At the end of the game, the five participants were given five different ranks - 1 through 5. The number of points awarded to the participants ranked 1, 2 and 3 were 10, 6 and 2 respectively. No points were awarded to the participants ranked 4 and 5. A total of 9 different players participated in the game over the span of five levels. The following table shows the total number of points garnered by each of the nine players.

Name of the Player	Points
A	10
B	10
C	16
D	4
E	10
F	12
G	8
H	20
I	0

The following information is also known:

(i) In Level 1, A, B, C, D and E participated in the game.
(ii) In Level 2, F replaced A.
(iii) In Level 3, G replaced B.
(iv) In Level 4, H replaced C.
(v) In Level 5, I replaced D.
(vi) Once a player was replaced by another player, he/she did not participate in the race in the subsequent levels.
(vii) H was the only participant who was awarded points in two consecutive levels.

11. Who got the 3rd rank in Level 1?

12. How many points did D get in Level 2?

13. If E got 2nd rank in Level 3 then what was the rank of G in the Level 5?

14. If E got 3rd rank in Level 3 then what was the rank of E in the Level 5?

15. Who got the 2nd rank in Level 2?

(a) F **(b)** E
(c) D **(d)** None of these

Directions for Questions 16 to 20: *Answer the questions on the basis of the information given below.*

Four teams T1-Delhi Daredevils (DD), T2-Kolkata Knight Riders (KKR), T3-Mumbai Indians (MI) and T4-Kings X1 Punjab (KP) participated in each of the four different years—Year-I, Year-II, Year-III and Year-IV—in India. Each team is owned by a different owner among Raman, Dinesh, Suresh and Rahul, in no particular order. None of the four teams ranked at the same position in more than two of the four years. In each year the four teams ranked 1, 2, 3 and 4. It is also known that:

(i) In Year-I, KKR ranked third and Rahul's team ranked first. Interestingly, in Year -II, KKR ranked first and Rahul's team ranked third.
(ii) In Year -IV, KKR ranked third and MI ranked fourth.
(iii) Suresh's team ranked at the same position in Year-I and Year-II, and also in Year-III and Year-IV.
(iv) In Year-IV, DD and MI interchanged the positions at which they had ranked in Year-II.
(v) In Year-III, MI ranked fourth and KP ranked second.
(vi) Raman's team did not rank first in any of the four years.

16. Who are the owners of MI and KP, respectively?

(a) Rahul and Raman **(b)** Suresh and Rahul
(c) Raman and Suresh **(d)** Can't be determined

17. Whose team ranked third in Year-IV?

(a) Raman
(b) Rahul
(c) Dinesh
(d) Either Raman or Suresh

18. If the team with the highest sum of ranks in the four years gets relegated to the second rung of teams, which team will get relegated?

(a) DD **(b)** KKR
(c) MI **(d)** KP

19. What is the sum of the ranks of KKR in year 1 and 4?

20. What is the absolute difference in the ranks of DD and MI in year 3?

2 Mock Test Paper

Directions for Questions 1 to 4:

(i) Five girls–Seema, Reema, Neeta, Mona and Veena have total five tickets at movie theatres–Priya, Chanakya, M2K, PVR Saket and Satyam, where movies–Gangster, Khiladi, Hero, Saalaam Namaste and Iqbal are currently playing. Each girl has one movie ticket to one of the five theatres.

(ii) The movie Gangster is running in Priya theatre whose ticket is not with Veena and Seema.

(iii) Mona had a ticket for Iqbal movie.

(iv) Neeta had ticket for the M2K theatre. Veena has the ticket of Satyam theatre where Khiladi is not running.

(v) In PVR Saket theatre Saalaam Namaste is running.

1. What is the correct combination of Theatre-Girl-Movie?

(a) M2K-Neeta-Hero
(b) Priya-Mona-Gangster
(c) Satyam-Veena-Iqbal
(d) PVR Saket-Seema-Saalaam Namaste

2. Which movie is running at Chanakya?

(a) Gangster **(b)** Iqbal
(c) Hero **(d)** Data is inadequate

3. Who has the ticket for the movie Hero?

(a) Reema **(b)** Veena
(c) Seema **(d)** Mona

4. Which movie is Neeta watching?

(a) Iqbal **(b)** Hero
(c) Salaam Namaste **(d)** Khiladi

Directions for Questions 5 to 8: *Read the following information and answer the questions.*

The owner of the house has been murdered. The visitors to the house were Aditya, Vijay and Puneet. The following additional information is also given:

(i) The murderer who was one of the three visitors, arrived at the house later than at least one of the other two visitors.

(ii) The driver of the house who was one of the three visitors, arrived at the house earlier than at least one of the two visitors.

(iii) The driver arrived at the house at midnight.

(iv) Neither Aditya nor Vijay arrived at the house after midnight.

(v) Between Vijay and Puneet, the one who arrived earlier was not the driver.

(vi) Between Aditya and Puneet, the one who arrived later was not the murderer.

5. Who arrived at the house earliest?

(a) Puneet **(b)** Aditya
(c) Vijay **(d)** Data insuflicient

6. Who arrived at the house last?

(a) Puneet **(b)** Aditya
(c) Vijay **(d)** Data insufficient

7. Who was the murderer?

(a) Aditya **(b)** Vijay
(c) Puneet **(d)** Cannot be determined

8. Who was the driver?

(a) Aditya **(b)** Vijay
(c) Puneet **(d)** Cannot be determined

Directions for Questions 9 to 13: *Answer the questions on the basis of the information given below.*

Five athletes - Sarah, Rinku, Simran, Jessica and Vandana participated in the sports day events at Netaji Subhas Chandra Bose National Institute of Sports, Patiala, and got top five ranks in two events, High jump and Long jump, not necessarily in the given order. No two athletes got the same rank in any event and no athlete got the same rank in both the events. The following information is also known:

(i) The number of athletes who got a better rank than Jessica in High jump is the same as the number of athletes who got a better rank than Vandana in Long jump.

(ii) Sarah got a better rank than Simran in at least one of the events.

(iii) Rinku's rank in High jump is better than her rank in Long jump.

(iv) In Long jump, Vandana got a better rank than Jessica.

(v) The sum of the ranks of Simran is 4 and the sum of the ranks of any other athlete is not 4.

(vi) The rank of Rinku in one of the events is the same as the rank of Jessica In the other event.

9. Who got the 3rd rank in High jump?
   (a) Sarah (b) Rinku
   (c) Jessica (d) Vandana
10. What is the rank of Vandana in Long jump?
11. How many athletes got a better rank than Simran in at least one of the two events?
12. What is the sum of the ranks of Rinku and Vandana in High jump?
13. Who got the highest sum of ranks?
   (a) Jessica (b) Sarah
   (c) Vandana (d) None of these

Directions for Questions 14 to 18: *Answer the questions on the basis of the information given below.*

During the track and field races during the 1982 New Delhi Asian Games, eight runners–Amit, Sumit, Hari, Manu, Mohit, Soham, Rahul and Ramesh–ran in eight different lanes on a track. The lanes were numbered 1 to 8 from left to right, in that order. In a strange coincidence, the finishing positions of all the riders were same as their lane numbers. E.g., the rider cycling in the lane numbered 1 finished first, the rider cycling in the lane numbered 2 finished second and so on. It is also known that:

(i) Exactly two riders finished between Hari and Rahul.
(ii) Manu finished just ahead of Rahul.
(iii) Soham finished just ahead of Amit.
(iv) Manu finished ahead of Hari.
(v) Neither Mohit nor Ramesh finished last.
(vi) Exactly two riders finished ahead of Manu.

14. Who could not have finished fifth in the race?
   (a) Amit (b) Mohit
   (c) Soham (d) Ramesh
15. Who finished seventh and eighth respectively in the race?
   (a) Rahul and Sumit (b) Hari and Sumit
   (c) Manu and Hari (d) Can't be determined
16. Who could not have finished first?
   (a) Amit (b) Soham
   (c) Ramesh (d) Mohit
17. How many possibilities are there for the lane numbers for all the runners?
18. How many people finished ahead of Rahul?

Directions for Questions 19 to 20: Mr. Bedi's family members went on a picnic. There were two grandfathers and four fathers and two grandmothers and four mothers in the group. There was at least one grandson or a granddaughter present in this group. There were two husband-wife pairs in this group. The single grandfather (whose wife was not present) had two grandsons and a son present in the party. The single grandmother (whose husband was not present) had two granddaughters present. A grandfather or a grandmother present with their spouses did not have any grandson or granddaughter present.

19. What was the minimum number of people present in this picnic group?
   (a) 14 (b) 10
   (c) 12 (d) 16
20. What is the minimum number of females present in the group?

3 Mock Test Paper

Directions for Questions 1 to 5: *The director of a drama group has to assign different roles to two artistes, Paramjeet and Kamaljeet, to play in a drama using four different symbols–@ for father, $ for wife, # for brother and * for daughter. There were four combinations decided by the director showing the following results. Answer the questions on the basis of results (i), (ii), (iii), (iv).*

(i) Paramjeet @ Kamaljeet stands for Paramjeet is father of Kamaljeet

(ii) Paramjeet $ Kamaljeet implies Paramjeet is the wife of Kamaljeet

(iii) Paramjeet # Kamaljeet stands for Paramjeet is brother of Kamaljeet

(iv) Paramjeet * Kamaljeet stands for Paramjeet is daughter of Kamaljeet

1. If Daljeet # Chiranjeet $ Baljeet, which of the following statements is true?
- **(a)** Daljeet is the brother of Baljeet
- **(b)** Daljeet is the father-in-law of Baljeet
- **(c)** Daljeet is the father of Baljeet
- **(d)** Daljeet is the brother-in-law of Baljeet

2. If Manjeet * Chiranjeet @ Daljeet @ Baljeet, which of the following is not true?
- **(a)** Manjeet is the mother of Baljeet
- **(b)** Chiranjeet is the grandfather of Baljeet
- **(c)** Manjeet and Daljeet are siblings
- **(d)** Manjeet is the aunt of Baljeet

3. If Abhijeet # Chiranjeet * Baljeet, which of the following is not true?
- **(a)** Baljeet is the parent of Abhijeet
- **(b)** Abhijeet and Chiranjeet are siblings
- **(c)** Abhijeet is the son of Baljeet
- **(d)** Baljeet is the mother-in-law of Chiranjeet

4. What does A*B*C*D#E definitely mean?
- **(a)** E is the uncle of C
- **(b)** C is the niece of E
- **(c)** B is the daughter of E
- **(d)** E is the grandfather of B

5. For the above question, how many males are there in the set of people?
- **(a)** 0 **(b)** 1
- **(c)** 2 **(d)** Cannot be determined

Directions for Questions 6 to 10: *Answer the questions on the basis of the information given below.*

There are five friends, Charlie, John, Bobby, Anderson and David. Each one of them belongs to one of the following nations: the UK, the USA, Australia, France and Spain. Each one plays a different game namely, football, cricket, hockey, tennis and polo. Charlie plays neither tennis nor polo and belongs either to the UK or Spain. David belongs to the USA and plays football. John belongs to Australia and plays neither polo nor cricket. Anderson plays hockey and belongs either to France or Spain. Bobby belongs neither to France nor the UK.

6. To which country does Bobby belong?
- **(a)** The UK **(b)** The USA
- **(c)** Australia **(d)** Spain

7. What game does Charlie play?
- **(a)** Football
- **(b)** Cricket
- **(c)** Polo
- **(d)** Hockey

8. What is the name of John's country and what game does he play?
- **(a)** The USA, cricket
- **(b)** The UK, polo
- **(c)** Australia, tennis
- **(d)** France, football

9. Which sport does the French man play?

10. If Charlie moves to the USA and the person who plays football shifts to Australia and John moves to the UK, then, the person who plays cricket lives in which country?

Directions for Questions 11 to 15: *Answer the questions on the basis of the information given below.*

There are 5 different surveying and mapping agencies – The Association of British Columbia Land Surveyors (ABCLS), United States Surveying and Land Information Group (USLIG), Hong Kong Institute of Surveyors (HKIS), Royal Institute of Survey (RIS) and Russian Central Survey Institute (RCSI), that have conducted their own surveys each year to find out the correct order of most polluted countries in the world. The agencies gave their respective orders of most polluted countries in the world as follows:

Surveying Agencies	The Most Polluted Country in				
	2023	2024	2025	2026	2027
ABCLS	China	United States	India	Russia	Japan
USLIG	Japan	China	India	United States	Russia
HKIS	China	United States	India	Japan	Russia
RIS	Russia	India	China	Japan	United States
RCSI	Japan	China	india	Russia	United States

If the order of any agency matches with the order which was surveyed by Unites Nations Surveying Agency (UNSA) in each year consecutively, then that agency will receive 10,000 Euros as prize money. If the surveying agency gives the correct order of only p ($p < 5$) but not all of the five years correctly, that agency will get ($p + 1$) thousand Euros as prize money. Further, it was found that each of the agencies won a different amount as prize money.

11. Which of the following country was the maximum polluted in 2023?
(a) China (b) Japan
(c) United States (d) Can't be determined

12. Which of the following agency won the least amount as prize money?
(a) USLIG (b) HKIS
(c) RIS (d) Can't be determined

13. Which of the following country was the maximum polluted in 2025?
(a) United States
(b) India
(c) Russia
(d) Can't be determined

14. How many agencies predicted the country having maximum pollution in 2023 correctly?

15. Which of the following countries had the maximum pollution in 2027?
(a) Japan (b) Russia
(c) Japan or Russia (d) None of these

Directions for Questions 16 to 20: *Answer the questions on the basis of the information given below.*

Six cricketers–Paresh, Kamal, Rahul, Suresh, Tarun and Usman were called for the selection trial for the opener's slot in the Indian cricket team. Each of them has a different surname among Kumar, Kamlesh, Sinha, Pandey, Vineet and Gupta, and was called on a different day of a week from Monday to Saturday. It was observed that the first letter of the name and that of the surname were not same for any of the six candidates. It is also known that:

(i) Kamal and Suresh were called on two consecutive days, in no particular order.
(ii) Gupta was called on the day next to the one on which Kumar was called.
(iii) Exactly three candidates were called between Kamal and Tarun.
(iv) Rahul Gupta was called on Friday. Paresh's surname is Kamlesh.
(v) Vineet and Kamlesh were called on two consecutive days, in no particular order.

16. Which of the following is the first name of Mr. Sinha?
(a) Tarun (b) Kamal
(c) Suresh (d) Can't be determined

17. Who among the following was called on Monday?
(a) Paresh (b) Usman
(c) Suresh (d) Can't be determined

18. Mr. Sinha was called on which of the following days?
(a) Saturday (b) Wednesday
(c) Friday (d) Tuesday

19. On which day was Mr. Kumar called?
(a) Monday (b) Tuesday
(c) Thursday (d) Friday

20. If the days are numbered from 1 to 6 for Monday to Saturday, then what is the sum of the days on which Tarun and Vineet were called?

4 Mock Test Paper

Directions for Questions 1 to 5: *Answer the questions based on the following information.*

In an institute there are five identical rooms having different items in them. Every identical looking room has a name indicating its contents. The details of the contents and the name of each room are as given below:

Contents	Name of Rooms
Two printers	Pashupatti
Two Computers	Chandrachud
Two Bags	Bagbahadur
One printer and one computer	Purnachandra
One bag and one computer	Biswachakra

One day somebody in the institute changed the name plate of every room such that no room contains the name correctly explaining its contents.

1. If supervisor of the institute opened a room named Biswachakra and found that one item was a bag, which of the following would definitely be correct?
   (a) The other item will be a bag
   (b) The other item will not be a bag
   (c) The other room named Bagbahadur will contain a bag
   (d) The other item is a computer
2. If it is known that room named Purnachandra does not contain either any printer or any computer, the room named Pashupatti does not contain any printer and room named Chandrachud contains one computer and one bag, which of the following will definitely be true if only one of the remaining rooms is opened?
   (a) It will have at least one computer and printer.
   (b) It will have two printers.
   (c) It will have at least one computer.
   (d) It will have at least one printer.
3. Someone opens rooms labeled Chandrachud and Pashupatti and finds 2 printers and 2 computers in those rooms, respectively, Which of the remaining rooms should they open in order to definitely find a bag?
   (a) Purnachandra
   (b) Biswachakra
   (c) Bagbahadur
   (d) They cannot have the guarantee of finding a bag in any single room.
4. Someone opens rooms labeled Chandrachud and Pashupatti and finds 2 printers and 2 computers in those rooms respectively, which of the remaining rooms should They open in order to definitely find a computer?
   (a) Purnachandra
   (b) Biswachakra
   (c) Bagbahadur
   (d) They cannot have the guarantee of finding a bag in any single room.
5. If it is known that Bagbahadur contains 2 printers and Pashupatti does not contain a bag, while Biswachakra contains 2 bags, which of the following would be definitely true if one of the remaining two rooms are opened?
   (a) It will have a bag
   (b) It will have 2 computers
   (c) It will have a computer
   (d) Not possible to determine

Directions for Questions 6 to 10: Pulkit, Qasim, Rahim and Shanti are Swimmer, Shooter, Footballer and Cricketer by profession, not necessarily in the same order. Each of them drives in a different color car among the four adjacent cars which are parked in a row. Each car has a distinct colour among red, green, blue and white in no particular order.

Additional Information:

(i) Pulkit is not a Cricketer and he drives the car at the extreme left of the row.
(ii) The shooter's car is parked beside the Footballer's car and the Swimmer's car.
(iii) Qasim is a Footballer and he has a green colored car which is parked beside the Cricketer's car.
(iv) Rahim drives in a white car and he is not a Shooter.

6. What is the profession of the person who drives the blue car?
(a) Swimmer (b) Cricketer
(c) Footballer (d) Can't be determined

7. Who is the Footballer among the four people?
(a) Rahim (b) Shanti
(c) Qasim (d) Can't be determined

8. Which of the following cannot be a possible combination of name, profession and car-colour?
(a) Pulkit → Swimmer → Red
(b) Shanti → Footballer → Blue
(c) Qasim → Footballer → Green
(d) Rahim → Cricketer → White

9. If Shanti does not have a blue car then what is the color of the car owned by the Shooter?

10. What is the profession of the person who owns a white car?

Directions for Questions 11 to 15: *These questions are based on the following information. Study it carefully and answer the questions.*

Seven athletes Ojasvi, Pandey, Qamar, Sachin, Virbhadra, Xenon and Zavi represent different countries in the Olympic games held in Paris. The countries they represent are India, Italy, Malaysia, Nepal, Pakistan, Sri Lanka and Egypt; each one competes for a different sport viz. Judo, Hockey, Weight Lifting, Wrestling, Swimming, Cycling and Basketball. The order of persons, countries and the games is not necessarily the same i.e., the orders of athlete, country and sports have been purposely jumbled in the above lists.

Qamar represents Italy in Hockey. Sachin represents India but not in Judo and neither in Weight Lifting. Someone from amongst the seven athletes represents Egypt and he/she competes in Swimming. Virbahdra competes in Judo but not for Malaysia. Ojasvi represents Sri Lanka in Cycling. The athlete from Pakistan competes in Wrestling. Xenon does not represent Malaysia or Egypt. Zavi competes in Weight Lifting.

11. The one who competes in Weight Lifting, represents which country?
(a) Nepal (b) Malaysia
(c) Egypt (d) India

12. Which of the following combinations is correct?
(a) Xenon-Wrestling-Nepal
(b) Zavi-Weight Lifting- Egypt
(c) Ojasvi-Wrestling-Sri Lanka
(d) Xenon-Wrestling-Pakistan

13. Who represents India?
(a) Virbhadra (b) Zavi
(c) Xenon (d) None of these

14. For which game does Sachin compete?
(a) Swimming (b) Basketball
(c) Wrestling (d) Cannot be determined

15. Virbhadra represents which country?
(a) Malaysia (b) Pakistan
(c) Egypt (d) None of these

Directions for Questions 16 to 19: *Answer the questions on the basis of the information given below.*

India and Pakistan played five different cricket matches over five years from 2011 to 2015. In a unique experiment sanctioned by the ICC–controlled wholly by India–the matches were 1-day, 2-day, 3-day, 4-day and 5-day long. However, the order in which the matches were played was random. Also, no match finished before its scheduled time frame. It is also known that:

(i) The match in 2012 was 1 day longer than the match played in Sialkot.
(ii) The match played in Delhi was played in the year consecutive to the match played in Kolkata.
(iii) The Bangalore match was played in the year next to the 1-day match.
(iv) The match in Delhi was not played in 2015 and was a match that was not the longest match scheduled.
(v) The match in 2013 lasted a day longer compared to the match in Nagpur.
(vi) The Bangalore match was played in 2012 and was not the longest match.

16. Which of the following combinations of the match length, venue and year is/are correct?
(i) 4 day - Nagpur - 2015
(ii) 2 day - Delhi - 2014
(iii) 5 day - Kolkata - 2013
(iv) 1 day - Bangalore - 2012
(a) (i) only (b) (i), (ii) and (iii)
(c) (i) and (iii) only (d) All of these

17. Which of the following is correct?
(a) The 5-day match was the third of the five matches.
(b) The 3-day match was played in 2012.
(c) The 4-day match was played in Nagpur.
(d) Both (a) and (c).

18. Which of the following statement(s) is/are false?
I. The Delhi match was played over 2 days.
II. The Kolkata match was played before the Nagpur match.
(a) Only I (b) Only II
(c) Both I and II (d) Neither I nor II

19. What is the sum of the number of days for the matches played in Sialkot and Delhi?

Directions for Question 20:

20. Six people are sitting in a row. They are Arun, Bhaskar, Chetan, Devarshi, Ebrahim and Farooq. It is also known that:

(i) There are as many people between Bhaskar and Devarshi as there are between Ebrahim and Devarshi.

(ii) The only person between Arun and Chetan is Devarshi.

(iii) Ebrahim is sitting somewhere to the right of Bhaskar.

Who amongst the following is definitely sitting at the end of the row?

(a) Bhaskar **(b)** Ebrahim

(c) Farooq **(d)** None of these

5 Mock Test Paper

Directions for Questions 1 to 5: *Study the information below and answer questions based on it.*

Five colleagues Neha, Priyanka, Rahul, Amita and Jaspreet have to be part of the welcoming committee for the president of Mindworkzz, which is India's leading online training and solutions company. Neha refuses to stand next to Priyanka because they have always competed against each other. Rahul and Amita are very good friends and would want to stand together always. Jaspreet on the other hand cannot get along well with Rahul, because they are competing for the same promotion. Hence, he does not stand next to him. Amita always wants to stand at the extreme right of the group–as it makes her look smarter.

1. If Neha is standing to the extreme left, who is standing next to Amita?
(a) Jaspreet **(b)** Priyanka
(c) Rahul **(d)** Can't say

2. If Priyanka stands to the extreme left, who stands next to her?
(a) Can't say **(b)** Priyanka
(c) Rahul **(d)** Jaspreet

3. If Amita decides that the position second from left is better for her and Neha decides to stand second from right, then who is standing on the extreme right?
(a) Rahul **(b)** Priyanka
(c) Can't say **(d)** Jaspreet

4. If the positions are numbered 1 to 5 from left to right, then what is the sum of all the places where Neha could be?

5. If Amita decides that the 2nd position from the left is actually her best position instead of the extreme right and Neha decides to stand in the 4th position from left, then who is standing exactly in the middle?

Directions for Questions 6 to 10: *Answer the questions on the basis of the information given below.*

Sam, Rahul, Qasim and Virat visited a party one at a time in the following manner.

(i) Qasim did not visit the party between Rahul and Virat.
(ii) At least one person visited the party between Sam and Rahul.
(iii) At least one of Qasim and Virat visited the party before Sam.

6. If Qasim was the last person to visit the party, then who visited the party first?
(a) Sam
(b) Virat
(c) Rahul
(d) Can't be determined

7. In how many ways could the four people visit the party?

8. Who could not be the last person to visit the party?
(a) Sam **(b)** Rahul
(c) Qasim **(d)** Virat

9. If it is known that Sam reached last, then which of the following is Definitely true?
I. Rahul visited first
II. Qasim visited 3rd
III. Qasim was never 2nd to visit
(a) Only I **(b)** Only II
(c) Both I and II **(d)** Only III

10. If Virat came first, then in which of the following order did the others visit?
I. Rahul
II. Sam
III. Qasim
(a) I, III, II **(b)** III, II, I
(c) I, II, III **(d)** III, I, II

Directions for Questions 11 to 15: *Study the following information carefully to answer these questions.*

Anil, Pritam, Sudesh, Rashmi, Mitali, Gitali and Yukta are sitting around a circle facing the centre. Anil is third to the left of Yukta and to the immediate right of Rashmi. Pritam is second to the left of Gitali who is not an immediate neighbour of Mitali.

11. Who is to the immediate left of Pritam?
(a) Mitali
(b) Sudesh
(c) Yukta
(d) Cannot be determined

12. Who is second to the right of Rashmi?
   (a) Anil (b) Mitali
   (c) Pritam (d) Sudesh
13. Which of the following pairs of persons has the first person sitting to the immediate right of the second person?
   (a) Rashmi-Mitali (b) Anil-Gitali
   (c) Sudesh-Pritam (d) None of these
14. Which of the following groups has the first person sitting between the other two?
   (a) Mitali-Anil-Gitali
   (b) Sudesh-Rashmi-Gitali
   (c) Yukta-Pritam-Rashmi
   (d) None of these
15. Which of the following is the correct position of Anil with respect to Pritam?
   I Second to the left
   II Third to the left
   III Fifth to the right
   IV Fourth to the right
   (a) (I) only (b) (II) only
   (c) Both (I) and (II) (d) Both (I) and (III)

Directions for Questions 16 to 20: In a coaching institute there are five students - Aman, Baman, Chaman, Daman, and Ehsaan each of whose height (in feet) is a distinct integer, with the highest being 6 feet long and the smallest being 2 feet long. They all are studying in 5 different schools - P, Q, R, S and T. The following information is also known:

(i) The tallest student studies in school P and the shortest student studies in school S.
(ii) Baman's height is half of the sum of heights of Aman and Daman.
(iii) Aman is shorter than Baman.
(iv) At most three students are shorter than Daman and at least one student is shorter than Aman.
(v) Chaman is not the tallest and Ehsaan is not the smallest.
(vi) The height of the student who studies in R is more than the student who studies in Q but less than that of the person who studies in T.

16. What is the name of the student who studies in T?
17. In which school does Ehsaan study?
18. In which of the schools does the student of height 5 feet study?
19. Which of the following school-student combination is not correct?
   (a) Daman–T (b) Baman–R
   (c) Chaman–S (d) Ehsaan–R
20. If E and B exchange schools, then what is the sum of the heights of people studying in P and S?

6 Mock Test Paper

Directions for Questions 1 to 5: *Read the text and the numbered statements carefully and answer the questions given at the end.*

Four people of different nationalities live on the same side of a street in four houses each of different color. Each person has a different favorite drink. The following additional information is also known:

(i) The Englishman lives in the red house.
(ii) The Italian drinks tea.
(iii) The Norwegian lives in the first house on the left.
(iv) In the second house from the right they drink milk.
(v) The Norwegian lives adjacent to the blue house.
(vi) The Spaniard drinks fruit juice.
(vii) Tea is drunk in the blue house.
(viii) The white house is to the right of the red house.

1. The color of the Norwegian's house is
(a) Yellow **(b)** White
(c) Blue **(d)** Red

2. Milk is drunk by
(a) Norwegian **(b)** Englishman
(c) Italian **(d)** None of the above

3. The Norwegian drinks
(a) Milk **(b)** Cocoa
(c) Tea **(d)** Fruit Juice.

4. Which of the following is not true?
(a) Milk is drunk in the red house.
(b) The Italian lives in the blue house.
(c) The Spaniard lives in a corner house.
(d) The Italian lives next to the Spaniard.

5. What does the person from the white colored house drink?

Directions for Questions 6 to 10: A chess tournament has nine players, five from India and rest from China. The five Indian players are A, B, C, D and E. The four Chinese players are W, X, Y and Z. Before the start of the tournament, the international chess federation released the ranking of different players. The five Indian players were ranked from 1 to 5 in the given order of their names and the four Chinese players were ranked from 6 to 9, again in the given order of their names.

The tournament was played in four rounds. In the first round, each Indian player played a match against every other Indian player and the same was true for Chinese players. Top three Indian and top two the Chinese players advanced to the next round. In the second round each player irrespective of his nationality played a match with each of the other players who had reached that round. The top four players from this round advanced to the third round. In the third round two matches were played, the 1st match was played between the highest and the lowest ranked player and the second match was played between the other two players. The winner of these two matches advanced to the 4th round. The winner of this round was declared the winner of the tournament. The following information is also known:

(i) In the 3rd round each match was played between an Indian and a Chinese player.
(ii) The player who was ranked 1 before the start of the tournament, did reach the third round, but won at most one match in the second round.
(iii) In the whole tournament no match ended in a draw.
(iv) W was the winner of the tournament.
(v) C and E won three matches each and were the top two players at the end of the first round.
(vi) Among the Chinese players, players with odd numbered rankings did not make it to the 2nd round.
(vii) Three players, none of them either ranked 1 or was the top player of the second round, won an equal number of matches in the second round.

6. Which of the following players played the final?
(a) A **(b)** C
(c) E **(d)** Either C or Y

7. Who among the following reached in the 3rd round?
(a) C **(b)** Y
(c) E **(d)** All of them

8. What is the sum of number of matches played by C and Y?

9. How many matches were played between C and E, during the whole tournament?

10. Who did W beat in the 3rd round?

(a) A (b) C
(c) E (d) B

Directions for Questions 11 to 15: *Study the following information carefully to answer these questions.*

Abhi, Binoy, Chintan, Dev, Esha, Freni and Gautam are members of the Genesis sports club. Each of them plays one of seven different games: Cricket, Swimming, Trekking, Kabbadi, Snooker, Chess and Golf, but not necessarily in the same order. Each one of them plays a different musical instrument from amongst Shehnai, Drum, Harmonium, Flute, Sarod, Manjira and Sarangi, not necessarily in the same order. Binoy plays Cricket and Manjira. Esha likes to play Kabbadi but not Harmonium or Sarod. The one who plays Snooker plays Shehnai. Freni plays Drums but does not Swim or play Golf. Abhi trekks and plays Flute. The one who plays Golf does not play Sarod. Gautam plays the sport of Snooker and Chintan plays Harmonium.

11. Who plays the Sarod?

(a) Dev (b) Abhi
(c) Esha (d) Dev or Esha

12. Esha plays which game?

(a) Swimming (b) Golf
(c) Chess (d) None of these

13. Which of the following combinations of game-person-musical instrument is definitely correct?

(a) Trekking - Binoy - Flute
(b) Swimming - Esha - Sarangi
(c) Golf - Dev - Sarod
(d) Swimming - Dev - Sarod

14. Who plays Chess?

(a) Chintan (b) Dev
(c) Gautam (d) Freni

15. Who is the swimmer?

(a) Chintan (b) Freni
(c) Dev (d) Cannot be determined

Directions for Questions 16 to 20:

16. At a circus, there were five enclosures with animals trained by Amar, Bhaskar, Chetan, Divyansh and Eknath. The enclosures were named Allahabad, Bharuch, Chandigarh, Delhi and Egmore (based on the places from where the animals in the enclosures were sourced). The five enclosures contained distinct numbers of animals ranging from 1 to 5. The only enclosure having fewer animals than Amar's enclosure was named Bharuch. Neither Divyansh's nor Bhaskar's enclosure had the highest number of animals among the five enclosures. The sum of the number of animals in Divyansh's enclosure and Amar's enclosure was equal to the number of animals in the enclosure named Chandigarh, which was Bhaskar's enclosure. If Egmore had 1 animal more than Eknath's enclosure, then who trained the animals in the Delhi enclosure?

(a) Amar (b) Bhaskar
(c) Eknath (d) Can't be determined

17. For the above question, how many animals were there in the Bharuch enclosure?

(a) 1 (b) 2
(c) 3 (d) Can't be determined

18. What is the difference in the number of animals in Chandigarh and with Chetan?

19. Which trainer had the maximum number of animals?

(a) Amar (b) Divyansh
(c) Eknath (d) Cannot be determined

20. How many animals were there in the Egmore enclosure?

7 Mock Test Paper

Directions for Questions 1 to 5: *Study the information below and answer the questions based on it*:

P said to Q "You are as old as R was when I was three times as old as S, and will be as old as T was when he was as old as R was 1 year ago". Q said to P "You may be older than U but V is as old as I was when you were as old as V is." Both of them then simultaneously tell each other: " S will be as old as U was when U will be as old as V is".

1. Who is the second oldest person in the group of P, Q, R, S, T, U and V?

(a) P **(b)** T
(c) R **(d)** Can't be determined

2. Who is the fourth youngest in the group of P, Q, R, S, T, U and V?

(a) Q **(b)** S
(c) U **(d)** P or Q

3. Who is the third youngest person?

(a) V **(b)** R
(c) Q **(d)** Can't be determined

4. Which of the following is/are not definitely true?

(a) U has 5 people older than him in the group of 7 people.
(b) P has three people older than him in the group of 7 people
(c) Q is older than S, but younger than R.
(d) All of these are true.

5. Which two people are equal in age?

(a) P and R **(b)** R and S
(c) P and Q **(d)** P and V

Directions for Questions 6 to 10: *In UEFA 2025, Barcelona played five matches with Manchester United, of which three matches were played in London and two in Manchester. Barcelona scored a different number of goals in each match viz: 8, 1, 4, 5 and 6 and conceded different number of goals among 6, 4, 2, 1 and 0 in the five matches (not necessarily in that order). It is also known that*:

(i) Compared to the 1st match, in the 2nd match the number of goals conceded by Barcelona is 2 more, but number of goals scored is 2 less.

(ii) Manchester United scored 4 goals in one of the matches in London.

(iii) Compared to the 5th match, the number of goals scored by Barcelona in one of the other matches is twice of the number of goals scored in the 5th match and the number of goals conceded by Barcelona in the other match is also twice the number of goals conceded in the 5th match.

(iv) Barcelona won the match in which it scored only one goal.

(v) The match in which, Manchester United scored no goal was played in London but it was not the 5th match.

(vi) The 5th match was played in London and the 3rd match was played in Manchester.

(vii) The number of goals Barcelona conceded in one of the matches is thrice the number of goals it conceded in the match in which it scored 4 goals.

6. How many goals did Barcelona score in its 3rd match?

7. In which match did Manchester United score the maximum number of goals?

8. Which of the following combinations is true of the goals scored by Manchester United?

(a) 1st match–1 **(b)** 2nd match–6
(c) 3rd game–0 **(d)** 4th game–2

9. The total number of goals scored by both the teams in all the matches that are played in London is ____.

10. If it is mentioned that the team who won the match would gain 3 points, a draw would result in 1 point and loss would be 0 points, then in UEFA 2025, Barcelona gained how many points by playing against Manchester United?

(a) 12 **(b)** 13
(c) 14 **(d)** 11

Directions for Questions 11 to 15: *Study the following information carefully and answer the questions.*

Atul, Binish, Charlie, Danish, Emy, Furqan, Gopal and Hina are sitting around a circle, facing the centre. Emy and Gopal always sit next to each other. Danish sits third to the right of Charlie. Furqan sits to the left of Hina. Charlie never sits next to Atul while Danish never sits next to Gopal. Hina is not the neighbour of Danish and Charlie while Danish is not the neighbour of Furqan.

11. Who sits to the immediate right of Furqan?

(a) Danish **(b)** Charlie
(c) Binish **(d)** None of these

12. Three of the following are alike in a certain way based on their positions in the seating arrangement and so form a group. Which pair among the following does not belong to that group?

(a) Charlie-Hina **(b)** Binish-Atul
(c) Furqan-Emy **(d)** Atul-Gopal

13. Which of the following pairs sits between Binish and Emy?

(a) Hina-Binish **(b)** Furqan-Danish
(c) Binish-Gopal **(d)** Gopal-Charlie

14. Who sits second to the left of Binish?

(a) Furqan **(b)** Gopal
(c) Atul **(d)** Emy

15. Who sits between Atul and Danish?

(a) Binish **(b)** Emy
(c) Charlie **(d)** Nobody

Directions for Questions 16 to 20: *Answer the questions on the basis of the given information.*

Six students A, B, C, D, E and F study in six different classes in a school. The classes are Class 5, Class 6, Class 7, Class 8, Class 9 and Class 10. The order of students and their classes is random. It is also known that:

(i) E studies in neither Class 7 nor Class 10.
(ii) B and D are in Classes 5 and 9, but not necessarily in that order.
(iii) The product of the Classes of E and A is either 56 or 60.
(iv) C is not the oldest amongst the students and hence it is known that he does not study in Class 10.

16. If it is known that E studies in Class 6, then in which class does C study?

(a) Class 7 **(b)** Class 8
(c) Class 10 **(d)** Either (a) or (b)

17. If F studies in Class 10, then in which class does A study?

(a) 7 **(b)** 8
(c) 9 **(d)** 10

18. What is the sum of all the classes which C could be a part of?

19. Who could be the oldest among the six people (assuming higher the class, higher the age)?

(a) A **(b)** B
(c) C **(d)** D

20. What is the maximum difference between the classes of A and B?

8 Mock Test Paper

Directions for Questions 1 to 5: *Read the following passage carefully and answer the questions that follow.*

Five flags, each with a distinct symbol, namely, Panther, Tiger, Rose, Swan and Quail, have been arranged in the following order:

(i) Panther is next to Quail and Swan is next to Rose.
(ii) Swan is not next to Tiger, Tiger is on the extreme left hand side, and Rose is on the second position from the right hand side.
(iii) Panther is on the right hand side of Quail and to the right side of Tiger.
(iv) Panther and Rose are together.

1. Which of the following statements is true?
(a) (iii) and (iv) are contradicting.
(b) Either (iii) or (iv) is redundant.
(c) (iii) is redundant
(d) (iv) is redundant

2. _______ is on the extreme right and _______ is on the extreme left.
(a) Tiger and Rose **(b)** Quail and Tiger
(c) Swan and Tiger **(d)** Tiger and Swan

3. _______ is in the middle and _______ is on its right.
(a) Panther and Swan
(b) Rose and Swan
(c) Panther and Rose
(d) Quail and Panther

4. Which flag is next to Quail?
(a) Only Tiger **(b)** Only Panther
(c) Tiger and Panther **(d)** Panther and Rose

5. It is known that after a couple of hours, the flags are shuffled and the new shuffling has Rose in the place of Quail, and vice versa. Also, if Swan and Panther are interchanged, then which flag is next to Quail?
(a) Only Panther **(b)** Only Swan
(c) Panther and Swan **(d)** Panther and Tiger

Directions for Questions 6 to 9: *Answer the questions on the basis of the information given below.*

A, B, C, D, E, F and G are the seven members of a family, comprising two lawyers, two MBAs, one entrepreneur, one executive and one author. It is also known that:

(i) There are exactly two married couples in the family.
(ii) D, who is an author, is married to an MBA.
(iii) No female member of the family is either an author or an executive.
(iv) C, who is a lawyer, is married to A, an MBA.
(v) Both the lawyers are females.
(vi) G is married to D.
(vii) It is a male in the family who has ventured into the risk-taking domain of entrepreneurship.
(vii) Neither B nor F is a lawyer.

6. How many male members are there in the family?
(a) 4 **(b)** 3
(c) 2 **(d)** None of these

7. Which of the following combinations of the member and his/her profession can be correct?
(a) B - MBA **(b)** B - Executive
(c) F - Entrepreneur **(d)** Both (b) and (c)

8. Which pair has the same profession?
(a) D and G **(b)** A and B
(c) C and E **(d)** B and F

9. Who could be an executive?
(a) A **(b)** B
(c) C **(d)** D

Directions for Questions 10 to 15: *Study the following information carefully and answer the questions.*

Anu, Bhavesh, Chintu, Durgesh, Esha, Farman, Ganesh and Hitesh are sitting around a circle, facing the centre. Anu sits fourth to the right of Hitesh while second to the left of Farman. Chintu is not the neighbour of Farman and Bhavesh. Durgesh sits third to the right of Chintu. Hitesh never sits next to Ganesh.

10. Who amongst the following sits between Ganesh and Durgesh?
(a) Ganesh **(b)** Farman
(c) Hitesh **(d)** Anu

11. Which of the following pairs sit between Esha and Farman?
(a) Bhavesh-Hitesh **(b)** Esha-Farman
(c) Chintu-Esha **(d)** Durgesh-Bhavesh

12. Three of the following are alike in a certain way based on their positions in the seating arrangement and so form a group. Which is the one that does not belong to that group?
(a) Durgesh-Chintu (b) Hitesh-Farman
(c) Bhavesh-Durgesh (d) Ganesh-Esha

13. Who is to the immediate left of Anu?
(a) Chintu (b) Durgesh
(c) Ganesh (d) Data inadequate

14. Who sits second to the right of Durgesh?
(a) Anu (b) Chintu
(c) Bhavesh (d) Esha

15. What is the position of Farman with respect to Esha?
I. Second to the right
II. Sixth to the left
III. Third to the left
IV. Fifth to the right
(a) Only II (b) Only II and III
(c) Only I and IV (d) Both III and IV

Directions for Questions 16 to 20:

P, Q, R, S, T, U, V, and W are eight students of a primary school. P is heavier than W and his height is more than that of V. T is heavier than P and lighter than V and his height is more than that of P and less than that of S. U is lighter than Q and heavier than V and his height is more than that of S. W is heavier than R and shorter than V and R. Q is taller than U. Q is lighter than S and his height is more than R. U is shorter than R.

16. Who among the following is shortest?
(a) P (b) S
(c) T (d) W

17. Who among the following is lightest?
(a) P (b) R
(c) T (d) U

18. How many are shorter than P but heavier than Q?

19. If the people are ranked based on their height and Weight with the heaviest and tallest getting rank 1, then what is the difference between the rank of R in both the categories?

20. How many people ranked similar in both the categories?

9 Mock Test Paper

Directions for Questions 1 to 4: *Answer the questions based on the following information.*

Four persons (1) Mohit, (2) Monohar, (3) Prasant and (4) Dinesh, each, had some initial money with them. They all were playing bridge in a way that the loser doubles the money of each of the other three persons from his share. They played four rounds and each person lost one round in the order 1, 2, 3 and 4 as mentioned above. At the end of the fourth round each person had ₹ 32000.

1. What was the amount with Mohit to start with?

(a) ₹ 60000 **(b)** ₹ 34000
(c) ₹ 66000 **(d)** ₹ 28000

2. What was the amount with Monohar at the end of the first round?

(a) ₹ 68000 **(b)** ₹ 72000
(c) ₹ 64000 **(d)** ₹ 80000

3. Who has the lowest amount at any round of play throughout the tournament?

(a) Mohit **(b)** Monohar
(c) Prasant **(d)** Dinesh

4. What was the amount with Prasant at the end of the second round?

(a) 36000 **(b)** 72000
(c) 16000 **(d)** 68000

Directions for Question 5:

5. The VC (Vice-Chancellor) of a university has to select four professors, out of eight professors for a committee. The VC decided to select these four professors in such a manner that each selected professor has a habit common with at least one of the other three professors selected. The selected professors must also hate at least one of the likes of the other professors.

Professor Arora likes surfing and smoking but hates gambling.
Professor Bhalla likes smoking and drinking but hates surfing.
Professor Chadha likes gambling but hates smoking.
Professor Dhyani likes movies but hates drinking.
Professor Eswar likes drinking but hates smoking and movie.
Professor Fazil likes surfing but hates smoking and movie.
Professor Goyal likes gambling and movies, but hates surfing.
Professor Hooda likes smoking and gambling but hates movies.

Who are the four professors selected by the VC for the committee?

(a) Prof. Chadha, Prof. Dhyani, Prof. Eswar, Prof. Goyal
(b) Prof. Arora, Prof. Bhalla, Prof. Eswar, Prof. Fazil
(c) Prof. Bhalla, Prof. Chadha, Prof. Goyal, Prof. Hooda
(d) Prof. Dhyani, Prof. Eswar, Prof. Fazil, Prof Hooda

Directions for Questions 6 to 10: *Study the following information carefully to answer these questions.*

Seven actors Om, Puri, Qadir, Ruk Ruk, Sanjay, Tina and Usman from a TV show have to visit seven different places for promotional activities of their show. The places to be visited are: Agra, Mumbai, Indore, Chandigarh, Bhopal, Bangalore and Gandhinagar. The order of actors and cities may not be necessarily the same. Each one is supposed to fly by a different airline: Go Air, Kingfisher, MDLR Airlines Express, Jetlite, Air Deccan, Indigo Airlines, MDLR Airlines, not necessary in the same order.

Qadir goes to Mumbai but not by MDLR Airlines Express or Jetlite Airlines. Ruk Ruk flies to Bangalore by MDLR Airlines. The one who goes to Gandhinagar does not travel by Air Deccan or MDLR Airlines Express. Sanjay travels by Air Deccan. Om does not go to Agra. Tina travels by Go Air to Bhopal. Puri goes to Chandigarh by Kingfisher. Sanjay does not go to Agra. Usman does not go to Gandhinagar.

6. Who travels by MDLR Airlines Express?

(a) Om **(b)** Qadir
(c) Usman **(d)** Can't be determined

7. Who goes to Gandhinagar?

(a) Om **(b)** Sanjay
(c) Usman **(d)** Ruk Ruk

8. The one who travels by Air Deccan, visits which place?
   (a) Agra (b) Indore
   (c) Chandigarh (d) Bangalore
9. Which of the following actor-city-airline combination is definitely true:
   (a) Om - Gandhinagar - Indigo
   (b) Puri - Chandigarh - MDLR Airlines
   (c) Ruk Ruk - Bangalore - MDLR Airlines
   (d) Tina - Bhopal - Indigo
10. The person traveling to Agra prefers which airline?

Directions for Questions 11 to 15: *Study the following information carefully to answer these questions.*

Seven friends Gimi, Harish, Javed, Kandarp, Luv, Moni and Nitin are working in different cities viz. Kolkata, Lucknow, Chandigarh, Gandhinagar, Delhi, Agra, and Bhopal not necessarily in the same order. Each one of them has a different profession from amongst Teacher, Photographer, Auditor, Fashion Designer, Builder, Choreographer and Painter not necessarily in the same order.

Harish is a Choreographer and he works in Gandhinagar. Kandarp is a Photographer and he does not work in Kolkata. The Teacher works in Lucknow. Moni works in Delhi. The Painter works in Bhopal. Luv is a Builder and he works in Chandigarh. Gimi is a Fashion Designer. Javed does not work in Lucknow.

11. Who is the Auditor?
    (a) Javed (b) Nitin
    (c) Kandarp (d) Moni
12. Which of the following combinations of person, profession and city is definitely correct?
    (a) Gimi-Fashion Designer-Chandigarh
    (b) Kandarp-Painter-Bhopal
    (c) Luv-Builder-Lucknow
    (d) None of the above
13. Who is working in Lucknow?
    (a) Javed (b) Kandarp
    (c) Moni (d) Nitin
14. The Fashion Designer works in which city?
    (a) Agra (b) Kolkata
    (c) Lucknow (d) Chandigarh
15. Who is the Builder?
    (a) Nitin (b) Javed
    (c) Moni (d) None of these

Directions for Questions 16 to 20:

Five friends Satish, Rajesh, Rehman, Rakesh and Vineet– each present one paper to their class on Physics, Zoology, Botany, English, Geology (in any order) one day in a week, Monday through Friday.

(i) Vineet does not present English and does not give his presentation on Tuesday.
(ii) Rajesh makes the Geology presentation and does not do it on Monday or Friday.
(iii) The Physics presentation is made on Thursday.
(iv) Rehman makes his presentation which is not in English on Wednesday.
(v) The Botany presentation is on Friday and not by Rakesh.
(vi) Satish makes his presentation on Monday.

16. What day is the English presentation made?
    (a) Friday (b) Monday
    (c) Tuesday (d) Wednesday
17. What presentation does Vineet do?
    (a) English (b) Geology
    (c) Physics (d) Botany
18. Rakesh makes his presentation on:
    (a) Monday (b) Tuesday
    (c) Wednesday (d) Thursday
19. Who makes their presentation on Friday?
    (a) Satish (b) Rajesh
    (c) Rehman (d) Vineet
20. Which subject is presented on Wednesday?
    (a) English (b) Geology
    (c) Zoology (d) Botany

10 Mock Test Paper

Directions for Questions 1 to 5: *Answer the questions on the basis of the information given below.*

There was an effort to study the relative importance that beneficiaries of five states assigned to five different development programmes implemented by their governments. The programmes were Jawahar Rozgar Yojana (JRY), Indira Awas Yozna (IAY), Mid-Day Meal (MDM), Rural Health Mission (RHM), National Rural Employment Guarantee Scheme (NREG). The level of dissimilarity between two states is the maximum difference in the rank allotted by the two states to any five programmes. The following table indicates the rank order of the five programmes for each state.

Rank	Orissa	Bihar	Rajasthan	Kerala	Karnataka
1	JRY	MDM	IAY	NREG	NREG
2	RHM	JRY	MDM	IAY	JRY
3	MDM	RHM	JRY	RHM	MDM
4	NREG	IAY	NREG	JRY	RHM
5	IAY	NREG	RHM	MDM	IAY

1. Which of the following states is least dissimilar to Orissa?
   (a) Bihar (b) Rajasthan
   (c) Kerala (d) Karnataka
2. Which of the following states is most dissimilar to Orissa?
   (a) Bihar (b) Rajasthan
   (c) Kerala (d) Karnataka
3. Three of the following four pairs of states have identical levels of dissimilarity. Which is the odd one out?
   (a) Kerala and Bihar
   (b) Bihar and Karnataka
   (c) Rajasthan and Kerala
   (d) Karnataka and Rajasthan
4. When compared to the JRY Program in Orissa, which state has the highest level of dissimilarity for its JRY program?
   (a) Kerala (b) Rajasthan
   (c) Karnataka (d) Bihar
5. How many instances of dissimilarity level of 4 can be seen in the table?
   (a) 1 (b) 2
   (c) 3 (d) 4

Directions for Questions 6 to 11: In the ancient Olympics held in the village of Porustistan in Greece, there was a competition between 8 teams from 8 villages. The villages were: Austricht (Aus), Entricht (En), Inswitch (In), Saberwitch (Sab), Patricht (Pat), Sriticht (Sr), Nervoushitch (Nh) and Badwarditch (Bd). The winner of the competition was awarded a golden ball, the team coming in second was awarded a silver ball, the teams coming in third and fourth were awarded platinum balls, while the last 4 teams were all awarded copper balls.

Since the competition was hotly contested, eight experts Amberhitch, Bamberhitch, Camberhitch, Damberhitch, Embermitch, Fannerfitch, Gangertitch and Handkerchief were called in before the competition – in order to guess which village team would win which ball. Let's just call them A, B, C, D, E, F, G and H for simplicity. They came up with the following predictions:

Name of the Person	Prediction							
	Golden Ball	Silver Ball	Platinum Ball		Copper Ball			
A	In	Pat	Aus	Sab	Nh	Bd	En	Sr
B	En	Bd	Aus	Sr	Sab	Pat	Nh	In
C	Pat	Nh	In	Sab	Bd	Aus	En	Sr
D	En	Bd	Aus	In	Sab	Nh	Pat	Sr
E	Sr	Sab	Aus	In	Bd	Pat	Nh	En
F	En	Aus	Sr	Bd	Pat	Sab	Nh	In
G	Aus	Pat	Bd	Nh	Sab	In	En	Sr
H	Aus	Sr	Eng	Bd	Pat	In	Sab	Nh

After the end of the tournament it was found that only three persons correctly predicted the 4 teams who got a copper ball. No two experts correctly predicted the final ball rewarded for the same number of teams.

6. Which team received the golden ball?
7. Who is the person who got all his predictions right?
8. Who is the person who got 5 predictions right?
9. How many persons correctly predicted the ball received by Sriticht?
10. Who was the person to get all his predictions incorrect?
    (a) B (b) C
    (c) D (d) F
11. What were the incorrect predictions of B?
    (a) Silver ball BD and Platinum ball Aus
    (b) Copper Ball Pat and Nh
    (c) Gold ball En
    (d) Silver ball NH

Directions for Questions 12 to 15: During the selection of Indian cricket team, four different selectors - Subroto, Sona, Sudhir and Sobraj, were invited to the team selection meeting.

There were four players who were voted by those selectors in the selection meeting. These four players are: Elex, Cariappa, Laxman, Tariq.

Each of the selectors either vote for or against each of the players. The following information is also known:

(i) Sudhir voted against Laxman but voted in favour of Cariappa.
(ii) Each selector voted for exactly two players.
(iii) Elex and Tariq were voted for by exactly two selectors. Cariappa was selected by three and Laxman was selected by only one.
(iv) Sona voted against Elex and Subroto voted for Tariq.
(v) No selector who voted for Tariq voted for Laxman.

12. If all the selectors who voted for Tariq also voted for Cariappa, then which of the following statement is also true? Assume, nobody voted for Cariappa and Laxman.
    (a) The selector who voted for Laxman did not vote for Elex.
    (b) The selector who voted for Laxman also voted for Cariappa.
    (c) Exactly one selector voted for Elex as well as Tariq.
    (d) Exactly one selector voted for Elex as well as Laxman.
13. If Subroto voted against Cariappa then which of the following statement cannot be true?
    (a) Both Sona and Sudhir voted against Laxman.
    (b) Both Sudhir and Sobraj voted for Elex.
    (c) Both Sobraj and Sona voted against Tariq.
    (d) Both Subroto and Sudhir voted for Elex.
14. If all selectors who voted for Tariq also voted for Cariappa, and nobody voted for Cariappa and Laxman, then which of the following is true?
    I. Subroto did not vote for Elex and Tariq
    II. Subroto voted for Cariappa and Laxman
    III. Sudhir voted for Elex and Cariappa
    (a) only I (b) only II
    (c) only III (d) all 3.
15. If Subroto voted against Cariappa, then which of the following statements can be true?
    (a) Sona voted for both Laxman and Tariq
    (b) Sudhir voted for both Tariq and Elex
    (c) Sobraj voted for any one of Elex, Laxman or tariq.
    (d) The selector who definitely voted for Elex also voted for Cariappa.

Directions for Questions 16 to 20:
Anubhav watched four movies of different genres action, romance, comedy, sci-fi. The movies were shown by four different channels PIX, ZEE, WB, HBO, not necessarily in the same order. These movies were telecasted on different days on Monday, Tuesday, Thursday, and Friday, not necessarily in the same order. The following information is also known:

(i) The movie by PIX was shown on Friday.
(ii) Action movie was shown on Monday.
(iii) Sci-fi movie was shown by WB and not telecasted on Thursday.
(iv) The comedy film was shown by HBO.

16. On Tuesday Anubhav watched:
    (a) A SCI-FI movie
    (b) A comedy movie
    (c) An action movie
    (d) A romantic movie
17. ZEE telecasted:
    (a) The comedy movie on Friday.
    (b) The sci-fi on Thursday.
    (c) The romantic movie on Monday.
    (d) The action movie on Monday.
18. Which of the following combination is true?
    (a) PIX- Action
    (b) HBO-Thursday
    (c) sci-fi- Thursday
    (d) None of these
19. Which genre runs on Friday?
    (a) Romantic (b) Action
    (c) Sci-fi (d) Comedy
20. Which channel telecasts comedy?

11 Mock Test Paper

Directions for Questions 1 to 5: *Answer the questions based on the following information.*

In a motor race competition certain rules are given for the participants to follow. To control direction and speed of the motorists, guards are placed at different signal points with caps of different colour. The guard with red cap indicates the direction of participant's movement and the guard with green cap indicates the speed of the participant's movement. At any signal point presence of three guards, two guards and one guard with red cap means the participant must stop, turn left and turn right, respectively. Signal points with three guards, two guards and one guard with green cap mean the participants must move at 10, 4 and 2 km/hours respectively.

Kartikay, one of the participants, starts at a point where his car was heading towards north and he encountered signals as follows: at start point one guard with green cap; after half an hour two guards with red caps and two guards with green caps at the first signal; after fifteen minutes one guard with red cap at second signal; after half an hour one guard with red cap and three guards with green caps at the third signal; after 24 minutes two guards with red caps and two guards with green caps at fourth signal; after 15 minutes three guards with red caps at fifth signal (time mentioned in each case is applicable after crossing the previous signal).

1. The total distance travelled by Kartikay from starting point till the last signal is:
   (a) 9 km **(b)** 10 km
   (c) 8 km **(d)** 12 km
2. What would be the final position of Kartikay if one guard with red cap and two guards with green caps were placed at the first signal point after the starting point?
   (a) 3 km to the west and 2 km to the south
   (b) 3 km to the west and 4 km to the north
   (c) 5 km to the east and 4 km to the north
   (d) 2 km to the west and 4 km to the south
3. If at the starting point Kartikay was heading towards south what would be his final position?
   (a) 3 km to the east and 4 km to the south
   (b) 5 km to the east and 4 km to the south
   (c) 3 km to the west and 4 km to the south
   (d) 5 km to the west and 2 km to the north
4. What would be the change in distance traveled if Kartikay had terminated the race after reaching the third signal?
5. If the guards at the third and the fourth signal exchange their positions, then what would be the change in distance traveled by Kartikay?

Directions for Questions 6 to 10: *Answer the questions on the basis of the information given below.*

130 cricketers of Green Park Cricket Academy, Kanpur, had to learn exactly one skill amongst batting and bowling. There are two groups of cricketers - Group A and Group B. At the end of the year the head coach decides whether a player is properly skilled or not in the chosen skill. At the end of the year the head coach gets the following information:

(i) Number of Group A cricketers who were skilled in batting is equal to the number of Group B cricketers who remained unskilled in bowling.

(ii) 44 Group A cricketers remained unskilled in batting and 26 Group B cricketers were skilled in bowling.

(iii) The number of Group B cricketers in the school is exactly two less than the number of Group A cricketers.

(iv) The number of Group B cricketers who were skilled in batting is less than the number of Group A cricketers who were skilled in bowling.

**In the above information, if it is given that any cricketer was unskilled in a particular skill then that cricketer must have chosen that particular skill in which he was unskilled.*

Answer the following questions based on the above data:

6. What is the total number of players who opted to learn batting?
7. What is the total number of players who opted to learn bowling?
8. Which of following statements is definitely wrong?
   (a) Number of Group B cricketers who remained unskilled in bowling is less than the number of Group A cricketers who were skilled in bowling.

(b) The number of Group B cricketers who were skilled in bowling is more than the number of Group A cricketers who were skilled in bowling.
(c) The number of Group A cricketers who remained unskilled in batting is more than the number of Group B cricketers who were unskilled in bowling.
(d) The number of Group A cricketers who remained unskilled in bowling is more than the number of Group B cricketers who remained unskilled in batting.

9. If the number of Group B cricketers who remained unskilled in bowling was more than 6, then what was the maximum possible number of Group A cricketers who remained unskilled in bowling?
10. What is the maximum possible difference between Group B players who are skilled in batting to group A players who are skilled in bowling?

Directions for Questions 11 to 15: *These questions are based on the following information. Study it carefully to answer the questions.*

Seven officers Lina, Mini, Nita, Pia, Queen, Rita and Sumant work in three different shifts I, II and III with at least two persons working in each shift. Each one of them has a different weekly off from Monday to Sunday (not necessarily in the same order). Mini works in the second shift only with Rita whose weekly off is on Friday. Queen's weekly off is on the next day of Lina's weekly off and both of them work in different shifts. Pia works in the third shift and her weekly off is on Saturday. Sumant has a weekly off on Monday and he works in the first shift. The one who has a weekly off on Sunday works in the first shift. Lina and Pia do not work in the same shift, Lina's weekly off is on Tuesday.

11. Whose weekly off falls on Sunday?
(a) Lina
(b) Mini
(c) Can't be determined
(d) None of these
12. Which of the following combinations of shift, person and weekly off is definitely correct?
(a) II, Mini, Saturday (b) III, Nita, Thursday
(c) III, Pia, Sunday (d) I, Lina, Tuesday
13. Whose weekly off is on Thursday?
(a) Lina (b) Mini
(c) Nita (d) Queen
14. On which day is Sumant's weekly off?
(a) Monday (b) Wednesday
(c) Sunday (d) Tuesday
15. Which of the following group of officers work in shift I?
(a) Lina, Nita, Sumant
(b) Lina, Sumant
(c) Nita, Sumant
(d) Lina, Pia, Sumant

Directions for Questions 16 to 20:

Six books are kept one on the top of another. The Physics book is just above the Chemistry book. The Math book is between Economics and Geography. Computer Science is between Physics and Economics.

16. Which book is between the Math and Computer Science books?
(a) Chemistry (b) Physics
(c) Geography (d) None of these
17. Which book is at the bottom?
(a) Chemistry (b) Economics
(c) Geography (d) Can't be determined.
18. Which book is at the top?
(a) Economics (b) Geography
(c) Chemistry (d) None of these
19. If the books are numbered from 1 to 6 from top to bottom, then what is the difference between the position of Geography and Physics?
20. How many books are there between Computer Science and Chemistry?

12 Mock Test Paper

Directions for Questions 1 to 5: *Read the following information and answer the Questions.*

Four students, Promilla, Qadir, Rita and Sridhar, each working under the guidance of one of the four professors–Anand, Bose, Chandrashekharan, and Deshpande, made their final year MBA project presentations one by one, one each in the area of Finance, Marketing, Systems, and Human Resource Management (HRM). Each professor is an expert in only one of the above areas, and has supervised exactly one of the above students in her/his own area. The following clues are provided.

(i) The first presentation was made by Rita.
(ii) Prof. Bose works in Finance.
(iii) Prof. Deshpande was Promilla's supervisor.
(iv) The last presentation was in the Systems area.
(v) Sridhar's project was in HRM area.
(vi) Prof. Bose's student's presentation followed Prof. Chandrashekharan's student's presentation.

1. In which area was Rita's project?
(a) Marketing **(b)** Finance
(c) Systems **(d)** Can't be determined

2. What is Prof. Deshpande's area of expertise?
(a) Marketing **(b)** HRM
(c) Systems **(d)** Can't be determined

3. Which student completed her/his project under Prof. Bose's supervision?
(a) Qadir **(b)** Rita
(c) Sridhar **(d)** Can't be determined

4. In which area was Qadir's Project?
(a) Marketing **(b)** Systems
(c) HRM **(d)** None of these

5. Which student completed his/her project under Professor Anand?
(a) Promilla **(b)** Qadir
(c) Rita **(d)** Rita or Sridhar

Directions for Questions 6 to 10: *Answer the questions on the basis of the information given below.*

The following table gives details related to the number of marks scored by four students - Ketty, Kaamini, Clara and Kriti - in four different exams - Physics, Chemistry, Maths and Biology. However, the names of the students are disguised as 1, 2, 3, 4 and the names of the exams are disguised as A, B, C, D, not necessarily in the same order.

	1	2	3	4
A	450	600	500	700
B	500	650	550	800
C	550	500	600	250
D	600	550	400	400

The following information is also known:

(i) The total number of marks scored by the 4 students, put together, in Chemistry was greater than that in the other three exams.
(ii) The absolute difference between the total marks scored in Chemistry and Biology and the total marks scored in Maths and Physics by the four students was 200.
(iii) When the total marks scored by individual students in the four exams, put together, are arranged in descending order Kriti and Ketty occupy the top two positions.

6. Kaamini's second highest score was in
(a) Chemistry **(b)** Biology
(c) Either (a) or (b) **(d)** None of these

7. If Clara's 2nd highest score was in Biology then Kaamini's 3rd highest score was in:
(a) Maths **(b)** Physics
(c) Biology **(d)** Can't be determined

8. If Kaamini's lowest score was 50% of Ketty's highest score then total marks obtained by Clara was?

9. If Clara's lowest score was 50 more than Kaamini's lowest score then Clara's score in Biology was?

10. What was the average of the total marks scored by Clara and Kriti?
(a) 2200 **(b)** 2175
(c) 2100 **(d)** cannot be determined

Directions for Questions 11 to 15: *Answer the questions on the basis of the information given below.*

At a party, seven friends are sitting on seven chairs arranged in a row. The friends are: Suresh, Neha, Mukesh,

Ravi, Kashif, Mayank and Prateek, and they are sitting not necessarily in the same order. It is also known that:

(i) Neha is sitting beside Kashif.
(ii) Prateek is the best friend of the party's host and so he is sitting in the middle of the row.
(iii) Either of Suresh or Ravi, but not both, is sitting at one of the ends of the row.
(iv) Mukesh and Mayank are sitting as far as possible from each other, keeping in mind all the conditions of the problem.

11. Which of the following represents the number of people who could not be sitting between Mukesh and Suresh?

(a) 0 **(b)** 2
(c) 3 **(d)** 5

12. Which two of the friends, among the given pairs, cannot sit adjacent to each other?

(a) Mayank and Ravi
(b) Mukesh and Neha
(c) Ravi and Kashif
(d) Each of the given pairs in the first three options could be sitting next to each other.

13. If Mayank is sitting at one of the ends, then who occupies the other end of the row?

14. If Mukesh and Suresh occupy the ends, then which pair is sitting adjacent to each other?

(a) Mayank and Ravi **(b)** Suresh and Prateek
(c) Ravi and Kashif **(d)** Suresh and Kashif

15. If Ravi is not sitting at the end, then who is sitting between Mayank and Prateek?

Directions for Questions 16 to 20:

Each of the person - A, B, C, D like four different games Cricket, Football, Chess, Tennis (not necessarily in the same order). They live in four different cities Delhi, Patna, Nagpur, and Chennai, in any order. The following information is also known:

(i) Neither D nor the person from Chennai likes Cricket.
(ii) B likes either Football or Chess.
(iii) A is from Patna.
(iv) A likes either Chess or Tennis.
(v) The person who likes Tennis is from Nagpur.

16. Who lives in Chennai?

(a) B **(b)** C
(c) D **(d)** None of these

17. The person who lives in Delhi likes which of the following sports?

(a) Cricket **(b)** Chess
(c) Football **(d)** None of these

18. Which of the following statement is true?

(a) B is from Delhi **(b)** C likes Football
(c) D is from Nagpur **(d)** None of these

19. The person who likes Chess is from which city?

(a) Patna **(b)** Chennai
(c) Delhi **(d)** Nagpur

20. Who plays Tennis?

1 Mock Test Paper

LEVEL OF DIFFICULTY (II)

Directions for Questions 1 to 5: A train left Ludhiana Station for Kanpur Station and passed through seven train stations on its way - Ambala, Saharanpur, Roorkee, Moradabad, Bareilly, Lucknow and Unnao - not necessarily in the same order. The distance between any two consecutive stations was the same. The train always moved with a constant speed, which was either 100 kmph or 200 kmph, between two consecutive stations. It was also noticed during the journey that:

High Yield Questions

Scan this QR code to access a video explanation of questions 1-5

(i) The time taken by the train to reach Moradabad from Ambala was the same as the time taken to reach Saharanpur from Bareilly.

(ii) There was exactly one station between Moradabad and Unnao.

(iii) The distance between Ambala and Saharanpur was the same as that between Saharanpur and Bareilly.

(iv) Lucknow was not the first station and Roorkee came after Lucknow.

1. Which among the seven was the first station?

(a) Bareilly **(b)** Ambala

(c) Unnao **(d)** Can't be determined

2. If Roorkee is the last station then which of the following can be true?

(a) Unnao is the middle station.

(b) Moradabad is the middle station.

(c) Either (a) or (b) is correct.

(d) None of these.

3. Which among the these stations was the last station?

(a) Moradabad **(b)** Roorkee

(c) Unnao **(d)** Can't be determined

4. If the average speed of the train between Ambala and Moradabad was different from the average speed of the train between Bareilly and Saharanpur, then which train station was immediately after Moradabad?

(a) Ambala **(b)** Roorkee

(c) Unnao **(d)** Saharanpur

5. If Unnao was the last station before Kanpur, then which of the following is true?

(a) The station just after Lucknow was Saharanpur

(b) Moradabad was not one of the stations before Unnao

(c) The station just before Unnao was Lucknow

(d) There were 3 stations between Ambala and Unnao

Directions for Questions 6 to 10: *Answer the following questions based on the given information:*

Five students A, B, C, D, E (where A, B are males and C, D and E are females) studied in IIT-Kanpur in different branches ECE, CS, IT, Chemical, and Mechanical not necessarily in the same order and these boys were from different states Punjab, U.P., M.P., Gujrat, Kerala (in any order). After completing their graduation they placed in different companies Microsoft, Google, Yahoo, Amazon, Oracle (in any order). Package offered by Microsoft, Google, Yahoo, Amazon, and Oracle were 80 lacs, 70 lacs, 60 lacs, 50 lacs, and 40 lacs respectively. We have the following additional information:

(i) Google hired the student who was from C.S. department.

(ii) D was not from Mechanical branch.

(iii) C was from Punjab.

(iv) B placed in Oracle was not from Gujarat and the student who was from Gujarat was a student of ECE department.

(v) A who is from I.T. was not hired by Amazon. A is not from Kerala.

(vi) The female student who was from U.P. placed in Yahoo but she was not from Chemical Engineering department.

6. Which of the students was from U.P.?

7. The Gujarati student was placed in which company?

8. Find the sum of salaries of student B and C (in lacs).

9. Find the absolute difference of the salaries of E and the student from Kerala (in lacs).
10. Find the sum of salaries of the student who belongs to UP and the student who works in Amazon (in lacs)

Directions for Questions 11 to 15: *Answer the questions on the basis of the information given below.*

Michel wants to distribute his profit among his four employees - Simon, Kriti, Lehman and Peter. While distributing the profit he considered three parameters - age, job experience and annual salary.

The following information is also known:

(i) For each of the three parameters, the profit allocated to that parameter was distributed among the four employees in the ratio 1:2:3:4.
(ii) On the age front, the youngest employee got the least amount, the second youngest the second least, and so on.
(iii) On the job experience front, the most experienced employee got the highest amount, the second most experienced the second highest, and so on.
(iv) On the salary front, the employee with least salary got the highest amount, with the second least salary the second highest, and so on.
(v) The total profit that Mr. Michel distributed among his employees was ₹ 4 crore.
(vi) The ratio in which he distributed his profit along the three parameters (age, job experience and annual salary), in the given order, was 5:3:2.

11. If the profit share of Lehman is 132 lakhs and his age share is 60 lakh, then what is his job experience share (in lakhs)?
12. If the share (Rs in lakhs) of Simon, Kriti, Lehman and Peter was 112, 68, 132 and 88 respectively, then whose salary was the least?
(a) Peter (b) Simon
(c) Lehman (d) Can't be determined
13. In the previous question what is the job experience share of Simon (in Lakh)?
14. If Peter was the oldest but not the most experienced, then the share (in Rs. Lakh) of Peter could not be equal to
(a) 148 (b) 144
(c) 132 (d) 136
15. If the share (Rs in lakh) of Simon, Kriti, Lehman and Peter was 112, 68, 132, and 88, then whose salary was the maximum?
(a) Peter (b) Simon
(c) Lehman (d) Cannot be determined

Directions for Questions 16 to 20: The staff of Mindworkzz presently consists of three senior faculty–A, B and C and five junior faculty–U, V, W, X and Y. Mr Arun Sharma, CEO of Mindworkzz, is planning to open a new office in another city using two senior faculty and three junior faculty of the present staff. To do so he plans to separate certain individuals who do not fuction well as a team. The following guidelines were established to set up the new office:

(i) Since U and X have been competing for promotion, they should not be a team.
(ii) Senior faculty A and C are constantly finding fault with one another and should not be sent to the new office as a team.
(iii) C and V function well alone but not as a team. Hence, they should be separated.
(iv) U and X have not been on speaking terms for many months. They should not be put together.

16. If A is to be moved as one of the senior faculty, which of the following cannot be a possible working unit?
(a) ABUVY (b) ABVWY
(c) ABUXY (d) ABVXY
17. If C and W are moved to the new office, how many teams are possible?
(a) 1 (b) 2
(c) 3 (d) 4
18. If C is sent to the new office, which member cannot go with C?
(a) B (b) U
(c) V (d) X
19. Given the conditions in the passage, which of the following must go to the new office?
(a) B (b) U
(c) V (d) T
20. If U goes to the new office, which of the following is/are true?
(i) X cannot go with him
(ii) A cannot go with him
(iii) B is another faculty to go with him
(a) (i) only
(b) (iii) only
(c) Both (i) and (iii) only
(d) None of these

2 Mock Test Paper

Directions for Questions 1 to 5: Chandramohan and his wife Kamini have a family of three generations comprising thirteen members of whom six are female members. Some of Chandramohan's children are married, but none of his grandchildren are married.

(i) Kamni has a daughter-in-law named Fullara and two sons-in-law, one being Geshwaran.
(ii) Harihar's brother is Devesh, who has two nephews and two nieces–one being Leela.
(iii) Bandana, Devesh's sister has two children.
(iv) Fullara, who is sister-in-law to Devesh has four nephews and nieces.
(v) Manohar, who is married to Geeta in the family has a daughter, Indira, and a son.
(vi) Joy has a sister and two cousins, Akash and Indira.

1. Amongst the following, which one is false?
(a) Bandana is Kamini's child.
(b) Joy is Geeta's child.
(c) Akash is Harihar's nephew.
(d) Geeta has less than two nephews.

2. Leela is the niece of
(a) Bandana **(b)** Geshwaran
(c) Harihar **(d)** Kamini

3. Akash is the son of
(a) Geeta **(b)** Harihar
(c) Devesh **(d)** Bandana

4. Which of the following pairs is a brother and a sister?
(a) Manohar and Fullara
(b) Devesh and Geeta
(c) Joy and Indira
(d) Eeshwaran and Bandana

5. Statements:
(i) Fullara is Harihar's wife.
(ii) Harihar's son's name is Akash.
(iii) Bandana is Leela's mother.
Based on the above facts, which of the following is true?
(a) (i) and (ii) only, but not (iii)
(b) (i) and (iii) only, but not (ii)
(c) (ii) and (iii) only, but not (i)
(d) All of (i), (ii) and (iii)

Directions for Questions 6 to 10: Twelve friends, comprising eight males–Alok, Charan, Vikram, Vinay, Mohit, Sunny, Vijay and Suraj and four females, viz. Reena, Rani, Nikita and Rohini planned to visit Agra from Lucknow. They booked three jeeps for the purpose. The group had three married couples. The jeeps belonged one to each–Alok, Vinay and Reena. The jeeps left the place at different times–viz at: 5:00 AM, 6:00 AM and 7:00 AM. The following information is also known:

High Yield Questions
Scan this QR code to access a video explanation of questions 6-10

(i) Nikita whose husband was the owner of one of the jeeps, went in the jeep that left at 5:00 AM.
(ii) At least one married couple went in Reena's jeep.
(iii) Rani and Sunny were a married couple and they left the place after the jeep that had Vikram in it.
(iv) Alok was unmarried and did not go in the jeep that left at 7:00 AM.
(v) Each jeep could carry a maximum of five passengers.
(vi) Each jeep had a distinct number of passengers.
(vii) The number of married couples in each jeep was also distinct.
(viii) The owner of the jeeps travelled in his/her own vehicle.
(ix) All married couples travelled together.
(x) Charan went in the jeep, which did not have any married couple.
(xi) Rohini went in a jeep, which had total four persons in it.
(xii) Suraj did not go with Mohit and Vikram, Mohit and Vikram went in two different vehicles.
(xiii) Nikita and Vikram did not go in the same jeep.
(xiv) Suraj and Rani went in the same jeep.

6. Which of the following was definitely a married couple?
(a) Suraj-Reena **(b)** Mohit-Rohini
(c) Nikita-Vinay **(d)** None of these

7. How many passengers were there in the jeep, which left at 7:00 AM?
(a) 3 (b) 4
(c) 5 (d) Either 3 or 5
8. How many married couple/s were there in the jeep, which left at 5:00 AM?
(a) 0 (b) 1
(c) 2 (d) Either 1 or 2
9. Who was the husband of Rohini, if she were married?
(a) Mohit (b) Vijay
(c) Vikram (d) Can't be determined
10. For how many jeeps can we exactly determine the number of married couples in that jeep?

Directions for Questions 11 to 15: *Answer the questions on the basis of the information given below.*

Eight athletes - Alan, Binny, Chris, Danny, Emmy, Fahim, Granny, and Harry - have opted for two sports each, from among eight sports - Cricket, Football, Hockey, Handball, Tennis, Polo, Squash and Chess - such that each of these sports was opted for by at least one athlete and no two athletes opted for the same combination of sports. Further, it is known that,

(i) Any person who opted for Cricket opted for neither Squash nor Hockey.
(ii) Harry, who opted for Hockey, opted for neither Tennis nor Handball.
(iii) Any person who opted for Polo did not opt for any of Handball, Football and Squash.
(iv) No other athlete chose any of the sports chosen by Binny.
(v) None of the sports was chosen by more than three persons and Cricket is one of the sports chosen by Danny.
(vi) Chris, Emmy and Fahim have opted for no sport in common with each other and none of them opted for Polo.
(vii) Alan opted for Squash and Chris opted for Hockey.
(viii) Any person who opted for Football opted for neither Cricket nor Hockey.
(ix) Fahim opted for Tennis and Granny opted for Handball.
(x) Except the sports chosen by Binny, every other sport was chosen by at least two athletes.

11. Which of the following sports are chosen by Emmy?
(a) Football and Squash
(b) Handball and Squash
(c) Handball and Football
(d) Handball and Cricket
12. Which of the following player chose tennis?
(a) Alan (b) Binny
(c) Chris (d) None of these.
13. Who among the following has opted for both Handball and Football?
(a) Emmy (b) Chris
(c) Danny (d) Granny
14. Which of the following sports was opted for by more than two persons?
(a) Handball (b) Hockey
(c) Tennis (d) Football
15. How many people opted for either Squash or Tennis or Both?

Directions for Questions 16 to 20: *A wooden cuboid of dimensions 9 × 7 × 5 unit is painted in a fixed pattern.*

(i) The two opposite faces in the front and back are painted in red with 9 × 7 cuts.
(ii) The other two opposite faces on the sides are painted in green with 9 × 5 cuts.
(iii) The remaining top and bottom faces are painted in blue.

The cuboid is cut into 315 small cubes.

16. How many cubes have all the three faces coloured?
(a) 8 (b) 32
(c) 24 (d) None of these
17. How many cubes have two faces coloured?
(a) 60 (b) 142
(c) 105 (d) None of these
18. How many cubes have one face coloured?
(a) 142 (b) 105
(c) 71 (d) None of these
19. How many cubes have no face coloured?
(a) 142 (b) 60
(c) 105 (d) None of these
20. How many cubes have two faces coloured, that too in red and green?
(a) 14 (b) 28
(c) 32 (d) None of these

3 Mock Test Paper

Directions for Questions 1 to 5: Amit, Balvinder, Chetan, and Deepak are employed in a company, where they have to share the work load, that consists of six tasks A, B, C, D, E, and F. The following statements identify their preferences for the different tasks:

(i) All those who like Task B also like Task E.
(ii) All those who like Task C also like Task D.
(iii) All those who like Task E do not like Task C, and vice-versa.
(iv) Some of those who like Task E also like Task A.
(v) Some of those who like Task D also like Task E.
(vi) All those who like Task D also like Task F.

1. Amit enjoys the Task D. Which of the following must be true?
(a) He may or may not like Task C.
(b) He does not like Task B.
(c) He likes Task A.
(d) He likes Task C.

2. Balvinder likes Task B. He may also like any of the following tasks, except
(a) Task A **(b)** Task C
(c) Task D **(d)** Task E

3. Chetan likes Task C. Which of the following must be false?
(a) He does not like Task A.
(b) He likes Task F.
(c) He does not like Task B.
(d) He may like Task E

4. Which of the following can be a combination of tasks for a given person?
(a) A, B, C **(b)** C, D, E
(c) C, D, B **(d)** C, D, F

5. If Deepak does not want to take task E, then which task should he take voluntarily so that no one could force Task E on him?
(a) A **(b)** B
(c) C **(d)** D

Directions for Questions 6 to 10: Four children A, B, C and D had 400 marbles, which they had to distribute between one another. At the time of distribution, they considered three parameters–academic grades, seniority and family wealth. The ratio in which they distributed the amount along the three parameters, in the given order, was 5:3:2. The following information is also known:

High Yield Questions
Scan this QR code to access a video explanation of questions 6-10

(i) For each of the three parameters, the number of marbles allocated to that parameter was distributed among the four children in the ratio 1:2:3:4.
(ii) On the academic grades front, the child with highest academic grades got the highest amount, the second highest academic grade got the second highest amount and so on.
(iii) On the seniority in school parameter, higher the seniority higher the number of marbles received by the child.
(iv) On the family wealth front, more the total wealth lesser the number of marbles received by the child.

6. If the number of marbles received by A, B, C and D were 112, 68, 132 and 88 respectively, then whose total family wealth was the highest?

7. If D had the highest academic grades in his name, but his seniority is not the highest among the given children, then which of the following, could not be the number of marbles received by D?
(a) 136 **(b)** 132
(c) 148 **(d)** 144

8. If C's share was 92 marbles, then what rank was not possible for C in his seniority among the given children?

9. If the number of marbles received by A, B, C & D were 112, 68, 132 and 88 respectively, then how many marbles did B and D together receive for their family wealth?

10. If the number of marbles received by A, B, C and D were 112, 68, 132 and 88 respectively, and C gave half of his marbles to B distributing the marbles as per the ratio he has the marbles in, then who had the maximum marbles for seniority?

(a) A (b) B
(c) D (d) B or D

Directions for Questions 11 to 15: *Answer the questions on the basis of the information given below.*

Six tennis players Parmesh, Quran, Rahim, Salim, Tariq and Ulaal played in a tennis tournament. Each of the players played with every other player exactly once. Every game resulted in a win/loss. The player who won, gets as many gold coins as the number of points. Each player could score points in between 1 to 6 and the person who scored more points won the game. The total number of games won by each player is distinct. The following information is also known:

(i) Quran won his game against Parmesh.
(ii) Rahim won the maximum number of coins, more than anyone else.
(iii) Ulaal lost only two games, one against Salim and the other against Rahim.
(iv) Tariq did not lose more than three games.

11. How many games did Parmesh win?

12. Which of the following statements is necessarily true?
(a) Tariq won 5 games
(b) Rahim won 5 games
(c) Salim won 5 games
(d) None of these

13. Rahim won 11 coins and all other players won lesser coins than Rahim. He lost one game. If the total coins won by the different players in the tournament is 47, then the number of coins won by Tariq was:

14. In the above question, Quran got _ gold coins.

15. Apart from Parmesh, who lost the match against Tariq?

Directions for Questions 16 to 20: *Read the following information and answer the questions given below.*

(i) Mark, a management representative (M. R.) from Mindworkzz Solutions Inc., has to meet 7 managers A, B, C, D, E, F and G on a particular day between 9 am and 4 pm.
(ii) He takes 30 minutes with each manager and keeps a gap of 25 minutes between two appointments for travel and preparation except after the fifth visit, when he takes 50 minutes' break for lunch, travel and preparation.
(iii) He has to meet manager A immediately before E but immediately after F, who is the third manager to be met.
(iv) G does not give time for M.R. before 9.30 am and after 10.30 am. D and B meet M.R. between 2 pm and 3:30 pm only.

16. Who among the following is likely to be the first manager of that day?
(a) G (b) C
(c) F (d) E

17. If manager F asks him to visit again 25 minutes after his scheduled seventh visit is over, then at what time can he meet manager F?
(a) 3.55 pm (b) 3.40 pm
(c) 3.25 pm (d) None of these

18. At what order number does Mark meet A?

19. When does Mark meet B?
(a) Between 9 am & 10 am
(b) Between 11 am & 12 pm
(c) Between 2.15 pm & 3.15 pm
(d) Between 12 pm & 1 pm

20. Who does Mark meet after his meeting with C?
(a) A (b) B
(c) C (d) G

4 Mock Test Paper

Directions for Questions 1 to 5: *Answer the questions based on the following information.*

High Yield Questions

Scan this QR code to access a video explanation of questions 1-5

Five women decided to go for shopping in South Extension, New Delhi. They arrived at the designated meeting place in the following order: 1. Aradhana, 2. Chandrima, 3. Deepika, 4. Heena and 5. Sumitra. Each of them spent at least ₹ 1000. The woman who spent ₹ 2234 arrived before the woman who spent ₹ 1193. One of them spent ₹ 1340 and she was not Deepika. One woman spent ₹ 1378 more than Chandrima. One of them spent ₹ 2517 and she was not Aradhana. Heena spent more than Deepika. Sumitra spent the largest amount and Chandrima the smallest.

1. What was the amount spent by Heena?

(a) ₹ 1193 **(b)** ₹ 1340
(c) ₹ 2234 **(c)** ₹ 2517

2. Which of the following amount is spent by one of the women?

(a) ₹ 1139 **(b)** ₹ 1378
(c) ₹ 2571 **(d)** ₹ 2518

3. The lady who spent ₹ 1193 is:

(a) Aradhana **(b)** Chandrima
(c) Deepika **(d)** Heena

4. What is the difference in amount spent by Deepika and Sumitra?

5. Who spent the second highest amount?

Directions for Questions 6 to 10: In Green Park stadium's cricket club (in Kanpur) there was a bowling machine, which worked for 6 hours a day, from 12 PM to 3 PM, and from 3:30 PM to 6:30 PM, every day from Monday to Saturday. The bowling machine was used by three batsmen, A, B and C with two hours of practice by each batsman on each day. The following information is also known about their practice sessions:

(i) There are a total of 6-slots for practice and each slot had a length of 1 hour. Slots start from 12 PM and each batsman was allotted two slots according to his comfort.

(ii) C took at least a one-hour break after his every practice session.

(iii) 'A' who did not take the last slot on any day, took his practice slots continuously without a break.

(iv) A took the 1st and 2nd slots on Wednesday and Friday.

(v) 'C' took the 3rd slot on four days and the 1st slot on 3 days of the week.

(vi) The slot-schedule allotted to any batsman was not identical for more than 2 days of the week.

(vii) 'B' took the 4th slot from Wednesday to Saturday. He was allotted the last slot only on three days–Monday, Wednesday and Friday.

(viii) A's slots allocation were identical on Thursday and Saturday.

6. On how many days did B take both of his slots before 3:30?

7. Who took the 12 PM to 1 PM slot on Saturday?

8. In a week on how many days did both the practice slots of B precede the slots of C?

9. Who took the 4:30–5:30 PM slot on Friday?

10. On which day did B have slots which were furthest?

Directions for Questions 11 to 15: *Answer the questions on the basis of the information given below.*

Five businessmen - Alan, Ben, Chris, David, Elec started their businesses in five different cities - Raigad, Brindapur, Manakpur, Kamalpur and Palampur, not necessarily in that order. They started their businesses with an amount which is a multiple of 4. The minimum investment was Rs. 16 lakh and maximum investment was Rs. 36 lakh. At the end of one year of their business their revenues were 96, 112, 64, 80 and 72 (in lakhs Rs), in no particular order.

$$\text{Profit Ratio} = \frac{\text{Total sale at the end of the year}}{\text{Total investment at the beginning}}$$

The following information is also known:

(i) Profit Ratio is an integer.

(ii) Profit Ratio ≤ 4.

(iii) Total sales of the businessman who started his business in Manakpur is 24 lakhs more than the total sales of Chris.

(iv) The difference in sales of David and Elec is twice of the difference of sales by the businessman who started their businesses in Brindapur and Raigad.

(v) The businessman whose sales was Rs. 16 lakh less than the businessman of Kamalpur had worst profit ratio.

(vi) Elec did not setup his business in Manakpur.

(vii) Ben invested the least amount and his sales value is Rs. 8 lakh more than a businessman, who did not setup his business in Brindapur.

11. Who among the following set his business in Palampur?

(a) Ben (b) Chris
(c) David (d) Elec

12. What was the difference between the sales value (in lakhs) of businessman who set up his business in Kamalpur and that of the businessman who setup his business in Raigad?

13. What was the amount invested (in Lakhs) by the businessman who setup his business in Kamalpur?

14. Who set up his business in Raigad?

(a) Ben (b) Chris
(c) David (d) Elec

15. If the Profit Ratio of Chris was not less than that of David, then what is the absolute difference between the amount Invested by both of them?

Directions for Questions 16 to 20:

Six techies- A, B, C, D, E, F attended a Tech-conference in Mumbai. Each of them was working in different companies Microsoft, Yahoo, Google, FB, Cisco, TCS in any order and each of them attended the conference on a different day among- Monday, Tuesday, Wednesday, Thursday, Friday, and Saturday, not necessarily in the same order. The following information is also given:

(i) A attended the conference on Monday and the person who works in Microsoft attended the conference on Saturday.

(ii) B and D attended the conference on consecutive days.

(iii) Exactly one person attended the conference between E and C and C was working in Google.

(iv) F was working in Yahoo.

(v) C attended the conference on the next day of FB employee.

(vi) The person who was working in Cisco attended the conference on Friday.

16. Which of the following person was working in TCS?

(a) B (b) C
(c) D (d) E

17. Which of the following person attended the conference on Friday?

(a) E
(b) D
(c) B
(d) Can't be determined

18. If Microsoft, Google, Yahoo, FB, Cisco, TCS were offering 1 Lac, 2 Lac, 3Lac, 4 Lac, 5 Lac & 6 Lac dollars per annum salary packages in the same order at the time of conference then find the average salary package (in Lacs of Dollars) of B, D and E.

19. Who works in TCS?

20. Which company definitely has a working day on Monday?

5 Mock Test Paper

Directions for Questions 1 to 4: *Answer the questions based on the following information.*

Mr. Mansingh has five sons - Arun, Mahi, Rohit, Nilesh and Saurav, and three daughters - Tamanna, Kuntala and Janaki. Three sons of Mr. Mansingh were born first, followed by two daughters. Saurav is the eldest child and Janki is the youngest. Three of the children are studying at Trinity School and three are studying at St. Stefan. Tamanna and Rohit study at St. Stefan school. Kuntala, the eldest daughter, plays chess. Mansorover school offers cricket only, while Trinity school offers chess. Besides these the schools offer no other games. The children who are at Mansorover school have been born in succession. Mahi and Nilesh are cricketers while Arun plays football. Rohit who was born just before Janki, plays hockey.

1. Arun is the __________ child of Mr. Mansingh.
   (a) 2nd (b) 3rd
   (c) 6th (d) 5th
2. Saurav is a student of which school?
   (a) Trinity (b) St. Stefan
   (c) Mansorover (d) Can't be determined
3. What game does Tamanna play?
   (a) Cricket (b) Hockey
   (c) Football (d) Can't be determined
4. Which of the following pairs was not born in succession (ignore the order)?
   (a) Mahi and Nilesh
   (b) Kuntala and Arun
   (c) Rohit and Janki
   (d) Arun and Rohit

Direction for Question 5:

5. Among Anil, Bibek, Charu, Debu, and Eswar, Eswar is taller than Debu but not as fat as Debu. Charu is taller than Anil but shorter than Bibek. Anil is fatter than Debu but not as fat as Bibek. Eswar is thinner than Charu, who is thinner than Debu. Eswar is shorter than Anil. Who is the thinnest person?
   (a) Bibek (b) Charu
   (c) Debu (d) Eswar

Directions for Questions 6 to 10: In the international mathematics Olympiad quiz, held recently at Reykjavik, two countries–USA and UK, qualified for the final round. Each team has five students amongst–Jackie, Bindu, Jake, Jorry, Luke, Chris, Kevin, Rashid, Oliver and Ozeal, not necessarily in the same order. A student can either get 2 points for his team by answering a basic level question or score 3 points by answering an advanced level problem. The following information is also known:

High Yield Questions
Scan this QR code to access a video explanation of questions 6-10

(i) Oliver and Rashid were in the same team and Jorry and Bindu are not in the same team.
(ii) Oliver and Rashid both obtained exactly 4 points each.
(iii) Kevin, Jake and Jackie obtained 7, 8 and 9 marks respectively.
(iv) No one scored more than Luke, who did not answer any basic level question and his team scored a total of 25 points.
(v) Students with the same initials belonged to the same team.
(vi) Each student answered at least one question correctly.
(vii) There were two students in the USA team and one student in the UK team who did not answer any advanced level question correctly.
(viii) The sum of the total number of correct answers given by the two countries is 22.
(ix) The sum of the total marks obtained by the two countries is 56.
(x) Jorry and Bindu answered exactly one question correctly. Jorry answered exactly one basic level question and Bindu answered one advanced level question.

6. What are the total marks scored by team UK?
7. Which of the following pair is in the same team?
   (a) Ozeal and Jorry (b) Jackie and Luke
   (c) Jake and Chris (d) None of these

8. How many total points were scored by team USA by answering only advance level questions?
9. What was the ratio of the total marks scored by Oliver, Ozeal and Rashid?
10. Find the sum of total marks scored by Jake and Jackie by answering only basic level questions.

Directions for Questions 11 to 15: *Read the following information carefully and answer the questions given below:*

Sachin, Saurav, Rahul, Yuvraj, Mahendra and Suresh, six enemies of different heights and wearing different coloured jackets of red, blue, white, orange, yellow and green, are standing on either sides of a road with three on each side. Mahendra, who is the tallest, is exactly opposite the person wearing red-coloured jacket. The shortest person is exactly opposite the person wearing green coloured jacket. Suresh is the person wearing orange-coloured jacket and is standing between Sachin and Yuvraj.

Rahul, who is wearing yellow-coloured jacket, is exactly opposite Sachin. Saurav who is wearing green-coloured jacket, is exactly opposite Suresh. Sachin, wearing the white-coloured jacket, is taller than Rahul but shorter than Yuvraj and Saurav.

11. What is the colour of the jacket of Yuvraj?
    (a) Red (b) Blue
    (c) Red or blue (d) None of these
12. What is the position of Sachin from top when the persons are arranged in descending order of their heights?
    (a) Third (b) Second
    (c) Fourth (d) None of these
13. Who is the tallest person of the group?
14. Who lives opposite the person living in the red colored house?
15. What is the color of Sachin's jacket?
    (a) Yellow (b) Green
    (c) Blue (d) White

Directions for Questions 16 to 20: *Answer the questions on the basis of the information given below.*

In an international level badminton tournament, there were 5 badminton teams that participated - China, Japan, South Korea, Singapore and Thailand together played 80 games and the number of games played by each team was between 8 and 24. The team from Japan and the one headed by Captain Paulie played an equal number of games. It is also known that:

(i) Team Thailand played 2 games more than the one headed by Captain Chang and 12 more than Team Singapore.
(ii) Team China played 10 games more than Team Singapore and is not headed by Captain Karen.
(iii) The team headed by Captain Karen played 14 games.
(iv) The team that played the minimum number of games was not headed by Captain Chang but by Captain Brock.
(v) The number of games played by team Thailand was 22.

16. How many games were played by the team that played double the number of matches as played by the team who played the least number of matches?
    (a) 24 (b) 28
    (c) 12 (d) 20
17. Which of the following combinations is wrong?
    (a) China – Chang –20
    (b) South Korea – Paulie –14
    (c) South Korea – Paulie –20
    (d) Singapore – Brock –10
18. What is the difference in the number of games played by Japan and South Korea?
19. Who was the captain of China?
    (a) Chang (b) Karen
    (c) Paulie (d) Brock
20. How many matches were played by Singapore?

6 Mock Test Paper

Directions for Questions 1 to 5: *Answer the questions based on the following information.*

Mr. Bankatlal acted as a judge for a beauty contest. There were four participants, viz. Ms. Andhra Pradesh, Ms. Uttar Pradesh, Ms. West Bengal and Ms Maharashtra. Mrs. Bankatlal, who was very anxious about the result, asked him about it as soon as he was back home. Mr. Bankatlal told her that the woman who was wearing the yellow saree won the contest. When Mrs. Bankatlal pressed for further details, he elaborated as follows:

High Yield Questions

Scan this QR code to access a video explanation of questions 1-5

(i) All of them were sitting in a row.

(ii) All of them wore sarees of different colours, viz. green, yellow, white, red.

(iii) There was only one runner-up and she was sitting beside Ms. Maharashtra.

(iv) The runner-up was wearing the green saree.

(v) Ms. West Bengal was not sitting at the ends and was not the runner up.

(vi) The winner and the runner-up are not sitting adjacent to each other.

(vii) Ms. Maharashtra was wearing white saree.

(viii) Ms. Andhra Pradesh was not wearing the green saree.

(ix) Participants wearing yellow saree and white saree were at the ends.

1. Who wore the red saree?
(a) Ms. Andhra Pradesh
(b) Ms. West Bengal
(c) Ms. Uttar Pradesh
(d) Ms. Maharashtra

2. Ms. West Bengal was sitting adjacent to
(a) Ms. Andhra Pradesh and Ms. Maharashtra
(b) Ms. Uttar Pradesh and Ms. Maharashtra
(c) Ms. Andhra Pradesh and Ms. Uttar Pradesh
(d) Ms. Uttar Pradesh

3. Which saree was worn by Ms Andhra Pradesh?
(a) Yellow **(c)** Red
(c) Green **(d)** White

4. Who was the runner-up?
(a) Ms. Andhra Pradesh
(b) Ms. West Bengal
(c) Ms. Uttar Pradesh
(d) Ms. Maharashtra

5. What was the color of the saree worn by the person sitting adjacent to the winner of the competition?

Directions for Questions 6 to 10: Seven players Nadal, Djokovic, Rogers, Andre, William, Chris and Murray are participating in ATP Masters Tennis Tournament 2023 in Dubai. According to the rules of the tournament, each player plays exactly once against the rest of the six players. The tournament starts on Thursday and finishes on Saturday. The following information is also given:

(i) An equal number of matches are played on each of these three days and all the players win different number of matches.

(ii) None of the matches ends in a draw.

(iii) On Thursday, Chris loses to Rogers, Andre, William and Murray.

(iv) On Saturday, Chris loses to Nadal and Djokovic.

(v) Djokovic wins against Rogers, Andre and William on Friday.

(vi) William loses to Nadal and Rogers on Friday.

(vii) On Saturday, Murray loses to Djokovic but wins against Nadal and Rogers.

(viii) Murray wins exactly two matches on Friday.

(ix) On Saturday, Andre wins against Rogers and William.

(x) Only one player, who is not Rogers, wins more than one match on Thursday.

6. The sum of the total number of matches won by Andre and Nadal together = ?
(a) 6 **(b)** 7
(c) 8 **(d)** None of these

7. The total number of matches won by Rogers is....

8. On how many days during the tournament does at least one player win more than two matches? (Type 3 if we cannot determine the answer)

9. According to the rules of the tournament the player who wins the most number of matches, is declared as the winner of the tournament. Who would be the winner of the tournament?

10. What happened between the match of Nadal and Andre?

(a) Nadal won **(b)** Andre won
(c) None of these **(d)** Cannot be determined

Directions for Questions 11 to 15: *Study the following information carefully and answer the questions given below:*

Amar, Biswas, Calvin, Devendra, Ekta, Firoz and Gavli are seven persons who travel to office everyday by a local train which stops at five stations-Kalyan, Thane, Kurla, Dadar and Mumbai Central, respectively, after it leaves base station.

(i) Three among them get in the train at the base station.
(ii) Devendra gets down at the next station at which Firoz gets down.
(iii) Biswas does not get down either with Amar or Ekta.
(iv) Gavli alone gets in at station Kurla and gets down with Calvin after having passed one station.
(v) Amar travels between only two stations and gets down at Mumbai central.
(vi) None of them gets in at Thane.
(vii) Calvin gets in with Firoz but does not get in with either Biswas or Devendra.
(viii) Ekta gets in with two others and gets down alone after Devendra.
(ix) Biswas and Devendra work in the same office and they get down together at Kurla.
(x) None of them gets down at Kalyan.

11. At which station does Ekta get down?

(a) Thane **(b)** Kurla
(c) Dadar **(d)** None of these

12. After how many stations does Ekta get down?

(a) One **(b)** Two
(c) Three **(d)** Four

13. Who got down with Biswas?

(a) Devendra **(b)** Ekta
(c) Amar **(d)** No one

14. At which station did Amar board the train?

(a) Thane **(b)** Kalyan
(c) Base **(d)** Dadar

15. How many stations did Gavli pass during her journey?

Directions for Questions 16 to 20: *Answer the questions on the basis of the information given below.*

Four friends - Kishore, Lokesh, Mayank and Neelam, from the same batch of IAS have been working since very long in different states of India, namely - U.P., Maharashtra and M.P. The number of years for which they have worked is an integral unit. The sums of the number of years spent in the three states together were distinct for the four friends. The sums of the number of years spent by the four friends together in the U.P., Maharashtra and M.P. were 22, 26 and 26 respectively. No friend spent an equal number of years in any two states. No two friends spent an equal number of years in any states. It is also known that:

(i) The number of years spent by Kishore and Mayank in M.P were 8 and 2, respectively.
(ii) The sum of the number of years spent in the three states together by Mayank was not less than that of Kishore.
(iii) The sum of the number of years spent in the three states together by Lokesh was 30.
(iv) The absolute difference between the numbers of years spent by Kishore in U.P. and the number of years spent by Mayank in Maharashtra was 4.
(v) Among the three states, Neelam spent the least amount of time in Maharashtra and the maximum in M.P.

16. What is the difference in the number of year(s) spent by Kishore in U.P. and Maharashtra?

(a) 4 **(b)** 2
(c) 8 **(d)** 6

17. What was the sum of the numbers of years spent by Mayank in U.P., Kishore in Maharsahtra, Lokesh in U.P. and Neelam in M.P?

(a) 24 **(b)** 32
(c) 26 **(d)** 36

18. Among the four friends, who spent the least amount of time in M.P and Maharashtra?

(a) Mayank and Neelam
(b) Lokesh and Kishore
(c) Kishore and Neelam
(d) Neelam and Lokesh

19. Who spent the maximum number of years in any state?

(a) Kishore
(c) Lokesh
(b) Mayank
(d) Neelam

20. What is the total number of years spent by the four people in all the four states combined?

7 Mock Test Paper

Directions for Questions 1 to 5: *Read the information given below and answer the questions that follow the information.*

High Yield Questions

Scan this QR code to access a video explanation of questions 1-5

A parking lot can accommodate only six cars. Six cars are parked in two rows in such a way that the front of the three cars parked in one row is facing the other three cars in the other row.

(i) The Alto is not parked in the beginning of any row.

(ii) The Esteem is second to the right of *i*10.

(iii) Punto, which is the neighbour of Alto is parked diagonally opposite the *i*10.

(iv) Swift is parked in front of Alto.

(v) SX4 is parked to the immediate right of Alto.

1. If the SX4 and Esteem exchange their positions mutually then car(s) adjacent to Esteem is(are)?

(a) i10 and Swift **(b)** Only Swift

(c) Only Alto **(d)** Alto and Punto

2. If Alto changes position with i10 and Punto changes position with SX4 and Swift shifts one position to the right to accommodate Beatle then the car(s) parked adjacent to Beatle is(are)?

(a) Punto only **(b)** i10 and SX4

(c) Punto and Alto **(d)** Alto and Swift

3. In the original parking scheme four new cars enter the parking lot such that Wagon-R is second to the right of i10 and Zen is second to the left of SX4. Jazz is parked second to the left of Wagon-R and Beat is parked to the right of Alto, then the cars that moved out are?

(a) Esteem and Swift **(b)** Punto and Alto

(c) i10 and Alto **(d)** Punto and SX4

4. In the previous question, if Wagon-R had to switch positions with Swift, then which of the following is true?

I. Before the switch, WagonR was next to Jazz, and after the shift, Swift is next to Jazz

II. Before the switch, Swift was in the middle of WagonR and Jazz, but now Jazz is in the middle

III. After the switch, Alto is next to WagonR

(a) Only I **(b)** Only 3

(c) All 3 **(d)** None of these.

5. After the entry of the 4 new cars as indicated, if Alto is replaced by Nexon, and Nexon switches its position with Zen, then which of the following car(s) is/are next to Zen?

(a) Only Wagon-R **(b)** Only Swift

(c) Nexon and Beat **(d)** Only Nexon

Directions for Questions 6 to 10: Four persons Alan, Bipul, Chris and David are from four distinct cities -Durban, Mumbai, Chicago and Karachi (not necessarily in the same order). Each person teaches in a different college amongst FMS, CRS, CHS and HMS, in any order. Each person is married to a different girl amongst Ervin, Croony, Jany and Alexa (in any order).

The following additional information is also known:

(i) Ervin's husband teaches in CHS and Jany's husband is from Durban.

(ii) Bipul is neither from Durban nor from Mumbai and he does not teach in FMS, and he is not married to Ervin.

(iii) Alan is neither from Mumbai nor from Karachi andhe does not teach in CHS. He is not married to Croony.

(iv) Alexa's husband is from Karachi and does not teach in HMS.

6. Which of the following statement/s is required to complete the arrangement (i.e Person, City, College, Wife):

1. Alan belongs to Durban.

2. David is from Chicago but does not teach in CHS.

3. Alan does not teach in FMS.

(a) Only 1 and 3 **(b)** Only 2 and 3

(c) Only 2 **(d)** None of these

7. If David teaches in FMS and Bipul is not from Chicago, then who teaches in HMS?

8. If Chris teaches in CHS and David is from Chicago then which of the following statements is true?

(a) Alan teaches in HMS

(b) David teaches in FMS

(c) Bipul teaches in CRS
(d) All of the above

9. If Chris is from Karachi, then which of the following statements is FALSE?
(a) The person from Durban teaches in CRS.
(b) Croony's husband is from Chicago.
(c) The person who teaches in CRS is not from Mumbai.
(d) None of these

10. If Chris teaches in CHS and David is from Chicago, who is married to Croony?

Directions for Questions 11 to 15: *Study the following information carefully and answer the questions given below it:*

Yudhishter passes through seven lanes to reach his school. He finds that 'Truth Lane' is between his house and 'Lie Lane'. The third lane from his school is 'Karma Lane'. 'Dharma Lane' is immediately before the 'Yog Lane'. He passes 'Salvation Lane' at the end, 'Lie Lane' is between 'Truth Lane' and "Dharma Lane', and the sixth lane from his house is 'Devotion Lane'.

11. How many lanes are there between 'Lie Lane' and 'Devotion Lane'?
(a) One (b) Two
(c) Three (d) Four

12. If from the house of Yudhishter, each lane and his school are equidistant and he takes two minutes to pass one lane, then how long will he take to reach school from his house?
(a) 18 minutes (b) 16 minutes
(c) 14 minutes (d) None of these

13. How many lanes are there between Yog and Salvation lanes?

14. Which lane is exactly in between 'Lie Lane' and Yudhishthir's school?
(a) Truth (b) Dharma
(c) Yog (d) Karma

15. Which lane is adjacent to 'Dharma Lane'?
(a) Lie (b) Karma
(c) Devotion (d) Salvation

Directions for Questions 16 to 20: *Answer the questions on the basis of the information given below.*

ABC paints have come up with a brilliant marketing campaign for 6 of their new products. They plan to launch their campaign in 6 different countries - South Africa, USA, UK, Australia, Ivory Coast and Brazil. In order to launch the campaign in the best of fashion that goes in accordance to the trends in those countries, they have tied up with 6 different advertising agencies in these nations - Maxwell Advertising, La-Nina Ltd., Sonya Advertisers, D-Damsels, Rated-R Agencies and Phoenix, not in a particular order. These 6 different campaigns were decided to be launched at 6 different dates in these nations - 1st January, 5th February, 23rd March, 29th April, 22nd May and 14th June, in no fixed order. The 6 products were - ABC Dylex, ABC Velvet, ABC Duplex, ABC Ivory, ABC Emulsion and ABC Putty. It is also known that:

(i) Sonya worked on the campaign to be held in USA and the launch date was 5th February. Maxwell decided to launch the product on 23rd March.
(ii) Rated-R is dealing with Emulsion. It will be launched after the launch in UK and the date of launch was not 14th June.
(iii) La-Nina would be launching Velvet but not in UK. La-Nina would make the launch before any launch in South Africa, but not in January.
(iv) Phoenix would be launching Duplex in Ivory Coast. Launch is not in January.
(v) D-Damsels would launch either in Australia or South Africa.
(vi) Neither Sonya nor Maxwell would be launching Ivory.

16. Rated-R would launch the campaign in which country?
(a) USA (b) Australia
(c) Brazil (d) South Africa

17. Which of the following is a correct combination of the country and the launch date?
(a) UK - 1st January
(b) South Africa - 14th June
(c) Brazil - 29th April
(d) None of these

18. Which product will be launched on 14th June?
(a) Emulsion (b) Dylex
(c) Duplex (d) Either (a) or (c)

19. Which product was launched on New Year's day?
(a) Putty (b) Dylex
(c) Velvet (d) Ivory

20. Which agency launched a product just after Velvet was launched?
(a) Rated-R (b) Phoenix
(c) La-Nina (d) Sonya

8 Mock Test Paper

Directions for Questions 1 to 5: *Read the information given below and answer the next five questions that follow:*

(i) Six friends Rahul, Kabeer, Anup, Raghu, Amit and Alok were engineering graduates. All six of them were placed in six different companies and were posted in six different locations, namely Tisco-Jamshedpur, Telco-Pune, Wipro-Bangalore, HCL-Noida, Mecon-Ranchi and Usha Martin-Kolkata. Each of them has their personal e-mail id with different email providers, i.e., Gmail, Indiatimes, Rediffmail, Yahoo, Hotmail, Sancharnet, and though not necessarily in the same order.

(ii) The one having e-mail account with Sancharnet works in Noida and the one having an e-mail account with Indiatimes works for Tisco.

(iii) Amit does not stay in Bangalore and does not work for Mecon, the one who works for Mecon has an e-mail id with Gmail.

(iv) Rahul has an e-mail id with Rediffmail and works at Pune.

(v) Alok does not work for Mecon and the one who works for Wipro does not have an e-mail account with Yahoo.

(vi) Kabeer is posted in Kolkata, and does not have an account with Hotmail.

(vii) Neither Alok nor Raghu work in Noida.

(viii) The one who is posted in Ranchi has an e-mail id which is not an account of Rediffmail or Hotmail.

(ix) Anup is posted in Jamshedpur.

1. The man who works in Wipro has an e-mail account with:

(a) Sancharnet **(b)** Yahoo
(c) Rediffmail **(d)** None of these

2. Which of the following e-mail-place of posting-person combination is correct?

(a) Kabeer-Kolkata-Rediffmail
(b) Alok-Bangalore-Indiatimes
(c) Amit-Noida-Yahoo
(d) Raghu-Ranchi-Gmail

3. Which of the following is true?

(a) Amit is posted at Ranchi.
(b) Raghu is posted at Jamshedpur.
(c) Kabeer has an e-mail id with Yahoo.
(d) Rahul has an e-mail id with Indiatimes.

4. Which of the following sequences of location represent Alok, Kabeer, Anup, Rahul, Raghu and Amit in the correct order?

(a) Bangalore, Noida, Pune, Jamshedpur, Ranchi, Kolkata
(b) Bangalore, Kolkata, Jamshedpur, Pune, Noida, Ranchi
(c) Kolkata, Bangalore, Jamshedpur, Pune, Noida, Ranchi
(d) None of these

5. People who have an e-mail account with Indiatimes, Sancharnet and Yahoo work for which companies, (in the same sequence as the e-mail accounts mentioned)?

(a) Usha Martin, HCL, Wipro
(b) Tisco, Wipro, Usha Martin
(c) HCL, Tisco, Wipro
(d) Tisco, HCL, Usha Martin

Directions for Questions 6 to 10: A and B are participating in a "Brain Games" tournament organised by Discovery India.

In the game they have to pick the coins kept on the table. The rules of the game say that:

(i) Each person has to pick up at least one coin in his turn.

(ii) A person can pick maximum 6 coins in each turn.

The player who picks up the last coin wins the match.

High Yield Questions
Scan this QR code to access a video explanation of questions 6-10

6. If at one stage there are total 19 coins on the table and it's A's turn to pick up the coins, how many coins should he pick to ensure his win, if both play rationally from that point?

7. At a time in the game, it was A's turn and there were 39 coins on the table. Without A realising it, B wanted to remove some coins from the table. How many coins should be removed to ensure B's win if both A and B play rationally from that point on?

8. If the person picking the last coin is the loser, then how many coins should A pick up to ensure a win, if he is faced with a situation where he has 45 coins in front of him at the start of the game. Assume both play rationally.
9. If at one point, it was B's turn and there are a total of 34 coins on the table, how many coins should B pick so that he wins the game?
10. If the last person loses, and there are 20 coins on the table and It's A's turn. How many coins should A pick so that he wins the game?

Directions for Questions 11 to 15: *Answer the questions on the basis of the information given below.*

Five friends - Aman, Beenu, Chandni, Danish and Eklavya - have some sweets with them. The total number of sweets is 450. Also, it is given that:

(i) At least 30 sweets are there with each of them.
(ii) The total number of sweets that Aman has is twice the square of a natural number and is over 100.
(iii) Danish and Eklavya have the sweets in the ratio of 3:5.
(iv) Chandni, who has the maximum number of sweets, has 4 more sweets than thrice the square of a natural number.
(v) Total sweets with Danish and Eklavya are equal to the number of sweets with Aman.
(vi) Beenu has an odd number of sweets.

11. Who among the five friends has the 2nd highest number of sweets?
(a) Eklavya (b) Beenu
(c) Chandni (d) Aman
12. What can be the difference between the number of sweets with Beenu and Chandni?
(a) 176 (b) 108
(c) 157 (d) None of these
13. The sum of the number of sweets with Aman and Danish is
(a) 104 (b) 166
(c) 176 (d) 108
14. Who has the least number of sweets?
(a) Aman (b) Beenu
(c) Chandni (d) Danish
15. What is the difference between the highest and the lowest number of sweets?

Directions for Questions 16 to 20: *Answer the questions on the basis of the information given below.*

Twelve friends - Amar, Bhawna, Chandni, Dishanth, Eshant, Faiz, Gaurank, Himesh, Inderjeet, Jaspreet, Kamlesh and Lokendra, who after being successful in their respective professions, decided to have a get together after a long time. They all decided to meet in Delhi for their reunion. Since they all were coming from different places, they decided to reach their nearest airports at three different locations - Mumbai, Bangalore and Kolkata, from where they would be reaching Delhi. Exactly four of them were reaching at the same airport. Four of the twelve are doctors, four are engineers and four are pilots. It is also known that:

(i) Amar is not a doctor and will not arrive at Mumbai.
(ii) Bhawna is an engineer and Faiz is a pilot.
(iii) Either Chandni or Gaurank will arrive where Faiz will be reaching.
(iv) Kamlesh is an engineer who will be meeting Dishanth. The place is not Kolkata.
(v) Himesh is a doctor who will reach Mumbai.
(vi) Jaspreet is an engineer and Inderjeet is a doctor and both of them will reach Kolkata.
(vii) Lokendra is a pilot and Bhawna is an Engineer. Both of them will arrive at Bangalore.
(viii) Gaurank will reach Mumbai and Faiz will reach Bangalore.
(ix) The number of engineers who will arrive at Mumbai is two.
(x) Each of the airports has at least 1 person of every profession.

16. Who among the following is a doctor and will arrive at Bangalore?
(a) Eshant (b) Amar
(c) Chandni (d) Gaurank
17. Who are the two engineers who will arrive at Mumbai?
(a) Kamlesh and Gaurank
(b) Kamlesh and Dishanth
(c) Kamlesh and Bhawna
(d) Can't be determined
18. What is the correct profession, destination combination for Eshant?
(a) Doctor, Bangalore (b) Pilot, Mumbai
(c) Pilot, Kolkata (d) Doctor, Kolkata
19. Who was the doctor flying to Mumbai?
(a) Inderjeet (b) Himesh
(c) Chandni (d) Eshant
20. Which pair had the same profession and destination?
(a) Faiz & Lokendra
(b) Gaurank & Himesh
(c) Chandni & Dishanth
(d) Eshant & Himesh

9 Mock Test Paper

Directions for Questions 1 to 5: *Answer the following questions based on the given information:*

High Yield Questions

Scan this QR code to access a video explanation of questions 1-5

During ICC T-20 World Cup 2020, five persons A, B, C, D, and E came to India to watch the India-Pakistan match in Mohali. Their countries, languages, professions are all different from each other. These persons were from different countries (India, China, USA, UAE, UK in any order) and they spoke different languages (P, Q, R, S, T in any order) and they were engineer, doctor, businessman, painter, cricketer by profession, in any order. We have the following additional information:

(i) A is a businessman but E was not from UAE.

(ii) The person who was from UAE was a doctor.

(iii) D didn't speak language S and the painter also didn't speak language S.

(iv) The person who was from the USA neither spoke S nor T and he was not a painter by profession.

(v) C was from India and he was neither a painter nor an engineer.

(vi) The person who spoke language Q was a cricketer.

(vii) The person from UK spoke language P.

(viii) B spoke language R.

1. A belonged to which country?

(a) UAE **(b)** China

(c) USA **(d)** UK

2. Who spoke language Q?

3. Who is a doctor by profession?

4. How many of the following combination/s is correct?

(i) India - Engineer

(ii) D - Painter

(iii) UK - Painter

Type 1 if only 1 combination is correct, Type 2 if 2 combinations are correct; Type 3 if 3 combinations are correct; Type 4 if 0 combinations are correct.

5. Which country did the cricketer come from?

Directions for Questions 6 to 10: There were only four politicians in a town – P, Q, R, S. They all had aspirations of being the MLA of their town. Hence, they were all standing in the election for the MLA. Initially each of the four names was proposed by exactly one person of the town and supported by exactly two other persons of the town and none of P, Q, R and S was allowed to propose or support any other politician. Any person of the town was allowed to either propose or support only a single politician.

There were three rounds in the election:

None of the four politicians are eligible to vote until they are left in the fray. In any round the candidate getting the lowest votes gets eliminated from the election. The process was repeated in each and every round and the survivor after the 3rd round won the election.

A candidate is not eligible to vote in the election as long as he is in the fray. Only if he is eliminated, does he become eligible to vote. Any person who initially proposed or supports a particular politician must vote for that politician in all rounds. If that politician gets eliminated in any round then the person who proposed or supported that particular politician, becomes ineligible to vote in subsequent rounds.

All people who are eligible to vote in any round have to vote for exactly one of the politicians in that round.

In all, a person can vote for at most 2 candidates in all rounds of voting put together and a person becomes ineligible to vote if both the politicians (voted by him) are eliminated.

All those who voted the politician Q and S in any rounds, voted for the same politician as long as they were in the contest. 3 out of 5 of those who voted for R in round 1, voted for him in round 2.

In the final round the loser got 7 votes less than the winner.

If a person is eligible to vote, he must vote in the election – abstaining or absenting oneself from the election is not an option for any voter.

The following table gives the partial information about the number of votes gained by the candidate.

Rounds	Total Votes	Maximum Votes		Minimum Votes	
		Candidate	No. of Votes	Candidate	No. of Votes
1		Q	36	P	20
2	110	S	45	R	29
3	95				

6. If all people were part in election process, then find the population of the town.

7. Find the number of votes got by R in the 1st round.

8. How many people voted for P in round 1 and voted for S in round 2?

9. How many voters, including P, voted for P in the first round but for R in the 2nd round?

(a) 20 **(b)** 14
(c) 16 **(d)** 12

10. What was the winning margin in terms of the number of votes?

(a) 11 **(b)** 9
(c) 7 **(d)** 5

Directions for Questions 11 to 15: *Answer the questions on the basis of the information given below.*

In the ICC cricket tournament, eight cricket teams – Australia, India, Zimbabwe, Pakistan, Kenya, West Indies, England and New Zealand – participated where each team played against every other team exactly once. Every win earned three points for the teams and a loss earned 0. If there was a draw, each team was rewarded only one point. Now, as per the fixtures, following are some of the observations:

(i) Out of the seven matches played by India, it won five and the other two matches were drawn.
(ii) Kenya won the match against Pakistan and West Indies but lost the match against Zimbabwe and India.
(iii) Australia drew a match against Pakistan, India and Kenya.
(iv) None of the teams lost all the matches.

11. If India won the match against Pakistan, what could have been the maximum score of Pakistan?

(a) 11 **(b)** 10
(c) 14 **(d)** 13

12. What could be the minimum absolute difference between the scores of Kenya and India?

(a) 1 **(b)** 3
(c) 4 **(d)** 0

13. What could be the maximum difference between points of India & Zimbabwe?

14. What could be the maximum sum of points of India & Zimbabwe?

15. What could be the lowest position of Australia?

Directions for Questions 16 to 20:

Five athletes Pulkit, Qadir, Rahim, Saqlain, and Tariq participated in a 100 meters race. They got different ranks from 1 to 5 in the race (1 being the fastest). The following information is also known:

(i) Pulkit is not the person who finished the race first.
(ii) Rahim did not get 5th rank but he finished the race after Pulkit.
(iii) Saqlain's finished the race after Qadir.
(iv) The sum of ranks of Pulkit and Tariq was equal to the sum of ranks of Rahim and Saqlain.

16. Who finishes the race at the end?

(a) Rahim **(b)** Saqlain
(c) Tariq **(d)** None of these

17. What is the maximum possible value of sum of ranks of Qadir and Saqlain?

18. If sum of ranks of Tariq and Rahim is 8 then who got the 4th rank?

(a) Pulkit **(b)** Saqlain
(c) Tariq **(d)** None of these

19. What is the difference between the ranks of Qadir and Pulkit?

20. Who couldn't have finished after Rahim?

(a) Pulkit **(b)** Saqlain
(c) Tariq **(d)** Cannot be determined

10 Mock Test Paper

Directions for Questions 1 to 5: *Answer the following questions based on the given information:*

High Yield Questions

Scan this QR code to access a video explanation of questions 1-5

We have 12 different words– Fore, Harshal, Hobby, Indira, Love, Man, Singer, Smartest, Tune, Turn, Wonder, and Wolf. We have a 3 × 4 matrix as shown in the diagram given below. Each element of the matrix is represented by a code m × n, where m represents the row number and n represents the column number. (1 × 1 means this element is in 1st row and 1st column).

1 × 1	1 × 2	1 × 3	1 × 4
2 × 1	2 × 2	2 × 3	2 × 4
3 × 1	3 × 2	3 × 3	3 × 4

We have following clues regarding to the position of letters:

(i) The word in 3 × 3 is made up of an even number of letters.

(ii) Wonder is immediately above Love and Hobby is immediately right of Love.

(iii) Fore is neither in the 2nd column nor in the 4th column and it is to the immediate right of Wolf.

(iv) Tune and Singer are in the same vertical column and Singer is above Tune.

(v) The words in 2 × 1 and in 3 × 1 have the same number of letters.

(vi) Smartest is in the box labeled 2 × 3.

(vii) The word in 2 × 4 is shorter than the word in 1 × 2.

(viii) Turn is separated horizontally from Indira only by the word Harshal.

1. Which is the word in the box labeled 3 × 2?

2. If the word Indira is in the m × n block then numerical value of m × n is?

3. Which box has the word 'Turn'?

4. Which of the following words are placed side by side in the matrix?

(a) Wonder-Fore **(b)** Indira-Tune
(c) Harshal-Tune **(d)** None of these

5. Which box has the word 'Smartest'?

Directions for Questions 6 to 10: Six friends, Abhishek, Deepak, Mridul, Pritam, Ranjan and Salil married within a year in the months of February, April, July, September, November and December and in the cities of Ahmedabad, Bengaluru, Chennai, Delhi, Mumbai and Kolkata, but not necessarily following the given order.

The brides' names were Geetika, Jasmine, Hema, Brinda, Ipsita, and Veena, once again not following any order. The following are some facts about their weddings.

(i) Mridul's wedding took place in Chennai; however he is not married to Geetika or Veena.

(ii) Abhishek's wedding took place in Ahmedabad and Ranjan's in Delhi; however neither of them is married to Jasmine or Brinda.

(iii) The wedding in Kolkata took place in February.

(iv) Hema's wedding took place in April, but not in Ahmedabad.

(v) Geetika and Ipsita got married in February and November and in Kolkata and Chennai, necessarily in that order

(vi) Pritam visited Bengaluru and Kolkata *only* after his marriage in December.

(vii) Salil got married to Jasmine in September.

6. Hema's husband is

(a) Abhishek **(b)** Deepak
(c) Ranjan **(d)** Pritam

7. Deepak's wedding took place in

(a) Bengaluru **(b)** Mumbai
(c) Kolkata **(d)** Delhi

8. In Mumbai, the wedding of one of the friends took place in the month of

(a) April **(b)** September
(c) November **(d)** December

9. Salil's wedding was held in

(a) Bengaluru **(b)** Chemlai
(c) Kolkata **(d)** Delhi

10. Ipsita's wedding took place in

(a) Ahmedabad **(b)** Bengaluru
(c) Mumbai **(d)** Chennai

Directions for Questions 11 to 15: *Answer the questions on the basis of the information given below.*

The annual turnovers (in '000 crores) of six software companies –Infosys, TCS, Accenture, HCL, IBM and HP– are 9, 12, 18, 24, 30 and 48, in no particular order. Each organisation saves a different percentage of its annual turnover among 10%, 20%, 25%, 35%, 40% and 60%, and invests it in 6 different departments - R&D, HR, Operations, Sales, Marketing and Services, in no particular order. It is also known that:

(i) The average of the annual turnovers of Infosys, TCS and HCL is ₹18000 crore.

(ii) The company which earns the highest saves ₹16800 crores and invests it in Sales. Accenture saves 25% of its annual turnover.

(iii) The annual turnover of IBM is the least among the six. It saves one-twelfth of the amount saved by the company which invests in Operations.

(iv) The sum of the annual turnovers of the company which invests in R&D and the company which saves 20% is equal to the sum of the annual turnovers of Infosys and the company which saves 60%.

(v) TCS invests in Marketing. The company which saves 40% does not invest in HR.

11. What is the difference (in '000 crores) between the savings of Infosys and HCL?

(a) 6.6 (b) 9.9
(c) 1.2 (d) 7.2

12. Which company among the following invests its savings in Sales?

(a) Infosys (b) Accenture
(c) HCL (d) HP

13. What is the annual turnover (in '000 crores) of Infosys?

(a) 12 (b) 24
(c) 48 (d) 18

14. Which company has the highest percentage savings?

(a) Infosys (b) TCS
(c) HCL (d) IBM

15. Which company invests in services?

(a) Infosys (b) TCS
(c) HCL (d) IBM

Directions for Questions 16 to 20:

There are 5 students- A, B, C, D, E in class IX A of the Millennium School. Each student possesses a different number of books from the class IX portion. The books belong to the subjects Hindi, English, Physics, Chemistry, Biology (there is 1 book each on each of these subjects in the portion). Each subject's books are possessed by a different number of students and it is possible that there is a book not possessed by any of the students and there is a student who does not possess any of the books. The following information is also known:

(a) E has lesser number of books than B but he has a Physics book.

(b) B has lesser number of books than C. C does not have the Hindi book.

(c) D has lesser number of books than A. A does not have the maximum number of books.

(d) E has two more books than the student who has the least number of books.

(e) B has a Biology book and E has a Chemistry book.

16. Who has the 3rd highest number of books?

(a) C (b) B
(c) D (d) E

17. Find the sum of number of books possessed by A and B?

18. How many students possess the Biology book?

19. Which student has an English Book?

(a) A (b) B
(c) C (d) D

20. What is the difference in the number of Hindi books and the number of books that E has?

1 Mock Test Paper

LEVEL OF DIFFICULTY (III)

Directions for Questions 1 to 5: *Answer the questions on the basis of the information given below.*

High Yield Questions

Scan this QR code to access a video explanation of questions 1-5

Each of the seven movie stars - Aryaman, Bimlesh, Chiranjeev, Devesh, Eesha, Falguni and Gitendra – acted in different movies among *Raaz*, *Dhoom*, *Mann*, *Garv*, *Karz*, *Boss* and *Hum* not necessarily in the same order. It is also known that:

(i) There is exactly one pair of stars who share the same date and year of birth and hence are to be considered to have the same age.

(ii) Bimlesh acted in *Boss* and Aryaman acted in *Garv*.

(iii) Those who acted in *Dhoom*, *Mann* and *Karz* are younger to Devesh, who is not the oldest among the seven.

(iv) Eesha is younger to Chiranjeev, who is younger to Falguni.

(v) The oldest and the youngest of the stars acted in *Mann* and *Garv*, in no particular order.

(vi) The one who acted in *Raaz* has exactly four stars elder to him/her and the one who acted in *Hum* has exactly four stars younger to him/her.

(vii) The ones who acted in *Boss* and *Hum* were of different ages

1. In which of the following movies did Falguni act?
(a) *Raaz* **(b)** *Karz*
(c) *Dhoom* **(d)** Either (b) or (c)

2. Who among the following is the pair of the stars having the same age?
(a) Chiranjeev and Eesha
(b) Falguni and Gitendra
(c) Chiranjeev and Gitendra
(d) Devesh and Gitendra

3. Who acted in *Raaz*?
(a) Gitendra **(b)** Eesha
(c) Chiranjeev **(d)** Can't be determined

4. In which movie did the oldest person act?
(a) Boss **(b)** Hum
(c) Garv **(d)** Raaz

5. How many people are older than the person who acted in *Hum*?

Directions for Questions 6 to 10: Four persons A, B, C, D participated during the Indian Defence Meet - 2025. They sat on four different chairs 1, 2, 3, 4 (placed from left to right) in random order.

Chair 1	Chair 2	Chair 3	Chair 4

These four men are from different departments–MEA, IB, IT, CBI (in any order). Ages of these four persons are 36, 38, 40, 42 years in random order. During the meet they gave their lectures in different orders. We have the following additional information:

(i) C sat somewhere to the left of, (but definitely not exactly next to) the man who was from CBI, who gave his lecture before C and who is 2 years younger than C.

(ii) B is four years younger than the man who was from IB and who was next to and to the left of B.

(iii) The man in chair 1 was not A and gave his lecture next after the 42 year-old.

(iv) The 40 year old sat next to and right of the man who was from the MEA and gave his lecture next but one after him.

(v) The man from IT gave his lecture next after the man who sat on chair-4 (who didn't speak first); he is older than both the latter & D.

(vi) The man who gave the 2nd lecture, sat next to the one who gave the 4th lecture, who is more than 2 years older than the one who spoke 2nd.

6. Who delivered the second lecture?

7. What is the Age of the person who spoke at the end?

8. The Sum of ages of the person who gave the 3rd lecture and who sat on Chair 3 was equal to?

9. Out of these four members who is eldest in age?
10. Which department did the person who gave the final lecture belong to?

Directions for Questions 11 to 15: *Sixteen teams have been invited to participate in the ABC Gold Cup cricket tournament. The tournament is conducted in two stages. In the first stage, the teams are divided into two groups. Each group consists of eight teams, with each team playing every other team in its group exactly once. At the end of the first stage, the top four teams from each group advance to the second stage while the rest are eliminated. The second stage comprises several rounds. Each round involves one match for each team. The winner of a match in a round advances to the next round, while the loser is eliminated. The team that remains undefeated in the second stage is declared the winner and claims the Gold Cup.*

The tournament rules are such that each match results in a winner and a loser with no possibility of a tie. In the first stage, a team earns one point for each win and no points for a loss. At the end of the first stage, teams in each group are ranked on the basis of total points to determine the qualifiers advancing to the next stage. Ties are resolved by a series of complex tie-breaking rules so that exactly four teams from each group advance to the next stage.

11. What is the total number of matches played in the tournament?
    (a) 28 (b) 55
    (c) 63 (d) 35
12. The minimum number of wins needed for a team in the first stage to guarantee its advancement to the next stage is:
    (a) 5 (b) 6
    (c) 7 (d) 4
13. What is the highest number of wins for a team in the first stage in spite of which it would be eliminated at the end of first stage?
    (a) 1 (b) 2
    (c) 3 (d) 4
14. What is the number of rounds in the second stage of the tournament?
    (a) 1 (b) 2
    (c) 3 (d) 4
15. Which of the following statements is true?
    (a) The winner will have more wins than any other team in the tournament.
    (b) At the end of the first stage, no team eliminated from the tournament will have more wins than any of the teams qualifying for the second stage.
    (c) It is possible that the winner will have the same number of wins in the entire tournament as a team eliminated at the end of the first stage.
    (d) The number of teams with exactly one win in the second stage of the tournament is 4.

Directions for Questions 16 to 20: *Answer the questions based on the given information.*

In the G-4 security summit 2015 four countries USA, UK, France, China sent five foreign secretaries Alex, Borris, Chris, Danial, Eva and six MEA officers Peter, Qutub, Rambo, Steve, Tim, and Utova to discuss the strategies to combat with terrorism. The following information is also known:

(i) Each country sent a different number of candidates.
(ii) Alex and Eva are the only secretaries from their respective countries.
(iii) Only Tim and Utova were from France.
(iv) Alex is not from the country, which sent the maximum number of delegates.
(v) Executives came from more number of countries than officers did.
(vi) The number of executives from China is more than that of USA.
(vii) No officer was from USA.

16. Which secretary/ies was/were from the USA?
17. The number of officers sent from China?
18. How many executives did UK sent?
19. What is the difference between the number of delegates sent from UK and the number of delegates that China and USA sent together?
20. Which of the following persons was not from the UK?
    (a) Peter
    (b) Qutub
    (c) Rambo
    (d) Borris

2 Mock Test Paper

Directions for Questions 1 to 5: *Study the following information carefully and answer the questions.*

Four houses Blue, Green, Red and Yellow are located in a row in the given order. Each of the houses is occupied by a person earning a fixed amount of a salary. The four persons are Paul, Krishna, Laxman and Som.

(i) Paul lives between Som and Krishna.
(ii) Laxman does not stay in the Blue house.
(iii) The person living in the Red house earns more than the person living in the Blue house.
(iv) The salary of Som is more than that of Paul but lesser than that of Krishna.
(v) One of the person earns ₹ 80,000.
(vi) The person earning ₹ 110,000 is not Laxman.
(vii) The salary difference between Laxman and Som is ₹ 30,000.
(viii) The house in which Krishna lives is located between the houses with persons earning salaries of ₹ 30,000 and ₹ 50,000.
(ix) Krishna does not live in the Yellow house, and the person living in yellow house is not earning the lowest salary among the four persons.

1. Who lives in the Red house?
   (a) Paul (b) Krishna
   (c) Laxman (d) Som
2. Which house is occupied by the person earning the highest salary?
   (a) Blue (b) Green
   (c) Red (d) Yellow
3. What is the salary earned by the person living in the Green house?
   (a) ₹ 30,000 (b) ₹ 50,000
   (c) ₹ 80,000 (d) ₹ 110,000
4. Whose salary is the second lowest amongst all and in which color of house is he living in?
   (a) Laxman, Red
   (b) Laxman, Yellow
   (c) Som, Blue
   (d) Krishna, Yellow
5. Which of the following combinations are true?
   I. Som, in blue house, with a salary of 30,000
   II. Paul in red house, with a salary of 50,000
   III. Laxman in Yellow house, with a salary of 50,000
   (a) Only I (b) All 3 statements
   (c) Only III (d) both I and III

Directions for Questions 6 to 10: Five boys Alan, Brad, Chris, Dom and Ehsaan bought five lottery tickets. The numbers of their lottery tickets were 2, 3, 4, 5 and 6 (not necessarily in the same order). While declaring the winners of the lotteries the lottery shop owner called 7 distinct positive integers, one at a time. If any of the boys has the same lottery number as the number that was called by the owner, then he would get Rs. 100 as a prize money. But, if any boy's lottery number is the factor of the number called by the lottery shop owner then he would get Rs. 10. On each call, only the boys whose assigned number was a factor of the called number raised their lottery tickets. The following information is also known:

High Yield Questions
Scan this QR code to access a video explanation of questions 6-10

(i) The sum of these seven numbers called out is 100 and each of them is greater than 2.
(ii) The sum of first two numbers he called out was 30.
(iii) The owner did not call the numbers 6 and 7.
(iv) The owner called only one single digit number.

The table given below shows the response of these boys upon the call by the owner. Here, Y denotes that the boy raised his lottery tickets and N denotes that he did not respond to the call.

	Call-1	Call-2	Call-3	Call-4	Call-5	Call-6	Call-7
Alan	Y	Y	N	N	Y	Y	Y
Brad	N	N	Y	N	N	Y	N
Chris	N	Y	N	N	Y	N	N
Dom	Y	Y	N	N	Y	N	N
Ehsaan	Y	Y	N	N	Y	N	N

6. What was the sum of the numbers called in 4th and 7th call?
7. Who won 100 rupees as the prize money on a single call?

8. What is the number called in Call-4?
9. If the owner called the number 45 in Call-8, then which of the following would raise their lottery tickets?
   (a) Only Alan (b) Alan and Dom
   (c) Brad and Dom (d) Can't be determined
10. What is the difference between the highest and lowest number called out?

Directions for Questions 11 to 15: *Answer the questions on the basis of the information given below.*

A, B, C, D, E, F, G and H are eight cars of different brands C1, C2, C3, C4, C5, C6, C7, C8 (not in the same order). They are parked in a circular ground– such that four of them are parked facing the inside of the circle and four of them are parked facing the outside of the circle. Each of them has different colours - blue, red, green and yellow. A and H are diametrically opposite each other and have the same colour. No other pair of cars parked diametrically opposite each other have the same colour. It is also known that:

(i) H from C1 is green. It is parked immediately to the left of both C from C2 and B from C3.
(ii) The car parked diametrically opposite the car from C2 faces inside.
(iii) G from C5 is parked immediately to the left of A from C4.
(iv) C and both its immediate neighbours face inside.
(v) D from C6 is parked diametrically opposite E.
(vi) The colours of B and C are yellow and blue respectively.
(vii) D, which is yellow, is parked third to the left of the car from C8.
(viii) The car from C7 is red and is the only car parked between the two cars of blue colour.
(ix) There are 2 cars each of each of the 4 colors.

11. Who is from C8 and has which colour?
    (a) F, Yellow (b) D, blue
    (c) F, blue (d) Can't be determined
12. How many of the following combinations is/are correct?
    (i) G - Blue - facing inwards
    (ii) D - yellow - facing outwards
    (iii) E - red - facing inwards
    (iv) A - green - facing outwards
    (a) 4 (b) 3
    (c) 2 (d) 1
13. Which colored car is to the right of the Blue colored car?
    (a) Red (b) Green
    (c) Blue (b) Yellow
14. What is the number of the car which is opposite to H?
    (a) C3 (b) C4
    (c) C5 (d) C6
15. What is the color of C5?
    (a) Red (b) Green
    (c) Blue (d) Yellow

Directions for Questions 16 to 20: *Answer the following questions based on the given information.*

Six gamblers A, B, C, D, E, F go to a casino every evening and sit around a circular table and play teen-patti together. Every evening they sit around the circular table such that they sit on different seats from the previous evening and they sit neither adjacent nor opposite to the seat they sat on the previous evening.

16. If seats are numbered from 1 to 6, and on the first day, A sits on the 1st seat and E sits on the 3rd seat and all the gamblers came to the casino and played teen patti for 10 consecutive evenings, then how many times would A and E sit adjacent to each other during these 10 evenings?
17. If they came to the casino and played teen-patti over seven consecutive evenings and on the 7th evening the order they sat in was B, E, C, F, A, D in the clockwise direction, then how many possible combinations are available for the number of ways they could have sat on the first day?
18. If they came to the casino on 10 consecutive evenings, then at least how many times would C have to sit at the same place?
19. If they came to the casino on 11 consecutive nights then at most how many times would A have to sit at the same place?
20. If seats are numbered from 1 to 6, in clockwise direction and D cannot sit in seat 6 and B cannot sit in seat 3. If the order they sat on the 11th evening was E, D, C, A, B, F in seats 1 to 6 respectively, then who sat on seat 5 on the 3rd evening?

3 Mock Test Paper

Directions for Questions 1 to 5: *Read the following information and choose the right alternative in the questions that follow.*

During the cultural week of an institute six competitions were conducted. The cultural week was inaugurated on the morning of 19th October, Wednesday and continued till 26th October. In the span of 8 days, six competitions namely debate, folk dance, fash-p, street play, rock band, and group song, were organized along with various other cultural programs. The information available from the institute is:

(i) Only one competition was held in a day.
(ii) Rock band competition was not conducted on the closing day.
(iii) Fash-p was conducted on the day prior to the debate competition.
(iv) Group song competition was conducted neither on Wednesday nor on Saturday.
(v) None of the competitions was conducted on Thursday and Sunday.
(vi) The street Play competitions was held on Monday.
(vii) There was a gap of two days between the debate competition and the group song competition.

1. The cultural week started with which competition?
(a) Fash-p competition
(b) Debate competition
(c) Street play competition
(d) Rock band competition

2. How many days gap is there between rock band competition and group song competition?
(a) Two **(b)** Three
(c) Four **(d)** Five

3. Which pair of competitions was conducted on Wednesday?
(a) Rock band competition and debate competition
(b) Debate competition and fash-p competition
(c) Rock band competition and Folk dance competition
(d) None of these

4. Which competition exactly precedes the street play competition?
(a) Rock band competition
(b) Group song competition
(c) Debate competition
(d) Fash-p competition

5. The Fash-p competition follows which competition?
(a) Debate competition
(b) Street play competition
(c) Rock band competition
(d) None of these

Directions for Questions 6 to 10: *Two people out of Sachin, Laxman and Rahul made centuries while playing a test match against Pakistan at Mohali, Chandigarh. The shorter of Sachin and Laxman is the older of the two century hitters. The younger of Laxman and Rahul is the shorter of the two century hitters. The taller of Sachin and Rahul is the younger of the two century hitters.*

High Yield Questions
Scan this QR code to access a video explanation of questions 6-10

6. Who is older between the two century makers?
(a) Sachin **(b)** Laxman
(c) Rahul **(d)** Can't be determined

7. Who is younger between the two century hitters?
(a) Sachin **(b)** Laxman
(c) Rahul **(d)** Can't be determined

8. Who is taller between the two century makers?
(a) Sachin **(b)** Laxman
(c) Rahul **(d)** Can't be determined

9. Who is shorter between the two century makers?
(a) Sachin **(b)** Laxman
(c) Rahul **(d)** Can't be determined

10. Who among the three did not hit a century?
(a) Sachin **(b)** Laxman
(c) Rahul **(d)** Can't be determined

Directions for Questions 11 to 16: *Answer the questions on the basis of the information given below:*

Five friends - Aman, Bob, Chris, Malini and Tariq - wearing five different brands of T-shirts among

Reebok, Nike, Puma, Roadster and Levis, not necessarily in the same order, are standing in a queue at a party. The colors of the T-shirts are Black, Red, Silver, Violet and White, in no particular order. It is also known that:

(i) The person who wears the Reebok T-shirt is standing ahead of the person who wears the Roadster T-shirt and thecolour of the Reebok T-shirt is not Red.

(ii) Bob does not wear Nike and he is standing behind Malini.

(iii) The color of the Levis T-shirt is violet, Tariq does not wear the Levis T-shirt.

(iv) Aman stands behind the person who wears the white T-shirt and the colour of Aman's T-shirt is not silver.

(v) Chris does not wear the Reebok T-shirt and he is immediately ahead of the person who wears Black T-shirt.

(vi) Bob wears the Red T-shirt and he is ahead of three other persons.

(vii) There is only one person between the person who wears Puma and the person who wearsthe Roadster T-shirt and that person wears White T-shirts.

(viii) Malini does not wear Silver colour T-shirt. The Roadster T-shirt is not Black in colour.

11. Who wears the Nike T-shirt?

(a) Aman **(b)** Chris

(c) Malini **(d)** Tariq

12. Which T-shirt does Tariq wear?

(a) Roadster **(b)** Nike

(c) Reebok **(d)** PUMA

13. Which brand T-shirt does Malini wear?

14. Which brand T-shirt does Bob wear?

15. Which colour T-shirt does Malini wear?

16. Which of the following is 4th from the front?

(a) Aman

(b) Chris

(c) Malini

(d) Tariq

Directions of Questions 17 to 20: *Read the given information and answer the given question:*

A group of fast bowlers is to be selected from among ten bowlers- Piku, Qadir, Ram, Shahir, Tinku, Umesh, Varun, Waqar, Xavier, Yusuf. Following conditions are also applicable while choosing the team

(i) If Umesh is selected, then Yusuf cannot be selected.

(ii) Exactly one among Piku and Ram must be selected.

(iii) Unless Piku is selected, Tinku cannot be selected.

(iv) Shahir must not be selected if and only if Varun is selected.

(v) If Shahir is not selected then Waqar must be selected.

(vi) Exactly two among Tinku, Xavier, Yusuf and Ram must be selected.

17. If Tinku is in the team then find the number of possible ways to select a six player team.

18. If Umesh and Waqar are in the team then find the difference between the maximum and minimum number of players possible in the team.

19. What is the maximum number of players in the team?

20. In how many ways can we choose the team with maximum number of possible players?

4 Mock Test Paper

Directions for Questions 1 to 5: *Answer the following questions based on the given information:*

Anand, Bhuvan, Charan, and Dhawan are four friends who live in India and each person belongs to one of the three states–Abra, Cadabra and Hoola Boola. A person who is from Abra always speaks the truth. A person from Cadabra can speak the truth or false in alternate statements and the persons from Hoola Boola always lie. Anand, Bhuwan, Charan, Dhawan are engineer, doctor, businessman, painter not necessarily in the same order. Once a police man arrests them late at night in a rash driving case and asked them a few questions about their states and professions. Then each of them made exactly three statements. Bhuwan, Charan, Dhawan made their statements in English but Anand made one statement in English and the rest two statements in his local language.

High Yield Questions

Scan this QR code to access a video explanation of questions 1-5

There is at least 1 person from each of the three states.

Anand:

1. Anna Chappi Ille.
2. Both of my statements in my native language are not true.
3. Kinna paro sa.

Bhuwan:

1. According to Anand's first statement - Charan is either a businessman or a doctor.
2. Charan is lying about me.
3. Anand is a painter.

Charan:

1. Bhuwan is a doctor.
2. According to Anand's third statement, Dhawan always speaks the truth.
3. Dhawan is neither a Businessman nor a painter.

Dhawan:

1. Charan made exactly two statements false.
2. Exactly two of us always speak truth.
3. Charan is a doctor or a businessman.

1. Which of the following is a businessman?
   (a) Anand (b) Bhuwan
   (c) Charan (d) Dhawan
2. Find the profession of the person who always speaks the truth.
   (a) Engineer (b) Doctor
   (c) Businessman (d) Painter
3. What is the profession of Anand?
   (a) Engineer (b) Doctor
   (c) Businessman (d) Painter
4. Which of the following statements is true?
   (a) Anand is from Abra.
   (b) The Painter is a liar.
   (c) Charan's third statement is false.
   (d) None of these.
5. Who is from Cadabra?

Directions for Questions 6 to 10: *Abdul, Balwinder, and Charu go for dinner to Domino's, a famous restaurant at C.R. Park. Each orders either Paneer Tikka or Roasted Chicken.*

(i) If Abdul orders Paneer Tikka, then Balwinder orders what Charu had ordered.
(ii) If Balwinder orders Paneer Tikka, then Abdul orders the dish that Charu doesn't order.
(iii) If Charu orders Roasted Chicken, then Abdul orders the dish that Balwinder ordered.

6. Who among the three always orders the same dish?
   (a) Abdul (b) Balwinder
   (c) Charu (d) Data inadequate
7. If Charu ordered Roasted chicken, what is the dish ordered by Balwinder?
   (a) Roasted Chicken (b) Paneer Tikka
   (c) Data Inadequate (d) None of these
8. If on Tuesday, Balwinder, a devotee of Lord Hanuman eats only vegetarian food, what will Charu eat on Tuesday?
   (a) Paneer Tikka (b) Roasted Chicken
   (c) None of these (d) Data inadequate
9. What is the dish ordered by Abdul?

10. If the dish ordered by Abdul & Charu is different, then what dish was ordered by Balwinder?
    (a) Roasted Chicken
    (b) Paneer Tikka
    (c) None of these
    (d) Cannot be determined.

Directions for Questions 11 to 15: *Answer the questions on the basis of the information given below.*

At the ICC players meet, there are 8 invitees, 4 each from the full ICC members and associate members L, M, N, P, Q, R, S and T. The four members from each group hold different posts among CCC (Chief Cricket Consultant), CFTP (Chief Future Tour Planner), CFO (Chief Financial officer) and CEO (Chief Executive Officer), in no particular order. During a board meeting, the eight members sit at a square table such that there are two members along each side of the table. It is also known that:

(i) No member has any of his fellow group members as neighbours.
(ii) No two members sitting along the same side of the table hold the same post in their respective groups.
(iii) L, who is a CFTP, and P sit along the same side of the table.
(iv) The two neighbours of N are the ICC full members' CFTP and S.
(v) R is a CCC and exactly one person sits between him and the associate members' CFO.
(vi) Q, who is a CFTP, is the third person to the right of L.
(vii) M, who is a CCC, sits diagonally opposite S. A CFO sits to the immediate right of S.

11. Who among the following can be the Full Members' CEO?
    (a) S (b) T
    (c) M (d) None of these
12. Which two members among the given pairs can be neighbours?
    (a) T and R (b) T and N
    (c) S and Q (d) L and T
13. If the two CCCs are neighbors, who could be the full members' CEO?
    (a) S (b) P
    (c) Either S or P (d) S, P or M
14. Who sits between two Associate members?
    (a) Q (b) L
    (c) P (d) Cannot Be Determined
15. Who sits between Full Members CXOs (CEOs or CFOs)?
    (a) R (b) L
    (c) P (d) Both options (a) or (b)

Directions for Questions 16 to 20: *Read the given information and answer the following questions:*

In IIT Kanpur, the Electrical Engineering department has exactly five different branches VLSI, Communication, Control, Power Electronics and Digital Electronics. Number of students enrolled in these five branches is 60, 70, 80, 64, 49, respectively. There are six classrooms in the department from 101 to 106. The capacities of room number 101, 102, 103, 104, 105, 106 are 128, 110, 80, 108, 90, 60, respectively. It is also known that:

(i) On a given day only one room is allotted to each branch.
(ii) A branch conducts the class if it has at least 80% attendance.
(iii) A department allows the branch head to conduct the class in a particular classroom if the total attendance is 50% or more than the strength of the classroom. But this rule is not applicable on classroom number 102.
(iv) A branch cannot conduct a class in a classroom if the attendance is more than that of the strength of the classroom.
(v) Room 102, can be used by all branches except Digital but it must be used only those days when any other room is shut for cleaning purpose.
(vi) All branches conduct a class every day.
(vii) Not more than one room is shut for cleaning purpose on any given day.

16. If on a certain given day classroom 102 was shut for cleaning purpose and there are 64 students in classroom 103, then which branch was in room 103?
17. If room number 106 has 50 students on a certain day, then which classroom would definitely not be closed for cleaning on the day?
18. If class 104 was shut for cleaning purpose for a particular day then maximum possible difference between number of students of class 101 and 106?
19. If Class 103 carries 50 students on a particular day, and 101 is not the one classroom that is shut down for cleaning, and the communication class is not held in an even numbered classroom, then the power electronics class will be conducted in which class room?
    (a) 102 (b) 104
    (c) 105 (d) Either (a) or (b)
20. For the question above, which classroom would be closed for cleaning?

5 Mock Test Paper

Directions for Questions 1 to 5: *Answer the following questions based on the given information:*

In the Lok Sabha elections five candidates A, B, C, D, E were planning for a rally in five different states U.P., M.P., Gujarat, Delhi, A.P. (not necessarily in the same order) on different days Monday, Tuesday, Wednesday, Thursday, Friday (not necessarily in the same order). Election symbol of these candidates were X, Y, Z, P, Q in any order. We have the following additional information:

(i) D's symbol was Y and he organised his rally on Thursday.

(ii) The man whose symbol was Q organised the rally a day before the person who organised his rally in A.P. and the person who organised rally in A.P. did not use 'P' as symbol.

(iii) The Rally in M.P. was organised on Wednesday.

(iv) Rally in U.P. was organised before the rally of A.

(v) The candidate who organised his rally in Gujarat used 'X' as his symbol and he organised his rally two days earlier than E.

(vi) The person with symbol Z organised his rally on Tuesday but this was not B.

(vii) B did not organise his rally in Delhi.

1. B organised his rally in which state?

2. Who used Z as his symbol?

3. A organised his rally on which day?

4. Who organised his rally in A.P.?

5. On which day did the person with symbol Z organize their rally?

Directions for Questions 6 to 11: *Five different film actors namely Amit, Shahrukh, Anil, Sunil, and Akshay are engaged in the shooting of five different movies with five different actresses Madhuri, Kareena, Aishwarya, Shilpa, and Juhi (not necessarily in the same order), in different studios. The studios were 415 to 419 in that order.*

The director of each film decided to set a record by making the films as early as possible.

> **High Yield Questions**
> Scan this QR code to access a video explanation of questions 6-11

(i) Aishwarya's studio is between Amit's and Akshay's studios.

(ii) Shahrukh's director who doesn't have Aishwarya as an actress in the shooting took three fourths as many as the number of days taken by Sunil's director.

(iii) Akshay's studio number is 417.

(iv) Anil's film took more days than Amit's, while Amit's film took more days than Aiswarya's to get finalised.

(v) The director from studio number 418 took 16 days lesser then the director from studio number 415, to complete his film.

(vi) Shilpa's film took 8 days more than Amit's and two days more than Juhi's.

(vii) Madhuri's studio number is 416.

(viii) Madhuri's film took 8 day less then Aishwarya's film. and Anil's films took maximum number of days for completion.

6. Who is the opposite of Kareena in her film?

(a) Amit (b) Shahrukh
(c) Akshay (d) Sunil

7. Which of the following pairs is correct for the film in studio number 418?

(a) Akshay and Shilpa
(b) Anil and Aishwarya
(c) Shahrukh and Aishwarya
(d) None of these

8. The director of which studio made the film in the least number of days?

(a) Studio No. 415 (b) Studio No. 416
(c) Studio No. 417 (d) Studio No. 418

9. Name the actress of studio No. 417.

(a) Kareena (b) Aishwarya
(c) Juhi (d) None of these

10. Sunil's film was completed in:

(a) 44 days (b) 40 days
(c) 32 days (d) None of these

11. Anil's opposite was:

(a) Juhi (b) Shilpa
(c) Aishwarya (d) Madhuri

Directions for Questions 12 to 15: *A quiz has three rounds of two questions each. In the first round, each correct answer carries 20 points; each incorrect answer carries a penalty of 10 points. If both the questions are answered correctly, a bonus of 10 points is awarded. In the second round, each correct and incorrect answer carries the same number of points as in the first round. However, an additional penalty of 10 points is awarded if both the questions were answered incorrectly. In the final round, each correct answer carries 40 points and an incorrect one carries a penalty of 20 points.*

12. In how many ways can a score of 40 be achieved in the quiz?
(a) 4 **(b)** 1
(c) 3 **(d)** 2

13. What is the probability of scoring 100 in the quiz?
(a) 2/9 **(b)** 2/27
(c) 4/27 **(d)** 1/9

14. If only two answers were correct, what is the probability that the score would be 20?
(a) 1/3 **(b)** 1/6
(c) 2/3 **(d)** 0

15. If two answers are incorrect, the minimum possible score is:
(a) 50 **(b)** 60
(c) 70 **(d)** 80

Directions for Questions 16 to 20: *Read the given information and answer the following questions:*

In an international science quiz competition students of five different countries *viz.* India, UAE, USA, UK, and China participated in five different disciplines: Physics, Chemistry, EVS, Biology, and Math. Further the following information is known:

(i) Number of students who participated in Math is same for each country other than India.
(ii) Each country sent maximum ten students in all.
(iii) No student participated in more than one subject quiz.
(iv) At least one student from each country other than UK participated in Physics quiz, while in each subject other than physics at least one student from UK participated.
(v) Out of the total number of students from UK who participated in different subject quizzes, the maximum number of students participated in Biology.
(vi) At least one student from each country participated in Biology and Chemistry.
(vii) The total number of students from India is two more than that of China.
(viii) Total number of students from China is one more than that of USA.
(ix) Total number of students from USA is one more than that of UAE.
(x) Total number of students from UAE is one more than that of UK.
(xi) The number of students who participated in each subject other than physics is two times the number of students who participated in physics quiz.
(xii) The number of students who participated from India in different subjects in different.
(xiii) No student of India participated in EVS quiz.
(xiv) Number of students from China participating in Chemistry, EVS, Biology are equal.

16. What is the total number of participants in all the quizzes?

17. In which subject maximum number of students from USA participated?

18. How many students from USA participated in the Biology quiz?

19. Which country had the maximum number of students in Chemistry and what is the maximum number of students that participated in Chemistry from a single country?

20. Find the sum of the maximum participants (from any country) for all the subjects?

6 Mock Test Paper

Directions for Questions 1 to 5: *Answer the following questions based on the given information:*

In Mayur Vihar there are 5 men A, B, C, D, E who live with their wives P, Q, R, S, T (not necessarily in the same order). These men are engineer, doctor, painter, salesman, boxer (in any order) by profession. Flat numbers of these men were G-13, K-1, K-2, X-1, X-2 (in any order). We have the following additional information:

(i) The person whose wife is T does not live in K-2.
(ii) The starting letter of the flat number of B is earlier in the alphabet than that of the flat number of the engineer.
(iii) The Flat number of the engineer is not X-1.
(iv) The owner of X-2 is a doctor.
(v) A is not a doctor.
(vi) R is the wife of D.
(vii) Q is not the wife of E who is a salesman.
(viii) P lives in flat number G-13.
(ix) S is not the wife of C who lives in flat number K-1.
(x) The husband of S is a painter.

1. What is the occupation of A?
2. Who is a boxer by profession?
3. Which husband wife pair lives in flat number X-1?
4. Who is the wife of A?
5. What is the profession of the couple living in X2?

Directions for Questions 6 to 11: *Six cricketers from six different nations stay in a five star hotel in different rooms. Each of them eats a different variety of food in a meal and hits different number of sixes in an average match. Now read the given clues carefully.*

(i) The player in room No. 142 eats twice as much as the number of varieties eaten by the player, who hits an average of 8 sixes per match, in a meal.
(ii) The player from New Zealand and the player in room No. 146 eat a combined 40 varieties in a meal.

High Yield Questions

Scan this QR code to access a video explanation of questions 6-11

(iii) The player from India eats 8 varieties less than the player from England but hits 10 more sixes in an average match.
(iv) Four times the number of varieties in a meal eaten by the player in room No. 144 is lesser than the number of sixes hit by him in an average match. There is only one such player.
(v) The player in room No.143 eats 12 varieties per meal and hits 8 sixes on an average in each match.
(vi) The player who eats 16 varieties per meal hits 24 sixes per match on an average.
(vii) The player in room No. 145 eats 8 varieties per meal and hits 2 sixes less than the player from Pakistan on an average in a match.
(viii) The Australian player is staying two rooms after the English who is staying two rooms after the Pakistani player.

6. In which room is the Australian player staying?
   (a) Room No. 142 (b) Room No. 143
   (c) Room No. 144 (d) Room No. 145
7. What is the average number of sixes hit by the Indian player?
   (a) 8 (b) 16
   (c) 18 (d) 24
8. How many varieties of food is eaten by the English player in his meal?
   (a) 8 (b) 12
   (c) 16 (d) 20
9. The player of which country is staying in room No. 146?
   (a) India (b) Pakistan
   (c) Sri Lanka (d) England
10. The player of which country hits 24 sixes on an average?
   (a) India (b) New Zealand
   (c) Pakistan (d) Sri Lanka
11. The player of which country eats the highest number of varieties of food in a meal?
   (a) India (b) New Zealand
   (c) England (d) Sri Lanka

Directions for Question 12 to 15: *Answer the questions based on the information given below.*

Times Celebex a famous Bollywood magazine analysed the careers of six Bollywood stars Akshay, Ranbir, Hritik, Aamir, Shahrukh, Salman from 2010 to 2015 and after the analysis it provide them a proper star rating. According to the magazine the star rating of any actor (in the given time period) is = Number of hits delivered by the actor- Number of flops delivered by the actor.

An actor is called a megastar if number of hits > number of flops.

An actor is called a super star if number of hits = number of flops.

An actor is called a flop star if number of hits < number of flops.

According to the magazine out of these six actors three are megastars, two are flop stars and one is a super star. Further it is known that:

(i) The number of hits delivered by Akshay, Ranbir, Hrithik, Aamir, Shahrukh, Salman are 0, 2, 3, 4, 6, 9, respectively.

(ii) The number of flops delivered by these actors are1, 2, 3, 5, 7, 8 not necessarily in the same order.

(iii) Star rating of Aamir or Shahrukh is neither +3 nor – 3.

(iv) Out of these six actors only for one actor is the ratio of $\frac{\text{number of hits}}{\text{number of flop}} = 3$.

(v) Star rating of any actor is neither less than – 6 nor greater than +6.

(vi) | Star rating | = 3 only for one actor.

12. Star rating of Salman is _.

13. Who delivered most number of flops?

(a) Akshay **(b)** Ranbir
(c) Hritik **(d)** Aamir

14. Star rating of how many actors can be greater than or equal to 3?

15. Find the value of number of flops delivered by Salman and Ranbir together – number of flops delivered by Aamir and Hritik together.

Directions for Questions 16 to 20: *Read the information provided and answer the questions which follow.*

Students in a college are discussing two proposals –

(i) A proposal by the authorities to introduce dress code on campus and

(ii) A proposal by the students to allow multinational food franchises to set up outlets on college campus.

A student does not necessarily support either of the two proposals. In an upcoming election for student union president, there are two candidates in fray: Sunita and Ragini. Every student prefers one of the two candidates. A survey was conducted among the students by picking a sample of 500 students. The following information was noted from this survey:

(i) 250 students supported proposal A and 250 students supported proposal B.

(ii) Among the 200 students who preferred Sunita as student union president, 80% supported proposal A.

(iii) Among those who preferred Ragini, 30% supported proposal A.

(iv) 20% of those who supported proposal B, preferred Sunita.

(v) 40% of those who did not support proposal B, preferred Ragini.

(vi) Every student who preferred Sunita and supported proposal B, also supported proposal A.

(vii) Among those who preferred Ragini, 20% did not support any of the proposals.

16. Among the students surveyed who supported proposal A, what percentage of the students preferred Sunita for student union president?

17. What percentage of the students surveyed who did not support proposal A, preferred Ragini as student union president?

18. What percentage of the students surveyed who supported both proposals A and B, preferred Sunita as student union president?

(a) 25 **(b)** 40
(c) 20 **(d)** 50

19. How many of the students surveyed, supported proposal B, did not support proposal A and preferred Ragini as student union president?

(a) 150 **(b)** 40
(c) 200 **(d)** 210

20. How many of the students surveyed supported proposal A, did not support proposal B and supported Ragini as student union president?

7 Mock Test Paper

Directions for Questions 1 to 5: *Answer the following questions based on the given information:*

Five different persons A, B, C, D, and E work in five different companies P, Q, R, S, T (not necessarily in the same order) and live in five different cities Kanpur, Mumbai, Mangalore, Delhi, Lucknow (in any order). They like different sports among cricket, football, hockey, tennis and boxing (in any order). We have the following additional information:

(i) E works in company P. A does not work in company R.
(ii) B does not live in Mumbai and does not like tennis.
(iii) D is from Mangalore. E does not live in Delhi.
(iv) A likes hockey and lives either in Mumbai or in Lucknow; the person who works in company S does not like tennis and he lives in the other city amongst Mumbai or Lucknow.
(v) The person who works in company T likes boxing and he does not live in Delhi.
(vi) The person who likes football lives in Kanpur.

1. A works in:
(a) P (b) Q
(c) R (d) S

2. Who likes cricket?

3. What sport does the person from Delhi like?

4. If A transferred to C's city and C is transferred to A's city, then the person who likes tennis works in which city?

5. Which of the following is true?
I. D is from Mangalore, likes boxing and works in company T.
II. A is from Mumbai, likes football and works in company Q.
(a) Only I (b) Only 2
(c) Both I and II (d) None of these

Directions for Questions 6 to 11: *Four bottles P, Q, R, and S are arranged side by side. Each contains a fixed amount of soft drink measured in litres. The different soft drinks are Pepsi, Coke, Limca, and Sprite.*

Read the following clues carefully:

(i) Pepsi is between Sprite and Coke.
(ii) The amount of Sprite is more than the amount of Pepsi, but lesser than that of Coke.
(iii) Limca is not in bottle R.
(iv) The bottle containing 2.2 ltr. of soft drink doesn't have Limca.
(v) Bottle R contains more amount than bottle P.
(vi) The difference between the amount contained by Limca and Sprite is 0.6 litres.
(vii) The bottle with Coke is between the bottles containing 0.6 ltr. and 1 l.
(viii) Bottle S doesn't contain Coke and doesn't have the least amount of soft drink in it.

Now answer Questions 6–11 based on the above clues:

6. What is the amount of soft drink in bottle Q.?
(a) 0.6 ltr. (b) 1 ltr.
(c) 1.6 ltr. (d) 2.2 ltr.

7. Which bottle contains 1.6 ltr. of soft drink?
(a) P (b) Q
(c) R (d) S

8. Bottle R contains:
(a) Pepsi (b) Coke
(c) Limca (d) Sprite

9. What is the amount of Limca in the bottle?
(a) 0.6 ltr. (b) 1.6 ltr.
(c) 1 ltr. (d) 2.2 ltr.

10. Which bottle contains the highest amount of soft drink?
(a) P (b) Q
(c) R (d) S

11. The amount of Sprite contained by the bottle is:
(a) 0.6 ltr. (b) 1 ltr.
(c) 1.6 ltr. (d) 2.2 ltr.

Directions for Questions 12 to 15: *Answer the questions based on the information given below.*

During the recent India– Australia bilateral 7 one-day international matches series Dhawan, Rohit and Kohli were in tremendous form and combined scored 7 centuries in these 7 games. Further it is also known about their scores in the series:

(i) In each game exactly one batsman scored a century.
(ii) Each of these three players scored at least one century and no two batsmen scored equal number of centuries.
(iii) Rohit did not score a century in the 2nd game and Kohli scored a century in the last game.
(iv) Dhawan did not score a century in the 1st and 4th game.
(v) The player who scored a century in the 2nd game did not score a century in the 5th game.
(vi) The player who scored a century in the 4th game also scored a century in the 6th game.
(vii) The player who scored a century in the 3rd game did not score a century in the 1st game.

High Yield Questions

Scan this QR code to access a video explanation of questions 12-15

12. How many centuries did Dhawan score?
(a) 2
(b) 4
(c) Either 1 or 2
(d) Either 1 or 4

13. If Rohit scored a century in the 3rd game in which game/s did Dhawan score a century:
(a) 2nd
(b) 5th
(c) Either 2nd or 5th
(d) None of these

14. If Rohit scored centuries in the 3rd and 5th games then which of the following option must be true?
(a) Kohli scored four centuries.
(b) Rohit scored a 100 in the 4th game too.
(c) Rohit scored four centuries.
(d) None of these.

15. If Kohli scored a century in the 2nd game but failed to score a century in the 4th game and his highest score in the games was 125, then what could be the maximum possible runs scored by Kohli in the series?

Directions for Questions 16 to 20: *Answer the following questions based on the given information:*

Five athletes Bolt, Jordon, Jackson, Wayne, and Phelps participated in the International Athletics Meet 2025. There were two types of races: 100 meters and 200 meters. Each athlete finished the races at a different time and each athlete got a rank according to his finishing time. The rank-1 athlete finished the race in the least time and the rank-5 athlete finished the race in the maximum time. Each athlete got top five ranks in these two races in any order. We have the following additional information:

(i) No athlete got the same rank in both races.
(ii) No two athletes got the same rank in any race.
(iii) Bolt finished at least one race earlier than Jackson.
(iv) Jordon's rank in the 100 meters race was better than his rank in the 200 meters race.
(v) Phelps finished the 200 meters race earlier than Wayne.
(vi) Sum of ranks of Jackson was 4 and the sum of ranks of any other athlete was not 4.
(vii) The rank of Jordon in one of the races is same as the rank of Wayne in other race.
(viii) The number of athletes who finished the 100 meters race earlier than Wayne was same as the number of athletes who finished the 200 meters race earlier than Phelps.

16. Phelps' rank in the 100 meters race is _.

17. Who got the 4th rank in the 100 meters race?
(a) Jackson **(b)** Bolt
(c) Jordon **(d)** Phelps

18. Sum of ranks of Phelps in both races =?

19. How many athletes got a better rank than Jordon in both races?
(a) 1 **(b)** 2
(c) 3 **(d)** 4

20. How many athletes got a better rank themselves in the longer race than in the shorter race?

8 Mock Test Paper

Directions for Questions 1 to 5: *Answer the following questions based on the given information:*

In R.K. Degree College, there are six hostels–101, 102, 103, 104, 105, and 106. These hostels are situated from left to right as shown in the diagram.

101	102	103	104	105	106

Number of students in these hostels is 51, 53, 55, 56, 57, 59 (in any order). These students are allotted from different courses among B.Tech, M.Sc., MBA, M.Tech., B.Sc., B.A. (in any order). All the students of any particular hostel have the same course. The names of mess managers of these hostels are Anand, Charan, Dharam, Dhiru, Lalu, Ramesh (in any order). We have the following additional information:

(i) Anand's hostel is immediately left to the one having B.Tech students and immediately right to the one which has 53 students.

(ii) Dharam is the manager of the hostel with B.A. students and Dharam's hostel is not next to the one which has 57 students.

(iii) The number of students in hostel-104 is four higher than that of the hostel managed by Lalu.

(iv) Hostel-101 has the least number of students and is not occupied by M Tech students.

(v) The 59 BSc students live somewhere left to the hostel managed by Ramesh, but not next to it.

(vi) The MBA students live in hostel-105 and the number of students in hostel-105 is not 56. The hostel having 56 students is next to the hostel managed by Dhiru, where the number of students is not 55.

1. The number of students in Dhiru's hostel is?

2. The BA students live in which hostel?

3. Ramesh is the mess manager of which hostel?

4. What is the sum of the number of students of Ramesh's hostel and hostel number 103?

5. What is the sum of the number of students who are studying B. Tech and MBA?

Directions for Questions 6 to 10: *Refer to the caselet below:*

Mr. Ahluwalia, Mr. Bhatia, Mr. Chopra, Mr. Dayal, and Mr. Eeshwar have first and middle names as per the following conditions (each of them has different first and middle names):

(i) Four of them have a first or middle name of Ram, three of them have first or middle name of Shyam, two of them have a first or middle name of Tram and one of them has a first or middle name of Alam.

High Yield Questions

Scan this QR code to access a video explanation of questions 6-10

(ii) Either Mr. Ahluwalia and Mr. Bhatia are both named Tram or Mr. Chopra and Mr. Dayal are both named Tram.

(iii) Of Mr. Bhatia and Mr. Chopra either both are named Shyam or neither is named Shyam.

(iv) Mr. Dayal and Mr. Eeshwar are both not named Ram.

6. Which of these is a possible combination of names?

(a) Tram Ram Ahluwalia

(b) Alam Ram Chopra

(c) Ram Shyam Chopra

(d) None of these

7. The two Trams are:

(a) Mr. Ahluwalia and Mr. Bhatia

(b) Mr. Chopra and Mr. Dayal

(c) Mr. Dayal and Mr. Ahluwalia

(d) Mr. Bhatia and Mr. Dayal

8. Who is named Alam?

(a) Mr. Ahluwalia **(b)** Mr. Bhatia

(c) Mr. Chopra **(d)** Mr. Dayal

9. Mr Eeshwar is known as:

(a) Ram Shyam **(b)** Tram Ram

(c) Shyam Alam **(d)** Tram Shyam

10. Which of these people have the same name?

(a) Mr. Bhatia and Mr. Chopra

(b) Mr. Chopra and Mr. Dayal

(c) Mr. Ahluwalia and Mr. Eeshwar

(d) There is no such pair

Directions for Question 11 to 15: *Answer the questions based on the information given below.*

In an interschool debate eight boys A, B, C, D. E. F, G, and H are sitting around a circular table. Each student is from different cities among Delhi, Mumbai, Pune, Chennai, Rajkot, Indore, Bhopal, Nagpur (not necessarily in the same order). The students are ranked according to their performance in the debate from 1 to 8. Also, it is known that:

(i) No two students got the same rank.
(ii) The rank 1 boy is not opposite to the rank 8 boy who is from Pune.
(iii) D is sitting to the immediate right of A and the boy opposite D is from Rajkot.
(iv) F got 7th rank and there is only one boy between F and 2nd rank boy.
(v) E is sitting opposite to the boy who is from Delhi and E is sitting two places away from A.
(vi) The sum of ranks of any two boys sitting opposite to each other is odd.
(vii) A got 4th rank and he is from Chennai and he is sitting opposite to the 5th rank boy who is from Nagpur.
(viiii) C is sitting opposite to B one of them is from Indore and other is from Mumbai.
(ix) The students from Delhi and Bhopal are sitting adjacent to each other.

11. Which boy is from Rajkot?

12. If the boy from Indore is adjacent to G, then which boy is 2nd to the left to the boy who is from Mumbai?

13. If G is sitting to the immediate left of the boy who is from Indore then which of the following person place or person -rank combination is definitely true?
(a) G- Nagpur
(b) C- 2nd rank
(c) H- 5th rank
(d) B- Mumbai

14. From which city does D come?

15. What is the rank of the person who sits between the one from Pune and the one who secured the 5th rank?
(a) 2nd (b) 3rd
(c) 7th (d) Cannot be determined

Directions for Questions 16 to 20:

P, Q, R, S and T took a photography class together. The assignment was to photograph animals, so they decided to take a safari for 10 days. A different pair took the pictures each day. Some days they didn't see any animals. But, they returned home with pictures of five animals, each taken on different days.

T was not involved with the picture of the anteater.

Q was one of the pair which took pictures of the emu.

No one was on the teams which took pictures of both the anteater and the deer.

One person captured the photo of both the crocodile and the emu.

One person took pictures of the bear. He also took photograph of an animal when he was out with S.

P and Q were successful on their day together as a team.

R and T, however, saw nothing on their day as a team.

Each man participated in the photographing of two animals.

Q, S and T together had a hand in photographing all five of the animals.

16. Which pair photographed the bear?
(a) P and T (b) P and Q
(c) R and S (d) Cannot be determined

17. Who among the following photographed the anteater?
(a) R (b) S
(c) T (d) P

18. Which animal is the odd one out?
(a) Anteater (b) Deer
(c) Emu (d) None of the above

19. Which of these animals did Q capture?
(a) Anteater (b) Bear
(c) Crocodile (d) Deer

20. Which of the following pairs was unsuccessful in capturing any animal's photograph?
(a) RS (b) PT
(c) ST (d) QS

ANSWER KEY

LEVEL OF DIFFICULTY (I)

MOCK TEST PAPER 1

1. (a)	2. (b)	3. 1	4. (a)	5. Kolkata	6. (c)	7. (d)
8. (a)	9. (b)	10. (a)	11. E	12. 2	13. 2	14. 2
15. (a)	16. (b)	17. (c)	18. (a)	19. 6	20. 1	

MOCK TEST PAPER 2

1. (d)	2. (b)	3. (b)	4. (d)	5. (c)	6. (a)	7. (a)
8. (a)	9. (d)	10. 2	11. 2	12. 7	13. (d)	14. (a)
15. (b)	16. (a)	17. 4	18. 3	19. (c)	20. 6	

MOCK TEST PAPER 3

1. (d)	2. (a)	3. (d)	4. (b)	5. (d)	6. (d)	7. (b)
8. (c)	9. Hockey	10. USA	11. (d)	12. (c)	13. (b)	14. 2
15. (c)	16. (a)	17. (d)	18. (a)	19. (c)	20. 8	

MOCK TEST PAPER 4

1. (a)	2. (d)	3. (a)	4. (c)	5. (c)	6. (d)	7. (c)
8. (b)	9. Red	10. Cricketer	11. (b)	12. (d)	13. (d)	14. (b)
15. (d)	16. (c)	17. (d)	18. (a)	19. 4	20. (c)	

MOCK TEST PAPER 5

1. (c)	2. (d)	3. (d)	4. 4	5. Rahul	6. (c)	7. 5
8. (d)	9. (d)	10. (a)	11. (a)	12. (b)	13. (d)	14. (b)
15. (d)	16. Daman	17. P	18. T	19. (d)	20. 6	

MOCK TEST PAPER 6

1. (a)	2. (b)	3. (b)	4. (d)	5. Fruit Juice	6. (d)	7. (d)
8. 18	9. 2	10. (c)	11. (a)	12. (d)	13. (d)	14. (d)
15. (c)	16. (d)	17. (a)	18. 1	19. (d)	20. 2	

MOCK TEST PAPER 7

1. (c)	2. (d)	3. (a)	4. (b)	5. (c)	6. 5	7. 2nd
8. (b)	9. 19	10. (b)	11. (d)	12. (a)	13. (d)	14. (a)
15. (d)	16. (d)	17. (a)	18. 21	19. (a)	20. 5	

MOCK TEST PAPER 8

1. (b)	2. (c)	3. (c)	4. (c)	5. (c)	6. (a)	7. (d)
8. (c)	9. (b)	10. (d)	11. (a)	12. (a)	13. (c)	14. (c)
15. (d)	16. (d)	17. (b)	18. 0	19. 6	20. 3	

MOCK TEST PAPER 9

1. (c)	2. (a)	3. (a)	4. (b)	5. (b)	6. (c)	7. (a)
8. (b)	9. (c)	10. MDLR Airlines Express		11. (d)	12. (d)	13. (d)
14. (b)	15. (d)	16. (b)	17. (d)	18. (d)	19. (d)	20. (c)

MOCK TEST PAPER 10

1. (a)	2. (b)	3. (c)	4. (a)	5. (d)	6. Entricht	7. Fannerfitch
8. Handkerchief	9. 2	10. (b)	11. (a)	12. (d)	13. (b)	
14. (c)	15. (c)	16. (a)	17. (d)	18. (b)	19. (a)	20. HBO

MOCK TEST PAPER 11

1. (a)	2. (a)	3. (c)	4. 5 Km	5. 900 meters	6. (82)	7. (48)
8. (d)	9. (14)	10. 22	11. (d)	12. (d)	13. (b)	14. (a)
15. (a)	16. (d)	17. (a)	18. (b)	19. 4	20. 1	

MOCK TEST PAPER 12

1. (a)	2. (c)	3. (a)	4. (d)	5. (d)	6. (c)	7. (d)
8. 2100	9. 550	10. (d)	11. (b)	12. (c)	13. Ravi	14. (a)
15. Ravi	16. (a)	17. (a)	18. (c)	19. (a)	20. D	

LEVEL OF DIFFICULTY (II)

MOCK TEST PAPER 1

1. (a)	2. (c)	3. (d)	4. (b)	5. (d)	6. E	7. Amazon
8. 110 lakhs	9. 20 lakhs	10. 110 lakhs	11. 48	12. (a)	13. (24)	14. (b)
15. (b)	16. (c)	17. (b)	18. (c)	19. (a)	20. (c)	

MOCK TEST PAPER 2

1. (b)	2. (c)	3. (a)	4. (b)	5. (b)	6. (c)	7. (c)
8. (d)	9. (a)	10. 1	11. (a)	12. (a)	13. (d)	14. (a)
15. 4	16. (a)	17. (a)	18. (a)	19. (c)	20. (b)	

MOCK TEST PAPER 3

1. (a)	2. (b)	3. (d)	4. (d)	5. (c)	6. A	7. (d)
8. 4th	9. 48	10. (d)	11. 0	12. (d)	13. 10	14. 6
15. Quran	16. (b)	17. (d)	18. 4	19. (c)	20. (d)	

MOCK TEST PAPER 4

1. (b)	2. (a)	3. (c)	4. 1324	5. Aradhana	6. 1	7. C
8. 1	9. C	10. Monday	11. (d)	12. (8)	13. (20)	14. (b)
15. 8 Lacs	16. (d)	17. (d)	18. 4	19. E	20. FB	

MOCK TEST PAPER 5

1. (c)	2. (a)	3. (d)	4. (b)	5. (d)	6. 31	7. (c)
8. 15	9. 4:5:4	10. 2	11. (a)	12. (c)	13. Mahendra	14. Mahendra
15. (d)	16. (d)	17. (c)	18. 0	19. (a)	20. 10	

MOCK TEST PAPER 6

1. (b)	2. (c)	3. (a)	4. (c)	5. Red	6. (b)	7. 2
8. 1	9. Djokovic	10. (d)	11. (c)	12. (d)	13. (a)	14. (d)
15. 1	16. (b)	17. (c)	18. (a)	19. (b)	20. 74	

MOCK TEST PAPER 7

1. (c)	2. (d)	3. (d)	4. (d)	5. (c)	6. (b)	7. Alan
8. (c)	9. (d)	10. David	11. (c)	12. (b)	13. 2	14. (d)
15. (a)	16. (d)	17. (c)	18. (c)	19. (d)	20. (a)	

MOCK TEST PAPER 8

1. (d)	2. (d)	3. (c)	4. (d)	5. (d)	6. 5	7. 4
8. 2	9. 6	10. 5	11. (d)	12. (b)	13. (c)	14. (b)
15. 108	16. (c)	17. (d)	18. (d)	19. (b)	20. (a)	

MOCK TEST PAPER 9

1. (b)	2. C	3. D	4. 1	5. India	6. 116	7. 25
8. 4	9. (b)	10. (c)	11. (d)	12. (c)	13. 14	14. 36
15. 8	16. (c)	17. 5	18. (b)	19. 1	20. (a)	

MOCK TEST PAPER 10

1. Harshal	2. 9	3. 3 × 1	4. (b)	5. 2 × 3	6. (c)	7. (c)
8. (d)	9. (a)	10. (d)	11. (c)	12. (d)	13. (b)	14. (c)
15. (a)	16. (d)	17. 4	18. 2	19. (c)	20. 2	

LEVEL OF DIFFICULTY (III)

MOCK TEST PAPER 1

1. (d)	2. (c)	3. (d)	4. (c)	5. 2	6. D	7. 40
8. 80	9. A	10. IT	11. (c)	12. (b)	13. (a)	14. (c)
15. (c)	16. Alex	17. 0	18. 1	19. 1	20. (d)	

MOCK TEST PAPER 2

1. (b) 2. (c) 3. (a) 4. (b) 5. (c) 6. 31 7. Brad
8. 17 9. (d) 10. 19 11. (c) 12. (b) 13. (a) 14. (b)
15. (a) 16. 0 17. 36 18. 4 19. 6 20. B

MOCK TEST PAPER 3

1. (d) 2. (d) 3. (c) 4. (c) 5. (c) 6. (b) 7. (a)
8. (a) 9. (b) 10. (c) 11. (a) 12. (c) 13. Levis 14. Puma
15. Violet 16. (b) 17. 7 18. 2 19. 7 20. 2

MOCK TEST PAPER 4

1. (a) 2. (d) 3. (c) 4. (d) 5. Anand 6. (a) 7. (a)
8. (a) 9. Roasted Chicken 10. (d) 11. (a) 12. (a) 13. (a)
14. (d) 15. (d) 16. Power 17. 103 18. 40 19. 102 20. 104

MOCK TEST PAPER 5

1. Gujarat 2. C 3. Friday 4. D 5. Tuesday 6. (a) 7. (d)
8. (b) 9. (c) 10. (c) 11. (b) 12. (d) 13. (b) 14. (d)
15. (b) 16. 36 17. EVS 18. 1 19. India, 3 20. 13

MOCK TEST PAPER 6

1. Painter 2. B 3. E-T 4. S 5. Doctor 6. (d) 7. (c)
8. (b) 9. (c) 10. (d) 11. (b) 12. 2 13. (d) 14. 0
15. 0 16. 64 17. 84 18. (d) 19. (a) 20. 40

MOCK TEST PAPER 7

1. (a) 2. B 3. Tennis 4. Mumbai 5. (a) 6. (a) 7. (a)
8. (b) 9. (c) 10. (c) 11. (c) 12. (c) 13. (a) 14. (d)
15. 745 16. 3rd 17. (c) 18. 5 19. (c) 20. 2

MOCK TEST PAPER 8

1. 57 2. 102 3. 106 4. 115 5. 112 6. (d) 7. (b)
8. (b) 9. (a) 10. (c) 11. F 12. F 13. (c) 14. Bhopal
15. (c) 16. (a) 17. (d) 18. (b) 19. (a) 20. (d)

SOLUTIONS AND SHORTCUTS

LEVEL OF DIFFICULTY (I)

MOCK TEST PAPER 1

Solutions for Questions 1 to 5:

In Group stage in one group the number of matches won by different teams were 3, 2, 1, 0 and number of games won by the teams of other group were 2, 2, 1, 1.

Kolkata lost exactly two games and qualified for the final match therefore it must have lost exactly one game in the group round and also lost the final game. This needs to happen since, if Kolkata had lost 2 games in the first stage, it would not have qualified for the semi finals from its' group. If Kolkata won two games, then the number of games won by Hyderabad, Pune, Chennai is same and equals to one (as we have only 3 teams winning 2 games and if Kolkata is one of them then we cannot have Hyderabad, Pune and Chennai winning 2 games each). As per the question Hyderabad won more games than Delhi. Hence, the total number of games won by Delhi is zero. As per the question Indore won one more game than Bangalore hence Indore won exactly three games and Bangalore won exactly two games.

Group 1: Indore (3), Bangalore (2), Hyderabad (1), Delhi (0)

Group 2: Kolkata (2), Mumbai (2), Pune (1), Chennai (1)

Semifinal could not be played between Indore and Mumbai because if Indore won the semifinal then Indore would play the final against Kolkata and it must have won the final. In this case Indore won all of its five games, which is not possible. If Mumbai won the semifinal then it would play the final against Kolkata, which violates statement (iii).

Semifinal 1: Kolkata- Indore/Mumbai

Semifinal 2: Bangalore- Mumbai/Indore

Final- Kolkata- Bangalore

Bangalore won the tournament.

1. Bangalore won 4 games, which is the most number of games won by any team. Option (a) is correct.
2. Delhi. Option (b) is correct.
3. Bangalore won 4 games and Kolkata won 3 games therefore the required difference = 4 – 3 = 1.
4. Out of the given options Indore is the only team, which could play the semifinal against Kolkata. Option (a) is correct.
5. Kolkata lost to Bangalore in the Finals.

Solutions for Questions 6 and 7:

6. Qatar, Russia and Spain lost their matches against Paraguay and won their matches against Turkey. If their points are equal when each of these teams won exactly one and lost exactly one of their remaining games.
   Hence, the required score = $2 \times 3 + 2 \times 1 = 8$.
   Hence, option (c) is correct.
7. Each team would have scored equal points when each team won exactly 2 matches and lost exactly 2 matches.
   Hence, the required score = $2 \times 3 + 2 \times 1 = 8$ points.
   Hence, option (d) is correct.

Solutions for Questions 8 to 10:

8. To maximise the points of Parguay and Qatar, we need to make sure they win all their matches against other teams and draw amongst each other to maximise the total. Hence Paraguay and Qatar both won 3 matches each, and Drew 1 Match. So the total would be $3 \times 3 + 2$ for both. Hence, The total number of points = 22. Option (a) is correct.
9. Russia will necessarily lose against Paraguay and Qatar, to maximise it's score it draws against Spain (given) and will need to win against Turkey. Hence, the answer would be $1 + 1 + 2 + 3 = 7$. Option (b) is correct.
10. As Turkey lost all the matches, the total number of points of Turkey would be 4. Option (a) is correct.

Solutions for Questions 11 to 15:

From statement (ii) and the given data, A got 1st rank in level 1.

From statement (iii): B participated in level 1 and level 2 and he got 10 points this is possible only when he got 1st rank in level 2.

From statement (iv): C participated in level 1, 2 and 3 and he got 16 points this is possible when he got 10 points in level 3 and 6 points in level 2 or level 1.

From statement (v): D participated in level 1, 2, 3 and 4 and he got only 4 points. This is possible when he got 3rd rank in any two of these four rounds.

From statement (iv): H was awarded 20 points and he participated in 4th and 5th round. Hence, he got 10 points in level 4 and level 5.

From statement (v): I got either 4th or 5th rank in level 5.

E got 2 points in any two levels and 6 points in one of the levels. But he got the points only in 1st, 3rd and 5th level.

G got 2 points in any one level and 6 points in one of the levels. But he got the points only in 3rd and 5th level.

F got 6 points each in two of the levels. But from the above analysis and the given data we can conclude that he got points in 2nd and 4th level.

From the above analysis we can get the following table:

	Level 1	Level 2	Level 3	Level 4	Level 5
1st Rank	A	B	C	H	H
2nd Rank	C	F	E/G	F	G/E
3rd Rank	E	D	G/E	D	E/G

11. E
12. 2
13. If E gets 2nd rank in Level 2, then the points of E in the 5th level = 10 – (2 + 6) = 2 points. In this case, G got 2nd rank.
14. If E gets 3rd rank in Level 2. Then, points of E in 5th level = 10 – (2 + 2) = 6 points. In this case, E got 2nd rank.
15. As can be seen from the table, F got the 2nd rank in Level 2
    Hence the answer is Option (a).

Solutions for Questions 16 to 20:

The following table structure would be derived after using all the information in the question:

	Year I	Year II	Year III	Year IV
1	KP	KKR	KKR	KP
2	MI	MI	KP	DD
3	KKR	KP	DD	KKR
4	DD	DD	MI	MI

We also know that KP is owned by Rahul, MI by Suresh, DD by Raman and KKR by Dinesh.

The answers would be:

16. (b)
17. (c)
18. (a)
19. KKR got the 3rd rank in both the years. Hence, the sum is 6
20. DD AND MI were placed 3rd and 4th respectively in year 3. Hence the absolute difference in the ranks of both the teams is 1.

MOCK TEST PAPER 2

Solutions for Questions 1 to 4:

The starting gird for this question set would involve three variables, viz: Girl name, Theatre and Movie.

Name	Movie	Theatre
Seema		
Reema		
Neeta		
Mona		
Veena		

We also know that the movie theatres are: P, C, M, PVR and S. Always make sure you use abbreviations for the names in solving reasoning questions, although in this question moving forward we would be showing the full names for your understanding.

Further, the movies are G, K, H, S and I.

Once we get to this point, we first look for direct clues that can directly fit into our solution grid. In this context, the easiest and most convenient clue to use are clues (iii) and (iv) which on using would change our grid to:

Name	Movie	Theatre
Seema		
Reema		
Neeta		M2K
Mona	Iqbal	
Veena	Not Khiladi means either Gangster/Hero/Salaam Namaste	Satyam

At this point in our solution grid, clue (ii) becomes usable. "Movie Gangster is running in Priya theatre whose ticket is not with Veena or Seema." This should be interpreted in the fashion that Gangster and Priya is a movie-theatre combination which has to be kept together and since it is not with Seema, looking at the grid the only place it can be fit inside the solution grid is in front of Reema. Thus, the solution grid changes to:

Name	Movie	Theatre
Seema		
Reema	Gangster	Priya
Neeta		M2K
Mona	Iqbal	
Veena	Hero/Salaam Namaste	Satyam

We can now directly use clue (v) and the grid would then fill out the details for Seema, and also since Salaam Namaste goes to Seema, Veena must be watching Hero. The grid would now become:

Name	Movie	Theatre
Seema	Salaam Namaste	PVR Saket
Reema	Gangster	Priya
Neeta		M2K
Mona	Iqbal	
Veena	Hero	Satyam

The missing values in the above grid can be filled up looking at what has not been used and the final answers can be read off the following table:

Name	Movie	Theatre
Seema	Salaam Namaste	PVR Saket
Reema	Gangster	Priya
Neeta	Khiladi	M2K
Mona	Iqbal	Chanakya
Veena	Hero	Satyam

1. Option (d) is correct.
2. Option (b) is correct.
3. Veena has the ticket to the Hero movie. Option (b) is correct.
4. Option (d) is correct.

Solutions for Questions 5 to 8:

From statements (i) and (ii): Murderer cannot be the 1st and the Driver cannot be the last to arrive.

From statements (iii), (iv), (v), (vi) we get that only the following case is possible.

Vijay arrived at the house earliest and Puneet arrived at the house last.

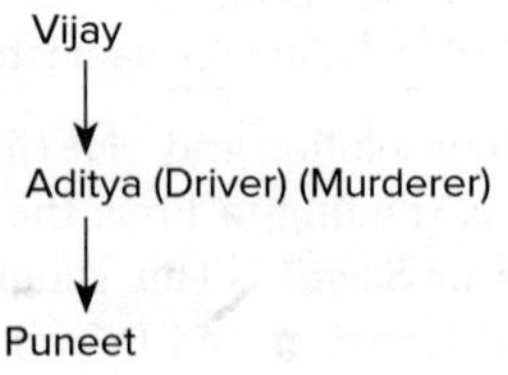

The answers would be:

5. (c)
6. (a)
7. As per the chart, Aditya is the murderer. Hence, option (a) is the answer
8. As per the chart, Aditya is the driver. Hence, Option (a) is the answer.

Solutions for Questions 9 to 13:

From statement (i), we can say that the rank of Jessica in High jump was the same as the rank of Vandana in Long jump. Let the rank of Jessica in high jump was a.

From statement (v), we can say that, the ranks of Simran are 1 and 3 (2 + 2 is not possible).

From statement (vi) and from the above analysis we can say that Jessica's rank in Long jump is the same as the Rinku's rank in High jump. Let it be (b).

From statement (iv) and a < b.

From statement (iii), b cannot equal to 5.

As Simran has neither a nor b as her rank and her ranks are 1 and 3. Thus, a = 2, b = 4.

From statement (iii), Rinku's rank in Long jump is 5.

From (ii), we can say that Sarah got the first rank in the event in which Simran got the third rank.

From (v) and the above analysis, the other rank of Sarah must not be 3.

It must be 5.

Rinku got the 5th rank in Long jump. Sarah got the 5th rank in High jump.

Finally, Vandana got the 3rd rank in High jump.

The results can be tabulated as below:

	Sarah	Rinku	Simran	Jessica	Vandana
High jump	5	4	1	2	3
Long jump	1	5	3	4	2
Total	6	9	4	6	5

9. Vandana. Hence, option (d) is correct.
10. The rank of Vandana in Long jump is 2.
11. In high jump no one got better rank than Simran. In long jump Sarah and Vandana got better ranks than Simran. Hence, the required answer 0 + 2 = 2.
12. Required sum = 4 + 3 = 7.
13. As per the table, Rinku had the highest sum of ranks, but since Rinku is not listed in the options, the answer is (d), none of these.

Solutions for Questions 14 to 18:

From Statements (ii) and (vi), Manu and Rahul were cycling in the lanes numbered 3 and 4 respectively. From Statements (i) and (iv), Hari was in the lane numbered 7. From Statements (iii) and (v), either Amit or Sumit was in the lane numbered 8. But since Hari was in the lane numbered 7, Amit could not have been in the lane numbered 8. Therefore, Sumit was in the lane numbered 8. Now two cases are possible:

Case I: Soham and Amit were in the lanes numbered 1 and 2 respectively. Mohit and Ramesh were in the lanes numbered 5 and 6, in no particular order.

Lane No.	1	2	3	4	5	6	7	8
Rider	Soham	Amit	Manu	Rahul	Mohit/Ramesh	Ramesh/Mohit	Hari	Sumit

Case II: Soham and Amit were in the lanes numbered 5 and 6 respectively. Mohit and Ramesh were in the lanes numbered 1 and 2, in no particular order.

Lane No.	1	2	3	4	5	6	7	8
Rider	Mohit/Ramesh	Ramesh/Mohit	Manu	Rahul	Soham	Amit	Hari	Sumit

14. (a) Amit
15. (b) Hari and Sumit
16. Among the four people mentioned above, Amit could not have finished first because Soham finished just ahead of Amit. Hence, Option (a) is the correct answer
17. In total, there could be 4 possibilities for the given problem set.
18. In both the possibilities, Rahul finishes 4th. Therefore, 3 people finished ahead of him.

Solutions for Questions 19 and 20:

19. The following table shows the possible solution with the minimum number of people in the group. In the table, a '+' denotes a male, a '–' denotes a female. Also, people in the same box with a comma separating them mean a husband wife pair, while people in the same box with no comma separating them would be siblings.

    Note: K, J and L could have been placed differently too.

Generation 1	A+, B–	C+	D–
Generation 2	K+	E+, J–	L–
Generation 3		F+G+	H–I–

The minimum number of people in the group would be 12. Option (c) is correct.

20. We can see from the table that there are a minimum of 6 women in the group.

MOCK TEST PAPER 3

Solutions for Questions 1 to 5:

1. Daljeet # Chiranjeet $ Baljeet means Daljeet is the brother of Chiranjeet who is the wife of Baljeet. Obviously this means that Daljeet is the brother-in-law of Baljeet. Option (d) is correct.
2. Manjeet * Chiranjeet @ Daljeet @ Baljeet shows us three relations. These are:

   Daljeet is the father of Baljeet. Chiranjeet is the father of Daljeet and Manjeet is the daughter of Chiranjeet. From these relationships we can confirm that the relations specified in options (b), (c) and (d) are true. Manjeet is the mother of Baljeet is the false statement as we can see that Manjeet being the daughter of Chiranjeet would be the sister of Daljeet. Hence, she is the aunt of Baljeet and not the mother. Option (a) is correct as we have to mark what is not true.
3. Abhijeet # Chiranjeet * Baljeet means that Chiranjeet is Baljeet's daughter and Abhijeet being Chiranjeet's brother it also means that Abhijeet and Chiranjeet are the son and daughter of Baljeet.

   Option (d) is not true and since that is what we are looking for, we can conclude that option (d) is the correct answer.
4. In this case A is B's daughter, B is C's daughter, C is D's daughter and D is E's brother. We can make out that C is the niece of E. Option (b) is correct.
5. D is the only male we definitely know of. E's gender is unknown and hence we can say that we do not know the exact number of males in the set of people mentioned. Hence, Option (d) is correct.

Solutions for Questions 6 to 10:

We can make the following table with the help of the given data:

Person	Country	Game
Charlie	(UK or Spain)	(X Tennis, X Polo)
John	Australia	(X Cricket, X Polo)
Bobby	(X France, X UK)	
Anderson	(France or Spain)	Hockey
David	USA	Foot ball

*X Cricket AND X USA means that person neither plays Cricket nor lives in the USA.

If we elaborate the above data table then we can get the following data table:

Person	Country	Game
Charlie	(UK or Spain)	(X Tennis, X Polo) (X Hockey, X Football)
John	Australia	(X Cricket, X Polo) (X Hockey, X Football)
Bobby	(X France, X UK) (X Australia , X USA)	
Anderson	(France or Spain)	Hockey
David	USA	Foot ball

From the analysis of the above data table we can get the following table:

Person	Country	Game
Charlie	UK	Cricket
John	Australia	Tennis
Bobby	Spain	Polo
Anderson	France	Hockey
David	USA	Foot ball

6. Spain. Hence, option (d) is correct.
7. Cricket. Hence, option (b) is correct.
8. Australia, Tennis. Hence, option (c) is correct.
9. From the table thus formed we can see that the French person plays Hockey

10. Charlie plays cricket and he lives in the USA after he shifted from the UK.

Solutions for Questions 11 to 15:

Since there are five countries, if an agency gets the correct order for the maximum polluted country for four years, then it would get the fifth year also correct. Hence, no agency can have 4 correct predictions. Hence, since, it is given that all the five surveying agencies got a different value for the number of countries in the correct order it must be 5, 3, 2, 1 and 0.

Assume the surveying agency - ABCLS got all of them correct, then the agencies - USLIG, HKIS, RIS and RCSI respectively 1, 3, 0 and 2 countries in the correct order. Similarly, checking for the order by the surveying agencies we arrive at the following two possibilities in the order in which the countries are considered to have the maximum pollution.

	Possibility 1	Possibility 2
Year	Country	Country
2023	China	Japan
2024	United states	China
2025	India	India
2026	Russia	United states
2027	japan	Russia

11. As per the given statement, China or Japan is the maximum polluted country in 2023. Option (d) is correct.
12. In either of the arrangements, surveying agency RIS got none of the most polluted countries in the world in the correct order. Hence, option (c) is correct.
13. (b)
14. When China were declared to be the most polluted country of world, then prediction of ABCLS and HKIS were correct. When Japan became the most polluted country USLIG and RCSI predicted the highest polluted country accurately. In both the cases, there were a total of 2 agencies that predicted the country having maximum pollution in 2023 correctly. Hence the correct answer is 2.
15. As per the table, either Japan or Russia got the highest pollution ranking in 2027.

Solutions for Questions 16 to 20:

Using the clues in the problem, we will get the following table:

Monday	Paresh Kamlesh or Suresh Pandey
Tuesday	Kamal Vineet
Wednesday	Suresh Pandey or Paresh Kamlesh
Thursday	Usman Kumar
Friday	Rahul Gupta
Saturday	Tarun Sinha

16. (a) Tarun
17. (d) It could be either Suresh or Paresh.
18. (a) Saturday
19. Mr. Usman Kumar was called for trials on Thursday. Hence, Option C is the correct answer.
20. Tarun Sinha was called on Saturday(6) and Kamal Vineet was called on Tuesday(2). Therefore the sum of days is 8.

MOCK TEST PAPER 4

Solutions for Questions 1 to 5:

The main thing you need to understand here is that once the name plates are interchanged, none of the room names would have the original items as given in the table of the question.

1. The room Biswachakrak would not have it's original contents, viz.: one bag and one computer. Thus, if the supervisor opens the room and finds a bag, the room must necessarily contain two bags (as there are only 2 possible combinations of items that include a bag). Thus, the other item must be a bag. Option (a) is correct.
2. If Purnachandra does not contain any printer or computer, it can only mean that Purnachandra contains 2 bags. Further, since Chandrachud contains one computer and one bag AND Pashupatti does not contain any printers, it must necessarily follow that Pashupatti contains two computers. In this case, the table of room names and contents would look like:

Pashupatti	Two computers
Purnachandra	Two bags
Chandrachud	One bag and one computer
Bagbahadur Biswachakrak	These rooms would have any of: 2 printers OR One printer and One Computer

If someone opens a room other than Pashupatti, Purnachandra and Chandrachud, it necessarily means that they would have opened either Bagbahadur or Biswachakrak. In either case, the room opened would have at least one printer. Option (d) is correct.

3. He can open Purnachandra and would be assured of a bag since it would contain either two bags or one bag and one computer. Option (a) is correct.

4. Bagbahadur would have either one printer and one computer or one bag and one computer. Hence, if he opens Bagbahdur, he is sure to find a computer. Option (c) is correct.
5. The last two rooms could contain two computers, a printer and a computer or a bag and a computer. Hence, a computer is guaranteed to be in one of the remaining rooms. Option (c) is correct.

Solutions for Questions 6 to 10:

The solution table would look as follows

Car Colour	Red/Blue	Blue/ Red	Green	White
Name	Pulkit	Shanti	Qasim	Rahim
Profession	Swimmer	Shooter	Footballer	Cricketer

6. Here, either Swimmer or Shooter drives the Blue car. Option (d) is correct.
7. (c)
8. (b)
9. Under the given condition, Shanti would have a red car and the blue car would be with Pulkit. Hence, the Shooter, Shanti would have a red car.
10. The Person with the white car is a cricketer.

Solutions for Questions 11 to 15:

After reading the first paragraph you would get the following structure for the grid:

Athlete	Country	Sport
Ojasvi		
Pandey		
Qamar		
Sachin		
Virbhadra		
Xenon		
Zavi		

Your first focus in the second paragraph should be to first fill in the direct clues into the grid. You get the following grid after using the clues:

Qamar represents Italy in Hockey. Sachin represents India. Virbhadra competes in Judo. Ojasvi represents Sri Lanka in Cycling. Zavi competes in Weight Lifting.

Athlete	Country	Sport
Ojasvi	Sri Lanka	Cycling
Pandey		
Qamar	Italy	Hockey
Sachin	India	
Virbhadra		Judo
Xenon		
Zavi		Weightlifting

At this point the following clues are left to be used:

Sachin represents India (used) but not in Judo and neither in Weight Lifting. Someone from amongst the seven athletes represents Egypt and he/she competes in Swimming. Virbhadra competes in Judo (used) but not for Malaysia. The athlete from Pakistan competes in Wrestling. Xenon does not represent Malaysia or Egypt.

Also, the countries/sports and country/sport combinations still to be filled in are: Malysia; Pakistan-wrestling; Egypt- Swimming; Nepal- Basketball.

Also, from the grid we have reached at this point of our solving, we know that the two combinations of country sport listed above have to be allocated to Pandey and Xenon. Based on this, we can make the following deductions which would help us complete the solution grid:

Deduction (i): Sachin cannot be matched with Swimming or Wrestling. This leaves only Basketball for Sachin.

Deduction (ii): Zavi and Virbhadra cannot be from either Pakistan or Egypt. Hence, they must be from either Malaysia or Nepal. Further, it is given to us that Virbahdra is not from Malaysia. Hence, we can pair Virbhadra for Nepal and Zavi for Malaysia.

Deduction (iii): At this point, we are only left with deciding about the combinations of Egypt-Swimming AND Pakistan-Wrestling and allocating these between Pandey and Xenon.

Since, we know that Xenon does not represent Egypt, we can easily decide the following combinations:

Pandey-Egypt-Swimming and Xenon-Pakistan- Wrestling.

Athlete	Country	Sport
Ojasvi	Sri Lanka	Cycling
Pandey (Deduction iii)	Egypt	Swimming
Qamar	Italy	Hockey
Sachin	India	Basketball (Deduction i)
Virbhadra	Nepal (Deduction ii)	Judo
Xenon (Deduction iii)	Pakistan	Wrestling
Zavi	Malysia (Deduction ii)	Weightlifting

The answers for questions 11 to 15 can be read off the table:

11. Zavi who competes in weightlifting represents Malaysia. Option (b) is correct.
12. Option (d) can be seen to be correct.

13. It can be seen that it is Sachin who represents India. Option (d) is correct.
14. Sachin competes in Basketball. Option (b) is correct.
15. Virbhadra represents Nepal. Option (d) is correct.

Solutions for Questions 16 to 20:

The following table represents the correct combinations:

The answers are:

Year	Number of Days	Played at
2011	1	SIALKOT
2012	2	BANGALORE
2013	5	KOLKATA
2014	3	DELHI
2015	4	NAGPUR

16. (c)
17. (d)
18. (a)
19. The match at Sialkot was played for 1 day and that for Delhi is 3.
    Hence, the answer is 4.
20. The arrangement would look like:

Bhaskar	Arun/ Chetan	Devarshi	Chetan/ Arun	Ebrahim	Farooq

Or

Farooq	Bhaskar	Arun/ Chetan	Devarshi	Chetan/ Arun	Ebrahim

In both cases, it is a must that Farooq is at one end of the row. Hence, Option (c) is the correct answer.

MOCK TEST PAPER 5

Solutions for Questions 1 to 5:

Based on the clues in the question, we can make the following deductions:

Deduction 1: Neha and Priyanka can't stand together.

Deduction 2: Rahul and Amita always stand together.

Deduction 3: Jaspreet and Rahul can't stand together

Deduction 4: Amita stands at the extreme right.

From deductions 2 and 4:

			Rahul	Amita

From deductions 1 and 3, the following arrangements are possible:

Arrangement 1:

Priyanka	Jaspreet	Neha	Rahul	Amita

Arrangement 2:

Neha	Jaspreet	Priyanka	Rahul	Amita

Hence the answers are:

1. Rahul. Hence, option (c) is correct
2. Jaspreet. Hence, option (d) is correct
3.

Priyanka	Amita	Rahul	Neha	Jaspreet

From statement (i) From statement (ii)

Hence, option (d) is correct.

4. Neha could take positions 1 and 3. Therefore sum = 4.
5. In this case Rahul is standing in the middle.

Solutions for Questions 6 to 10:

The following five cases are possible:

Possibility 1: (Qasim, Sam, Virat, Rahul)

Possibility 2: (Rahul, Virat, Sam, Qasim)

Possibility 3: (Rahul, Virat, Qasim, Sam)

Possibility 4: (Qasim, Rahul, Virat, Sam)

Possibility 5: (Virat, Rahul, Qasim, Sam)

6. If Qasim is the last person to visit, then from Case 2 we can say that Rahul visited the party first. Hence, option (c) is correct.
7. 5
8. Virat can never be the last person to visit the party. Hence, option (d) is correct.
9. The answer is d as in the 3 possible outcomes when sam is last to visit, only the possibility that Qasim visiting 2nd is not possible, hence it is definitely true.
10. We know as per our possibility list that Virat visiting first is only true in possibility number 5, which means the order of visit is Virat, Rahul, Qasim and Sam. This is expressed in option (a), hence (a) is the answer.

Solutions for Questions 11 to 15:

Based on the information in the question we can start off with a circular figure with 7 blank seats as shown below.

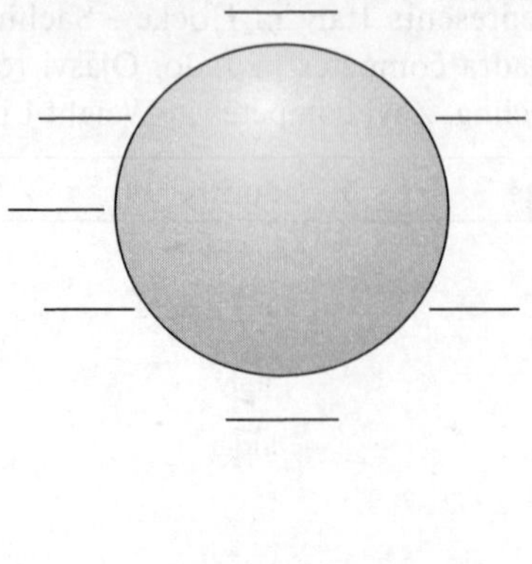

Based on the clue "Anil is third to the left of Yukta and to the immediate right of Rashmi" we get:

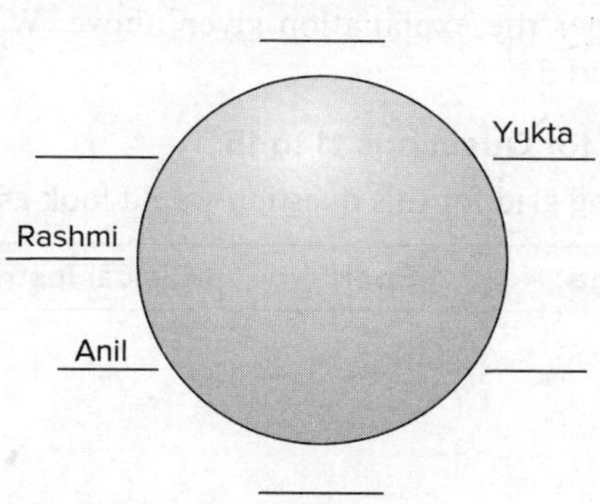

From this point we can use the clue:
"Pritam is second to the left of Gitali who is not an immediate neighbour of Mitali." This gives us only one way to complete the seating arrangement as shown below:

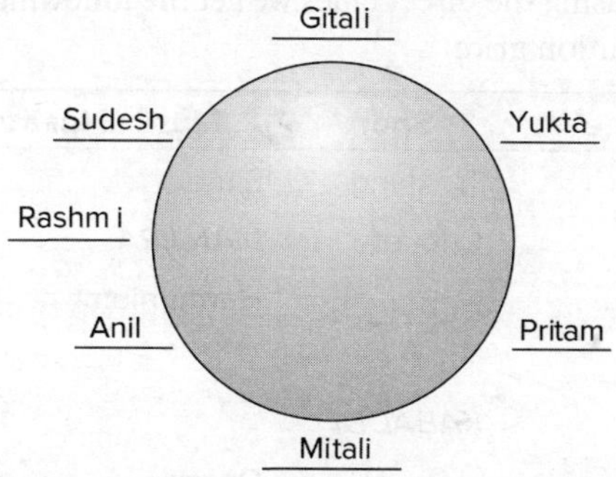

The answers can then be read off the final seating grid.

11. Mitali is to the immediate left of Pritam. Option (a) is correct.
12. Mitali is second to the right of Rashmi. Option (b) is correct.
13. None of the given pairs satisfies the condition. Option (d) is correct.
14. Sudesh is sitting between Rashmi and Gitali. Option (b) is correct.
15. Anil is second to the left and fifth to the right of Pritam. Option (d) is correct.

Solutions for Questions 16 to 20:

The heights are 2, 3, 4, 5 and 6 feet.

Let the heights of Aman, Baman, Chaman, Daman, Ehsaan are A, B, C, D, E respectively.

Solution: From statement (i): The student whose height is 6 feet studies in school P and the student whose height is 2 feet studies in school S.

From statement (ii): A + D = 2B.

From statement (iii): B > A, now following possibilities are there:

1. A = 2, D = 6, B = 4
2. A = 2, D = 4, B = 3
3. A = 3, D = 5, B = 4
4. A = 4, D = 6, B = 5

From statement (vi): T > R > Q
T = 5, R = 4, Q = 3.

From statement (v): $C \neq 6$, $E \neq 2$.

From statement (iii): Daman is not the tallest and Ehsaan is not the shortest.

The above analysis can be tabulated in the following table:

School	Height (in feet)	Case 1	Case 2	Case 3	Case 4
P	6	D		E	B
T	5			D	D
R	4	B	D	B	A
Q	3		B	A	
S	2	A	A	C	

Now from the clue (iv) which states: 'At most three students are shorter than Daman and at least one student is shorter than Aman' we can eliminate cases 1, 2 and 4 as possibilities. This leaves us only with Case 3, and the definite table looks as follows:

School	Height (in feet)	Case 3
P	6	E
T	5	D
R	4	B
Q	3	A
S	2	C

The answers would be:

16. Daman
17. P
18. T
19. Ehsaan–R is not correct. Hence, option (d) is the correct answer.
20. After exchange, P has student of height 4 and S has the student with height 2. Therefore, the answer would be 4 + 2 = 6.

MOCK TEST PAPER 6

Solutions for Questions 1 to 5:

Person	Colour	Drink
Englishman	Red	
Italian	Blue	Tea
Spain		Fruit Juice
Norway (x Blue)		

From statements (i), (iii), (v) and (viii) & from above analysis we get the following arrangements:

Norway	Italian	Englishman	Spaniard
Norway	Italian	Englishman	Spainand
Yellow	Blue	Red	White
(Cocoa)	(Tea)	(Milk)	(Fruit Juice)

The answers are:

1. (a)
2. (b)
3. (b)
4. (d)
5. The person drinks Fruit Juice.

Solutions for Questions 6 to 10:

From statements (ii), (v) and (vi), we can deduce that C, E, A (ranked 1 player), W and Y advanced to the second round.

Total number of matches played in the second round $= {}^5C_2 = 10$.

From statements (iii), (vi) and (vii), we can deduce that the following three combinations of number of matches won by the five players in the 2nd round are possible – (2, 2, 2, 3, 1), (2, 2, 2, 4, 0), (3, 3, 3, 1, 0).

The last combination (3, 3, 3, 1, 0) is not possible, because in this case, the top player of the second round would come from the 3 players who won an equal number of matches – this would be a contradiction of the 7th statement.

From statement (ii), A won at most one match in the second round, so he could not advance to the 3rd round. Therefore, we can deduce that C, E, W and Y advanced to the 3rd round. Out of these four players the top seeded player was C (3rd) and bottom seeded player was Y (8th). The first match of the 3rd round was played between C and Y and the second match was played between E and W.

W is the winner of the tournament so he must have beaten E in the 3rd round, but we cannot decide who won the 1st match of 3rd round. So W played the final round against either C or Y.

The answers then would be:

6. (d)
7. (d)
8. Total matches played by C till the start of the 4th round $= 4 + 4 + 1 = 9$

   Total matches played by Y till the start of the 4th round $= 3 + 4 + 1 = 8$

   Either C or Y qualified for the final. So, the sum of the total matches played by them together $= 9 + 8 + 1 = 18$.
9. C and E played against each other only in the 1st and 2nd round. Hence, the required answer is $1 + 1 = 2$.
10. As per the explanation given above, W beat E in round 3.

Solutions for Questions 11 to 15:

The starting grid for this question would look as follows:

Name	Sport	Musical Instrument
Abhi		
Binoy		
Chintan		
Dev		
Esha		
Freni		
Gautam		

After using the direct clues we get the following position in the solution grid:

Name	Sport	Musical Instrument
Abhi	Trekking	Flute
Binoy	Cricket	*MANJIRA*
Chintan		Harmonium
Dev		
Esha	*KABADDI*	
Freni		Drums
Gautam	Snooker	*SHEHNAI*

At this point in our solution, we have to still fit in the following sport/musical instrument or sport-musical instrument combination.

Swimming, chess, golf, *SAROD* and *SARANGI*.

From this point the following deductions help us get to the final answers:

Deduction 1: Since Esha does not play *SAROD*, she must be playing *SARANGI*. Consequently, Dev plays *SAROD*.

Deduction 2: Since Freni does not swim or play golf, her sport must be Chess.

The grid would become as follows:

Name	Sport	Musical Instrument
Abhi	Trekking	Flute
Binoy	Cricket	*MANJIRA*
Chintan		Harmonium
Dev		*SAROD*
Esha	*KABADDI*	*SARANGI*

Name	Sport	Musical Instrument
Freni	Chess	Drums
Gautam	Snooker	*SHEHNAI*

Now, since the one who plays golf does not play Sarod, Golf can only go to Chintan. The final table will look as follows:

Name	Sport	Musical Instrument
Abhi	Trekking	Flute
Binoy	Cricket	*MANJIRA*
Chintan	Golf	Harmonium
Dev	Swimming	*SAROD*
Esha	*KABADDI*	*SARANGI*
Freni	Chess	Drums
Gautam	Snooker	*SHEHNAI*

The answers can now be read off the above table:

11. Dev plays *SAROD*. Option (a) is correct.
12. Esha plays *KABADDI*. Option (d) is correct.
13. Option (d) is correct.
14. Freni plays Chess. Option (d) is correct.
15. Dev is the swimmer. Option (c) is correct.

Solutions for Questions 16 to 20:

Enclosure	Allahabad	Bharuch	Chandigarh	Delhi	Egmore
Trainer	Amar/Eknath	Divyansh	Bhaskar	Eknath/Amar	Chetan
Number of Animals	4 or 5	1	3	4 or 5	2

16. (d) We get the following structure based on our solving of the clues in the question:
    We cannot uniquely determine who trains the animals in the Delhi enclosure.
17. (a) the Bharuch enclosure had 1 animal.
18. 3 animals in Chandigarh and 2 animals with Chetan. Hence the difference is 1.
19. Any one between Amar and Eknath could have 5 animals. Hence Option (d) is the correct answer.
20. In the Egmore enclosure there were 2 animals.

MOCK TEST PAPER 7

Solutions for Questions 1 to 5:

Looking at the questions, we realise that the only thing we need to do is order the people in terms of their age.

From the statements we can infer that:

From the first statement: R > Q; P > S; T > R; T > Q

From the second statement: P > U; Q > V; P > V; U > S and V > U

Looking at the arrangements for the seven people we can identify: T > R> Q > V > U > S; Also P is greater than S, U and V.

Further, from the statement of Q: "*V is as old as I was when you were as old as V is*" we get: P = Q – since V has the same relationship with each of P and Q.

Thus, the correct order is:

T > R > Q = P > V > U > S

1. Option (c) is correct.
2. Option (d) is correct.
3. Option (a) is correct.
4. Option (b) is correct.
5. From the arrangement we can see that P & Q are equal in age. Hence, Option C is the correct answer.

Solutions for Questions 6 to 10:

From statement (iv), we can deduce that the score in one of the matches is (Barcelona) 1 – 0 (Manchester United);

From statement (vii), we can deduce that the score in one of the five matches is (Barcelona) 4 – 2 (Manchester United) – since the only numbers in the numbers of goals conceded by Barcelona, that have a ratio of 3:1 are 6 and 2.

From statement (i), we can deduce that the 1st match score is – (Barcelona) 8 – 4 (Manchester United), while the score in the second match would be (Barcelona) 6 – 6 (Manchester United).

From statements (vii) & (iii), the score of 4 – 2 would be in the 5th match.

As the 3rd match was played in Manchester and from statement (v), 1 – 0 must be the score of the match in London (4th match). Hence, the score of the 3rd match was (Barcelona) 5 – 1 (Manchester United).

The following table emerges:

Match	Barcelona	Manchester United	Venue
1st	8	4	London
2nd	6	6	Manchester

Match	Barcelona	Manchester United	Venue
3rd	5	1	Manchester
4th	1	0	London
5th	4	2	London

The answers can then be read off the table:

6. 5
7. 2nd
8. (b)
9. Required number of goals = 8 + 4 + 1 + 0 + 4 + 2 = 19.
10. As can be seen from the table, Barcelona won 4 matches and drew 1 match against Manchester united. So the total points gained by Barcelona would be 3 + 3 + 3 + 3 + 1 = 13.
    Hence the answer is (b)

Solutions for Questions 11 to 15:

Since there are 8 people sitting around the circle, we can look at creating the following picture:

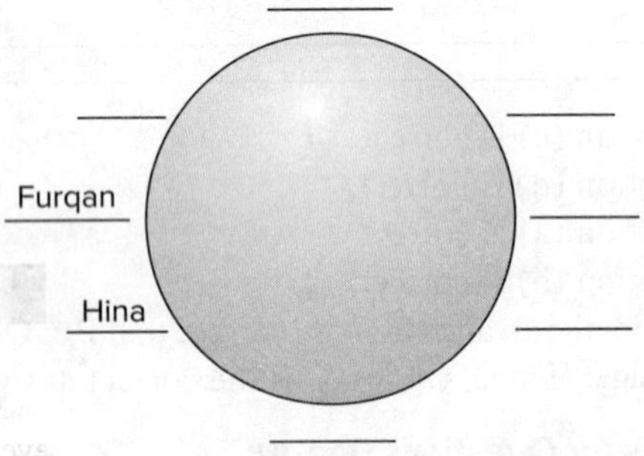

From this point, if we use the clue: Danish sits third to the right of Charlie and Hina is not the neighbour of Danish and Charlie we get only the following possible placement for the eight people.

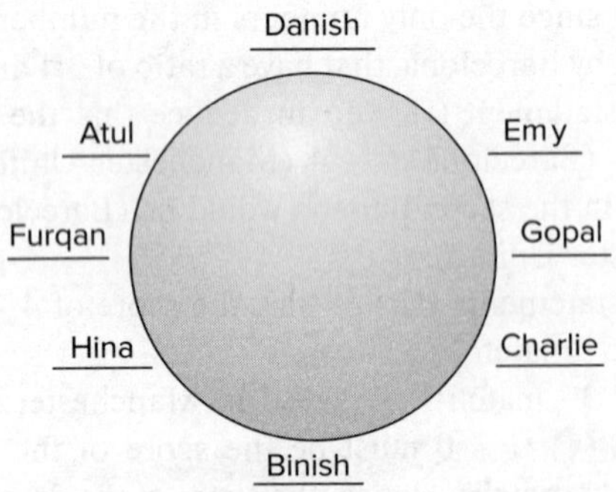

The answers can be read off the above figure.

11. Hina sits to the right of Furqan. Option (d) is correct.
12. Apart from the pair of Charlie-Hina, in each of the other pairs the second person is sitting 3 places to the left of the first person. Option (a) is the one that does not belong to the group and hence option (a) is correct.
13. Option (d) is the correct answer.
14. Option (a) is correct.
15. Option (d) is correct.

Solutions for Questions 16 to 20:

From Statements (i) and (iii), two cases are possible:

16. (d)
17. (a)
    There are two cases for the arrangements between student and class:

Case 1:

Student	B/D	C	A	E	D/B	F
Class	5	6	7	8	9	10

Case 2:

Student	B/D	E	C/F	F/C	D/B	A
Class	5	6	7	8	9	10

Question 16:
We refer to Case 2 and in that situation we can see that C studies in Class 7 or 8. Hence, Option (d) is correct.

Question 17:
We refer to Case 1, where A studies in Class 7. Option (a) is correct.

18. C could study in classes 6,7 & 8. Hence, the sum is 21.
19. Only A or F could be studying in class 10. Hence, Option (a) is the correct answer.
20. Possibilities for A = 7 & 10. Possibilities for B = 5 & 9. Hence the maximum difference is 10 – 5 = 5

MOCK TEST PAPER 8

Solutions for Questions 1 to 5:

From statement (i), (ii) and (iii) the following arrangement is possible.

Tiger	Quail	Panther	Rose	Swan

We can get the above arrangement from statement (i), (ii) and (iv) also.

1. (b)
2. (c)
3. (c)
4. As per the arrangement, Panther and Swan are next to Quail.
5. The new arrangement is as follows: T - R - S - Q - P
   According to this, Panther and Swan are next to Quail.

Solutions for Questions 6 to 9:

The structure of the family would look something like this:

Married couple 1: C (female, lawyer) – A (male, MBA)

Married couple 2: D (author, Male) – G (MBA, Female)

E- (female, lawyer); B/F (Male, entrepreneur); F/B (Male, executive)

The answers are:

6. (a) (There are 4 male members in the family.)

7. (d) (B and F share the professions of executive and entrepreneur. Hence, both the Options (b) and (c) can be correct. Hence, Option (d) is the correct answer.)

8. Among the pairs given, C & E are lawyers. Hence, option (c) is the correct answer.

9. For the executive position we have only 2 possibilities, B & F. Hence, Option (b) is the correct answer.

Solutions for Questions 10 to 15:

From the clue: Anu sits fourth to the right of Hitesh while second to the left of Farman we get:

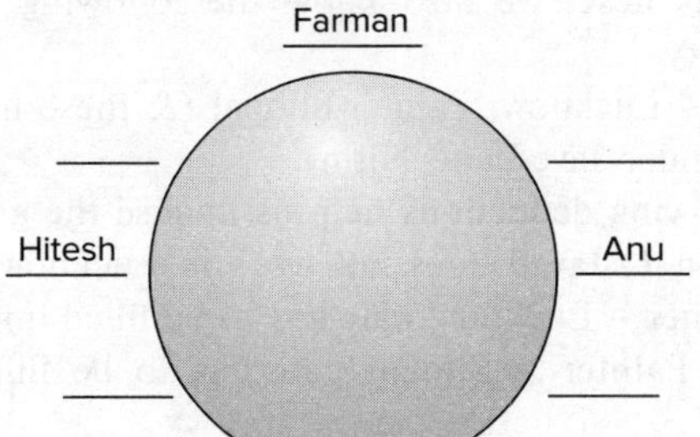

From this point if we further use the clues that: Chintu is not the neighbour of Farman and Bhavesh and Durgesh sits third to the right of Chintu we would have only one position to place Chintu and Durgesh in. Subsequently, the other people would each have only a single position to get placed in. The solution would be as shown by the figure given below:

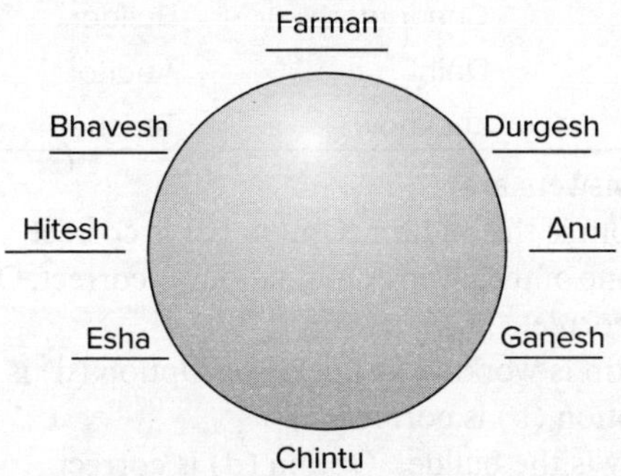

The answers to Questions 21 to 26 can then be read off the final solution figure:

10. Anu sits between Ganesh and Durgesh. Option (d) is correct.
11. Hitesh and Bhavesh sit between Esha and Farman. Option (a) is correct.
12. Apart from the Durgesh Chintu pair, all other pairs are separated only by one person in between them. Hence, option (a) is correct.
13. Ganesh is to the immediate left of Anu. Option (c) is correct.
14. Bhavesh sits second to the right of Durgesh. Option (c) is correct.
15. Farman is third to the left of Esha and is also fifth to the right of Esha. Option (d) is correct.

Solutions for Questions 16 to 20:

If you use all the clues, the following orders emerge:

Order of weight: S > Q > U > V > T > P > W > R

Order height: Q > R > U > S > T > P > V > W

16. W is shortest. Option (d) is correct.
17. R is lightest. Option (b) is correct.
18. People shorter than P are V&W, both of whom are lighter than Q. Hence the answer is 0.
19. R's rank in height = 2; R's rank in weight = 8; Difference = 6
20. U, T and P are the only 3 people who ranked similar in both the categories.

MOCK TEST PAPER 9

Solutions for Questions 1 to 5:

These kind of questions are best solved in the reverse order by progressively doubling the money of the individuals depending on who lost the game. The following table is self explanatory:

After Round	Mohit	Monohar	Prasant	Dinesh	Loser in Round
4	32000	32000	32000	32000	Dinesh
3	16000	16000	16000	80000	Prasant
2	8000	8000	72000	40000	Monohor
1	4000	68000	36000	20000	Mohit
Starting values	66000	34000	18000	10000	

The solutions can then be read off the table:

1. Mohit had ₹66000 to start with. Option (c) is correct.

2. Monohar had ₹68000 at the end of the first round. Option (a) is correct.

3. Mohit had ₹4000 at the end of the first round and that is the lowest value throughout the tournament. Option (a) is correct.

4. Prasant had ₹72000 at the end of the second round. Option (b) is correct.
5. The only combination amongst those given in the options that satisfies the given condition is the combination of Prof. Arora, Prof. Bhalla, Prof. Eswar and Prof. Fazil. In this combination of 4 professors, each professor has a habit which is common with at least 1 of the other three professors selected. Also, the selected professors can be seen to share at least one non-common habit of any of the other three professors selected. Option (b) is correct.

Solutions for Questions 6 to 10:

After putting the given data in, the appropriate grid for this question would look as follows:

Actor	City	Airline
Om		
Puri	Chandigarh	Kingfisher
Qadir	Mumbai	
Ruk Ruk	Bangalore	MDLR Airlines
Sanjay		Air Deccan
Tina	Bhopal	Go Air
Usman		

At this point, the missing pieces pertain to the following cities/airlines:

Cities left: Agra, Indore, Gandhinagar

Airlines left: Indigo Airlines, MDLR Airlines Express, Jetlite.

Since we know that Agra cannot be Om and neither Sanjay, it leaves us only Usman who can go to Agra. Also, the one traveling to Gandhinagar does not travel by Air Deccan. This can only mean that Air Deccan (and Sanjay) must be going to Indore and hence, Om would be going to Gandhinagar.

Since, Om is going to Gandhinagar, he cannot be going by MDLR Airlines Express.

The table converts to the following

Actor	City	Airline
Om	Gandhinagar	Jetlife
Puri	Chandigarh	Kingfisher
Qadir	Mumbai	Indigo
Ruk Ruk	Bangalore	MDLR Airlines
Sanjay	Indore	Air Deccan
Tina	Bhopal	Go Air
Usman	Agra	MDLR Airline Express

The answers can be read off this table:

6. Usman. Hence, option (c) is correct.
7. Om goes to Gandhinagar. Option (a) is correct.
8. Sanjay who goes by Air Deccan visits Indore. Option (b) is correct.
9. Option (c) is correct.
10. From the table we can see it is MDLR Airlines Express.

Solutions for Questions 11 to 15:

The starting grid in this question (after using the direct information in the question) would look as follows:

Person	City	Profession
Gimi		Fashion Designer
Harish	Gandhinagar	Choreographer
Javed		
Kandarp		Photographer
Luv	Chandigarh	Builder
Moni	Delhi	
Nitin		

At this point we have to place the following: Kolkata, Lucknow, Agra, Bhopal, Auditor, Painter and Teacher.

Amongst these, we also know the following pairs are mandatory:

Teacher – Lucknow; Painter-Bhopal (& these have to be placed under Javed and Nitin).

The following deductions help us finalise the grid:

Deduction 1: Javed does not work in Lucknow – hence the Teacher – Lucknow pair has to be filled under Nitin and the Painter – Bhopal pair has to be filled under Javed.

Deduction 2: Kandarp does not work in Kolkata – hence he can only work in Agra while Gimi must be working in Kolkata. The finalized grid would look as below:

Person	City	Profession
Gimi	Kolkata	Fashion Designer
Harish	Gandhinagar	Choreographer
Javed	Bhopal	Painter
Kandarp	Agra	Photographer
Luv	Chandigarh	Builder
Moni	Delhi	Auditor
Nitin	Lucknow	Teacher

The answers are:

11. Moni is the auditor. Option (d) is correct.
12. None of the given combinations is correct. Option (d) is correct.
13. Nitin is working in Lucknow. Option (d) is correct.
14. Option (b) is correct.
15. Luv is the builder. Option (d) is correct.

Solutions for Questions 16 to 20:

The given information can be tabulated in the following manner:

Person	Subject	Day
Satish		Monday
Rajesh	Geology	(X Monday, X Friday)
Rehman	(X English)	Wednesday
Rakesh	(X Botany)	(x Friday)
Vineet	(X English)	(X Tuesday)

From Statement-(v) it is clear that Vineet presents Botany paper on Friday and Rakesh presents Physics on Thursday.

Person	Subject	Day
Satish	English	Monday
Rajesh	Geology	Tuesday
Rehman	Zoology	Wednesday
Rakesh	Physics	Thursday
Vineet	Botany	Friday

16. Monday. Option (b) is correct.
17. Botany. Option (d) is correct.
18. Thursday. Option (d) is correct.
19. From the table it is clear that Vineet presents on Friday. Hence, Option (d) is the correct answer.
20. On Wednesday, Rehman makes a presentation on Zoology. Hence, option (c) is the correct answer.

MOCK TEST PAPER 10

Solutions for Questions 1 to 5:

In order to solve this question, you need to be clear about what level of dissimilarity means. As stated in the question set, the level of dissimilarity is the 'maximum difference of ranks' allotted by the two states to any of the five attributes.

Thus, for instance, if we look at the level of dissimilarity between Orissa and Rajasthan the rank given to IAY by Orissa is 5th and by Rajasthan is 1st. Hence, their level of dissimilarity is 4, as no other pair can have a level of dissimilarity higher than 4.

1. The level of dissimilarity between Orissa and Bihar is 2 as the maximum difference in ranks allotted is for MDM (2). Orissa and Rajasthan have a dissimilarity of 4, while Kerala and Karnataka have a dissimilarity of 3 with Orissa. Thus, Bihar is least dissimilar to Orissa and option (a) is correct.
2. As already seen in the question above, Rajasthan has a dissimilarity of 4 with respect to Orissa and hence is the most dissimilar to Orissa. Option (b) is correct.
3. Kerala and Bihar; Bihar and Karnataka AND Karnataka and Rajasthan have a dissimilarity of 4 each. Only the pair of Rajasthan and Kerala have a dissimilarity of 3 and hence this pair is the odd pair out of the four pairs. Option (c) is correct.
4. We can see from the table given to us that the ranks between Orissa and Kerala is the highest for the levels of dissimilarity as 3, hence Kerela is the answer.
5. The question is asking us the number of instances of rank difference of 4, in the table, We can see 4 such instances as listed here:
   (i) Orissa IAY and Rajasthan IAY
   (ii) Bihar MDM and Kerala MDM
   (iii) Bihar NREG and Kerala NREG
   (iv) Kerala IAY and Karnataka IAY.
   Hence, the answer is 4. Option (d) is correct.

Solutions for Questions 6 to 11:

According to the question, only three persons correctly predicted the four teams who got a copper ball. According to the table, only B, F and H are the four teams receiving the copper ball the same.

As no two persons correctly predicted the final position of the same number of teams – so the number of correct predictions must have been 8, 6, 5, 4, 3, 2, 1 and 0. Note here that nobody could get exactly 7 predictions correct, since if someone had 7 correct predictions, his eighth prediction would automatically come correct.

Based on our observation that there are only 3 people who predicted the copper balls correctly – it has to be one of these 3 who got all 8 predictions correct.

If we look at these three cases one by one, we see:

Case 1: B predicted all of the team's positions correctly – then D and F would have six of the predictions correct which is not possible. Hence, we reject this case.

Case 2: If H predicted all the teams correctly then B and G would have got exactly four predictions correct which is not possible again.

So the only possibility left is that F got all his predictions correct. In this case the number of correct predictions for the persons are as following:

A	1
B	6
C	0
D	4
E	2
F	8
G	3
H	5

6. Entricht
7. Fannerfitch
8. Handkerchief
9. 2 people predicted the platinum ball for Sriticht

10. As per the table, we can see that C had all of his predictions as incorrect. Option (b) is incorrect.
11. Since F got all the correct predictions, and comparing F's predictions, we can see that the incorrect predictions of B were for the Silver ball BD and Platinum ball Aus. Hence, option (a) is correct.

Solutions for Questions 12 to 15:

The given information can be tabulated in the following table:

Person	Players			
	Elex	Laxman	Cariappa	Tariq
Subroto		N		Y
Sona	N			
Sudhir		N	Y	
Sobraj				

Y: Voted in favour
N: Voted against.

Subroto must have voted against Laxman (From statement (v), no person who voted for Tariq voted for Laxman.)

12. All the selectors who voted for Tariq also voted for Cariappa.

Subroto must have voted for Cariappa but not voted for Elex.

Sudhir voted for Elex but not for Tariq. Sobraj voted for Elex.

Sona must have voted for two players among Laxman, Cariappa and Tariq. However, he could not have voted for Laxman and Tariq at the same time - as if he voted for Tariq he would have voted for Cariappa also.

Person	Players			
	Elex	Laxman	Cariappa	Tariq
Subroto	N	N	Y	Y
Sona	N	N	Y	Y
Sudhir	Y	N	Y	N
Sobraj	Y	Y	N	N

Option (d) is correct.

13. Subroto voted against Cariappa, then:

Person	Players			
	Elex	Laxman	Cariappa	Tariq
Subroto	Y	N	N	Y
Sona	N		Y	
Sudhir		N	Y	
Sobraj			Y	

From the above table we can deduce that only one of Sudhir and Sobraj voted for Elex. Option (b) cannot be true.

14. As per the table, we know that Sudhir voted for Elex and Cariappa, hence the third statement is true. Option (c) is correct.
15. As per the table, only option (c) can be true.

Solutions for Questions 16 to 20:

The given information can be tabulated as following table:

Channel	Movie genre	Day
PIX		Friday
ZEE		
WB	Sci-fi	(X Thursday)
HBO	Comedy	

As per the question action is telecasted on Monday.

Channel	Movie genre	Day
PIX	Romantic	Friday
ZEE	Action	Monday
WB	Sci-fi	Tuesday
HBO	Comedy	Thursday

16. (a)
17. (d)
18. (b)
19. From the table it is clear that the romantic genre is telecasted on Friday. Option (a) is correct.
20. HBO telecasts the comedy genre.

MOCK TEST PAPER 11

Solutions for Questions 1 to 5:

1. The basic structure of the movement that Kartikay would exhibit would look as follows:

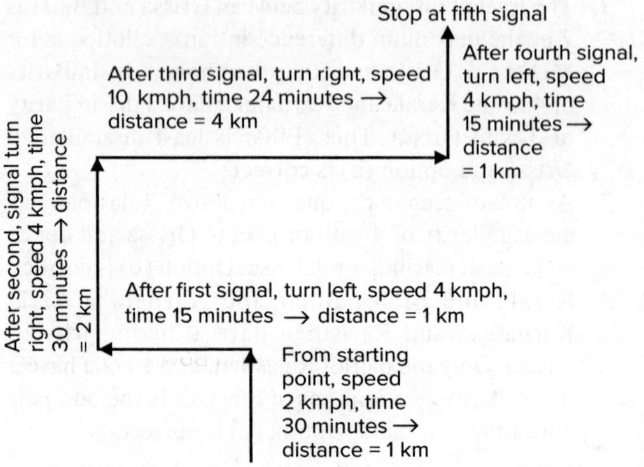

Thus, the total distance he would travel would be 9 km. Option (a) is correct.

2. If the first signal had 1 guard with red cap and 2 guards with green caps he would need to turn right at the first signal. His speed for this part of the journey would not get affected. Also, it would not affect his subsequent turns and his subsequent distances too.
His journey path would look as below and it can be clearly seen that he would be 3 km west and 2 km south at the end of his journey.

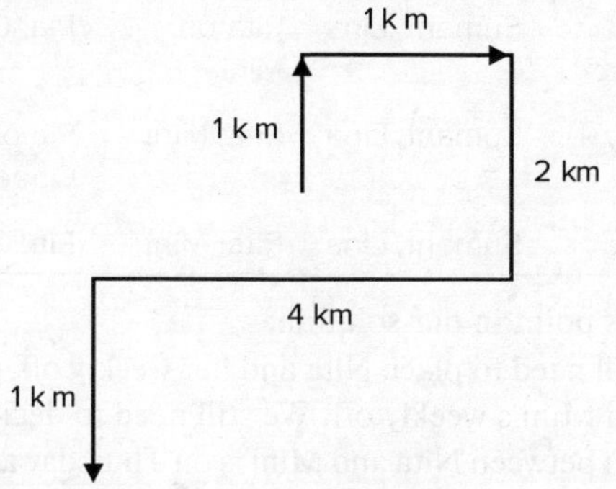

Option (a) is the correct answer.

3. If he were heading south the figure would change from the figure in the 14th question and it would just be the inverse of the figure in the 14th question, i.e., everytime he is moving north in the figure for the 14th question he would move south for this question and every time he is moving east he would now be moving west. Also, every time he is moving west he would now be moving east. Hence, the final result would also be the opposite of the final position in question 14. In the figure for question 14 it can be seen that Kartikay ends up 4 km north and 3 km east. Hence, for this question his final position would be 3 km west and 4 km south. Option (c) is correct.
4. Distance traveled till third signal = 4 km
Total distance = 9 Km
Difference = 5 Km
5. Old Scenario:
Total distance after third signal = 5 km
New Scenario:
Total distance after third signal = 1.6 + 2.5 = 4.1 km
Net change = 900 meters

Solutions for Questions 6 to 10:

The cricketers of Group A and Group B can each be divided into 4 kinds as follows:

Group A Cricketers (66)		Group B Cricketers (64)	
Skilled in Batting	A	Skilled in Batting	r
Unskilled in Batting	44	Unskilled in Batting	s
Skilled in Bowling	q	Skilled in Bowling	26
Unskilled in Bowling	p	Unskilled in Bowling	A

We can make the following deductions in order to get to the answers of the questions asked based on these variables:

From statement (i):

Number of Group A players who were skilled in batting = Number of Group B players who were unskilled in bowling = A.

From the above table:

$p + q + A + 44$ = Total number of Group A players.

Total number of Group B players = $r + s + 26 + A$.

From statement (iii):

Number of Group A players = 66

Number of Group B players = 64

From the above table:

$p + q + A + 44 = 66$

$p + q + A = 22$ (1)

Similarly: $r + s + A = 38$ (2)

6. Number of players who opted to learn batting = $r + s + A + 44 = 38 + 44 = 82$.
7. Number of players who opted to learn bowling = $130 - 82 = 48$.
8. As per option (a):
$A < q$
From statements (i), (ii) & (iii) this can either be true or false.
Option (b): $q < 26$, from statement (i) it is true.
Option (c): $A < 44$, from statement (i) this is true.
Option (d): From statement (4) => $q > r$
From equations 1 & 2:
$p + q + A < r + s + A$
$p + q < r + s$
As, $q > r$
∴ $p < s$ (which contradict option (d)).
Hence, option (d) is correct.
9. Given that: $A > 6$.
Number of Group A player who remained unskilled in bowling = p
From equation (1):
$p + q + A = 22$
To maximize the value of p, we need to minimize the value of A.
Minimum value of A = 7.
$p + q = 11 - A = 22 - 7 = 15$
Minimum value of q = 1 (Because $q > r$ so if $r = 0$ then minimum value of q = 1)
$p = 15 - 1 = 14$
10. The minimum value of r (group B, skilled in batting) is 0, while the maximum value of q (Group A, skilled in bowling) is 22. Thus, the maximum possible difference between the two is $22 - 0 = 22$.

Solutions for Questions 11 to 15:

The ideal starting grid structure for this question would be:

	Shift I	Shift II	Shift III
Monday			
Tuesday			
Wednesday			
Thursday			
Friday			
Saturday			
Sunday			

We have direct information about the shifts of Mini, Pia, Rita and Sumant. We also have direct information about the weekly offs of Sumant, Rita and Pia. Placing this information into the above table we would get:

	Shift I	Shift II	Shift III
Monday	Sumant off	Rita, Mini	Pia
Tuesday	Sumant	Rita, Mini	Pia
Wednesday	Sumant	Rita, Mini	Pia
Thursday	Sumant	Rita, Mini	Pia
Friday	Sumant	Rita off, Mini	Pia
Saturday	Sumant	Rita, Mini	Pia
Sunday	Sumant	Rita, Mini	Pia off

At this point we should be thinking about the following:

(i) The shifts and weekly offs for Lina, Nita and Queen and

(ii) The weekly off for Mini

(iii) We also realize that of the remaining 3 people who have to be allocated to shifts, each of them has to be allocated only to either shift I or shift III (as it is given that shift II has only Mini and Rita.)

(iv) Of the remaining 3 people whose shifts have to be decided, two would need to go into any one of the two remaining shifts while the third would go to the other shift. Thus, between shifts I and III, one of them would have to have 2 people working in it while the other shift would have 3 people working in it.

(v) The weekly offs for 4 people - hence for four days is still not known. These are Tuesday, Wednesday, Thursday and Saturday.

In order to move ahead in completing the table we have:

Lina and Pia do not work in the same shift - meaning that Lina should be working in shift I and her weekly off is Tuesday. Also, Queen's weekly off being on the next day to Lina's weekly off, her weekly off must be on Wednesday. Further Queen should be working in a shift different from Lina–so since Lina is in shift I, Queen would be in shift III (remember that shift II has been completely filled up).

With this information placed, the solution grid would become as below:

	Shift I	Shift II	Shift III
Monday	Sumant off, Lina	Rita, Mini	Pia, Queen
Tuesday	Sumant, Lina off	Rita, Mini	Pia, Queen
Wednesday	Sumant, Lina	Rita, Mini	Pia, Queen off
Thursday	Sumant, Lina	Rita, Mini	Pia, Queen
Friday	Sumant, Lina	Rita off, Mini	Pia, Queen
Saturday	Sumant, Lina	Rita, Mini	Pia off, Queen
Sunday	Sumant, Lina	Rita, Mini	Pia, Queen

At this point in our solution:

We still need to place Nita and her weekly off, as well as decide on Mini's weekly off. We still need to decide whose weekly off between Nita and Mini is on Thursday and whose is on Sunday. We also need to decide the one shift that has 3 people working.

Note: Since there are 7 officers and 3 shifts with a minimum of 2 officers per shift- it means that one of the shifts would have 3 officers and the other two would have 2 officers each.

The clue that helps us decide on these unknowns in the table is:

The one who has a weekly off on Sunday works in the first shift.

This means that Mini cannot have her weekly off on Sunday–hence her weekly off is on Thursday. Also, Nita must be a first shift worker and her weekly off is on Sunday. The solution grid gets completed as below:

	Shift I	Shift II	Shift III
Monday	Sumant off, Lina, Nita	Rita, Mini	Pia, Queen
Tuesday	Sumant, Lina off, Nita	Rita, Mini	Pia, Queen
Wednesday	Sumant, Lina, Nita	Rita, Mini	Pia, Queen off
Thursday	Sumant, Lina, Nita	Rita, Mini off	Pia, Queen
Friday	Sumant, Lina, Nita	Rita off, Mini	Pia, Queen
Saturday	Sumant, Lina, Nita	Rita, Mini	Pia off, Queen
Sunday	Sumant, Lina, Nita off	Rita, Mini	Pia, Queen

The answers can now be read off the above table:

11. It is Nita whose weekly off is on Sunday. Option (d) is correct.
12. Option (d) is correct.
13. Mini's weekly off is on Thursday. Option (b) is correct.
14. Option (a) is correct.
15. Option (a) is correct.

Solutions for Questions 16 to 20:

We can make the following order based on the information provided:

Subject	Order
Geography	1
Math	2
Economics	3
Computer Science	4
Physics	5
Chemistry	6

16. Economics. Option (d) is correct.
17. Chemistry. Option (a) is correct.
18. Geography. Option (b) is correct.
19. Position of Geography = 1; Position of Physics = 5
    Difference = 4
20. There is 1 book between Computer Science & Chemistry.

MOCK TEST PAPER 12

Solutions for Questions 1 to 5:

Let's represent Promila, Qadir, Rita and Sridhar by P, Q, R and S and Anand, Bose, Chandra Shekhran and Deshpande by A, B, C, D.

Student	Professor	Area
P	D	
Q		
R		
S		HRM

From statement (ii) & (v) it is clear that Promila's area is neither Finance nor HRM.

From Statements (i) & (iv), it is clear that Rita's Area is Marketing and Promila's area is system.

The above analysis can be tabulated as below:

Student	Professor	Area
P	D	System
Q	B	Finance
R		Marketing
S		HRM

1. Marketing. Option (a) is correct.
2. Systems. Hence, option (c) is correct.
3. Qadir. Hence, option (a) is correct.
4. As per the table, Qadir's project is in Finance, but since Finance is not in the options, the answer is (d), none of these.
5. According to the table, Rita or Sridhar could've completed their project under Anand as it's a multiple possibility structure in the final table, hence the answer is (d).

Solutions for Questions 6 to 10:

	1	2	3	4	Total Marks in the Exam
A	450	600	500	700	2250
B	500	650	550	800	2500
C	550	500	600	250	1900
D	600	550	400	400	1950
Total Marks by Student	2100	2300	2050	2150	

From statement (i): B is Chemistry.

From the above table: B + C – (A + D) = 2500 + 1900 – (2250 + 1950) = 200

C must be Biology. A and D were Maths and Physics in any order.

From statement (iv): Kriti and Ketty were 2 and 4. Kaamini and Clara were 1 and 3 in any order.

	1 (Clara/Kaamini)	2 (Kriti)	3 (Kaamini/Clara)	4 (Ketty)	Total Marks in the Exam
A (Maths/Physics)	450	600	500	700	2250
B (Chemistry)	500	650	550	800	2500
C (Biology)	550	500	600	250	1900
D (Physics/ Maths)	600	550	400	400	1950
Total Marks by Student	2100	2300	2050	2150	

6. If Kaamini was 1 then Kaamini's second highest score was in C (Biology). If Kaamini was 3 then Kaamini's second highest score was in B (Chemistry). Hence, option (c) is correct.
7. If Clara's second highest score was in Biology then Clara must be 1. Hence, Kaamini must be 3 and her 3rd highest score was in A which was either Maths or Physics. Hence, option (d) is correct.
8. If Kaamini's lowest score was 50% of Ketty's highest score (800). In this case, Kaamini lowest score = 400. Hence, Kaamini must be 3 and Clara must be 1. Clara's total score = 2100.
9. Clara's lowest score was 50 more than Kaamini's lowest score. It is possible only when Clara was 1 and Kaamini was 3. Hence, Clara's score in Biology = 550.
10. As per the table, the average can be either 2200 or 2175, since it is not certain without additional clues, hence the answer is option (d), cannot be determined

Solutions for Questions 11 to 15:

11. Based on the information provided you can visualise each of the following situations for arranging the people in the row:

Number of people between Suresh and Mukesh = 0

Ravi	Mukesh	Suresh	Prateek	Kashif	Neha	Mayank

Number of people between Suresh and Mukesh = 3

Ravi	Mayank	Suresh	Prateek	Kashif	Neha	Mukesh

Number of people between Suresh and Mukesh = 5

Suresh	Mayank	Ravi	Prateek	Kashif	Neha	Mukesh

It is not possible to have 2 people sitting between Suresh and Mukesh. Hence, Option (b) is the correct answer.

12. Ravi and Kashif cannot be next to each other and hence, option (c) is correct.
13. In the only possibility where Mayank sits at one of the ends, the person occupying the other end is Ravi.
14. In the possibility where Mukesh & Suresh occupy the ends, then the only pair sitting adjacent to each other from the given options is Mayank & Ravi. Hence, Option (a) is the correct answer.
15. In the possibility where Ravi does not sit at any of the ends, The person sitting between Mayank & Prateek is Ravi.

Solutions for Questions 16 to 20:

The given information can be tabulated in the following manner:

Persons	Sports	Cities
A	Chess or Tennis	Patna
B	Football or Chess	
C		
D	(X Cricket)	

From the statement-(v) it is clear that A likes Chess. Therefore B likes Football. From the statement (i), C likes Cricket, B lives in Chennai and D likes Tennis and lives in Nagpur.

Persons	Sports	Cities
A	Chess	Patna
B	Football	Chennai
C	Cricket	Delhi
D	Tennis	Nagpur

16. B. Option (a) is correct.
17. Cricket. Option (a) is correct.
18. Option (c) is correct.
19. A likes Chess and is from Patna. Hence, Option (a) is the correct answer.
20. Tennis is played by D in Nagpur.

LEVEL OF DIFFICULTY (II)

MOCK TEST PAPER 1

Solutions for Questions 1 to 5:

Ludhiana _ _ _ _ _ _ _ Kanpur

From statements (i) and (iii) we can say that Saharanpur was exactly in the middle of Ambala and Bareilly and the order of the three was 'Bareilly Saharanpur Ambala' (as he is going Saharanpur from Bareilly).

Now, three cases are possible:

Case 1: There were two stations between Bareilly and Saharanpur.

Case 2: There was no station between Bareilly and Saharanpur.

Case 3: There was exactly one station between Bareilly and Saharanpur.

Case 1: There were two stations between Bareilly and Saharanpur.

Bareilly _ _ Saharanpur _ _ Ambala.

From statement (i) which states that the train reached Moradabad from Ambala. This situation is not possible.

Case 2: There was no station between Bareilly and Saharanpur.

(a) Bareilly Saharanpur Ambala _ _ _
Two arrangements are possible:
Bareilly Saharanpur Ambala Moradabad Lucknow Unnao Roorkee
and
Bareilly Saharanpur Ambala Lucknow Moradabad Roorkee Unnao

(b) _ Bareilly Saharanpur Ambala _ _ _
This violates statement (iv).

(c) _ _ Bareilly Saharanpur Ambala _ _
This violates statement (ii).

(d) _ _ _ Bareilly Saharanpur Ambala _
This violates statement (i) and (iv).

(e) _ _ _ _ Bareilly Saharanpur Ambala
This violates statement (i) and (iv).

Case 3: There was exactly one station between Bareilly and Saharanpur.

(a) Bareilly _ Saharanpur _ Ambala _ _
Only one arrangement is possible:
Ludhiana Bareilly Lucknow Saharanpur Unnao Ambala Moradabad Roorkee Kanpur

(b) _ Bareilly _ Saharanpur _ Ambala _
This violates statements (i) and (iv) both.

(c) _ _ Bareilly _ Saharanpur _ Ambala
This violates statement (i) which states that the train reached Moradabad from Ambala.

From the above analysis following orders are possible:

I. Ludhiana Bareilly Lucknow Saharanpur Unnao Ambala Moradabad Roorkee Kanpur
II. Ludhiana Bareilly Saharanpur Ambala Moradabad Lucknow Unnao Roorkee Kanpur
III. Ludhiana Bareilly Saharanpur Ambala Lucknow Moradabad Roorkee Unnao Kanpur

1. Bareilly. Hence, option (a) is correct.
2. Either (a) or (b) is correct. Hence, option (c) is correct.
3. Option (d) is correct.
4. According to the question and statement (i), the distance between Ambala and Moradabad was not the same as that between Bareilly and Saharanpur. In this case the following arrangements are possible.
   I. Ludhiana Bareilly Lucknow Saharanpur Unnao Ambala Moradabad Roorkee Kanpur
   II. Ludhiana Bareilly Saharanpur Ambala Lucknow Moradabad Roorkee Unnao Kanpur
   For both the arrangements the station immediately after Moradabad was Roorkee. Hence, option (b) is correct.
5. As per the given possibilities, Unnao was the last station in Case 3, and in case 3, there were 3 stations between Ambala and Unnao, hence option (d) is correct

Solutions for Questions 6 to 10:

There are 4 aspects to the information, *viz*: Person, Department, Place and Company placed in. The possibility matrix given below would be the best way to start solving this:

> **Note:** M/G/Y/A/O represent Microsoft, Google, Yahoo, Amazon and Oracle (in that order). Also, P/UP/G/MP/K represent Punjab, UP, Gujarat, MP and Kerala in that order.

			M/G/Y/A/O P/UP/G/MP/K ECE	M/G/Y/A/O P/UP/G/MP/K CS	M/G/Y/A/O P/UP/G/MP/K IT	M/G/Y/A/O P/UP/G/MP/K Chemical	M/G/Y/A/O P/UP/G/MP/K Mech
M/G/Y/A/O	P/UP/G/MP/K	A					
M/G/Y/A/O	P/UP/G/MP/K	B					
M/G/Y/A/O	P/UP/G/MP/K	C					
M/G/Y/A/O	P/UP/G/MP/K	D					
M/G/Y/A/O	P/UP/G/MP/K	E					

Since most of the clues are directly given in the problem, we can start off the table with the following modifications on our first iteration with the clues:

			M/Y/A/O	G	M/Y/O	M/Y/A/O	M/Y/A/O
			G	P/UP/MP/K	P/UP/MP	P/UP/MP/K	P/UP/MP/K
			ECE	CS	IT	Chemical	Mech
M/G/Y	UP/G/MP	A	NO	NO	YES	NO	NO
O	UP/MP/K	B			NO		
M/G/Y/A	P	C			NO		
M/G/Y/A	UP/G/MP/K	D			NO		NO
M/G/Y/A	UP/G/MP/K	E			NO		

Oracle not Gujarat; Also from clue (vi): UP and Y have to be together and this combination is not in Chemical Engineering. So we can eliminate UP and Y from the Chemical column. Also A cannot be from Gujarat as Gujarat is ECE and A is from IT.

			M/Y/A	G	M/Y/O	M/A/O	M/Y/A/O
			G	P/UP/MP/K	P/UP/MP	P/MP/K	P/UP/MP/K
			ECE	CS	IT	Chemical	Mech
M/G/Y	UP/MP	A	NO	NO	YES	NO	NO
O	UP/MP/K	B			NO		
M/G/Y/A	P	C			NO		
M/G/Y/A	UP/G/MP/K	D			NO		NO
M/G/Y/A	UP/G/MP/K	E			NO		

At this stage it is evident that the UP- Yahoo combine can only be from the Mechanical department.

			A	G	M	O	Y
			G	P	MP	K	UP
			ECE	CS	IT	Chemical	Mech
M	MP	A	NO	NO	YES	NO	NO
O	K	B	NO	NO	NO	YES	NO
G/Y/A	P	C			NO		
G/Y/A	UP/G/K	D			NO		NO
G/Y/A	UP/G/K	E			NO		

At this stage of the matrix, we know that the UP–Yahoo combination has to go to either D or E. Since Mech is ruled out for D, it has to be E. This gets us to the final table as shown below.

			A	G	M	O	Y
			G	P	MP	K	UP
			ECE	CS	IT	Chemical	Mech
M	MP	A	NO	NO	YES	NO	NO
O	K	B	NO	NO	NO	YES	NO
G	P	C	NO	YES	NO	NO	NO
A	G	D	YES	NO	NO	NO	NO
Y	UP	E	NO	NO	NO	NO	YES

The answers for 124 to 127 then are:

6. E
7. Amazon
8. B works in Oracle and C in Google at salaries of 40 lakhs and 70 lakhs respectively. Sum of their salaries = 110 lakhs.
9. E works in Yahoo at 60 lakhs while the student from Kerala is B, who works for Oracle at 40 lakhs. The required difference is 20 lakhs.
10. The salary of the student who belongs to UP is 60 Lakhs and the student who works at Amazon has a salary of 50 Lakhs. Hence the sum would be 110 Lakhs.

Solutions for Questions 11 to 15:

From the statement (vi):

Amount distribution on the basis of age:

$$400 \times \frac{5}{5+3+2} = 200 \text{ lakhs}$$

Amount distribution on the basis of experience:

$$400 \times \frac{5}{5+3+2} = 120 \text{ lakhs}$$

Amount distribution on the basis of salary:

$$400 \times \frac{5}{5+3+2} = 80 \text{ lakhs}$$

From statement (i) we get the following table:

Parameter	Age (2 Crore)	Job Experience (1.2 Crore)	Salary (0.8 Crore)
Share along descending order of values of the parameters (in lakhs)	80	48	32
	60	36	24
	40	24	16
	20	12	8
Total (in lakhs)	200	120	80

11. The share of Lehman, whose share was Rs. 132 Lakh, could be obtained in two ways.
    Case I: When 132 = 60 + 48 + 24.
    Case II: When 132 = 80 + 36 + 16.
    If 60 lakh is the profit share based on age then 48 lakh is the Job share experience. Hence, the correct answer is 48 lakh.
12. The share of Lehman, whose share was Rs. 132 Lakh, could be obtained in two ways.
    Case I: When 132 = 60 + 48 + 24.
    The table given below gives the shares of the four employees along the three parameters.

Name	Age Share (in Lakhs)	Job Experience (in Lakhs)	Salary (in Lakhs)	Total (in Lakhs)
Lehman	60	48	24	132
Simon	80	24	8	112
Peter	20	36	32	88
Kriti	40	12	16	68

In this case, Peter's salary is least since, the person with the least salary gets the maximum share of profit based on salary.

Case II: When 132 = 80 + 36 + 16.
The distribution of shares along the three parameters for other employees of Mr. Michel cannot be found. So this case is not possible.
Hence, Peter's salary is the least. Option (a) is correct.

13. 24 lakhs.
14. Possible shares of Peter along the three parameters.

Parameter	Age	Job experience	Salary
Share (in Lakh)	80	12 or 24 or 36	8 or 16 or 24 or 32

From the above table, it can be observed that a sum of 144 cannot be obtained in any of the cases.
Hence, option (b) is correct.

15. As Simon's salary is the highest (8) since the person with the least salary gets the highest share, hence, option B is the right answer

Solutions for Questions 16 to 20:

Solve using constraints and checking the options for each constraint:
Constraint 1: The constraints are U and X not together
Constraint 2: A and C not together.
Constraint 3: C not with V

16. ABUXY contradicts constraint 1. Hence, this team is not possible. Thus Option (c) is correct.
17. C AND W are compulsory. Hence, of the senior faculties we need to take B. The teams possible then are: BC-WUY and BC-WXY. Hence, only 2 teams are possible. Option (b) is correct.
18. Constraint 3 clearly defines that V cannot go with C. Hence, Option (c) is correct.
19. B must compulsorily go to the new office as we can select only one out of A and C. Hence, Option (a) is correct.
20. Both i and iii are true. Hence, Option (c) is correct.

MOCK TEST PAPER 2

Solutions for Questions 1 to 5:

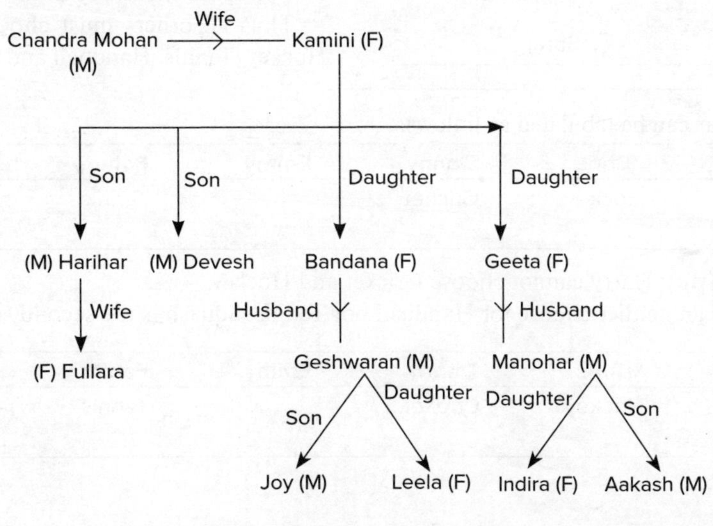

1. (b) Joy is not Geeta's child. Hence, option (b) is correct.
2. (c) Harihar. Hence, option (c) is correct.
3. (a) Geeta. Hence, option (a) is correct.
4. (b) Devesh and Geeta. Hence, option (b) is correct.
5. (b) (i) and (iii). Hence, option (b) is correct.

Solutions for Questions 6 to 10:

As each jeep had a distinct number of passengers and married couples, so we can say that each jeep must have 3, 4 or 5 passengers and must have either 0, 1 or 2 couples in it. From statement (iii), (xi) and (xiv) we can deduce that Suraj, Rani and Sunny went in the same jeep. From statements (xi), (xiii) and (xiv) we can deduce that Nikita went with Mohit. From statement (ii) and (iv) we can deduce that Alok, Vikram and Charan went in the same jeep. Further analysis leads us to a situation, where the people in the three jeeps with the definite married couples are:

5 AM – Owned by Vinay – Passengers: Vinay – Nikita, Mohit, Rohini; Number of married couples 1 or 2
6 AM – Owned by Alok – Passengers: Vikram, Alok, Charan; Number of married couples 0
7 AM – Owned by Reena – Passengers: Reena, Rani Sunny, Suraj, Vijay; Number of married couples 1 or 2

From this point based on, where we place the third married couple, it gives us three cases:

Case I: The third married couple is Suraj-Reena

5: 00 AM Bus	6: 00 AM Bus	7: 00 AM Bus
Nikita-Vinay	Vikram	Rani-Sunny
Mohit	Alok	Suraj-Reena
Rohini	Charan	Vijay

Case II: The third married couple is Vijay-Reena

5: 00 AM Bus	6: 00 AM Bus	7: 00 AM Bus
Nikita-Vinay	Vikram	Rani-Sunny
Mohit	Alok	Vijay-Reena
Rohini	Charan	Suraj

Case III: The third married couple is Mohit-Rohini

5: 00 AM Bus	6: 00 AM Bus	7: 00 AM Bus
Mohit-Rohini	Vikram	Rani-Sunny
Nikita-Vinay	Alok	Reena
	Charan	Vijay
		Suraj

The answers would then be read off the three tables and would be

6. Nikita-Vinay. Option (c) is correct.
7. 5. Option (c) is correct
8. Either 1 or 2, option (d)
9. If Rohini were married, it is definite that she would be married to Mohit. Option (a) is correct.
10. We know that the jeep which left at 6 am had 0 married couples. For the remaining 2 jeeps we do not know exactly how many couples were there. Hence, the correct answer is 1.

Solutions for Questions 11 to 15:

From statement (iv): No other athlete has opted for the sports chosen by Binny. All other athletes chose their sports from the remaining six sports.

From statement (vi): Chris, Emmy and Fahim have opted for no sport in common. Hence, each of Binny, Chris, Emmy and Fahim chose different sports.

Hence, Chris, Emmy, Fahim and Binny chose different sports.

From statement (vi): None of Chris, Emmy and Fahim chose Polo, it must be one of the sports chosen by Binny.

From statement (vi) & (iii): Binny chose Polo. Binny cannot choose any of Handball, Football and Squash.

Binny cannot chose Hockey (chosen by Harry), Cricket (Danny), Tennis (Opted by Fahim), Handball, Football and Squash (from statement (iii)). Hence, Chess must be the second sport chosen by Binny.

Thus all others must choose from Cricket, Football, Hockey, Tennis, Handball and Squash.

The results obtained so far can be tabulated as follows.

Alan	Binny	Chris	Danny	Emmy	Fahim	Granny	Harry
Squash	Polo Chess	Hockey	Cricket		Tennis	Handball	Hockey

From statement (i), (ii) and (viii): Harry cannot choose Cricket and Hockey.

From statement (iii): Harry can neither choose for Handball nor Tennis. Squash is the second sport chosen by Harry.

Alan	Binny	Chris	Danny	Emmy	Fahim	Granny	Harry
Squash	Polo Chess	Hockey	Cricket		Tennis	Handball	Hockey Squash

As no two athletes chose the same combination of sports, Chris cannot opt Squash. From statement (i) and (viii), Chris cannot choose any of Football and Cricket. As Fahim opted for Tennis, he cannot choose the same, from statement (vi): Handball is the second sport chosen by Chris.

From the above analysis, Emmy must have chosen two sports from Cricket, Football and Squash. However, from statement (i) and (ii), he can neither choose Football nor choose Squash, if he choose Cricket : Football and Squash are the sports chosen by him. From above, Cricket must be the second sport chosen by Fahim.

The analysis can be tabulated as below:

Alan	Binny	Chris	Danny	Emmy	Fahim	Granny	Harry
Squash	Polo	Hockey	Cricket	Football	Tennis	Handball	Hockey
	Chess	Handball		Squash	Cricket		Squash

From statements (i) and (viii): Danny cannot choose any of Squash, Hockey and Football. He chose either Handball or Tennis. As Fahim already chose Tennis - Cricket combination. Danny must choose Handball.

As all sports except Polo and Chess are chosen by at least two persons, Football and Tennis must be chosen by Granny and Alan. Alan can neither choose Football nor choose Hockey as Emmy has a combination of Squash - Football and Harry has a combination of Squash - Hockey and from statement (i), he cannot choose Cricket, his second sport must be Tennis. Thus Granny must choose Football.

The above analysis can be tabulated as shown below:

Alan	Binny	Chris	Danny	Emmy	Fahim	Granny	Harry
Squash	Polo	Hockey	Cricket	Football	Tennis	Handball	Hockey
Tennis	Chess	Handball	Handball	Squash	Cricket	Football	Squash

11. Football and Squash. Hence, option (a) is correct.
12. Alan. Hence, option (a) is correct.
13. Granny opted for Handball and Football Hence, option (d) is correct.
14. Handball was chosen by three persons. Hence, option (a) is correct.
15. From the table we can see that, 3 people opted for squash, and 2 people opted for Tennis. However, Alan opted for both the sports. Hence the answer would be 4.

Solutions for Questions 16 to 20:

The six surfaces can be visualized as three surfaces of 9×7, 9×5 and 7×5 (rows and columns) as shown in the figures below:

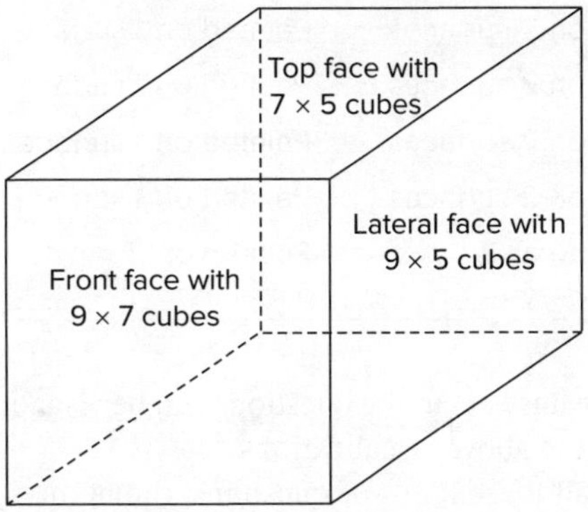

The individual surfaces would look as below:
9 rows × 7 columns (two surfaces)

Painted on all three surfaces	Painted on 2 surfaces	Painted on 2 surfaces	Painted on 2 surfaces	Painted on 2 surfaces	Painted on 2 surfaces	Painted on all three surfaces
Painted on 2 surfaces	Painted on 1 surface	Painted on 1 surface	Painted on 1 surface	Painted on 1 surface	Painted on 1 surface	Painted on 2 surfaces
Painted on 2 surfaces	Painted on 1 surface	Painted on 1 surface	Painted on 1 surface	Painted on 1 surface	Painted on 1 surface	Painted on 2 surfaces
Painted on 2 surfaces	Painted on 1 surface	Painted on 1 surface	Painted on 1 surface	Painted on 1 surface	Painted on 1 surface	Painted on 2 surfaces
Painted on 2 surfaces	Painted on 1 surface	Painted on 1 surface	Painted on 1 surface	Painted on 1 surface	Painted on 1 surface	Painted on 2 surfaces
Painted on 2 surfaces	Painted on 1 surface	Painted on 1 surface	Painted on 1 surface	Painted on 1 surface	Painted on 1 surface	Painted on 2 surfaces
Painted on 2 surfaces	Painted on 1 surface	Painted on 1 surface	Painted on 1 surface	Painted on 1 surface	Painted on 1 surface	Painted on 2 surfaces

Painted on 2 surfaces	Painted on 1 surface	Painted on 1 surface	Painted on 1 surface	Painted on 1 surface	Painted on 1 surface	Painted on 2 surfaces
Painted on all three surfaces	Painted on 2 surfaces	Painted on 2 surfaces	Painted on 2 surfaces	Painted on 2 surfaces	Painted on 2 surfaces	Painted on all three surfaces

9 rows × 5 columns (two surfaces)

Painted on all 3 surfaces	Painted on 2 surfaces	Painted on 2 surfaces	Painted on 2 surfaces	Painted on all 3 surfaces
Painted on 2 surfaces	Painted on 1 surface	Painted on 1 surface	Painted on 1 surface	Painted on 2 surfaces
Painted on 2 surfaces	Painted on 1 surface	Painted on 1 surface	Painted on 1 surface	Painted on 2 surfaces
Painted on 2 surfaces	Painted on 1 surface	Painted on 1 surface	Painted on 1 surface	Painted on 2 surfaces
Painted on 2 surfaces	Painted on 1 surface	Painted on 1 surface	Painted on 1 surface	Painted on 2 surfaces
Painted on 2 surfaces	Painted on 1 surface	Painted on 1 surface	Painted on 1 surface	Painted on 2 surfaces
Painted on 2 surfaces	Painted on 1 surface	Painted on 1 surface	Painted on 1 surface	Painted on 2 surfaces
Painted on 2 surfaces	Painted on 1 surface	Painted on 1 surface	Painted on 1 surface	Painted on 2 surfaces
Painted on all 3 surfaces	Painted on 2 surfaces	Painted on 2 surfaces	Painted on 2 surfaces	Painted on all 3 surfaces

AND 7 rows × 5 columns (two surfaces)

Painted on all 3 surfaces	Painted on 2 surfaces	Painted on 2 surfaces	Painted on 2 surfaces	Painted on all 3 surfaces
Painted on 2 surfaces	Painted on 1 surface	Painted on 1 surface	Painted on 1 surface	Painted on 2 surfaces
Painted on 2 surfaces	Painted on 1 surface	Painted on 1 surface	Painted on 1 surface	Painted on 2 surfaces
Painted on 2 surfaces	Painted on 1 surface	Painted on 1 surface	Painted on 1 surface	Painted on 2 surfaces
Painted on 2 surfaces	Painted on 1 surface	Painted on 1 surface	Painted on 1 surface	Painted on 2 surfaces
Painted on 2 surfaces	Painted on 1 surface	Painted on 1 surface	Painted on 1 surface	Painted on 2 surfaces
Painted on all 3 surfaces	Painted on 2 surfaces	Painted on 2 surfaces	Painted on 2 surfaces	Painted on all 3 surfaces

The answers to the questions can be visualized based on the above visualizations:

16. In all these kinds of questions, the number of cubes which would be painted on three sides would always be the corner cubes. There would be 8 corner cubes.
Option (a) is correct.

17. The two faces colored cubes would be the cubes along each edge (except for the corner cubes). It can be visualized that the top edges of the cube would have $7 + 7 + 3 + 3 = 20$ cubes and the bottom edges would also have the same number (i.e. 20 cubes).
The vertical edges would have a further $7 + 7 + 7 + 7 = 28$ cubes.
Out of the total of 68 cubes which are on the edges, 8 cubes would be corner cubes. Hence, the number of cubes painted on two sides would be $68 - 8 = 60$.
Option (a) is correct.

18. The number of one face colored cubes would be:
On the front and back surfaces: $7 \times 5 + 7 \times 5 = 70$ cubes. (you can remember this as (m-2) × (n-2) where m and n are the number of rows and columns on the surface in question)
On the top and bottom surfaces: $5 \times 3 + 5 \times 3 = 30$ cubes.
On the lateral surfaces: $7 \times 3 + 7 \times 3 = 42$ cubes.
Thus a total of 142 cubes would have one side painted.
Option (a) is correct.

19. The number of cubes with no face colored would be given by $7 \times 5 \times 3 = 105$ [which can again be remembered as (m-2)(n-2)(p-2) where m, n and p are the number of parts in which the cube surfaces have been cut - in this case m = 9, n = 7 and p = 5].
Alternately, you could also have solved this using: All cubes - cubes with 3 sides colored - cubes with 2 sides colored - cubes with 1 side colored = 315 - 8 - 60 - 142 = 105.
Option (c) is correct.

20. The cubes along the vertical edges would be painted both red and green. There are 7 such cubes (with 2 faces colored) on each of the 4 edges of the cuboid. Thus, the total number of cubes which would be

painted on two sides (in red and green) would be $7 \times 4 = 28$. Option (b) is correct.

Short cut: No. of cubes with no color = (m - 2)(n - 2)(p - 2) where m, n, p are the number of cuts on each side where m, n and $p \geq 3$

No. of 1 side colored cubes: $2 \times ((m - 2)(n - 2) + (n - 2)(p - 2) + (p - 2)(m - 2))$

MOCK TEST PAPER 3

Solutions for Questions 1 to 5:

1. From statement (ii) all those who like Task C also like task D but the reverse may or may not be true. Hence, option (a) is correct.
2. From statement (i) and (iii), all those who like B also like E and those who like task E do not like task C. Hence, option (b) is correct.
3. From statement (iii), option d must be false. Hence, option (d) is correct.
4. All those who have C would have D. And all those who have D will also have F. Hence from the options given, Option (d) satisfies the given conditions.
5. Since task E & C do not go together as given in the condition, Deepak should take task C. Hence, Option (c) is the correct answer.

Solutions for Questions for 6 to 10:

Total number of marbles distributed according to the academic grades = $400 \times \frac{5}{5+3+2} = 200$.

Out of these 200 marbles, 80, 60, 40 and 20 marbles were distributed amongst the four children, in decreasing order of their academic grades.

Similarly for the parameter of seniority: total marbles allotted were 120, with distribution of 48, 36, 24 and 12 marbles among the children in decreasing orer of seniority.

Similarly for the family wealth parameter, the total number of marbles allotted were 80, with distribution of 32, 24, 16 and 8 marbles among the children in increasing order of family wealth.

6. According to the question, the number of marbles received by C was 132. This amount could be obtained in the following ways:
   132 = 60 + 48 + 24 or 80 + 36 + 16.
   Case I: For the distribution 132 = 60 + 48 + 24. Thinking through the other numbers available, we can build 112 of A only by 80 + 24 + 8. This leaves only 20 + 36 + 32 = 88 (the only way to build 88 for D). Consecutively, the numbers for B would be 40 + 12 + 16. The following table gives the share of the four children along the given parameters.

Name	Academic Grades	Seniority	Family wealth	Total
A	80	24	8	112
B	40	12	16	68
C	60	48	24	132
D	20	36	32	88

In this case A's share of the number of marbles distributed based on the parameter of family wealth is the least. Hence, A's family wealth must be the highest.

Case II: The distribution 132 = 80 + 36 + 16 is not possible at all because in this case the distribution break up of the 112 marbles for A, cannot be created in any way.

Thus, only one of the two cases exists and hence, the only person whose family wealth can be the highest is A.

7. If D had the highest academic grades, then because of this he will get 80 marbles. As his seniority is not the highest one, so possible share because of his seniority was 12 or 24 or 36. As we have no information about the family wealth of D so possible share because of his family wealth was 8 or 16 or 24 or 32 (in lakh).
   From the above analysis, we can observe that a total 144 marbles for D is not possible here. So this is the correct option.
8. As C's share was 92 marbles, this can be achieved by the following way:
   92 = 60 (academic grades) + 24 (Seniority) + 8 (family wealth)
   92 = 40 (academic grades) + 36 (Seniority) + 16 (family wealth)
   92 = 20 (academic grades) + 48 (Seniority) + 24 (family wealth)
   Here we can see that C's share because of his seniority was 24, 36 or 48. Since, higher the seniority, more the number of marbles allocated, it is clear that since C cannot be allocated 12 marbles, his seniority position cannot be 4th amongst the 4 students.
9. Under the given condition, B & D would receive 16 and 32 for their family wealth respectively. Hence, the answer is 16 + 32 = 48.
10. After C gives the marbles to B, B would have 36 marbles for seniority but D also has 36 marbles. Hence, option (d) is the correct answer.

Solutions for Questions 11 to 15:

Let we represent Parmesh, Quran, Rahim, Salim, Tariq, Ulaal by P, Q, R, S, T, U respectively. Each player played 5 games.

According to the question the number of games won by each person is distinct, therefore P, Q, R, S, T and U won 5, 4, 3, 2, 1 and 0 games in the whole tournament not necessarily in that particular order.

The player who won 5 games has won against all the other players. The player who won 4 games won against all the players except the player who won 5 games. Similarly, the player who won 3 games has won against the players who won 2, 1 and 0 games.

From statement (iii): U lost against S and R. Hence, U won only 3 games.

R and S must have won 4 and 5 games not necessarily in the same order.

From statement (iv): T won 2 or more games. So, we can conclude that U won 3 games and T won 2 games. Hence, P and Q won 0 and 1 game (in any order).

From statement (i): Q won its game against P. So, Q won 1 game and P won 0 games.

From the above analysis we can draw the following table:

Player	Numbers of Games Won
Parmesh	0
Quran	1
Rahim	4 or 5
Salim	5 or 4
Tariq	2
Ulaal	3

11. The number of games won by Parmesh is 0.
12. Either Rahim or Salim won 5 games. Hence, option (d) is correct.
13. Given that Rahim won four games and got 11 coins and won exactly four games in the whole tournament. Parmesh got no coin because he did not win the game. Since, S won all the five games then he must have necessarily got 10 coins. (Two coins in each game because in all the games minimum point scored by the losing player was 1).
    $47 = 0 + 11 + 10 + T + U + Q$
    $\Rightarrow T + U + Q = 26$ which is only possible when Tariq gets 10 coins, Quran gets 6 coins and Ullal gets 10 coins. Hence, Tariq got 10 coins.
14. Quran got 6 coins.
15. From the data obtained, we see that Tariq won against Quran & Parmesh. Hence, the answer for the question is Quran.

Solutions for Questions 16 to 20:

16. The questions are approached by tabulating all the indirect and direct clues in the following table:

Order	Manager	Duration of Meeting	Gap taken by Mark
1	C	9:00 AM TO 9:30 AM	25
2	G	9:55 AM TO 10:25 AM	25
3	F	10:50 AM TO 11:20 AM	25
4	A	11:45 AM TO 12:15 PM	25
5	E	12:40 PM TO 1:10 PM	50
6	D/B	2:00 PM TO 2:30 PM	25
7	B/D	2:55 PM TO 3:25 PM	-

Now we can answer the questions:

Hence option (b) is the correct answer.

17. The time will be 3:50 pm. Hence option (d) is the correct answer.
18. Mark meets A at number 4.
19. Mark could have possibly met with B between 2 pm & 3:30 pm. Hence, Option (c) is the correct answer.
20. Mark meets G after C. Hence, Option (d) is the correct answer.

MOCK TEST PAPER 4

Solutions for Questions 1 to 5:

From the given information it is clear that four numbers which must have been the values of money spent would be: 2517 (clue 4), 2234 (clue 1), 1340 (clue 2) and 1193 (clue 1 again).

We need to work out the fifth value.

Also, since Chandrima is the least and Sumitra is the max and since one woman spent 1378 more than Chandrima a little bit of introspection will give you the following possibilities for the five numbers:

Possibility 1: If 1193 is the least value

A The five numbers are:

1193, 1340, 2234, 2517 and 2571 (since $2571 = 1193 + 1378$)

Possibility 2: If 2517 is the maximum value

1139 (since $1139 = 2517 - 1378$), 1193, 1340, 2234 and 2517

Accordingly we have the following possible arrangements for the five women and the amount they spent:

	Possibility 1	Possibility 2
A (x 2517)	2234	
C (least)	1193	
D (x 1340)	2517	
H	1340	
S (Max)	2571	

Note: The thought structure for placing the 5 values with 5 women in the case of possibility 1, goes as follows:

Step 1:

A	
C	1193
D	
H	
S	2571

After Placing the least and maximum.

Step 2: 2234 should be before 1193 and Deepika has not spent 1340.

A	2234
C	1193
D	2517
H	1340
S	2571

A close look at the above table shows that clue 5 (H > D) is not obeyed by this arrangement. Hence, this solution is wrong.

We thus move into possibility 2 i.e.:

1139, 1193, 1340, 2234, 2517, are the five values. The thought structure for placing the five numbers for the five women goes as:

Step 1: Place the maximum and least values for S and C respectively.

A	(x 2517)	
C	(Least)	1139
D	(x 1340)	
H		
S	(Maximum) 2517	

This leaves us with 1340, 1193 and 2234 to place.

Step 2: We need to keep 2 constraints in mind while doing this.

(a) 2234 has to come before 1193 (remember not = immediately before). At the same time H > D. (Clue 5)

We can arrange 2234 before 1193 in 3 ways as shown below and then 1340 automatically falls into the vacant space.

1

A	2234
C	1139
D	1193
H	1340
S	2517

2

(Not possible since Deepika cannot be 1340)

A	2234
C	1139
D	1340
H	1193
S	2517

3

(Not possible since H should be greater than D).

A	1340
C	1139
D	2234
H	1193
S	2517

Hence, the only possible arrangement is as in (1) above.

Hence the answers are:

1. (b) Heena spent ₹ 1340.
2. (a) ₹ 1139
3. (c) Deepika
4. Amount spent by Deepika = 1193
   Amount spent by Sumitra = 2517
   Difference = 1324
5. Aradhana spent ₹ 2234 which was the second highest amount.

Solutions for Questions 6 to 10:

Information in statements (ii) to (vii) can be tabulated in the following form:

Slot Timing	Monday	Tuesday	Wednesday	Thursday	Friday	Saturday
12:00-1:00			A		A	
1:00- 2:00			A		A	
2:00-3:00			C		C	
3:30-4:30			B	B	B	B
4:30-5:30			C		C	
5:30-6:30	B		B		B	

From statement (iii), ('A' did not take the last slot on any day), the last slot on Tuesday, Thursday and Saturday must have been taken by C. Consequently, C cannot take the 5th slot on Thursday and neither can it go to A (since A would always need two consecutive slots). Hence, we can slot in B for Thursday's fifth slot. After this, if we look through the remaining slots on Thursday, we would see that A can only be on the 2nd and 3rd slots (as we cannot allocate the 1st and 2nd slots to A on Thursday, since 1 and 2 have already been allocated to A on Wednesday and Friday). Also, since A has the same slots on Thursday and Saturday we can put A's slots on Saturday too. Exactly, the same thinking for Saturday, gives us the following table:

Slot Timing	Monday	Tuesday	Wednesday	Thursday	Friday	Saturday
12:00-1:00			A	C	A	C
1:00- 2:00			A	A	A	A
2:00-3:00			C	A	C	A
3:30-4:30			B	B	B	B
4:30-5:30			C	B	C	B
5:30-6:30	B	C	B	C	B	C

We can now focus on finding the schedules for Monday and Tuesday. The following deductions follow:

(i) We know that C took the third slot on four days. Consequently, C must be fitted into the third slot on Monday and Tuesday.

(ii) Consequently, two A's can only be scheduled in the 4th and 5th slot on these days.

(iii) Then we get the order of the first two sessions as C, B on Monday and B, B on Tuesday.

The final table will look as follows:

Slot Timing	Monday	Tuesday	Wednesday	Thursday	Friday	Saturday
12:00-1:00	C	B	A	C	A	C
1:00- 2:00	B	B	A	A	A	A
2:00-3:00	C	C	C	A	C	A
3:30-4:30	A	A	B	B	B	B
4:30-5:30	A	A	C	B	C	B
5:30-6:30	B	C	B	C	B	C

The answers are:

6. 1
7. C
8. On 1 day (Tuesday)
9. C
10. On Monday, B had the second and the last slot which were furthest during the given period. Hence, the answer is Monday.

Solutions for Questions 11 to 15:

Possible investment values: 16, 20, 24, 28, 32, 36 (in Lakhs). Sales values: 96, 112, 64, 72, 80 (in Lakhs) from information (i) & (ii), we get the following table:

Sales (in Lakh)	Investment (in Lakh)	Profit Ratio
96	24/32	4/3
112	28	4
64	16/32	4/2
72	24/36	3/2
80	20	4

From statement (iii):

The sales of businessman of Manakpur was 96 lakhs and sales of Chris was 72 lakhs.

From statement (vii): Ben's sales is either 72 lakhs or 80 lakhs. (72 = 64 + 8, 80 = 72 + 8).

But from statement (vii): Ben's invested the least amount which could be either 16 or 20.

If Ben's investment was 16 lakhs then his profit Ratio would greater than 4 (72/16 > 4 and 80/16 > 4). So this condition is not possible.

If Ben's invested 20 lakhs then his sales must be 80 lakhs.
Hence, Ben's investment = 20 lakhs.
Ben's sales = 80 lakhs.
Every other businessman invested more than Rs. 20 lakhs.
Hence, the person whose sales was 64 lakhs invested Rs. 32 lakhs.

From the above discussion we can draw the following table:

Sales (in lakh)	Investment (in lakhs)	Profit Ratio
96	24/32	4/3
112	28	4
64	32	2
72	36/24	2/3
80	20	4

From statement (v):

Sales of businessman of Kamalpur = 80 lakhs.

From statement (iv):

The sales value of the businessmen of Brindapur and Raigad were any two among 64, 72 and 112 (lakhs).

The sales value (in lakhs Rs.) of David and Elec any two among 64, 96 and 112.

We can conclude that sales value of businessmen of Brindapur and Raigad were 64 lakhs or 72 lakhs (in any order).

Sales of David and Elec were 96 and 112 lakhs (in any order).

From statement (vi): Elec was not from Manakpur. So David was from Manakpur and earned 96 lakhs.

⇒ Elec earned 112 lakhs.
Alan earned 64 lakhs.
Chris must have setup his business in Raigad.

⇒ Elec setup his business in Palampur.

From the above analysis, we can draw the following table.

Businessman	Place of Business	Amount Earned	Amount Invested
Alan	Brindapur	64 lakhs	32 lakhs
Ben	Kamalpur	80 lakhs	20 lakhs
Chris	Raigad	72 lakhs	36/24 lakhs
David	Manakpur	96 lakhs	24/32 lakhs
Elec	Palampur	112 lakhs	28 lakhs

11. Elec. Hence, option (d) is correct.
12. 80 - 72 = 8 lakhs.
13. 20 lakhs.
14. Chris. Hence, option (b) is correct.
15. This scenario is only possible if the Amount invested by Chris is 24L and that by David is 32L. Therefore, the difference in amount is 8L. Hence, the answer is 800000.

Solutions for Questions 16 to 20:

From statements (i) and (vi):

Day	Person	Company
Monday	A	
Tuesday		
Wednesday		
Thursday		
Friday		Cisco
Saturday		Microsoft

From statement (ii) and (iii): There are two cases possible:

	Tuesday	Wednesday	Thursday	Friday	Saturday
Case1	B/D	D/B	E/C	F	C/E
Case2	E/C	F	C/E	B/D	D/B

F was working in Yahoo therefore case 1 is not possible. We can tabulate the above analysis in the following manner:

Day	Person	Company
Monday	A	
Tuesday	E/C	
Wednesday	F	Yahoo
Thursday	C/E	
Friday	B/D	Cisco
Saturday	D/B	Microsoft

From statement (v): C attended the conference just after the person who was working in FB.

Day	Person	Company
Monday	A	FB
Tuesday	C	Google
Wednesday	F	Yahoo
Thursday	E	TCS
Friday	B/D	Cisco
Saturday	D/B	Microsoft

16. E was working in TCS. Option (d) is correct.
17. Either B or D. Option (d) is correct.
18. Required average = $(1 + 5 + 6)/3 = 4$.
19. E works in TCS.
20. A goes to work at FB on Monday.

MOCK TEST PAPER 5

Solutions for Questions 1 to 5:

Based on an initial reading of the question set it is clear that there are three variables, which are being measured. These are the order in which the children are born, the game they play and the School they go to. Besides, the sex of the child is another variable being measured. Also, the boys can be represented by A, M, R, N, S while the girls can be represented by T, K, J. Based on these realisations, the starting grid structure for the given question would look like below:

Order of Birth	Name of Child	Sex of Child	Sport	School
1				
2				
3				
4				
5				
6				
7				
8				

With this starting point we start using the information in the question. The first direct clue is Saurav is the eldest while Janki is the youngest. Besides, we also know that Mr. Mansingh first had three sons and then had two daughters in succession. With this information placed into the grid, we would get the following:

Order of Birth	Name of Child	Son/ Daughter	Sport	School
1	Saurav	Son		
2		Son		
3		Son		
4		Daughter		
5		Daughter		
6		Son		
7		Son		
8	Janaki	Daughter		

We then know that Kuntala is the eldest daughter and she plays chess and that Rohit was born just before Janaki, and he plays hockey. Also, Tamanna and Rohit study at St. Stefan.

Order of Birth	Name of Child	Son/ Daughter	Sport	School
1	Saurav	Son		

Order of Birth	Name of Child	Son/ Daughter	Sport	School
2		Son		
3		Son		
4	Kuntala	Daughter	Chess	
5	Tamanna	Daughter		St. Stefan
6		Son		
7	Rohit	Son	Hockey	St. Stefan
8	Janaki	Daughter		

At this point, from the statement that three of the children are studying at Trinity school and three are studying at St. Stefan, we also know that two students are studying at Mansarovar. Also, we know that these two must be born in succession and since Mansarovar school offers only cricket it follows that Mahi and Nilesh must be from the Mansarovar school and that they must be placed second and third in the birth order. This also means that Arun's position gets fixed as the sixth child.

We also know that Trinity only offers chess (as it is given that "these schools offer no other games.) The table evolves to:

Order of Birth	Name of Child	Son/ Daughter	Sport	School
1	Saurav	Son	Chess	Trinity
2	Mahi/ Nilesh	Son	Cricket	Mansarovar
3	Nilesh/ Mahi	Son	Cricket	Mansarovar
4	Kuntala	Daughter	Chess	Trinity
5	Tamanna	Daughter		St. Stefan
6	Arun	Son	Football	St. Stefan
7	Rohit	Son	Hockey	St. Stefan
8	Janaki	Daughter	Chess	Trinity

The answers can be read off the table:

1. Arun was born sixth. Option (c) is correct.
2. Saurav studies at Trinity. Option (a) is correct.
3. Tamanna's game we cannot determine. Option (d) is correct.
4. Kunatala and Arun were not born in succession. Option (b) is correct.
5. Since the question is asking us to find out the thinnest person we can keep our processing focused on doing so; hence we concentrate on the fatter/thinner clues ignoring the taller/shorter clues.

In terms of fatness/thinness, the following structures exist:

D > E (from the first sentence in the question)

Also, B > A > D (from the second sentence in the question)

Combining the two we get:

B > A > D > E

The third sentence tells us that Eswar is thinner than Charu, who is thinner than Debu. This means D > C > E.

Combining these we get:

B > A > D > C > E

Hence, Eswar is the thinnest. Option (d) is correct.

Solutions for Questions 6 to 10:

From (i), (ii), (v) and (x) we can deduce that Jackie, Jake, Jorry belonged to the same team, while Ozeal, Oliver, Rashid and Bindu belonged to the other team.

From statement (iii) and (x): Sum of total marks scored by Jackie, Jake and Jorry = 2 + 8 + 9 = 19.

Sum of total marks scored by Oliver, Rashid and Bindu = 4 + 4 + 3 = 11.

As we know no one scored more than Luke, so he must have scored at least 9 points. From statement (iv) his team obtained 25 points, so he must have been a member of the team that comprised Oliver, Ozeal, Rashid and Bindu. From here we can deduce the members of the two teams:

USA: Oliver, Ozeal, Rashid, Bindu and Luke.

UK: Jackie, Jake, Jorry, Kevin and Chris.

Let the number of 2 marks and 3 marks questions answered by both the teams be x and y respectively.

From statements (viii) and (ix): $x + y = 22$ and $2x + 3y = 56$. By solving, the two equations we get: $x = 10$, $y = 12$.

The above analysis and the statements (i), (ii), (iii) and (x) can lead us to the following tables:

Team USA:

Name of player	Total number of 2 marks questions answered correctly	Total number of 3 marks questions answered correctly	Total score
Oliver	2	0	4
Ozeal			
Rashid	2	0	4
Bindu	0	1	3
Luke			

Team UK:

Name of player	Total number of 2 marks questions answered correctly	Total number of 3 marks questions answered correctly	Total score
Jackie	3 or 0	1 or 3	9
Jorry	1	0	2
Jake	4 or 1	0 or 2	8
Kevin	2	1	7
Chris			

Total marks scored by Luke, Ozeal and Chris = 56 – (4 + 4 + 3 + 9 + 2 + 8 + 7) = 56 – 37 = 19.

From statement (iv), Luke answered only advanced level question, so he must have scored either 9, 12 or 15.

From statement (vii), there are only three students who did not answer any advanced level question and these students must have been Oliver, Rashid and Jorry.

So Ozeal and Chris scored at least one advanced level question each i.e. 6 marks. So Luke scored only 9 marks (because if he scored 12 marks, then Ozeal and Chris scored 7 marks together which is not possible with this constraint. If Luke scored 15 marks then rest of two must have scored 4 marks together which is again not possible because Chris and Ozeal scored 6 marks together just by answering advanced level questions).

Marks obtained by Ozeal = 25 – (4 + 4 + 3 + 9) = 5.

Marks obtained by Chris = 56 – 25 – (9 + 2 + 8 + 7) = 5.

Based on these deductions, we have the final tables that look as follows:

Team USA:

Name of player	Total number of 2 marks questions	Total number of 3 marks questions	Total score
Oliver	2	0	4
Ozeal	1	1	5
Rashid	2	0	4
Bindu	0	1	3
Luke	0	3	9

Team UK:

Name of player	Total number of 2 marks questions	Total number of 3 marks questions	Total score
Jackie	0	3	9
Jorry	1	0	2
Jake	1	2	8
Kevin	2	1	7
Chris	1	1	5

The answers can then be read off the tables:

6. $9 + 2 + 8 + 7 + 5 = 31$

7. (c)

8. $3 \times (1 + 1 + 3) = 15$

9. 4 : 5 : 4

10. $2 \times (0 + 1) = 2.$

Solutions for Questions 11 to 15:

In these questions there are two types of clues given, since there are multiple objects in the questions which are to be arranged in a particular fashion. First are the primary clues and then are the secondary clues.

To solve the questions first use all the primary clues to create a clear structure of the situation in the following manner:

Let heights be H1 to H6. Where H1 being the tallest and H6 being the shortest.

Since Suresh is wearing orange coloured jacket, he is standing between Sachin and Yuvraj, positions of all the three can be [Sachin, Suresh, Yuvraj] or [Yuvraj, Suresh, Sachin]. Now since Rahul is wearing yellow-coloured jacket and is exactly opposite Sachin and Saurav, the person wearing the green coloured jacket is exactly opposite Suresh, the positions of the persons may be given as:

Possibility 1

Rahul (Yellow)	Saurav (Green)	Mahendra (Blue)
	ROAD	
Sachin (White)	Suresh (Orange)	Yuvraj (Red)

Possibility 2

Mahendra (Blue)	Saurav (Green)	Rahul (Yellow)
	ROAD	
Yuvraj (Red)	Suresh (Orange)	Sachin (White)

It is evident that Mahendra is opposite to Yuvraj. Now, since Mahendra is opposite to the person wearing red-coloured jacket, it is given that Sachin is wearing white coloured jacket hence, by elimination Mahendra is the person wearing blue-coloured jacket.

Delving into the heights of the six enemies, the height of Mahendra is H1. The shortest person is Suresh because he is opposite to the person wearing green jacket. Hence Suresh is the shortest i.e. H6.

As Sachin is taller than Rahul but shorter than Yuvraj and Saurav this means that Rahul and Sachin are H5 and H4. But heights of Saurav and Yuvraj are still unknown.

We can tabulate all the information into a table:

Person	Colour	Height
Sachin	White	H4
Saurav	Green	H2/H3
Rahul	Yellow	H5
Yuvraj	Red	H3/H2
Mahendra	Blue	H1
Suresh	Orange	H6

11. Hence, option (a) is the correct answer.
12. Option (c) is the correct answer.
13. From the table, it is clear that Mahendra was the tallest person.
14. In both the possibilities, Mahendra lives opposite the person who lives in a red colored house.
15. Sachin wears a white colored jacket. Hence, option (d) is the correct answer.

Solutions for Questions 16 and 20:

From Statements (i), (iii) and (v), the number of games played by three of the teams were 14, 20 and 22.

Thus, the sum of the number of games played by the other two teams = 80 - 14 - 200 - 22 = 24.

Since two of the teams played an equal number of games, the games played by the five teams were either 10, 14, 14, 20 and 22 or 12, 12, 14, 20 and 22.

From Statement (ii), China played 10 games more than Singapore; therefore, the number of games played by China was either 20 or 22. However, from Statement (v), Thailand played 22 games. Therefore, the number of games played by China was 20 and Singapore was 10.

The teams headed by Captain Karen and Captain Paulie played 14 games each and the one headed by Captain Chang played 20 games. From Statement (iv), Captain Brock's team must have played 10 games.

The final table is given below:

Teams	China	Japan	South Korea	Singapore	Thailand
Number of games	20	14	14	10	22
Captain	Chang	Karen	Paulie	Brock	.

16. (d) China played 20 matches which is double of what Singapore played, i.e.,10.
17. (c) South Korea - Paulie - 20 is the wrong combination.
18. Both these countries played an equal number of matches. Hence, the difference is 0
19. Chang captained China. Hence, Option (a) is the correct answer.
20. Singapore played 10 matches.

MOCK TEST PAPER 6

Solutions for Questions 1 to 5:

From statement C it is clear that Ms. Maharashtra was definitely not runner-up and from statements D, H and E, Ms. West Bengal and Ms. Andhra were not the runner-up. Hence, Ms. Uttar Pradesh was the runner-up and she wore the green saree. From statements E and I, Ms West Bengal does not wear the yellow saree. Hence, Ms Andhra wore the yellow Saree. From the above analysis we can form the following table:

Contestant	Color of Saree
Andhra Pradesh	Yellow
Uttar Pradesh	Green
West Bengal	Red
Maharashtra	White

According to the question who wore yellow saree won the contest hence, Ms. Andhra won the contest.

From statement (vi) and (ix) following two combinations are possible.

1	2	3	4	
Maharashtra	UP	West Bengal	Andhra Pradesh	Possibility 1
Andhra Pradesh	West Bengal	UP	Maharashtra	Possibility 2

1. Ms. West Bengal. Hence, option (b) is correct.
2. Ms. Uttar Pradesh and Ms. Andhra Pradesh. Hence, option (c) is correct.
3. Yellow. Hence, option (a) is correct.
4. Ms. Uttar Pradesh. Hence, option (c) is correct.
5. In both the possibilities, Ms West Bengal was sitting adjacent to Ms Andhra, the winner, and she was wearing a red color saree. Hence, the answer is Red.

Solutions for Questions 6 to 10:

The Total number of games played in the tournament = $7c_2 = \frac{7!}{2!5!} = 21.$

According to the statement (i), an equal number of matches are played on each of these three days. Hence, the number of matches played on each day = 21/3 = 7.

Each player won a different number of matches, so they must be distinct integers from 0 to 6 i.e. somebody won all 6 matches, some won 5, someone else won 4, 3, 2, 1 and 0 respectively. Now we can form the following table from the information given in the question:

	Nadal	Djokovic	Rogers	Andre	William	Chris	Murray
Nadal					Win (Friday)	Win (Saturday)	Lose (Saturday)
Djokovic			Win (Friday)	Win (Friday)	Win (Friday)	Win (Saturday)	Win (Saturday)
Rogers		Lose (Friday)		Lose (Saturday)	Win (Friday)	Win (Thursday)	Lose (Saturday)
Andre		Lose (Friday)	Win (Saturday)		Win (Saturday)	Win (Thursday)	
William	Lose (Friday)	Lose (Friday)	Lose (Friday)	Lose (Saturday)		Win (Thursday)	
Chris	Lose (Saturday)	Lose (Saturday)	Lose (Thursday)	Lose (Thursday)	Lose (Thursday)		Lose (Thursday)
Murray	Win (Saturday)	Lose (Saturday)	Win (Saturday)			Win (Thursday)	

Here,

	B
A	Win (Thursday)

means A won against B on Thursday, which also means that B lost to A on Thursday.

From this point, the following deductions make us reach the answers:

Deduction 1: As per statement (viii), Murray wins two matches on Friday. Hence, these two matches must be against Andre and William (the only two players he has not played against on the other days).

Deduction 2: Nadal must have played against Djokovic, Rogers and Andre on Thursday as the information is given only about 4 matches for Thursday, while we already have the information about all 7 matches on Friday and Saturday.

Deduction 3: Rogers must have lost to Nadal as it is given that Rogers did not win more than 1 match on Thursday.

Deduction 4: Djokovic must have won against Nadal on Friday as each of the other six players has lost at least 1 game – hence only Djokovic can fill in the slot of the player who wins 6 matches.

From the above analysis we can conclude that the number of matches won by Murray, Chris, William, Djokovic and Rogers must be 5, 0, 1, 6 and 2, respectively. However, we cannot determine the winner of the game between Nadal and Andre as it could be won by either – without contradicting any of the conditions in the problem.

The final table would look as follows:

	Nadal	Djokovic	Rogers	Andre	William	Chris	Murray
Nadal		Lose (Thursday)	Win (Thursday)	Can't be determined	Win (Friday)	Win (Saturday)	Lose (Saturday)
Djokovic	Win (Thursday)		Win (Friday)	Win (Friday)	Win (Friday)	Win (Saturday)	Win (Saturday)
Rogers	Lose (Thursday)	Lose (Friday)		Lose (Saturday)	Win (Friday)	Win (Thursday)	Lose (Saturday)
Andre	Can't be determined	Lose (Friday)	Win (Saturday)		Win (Saturday)	Win (Thursday)	Lose (Friday)
William	Lose (Friday)	Lose (Friday)	Lose (Friday)	Lose (Saturday)		Win (Thursday)	Lose (Friday)
Chris	Lose (Saturday)	Lose (Saturday)	Lose (Thursday)	Lose (Thursday)	Lose (Thursday)		Lose (Thursday)
Murray	Win (Saturday)	Lose (Saturday)	Win (Saturday)	Win (Friday)	Win (Friday)	Win (Thursday)	

6. Required answer = 3 + 4 = 7. Hence, option (b) is correct.

7. 2.

8. On Friday Djokovic wins exactly three matches. On the rest of the days, no player wins more than two matches. Hence, the correct answer must be 1.

9. Djokovic.

10. As we don't have enough information, the answer is (d).

Solutions for Questions 11 to 15:

The clues in the questions that can be decoded directly for tabulation will lead to the following table:

Table 1 for Questions 11 and 12

Station	Get In	Get Down
Base Station	????	XXX
Kalyan	????	XXX
Thane	XXX	????
Kurla	Only Gavli	Biswas and Devendra
Dadar	Amar	Only Ekta
Mumbai Central	XXX	Amar, Gavli and Calvin

Now, from second clue Firoz gets down at Thane and he got in either at the base station or at Kalyan. Now Since Firoz got down at Thane and he had got in with Calvin then it means that both Calvin and Firoz got in either at base station or at Kalyan. As Biswas and Devendra got down at station Kurla then they too have got in either at the base station or at Kalyan. It is given that Ekta got in with two other persons i.e., in a group of three persons. So, Ekta must have got in at the base station.

We can tabulate the conclusions as:

Table 2 for Questions 11 and 12

Station	Get In	Get Down
Base Station	Ekta and (Calvin, Firoz) or (Biswas, Devendra)	XXX
Kalyan	(Calvin, Firoz) or (Biswas, Devendra)	XXX
Thane	XXX	Only Firoz
Kurla	Only Gavli	Biswas and Devendra
Dadar	Amar	Only Ekta
Mumbai Central	XXX	Amar, Gavli and Calvin

Now we can answer the questions:

11. Option (c) is the correct answer.
12. Ekta travels from base station to Kalyan, Thane, Kurla and gets down at Dadar. Hence, option (d) is correct.
13. Devendra got down with Biswas at Kurla. Hence, option (a) is the correct answer.
14. Amar boarded the train at Dadar. Hence, option (d) is the correct answer.
15. Gavli passed only through Dadar. Hence, the answer is 1.

Solutions for Questions 16 to 20:

As no friend spent an equal number of years in any two states, each friend must have spent at least 12 years (2 + 4 + 6) in the three states together.

The total number of years spent by the four friends in the three states = 22 + 26 + 26 = 74. From Statement (iii), Lokesh spent 30 years in the three states together, therefore, the total number of years spent by the other three friends was 74 - 30 = 44. From Statement (i), Kishore must have spent at least 14 years in the three states together as he had spent 8 years in M.P alone. From Statement (ii), the total number of years spent by Mayank in the three states together was not less than that of Kishore. The only possibility is that Kishore spent 14 years, and Mayank and Neelam spent 18 years and 12 years respectively.

Using Statements (v), (iv) and (i) in that order along with the conclusions drawn above, the final distribution can be tabulated as given below.

States/Friends	U.P.	Maharashtra	M.P.	Total
Kishore	2	4	8	14
Lokesh	6	14	10	30
Mayank	10	6	2	18
Neelam	4	2	6	12
Total	22	26	26	74

16. (b)
17. (c)
18. (a)
19. Lokesh spent 14 years in Maharashtra. Hence, Option (b) is the correct answer.
20. The four people spent a total of 74 years.

MOCK TEST PAPER 7

Solutions for Questions 1 to 5:

Again for this question, the first thing you should do is to create the visual structure of the problem situation. The following grid would define the situation.

First Row			
Second Row			

Using clues (iii) and (v), we get that SX4, Alto and Punto are parked in one row. Also, we know from Clue (iii) that Punto is diagonally opposite *i*10. This gives rise to two essential possibilities:

Possibility 1:

First Row			*i*10
Second Row	Punto	Alto	SX4

Possibility 2:

First Row	SX4	Alto	Punto
Second Row	*i*10		

> **Note:** We have been able to deduce that Alto is in the middle parking of it's row using the combination of clues (iii) and (v). Although Clue (i) also tells us that, we really do not need that clue and this you should recognize as a case of what can be called redundant information.

To the current grid if we add the information we get from Clue (ii) that tells us that Esteem is second to the right of *i*10, and from Clue (iv) which tells us that Swift is in front of Alto, we can complete the picture as follows:

Possibility 1:

First Row	Esteem	Swift	*i*10
Second Row	Punto	Alto	SX4

Possibility 2:

First Row	SX4	Alto	Punto
Second Row	*i*10	Swift	Esteem

From this point we can move into the questions as we have already used up all the information given in the clues.

1. If SX4 and Esteem interchange their position, then the car(s) adjacent now to SX4 would become adjacent to Esteem.
   Since, Alto is adjacent to SX4 currently (in both the possibilities), we can conclude that only Alto would be adjacent to Esteem after the switch. The situation can be visualised as follows:

   Possibility 1:

First Row	SX4	Swift	*i*10
Second Row	Punto	Alto	Esteem

   Possibility 2:

First Row	Esteem	Alto	Punto
Second Row	*i*10	Swift	SX4

   Option (c) is the correct answer.
2. After the interchanges as defined: Alto with i10 and Punto with SX4, the possibility grids would look as below:

   Possibility 1:

First Row	Punto	Swift	Alto
Second Row	SX4	*i*10	Esteem

   Possibility 2:

First Row	Esteem	*i*10	SX4
Second Row	Alto	Swift	Punto

   From this position if Swift shifts right it would obviously have to displace Punto from the parking lot and the Beatle would take the position which Swift is currently occupying. The new grid after this change would look like:

   Possibility 1:

First Row	Swift	Beatle	Alto
Second Row	SX4	*i*10	Esteem

   Possibility 2:

First Row	Esteem	*i*10	SX4
Second Row	Alto	Beatle	Swift

   In this situation we can clearly see that Alto and Swift are next to the Beatle.
   Option (d) is the correct answer.
3. Wagon-R replaces Esteem, *i*10 gets replaced by Jazz, Zen replaces the Punto and Beat replaces the SX4. The figures now look like:

   Possibility 1:

First Row	Wagon-R	Swift	Jazz
Second Row	Zen	Alto	Beat

   Possibility 2:

First Row	Beat	Alto	Zen
Second Row	Jazz	Swift	Wagon-R

   In both cases, the Alto and the Swift are two cars which remain in the parking lot. Thus, options (a), (b) and (c) cannot be true with respect to the cars which moved out. Hence, we select option (d) as the correct answer.
4. We can clearly see that none of the following is true as per the two possibilities of the previous question, hence the answer is (d)
5. If we replace Alto by Nexon, and Nexon switches its position with Zen, then in both cases, Zen would be between Nexon and Beat. Hence, option (c) is correct.

Solutions for Questions 6 to 10:

The information given in the question leads to the following deductions, which can be tabulated as shown in the following table (Note: for questions like these, the key is to identify the correct table structure to get to the answer):

(i) According to the question Alan does not teach in CHS, so he is not the husband of Ervin.

(ii) Since Alan is not from Karachi, he cannot be the husband of Alexa, Alan must be the husband of Jany and he is from Durban.

(iii) Since Bipul is not the husband of Ervin, he does not teach in CHS.

	Alan	Bipul	Chris	David		
Mumbai	**No**	**No**				
Durban	**Yes**	**No**	**No**	**No**		
Chicago	**No**					
Karachi	**No**					
Ervin	**No**	**No**			**CHS**	
Croony	**No**					
Jany	**Yes**	**No**	**No**	**No**		**Durban**
Alexa	**No**				**No HMS**	**Karachi**
	No CHS	**No FMS and No CHS**				

6. Statement (i) is already known. Hence, it cannot be part of the answer.

Statement (ii): 'David is from Chicago but does not study in CHS' leads to the following deductions:

Bipul must be from Karachi and Chris must be from Mumbai.

If Bipul is from Karachi then he must be the husband of Alexa and does not teach in HMS. So, he must teach in CRS.

Since David does not teach in CHS, he cannot be the husband of Ervin.

Chris must be the husband of Ervin and he teaches in CHS. David must be married to Croony.

(**Note:** The fresh deductions are shown in bold in the table):

	Alan	Bipul	Chris	David		
Mumbai	No	No	**Yes**	No		
Durban	Yes	No	No	**No**		
Chicago	No	**No**	**No**	**Yes**		
Karachi	No	**Yes**	**No**	**No**		
Ervin	No	No	**Yes**	**No**	CHS	
Croony	No	**No**	**No**	**Yes**		
Jany	Yes	No	No	No		Durban
Alexa	No	**Yes**	**No**	**No**	No HMS	Karachi
	HMS/ FMS	**CRS**	**CHS**	FMS/ HMS		

Statement (iii): 'Alan does not teach in FMS.' So David teaches in FMS and Alan teaches in HMS. This will complete the table.

So we can see that statements (ii) and (iii) are necessary to get the complete arrangement. Option (b) is correct.

7. If David teaches in FMS and Bipul is not from Chicago, then the deductions given below would make the table look like the following:

If David teaches in FMS, he cannot be the husband of Ervin. Chris must be the husband of Ervin and he teaches in CHS.

Bipul is not from Chicago so he must be from Karachi. He must be the husband of Alexa and teaches in CRS.

(**Note:** The fresh deductions are shown in bold in the table):

	Alan	Bipul	Chris	David		
Mumbai	No	No				
Durban	Yes	No	No	No		
Chicago	**No**	No				
Karachi	**No**	**Yes**	**No**	**No**		
Ervin	No	No	**Yes**	**No**	CHS	
Croony	No	**No**	**No**	**Yes**		
Jany	Yes	No	No	No		Durban
Alexa	No	**Yes**	**No**	**No**	No HMS	Karachi
	HMS	**CRS**	**CHS**	**FMS**		

Hence, Alan teaches in HMS.

8. Chris teaches in CHS and David is from Chicago leads to the following table.

(**Note:** The fresh deductions are shown in bold in the table):

	Alan	Bipul	Chris	David		
Mumbai	No	No	**Yes**	**No**		
Durban	Yes	No	No	No		
Chicago	No	**No**	**No**	**Yes**		
Karachi	No	**Yes**	**No**	**No**		
Ervin	No	No	**Yes**	**No**	CHS	**Mumbai**
Croony	No	No	No	Yes		**Chicago**
Jany	Yes	**No**	**No**	**No**		Durban
Alexa	No	Yes	No	No	No HMS	Karachi
	?	**CRS**	**CHS**	?		

Bipul teaches in CRS and Chris teaches in CHS. Option (c) is correct.

9. If Chris is from Karachi and David is the husband of Ervin the deductions can be seen in bold in the table:

	Alan	Bipul	Chris	David		
Mumbai	No	No	**No**	**Yes**		
Durban	Yes	No	No	No		
Chicago	No	**Yes**	**No**	**No**		
Karachi	No	**No**	**Yes**	**No**		
Ervin	No	No	**No**	**Yes**	CHS	
Croony	No	**Yes**	**No**	**No**		
Jany	Yes	No	No	No		Durban
Alexa	No	**No**	**Yes**	**No**	No HMS	Karachi
	No CHS	No FMS and No CHS	**No HMS**	**CHS**		

It can be verified that each of the first three options may be true. The question has asked us which option is false. Hence, we would choose none of these.

10. From the solution table, we can see that Croony was married to David. Hence, the answer is David.

Solutions for Questions 11 to 15:

House	Truth	Lie	Dharma	Yog	Karma	Devotion	Salvation	**School**

Now, we answer the questions:

11. Option (c) is the correct answer.
12. Option (b) is the correct answer.
13. There are 2 lanes between Yog and Salvation.
14. The Karma Lane is exactly in between Lie Lane and the school. Hence, option (d) is the correct answer.
15. Dharma Lane lies between Lie and Yog lane. Hence, option (a) is the correct answer.

Solutions for Questions 16 to 20:

Since the launch in U.K. will not be done by Sonya, La-Nina, Rated-R, Phoenix and D-Damsels, then the product launch in U.K must be done by Maxwell on 1st January. As none of Sonya, Rated-R, La-Nina, Phoenix and Maxwell would launch the product on 1st January, D-Damsels must have launched the product on 1st January.

From Statements (iii) and (IV), we can conclude that D-Damsels launched the product in Australia.

Since none of the agencies–Sonya, La-Nina, Phoenix, D-Damsels, and Maxwell have launched the products in South Africa, Rated-R must have launched the product in South Africa.

As Sonya would be launching in USA and Phoenix would launch the product in Ivory Coast, La-Nina must have launched the product in Brazil.

Since none of the agencies–Sonya, Rated-R, La-Nina, D-Damsels and Maxwell launched the product on 14th June, Phoenix must have launched the ABC Duplex in Ivory Coast on 14th June.

From Statement (iii), La-Nina launched the product before any launch in South Africa. Hence, in South Africa the launch would be done by Rated-R and on 22nd May. La-Nina launched the product in Brazil on 29th April.

Agency	**Country**	**Launch Date**	**Product**
Maxwell	UK	23rd March	Putty/ Dylex
La-Nina	Brazil	29th April	Velvet

Agency	Country	Launch Date	Product
Sonya	USA	5th February	Dylex/ Putty
D-Damsels	Australia	1st January	Ivory
Rated-R	South Africa	22nd May	Emulsion
Phoenix	Ivory Coast	14th June	Duplex

16. (d)
17. (c)
18. (c)
19. Ivory was launched on 1st January. Hence, Option (d) is the correct answer.
20. Rated-R launched Emulsion just after Velvet. Hence, Option (a) is the correct answer.

MOCK TEST PAPER 8

Solutions for Questions 1 to 5:

Again like for all puzzle questions, the key is to define the visual structure of the solution. Clue (i) gives you the input as to how you would need to structure the solution grid. The starting solution grid should look something like below:

Name	Company	Location	Email Provider
	TISCO	Jamshedpur	
	Telco	Pune	
	Wipro	Bangalore	
	HCL	Noida	
	Mecon	Ranchi	
	Usha Martin	Kolkata	

From this point first try to fix the positioning of the direct clues into the grid.

Clues (iv), (vi) and (ix) are usable directly in the above table.

These clues about Rahul, Kabeer and Anup help us move further into our solution grid which would now look as below.

Name	Company	Location	Email Provider
Anup	TISCO	Jamshedpur	
Rahul	Telco	Pune	Rediffmail
	Wipro	Bangalore	
	HCL	Noida	
	Mecon	Ranchi	
Kabeer	Usha Martin	Kolkata	Not Hotmail

From this point you realise that since we have to place only 3 more people in their correct cities/companies we can use the clue (vii) in order to realise that since neither Alok nor Raghu work in Noida it only leaves us with Amit who must be in Noida. The table modifies to:

Name	Company	Location	Email Provider
Anup	TISCO	Jamshedpur	
Rahul	Telco	Pune	Rediffmail
	Wipro	Bangalore	
Amit	HCL	Noida	
	Mecon	Ranchi	
Kabeer	Usha Martin	Kolkata	Not Hotmail

Now use clue (v) to place Alok and Raghu in the two remaining places. Since Alok does not work for Mecon, he must be working for Wipro and consequently Raghu would be working for Mecon.

The solution grid now becomes:

Name	Company	Location	Email Provider
Anup	TISCO	Jamshedpur	
Rahul	Telco	Pune	Rediffmail
Alok	Wipro	Bangalore	Not Yahoo
Amit	HCL	Noida	
Raghu	Mecon	Ranchi	
Kabeer	Usha Martin	Kolkata	Not Hotmail

We should now concentrate on fixing the email providers for the six people.

For this Clue (i) is very useful at this point as it helps us fix two email providers in the above grid. We can also use clue (viii) at this point to fix that Ranchi-Mecon-Raghu is not Hotmail.

The solution grid now becomes:

Name	Company	Location	Email Provider
Anup	TISCO	Jamshedpur	Indiatimes
Rahul	Telco	Pune	Rediffmail
Alok	Wipro	Bangalore	Not Yahoo
Amit	HCL	Noida	Sancharnet
Raghu	Mecon	Ranchi	Not Hotmail
Kabeer	Usha Martin	Kolkata	Not Hotmail

Analysing the above situation we can clearly see that three of the six email providers are now fixed leaving the other three to be fixed. These are Hotmail, Yahoo and Gmail.

Also we can see in our solution grid at this point that Hotmail cannot be put for Raghu-Mecon-Ranchi nor for Kabeer-Usha Martin-Kolkata and that leaves us with only Alok-Wipro-Bangalore where Hotmail can be matched.

The solution grid now becomes:

Name	Company	Location	Email Provider
Anup	TISCO	Jamshedpur	Indiatimes
Rahul	Telco	Pune	Rediffmail
Alok	Wipro	Bangalore	Hotmail
Amit	HCL	Noida	Sancharnet
Raghu	Mecon	Ranchi	Yahoo/Gmail
Kabeer	Usha Martin	Kolkata	Gmail/Yahoo

Clue (iii) helps us place that Gmail is for Mecon. Thus the final solution becomes:

Name	Company	Location	Email Provider
Anup	TISCO	Jamshedpur	Indiatimes
Rahul	Telco	Pune	Rediffmail
Alok	Wipro	Bangalore	Hotmail
Amit	HCL	Noida	Sancharnet
Raghu	Mecon	Ranchi	Gmail
Kabeer	Usha Martin	Kolkata	Yahoo

The answers can now be read off the above table:

1. The man who works for Wipro has an email account with Hotmail. Option (d) is the correct answer.
2. Raghu-Ranchi-Gmail is the only correct combination amongst the 4 options. Option (d) is the correct answer.
3. Kabeer has an email-id with Yahoo is the correct statement. The other options are incorrect. Option (c) is the correct answer.
4. Option (a) is incorrect as Kabeer is in Kolkata and not in Noida.
   Option (b) is incorrect as Amit is in Noida and not in Ranchi as this options says.
   Option (c) is incorrect as Alok is in Bangalore and not in Kolkata.
   Thus, option (d) is the correct answer.
5. The person with the Indiatimes email-id works for TISCO while the one with the Sancharnet email account works for HCL and the one with the Yahoo email-id works for Usha Martin.
   Option (d) is the correct answer.

Solutions for Questions 6 to 10:

The person who picks the last coin is a winner. In order to ensure a win for oneself, one needs to leave 7 coins for the opponent after one's second last move. If one does so, whatever the opponent does, one would be able to win the game by picking up the remaining coins.

The crux of such games is that both the players are intelligent. Hence, if one person can analyse that he would win by leaving 7 coins on the table, so can the other person analyse the same. Hence, the key to the game is not to allow one's opponent to leave 7 coins on the table. This would mean that if we leave anything between 8 and 13 coins on the table after one of our moves, the opponent would pick up an appropriate number (between 1 and 6) and leave us 7 coins on the table - and hence we would lose.

However, if one leaves 14 coins on the table after one's move, the opponent would have no option but to leave us between 8 and 13 coins, and that would mean that we would win. Similar analysis carried forward would tell us that someone who leaves 21 coins on the table cannot lose.

Thus, an analysis leaves us with the realisation that anyone who manages to leave 7n coins on the table at any stage of the game, would win the game.

6. If A picks up 5 coins from 19, he would leave 14 coins for B. B cannot win from this point.
7. To ensure his win, B needs to leave 7n coins on the table for A. Hence, his target should be 35 coins. If he picks up 4 coins he would leave 35 coins for A. Hence, he should pick up 4 coins.
8. If the last person loses, the target shifts from making it '0' on the table to making it '1' on the table so that the opponent has no option but to pick up the last coin. In such a situation, the person who makes it 7n + 1 would be the winner. Thus, from 45 coins, if A picks up 2 coins, there would be 43 coins left on the table and B cannot win.
9. To ensure the win, you need to leave $7n$ Coins on the table. If he leaves 28 coins, he wins. Hence, he picks 6 coins.
   Therefore, 6 is the correct answer.

10. To ensure A's win, he needs to leave $7n + 1$ coins on the table as the motive is to leave 1 coin on the table. Hence, he needs to pick 5 coins as 15 is the closest to $7n + 1$.

    Therefore, 5 is the correct answer

Solutions for Questions 11 to 15:

Let 3x and 5x be the number of sweets with Danish and Eklavya respectively, where x is a natural number.

Then, the number of sweets with Aman = $3x + 5x = 8x$

Since the number of sweets with Aman is twice a perfect square greater than 100, the value of 8x is 128 or 200.

$x = 16$ or 25

Now, $x = 25$ is not possible. In this case the total number of sweets will exceed 450. Therefore, only $x = 16$ satisfies all the given conditions.

Hence, the number of sweets with Aman, Danish and Eklavya are 128, 48, and 80.

The number of sweets with Beenu and Chandni together $= 450 - (128 + 48 + 80) = 194$

As Beenu has an odd number of sweets, the number of sweets with Chandni must be also be odd.

The number of sweets with Chandni is 151 and so the number of sweets with Beenu is 43.

The conclusions drawn above can be tabulated as shown below.

Friend	Aman	Beenu	Chandni	Danish	Eklavya
No. of Sweets	128	43	151	48	80

11. (d) Aman 2nd highest number of sweets.
12. (b) The difference between the number of sweets with Beenu and Chandni is $151 - 43 = 108$
13. (c) The sum of the number of sweets with Aman and Danish $= 128 + 48 = 176$.
14. Option (b) is the correct answer.
15. Highest = 151; Lowest = 43; Difference = 108

Solutions for Questions 16 to 20:

The given information can be tabulated as shown below.

Name	Profession	Destination
Amar	-	-
Bhawna	Engineer	-
Chandni	-	Bangalore
Dishanth	-	-
Eshant	-	-
Faiz	Pilot	Bangalore
Gaurank	-	Mumbai
Himesh	Doctor	Mumbai
Inderjeet	Doctor	Kolkata
Jaspreet	Engineer	Kolkata
Kamlesh	Engineer	-
Lokendra	Pilot	Bangalore

It can be easily deduced that the number of different professionals who will arrive at the three meeting points is as given below:

	Kolkata	Bangalore	Mumbai
Doctor	2	1	1
Engineer	1	1	2
Pilot	1	2	1

As the three people who would be reaching Bangalore are already known, Kamlesh and Dishanth must reach Mumbai. As Jaspreet who's an engineer will reach Kolkata, Bhawna must reach Bangalore, so Amar and Eshant must reach Kolkata. As Amar is not a doctor, he must be a pilot and eshant must be a doctor. Therefore, Chandni also must be a doctor. Hence, one among Gaurank and Dishanth is an engineer and the other is pilot. The final table can be shown as given below.

Name	Profession	Destination
Amar	Pilot	Kolkata
Bhawna	Engineer	Bangalore
Chandni	Doctor	Bangalore
Dishanth	Engineer/Pilot	Mumbai
Eshant	Doctor	Kolkata
Faiz	Pilot	Bangalore
Gaurank	Pilot/Engineer	Mumbai
Himesh	Doctor	Mumbai
Inderjeet	Doctor	Kolkata
Jaspreet	Engineer	Kolkata
Kamlesh	Engineer	Mumbai
Lokendra	Pilot	Bangalore

16. (c) Chandni is a doctor who will be reaching Bangalore.
17. (d) Apart from Kamlesh, either Dishanth or Gaurank could be the other engineer who will reach Mumbai
18. (d) Eshant is a doctor who will reach Kolkata.
19. Himesh is the doctor who was going to Mumbai. Hence, Option (b) is the correct answer.
20. Faiz & Lokendra were pilots traveling to Bangalore. Hence, Option (a) is the correct answer.

MOCK TEST PAPER 9

Solutions for Questions 1 to 5:

By using the clues in the problem, the following table can be formed using persons (A/B/C/D/E) occupations (En/Do/Bu/Pa/Cr); languages (P/Q/R/S/T) and countries (I/Ch/USA/UK/UAE):

Person	A	B	C	D	E	Left to be Placed
Occupation	Bu		Pa× En×	Pa×		En/Do/Pa/Cr
Language		R		S×		P/Q/S/T
Country			I		UAE×	Ch/USA/UK/UAE

The first round of reading will also give us the following cross referenced clues to be used to move further in the problem: Unused cross referenced clues: 'Pa' Not 'S'; 'UAE' = 'Do'; 'USA' Not 'S', Not 'T' Not 'Pa'; 'Q' = 'Cr'; 'UK' = 'P'; D not Pa (from clue (iii)).

At this point of the table, we can make the following deductions:

Deduction 1: UAE = Do, so Do gets deleted from C and E.

Deduction 2: This then leads us to the conclusion that C has to be a cricketer (as that is the only option left for C's occupation). Also, since the cricketer's language is Q, we can say that C's language would also be Q.

Deduction 3: Since UK = P, B cannot be from UK.

Deduction 4: Since UAE = Do, A cannot be from UAE (as A is a businessman).

The table then evolves to:

Person	A	B	C	D	E	Left to be Placed
Occupation	Bu		Cr	Pa×	Do×	En/Do/Pa
Language	P/S/T	R	Q	S×. Hence P/T	P/S/T	P/S/T
Country	UAE×	UK×	I		UAE×	Ch/USA/UK/UAE

The list of unused cross referenced clues now becomes: 'Pa' Not 'S'; 'UAE' = 'Do'; 'USA' Not 'S', Not 'T' Not 'Pa'; 'UK'='P'; D not Pa.

Deductions at this stage:

1. At this stage, we can clearly see that the UAE = Do combination has two possible positions in the grid–Column B and Column D.
2. We also see that the UK = P combination has three possible positions in the grid–Columns A, D and E.
3. From the clue: 'USA' Not 'S', Not 'T' Not 'Pa', we can clearly see that if we place UK = P in any of the columns A, D or E, USA cannot go into any of these three columns, as UK = P, would block USA's combination with P, while USA's combinations with S and T are already ruled out by this clue.
4. Hence we can conclude the B is from USA and D would be a doctor from UAE.

Person	A	B	C	D	E	Left to be Placed
Occupation	Bu		Cr	Do		En/Pa
Language	P/S/T	R	Q	P/T	P/S/T	P/S/T
Country		USA	I	UAE		Ch/UK

Consequently, B cannot be a painter (as he is from USA). So B is an engineer and E must be a painter. This would also mean that E's language cannot be S. Hence, D's and E's language would be shared between P and T.

Thus, S must be A's language. Also, UK = P, can only be placed under E. The final table would be as follows:

Person	A	B	C	D	E
Occupation	Businessman	Engineer	Cricketer	Doctor	Painter
Language	S	R	Q	T	P
Country	China	USA	I	UAE	UK

The answers are:

1. China. Option (b) is correct.
2. C
3. D
4. 1
5. From the table above, we can see that cricketer C comes from India.

Solutions for Questions 6 to 10:

According to the question, a politician can be eligible to participate in the voting process if and only if he is eliminated. This means that in the second round, we would have P eligible to vote, while in the third round we would have R eligible to vote. However, we are also told after every round the proposer and the supporters of the eliminated politician become ineligible to vote. This means that going from the first round to the second round - there would be 1 new voter (P) who becomes eligible to vote and 3 existing voters who would become ineligible to vote. So the total votes cast in each round comes down by 2.

So, the total votes in the 1st round = 110 + 2 = 112.

This means that R + S = 56 in the first round - with each of them getting more than 20 and less than 36. (as P is getting the minimum of 20 votes and getting eliminated in the first round, while Q gets the maximum number of 36 votes in the first round).

From the statement: '3 out of 5 of those who voted for R in round 1, voted for him in round 2' we get that:

R's number of votes must be a multiple of 5 and greater than 20, but less than 36.

This leaves us with 3 possibilities for R and S in round 1.

	R	S	People who continued to vote for R in the second round
Case 1	35	21	21
Case 2	30	26	18
Case 3	25	31	15

However, more information needs to be processed to decide the values of R and S in the first round. Consider the following analysis:

In the third round, there is a net drop of 15 voters. We know that there is a drop of 2 voters in every round. Thus, there should have been 108 voters in the third round.

However, since there are only 95 voters in the third round, it means that there must have been 13 more voters who would have become ineligible to vote in the third round.

Apart from what we have discussed above, becoming ineligible to vote could only occur if someone voted for P in the first round and voted for R in the second round – since both of them are not in the fray in the third round.

Thus, it means that there are 13 people who voted for P in the first round and voted for R in the second round. However, we know from the table in the question that there were only 29 votes for R in round 2. Hence, from the 3 cases listed above, we can eliminate cases 1 and 2. Case 3 becomes the only possibility left. We can infer from this that the table in the question would break down in the following way:

Rounds	Total Votes	Maximum Votes		Minimum Votes					
		Candidate	No. of Votes	Candidate	No. of Votes	Candidate	No. of Votes	Candidate	No. of Votes
1	112	Q	36	P	20	S	31	R	25
2	110	S	45 (31 retained + 4 from P + 10 from R)	R	29 (15 retained + 13 from P + P himself)	Q	36 (all retained)		
3	95		51		44				

Note:

(i) Q retained all his 36 votes;

(ii) Out of 20 voters for P in round 1, 13 transferred to R, 4 transferred to S and 3 became ineligible (1 proposer and 2 supporters of P).

(iii) This means that the 10 voters R was not able to retain in round 2, went on to vote for S in round 2.

(iv) From the above analysis we can deduce that S got 51 votes in the 3rd round (as the number of votes received by S cannot decrease). This means that out of 15 votes retained by R in round 2, 12 voters would have transferred to either S or Q and 3 voters (1 proposer of R and 2 supporters of R) would not be voting in round 2. Thus, the total number of votes in round 3 would be 45 + 36 + 12 = 93. We can also perceive that the remaining 2 voters in round 3 would have been P and R themselves, thus making it 95 votes in round 3. However, we would not be sure of who these additional 14 people would vote for.

Thus the final table would be:

Rounds	Total Votes	Maximum Votes		Minimum Votes					
		Candidate	No. of Votes	Candidate	No. of Votes	Candidate	No. of Votes	Candidate	No of Votes
1	112	Q	36	P	20	S	31	R	25
2	110	S	45 (31 retained + 4 from P + 10 from R)	R	29 (15 retained + 13 from P + P himself)	Q	36 (all retained)		
3	95	S	51	Q	44				

6. Total population = 112 + 4 (4 politicians) = 116.
7. R would have got 25 votes in round 1.
8. 4
9. As per the table given above, the answer is 13 + 1 (P's vote) = 14. Option (b) is correct.
10. The winning margin is 7 votes. Option (c) is correct.

Solutions for Questions 11 to 15:

11. (d) As Pakistan lost the matches against India and Kenya and drew against Australia, it could have won at most 4 matches.
    Hence, its maximum score could be $4 \times 3 + 1 = 13$.
12. (c) India's score = 3 + 3 + 3 + 3 + 3 + 1 + 1 + 1 = 17.
    In order to minimise the absolute difference between the scores of India and Kenya, we need to make Kenya's score as close as possible to 17.
    Since Kenya lost against Zimbabwe and India and drew against Australia, if it wins the rest of its matches its score would be = 1 + 3 + 3 + 3 + 3 = 13.
    Required minimum difference = 17 – 13 = 4.
13. India scores 17 points. Now, Zimbabwe will have a minimum of 3 points. Hence the maximum difference could be 14 points.
14. India scores 17 points. Now, Zimbabwe could have reached 18 or 19 points depending on the result of India vs Zimbabwe. Hence, the maximum sum could be 36 points.
15. Australia could have come 8th if it loses its remaining 4 matches.

Solutions for Questions 16 to 20:

From statements (i) and (ii): Pulkit got either 2nd or 3rd rank and Rahim got either 3rd or 4th rank.

From statement (iii): Qadir cannot finish the race at the end and Saqlain cannot get 1st rank.

Person	Possible ranks
Pulkit	2nd, 3rd
Qadir	1st, 2nd, 3rd, 4th
Rahim	3rd, 4th
Saqlain	2nd, 3rd, 4th, 5th
Tariq	1st, 2nd, 3rd, 4th, 5th

From statement (iv): P + T = R + S

The above equation is possible only when P = 2, T = 5 and R = 3/4 and S = 4/3

16. Tariq finished the race at the end. Option (c) is correct.
17. Qadir got the first rank and maximum possible rank of Saqlain is 4. Therefore the required maximum possible sum = 1 + 4 = 5.
18. T + R = 8 or 5 + R = 8 => R = 3.
    If R = 3 then S = 4, therefore Saqlain got the 4th rank. Option (b) is correct.
19. Qadir finished first and Pulkit came second. Hence the answer is 1.
20. Pulkit couldn't have lost to Rahim. Hence, Option (a) is the correct answer.

MOCK TEST PAPER 10

Solutions for Questions 1 to 5:

We can first make a list of the words in the context of their number of letters.

3-letter word: Man; 4-letter words: Fore, Love, Tune, Turn, Wolf.

5-letter word: Hobby; 6-letter words: Indira, Singer, Wonder.

7-Letter word: Harshal; 8-Letter word: Smartest.

Clue (vi) is a direct clue, while clue (i) tells us indirectly, that the box 3 × 3 contains a word with an even number of letters.

1 × 1	1 × 2	1 × 3	1 × 4
2 × 1	2 × 2	2 × 3 Smartest	2 × 4
3 × 1	3 × 2	3 × 3 Even number of letters	3 × 4

Clue (ii) tells us that the following structure needs to be placed in the grid:

WONDER	
LOVE	HOBBY

Given the condition of the table currently, this can only be done by placing the word Wonder in the 1 × 1 or the 2 × 1 box. However, if we place the word Wonder in the 2 × 1 box, it would result in a contravention of clue (v).Thus, Wonder can only be placed in the 1 × 1 box. The grid would look as follows after this change:

1 × 1 WONDER	1 × 2	1 × 3	1 × 4
2 × 1 LOVE	2 × 2 HOBBY	2 × 3 SMARTEST	2 × 4
3 × 1	3 × 2	3 × 3 Even number of letters	3 × 4

At this stage the words left to be placed are:

Fore, Harshal, Indira, Man, Singer, Tune, Turn, Wolf. The following deductions can now be made;

1. Clue (iii) tells us that Wolf–Fore would be placed next to each other in that order. Currently, these can only be placed side by side in the 2nd and 3rd columns in the first or the third row.
2. Also, since Singer is somewhere above Tune, in the same vertical column–these two cannot be placed in the first column or the 2nd and 3rd columns either.

Hence, Singer and Tune have to be placed in the 4th column only with Singer somewhere above Tune.

Note: This happens because after placing Wolf-Fore in the first or the third row we would not have the space to accommodate 2 words in the same vertical column except in the 4th column.

3. Also, since 'The words in 2 × 1 and in 3 × 1 have same number of letters' from Clue (v), Turn is the only 4 letter word for the 3 × 1 box.
4. From Clue (vii), we get that the word in 2 × 4 would be Man. This also determines the Singer & Tune placement.
5. Clue (viii) can also be directly applied at this point to place Harshal and Indira to the right of Turn in the bottom row.
6. This placement, then consequently fixes the positions of Wolf-Fore in the top row.

The final table would look as follows:

1 × 1 WONDER	1 × 2 WOLF	1 × 3 FORE	1 × 4 SINGER
2 × 1 LOVE	2 × 2 HOBBY	2 × 3 SMARTEST	2 × 4 MAN
3 × 1 TURN	3 × 2 HARSHAL	3 × 3 INDIRA	3 × 4 TUNE

The answers to 1 to 4 would then be:

1. Harshal
2. 9
3. 3 × 1
4. (b)
5. As per the table, Box labelled 2 × 3 has the word 'smartest' in it.

Solutions for Questions 6 to 10:

From the given data we can make the following table:

Name	Bride	Marriage month	City
Abhishek	(X Jasmine, XBrinda) (XHema)		Ahmedabad
Deepak			
Mridul	(XGeetika, XVeena)		Chennai
Pritam		December	(X Bengaluru, X Kolkata)
Ranjan			Delhi
Salil	Jasmine	September	

From the above table and the given data we can get the following points:

- Pritam is from Mumbai.
- From the 6th & 7th statements, Salil is from Bengaluru.
- From the 3rd statement, Deepak married in February and from 6th statement Mridul married in November.
- From the 4th statement and the above analysis we infer that Abhishek married in July and Ranjan married in April with Hema.
- From 5th statement and above analysis we get that Geetika married in Kolkata and Ipsita married in Chennai.

From the above analysis we can get the following table:

Name	Bride	Marriage month	City
Abhishek	Veena	July	Ahmedabad
Deepak	Geetika	February	Kolkata
Mridul	Ipsita	November	Chennai
Pritam	Brinda	December	Mumbai
Ranjan	Hema	April	Delhi
Salil	Jasmine	September	Bengaluru

6. Ranjan. Hence, option (c) is correct.
7. Kolkata. Hence, option (c) is correct.
8. December. Hence, option (d) is correct.
9. Bengaluru. Hence, option (a) is correct.
10. Chennai. Hence, option (d) is correct.

Solutions for Questions 11 to 15:

From Statement (i), the annual turnovers (in '000 crores) of Infosys, TCS and HCL are 12, 18 and 24, not necessarily in that order. From Statement (ii), the company which earns the highest saves 35% of its turnover and Accenture saves 25% of its turnover. However, from Statement (iii), IBM's turnover is the least, i.e., 9000 crores. Hence, the turnovers of Accenture and HP are 30,000 crores and 48,000 crores respectively.

From Statement (iii), IBM's turnover is 9,000 crores and its savings are one-twelfth of the savings of the company which invests in Operations; this is possible only if IBM saves 10% because if it is more than 10%, the savings of any other company cannot be twelve times that of IBM's savings. Thus, we can conclude that the company which invests its savings in Operations earns 18,000 crores and saves 60% of its income.

Name	Income (in '000crores)	Percentage Savings	Savings (in '000crores)	Instrument
Infosys	24	40	9.6	Services
TCS	12	20	2.4	Marketing
Accenture	30	25	7.5	R&D
HCL	18	60	10.8	Operations
IBM	9	10	0.9	HR
HP	48	35	16.8	Sales

Now, from Statements (i), (iv) and (v), the following conclusions can be drawn.

HCL		Infosys		TCS		Accenture
↓		↓		↓		↓
18 (60%)	+	24 (40%)	=	12(20%)	+	30 (25%)
↓		↓		↓		↓
Operations		**Services**		**Marketing**		**R&D**

The final arrangement can then be tabulated.

11. (c) The difference = 10.8 – 9.6 = 1,200 crores
12. (d) HP invests its savings in Sales.
13. (b) The annual turnover of Infosys is 24,000 crores.
14. From the solution table it is clear that HCL has the highest savings percentage. Hence, Option (c) is the correct answer.
15. Option (a) is the correct answer.

Solutions for Questions 16 to 20:

From statements (i), (ii), (iii): In terms of number of books: C > B > E and A > D.

From statement-(iii), A does not have maximum number of books. Therefore C must have maximum number of books. C does not have the Hindi book and as per the question each student has different number of books therefore C must have four books and the rest four students must possess 3, 2, 1, 0 books.

C-English, Physics, Chemistry, Biology.

E must have two books and one of these books is Physics and the other one is Chemistry. Also, then D would have the least number of books and that would be equal to 0 books.

So, D has no book.

According to the question each subject book is possessed by different number of students. Therefore no one should possess Hindi book (as there is at least 1 person possessing the books of each of the other subjects).

Based on these deductions, we can create the following table:

	Hindi (0)	English (1)	Physics (3 or 4)	Chemistry (3 or 4)	Biology (2)
A (1)	N	N	Y/N	N/Y	N
B (3)	N	N	Y	Y	Y
C (4)	N	Y	Y	Y	Y
D (0)	N	N	N	N	N
E (2)	N	N	Y	Y	N

16. E. Option (d) is correct
17. Required sum = 1 + 3 = 4
18. 2 students possess the Biology book.
19. C has a book on English. Hence, Option (c) is the correct answer.
20. Number of Books that E has = 2; Number of Hindi Books = 0; Difference = 2.

LEVEL OF DIFFICULTY (III)

MOCK TEST PAPER 1

Solutions for Questions 1 to 5:

The best way to think in this question is to look at the age-wise order of the seven stars. The blank table would look something as follows:

Name of movie	Name of Star	Age wise order
		Oldest
		Youngest

The first thing to think of in this table is, using Clues (iii) and (v), we get that the star who acted in *Mann* cannot be the oldest star (as the star who acted in *Mann* should be younger to D). Further, if we use the information in Clue (vi) which is direct, the table transforms to:

Name of movie	Name of Star	Age wise order
Garv	A	Oldest
Hum		
Raaz		
Mann		Youngest

At this point, we have to place three more movies - *viz*: *Dhoom*, *Karz* and *Boss*. Using Clue (iii) again, those who acted in *Dhoom* and *Karz* have to be younger than D–we realise that of the three blanks, *Dhoom* and *Karz* would have to occupy the lower two. Thus, *Boss* must be for the second oldest star. Using Clue (ii) we know that B acted in *Boss*. We also know that D is not acting in any of *Dhoom*, *Mann* or *Karz*. Hence, D must be in *Hum*. The table now becomes:

Name of Movie	Name of Star	Age-wise order
Garv	A	Oldest
Boss	B	Second
Hum	D	Third
Dhoom/Karz	F	Fourth
Raaz	C/G	Fifth
Karz/Dhoom	G/C	Fifth
Mann	E	Youngest

At this point, we are left with two movies - *Dhoom* and *Karz* and also left with 4 people C, E, F and G to place. Since F>C>E and the *Raaz* star necessarily has to be younger than 4 of the stars, we get that F must be in the fourth place and E must be the youngest and between C and G, their age would be the same.

The answers are:

1. (d)
2. (c)
3. (d)
4. A acted in *Garv*. Hence, option (c) is the correct answer.
5. D is the third oldest person. Hence 2 people are older than D.

Solutions for Questions 6 to 10:

The first thing you do in this question is to recognise that there are 5 variables in the question. Hence, the starting possibility matrix in the question would be:

				36/38/40/42	36/38/40/42	36/38/40/42	36/38/40/42
				MEA/IT/IB/CBI	MEA/IT/IB/CBI	MEA/IT/IB/CBI	MEA/IT/IB/CBI
				A/B/C/D	A/B/C/D	A/B/C/D	A/B/C/D
				Chair 1	Chair 2	Chair 3	Chair 4
36/38/40/42	MEA/IT/IB/CBI	A/B/C/D	Lecture1				
36/38/40/42	MEA/IT/IB/CBI	A/B/C/D	Lecture 2				
36/38/40/42	MEA/IT/IB/CBI	A/B/C/D	Lecture3				
36/38/40/42	MEA/IT/IB/CBI	A/B/C/D	Lecture 4				

Initially all the possibilities for all the variables exist.

A quick glance through the clues tells us that there are no direct clues in the question. Hence, the only option left to start the question is to start eliminating the possibilities from the given clues. Let us now consider the first clue:

Clue (i): C sat somewhere to the left of, (but definitely not exactly next to) the man who was from CBI, who gave his lecture before C and who is 2 years younger than C.

Reaction 1: C was not in Chair 4 or Chair 3.

Reaction 2: The man from the CBI was not in Chairs 1 or 2.

Reaction 3: C is not the 36 year old.

Reaction 4: The man from the CBI is not 42 years old.

Reaction 5: The man from the CBI did not give lecture 4 and C did not speak first.

Clue (ii): B is four years younger than the man who was from IB and who was next to and to the left of B.

Reaction 1: B is either 36 or 38 years old.

Reaction 2: The man from IB is either 40 or 42 years old.

Reaction 3: B is not on Chair 1; The man from IB is not on Chair 4.

Clue (iii): The man in chair 1 was not A and gave his lecture next after the 42 year-old; gives us the following reactions:

Reaction 1: The man in chair 1 was not 42 years old and obviously the man in Chair 1 is not A.

Reaction 2: The man in Chair 1, did not give the first lecture.

Reaction 3: The 42 year old did not give the 4th lecture.

Using these clues the possibility matrix changes to:

				36/38/40	36/38/40/42	36/38/40/42	36/38/40/42
				MEA/IT/IB	MEA/IT/IB	MEA/IT/IB/CBI	MEA/IT/CBI
				C/D	A/B/C/D	A/B/D	A/B/D
				Chair 1	Chair 2	Chair 3	Chair 4
36/38/40/42	MEA/IT/IB/CBI	A/B/D	Lecture 1	NO			
36/38/40/42	MEA/IT/IB/CBI	A/B/C/D	Lecture 2				
36/38/40/42	MEA/IT/IB/CBI	A/B/C/D	Lecture 3				
36/38/40	MEA/IT/IB	A/B/C/D	Lecture 4				

Also, we have a couple of cross-referenced deductions that we would need to carry with us from this point in a visual form: These are:

C not 36

CBI not 42

B = 36 or 38

IB = 40 or 42

C----------CBI

SEATING

IB-B

lecture order: 42 year old followed by Chair 1

To this information, we can now start adding the deductions from clues (iv) and (v):

Clue (iv): The 40 year old sat next to and right of the man who was from the MEA and gave his lecture next but one after him.

Reaction 1: The 40-year-old was not in Chair 1.

Reaction 2: The man from the MEA was not in Chair 4.

Reaction 3: The 40-year-old spoke either 3rd or 4th. The MEA man either spoke first or second.

Clue (v): The man from IT gave his lecture next after the man who sat on Chair-4 (who didn't speak first); he is older than both the latter and D.

Reaction 1: The IT man did not speak first.

Reaction 2: The IT man did not sit in Chair 4.

Reaction 3: Chair 4 did not speak first. Chair 4 also did not speak last.

Reaction 4: D was not in Chair 4.

Reaction 5: The man from IT is either 40 or 42 years old.

				36/38	36/38/40/42	36/38/40/42	36/38/40/42
				MEA/IT/IB	MEA/IT/IB	MEA/IT/IB/CBI	CBI
				C/D	A/B/C/D	A/B/D	A/B
				Chair 1	Chair 2	Chair 3	Chair 4
36/38/42	MEA/IB/CBI	A/B/D	Lecture 1	NO			NO
36/38/42	MEA/IT/IB/CBI	A/B/C/D	Lecture 2				
36/38/40/42	IT/IB/CBI	A/B/C/D	Lecture 3				
36/38/40	IT/IB	A/B/C/D	Lecture 4				NO

Cross referenced deductions:

MEA not 40 year old

C----------CBI

SEATING

IB-B

C not 36

CBI not 42

B = 36 or 38

IB = 40 or 42

Lecture order: 42 year old followed by Chair 1

Man from IT = 40 or 42

Lecture order: 40 year old after MEA person

(with 1 person speaking between them)

Lecture order: Chair 4 followed by Man from IT

From this point we can start to use the cross referenced deductions and make the following modifications to the possibility matrix:

Since we have fixed that the Man from CBI is in Chair 4, we can delete him from Chair 3. We can also delete the possibility of the Chair 4 man being 42 years old.

The IB or the IT man cannot be in Chair 1 as the person in Chair 1 should be either 36 or 38 years old. Hence, B cannot be in Chair 2 (as he is sitting immediately right of the IB man).

Also, the removal of IB and IT from Chair 1's possibilities freezes that it is the MEA man who is in Chair 1. Consequently, we can delete the possibility of the MEA man being in either Chair 2 or Chair 3.

Further, since the IT and the IB men share the ages of 40 and 42 years, the CBI man in Chair 4 cannot be 40 years too.

Also, since we have the cross reference of the 40 year old sitting to the right of the man from MEA we can freeze the Chair 2 Man to be a 40 year old. This would leave Chair 3 with only one age possibility, i.e., 42 years.

At this stage the possibility matrix would look as below:

				36/38	40	42	36/38
				MEA	IT/IB	IT/IB	CBI
				C/D	A/C/D	A/B/D	A/B
				Chair 1	Chair 2	Chair 3	Chair 4
36/38/42	MEA/IB/CBI	A/B/D	Lecture 1	NO			NO
36/38/42	MEA/IT/IB/CBI	A/B/C/D	Lecture 2				
36/38/40/42	IT/IB/CBI	A/B/C/D	Lecture 3				
36/38/40	IT/IB	A/B/C/D	Lecture 4				NO

Cross referenced deductions:

MEA not 40 year old

C----------CBI

SEATING

IB-B

C not 36

CBI not 42

B = 36 or 38

IB = 40 or 42

Lecture order: 42 year old followed by Chair 1

Man from IT = 40 or 42

Lecture order: 40 year old after MEA person

(with 1 person speaking between them)

Lecture order: Chair 4 followed by Man from IT

At this point, we further have that the since the 40 year old spoke two slots after the man from the MEA and in the table we can have the man from the MEA speaking earliest at the second position, we get that the MEA man must have spoken 2nd and the 40 year old in Chair 2 would have spoken last.

This leaves Chair 4 to speak 3rd and Chair 3 to speak first

				36/38	40	42	36/38
				MEA	IT/IB	IT/IB	CBI
				C/D	A/C/D	A/B/D	A/B
				Chair 1	Chair 2	Chair 3	Chair 4
36/38/42	MEA/IB/CBI	A/B/D	Lecture 1	NO	NO	YES	NO
36/38/42	MEA/IT/IB/CBI	A/B/C/D	Lecture 2	YES	NO	NO	NO
36/38/40/42	IT/IB/CBI	A/B/C/D	Lecture 3	NO	NO	NO	YES
36/38/40	IT/IB	A/B/C/D	Lecture 4	NO	YES	NO	NO

At this point Clue (vi) becomes usable to complete the table: Clue (vi) says: The man who gave the 2nd lecture, sat next to the one who gave the 4th lecture, who is more than 2 years older than the one who spoke 2nd.

Reaction 1: Chair 1 can only be 36 since Chair 2 is 40.

Also, since Chair 4 is followed by the Man from IT, Chair 2 would be the man from IT and Chair 3 would be the man from IB.

Consequently, B would be in Chair 4.

The table now becomes:

				36	40	42	38
				MEA	IT	IB	CBI
				C/D	A/C/D	A/D	B
				Chair 1	Chair 2	Chair 3	Chair 4
36/38/42	MEA/IB/CBI	A/B/D	Lecture 1	NO	NO	YES	NO
36/38/42	MEA/IT/IB/CBI	A/B/C/D	Lecture 2	YES	NO	NO	NO
36/38/40/42	IT/IB/CBI	A/B/C/D	Lecture 3	NO	NO	NO	YES
36/38/40	IT/IB	A/B/C/D	Lecture 4	NO	YES	NO	NO

To this, if we add that the man from CBI is 2 years younger than C (cross referenced from clue (i)), we get that C must be in Chair 2.

Consequently, D is in Chair 1 and A must be in Chair 3. The final matrix looks as follows:

	36	40	42	38
	MEA	IT	IB	CBI
	D	C	A	B
	Chair 1	Chair 2	Chair 3	Chair 4
Lecture 1	NO	NO	YES	NO
Lecture 2	YES	NO	NO	NO
Lecture 3	NO	NO	NO	YES
Lecture 4	NO	YES	NO	NO

The answers can now be read off the table:

6. D
7. 40 years
8. 38 + 42 = 80
9. A is the eldest.
10. The final lecture was given by C and he belonged to the IT department.

Solutions for Questions 11 to 15:

11. There will be $8C_2$ + $8C_2$ + 4 quarter finals + 2 semifinals + 1 final = 63 matches. Option (c) is correct.
12. A team can be eliminated even if it wins 5 of its 7 matches (as 5 teams can possibly win 5 matches each) The logic for this is that in each group there are 8C2 = 28 matches, hence 28 winners. Thus, it is not possible for 5 teams to win 6 matches each. Hence if a team wins six matches it is safe. However, if a team wins 5 matches, 4 more teams could also have won 5 matches each and in that case the team would get eliminated. Hence, advancement is not guaranteed with 5 wins.
13. In this question we need to guarantee elimination. With 2 wins a team could still qualify (And hence elimination is not guaranteed) since there could be a scenario of (7 + 6 + 5 + 2 + 2 + 2 + 2 + 2) wins giving a situation wherein at least one of the teams with 2 wins needs to qualify. Hence, only if a team has 1 win, it's elimination is guaranteed. Option (a) is correct.
14. Quarter finals, semifinals and finals. Hence 3, option (c) is correct.
15. Option (c) is possible.

It is not necessary for the winner to have more wins than any other team. Since it is possible that a team with 2 wins in the first phase and 3 more wins (Quarterfinal, semifinal and final) in the 2nd stage wins the tournament and a team with 7 wins in the first phase loses the Quarterfinal. Hence (a) is not true.

Option (b) is also eliminated as it could happen that in one group a team with 5 wins is eliminated while in the other group a team with 2 wins advances.

Option (d) is also incorrect, since in the second stage of the tournament 4 teams who lose the quarterfinal will have no wins, 2 teams which lose the semifinals will have 1 win, 1 team which loses the final will have 2 wins and the team which wins the tournament will have 3 wins.

Option (c) could happen if a team is eliminated with 5 wins in the first stage and another team from the other group goes through to the second stage with 2 wins and then wins the 3 rounds in the second stage to emerge the winner with a total of 5 wins.

Solutions for Questions 16 to 20:

Each country sent a different number of candidates and the total number of candidates is 11.

Therefore 1, 2, 3, 5 candidates are sent from these countries in any order.

Let Alex, Borris, Chris, Danial, Eva, Peter, Qutub, Rambo, Steve, Tim, Utova be represented by A, B, C, D, E, P, Q, R, S, T, U, respectively.

According to the statement (iii) only Tim and Utova are from France.

Country	USA	UK	France	China
Number of candidates			2	
Name of the candidates			Tim, Utova	

Here we can see that France sent only officers. According to the statement (v) executives came from more number of countries than officers did. It implies that in the remaining three countries, all of them could not send officers and executives might have come from at most three countries therefore only one more country except France sent all the remaining four officers. Therefore, the country, which sent five candidates, sent all these four officers.

At this point, using the clue that, Alex and Eva were the only secretaries from their respective countries (Statement (ii)) and the number of executives from China is more than that of USA (Statement (vi)) we get that, UK and USA both have only one executive each (either Alex or Eva) and rest of the executives were from China.

Country	USA	UK	France	China
Number of candidates			2	3
Name of candidate			Tim, Utova	Borris, Chris, Danial

According to the statement-(vii) no officer was from USA. Therefore UK sent all the remaining officers. From statement-(iv) Alex is not from the UK. Hence Eva was from UK and Alex from USA.

Country	USA	UK	France	China
Number of candidates	1	5	2	3
Name of candidate	Alex	Peter, Qutub, Rambo, Steve, Eva	Tim, Utova	Borris, Chris, Danial

16. Alex
17. 0
18. 1
19. 1
    Total candidates sent by UK = 5; Total candidates sent by USA and China together = 1 + 3 = 4. Hence, 5 − 4 = 1.
20. Borris was from China. Hence, Option (d) is the correct answer.

MOCK TEST PAPER 2

Solutions for Questions 1 to 5:

In order to solve any puzzle kind of question, the first thing you have to think about is the best pictorial representation which would make it convenient to solve the question.

In this context, you realise when you read the question set that there are essentially 4 variables in this question viz: The house position and the house colour, the person's name and the salary of the individual. Out of these you realise from the starting statement of the problem itself that the relationship between the house colour and position is fixed ("Four houses Blue, Green, Red and Yellow are located in a row in the given order.")

Accordingly, your starting grid structure should look like this:

Position	1st	2nd	3rd	4th
Colour of house	Blue	Green	Red	Yellow
Name of person				
Salary				

Note that the 1st and 4th houses in the row are corner houses and have only 1 neighbour.

Once you create this grid structure, you need to first look at any direct clues within the clues provided. Scanning the 9 clues at this point you can see that all the clues are indirect clues and cannot be used directly in the current grid structure. The next thing you try to do is to try to use two clues in combination with each other. The first and second clues used together provide you with this opportunity.

Analysis of clues (I) and (II):

The first clue tells us that "Paul lives between Som and Krishna".

This gives us an initial thought that these three can occupy the houses 1, 2, 3 in the row with Paul occupying the 2nd house and Som and Krishna sharing houses 1 and 3 in no particular order. In this case Laxman has to occupy the 4th house, i.e. the Yellow house.

OR they can occupy the houses 2, 3, 4 with Paul occupying the 3rd house and Som and Krishna sharing houses 2 and 4 in no particular order. In this case Laxman has to occupy the 1st house, i.e. the Blue house. However, since we know from Clue (II) that Laxman does not stay in the Blue house we reject this possibility.

Consequently, we can fix the position of Paul and Laxman in the Green and Yellow houses respectively.

Position	1st	2nd	3rd	4th
Colour of house	Blue	Green	Red	Yellow
Name of person	Som/ Krishna	Paul	Krishna/ Som	Laxman
Salary				

At this point if we use Clue (VIII), we see that since "Krishna lives in between two houses" he cannot be in the first house. Hence, Krishna takes the third house and Som takes the 1st one.

Thus, the grid converts to:

Position	1st	2nd	3rd	4th
Colour of house	Blue	Green	Red	Yellow
Name of person	Som	Paul	Krishna	Laxman
Salary				

From this point we need to focus on fixing the values of the salaries of the 4 individuals.

The values of the four salaries can first be identified as 30000, 50000 (from Clue VIII), 80000 (Clue V) and 110000 (Clue VI). We also know from Clue VIII that Krishna lives between the people earning 30000 and 50000 which means that 30000 and 50000 could be Laxman and Paul's salary.

Further, the salary difference between Laxman and Som being 30000, their salaries would have to be 50000 and 80000, with Laxman getting 50000 and Som getting 80000. Consequently Paul gets 30000 and Krishna would earn 110000. The solution grid would then look like below:

Position	1st	2nd	3rd	4th
Colour of house	Blue	Green	Red	Yellow
Name of person	Som	Paul	Krishna	Laxman
Salary	80000	30000	110000	50000

The solutions can then be read off from the above as:

1. Krishna lives in the red house. Option (b) is correct.
2. The person earning the highest salary is Krishna and he lives in the Red house. Option (c) is correct.
3. The salary of the person in the green house is ₹ 30000. Option (a) is correct.
4. As the salary of Laxman is the second lowest (50,000) and he lives in the yellow house, option (b) is correct.
5. As per the table, we can see that only statement 3 is correct, hence the correct answer is (c).

Solutions for Questions 6 to 10:

Let the numbers called by the owner were p, q, r, s, t, u & v in the order of the calls made.

Let the lottery numbers assigned to Alan, Brad, Chris, Dom & Ehsaan be a, b, c, d & e respectively.

According to the statement (ii): $p + q = 30$. From the given table it is clear that out of 2, 3, 4, 5 and 6, 3 numbers (a, d and e) divide p and 4 numbers (a, c, d and e) divide q.

Now if we assume that p and q are divisible by 5, then p and q take the values 5 and 25 or 10 and 20 in any order but for these values of p and q the numbers would not be divisible by 3 or 4 of 2, 3, 4, 5 or 6. So we can conclude that p and q must not be divisible by 5.

Hence, $b = 5$.

a, c, d and e must be 2, 3, 4 and 6 (not necessarily in the same order).

From the above analysis we can conclude that p and q must be multiples of 6 (LCM of 2, 3 and 6) and 12 (LCM of 2, 3, 4 and 6) respectively.

p must be divisible by 2, 3 and 6 and q must be divisible by 2, 3, 4 and 6. Hence, p and q must be 18 and 12 respectively.

From the given table and the above analysis we can conclude that $c = 4$. (As c is a factor of 12 but not of 18). We are now sure about b and c being 5 and 4 respectively.

a, d and e must be 2, 3 and 6 (not necessarily in the same order).

According to the statement (i), $p + q + r + s + t + u + v = 100$

or $r + s + t + u + v = 100 - 30 = 70$ ...(1)

According to the statement (iv), owner called only 1 single digit number, therefore four of the above five (r, s, t, u, v) must be double digit numbers. Hence, none of those double digit numbers is greater than 30 because if any one of them is greater than 30 then there must be two single digit numbers which is a contradiction of the situation.

At this stage, if we look at Call 5, we see that Call 5 must be a number that has 2, 3, 4 and 6 as its factors, and 5 must not be its factor. Hence Call 5 (t) = 24. This leaves us with: r + s + u + v = 46.

Now by analysis of the given table it is clear that a = 2

Note: This can come from the analysis of the Call 7, where only A has raised his hand. Hence, the number in Call 7 must be a multiple of only one of the numbers amongst 2, 3 and 6.

But any number with a factor of 6, would also have 2 and 3 as its factors. Hence, a cannot be 6. This leaves a = 3 or a = 2. Analysing the possible values of Call 7 if a = 3, we get that Call 7 'v' could be: 9, 21 or 27 - multiples of 3, that are below 30, and are not divisible by 2, 4, 5, 6. Also, if a = 3, then Call 6, has to be a multiple of 5 and 3 and of course below 30 → Call 6 = u = 15. This leaves us with r + s + v = 31. You cannot fit any of the three values of v into this situation, while keeping s as prime and only one number being a single digit number. Thus, we conclude that a must be 2.).

This leaves us with d and e sharing 3 and 6.

From the table it is clear that only Brad raised his lottery ticket on the Call 3. Hence r must be a multiple of 5, hence r must be 5.

From the table it is clear that no one raised his lottery ticket on the 4th call hence 's' must be a double digit prime number less than 30.

'u' is a multiple of 5 and 2 hence, it must be 10.

'v' is a multiple of 2 but it is not a multiple of 3, 4, 5 and 6. As 'v' is greater than 10 and less than 30 so 'v' can take only three values 14, 22 or 26.

Now by putting all the known values in equation 1 we get: 5 + s + 24 + 10 + v = 70 or s + v = 31.

The only possible values 's' and 'v' can take are 17 and 14 respectively.

6. 31
7. Brad
8. 17
9. Brad would definitely raise his lottery ticket and one person out of Dom and Ehsaan (whoever held ticket 3) would also raise his lottery ticket. Hence, we cannot determine the answer. Option (d) is correct.
10. From the above solution, we see that the highest number is 24 and the lowest is 5. Hence, the answer is 24 - 5 = 19.

Solutions for Questions 11 to 15:

The first thing you should realise about this question is that there are 8 cars parked in a circle, 4 of which face inside and 4 face outside.

Based on this, you can start with the following figure before you start putting in the information:

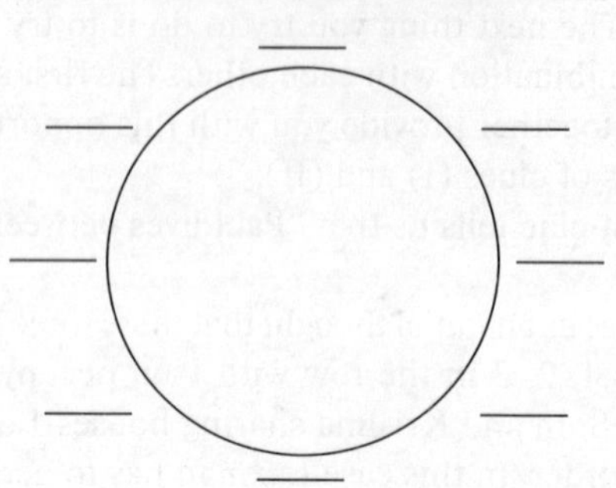

Using the fact that A and H are opposite each other and the information given in Statement (i) we get:

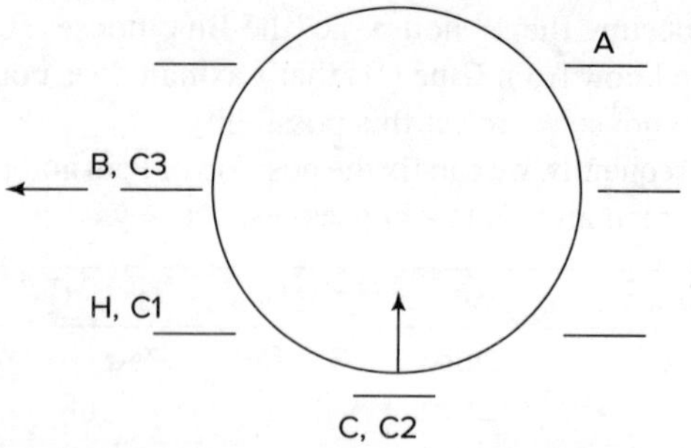

Using the information of Statements (ii) and (iv), the figure can be completed for which slot's car is facing in which direction and will look as given here:

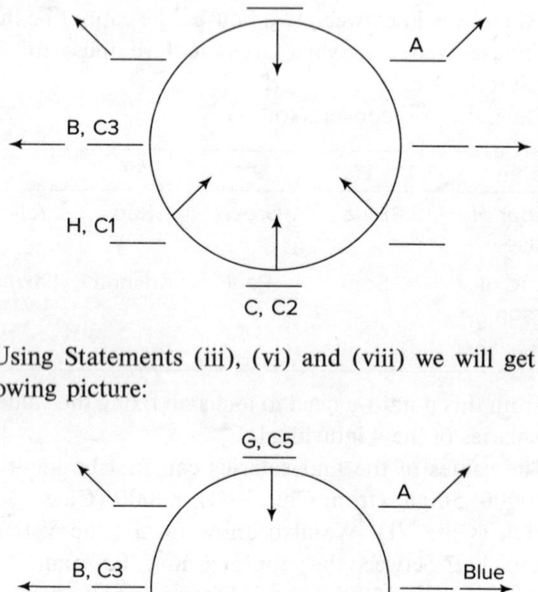

Using Statements (iii), (vi) and (viii) we will get the following picture:

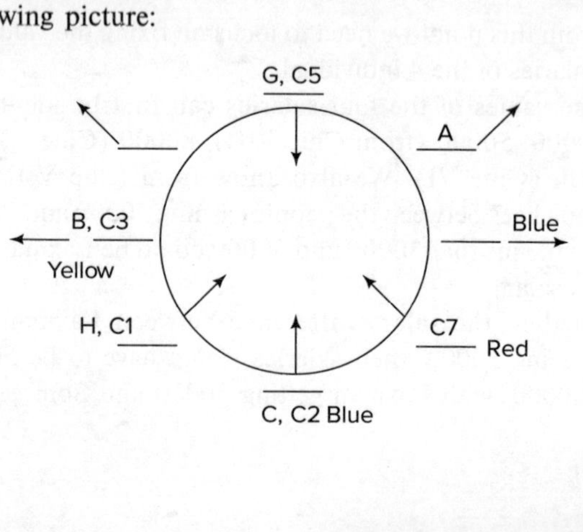

Using the remaining clues, we will get the final figure as follows:

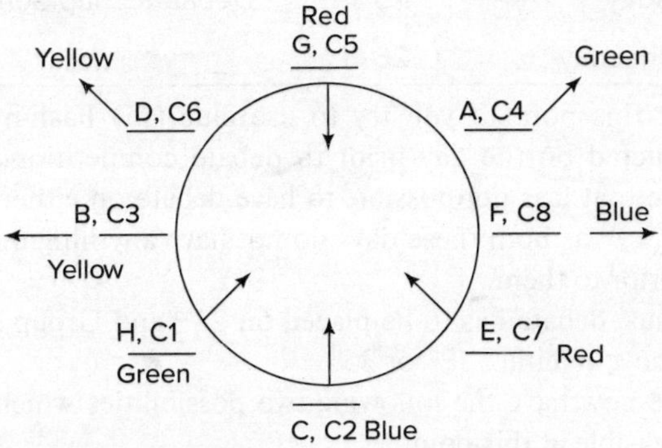

The Answers are:

11. (c)
12. (b)
13. A red car is to the right of the blue colored car. Hence, Option (a) is the correct answer.
14. A with C4 is opposite H. Hence, Option (b) is the correct answer.
15. C5 is a red colored car. Hence, Option (a) is the correct answer.

Solutions for Questions 16 to 20:

16. 0
    If A is sitting on the first seat on the first day, he can either go to the 3rd or the 5th seat on the second day. Likewise, if E is sitting on seat 3 on the first day, he would go to either seat 1 or seat 5 on the second day. It can be seen that both A and E would occupy odd numbered seats on all 10 days. On the other hand adjacent seats need to be a combination of consecutive integers – one odd and one even. Such a case would never occur for either A or for E, as they would be alternating within the three odd numbered seats only. Hence, the correct answer to this question is 0.
17. 36
    If you were to consider the seats to be numbered 1 to 6, in the clockwise fashion, then you realise from the solution of the previous question, that B,C and A are always going to be on the odd numbered seats, while D, E and F are always going to be on the even numbered seats. Hence, on the first day too, A,B and C would be on odd numbered seats 1,3 and 5 (a total of $3! = 6$ combinations); D, E and F would also be on the even numbered seats (a total of $3! = 6$ combinations). Hence, there would be a total possibility of $6 \times 6 = 36$ seating arrangements.
18. 4
    C has only three places to sit. If we try to minimise the number of times, for which he sat on any seat, we would need to distribute 10 sittings among three parts as equally as possible. This can be achieved with a distribution of $10 = 4 + 3 + 3$. Therefore he would need to sit on any one position a minimum of 4 times.
19. If A sat initially at a particular position on the 1st evening, then in order to sit at the same position the maximum number of times he would have to repeat his position on the 3rd, 5th, 7th, 9th, 11th evenings. Therefore the required value is 6.
20. D's seating would alternate between seats 2 and 4 and he would be on seat 2 (his position on the 11th evening) every alternate day. Hence, D would be on seat 2 on the 9th, 7th, 5th and 3rd evenings. Likewise, the position of B, would be the same on the 11th, 9th, 7th, 5th and 3rd evenings. Since, B is on seat 5 on the 11th evening, he must be on seat 5 on the 3rd evening too.

MOCK TEST PAPER 3

Solutions for Questions 1 to 5:

The first thing you should do in this case is to build the most relevant structure to place the information. Since, the question talks about the week from 19th October to 26th October, we can build the following starting grid in order to place the information of the question:

Day	Date	Competition
Wednesday	19	
Thursday	20	
Friday	21	
Saturday	22	
Sunday	23	
Monday	24	
Tuesday	25	
Wednesday	26	

Once you have visualised the above table, you can now move on to the direct clues which can be fit into the table at this point. These are:

Clue number (v): No Competition conducted on Thursday and Sunday.

Clue number (vi): Street Play conducted on Monday.

Putting these two clues in the above grid you would get the following:

Day	Date	Competition
Wednesday	19	
Thursday	20	XXXX
Friday	21	
Saturday	22	

Day	Date	Competition
Sunday	23	xxxx
Monday	24	Street Play
Tuesday	25	
Wednesday	26	

Once you have placed this information inside the grid you should look for the next clues that are usable directly at this point. In case you cannot use exactly one clue directly:

You should first look for a mixture of two clues which can give you some direct information to move ahead with your solution;

OR if such a thing cannot be found;

You should look for a clue that gives you multiple possibilities and move ahead with your solution process by considering each of the possibilities from that point. For instance, clue (vii) at this point gives you 4 possibilities of placing debate competition and group song as it says that there is a gap of 2 days between the two. These possibilities can be seen as under:

Possibilities 1 and 2 arise out of placing group song and debate on 19th and 22nd as shown below:

Day	Date	Competition
Wednesday	19	Group Song/Debate
Thursday	20	xxxx
Friday	21	
Saturday	22	Debate/Group Song
Sunday	23	xxxx
Monday	24	Street Play
Tuesday	25	
Wednesday	26	

Possibilities 3 and 4 arise out of placing group song and debate on 22nd and 25th as shown below:

Day	Date	Competition
Wednesday	19	
Thursday	20	xxxx
Friday	21	
Saturday	22	Group Song/Debate
Sunday	23	xxxx
Monday	24	Street Play
Tuesday	25	Debate/Group Song
Wednesday	26	

At this point if you try to use clue (iii) Fash-p was conducted on the day prior to debate competition, you realise that it is not possible to have debate on either 25th or on 19th as both these days do not have anything on the day prior to them.

Thus, debate has to be placed on 22nd and Group song can move to either 19th or 25th.

We now have the following two possibilities which are still feasible at this point:

Possibility 1:

Day	Date	Competition
Wednesday	19	
Thursday	20	xxxx
Friday	21	Fash-p
Saturday	22	Debate
Sunday	23	xxxx
Monday	24	Street Play
Tuesday	25	Group Song
Wednesday	26	

Possibility 2:

Day	Date	Competition
Wednesday	19	Group Song
Thursday	20	xxxx
Friday	21	Fash-p
Saturday	22	Debate
Sunday	23	xxxx
Monday	24	Street Play
Tuesday	25	
Wednesday	26	

But Possibility 2 can be rejected due to the fact that it contradicts clue (iv).

Thus, we get the following definite structure:

Day	Date	Competition
Wednesday	19	
Thursday	20	xxxx
Friday	21	Fash-p
Saturday	22	Debate
Sunday	23	xxxx

Day	Date	Competition
Monday	24	Street Play
Tuesday	25	Group Song
Wednesday	26	

This can be further completed by using clue (ii) at this point, viz: Rock band is not conducted on the closing day. With this the table gets completed.

Day	Date	Competition
Wednesday	19	Rock Band
Thursday	20	XXXX
Friday	21	Fash-p
Saturday	22	Debate
Sunday	23	XXXX
Monday	24	Street Play
Tuesday	25	Group Song
Wednesday	26	Folk Dance

The answers can now be read off from the above table.

1. The fashion week started with the Rock Band competition. Option (d) is the correct answer.
2. There are 5 days between the rock band and group competition. Option (d) is the correct answer.
3. The two Wednesdays are 19th and 26th and on these days the Rock band competition and the Folk Dance competition were held. Option (c) is the correct answer.
4. The Debate competition precedes the Street play competition. Option (c) is the correct answer.
5. Fash-p competition follows the Rock Band competition. Option (c) is the correct answer.

Solutions for Questions 6 to 10:

In this question there are essentially three clues.

When we use the first clue (The shorter of Sachin and Laxman is the older of the two century hitters) we get two main possibilities depending on who is shorter between Sachin and Laxman. We get the following options:

Possibility 1		Possibility 2
L		S
S	Older century Hitter	L

If we introduce Rahul on the basis of his height into the above figure, we would get six possible arrangements on the basis of height.

Possibility 1	Possibility 2	Possibility 3	Possibility 4	Possibility 5	Possibility 6	
		R			R	
L	L	L	S	S	S	
	R			R		
S	S	S	L	L	L	Older Century Hitter
R			R			

At this point if we use the third clue (*viz*: Taller of Sachin and Rahul is the younger century hitter) the table above would modify to:

Possibility 1	Possibility 2	Possibility 3	Possibility 4	Possibility 5	Possibility 6	
		R^Y			R^Y	
L	L	L	S^Y	S^Y	S	
	R^Y			R		
S^Y	S	S	L	L	L	Older Century Hitter
R			R			

(In the above table Y denotes the younger century hitter)

At this stage and the constraint of clue (ii) (*viz*: The younger of Laxman and Rahul is the shorter of the two century hitters.) Looking at individual possibilities of following deductions would emerge:

Possibility 1: Ruled out – Sachin is the older as well as the younger century hitter – not possible

Possibility 2 and 3: Rule out – The shorter century hitter has to come out of Laxman or Rahul, but in this case the shorter century hitter is Sachin.

Possibility 6: Ruled out: The younger of Rahul and Laxman has to be the shorter century hitter. But in this case Rahul is the younger century hitter while Laxman is the older century hitter (thus Rahul is younger than Laxman) yet is the taller one of the 2 century hitters also.

Possibilities 4 and 5 cannot be eliminated as they obey all 3 clues.

Thus Sachin is the younger century hitter while Laxman is the older century hitter (a conclusion which is consistent in both possibilities 4 and 5).

The answers are:

6. (b) Laxman
7. (a) Sachin
8. (a) Sachin
9. (b) Laxman
10. (c) Rahul

Solutions for Questions 11 to 16:

- From statement (vi): Bob is the second from the front and his T-shirt colour is Red.
- From statement (ii): Bob is standing behind Malini, who must be in the first position from the front. Now, Malini's T-shirt is not Red in colour.
- From statement (v): Malini's T-shirt is not Black in colour as Chris can not be ahead of Malini.
- From statement (vii): Malini's T-shirt is not White in colour.
- From statement (viii): Malini's T-shirt is not Silver in colour.
- From statement (iii): It can be concluded that Malini wears the Violet coloured Levis T-shirt.

Then we get, Bob does not wear the Levis T-shirt.

- From statement (i): Bob does not wear the Reebok T-shirt as it is not Red in colour.
- From statement (ii): Bob does not wear the Nike T-shirt.
- From statement (vii): Bob does not wear the Roadster T-shirt as it must be behind at least 2 persons.

Therefore, it can be concluded that Bob wears Puma. Further analysis leads to the following table:

Name	T-shirt	Colour
Malini	Levis	Violet
Bob	Puma	Red
Tariq	Reebok	White
Chris	Roadster	Silver
Aman	Nike	Black

11. Aman. Hence, option (a) is correct.
12. Reebok. Hence, option (c) is correct.
13. Levis.
14. Puma.
15. Violet.
16. Chris. Hence, option (b) is correct.

Solutions for Questions 17 to 20:

Let Piku, Qadir, Ram, Shahir, Tinku, Umesh, Varun, Waqar, Xavier,Yusuf be represented by P, Q, R, S, T, U, V, W, X, Y.

Possible groups of T, X, Y, R which could be in the selected team: TX/TY/TR/XY/XR/YR.

17. If T is in the team then P must be in the team (Condition- 3). If P is in the team then R cannot be in the team (Condition- 2).Now a team of 6 can be selected in the following ways:
1. T, P, X, U, S, Q
2. T, P, X, V, W, Q
3. T, P, X, S, W, Q
4. T, P, X, U, V, W
5. T, P, X, U, S, W
6. T, P, Y, V, W, Q
7. T, P, Y, S, W, Q

The required answer = 7

18. If Umesh is in the team then Yusuf cannot be in the team (Condition-1).
Among T, X, R TX/ TR/ XR are possible in the team.
Among V and S only one is selected.
Therefore minimum number of players possible in the team = 5 and maximum possible size of the team = 7.
Required value = 7 – 5 = 2.

19. To maximise the number of players in the team Yusuf must not be in the team because if Yusuf is in the team then according to the 6th condition two among Tinku, Xavier, Ram cannot be in the team and according to the 1st condition Umesh must not be in the team.
To maximize the size of the team Ram must not be in the team because if Ram is in the team then according to the 6th condition two among Tinku, Xavier, Yusuf cannot be in the team and according to the 2nd condition Piku must not be selected in the team.
According to the 4th condition only one among Varun and Sahir can be selected.
Hence maximum possible number of players in the team is 7.

20. If the team has maximum number of players then we can choose the team in the following ways:
1. PQSTWXY 2. PQTVWXY
Therefore two ways are possible.

MOCK TEST PAPER 4

Solutions for Questions 1 to 4:

If we consider the second statement of Anand, we can analyse the three cases:

(a) If the statement was made by a person who always speaks the truth: Not possible, since a person who is always true cannot make such a statement—as the statement would need to be true and if the statement is true, he would not be speaking the truth all the time. There is an internal contradiction in this statement, if spoken by a person who always speaks the truth.

(b) If the statement was made by a person who speaks the truth and lies (both): This is possible, as this statement could be true making him a liar in certain cases and a truth teller in certain cases.

(c) If a person who always lies made the statement: If the person always lies, by that condition, this statement would be false. However, if you look at the logic of what is said in this statement, the statement would become true—which is a contradiction of the premise that Anand always lies. Hence, this is not possible. We can conclude that Anand must be from Cadabra, his statement 2 can be true or false. His remaining statements must then be false or true.

	Statement 1	Statement 2	Statement 3	State	Profession
Anand	F/T	T	F/T	Cadabra	
Bhuwan					
Charan					
Dhawan					

If Dhawan's first statement is true then Bhuwan's second statement must be true and in that case none of them can be from Hoola Boola (since everyone would have at least one statement true). Therefore Dhawan's first statement must be false.

	Statement 1	Statement 2	Statement 3	State	Profession
Anand	F/T	T/F	F/T	Cadabra	
Bhuwan					
Charan					
Dhawan	F				

From the second statement of Bhuwan at most one of Bhuwan and Charan is from Abra (i.e. at most one amongst Bhuwan and Charan always speaks the truth). Therefore Dhawan's 2nd statement saying 'Exactly two of us always speak truth' must be false—since amongst the four people, Anand and Dhawan are already determined as to be not from Abra and if Bhuwan's second statement is true Charan is not from Abra. If Bhuwan's second statement is false, then he himself cannot be from Abra. Hence, Dhawan must be a liar—as his first two statements are false.

	Statement 1	Statement 2	Statement 3	State	Profession
Anand	F/T	T/F	F/T	Cadabra	
Bhuwan					
Charan					
Dhawan	F	F	F	Hoola Boola	

Since Dhawan's second statement is false, there must be exactly 1 person from Abra, who always speaks the truth. This person can be either Bhuwan or Charan.

Suppose Bhuwan was always true, then Charan was either always false or alternating between truth and false. Also, Bhuwan's three statements were true, then Anand would be a painter (Statement 3); Charan would be either a businessman or a doctor. This can be represented as shown below (with the suppositions and the consequent deductions in italics)

	Statement 1	Statement 2	Statement 3	State	Profession
Anand	F/T	T/F	F/T	Cadabra	*Painter*
Bhuwan	T	T	T		
Charan					
Dhawan	F	F	F	Hoola Boola	

This gives us the following three scenarios:

Scenario 1 under Bhuwan is true: Charan is always false:

	Statement 1	Statement 2	Statement 3	State	Profession
Anand	F/T	T/F	F/T	Cadabra	Painter
Bhuwan	*T*	*T*	*T*		Doctor
Charan	F	F	F		Engineer
Dhawan	F	F	F	Hoola Boola	Businessman

The following deductions follow: 1. Dhawan would be a businessman or a Painter (Charan's 3rd statement being false); However, he is not the painter as Anand is the painter. Hence, he would be the Businessman. Thus, Charan would be the engineer and Bhuwan the doctor as Dhawan's third statement being false, rules out Charan as a doctor. However, this makes Charan's first statement true–which we have already assumed to be false. Hence, scenario 1 can be ruled out.

Scenario 2 under Bhuwan is true: Charan is F, T, F.

This scenario cannot exist, since, this would make Dhawan's 1st statement true–something we already deduced is false.

Scenario 3 under Bhuwan is true: Charan is T, F, T.

Bhuwan is a doctor, hence Charan should be the businessman and Dhawan should be the Engineer. The table becomes:

	Statement 1	Statement 2	Statement 3	State	Profession
Anand	F/T	T/F	F/T	Cadabra	Painter
Bhuwan	T	T	T		Doctor
Charan	T	F	T		Businessman
Dhawan	F	F	F	Hoola Boola	Engineer

However, this scenario makes Dhawan's 3rd statement true, which is not possible.

Hence, we are left with no cases where Bhuwan could be always true. So we can conclude that it must be Charan who is always true. So we go back to the Y-junction in the problem and work with Charan's three statements being true. This leads to the following deductions:

	Statement 1	Statement 2	Statement 3	State	Profession
Anand	F/T	T/F	F/T	Cadabra	
Bhuwan					Doctor
Charan	T	T	T	Abra	
Dhawan	F	F	F	Hoola Boola	Engineer

Again from this point we have three scenarios for Bhuwan's statements–F, F, F; F, T, F or T, F, T. Testing each one:

	Statement 1	Statement 2	Statement 3	State	Profession
Anand	F/T	T/F	F/T	Cadabra	Businessman
Bhuwan	F	F	F	Hoola Boola	Doctor
Charan	T	T	T	Abra	Painter
Dhawan	F	F	F	Hoola Boola	Engineer

There are no contradictions in this solution and hence we can conclude the answers from this table.

Note: You can check the other two scenarios and try to find the contradictions.

1. Anand. Option (a) is correct.
2. Painter. Option (d) is correct.
3. Businessman. Option (c) is correct.
4. (d)
5. From the final solution table we can see that Anand belonged to Cadabra. Hence the correct answer is Anand.

Solutions for Questions 6 to 10:

There are originally (by default) eight possibilities to distribute the three dishes amongst A, B and C.

(PT = Paneer Tikka, RC = Roasted Chicken)

These are:

	A	B	C
Possibility 1	PT	PT	PT
Possibility 2	PT	RC	PT
Possibility 3	PT	PT	RC
Possibility 4	RC	PT	PT
Possibility 5	RC	RC	PT
Possibility 6	RC	PT	RC
Possibility 7	PT	RC	RC
Possibility 8	RC	RC	RC

The three constraints are:

1. If A = PT, B = C
2. If B = PT, $A \neq C$
3. If C = RC, A = B

If we analyse the eight possibilities with respect to the constraints, the following results emerge:

	A	B	C	Result
Possibility 1	PT	PT	PT	Rejected, constraint 2
Possibility 2	PT	RC	PT	Rejected, constraint 1
Possibility 3	PT	PT	RC	Rejected, constraint 1
Possibility 4	RC	PT	PT	No contradiction with any constraint
Possibility 5	RC	RC	PT	No contradiction with any constraint
Possibility 6	RC	PT	RC	Rejected, constraint 2
Possibility 7	PT	RC	RC	Rejected, constraint 3
Possibility 8	RC	RC	RC	No contradiction with any constraint

This gives us the possibility matrix for what is possible:

	A	B	C
Final Possibility 1 (Possibility 4 in the table above)	RC	PT	PT
Final Possibility 2 (Possibility 5 in the table above)	RC	RC	PT
Final Possibility 3 (Possibility 8 in the table above)	RC	RC	RC

Hence the answers are:

6. (a) Abdul always orders RC
7. If C orders RC (Final possibility 3), B orders RC. Hence option (a) is correct.
8. If B = PT (Final possibility 1) then Charu would also eat PT. Hence (a)
9. Abdul always orders a Roasted Chicken irrespective of what the other two order.
10. In the situation given above, Balwinder can order a Roasted Chicken or Paneer Tikka. Hence, Option (d) is the correct answer.

Solutions for Questions 11 to 15:

We get two combinations of possibilities. These are:

CASE I:

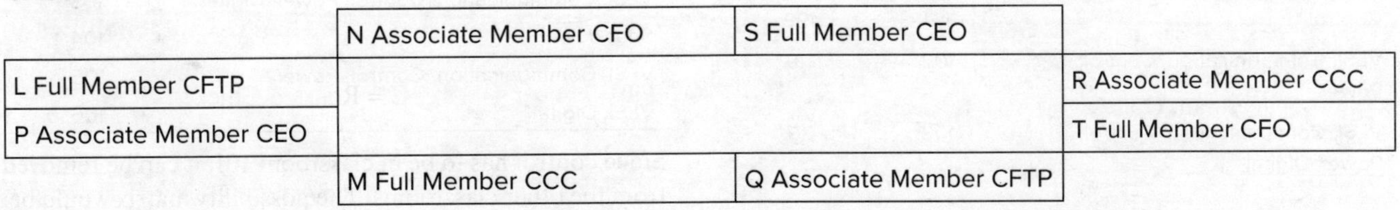

CASE II:

	N Associate Member CFO	S Full Member CEO	
Q Full Member CFTP			L Associate Member CFTP
R Associate Member CCC			P Full Member CFO
	M Full Member CCC	T Associate Member CEO	

The answers can be read off the possible tables:

11. (a)
12. (a)
13. (a) This would mean Case II and in that case, S will be the full members' CEO.
14. Q, L, P could each sit between two Associate members. Hence, Option (d) is the correct answer.
15. Both R & L could be sitting between Full Members CXOs. Hence, Option (d) is the correct answer.

Solutions for Questions 16 to 20:

From clue (ii):

Branch	Number of students
VLSI	48-60
Communication	56-70
Control	64-80
Power electronics	52-64
Digital electronics	40-49

From Clue (v):

Branches	Class room	Capacities
	101	128
VLSI, Communication, Control, Power	102	110
	103	80
	104	108
	105	90
	106	60

From Clues (iii), (iv), we can draw up the following possibility matrix:

Branches	Class room	Capacities
Control	101	128
VLSI, Communication, Control, Power	102	110
VLSI, Communication, Control, Power, Digital	103	80
Communication, Control	104	108
VLSI, Communication, Control, Power	105	90
VLSI, Digital	106	60

16. Power

If there are 64 students in classroom 103, then classroom 103 should have – either communication, control or power. This means that we have only 106 for digital – hence the digital lecture should be in 106. Control should be held in 101 and communication should be held in 104. That leaves us with Power in classroom 103 and VLSI in 105.

Branches	Class room	Capacities
Control	101	128
Shut down	102	110
Power,	103	80
Communication,	104	108
VLSI	105	90
Digital	106	60

17. 103

50 students can only be from the VLSI branch. Hence, the VLSI lecture must be held in room 106. This means that the Digital lecture has only 1 possible classroom left – i.e., 103. Hence, Classroom 103 cannot be shut for cleaning on that day.

18. 40

If 104 is closed down, the possibility matrix would look as below:

Branches	Class room
Control	101
VLSI, Communication, Control, Power	102
VLSI, Communication, Control, Power, Digital	103
Shut down	104
VLSI, Communication, Control, Power	105
VLSI, Digital	106

Since control has to be in classroom 101, it can be removed from the other classrooms. The possibility matrix would be:

Branches	Class room
Control	101
VLSI, Communication, Power	102
VLSI, Communication, Power, Digital	103
Shut down	104
VLSI, Communication, Power	105
VLSI, Digital	106

The number of students in 101 would be between 64 and 80. The number of students in classroom 106 would be between 40 and 60. The maximum possible difference would be 80 - 40 = 40.

19. 102
50 students can only come from the VLSI branch. Hence, classroom 103 should have a lecture of the VLSI branch. Then Digital should be in classroom 106. Also, since 101 is not shut down, Control should be held there. Further, since the Communication class is not held in 102 or 104, then 104 should be shut down and the communication class should be held in 105 - leaving Power to be held in Classroom 102.

Branches	Class room
Control	101
Power	102
VLSI,	103
Shut down	104
Communication	105
Digital	106

20. 104
104 is closed as seen from the previous solution.

MOCK TEST PAPER 5

Solutions for Questions 1 to 5:

The variables in the problem are:
Persons A/B/C/D/E
Date of Rally M/T/W/Th/F
Rally States UP/MP/G/D/AP
Symbol X/Y/Z/P/Q

Based on the starting clues in the problem, the following possibility matrix can be made using only the direct clues in the problem:

While making this table we have made the following deductions:

1. A's rally was not in UP and also was not on Monday (interpreted from clue (iv)).
2. B's rally is not in Delhi, his rally was not on Tuesday and his symbol was not Z (combination of clues (vi) and (vii)).

Person	A	B	C	D	E	Left to be Placed
States	UP×	Del×		G×/MP×		UP/MP/G/D/AP
Date	M×	T×		Th		M/T/W/F
Symbol		Z×		Y		X/Z/P/Q

The cross referenced clues at this stage are:

1. Q NOT F and Q should be 1 day before AP not M not P. (Interpreted from clue (ii))
2. MP = W.
3. UP not Friday.
4. G = X and G not in Column E. Also, the candidate whose rally was in Gujarat had his rally two days before E. This means E's rally could not be before Tuesday. Thus, E's rally can be only on Wednesday or Friday. Consequently, Gujarat = Monday/Wednesday. But since MP = W (given clue (iii)), Gujarat's rally could only be on Monday and hence, E's rally would be on Wednesday. Again since MP = W, E's rally is on Wednesday in MP. The table evolves to:

Person	A	B	C	D	E	Left to be Placed
States	UP×	Del×		G×/MP×	MP	UP/G/D/AP
Date	M×	T×		Th	W	M/T/F
Symbol		Z×		Y		X/Z/P/Q

At this stage the following deductions can be made:

1. Since Gujarat is on Monday, A's rally cannot be in Gujarat

Person	A	B	C	D	E	Left to be Placed
States	UP×Guj×	Del×		G×/MP×	MP	UP/G/D/AP
Date	M×	T× so M/F		Th	W	M/T/F
Symbol		Z×		Y		X/Z/P/Q

At this stage, we can use the clue (iv). According to that, the rally in UP is before the rally of A. We have already used one implication of this clue, by saying that A's rally is not in UP. However, there is a second connotation of this clue that comes out at this stage of the table, i.e., if we look for possible dates of the UP rally and A's rally, the apparent possibilities are Monday-Tuesday; Monday-Friday (Since Wednesday and Thursday cannot be A's rally date); Tuesday-Friday; Wednesday-Friday or Thursday-Friday. However, out of these possibilities, the possibility of UP's rally on Monday does not exist, as we have already found out that it is Gujarat's rally on Monday. Also, Wednesday-Friday is also not a possible combination, as Wednesday is fixed for MP and hence cannot be allocated to UP. Thus, all the possibilities for A's rally point out to only one date–viz. Friday for A's rally. Further, UP's rally is on Tuesday or Thursday.

So A's rally is on Friday, which also means that B's rally must be on Monday (and hence must be in Gujarat). Also since Gujarat = Monday = Symbol X, and since Z is on Tuesday (clue (vi)) the table evolves to:

Person	A	B	C	D	E	Left to be Placed
States	UP × so D/AP	G			MP	UP/D/AP
Date	F	M	T	Th	W	
Symbol		X	Z	Y		P/Q

Now, since we know that Friday is not the date for Symbol Q (clue (ii)'s interpretation), Q can only be E's symbol and P is A's symbol.

The table becomes:

Person	A	B	C	D	E	Left to be Placed
States	UP × so D/AP	G			MP	UP/D/AP
Date	F	M	T	Th	W	
Symbol	P	X	Z	Y	Q	

Then, we have that A's rally is not in UP and AP is not the state for the rally of the symbol P, which means that A's rally can only be in Delhi. Also, clue (ii) gives us that the AP rally is one day after symbol Q's rally. Hence, the AP rally would be on Thursday. The table then gets completed as below:

Person	A	B	C	D	E
States	D	G	UP	AP	MP
Date	F	M	T	Th	W
Symbol	P	X	Z	Y	Q

The answers are:

1. Gujarat
2. C
3. Friday
4. D
5. Symbol Z is associated with C and he organized his rally on Tuesday.

Solutions for Questions 6 to 11:

We start off by making a grid as follows (Note: in this grid we have used clues numbered (iii) and (vii))

	416 Madhuri	Kareena	Aishwarya	Shilpa	Juhi
Amit					
Shahrukh					
Anil					
Sunil					
417 Akshay		×			

From clue (iv) we get that Anil and Amit are in different films than Aishwarya. We also know from clue (ii) that Shahrukh and Aishwarya are not together and from clue (i) that Aishwarya is not with Akshay too. Also since Aishwarya is between Akshay and Amit, Aishwarya's number could only by 418 (As 416 is Madhuri) and Amit must be 419). Also, clue (vi) gives us that neither Shilpa nor Juhi have acted with Amit. Based on these realisations, the grid above transforms into:

	416 Madhuri	419 Kareena	418 Aishwarya	Shilpa	Juhi
419 Amit	×	✓	×	×	×
Shahrukh		×	×		
Anil		×	×		
418 Sunil	×	×	✓	×	×
417 Akshay	×	×	×		

At this point we need to concentrate on the time of film completion to move further in the question.

From clue (ii)

Shahrukh's film takes 3/4th the time of Sunil's film. (But we know that Sunil's film has Aishwarya). Hence, we conclude (from clue (ii) and clue (iv))

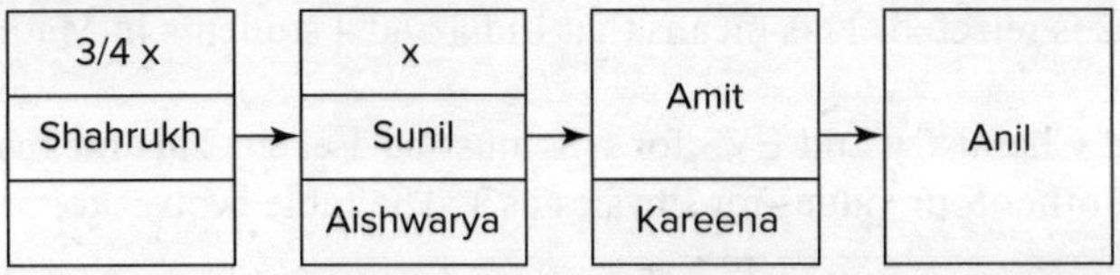

If we add the information from clue (vi) to this, we realise that Shilpa and Juhi must be after Amit. Thus, only Madhuri is left for Shahrukh. Also, since Anil's film took maximum number of days Anil must be with Shilpa. We then get the following chronological figure:

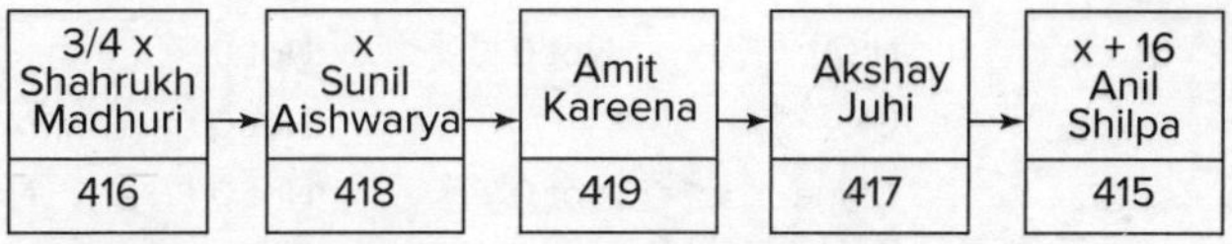

Also from clue (viii), we get that x must be 32 days (Sunil's film) and Shahrukh's film must be 24 days and Anil's film 48 days.

The answers are:

6. Amit (a)
7. Sunil and Aishwarya (d)
8. 416 (b)
9. Juhi (c)
10. 32 days (c)
11. Shilpa (b)

Solutions for Questions 12 to 15:

Solve on the basis of the following table:

I round			II round			III round		
C	W	Net score	C	W	Net score	C	W	Net score
2	–	50	2	–	50	2	–	80
1	1	10	1	1	10	1	1	20
0	–2	–20	0	2	–30	0	2	–40

12. 40 can be scored by:
    (1) 50 - 30 + 20
    or (2) 10 + 10 + 20.
    Hence option (d) is correct.
13. There are 3 × 3 × 3 = 27 possible scores. Out of these three there are only 2 ways of scoring 100.
    Hence 2/27. option (b)
14. There are only two ways of scoring 20 from the table *viz.*: 50 + 10 - 40 or 10 + 50 - 40. In both cases there are three right answers. Hence, the required probability is zero. option (d) is correct.
15. The maximum Penalty for 2 incorrect answers would occur when they happen in the last round. Hence, the score would be 50 + 50 - 40 = 60
    Hence option (b) is correct.

Solutions for Questions 16 to 20:

We can start thinking about the solution with the following table, using the direct clues given in the question:

	Physics	Chemistry	EVS	Biology	Math	Total
India			0			C+2
UAE					x	C-2
USA					x	C-1
UK					x	C-3
China					x	C
	P	2P	2P	2P	2P	9P = 5C-4

From the information that the number of students in each subject for India was different, we can deduce that India has 0, 1, 2, 3 and 4 students in the five subjects in some order. This means that C + 2 = 10. Consequently the table changes to:

	Physics	Chemistry	EVS	Biology	Math	Total
India	Not 0	Not 0	0	Not 0		10
UAE	Not 0	Not 0		Not 0	x	6

USA	Not 0	Not 0		Not 0	x	7
UK		Not 0	Not 0	Not 0(Max for UK)	x	5
China	Not 0	Not 0	Not 0	Not 0	x	8
	4	8	8	8	8	36

At this point the following deductions occur:

1. Since India's number in Math cannot be 0, the value of $x = 2$ is rejected. This means that India had 4 students in Math and the value of $x = 1$.
2. Since UK's maximum value is for Biology, it must be 2 and Chemistry and EVS for UK must be 1 each. This means that UK's value for Physics would be 0, making each of the other four values for Physics as 1. The table evolves to:

	Physics	Chemistry	EVS	Biology	Math	Total
India	1	Not 0	0	Not 0	4	10
UAE	1	Not 0		Not 0	1	6
USA	1	Not 0		Not 0	1	7
UK	0	1	1	2	1	5
China	1	Not 0	Not 0	Not 0	1	8
	4	8	8	8	8	36

At this point we are given that, for China Chemistry, EVS and Biology are all equal. Since the total for China is 8, each of these values must be 2 each. This gives us the India cannot have 3 students for Biology. So, Biology for India = 2.

Thus, Chemistry for India = 3 and Chemistry for USA and UAE would be 1 each. We can then complete the total, which would give us the final table.

	Physics	Chemistry	EVS	Biology	Math	Total
India	1	3	0	2	4	10
UAE	1	1	2	1	1	6
USA	1	1	3	1	1	7
UK	0	1	1	2	1	5
China	1	2	2	2	1	8
	4	8	8	8	8	36

The answers can be read off from the table:

16. Total number of students = 36
17. Maximum number of students from USA participated in EVS quiz.
18. Number of students from USA participated in Biology quiz = 1
19. India had maximum number of students in Chemistry and the number of students is 3.
20. The required sum is 1 + 3 + 3 + 2 + 4 = 13.

MOCK TEST PAPER 6

Solutions for Questions 1 to 5:

Represent the professions as En/Do/Pa/Sa/Bo. The starting matrix would look as follows:

			En/Do/Pa/Sa/Bo	En/Do/Pa/Sa/Bo	En/Do/Pa/Sa/Bo	En/Do/Pa/Sa/Bo	En/Do/Pa/Sa/Bo
			G13/K1/K2/X1/X2	G13/K1/K2/X1/X2	G13/K1/K2/X1/X2	G13/K1/K2/X1/X2	G13/K1/K2/X1/X2
			P	Q	R	S	T
En/Do/Pa/Sa/Bo	G13/K1/K2/X1/X2	A					
En/Do/Pa/Sa/Bo	G13/K1/K2/X1/X2	B					

			En/Do/Pa/Sa/Bo	En/Do/Pa/Sa/Bo	En/Do/Pa/Sa/Bo	En/Do/Pa/Sa/Bo	En/Do/Pa/Sa/Bo
En/Do/Pa/ Sa/Bo	G13/K1/K2/ X1/X2	C					
En/Do/Pa/ Sa/Bo	G13/K1/K2/ X1/X2	D					
En/Do/Pa/ Sa/Bo	G13/K1/K2/ X1/X2	E					

Using the direct clues from (iv) to (x), the possibility matrix transforms to the one shown below (through the following chain of deductions):

1. From Clues (iv) and (v): A is not in X-2 as he is not a doctor. So, we cancel out the possibilities X2 and Doctor from A.
2. Clue (vi) gives us: R is the wife of D, is placed directly in the grid, thus ruling out the entire set of other possibilities in the R column and the D row.
3. Clue (vii) tells us to rule out the intersection of E & Q. Also, it tells us that E is a Salesman. Consequently, Salesman as a profession gets deleted from A to D. It also deletes the possibility of Sa (Salesman) for Q.
4. From Clues (viii) to (x): we get P lives in flat G-13 (so we delete G13 from Q, R, S and T); C lives in K-1 (so we delete K1 from A, B, D and E). Also, the intersection of C and S is rejected. S's husband is a painter–hence we can delete the possibility of Pa (Painter) from the possibilities of P, Q, R and T.

			En/Do/Sa/Bo	En/Do/Bo	En/Do/Sa/Bo	Pa	En/Do/Sa/Bo
			G13	K1/K2/X1/X2	K1/K2/X1/X2	K2/X1/X2	K1/K2/X1/X2
			P	Q	R	S	T
En/Pa/Bo	G13/K2/X1	A			NO		
En/Do/Pa/Bo	G13/K2/X1/X2	B			NO		
En/Do/Bo	K1	C			NO	NO	
En/Do/Bo	G13/K2/X1/X2	D	NO	NO	YES	NO	NO
Sa	G13/K2/X1/X2	E		NO	NO		

The next set of deductions, are as follows:

1. From Clue (i), we can delete K2 from T;
2. From Clue (ii), we can delete X1 and X2 from B's possibilities; Also, B is not an engineer.
3. From Clues (ii) and (iii), we get that the flat number of the engineer is either K1, K2 or X2. This deduction cannot be used to transform the table at this point, so we should keep this aside as a cross-referenced clue.
4. Since E is a Salesman and S's husband is a Painter, E cannot be S's husband.
5. Since C is in K-1 and P is in G-13, P cannot be C's wife.
6. We can also delete Sa (Salesman) from R (since R is D's wife, while the salesman is E).
7. We can delete Do (Doctor) from B and C (as Do has to be matched with X2, but X2 is no longer a possibility for B and C).

The matrix transforms to the following:

Cross Referenced Clue: Engineer is in either K1, K2 or X2.

			En/Do/Sa/Bo	En/Do/Bo	En/Do/Bo	Pa	En/Do/Sa/Bo
			G13	K1/K2/X1/X2	K1/K2/X1/X2	K2/X1/X2	K1/X1/X2
			P	Q	R	S	T
En/Pa/Bo	G13/K2/X1	A			NO		
Pa/Bo	G13/K2	B			NO		
En/Bo	K1	C	NO		NO	NO	
En/Do/Bo	G13/K2/X1/X2	D	NO	NO	YES	NO	NO
Sa	G13/K2/X1/X2	E		NO	NO	NO	

A close look at the matrix now shows that amongst the men, it is only D who could be the doctor. This moves the matrix forward in the following ways:

1. Do (Doctor) and X2 get fixed for D. Consequently, Do (Doctor) and X2 also get fixed for R. Thus, X2 gets deleted from Q, S and T. Do, gets deleted from P, Q and T.
2. X2 gets deleted from E.

			En/Sa/Bo	En/Bo	Do	Pa	En/Sa/Bo
			G13	K1/K2/X1	X2	K2/X1	K1/X1
			P	Q	R	S	T
En/Pa/Bo	G13/K2/X1	A			NO		
Pa/Bo	G13/K2	B			NO		
En/Bo	K1	C	NO		NO	NO	
Do	X2	D	NO	NO	YES	NO	NO
Sa	G13/K2/X1	E		NO	NO	NO	

1. At this stage, the possibility matrix shows us that the Engineer is either in K1 or K2. Using Clue (ii) again at this point, we get that B's starting letter, (flat number) can only be G. Hence, B lives in flat G-13. Thus, P is B's wife.
2. Also, B can only be a boxer since the list of profession possibilities for B is Pa/Bo and for P is En/Sa/Bo. The only intersecting possibility is Bo. So P is also G13 and Bo. So we can delete En and Sa from P.
3. Bo can then be deleted from C, giving us that C is an Engineer. Bo can also be deleted from Q, giving us that Q's husband is the engineer. Consequently, Q's husband should be C and they live in the flat K1.
4. Bo and En can also be deleted from T and A at this point.
5. The only possibility left for E's wife is T and consequently, A's wife is S.
6. The final deduction at this point is that E and T must be in X1 (as that is the only intersecting possibility for flat number for E and T). This leaves K2 for S and her husband A.

The possibility matrix reaches its final point shown below:

			Bo	En	Do	Pa	Sa
			G13	K1	X2	K2	X1
			P	Q	R	S	T
Pa	K2	A	NO	NO	NO	YES	NO
Bo	G13	B	YES	NO	NO	NO	NO
En	K1	C	NO	YES	NO	NO	NO
Do	X2	D	NO	NO	YES	NO	NO
Sa	X1	E	NO	NO	NO	NO	YES

The answers are:

1. Painter
2. B
3. E-T
4. S
5. It is clear from the table that the couple who lives in X2 are Doctors.

Solutions for Questions 6 to 11:

For this question if you try to refer to the information with respect to the country of the player you will not get any headway, but if you try to reference the information with respect to the room number you will find it easier.

An obvious question that might crop up in your mind will obviously be - "But how do I know that?" and indeed "How do I decide what variable to reference for solving a complex question like this? The answer is simple really while reading the question for the first time, try to focus on spotting the variable with respect to which the maximum number of direct clues are associated.

In this question it is clear that the maximum number of direct clues here are associated with the room number and hence we try to associate things with the room number.

From clue number (v):

Room No. 143 → 12 m and 8 Sixes (meal = m and sixes = S)

From clue no. (vii): Room No. 145 → 8 m and (P-2S) (Where P is the number of sixes hit by the Pakistan player).

From clue (viii): Pakistan, England and Australia can either be 141, 143 and 145 or 142, 144 and 146. But from question 6 (and it's options) it is clear that Australia cannot be in Room 146. Thus, we get the following situation at this stage.

141	Pakistan	
142		
143	England	(12 m, 8 s)
144		
145	Australia	(8 m, P–2s)
146		

We also have the following information:

From clue (i): Room No. 142 → 24 m (twice the player who hits 8 sixes).

From clue (iii) we have that the Indian is 8 less than the English (Meals) and 10 more than the English (Sixes). This means that the Indian is 4 m and 18 S.

From clue (ii): NZ + Room No. 146 = 40 (Meals).

From clue (vi): someone has (16 m and 24 S).

Now since we have to adjust New Zealand, India and Sri Lanka (which we discover from options to question 10) and all the above facts the only way to do so is as shown below.

141	Pakistan	
142	New Zealand	(24 m,)
143	England	(12 m, 8 S)
144	India	(4 m, 18 S)
145	Australia	(8 m, P – 2 S)
146	Sri Lanka	(16 m, 24 S)

This arrangement also satisfies clue (iv).

The answers:

6. 145 (d)
7. 18 (c)
8. 12 (b)
9. Sri Lanka (c)
10. Sri Lanka (d)
11. New Zealand (b)

Solutions for Questions 12 to 15:

The basic premises in this question provide us with the following constraints.

There have to be 3 actors for whom the number of hits > Number of flops;

1 actor should have hits = flops; 2 actors should have hits < flops.

The other conditions to be remembered are:

Constraint 1: $\frac{\text{number of hits}}{\text{number of flops}} = 3$ only for 1 actor;

| Star rating | = 3 only for one actor and

Nobody's star rating > 6 or < –6.

Based on these conditions we can tabulate the given information to start thinking clearly:

Actor	Hits	Flops (1, 2, 3, 5, 7, 8)
Akshay	0	
Ranbir	2	
Hrithik	3	
Aamir	4	Not 1, not 7
Shahrukh	6	
Salman	9	

Using constraint 2: We get that there are two actors for whom: | Star rating | = 3 is possible. These are Akshay if he has 3 flops and Ranbir if he has 5 flops.

Also, there are only two cases of the superstar possible (Ranbir or Hrithik being the only two actors with a possibility for number of hits = number of flops).

This gives rise to 2 possible cases as:

Case 1: | Star rating | = 3 for Akshay and Superstar = Ranbir and $\frac{\text{number of hits}}{\text{number of flops}} = 3$ for Shahrukh;

In this case, since 3 and 2 flops would get allocated to Akshay and Ranbir respectively, it would mean that the $\frac{\text{number of hits}}{\text{number of flops}} = 3$ would only be possible for Hrithik.

So we have to allocate to him 1 flop. Then, if we try to look for the number of Flop stars and megastars, we would need to make two of Aamir, Shahrukh and Salman Megastars. Since, the number of flops left to be allocated would be 5, 7 and 8, Aamir cannot be a megastar. Hence, Shahrukh should be a megastar – which is only possible if he has 5 flops. Then Aamir would have 8 flops (as he cannot have 7 by flops by definition) and Salman would have 7 flops.

Case 2: | Star rating | = 3 for Ranbir and Superstar = Hrithik and $\frac{\text{number of hits}}{\text{number of flops}} = 3$ for Salman or Shahrukh;

In this case, the superstar with hits = flops can only be Hrithik. Further, the two flop stars in this case would get fixed as Akshay and Ranbir. This means that Aamir, Shahrukh and Salman would all be Mega stars. But for that to be true, Aamir would need to have 2 flops – and the moment you do that the other constraint in the problem of $\frac{\text{number of hits}}{\text{number of flops}} = 3$, would have no resolution as you can create neither the 6/2 nor the 9/3 pairs for Shahrukh or Salman.

Actor	Hits	Flops (1, 2, 3, 5, 7, 8)	Case 1	Case 2
Akshay	0		3 (F)	(F)
Ranbir	2		2 (S)	5 (F)

Actor	Hits	Flops (1, 2, 3, 5, 7, 8)	Case 1	Case 2
Hrithik	3		1 (M)	3 (S)
Aamir	4	Not 1, not 7	8 (F)	2 (M)
Shahrukh	6		5 (M)	1/7 or 8 (M)
Salman	9		7 (M)	1/7 or 8 (M)

Thus, Case 1 is the only possibility. The answers then can be read from the completed table for Case 1.

12. 2
13. Aamir
14. 0
15. 0

Solutions for Questions 16 to 20:

The first thing you need to recognize in this set is the variables involved. From the first two paragraphs, it is amply clear that we need to make a Venn diagram between people who support proposal A and those who support proposal B. Also, there is a two way split of every area of the Venn diagram, between people who prefer Sunita (S) and those who prefer Ragini (R). It might help to point out here that there are two things to note in the starting instructions–

(i) There may be people who prefer both proposals A and B, people who prefer only A, people who prefer only B and also those who prefer neither A nor B. (hence, the Venn diagram between A and B).

(ii) Amongst the 500 people surveyed, everyone prefers either S or R for president (hence, the division of the 500 amongst those who prefer S or R would be tabular and not a Venn diagram).

The initial figure with the visualization of the variables involved would look as follows:

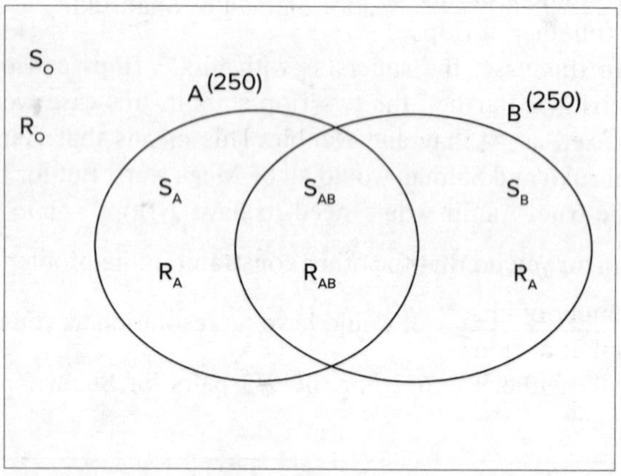

At this point, you should be aware from clues 2 and 3, that:

$$S_A + S_B + S_{AB} + S_O = 200 \quad (1)$$
$$R_A + R_B + R_{AB} + R_O = 300 \quad (2)$$
$$S_A + S_{AB} = 80\% \text{ of } 200 = 160 \quad (3)$$
$$R_A + R_{AB} = 30\% \text{ of } 300 = 90 \quad (4)$$

From the clue 4, '20% of those who supported Proposal B, preferred Sunita', we get $S_B + S_{AB} = 50$.

This also means that there are 200 people amongst those who support B, who prefer Ragini. At this point, the clues seem to be taking us in circles. But clue 6, is what helps us to move out of the puzzle as it says, "Every student who preferred Sunita and supported proposal B also supported proposal A.", which essentially should be interpreted as: $S_B = 0$. Using the equations, we have created above and starting with $S_B = 0$, we get the following chain → $S_{AB} = 50$ (from equation 5) → $S_A = 110$ (from equation 3) → $S_O = 40$ (from equation 1).

Also, from the clue 7 we have that: $R_O = 60$. Hence, from equations 2 and 4, we get $R_A = 300 - 60 - 90 = 150$. Subsequently, from the B circle in the figure, we can deduce that $R_{AB} = 50$ and then from equation 2, we get $R_B = 40$. The final picture looks as follows:

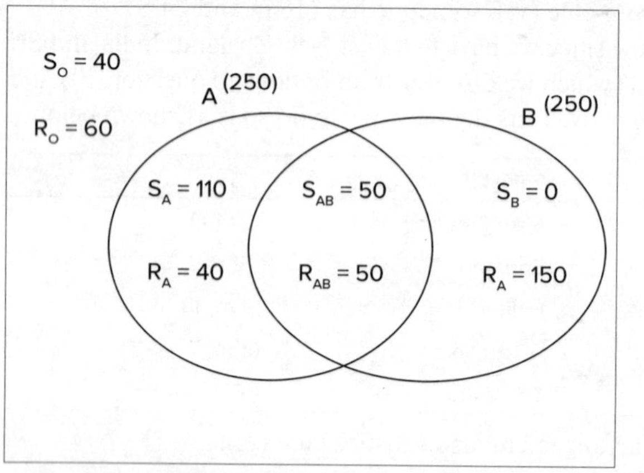

The answers can be read off from here.

16. A total of 250 students support proposal A. Out of these, 160 prefer Sunita. 160 out of 250 = 64%.
17. A total of 250 people did not support proposal A. Out of these 210 preferred Ragini. Hence, the required percentage is 210/250 = 84%.
18. 100 people support both proposals. Out of these, 50 prefer Sunita. 50 out of 100 = 50%. Hence, option (d).
19. There are 150 students who support only B and prefer Ragini. Hence, option (a) is correct.
20. From the solution figure, this number is 40.

MOCK TEST PAPER 7

Solutions for Questions 1 to 5:

The starting grid would look as follows: The cities Kanpur, Mumbai, Mangalore, Delhi and Lucknow can be represented by K/Mu/Ma/De/L while the sports Cricket, Football, Hockey, Tennis and Boxing can be represented as Cr/F/H/Te/Bo. The starting possibility matrix would look as follows:

			Cr/F/H/Te/Bo	Cr/F/H/Te/Bo	Cr/F/H/Te/Bo	Cr/F/H/Te/Bo	Cr/F/H/Te/Bo
			K/Mu/Ma/De/L	K/Mu/Ma/De/L	K/Mu/Ma/De/L	K/Mu/Ma/De/L	K/Mu/Ma/De/L
			P	Q	R	S	T
Cr/F/H/Te/Bo	K/Mu/Ma/De/L	A					
Cr/F/H/Te/Bo	K/Mu/Ma/De/L	B					
Cr/F/H/Te/Bo	K/Mu/Ma/De/L	C					
Cr/F/H/Te/Bo	K/Mu/Ma/De/L	D					
Cr/F/H/Te/Bo	K/Mu/Ma/De/L	E					

We can now start looking at the clues in the problem. Using the direct information in the clues, the grid would start looking as follows:

			Cr/F/H/Te	Cr/F/H/Te	Cr/F/H/Te	Cr/F/H	Bo
			K/Mu/Ma/De/L	K/Mu/Ma/De/L	K/Mu/Ma/De/L	Mu/L	K/Mu/Ma/L
			P	Q	R	S	T
H	Mu/L	A	NO		NO		
Cr/F/Bo	K/De/L	B	NO				
Cr/F/Te/Bo	K/Mu/De/L	C	NO				
Cr/F/Te/Bo	Ma	D	NO				
Cr/F/Te/Bo	K/Mu/L	E	YES	NO	NO	NO	NO

Cross-referenced clue: Football – Kanpur

The following deductions can then be made based on the current state of the table:

1. As D is from Mangalore, he cannot work in company S (because Mangalore has been deleted from the list of possibilities for S).
2. T cannot be the company of A (as the person working in T likes Boxing and A likes Hockey).
3. We can delete F (football) from the list of possibilities for Company S since Football & Kanpur are together and the possibility for Kanpur for Company S has already been deleted. By the opposite logic we can delete Kanpur (K) from Company T's possibilities.
4. Since Mumbai (Mu) and Lucknow (L), are to be shared between person A and Company S (and they are separate people), and since A likes Hockey, the person in Company S cannot like Hockey. Hence, that person must like Cricket.
5. Also, H (Hockey) can be deleted from Company P and R's possibilities as H belongs to Person A, who is clearly not working in either company P or R.
6. This leaves only 1 possibility for H (Hockey), i.e., the person from Company Q must like H (Hockey).

These deductions convert the table to:

			F/Te	H	F/Te	Cr	Bo
			K/Mu/Ma/D/L	K/Mu/Ma/D/L	K/Mu/Ma/D/L	Mu/L	Mu/Ma/L
			P	Q	R	S	T
H	Mu/L	A	NO	YES	NO	NO	NO
Cr/F/Bo	K/D/L	B	NO	NO			
Cr/F/Te/Bo	K/Mu/D/L	C	NO	NO			
Cr/F/Te/Bo	Ma	D	NO	NO		NO	
Cr/F/Te/Bo	K/Mu/L	E	YES	NO	NO	NO	NO

The following deductions can now be made on this table:

1. Since A is working in company Q, Q must be from Mu or L. Consequently, Mu (Mumbai) and L (Lucknow) have to get shared between Companies Q and S.
2. Hence, the possibilities of Mu (Mumbai) and L (Lucknow) have to be removed from Companies P, R and T.

3. Consequently, Mu and L also has to be removed from Person E–leaving only Kanpur (and consequently Football) for Person E. Football–Kanpur can then be deleted from everywhere else *viz.*: persons A, B, C and D as well as Companies Q, R, S and T.
4. Since Company T had only 3 possibilities with regards to their cities, this leaves us only with Mangalore (Ma) for Company T. Since D is from Mangalore, D must be in company T. D must like Boxing then–as Boxing has already been frozen as the preferred sport for the person from Company T.

The table becomes the following after this set of deductions:

			F	H	Te	Cr	Bo
			K	Mu/L	De	Mu/L	Ma
			P	Q	R	S	T
H	Mu/L	A	NO	YES	NO	NO	NO
Cr	De/L	B	NO	NO			NO
Cr/Te	Mu/De/L	C	NO	NO			NO
Bo	Ma	D	NO	NO	NO	NO	YES
F	K	E	YES	NO	NO	NO	NO

From the above table the next set of deductions that emerges is:

1. Since Cricket (Cr) has got frozen for Person B and Company S, Person B belongs to Company S. Also, this person cannot be in Mumbai or Delhi (as Person B has Delhi but not Mumbai as a possibility while Company S has Mumbai but not Delhi as a possibility). So, B is from Lucknow (L).
2. This means that Person C must be in Company R.
3. It also means that Person A of Company Q must be from Mumbai.

			F	H	Te	Cr	Bo
			K	Mu	De	L	Ma
			P	Q	R	S	T
H	Mu	A	NO	YES	NO	NO	NO
Cr	L	B	NO	NO	NO	YES	NO
Te	De	C	NO	NO	YES	NO	NO
Bo	Ma	D	NO	NO	NO	NO	YES
F	K	E	YES	NO	NO	NO	NO

The answers can be read off this table:

1. A works in Company P.
2. B likes cricket.
3. Tennis.
4. C who likes tennis would then be working in Mumbai.
5. As per the given table, only Statement I is correct.

Solutions for Questions 6 to 11:

We can make the following visual representations in order to represent the information:

Clue (i) Coke - Pepsi - Sprite OR Sprite - Pepsi - Coke

Clue (ii) Coke
↑
Sprite
↑
Pepsi

Clue (iii) Limca $\rightarrow \times$ R

Clue (iv) Limca $\rightarrow \times$ 2.2

Clue (v) R > P

Clue (vi) (and clue (ii)) Sprite and Limca will share 1 litre and 1.6 litre amongst themselves (we get the values of the 4 quantities from clue (vii) and from the options to question 6).

Clue (vii) 0.6 litre - Coke - 1 litre

Clue (viii) S $\rightarrow \times$ Coke and S $\rightarrow$ Not 6 Litre

At this stage we can make the first deduction:

Since Coke is neither 0.6 nor 1 litre nor 1.6 litre, Coke must be 2.2 and since 1 litre and 1.6 litre are shared between Limca and Sprite, Pepsi must be 0.6 litre.

This gives us 2 possibilities for distributing the 4 quantities:

Possibility 1: Pepsi (0.6), Limca (1.6 litre), Sprite (1 litre) and Coke (2.2)

OR

Possibility 2: Pepsi (0.6), Limca (1 litre), Sprite (1.6 litre) and Coke (2.2).

We now try to place both arrangements in order in terms of the bottles P, Q, R, S by obeying the constraints of the question.

Considering possibility 1 above and clue (vii), we get:

	Pepsi	Coke	Sprite
or	Sprite	Coke	Pepsi

as the two possible arrangements such that Coke comes between 0.6 litres and 1 litre.

However, according to clue (i), Pepsi is between Sprite and Coke and possibility 1 clearly violates this condition. Hence, we reject possibility 1.

Thus, we have possibility 2 as the only possibility left i.e.:

Pepsi = 0.6
Limca = 1
Sprite = 1.6
Coke = 2.2

We just need to arrange the placement of these 4 cold drinks in the right order.

We need to realise at this point that both Coke and Pepsi cannot be extremes. Hence, the extremes have to be made up of Limca and Sprite. This can be done in two ways:

(A)

P	Q	R	S
Limca			Sprite
(1)			1.6

In this case we need to place Coke between 0.6 and 1. Thus we get:

P	Q	R	S
Limca	Coke	Pepsi	Sprite
(1)	2.2	0.6	1.6

But, we can see that clue (v) is violated. (R > P)

Hence, we reject this arrangement and go to the next possibility:

(B)

P	Q	R	S
Sprite	Pepsi	Coke	Limca
1.6	0.6	2.2	1

This arrangement meets all constraints and gives us the answers as:

6. 0.6 litre (a)
7. Bottle P (a)
8. Coke (b)
9. 1 litre (c)
10. R (c)
11. 1.6 litre (c)

Solutions for Questions 12 to 15:

From statement (i) and (ii) it is clear that these three batsmen scored 1, 2, 4 centuries in any order. From the remaining information we could form the following table:

	1	2	3	4	5	6	7
Dhawan	N			N		N	N
Rohit		N					N
Kohli							C

'N' represents a less than 100 score. 'C' represents a century.

12. (c)

From the given table it is clear that Dhawan scored either 1 or 2 centuries.

13. (a)

It is given that Rohit scored a century in the 3rd game, therefore, he did not score a century in the 1st game. Hence Kohli scored a century in the 1st game. Now Dhawan scored a 100+ in either the 2nd or the 5th game.

	1	2	3	4	5	6	7
Dhawan	N		N	N		N	N
Rohit	N	N	C				N
Kohli	C		N				C

Case 1: Dhawan scored a century in the 5th game.
In this case it is not possible that he scored a century in the 2nd game (according to the 5th condition), hence Kohli scored a century in the 2nd game. If Kohli scored a century in the 4th game he must score a 100 in 6th game as well, which is not possible because in this case he scored 5 centuries, which is not possible. If Rohit scored a 100 in the 4th game then he must score a century in the 6th game as well which is again not possible because in this case two batsmen scored equal number of centuries. (Kohli and Rohit would have 3 centuries each). Thus, we reject Dhawan scoring a century in game 5. He could not have scored a century in game 5.

Case 2: Dhawan scored a century in the 2nd game. In such a case, the table would look as below:

	1	2	3	4	5	6	7
Dhawan	N	C	N	N	N	N	N
Rohit	N	N	C				N
Kohli	C	N	N				C

From the above table it is clear that out of the 4th, 5th and 6th games, Kohli scored a century in either 0 or 2 games and Rohit scored a century in either 1 or 3 games.

Case 2(a): When Kohli did not score a century in 4th, 5th, 6th games. Then Rohit scored centuries in all three games (4th, 5th, 6th).

	1	2	3	4	5	6	7
Dhawan	N	C	N	N	N	N	N
Rohit	N	N	C	C	C	C	N
Kohli	C	N	N	N	N	N	C

Case 2(b): When Kohli scored centuries in the 4th and 6th games: Note- It is not possible that Kohli scored a 100 in the 4th, 5th or 5th, 6th games that contradicts clue (vi). Then, Rohit scored a century in the 5th game. The table would become as follows:

	1	2	3	4	5	6	7
Dhawan	N	C	N	N	N	N	N
Rohit	N	N	C	N	C	N	N
Kohli	C	N	N	C	N	C	C

Therefore, Dhawan scored a 100 in only the 2nd game. Option (a) is correct.

14. (d)

From case 2(a) and case 2(b) of the above question we get that Kohli and Rohit both could score 2 centuries as well as 4 centuries. Therefore, options a, c are not true. From case 2(b) it is also possible that when Rohit scored a century in the 3rd and 5th games, then he did not score a century in 4th game, therefore option (b) is wrong. Only option (d) is correct.

15.

If Kohli scored a century in the 2nd game but failed to score a century in 4th game, the table would become as follows:

	1	2	3	4	5	6	7
Dhawan	N	N		N		N	N
Rohit		N		C		C	N
Kohli		C		N	N	N	C

Now, Kohli could have scored a century in at most one of the 1st and 3rd games. Therefore, he scored at most 3 centuries. But 3 centuries for 1 player is not possible. Hence, for the maximum possible runs for Kohli, we would need to consider that he scored two centuries.

Maximum possible runs scored by Kohli = $125 \times 2 + 99 \times 5 = 745$

Solutions for Questions 16 to 20:

From clue (vi) and (i):

	Bolt	Jordon	Jackson	Wayne	Phelps
100 m			1 or 3		
200 m			3 or 1		
Sum of Ranks			4		

From clues (viii), (vii), (iv) and (v), we get:

	Bolt	Jordon	Jackson	Wayne	Phelps
100 m		M	1 or 3	N	
200 m			3 or 1	M	N
Total			4	6	

Deduction 1: M > N (as a numerical value) as, Phelps finishes the 200 m race earlier than Wayne.

Deduction 2: N cannot be equal to 1 or 3 as that would leave no space for Jackson to be 1st and 3rd or 3rd or 1st in the two races respectively. By the same logic M cannot be 3rd, as that would occupy the 3rd place in both the races, not allowing Jackson to come third in either race.

Deduction 3: N cannot be 4 as that would make M = 5, which would contradict clue (iv).

Thus, the only combination of values possible for N and M are 2 and 4 respectively. The table now becomes:

	Bolt	Jordon	Jackson	Waynze	Phelps
100 m		4	1 or 3	2	
200 m			3 or 1	4	2
Total			4	6	

From clue (iv) we get:

(2) Jordon must finish 5th in the 200 m race.

	Bolt	Jordon	Jackson	Wayne	Phelps
100 m		4	1 or 3	2	
200 m		5	3 or 1	4	2
Total		9	4	6	

If we try to put Jackson as 3rd in the 100 m race, the following logic string follows that leads to a contradiction of positions:

Jackson's ranks: 3rd in 100 m and 1st in 200 m. Thus, Bolt can only be 3rd in the 200 m race and according to clue (iii), he should be 1st in the 100 m race - leading to a contradiction of Bolt's sum of ranks becoming 4 - which contradicts clue (vi) as can be seen from the table below.

	Bolt	Jordon	Jackson	Wayne	Phelps
100 m	1	4	3	2	
200 m	3	5	1	4	2
Total	4 (Contradicts clue (vi))	9	4	6	

Thus, put Jackson as 3rd in the 200 m race, the following logic string follows that leads to the final table:

Jackson 1st in 100 m and 3rd in 200 m. Bolt 1st in 200 m and 5th in 100 m (as he cannot be 3rd there to make his sum of ranks as 4th). The final table that emerges is as follows:

	Bolt	Jordon	Jackson	Wayne	Phelps
100 m	5	4	1	2	3
200 m	1	5	3	4	2
Total	6	9	4	6	5

The answers are:

16. 3rd
17. Jordon
18. 5
19. Jackson, Wayne and Phelps. Hence, 3.
20. Bolt and Phelps secured better ranks in 200 m than they did in 100 m. Hence, 2.

MOCK TEST PAPER 8

Solutions for Questions 1 to 5:

There are 4 variables in this problem—*viz.* hostel number, mess manager, subject stream of students residing there and the number of students residing in each hostel. The starting possibility matrix we can make here can be something like:

	Mess Managers						Subjects						People					
	Anand	Charan	Dharam	Dhiru	Lalu	Ramesh	B Tech	M Sc	MBA	M Tech	B Sc	BA	51	53	55	56	57	59
101																		
102																		
103																		
104																		
105																		
106																		

Note: The critical decision here is to decide on putting the hostel numbers on the left side, stacked against the three other variables. This we do if we quickly glance through the clues, we realise that the maximum number of clues are directly associated with the hostel number.

From Clue (i): Anand's hostel is immediately left to the one having B. Tech students and immediately right to the one which has 53 students' we get the following reactions:

Reaction 1: Anand's hostel cannot be 101 or 106.
Reaction 2: The hostel with 53 students is not 106 or 105.
Reaction 3: The B. Tech hostel is not 101 or 102.
Reaction 4: This is a cross-referenced reaction and it is that we need to have a sequence of 53-Anand-B. Tech, that needs to be fit into 101 to 103 or 102 to 104 or 103 to 105 or 104 to 106. So essentially we have 4 options for fitting in this sequence of 3.
Using Clue (i) and the direct information in Clue (ii), the table converts to:

	Mess Managers						Subjects						People					
			BA															
	Anand	Charan	Dharam	Dhiru	Lalu	Ramesh	B Tech	M Sc	MBA	M Tech	B Sc	BA	51	53	55	56	57	59
101	NO						NO											
102							NO											
103																		
104																		
105														NO				
106	NO													NO				

From Clue (iii): 'The number of students in hostel-104 is four higher than that of the hostel managed by Lalu' we get:
Reaction 1: Number of students in hostel 104 is either 55, 57 or 59. So it is not 51, 53 or 55.
Reaction 2: Number of students in Lalu's hostel is 51, 53 or 55.
Adding the direct information from Clue (iv): 'Hostel-101 has the least number of students and is not occupied by M Tech students' we get the possibility matrix transforming to:

	Mess Managers						Subjects						People					
Cross Referenced Clues			BA		51 53 55													
	Anand	Charan	Dharam	Dhiru	Lalu	Ramesh	B Tech	M Sc	MBA	M Tech	B Sc	BA	51	53	55	56	57	59
101	NO						NO			NO			YES	NO	NO	NO	NO	NO
102							NO						NO					
103													NO					
104													NO	NO		NO		

	Mess Managers						Subjects						People					
105													NO	NO				
106	NO												NO	NO				

Reactions from Clue (v): 'The 59 B.Sc students live somewhere left to the hostel managed by Ramesh, but not next to it.'
Reaction: The 59 B.Sc students do not live in 105 or 106. Also, Ramesh is not in 101 or 102.
Reactions from Clue (vi): 'The MBA students live in hostel-105 and the number of students in hostel-105 is not 56. The hostel having 56 students is next to the hostel managed by Dhiru, where the number of students is not 55.'
Reaction:

	Mess Managers						Subjects						People					
Cross Referenced Clues			BA		51 53 55						59							
	Anand	Charan	Dharam	Dhiru	Lalu	Ramesh	B Tech	M Sc	MBA	M Tech	B Sc	BA	51	53	55	56	57	59
101	NO					NO	NO		NO	NO			YES	NO	NO	NO	NO	NO
102						NO	NO		NO				NO					
103									NO				NO					
104									NO				NO	NO		NO		
105							NO	NO	YES	NO	NO	NO	NO	NO		NO		NO
106	NO								NO		NO		NO	NO				NO

At this point, we can see that since the 3 *viz.*: 53-Anand-B. Tech, we can no longer place them in 101 to 103 (since 101 is occupied by '51' and hence, '53' cannot be placed in 101). Also, since 105 is occupied by MBA, we cannot place B. Tech in 105. Consequently, we cannot place '53' in 103. This leaves only 102 for 53. Consequently, 103 would be Anand and 104 would be B. Tech.
The table transforms to:

	Mess Managers						Subjects						People					
Cross Referenced Clues			BA		51 53 55						59							
	Anand	Charan	Dharam	Dhiru	Lalu	Ramesh	B Tech	M Sc	MBA	M Tech	B Sc	BA	51	53	55	56	57	59
101	NO					NO	NO		NO	NO			YES	NO	NO	NO	NO	NO
102	NO					NO	NO		NO				NO	YES	NO	NO	NO	NO
103	YES	NO	NO	NO	NO	NO	NO		NO				NO	NO				
104	NO						YES	NO	NO	NO	NO	NO	NO	NO		NO		
105	NO						NO	NO	YES	NO	NO	NO	NO	NO		NO		NO
106	NO						NO		NO		NO		NO	NO				NO

The 59 students of B.Sc, are not in 101, 102, 105 or 106 (as the 59 students are not in these slots). Also, the B.Sc Students are not in 104 or 105. This leaves, the 59 B.sc Students with only 1 slot, i.e., 103.

Additionally at this point, since we know that Dharam manages the hostel with the BA students, it follows that the possibilities 104 and 105 that have already been eliminated for the BA students can be eliminated for Dharam too.

Carrying out this deduction and its' associated reactions inside the table, we get the following transformed table:

	Mess Managers						Subjects						People					
Cross Referenced Clues					51 53													
			BA		55						59							
	Anand	Charan	Dharam	Dhiru	Lalu	Ramesh	B Tech	M Sc	MBA	M Tech	B Sc	BA	51	53	55	56	57	59
101	NO					NO	NO		NO	NO	NO		YES	NO	NO	NO	NO	NO
102	NO					NO	NO		NO		NO		NO	YES	NO	NO	NO	NO
103	YES	NO	NO	NO	NO	NO	NO	NO	NO	NO	YES	NO	NO	NO	NO	NO	NO	YES
104	NO		NO				YES	NO	NO	NO	NO	NO	NO	NO		NO		NO
105	NO		NO				NO	NO	YES	NO	NO	NO	NO	NO		NO		NO
106	NO						NO		NO		NO		NO	NO	NO	YES	NO	NO

At this point, we can add the information that the hostel managed by Ramesh is not next to the 59 BSc Students. Thus, Ramesh's hostel cannot be 104.

Also, from clue (vi) and the current table, we have that since Dhiru's hostel is next to the hostel having 56 students, his hostel must be 105.

The next set of transformations would give us the following table:

	Mess Managers						Subjects						People					
Cross Referenced clues				NOT 55 NOT 56	51 53													
			BA		55						59							
	Anand	Charan	Dharam	Dhiru	Lalu	Ramesh	B Tech	M Sc	MBA	M Tech	B Sc	BA	51	53	55	56	57	59
101	NO			NO		NO	NO		NO	NO	NO		YES	NO	NO	NO	NO	NO
102	NO			NO		NO	NO		NO		NO		NO	YES	NO	NO	NO	NO
103	YES	NO	NO	NO	NO	NO	NO	NO	NO	NO	YES	NO	NO	NO	NO	NO	NO	YES
104	NO		NO	NO		NO	YES	NO	NO	NO	NO	NO	NO	NO		NO		NO
105	NO	NO	NO	YES	NO	NO	NO	NO	YES	NO	NO	NO	NO	NO		NO		NO
106	NO	NO	NO	NO	NO	YES	NO		NO		NO		NO	NO	NO	YES	NO	NO

→ Next, since we know that Dhiru's hostel does not have 55 students, we can complete the hostels vis-à-vis people table as the 55 students must be in hostel 104.

→ This also, gives us that Lalu must be managing the hostel with 51 students (Hostel 101).

	Mess Managers						Subjects						People					
Cross Referenced Clues				NOT 55 NOT 56	51 53													
			BA		55						59							
	Anand	Charan	Dharam	Dhiru	Lalu	Ramesh	B Tech	M Sc	MBA	M Tech	B Sc	BA	51	53	55	56	57	59

	Mess Managers						Subjects						People					
101	NO			NO		NO	NO		NO	NO	NO		YES	NO	NO	NO	NO	NO
102	NO			NO		NO	NO		NO		NO		NO	YES	NO	NO	NO	NO
103	YES	NO	NO	NO	NO	NO	NO	NO	NO	NO	YES	NO	NO	NO	NO	NO	NO	YES
104	NO		NO	NO		NO	YES	NO	NO	NO	NO	NO	NO	NO		NO		NO
105	NO	NO	NO	YES	NO	NO	NO	NO	YES	NO	NO	NO	NO	NO		NO		NO
106	NO	NO	NO	NO	NO	YES	NO		NO		NO	NO	NO	NO	NO	YES	NO	NO

From this point, Clue (vi) gives us that since the hostel managed by Dhiru does not have not 55 students, the only possibility left is for the hostel 105 (the one managed by Dhiru) to have 57 students. Consequently, this fixes that Lalu must be managing the hostel with 51 students. This starts the chain of thought that completes the table:

	Mess Managers						Subjects						People					
	Anand	Charan	Dharam	Dhiru	Lalu	Ramesh	B Tech	M Sc	MBA	M Tech	B Sc	BA	51	53	55	56	57	59
101	NO	NO	NO	NO	YES	NO	NO	YES	NO	NO	NO	NO	YES	NO	NO	NO	NO	NO
102	NO	NO	YES	NO	NO	NO	NO	NO	NO	NO	NO	YES	NO	YES	NO	NO	NO	NO
103	YES	NO	NO	NO	NO	NO	NO	NO	NO	NO	YES	NO	NO	NO	NO	NO	NO	YES
104	NO	YES	NO	NO	NO	NO	YES	NO	NO	NO	NO	NO	NO	NO	YES	NO	NO	NO
105	NO	NO	NO	YES	NO	NO	NO	NO	YES	NO	NO	NO	NO	NO	NO	NO	YES	NO
106	NO	NO	NO	NO	NO	YES	NO	NO	NO	YES	NO	NO	NO	NO	NO	YES	NO	NO

The answers can now be read off this table:

1. 57
2. 102
3. 106
4. 56 + 59 = 115
5. As can be seen from the table, MBA Students are in hostel 105, and Btech students are in Hostel 104. Hostel 105 has a total of 57 students and Hostel 104 has a total of 55 students.
   So, the total sum would be 55 + 57 = 112.

Solutions for Questions 6 to 10:

A → Ahluwalia
B → Bhatia
C → Chopra
D → Dayal
E → Eshwar

Based on clue number (i) you realise that there are 10 first and middle names for the 5 people and these are distributed as:

4 Rams (R)
3 Shyams (S)
2 Trams (T)
1 Alam (A)

From clue (ii) we realise that we can put Tram in 2 ways:

Possibility (1) Both Ahluwalia (A) and Bhatia (B) are Trams (T)

T		Ahluwalia
T		Bhatia
		Chopra
		Dayal
		Eeshwar

Or

Possibilty (2) Both Chopra and Dayal are Trams

		Ahluwalia
		Bhatia
T		Chopra
T		Dayal
		Eeshwar

We now look at possibility 1 above:

Using clue (iii), we can place both B and C as Shyam or neither B and C as Shyam (in which case the 3 Shyams must go to A, D and E)

Thus we have two further possibilities emerging out of possibility 1 above:

Possibility (A) for Possibility 1:

T		Ahluwalias
T	S	Bhatia

	S	Chopra
		Dayal
		Eeshwar

Possibility (B) for Possibility 1:

T	S	Ahluwalia
T		Bhatia
		Chopra
	S	Dayal
	S	Eeshwar

In each of the above scenarios we now have to place the 4 Rams.

However, in both cases both Dayal and Eshwar get named Ram, and this contradicts Clue (iv). Hence, we rule out this possibility.

Moving on to possibility 2 and using clue (iii), the following possibilities emerge:

Possibility (A) for Possibility 2:

		Ahluwalia
	S	Bhatia
T	S	Chopra
T		Dayal
		Eeshwar

Possibility (B) for Possibility 2:

	S	Ahluwalia
		Bhatia
T		Chopra
T	S	Dayal
	S	Eeshwar

In possibility A above, when we place the 4 Rams, we again contradict clue (iv) (since both D and E are named Ram).

Hence, only possibility B remains and the final names are:

R	S	Ahluwalia
A	R	Bhatia
T	R	Chopra
T	S	Dayal
R	S	Eeshwar

Hence the answers are:

6. (d) None of the 3 name combination appears.
7. (b) Chopra and Dayal
8. Mr. Bhatia (b)
9. Ram Shyam (a)
10. Mr. Ahluwalia and Mr. Eeshwar are both named Ram Shyam. Hence, (c)

Solutions for Questions 11 to 15:

From clues (iii) and (vii) we get the following starting figure

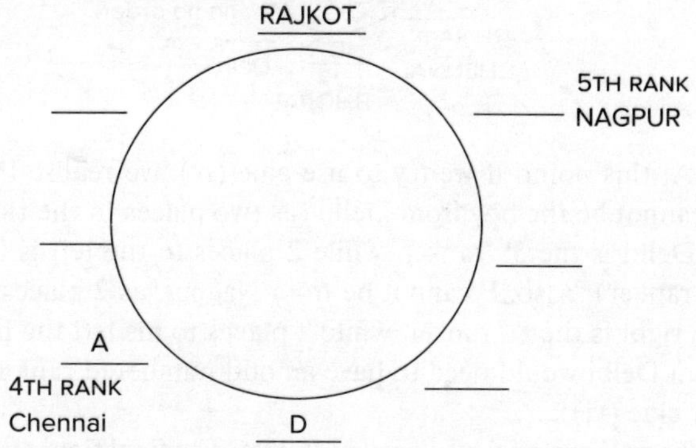

Using Clues (v) and (viii) at this point, we get the following addition to this figure:

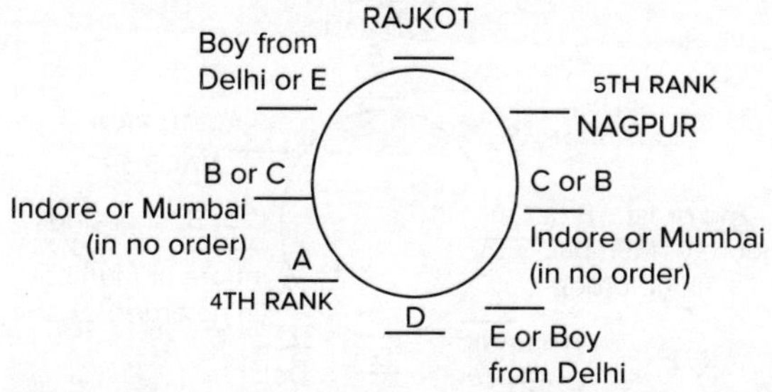

At this point, using clue (ix), it is evident that D must be from Bhopal and the person on his right should be from Delhi. When we use these deductions to modify the figure, the figure changes to:

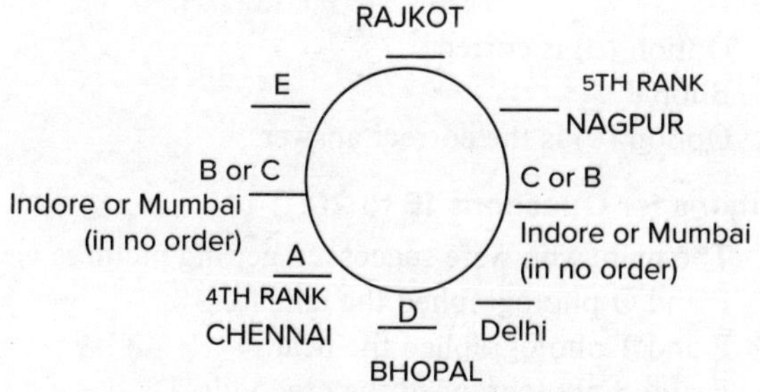

This leaves Pune only one position in the figure - i.e., E must be the 8th ranker from Pune (Clue (ii) used for the boy from Pune being the 8th ranker). Also, the boy from Delhi cannot be first. The figure now becomes:

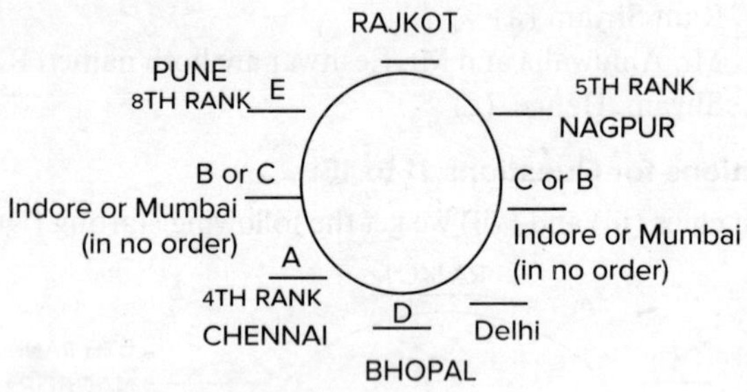

At this point, if we try to use clue (iv), we realise that F cannot be the boy from Delhi (as two places to the right of Delhi is the 5th ranker, while 2 places to the left is the 4th ranker). Also, F cannot be from Nagpur, as 2 places to the right is the 8th ranker, while 2 places to his left the boy from Delhi would need to have an odd numbered rank (as per clue (vi)).

Thus F can only by placed in Rajkot. The final figure now comes out as shown:

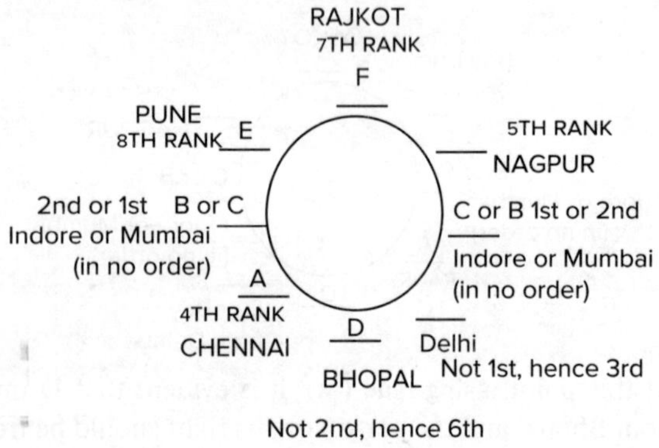

The answers can be interpreted from the above figure.

11. F
12. F
13. Option (c) is correct.
14. Bhopal
15. Option (c) is the correct answer.

Solutions for Questions 16 to 20:

16. The pairs who were successful getting pictures were:
 P and Q photographed the anteater.
 P and T photographed the bear.
 R and S photographed the crocodile.
 S and T photographed the deer.
 Q and R photographed the emu.
 There are 10 possible pairs. Each person went out four times, each time with a different partner. Each person got a photograph twice and got nothing twice. First, to determine which pairs photographed an animal and which didn't, make a 5 × 5 matrix with row and column headings of P, Q, R, S and T. Since we don't always know what animal was photographed, assign the animals a number, 1 through 5.
 Everybody took photographs of two animals. So, you can assign animal 2 to P [(P, RST) = 2] and you can assign animal 3 to Q [(Q, RST) = 3] in the matrix. Then you are left with assigning animal 4 to S and animal 5 to T [(R, S) = 4 and (S, T) = 5.]
 As S has both animals 4 and 5, S cannot have animals 2 and 3. That means that we can assign 2 to R and 3 to T.
 The pairs who were successful were–(P, Q), (P, T), (Q, R), (R, S) and (S, T).
 Next, we need to determine which pair photographed which animal. We know that:
 - The Emu is animal 1 or 3
 - The Anteater is not 2 and 5.
 - The Bear is not 4 and 5. Therefore, the bear is 2 or 3.

 Consider these cases separately: (Emu, Bear) = (1, 2), (1, 3) and (3, 2). The first two cases lead to contradictions. Therefore, (Emu, Bear) = (3, 2) which leads to Crocodile = (4)
 Then, since T did not photograph the Anteater, the Anteater cannot be 2 or 5. So the Anteater must be (1)
 Then, the Deer is 5.
17. The anteater was photographed by P & Q. Hence the correct answer is Option (d).
18. Anteater and Emu were both photographed by Q. However, Deer does not have any photographers in common. Hence, Option (b) is the correct answer.
19. Q captured Anteater & Emu. Hence, Option (a) is the correct answer.
20. QS did not photograph any animal on their day out. Hence, Option (d) is correct.

PART II

Reasoning Question Types from Other MBA Exams

SECTION 1
General Reasoning and Intelligence

Scan this QR code to access a video on this section's chapters, their importance and weightage in the examination!

CHAPTER 1

Sequences and Series

Chapter Launchpad
Scan this QR code for an introductory video on Sequences and Series

Sequences and series (as the name suggests) consists of questions where you are supposed to understand the logic behind a given sequence or series of number/alphabets. Based on this understanding you are supposed to determine either:

(a) A continuation to the series

(b) The immediate next term of the series

or

(c) A missing term/terms within the series.

While preparing yourself to solve such questions, you should improve your ability to spot a particular relationship between terms within the series. The common logical premises used for questions are given here.

SERIES BASED ON NUMBERS

1. Squares
2. Squares + something or squares–something e.g. next term in the series
   24, 35, 48, 63, 80... will be 99 since the series is $(5^2 + 1)$, $(6^2 + 1)$, etc.
3. Cubes, cubes + something, cubes–something
4. Geometric series
5. Arithmetic series
6. Harmonic series
7. Series of constantly changing additions or multiplications, e.g.,
   (i) 2, 6, 24, 120,.......... (The terms are got by × 3, ×4, × 5, and so on.)
   (ii) 11, 16, 22, 29, 37,.......... (The series follows a logic of +5, +6, +7, +8, and so on.)
8. Binary numbers systems or number systems with other bases like Base 3, Base 4, etc.
9. Intermingled series–
   e.g., 2, 5, 6, 10, 18, 15, 54
   In this series alternate terms starting with the first form a GP with common ratio 3, while the 2nd, 4th, 6th terms form an AP 5, 10, 15........

SERIES BASED ON ALPHABETS

In such series, the most crucial aspect is to know the position of each alphabet in the alphabet series A to Z both from start to end.

Thus, the following reference numbers for each alphabet become important:

Going Forward	1	2	3	4	5	6	7	8	9	10	11	12	13
Alphabet	A	B	C	D	E	F	G	H	I	J	K	L	**M**
Going Back from Z	26	25	24	23	22	21	20	19	18	17	16	15	**14**

Going Forward	**14**	15	16	17	18	19	20	21	22	23	24	25	26
Alphabet	**N**	O	P	Q	R	S	T	U	V	W	X	Y	Z
Going back from Z	**13**	12	11	10	9	8	7	6	5	4	3	2	1

Notice that M and N are the two middle points of this series. Let us now look at a few solved examples before we go into the practice exercise.

WORKED-OUT PROBLEMS

Illustration 1: Which of the numbers given below would come next in the series of numbers?

1, 9, 25, __

(a) 36 (b) 25
(c) 49 (d) None of these

Solution: The first number is 1, second is 9 and third is 25. We can easily observe that the numbers in the series are squares of consecutive odd numbers. Hence, the next number would be the square of 7 which would be 49. Thus Option (c) is correct.

Illustration 2: Which of the following letters would come next in the series of letters?

Z, W, R, K, __

(a) A (b) C
(c) B (d) D

Solution: In the given series from the end of the alphabet series, Z is the 1st alphabet, W is the 4th alphabet, R is the 9th alphabet and K is the 16th alphabet. Thus the next letter in the series will be the 25th alphabet from the end or the second from the start. Hence, the next alphabet must be B. Thus, (c) is the correct option.

Illustration 3: What would come next in the following series of numbers?

1, 2, 10, 37, __

(a) 62 (b) 91
(c) 101 (d) None of these

Solution: The series is following the +1, +8, +27 routine. Hence, the next number must be at an interval of +64 and should be 101. Thus Option (c) is the correct answer.

Illustration 4: What would come next in the following series?

A_{10}, D_{15}, G_{20}, J_{25} —

(a) N_{18} (b) O_{20}
(c) M_{16} (d) None of these

Solution: In the series of letters represented above there is a gap of 2 letters between every two consecutive terms and hence, the next letter will be M (after skipping K and L). Thus, the correct answer should be M_{30}. Thus Option (d) is correct.

Illustration 5: What should come next in the series below?

122343456________

(a) 45678 (b) 6789
(c) 34567 (d) None of these

Solution: We can see that the series is a group of joined series as 12, 234, 3456 and hence the next terms should be 45678. Thus Option (a) is correct.

EXERCISE

Directions for Questions 1 to 40: *Find out the missing term:*

1. 0, 3, 8, 15, 24, 35, 48, ?
   (a) 53 (b) 63
   (c) 80 (d) None of these
2. 256, 64, 16, 4, ?
   (a) 1 (b) 1/4
   (c) 1/16 (d) None of these
3. Obtain the missing term
   B, G, K, ?
   (a) N (b) P
   (c) M (d) L
4. 7,15, 27, ?, 63
   (a) 42 (b) 43
   (c) 38 (d) None of these
5. ?, 425, 600, 825, 1100, 1425
   (a) 225 (b) 300
   (c) 250 (d) None of these
6. 1, 121, 12321, 1234321, ___?
   (a) 123454321 (b) 12344321
   (c) 12345654321 (d) None of these
7. 0.005, 0.05, ?, 5
   (a) 5.50 (b) 0.05
   (c) 0.5 (d) None of these
8. 31, 32, 36, 45, ?
   (a) 55 (b) 56
   (c) 61 (d) 62
9. 1, 5, 2, 25, 3, 125, 4, ?
   (a) 144
   (b) 36
   (c) 625
   (d) 500
10. 83, 82, 80, 77, ?
    (a) 74
    (b) 73
    (c) 75
    (d) 76

High Yield Questions

Scan this QR code to access video explanations of questions 5, 15, 35, 45, 59 and 60

11. $2/\sqrt{3}$, $3/\sqrt{4}$, $4/\sqrt{5}$, ?
    (a) $5/\sqrt{6}$
    (b) $5/\sqrt{5}$
    (c) $6/\sqrt{5}$
    (d) None of these
12. 1, 1, 5, 49, 11, 169, 19, ?
    (a) 256 (b) 289
    (c) 324 (d) 361
13. 5, 36, 253, ?
    (a) 1749 (b) 1750
    (c) 1772 (d) 1771
14. 45678912, 5678912, 567891, ?
    (a) 56789 (b) 67891
    (c) 567891 (d) None of these
15. ABCDEFG, GABCDEF, FGABCDE, ?
    (a) EFGABCD (b) GABCDEF
    (c) EFGABCDE (d) FGABCDE
16. (1, 1), (2, 16), (3, 81), ?
    (a) (4, 16) (b) (4, 64)
    (c) (4, 256) (d) None of these
17. 1, 4, 16, 64, ______ what will be the 8th term?
    (a) 1024 (b) 16384
    (c) 4096 (d) None of these
18. 40, 24, 16, 12, 10, 9, ?
    (a) 8.5 (b) 8
    (c) 7.5 (d) None of these

19. 7, 28, 70, 140, ?
(a) 240 (b) 250
(c) 245 (d) None of these

20. 729, 1331, 2197, ?
(a) 2180 (b) 2185
(c) 2196 (d) None of these

21. 0.7, 2.8, 11.2, 44.8, ?
(a) 178.2 (b) 177.2
(c) 179 (d) 179.2

22. 1, 5/4, 21/16, ______ what will be the nth term of the series?
(a) $[1 - (1/4)^n]/(3/4)$
(b) $[1 + (1/3)^n]/(2/3)^n$
(c) $[(1/3)^n + 1]/(2/3)$
(d) None of these

23. 600, 550, 450, 300, ?
(a) 50 (b) 0
(c) 100 (d) 150

24. 1, 2, 3, 6, 11, 20, 37, 68 ?
(a) 125 (b) 126
(c) 124 (d) 105

25. 12, 24, 36, 48, ?, 72
(a) 50 (b) 55
(c) 60 (d) 70

26. 1, 6, 11, ______ what will be its 15th term?
(a) 46 (b) 76
(c) 66 (d) 71

27. –3, 4, 23, 60, 121?
(a) 22 (b) 212
(c) 205 (d) None of these

28. 20, 26, 62, ?, 1574
(a) 125 (b) 150
(c) 278 (d) 200

29. 45, 40, 35, _____ which term will be the first negative term of the series?
(a) 10th term (b) 11th term
(c) 12th term (d) 13th term

30. 1/1, 4/8, 9/27, 16/64, 25/125, ?
(a) 36/49 (b) 49/64
(c) 36/216 (d) None of these

31. 1, 3, 2, 5, 3, 7, 4, 9, 5, 11, 6, ?
(a) 10 (b) 11
(c) 13 (d) 9

32. 1, 4, 27, ?
(a) 256 (b) 3125
(c) 2425 (a) None of these

33. What is the next term in the following series?
ABE, BCF, CDG, DEH, EFI, ______
(a) FGK (b) FGJ
(c) FGL (d) None of these

34. What is the next term in the following series?
ZYXWTSRQNMLK
(a) I (b) G
(c) H (d) J

35. What is the sum of infinite terms of the given series?
$4 + 4 \times 4^{1/2} + 4 \times 4^{1/2} \times 4^{1/4} +$ ______.
(a) 12 (b) 16
(c) 64 (d) Can't be determined

36. What is the next term in the following series?
1, 4, 3, 9, 5, 16, 7, 25, 9, 36, 11, ?
(a) 64 (b) 49
(c) 48 (d) 55

37. Calculate the sum of the series
1 + 1/4 + 1/16 + ______.
(a) 3/4 (b) 4/3
(c) 2 (d) None of these

38. Calculate the missing term.
625, 125, ?, 5, 1
(a) 1/5 (b) 1
(c) 5 (d) None of these

39. Obtain the missing term.
300, 296, 287, 271, ?, 210
(a) 246 (b) 250
(c) 244 (d) None of these

40. Obtain the missing term.
12, 15, 19, ?, 30, 37
(a) 35 (b) 34
(c) 37 (d) 24

Directions for Questions 41 to 47: *In each of the following number series a wrong number is given. Find out the wrong number.*

41. 31, 22, 30, –32, –89, –174
(a) 22 (b) 30
(c) –32 (d) –89

42. 4, 26, 163, 1149, 9201, 82809
(a) 26 (b) 163
(c) 82809 (d) 9201

43. 4, 39, 269, 1605, 8009, 32011
(a) 4 (b) 39
(c) 269 (d) 1005

44. 28, 84, 112, 196, 308, 504, 872
(a) 112 (b) 196
(c) 308 (d) 872

45. 14, 20, 369, 1288, 12961, 155432
(a) 14 (b) 20
(c) 369 (d) 1288

46. 14400, 7200, 4800, 3600, 2800, 2400
(a) 7200 (b) 4800
(c) 2800 (d) 2400

47. 300, 421, 592, 815, 1104, 1465
(a) 421 (b) 1104
(c) 815 (d) 592

Directions for Questions 48 to 52: *Study the following information carefully to answer the questions given below:*
S Q A 5 N % T 7 B 4 # J E $ 2 T D * 1 8 H 3 U @ 9 F W © K

48. How many such consonants are there in the above arrangement, each of which is immediately followed by a number but not immediately preceded by a number?

(a) One (b) Two
(c) Three (d) More than three

49. How many such consonants are there in the above arrangement, each of which is either immediately preceded by a vowel or immediately followed by a symbol but not both?

(a) None (b) One
(c) Two (d) Three

50. Which of the following is the seventh to the left of the fifteenth from the left end in the above arrangement?

(a) H (b) B
(c) 1 (d) 7

51. The letters skipped between adjacent letters is in the order of 1, 2, 3, 4, ... Which alternative follows this rule?

(a) EFJNS (b) EGJOS
(c) EGJNS (d) EGJNT

52. Which of the following will come in place of the question mark (?) in the following sequence?

16D7, 18G10, 21K14, 25P19, ?

(a) 30V20 (b) 30V25
(c) 30V24 (d) 29V25

Directions for Questions 53 to 60: *Complete the following series:*

53. BZ, HT, NN, ?, ZB

(a) LF (b) SX
(c) TH (d) TI

54. J2Z, K4X, I7V, ?, H16R, F22P

(a) G11T (b) G11S
(c) L12S (d) G11U

55. ane ____ ba ______ ebb ______ neb _____an ______ bb

(a) e b b a b (b) b B a b e
(c) B b a b e (d) b n a b e

56. In a row of children, Bali is seventh from the left and Moti is fourth from the right. When Bali and Moti exchange positions, Bali will be fifteenth from the left. What will be Moti's position from the right?

(a) Eighth (b) Fourth
(c) Eleventh (d) Twelfth

57. Which of the following cannot be a number of the series ....64, 125, 216, 343, 512 .....?

(a) 8 (b) 729
(c) 27 (d) 999

58. Complete the series

E-5, G-7, I-9, K-11, ?

(a) L-13, N-14 (b) M-13, O-15
(c) L-12, M-14 (d) K-12, M-14

59. An application was received by class teacher in the afternoon of a week day. Next day she forwarded it to the Student Coordinator, who was on leave that day. The Student Coordinator put up the application to the principal next day in the evening. The Principal studied the application and disposed off the matter on the same day, i.e, Saturday. Which day was the application received by the class teacher?

(a) Monday (b) Wednesday
(c) Tuesday (d) Thursday

60. Which letter should be the tenth letter to the left of the ninth letter from the right, if the first half of the alphabet of English are reversed?

(a) D (b) F
(c) E (d) I

Directions for Questions 61 to 68: *What will come in place of (?) in each of the given number series?*

61. 11, 12, 28, 93, 388, ?

(a) 1965 (b) 865
(c) 1956 (d) 2065
(e) None of these

62. 2, 7.5, 20.5, 67, 273.5, ?

(a) 1263 (b) 1373
(c) 1273 (d) 1337
(e) None of these

63. 8, 4.5, 5.5, 9.75, 21.5, ?

(a) 56.75 (b) 55.25
(c) 56.25 (d) 54.50
(e) None of these

64. 12, 22, 42, 82, 162, ?

(a) 332 (b) 304
(c) 302 (d) 322
(e) None of these

65. 3, 5, 16, 60, 260, ?

(a) 1330 (b) 1303
(c) 1203 (d) 1230
(e) None of these

66. 2, 3, 18, 115, 854, ?

(a) 7776 (b) 7767
(c) 6676 (d) 6667
(e) None of these

67. 20, 22, 29, 46, 78, ?

(a) 135 (b) 170
(c) 130 (d) 140
(e) None of these

68. 24, 27, 34, 47, 68, ?

(a) 96 (b) 97
(c) 98 (d) 99
(e) 100

Directions for Questions 69 to 73: *What will come in place of the questions mark (?) in the following numerical series?*

69. 9, 31, 73, 141, (?)

(a) 164 (b) 280
(c) 239 (d) 241

70. 35, 256, 451, 620, 763, (?)
(a) 680 (b) 893
(c) 633 (d) 880
(e) None of these

71. 2890, (?), 1162, 874, 730, 658
(a) 1684 (b) 1738
(c) 1784 (d) 1672
(e) None of these

72. 14, 1004, 1202, 1251.5, 1268, (?)
(a) 1267.5 (b) 1276.25
(c) 1324.5 (d) 1367.25
(e) None of these

73. 5, 7, 13, 25, 45, (?)
(a) 67 (b) 75
(c) 65 (d) 55
(e) None of these

Directions for Questions 74 to 76: *What will come in place of the questions mark (?) in the following numerical series?*

74. 4, 11, 25, 53, 109, (?)
(a) 221 (b) 234
(c) 212 (d) 222
(e) None of these

75. 15, 21, 33, 51, 75, (?)
(a) 113 (b) 103
(c) 105 (d) 115
(e) None of these

76. Find the 4th term of the following series:
3, 10, 101, ...

Directions for Questions 77 to 115: *What will come in place of the questions mark (?) in the following numerical series?*

77. 5, 12, 23, 50, 141, ?
(a) 488 (b) 473
(c) 425 (d) 392

78. 7, 13, 25, 45, ?
(a) 75 (b) 123
(c) 103 (d) 90

79. 4, 11, 19, 41, 79, ?
(a) 108 (b) 161
(c) 126 (d) 136

80. 5, 8, 28, 162, 1288, ?
(a) 12620 (b) 12870
(c) 13920 (d) 14112

81. 3, 5, 10, 20, 37, ?
(a) 76 (b) 77
(c) 63 (d) 64

82. 5, 7, 25, 131, 925, ?
(a) 5335 (b) 8335
(c) 8115 (d) 9665

83. 5, 7, 11, 37, 143, ?
(a) 720 (b) 721
(c) 723 (d) 749

84. 650, 647, 636, 605, ?
(a) 536 (b) 556
(c) 576 (d) None of these

85. 3, 2, 0, –9, –52, ?
(a) –285 (b) –235
(c) –275 (d) None of these

86. 7, 9, 13, 22, 50, ?
(a) 105 (b) 125
(c) 175 (d) 195

87. 40, 184, 668, 1692, ?
(a) 3256 (b) 3456
(c) 3156 (d) 3056

88. 59, 60, 68, 95, 159, ?
(a) 131 (b) 136
(c) 141 (d) None of these

89. 168, 86, 88, 134, 270, ?
(a) 667 (b) 657
(c) 676 (d) 677

90. 4, 13, 31, 67, 139, ?
(a) 211 (b) 243
(c) 263 (d) 283

91. 17, 40, 109, 224, ?
(a) 365 (b) 375
(c) 385 (d) None of these

92. 11, 14, 23, 50, 131, ?
(a) 372 (b) 374
(c) 376 (d) 378

93. 6, 11, 24, 49, 90, ?
(a) 151 (b) 161
(c) 172 (d) 181

94. 2, 10, 30, 68, 130, ?
(a) 192 (b) 222
(c) 246 (d) None of these

95. 11, 33, 30, 90, 87, ?
(a) 241 (b) 251
(c) 261 (d) None of these

96. 620, 613, 594, 557, ?
(a) 496 (b) 448
(c) 483 (d) None of these

97. 13, 36, 82, 151, ?
(a) 213 (b) 223
(c) 243 (d) 253

98. 78, 94, 69, 105, ?
(a) 76 (b) 66
(c) 56 (d) None of these

99. 17, 18, 37, 112, 449, ?
(a) 2246 (b) 2251
(c) 2236 (d) None of these

100. 35, 37, 40, 45, 52, ?
(a) 60 (b) 61
(c) 62 (d) 63

101. 21, 37, 73, 137, 237, ?
(a) 381 (b) 382
(c) 380 (d) None of these.

102. 17, 18, 37, 112, 449, ?
(a) 2251 (b) 2249
(c) 2174 (d) 2246

103. 14, 29, 74, 149, ?
(a) 251 (b) 252
(c) 253 (d) 254

104. 7, 35, 32, 160, 157, ?
(a) 780 (b) 785
(c) 787 (d) None of these

105. 52, 45, 66, 31, 80, ?
(a) 17 (b) 16
(c) 15 (d) None of these

106. 13, 17, 25, 41, 69, ?
(a) 110 (b) 113
(c) 116 (d) None of these

107. 2, 3, 10, 39, 172, ?
(a) 883 (b) 884
(c) 885 (d) None of these

108. 7, 9, 16, 25, 41, ?
(a) 65 (b) 64
(c) 66 (d) 63

109. 3, 5, 7, 25, 95, ?
(a) 839 (b) 840
(c) 841 (d) 842

110. 2, 2, 4, 9, 22, 60, ?
(a) 174 (b) 176
(c) 180 (d) 186

111. 120, 245, 461, 804, 1316, ?
(a) 2042 (b) 2043
(c) 2044 (d) 2045

112. 67, 92, 192, 417, ?
(a) 817 (b) 820
(c) 823 (d) None of these

113. 50, 90, 150, 240, 375, ?
(a) 570 (b) 577.5
(c) 580 (d) None of these

114. 4, 6, 16, 54, 224, ?
(a) 1125 (b) 1130
(c) 1135 (d) 1140

115. 2, 10, 30, 68, 130, ...?
(a) 225 (b) 224
(c) 223 (d) 222

ANSWER KEY

1. (b)	2. (a)	3. (a)	4. (b)
5. (b)	6. (a)	7. (c)	8. (c)
9. (c)	10. (b)	11. (a)	12. (d)
13. (c)	14. (b)	15. (a)	16. (c)
17. (b)	18. (a)	19. (c)	20. (d)
21. (d)	22. (a)	23. (c)	24. (a)
25. (c)	26. (d)	27. (b)	28. (c)
29. (b)	30. (c)	31. (c)	32. (a)
33. (b)	34. (c)	35. (d)	36. (b)
37. (b)	38. (d)	39. (a)	40. (d)
41. (b)	42. (c)	43. (a)	44. (d)
45. (c)	46. (c)	47. (c)	48. (a)
49. (b)	50. (d)	51. (c)	52. (b)
53. (c)	54. (a)	55. (d)	56. (d)
57. (d)	58. (b)	59. (d)	60. (b)
61. (a)	62. (b)	63. (c)	64. (d)
65. (a)	66. (b)	67. (c)	68. (d)
69. (d)	70. (d)	71. (b)	72. (b)
73. (b)	74. (a)	75. (c)	76. 10202
77. (a)	78. (a)	79. (b)	80. (b)
81. (c)	82. (b)	83. (b)	84. (a)
85. (a)	86. (c)	87. (b)	88. (d)
89. (d)	90. (d)	91. (c)	92. (b)
93. (a)	94. (b)	95. (c)	96. (a)
97. (c)	98. (c)	99. (a)	100. (d)
101. (a)	102. (d)	103. (d)	104. (b)
105. (a)	106. (b)	107. (c)	108. (c)
109. (c)	110. (d)	111. (d)	112. (a)
113. (b)	114. (b)	115. (d)	

SOLUTIONS AND SHORTCUTS

Solutions for Questions 1 to 40:

1. The series is following the pattern +3, +5, +7, +9, +11, +13 and hence, the next term should be 48 + 15 = 63. Answer is option (b).
2. The given series is a GP with common ratio $\frac{1}{4}$. Hence, option (a) is correct.
3. The series is defined by the 2nd, 7th, 11th term of the alphabet. Hence, the next term would be the 14th term i.e., N. Option (a) is the correct answer.
4. The series follows a pattern of +8, +12, +__, +20. Obviously we need to add 16 for the missing term. Hence, 43 i.e., option (b) is the correct answer.
5. The series follows a pattern of +175, +225, +275, +325. Hence, the first term should be 300, so the answer is option (b).
6. The series is representing the values of 1^2, 11^2, 111^2, 1111^2. Hence, the next value would be 11111^2 = 123454321, so option (a) is the answer.
7. A GP with common ratio 10. Hence, the missing term will be 0.5 i.e., option (c).
8. +1, +4, +9, thus +16 and hence the next term should be 61. Correct answer is option (c).
9. There are two series intermixed with one another. One of the series is placed at the odd places of the series and the other is placed at the even places. The series at the even places of the series is 5, 25, 125 and hence its next term should be 625. Option (c) is correct answer.
10. The logic of the series is −1, −2, −3 and hence, −4 should give us 73. So, the answer is option (b).
11. Obviously the answer has to be option (a).
12. There are two series intermingled in the given series of numbers. 1, 5, 11, 19 and the other series is 1^2, 7^2, 13^2 and 19^2 = 361. Hence, option (d) is the answer.
13. The series follows the pattern of × 7 + 1. Hence, the next number in the series is 253 × 7 + 1 = 1772. Option (c) is the answer.
14. We are consecutively deleting one digit from the left and then one digit from the right and then the next move has to be to delete one digit from the left. Hence, the answer is option (b).
15. The next term is formed by removing the last alphabet in the previous term and attaching it to the first alphabet of the next term. Hence, the next term in the series would be EFGABCD. So, the answer is option (a).
16. The relationship followed in each bracket is the fourth power of the first digit in the bracket. Hence, option (c) is correct.
17. 256,1024,4096,16384. Option (b) is correct.
18. The series follows a logic of −16, −8, −4, −2, −1. Hence, the next term in the series would be 9 − 0.5 = 8.5. Correct answer is option (a).
19. The addition between various terms of the series follows a logic of 7 × 3, 7 × 6, 7 × 10. Hence, the next addition should be 7 × 15. Hence, the next term in the series would be 140 + 105 = 245. So, the answer is option (c).
20. The series represents 9^3,11^3,13^3 and hence the next term should be 15^3; correct answer is (d).
21. GP with common ratio 4. Hence, the next term would be 179.2 i.e., option (d).
22. The formula for the nth term can be easily verified from the given terms of the series. Option (a) is correct.
23. The series follows the logic of −50, −100, −150 and hence the next term of the series should be 300 − 200 = 100. Correct answer is option (c).
24. Beginning with 6, each term of the series is the sum of the previous 3 terms. Hence, the next term would be 125. So, the answer is option (a).
25. AP with common difference 12. Hence, the unknown term is 12. So option (c) is the answer.
26. AP with common difference 5. Hence, 15th term is 71. Answer is option (d).
27. +7, +19, +37, +61. Hence, the next term in the series would be 121 + 91 = 212, answer is (b).
28. We are consecutively adding increasing powers of 6. Hence, option (c) is correct.
29. The first negative term will be −5 (11th term). Hence, option (b) is the answer.
30. The numerator is represented by n^2 and the denominator is represented by n^3. Hence, the next term in the series would be 36/216, option (c) is the answer.
31. Two series are intermixed. 1, 2, 3, 4, 5, 6 and 3, 5, 7, 9, 11. Hence, the next term should be 13. So option (c) is the answer.
32. The general term of the series is n^n. Hence, the next term in the series would be 4^4 = 256. Option (a) is the answer.
33. The next term in the series would be FGJ. Hence, option (b) is the answer.
34. The given series starts with the last 4 alphabets of the English language and then gives a break of 2 alphabets, followed by the next four alphabets and so on. Hence, the next term in the series would be H (after skipping J and I). So, option (c) is the answer.
35. We cannot work out the logic of this series as we do not have enough information of what the next term of this series would be. Hence, the correct answer cannot be determined. Option (d) is correct.

36. Two series are intermingled with each other as 1, 3, 5, 7, 9, 11 and 2^2, 3^2, 4^2, 5^2, 6^2. Hence, the next term in the series would be $7^2 = 49$, so the correct answer is option (b).
37. Infinite GP with common ratio $\frac{1}{4}$. Hence, Sum to infinity = 1/(3/4) = 4/3. Answer is option (b).
38. GP with common ratio 1/5. Hence, option (d) is correct.
39. The series follows the logic of –4, –9, –16 and hence the missing term must be 271 – 25 = 246. So option (a) is correct.
40. The series follows the logic of +3, +4, +5, +6 and +7. Hence, the missing term would be 19 + 5 = 24. So option (d) is the correct answer.

Solutions for Questions 41 to 47:

41. Obviously 30 is the misplaced number because all other terms are in a reducing series here. Option (b) is correct.
42. The logic followed in this series is 4 × 5 + 6 = 26; 26 × 6 +7 = 163; 163 × 7 + 8 =1149; 1149 × 8 + 9 = 9201. Only the last number in the series (82809) breaks this trend. Instead the correct value should have been 9201 × 9 + 10 = 82819. Thus, Option (c) is correct.
43. The logic followed in this series is 39 × 7 – 4 = 269; 269 × 6 – 9 = 1605; 1605 × 5 –16 = 8009; 8009 × 4 – 25 = 32011. Only the movement from 4 to 39 is unexplained by this trend. Thus, 4 is the incorrect number in the series. Option (a) is correct.
44. The logic of this series is that the sum of two numbers makes the third one in the series. This we can observe by seeing 28 + 84 = 112, 84 + 112 = 196 and so on. The only number that does not satisfy this logic is 308 + 504, which should be 812 and not 872. Thus, 872 is the wrong number in the series.
45. The logic is 14 × 4 – 36 = 20; 20 × 6 + 49 = 169; 169 × 8 – 64 = 1288, 1288 × 10 + 81 = 12961; 12961 ×12 – 100 = 155432. Obviously, the incorrect value in the series is 369 and Option (c) is the correct answer.
46. The logic of the series is 14400 × ½ = 7200, 7200 × 2/3 = 4800, 4800 × 3/4 = 3600, 3600 × 4/5 = 2880. Obviously the number 2800 is out of place. Option (c) is correct.
47. The logic of the additions are 121,171, 221, 291, 361 and so on. Thus, the number series should be 300, 421, 592, 813, 1104,1465. The number 815 is misplaced in the above series and hence Option (c) is incorrect.

Solutions for Questions 48 to 50:

48. T7 is the only instance of a consonant followed by a number and not preceded by a number. Option (a) is correct.
49. 5N% is the only instance of a consonant either followed by a symbol or preceded by a vowel but not both. Option (b) is correct.
50. The fifteenth from the left is '2' while the 7th to the left of 2 is '7' itself. Option (d) is correct.
51. EGJNS follows the skipping of 1, 2, 3 and 4 letters respectively as we can see in:
EFGHIJKLMNOPQRS
52. There are three series in the sequence. The numbers to the left of the letter–16, 18, 21, 25 are increasing continuously by 1 more than the previous increase, i.e., the series of increases in these numbers are +2, +3, +4 and the next number should be +5; thus 25 + 5 = 30.
The letters DGKP form a series where 2, 3 and 4 letters are skipped every time. Hence, the next letter would be V. Similarly, 7, 10, 14, 19 would give 25 as the next term. Thus, the correct answer would be 30V25, i.e., option (b).

Solutions for Questions 53 to 55:

53. For the first alphabet add 6 to the position number to get the next first alphabet of the next element of the series and for the second alphabet subtract 6 from the position and we'll get the required number. Option (c) is correct.
54. For the first alphabet we jump from one alphabet to the next alphabet and then to the alphabet right before the first jump. The numbers move with a gap of 2,3,4... .For the last alphabet count from Z leaving one alphabet in the count.
G11T would be correct. Option (a) is correct.
55. It is a repetition of the string: anebb. The missing alphabets in the blanks are: bnabe. Option (d) is correct.

Solutions for Questions 56 to 60:

56. Since, Bali's count from the left goes up by 8, Moti's count from the right would go down by 8 too. Option (d) is correct.
57. All the numbers in the series are perfect cubes. 999 is not a cube of any natural number. Hence, Option (d) does not belong to the series.
58. M13 and O15 should be the correct terms. Option (b) is correct.
59. A gap of two days is there in receiving and the disposal of the application. Thursday would be the correct answer option (d).
60. We are looking for the 19th letter from the right in the series:
MLKJIHGFEDCBA NOPQRSTUVWXYZ.
The letter would be F as can be counted from the above series. Option (b) is correct.

Solutions for Questions 61 to 68:

61. $12 = 11 \times 1 + 1^2$
$28 = 12 \times 2 + 2^2$
$93 = 28 \times 3 + 3^2$
$388 = 93 \times 4 + 4^2$
$388 \times 5 + 5^2 = 1965$

62. $7.5 = 2 \times 1 + 5.5$
$20.5 = 7.5 \times 2 + 5.5$
$67 = 20.5 \times 3 + 5.5$
$273.5 = 67 \times 4 + 5.5$
$273.5 \times 5 + 5.5 = 1373$

63. $8 \times 0.5 + 0.5 = 4.5$
$4.5 \times 1 + 1 = 5.5$
$5.5 \times 1.5 + 1.5 = 9.75$
$21.5 = 9.75 \times 2 + 2$
$21.5 \times 2.5 + 2.5 = 56.25$

64. $22 = 12 \times 2 - 2$
$22 \times 2 - 2 = 42$
$42 \times 2 - 2 = 82$
$82 \times 2 - 2 = 162$
$162 \times 2 - 2 = 322$

65. $3 \times 1 + 1 \times 2 = 5$
$5 \times 2 + 2 \times 3 = 16$
$16 \times 3 + 3 \times 4 = 60$
$60 \times 4 + 4 \times 5 = 260$
$260 \times 5 + 5 \times 6 = 1330$

66. $3 = 2 \times 1 + 1^2$
$18 = 3 \times 3 + 3^2$
$115 = 18 \times 5 + 5^2$
$854 = 115 \times 7 + 7^2$
$854 \times 9 + 9^2 = 7686 + 81 = 7767$

67. $20 + 2 = 22$
$22 + (1 \times 5) + 2 = 22 + 7 = 29$
$29 + (2 \times 5) + 7 = 46$
$46 + (3 \times 5) + 17 = 78$
$78 + (4 \times 5) + 32 = 130$

68. $24 + 3 = 27$
$27 + 3 + 4 = 34$
$34 + 3 + 4 + 6 = 47$
$47 + 3 + 4 + 6 + 8 = 68$
$68 + 3 + 4 + 6 + 8 + 10 = 99$

Solutions for Questions 69 to 73:

69. The pattern is:
$2^3 + 1^2 = 9$
$3^3 + 2^2 = 31$
$4^3 + 3^2 = 73$
$5^3 + 4^2 = 141$
$6^3 + 5^2 = 241$

70. The pattern is:
$35 + 221 = 256$
$256 + (221 - 26) = 451$
$451 + 169\ (195 - 26) = 620$
$620 + 143\ (169 - 26) = 763$
$763 + 117 = 880$

71. The pattern is:
$658 + 72 = 730$
$730 + 144 = 874$
$874 + 288 = 1162$
$1162 + 576 = 1738$

72. The pattern is:
$14 + 990 = 1004$
$1004 + 990/5 = 1004 + 198 = 1202$
$1202 + 198/4 = 1202 + 49.5 = 1251.5$
$1251.5 + 49.5/3 = 1251.5 + 16.5 = 1268$
$1268 + 8.25 = 1276.25$

73. The pattern of the number series is:
$5 + 1 \times 2 = 7$
$7 + 2 \times 3 = 13$
$13 + 3 \times 4 = 25$
$25 + 4 \times 5 = 45$
$45 + 5 \times 6 = 75$

Solutions for Questions 74 to 75:

74. The pattern of the number series is:
$4 + 1 \times 7 = 11$
$11 + 2 \times 7 = 25$
$25 + 4 \times 7 = 53$
$53 + 8 \times 7 = 109$
$109 + 16 \times 7 = 221$

75. The pattern of the number series is:
$15 + 6 \times 1 = 21$
$21 + 6 \times 2 = 33$
$33 + 6 \times 3 = 51$
$51 + 6 \times 4 = 75$
$75 + 6 \times 5 = 105$

76. Each term of the series is obtained by adding 1 to the square of the preceding term.
4th term of the series = $(101)^2 + 1 = 10202$

Solutions for Questions 77 to 115:

77.
$$5 \xrightarrow{+7} 12 \xrightarrow{+11} 23 \xrightarrow{+27} 50 \xrightarrow{+91} 141$$
Differences of the differences: +4, +16, +64

Hence, the next term = 141 + 91 + 256 = 488.

Hence, option (a) is correct.

78. $7 + 2 \times 3 = 13$
$13 + 3 \times 4 = 25$
$25 + 4 \times 5 = 45$
$45 + 5 \times 6 = 75$
Hence, option (a) is correct.

79. $11 = 4 \times 2 + 3$
$19 = 11 \times 2 - 3$
$41 = 19 \times 2 + 3$
$79 = 41 \times 2 - 3$
$? = 79 \times 2 + 3 = 161$

80. $8 = 5 \times 2 - 2$
$28 = 8 \times 4 - 4$
$162 = 28 \times 6 - 6$
$1288 = 162 \times 8 - 8$
$? = 1288 \times 10 - 10 = 12870$
Hence, option (b) is correct.

81. $5 = 3 + (1^2 + 1)$
$10 = 5 + (2^2 + 1)$
$20 = 10 + (3^2 + 1)$
$37 = 20 + (4^2 + 1)$
$? = 37 + (5^2 + 1) = 63.$
Hence, option (c) is correct.

82. $7 = 5 \times 1 + 2$, $25 = 7 \times 3 + 4$, $131 = 25 \times 5 + 6$, $925 = 131 \times 7 + 8$, $? = 925 \times 9 + 10 = 8335$
Hence, option (b) is correct

83. $7 = 5 \times 1 + 2$
$11 = 7 \times 2 - 3$
$37 = 11 \times 3 + 4$
$143 = 37 \times 4 - 5$
$? = 143 \times 5 + 6 = 721$
Hence, option (b) is correct.

84. $647 = 650 - (1^3 + 2)$
$636 = 647 - (2^3 + 3)$
$605 = 636 - (3^3 + 4)$
$? = 605 - (4^3 + 5) = 536.$
Hence, option (a) is correct

85. $2 = 3 \times 1 - 1^2$, $0 = 2 \times 2 - 2^2$, $-9 = 0 \times 3 - 3^2$, $-5^2 = -9 \times 4 - 4^2$
$? = -52 \times 5 - 52,$
Hence, option (a) is correct.

86. $9 = 7 + 1! + 1$, $13 = 9 + 2! + 2$, $22 = 13 + 3! + 3$, $50 = 22 + 4! + 4$ $? = 50 + 5! + 5 = 175$
Hence, option (c) is correct.

87. $184 = 40 + 12^2$, $668 = 184 + 22^2$, $1692 = 668 + 32^2$, $? = 1692 + 42^2 = 3456.$
Hence, option (b) is correct

88. $60 = 59 + 13$, $68 = 2^3$, $95 = 68 + 3^3 = 159 = 95 + 4^3$, $? = 159 + 5^3 = 284$
Hence, option (d) is correct

89. $86 = 168 \times 0.5 + 2$, $88 = 86 \times 1 + 2$, $134 = 88 \times 1.5 + 2$
$270 = 134 \times 2 + 2$, $? = 270 \times 2.5 + 2 = 677.$
Hence, option (d) is correct.

90. $13 = 4 \times 2 + 5$, $31 = 13 \times 2 + 5$, $67 = 31 \times 2 + 5$
$139 = 67 \times 2 + 5$, $? = 139 \times 2 + 5 = 283$
Hence, option (d) is correct.

91. $40 = 17 + 23 \times 1$
$109 = 40 + 23 \times 3$
$224 = 109 + 23 \times 5$
$? = 224 + 23 \times 7 = 385$
Hence, option (c) is correct.

92. $14 = 11 + 3^1$, $23 = 14 + 3^2$, $50 = 23 + 3^3$, $131 = 50 + 3^4$,
$? = 131 + 3^5 = 374.$
Hence, option (b) is correct.

93. $11 = 6 + 1^2 + 2^2$
$24 = 11 + 2^2 + 3^2$
$49 = 24 + 3^2 + 4^2$
$90 = 49 + 4^2 + 5^2$
$? = 90 + 5^2 + 6^2 = 151.$
Hence, option (a) is correct.

94. $2 = 1^3 + 1$, $10 = 2^3 + 2$, $30 = 3^3 + 3$, $68 = 4^3 + 4$
$130 = 5^3 + 5$, $? = 6^3 + 6 = 222.$
Hence, option (b) is correct.

95. $33 = 11 \times 3$, $30 = 33 - 3$, $90 = 30 \times 3$, $87 = 90 - 3$,
$? = 87 \times 3 = 261$
Hence, option (c) is correct.

96. $613 = 620 + 1^3 - 2^3$
$594 = 613 + 2^3 - 3^3$
$557 = 594 + 3^3 - 4^3$
$? = 557 + 4^3 - 5^3 = 496.$
Hence, option (a) is correct.

97. $36 = 13 + 23 \times 1$
$82 = 36 + 23 \times 2$
$151 = 82 + 23 \times 3$
$? = 151 + 23 \times 4 = 243.$
Hence, option (c) is correct.

98. $94 = 78 + 4^2$, $69 = 94 - 5^2$, $105 = 69 + 6^2$,
$? = 105 - 7^2 = 56.$
Hence, option (c) is correct.

99. $18 = 17 \times 1 + 1$
$37 = 18 \times 2 + 1$
$112 = 37 \times 3 + 1$
$449 = 112 \times 4 + 1$
$? = 449 \times 5 + 1 = 2246.$
Hence, option (a) is correct.

100. $37 = 35 + 2$, $40 = 37 + 3$, $45 = 40 + 5$, $52 = 45 + 7$,
$? = 52 + 11 = 63.$
Hence, option (d) is correct.

101. $37 = 21 + 4^2$
$73 = 37 + 6^2$
$137 = 73 + 8^2$
$237 = 137 + 10^2$
$? = 237 + 12^2 = 381.$
Hence, option (a) is correct.

102. $18 = 17 \times 1 + 1$, $37 = 18 \times 2 + 1$, $112 = 37 \times 3 + 1$, $449 = 112 \times 4 + 1$,

? = 449 × 5 + 1 = 2246.
Hence, option (d) is correct.

103. 29 = 14 + 15 × 1, 74 = 29 + 15 × 3, 149 = 74 + 15 × 5,
? = 149 + 15 × 7 = 254.
Hence, option (d) is correct.

104. 35 = 7 × 5, 32 = 35 − 3, 160 = 32 × 5, 160 − 3 = 157,
? = 157 × 5 = 785.
Hence, option (b) is correct.

105. 45 = 52 − 7 × 1, 66 = 45 + 7 × 3, 31 = 66 − 7 × 5, 80 = 31 + 7 × 7
? = 80 − 7 × 9 = 17.
Hence, option (a) is correct.

106. 17 = 13 + 4 × 1
25 = 17 + 4 × 2
41 = 25 + 4 × 4
69 = 41 + 4 × 7
? = 69 + 4 × 11 = 113.
Hence, option (b) is correct.

107. 2 × 1 + 1 = 3, 3 × 2 + 4 = 10, 10 × 3 + 9 = 39,
39 × 4 + 16 = 172, 172 × 5 + 25 = 885.
Hence, option (c) is correct.

108. 7 + 9 = 16, 16 + 9 = 25, 25 + 16 = 41, 41 + 25 = 66
Hence, option (c) is correct.

109. 3 × 1 + 2 = 5, 5 × 2 − 3 = 7, 7 × 3 + 4 = 25, 25 × 4 − 5 = 95,
95 × 5 + 6 = 841.
Hence, option (c) is correct.

110. 2 × 0.5 + 1 = 2, 2 × 1 + 2 = 4, 4 × 1.5 + 3 = 9,
9 × 2 + 4 = 22.
22 × 2.5 + 5 = 60, 60 × 3 + 6 = 186.
Hence, option (d) is correct.

111. $120 + 5^3 = 245$, $245 + 6^3 = 461$, $461 + 7^3 = 804$
$804 + 8^3 = 1316$, $1316 + 9^3 = 2045$.
Hence, option (d) is correct.

112. 92 = 67 + 25 × 1, 192 = 92 + 25 × 4, 417 = 192 + 25 × 9
? = 417 + 25 × 16 = 817.
Hence, option (a) is correct.

113. 90 = 50 + 40, 150 = 90 + 60, 240 = 150 + 90
375 = 240 + 135.
We can see à 60 = 40 × 1.5, 90 = 60 × 1.5,
135 = 90 × 1.5,
Hence, the required term = 375 + 135 × 1.5 = 577.5
Hence, option (b) is correct.

114. 6 = 4 × 1 + 2, 16 = 6 × 2 + 4, 54 = 16 × 3 + 6,
224 = 54 × 4 + 8,
? = 224 × 5 + 10 = 1130.
Hence, option (b) is correct.

115. $1^3 + 1 = 2$; $2^3 + 2 = 10$,
$3^3 + 3 = 30$; $4^3 + 4 = 68$
$5^3 + 5 = 130$; $6^3 + 6 = 222$
Hence, option (d) is correct.

CHAPTER 2

Blood Relations

Chapter Launchpad
Scan this QR code for an introductory video on Blood Relations

Questions on blood relations are common under the Logical Reasoning section of aptitude exams. As the name suggests, questions on blood relations involve working out the familial relationships between people in a family.

There are essentially two kinds of questions that can be classified under this area: *viz*

(A) Puzzle type questions with a family relationship component

(B) Statement-based relationship questions

Let us look at these one by one:

(A) Puzzle type Questions: This question type normally involves situations where there is some family relationship that is part of the puzzle. The following illustrations would make it clear to you:

WORKED-OUT PROBLEMS

Illustration 1: In a family of six persons–Abhay, Banta, Cathy, Deepak, Emily and Fatima, there are three males and three females. There are two married couples and two persons are unmarried. Each one of them likes different cold drinks.

Emily, who likes Coke, is the mother-in-law of Abhay, who is the wife of Cathy. Deepak is the father of Fatima and he does not like Thums Up or Pepsi; Banta likes Limca and is the sister of Fatima who likes Sprite. Cathy does not like Pepsi. Fanta is another cold drink.

1. Who among the following likes Thums Up?
(a) Cathy
(b) Deepak
(c) Abhay
(d) Data inadequate

2. How is Fatima related to Emily?
(a) Brother (b) Son
(c) Father (d) Daughter

3. One of the married couples is:
(a) Deepak-Banta
(b) Deepak-Emily
(c) Banta-Fatima
(d) Emily-Fatima

4. Which of the following cold drinks is liked by Abhay?
(a) Thums Up
(b) Fanta
(c) Pepsi
(d) Data inadequate

5. How many sons does Emily have?
(a) Four (b) Three
(c) Two (d) One

Illustration 2: In a family gathering, there are two males who are grandfathers and four males who are fathers. In the same gathering there are two females who are grandmothers and four females who are mothers. There is at least one grandson or a granddaughter present in this gathering. There are two husband-wife pairs in this group. These can either be a grandfather and a grandmother, or a father and a mother. The single grandfather (whose wife is not present) has two grandsons and a son present. The single grandmother (whose husband is not present) has two granddaughters present. A grandfather or a grandmother present with their spouses does not have any grandson or granddaughter present.

6. What is the minimum number of people present in this gathering?
(a) 10 (b) 12
(c) 14 (d) 16

Illustration 3: Directions for Questions 7 to 9: Read the following information carefully and answer the questions given below.

In a joint family of seven persons L, M, N, O, P, Q and R two are married couples.

'R' is a housewife and her husband is a lawyer. 'N' is the wife of 'M', 'L' is an engineer and is the granddaughter of 'R', and 'O' is the father-in-law of 'N', a doctor, and father of 'P', a professor. 'Q' is L's brother and M's son.

7. How is P related to M?
   (a) Son (b) Brother
   (c) Daughter (d) Data inadequate
8. How is Q related to O?
   (a) Grand-father (b) Uncle
   (c) Grand-son (d) Data inadequate
9. Who is M's father?
   (a) O (b) R
   (c) N (d) Data inadequate

Illustration 4: Directions for Questions 10 to 13: Answer the questions based on the following information:

Hello, Ciao and Vanakkam are related to each other.

(i) Among the three, one is Hello's legal spouse, another is Ciao's sibling and the third is Vanakkam's sister-in-law.
(ii) Hello's legal spouse and Ciao's sibling are of the same sex.

(Assume: There are no gay marriages.)

10. Who is the married man?
    (a) Hello (b) Ciao
    (c) Vanakkam (d) Can't be determined
11. Who is the married woman?
    (a) Hello (b) Ciao
    (c) Vanakkam (d) Can't be determined
12. The number of males amongst the group is
    (i) 1 (ii) 2
    (a) (i) (b) (ii)
    (c) (i) or (ii) (d) Neither (i) nor (ii)
13. Who is Ciao's sibling?
    (a) Hello (b) Ciao
    (c) Vanakkam (d) Can't be determined

Solutions:

Illustration 1:

While solving logical reasoning questions, always try to place the direct information first and keep any indirect clues aside for later use.

In this question you will find that:
Emily likes Coke → Direct clue
Deepak is the father of Fatima → Direct clue
Deepak does not like Thum up or Pepsi → Indirect clue,.... and so on.

Keep in mind the following points while solving all questions on logical reasoning:

1. First use the direct clues.
2. In the case of a family tree the diagram should essentially be a multilevel diagram to ensure clarity of being able to see multiple generations on the same diagram.
3. Males and females should be marked separately with some symbols. One suggestion is the females can be marked inside a circle/bracket or with an underlined letter as A or alternately males can be marked with a + sign and females with a - sign.
4. Relationships should be marked using horizontal links or vertical links.

The following diagrams will emerge from the clues

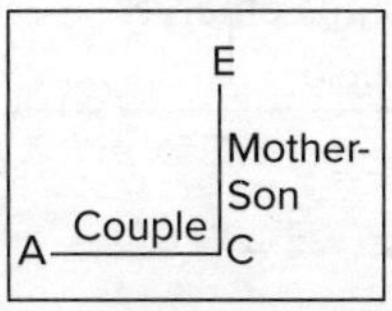

Figure 1

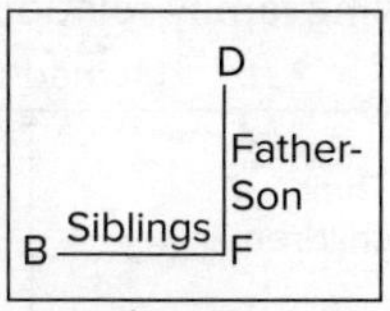

Figure 2

At this stage, you know that A, B and E are the three females and C, D and F are the three males; you also know that A and C are one of the two couples.
Hence, the other couple must be D and E. (They must be married to each other since they have children.)

This leads to a combined diagram which looks as below:

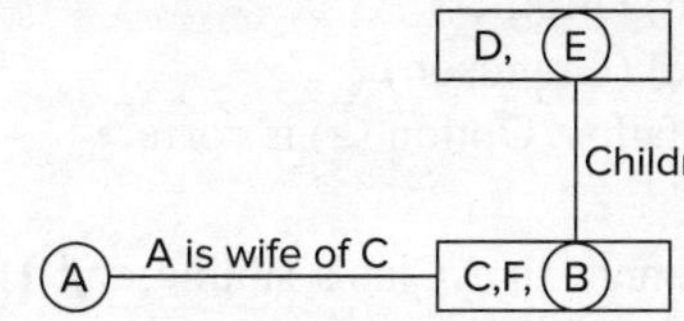

To this information, add the likes and dislikes of individuals as follows:

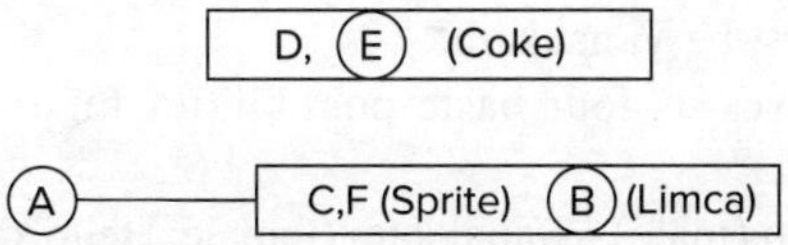

Further, D does not like Thums Up or Pepsi, hence he must like Fanta; Cathy does not like Pepsi (hence Thums Up) and Abhay likes Pepsi.
The answers are:

1. Cathy
2. Fatima is Emily's son
3. Deepak-Emily is a married couple
4. Pepsi
5. Two sons (C and F).

Illustration 2:

The family needs to have a minimum of 12 people.
GF1-GM1, GF2, GM2
F1-M1, F2, M2

Generation 1	Grandfather 1 and his wife grandmother 1	Single grandfather 1	Single grandmother 1
Generation 2	Father-Mother (husband-wife pair)	Father	
Generation 3		Two boys	Two girls

The above table gives us a total of 11 people who are compulsorily present. We need to add 1 more female (who is a mother) to this group as there are 4 mothers in the gathering. Thus a total of 12 people.
Option (b) is correct.

Illustration 3:

The following family relationships emerge

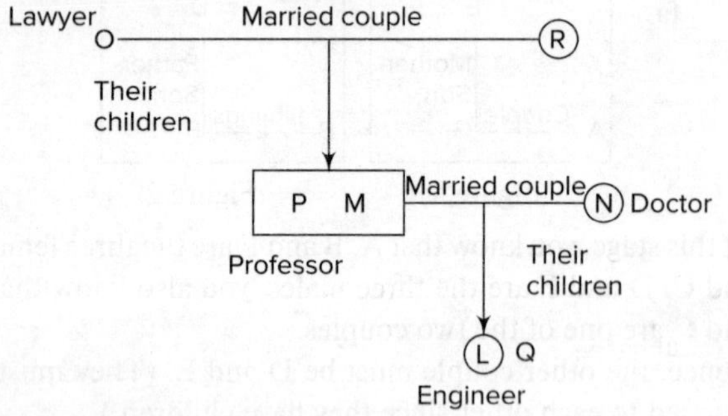

The answers are:

7. Option (b) (Brother)
8. Option (c) (Grandson)
9. O is M's father. Option (a) is correct.

Illustration 4:

From the statement that Ciao's sibling and Hello's legal spouse are of the same sex, we can conclude that Hello cannot be the sibling of Ciao (because Hello's sex would be different from his/her legal spouse's sibling). Hence, Ciao's sibling must be Vanakkam.

This gives us four basic possibilities for the husband wife pair:

(1) Hello (male) - Vanakkam (female; Hello's wife as well as Ciao's sibling); Ciao (Vanakkam's sibling; sex not known). In this case, the situation does not allow for Vanakkam's sister-in-law. Hence, we can reject this as a possible solution to the situation.

(2) Hello (female) - Vanakkam (male; Hello's husband as well as Ciao's sibling); Ciao (Vanakkam's sibling - sex not known). In this case again, the situation does not allow for Vanakkam's sister-in-law. Hence, we can reject this as a possible solution to the situation.

(3) Hello (male) - Ciao (female; Hello's wife as well as Vanakkam's sibling); Vanakkam (Ciao's sibling - female as she has to be the same sex as Hello's spouse). In this case, again the situation does not allow for Vanakkam's sister-in-law. Hence, we can reject this as a possible solution to the situation.

(4) Hello (female) - Ciao (male; Hello's husband as well as Vanakkam's sibling); Vanakkam (Ciao's sibling - male as she has to be the same sex as Hello's spouse). In this case, the last condition of Vanakkam's sister-in-law is met because Hello is the sister-in-law of Vanakkam. Thus, we conclude that this is the only possible solution given the clues. The answers then become:

10. Ciao is the married man–Option (b).
11. Hello is the married woman–Option (a).
12. There are exactly 2 males–Ciao and Vanakkam–Option (b).
13. Vanakkam–Option (c).

(B) Statement-based relationship finding questions: In this question type, we typically have to determine the relationship between two individuals whose relationship is mentioned in a roundabout manner.

In such questions, it is advisable to look at a problem from one's own perspective, i.e., if you place yourself as the central figure in the relationship matrix, the solving of the question becomes much easier as the solution anchors itself to pre-existing relationships in your own mind. The following examples would make things clear to you.

Example 1:

1. Introducing a boy, Ralf said, "His mother is the only daughter of my mother-in-law." How is Ralf related to the boy?

   (a) Uncle (b) Father
   (c) Brother (d) Husband

Example 2:

2. Pointing to a man in a photograph, a woman said, "His brother's father is the only son (and child) of my grandfather." How is the woman related to the man in the photograph?

   (a) Mother (b) Sister
   (c) Aunt (d) Daughter

Example 3:

3. If Nina says, "Anna's father Rick is the only son of my father-in-law Mick." Then how is Bridgette, who is the sister of Anna, related to Mick?

   (a) Daughter (b) Wife
   (c) Daughter-in-law (d) None of these

Example 4:

4. 'X + Y' means 'X is the father of Y', 'X - Y' means 'X is the wife of Y', 'X x Y' means 'X is the brother of Y', 'X ÷ Y' means ,'X is the mother of Y' and 'X = Y' means 'X is the sister of Y'. On the basis of this information, what does X + Y – Z mean?

   (a) X is the father-in-law of Z
   (b) Z is the father of X
   (c) Z is the neice of X
   (d) X is the brother of Z

Solutions:

Example 1: Mother-in-law's only daughter means wife. Thus the statement could be read as "His mother is my wife." Thus, Ralf must be the father of the boy.

Example 2: Read this as "his father" is my grandfather's only child. Obviously this means that the woman would be the sister of the man in the photograph. Option (b) is correct.

Example 3: From the statement, it is clear that Mick is Rick's father and Rick is Anna's father. Bridgette and Anna would thus be granddaughters of Mick. Option (d) is correct.

Example 4: X + Y means that X is the father of Y and Y - Z means that Y is the wife of Z. Thus, X is the father-in-law of Z. Option (a) is correct.

The key skills involved in solving questions on blood relations include:

(i) The ability to structure the family tree in terms of visualising the number of generations, the number of people in each generation, etc.

(ii) The ability to understand and use vital clues leading to information such as: husband-wife relationships, father-son relationships, mother-son relationships, sibling relationships

(iii) The ability to keep count of the number of people being talked about in the problem

(iv) The ability to convert clues written in language form into visual cues so that you do not need to read the text again and again. Also, converting the language clues to visual cues is critical for the purpose of being able to 'see' all the clues at one go.

EXERCISE

Directions for Questions 1 to 7:

High Yield Questions

Scan this QR code to access video explanations of questions 1, 3, 7, 24-25 and 55-60

1. Pointing to a lady on the stage, Devika said, "She is the sister of the son of the wife of my husband". How is the lady related to Devika?
   (a) Sister-in-law
   (b) Sister
   (c) Daughter
   (d) Cousin
2. Arvind said, "This girl is the sister of the grandson of my mother". How is this girl related to Arvind?
   (a) Daughter
   (b) Niece
   (c) Sister
   (d) Can't be determined
3. Pointing to a lady, a man said, "Her husband is the only son of my mother". How is the lady related to man?
   (a) Wife (b) Daughter
   (c) Father-in-law (d) None of these
4. Arun told Meesum, "Yesterday I met the son of my wife's father-in-law". How is Arun related to that man?
   (a) Brother (b) Father
   (c) Son-in-law (d) Niece
5. Pointing to a man, Manisha said, "He is the youngest son of my father-in-law's only son". How is Manisha related to this youngest son's father?
   (a) Daughter (b) Sister
   (c) Wife (d) Can't be determined
6. A family consists of a husband and wife, their three sons and two daughters, three wives of three sons. How many females are in this family?
   (a) 5 (b) 6
   (c) 7 (d) none of these
7. A man has two wives *A* and *B*. *A* is Sunny's step-mother. How is Sunny related to *B*?
   (a) Step-daughter
   (b) Sister-in-law
   (c) Son
   (d) Can't be determined

Directions for Questions 8 to 10: *If a + b means a is sister of b,*

a - b means a is brother of b,

a × b means a is daughter of b,

a ÷ b means a is mother of b.

8. Which of the following relationship shows that l and n are wife and husband?
   (a) $l \div m \times n$ (b) $l - m \times n$
   (c) $l + m \times n$ (d) None of these
9. How many females does this relationship shows? $l + m - n + o - p \times q$
   (a) 2 (b) 3
   (c) 4 (d) Can't be determined
10. The relationship $p + q - r \times s \div t$ shows that
    (a) p, q, r, s are children of t
    (b) p, q, r, t are children of s
    (c) p, q, r are children of t and s
    (d) p, q, r, s, t are all siblings.

Directions for Questions 11 to 15: *If a + b means a is daughter of b,*

a - b means a is husband of b,

a × b means a is brother of b.

11. What does the relation $p \times q - r$ show?
    (a) p is son-in-law of r
    (b) p is brother of r
    (c) r is wife of p
    (d) None of these
12. If $h + i \times j + k \times l + m \times n$, then what is the present generation of h. Assume that the oldest generation in this group is the first generation?
    (a) 2nd (b) 3rd
    (c) 4th (d) None of these

13. Which of the following statements does not hold?
(a) $a + b \times c$ (b) $a - b \times c$
(c) $a + b + c$ (d) $a + b - c$

14. From the statement $a \times b \times c \times d$, which of the following statement is not necessarily true?
(a) b is the brother of a
(b) c is the brother of a
(c) d is brother of c
(d) a, b, c are male

15. From the statement $p - q + r \times s$, how is q related to s?
(a) Niece (b) Sister
(c) Mother (d) None of these

16. Anwar's father is the only son of Mahesh's father. How is Mahesh related to Anwar?
(a) Father
(b) Brother
(c) Can't be determined
(d) None of these

17. Rahul has two mothers. Shalini is the step-daughter of Seema and step-sister of Rahul. How is Seema related to Rahul?
(a) Step-mother
(b) Mother
(c) Can't be determined
(d) None of these

18. If
I. A is brother of B
II. B is brother of C
III. C is brother of D
IV. D is sister of E.
Then which of the following statements is not necessarily true?
(a) D is sister of C
(b) B and C are brothers
(c) A, B, C are male and D is a female
(d) D and E are sisters

19. Pointing to a photograph, Vandana says, "She is the elder daughter of my mother's husband". How is person in photograph related to Vandana?
(a) Sister (b) Mother
(c) Sister-in-law (d) None of these

20. Pointing to the man in the platform, Siddhartha said, "He is the brother of the father of my mother's son". How is this man on the platform related to Siddhartha?
(a) Nephew (b) Father
(c) Brother (d) None of these

Directions for Questions 21 to 23:

a * b means a is the brother of b.
a @ b means a is the daughter of b.
a $ b means a is the sister of b.

21. Which of the following shows the relationship p is the paternal uncle of n?
(a) $n\$o@p$ (b) $n@o\$p$
(c) $n@o*p$ (d) None of these

22. From the following statement, what is the relationship between n and s?
$n\$o@p*q\$r*s$
(a) Grandmother (b) Grandfather
(c) Aunt (d) Can't be determined

23. If $a\ \$b\$c@d@e*f*g$, then how many males and females are there respectively?
(a) 4, 3 (b) 3, 4
(c) 5, 2 (d) Can't be determined

Directions for Questions 24 to 45: *P, Q, R, S, T went on a picnic. P is the son of Q but Q is not the father of P. R is the son of S, who is the brother of P. T is the wife of S.*

24. How is P related to S?
(a) Nephew (b) Brother
(c) Father (d) None of these

25. How many males are present in this group?
(a) 1 (b) 2
(c) 3 (d) 4

26. Genuflecting (bending) in front of a portrait , Raman said, "She is the only daughter of the mother of my brother's sister". How is that person related to Raman?
(a) Uncle (b) Father
(c) Mother (d) None of these

27. Pointing towards a lady in a polaroid, Victor said, "She is the daughter of the father of the sister of my brother". How is the lady in photograph related to Victor?
(a) Daughter (b) Wife
(c) Mother (d) None of these

28. A woman, pointing towards a man said, "He is my mother's mother's only son". How is the woman related to the man?
(a) Mother (b) Cousin
(c) Niece (d) Aunt

29. A woman presents a man as the son of the brother of her mother. How is the man related to the woman?
(a) Nephew (b) Son
(c) Cousin (d) Uncle

30. Pointing towards a boy, Aruna said to Pushpa, "The mother of his father is the wife of your grandfather (Mother's father)". How is Pushpa related to that boy?
(a) Sister (b) Niece
(c) Cousin sister (d) Wife

31. Looking at a man, Darren said, "Your only brother is the father of my daughter's father". How is the gentleman related to Darren?
(a) Father (b) Grandfather
(c) Brother-in-law (d) Uncle

32. Pointing to a lady, a person says to his friend, "She is the granddaughter of the elder brother of my father". How is the girl in the photograph related to the man?
(a) Niece (b) Sister
(c) Aunt (d) Sister-in-law

33. Pointing to a man in a photograph Amelia said, "His mother's only daughter is my mother". How is Amelia related to that man?
(a) Nephew (b) Sister
(c) Niece (d) Wife

34. While discussing Pam's ancestry, Rick quizzes Pam while pointing towards a man, "His mother is the only daughter of your father." How is Pam related to that person?
(a) Aunt (b) Mother
(c) Daughter (d) None of these

35. Pointing to a man in a photograph, a woman said, "His brother's father is the only son of my grandfather". How is the woman related to the man in the photograph?
(a) Mother (b) Sister
(c) Aunt (d) Daughter

36. Facing a man in the eye, Nero said, "Your son is my son's uncle." How is the man related to Nero?
(a) Brother (b) Father
(c) Uncle (d) Grandfather

37. Nikky, who is Roland's daughter, says to Irene, "Your mother Rita is the younger sister of my father, who is the third child of Sylvester". How is Sylvester related to Irene?
(a) Maternal-uncle (b) Father
(c) Grandfather (d) Father-in-law

38. A woman said, "His wife is the only daughter of my father", after introducing a man. How is that man related to the woman?
(a) Husband (b) Brother
(c) Father-in-law (d) None of these

39. Showing the woman in the park, Veronica said, "She is the daughter of my grandfather's only son." How is Veronica related to that woman?
(a) Cousin (b) Sister
(c) Father (d) Uncle
(e) None of these

40. A is the brother of B and C. D is C's mother. E is A's father. Which of the following statement cannot be definitely true?
(a) B is E's son
(b) E is B's father
(c) D is A's mother
(d) A is D's son

41. If X says that his mother is the only daughter of Y's mother, how is Y related to X?
(a) Aunt (b) Father
(c) Brother (d) Uncle

42. Jack said, "This girl is the wife of the only grandson of my mother." How is Jack related to the girl?
(a) Father (b) Father-in-law
(c) Grandfather (d) Husband

43. A woman Manpreet asks a man Harpreet, "You are the brother of my uncle's daughter. How are you related to me?". What was the man's answer?
(a) Cousin (b) Son
(c) Brother-in-law (d) Nephew

44. Allen told Beatrix, "Yesterday, I met the only brother of the daughter of my grandmother." Whom did Allen meet?
(a) Cousin (b) Brother
(c) Nephew (d) Father

45. A woman presents a man as the son of the brother of her mother. How is the man related to the woman?
(a) Nephew (b) Son
(c) Cousin (d) Uncle

Directions for Questions 46 to 47: *Study the following information carefully and answer the questions given below.*

Raina, Murli, Haiden, Patel, Gony, Balaji and Morkel are seven members in a family, out of which there are three females and four males. There are two managers, two lawyers, one teacher, one engineer and one doctor. No lady is either a teacher or an engineer. Haiden is a lawyer and is married to Raina, who is a teacher. Balaji, the engineer, is married to Patel, who is neither a lawyer nor a doctor. No two ladies have the same profession. Murli is the sister of Morkel, who is a manager.

46. What is Gony's profession?
(a) Manager
(b) Lawyer
(c) Manager or Lawyer
(d) Data inadequate

47. Which of the following is the group of males?
(a) Raina, Murli, Balaji and Morkel
(b) Gony, Balaji, Patel and Morkel
(c) Raina, Haiden, Gony and Balaji
(d) Raina, Gony, Balaji and Morkel

Directions for Questions 48 to 49: *Study the following information carefully and answer the questions given below.*

P, Q, R, S, T, U and V are seven members of a family belonging to three generations. There are two married couples–one each of first and second generation respectively. They travel in three different cars–Bentley, Lamborghini and Ferrari so that no car has more than three members and there is at least one female in each car. R, who is a granddaughter, does not travel with her grandfather and grandmother. Q travels with his father T in Lamborghini. U travels with her granddaughter S in Bentley. P travels with her daughter in Ferrari.

48. How many female members are there in the family?
(a) Three (b) Four
(c) Five (d) None of these

49. Which of the following is one of the married couples?
(a) PS (b) PR
(c) TU (d) None of these

Directions for Question 50: *Read the information given carefully and answer the question.*

In a family of six persons–Pranay, Qayamat, Ravi, Shashi, Tanveer, and Umed, there are three males and three females. There are two married couples and two persons are unmarried. Each one of them reads different magazines, which are *Cosmopolitan, Vogue, India Today, Economist, Stardust* and *Femina.*

The following facts about the family members are also known:

Tanveer, who reads *Cosmopolitan*, is mother-in-law of Pranay, who is wife of Ravi. Shashi is the father of Umed and he does not read Vogue or *Femina*. Qayamat reads *Stardust* and is the sister of Umed, who reads *India Today*. Ravi does not read *Femina*.

50. Who among the following reads *Vogue* and what is the relation between the person who reads *Vogue* and *Qayamat*?
(a) Ravi, Sister (b) Ravi, Father
(c) Umed, sister (d) Shashi, Father

Directions for Questions 51 to 54: *There are six persons in a room namely - A, B, C, D, E and F. A and E are brothers, B and D are daughters of the brother of C's father. F is the sister of E, C is the only son of A's uncle.*

51. How many male persons are there amongst A, B, C, D, E and F?
(a) 5 (b) 3
(c) 1 (d) 0

52. How is C related to F?
(a) Uncle (b) Cousin
(c) Aunt (d) None of these

53. How many female persons are there?
(a) 0 (b) 1
(c) 2 (d) 3

54. How is D related to A?
(a) Uncle (b) Father
(c) Cousin (d) Mother

Directions for Questions 55 to 60: *A, B, C, D, E and F are six members of a family. C is not the mother of B but B is the son of C. A and C are a married couple. E is the brother of C. F is the brother of B. D is the daughter of A.*

55. E is D's ____.
(a) Uncle (b) Mother
(c) Brother (d) Father

56. Which of the following is a pair of females?
(a) A, D (b) B, D
(c) C, A (d) B, A

57. E's wife is ____.
(a) A (b) C
(c) F (d) Can't be determined

58. How many kids does A have?
(a) 0 (b) 1
(c) 2 (d) 3

59. How many female members are there in the family of 6?
(a) 0 (b)
(c) 2 (d) 3

60. B's mother is ____.
(a) A (b) E
(c) F (d) D

Directions for Questions 61 to 65: *There are six members - A, B, C, D, E and F in a family. There are two married couples. B is Indian and is the father of E. F is the grandfather of C. F is from America. D is the grandmother of E and D is from U.K. There is one Indian, one American, one British, one French and two Germans in the family. The French person is a female and married. Nobody who is a grandchild is married.*

61. Which of following two are married couples?
(a) AB, FD (b) AD, BF
(c) AC, BD (d) AF, BC

62. Who is the husband of A?
(a) B (b) F
(c) D (d) C

63. Who is the sister of E?
(a) C (b) B
(c) D (d) Can't be determined

64. Which of the following is a group of male members?
(a) D, A (b) B, F
(c) D, F (d) A, B

65. A is a/an ______.
(a) German (b) French
(c) UK (d) Can't be determined

Directions for Questions 66 to 69: *Answer the questions on the basis of the information given below:*

A family consists of 6 members namely P, Q, R, S, T and U. Q is the brother-in-law of R's mother. R is father of U. S is father of P and U is grandson of S. There are two female members in the family.

66. Who is the mother of R?
(a) Q (b) T
(c) P (d) Can't be determined

67. Which of the following pairs represents the female members in the family?
(a) P and T (b) Q and R
(c) R and S (d) Can't be determined

68. The members of the family belong to how many generations?
(a) Four
(b) Two
(c) Three
(d) Either two or three

69. S has two children. One is P and who is the other one?
(a) T (b) R
(c) Q (d) U

Directions for Questions 70 to 72: *Answer the questions on the basis of the information given below:*

C + D means C is father of D.
C - D means C is sister of D.
C × D means C is husband of D.
C ÷ D means C is wife of D.

70. Which of the following means S is granddaughter of R?
(a) R + P ÷ Q + S
(b) K ÷ R + P × Q - L + S
(c) K ÷ R + P ÷ Q + S L
(d) Can't be determined

71. Which of the following means P has a blood relationship with Q?
(a) R ÷ P + K × L - M + Q
(b) R ÷ P + K ÷ L + Q - M
(c) R ÷ P + K - L × M - N + Q
(d) R ÷ P + K × L - Q

72. Which of the following means P is the grandmother of Q?
(a) P ÷ R + S × T - U × Q
(b) P ÷ R + S + T ÷ Q
(c) P ÷ R + S + B + K - L - Q
(d) P ÷ R + S - T + Q - U

Directions for Questions 73 to 74: *Read the following information to answer the questions:*

E + F means E is brother of F.
E - F means E is sister of F.
E × F means E is father of F.
E ÷ F means E is mother of F.

73. If P ÷ Q - R × S, then P is S's
(a) Grandmother (b) Maternal grandmother
(c) Maternal aunt (d) Sister

74. Which of the following shows that T is the grandmother of W?
(a) T × U + V ÷ W (b) T + U - V ÷ W
(c) T + U ÷ V × W (d) T ÷ U - V × W

Directions for Questions 75 to 80: *Charan and his wife Kirti have a family of three generations comprising thirteen members of whom six are female and rest are male members. Some of Charan's children are married, but none of his grandchildren are married.*

(i) Kirti has a daughter-in- law named Fatima and two sons-in-law, one being Chatur.
(ii) Harman's brother is David, who has two nephews and two nieces.-one being Leela.
(iii) Barima, David's sister has two children.
(iv) Fatima, who is sister-in-law to David has four nephews and nieces.
(v) Manohar who is married to Garima in the family has a daughter, Ishika and a son.
(vi) Jairam has a sister and two cousins, Akash and Ishika.

Answer the following questions based on the above data:

75. Who is Garima's son?
76. Who is the niece of Chatur?
77. Who is the sister of Jairam?
78. How many sons does Harman have?
79. How many children does Kirti have?
80. Akash is the son of:
(a) Garima (b) Harman
(c) David (d) Barima

ANSWER KEY

1. (c)	2. (d)	3. (a)	4. (a)
5. (c)	6. (b)	7. (d)	8. (a)
9. (d)	10. (b)	11. (d)	12. (c)
13. (b)	14. (c)	15. (a)	16. (a)
17. (b)	18. (d)	19. (a)	20. (d)
21. (c)	22. (d)	23. (d)	24. (b)
25. (c)	26. (d)	27. (d)	28. (c)
29. (c)	30. (c)	31. (d)	32. (a)
33. (c)	34. (b)	35. (b)	36. (b)
37. (c)	38. (a)	39. (b)	40. (a)
41. (d)	42. (b)	43. (a)	44. (d)
45. (c)	46. (b)	47. (d)	48. (c)
49. (c)	50. (a)	51. (b)	52. (b)
53. (d)	54. (c)	55. (a)	56. (a)
57. (d)	58. (d)	59. (c)	60. (a)
61. (a)	62. (a)	63. (d)	64. (b)
65. (b)	66. (b)	67. (a)	68. (c)
69. (b)	70. (c)	71. (b)	72. (d)
73. (a)	74. (d)	75. Akash	76. Ishika
77. Leela	78. 0	79. 4	80. (a)

SOLUTIONS AND SHORTCUTS

Solutions for Questions 1 to 7:

1. From Devika's perspective, wife of my husband means me. Then, my son's sister means my daughter. Hence, option (c) is correct.
2. The girl could be Arvind's niece or daughter. Hence, option (d) is correct.
3. Only son of my mother, means me. Hence, the situation transforms into I am her husband. Hence, the lady is the man's wife. So the correct option is (a).
4. The son of my wife's father-in-law would be either me or my brother. Since Arun says that he met this person it must be the brother. Hence, option (a) is the answer.
5. Looking at it from Manisha's perspective, "my father-in-law's only son" would be my husband. Thus the youngest son of this person would also be Manisha's son. Hence, this person's father would be Manisha's husband and Manisha would be the wife. Option (c) is the answer.
6. Wife + two daughters + 3 wives of the three sons = 6. Hence, option (b) is the answer.
7. Sunny could be B's son or daughter. Hence, option (d) is correct.

Solutions for Questions 8 to 10:

8. Go through the options, $l \div m$ means l is the mother of m. $m \times n$ means m is the daughter of n. Thus, m must be the daughter of l and n. Hence, (a) is the correct option.
9. $l + m - n + o - p \times q$ can be read as l is the sister of m, m is the brother of n, n is the sister of o, o is the brother of p and p is the daughter of q. Thus, l, n and p are females, m and o are males and we do not know about q's sex. Hence, we cannot be sure about the number of females in this relationship string. Thus, option (d) is correct.
10. $p + q - r \times s \div t$ reads as: p is the sister of q, q is the brother of r, r is the daughter of s and s is the mother of t. Thus, option (b) is correct.

Solutions for Questions 11 to 15:

11. $p \times q - r$ can be read as p is the brother of q and q is the husband of r. Thus p must be the brother-in-law of r. Hence, option (d) is correct.
12. $h + i \times j + k \times l + m \times n$ means h is the daughter of i, i is the brother of j, j is the daughter of k, k is the brother of l, l is the daughter of m and m is the brother of n. Thus, if m and n are the first generation, k and l are the second, i and j are the third generation, h is the fourth generation. To solve this question in short, you only need to realise that the use of the + sign signifies a generation change. Since the + sign is used thrice, h must be the fourth generation. Hence, option (c) is the answer.
13. Option (b) says: $a - b \times c$, this does not hold since a must be the husband of b (who is a female) and b is the brother of c (which cannot happen). Hence, option (b) is the answer.
14. $a \times b \times c \times d$ means a is the brother of b, b is the brother of c and c is the brother of d. This makes options (a), (b) and (d) as correct. Only option (c) is not necessarily true since d could be b's sister too. Hence, (c) is the answer.
15. $p - q + r \times s$ reads as p is the husband of q, q is the daughter of r and r is the brother of s. Thus, q must be s's niece. Hence, option (a) is the correct answer.

Solutions for Questions 16 to 20:

16. Anwar's father being the only son of Mahesh's father, means that Mahesh must be Anwar's father. Option (a) is the answer.
17. Mother, hence, option (b) is correct.
18. *A*, *B*, *C* are siblings and brothers of each other. *D* is their sister but we cannot say anything about *E*'s sex (whether *E* is male or female and hence brother or sister is unknown). Hence, (d) is correct.
19. Sister. Hence, option (a) is the answer.
20. My mother's son means me or my brother, father of my mother's son means my father. Brother of my father means my uncle. Hence, option (d) is correct.

Solutions for Questions 21 to 23:

21. $n@o*p$ reads, n is the daughter of o and o is the brother of p. Hence, p becomes n's paternal uncle. So, option (c) is correct.
22. It is clear that s's sex cannot be determined. Hence, the relationship between n and s cannot be determined. Option (d) is the answer.
23. Again here, g's sex is indeterminable. Hence, the answer cannot be determined. Option (d) is the answer.

Solutions for Questions 24 to 25:

P is the son of *Q* but *Q* is not the father of *P* means that *Q* must be the mother of *P*. Also, *R* is the son of *S*, who is the brother of *P* means that *S* and *P* must be brothers and *R* is *S*'s son. Also, since *T* is the wife of *S*, *R* must be *T*'s son also.

Consolidating these relationships we get:

Q mother of *S* and *P* (brothers). Also, *S*'s wife is *T* and their son is *R*.

24. *P* is *S*'s Brother. Hence, (b) is correct option.
25. *S*, *P* and *R* are males. Hence, option (c) is correct.

Solutions for Questions 26 to 45:

26. Raman's brother's sister would be same as Raman's sister. This makes Raman son of the mother and the brother of the person, while that person would become Raman's sister. Hence Option (d) is the correct answer.
27. Victor's brother's sister's father will be Victor's father as well and the daughter of the father will be Victor's sister. Hence, Option (d).
28. It makes the man the brother of the woman's mother, that makes the woman the man's niece. So Option (c) is the correct answer.
29. The man is the son of the woman's mother's brother, that makes the man and the woman cousins. So option (c) is correct.
30. The father of the boy is brother of Pushpa's mother. That makes Pushpa that boy's cousin sister. Hence (c) is the correct option.
31. According to the clue the man is brother of Darren's father. This makes the gentleman Darren's uncle. Hence, Option (d).
32. It would make the man uncle of the lady, as he would be the son of her grandfather's brother. Therefore (a) is the correct option.
33. Amelia's mother is that man's sister. It makes Amelia that man's niece. So (c) is correct.
34. Option (a) could have been correct but, it has been mentioned that the mother is the only daughter. This only means that Pam must be the mother of that person. Hence, (b).
35. According to the clue, the man is also grandson of the woman's grandfather. So (b) is the correct option.
36. The uncle of Nero's son is Nero's brother that makes the man Nero's father. Hence Option (b).
37. Rita's father is Sylvester who is Roland's father. It makes Irene Sylvester's granddaughter. So (c) is the right option.
38. Has to be the husband. Hence, Option (a) is correct.
39. This means Veronica and the woman have the same father. It makes them sisters. Hence Option (b) is correct.
40. The gender of B is not there in the question. Therefore (a) is the correct option.
41. Y must be a man as his sister is the only daughter of his mother. So Y is X's uncle. Therefore (d) is correct.
42. The grandson is Jack's son, so it makes Jack this girl's father-in-law. Hence, Option (b) is correct.
43. The man is the son of the woman's uncle, i.e., the man is the woman's cousin. Hence (b) is correct.
44. The clue makes the man son of Allen's grandmother i.e., the man can be Allen's father or uncle. Since, the options do not contain uncle, we have to conclude it is the father. So, (d) is the right option.
45. The man is the son of the woman's mother's brother, that makes the man and the woman cousins. Therefore, (c) is the correct answer.

Solutions for Questions 46 to 47:

From the clues we can see that no lady is either a teacher or an engineer. Hence these have to be males. Now since Raina is a male, Haiden is a female because Haiden is a lawyer and is married to Raina. Balaji the engineer is married to Patel. Hence Balaji is a male and Patel is a female so Patel cannot be teacher or engineer. It is also given that she is neither a lawyer or a doctor. Thus, she is a manager.

Again, Murli is sister of Morkel who is the manager. Morkel is a male because no two females have the same profession and Patel is a female and a manager. On the same grounds, Murli cannot be lawyer hence she is a doctor. By elimination of clues Gony is a lawyer and a male.
Now, let us tabulate all the conclusions in a table:

Person	Profession	Gender
Raina	Teacher	Male
Murli	Doctor	Female
Haiden	Lawyer	Female
Patel	Manager	Female
Gony	Lawyer	Male
Balaji	Engineer	Male
Morkel	Manager	Male

Now we can answer the questions.

46. Option (b)
47. Option (d)

Solutions for Questions 48 to 49:

On the basis of the given clues we get the following information:

Car	Persons travelling in car
Bentley	U(F), S(F)
Lamborghini	Q(M), T(M)
Ferrari	P(F), ?(F)

Besides this we came to know that R is a female but we still do not know the gender of V. But it is given that there is at least one female in each car. The above table shows that Lamborghini has a vacant seat for a female passenger. Hence, the seventh person must be a female to fulfill the condition. Hence, V is a female. But we still do not know in which car R and V are travelling knowing that both are not in the same car. Now we need to construct a family tree:

[T(M)↔U (F)] ----> [Q(M)↔ P(F)] ----> [R(F) + S(F)]

FIRST SECOND THIRD

Since R does not travel with her grandfather and grandmother, R is not in Bentley, hence R is in Lamborghini. We are still not aware of V's position in the family tree.

48. Option (c)
49. Option (c)

Solution for Question 50:

50. From the given information of the readership, we can build a table as follows:

	Payal	Qayamat	Ravi	Shashi	Tanveer	Umed
Cosmo-politan	X	X	X	X	√	X
Vogue	X	X	√	X	X	X
India Today	X	X	X	X	X	√
Economist	X	X	X	√	X	X
Stardust	X	√	X	X	X	X
Femina	√	X	X	X	X	X

(a) Tanveer and Shashi are a couple.
(b) Pranay and Ravi are a couple.
(c) Ravi, Umed and Qayamat are brothers and sisters.
Hence Option (a) is the correct answer.

Solutions for Questions 51 to 54:

The following figure would show us the family tree

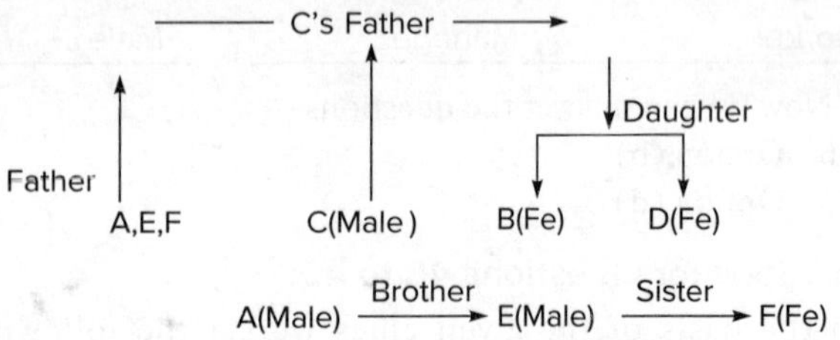

51. 3
52. C is the cousin of F.
53. 3
54. D is A's cousin.

Solutions for Questions 55 to 60:

B is the son of C but C is not his mother means C is his father and A is C's wife or B's mother.

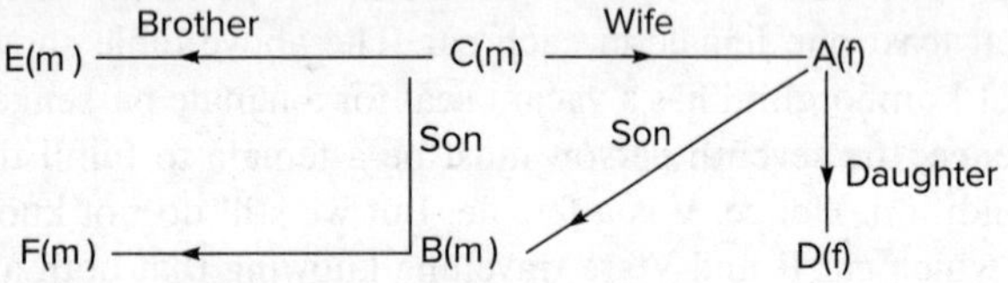

55. E is D's uncle
56. A, D
57. Can't be determined
58. 3. B, D and F are all children of A.
59. A and D are the only female members in the family of 6. Hence, the correct answer would be 2.
60. A

Solutions for Questions 61 to 65:

As there are only two married couples and B is the father of E and F is the grandfather of C. It means F is father of B and C is B's child. A is B's wife.

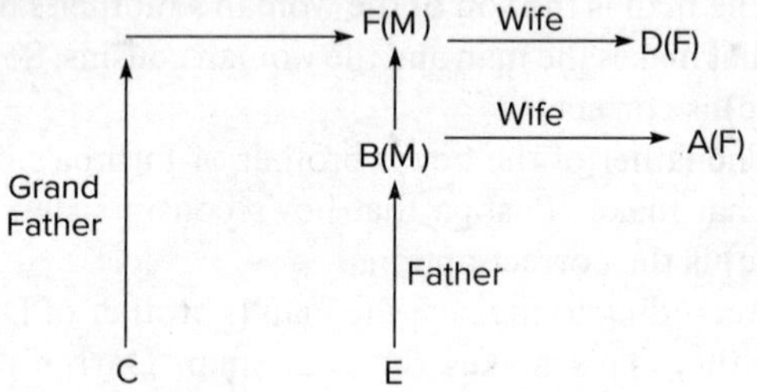

61. (a)
62. B
63. Can't be determined
64. B, F
65. As D is female and she is from UK. So the French married lady must be A.

Solutions for Questions 66 to 69:

From the information given in the question we can form the following relation chart:

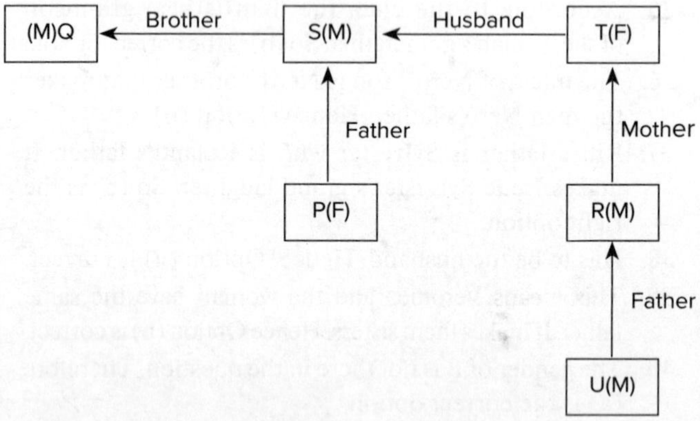

66. T is the mother of R. Option (b) is correct.
67. P and T represent the female members of the family. Option (a) is correct.
68. Members of the family belong to three different generations. Option (c) is correct.
69. P, R are the two children of S. Option (b) is correct.

Solutions for Questions 70 to 72:

70. We can solve this problem just by checking the options: In option (c) we have: K ÷ R + P ÷ Q + S – L and R + P ÷ Q + S – L represent S is sister of L it means S is a female. Q is the father of S, P is the wife of Q and R is the father of P. It means S is the granddaughter of R. Hence, option (c) is correct.
71. For this question, again check the options to identify the correct answer. In Option (b): R ÷ P + K ÷ L + Q – M, if we start to analyse the relationships from the right to the left we get:
Q is the sister of M, L is the father of Q, K is the wife of L, P is the father of K. This means that P is the grand father of K, which implies a blood relationship. Note: A blood relation means a relationship through blood. For example, husband-wife is not a blood relation.
72. Option (d): P ÷ R + S – T + Q × U means P is the grandmother of Q.

Solutions for Questions 73 to 74:

73.

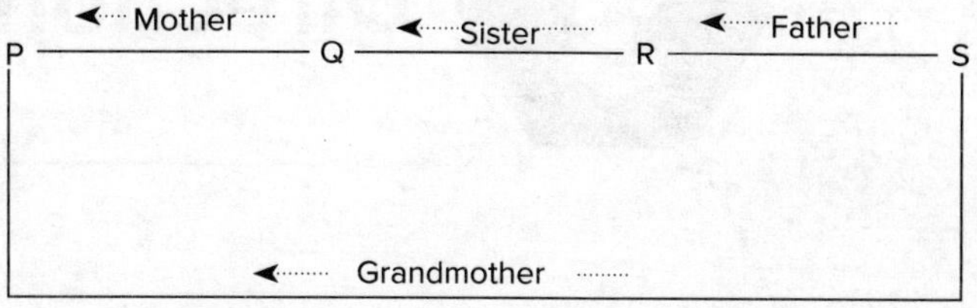

P ÷ Q – R × S means P is S's grandmother. Hence, option (a) is correct.

74. You would need to check the options in order to solve this question. When you check option (d), you get:

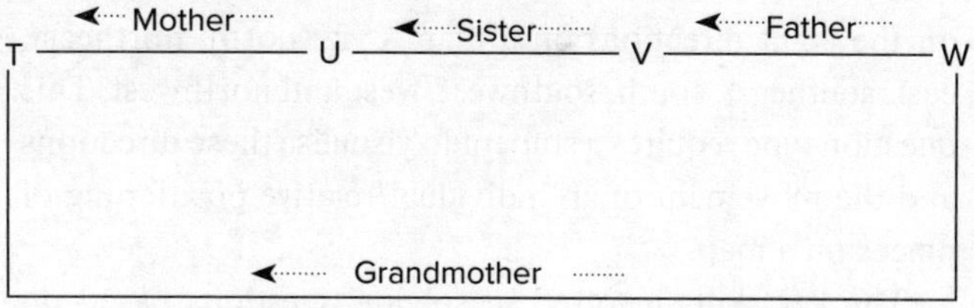

T ÷ U – V × W represents T is grandmother of W. Hence, option (d) is correct.

Solutions for Questions 75 to 80:

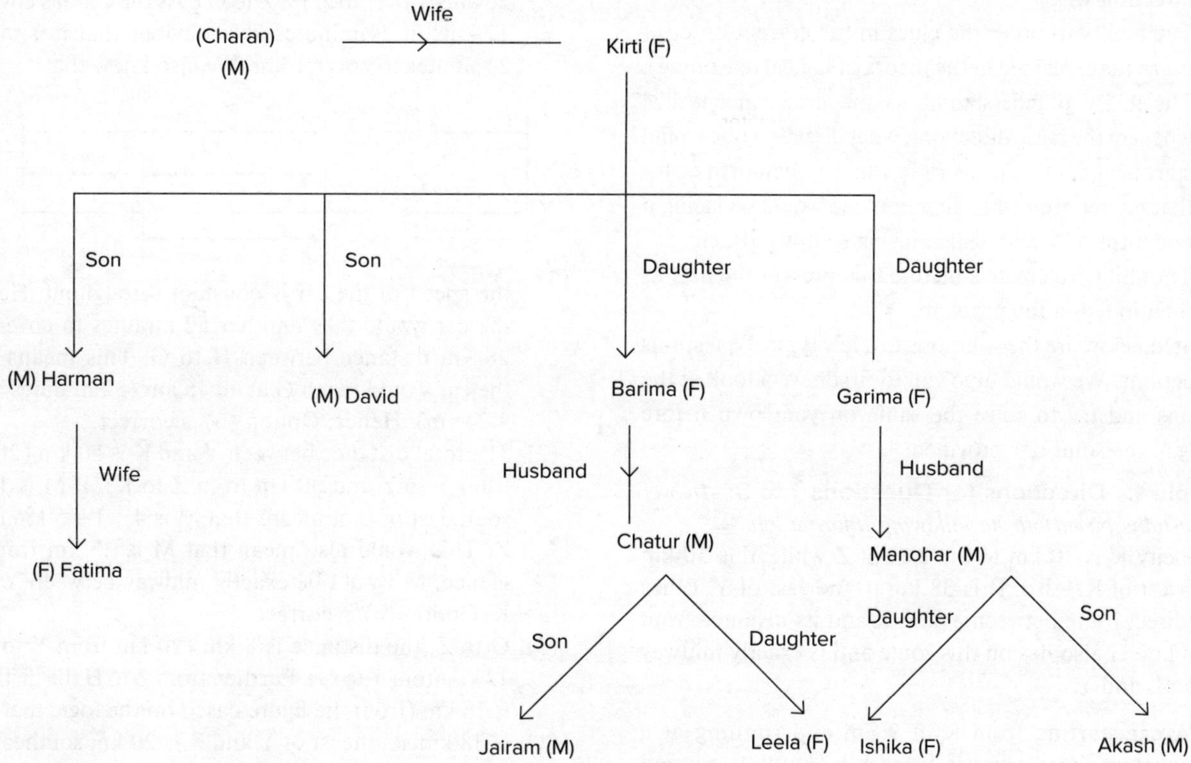

75. Akash
76. Ishika
77. Leela
78. 0
79. 4
80. (a)

CHAPTER 3

Direction Test

Chapter Launchpad

Scan this QR code to access an introductory video on Direction Test

Questions on directions are standard ones that are asked in most aptitude exams, hence are a common component in the study of reasoning. As the name itself suggests, questions about directions would involve reasoning based on the eight directions on a map - viz: north, northeast, east, southeast, south, southwest, west and northwest. This question type requires a student to visualise these directions and the movement of an individual/relative positioning of places on a map.

The key skills involved in solving questions based on directions are the following:

(i) The ability to understand and interpret the clues written in plain language in terms of what it means direction wise.

(ii) The ability to order the clues in the correct order of usage (as explained in the theory of logical reasoning).

(iii) The ability to understand basic mapping concepts like what are the basic directions, what direction one would start facing if one turns right while going north or for that matter even what direction one would be facing if one turns 45° right while moving southwards, etc.

(iv) The ability to create a picture to represent the flow as mentioned in the problem.

Illustrated below are the solutions to a few typical questions on directions. We would urge you to first have a look at the questions and try to solve the same on your own before looking at the solutions provided.

Example 1: Directions for Questions 1 to 3: *Answer the questions based on the following information.*

The city K is 30 km to the east of Z while Y is 50 km to the west of K. Also, H is 38 km to the east of Y. L lies in the direct route between Y and K and its distance from H is 14 km. G also lies on this route and is exactly midway between L and Y.

1. A car starting from K at 9 am and running at a constant speed towards Y reaches H at 9:24 am and then reaches G at

(a) 9:18 am (b) 10:16 am
(c) 10:36 am (d) 10:42 am

2. If M is 1 km to the east of L, then it is exactly midway between

(a) H and L (b) Y and K
(c) H and Z (d) None of these

3. The distance from G to H is

(a) 26 km (b) 24 km
(c) 12 km (d) 16 km

Solutions to Example 1: The figure below shows the respective positioning of the cities K, H, L, Z, G and Y.

From the figure we can deduce the answers using the following thinking:

(1) The car covers K to H–a distance of 12 kms in 24 minutes according to the figure (starting at 9 am and reaching at 9:24 am). From H to G, the distance is 26 kms. (18 H to Z + 8 Z to G). As the car has covered 12 kms in 24 minutes, it is obvious that it is taking 2 minutes to cover 1 km. We also know that

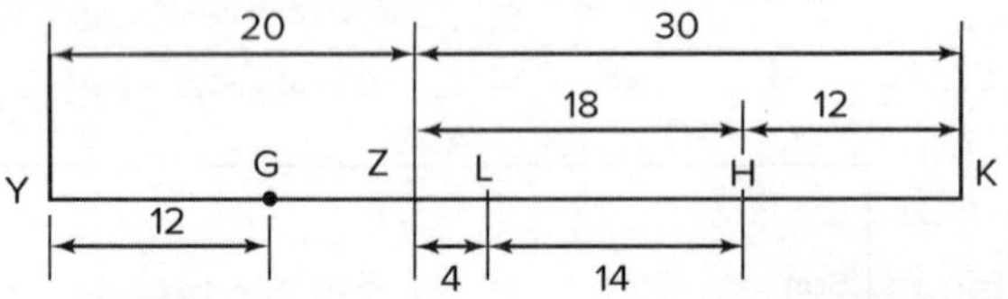

the speed of the car is constant throughout. Hence, the car would take another 52 minutes to cover the 26 km distance between H to G. This means that the car would reach G at 10:16 am (52 minutes after 9:24 am). Hence, Option (b) is correct.

(2) The total distance between Y and K is 50 km (20 km from Y to Z and 30 km from Z to K). If M is 1 km southeast of L, it means that M is 4 + 1 = 5 km from Z. This would also mean that M is 25 km from Y. Hence, M would be exactly midway between Y and K. Option (b) is correct.

(3) G to Z, the distance is 8 km (20 km from Y to Z - 12 km from Y to G). Further, from Z to H the distance is 18 km (from the figure based on the logic that if H is 38 km southeast of Y and Z is 20 km southeast of Y, the distance from Z to H would be 38 - 20). Total distance would be 8 + 18 = 26 km. Option (a) is correct.

Example 2: Directions for Questions 4 to 6: Refer to the information given below.

There are six cities viz., Amsterdam, Bhubaneshwar, Calgary, Denver, El Dorado and Frankfurt. Their positions with respect to one another on a map are described through the five clues given below.

Calgary is to the south of Frankfurt, but to the west of Denver.

Frankfurt is to the south of El Dorado which is east of Denver.

Amsterdam is south of Bhubaneshwar which is west of Frankfurt.

El Dorado is south of Amsterdam which is west of Calgary.

Denver is south of Frankfurt which is west of Amsterdam.

4. Which of the following are situated to the northeast of at least one other city?
   (a) Bhubaneshwar, Amsterdam and El Dorado
   (b) Amsterdam and El Dorado
   (c) Bhubaneshwar, Amsterdam
   (d) Amsterdam, Frankfurt and Denver
5. Which of the following are to the northeast of Frankfurt?
   (A) Amsterdam (B) El Dorado (C) Calgary
   (a) A only (b) B only
   (c) A and C (d) A and B
6. Which of the following statements cannot be derived from the given information?
   (a) Bhubaneshwar is to the west of Amsterdam.
   (b) Denver is to the south of Amsterdam.
   (c) Denver is to the south of Calgary.
   (d) Amsterdam is to the west of El Dorado.

Solutions to Example 2: It can be concluded that the northsouth distribution of the cities would be one of the following:

Possibility 1	Possibility 2
Bhubaneshwar	Bhubaneshwar
Amsterdam	Amsterdam
El Dorado	El Dorado
Frankfurt	Frankfurt
Denver	Calgary
Calgary	Denver

The eastwest placement would be as follows:

Bhubaneshwar	Frankfurt	Amsterdam	Calgary	Denver	El Dorado

The grid possibilities based on these two arrangements would be as follows:

Possibility 1:

Bhubaneshwar					
		Amsterdam			
					El Dorado
	Frankfurt				
				Denver	
			Calgary		

Possibility 2:

Bhubaneshwar					
		Amsterdam			
					El Dorado
	Frankfurt				
			Calgary		
				Denver	

Based on these we can answer the questions as follows:

4. Looking at the above tabular picture of the placement of the cities as northsouth or eastwest, we can see that El Dorado and Amsterdam are the only cities that satisfy this condition. Denver and Calgary could be northeast to each other depending on which possibility we consider–in Possibility 1 Calgary is not northeast of any city and hence we can eliminate the possibility of Calgary being northeast of at least one other city. Similarly on the basis of Bhubaneshwar being west most cannot be to the northeast of any city (as Denver would. Option (b) is correct.
5. Both A and B. Hence, Option (d) is correct.
6. Option (c) cannot be concluded from the information as we cannot decide on the northsouth placement between Calgary and Denver.

Example 3:

7. Jack runs 10 m south from his flat, turns left and walks 23 m, again turns left and walks 40 m, then turns right and walks 5 m to reach his office. In which direction is the office from his house?
   (a) East (b) Northeast
   (c) Southwest (d) North

Solution to Example 3:

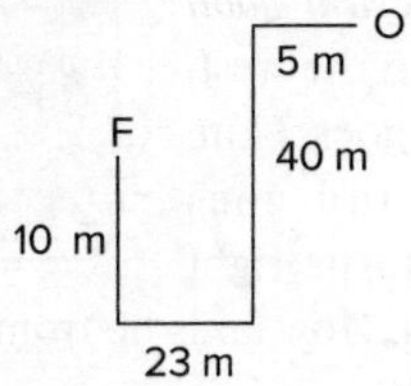

When we will look from F (Flat) to O (office) in the figure it can be observed that the direction is northeast. Option (b) is correct.

Example 4:

8. I am facing north. I turn 90° in the clockwise direction and then 135° in the same direction and then 270° anti-clockwise. Which direction am I facing now?
   (a) Southwest
   (b) South
   (c) West
   (d) Northwest

Solution to Example 4: After turning 90° I am looking in the east direction, then after turning 135° in the same direction I would be facing the southwest direction. At last after turning 270° anticlockwise I would be facing the northwest direction. Option (d) is correct.

Example 5: Two cars start from the opposite points of straight part of the National Higway 8, 100 km apart. The first car runs for 20 km. It then takes a detour–takes a right turn goes straight for 15 km. It then turns left, runs for another 25 km and then takes the straight connecting road to reach back on the main road. In the meantime, due to a minor breakdown, the other car has run only 35 km along the main road. What would be the distance between the two cars at this point?
   (a) 20 km
   (b) 30 km
   (c) 45 km
   (d) 10 km

Solution to Example 5:

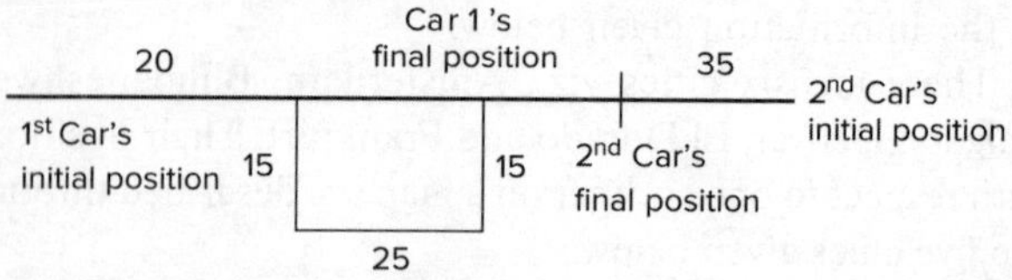

From the above figure it is clear that Car 1 would move 45 kms along the highway while Car 2 would run 35 kms along the same highway. Naturally, the distance between the two cars at this time would be 20 km. Option (a) is correct.

Example 6: A messenger was returning to his base station which was in front of him to the north. When his base station was 100 m away from him, he turned to the left and moved 50 m to deliver the last message to the Peshwa's troops. He then moved in the same direction for 40 m, turned to his right and moved 100 m. How many meters away he was now from his base station?
   (a) 0 (b) 150
   (c) 90 (d) 100

Solution to Example 6:

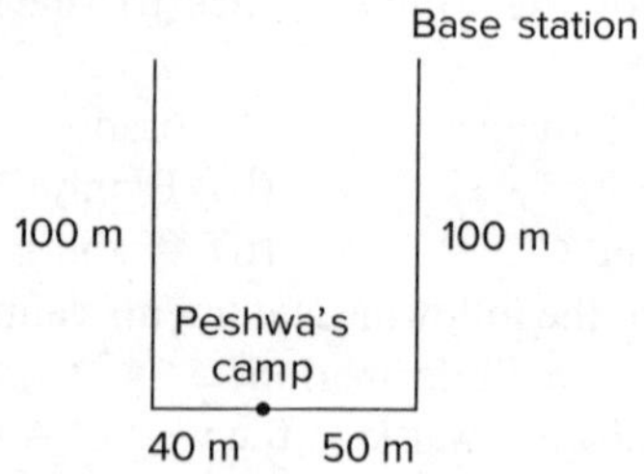

Option (c) is correct.

EXERCISE

Directions for Questions 1 to 4: *Answer the questions independent of each other.*

1. A watch in Huckleberry Finn's house reads 4·30. If the minute hand points towards the West, in which direction does the hour hand point?
   (a) Northeast
   (b) Southwest
   (c) Northwest
   (d) North
2. Hanuman, while looking for the *Sanjeevani booti* travels 3 km to the west, turns left and goes 3 km, turns right and goes 1 km, again turns right and goes 3 km. How far is he from the starting point?
   (a) 7 km (b) 6 km
   (c) 5 km (d) 4 km

High Yield Questions
Scan this QR code to access video explanations of questions 5-9, 12-14, 29, 30 and 31

3. Raveena walks 10 km south from her house, turns left and walks 25 km, again turns left and walks 40 km, then turns right and walks 5 km to reach her office. In which direction was the office from her house?
   (a) Southwest (b) Northeast
   (c) East (d) North
4. For the above question, what is the distance of her office from her home?
   (a) 30 (b) 30×2^{½}
   (c) 45×2^{½} (d) None of these

Directions for Questions 5 to 9: *These questions are based on the diagram given below, showing four persons Amar, Bhushan, Chandu and Dilip stationed at the four corners of a square piece of plot as shown.*

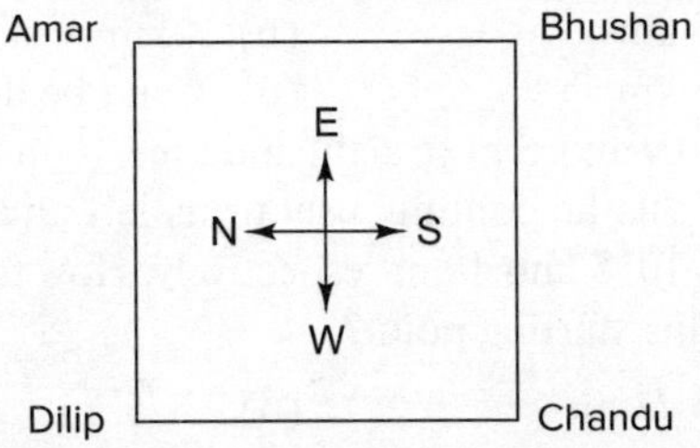

5. Amar starts crossing the plot diagonally. After walking half the distance, he turns right 90°, walks some distance and turns left. Which direction is he facing now?
(a) Northeast (b) North
(c) Northwest (d) Southeast

6. From the original position given in the above figure, Amar and Chandu move one side length clockwise and then cross over to the corner diagonally opposite; Bhushan and Dilip move one side length anticlockwise and cross over to the corner diagonally opposite. The original configurations Amar-Bhushan-Chandu-Dilip (ABCD) has now changed to
(a) CBDA (b) DCBA
(c) BDAC (d) ACBD

7. From the original position, Bhushan and Dilip move one and a half length of sides clockwise. Which one of the following statements is now true?
(a) Bhushan and Dilip are both at the midpoints between Amar and Chandu.
(b) Bhushan is at the midpoint between Amar and Chandu, and Dilip is at the corner originally occupied by Amar.
(c) Bhushan and Chandu are at the same point.
(d) Dilip is closer to Amar than he is to Chandu and Bhushan is closer to Chandu than he is to Amar.

8. From the positions in the original figure, Bhushan and Amar move diagonally to opposite corners and then one side each clockwise and anticlockwise respectively. Chandu and Dilip move three sides each anticlockwise and clockwise respectively. Where is Amar now?
(a) At the northwest corner
(b) At the southeast corner
(c) At the northeast corner
(d) At the southwest corner

9. After the movements given in the above questions, who is at the northwest comer?
(a) Amar (b) Chandu
(c) Bhushan (d) Dilip

10. A road network has parallel and perpendicular roads running northsouth or eastwest only. Junctions/Intersections on this road network are marked as A, B, C, D... All roads are at exactly half a kilometer distance from each other. The following is known about junctions A, B, C, H and X.
'A' is east of 'B' and west of 'C', 'H' is southwest of 'C' and southeast of B. 'B' is southeast of 'X'. Which junctions are the farthest south and the farthest east?
(a) H, B (b) H, C
(c) C, H (d) B, H

11. The Suvarna Rekha river flows from west to east and on the way turns left and goes in a quarter circle around a Shiv temple, and then turns left in right-angles. In which direction is the river finally flowing?
(a) North (b) South
(c) East (d) West

Directions for Questions 12 to 14: *Read the situation given below to answer these questions.*

j, k, l, m, n, o, p, q and r are nine huts. l is 2 km east of k. j is 1 km north of k and q is 2 km south of j. p is 1 km west of q while m is 3 km east of p and o is 2 km north of p. r is situated just in middle of k and l while n is just in middle of q and m.

12. Distance between k and l is:
(a) 2 km (b) 1 km
(c) 5 km (d) 1.5 km

13. Distance between k and r is:
(a) 1.41 km (b) 3 km
(c) 2 km (d) 1 km

14. Distance between p and q is:
(a) 4 km (b) 2 km
(c) 1 km (d) 3 km

Directions for Questions 15 to 19: *Study the following information carefully to answer these questions.*

All the streets of a city are either perpendicular or parallel to one another. The streets are all straight. Streets N, O, P, Q and R are parallel to one another. Streets S, T, U, V, W, X and Y are parallel to one another.
(i) Street N is 1 km east of Street O.
(ii) Street O is 1/2 km west of Street P.
(iii) Street Q is 1 km west of Street R.
(iv) Street S is 1/2 km south of Street T.
(v) Street U is 1 km north of Street V.
(vi) Street W is 1/2 km north of Street X.
(vii) Street W is 1 km south of Street Y.

15. If W is parallel to U and W is 1/2 km south of V and 1 km north of T, then which two streets would be 1 and 1/2 km apart?
(a) U and W
(b) V and S
(c) V and X
(d) W and V

16. Which of the following possibilities would make two streets coincide?
(a) X is 1/2 km north of U
(b) P is 1 km west of Q
(c) Q is 1/2 km east of N
(d) R is 1/2 km east of O

17. If street R is between O and P, then distance between N and Q is:
(a) 1/2 km (b) 1 km
(c) 1.5 km (d) 1.5–2 km

18. If R is between O and P, then which of the following is false?
(a) Q is 1.75 km west of N
(b) P is less than 1 km from Q
(c) R is less than 1 km from N
(d) Q is less than 1 km from O

19. Which of the following is necessarily true (given the basic clues)?
(a) R and O intersect
(b) Q is 2 km west of O
(c) Q is at least 2 km west of N
(d) Y is 1.5 km north of X

20. Usain runs 100 m south from his house, turns left and runs 250 m, again turns left and runs 400 m, then turns right and runs 50 m to reach to the stadium. In which direction is the stadium from his house?
(a) Southwest (b) Northeast
(c) East (d) North

21. The front door of Kiran's house is towards the south. From the backside of her house she walks 50 m straight then turns towards the left and walks 100 m and after that turns right and stops after walking 100 m. Now Kiran is facing which direction?
(a) East (b) South
(c) West (d) North

22. A boy starts walking straight towards the north and walks 10 feet, then he turns to his left and walks 5 feet, then he turns to his left and walks another 5 feet, then again he turns to his left and walks 10 feet and then he turns to his right and walks 2 feet. How far is he now from his starting point?
(a) 5 feet (b) 2 feet
(c) $\sqrt{34}$ feet (d) 7 feet

23. A policeman goes 20 km east and then turning to the south he goes 30 km and then again turns to his left and goes 10 km. How far is he from his starting point?
(a) 30 km (b) 20 km
(c) $30\sqrt{2}$ km (d) 40 km

24. I walk 1 km to my east, then I turn to the south and walk for 5 km. Next, I turn east and walk 2 km. After this I turn to the north and walk for 9 km. How far am I from my starting point?
(a) 5 km (b) 4 km
(c) 6 km (d) Can't be determined

25. A man walks 5 m straight and then 10 m to the right. After this he continuously turns left and every time walks 10, 5 and 10 m respectively. How far is he now from his starting point?
(a) $5\sqrt{3}$ m (b) $3\sqrt{5}$ m
(c) $5\sqrt{2}$ m (d) 10 m

26. Karan's house is south facing. From the front door of his house Karan started walking and after walking 20 m straight he turned to his left and walked 50 m. After this he turned to his right and walked 80 m. Find the distance between the point from where he finished his walk and the door of his house.
(a) $50\sqrt{5}$ m (b) $5\sqrt{50}$ m
(c) 100 m (d) 120 m

27. A man started walking towards north, he walks 10 m and then turns to his right, walks 5 m and turns to his right again and walks 10 m and turns to his left, walks 7 m and then turns to his right. At this point in which direction is he facing?
(a) East (b) South
(c) Southeast (d) Southwest

28. If Southeast becomes east and Northwest becomes west and all the other directions are changed in the same direction. Then what will be the direction for north?
(a) Northwest (b) Southeast
(c) Southwest (d) Northeast

29. If Northwest becomes south and southwest becomes east and all the other directions change in the similar manner, then what will be the direction for north?
(a) Southeast (b) Northeast
(c) North (d) None of these

30. At a crossing there was a direction pole, which was showing all the four directions in correct manner. But due to wind it turns in such a manner that now west pointer is showing South. A man went to the wrong direction thinking that he was traveling East. In what direction he was actually traveling?
(a) South (b) West
(c) North (d) Can't say

31. A direction pole at a crossing, due to an accident turns in such a manner that now east pointer is showing southwest. A traveler went to wrong direction thinking that he was travelling south. In what direction was he actually traveling?
(a) Southwest (b) Westnorth
(c) Northeast (d) Eastsouth

32. Aman, Raman, Saman and Chaman are standing on the four corners of a square carpet as shown in the figure here.

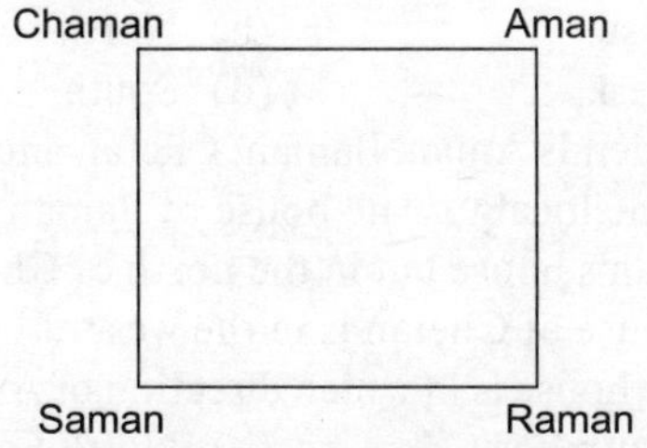

Aman starts walking towards Saman diagonally. After walking half the diagonal he turns to his left. What direction is Aman facing now?

(a) Northwest (b) East
(c) South (d) Southeast

33. If Ram is in the West of Shyam and Kareem is in the North of Shyam, in what direction is Kareem with respect to Ram?

(a) Northeast (b) Southwest
(c) Northwest (d) Southeast

Directions for Questions 34 to 35: *Alok starts walking from his school toward his house as shown in the figure here. He starts from the front gate of his school, walks 5 km, turns left, walks 2 km, then turns left again and walks 4 kms, then he turns to his right and walks 3 km and then turns left, walks 1 km and then turns to his left again to walk 4 km and then to his right and walks 10 km and finally turns right, walks 3 km and thus reaches the front gate of his house.*

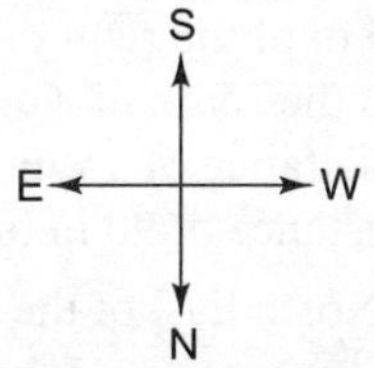

34. If Alok's house is South facing, in which direction did he start walking?

(a) West (b) North
(c) South (d) None of these

35. Alok's house is in what direction with respect to his school?

(a) Northwest (b) Southwest
(c) South (d) Cannot be determined

36. Sheela walks from A to B which is 2 km away, turns right at 90° and walks for 3 km to point C, turns right at 90° and walks to D which is 8 km away, turns 90° right and goes 3 km to point K. Then, once again she turns right at 90° and walks 4 km to point F. How far is it from A to F?

(a) 2 km (b) 4 km
(c) 6 km (d) 8 km

37. Mohan starts from point A and walks 1 km towards south, turns right and walks 1 km. Then he turns right again and walks 1 km. Now he is facing

(a) East
(b) West
(c) North
(d) South-west

38. Sohan started from point X and travelled forward 8 km up to point Y, then turned towards right and travelled 5 km up to point Z. then turned right and travelled 7 km up to point A and then turned towards right and travelled 5 km up to B. What is the distance between point B and X?

(a) 1 km (b) 2 km
(c) 3 km (d) 4 km

39. A child is looking for his father. He went 90 m in the east before turning to his right. He went 20 m before turning to his right again to look for his father at his uncle's place 30 m from this point. His father was not there. From here he went 100 m to his north before meeting his father in a street. How far did the son meet his father from the starting point?

(a) 90 m (b) 100 m
(c) 260 m (d) 140 m

40. K is a place which is located 2 km away in the northwest direction from the capital P. R is another place that is located 2 km away in the south-west direction from K. M is another place and that is located 2 km away in the north-west direction from R. T is yet another place that is located 2 km away in the southwest direction from M. In which direction T is located in relation to P?

(a) South-west (b) North-west
(c) West (d) North

41. Vijit walks 10 m westward, then turns left and walks 10 m. He then takes a 45 degree turn rightwards and walks straight. In which direction is he walking now?

(a) South (b) West
(c) South-East (d) South-West

42. Sanmitra walked 8 m towards the north. He turned to his right and walked 16 m, then turned to his left and walked 5 m and again he turned to his left and walked 16 m. Now how far is he from his starting point?

(a) 32 m (b) 23 m
(c) 13 m (d) 16 m

43. Leela starts from a point and walks 1 km east and then turns left and walks 2 km and turns right and walks 2 km again. She then starts towards a point 2 km towards her right, from where again she walks 1 km left. How far is she from the starting point?

(a) 3 km (b) 4 km
(c) 5 km (d) 2 km

44. Shaurya facing towards east moved straight 2 km and from there turned to his left 90° and travelled 2 km. Then he took a 45° turn to his right and travelled 1 km. Where would he be now with respect to the starting point?

(a) South region
(b) South-east region
(c) North-west region
(d) South-west region

45. Raju is Ramu's neighbour and he stays 100 m away towards southeast. Venu is Raju's neighbour and he stays 100 m away towards southwest. Khader is Venu's neighbour and he stays 100 m away towards northwest. Where is the position of Khader's home in relation to Ramu's?

(a) South-East (b) South-West
(c) North-West (d) North

46. Vandana walks 4 kms towards the north, turns right and walks 5 km. Then she turns towards south and walks 2 km. Again she takes a turn towards west walks 3 km and stops for a while. Then she further walks 2 km. What is her distance from the starting point?

(a) 16 km (b) 2 km
(c) 4 km (d) 3 km

47. A child is looking for his father. He went 90 m to the east before turning to his right. He went 20 m before turning to his right again to look for his father at his uncle's place 30 m from this point. He met his father there. How far did the child meet his father from his starting point?

(a) 80 m (b) 90 m
(c) $20\sqrt{10}$ meters (d) None of these

48. One day, Raviraj left home and cycled 20 km southwards, turned right and cycled 10 km and turned left and cycled 20 km and turned right and cycled 20 km. How many kilometers will he have to cycle to reach his home straight?

(a) 50 km (b) 30 km
(c) 40 km (d) 60 km

49. Gaurav walks 20 m towards North. He then turns left and walks 40 m. He again turns left and walks 20 m. Further, he moves 20 m after turning to the right. How far is he from his original position?

(a) 40 m (b) 50 m
(c) 60 m (d) 70 m

50. A confused dog runs 20 m towards the east and turns right, runs 10 m and turns to his right, runs 9 m and again turns to his left, runs 5 m and then turns to his left, runs 12 m and finally turns to his left and runs 6 m. Now which direction is the dog facing?

(a) East (b) North
(c) West (d) South

51. Four friends Aman, Baman, Chetan and Dolly live in the same locality. The house of Baman is in the east of Aman's house but in the north of Chetan's house. The house of Chetan is in the west of Dolly's house. Dolly's house is in which direction of Aman's house?

(a) South-East (b) North-East
(c) East (d) Data is inadequate

52. Malini directly went from P, to Q which is 9 meters distant. Then she turned to the right and walked 4 m. After this she turned again to the right and walked a distance, which is equal to the distance from P to Q. Finally she turned to the right and walked 3 m. How far is she now from P?

(a) 6 m (b) 5 m
(c) 1 m (d) 0 m

53. Babita walks 5 m towards East and then turns left and walks 6 m. Again she turns right and walks 9 m. Finally she turns to her right and walks 6 m. How far is she from the starting point?

(a) 26 m (b) 21 m
(c) 14 m (d) 9 m

Directions for Questions 54 to 55: *Don, Kumar, Nikhil, Amit and Pulkit are standing facing to the North in a playground such as given below:*

(i) Kumar is at 40 m to the right of Amit.
(ii) Don is 60 m to the south of Kumar.
(iii) Nikhil is at a distance of 25 m to the west of Amit.
(iv) Pulkit is at a distance of 90 m to the North of Don.

54. Who is in the North-East of the person who is to the left of Kumar?

(a) Don (b) Nikhil
(c) Amit (d) Pulkit

55. Rishi starting from Nikhil's position, met Amit and then moved onto Kumar and after this he went to Don and then to Pulkit and for the whole time he walked in straight lines, then what is the total distance how much total distance did he cover?

(a) 215 m (b) 155 m
(c) 245 m (d) 185 m

Directions for Questions 56 to 59:

(i) Six rooms in a hotel in two rows facing North and South are allotted to A, B, C, D, E and F.
(ii) B gets a North facing room and is not next to D.
(iii) D and F get diagonally opposite flats.
(iv) C who is next to F, gets a south facing flat and E gets a North facing flat.

56. If the flats of A and E are interchanged then whose flat will be next to that of F?
(a) A (b) B
(c) C (d) E

57. Which of the following combinations get south facing flats?
(a) BED (b) FAE
(c) FCA (d) Data is inadequate

58. The flats of which of the other pair than DF, are diagonally opposite to each other?
(a) BA (b) BC
(c) AE (d) ED

59. Whose flat is between B and D?
(a) E (b) F
(c) C (d) A

Directions for Question 60:

(i) P # Q means Q is at 1 metre to the right of P
(ii) P $ Q means Q is at 1 metre to the North of P
(iii) P * Q means Q is at 1 metre to the left of P
(iv) P @ Q means Q is at 1 metre to the south of P
(v) In the given question first person from the left is facing North.

60. According to C @ B * A, A is in which direction with respect to C ?
(a) North (b) South
(c) North East (d) South West

Directions for Questions 61 to 65: *John goes for a run in the evening. He started from point A towards north and reached B after jogging 100m. At B he turned towards his right and jogged 60 meters to reach point C. From C he takes a left turn and jogged 40 meters to reach D. From D he turned to his right and after jogging for 50 meters, he reached a point E. From E he turns towards his right and jogged 140 m to reach point F. After jogging 50 meters from F to his right, he finally reached his destination.*

61. What is the shortest distance between john's final position and point A?
(a) 40 m (b) 80 m
(c) 100 m (d) 60 m

62. In which direction is point C with respect to John's final position?
(a) North (b) North West
(c) South West (d) West

63. What is the total distance travelled by John?
(a) 410 m (b) 430 m
(c) 440 m (d) 420 m

64. If John covered the distance till E with a speed of 10 m/s and rest of the distance with a speed of 20 m/s, then what is the total time taken (in seconds) by John to reach at the final position?
(a) 34 (b) 35
(c) 34.5 (d) 40

65. In which direction is point F with respect to A?
(a) North East (b) North West
(c) South West (d) East

Directions for Questions 66 to 70: *Study the following information and answer the questions given below:*

There is an AB axis in such a way that A is in the north and B is in the south direction. There is an XY axis in such a way that X is in the west direction and Y is in the east direction. The AB axis and the XY axis intersect at a point O in such a way that AO is 20 m, OB is 30 m, OX is 24 m, OY is 36 m.

While facing towards south direction at point O, Priya takes a right turn and walks 10 m to reach point E and then she takes left turn and walks 30 m and reached point C. While facing towards north direction from point C, Rashmi walks 10 m and reached at point D and from there she takes right turn and walks 18 m to reach point F and then finally takes a left turn and walks 26 m to reach her destination G.

66. Point X is in which direction with respect to Rashmi's final point?
(a) South (b) South East
(c) South West (d) West

67. Point D is in which direction with respect to Rashmi's starting position?
(a) South West (b) East
(c) North East (d) North West

68. What is the shortest distance between point G and point O?
(a) 12 m (b) 6 m
(c) 8 m (d) 10 m

69. Priya's starting position is in which direction with respect to Rashmi's final position?
(a) South West (b) East
(c) North East (d) North West

70. What is the shortest distance between point A and point E?
(a) 8 m (b) 6 m
(c) 12 m (d) None of these

ANSWER KEY

1. (b)	2. (d)	3. (b)	4. (b)
5. (d)	6. (b)	7. (d)	8. (b)
9. (b)	10. (b)	11. (a)	12. (a)
13. (d)	14. (c)	15. (a)	16. (d)
17. (d)	18. (d)	19. (d)	20. (b)
21. (d)	22. (c)	23. (c)	24. (a)
25. (c)	26. (a)	27. (b)	28. (a)
29. (d)	30. (c)	31. (b)	32. (d)
33. (a)	34. (d)	35. (d)	36. (a)

37. (c)	38. (a)	39. (b)	40. (c)
41. (d)	42. (c)	43. (b)	44. (d)
45. (b)	46. (b)	47. (c)	48. (a)
49. (c)	50. (b)	51. (a)	52. (c)
53. (c)	54. (d)	55. (a)	56. (c)
57. (c)	58. (a)	59. (a)	60. (d)
61. (d)	62. (a)	63. (c)	64. (c)
65. (d)	66. (c)	67. (a)	68. (d)
69. (a)	70. (d)		

SOLUTIONS AND SHORTCUTS

Solutions for Questions 1 to 4:

1. If minute hand is pointing towards west, there will be a difference of 45 degrees in the minute hand and the hour hand at 4:30. And that difference would be in the anticlockwise direction. So, southwest. Option (b) is correct.
2. 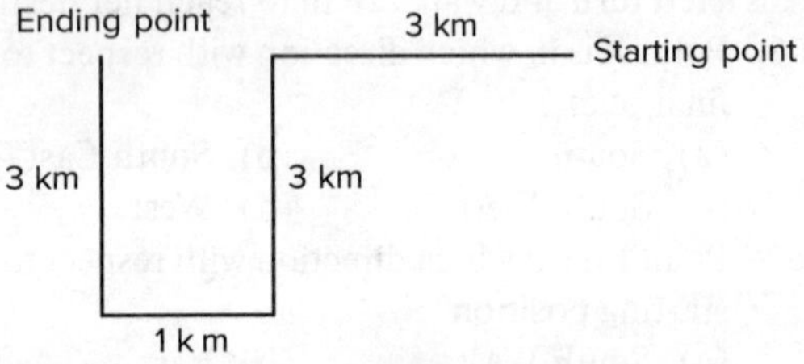

From the figure it is evident that the distance is 4 kms. Option (d) is correct.
3. 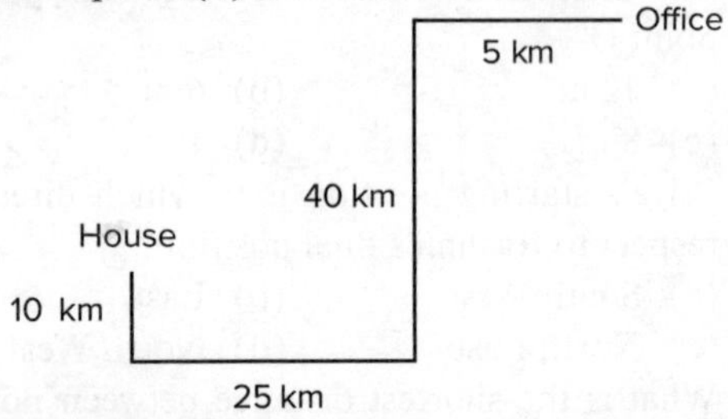

The journey would be as per the figure. Her office would be northeast from her house.
Option (b) is correct.
4. The distance $d^2 = 30^2 + 30^2 = 1800$. $d = 30 \times 2^{1/2}$.
Option (b) is correct.

Solutions for Questions 5 to 9:

5. To get to the answer we must assume Amar to be at the point of dissection of the two direction lines. After walking half the distance, Amar will reach the mid of the diagonal, then turn right and face northwest and after that would face the southwest direction when he turns left. (Note that the directions in the figure are different from the usual north, south, east, west directions as the north is in the east position.) Option (d) is correct.
6. Amar would be at Dilip's position, Chandu would be at Bhushan's position, Bhushan would be at Chandu's position and Dilip would be at Amar's position. Thus, the final positioning would be Dilip-Chandu-Bhushan-Amar. DCBA (Option b) is correct.
7. The final positions would be:

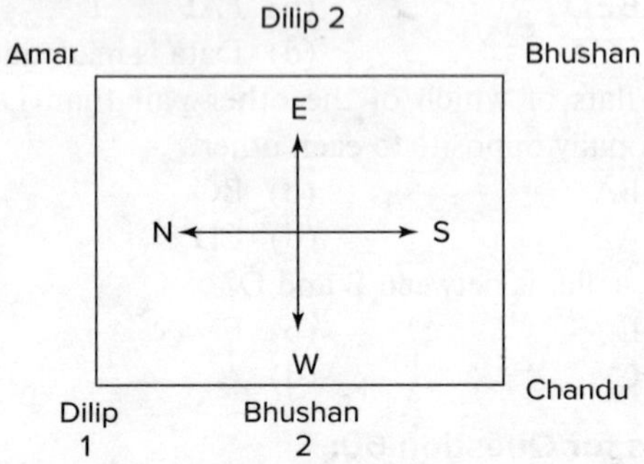

Option (d) can be seen to be correct.
8. Amar would reach Bhushan's original position as seen in the figure for the final positions. He would be at the southeast corner.

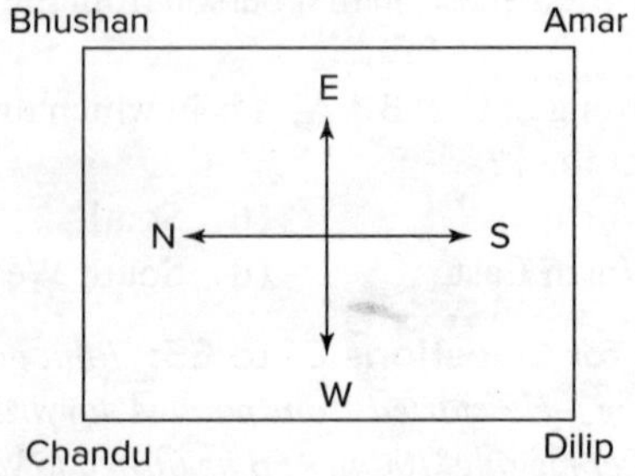

Option (b) is correct.
9. Chandu would be at the northwest corner from the solution figure to the previous question.
10. It can be inferred from the figure below that H is the farthest south and C is the farthest east.

X
B A C
H

Option (b) is correct.
11. 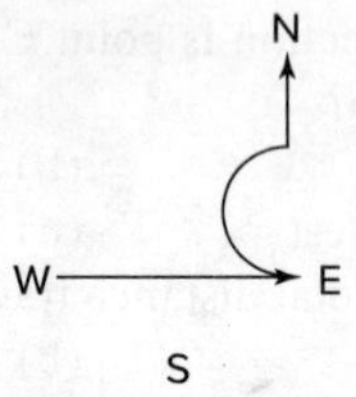

From the given figure it is clear that the river would be flowing north.
Option (a) is correct.

Solutions for Questions 12 to 14: The following figure represents the positioning of the nine huts:

o j
k r l
p q n m

The answers are:
12. (a)
13. (d)
14. (c)

Solutions for Questions 15 to 19: The vertical North South streets are N, O, P, Q, R. From the basic information we have two relative positions are available–one between O, P and N and the other between Q and R.

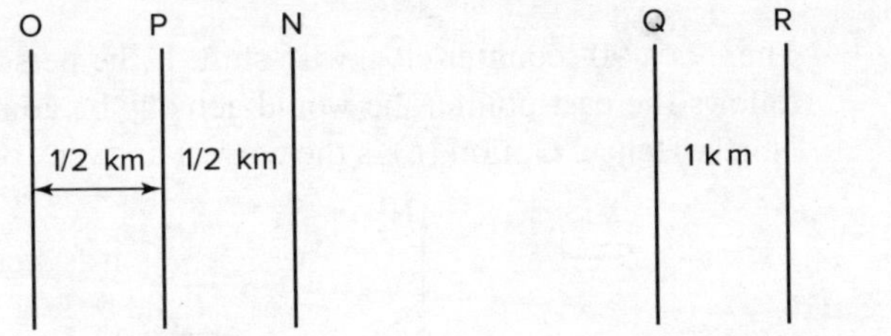

Figure for O, P and N Figure for Q and R

The horizontal eastwest streets are: S, T, U, V, W, X, Y. Of these seven streets the relative positioning is given in 3 distinct parts as shown here.

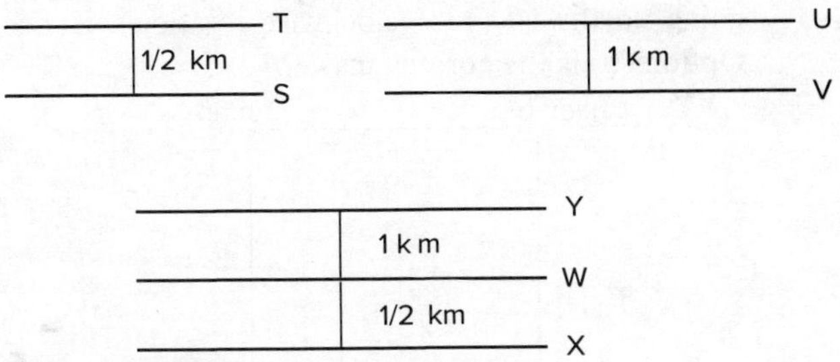

15. The solution is visible from the figure below. Option (a) is correct.

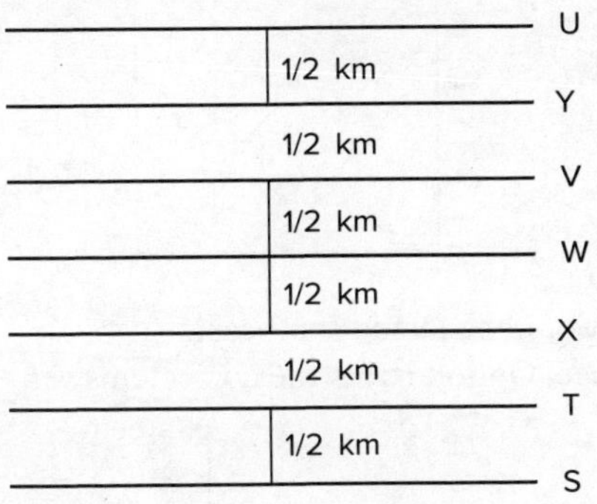

16. If R is 1/2 km east of O, then R and P would coincide. Option (d) makes two streets coincide.

17. If R is placed between O and P, Q to N would be a minimum of 1.5 and a maximum of 2 kms. Option (d) is correct.

18. If R is between O and P, then Q being 1 km to the west of R, would be more than 1.5km but less than 2 km west of north. Option (d) is correct.

19. Y is 1.5 km north of X is correct in all cases as the figure between X, W and Y shows. Option (d) is correct.

20. The stadium is northeast with respect to the house. Option (b) is correct.

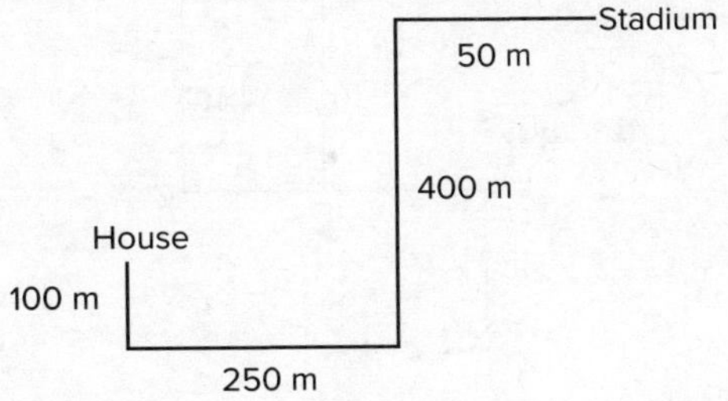

21. Since her house faces towards the south, when she starts from the back side of her house she would go 50 m north. After this when she turns left, she would be going west and when she again turns right she would be facing the north again. Hence, Option (d) is the correct answer.

22.

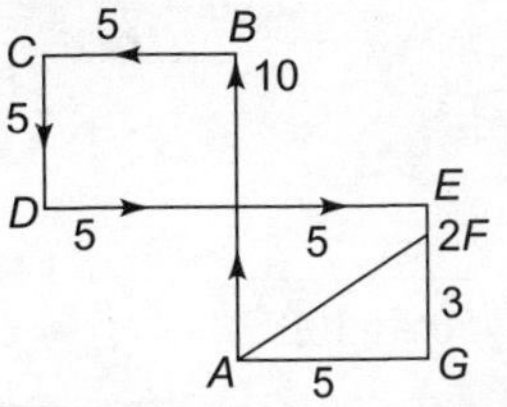

From the figure, he starts at A goes through $BCDEF$ and his final distance from A is given by the distance $A = \sqrt{(5)^2 + (3)^2} = \sqrt{34}$. Hence, Option (c) is the correct answer.

23.

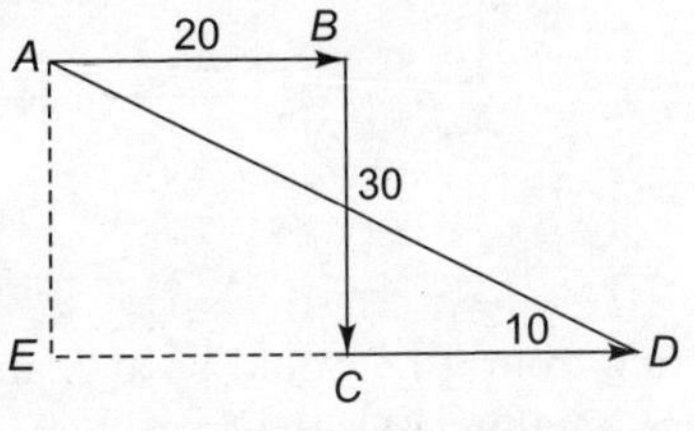

Distance AD = $\sqrt{1800} = 30\sqrt{2}$

Hence, Option (c) is the correct answer.

24.

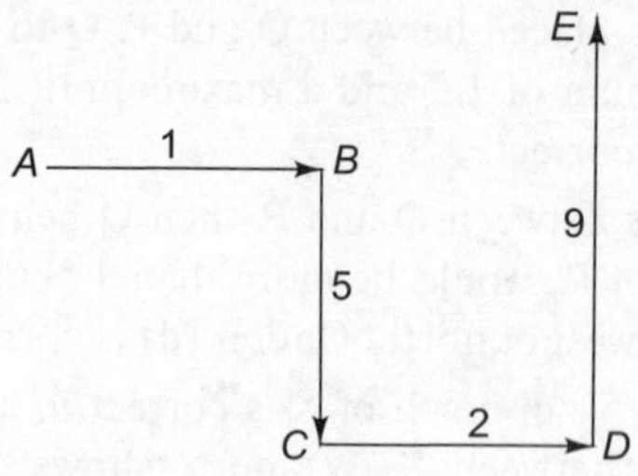

$d(AE) = \sqrt{3^2 + 4^2} = 5$ km

Hence, Option (a) is the correct answer.

25.

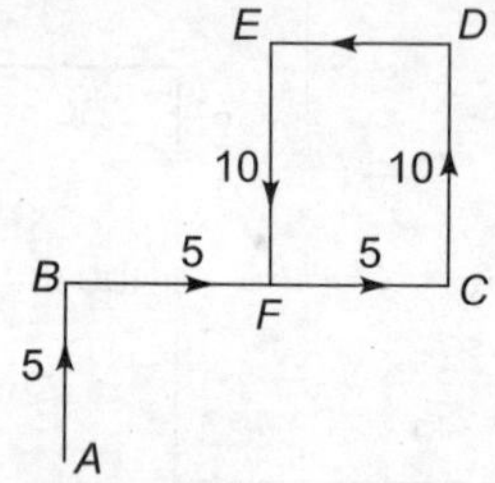

If A is the starting point:
The required distance is seen on $AF = \sqrt{50} = 5\sqrt{2}$.
Hence, Option (c) is the correct answer.

26.

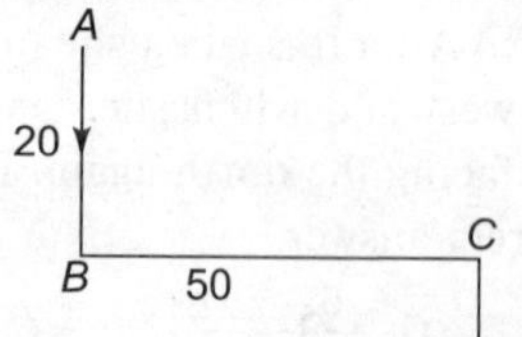

$d/AD = \sqrt{50^2 + 100^2}$

$\sqrt{12500} = 50\sqrt{5}$ m

Hence, Option (a) is the correct answer.

27.

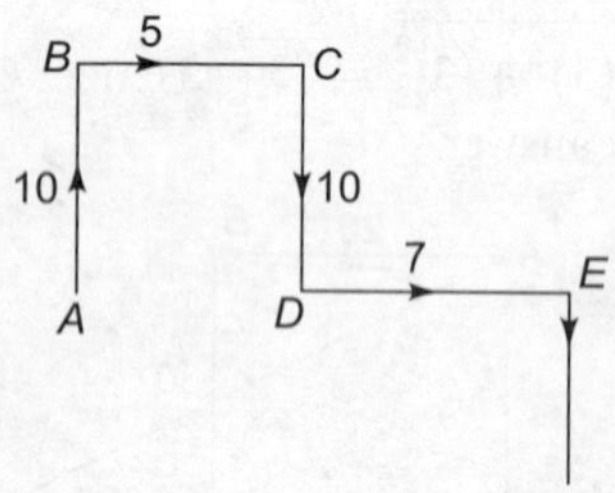

Starting from A he would be at E and facing South.
Hence, Option (b) is the correct answer.

28.

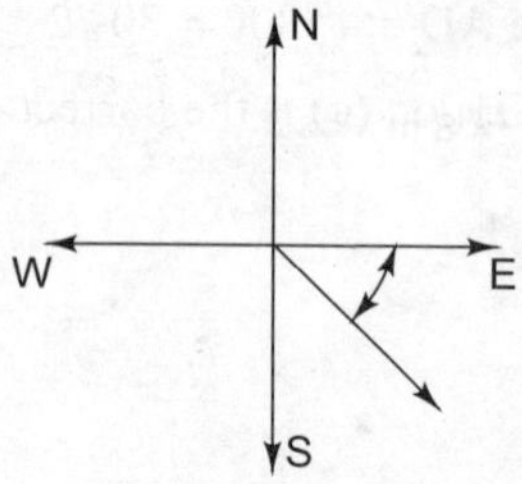

From this figure it is clear that there has to be a 45° counter clockwise rotation. Hence, North would become northwest. Hence, Option (a) is the correct answer.

29. Similar to the above question it would be southwest. Hence, Option (d) is the correct answer.

30.

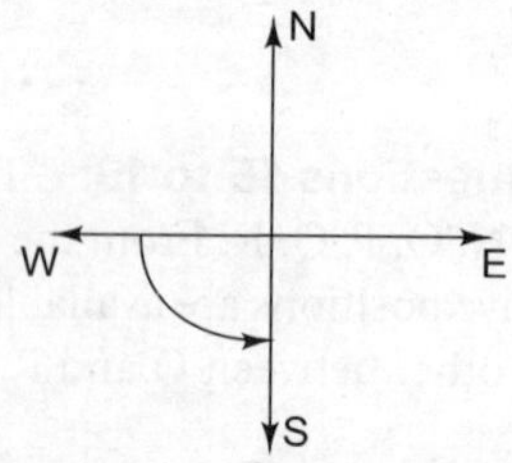

There is a 90° counter clockwise shift. If the person follows the east pointer, he would actually be going North. Hence, Option (c) is the correct answer.

31.

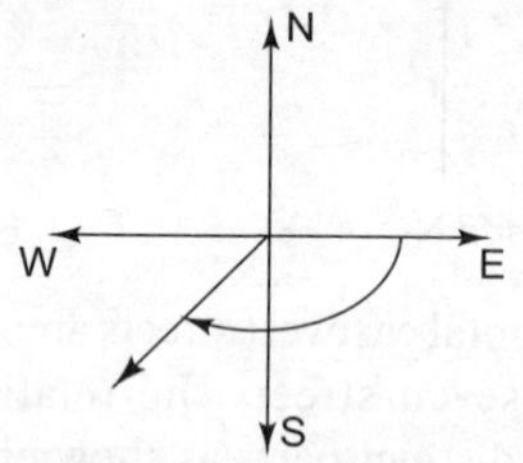

Since east is showing southwest, south would be going northwest (135° clockwise rotation). Hence, Option (b) is the correct answer.

32.

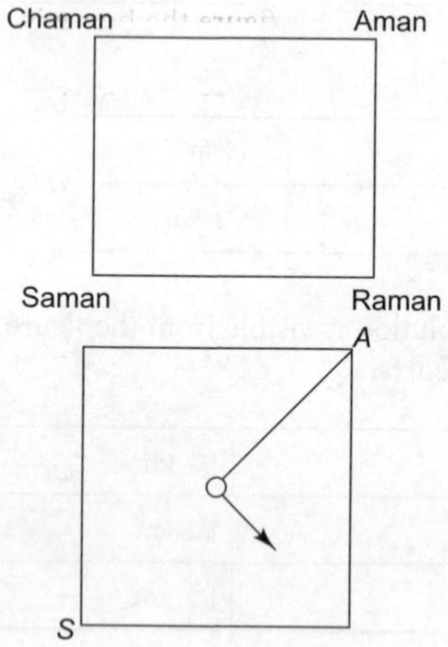

He would be facing southeast.
Hence, Option (d) is the correct answer.

33.

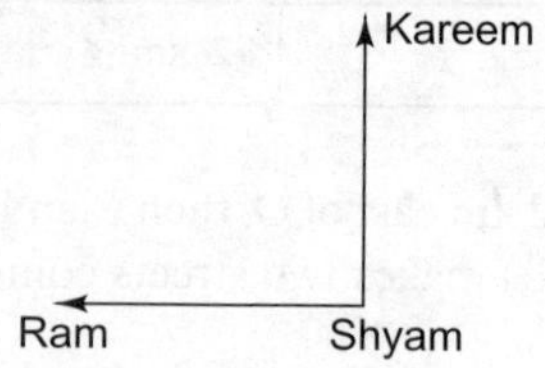

He will be northeast. Hence, Option (a) is the correct answer.

Solutions for Questions 34 to 35:

34.

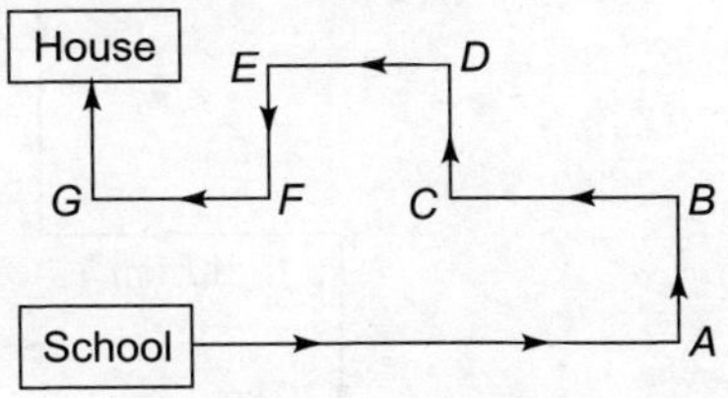

We need to just work out the direction for this question. Since Alok's house is south facing, the above figure will describe his journey correctly. Hence, the school faces east. Hence, Option (d) is the correct answer.

35.

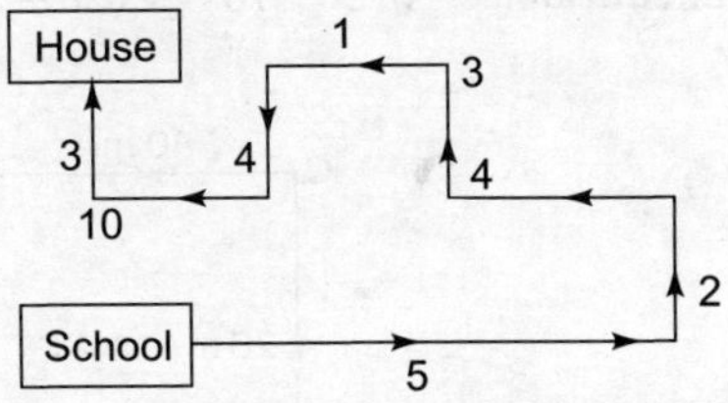

According to this figure the house is North-west.

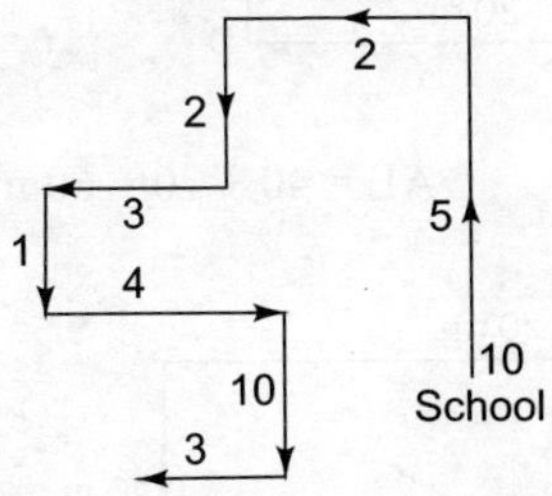

According to this figure the house is southwest. Since we do not know the starting direction, we cannot determine the answer. Hence, Option (d) is the correct answer.

36.

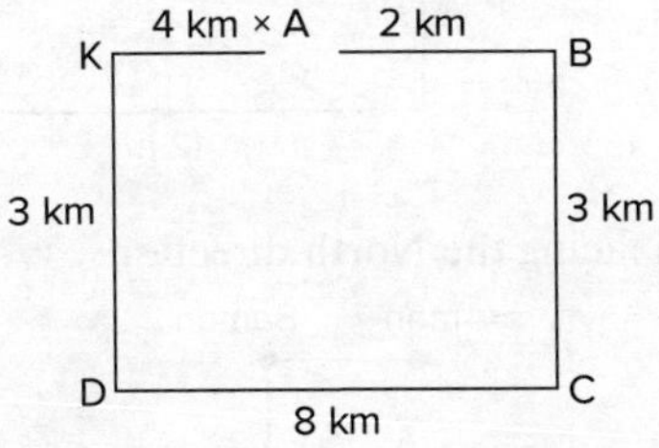

The path of Sheela is shown in the diagram above.

AF = 8 – 4 – 2 = 2 km

37. The travelling path of Mohan is shown in the diagram given below:

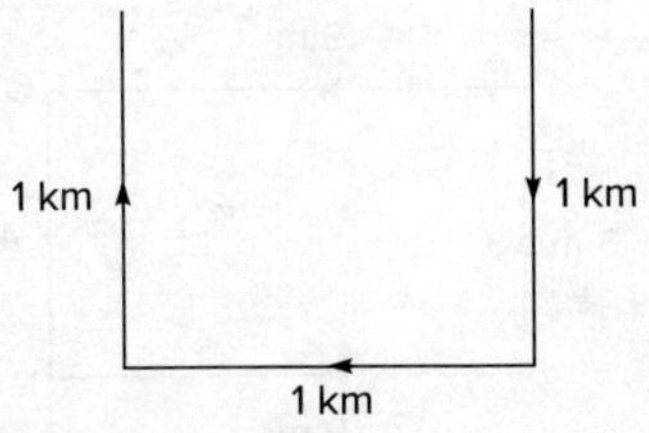

From the above diagram it is clear that Mohan is facing North.

38.

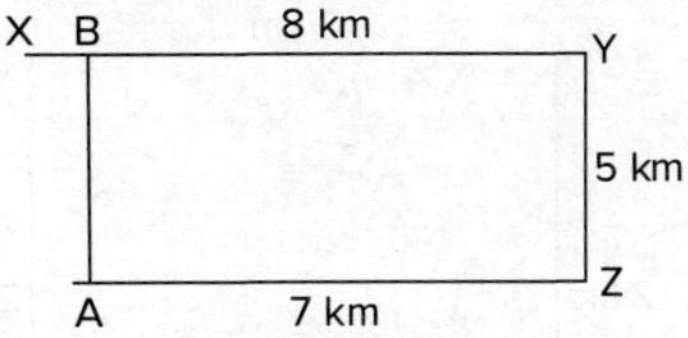

BX = 8 – 7 = 1 km

39.

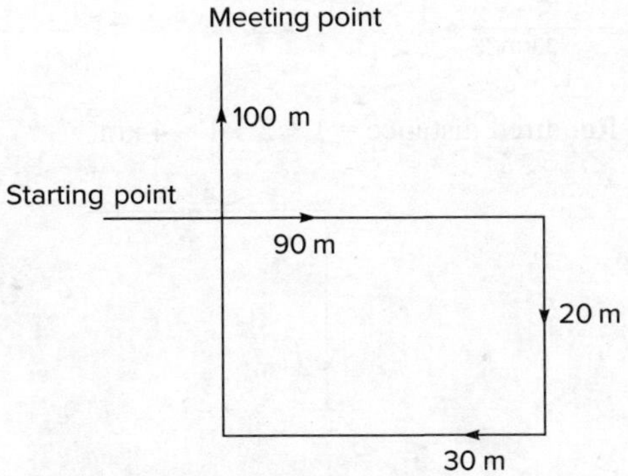

$$\text{Required distance} = \sqrt{(90-30)^2 + (100-20)^2} = 100 \text{ m}$$

40.

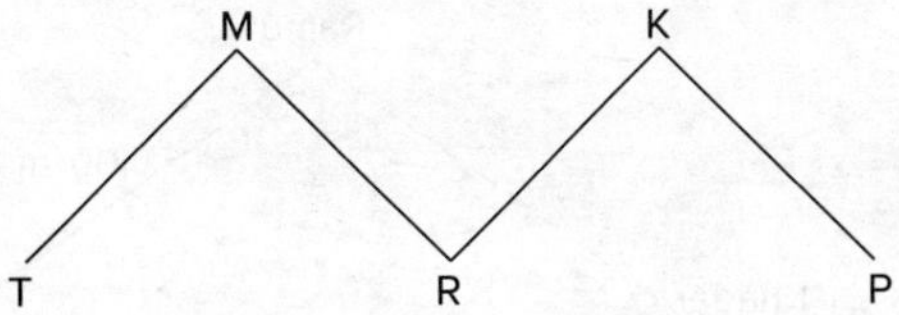

T is located at west of P.

41.

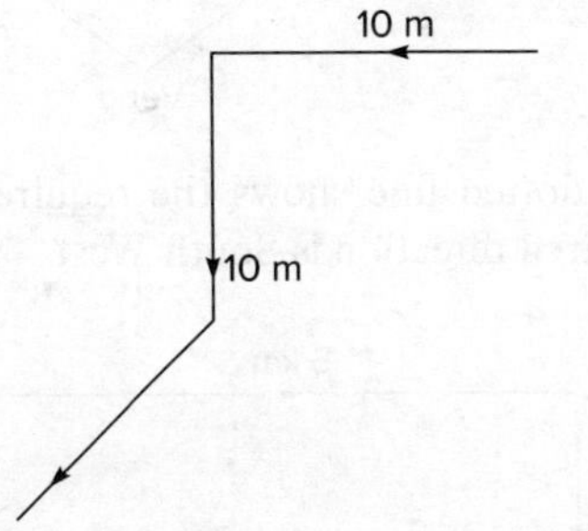

He is walking in South-west direction.

42.

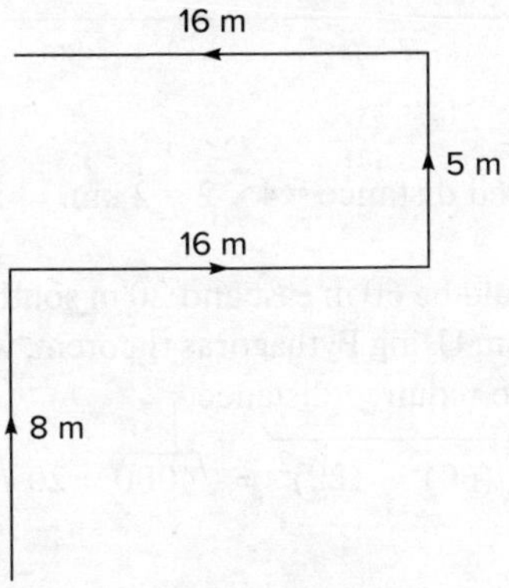

Required distance = 8 + 5 = 13 m.

43.

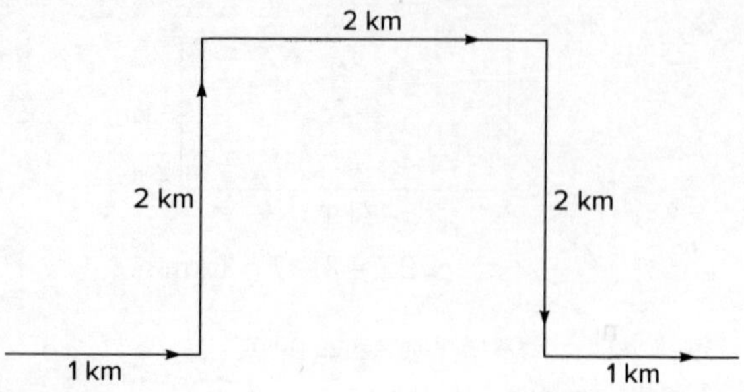

Required distance = 1 + 2 + 1 = 4 km.

44.

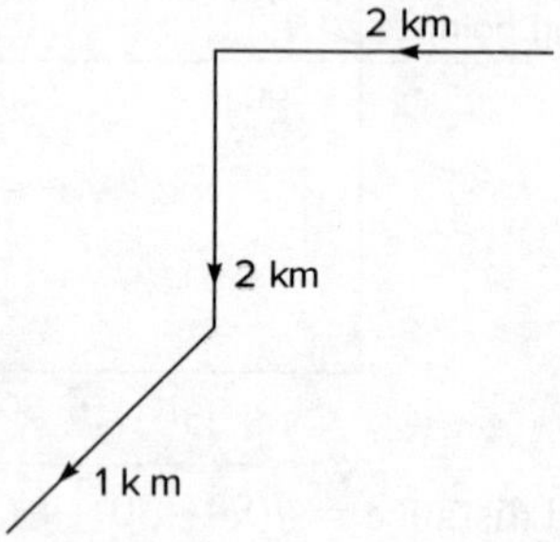

The required direction is South-west.

45.

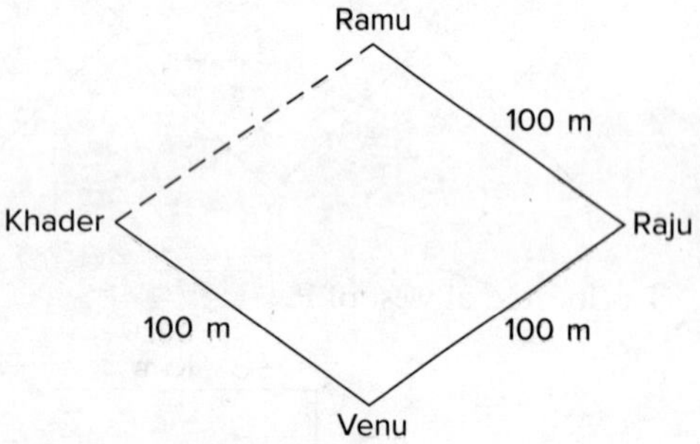

The dotted line shows the required direction. The required direction is South West.

46.

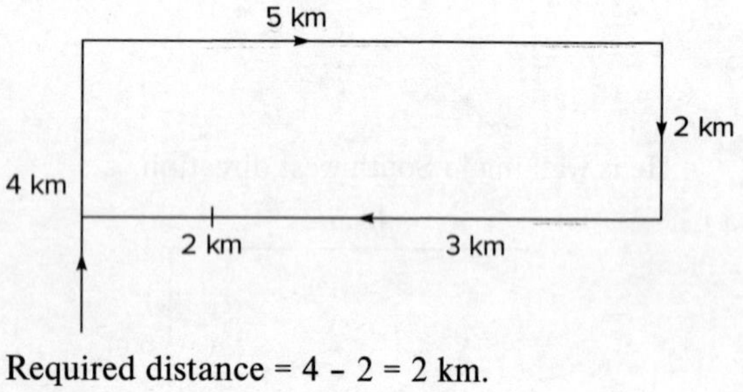

Required distance = 4 – 2 = 2 km.

47. He would be 60 m east and 20 m south of his original position. Using Pythagoras theorem, we can work out that the required distance =

$$\sqrt{(60)^2 + (20)^2} = \sqrt{4000} = 20\sqrt{10}$$

48.

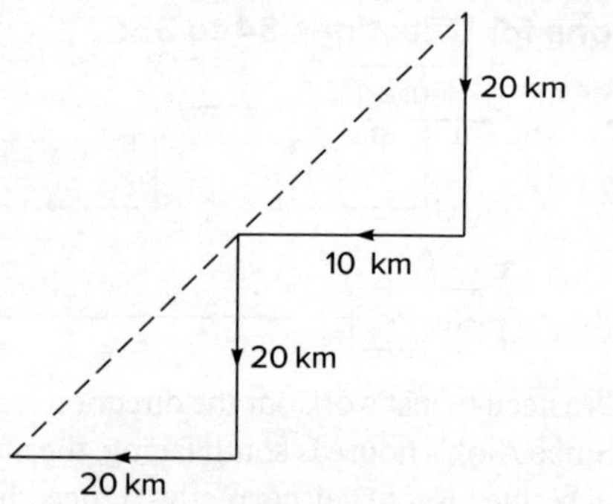

Required distance = $\sqrt{(20+10)^2 + (20+20)^2} = 50$ km

49.

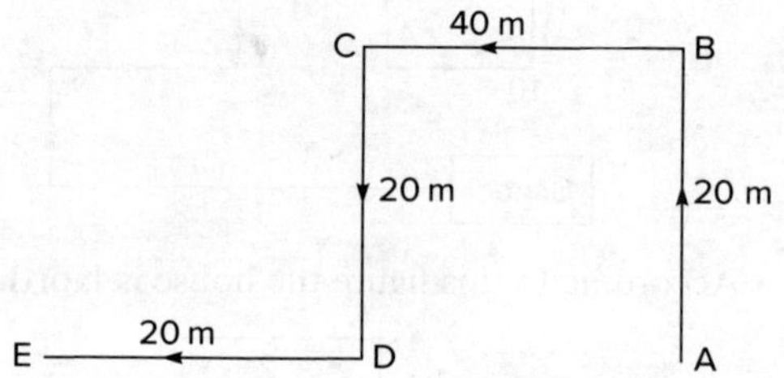

AE = 40 + 20 = 60 m

50.

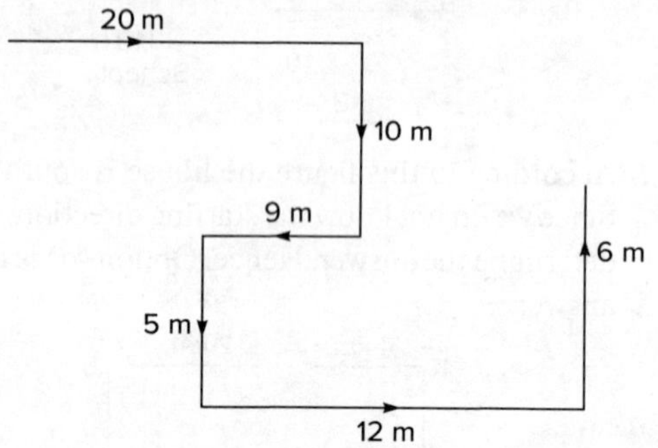

Dog is facing the North direction.

51.

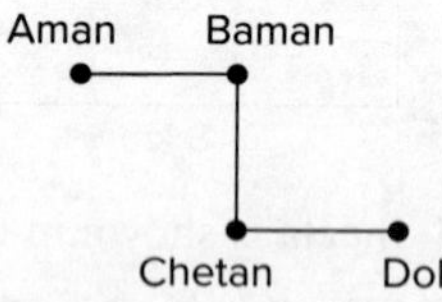

Therefore, Dolly's house is in the South-East direction of Aman. Hence, option (a) is correct.

52.

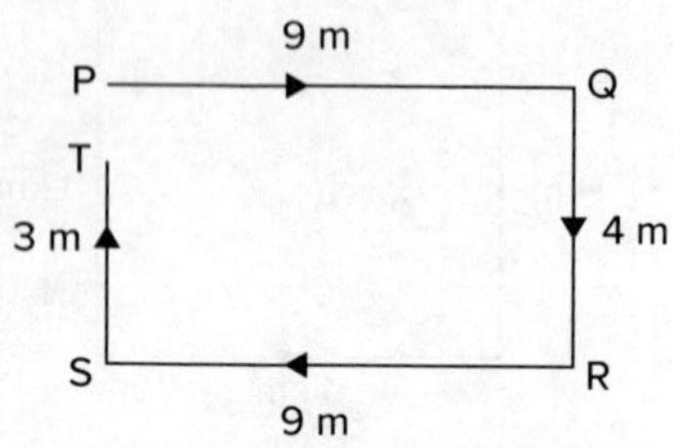

So the required distance = 4m - 3m = 1m. Hence, Option (c) is correct.

53. Let the initial position of Babita be A and her final position be B.

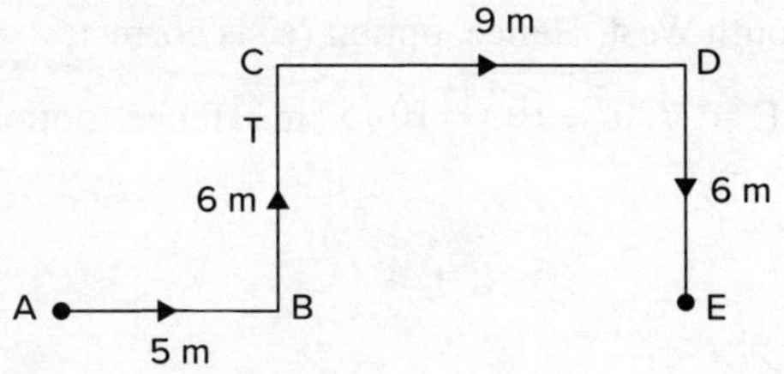

Required distance = EA = 9 + 5 = 14 m. Hence, option (c) is correct.

Solutions for Questions 54 to 55:

54.

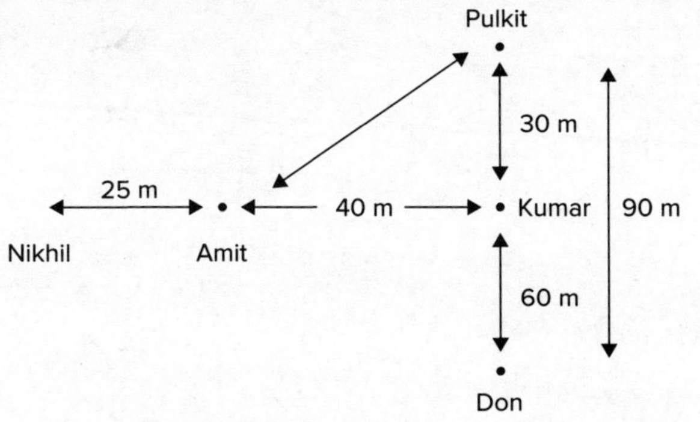

Amit is standing to the left of Kumar. Hence, Pulkit is to the North-East of Amit. Hence, option (d) is correct.

55. Required distance = 25 m + 40 m + 60 m + 90 m
Required distance = 215 m. Hence, option (a) is correct.

Solutions for Questions 56 to 59:

56.

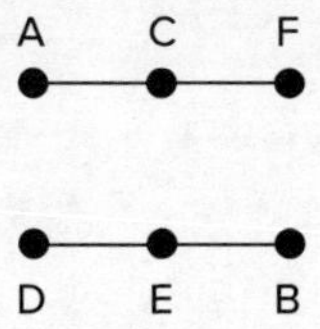

Now after interchanging flats A and E. The new arrangement will be like the following diagram:

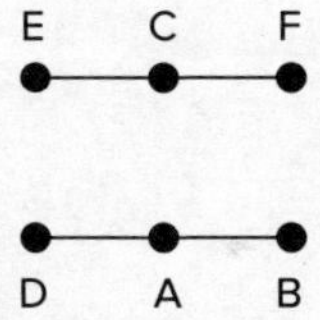

So the flat of C will be next to F. Hence, option (c) is correct.

57.

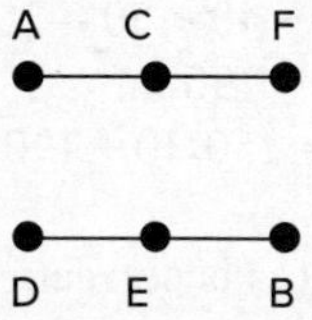

Hence the combination of FCA gets south facing flats. Hence, option (c) is correct.

58. BA is diagonally opposite to each other. Hence, option (a) is correct.

59. The flat of E is between B and D. Hence, option (a) is correct.

Solution for Question 60:

60. According to C @ B * A

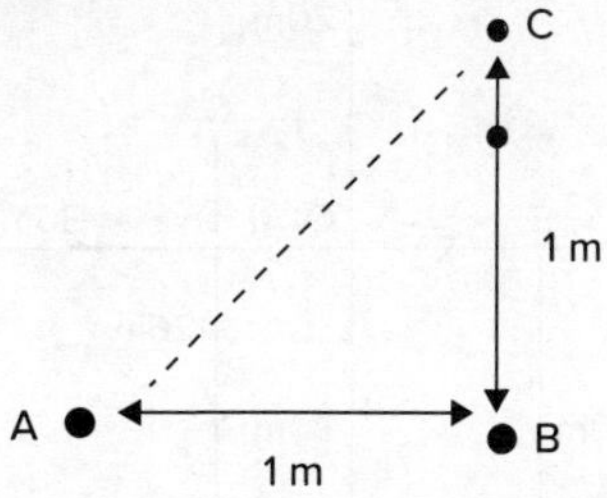

Hence A is to the South-West of C. Hence, option (d) is correct.

Solutions for Questions 61 to 65:

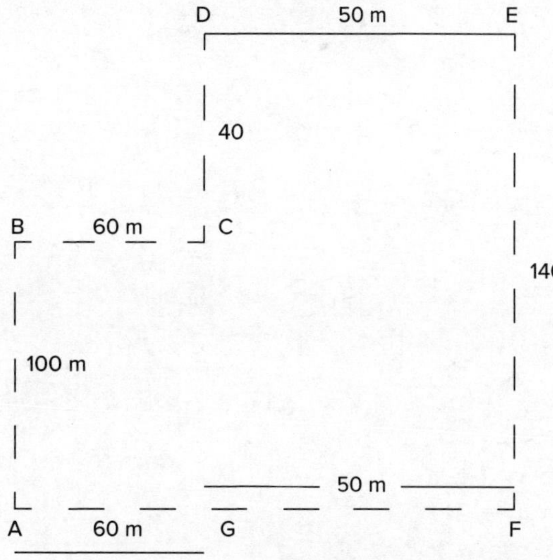

61. Shortest distance between John's final position and point A = 60 m. Hence, option (d) is correct

62. From the solution figure we can see that Point C is exactly to the north of his finishing point.
Hence, option (a) is correct.

63. Total distance travelled by John = 100 + 60 + 40 + 50 + 140 + 50 = 440 m. Hence, option (c) is correct.

64. AE = 100 + 60 + 40 + 50 = 250 m.
    EG = 140 + 50 = 190 m.
    Required time= 250/10 + 190/20 = 25 + 9.5
    = 34.5 seconds.
    Hence, option (c) is correct.
65. Point F is to the East of A. Hence, option (d) is correct.

Solutions for Questions 66 to 70:

O: Priya Initial point
C: Priya Final point
C: Rashmi initial point
G: Rashmi Final point

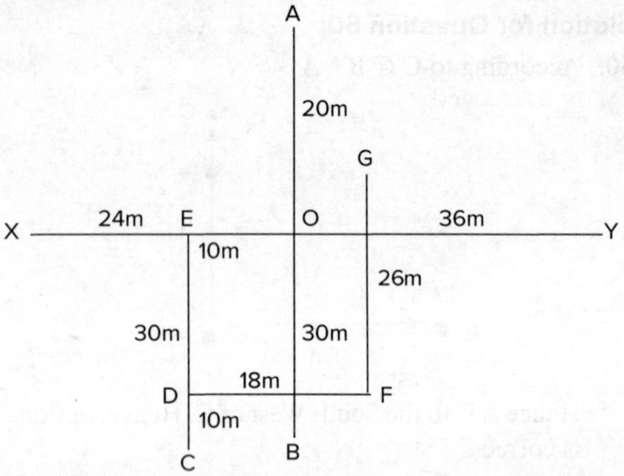

66. The point X is South West of G,. Hence, option (c) is correct.
67. North. Hence, option (a) is correct.
68. GO = $\sqrt{6^2+8^2}$ = 10 m. Hence, option (d) is correct.
69. South-West. Hence, option (a) is correct.
70. AE = $\sqrt{20^2+10^2}=10\sqrt{5}$ m. Hence, option (d) is correct.

CHAPTER 4

Statement and Conclusions

Chapter Launchpad

Scan this QR code for an introductory video on Statement and Conclusions

Conclusions are inferences that can be drawn on the basis of the information contained in a paragraph/statement. A conclusion in other words is also an inference that follows the given information. Drawing conclusions is something we all do regularly. The wmain difference between a conclusion which we saw in the last chapter and an assumption is that while an assumption precedes the information, a conclusion follows it.

The following solved examples will help you better understand conclusions:

Directions: In each of the following questions, a statement is given followed by two conclusions. Give answer

(a) If only conclusion I follows.
(b) If only conclusion II follows.
(c) If both conclusions I and II follow.
(d) If neither I nor II follows.

Example 1:

Statement:

Ahmedabad has a lower population and hence is a safer place to live.

Conclusions:

I. A city which has less population is a better place to live.
II. Ahmedabad has lower number of crimes than Bombay.

Solution: Both the conclusions do not follow. The first conclusion statement is in fact an assumption on which the argument statement is based. It is not a conclusion which can be derived from the statement. Similarly, we have no information about crime rates in Bombay in the statement and hence conclusion II also does not follow. Hence, option (d) is correct.

Example 2:

Statement:

All students of my class have a bright chance in their examination.

Conclusions:

I. I teach them the whole syllabus thoroughly.
II. All the students are intelligent.

Solution: A teacher can claim that his/her students have a bright chance in the examination only if he teaches the syllabus thoroughly. However this is an assumption that must be valid for the statement to be made (and is not a conclusion). Hence conclusion I is invalid. Conclusion II is also invalid because the 'students' who are being referred to are not defined clearly. Hence, option (d) is correct.

Example 3:

Statement:

Anyone who manages an engineering organisation like Tata Motors can only be successful if they have the knowledge of the professional work that is carried on in the organisation.

Conclusions:

I. If you want to run any company, it is essential that you should know the professional work associated with it.
II. In order to manage an engineering organisation like Tata Motors, it is essential to have an engineering education background.

Solution: The statement particularly talks about engineering organisations like Tata Motors. The first conclusion is generalising the statement and is hence not valid as a conclusion. The second conclusion follows. Hence option (b) is correct.

Example 4:

Statement:

According to Baba Ramdev "Values, integrity and peace of mind are essential for a beautiful life."

Conclusions:

I. Baba Ramdev believes that each of values, integrity and peace of mind are essential for a beautiful life.
II. Baba Ramdev believes that materialistic persons can not have a beautiful life.

Solution: Conclusion I follows since that is what is meant by the statement. Materialism is generally anti values and integrity and hence, we can draw the second conclusion. Thus, option (c) is correct.

Example 5:

Statement:

India won the second test match against Pakistan by one innings and two hundred and three runs. The greatest contribution was from the bowlers.

Conclusions:

I. Most of the Indian players are bowlers.

II. It was India's biggest win against Pakistan.

Solution: Both conclusions are invalid. Hence, option (d) is correct.

EXERCISE

Directions for Questions 1 to 16: *In the following questions there is a statement followed by two conclusions. You have to choose:*

(a) If only conclusion I follows.

(b) If only conclusion II follows.

(c) If conclusions I and II both follow.

(d) If neither I nor II follows.

High Yield Questions

Scan this QR code to access video explanations of questions 13 & 14

1. **Statement:** A degree in law is one of the most wanted degrees by youth in India.

   Conclusions: **I.** A degree in law guarantees a good profession.

   II. A degree in law is the first choice for youth in India.

2. **Statement:** Protinex is beneficial for a muscular body.

   Conclusions: **I.** All athletes take Protinex.

   II. We should take Protinex for muscular body.

3. **Statement:** Most students of the LU BMS program are bright.

   Conclusions: **I.** Many companies visit the LU BMS program for campus placements.

   II. Some of the students of LU BMS are not bright.

4. **Statement:** India is the largest exporter of Lichi.

   Conclusions: **I.** India only exports Lichi.

   II. China and Japan are the most important customers of Lichi from India.

5. **Statement:** SRK is a famous filmstar. SRK earns handsome amounts every year through advertisements of products he endorses.

   Conclusions: **I.** All famous filmstars earn handsome amount through advertisements.

   II. SRK, being famous, endorses only famous brands.

6. **Statement:** Reputed management institutes focus on both quality and advertisement.

   Conclusions: **I.** There are only two important factors for a reputed management institute: quality and advertising.

   II. Small management institutes focus on only one of quality and advertising.

7. **Statement:** The Australian Cricket team scored 300 runs, out of which Andrew Symonds scored 151 runs.

   Conclusions: **I.** Andrew Symonds was the highest run scorer of the match.

   II. Symonds scored 66 runs in singles only.

8. **Statement:** Due to the onset of monsoon there is a sharp hike in the price of alphonso mangoes.

   Conclusions: **I.** Alphonso mangoes are in demand at any price.

   II. The onset of monsoons affects the market for alphonso mangoes.

9. **Statement:** What is an RDX explosive? From the outside it looks like a simple harmless object, but its real contents are so deadly that they are sufficient to blast off an entire compartment of a train or even a plane.

   Conclusions: **I.** The RDX explosive can cause massive destruction by killing a number of persons with a single explosion.

   II. The RDX explosive is only used to blast planes/trains as it is difficult to recognise in such settings.

10. **Statement:** Don't park here. If you violate this no-parking sign, a penalty of ₹ 5000 will be charged.

    Conclusions: **I.** The same penalty is charged for every wrong parking offence.

    II. This warning is written outside all non-parking zones.

11. **Statement:** Whenever there is a match between India and Pakistan, Mr. Sahai takes

leave from his office. Mr. Sahai is in office today.

Conclusions: **I.** Today there is no match between India and Pakistan.

II. Mr. Sharma always goes to his office except on India–Pakistan match days.

12. Statement: All the male members of my family are either software engineers or MBAs.

Conclusions: **I.** Mrs. Meena is a member of my family. She is either a software engineer or an MBA.

II. Mr. Prakash is a member of my family. He is either a software engineer or an MBA.

13. Statement: All politicians are honest. Radha Devi is an honest lady.

Conclusions: **I.** She is a politician.

II. She is not interested in politics.

14. Statement: If the temperature remains constant the wind speeds will be below 100 kmph. Wind speeds were above 100 kmph.

Conclusions: **I.** Temperature was not constant.

II. Temperature was fluctuating.

15. Statement: Without abundant rains, there will be a decline in the water level beneath the earth. This year, the rains were deficient.

Conclusions: **I.** The water level must have declined.

II. Millions of people were in trouble because of shortage of water.

16. Statement: Any student who is caught red-handed using unfair means discredits his parents and teachers.

Conclusions: **I.** Such students try to show that their teachers don't teach properly in the class.

II. Stringent actions must be taken against such students.

Directions for Questions 17 to 20: *Choose the correct conclusion for the given statement/s.*

17. Statement: Laughter is the best medicine.

Conclusions: (a) All medicines have Benzene enzymes.

(b) Laughter is good for health.

(c) All medicines that make you laugh are good.

(d) Stand up comedy shows on television are a good source of laughter.

18. Statement: 1. Private companies employees work for five working days with 9 working hours every day.

2. IOC's employees work for 6 working days a week and 8 working hours a day.

Conclusions: (a) IOC's employees are better than private companies employees.

(b) IOC's employees work more than Private companies employees.

(c) Private companies employees work more than IOC's employees.

(d) IOC's employees are more efficient than that of private companies.

19. Statement: 1. All athletes in the Asian athletics teams are talented.

2. All Indian athletes are now in the Asian athletics team.

Conclusions: (a) Some Indian athletes are talented.

(b) All Indian athletes are talented.

(c) India does not have any athletics team.

(d) India has more cricketers than athletes.

20. Statement: 1. Next year, salary of all people working in the Bata Hindicom will increase by ₹ 1 lac per year.

2. The current income difference between two employees of Bata Hindicom, Arun and Subhash is ₹ 2 lacs.

Conclusions: (a) Arun's salary will be higher after the increment in salary.

(b) Subhash's salary will be higher than Arun's from the next year.

(c) The difference between Arun and Subhash's salary will remain constant.

(d) None conclusion follows.

Directions for Questions 21 to 25: *In the following questions there are given some statements followed by conclusions that can be drawn from them. Choose the answer for each question independently.*

21. Bombay is more expensive than Delhi. Delhi is more expensive than Calcutta. Bombay is more expensive than Calcutta.

(a) True (b) Probably true
(c) False (d) Can't say

22. Basket ball players are generally tall. Jeevan is a basketball player. So Jeevan is tall.

(a) False (b) Probably false
(c) True (d) Can't say

23. Statement: 1. Some actors are dancers.
2. All those, who are dancers, are paid well.

Conclusions: Some actors are paid well.

(a) True (b) Probably true
(c) False (d) Can't say

24. Statement: Teachers punish students when they do not complete their homework. Ravi (a teacher) punished Soni in school today.

Conclusions: Soni did not do her homework.

(a) Definitely true
(b) Definitely false
(c) Can't say
(d) Conclusion is irrelevant

25. Statement: Smart managers are those who hire smart employees.

Conclusions: To be a smart manager, I just have to hire smart employees.

(a) True
(b) False
(c) Either probably true or probably false
(d) Can't say

ANSWER KEY

1. (d)	2. (b)	3. (b)	4. (d)	5. (d)	6. (d)	7. (d)
8. (b)	9. (a)	10. (d)	11. (a)	12. (b)	13. (d)	14. (c)
15. (d)	16. (b)	17. (b)	18. (b)	19. (b)	20. (c)	21. (a)
22. (d)	23. (a)	24. (c)	25. (d)			

SOLUTIONS AND SHORTCUTS

Solutions for Questions 1 to 16:

1. The first conclusion is not necessarily true. Similarly we cannot comment definitely about the first choice of youth. Hence, option (d) is correct as neither conclusion follows.
2. The second conclusion is what is hinted at by the statement. Hence, option (b) is correct.
3. Conclusion II follows. Hence, option (b) is correct.
4. Neither conclusion can be drawn from the statement. Hence, option (d) is correct.
5. Neither conclusion can be drawn from the statement. Hence, option (d) is correct.
6. We cannot say that there are only 2 important factors for reputes management institutes as there could be more factors present too. Similarly, we cannot draw any conclusion about small management institutes. Thus, neither conclusion can be drawn from the statement. Hence, option (d) is correct.
7. Neither conclusion can be drawn. Hence, option (d) is correct.
8. Conclusion I is irrelevant to the argument while conclusion II follows. Hence, option (b) is correct.
9. Only the first conclusion can be drawn. It is clear from the statement that the RDX explosive can cause massive destruction and can kill a number of persons with one explosion. The second conclusion cannot be drawn since we have no indication to conclude that RDX is used only to blast planes or trains. Hence, option (a) is correct.
10. Neither conclusion is valid. Hence, option (d) is correct.
11. Conclusion I follows while the second one does not. Hence, option (a) is correct.
12. Conclusion II can be drawn. Hence, option (b) is correct.
13. Just because all politicians are honest and Radha Devi is also honest does not mean that Radha Devi is a politician–she might not be a politician and still be honest. Conclusion 1 would have followed if it had been mentioned that only politicians are honest. Similarly, we cannot draw any conclusion about her interest in politics. Hence, option (d) is correct.
14. Both the conclusions are correct. Hence, option (c) is correct.
15. We cannot conclude either conclusion I or conclusion II since we cannot comment on the decline of water level we do not know whether water level declines immediately if the rains are deficient. Thus just because the rains were deficient in this year we cannot conclude that the water level must have already fallen–for all you know it could fall later. Similarly, conclusion II is not valid because we do not know anything about the trouble-deficient rain causes to millions of people. Hence, option (d) is correct.

16. Conclusion II follows while the first one does not–we cannot be certain that such students are trying to show that their teachers do not teach properly. Hence, option (b) is correct.

Solutions for Questions 17 to 20:

17. A medicine is something that is beneficial for health. Hence, we can conclude that conclusion (b) follows from the statement. Options (a), (c) and (d) are irrelevant conclusions.
18. Options (a) and (d) do not follow as we do not know anything about who is better. From the two statements it is easy to conclude that IOC's employees work more than Private company employees. Hence, option (b) is correct.
19. Obviously conclusion (b) follows.
20. Obviously conclusion (c) is correct. We cannot say anything about whose salary is higher.

Solutions for Questions 21 to 25:

21. Clearly the conclusion holds true. Hence, option (a) is correct.
22. Clearly we cannot claim that every basket ball player is tall. However, we cannot also say for sure that Jeevan is not tall. Hence, option (d) is correct.
23. Definitely true. Option (a) is correct.
24. From the given statement it is not clear as to why Ravi punished Soni. While her not doing her homework could have been a reason it could equally well not have been the reason too. Hence, we cannot say anything about this. Option (c) is correct.
25. We cannot say for sure whether this conclusion is true or false. It might be true and at the same time might be false if there are more things that are needed to be done for being a smart manager. Hence, option (d) is correct.

CHAPTER 5

Statement and Assumptions

Chapter Launchpad
Scan this QR code for an introductory video on Statement and Assumptions

Whenever we say something (in any conversation) there are certain assumptions which must be true for the statement to make sense. In other words an assumption is something that is 'taken for granted' in the context of a statement.

Most questions on Statement and Assumptions give you a statement and follow it up with two further statements which have to be tested for whether they are implied in the original statement or not. In order to identify whether an assumption is implied in a statement, the best way to do so is to look at the original statement in the question by negating the assumption which is being tested. In case the assumption being tested is implied, negating it will have the effect of weakening the argument of the original statement.

Directions: In each question below is given a statement followed by two assumptions numbered I and II. Consider the statement and decide which of the given assumption is implicit.

Given answer

(a) If only assumption I is implicit.
(b) If only assumption II is implicit.
(c) If both I and II are implicit.
(d) If neither I nor II is implicit.

Example 1:

Statement:

Strong programming skills cannot be the only criteria for a successful career in the field of Information Technology.

Assumptions:

1. Bright careers in Information Technology are not linked only with strong programming skills.

II. If a person has excellent communication skills as well as strong programming skills, only then would he be successful.

Solution: Clearly, there should be some other skills such as interpersonal skills, communication skills, negotiation skill, etc., for a successful career. Hence, Assumption I is implicit. Assumption II is not implicit because it talks only about communication and technical skills. Hence option (a) is correct.

Note: Try the negation test in this question. If Assumption 1 is not true, i.e. "Bright careers in Information Technology are not linked only with strong programming skills" is untrue, then the argument contained in the statement "Strong programming skills cannot be the only criteria for a successful career in the field of Information Technology" loses its strength. Hence, this assumption is implicit in the statement.

Example 2:

Statement:

The maximum IAS exam selection will be from our institute–A director of a coaching institution.

Assumptions:

I. Most of the students who study in this institute are genius.

II. Teachers of the coaching institution are preparing their students thoroughly.

Solution: Assumption I is irrelevant because there might be some other genius students who are studying in other coaching institutions. Assumption II is implicit.

A coaching institution can only claim such statements if it is preparing its students thoroughly. Hence, option (b) is correct.

Example 3:

Statement:

Over a cricketing career most players would do well to remember that there is only one thing that overcomes hard luck–hard work.

Assumptions:

I. If a cricketer is hardworking, he/she can easily tackle the toughest phases of his cricketing career.

II. A cricketer writes his/her own destiny by hard work.

Solution: Both the statements are implicit. All cricket players face difficult times in their careers, but only those succeed, who confront these phases bravely and work hard to overcome them. In this way, hard luck becomes insignificant for a cricketer. Hence, option (c) is correct.

Example 4:

Statement:

The case of Marion Jones clearly indicates that if taking drugs play a vital role in the performance of athletes, there is absolutely no use of spending time to watch the athletics in the Olympics.

Assumptions:

I. Cricketers, hockey players and footballers are not involved in doping. So we can spend time to watch such games.

II. Asian athletes do not win medals because they refrain from taking drugs.

Solution: Both the assumptions are irrelevant. In the statement nothing is said about other games and as such negating that assumption has no effect on the strength of the argument in the statement. Besides, the performance of Asian athletes is irrelevant to the argument. Hence, option (d) is correct.

Example 5:

Statement:

A Reliance Fresh Retail store was attacked by vegetable vendors in Ranchi.

Assumptions:

I. Reliance Fresh has affected the livelihood of local vegetable vendors.

II. Reliance Fresh stores are built in thickly populated areas.

Solution: Assumption I is implicit because somewhere down the line, Reliance Fresh is affecting the local vendors. That is why they have been violent. Assumption II is irrelevant because nothing is mentioned regarding the location of the stores. Hence, option (a) is correct.

EXERCISE

Directions for Questions 1 to 25:

(a) If only assumption I is implicit.

(b) If only assumption II is implicit.

(c) If both I and II are implicit.

(d) If neither I nor II is implicit.

High Yield Questions

Scan this QR code to access video explanations of questions 17, 22 and 25

1. Statement: UPSC is tougher than MPPSC. So, I will appear in MPPSC.

Assumptions: **I.** Every graduate should appear in MPPSC.

II. One should avoid tougher things because one might fail in them and failure might lead to a loss of time. On the other hand, if something is easy the chances of succeeding are high.

2. Statement: Rahim is a tall boy

Assumptions: **I.** Rahim's father's height is 6 feet 7 inches.

II. Any height above 6 feet is considered to be tall.

3. Statement: What is the distance of my home from my office?

Assumptions: **I.** My home is at the centre of the city.

II. My office is 10 km away from the park, which is 1 km away from my home.

4. Statement: A says to B "refer to the Cambridge dictionary instead of the Oxford dictionary to be good at English."

Assumptions: **I.** B wants to be good at English.

II. A is a good advisor.

5. Statement: Narayan, the CEO of the company, says to his employee, "achieve the targets we have set for you or I will fire you."

Assumptions: **I.** With Narayan's statement, the employee will work hard to achieve his targets.

II. All bosses are in the habit of intimidating their employees.

6. Statement: In the last year, Lucknow University has launched a number of management courses for the better future of its students.

Assumptions: **I.** These courses may attract students.

II. Lucknow University is conscious about the future of students.

7. Statement: "We should take permission from the director of the college in order to organise the annual fest." One student said this to another.

Assumptions: **I.** Without the director's permission we can't organise the annual fest.

II. The director does not want to celebrate annual fests.

8. Statement: "If you want to specialise in Human Resource Management in India, join XLRI."

Assumptions: **I.** XLRI provides specialisation in HRM.

II. XLRI has the best HRM course in India.

9. Statement: Most rural folks are uneducated and therefore superstitious.

Assumptions: **I.** Education increases rational thinking.

II. Rural folks don't go to school.

10. Statement: Since the exam is held on the third Sunday of November it is going to be held on 18th November this year.

Assumptions: **I.** This year it will not be held on 15th, 19th, 20th or 21st of November.

II. This year it will not be held on 16th or 17th November.

11. Statement: "See it first only on our channel", an advertisement of a news channel.

Assumptions: **I.** Advertising is the first and most important thing for every channel.

II. Other news channels do not want to show things first.

12. Statement: To keep my knowledge about world affairs strong I always read *The Economist* magazine.

Assumptions: **I.** There is no other magazine except *The Economist* for world affairs.

II. *The Economist* is a cheap magazine.

13. Statement: The present condition of law and order is the worst of all time.

Assumptions: **I.** The present government does not pay heed to the requirements of maintaining law and order.

II. In earlier days, the law and order condition was better.

14. Statement: India's contribution to the growing global market of management consultancy may touch $5 billion by 2030, which is 10 per cent of the current export size.

Assumptions: **I.** The current export size is $50 billion.

II. The current year is 2010.

15. Statement: A Harvard University study raises fresh concerns about the anti-allergy drug Crocin which is prescribed to patients following antibiotic medication. Compared with other two anti-allergy drugs (one of the three must be prescribed), this study shows that Crocin significantly raises the risk of adverse side effects following antibiotic medication.

Assumptions: **I.** There is no risk if one of the two other anti-allergy drugs are administered.

II. It is necessary to take an anti-allergy drug after antibiotic medication.

16. Statement: Children whose mothers eat more Frito Lays during pregnancy have higher motor skills and more athletic capability than those whose mothers eat little, according to a new British study.

Assumptions: **I.** Those whose mothers don't eat Frito Lays have zero motor skills and athletic capability.

II. It is essential for pregnant women to have Frito Lays in order to have children with higher motor skills and more athletic capability.

17. Statement: Many students were caught red-handed and rusticated while using unfair means during the recent university examinations.

Assumptions: **I.** The University authorities have never taken such strong actions earlier.

II. The examination administration committee had prior knowledge about this issue.

18. Statement: The parents of majority of the students of IIM Ahmedabad have decided to withdraw their wards from the institute to protest against the sharp fee hike.

Assumptions: **I.** It is likely that such attempts will make the IIM Ahmedabad authority to rethink the sharp fee hike.

II. The institution will be closed after 10th of June.

19. Statement: In the absence of Ravi, Sunil will be teaching mathematics in AMS.

Assumptions: **I.** AMS has only two teachers of mathematics.

II. Ravi is better than Sunil.

20. Statement: It is clear from the past records of the gym that most people who exercise at the gym regularly maintain the perfect correlation between height and weight.

Assumptions: I. Exercise at the gym is essential for everyone.

II. If one wants to have weight according to his height, he should exercise at the gym regularly.

21. Statement: "Please switch off your mobile phones while you are in class", mentions a notice outside a classroom in XYZ.

Assumptions: I. Every student of XYZ keeps mobile phones.

II. Switched on mobile phones might distract the atmosphere of the class.

22. Statement: If you have the desire to excel, we have a job for you.

Assumptions: I. If you don't have a desire to excel, you will not get a job with us.

II. Every job requires the desire to excel.

23. Statement: "Please submit your fee well before 10th February", mentions a notice at a coaching institution.

Assumptions: I. Unless they are instructed through a notice, a number of students will not submit their fee.

II. The institute will be closed after 10th of February.

24. Statement: The telephone department has started going home to home to collect bills.

Assumptions: I. A substantial number of customers fail to pay their bills in the telephone department.

II. There has been a high default rate in the case of telephone bill payments.

25. Statement: Use Brylcream to look handsome.

Assumptions: I. People want to look handsome.

II. Only ugly people will purchase this product.

ANSWER KEY

1. (b)	2. (d)	3. (d)	4. (a)	5. (a)	6. (c)	7. (a)
8. (c)	9. (a)	10. (c)	11. (d)	12. (d)	13. (c)	14. (a)
15. (b)	16. (b)	17. (d)	18. (a)	19. (d)	20. (d)	21. (b)
22. (a)	23. (a)	24. (c)	25. (a)			

SOLUTIONS AND SHORTCUTS

Solutions for Questions 1 to 25:

1. Only Assumption II is relevant here as it justifies the argument in the statement of going for easier things rather than tougher things.
2. Both assumptions are invalid and not implied. Hence, option (d) is correct.
3. Neither assumptions are valid. Hence, option (d) is correct.
4. This advice will only be given if Assumption I is true. We cannot assume anything about A's advisory skills hence assumption II is not necessary for the statement.
5. Assumption I is implied as the boss would want (and assumes) this reaction from the employee. The second assumption is invalid.
6. Assumption I is an assumption since the University has launched the courses with this intention. Assumption II is also valid since the launching of these courses shows that the Lucknow University is conscious about the future of its students.
7. Assumption I is obvious while Assumption II is something that we know nothing about.
8. Both assumptions are implied.
9. Assumption I supports the basic conclusion that is drawn in the statement and is hence implied but Assumption II is something that we cannot make a judgement about since it is possible to be uneducated even if you have gone to school.
10. Both Assumptions are implied.
11. The first Assumption is irrelevant while the second is also not implied in the statement since we cannot judge about the intentions of every other news channel on the basis of the statement.
12. Neither Assumption is implied.
13. If the present condition is the worst ever, obviously law and order being the responsibility of the government it must be the case that the present government does not pay heed to the requirements of maintaining law and order. Besides, we can also assume that the condition must have been better earlier.

14. We cannot say anything about the current year.
15. Since one of the three must be prescribed, Assumption II must be implied.
16. We cannot assume that those children whose mothers do not eat Frito Lays have zero motor skills and athletic capability. Hence, assumption I is invalid. However, assumption II is valid.
17. Neither assumption is implied.
18. Assumption I is implicit while the second one is irrelevant to the statement.
19. Neither of the two assumptions are implied in the statement.
20. There could be many different ways of maintaining the perfect correlation between height and weight. Neither assumption is valid.
21. Obviously only assumption II is implied in the statement.
22. Assumption I is directly implied in the statement.
23. This notice will only be required if the institute feels that Assumption I is true. The second assumption is irrelevant.
24. Both assumptions are valid since only when I and II are true will the telephone department feel the need to go house to house for bill payments.
25. This assertion assumes that people would want to look handsome, but the second assumption is not necessary for this assertion.

CHAPTER 6

Assertion and Reason

Chapter Launchpad
Scan this QR code for an introductory video on Assertion and Reason

An Assertion is an affirmation, a declaration or a strong statement. Normally, assertions have reasons. In this question type, an assertion is given first followed by a reason. You are supposed to first judge whether the Assertion (A) is true and then decide on whether the Reason (R) is true and in case both A and R are true then we need to see whether the reason is the correct explanation of the Assertion.

The following solved examples will help you get a clearer understanding of this question type.

Examples:

For the Assertions (A) and Reasons (R), choose the correct alternative from the following.

(a) Both A and R are true and R is the correct explanation of A.
(b) Both A and R are true but R is not the correct explanation of A.
(c) A is true but R is false.
(d) A is false but R is true.
(e) If both A and R are false.

1. **Assertion:** Crude oil is abundantly found in nature.
Reason: It is the main raw material for all automobiles.
Solution: Both Assertion and Reason are true but the Reason does not explain the Assertion. Hence, (b) is the answer.

2. **Assertion:** Anil Kumble lost his place in the Indian ODI squad sometime back.
Reason: In spite of being India's best spinner he was considered to be too old for ODIs.
Solution: Both Assertion and Reason are right and the reason correctly explains the assertion. Hence (a) is the right answer.

3. **Assertion:** Over the past few decades, there has been drastic global warming.
Reason: The push for economic development has increased to dangerous proportions the emission of greenhouse gases into the atmosphere.
Solution: Green house gases are the root cause of global warming. Hence both A and R are true and R explains A. Hence, option (a) is correct.

4. **Assertion:** Kerala is the largest state in India.
Reason: Some of the leading car manufacturing companies of the world are Japanese.
Solution: The Assertion is false because Kerala is not the largest state in India. R is true but it is not related to Assertion. Hence, option (d) is correct.

5. **Assertion:** The filament inside a bulb is made of copper.
Reason: Usually there is vacuum in the bulb.
Solution: A is false because a bulb's filament is made of tungsten and not copper. R is also false because inert gases or nitrogen are filled inside the bulb and there is no vacuum in the bulb. Hence, option (e) is correct.

EXERCISE

Directions for Questions 1 to 25: *For the Assertion (A) and Reason (R) below, choose the correct alternative from the following.*

High Yield Questions
Scan this QR code to access video explanations of questions 11, 14 and 18

(i) Both A and R are true and R is the correct explanation of A.
(ii) Both A and R are true but R is not the correct explanation of A.
(iii) A is true but R is false.
(iv) A is false but R is true.

1. **Assertion:** In medical parlance with respect to blood groups, a person with a blood group of 'O' is called Universal Donor.
Reason: A person with the 'AB' blood group can accept blood of all types, i.e., A, B, AB and O.

2. **Assertion:** The Ozone layer present in the upper atmosphere of earth is beneficial for sustaining life on earth.
Reason: The Ozone layer blocks the harmful ultraviolet rays from the Sun and thus protects life on earth.

3. **Assertion:** Mahatma Gandhi is considered to be the father of the Indian Nation.
Reason: The name 'India' was coined by Mahatma Gandhi.

4. **Assertion:** Diesel oil is cooking medium.
Reason: It is also used in diesel cars.

5. **Assertion:** Water is essential for life.
Reason: It is formed using three parts of hydrogen and one part of oxygen.

6. **Assertion:** The phenomena of nuclear fission generates great energy.
Reason: The process in which a nucleus is broken into two parts is called nuclear fission.

7. **Assertion:** India is a sovereign country.
Reason: Its parliament is based in Delhi.

8. **Assertion:** When velocity is kept constant and wavelength is halved, then the frequency is doubled.
Reason: Velocity = Frequency × wavelength

9. **Assertion:** An object immersed in a bottle of water appears larger than it actually is.
Reason: It is because of refraction.

10. **Assertion:** Four stroke engines are more efficient than two stroke engines as far as fuel consumption is concerned.
Reason: Four stroke engines have lower wastage of petrol in their operation.

11. **Assertion:** One should not take medicines without a prescription.
Reason: Taking medicines without prescription is dangerous because only the doctor knows the actual components in a medicine and the possible side effects due to taking the medicine.

12. **Assertion:** Harshad Mehta was responsible for a major bull run in the Indian Stock market.
Reason: Harshad Mehta was known as the "big bull".

13. **Assertion:** It has been observed that buffaloes like to remain in the water during the summer.
Reason: Contact with water cools the body in the summer.

14. **Assertion:** Iron is a good conductor of electricity.
Reason: If you touch an iron rod which is exposed to electric current, you will get an electric shock.

15. **Assertion:** If you touch an iron rod which is exposed to electric current, you will get an electric shock.
Reason: Iron is a good conductor of electricity.

16. **Assertion:** The price of a stock is determined on the basis of the demand and supply of the stock.
Reason: The value of the sensex increases whenever there is a heavy demand for the stocks which form the Sensex.

17. **Assertion:** In the Indian democratic system, the cabinet ministers are appointed by the President.
Reason: The Prime minister plays an advisory role.

18. **Assertion:** India is a country of diverse cultures, customs and languages.
Reason: What we now call India is the modern version of Bharat.

19. **Assertion:** India's President is appointed on a five-year term.
Reason: Pratibha Patil was appointed as India's first woman president in 2007.

20. **Assertion:** The World Bank is a leading international financial institution.
Reason: Ever since its formation, it has played a major role in disbursing aid and support to economies across the world.

21. **Assertion:** India won the inaugural 20-20 world cup cricket tournament.
Reason: A young team played fearless and brilliant cricket to win the inaugural T20 world cup.

22. **Assertion:** As the pressure increases, the volume decreases if the temperature is constant.
Reason: When temperature is constant, pressure and volume are inversely proportional to each other.

23. **Assertion:** The Y2k problem had the entire computer industry in a fix towards the end of the 20th century.

Reason: The Y2k problem emerged due to the fact that the date field in computers had only two digits.

24. Assertion: Amartya Sen was awarded the Nobel Prize for Economics.

Reason: Amartya Sen has made an invaluable contribution in the field of developmental economics.

25. Assertion: Manmohan Singh is widely recognised as the chief architect of liberalisation in India.

Reason: Manmohan Singh was the finance minister who first started opening up the Indian economy in 1991.

ANSWER KEY

1. (b)	2. (a)	3. (c)	4. (d)	5. (c)	6. (b)	7. (b)
8. (a)	9. (a)	10. (a)	11. (a)	12. (b)	13. (a)	14. (b)
15. (a)	16. (b)	17. (b)	18. (b)	19. (b)	20. (a)	21. (a)
22. (a)	23. (a)	24. (a)	25. (a)			

SOLUTIONS AND SHORTCUTS

Solutions for Questions 1 to 25:

1. Both A and R are true, but R is not the reason for A. Hence, option (b) is correct.
2. Both A and R are true, and R is the reason for A. Hence, option (a) is correct.
3. A is true but R is false. Hence, option (c) is correct.
4. A is false but R is true. Hence, option (d) is correct.
5. A is true but R is false. Hence, option (c) is correct.
6. Both A and R are true, but R is not the reason for A. Hence, option (b) is correct.
7. Both A and R are true, but R is not the reason for A. Hence, option (b) is correct.
8. Both A and R are true, and R is the reason for A. Hence, option (a) is correct.
9. Both A and R are true, and R is the reason for A. Hence, option (a) is correct.
10. Both A and R are true, and R is the reason for A. Hence, option (a) is correct.
11. Both A and R are true, and R is the reason for A. Hence, option (a) is correct.
12. Both A and R are true, but R is not the reason for A. Hence, option (b) is correct.
13. Both A and R are true, and R is the reason for A. Hence, option (a) is correct.
14. Both A and R are true, but R is not the reason for A. Hence, option (b) is correct.
15. Both A and R are true, and R is the reason for A. Hence, option (a) is correct.
16. Both A and R are true, but R is not the reason for A. Hence, option (b) is correct.
17. Both A and R are true, but R is not the reason for A. Hence, option (b) is correct.
18. Both A and R are true, but R is not the reason for A. Hence, option (b) is correct.
19. Both A and R are true, but R is not the reason for A. Hence, option (b) is correct.
20. Both A and R are true and because of the reason the assertion is true. Hence, option (a) is correct.
21. Both A and R are true and because of the reason the assertion is true. Hence, option (a) is correct.
22. Both A and R are true and because of the reason the assertion is true. Hence, option (a) is correct.
23. Both A and R are true and because of the reason the assertion is true. Hence, option (a) is correct.
24. Both A and R are true and because of the reason the assertion is true. Hence, option (a) is correct.
25. Both A and R are true and because of the reason the assertion is true. Hence, option (a) is correct.

CHAPTER 7

Statement–Courses of Action

Chapter Launchpad

Scan this QR code for an introductory video on Statement–Courses of Action

Most situations that we face in life throw up the possibility of creating an improvement by following certain courses of action. In fact, deciding on a course of action in a given situation is a primary responsibility in any managerial job.

This question type tests you on your ability to decide on how a situation can be tackled/improved/followed up. Look through the following solved examples to get this question type clear.

Directions: In each of the following questions a statement is given followed by two courses of action. A course of action is taken for improvement, follow up, etc. Read the statement carefully and give your answer as

(a) If only course of action I follows.
(b) If only course of action II follows.
(c) If both I and II follow.
(d) If neither course of action I nor II follows.

Example 1:

Statement:

The presence of mafiosi in the education system of UP has increased drastically.

Courses of Action:

I. There should be a special taskforce constituted to clean the system of its ills.
II. The U.P. government should resign immediately.

Solution: Course of action I follows because it is necessary to tackle such antisocial elements.

Course of action II does not follow because the resignation of the government is unlikely to improve the situation. Hence, option (a) is correct.

Example 2:

Statement:

In a recent survey by the National Health mission it was showed that fruits and vegetables which contain certain vitamins have a higher effect on human health than capsules marketed by private companies that contain the same vitamins.

Courses of Action:

I. Such vitamin capsules marketed by private companies should be banned with immediate effect.
II. People should prefer fruits and vegetables to capsules marketed by private companies.

Solution: Course of action I does not follow because we are only making a comparison between the effects of food and vegetables against the effect of capsules. Capsules have just been found to be less effective and it does not mean that they are harmful.

Course of action II follows because fruits and vegetables are preferable to capsules for their positive effect on health. Hence, option (b) is correct.

Example 3:

Statement:

It has been reported that water level is declining rapidly in India.

Courses of Action:

I. There should be a public campaign to educate people about the need to reduce and eliminate the wastage of water.
II. New technologies should be researched and utilised to store rain water.

Solution: Both the courses of action are logical steps that could be taken to address the problem. Hence, option (c) is correct.

Example 4:

Statement:

Reliance Telecommunications is playing dirty tricks with its competitor Tata Indicom.

Courses of Action:

I. Tata Indicom should also do the same.
II. Tata Indicom should decrease the tariff rate of phone calls.

Solution: Both the courses of action do not follow. Tata Indicom should not start playing dirty tricks but should approach the government and its regulatory bodies to help. The II course of action is also not valid because it will do nothing to stop the dirty tricks. Hence option (d) is correct.

Example 5:

Statement:

There is a proposal for the Maharashtra government to clear the slum areas in Mumbai for beautification and economic development.

Courses of Action:

I. The Maharashtra Government should compensate the affected persons with reasonable amount.

II. The Maharashtra Government should stop beautification and economic development work immediately.

Solution: Only course of action I follows. Government should take care of affected people. It should pay reasonable amount to affected persons. Second course of action does not follow because it is illogical. Hence, option (a) is correct.

EXERCISE

Directions for Questions 1 to 25: *In each question below a statement is given followed by two courses of action numbered I and II. You have to assume everything in the statement to be true. Then, decide which of the two suggested courses of action logically follows for pursuing.*

High Yield Questions

Scan this QR code to access video explanations of questions 1, 3 and 7

Given Answers

(a) If only I follows
(b) If only II follows
(c) If both I and II follow
(d) If neither I nor II follows

1. **Statement:** A sting operation conducted by a TV news channel proved to be a total failure as the reporter who carried out the sting was found to have created a fake sting in order to gain publicity and money.

   Courses of Action:
   I. Disciplinary action must be initiated immediately against the reporter.
   II. The TV channel should be penalised and taken off air for a short period of time.

2. **Statement:** Across the globe there is an increasing tendency to use child soldiers for terrorist activities.

   Courses of Action:
   I. The United Nations Security Councilshould try to address this problem by asking its member states to crack down heavily on terrorist groups.
   II. The U.S. led forces must attack such terrorist groups.

3. **Statement:** A state-wide bandh called by opposition parties in Bihar led to a total shut down of normal activities of Bihar's people.

   Courses of Action:
   I. The government should call a meeting with opposition parties to work out an approach that does not affect the common man.
   II. Opposition Parties must continue their agitation.

4. **Statement:** There is a shortage of power in India.

   Courses of Action:
   I. There should be more power projects initiated by the government.
   II. The government should encourage private investment in power projects.

5. **Statement:** The reduction of the tax rates has led to an increase in the tax collection as there has been higher compliance.

   Courses of Action:
   I. It should be made compulsory every Indian to pay tax.
   II. Tax rates should be further reduced and a further increase in tax collections can be expected on doing so.

6. **Statement:** The number of people who die on the roads every year is so alarming that the numbers every year are close to the numbers which can be attributed to the major diseases of the world.

   Courses of Action:
   I. There should be an active campaign for sensitising people towards road safety norms.
   II. There should be an increased emphasis on enforcing speed limits, road safety rules and traffic management on roads across the world.

7. **Statement:** In each of the three years from 2000–2002, shareholders of India's Sensex lost between 15 to 30 per cent of the value of their assets. Yet the

average value of the CEO's package of the 30 companies that formed the Sensex was higher in 2002 than in 2000 by almost 50 per cent.

Courses of Action:
I. Companies should include greater transparency of compensation packages.
II. If a company is in loss, top executives should not get pay hikes.

8. Statement: An unacceptable number of children die during the first year of their lives. The high incidence of infant deaths is a major cause for concern for the health ministry.

Courses of Action:
I. All government hospitals should be privatised to improve health care facilities.
II. Governments should commit higher levels of their budget to health services.

9. Statement: The cream of India's cricket team is likely to retire in the next three years leaving a vacuum which the Indian cricket team is going to struggle to overcome.

Courses of Action:
I. The BCCI should start to induct youngsters into the team and start to give them exposure to pressure situations.
II. There should be a rotation policy adopted for senior players in order to prolong their careers and keep them injury free.

10. Statement: Amartya arrived an hour late for the examination. The cut off time to enter the exam hall is maximum 15 minutes late.

Courses of Action:
I. A rule is for everyone, so Amartya should not be allowed to enter the exam hall and take the exam.
II. Amartya should be rusticated from his college for violating the rule.

11. Statement: Studies of global warming show that the earth could be hotter by at least 6°C in the next 100 years, thanks to huge greenhouse gas emission.

Courses of Action:
I. Since greenhouse gases are responsible for global warming, steps should be taken to control their emission immediately.
II. All new industries should be immediately stopped from starting to control environmental damage.

12. Statement: "New students of our college get frightened by ragging. The ragging prevalent in our college is also creating a bad name for our college".

Courses of Action:
I. The college authorities take stringent action against those who are involved.
II. A strict anti ragging law should be passed to control ragging in our college.

13. Statement: A lot of unscrupulous and non-affiliated colleges have started to lure unsuspecting students by giving attractive advertisements.

Courses of Action:
I. Students should make appropriate enquiries while enrolling in any course.
II. The government should initiate strict action against such college authorities.

14. Statement: Higher education in America is very expensive. This is perhaps because more and more graduates from across the world try to go to America for higher education.

Courses of Action:
I. The American government should stop such migration of students from other countries.
II. The American government should clamp down heavily on such institutions and universities which charge high for higher education.

15. Statement: The lives of millions of people are likely to be endangered in the future as thousands of active landmines are still undiscovered in the fields of Africa.

Courses of Action:
I. The international community should immediately take action so that no more landmines are laid down across the world.
II. It should be an offence against all humanitarian norms to continue using these landmines.

16. Statement: There is an alarming and increasing trend of engineering and technical graduates to opt for jobs rather than doing research.

Courses of Action:
I. Universities must make research in engineering subjects more attractive.
II. It should be made compulsory to pursue research after an engineering degree.

17. Statement: The colony has suffered major thefts and break-ins due to lax security systems.

Courses of Action:
I. Security should be strengthened in the colony.
II. Residents and regular visitors and their vehicles should be provided with identity cards and stickers for better control of who is coming and going into the colony.

18. Statement: The lack of employment and income during economic depression leads to an increase in the crime rates.

Courses of Action:
I. The government should provide an unemployment compensation as done in advanced countries.
II. The government should encourage greater economic activity and increase the number of industries in order to reduce crime rates.

19. Statement: The appreciation of the rupee has reduced the impact of the oil price rise on the Indian economy although it has also created a problem for exporters.

Courses of Action:
I. The government should allow a further rise in the value of the rupee.
II. The government should provide some additional incentives to exporters.

20. Statement: The U.S. and its allies have been claiming that Iran is developing dangerous chemical, biological and nuclear weapons.

Courses of Action:
I. The international community should boycott Iran.
II. The U.S. should wage war against Iran just as it did against Iraq a few years ago.

21. Statement: Fordon Motors has found that its managerial manpower is not efficient.

Courses of Action:
I. It should fire all its managers.
II. It should organise training programs for its managers.

22. Statement: The TV channel Kal Tak has shown a video recording of some policemen taking bribes from car drivers.

Courses of Action:
I. The cops should be suspended after an inquiry.
II. The guilty cops should be warned for future.

23. Statement: The Maharashtra State Electricity Board has been unable to provide 24 hours electricity leading to tremendous economic loss.

Courses of Action:
I. The Government must provide for increasing electricity consumption.
II. The government should check the electricity theft cases.

24. Statement: The flood relief sanctioned for the purpose never reached the intended beneficiaries.

Courses of Action:
I. Those who are responsible should be checked and suspended.
II. The Government of India should resign taking moral responsibility for the same.

25. Statement: It has been observed that commercial banks refrain from giving loans to people from poor backgrounds because they cannot provide assets for security.

Courses of Action:
I. The finance ministry must look into the matter immediately.
II. The finance minister should initiate an enquiry into the matter.

ANSWER KEY

1. (c)	2. (a)	3. (a)	4. (c)	5. (b)	6. (c)	7. (c)
8. (b)	9. (c)	10. (a)	11. (a)	12. (c)	13. (c)	14. (d)
15. (c)	16. (a)	17. (c)	18. (c)	19. (b)	20. (d)	21. (b)
22. (a)	23. (a)	24. (a)	25. (c)			

SOLUTIONS AND SHORTCUTS

1. Both the courses of action are logical. Hence, option (c) is correct.
2. Only the first course of action is logical in this situation as a crack down on terrorist organisations is the responsibility of every country. US attacking terrorist groups across the world is an infeasible solution. Hence, option (a) is correct.
3. The first course of action follows since it is the responsibility of all parties concerned to ensure that the common man is not affected. The second course of action does not follow as it is opposite what should happen. Hence, option (a) is correct.
4. Both the courses of action follow logically in order to solve the power crisis. Hence, option (c) is correct.
5. Only the second course of action fits in. Hence, option (b) is correct.
6. Both courses of action are correct. Hence, option (c) is correct.
7. Both courses of action are correct. Hence, option (c) is correct.
8. Only the second course of action is logical. Hence, option (b) is correct.
9. Both courses of action are likely to help the Indian cricket team transit from one generation to the next smoothly. Hence, option (c) is correct.
10. Only the first course of action is valid. The second is too drastic. Hence, option (a) is correct.
11. Only the first course of action is valid. We need to take immediate steps to control the emission of green house gases. The second is too drastic. Hence, option (a) is correct.
12. Obviously we need to control the ragging menace. In such a case both options are correct. Hence, option (c) is the answer.
13. Both the courses of action are logical and recommended in the given situation. Hence, option (c) is correct.
14. Neither of the two courses of action are valid since the government should just allow the market economics to prosper. Hence, (d) is the correct option.
15. Both the courses of action are valid logically. Hence, option (c) is correct.
16. Only course of action I is correct. Hence, option (a) is correct.
17. Both courses of action are logical and would help in the improvement of security in the colony. Hence, option (c) is the answer.
18. Both the courses of action are valid. Hence, option (c) is correct.
19. The first course of action will further affect exporters and will make Indian exports unviable in the international markets. Providing some support to exporters at this juncture might be a good idea since it will have to improve the position of Indian exporters which has been jolted by the rupee appreciation. Hence, option (b) is correct.
20. Neither course of action is logical because both are too drastic just on the basis of claims made by one party against the other. Hence, option (d) is correct.
21. Course of action II is logically correct as training is likely to improve the efficiency of the managers. Firing all the managers is illogical and likely to be counterproductive. Hence, option (b) is correct.
22. Course of action I follows, II does not. Hence, option (a) is the answer.
23. Only course of action I follows as the government must make provisions to increase the generation of power. However the course of action II does not follow because the government cannot be expected to check electricity theft cases since that is the work of the Electricity Board and not the government. Hence, option (a) is the answer.
24. Course of action I is logical. Hence, option (a) is the answer.
25. Both the courses of action are logical. Option (c) is correct.

CHAPTER 8 Mathematical Operations

Chapter Launchpad
Scan this QR code for an introductory video on Mathematical Operations

Questions on Mathematical operations will first start with either defining a new meaning to existing symbols or define a new symbol and its mathematical meaning.

You are then required to evaluate the value of an expression by assuming the meaning of the symbols as defined in the question. The following questions will make this question type clear to you.

WORKED-OUT PROBLEMS

Illustration 1: If '+' means '–', '–' means '×', '×' means '÷', and '÷' means '+' then which of the following will be the value of the expression?

$32 + 8 \times 2 - 3 \div 4$

(a) 12 (b) 20
(c) 0 (d) 24

Solution: Putting the changed signs, the expression can be rewritten as

$32 - 8 \div 2 \times 3 + 4$

Using BODMAS rule, we have

$= 32 - 4 \times 3 + 4$

$= 32 - 12 + 4 = 24$

Hence, the correct option is (d).

Illustration 2: If *A* implies '+', *B* implies '–', *C* implies '×', *D* implies '÷', then calculate the value of the expression 2*A*3*B*4*C*5*D*1.

(a) 15 (b) 0
(c) –15 (d) –12

Solution: Using the proper signs, the above expression can be written as

$2 + 3 - 4 \times 5 \div 1$

$= 5 - 20 = -15$

Hence, option (c) is correct.

Illustration 3: Which of the following changes would make the given expression correct?

$4 + 4 \times 4 - 4 \div 4 = 4$

(a) '+' and '×' (b) '–' and '÷'
(c) '+' and '÷' (d) both 'b' and 'c'

Solution: By making inter-changes given in 'a' we get the expression as:

$4 \times 4 + 4 - 4 \div 4 = 4$ which is false.

By making interchanges given in 'b', we get expression as

$4 + 4 \times 4 \div 4 - 4 = 4$ which is true.

By making interchanges given in option 'c', we get the expression as

$4 \div 4 \times 4 - 4 + 4 = 4$ which is also true.

Hence, option (d) is correct.

Illustration 4: If *A*"*B* means add *B* to *A*, *A*'*B* implies subtract *B* from *A*, *A*@ *B* implies divide *A* by *B*, *A***B* means multiply *A* with *B*.

If a train travels with a speed of S_1 from point *A* to *B* and returns with a speed of S_2. The average speed will be represented using the above explained notations?

(a) $(2*S_1"S_2)/(S_1"S_2)$
(b) $(2*S_1*S_2)/(S_1"S_2)$
(c) $(2*S_1"S_2)/(S_1'S_2)$
(d) $(2*S_1@S_2)/(S_1'S_2)$

Solution: We know that the formula for average speed is given by

$2S_1S_2/(S_1 + S_2)$

Hence the correct option is (b).

Illustration 5: If (*l*, *m*, *n*) is represented as $\sqrt{[(l+1)(m+1/(n+1))]}$:

What is the value of (48, 63, 80)?

(a) 56/9 (b) 55/9
(c) 6 (d) 7

Solution: Putting the value in the above equation we get

$$\sqrt{[(48+1)(63+1)/(80+1)]}$$

$$= \sqrt{(49 \times 64/81)} = (7 \times 8)/9 = 56/9$$

Hence, the correct option is (a).

EXERCISE

Directions for Questions 1 to 5: If a + b implies a – b
$a - b$ implies $a \times b$
$a \times b$ implies $a \div b$
$a \div b$ implies $a + b$

High Yield Questions

Scan this QR code to access video explanations of questions 1-5, 9-12 and 22-25

1. Calculate $5 + 8 - 25 \times 5 \div 40$
(a) 5
(b) –5
(c) 0
(d) 10

2. With which statement can you find the value of 8?
(a) $1 + 2 - 6 \times 3 \div 8$ (b) $1 - 2 + 6 \times 3 \div 8$
(c) $1 - 2 \times 6 + 3 \times 8$ (d) None of these

3. Which of the following is true?
(a) $6 + 2 - 3 \times 1 \div 4 = 12$
(b) $10 + 4 - 3 \times 1 \div 2 = 5$
(c) $6 + 4 - 2 \times 2 \div 1 = 3$
(d) None of these

4. Which of the following is true?
$(1 + 2 - 3 \times 1 \div 4)/(4 + 5 - 4 \times 2 \div 1) =$
(a) –1/5 (b) 1/5
(c) 1 (d) None of these

5. Find the value of
$(4 + 3 - 5 \times 1 \div 4) \times (5 + 2 - 3 \times 1 \div 4)$
(a) –7/3 (b) –8/3
(c) 1 (d) None of these

Directions for Questions 6 to 8: If 'a' means +, 'b' means –, 'c' means × and 'd' means ÷

6. Calculate the value of $6a7b8c8d2$
(a) –17 (b) 12
(c) –19 (d) None of these

7. Calculate $(8c7)c(7a5)b(6d3)d(3b2)$
(a) 650 (b) 375
(c) 670 (d) None of these

8. What is the value of $9a10b11c15d0$?
(a) 1 (b) 2
(c) 3 (d) Undefined

Directions for Questions 9 to 18: In each of the following questions if the given interchanges are made in signs and numbers, which one of the four equations would be correct?

9. Given interchanges, signs '–' and '÷' and numbers 4 and 8 (on the LHS)
(a) $4 - 8 \div 12 = -23/4$
(b) $4 \div 8 - 2 = 8$
(c) $8 \div 2 - 4 = -15/4$
(d) None of these

10. Given interchanges: 3 and 2, ÷ and –
(a) $1 + 3 \times 4 - 2 \div 1 = 5$
(b) $1 + 2 - 3 \times 8 \div 4 = 9$
(c) $3 - 1 \times 4 + 2 \div 1 = 11$
(d) None of these

11. Given interchanges: 0.4 and 0.04,
(a) $1 + 2 - 0.04 \times 0.4 = 1$
(b) $0.4 + 0.04 - 2 \times 2 = 1.76$
(c) $0.04 \times 0.4 - 1 = 0.18$
(d) None of these

12. Given interchanges, × and +, 10, 1
(a) $5 \times 1 + 10 - 2 = 5$
(b) $8 + 8 - 10 \times 1 = 75$
(c) $4 - 6 \times 10 + 1 = 6$
(d) $3 + 4 - 12 \times 1 \div 10 = 10$

13. Find out the two signs to be interchanged for making the following equation to be correct:
$5 + 3 - 5 \times 5 \div 1 = 15$
(a) × and – (b) × and +
(c) ÷ and – (d) + and –

14. Which of the following two signs need to be interchanged to make the given equation correct?
$4 + 2 - 5 \times 7 \div 12 = -21$
(a) ÷ and – (b) ÷ and +
(c) × and + (d) × and –

15. Insert proper arithmetical signs between the figures in the following equation
12_4_2_1 = 24
(a) –, ÷, × (b) ×, ÷, ×
(c) +, ×, ÷ (d) None of these

16. If '*a*' implies '+', '*b*' implies '–', '*c*' implies '×' and '*d*' implies '÷', insert proper letter between the figures in the following equation
40__ 20__ 30__6 = 55
(a) *a*, *b*, *c* (b) *b*, *c*, *d*
(c) *a*, *b*, *d* (d) *d*, *b*, *a*

17. If '+' implies '–', '–' implies '×', '×' implies '÷' and '÷' implies '+' , then insert the proper signs between the figures in the given equation
12__8__4__2__1 = 12
(a) ÷, ×, –, + (b) ÷, –, +, ×
(c) +, –, ×, ÷ (d) –, +, ÷, ×

18. If $\alpha = +$, $\beta = -$, $\gamma = \times$, $\delta = \div$
Insert the proper notations between the figures in the following sum
10__8__6__4__2 = 6
(a) β, α, δ, γ (b) α, β, γ, δ
(c) β, δ, γ, α (d) None of these

Directions for Questions 19 to 21: If

12 + 2 = 6,

27 + 9 = 3 and

15 + 5 = 3

19. Calculate the value of 182 + 13
(a) 14 (b) 1.4
(c) 0.14 (d) None of these

20. Calculate the value of 50 + [50 + 10]
(a) 10 (b) 100
(c) 110 (d) 5

21. Calculate (10 + (6 + (3 + (2 + 1))))
(a) 4 (b) 5
(c) 8 (d) None of these

Directions for Questions 22 to 25: If

3 × 4 = 5

5 × 12 = 13

Then solve the following questions.

22. Calculate the value of 7 × 24
(a) 12 (b) 48
(c) 10 (d) None of these

23. Calculate the value of 8 × 9
(a) 145 (b) $\sqrt{145}$
(c) 12 (d) 12.5

24. 9 × ? = 41
(a) 35 (b) 30
(c) 40 (d) None of these;

25. Obtain {3 × (5 × 6)} = ?
(a) 5 (b) $\sqrt{70}$
(c) $5\sqrt{3}$ (d) None of these

Directions for Questions 26 to 30: If

M means greater than

N means equal to

O means not less than

P means less than

Q means not equal to

and R means not greater than

26. If yPz and zNa, then which of the following is true?
(a) yMa (b) yPa
(c) yOa (d) None of these

27. If 10aM6b and 12bM20c
(a) 5aMc (b) aM5c
(c) aNc (d) None of these

28. If aP0 and b+2Pa, then which of the following is true?
(a) bM – 2 (b) bN – 2
(c) bP – 2 (d) None of these

29. If sOt, tRu and tRv then which of the following could be true about s and u/v or u and v?
(a) sMu (b) sPv
(c) uNv (d) can't be determined

30. If $|t - u|$ M0, then which of the following is/are true?
(a) sMt (b) tMs
(c) sNt
(d) (a), (b) and (c) could be true

Directions for Questions 31 to 33: If

aAb implies $a + b$

aMb implies $a - b$

aPb implies $a \times b$

aQb implies $a \div b$

31. Which of the following equations is correct?
(a) 30Q10A4P2M2 = 15
(b) 5P2A4Q2P2 = 14
(c) 2Q3B5P6A7 = –5
(d) None of these

32. Calculate 5A6M3P4Q8
(a) 10 (b) 9
(c) 9.5 (d) 10.5

33. Calculate (2A3M4P5)P(5M6P8Q4)
(a) –105 (b) –120
(c) 120 (d) None of these

Directions for Questions 34 to 36:

A"B implies A + B

A'b implies A – B

A@B implies A ÷ B

A*B implies A × B

34. A man travels with a speed of f from *A* to *B* and returns from *B* to *A* with speed h. What is the average speed of the man over the entire journey?
(a) 2f'h/f"h (b) 2f@h/f"h
(c) 2f*h/f@h (d) None of these

35. Jadugar has a jadoo box which has a length, breadth and height which can be represented by '*x*', '*a*', '*c*' respectively. What is the formula for its total surface area?
(a) 2[(*x*'*a*)*(*a*"*c*)*(*x*"*c*)]
(b) 2[(*x***a*)"(*a***c*)"(*x***c*)]
(c) 2[(*x*'*a*)*(*a***c*)*(*x***c*)]
(d) None of these

36. At the Wave cinemas in Sector 18 in Noida, charges for parking are as follows
1. For cycles ₹ 2
2. For scooters ₹ 5
3. For cars ₹ 20

On a particular day there were '25' cycles, '40' scooters and '100' cars parked at the stand, what was the amount collected in that particular day?
(a) (25"2)*(40"5)*(100"20)
(b) (25'2)@(40'5)@(100'20)
(c) (25*2)"(40*5)"(100*20)
(d) None of these

Directions for Questions 37 to 41: If

AXB implies $A^2 + B^2$
AYB implies $A^2 - B^2$
AZB implies $(A + B)^2$
AMB implies $(A - B)^2$

37. Calculate the value of (4X5)Y(6X7)
(a) 5544 (b) –5544
(c) 500 (d) None of these

38. Calculate the value of (373)M(413)
(a) 1600 (b) 900
(c) 400 (d) 2500

39. If $(AMB) = (AZB)$ then which of the following is true.
(a) $A - B = 0$ (b) $A^2 = B^2$
(c) $A.B = 0$ (d) $A = 0$

40. Calculate (3Z4) – (5M5)
(a) 49 (b) 25
(c) 64 (d) None of these

41. Calculate the value of (2Z2)M(4Y4)
(a) 16 (b) 256
(c) 25 (d) None of these

Directions for Questions 42 to 43:

If '*' indicates either '+' or '×', solve the following questions.

42. What is the maximum value of
1*2*3*4*5*6*7
(a) 5040 (b) 5041
(c) 7!/2 (d) None of these

43. What is the minimum value of
1*2*3*4
(a) 10 (b) 9
(c) 11 (d) 14

Directions for Questions 44 to 46: If

A indicates >
B indicates <
C indicates =
D indicates ≠
E indicates +
F indicates –
G indicates *
H indicates ÷

44. Which of the following is false?
(a) (5E7)A(4E3)A(1E2)
(b) (5E6)A(6E12)A(13E6)
(c) (12H3)C(40H10)C(60H15)
(d) All of these are false

45. Calculate (32H(2H(6H3)))
(a) 16 (b) 32
(c) 8 (d) None of these

46. Calculate 5E3F4G6H2
(a) 1.5 (b) 1
(c) –4 (d) None of these

Directions for Questions 47 to 50:

"x" means greater than.
"Y" means less than.
"Z" means not greater than.
"A" means not less than.
"B" means equal to.

47. If P(x)2R and 2P(B)3Q then
(a) RYQ (b) RAQ
(c) RXQ (d) RBQ

48. If 3PXQ and 3QX2R, then
(a) 3PX2R/3 (b) 5PxR
(c) 2P B R (d) 3PA R

49. QB2R and 3RZP, then
(a) QA2P (b) QBP
(c) 3QZ2P (d) QYP

50. If 3RA2P and QXR then
(a) 2Px3Q (b) 3Qx2P
(c) QBP (d) 3Q B 2P

Directions for Questions 51 to 55:

"P$Q" means "P is not smaller then Q".
"P@Q" means "P is neither smaller than nor equal to Q".
"P#Q" means "P is neither greater than nor equal to Q".
"P&Q" means "P is neither greater than nor smaller than Q".
"P*Q" means "P is not greater than Q".

51. Statements: H@T, T#F, F&E, E*V
Conclusion:
I. V$F
II. E@T
III. H@V
IV. T#V
(a) Only I II and III are true
(b) Only I II and IV are true
(c) Only II III and IV are true
(d) Only I III and IV are true
(e) All I II III and IV are true

52. Statement: D#R, R*K, K@F, F$J
Conclusions:
I. J#R
II. J#K
III. R#F
IV. K@D
(a) Only I II and III are true
(b) Only II and IV are true
(c) Only I III and IV are true

(d) All I II III and IV are true
(e) None of these

53. Statement: N&B, B$W, W#H, H*M
Conclusion:
I. M@W
II. H@N
III. W&N
IV. W#N
(a) Only I is true
(b) Only III is true
(c) Only either III or IV are true
(d) Only either III or IV and I are true
(e) None of these.

54. Statement: R*D, D$J, J#M, M@K
Conclusion:
I. K#J
II. D@M
III. R#M
IV. D@K
(a) None is true
(b) Only I is true
(c) Only II is true
(d) Only III is true
(e) Only IV is true

55. Statement: M$K, K@N, N*R, R#W
Conclusion:
I. W@K
II. M$R
III. K@W
IV. M@N
(a) Only I and II are true
(b) Only III and IV are true
(c) Only III or IV are true
(d) Only II III and IV are true
(e) None of these

Directions for Questions 56 to 60:

"A%B" means "A is not smaller than B"
"A@B" means "A is neither smaller than nor equal to B"
"A$B" means "A is neither greater than nor equal to B"
"A*B" means "A is neither greater than nor less to B"
"A#B" means "A is not greater than B".

56. Statements: F@J, J#R, R*L, L%M
Conclusions:
I. F$R
II. M#R
III. M%J
(a) None is true
(b) Only III is true
(c) Only II is true
(d) Only either II or III is true
(e) All are true

57. Statements: T#W, W$Q, Q%D, D@J. Given T and J are not equal.
Conclusions:
I. J$T
II. T$J
III. T$Q
(a) Only I and III are true
(b) Only either I or II is true
(c) Only II and III are true
(d) Only III and either I or II are true
(e) None of these

58. Statements: L#V, V$E, E%U, U@B
Conclusions:
I. B$E
II. L$E
III. B*L
(a) Only I and II are true
(b) Only III is true
(c) Only either I or II is true
(d) All are true
(e) None of these

59. Statements: M$T, T*R, R@H, H#G
Conclusions:
I. M$H
II. R@G
III. M#R
(a) Only I is true
(b) Only II is true
(c) Only III is true
(d) All are true
(e) None is true

60. Statements: H%R, R@W, W*F, J$F
Conclusions:
I. H@F
II. J$W
III. F@J
(a) Only I and II are true
(b) Only II and III are true
(c) Only III are true
(d) Only either I and III is true
(e) All are true

ANSWER KEY

1. (a)	2. (b)	3. (c)	4. (b)
5. (a)	6. (c)	7. (c)	8. (d)
9. (d)	10. (b)	11. (d)	12. (d)
13. (a)	14. (b)	15. (b)	16. (c)
17. (a)	18. (b)	19. (a)	20. (a)
21. (d)	22. (d)	23. (b)	24. (c)
25. (b)	26. (b)	27. (d)	28. (c)
29. (d)	30. (d)	31. (b)	32. (c)

33. (d)	34. (d)	35. (b)	36. (c)
37. (b)	38. (a)	39. (c)	40. (a)
41. (b)	42. (b)	43. (b)	44. (b)
45. (b)	46. (c)	47. (a)	48. (a)
49. (c)	50. (b)	51. (b)	52. (b)
53. (d)	54. (a)	55. (e)	56. (c)
57. (d)	58. (a)	59. (e)	60. (e)

SOLUTIONS AND SHORTCUTS

Solutions for Questions 1 to 5:

1. The expression will become 5 – 8 × 25 ÷ 5 + 40. Using the BODMAS rule we will get:
   5 – 40 + 40 = 5. Hence, option (a) is correct.
2. Looking at option (b), we will get, 1 – 2 + 6 × 3 ÷ 8 becomes 1 × 2 – 6 ÷ 3 + 8 = 8. Hence, option (b) is the correct answer.
3. Option (c) gives us 6 – 4 × 2 ÷ 2 + 1= 3. Hence, this is correct.
4. (1 + 2 – 3 × 1 ÷ 4)/(4 + 5 – 4 × 2 ÷ 1) = (1 – 2 × 3 ÷ 1 + 4)/(4 – 5 × 4 ÷ 2 + 1) = –1/–5 = 1/5. Hence, (b) is the answer.
5. (4 + 3 – 5 × 1 ÷ 4) × (5 + 2 – 3 × 1 ÷ 4) = (4 – 3 × 5 ÷ 1 + 4) ÷ (5 – 2 × 3 ÷ 1 + 4) = –7/3. Hence, option (a) is the answer.

Solutions for Questions 6 to 8:

6. $6a7b8c8d2$ = 6 + 7 – 8 × 8 ÷ 2 = –19. Hence, (c) is the answer.
7. $(8c7)c(7a5)b(6d3)d(3b2)$ becomes 56 × 12 – 2 ÷ 1 = 670. Option (c) is the answer.
8. The expression contains a division by 0, hence is undefined. Option (d) is the answer.

Solutions for Questions 9 to 18:

9. None of these, i.e. option (d) is correct.
10. The given expression will become 1 + 3 ÷ 2 × 8 – 4 = 9. Option (b) is the answer.
11. Checking each of the four options we will get none of these the answer. Hence, option (d) is the answer.
12. Option (d) bwwecomes correct.
13. If the signs are changed according to the first option the equation is satisfied. Hence, option (a) is correct.
14. If the signs are changed according to the second option the equation is satisfied. Hence, option (b) is correct.
15. Insertion of ×, ÷, × in that order will make 12 × 4 ÷ 2 × 1 = 24. Hence, option (b) is correct.
16. 40 + 20 – 30 ÷ 6 = 60 – 5 = 55. Hence, *a*, *b*, *d*. Option (c) is correct.
17. 12 ÷ 8 × 4 – 2 + 1 would mean 12 + 8 ÷ 4 × 2 – 1 = 12 + 1 – 1 = 12. Hence, the order given in option (a) is correct.
18. Option (b) is correct.

Solutions for Questions 19 to 21:

It is clear that the + sign means ÷ Hence,

19. 182 + 13 would give us a value of 14. Hence, (a) is the answer.
20. 50/5 = 10. Hence, (a) is the answer.
21. 10/4 = 2.5. Hence, correct option is (d).

Solutions for Questions 22 to 25:

The relationship that is defined through $a \times b = \sqrt{(a^2 + b^2)}$

Thus, $3 \times 4 = \sqrt{25} = 5$ and $5 \times 12 = \sqrt{(25+144)} = 13$.

22. $7 \times 24 = \sqrt{625} = 25$. Hence, option (d) is the answer.
23. $8 \times 9 = \sqrt{(64+81)} = \sqrt{145}$. Hence, option (b) is the answer.
24. The required value will be got by the square root of the difference between 41^2 and $9^2 \rightarrow 1681 - 81 = 1600$. Hence, the required answer is 40. Correct answer is option (c).
25. The required value would be square root of 61 + 9 = $\sqrt{70}$. Hence, option (b) is the answer.

Solutions for Questions 26 to 30:

26. yPz means that y is less than z and zNa means $z = a$. Thus, y is less than a → yPa. Option (b) is correct.
27. 10a is greater than 6b. and 12b is greater than 20c → 6b is greater than 10c. Thus 10a is greater than 10c or a is greater than c. Option (d) is correct.
28. a is negative and $b + 2$ is less than a implies that b must be below –2. Hence, option (c) is correct.
29. Nothing can be said about the relationships between s, u or v or for that matter about u and v. Hence, cannot be determined. The correct answer is option (d).
30. Since the modulus value is always positive, all the three, i.e. the first, second and third relationships are possible. Hence, option (d) is correct.

Solutions for Questions 31 to 33:

31. Option (b) is correct since we will get 10 + 4 = 14.
32. 11 – 1.5 = 9.5. Option (c) is correct.
33. (–15)(–7) = 105. Hence, option (d) is correct.

Solutions for Questions 34 to 36:

34. It can be seen that none of these is correct. Hence, (d) is the answer.
35. The surface area of a cuboid box is equal to twice the areas of each of the sides. Hence, option (b) is correct.

36. The correct answer is option (c).

Solutions for Questions 37 to 41:

37. $41^2 - 85^2 = 1681 - 7225 = -5544$. Hence, option (b) is correct answer.
38. $(-40)^2 = 1600$. Hence, option (a) is correct answer.
39. The given expression tells us that $(A - B)^2 = (A + B)^2$. This can only occur when $2AB = -2AB = 0$. Hence, option (c) is correct.
40. $7^2 = 49$. Hence, correct answer is option (a).
41. $16^2 = 256$. Hence, correct answer is option (b).

Solutions for Questions 42 to 43:

42. The maximum value will be obtained when we use multiplication between 2 to 7 and addition between 1 and 2. Hence, option (b) is the answer.
43. The minimum value will be got if we use a multiplication between 1 and 2 and addition between 2, 3, and 4. The value will be $1 \times 2 + 3 + 4 = 9$. Hence, option (b) is the answer.

Solutions for Questions 44 to 46:

44. It can be seen that options (a) and (c) are correct, but option (b) is wrong. Hence, option (b) is the correct answer.
45. 32/1 = 32. Hence, option (b) is correct.
46. 5 + 3 – 12 = –4. Hence, option (c) is correct.

Solutions for Questions 47 to 50:

According to the problem, we know

X is >, Y is <, Z is ≤, A is ≥ & B is =.

47. P > 2R and 2P = 3Q
    2P > 4R and 2P = 3Q
    3Q > 4R
    Q > 4R/3 or Q>R or R<Q
    RYQ
48. 3P > Q, 3Q > 2R
    3P > Q, Q > 2R/3
    3P > 2R/3
49. Q = 2R and 3R ≤ P
    3Q = 6R and 6R ≤ 2P
    This means that 3Q ≤ 2P or 3QZ2P
50. 3R ≥ 2P and Q > R or 3Q > 3R
    3Q > 3R ≥ 2P
    3Q > 2P → 3QX2P

Solutions for Questions 51 to 55:

In this question, the terminology is as follows: $ is ≥; @ is >; # is <; & is = AND * is ≤

51. H @ T, T # F, F & E, E * V
    H > T, T < F, F = E, E ≤ V
    H > T < F = E ≤ V
    Conclusions: V $ F → V ≥ F True
    E @ T → E > T True
    H @ V → H > V Can't be determined
    T # V → T < V True
    Conclusions I, II, IV are true.
    Option (b) is correct.
52. D < R, R ≤ K, K > F, F ≥ J
    D < R ≤ K > F ≥ J
    Conclusions: J < R can't be determined
    J < K True
    R < F Can't be determined
    K > D True
    II, IV conclusions are true.
    By using the same method mentioned above, we can solve the rest of the problems:
53. (d)
54. (a)
55. (e)

Solutions for Questions 56 to 60:

% is ≥; @ is >; $ is <; * is = AND # is £.

56. F > J ≤ R = L ≥ M
    Conclusions: F < R → can't be determined
    M ≤ R → True
    M ≥ J → Can't be determined
    Option (c) is true.
57. T ≤ W < Q ≥ D > J
    Conclusion: I-J < T Can't be determined
    II-T < J Can't be determined
    III-T < Q True
    Both I and II can't be determined. But if one of these statements is correct the other must be wrong. Hence, the correct answer is option (d) (Only III and either I or II are true).
    The other questions can be solved in the same way to get the answers as follows:
58. (a)
59. (e)
60. (e)

CHAPTER 9

Coding Decoding

Chapter Launchpad
Scan this QR code for an introductory video on Coding Decoding

Questions on Coding Decoding start off with a clue/s to the given coding structure and logic. This is done by giving us a few words/sentences and their corresponding codes. By analysing these, we can identify the logic of the coding. Based on the logic identified, we have to answer the questions about other words/sentences.

A few solved examples will help you enter the groove with respect to this question type.

WORKED-OUT PROBLEMS

Illustration 1: If GLORIOUS is coded as GOLRIOSU, code 'JUDICIAL'?

Solution: The second and third letters are interchanged, again last two letters are also interchanged as shown below.

Using the same logic, the word J U D I C I A L is coded as J D U I C I L A.

Illustration 2: If PAINT is coded as 74128 and EXCEL is coded as 93596, then how would you encode ACCEPT?

Solution: In the given code the alphabets have been coded as follows:

P	A	I	N	T	E	X	C	L	
7	4	1	2	8	9	3	5	6	

Using this table, we can code ACCEPT as: 455978.

Illustration 3: If 'tee see pee' means 'drink fruit juice'; 'see kee lee' means 'juice is sweet' and 'lee ree mee' means 'he is intelligent', which word in that language means 'sweet'?

Solution: In the first and second statement, the common word is 'juice' and the common code word is 'see'. So, 'see' means 'juice'.

In the second and third statements, the common word is 'is' and the common code is 'lee'. So 'lee' means 'is'. Thus in the second statement, the remaining word 'sweet' is coded as 'kee'.

Illustration 4: In a certain code, '786' means 'study very hard', '958' means 'hard work pays' and '645' means 'study and work'. Which of the following is the code for 'very'?

(a) 8 (b) 6
(c) 7 (d) Can't be determined

Solution: Between the first and second sentences, the common word is hard and the common digit is 8. Hence, Hard = 8. Between the first and third sentences, the common word is study and the common digit is 6. Hence, Study = 6

Hence, the code for 'very' can be found out to be '7'

EXCERCISE

Directions for Questions 1 to 9:

High Yield Questions
Scan this QR code to access video explanations of questions 3, 5, 7, and 16-20

1. It in a certain language "AMBE" is coded as "BNCF". How is "CHENNAI" Coded in that language?
(a) DIFOOBJ
(b) BGDMMZH
(c) DGDMMZJ
(d) None of these

2. In a certain language "MUMBAI" is coded as "LTLAZH". How is "KANPUR" coded in that language?
(a) JZMOTQ (b) LBOQVS
(c) JBOOVS (d) None of these

3. In a certain language "LUCKNOW" is coded as "NWEMPQY". How is "SARK" coded in that language?
(a) UCTM (b) MCT
(c) CTUM (d) None of these

4. In a certain language "DELHI" is coded as " CFKIH". How is "SUDHIR" coded in that language?
(a) RVCIHS (b) TTCIHS
(c) RVCHHS (d) None of these

5. In a certain language "PARAMPARA" is written as "RAPPMAARA". How is "SUDHAKARA" coded in that language?
(a) DUSHAKARA (b) DUSKAHARA
(c) DUSHAKRAA (d) None of these

6. In a certain language.
"DELHI" is coded as "IHLED"
How is "SURAJ" coded in that language?
(a) P I S B K (b) U S J A R
(c) J A R U S (d) None of these

7. In a certain code "KARMPUTRA" is coded as "AKSNQVUAR". How is "BHILWARAM" is written in that code?
(a) HBJMXBSMA (b) HBJMXBSMN
(c) CIJMXBSBN (d) None of these

8. In a certain language "DELHI" is written as 451289. How is "MUMBAI" coded in that language?
(a) 132113219 (b) 5105108
(c) 76765 (d) None of these

9. How is "SHRI" coded in that language?
(a) 2091910 (b) 198189
(c) 209199 (d) None of these

Directions for Questions 10 to 11: *If ABHI is coded as 23910 and BIG is coded as 3108 then answer the following questions.*

10. How is "RAM" coded in the language.
(a) 19214 (b) 18113
(c) 17112 (d) None of these

11. If "AMAN" is coded as 3 and "BANANA" is coded as 5 and "KNIFE" is coded as 4 then "PARTNERSHIP" is coded as-
(a) 9 (b) 10
(c) 11 (d) 12

Directions for Questions 12 to 13: *In a certain code, if "ABHI" is written as 20 and "RAM" is written as 32, then answer the following questions:*

12. How will you code "SHIP"?
(a) 51 (b) 50
(c) 52 (d) 53

13. Which of the following word is coded as 50?
(a) OPS (b) RST
(c) VUX (d) None of these

14. If MISTER is coded as 131776218 then PAWAN will be coded as:
(a) 123251225 (b) 102532
(c) 2532 (d) 102532512

15. If No = 210, So = 285 then ANI = ?
(a) 126 (b) 258
(c) 185 (d) 512

Directions for Questions 16 to 20: *Study the following information to answer the given questions:*

In a certain code **'best way to win'** is written as **'ad mi ja no'**, **'the way to hell'** is written as **'ku ja ig ad'**. **'win of the day'** is written as **'be ku zo mi'** and **'to sell of night'** is written as **'be Ii ya ja'**.

16. What is the code for 'sell'?
(a) be (b) Ii
(c) ya (d) ja
(e) Can't be determined

17. Which of the following may represent 'hell is way'?
(a) ig ad no (b) ig py ya
(c) re ad be (d) ig li re
(e) ad re ig

18. 'mi' is the code for
(a) to (b) win
(c) way (d) of
(e) Can't be determined

19. What is the code for 'best'?
(a) ad (b) mi
(c) no (d) ja
(e) Can't be determined

20. Which of the following represents 'of the way'?
(a) ku be ad (b) rni be no
(c) ku be ya (d) mi ku be
(e) be mi ad

Directions for Questions 21 to 25: *Study the following information and answer the questions given.*

In a certain code language **"lu ja ka hu"** means **'we provide study material'**, **"fa ka la ju"** means **'we score maximum selection'**, **"la fu ja ju"** means **"study score the selection"** and **"ju lu na fu"** means **"selection of the material"**. Then:

21. What is the code of "score" in this code language?
(a) ju (b) la
(c) fa (d) ka
(e) Can't be determined

22. What is the code of "provide" in this code language?
(a) hu (b) lu
(c) ka (d) ja
(e) Can't be determined

23. What is the code of "provide of maximum"?
(a) na hu fu (b) fa hu na
(c) fu lu na (d) hu fa la
(e) Can't be determined

24. What is the code of "we the" in this code language?
(a) ka fu (b) na hu
(c) ka na (d) hu fu
(e) Can't be determined

25. What is the code of "material" in this code language?
(a) hu (b) lu
(c) ja (d) ka
(e) Can't be determined

26. In a certain code 'SUDHIR' is written as 'HIRSUD' How would 'VISHES' be written in that code?
(a) VISHSE (b) HESVIS
(c) VISEHS (d) HESIVS

27. In a certain code 'PURPOSE' is written as 'UPPRSOE'. How would 'SUDHI' is written in that code.
(a) USHDI (b) SUDIH
(c) USDIH (d) None of these

28. In a certain code 'SUDHIR' is written as 'QTBGGQ'. How would 'ARUN' be written in that code?
(a) QYSM (b) PQRS
(c) YQSM (d) None of these

29. If AMAN is written as 'BNBO' in a certain code then ARUN is written as
(a) BPTM (b) BSVM
(c) BVSM (d) None of these

30. If 'AMAN' is written as 'CLCM' in a certain code than in the same code 'ARUN' is written as:
(a) CQWO (b) CQVM
(c) CPWM (d) CQWM

31. In a certain code if '1000' is written as '1728' and '125' is written as '343'. In the same code '512' is written as:
(a) 729 (b) 343
(c) 216 (d) 1000

32. In a certain code 'SUDHIR' is written as '192104080918'. What should be the code of 'AMAN' in the same coding language?
(a) 01130114 (b) 01140114
(c) 01130113 (d) 01120112

33. In a certain code '12' is written as 'L' and '7' is written as G. Then what should be the code for 9?
(a) G (b) P
(c) I (d) M

34. In a certain code 'ALEX' is written as '001144025576' what should be the code for 'SUD' in the same code?
(a) 361144025 (b) 361
(c) 361144 (d) 361441016

35. In a certain code 'CHARAN' is written as 'AJYTYP'. What should be the code of 'AMAN' in the same coding?
(a) YOYP (b) YOPY
(c) YYYP (d) None of these

36. In a certain code 'VIMAL' is written as 'WKPEQ'. What should be the code of 'ARUN' in the same coding language?
(a) BTYR (b) BRTX
(c) BXTR (d) BTXR

37. In a certain coding language 'AMAN' is written as '114317'. What should be the code of 'ARUN' in the same coding language?
(a) 1192317
(b) 1182118
(c) 1202221
(d) None of these

38. In a certain code 'PINK' is written as 'JQLO'. What should be the code for 'BLUE'?
(a) XNEV (b) XNDU
(c) XNEU (d) XENU

39. In the previous question 'RED' is written as:
(a) HUI (b) HVU
(c) HIU (d) HUV

40. If in a certain code if 'GIRISH' is written as 70 and 'RAM' is written as 32. What should be the code of 'PIKU' in the same coding language?
(a) 57 (b) 55
(c) 56 (d) 58

41. In a certain code 'BIGB' is written as '2972' and 'ADO' is written as '146'. What should be the code for 'BINGO' in the same code?
(a) 29476 (b) 29176
(c) 29576 (d) 29976

42. In a certain code 'BISNU' is written as 'YRHMF'. What should be the code for 'PINK' in the same coding system?
(a) KRPM (b) KXYZ
(c) KRMP (d) KPMR

43. If in a certain coding language 'BABAR' is written as 'ABABQ'. Then what should be the code of 'PULKIT' in the same coding language?
(a) OVKLHV
(b) OVIHUH
(c) OVLKHU
(d) None of these

44. In a certain code 'RED' is written as 360, 'BOX' is written as '720'. What should be the code of 'BLUE' in the same coding language?
(a) 1440 (b) 780
(c) 2520 (d) None of these.

45. In a certain coding language 'SUDHIR' is coded as 1540 and 'PRAVIN' is coded as 1575. What should be the code for 'RAHOOL' in the same language?
(a) 1244 (b) 1236
(c) 1034 (d) 1134

ANSWER KEY

1. (a)	2. (a)	3. (a)	4. (a)
5. (b)	6. (c)	7. (a)	8. (a)
9. (b)	10. (a)	11. (b)	12. (c)
13. (a)	14. (d)	15. (a)	16. (e)
17. (e)	18. (b)	19. (c)	20. (a)
21. (b)	22. (a)	23. (b)	24. (a)
25. (b)	26. (b)	27. (a)	28. (c)
29. (d)	30. (d)	31. (d)	32. (a)
33. (c)	34. (d)	35. (a)	36. (d)
37. (a)	38. (c)	39. (d)	40. (a)
41. (c)	42. (c)	43. (d)	44. (c)
45. (d)			

SOLUTIONS AND SHORTCUTS

Solutions for Questions 1 to 15:

1. Each letter in the word is moved one step ahead to obtain the corresponding letter.
   Hence, CHENNAI = DIFOOBJ
2. Each letter in the word is moved one step backward to obtain the corresponding letter.
   Hence, KANPUR = JZMOTQ
3. Each letter in the word moves two steps ahead.
   Required answer: UCTM
4. Even place letters move one step ahead and odd place letter move one step backward.
   Following that pattern we get SUDHIR = RVCIHS
5. In this question, the first three letters are reversed in the coded word, the next three letters are also reversed and the last three letters are also reversed. Thus, in PAR-AMP-ARA, PAR become RAP, AMP become PMA and ARA becomes ARA.
   Thus for SUD-HAK-ARA, the corresponding word would be DUS-KAH-ARA
   Hence, SUDHAKARA = DUSKAHARA
6. We need to reverse the given order of the word.
   Hence the required answer is: JARUS.
7. 1st and 2nd letter are interchanged. Similarly 8th and 9th letters are interchanged with each other. Rest letters are moved one step ahead.
   Hence, the required answer is:
   HBJMXBSMA.
8. D is the 4th letter, E is the 5th, L is 12th and so on.
   Hence, MUMBAI is equivalent to 132113219.
9. The codes can be interpreted as follows:
   A , the 1st letter $1 + 1 = 2$; B, the 2nd letter $\rightarrow 2 + 1 = 3$; H, the 8th letter $\rightarrow 8 + 1 = 9$; J, the 9th letter $\rightarrow 9 + 1 = 10$. Hence,
   SHRI = $(19 + 1)(8 + 1)(18 + 1)(9 + 1)$
   = 2091910.
10. R - 18th letter $\rightarrow 18 + 1 = 19$; A - 1st letter - $1 + 1 = 2$; M - 13th letter - $13 + 1 = 14$
    RAM = 19214.
11. There are total 4 letters in AMAN, 6 in BANANA, 5 in KNIFE by observation we get to find that for the code of any word we just reduce the total number of letters by 1.
    Hence, PARTNERSHIP = 11 - 1 = 10.
12. ABHI = 1 + 2 + 8 + 9 = 20. Hence SHIP = 19 + 8 + 9 + 16 = 52
13. OPS = 15 + 16 + 19 = 50.
    RST = 18 + 19 + 20 = 57
    VUX = 22 + 21 + 24 = 67
    Option (a) is correct.
14. The coding scheme can be seen to be as follows:
    M $\rightarrow$ 26 - 13 = 13; I $\rightarrow$ 26 - 9 = 17; S $\rightarrow$ 26 - 19 = 7; T $\rightarrow$ 26 - 20 = 6; E $\rightarrow$ 26 - 5 = 21; R $\rightarrow$ 26 - 18 = 8
    Hence, in PAWAN we will have: P $\rightarrow$ 26 - 16 = 10; A $\rightarrow$ 26 - 1 = 25; W $\rightarrow$ 26 - 23 = 3; A $\rightarrow$ 26 - 1 = 25; N $\rightarrow$ 26 - 14 = 12
    Hence, PAWAN =102532512
15. NO $\rightarrow 14 \times 15 = 210$ (Note N = 14th letter & O is the 15th letter)
    SO $\rightarrow 19 \times 15 = 285$ (S is the 19th letter and O is the 15th letter)
    Hence, ANI $\rightarrow 1 \times 14 \times 9 = 126$.

Solutions for Questions 16 to 20: Based on our observation of the word patterns we can deduce the following about the various words that occur in the sentences:

Word	Code
night	li/ya
sell	ya/li
day	zo
of	be
hell	ig
the	ku
win	mi
to	ja
way	ad
best	no

16. (e)
17. (e)
18. (b)
19. (c)
20. (a)

Solutions for Questions 21 to 45: Based on our observation of the word patterns we can deduce the following about the various words that occur in the sentences:

Word	Code
of	na
the	fu
selection	ju
maximum	fa
score	la
material	lu
study	ja
provide	hu
we	ka

The answers can be read off the table:

21. (b)
22. (a)
23. (b)
24. (a)
25. (b)
26. SUD HIR

    HIR SUD

    Similarly: VISHES → HESVIS

    Hence, option (b) is correct.
27. Interchange the letter in the pair of two and keep the last letter as it is.

    SUDHI → USHDI

    Hence, option (a) is correct.
28. Solution:

    S U D H I R

    -2 -1 -2 -1 -2 -1

    Q T B G G Q

    A R U N

    -2 -1 -2 -1

    Y Q S M

    Hence, option (c) is correct.
29. A M A N

    +1 +1 +1 +1

    B N B O

    A R U N

    +1 +1 +1 +1

    B S V O

    Hence, option (d) is correct.
30. A M A N

    +2 -1 +2 -1

    C L C M

    A R U N

    +2 -1 +2 -1

    C Q W M

    Hence, option (d) is correct.
31. 1000 → 10^3

    1728 → $(10 + 2)^3$

    Similarly: $125 = 5^3$ & $343 = (5 + 2)^3$

    Therefore 512 = 83 and requires code = $(8 + 2)^3$ = 1000.

    Hence, option (d) is correct.
32. S → 19th letter

    U → 21st letter

    D → 4th letter

    H → 8th letter

    I → 9th letter

    R → 18th letter

    A M A N

    1 13 1 14

    01130114 is the required code.

    Hence, option (a) is correct.
33. L → 12th letter, G → 7th letter

    9 → 9th letter → I.

    Hence, option (c) is correct.
34. A → 1st letter → 1^2 = 001

    L → 12th letter → 12^2 = 144

    E → 5th letter → 5^2 = 025

    X → 24th letter → 24^2 = 576

S	U	D
19^2	21^2	4^2

SUD → 361441016

Hence, option (d) is correct.

35.

C	H	A	R	A	N
-2	+2	-2	+2	-2	+2
A	J	Y	T	Y	P

A	M	A	N
-2	+2	-2	+2
Y	O	Y	P

Hence, option (a) is correct.

36.

V	I	M	A	L
+1	+2	+3	+4	+5
W	K	P	E	Q

A	R	U	N
+1	+2	+3	+4
B	T	X	R

BTXR is the required code. Hence, option (d) is correct.

37. A → 1st letter → 1
M → 13th letter → 13 + 1 = 14
A → 1st letter → 1 + 2 = 3
N → 14th letter → 14 + 3 =17

A → 1
R → 18 + 1 = 19
U → 21 + 2 = 23
N → 14 + 3 = 17
Required code = 1192317.
Hence, option (a) is correct.

38. P → 16th letter → J → 10th letter $(26-16)^{th}$ letter
I → 9th letter → Q → 17th letter $(26-9)^{th}$ letter
N → 14th letter → L → 12th letter $(26-14)^{th}$ letter
K → 11th letter → O → 15th letter $(26-11)^{th}$ letter

B → 2nd letter → (26–2) → 24th letter → X
L → 12th letter → (26–12) = 14th letter → N
U → 21st letter → (26–21) = 5th letter → E
E → 5th letter → (26–5) = 21st letter → U
XNEU is the required code. Hence option (c) is correct.

39. R → 18th letter → (26–18) = 8th → H
E → 5th letter → (26–5) = 21st → U
D → 4th letter → (26–4) = 22nd → V
Hence, option (d) is correct.

40.

G	I	R	I	S	H
7	9	18	9	19	18

7 + 9 + 18 + 9 + 19 + 8 = 70

R	A	M
18	1	13

18 + 1 + 13 = 32

P	I	K	U
16	9	11	21

16 + 9 + 11 + 21 = 57
Hence, option (a) is correct.

41. B → 2
I → 9
N → 14 = 1 + 4 = 5
G → 7
O → 15 = 1 + 5 = 6
Hence, the required code 29576. Hence, option (c) is correct.

42. B → 2nd from start, Y → 2nd from end.
I → 9th from start, R → 9th from end.
S → 19th from start, H → 19th from end.
N → 14th from start, M → 14th from end.
U → 21st from start, F → 6th from end.

P → 16th from start, 16th from end → K
I → 9th from start, 9th from end → R
N → 14th from start, 14th from end → M
K → 11th from start, 11th from end → P
Hence, option (c) is correct.

43.

B	A	B	A	R
-1	+1	-1	+1	-1
A	B	A	B	Q

P	U	L	K	I	T
-1	+1	-1	+1	-1	+1
O	V	K	L	H	U

Hence, option (d) is correct.

44.

R → 18, E → 5, D → 4 ⟶ 18 × 5 × 4 = 360

B → 2, O → 15, X → 24 ⟶ 2 × 15 × 24 = 720

B → 2, L → 12, U → 21, E → 5 ⟶ 2 × 12 × 21 × 5 = 2520

Hence, option (c) is correct.

45.

S → 19, U → 21, D → 4; H → 8, I → 9, R → 18

(19 + 21 + 4) = 44 × (8 + 9 + 18) = 35 = 1540

P → 16, R → 18, A → 1; V → 22, I → 9, N → 14

35 × 45 = 1575

R → 18, A → 1, H → 8; O → 15, O → 15, L → 12

27 × 42 = 1134

Hence, option (d) is correct.

CHAPTER 10

Input Output

Chapter Launchpad

Scan this QR code for an introductory video on Input Output

The Input Output question type is a particular question type in reasoning where a machine takes an input of words and numbers and rearranges the input through a series of steps based on certain rules. The question starts with giving you a sample rearrangement sequence of a set of words and numbers. This rearrangement happens through a series of steps. You have to carefully study and identify the rules for the re-arrangements used in the given sequence and based on those rules identified you have to re-arrange another set of words/numbers given to you in the question.

This is best illustrated through a couple of examples. Please go through the examples carefully before moving on to the questions in the practice exercise that follows:

Example 1: Directions for Questions 1 to 3: Answer the questions based on the following information.

A word arrangement machine, when given a particular input, rearranges it following a particular rule. Following is the illustration of the input and the steps of arrangement:

Input: She was interested in doing art film
Step 1: Art she was interested in doing film
Step 2: Art was she interested in doing film
Step 3: Art was in she interested doing film
Step 4: Art was in film she interested doing
Step 5: art was in film doing she interested

Step 5 is the last step of the given input. Now study the logic and rules followed in the above steps and find out the appropriate step for the questions given below for the given input.

1. Which of the following will be the last step for the input given below?
   Input: he is going out to search air
   (a) Out is air to going search he
   (b) Out is air to search going he
   (c) Search he out is air to going
   (d) None of the above
2. If Step 2 of an input is not "not is the casino considering legal action", which step is: "not is casino action legal the considering?"
   (a) Step 3 (b) Step 6
   (c) Step 4 (d) None of the above
3. How many steps will be required to get the final output from the following input?
   Input: Father needs to check on the boy
   (a) Four (b) Five
   (c) Six (d) None of the above

Solutions for Questions 1 to 3: A close inspection of what the word arrangement machine is doing tells us that since "She was interested in doing art film" gets converted to "art was in film doing she interested" it is essentially arranging the words on the basis of the 'reverse alphabetical order arrangement' of the last alphabets in each word of the word string. If you look at the final output "art was in film doing she interested" the last alphabets of the words follow the order: t-s-n-m-g-e-d and is the reverse alphabetical order of the last letters in each of the seven words. Also notice that the standard move of the machine is to just get the appropriate word in its place in the string by just displacing the incorrect word which stands in it's place. This is contrary to the previous question where the standard move of the machine was to interchange the wrong word with the right word's position. Based on this understanding of the logic of the word series we can then move towards solving questions 1 to 3.

1. In the word string "he is going out to search air" the last alphabets are:
   e-s-g-t-o-h-r. Their reverse alphabetical order would be: t-s-r-o-h-g-e which means that the output string would be "out is air to search going he". Option (b) is the correct answer.
2. **Step 2** is "t-s-e-o-g-l-n" and we are asked to trace the step number for "t-s-o-n-l-e-g".
   Step 2: t-s-e-o-g-l-n;
   Step 3: t-s-o-e-g-l-n;
   Step 4: t-s-o-n-e-g-l;
   Step 5: t-s-o-n-l-e-g which means "not is casino action legal the considering".
   Thus the machine would reach the given situation in step 5 and hence option (d) is the correct answer.
3. "Father needs to check on the boy" can be looked at as Input: r-s-o-k-n-e-y (by looking at the last alphabet of each word in the given string). Now the objective of the machine is to put these letters in the reverse alphabetical order which means that the final output has to be: y-s-r-o-n-k-e.
   Then we have:

Input: r-s-o-k-n-e-y
Step 1: y-r-s-o-k-n-e
Step 2: y-s-r-o-k-n-e
Step 3: y-s-r-o-n-k-e.

Thus it can be seen easily that the machine would take exactly 3 steps to reach the output required.
Hence, option (d) is correct.

Example 2: **Directions for Questions 4 to 6:** Study the information given below and answer the questions.

A word arrangement machine, when given a particular input, rearranges it using a particular rule. The following is the illustration and the steps of the arrangement

INPUT:	Smile	Nile	Style	Mile	Shine	Wine	Mine	Swine	Bovine	Feline
STEP 1:	Smile	Nile	Style	Mile	Shine	Wine	Bovine	Feline	Mine	Swine
STEP 2:	Style	Mile	Smile	Nile	Shine	Wine	Bovine	Feline	Mine	Swine
STEP 3:	Style	Mile	Smile	Nile	Wine	Shine	Bovine	Feline	Mine	Swine
STEP 4:	Mile	Style	Nile	Smile	Wine	Shine	Feline	Bovine	Swine	Mine
STEP 5:	Nile	Smile	Mile	Style	Wine	Shine	Swine	Mine	Feline	Bovine
STEP 6:	Nile	Smile	Mile	Style	Wine	Shine	Feline	Bovine	Swine	Mine
STEP 7:	Mile	Style	Nile	Smile	Wine	Shine	Feline	Bovine	Swine	Mine

4. Which of the following will be step 14 for the given input?
(a) Style Mile Smile Nile Wine Shine Bovine Feline Mine Swine
(b) Smile Nile Style Mile Shine Wine Mine Swine Bovine Feline
(c) Mile Style Nile Smile Shine Wine Feline Bovine Swine Mine
(d) Style Mile Smile Nile Shine Wine Bovine Feline Mine Swine

5. Mark the arrangement that does not fall between step numbers 12 and 14.
(a) Style Mile Smile Nile Wine Shine Bovine Feline Mine Swine
(b) Mile Style Nile Smile Wine Shine Feline Bovine Swine Mine
(c) Style Mile Smile Nile Shine Wine Bovine Feline Mine Swine
(d) Smile Nile Style Mile Shine Wine Bovine Feline Mine Swine

6. If the arrangement is repeated, which of the steps will be the same as the INPUT row?
(a) Step 9 (b) Step 11
(c) Step 20 (d) Step 14

Solutions for Questions 4 to 6: The given input output string is such that in seven steps we get the following interchanges:

1, 2, 3, 4 are switched to 4, 3, 2, 1. 5, 6 becomes 6, 5 and 7, 8, 9 and 10 becomes 10, 9, 8, 7. Thus, by step 14 the same changes would occur again, i.e., reversal of each of the strings, viz: 4, 3, 2, 1 will become 1, 2, 3, 4, 6, 5 will become 5, 6 and 10, 9, 8, 7 will become 7, 8, 9, 10.

Based on this analysis we can solve the questions.

4. Consequently step 14 would go back to the original arrangement, viz: Smile, Nile, Style, Mile, Shine, Wine, Mine, Swine, Bovine, Feline.
Option (b) is correct.

5. Steps 12 to 14 would be the reverse order of steps 2,1 and input. Option (b) is not a part of any of steps 1 or 2 and is not the input too. Thus, Option (b) is the correct answer.

6. Step 14 would be the same as the input row as it would completely reverse all the changes that have happened from steps 1 to 7. Option (d) is correct.

EXCERCISE

Directions for Questions 1 to 5: *Study the following information carefully and answer the questions given below:*

A word and number arrangement machine when given an input line of words and numbers rearranges them following a particular rule in each step. The following is an illustration of input and rearrangement.

Input: 3 envelop orayot 6 7 from 4 5 haree seh
Step I: seh 3 envelop orayot 6 7 from 4 5 haree
Step II: orayot 6 seh3 envelop 7 from 4 5 haree

High Yield Questions
Scan this QR code to access video explanations of questions 1-5 and 16-20

Step III: haree 5 orayot 6 seh 3 envelop 7 from 4
Step IV: from 4 haree 5 orayot 6 seh 3 envelop 7
Step V: envelop 7 from 4 haree 5 orayot 6 seh3
Step V: is the last step of the above arrangement.

As per the rules followed in the steps given above, find out in each of the following questions the appropriate step for the given input.

Input: 6 prove hen 9 extreme following 4 rice 7 5 storme 3

1. Which of the following element is 6th from the right end in Step III?
   (a) Storme (b) 6
   (c) Hen (d) 7
2. How many steps will be required to complete the given arrangement ?
   (a) Five (b) Four
   (c) Seven (d) None of these
3. What is the position of '4' in the last step?
   (a) Third from the right
   (b) Fourth from the right
   (c) Fifth from the left
   (d) ninth from the left end
4. Which of the following element is sixth to right of 'prove' in Step II?
   (a) 7 (b) 4
   (c) 5 (d) 6
5. What is the position of ' hen' in the penultimate step?
   (a) Fifth from the right end
   (b) Fifth from the left end
   (c) Eight from the left end
   (d) Third from left end
   (e) None of these

Directions for Questions 6 to 10: *Study the following information carefully and answer the questions given below:*

A word and number arrangement machine when given an input line of words and numbers rearranges them following a particular rule in each step. The following is an illustration of input and rearrangement (all the numbers are two digits numbers).

Input: 54 ra ja 41 38 22 27 na ka ga
Step I: ga ra ja 41 38 22 27 na ka 54
Step II: ga ja ra 38 22 27 na ka 54 41
Step III: ga ja ka ra 22 27 na 54 41 38
Step IV: ga ja ka na ra 22 54 41 38 27
Step V: ga ja ka na ra 54 41 38 27 22
Step V is the last step of the above arrangement.

As per the rules followed in the steps given above, find out in each of the following questions the appropriate step for the given input.

Input: ba qa fa 51 42 16 31 ma za la 62 75

6. Which of the following represents the position of '51' in the fourth step?
   (a) Eighth from the left
   (b) Second from the left
   (c) Third from the right
   (d) Sixth from the right
7. Which of the following would be fourth to the left of second to the right of ma in Step III?
   (a) la (b) 62
   (c) fa (d) 42
8. How many steps will be required to complete the given arrangement?
   (a) Four (b) Five
   (c) Seven (d) Eight
9. How many elements (words or numbers) are there between 'fa' and '42' as they appear in the 4th step?
   (a) One (b) Eight
   (c) Six (d) Five
10. Which step number would be the following output?
    ba fa la ma qa za 75 62 51 42 31 16
    (a) Step V (b) Step II
    (c) Step VI (d) Step VII

Directions for Questions 11 to 15: *Study the given information and answer the questions:*

A word and number arrangement machine when given an input line of words and numbers rearrange them following a particular rule in each step. The following is an illustration of an input and rearrangement.

Input: more 11 rain 48 owe 29 donne 54 ban 35 bamm 36
Step I: bamm more rain 48 owe 29 donne 54 ban 35 36 12
Step II: 35 bamm more rain 48 owe 29 donne 54 35 12 ban
Step III: donne 35 bamm more rain 48 owe 54 35 12 ban 30
Step IV: 47 donne 35 bamm rain owe 54 35 12 ban 30 more
Step V: owe 47 donne 35 bamm rain 54 12 ban 30 more 36
Step VI: 53 owe 47 donne 35 bamm 12 ban 30 more 36 rain

And **Step VI** is the last step of the rearrangement of the above input.

As per the rules followed in the above steps, find out in each of the following questions the appropriate step for the given input.

Input: seneate 8 week 7 calf 24 not 29 sinchan 16 change 19

11. In which step are the elements "16 8 change" found in the same order?
    (a) Step I (b) Step II
    (c) Step III (d) Step V
12. In step IV, which of the following words would be at 6th to the left of the element which is 3rd from the right end?
    (a) Seneate (b) Calf
    (c) Week (d) None of these

13. How many steps are required to complete the above arrangement?
(a) III (b) IV
(c) VI (d) VII
14. Which of the following would be the step III after arrangement?
(a) seneate 24 not 7 calf week 16 8 change 20 sinchan 30
(b) seneate 23 not 7 calf week 16 8 change 21 sinchan 30
(c) seneate 23 not 7 calf week 16 8 change 20 sinchan 29
(d) None of these
15. What is the difference between the number which is third from left in Step IV and the number which is second from right in Step VI?
(a) 23 (b) 7
(c) 30 (d) 15

Directions for Questions 16 to 20: *Study the given information and answer the following questions:*

A word and number arrangement machine when given an input line of words and numbers rearranges them following a particular rule in each step. The following is an illustration of an input and rearrangement.

Input: mere 17 poor 48 on 29 counter 54 because 35 arrange 36

Step I: arrange mere poor 48 on 29 counter 54 because 35 36 18

Step II: 35 arrange mere poor 48 on 29 counter 54 35 18 because

Step III: counter 35 arrange mere poor 48 on 54 35 18 because 30

Step IV: 47 counter 35 arrange poor on 54 35 18 because 30 mere

Step V: on 47 counter 35 arrange poor 54 18 because 30 mere 36

Step VI: 53 on 47 counter 35 arrange 18 because 30 mere 36 poor

Step VI: is the last step of the rearrangement of the above input.

As per the rules followed in the above steps, find out in each of the following questions the appropriate step for the given input.

Input: throw 8 weed 7 bo 24 ne 29 sufficient 16 chaos 19

16. In which step are the elements "24 29 sufficient" found in the same order?
(a) Step I (b) Step II
(c) Step III (d) Step V
17. In step IV, which of the following words would be at 6th to the left of 3rd from the right end?
(a) 23 (b) bo
(c) 7 (d) None of these
18. How many steps are required for completing the above arrangement?
(a) Three (b) Four
(c) Six (d) Seven
19. Which of the following would be the step IV after arrangement?
(a) throw 24 ne 7 bo weed 16 8 chaos 20 sufficient 30
(b) throw 23 ne 7 bo weed 16 8 chaos 21 sufficient 30
(c) throw 23 ne 7 bo weed 16 8 chaos 20 sufficient 29
(d) 15 ne 7 bo throw weed 24 29 8 chaos 20 sufficient
20. What is the difference between the number which is third from left in Step IV and the number which is second from right in Step VI?
(a) 23 (b) 7
(c) 30 (d) 15

Directions for Questions 21 to 25: *When a word and number arrangement machine is given an input line of words and numbers, it arranges them following a particular rule. The following is an illustration of Input and rearrangement.*

Input: Stand 30 Worse Urge 41 52 Zoom 61 Xage 36 89 Veer

Step 1: Stand Urge 30 Worse 41 52 Zoom 61 Xage 36 89 Veer

Step 2: Stand Urge 89 61 30 Worse 41 52 Zoom Xage 36 Veer

Step 3: Stand Urge 89 61 Veer Worse 30 41 52 Zoom Xage 36

Step 4: Stand Urge 89 61 Veer Worse 52 41 30 Zoom Xage 36

Step 5: Stand Urge 89 61 Veer Worse 52 41 Xage Zoom 30 36

Step 6: Stand Urge 89 61 Veer Worse 52 41 Xage Zoom 36 30

Step 6: is the last step of the above input. As per the rules followed in the above step, find out the appropriate step for the given output.

Input: Oral 11 Micy 25 Pink 47 81 Pick 49 Vineet 16 Neenu

21. Which of the following term exactly comes between 49 and Pick in step 3?
(a) Pink (b) 11
(c) Vineet (d) Oral
22. How many elements are there between 25 and 47 in step 5?
(a) 0 (b) Three
(c) Two (d) Five

23. After step 6, if an additional step is introduced wherein from the output of step 6, Pick and Pink, 11 and 49 are interchanged. Then how many terms will be placed between Pick and 49?
(a) Two (b) Three
(c) Four (d) Six

24. What is the position of 25 from the left end in step 4?
(a) Eighth (b) Fourth
(c) Sixth (d) Fifth

25. Which of the following will be the 5th step of the given input?
(a) Micy Neenu 16 11 Oral Pick 25 47 Pink Vineet 49 81
(b) Pink Neenu 49 81 Pick Oral 47 25 Micy Vineet 16 11
(c) Micy Neenu 81 49 Oral Pick 25 47 Pink Vineet 11 16
(d) Micy Neenu 81 49 Oral Pick 47 25 Pink Vineet 11 16

Directions for Questions 26 to 30: *Study the following information to answer the given questions:*

A word and number arrangement machine when given an input line of words and numbers rearranges them following a particular rule in each step. The following is an illustration of input and rearrangement. (All the numbers are two-digit numbers and all are arranged as per some logic based on the value of the number.)

Input: toned 54 cort 61 to 71 laste 41 gallop 24
Step I: 41 54 cort 61 to 71 laste gallop 24 toned
Step II: 24 41 54 cort 61 to 71 gallop toned laste
Step III: 61 24 41 54 cort 71 gallop toned laste to
Step IV: 71 61 24 41 54 cort toned laste to gallop
Step V: 54 71 61 24 41 toned laste to gallop cort
Step V: is the last step of the arrangement the above input.

As per the rules followed in the above steps, find out in each of the following questions the appropriate steps for the given input.

Input: oyr 18 hts 71 btun 51 no 41 internet 25

26. In which step the elements "71 internet btun" are found in the same order?
(a) Step III (b) Step V
(c) Step I (d) Step II

27. Which of the following elements comes between 41 and 18, when there is only one element between them?
(a) 24 (b) oyr
(c) 51 (d) hts

28. In step II, which of the following element would be at 2nd to right of 4th from left position?
(a) hts (b) 71
(c) internet (d) 25

29. How many steps are required to complete the above arrangements?
(a) four (b) five
(c) six (d) seven

30. Which of the following is Step IV after the re-arrangement?
(a) 71 25 51 41 18 internet btun no oyr hts
(b) 25 51 41 18 hts 71 internet btunoyr no
(c) 51 25 41 18 hts 71 internet btun no oyr
(d) 25 41 51 18 hts 71 internet btun no oyr

Directions for Questions 31 to 34: *Answer the questions based on the following information.*

A number arrangement machine, when given a particular input, rearranges it following a particular rule. Illustrations of the input and the steps of arrangement are given below.

Input: 245, 316, 436, 519, 868, 710, 689
Step 1: 710, 316, 436, 519, 868, 245, 689
Step 2: 710, 316, 245, 519, 868, 436, 689
Step 3: 710, 316, 245, 436, 868, 519, 689
Step 4: 710, 316, 245, 436, 519, 868, 689
Step 4 is the last step for the given input.

31. If the input is given as "655, 436, 764, 799, 977, 572, 333", which of the following step will be "333, 436, 572, 655, 977, 764, 799"?
(a) Step 3 (b) Step 2
(c) Step 4 (d) None of the above

32. How many steps will be required to get the final output from the following input?
Input: 544, 653, 325, 688, 461, 231, 857
(a) 6 (b) 5
(c) 4 (d) None of the above

33. Step 3 for an input is "432, 433, 542, 666, 734, 355, 574" What will be the first step for the input?
(a) 666, 542, 432, 734, 433, 574, 355
(b) 542, 666, 734, 432, 433, 574, 355
(c) 355, 574, 433, 432, 734, 666, 542
(d) Can't be determined

34. What will be the third step for the following input?
Input: 653, 963, 754, 345, 364, 861, 541
A. 541, 345, 754, 963, 364, 816, 653
B. 541, 345, 364, 653, 963, 754, 861
C. 541, 345, 364, 963, 754, 861, 653
D. 541, 345, 364, 653, 861, 754, 963

ANSWER KEY

1. (c)	2. (d)	3. (a)	4. (c)
5. (d)	6. (c)	7. (c)	8. (b)
9. (b)	10. (a)	11. (c)	12. (b)

13. (c)	14. (d)	15. (a)	16. (c)
17. (b)	18. (c)	19. (d)	20. (a)
21. (d)	22. (a)	23. (a)	24. (a)
25. (d)	26. (a)	27. (b)	28. (b)
29. (b)	30. (a)	31. (a)	32. (b)
33. (d)	34. (c)		

SOLUTIONS AND SHORTCUTS

Solutions for Questions 1 to 5: The machine is creating an alphabetical order for the words - and simultaneously adding the number of letters to the word at the end of it. Also, words from the end are brought to the front (along with their attached numbers) if the alphabetical order suits them. The other move the machine makes is to re-arrange the alphabetical order of the words at the start in case, the words are not following the order.

Input: 6 prove hen 9 extreme following 4 rice 7 5 storme 3

Step I: storme 6 prove hen 9 extreme following 4 rice 7 5 3

Step II: rice 4 storme 6 prove hen 9 extreme following 7 5 3

Step III: prove 5 rice 4 storme 6 hen 9 extreme following 7 3

Step IV: hen 3 prove 5 rice 4 storme 6 9 extreme following 7

Step V: following 9 hen 3 prove 5 rice 4 storme 6 extreme 7

Step VI: extreme 7 following 9 hen 3 prove 5 rice 4 storme 6

1. (c)
2. (d)
3. (a)
4. (c)
5. (d)

Solutions for Questions 6 to 10: In this question, there are two alternate logics followed for words and numbers separately. For the Words arrangement, words are arranged according to alphabetical order (according to the English dictionary) from the left end, such that in the first step word with the lowest place value of the first letter is placed at the extreme left end and so on till the last step.

For number arrangement, numbers are arranged in decreasing order from the right end such that the highest number is placed to the extreme right in each step till the last step.

Input: ba qa fa 51 42 16 31 ma za la 62 75

Step I: ba fa qa 51 42 16 31 ma za la 75 62 (The words have started to get placed at the left end according to the alphabetical order; the numbers at the extreme right end have started to be arranged in descending order.)

Step II: ba fa la qa 42 16 31 ma za 75 62 51 (la comes after fa on the left side as the correct alphabetical order between the first three letters available amongst the words is b, f, l)

Step III: ba fa la ma qa 16 31 za 75 62 51 42

Step IV: ba fa la ma qa za 16 75 62 51 42 31

Step V: ba fa la ma qa za 75 62 51 42 31 16 (The arrangement is complete as the alphabetical order is complete as also the descending order for the numbers is complete)

The answers can be read off the above set of steps:

6. (c)
7. (c)
8. (b)
9. (b)
10. (a)

Solutions for Questions 11 to 15: If you read the machine outputs, the following are occurring. The words are sequentially arranged according to their alphabetical order - first word put at the extreme left, next word put at the extreme right. The process continues with alternate placing of words on the left side and the right side.

For the numbers, you first need to realize that there are three odd numbers and three even numbers.

The numbers on the other hand are being placed with changes in them. In the first step, the smallest odd number 11, is increased by 1 and placed on the extreme right. Next, the smallest even number 36 is placed on the extreme left with a decrease of 1 (thus, 36 becomes 35). The process is continued with odd numbers in increasing order (getting a +1) and going to the right end, while even numbers get a −1 and move to the extreme left. Based on these rules, the given input would go through the following steps:

Input: seneate 8 week 7 calf 24 not 29 sinchan 16 change 19

Step I: calf seneate 8 week 24 not 29 sinchan 16 change 19 8

Step II: 7 calf seneate week 24 not 29 sinchan 16 19 8 change

Step III: not 7 calf seneate week 24 29 sinchan 16 8 change 20

Step IV: 15 not 7 calf week 24 29 sinchan 8 change 20 seneate

Step V: sinchan 15 not 7 calf week 24 8 change 20 seneate 30

Step VI: 23 sinchan 15 not 7 calf 8 change 20 seneate 30 week

The answers can be read from the above outputs:

11. (c)
12. (b)

13. (c)
14. (d)
15. (a)

Solutions for Questions 16 to 20: You need to identify what is happening to the words and the numbers as the arrangement machine goes through its' steps. The words are sequentially arranged according to their alphabetical order - first word put at the extreme left, next word put at the extreme right. The process continues with alternate placing of words on the left side and the right side. Thus, 'arrange' goes to the extreme left first, followed by 'because' going to the extreme right next, then 'counter' moving to the extreme left and so on.

For the numbers, you first need to realize that there are three odd numbers and three even numbers.

The numbers on the other hand are being placed with changes in them. In the first step, the smallest odd number 11, is increased by 1 and placed on the extreme right. Next, the smallest even number 36 is placed on the extreme left with a decrease of 1 (thus, 36 becomes 35). The process is continued with odd numbers in increasing order (getting a +1) and going to the right end, while even numbers get a –1 and move to the extreme left. Based on these rules, the given input would go through the following steps:

Input: throw 8 weed 7 bo 24 ne 29 sufficient 16 chaos 19

Step I: bo throw 8 weed 24 ne 29 sufficient 16 chaos 19 8

Step II: 7 bo throw weed 24 ne 29 sufficient 16 19 8 chaos

Step III: ne 7 bo throw weed 24 29 sufficient 16 8 chaos 20

Step IV: 15 ne 7 bo throw weed 24 29 8 chaos 20 sufficient

Step V: throw 15 ne 7 bo weed 24 8 chaos 20 sufficient 30

Step VI: 23 throw 15 ne 7 bo 8 chaos 20 sufficient 30 weed

The answers can then be read off based on the above series of outputs:

16. (c)
17. (b)
18. (c)
19. (d)
20. (a)

Solutions for Questions 21 to 25: In step 1, two words are picked up and placed in the increasing alphabetical order at the left end of the arrangement. In step 2, two numbers are picked and arranged in the descending order, after the words that were arranged in the first step. Step 3, again sees two words picked and arranged next from the left side followed by 2 numbers in the descending order. The arrangement of the given input would go as follows:

Step 1: Micy Neenu Oral 11 25 Pink 47 81 Pick 49 Vineet 16

Step 2: Micy Neenu 81 49 Oral 11 25 Pink 47 Pick Vineet 16

Step 3: Micy Neenu 81 49 Oral Pick 11 25 Pink 47 Vineet 16

Step 4: Micy Neenu 81 49 Oral Pick 47 25 11 Pink Vineet 16

Step 5: Micy Neenu 81 49 Oral Pick 47 25 Pink Vineet 11 16

Step 6: Micy Neenu 81 49 Oral Pick 47 25 Pink Vineet 16 11

21. (d)
22. (a)
23. (a)
24. (a)
25. (d)

Solutions for Questions 26 to 30: In this arrangement, the words are taken to the extreme right and the numbers are taken to the extreme left. The words are arranged according to the last letter of each word. So, we have to see the last letter of each word while arranging the words.

For the number arrangement we have to add the sum of the digits of the given number and place them in the increasing order.

In the given input series last letter of given words are R, S, N, O and T. The alphabetical order of the letters are N, O, R, S, T. So the first word to be arranged from the right in step 1, should be 'btun' since it contains the letter 'n' as its last letter. The following steps would lead to the final output:

Input: oyr 18 hts 71 btun 51 no 41 internet 25

Step I: 41 oyr 18 hts 71 51 no internet 25 btun

Step II: 51 41 oyr 18 hts 71 internet 25 btun no

Step III: 25 51 41 18 hts 71 internet btun no oyr

Step IV: 71 25 51 41 18 internet btun no oyr hts

Step V: 18 71 25 51 41 btun no oyr hts internet

The answers can then be read off from the above steps.

26. (a)
27. (b)
28. (b)
29. (b)
30. (a)

Solutions for Questions 31 to 34: From the analysis of the input-output of the given string it is evident that what the machine is doing is essentially placing the numbers in such an order that the sum of digits of the numbers is placed from minimum to maximum. Also, it does so by first placing the number with the least sum of digits in the first place by switching its position with the first number in the string. The focus then shifts to put the number with the second least sum of digits in the second place and so on.

Based on an understanding of this logic we can solve the questions that follow based on the same logic.

31. 655, 436, 764, 799, 977, 572, 333 has sum of digits as 16, 13, 17, 25, 23, 14, 9.
    In the first step the string would become:
    655, 436, 764, 799, 977, 572, 333
    Step 1: 333, 436, 764, 799, 977, 572, 655
    Step 2: 333, 436, 572, 799, 977, 764, 655
    Step 3: 333, 436, 572, 655, 977, 764, 799
    which is the required string of numbers. Thus, the required step number is the third step.
32. 544, 653, 325, 688, 461, 231, 857 can be seen as: 13, 14, 10, 22, 11, 6, 20
    First step: 6, 14, 10, 22, 11, 13, 20
    Second step: 6, 10, 14, 22, 11, 13, 20
    Third step: 6, 10, 11, 22, 14, 13, 20
    Fourth step: 6, 10, 11, 13, 14, 22, 20
    Fifth step: 6, 10, 11, 13, 14, 20, 22.
33. The logic of this situation is such that the third step for an input as mentioned can be possible due to any of many possible inputs. Hence, answering this question definitively is not possible. Note that the question has asked, "What will be the first step of the input?" as against "what could be the first step of the input?" in which case it could have been one of the options which could have been checked to give us a third step as defined in the question.
34. 653, 963, 754, 345, 364, 861, 541 can be seen as 14, 18, 16, 12, 13, 15, 10 if we look at the sum of digits of the numbers. Then we have:
    First step: 10, 18, 16, 12, 13, 15, 14
    Second step: 10, 12, 16, 18, 13, 15, 14
    Third step: 10, 12, 13, 18, 16, 15, 14
    which means:
    541, 345, 364, 963, 754, 861, 653.
    Option (c) is the correct answer.

CHAPTER 11

Syllogisms

Chapter Launchpad

Scan this QR code for an introductory video on Syllogisms

SYLLOGISMS—THEORY

Syllogisms can be defined as a deductive scheme under which a formal argument is made. It consists of a major and a minor premise, leading up to a conclusion.

For example, let us look at the following example:

Major Premise: Every crime is deplorable;

Minor Premise: Eve teasing is a crime;

Conclusion: Eve teasing is deplorable.

Questions based on syllogisms always first state the premises and then ask you to derive the conclusion on the basis of the relationship existing between the different elements of the premises.

The best method for solving syllogisms involves the use of Venn Diagrams. We will first look at the main types of premises and then look in detail at the process to be used to solve questions of syllogisms.

PREMISES—VARIOUS PATTERNS

A premise is defined as a proposition antecedently supposed or proved as a basis of argument or inference. In other words: something assumed or taken for granted.

Type 1: All As are Bs (Or No A is not B):

There are two possible Venn diagrams for this situation. These are:

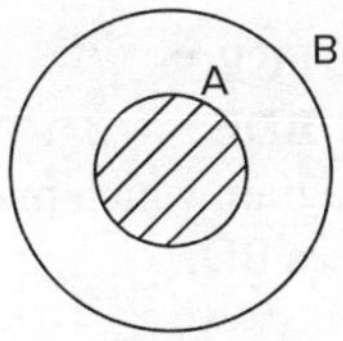

Figure A

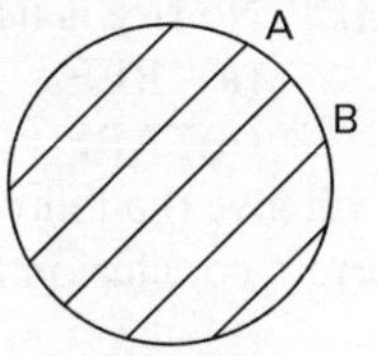

Figure B

The following reactions to the premise *All As are Bs* are valid:

(a) *Some Bs are As.* This is a definite conclusion. This is true in both Figures A and B.

(b) *Some Bs are not As.* This is a probable conclusion and will occur only if the conclusion *All Bs are As* is not true.

Hence, it can be stated that if *All As are Bs*, then either *All Bs are As* (No B is Not A) or Some B's are not As. As can be seen in the figures above, either *Some Bs are not As* (Figure A) or *All Bs are As* (as seen in Figure B).

Type 2: Some A's are B's

This premise is represented by the following figure:

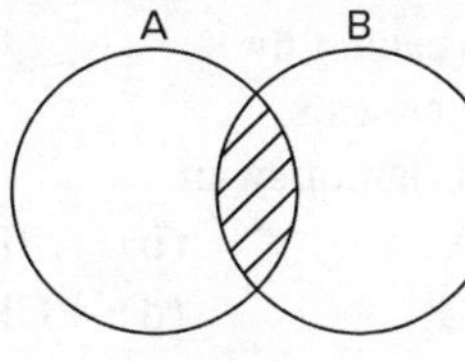

Figure A

The valid reaction to this premise is:

Some Bs are As

This is a definite conclusion (as can be seen clearly in figure A above.)

Although the above figure also supports the conclusion –some Bs are not As, this cannot be taken as a definite conclusion. This is because, when we say that *Some As are Bs,* it does not mean that there have to be some Bs that are not As.

Type 3: No A is B

This premise is represented by the following figure:

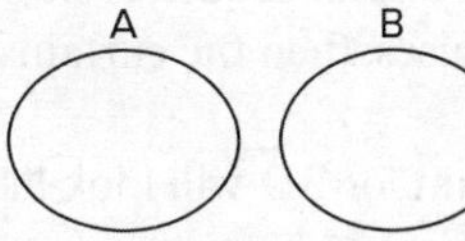

Figure A

The conclusion *No B is A* is a valid conclusion.

Type 4: Some As are not Bs (Or All As is not Bs)

There could be three possible Venn Diagrams in this case, as shown below:

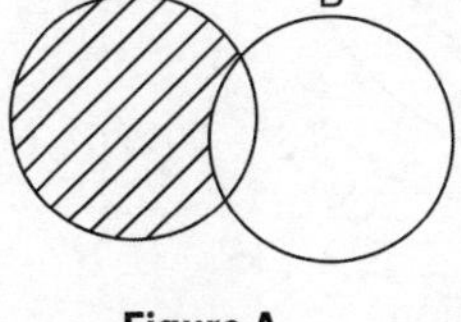

Figure A

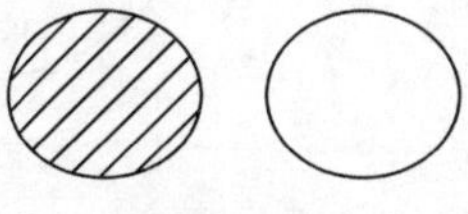

Figure B

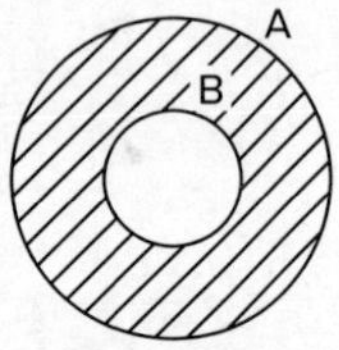

Figure C

STANDARD PROCESS FOR SOLVING SYLLOGISM QUESTIONS

The most logical process of solving Syllogism questions is through Venn diagrams. The following examples will make the process clear:

Example 1:

1. **(A) All tigers lay eggs**
   (B) All cats lay eggs
   (C) Some cats can fly
   (D) All tigers cannot fly
   (E) All tigers are cats
   (F) All tigers cannot swim
   (a) BEA (b) ABE
   (c) DEC (d) ECB

   In the above question, it can be clearly seen that the sequence BEA is the most appropriate since if all cats lay eggs is true and it is also true that all tigers are cats, then it will also be true that all tigers lay eggs.

2. **(A)** Some curtains are cloth
   (B) All cloth is wood
   (C) All that is wood is cloth
   (D) All cloth are curtains
   (E) All curtains are wood
   (F) Some curtains are wood
   (a) BED (b) BDF
   (c) FAB (d) FBA

BDF is the most logical sequence here since if we take B and D as the premises, then the curtains which are cloth, will also be wood.

The Venn Diagram for BD will look like this–

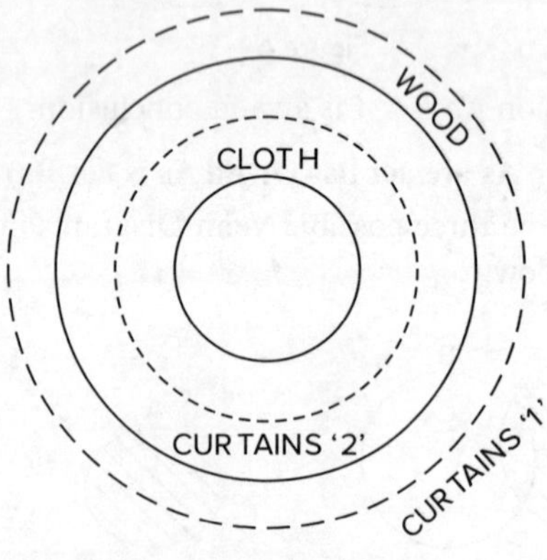

Hence, F is the correct conclusion.

3. **(A)** All balls are talls
   (B) Some talls are dolls
   (C) Some dolls are balls
   (D) Some talls are not balls
   (E) All talls are dolls
   (F) No talls are dolls
   (a) EAC (b) BCD
   (c) ABC (d) EDC

EA will give the following figure which will give C as the conclusion. Hence, the answer is (a).

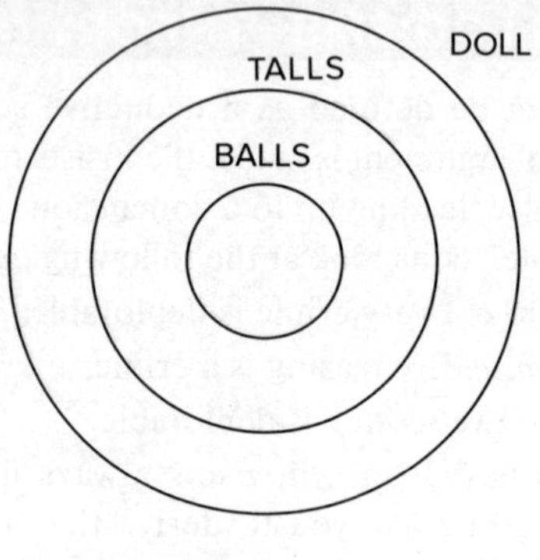

4. **(A)** Some stone is bone
   (B) All slipper is bone
   (C) All bone is stone
   (D) No stone is slipper
   (E) No bone is stone
   (F) Some bone is slipper
   (a) BCA (b) AFE
   (c) DEC (d) CEA

(A) is the obvious answer here, since if all bone is stone (C), then obviously, some stone is bone (A).

5. **(A)** No rice is a pest
   (B) All pest is lice
   (C) Some rice is lice
   (D) All rice is pest
   (E) All rice is lice
   (F) No rice is lice
   (a) BEF (b) FCB
   (c) ABF (d) BDE

BDE will give the following Venn Diagram which makes E the correct conclusion for the premises BD.

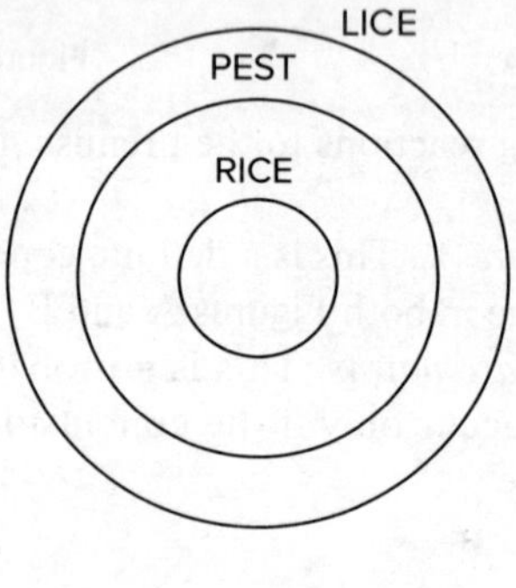

6. For this question, you have to base your conclusion on the three premises (viz: a, b and c). Identify the correct answer from amongst the options given to you:

Statements: **a.** Some cakes are bikes
b. Some bikes are hills
c. All laptops are bikes

Conclusions: **I.** All laptops are hills
II. Some laptops are cakes
III. Some cakes are hills
IV. Some laptops are not cakes

(a) Only I follows
(b) Only either II or IV follows
(c) Only I or III follow
(d) Only I and IV follows
(e) None of these

For the question above, the following Venn Diagram can be drawn:

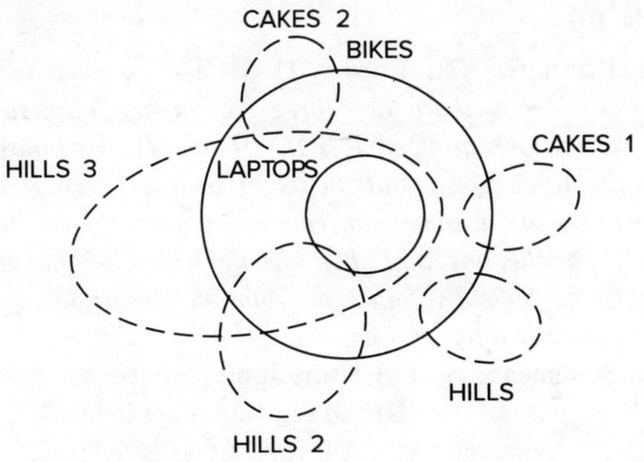

It is clear from the figure that the conclusion 'All Laptops are Hills' does not hold.

Similarly, some Cakes are hills is also not necessarily true. If we take a look at II & IV, we can conclude that one of them has to be true. Hence, the answer is (b).

7. **(A)** No hyenas laugh. Some who laugh are lions. Some lions are not hyenas.
(B) All ghosts are red. Some ghosts do not dance. Some dancers are not red.
(C) Australians indulge in swearing. Those who swear are fined. Some who are fined are not Australians.
(D) Some Europeans are Spanish. All Europeans are British. Some British are Spanish.

(a) A and B (b) Only C
(c) A and D (d) Only D

The following Venn Diagram can made for the sequence A:

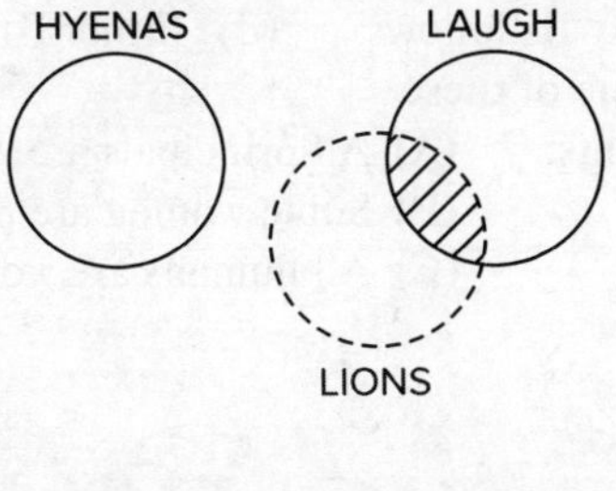

Obviously, the lions who laugh are not hyenas. Hence, the conclusion is justified.

The following Venn Diagram will be made for the sequence D:

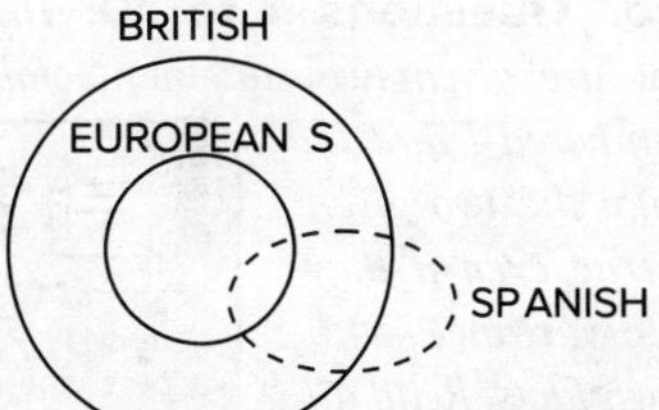

It is obvious that whatever circle we draw for Spanish (apart from the one shown) it will have to intersect the circle for Europeans. This in effect, means that, it has also to intersect with the British circle. Hence, the conclusion that 'Some British are Spanish' is justified.

8. **(A)** All Pakistanis are brave. All baskets are Pakistanis: All brave are baskets.
(B) No golfers are Asian. All golfers are athletic. Some Asians are pros.
(C) All burgers are chips. Some refreshments are burgers. Some refreshments are chips.
(D) Some bowlers are fast. All bowlers are spinners. Some spinners are fast.

(a) C and D (b) B and C
(c) Only A (d) Only C

The following Venn Diagram can be made for the sequence C:

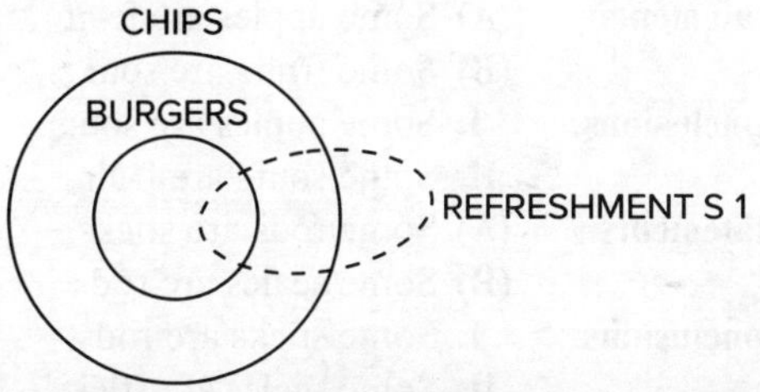

The conclusion for C is justified in exactly the same way as the one for the sequence D of Solved Example 7.

The following Venn Diagram can be made for sequence D:

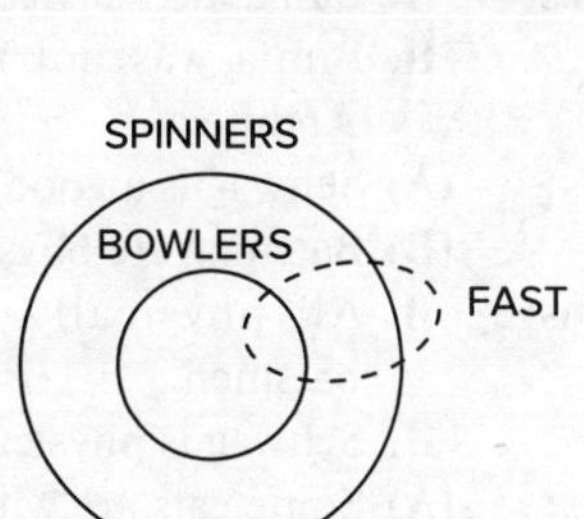

As is clear from the diagram above, the conclusion is justified on the basis of the same logic as for the last two diagrams.

EXERCISE

TYPE (I)

Directions for Questions 1 to 10: *In each of the questions below are given two statements followed by two conclusions numbered I and II. You have to take the two given statements as true even if they seem to be at variance with commonly known facts. Read all the conclusions and then decide which of the given conclusions logically follow(s) from the given statements, disregarding commonly known facts.*

High Yield Questions

Scan this QR code to access video explanations of questions 1, 3, 7, 13, 15, 51, 53 and 71

Give answers **(a)** *If only conclusion I follows*
(b) *If only conclusion II follows*
(c) *If either I or II follows*
(d) *If neither I nor II follows*
(e) *If both follow*

1. Statements: **(A)** All cats are dogs
(B) All dogs are brown
Conclusions: **I.** All cats are brown
II. All brown are dogs

2. Statements: **(A)** All computers are pentiums
(B) Some pentiums are machines
Conclusions: **I.** Some computers are machines
II. Some machines are computers

3. Statements: **(A)** Some apples are fruit
(B) Some fruits are sour
Conclusions: **I.** Some apples are sour
II. Some sours are fruit

4. Statements: **(A)** Some rods are sticks
(B) Some scales are rods
Conclusions: **I.** Some sticks are rods
II. Some scales are sticks

5. Statements: **(A)** Architects marry only fair girls
(B) Bimla is very fair
Conclusions: **I.** Bimla was married to an Architect
II. Bimla was not married to an Architect

6. Statements: **(A)** Sehwag is a good batsman
(B) Batsmen are physically powerful
Conclusions: **I.** All physically powerful are batsmen
II. Sehwag is physically powerful

7. Statements: **(A)** Some cats are white
(B) Milk is white
Conclusions: **I.** Some cat is milk
II. Some white is milk

8. Statements: **(A)** All pens are long
(B) All pencils are long
Conclusions: **I.** All pens are pencils
II. Some pens are pencils

9. Statements: **(A)** All resorts have scenery
(B) Mahabaleshwar is a resort
Conclusions: **I.** Mahabaleshwar has scenery
II. Places other than resorts don't have scenery

10. Statements: **(A)** All teenagers go to cinema
(B) Raveesh doesn't go to cinema
Conclusions: **I.** Raveesh is not a teenager
II. Going to cinema is not essential to be a teenager

TYPE (II)

Directions for Questions 11 to 50: *In each of the questions below there are three statements followed by four conclusions numbered I, II, III and IV. You have to take the three given statements to be true even if they seem to be at variance with commonly known facts. Read all the conclusions and then decide which of the given conclusions logically follow(s) from the given statements disregarding commonly known facts.*

11. Statements: **(A)** Some apples are fruits
(B) All vegetables are fruits
(C) All fruits are vegetables
Conclusions: **I.** Some apples are vegetables
II. All vegetables are fruits
III. All fruits are apples
IV. All vegetables are apples

(a) Only I and II follow
(b) Only II follows
(c) Only I and IV follow
(d) Only II and IV follow
(e) None of these

12. Statements: **(A)** Some cars are four wheelers
(B) All four wheelers are vehicles
(C) Some vehicles are SUVs
Conclusions: **I.** Some SUVs are four wheelers
II. Some vehicles are four wheelers
III. Some vehicles are cars
IV. Some SUVs are cars

(a) All follow (b) Only II & III follow
(c) Only III follows (d) Either III or IV follows
(e) None of these

13. Statements: **(A)** All principals are men
(B) Some women are principals
(C) All humans are women

Conclusions: **I.** All humans are men
II. Some humans are principals
III. Some men are principals
IV. All women are men

(a) Only I follows
(b) Only II follows
(c) Only I and III follow
(d) Only III follows
(e) None of these

14. Statements: **(A)** Most architects are writers
(B) No writer is a driver
(C) All drivers are architects

Conclusions: **I.** Some writers are architects
II. All architects are drivers
III. No driver is a writer
IV. Some drivers are writers

(a) Only I follows
(b) Only II and III follow
(c) Only I and III follow
(d) Either III or IV follows
(e) None of these

15. Statements: **(A)** All registers are books
(B) All books are written materials
(C) All written materials are novels

Conclusions: **I.** All books are novels
II. All written materials are registers
III. All registers are novels
IV. All novels are books

(a) Only I and II follow
(b) Only II and III follow
(c) Only I and III follow
(d) All follow
(e) None of these

16. Statements: **(A)** Some cats are animals
(B) Some animals are mammals
(C) Some mammals are earthlings

Conclusions: **I.** Some earthlings are cats
II. Some mammals are cats
III. Some earthlings are animals
IV. Some cats are earthlings

(a) None follow
(b) All follow
(c) Only I and II follow
(d) Only II and IV follow
(e) Only III and IV follow

17. Statements: **(A)** No apple is mango
(B) All mangoes are fruits
(C) All fruits are vegetarian

Conclusions: **I.** No fruit is apple
II. No vegetarian is apple
III. Some vegetarians are mango
IV. Some vegetarians are apples

(a) None follows
(b) All follow
(c) Either II or IV and III follow
(d) Either II or III and I follow
(e) None of these

18. Statements: **(A)** All pens are pencils
(B) Some pencils are markers
(C) All markers are ball points

Conclusions: **I.** Some markers are pens
II. Some ball points are pencils
III. Some ball points are pens
IV. Some pencils are pens

(a) None follows
(b) Only I and III follows
(c) All follows
(d) Only II and IV follows
(e) None of these

19. Statements: **(A)** Some dogs are cats
(B) Some cats are hounds
(C) Some hounds are animals

Conclusions: **I.** Some animals are dogs
II. Some hounds are dogs
III. Some animals are cats
IV. No animals are cats

(a) None follows
(b) Only III follows
(c) Only either I or IV and III follows
(d) Only either I or IV and II follows
(e) None of these

20. Statements: **(A)** All leaves are fruits
(B) No fruit is vegetable
(C) All vegetables are panthers

Conclusions: **I.** Some fruits are leaves
II. All fruits are leaves
III. Some panthers are vegetables
IV. All panthers are vegetables

(a) Only II and IV follow
(b) Only either I or II follow
(c) Only either III or IV follows
(d) All follow
(e) None of these

21. Statements: **(A)** Some panthers are cats
(B) All cats are mammals
(C) Some mammals are not panthers

Conclusions: **I.** Some mammals are panthers
II. All panthers are mammals
III. All cats are panthers
IV. All mammals are panthers

(a) None follows
(b) Only I follows
(c) Only I and II follow
(d) Only II and III follow
(e) All follow

22. **Statements:** **(A)** Some young are boys
(B) All boys are actors
(C) Some actors are cars
Conclusions: **I.** Some actors are young
II. Some cars are young
III. Some cars are boys
IV. Some boys are young
(a) None follows (b) Only IV follows
(c) Only I follows (d) Both I and IV follow
(e) None of these

23. **Statements:** **(A)** All actors are males
(B) Some artists are males
(C) All singers are artists
Conclusions: **I.** Some artists are actors
II. Some singers are males
III. Some males are actors
IV. No singers are male
(a) Only either II or IV and III follow
(b) Only either II or IV and I follow
(c) Only either I or II and IV follow
(d) None follows
(e) None of these

24. **Statements:** **(A)** All cats are drakes
(B) No drake is a mare
(C) All mares are animals
Conclusions: **I.** No cat is a mare
II. Some animals are mares
III. Some drakes are cats
IV. Some cats are mares
(a) All follow
(b) Only either I or II and both III and IV follow
(c) Only either I or IV and both II and III follow
(d) Only either I or IV and II follow
(e) None of these

25. **Statements:** **(A)** Some cars are vehicles
(B) Some vehicles are machines
(C) Some machines are mechanics
Conclusions: **I.** Some mechanics are machines
II. Some vehicles are cars
III. Some machines are cars
IV. Some mechanics are vehicles
(a) All follow
(b) Only I and II follow
(c) Only III and IV follow
(d) Only I and IV follow
(e) None follows

26. **Statements:** **(A)** All desks are boards
(B) All boards are flat
(C) All flats are white
Conclusions: **I.** All whites are desks
II. All boards are white
III. Some whites are flat
IV. Some flats are desks
(a) All follows
(b) Only I, II and IV follow
(c) Only III and IV follow
(d) II, III and IV follow
(e) None of these

27. **Statements:** **(A)** Some opels are televisions
(B) Some televisions are bulbs
(C) All tubes are bulbs
Conclusions: **I.** Some opels are tubes
II. Some opels are bulbs
III. No tube is opel
IV. All bulbs are tubes
(a) None follows
(b) Both III and II follow
(c) Only either II or III follows
(d) Only either I or III follows
(e) Only either I or IV follows

28. **Statements:** **(A)** Some trains are cars
(B) All cars are rivers
(C) Some roads are rivers
Conclusions: **I.** Some rivers are trains
II. Some roads are trains
III. Some roads are cars
IV. Some rivers are roads
(a) Both I and IV follows
(b) Only I and II follow
(c) Only either I or III follows
(d) Only either II or III follows
(e) Only either I or IV follows

29. **Statements:** **(A)** All cats are Lions
(B) Some lions are mice
(C) All mice are giraffes
Conclusions: **I.** Some mice are cats
II. Some giraffes are lions
III. Some giraffes are cats
IV. Some giraffes are mice
(a) Only I and II follow
(b) Only I and III follow
(c) Only II and III follow
(d) Both II and IV follow
(e) None of these

30. **Statements:** **(A)** All pencils are pens
(B) No pens are markers
(C) All markers are drawings
Conclusions: **I.** No pencil is a marker
II. No pencil is a drawing
III. Some drawings are pens
IV. Some markers are pencils
(a) Only I follows
(b) Only I and II follow
(c) Only II and III follow
(d) Only III and IV follow
(e) None of these

31. **Statements:** **(A)** Some apples are flowers
(B) No flower is a papaya
(C) All papayas are baskets
Conclusions: **I.** Some apples are baskets
II. Some baskets are papayas
III. Some baskets are apples
IV. Some flowers are apples
(a) All follow
(b) None follows
(c) Only II and IV follow
(d) Only II and III follow
(e) None of these

32. **Statements:** **(A)** Some cars are horses
(B) All horses are guns
(C) All guns are cows
Conclusions: **I.** Some cows are cars
II. Some cows are horses
III. Some cows are guns
IV. Some cars are guns
(a) None follows
(b) Only I and II follow
(c) Only II and III follow
(d) Only III and IV follow
(e) All follow

33. **Statements:** **(A)** Some desks are apartments
(B) All apartments are cars
(C) Some cars are trucks
Conclusions: **I.** Some desks are trucks
II. Some desks are cars
III. Some cars are apartments
IV. No truck is a desk
(a) None follows
(b) Only II and III follow
(c) Either only I or II, III and IV follow
(d) Either only I or IV, and II and III follow
(e) All follow

34. **Statements:** **(A)** All cats are cows
(B) All horses are cows
(C) Some cows are bulls
Conclusions: **I.** Some cats are horses
II. Some horses are bulls
III. Some bulls are cats
IV. All bulls are cows
(a) None follows
(b) Only I follows
(c) Only I and III follow
(d) Only II and IV follow
(e) All follow

35. **Statements:** **(A)** Some cats are elephants
(B) No elephant is river
(C) All rivers are roads
Conclusions: **I.** No cat is river
II. Some roads are rivers
III. Some elephants are cat
IV. Some cats are rivers
(a) Only I and II follow
(b) Either I or IV and II and III follow
(c) Only either I or IV and III follow
(d) Only I, II and III follow
(e) None of these

36. **Statements:** **(A)** All mirrors are phones
(B) Some phones are gadgets
(C) All gadgets are mirrors
Conclusions: **I.** Some gadgets are phones
II. Some gadgets are mirrors
III. Some gadgets are not mirrors
IV. Some mirrors are phones
(a) None follows
(b) I, II and IV follow
(c) Only II and III follow
(d) Either II or IV follows
(e) None of these

37. **Statements:** **(A)** No proud is animal
(B) Some sheeps are animals
(C) All cats are sheeps
Conclusions: **I.** No cat is proud
II. Some cats are animals
III. No animal is cat
IV. Some prouds are sheeps
(a) Only III follows
(b) Only either II or III follows
(c) Only I follows
(d) Only I and either II or III follow
(e) None of these

38. **Statements:** **(A)** All grapes are apples
(B) All papayas are apples
(C) Some apples are mangoes
Conclusions: **I.** No grape is mango
II. Some papayas are not mangoes
III. Some grapes are papayas
IV. All mangoes are grapes
(a) Only I follows
(b) Either I or III follows
(c) Only II and III follow
(d) Only I, II and III follow
(e) None of these

39. **Statements:** **(A)** Some bats are rackets
(B) Some rackets are bats
(C) Some bats are balls
Conclusions: **I.** Some balls are bats
II. Some balls are not bats
III. No racket is ball
IV. No bat is ball

(a) Only I and IV follow
(b) Only II follows
(c) Only I and III follow
(d) Only I follows
(e) None of these

40. Statements: **(A)** All stereos are cds
(B) Some stereos are cassettes
(C) Some cds are pens

Conclusions: **I.** Some pens are stereos
II. Some cds are cassettes
III. Some pens are cassettes
IV. All stereos are pens

(a) Either I or IV follows
(b) Only II and III follow
(c) Either I or IV and II follow
(d) Only II follows
(e) None of these

41. Statements: **(A)** Some sacks are backs
(B) All backs are bones
(C) No bone is muscle

Conclusions: **I.** Some sacks are not muscles
II. Some sacks are not bones
III. All sacks are bones
IV. No sack is muscle

(a) Only I follows
(b) None follows
(c) Only IV follows
(d) I and either II or III follow
(e) None of these

42. Statements: **(A)** All rackets are jackets
(B) No cow is cat
(C) Only cats are dogs

Conclusions: **I.** Some rackets are not cats
II. Some cats are jackets
III. Some rackets are cats
IV. No dog is a cow

(a) Only either I or II and IV follow
(b) Only II and IV follow
(c) Only III and IV follow
(d) Only I and IV follow
(e) None of these

43. Statements: **(A)** All stairs are lifts
(B) No lift is an escalator
(C) Some escalators are helicopters
(D) Some lifts are planes

Conclusions: **I.** No stairs is an escalator
II. Some helicopters are not escalators
III. Some stairs are planes
IV. Some helicopters are escalators

(a) Only I and either II or IV follow
(b) Only I and IV follow
(c) Either II or IV follows
(d) Only I, III or IV follows
(e) None of these

44. Statements: **(A)** All boxes are cartons
(B) All cartons are packages
(C) Some packages are letters
(D) No box is a parcel

Conclusions: **I.** All boxes are packages
II. Some boxes are not cartons.
III. All packages are letters.
IV. Some packages are not letters.

(a) Only I and either III or IV follow
(b) Only I, II and either III or IV follow
(c) Only I and II follow
(d) Only I follows
(e) None of these

45. Statements: **(A)** Most bulls are cows.
(B) No bull is horse.
(C) All horses are cows.

Conclusions: **I.** Some cows are not horses.
II. All cows are not horses.
III. Some bulls are cows.
IV. Some bulls are not horses.

(a) Only II, III and IV follow
(b) Either I or II and III and IV follow
(c) Only I, III and IV follow
(d) All follow
(e) None of these

46. Statements: **(A)** Many perfumes are diamonds.
(B) All aspirins are powder.
(C) No perfume is powder.

Conclusions: **I.** Some diamonds are not powders.
II. Some diamonds are powders.
III. No aspirins are perfume.
IV. Some diamonds are not aspirins.

(a) Only I, III and IV follow
(b) Either I or II and III and IV follow
(c) Only III and IV follow
(d) Only I and IV follow
(e) None of these

47. Statements: **(A)** All bulls are bells.
(B) Some bulls are cows.
(C) Some bells are chairs.

Conclusions: **I.** Some cows are chairs.
II. Some bells are bulls.
III. All bells are cow.
IV. All bells are bulls.

(a) All follow
(b) None follows
(c) Only II follows
(d) Only II and III follow
(e) None of these

48. **Statements:** **(A)** Some cakes are bikes
(B) Some bikes are hills
(C) All laptops are bikes
Conclusions: **I.** All laptops are hills
II. Some laptops are cakes
III. Some cakes are hills
IV. Some laptops are not cakes
(a) Only I follows
(b) Only either II or IV follows
(c) Only I or III follows
(d) Only I and IV follows
(e) None of these

49. **Statements:** **(A)** Some pots are pans
(B) Some pans are cookers
(C) Some cookers are rafts
Conclusions: **I.** Some rafts are pans
II. Some cookers are pots
III. Some rafts are pans
IV. Some pots are cookers
(a) All follow
(b) None follows
(c) Only I and III follow
(d) Only II and IV follow
(e) None of these

50. **Statements:** **(A)** Most chairs are tables
(B) No chairs are trolleys
(C) All trolleys are tables
Conclusions: **I.** Some tables are not trolleys
II. All tables are not trolleys
III. Some chairs are tables
IV. Some chairs are not trolleys
(a) Only II, III and IV follow
(b) Either I or II, III and IV follow
(c) Only I, III and IV follow
(d) All follow
(e) None of these

TYPE (III)

Directions for Questions 51 to 70: *Each question contains six statements, followed by four options of combinations of any three of the given sentences. Choose the option in which the combinations are logically related*

51. **(A)** All Martians eat sausages
(B) All those who eat sausages are not Martians
(C) All those who eat sausages are herbivorous
(D) All Martians are carnivorous
(E) All those who eat sausages are carnivorous
(F) Martians are herbivorous
(a) BCE (b) ABE
(c) ACD (d) ACF

52. **(A)** All lotuses have flowers
(B) All lotuses have nectar
(C) All plants with nectar have flowers
(D) All shrubs have lotuses
(E) All shrubs have nectar
(F) Some lotuses have flowers
(a) BEF (b) BCF
(c) BDE (d) ACF

53. **(A)** No summer is a season
(B) Some seasons are summers
(C) Some seasons are winters
(D) No seasons are winters
(E) Some summers are not winters
(F) All summers are winters
(a) DFA (b) BEF
(c) CEB (d) DEB

54. **(A)** All falcons fly high
(B) All falcons are blind
(C) All falcons are birds
(D) All birds are yellow
(E) All birds are thirsty
(F) All falcons are yellow
(a) ABC (b) CDF
(c) DEF (d) BCA

55. **(A)** No nails are wires
(B) Some hooks are wires
(C) All hooks are nails
(D) Some wires are not nails
(E) No wire is a hook
(F) All nails are hooks
(a) AED (b) BCF
(c) BEF (d) ACE

56. **(A)** Some dabba are cobra
(B) All dabba are chabi
(C) All cobra are dabba
(D) All cobra are not dabba
(E) Some chabi are dabba
(F) Some chabi are cobra
(a) AEF (b) BCF
(c) ABD (d) BCE

57. **(A)** No train is a claim
(B) All heads are claims
(C) No head is a train
(D) Some heads are not trains
(E) Some trains are heads
(F) Some claims are not trains
(a) ACD (b) ADF
(c) ABC (d) CDF

58. **(A)** All balls are Barbie
(B) All bats are Barbie
(C) All bats are balls
(D) Some bats are Barbie
(E) Some Barbie are balls
(F) No ball is Barbie

(a) CDE (b) CEF
(c) ACD (d) BEF

59. **(A)** Some apartments are not multistories
(B) Some multistories are not apartments
(C) No house is a skyscraper
(D) All multistories are houses
(E) Some multistories are apartments
(F) Some houses are not apartments
(a) ACE (b) BDF
(c) FDA (d) ACF

60. **(A)** All bows are arrows
(B) No arrow is a casket.
(C) No bow is a casket
(D) Some caskets are arrows
(E) Some bows are caskets
(F) No casket is a bow
(a) BDE (b) ACB
(c) CDF (d) ABF

61. **(A)** Some soaps are not shampoos
(B) Some shampoos are not soaps
(C) No oil is shampoo.
(D) All shampoos are oils
(E) Some shampoos are soaps
(F) Some who are oils are not soaps
(a) ACF (b) DEF
(c) ABC (d) BDF

62. **(A)** Some humans are late
(B) All humans are bad
(C) All late things are humans
(D) All late things are bad
(E) Some bad things are humans
(F) Some bad things are late
(a) AFE (b) BCF
(c) BCA (d) BCE

63. **(A)** All Shomes are bright
(B) No bright Shomes are Bands
(C) Some Shomes are Bands
(D) Some Bands are bright
(E) No Tom is a Band
(F) No Band is a Shome
(a) ABC (b) BEF
(c) ABF (d) CDA

64. **(A)** All sorcerors are hasty
(B) Some daredevils are hasty
(C) All sorcerors are daredevils
(D) All daredevils are hasty
(E) Some hasty are daredevils
(F) No sorceror is pasty
(a) BCD (b) CDA
(c) DEC (d) FEC

65. **(A)** No mango is a lingo
(B) All tangos are lingos
(C) No tango is a mango
(D) Some tangos are not mangoes
(E) Some mangoes are tangos
(F) Some lingos are not mangoes
(a) ABC (b) ACB
(c) DFA (d) BDA

66. **(A)** Some irons are made of steel
(B) All steel is made of copper
(C) All copper is used for making irons
(D) Some steel is copper
(E) Some irons are used for steel
(F) Some copper is used for steel
(a) ABC (b) CEF
(c) CDA (d) ABE

67. **(A)** No tiger is carnivorous
(B) All animals are carnivorous
(C) Cats are carnivorous
(D) No cat is a tiger
(E) No tiger is an animal
(F) All cats are animals
(a) ADC (b) ABE
(c) FBA (d) AFC

68. **(A)** No brother is a pro
(B) Some pros like to work
(C) No Indian is rude
(D) Some rude are pros
(E) Some pro are Indians
(F) All Indians like to work
(a) ABE (b) CED
(c) FEB (d) BEF

69. **(A)** Apples are fruits
(B) All apples are pears
(C) Some fruits are pears
(D) Some apples are pears
(E) All fruits are sweet
(F) Some pears are sweet
(a) DAC (b) CDA
(c) BCA (d) EFC

70. **(A)** Santros are RIMs
(B) Santros are cars
(C) RIMs are cars
(D) Fords are cars
(E) RIMs are Fords
(F) Fords are stable
(a) ACB (b) FED
(c) CEA (d) ABC

TYPE (IV)

Directions for Questions 71 to 97: *Each question contains four arguments of three sentences each. Choose the set in which the third statement is a logical conclusion of the first two.*

71. I. Some Xs are Ps. Some Ps are Ys. Some Xs are Ys
II. All Chandis are beautiful. Some beautiful are crazy. Some Chandis are crazy
III. No belief is strong. Only strong have muscles. No belief has muscles
IV. All orangutans are men. Some men are strong. Some orangutans are strong
(a) I and IV (b) Only III
(c) Only IV (d) None of these

72.
I. Some bikes are mopeds. All mopeds are scooters. Some bikes are scooters
II. All children are hairs. No hairs are red. No children are red
III. No pencil is pen. Some pens are markers. Some pencils are markers
IV. Every man has a wife. All wives are devoted. No devoted has a husband
(a) I, II and III (b) I and II
(c) III and II (d) I, II and III and IV

73.
I. No moon is not red. All stars are moon. All stars are red
II. All doors are open. No open is outdoors. All doors are not outdoors
III. No Japanese can fire. All Chinese are books. Japanese and Chinese can fire
IV. No A is B. No B is C. No A is C.
(a) Only I (b) Only II
(c) I and II only (c) Only IV

74.
I. All envelopes are rectangles. All rectangles are rectangular. All envelopes are rectangular
II. Some thin are smart. Some smart things are tiny. Some thin are tiny
III. Learneds are well read. Well read know. Learneds know.
IV. Dieting is good for health. Health foods are rare. Dieting is rare
(a) Only IV (b) Only III
(c) Both I and III (d) All of these

75.
I. Shahrukh is an actor. Some actors are pretty. Shahrukh is pretty
II. Some executives are soldiers. All soldiers are patriotic. Some executives are patriotic
III. All cricketers are patriotic. Some executives are soldiers. Some executives are patriotic
IV. All actors are pretty. Shahrukh is not an actor. Shahrukh is not pretty
(a) Only IV (b) Only II
(c) Only I (d) II and III

76. **Statements:** I. Some Cats are bats
II. All bats are rats
III. All tables are cats
IV. All mats are tables
Conclusions:
(a) Some Mats are Rats
(b) Some Tables are Bats
(c) Some Cats are Rats
(d) None of these

77. **Statements:** Some ships are boats. All boats are submarines. Some submarines are yatches
Conclusion: I. Some yatches are boats
II. Some submarines are boats
III. Some submarines are ships
IV. Some yatches are ships
(a) All follow (b) Only II and III follow
(c) Only III follows (d) Only IV follows

78. All Animals are birds. Some parrots are Animals. All crows are parrot
Conclusion: I. All crows are birds
II. Some crows are birds
III. Some birds are parrot
IV. All parrot are birds
(a) Only I follows
(b) Only II follows
(c) Only I and III follow
(d) Only III follows

79. **Statements:** Most CPUs are keyboards. No keyboard is a Mouse. All Mouses are CPU
Conclusion:
I. Some keyboards are CPU
II. All CPU's are Mouse
III. No Mouse is a keyboard
IV. Some Mouse are keyboard
(a) Only I follows
(b) Only II and III follow
(c) Only I and III follow
(d) Only II follows

80. **Statements:** A are B. All B are C. All C are D
Conclusion: I. All B are D
II. All C are A
III. All A are D
IV. All D are B
(a) Only I and II follow
(b) Only I and III follow
(c) Only II and III follow
(d) All follow

81. Statements: Some eyes are ears. Some ears are lungs. All lungs are hands.

Conclusion: **I.** Some hands are eyes
II. Some hands are ears
III. Some lungs are eyes
IV. No hand is eye

(a) None follow
(b) Only IV follows
(c) Only II follows
(d) Only III follows

82. Statements: All liquids are solids. Some solids are gases. All gases are clouds.

Conclusion: **I.** Some clouds are solids
II. Some clouds are liquids
III. Some gases are liquids
IV. Some solids are clouds

(a) None follows
(b) Only I and II follow
(c) Only III and IV follow
(d) Only I and IV follow

83. Statements: All A are B. No B is C. Some D are C

Conclusion: **I.** Some D are A
II. Some D are B
III. Some A are C

(a) Only I follows
(b) Only III follows
(c) None of these
(d) Only II and III follow

84. Statements: Some snaps are WhatsApp. All Hikes are WhatsApp. All WhatsApp are facebook.

Conclusion: **I.** Some Facebook are snaps
II. All hikes are Facebook
III. Some snaps are Hikes
IV. Some snaps are Facebook

(a) All follow
(b) Only I, II and III follow
(c) Only I, II and IV follow
(d) Only III and IV follow

85. Statements: Some cow is deer. No deer is dog. Some dog is fox.

Conclusions: **I.** Some cow are fox
II. Some fox are deer

(a) None follows
(b) Only I follows
(c) Either I or II follows
(d) Only II follows

86. Statements: All pen is copy. No copy is rough. All rough is note

Conclusions: **I.** All rough being note is a possibility
II. Some pen is rough

(a) None follows
(b) Only I follows
(c) Either I or II follows
(d) Only II follows

87. Statements: Some mono is metro. All metro is bus. No bus is bike.

Conclusions: **I.** Some mono is not bike
II. No metro is bike

(a) Both I and II follow.
(b) Only I follows
(c) Either I or II follows
(d) Only II follows

88. Statements: Some point is not scale. No scale is a circle. Some circle is triangle.

Conclusions: **I.** No point is circle
II. No triangle is point

(a) None follows
(b) Only I follows
(c) Either I or II follows
(d) Only II follows

89. Statements: Some leaves are fruits. All branches are fruits. Some roots are branches.

Conclusions: **I.** Some roots are fruits.
II. Some branches are leaves.
III. No leaf is branch
IV. Some leaves are roots

(a) Either II or III and I follow
(b) Only I follows
(c) Only either II or III follows
(d) Only I and III follow

90. Statements: Some kings are cars. Some cars are bottles. No bottle is a lemon.

Conclusions: **I.** Some cars are lemons.
II. No king is a lemon.
III. Some kings are bottles.
IV. All cars are either kings or bottles.

(a) Only I and II follow
(b) Only either 1 or II and III follow
(c) Only III or IV follows
(d) None of these

91. Statements: All cups are bottles. Some bottles are jugs. No jug is plate. Some plates are tables

Conclusions: **I.** Some tables are bottles
II. Some plates are cups
III. No table is bottle
IV. Some jugs are cups

(a) Only I follows
(b) Only III follows
(c) Only either I or III follows
(d) Only either II or IV follows

92. Statements: All birds are horses. All horses are tigers. Some tigers are lions. Some lions are monkeys.

Conclusion:
I. Some tigers are horses
II. Some monkeys are birds
III. Some tigers are birds
IV. Some monkeys are horses

(a) Only I and III follow
(b) Only I, II and III follow
(c) Only II, III and IV follow
(d) All I, II, III and IV follow

93. Statements: Some chairs are handles. All handles are pots. All pots are mats. Some mats are buses.

Conclusion:
I. Some buses are handles
II. Some mats are chairs
III. No bus is a handle
IV. Some mats are handles

(a) Only I, II and IV follow
(b) Only II, III and IV follow
(c) Only either I or III and IV follow
(d) Only either I or III and II and IV follow

94. Statements: Some sticks are lamps. Some flowers are lamps. Some lamps are dresses. All dresses are shirts

Conclusions:
I. Some shirts are sticks
II. Some shirts are flowers
III. Some flowers are sticks
IV. Some dresses are sticks

(a) Only I follows (b) Only II follows
(c) Only III follows (d) None follows

95. Statements: Some benches are walls. All walls are houses. Some houses are jungles. All jungles are roads

Conclusions:
I. Some roads are benches
II. Some jungles are walls
III. Some houses are benches
IV. Some roads are houses

(a) Only I and II follow
(b) Only III and IV follow
(c) Only I and III follow
(d) Only II, III and IV follow

96. Statements: Some trains are cars. All cars are branches. All branches are nets. Some nets are dresses

Conclusions:
I. Some dresses are cars
II. Some nets are trains
III. Some branchesare trains
IV. Some dresses are trains

(a) I and II follow
(b) II and III follow
(c) I and IV follow
(d) II, III and IV follow

97. Statements: All papers are clips. Some clips are boards. Some boards are lanes, All lanes are roads.

Conclusions:
I. Some roads are boards
II. Some lanes are clips
III. Some boards are papers
IV. Some roads are clips

(a) I and II follow
(b) I and III follow
(c) I, II and III follow
(d) I follows

Directions for Questions 98 to 102: *In each of the following questions. Some statements are given followed by conclusions/group of conclusions numbered I and II. Give the answer as*

(a) If only Conclusion I follows
(b) If none of the Conclusions I or II follows
(c) If only Conclusion II follows
(d) If both I and II follow

Statements: Some squares are circles. No circle is a triangle. No line is a square

98. Conclusions:
I. All squares can never be triangles
II. Some lines are triangles

99. Conclusions:
I. No triangle is a square
II. No line is a circle.

Statements: All songs are poems. All poems are rhymes. No rhyme is a paragraph

100. Conclusions:
I. No song is a paragraph
II. No poem is a paragraph

101. Conclusions:
I. All rhymes are poems
II. All songs are rhymes

102. Statements: Some dews are drops. All drops are stones

Conclusions:
I. At least some dews are stones
II. At least some stones are drops

ANSWER KEY

1. (a)	2. (d)	3. (b)	4. (a)
5. (c)	6. (b)	7. (b)	8. (d)
9. (a)	10. (a)	11. (a)	12. (b)
13. (d)	14. (c)	15. (c)	16. (a)
17. (c)	18. (d)	19. (a)	20. (e)
21. (b)	22. (d)	23. (a)	24. (c)
25. (b)	26. (d)	27. (d)	28. (a)
29. (d)	30. (a)	31. (c)	32. (e)
33. (d)	34. (a)	35. (b)	36. (b)
37. (b)	38. (e)	39. (d)	40. (d)
41. (d)	42. (a)	43. (b)	44. (a)
45. (d)	46. (a)	47. (c)	48. (b)
49. (b)	50. (d)	51. (d)	52. (c)
53. (a)	54. (b)	55. (d)	56. (b)
57. (c)	58. (a)	59. (b)	60. (d)
61. (d)	62. (b)	63. (c)	64. (b)
65. (a)	66. (c)	67. (b)	68. (c)
69. (a)	70. (a)	71. (b)	72. (b)
73. (c)	74. (c)	75. (b)	76. (c)
77. (b)	78. (d)	79. (c)	80. (b)
81. (c)	82. (d)	83. (c)	84. (c)
85. (a)	86. (b)	87. (a)	88. (a)
89. (a)	90. (d)	91. (c)	92. (a)
93. (d)	94. (d)	95. (b)	96. (b)
97. (d)	98. (a)	99. (b)	100. (d)
101. (c)	102. (d)		

SOLUTIONS AND SHORTCUTS

Solutions for Questions 1 to 10:

1.

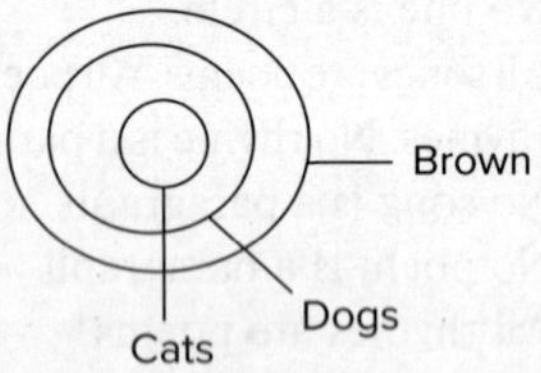

Only conclusion I is correct. Hence, option (a) is correct.

2.

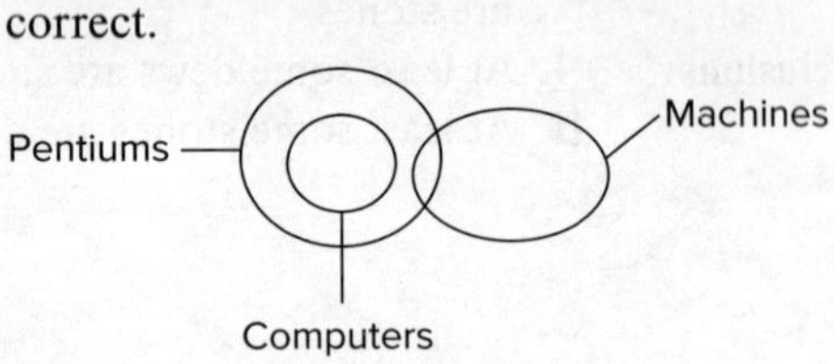

None of the given conclusions are necessarily true. Hence, option (d) is correct.

3.

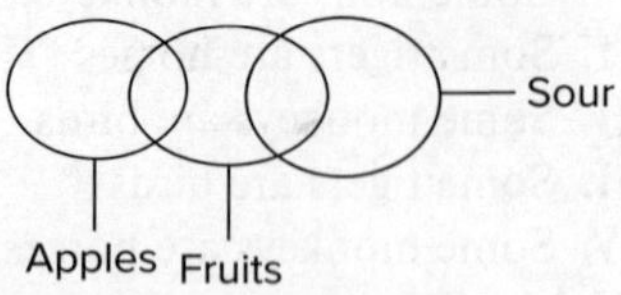

Only, conclusion II is true. Hence, option (b) is correct.

4.

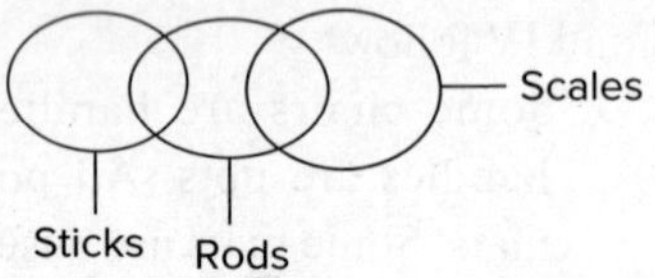

Only, conclusion I is always true. Hence, option (a) is correct.

5. For this question there is no need to draw a Venn diagram. It is self evident that either I or II would be correct – since Bimla could either be married or not married to an architect. Option (c) is correct.

6.

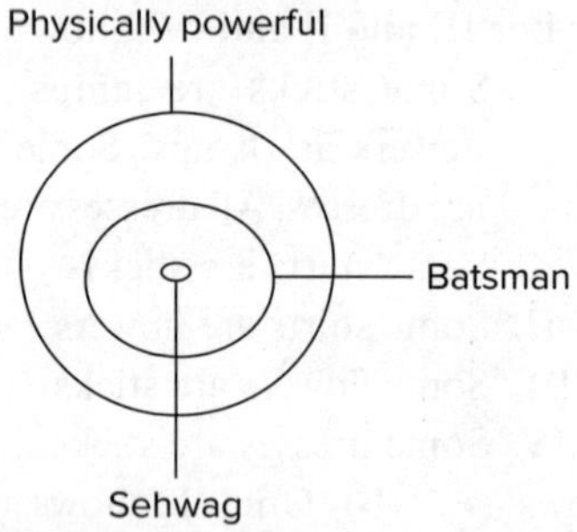

Only conclusion II is correct. Hence, option (b) is correct.

7.

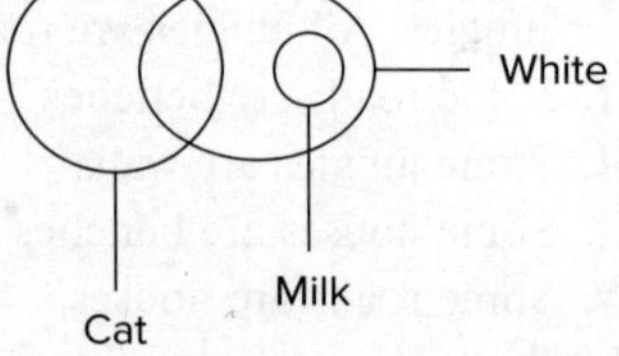

Conclusion II is always true. Hence, option (b) is correct.

8.

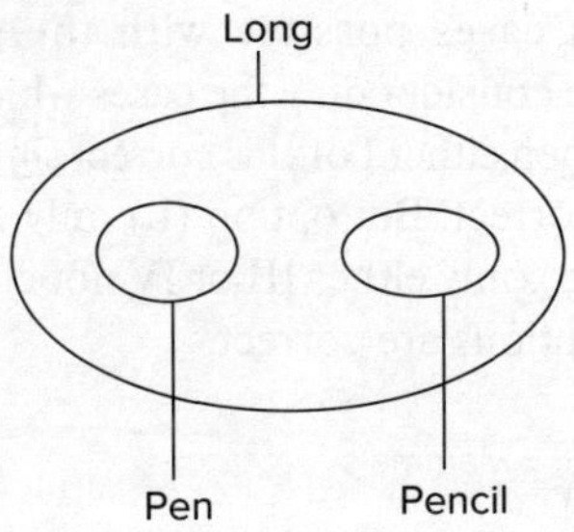

None of the given conclusion is true. Hence, option (d) is correct.

9.

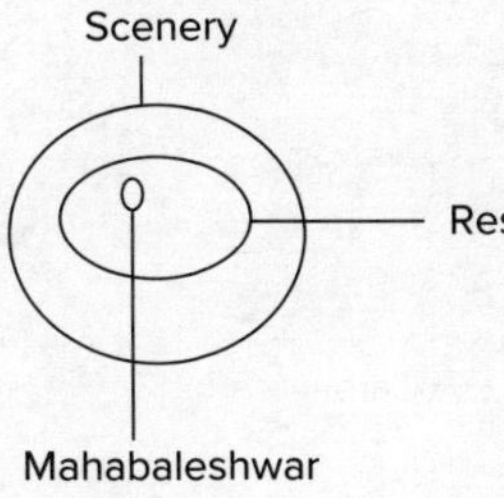

Conclusion I is always true but conclusion II is not necessarily true as we cannot say anything about it. Hence, option (a) is correct.

10.

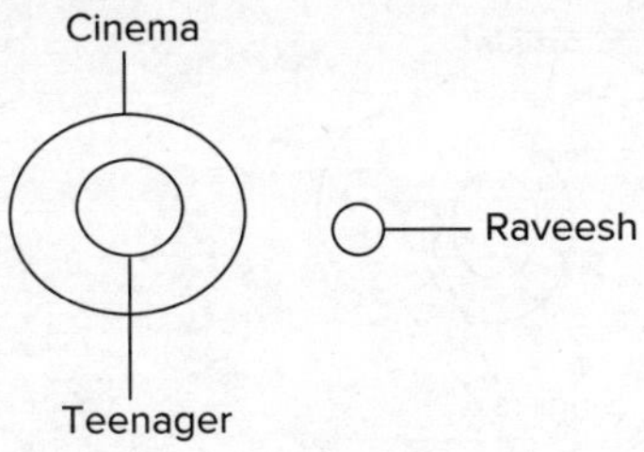

Conclusion (I) is always correct. Hence, option (a) is correct.

Solutions for Questions 11 to 50:

11.

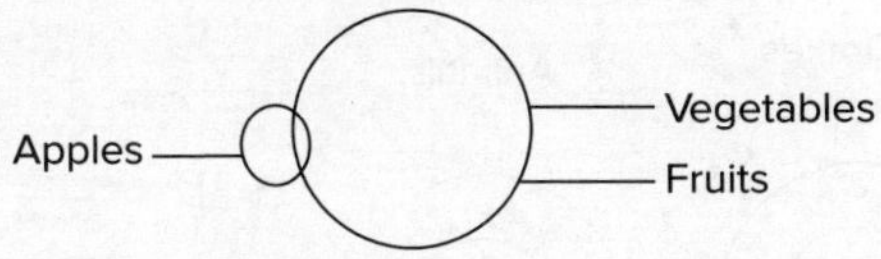

Only I and II follow

12.

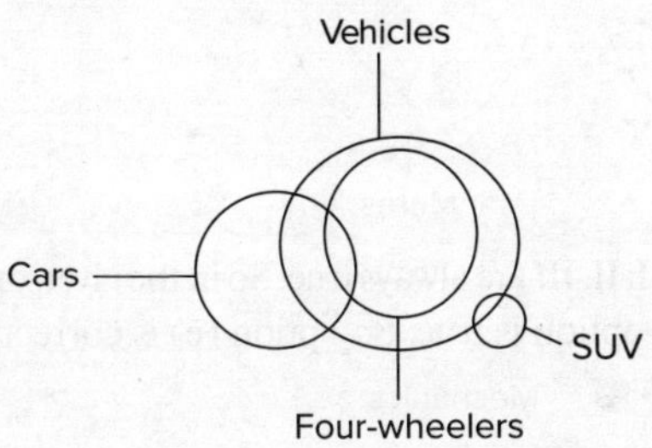

Only conclusion II and III follow

13.

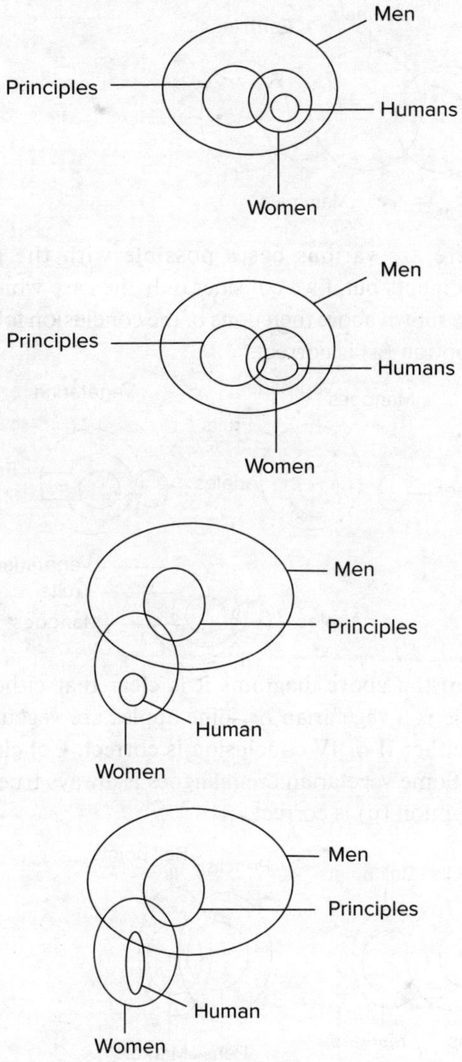

Only conclusion III follows

14.

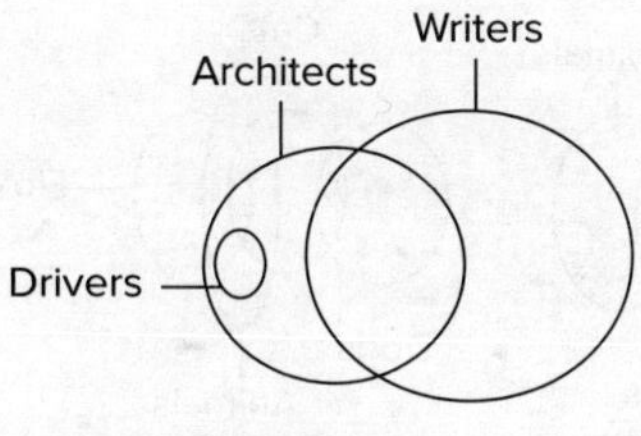

Only I and III follow

15.

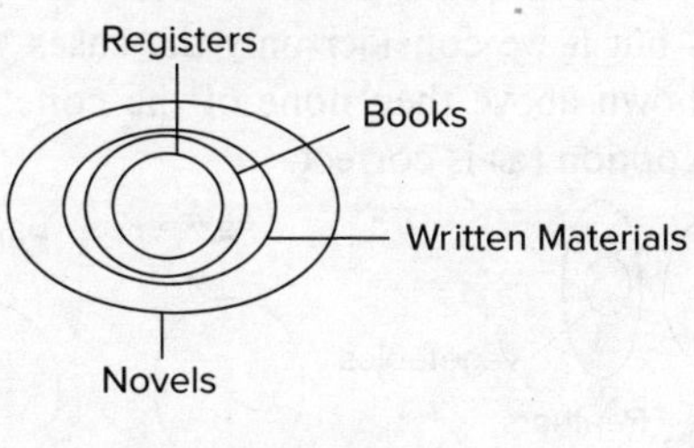

Only I and III follow

16. 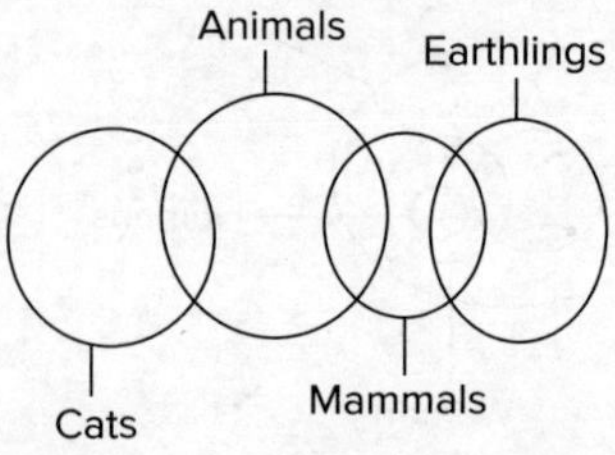

There are various cases possible with the given statements but if we consider only the case which we have shown above then none of the conclusion follows, so option (a) is correct.

17. 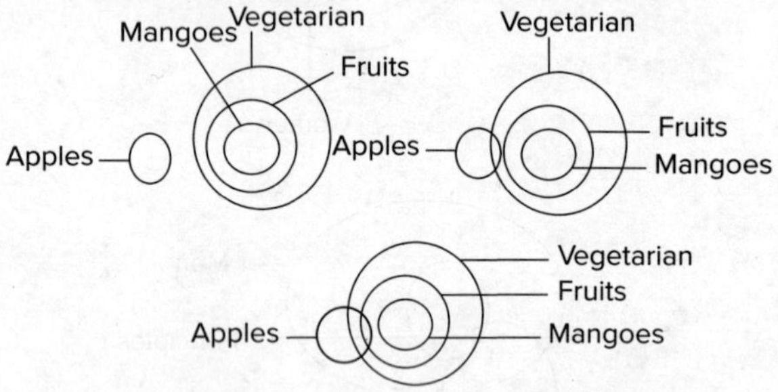

From the above diagrams it is clear that either no apple is a vegetarian or some apples are vegetarian. So either II or IV conclusion is correct. Conclusion III: Some vegetarian are mangoes is always true. So option (c) is correct.

18. 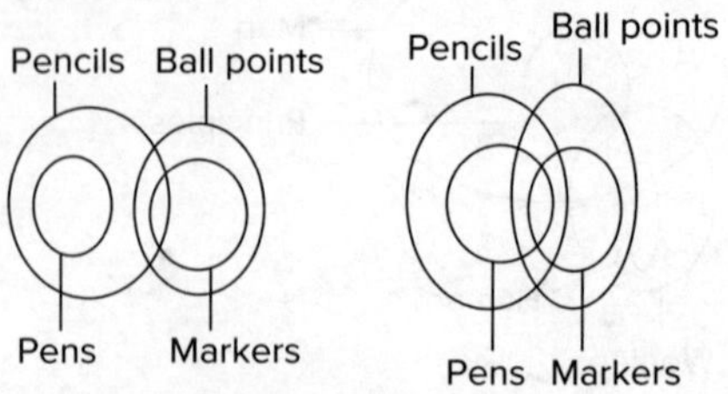

Only II and IV follow

19. 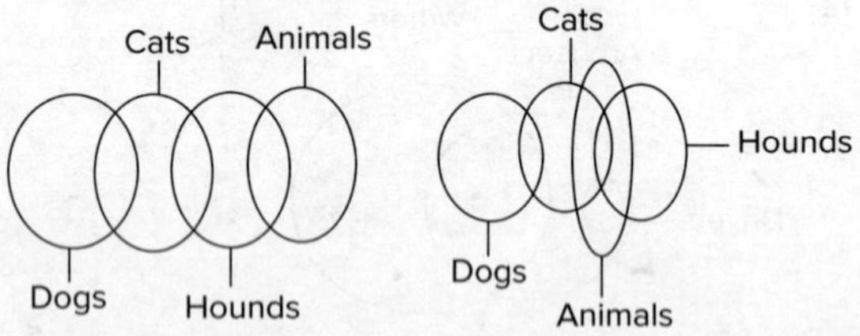

There are various cases possible with the given statements but if we consider only the cases which we have shown above then none of the conclusion follows, so option (a) is correct.

20. 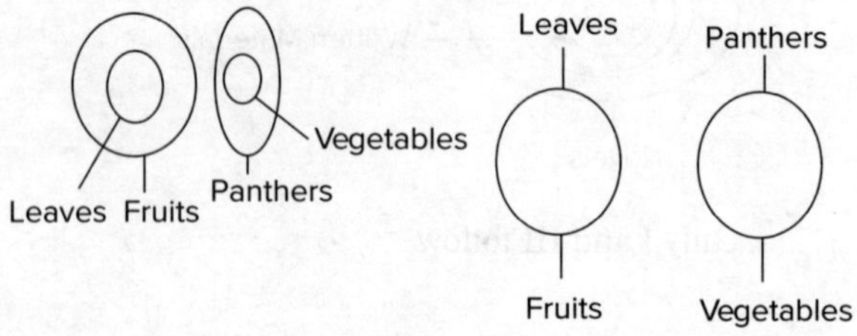

There are various cases possible with the given statements but if we consider only the cases which we have shown above then either I or II is correct similarly either III or IV is correct. But option (b) only either I or II and option (c) only either III or IV not correct because both the options are correct.

21. 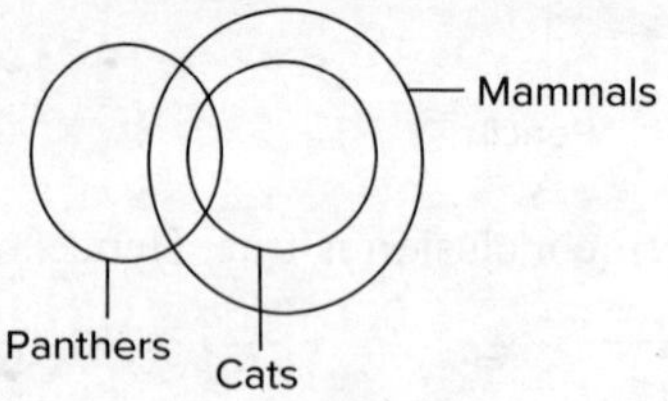

Only conclusion I follows

22. 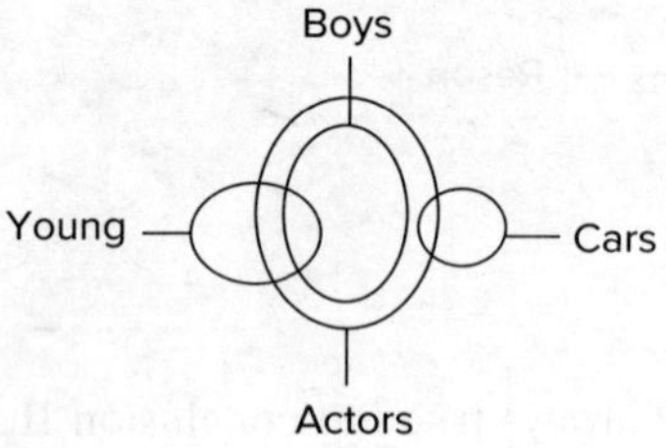

Conclusions I and IV are true. So option (d) is correct.

23. 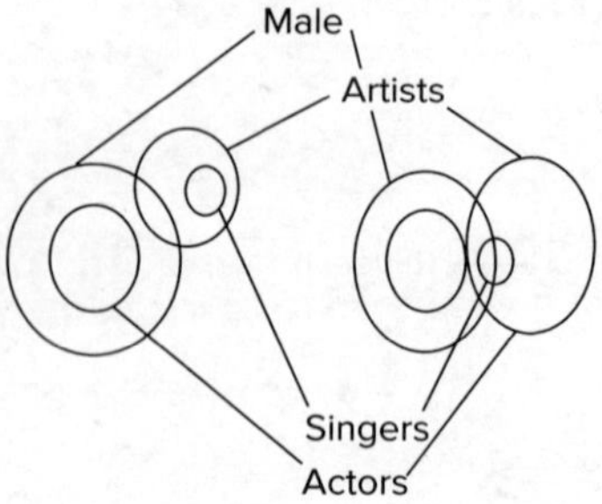

Conclusion III is true.
Either statement II or IV follows.
Option (b) is true.

24. 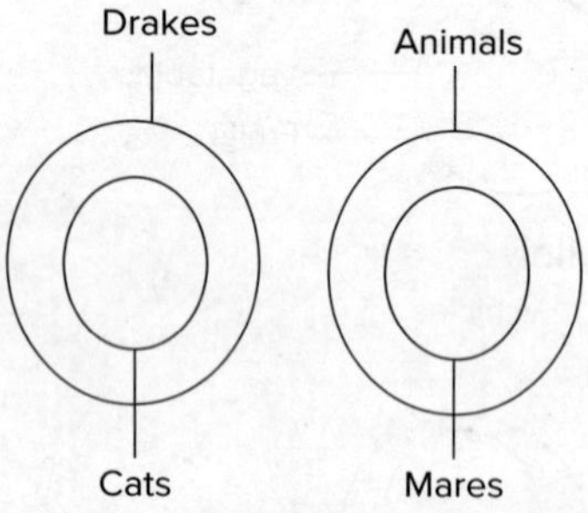

Conclusion I, II, III are always true. So in the given options none of the option is true. So option (e) is correct.

25. 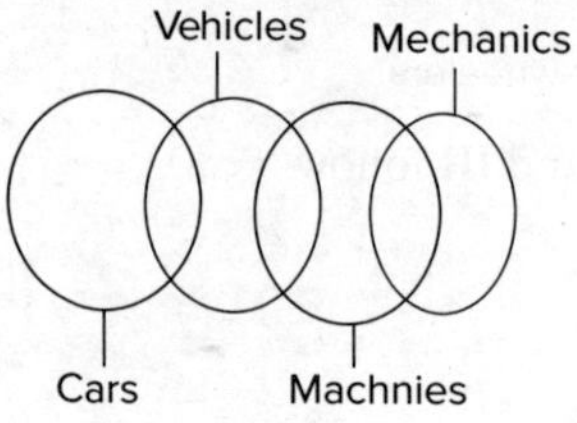

Conclusions I and II are true. So option (b) is correct.

26.

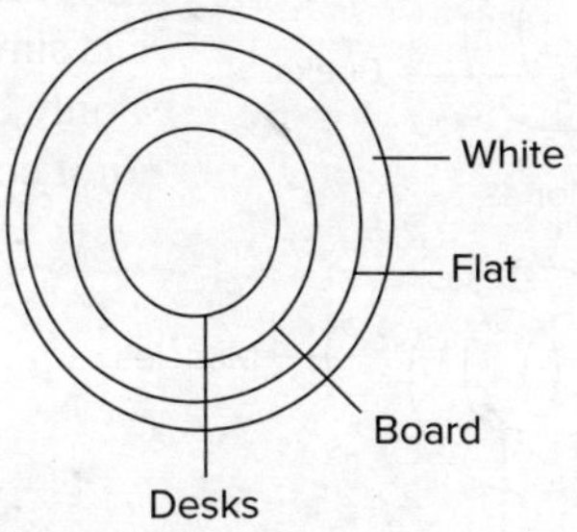

Conclusions II, III, IV are true. So option (d) is correct.

27.

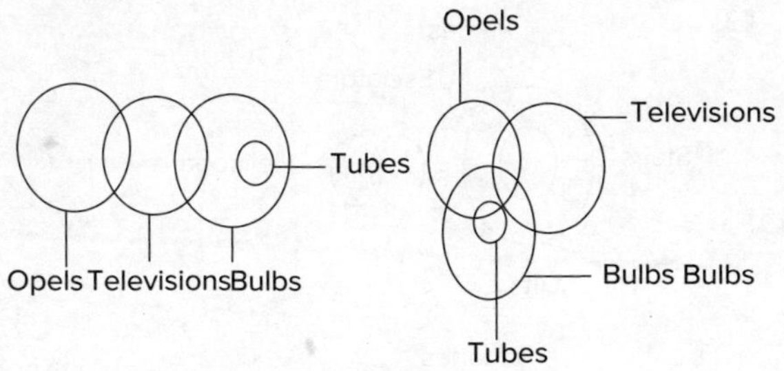

None of the given conclusions follows

28.

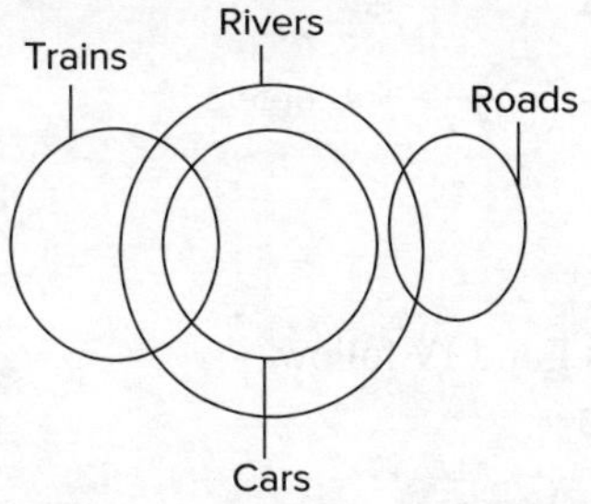

Both conclusions I and IV follow. Hence, option (a) is correct.

29.

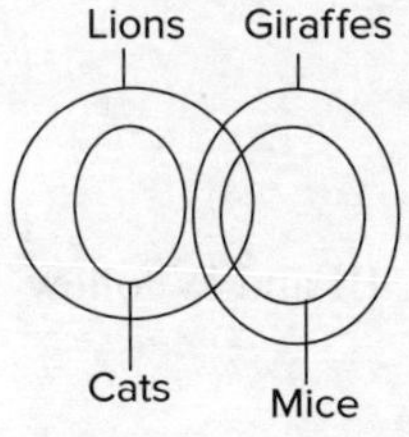

Conclusions II and IV follows. So option (d) is correct.

30.

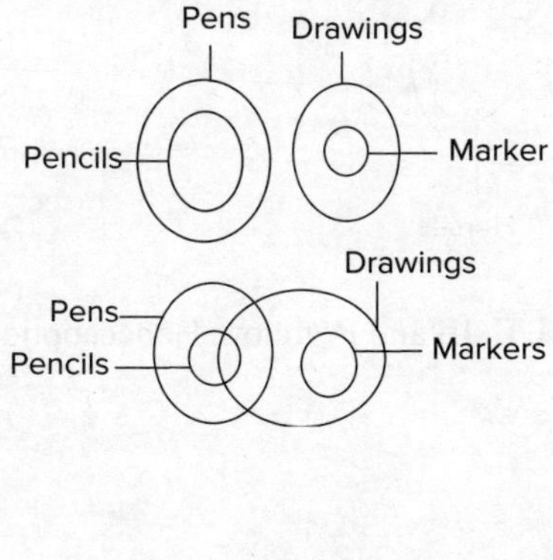

Only conclusion I follows

31.

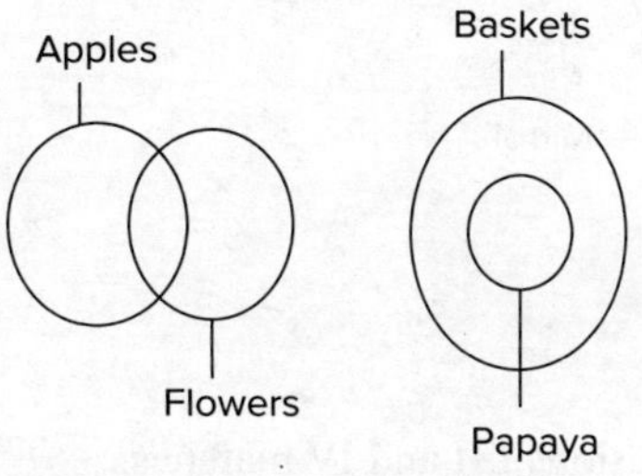

Only conclusions II and IV follow

32.

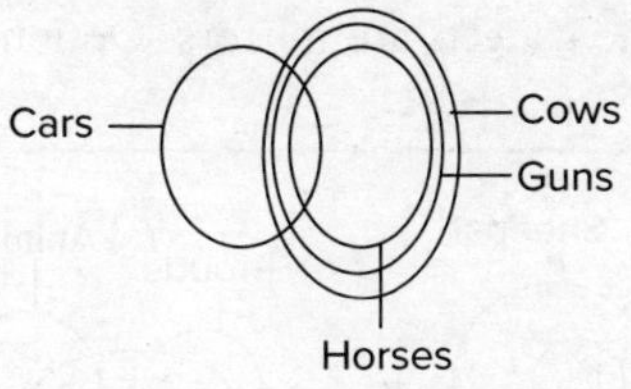

All the conclusions follow

33.

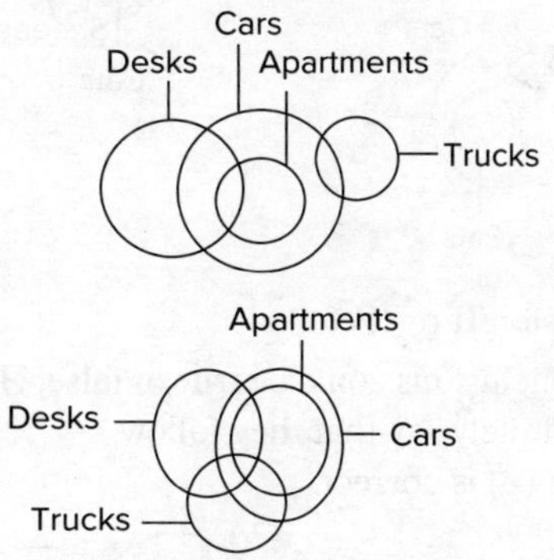

Conclusion II and III are true & either conclusion I or IV follows.

34.

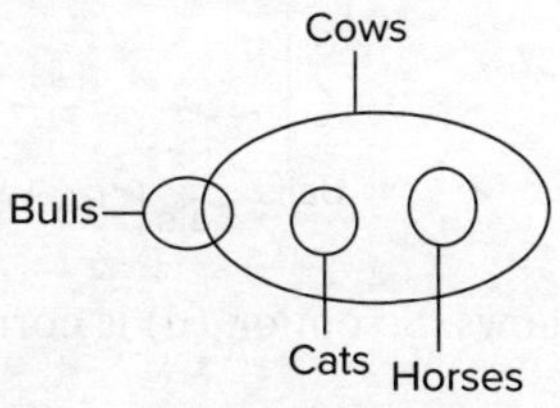

None of the given conclusions follows

35.

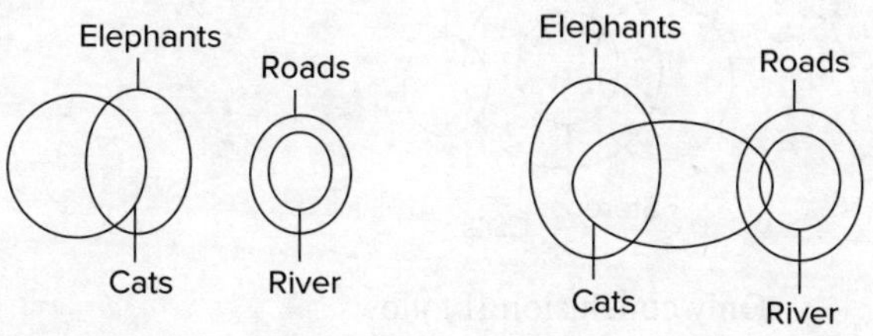

Only conclusions II, III follow. Also, either I or IV must be true. Option (b) is correct.

36.

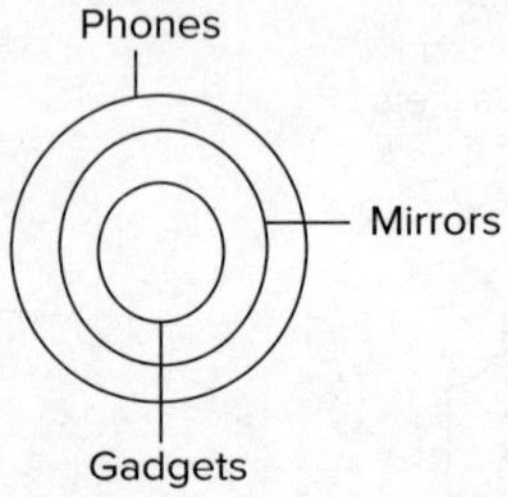

Each of conclusions I,II and IV matches.

Note: If all Gadgets are mirrors (as seen in the figure) it also means that some gadgets are mirrors. Option (b) is correct.

37.

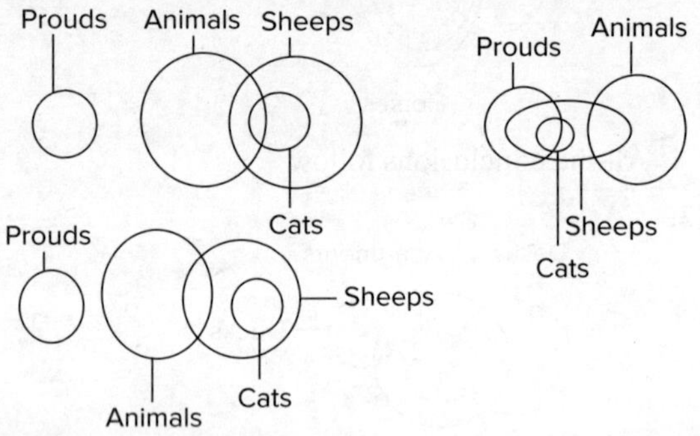

Either conclusion II or III follows

38. Each of the conclusions could be true or false. Hence, we cannot definitely say that they follow. Hence, option (e) is correct.

39.

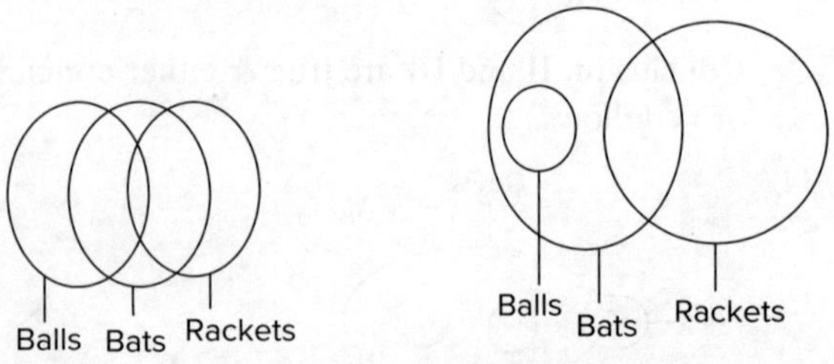

Only conclusion I follows. So option (d) is correct.

40.

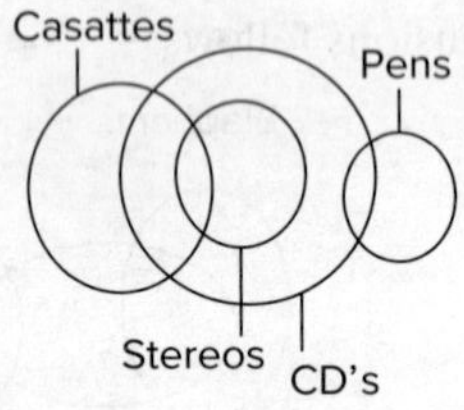

Only conclusion II follows

41.

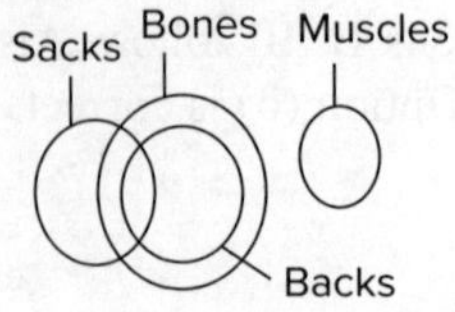

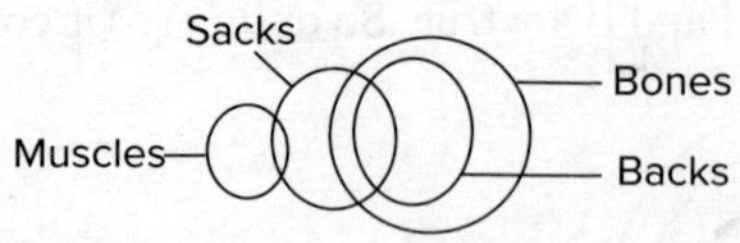

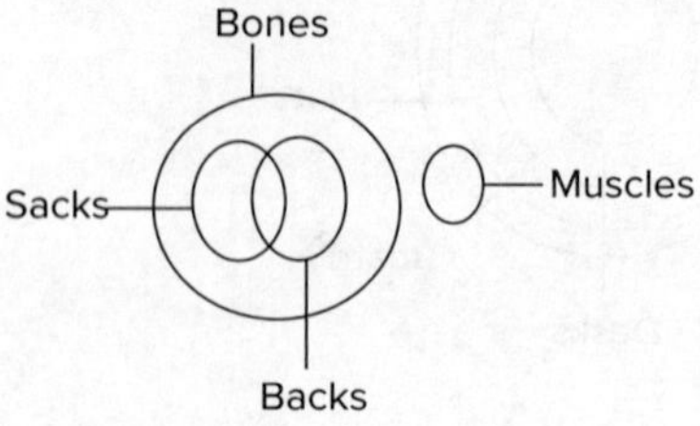

Option (d) is correct

42. Option (a) is correct.

43.

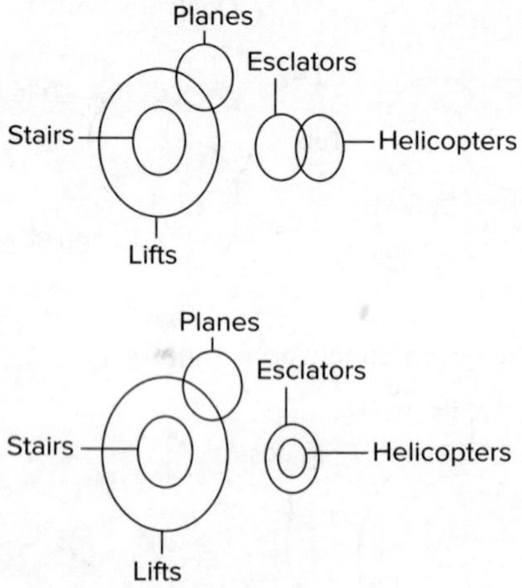

Only conclusions I and IV follow

44.

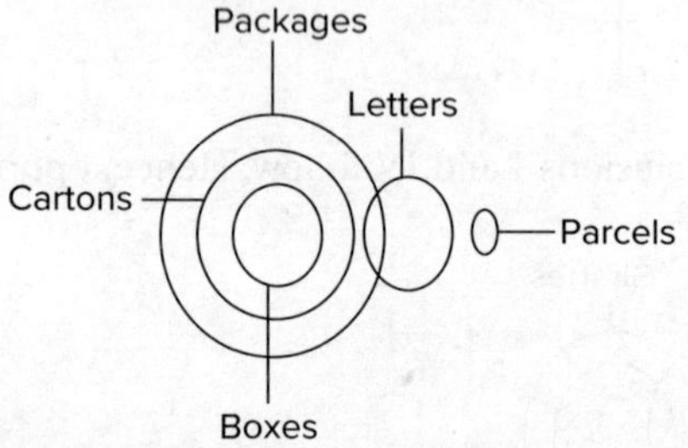

Only conclusion I and either III and IV follow

45.

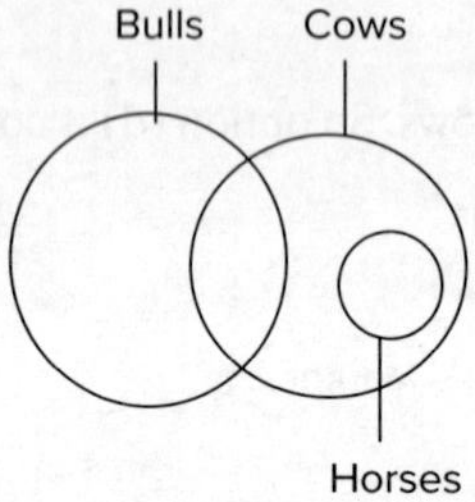

Conclusions I, II, III and IV follow. Hence, option (d) is correct.

46.

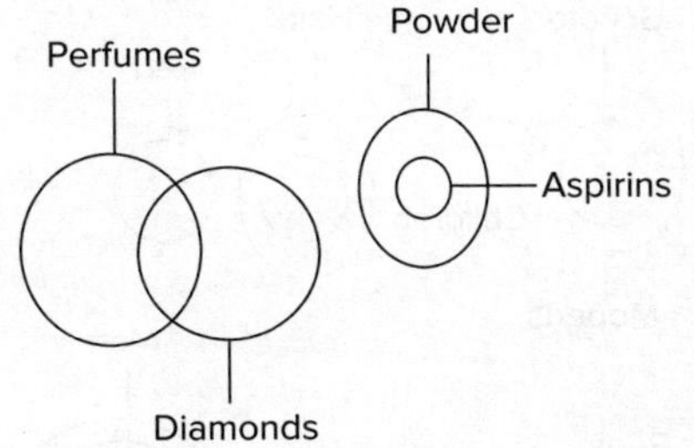

No perfume is powder so those diamonds which are perfumes cannot be powder. So conclusion I follows. Only I, III, IV follow

47.

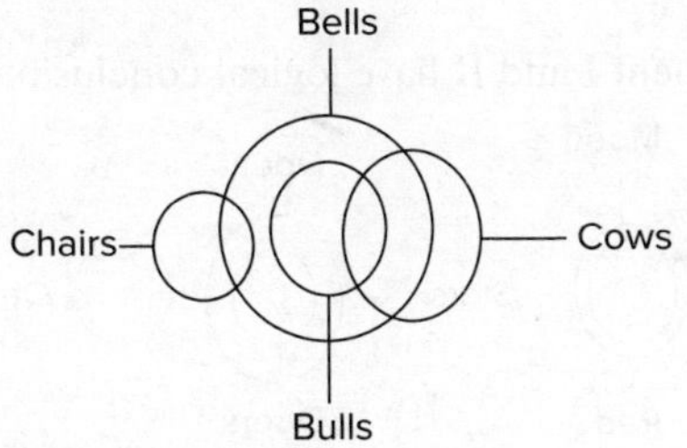

Only conclusion II follows

48.

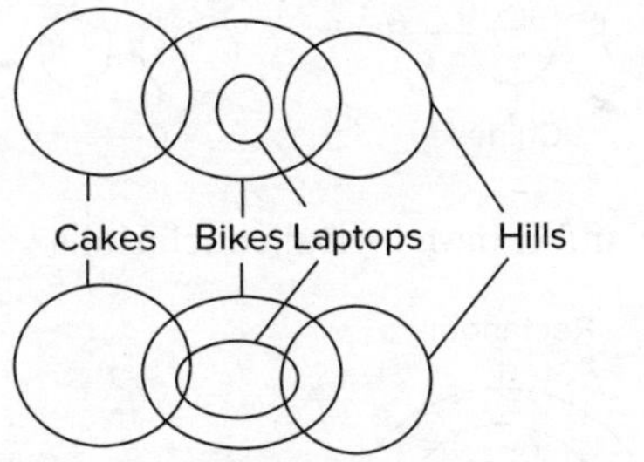

Either conclusion II or IV follows

49.

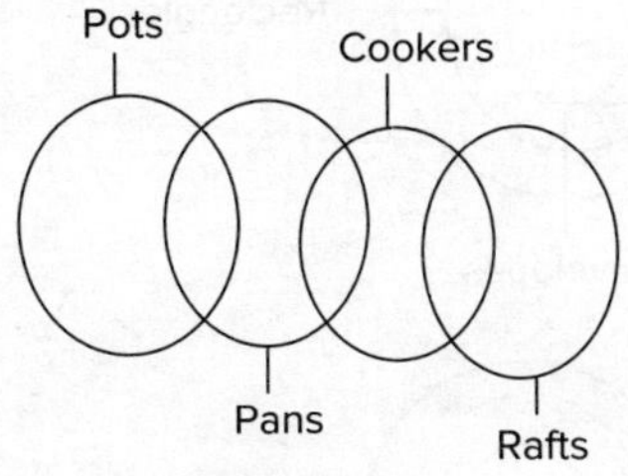

None of the conclusions follows

50.

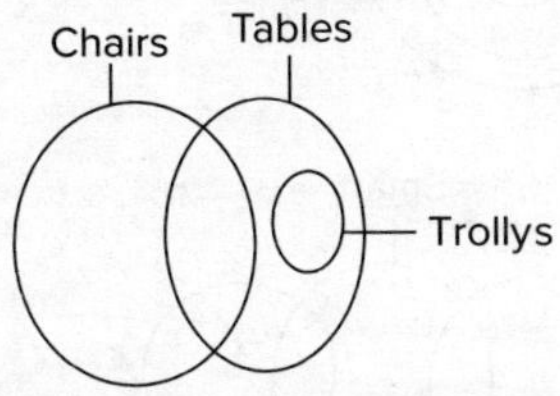

All the conclusions follow.

Solutions for Questions 51 to 70:

51. If all Martians eat sausages and all those who eat sausages are herbivorous then all Martians should be herbivorous.

52. If all lotus have nectar and all shrubs have lotuses then all shrubs have nectar.

53. If no season is winter and all summers are winters then no summer is a season.

54. All falcons are birds and all birds are yellow then all falcon should be yellow.

55.

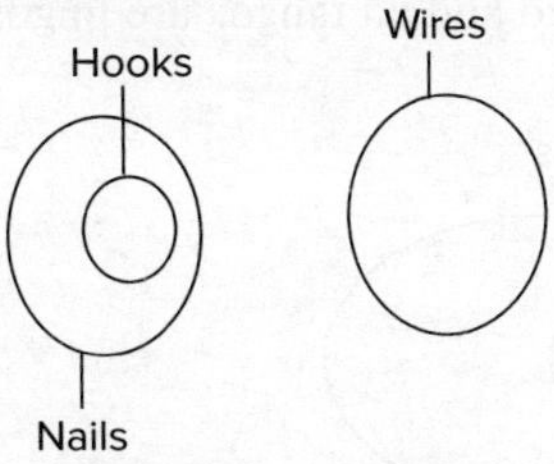

If no nail is a wire and all hooks are nails then no wire is a hook.

56. If all dabba are chabi and all cobra are not dabba then some chabi are dabba.

57. If no train is a claim and all heads are claims then it means no head is train.

58.

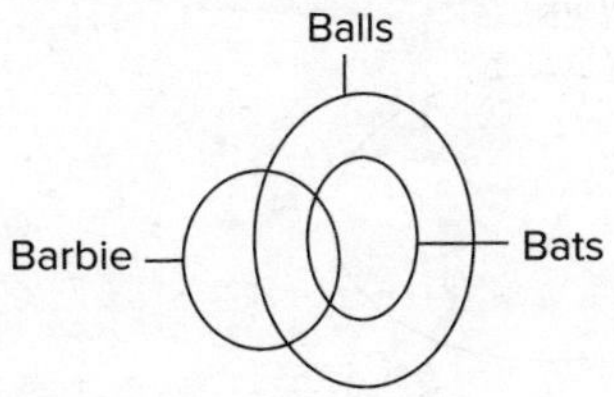

If all bats are balls and some bats are Barbie then some balls are Barbie.

59. If some multistories are not apartments and all multistories are houses then some houses are not apartments.

60. If no bow is a casket then no casket is a bow so option (d) is correct.

61. If some shampoos are not soaps all shampoos are oils then some who are oils are not soaps.

62.

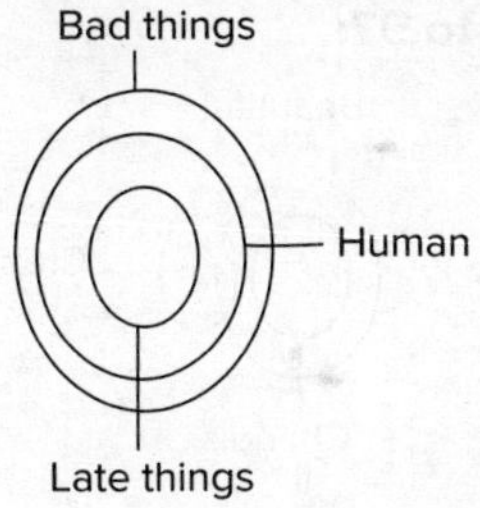

If all late things are human and all humans are bad things then some bad things are late things.

63. If all Shomes are bright and no bright Shomes is Band then no Band is a Shome.

64. If all sorcerers are daredevils and all daredevils are hasty then all sorcerers are hasty.

65.

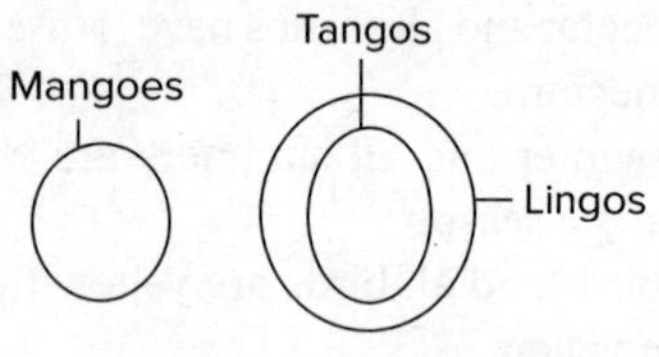

If no mango is a lingo and all tangos are lingos then no tango is a mango.

66.

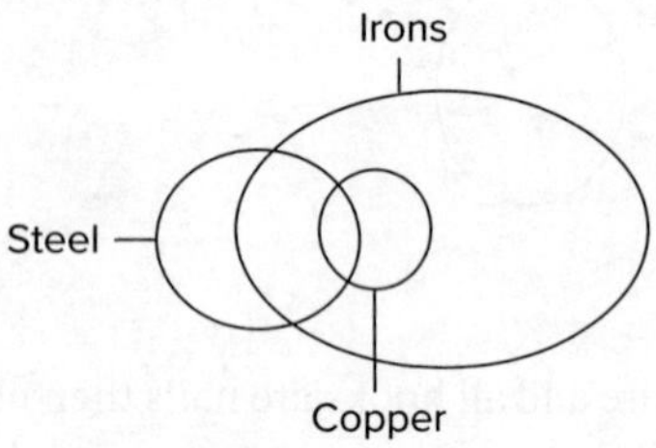

If all copper is used for making irons and some steel is copper then some irons are made of steel.

67. If no tiger is carnivorous and all animals are carnivorous then no tiger is an animal.

68.

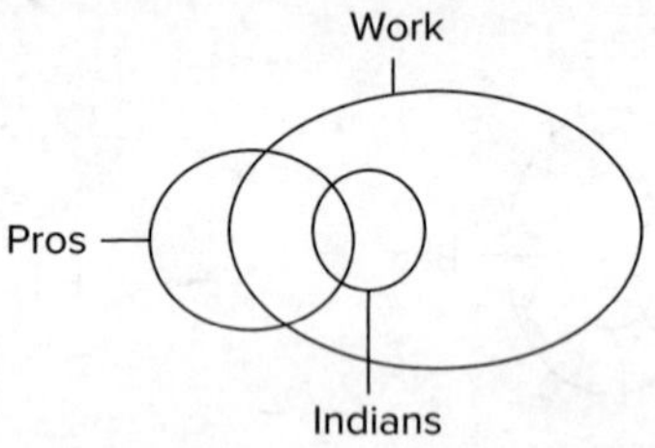

If all Indians like to work and some pro are Indians then some pros like to work.

69. Apples are fruits means all apples are fruits. So if some apples are pears and apples are fruits then some fruits are pears.

70. Santros are Rim means all Santros are Rim. So if all Santros are Rims and all Rims are cars then all Santros should be cars.

Solutions for Questions 71 to 97:

71.

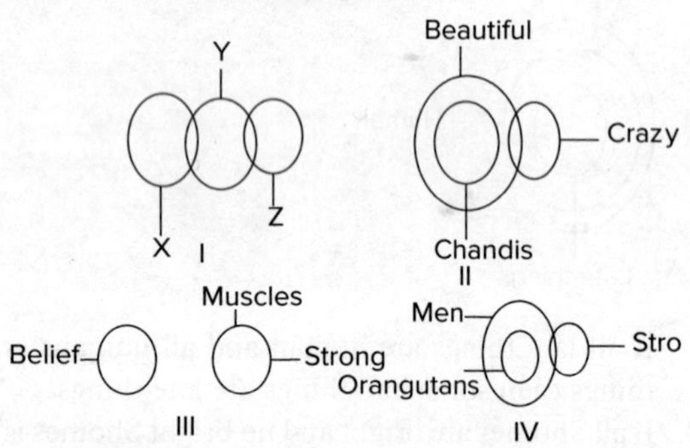

Only III argument is correct. If no belief is strong and only strong have muscles then it means all those are not strong have not muscles so no belief has muscle.

72.

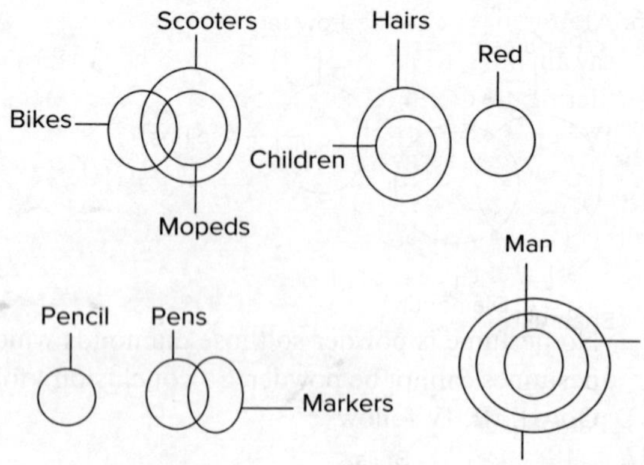

Only argument I and II have logical conclusions.

73.

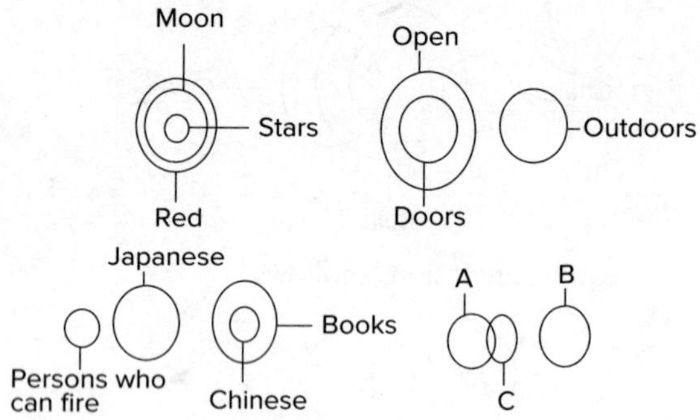

Arguments I and II have logical conclusions

74.

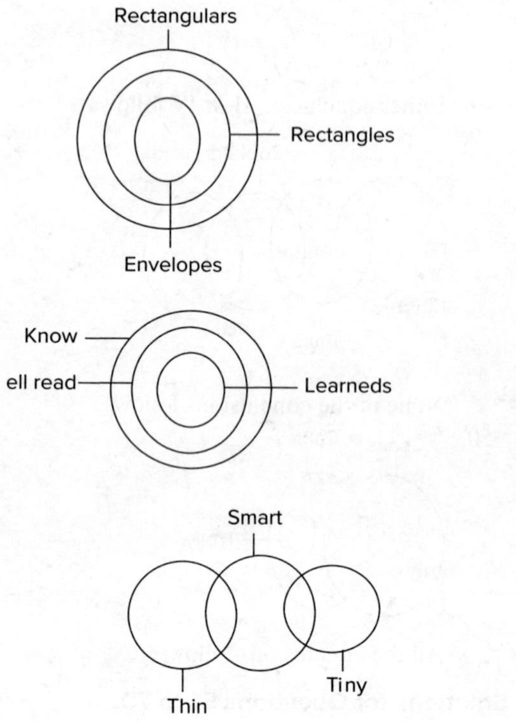

From the above Venn diagram it is clear that I and III are correct.

Argument IV says health foods are rare but it does not say anything about the relationship of health foods and dieting. So dieting is rare is not perfect conclusion. So IV is not correct.

75.

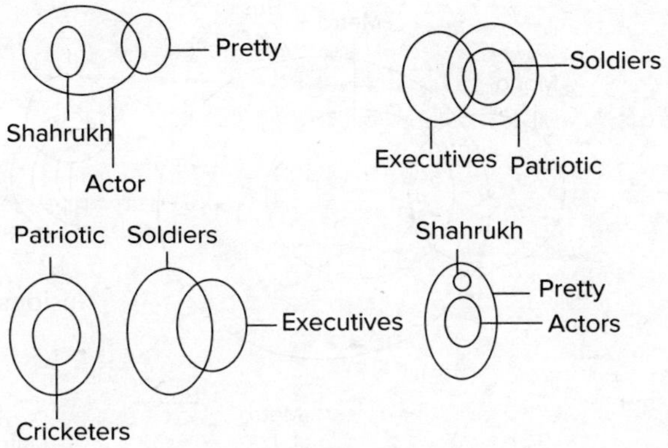

Only argument II has logical conclusion

76.

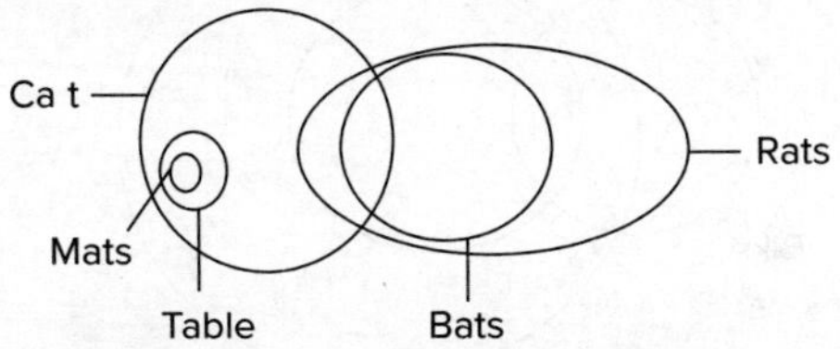

Only option (c) is correct

77.

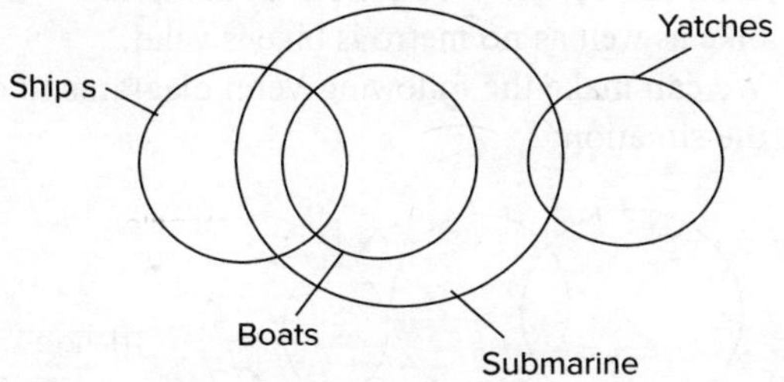

From the above venn diagram we can see that the statements II and III follow. Hence, option (b) is correct.

78.

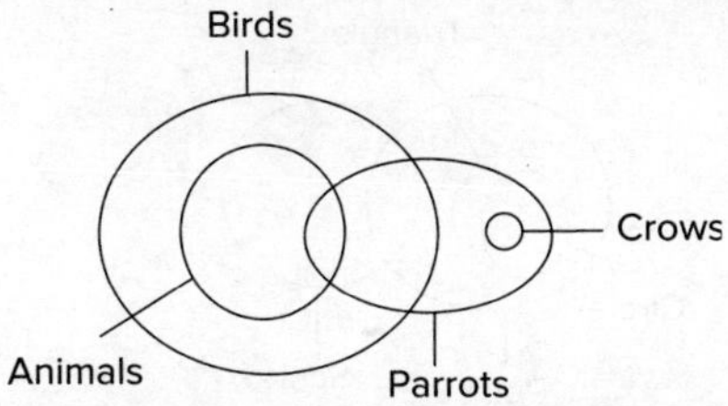

Only conclusion III follows. Hence, option (d) is correct.

79.

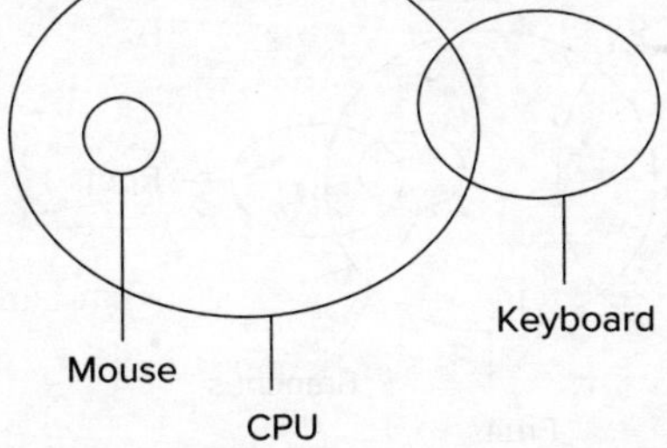

From the above venn diagram only I and III follows. Hence, option (c) is correct.

80.

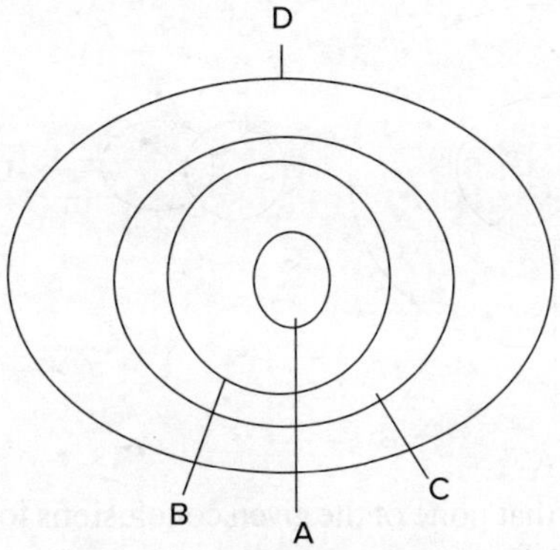

Only I and III follow. Hence, option (b) is correct.

81. There are multiple possibilities through which we can draw the Venn diagram for the given relationships:

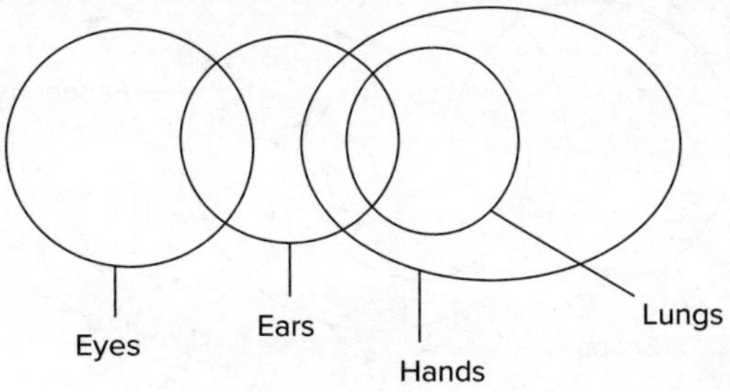

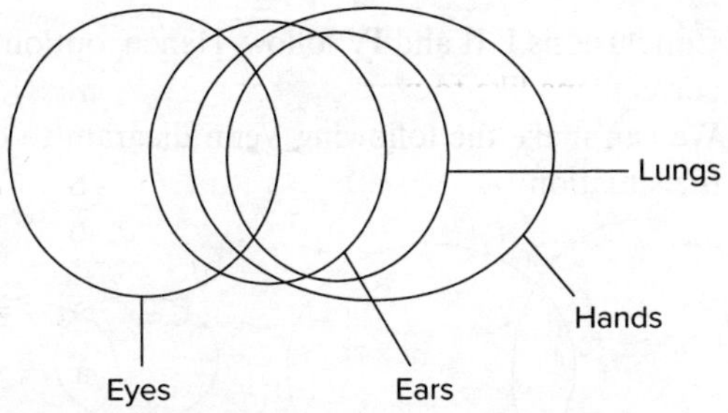

From the above venn diagrams, option (c) is correct.

82. We can make the following Venn diagram to depict the situation:

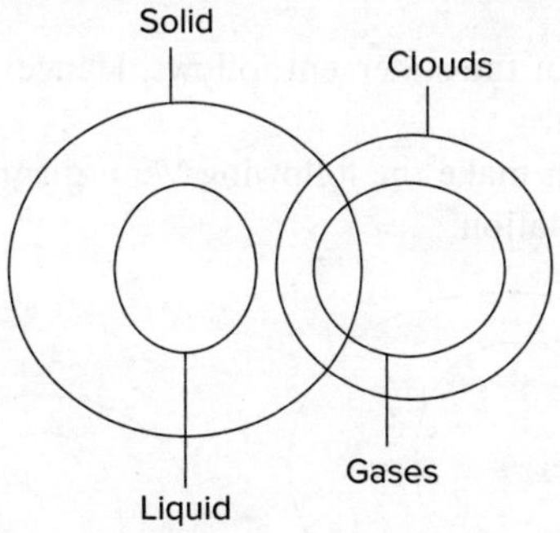

We can see that conclusions I and IV follow. Hence, option (d) is correct.

83. We can make the following Venn diagram to depict the situation:

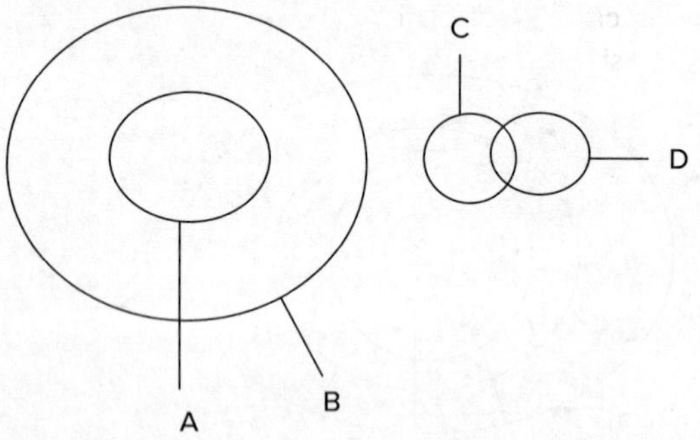

We can see that none of the given conclusions follows. Hence, option (c) is correct.

84. We can make the following Venn diagram to depict the situation:

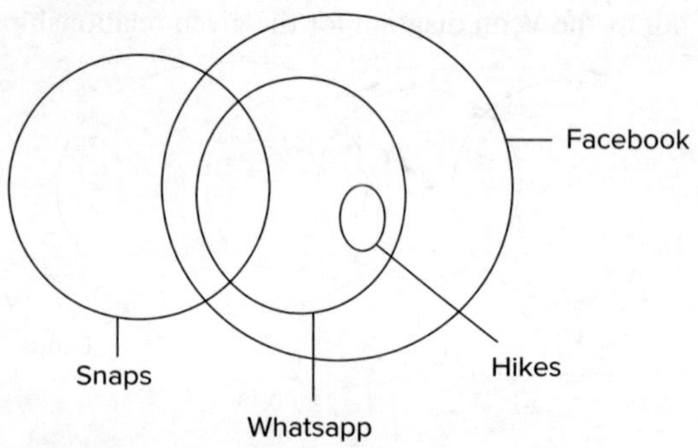

Conclusions I, II and IV follow. Hence, option (c) is correct.

85. We can make the following Venn diagram to depict the situation:

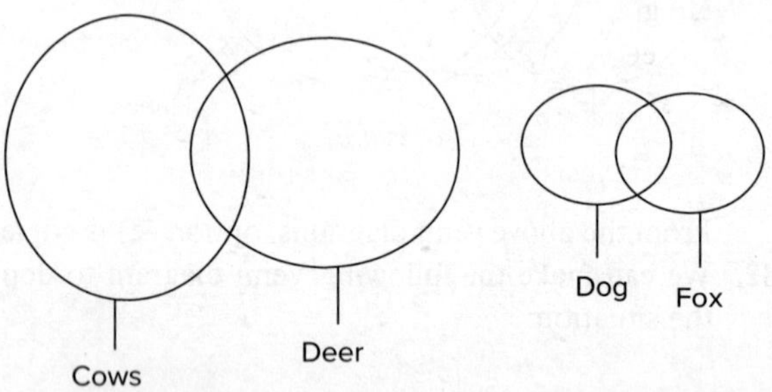

None of the statement follows. Hence, option (a) is correct.

86. We can make the following Venn diagram to depict the situation:

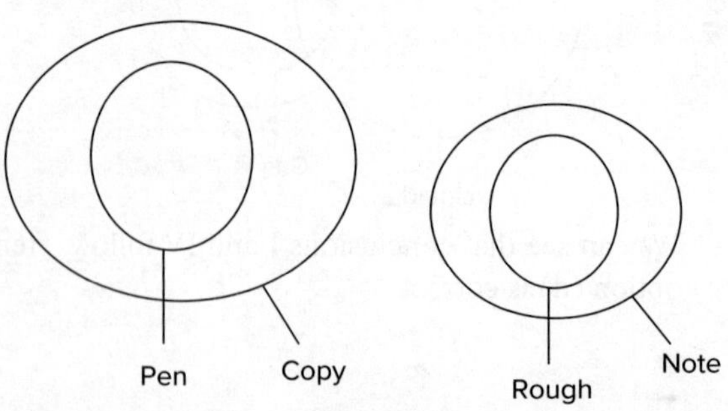

Conclusion I is definitely a possibility.

Conclusion II is not possible. Hence, option (b) is correct.

87. We can make the following Venn diagrams to depict the situation:

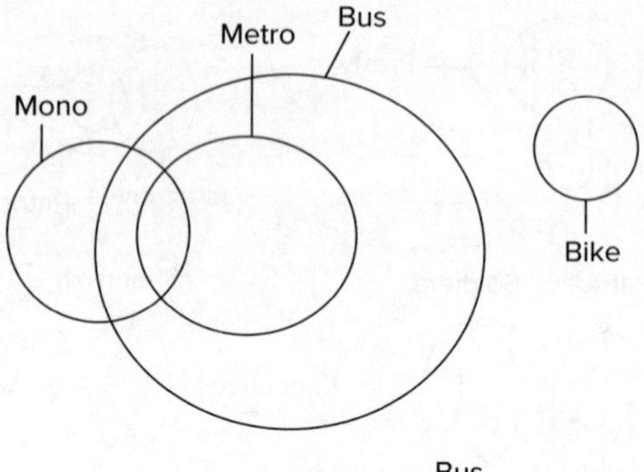

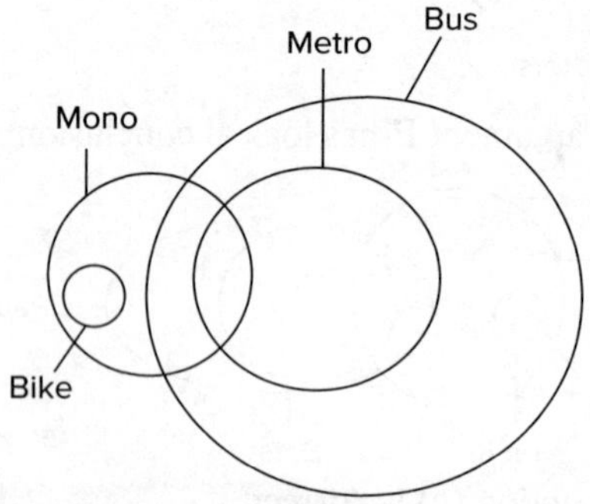

Both the conclusions follow -as some mono are not bike as well as no metro is bike is valid.

88. We can make the following Venn diagrams to depict the situation:

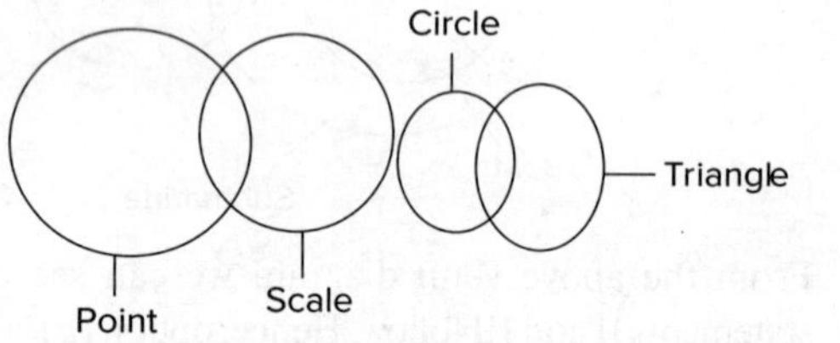

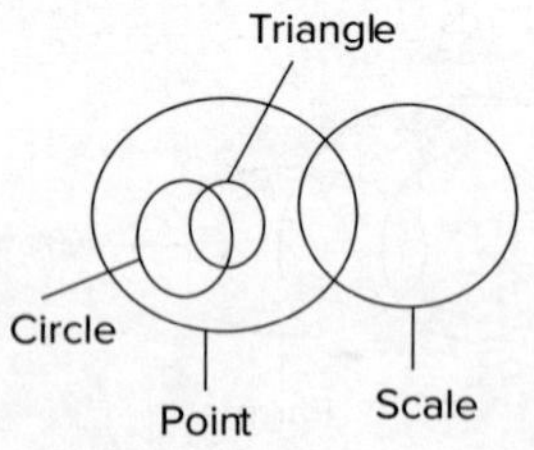

From 2nd venn diagram it is clear that none of the given conclusion is true. Hence, option (a) is correct.

89.

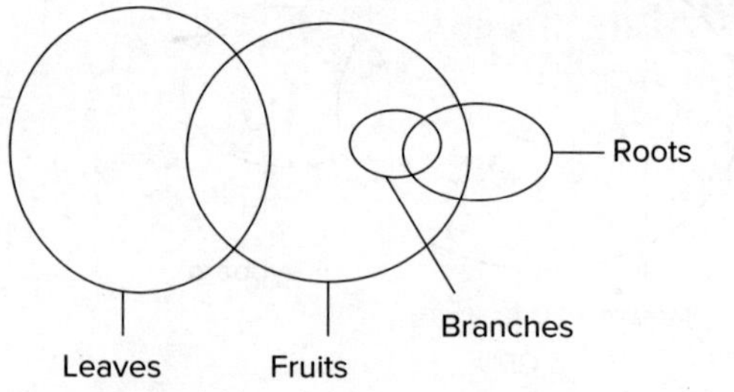

Conclusion 1 is correct

Either some branches are leaves or no branch is a leaf. Hence either conclusion 2 or 3 is correct. Hence option (a) is correct.

90.

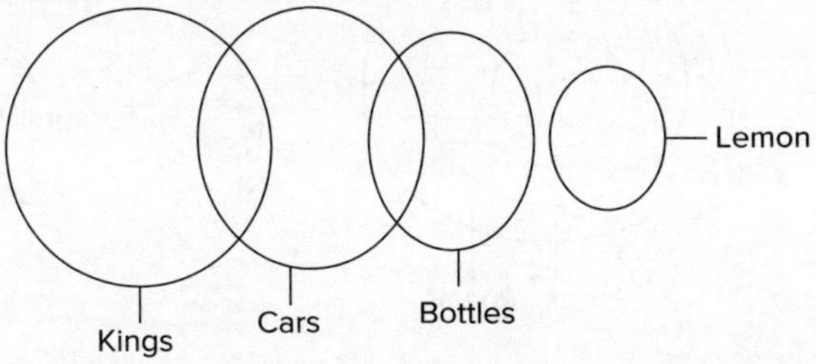

None of the given conclusions satisfy (Note: Conclusion II is not correct because we could have drawn the Lemon circle to intersect the King circle too). Hence, option (d) is correct.

91. We can make the following Venn diagram to depict the situation (note: in this diagram we could have drawn the table and plate circles intersecting the bottles circle too since, plates are only connected to jugs in the original premises. That leaves us free to change the relationship between plates and bottles, plates and cups and consequently bottles and tables and cups and tables):

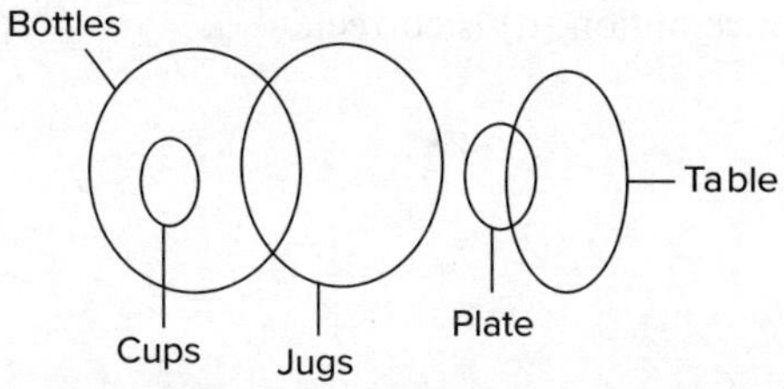

In this Venn diagram, we can have the Plate and table circles intersecting with the Bottles circle too. Hence, either some tables are bottles or no table is bottle. Hence option (c) is correct.

92.

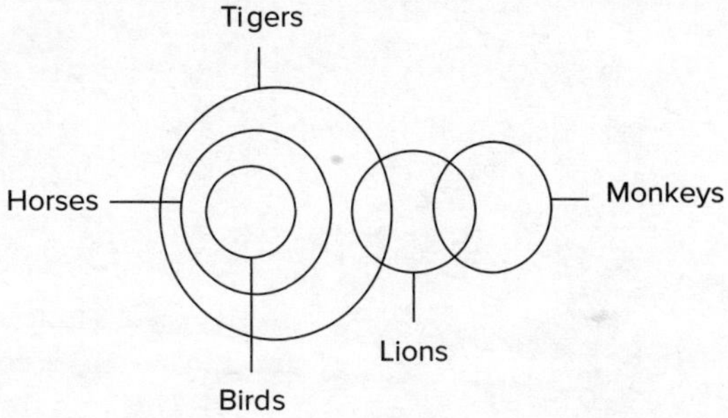

Only conclusions I and III follow. Hence, option (a) is correct.

93. We can make the following Venn diagram to depict the situation:

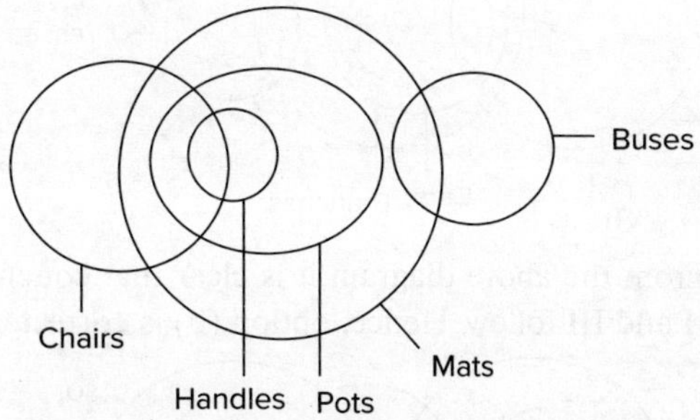

Either some buses are handles or no bus is a handle. Hence either of conclusions I and III is correct. Conclusions II and IV are always correct. Hence option (d) is true.

94. We can make the following Venn diagram to depict the situation:

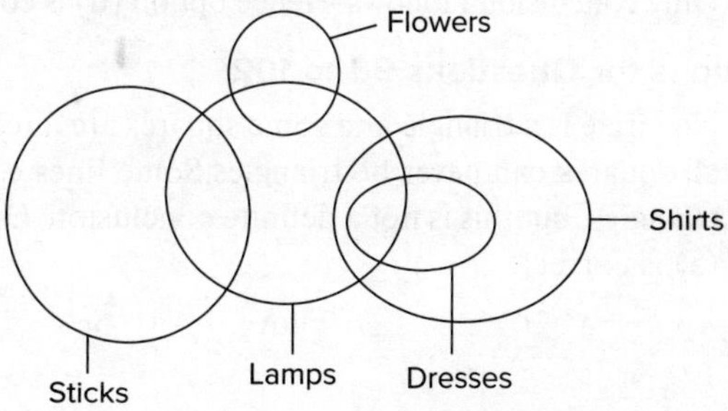

From the above diagram it is clear that none of the given conclusion follows. Hence, option (d) is correct.

95.

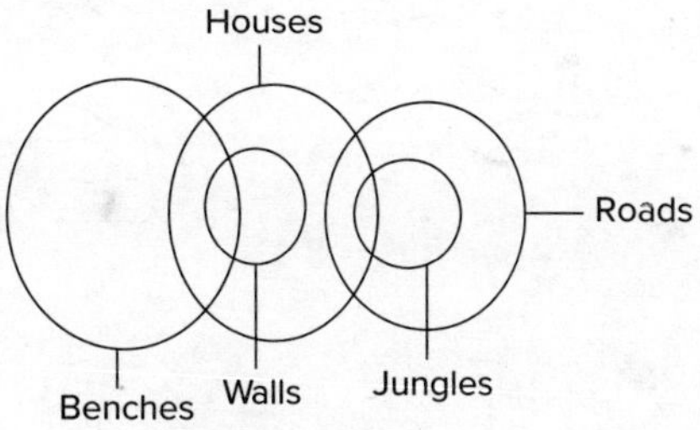

Only conclusions III and IV follow. Hence, option (b) is correct

96. We can make the following Venn diagram to depict the situation:

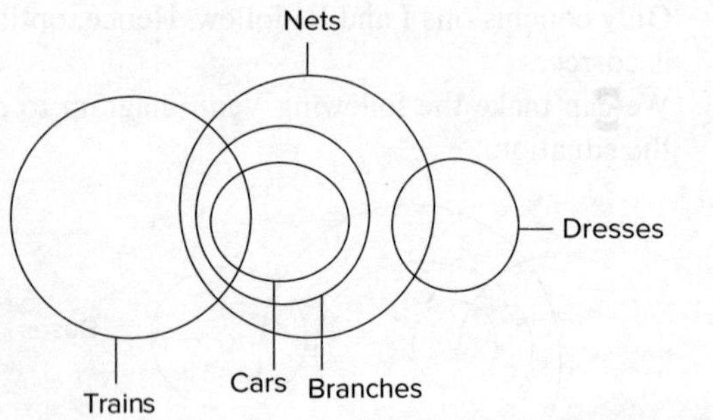

From the above diagram it is clear that conclusions II and III follow. Hence, option (b) is correct.

97.

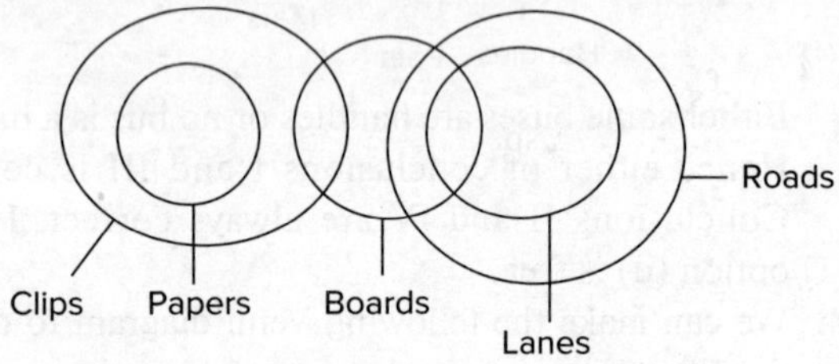

Only conclusion I follows. Hence option (d) is correct.

Solutions for Questions 98 to 102:

98. No circle is a triangle and some squares are circles so all squares can never be triangles.Some lines can be triangles, but this is not a definite conclusion. Option (a) is correct.

99. None of the given conclusions follow. Option (b) is correct.

100.

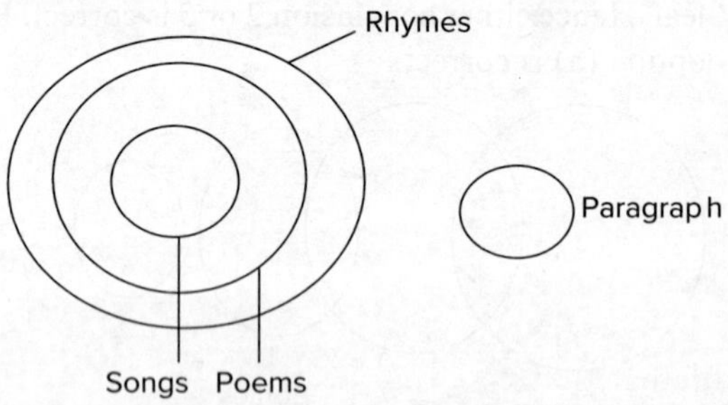

From the above diagram it is clear that no song is a paragraph and no poem is a paragraph. Hence, both the conclusions follow. Hence, option (d) is correct.

101. Only conclusion II follows. Option (c) is correct.

102.

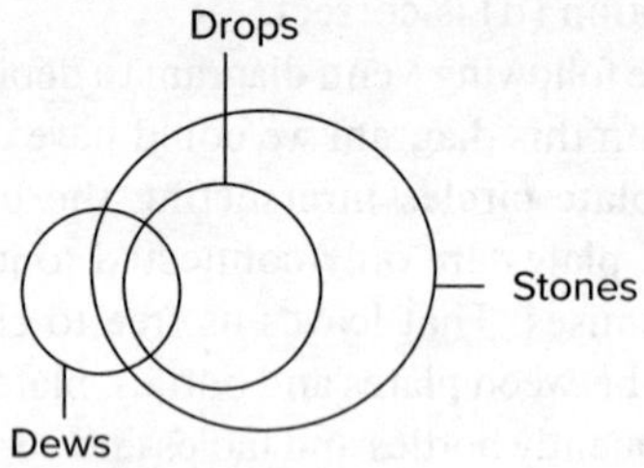

Both the conclusions follow the given statement. Hence option (d) is correct.

CHAPTER 12

Logical Deduction

Chapter Launchpad

Scan this QR code for an introductory video on Logical Deduction

As the name itself suggests, logical deduction questions require logical thinking. Every question starts off with a premise which might be of any one of the following types:

LOGICAL DEDUCTIONS PREMISES—VARIOUS PATTERNS

Type 1: If A Happens B Happens

This means that A leads to B, but does not mean the reverse, i.e., if B has happened, A must have happened. In such situations, A is a sufficient condition for B, but is not a necessary condition.

Let's look at the following example:

If I go to a movie, I enjoy myself.

This would mean, that if I have gone to the movie, I will definitely enjoy myself. However, it does not mean that if I have enjoyed myself, I must have gone to the movie–there are so many ways of enjoying yourself.

Another example of this type would be:

If Amitabh acts in a movie, he will earn money.

This does not mean that if he has earned money, he must have acted in a movie.

Type 2: Only If A Happens B Happens

In this case, A is a necessary and sufficient condition for the occurrence of B. In this case, there is reversibility of the logic, i.e., if B has happened, A must have happened.

Only if Saurav plays the match, will he get a hundred.

If Saurav has got a hundred, he must have played the match.

Type 3: If A Happens B does not Happen

In this case, if A has happened, B does not happen. The opposite is also true, i.e., if B has happened, A must not have happened.

If Martina plays well, Sania will not win.

Type 4: If A does not Happen B will Happen

Again in this case, the reverse might not be true.

If Anand does not come, Kasparov will. This does not mean that if Kasparov comes, Anand will not come.

Type 5: Either A or B will Happen

One of the two has to happen. At the same time, the two events are exclusive of one another. If one happens, the other will not happen.

Either he becomes a TV star or he becomes a movie star.

Let us look at a few solved examples:

1. Shahrukh either acts as a villain, or he acts as a hero.
   - **A.** Shahrukh acts like a hero.
   - **B.** Shahrukh does not act like a villain.
   - **C.** Shahrukh acts like a villain.
   - **D.** Shahrukh does not act like a hero.

   (a) Only CD (b) Only BA
   (c) CD and BA (d) None of these

This question is based on an EITHER-OR Premise. Thus, we can see that CD is correct. Therefore, if he acts like a villain–(Statement C) he will not act like a hero (Statement D).

Similarly, BA can also be seen to be true. Hence, option (c) is correct.

2. Whenever Martin goes to a movie, he has nightmares.
   - **A.** Martin did not have nightmares.
   - **B.** Martin went to a movie.
   - **C.** Martin had nightmares.
   - **D.** Martin did not go to the movie.

   (a) AD (b) DC
   (c) CB (d) DA

When A happens, B happens. However, if A does not happen, it is not necessary that B will not happen. Also, if B has happened, it is not necessary that A must have happened.

However, if B has not happened, it is necessary that A must not have happened.

Thus, AD is the only correct sequence.

3. If I talk to my girl friends, then I do not need to take a pill for heartache.
   A. I talked to my girl friends.
   B. I did not need to take a pill for heartache.
   C. I needed to take a pill for heartache.
   D. I did not talk to my girl friends.
   (a) Only AB (b) Only DC
   (c) Only CD (d) AB and CD

This question falls under the category of if A happens, then B does not happen. However, if B has not happened, it does not mean that A has happened.

AB and CD are both logically correct.

EXERCISE

Directions for Questions 1 to 30: *Each question has a main statement, followed by four statements labelled A, B, C, and D. Choose the ordered pair of statements, where the first statement implies the second, and the two statements are logically consistent with the main statement.*

High Yield Questions

Scan this QR code to access video explanations of questions 1, 3, 7 and 11

1. One gets a chocolate every time one visits the restaurant.
   (A) I got a chocolate.
   (B) I didn't get a chocolate.
   (C) I didn't visit the restaurant.
   (D) I visited the restaurant.
   (a) AD (b) BD
   (c) DA (d) AC
2. Whenever I get a flower, I feel loved.
   (A) I got a flower.
   (B) I felt loved.
   (C) I didn't get a flower.
   (D) I didn't feel loved.
   (a) BA (b) BC
   (c) CD (d) DC
3. I wear a cap every time I play.
   (A) I played.
   (B) I didn't play.
   (C) I wore a cap.
   (D) I didn't wear a cap.
   (a) BD (b) CA
   (c) DB (d) AD
4. I feel happy every time I see an innovation.
   (A) I didn't see an innovation.
   (B) I saw an innovation.
   (C) I felt happy.
   (D) I didn't feel happy.
   (a) BC (b) AD
   (c) CB (d) CD
5. If you once visit the USA, you become addicted to its openness.
   (A) I visited the USA.
   (B) I didn't get addicted to the USA's openness.
   (C) I got addicted to the USA's openness.
   (D) I didn't visit the USA.
   (a) BD (b) DB
   (c) CA (d) AB
6. Whenever the villain makes an entry, the viewers boo.
   (A) The villain made an entry.
   (B) The viewers didn't boo.
   (C) The villain didn't make an entry.
   (D) The viewers booed.
   (a) BC (b) CB
   (c) DA (d) None of these
7. I get cold feet whenever I see an examination paper.
   (A) I saw an examination paper.
   (B) I didn't see an examination paper.
   (C) I got cold feet.
   (D) I didn't get cold feet.
   (a) CA (b) BD
   (c) DB (d) BC
8. I remember her every time I see her photograph.
   (A) I remembered her.
   (B) I saw her photograph.
   (C) I didn't see her photograph.
   (D) I didn't remember her.
   (a) CD (b) DC
   (c) AB (d) None of these
9. Whenever Devdas comes, Paro sings.
   (A) Paro is singing.
   (B) Devdas has come.
   (C) Devdas hasn't come.
   (D) Paro is not singing.
   (a) AB (b) BA
   (c) BC (d) CD
10. Every player will become a champ.
    (A) Rajesh is a player.
    (B) Rajesh will become a champ.

(C) Rajesh is not a player.
(D) Rajesh will not become a champ.

(a) AD (b) DA
(c) CD (d) DC

11. You can see the star only if you go to the cinema.
(A) I went to the cinema.
(B) I didn't see the star.
(C) I saw the star.
(D) I didn't go to the cinema.

(a) BD (b) DB
(c) AB (d) CD

12. You can find Chinese toys only in China.
(A) I didn't find Chinese toys.
(B) I found Chinese toys.
(C) I went to the fair.
(D) I didn't go to China.

(a) CD (b) CB
(c) CA (d) DA

13. I will marry Vandana only if she wears my ring.
(A) I married Vandana.
(B) Vandana wore my ring.
(C) I could not marry Vandana.
(D) Vandana didn't wear my ring.

(a) BA (b) BC
(c) DC (d) CD

14. Only in Africa, can you see the African elephant.
(A) You went to Africa.
(B) You didn't go to Africa.
(C) You saw the African elephant.
(D) You didn't see the African elephant.

(a) AC (b) DB
(c) AD (d) BD

15. You cannot clear the CAT unless you are intelligent.
(A) You are intelligent.
(B) You can clear the CAT.
(C) You are not intelligent.
(D) You cannot clear the CAT.

(a) BD (b) AC
(c) CD (d) AB

16. Martina wins the tournament provided she plays the final.
(A) Martina played the final.
(B) Martina won the tournament.
(C) Martina did not win the tournament.
(D) Martina did not play the final.

(a) AB (b) BA
(c) CD (d) AC

17. You can drive over 100 km/h only on the freeway.
(A) You are on the freeway.
(B) You cannot drive over 100 km/h.
(C) You can drive over 100 km/h.
(D) You are not on the freeway.

(a) DB (b) AC
(c) BD (d) AB

18. The exam is either CAT or XAT.
(A) The exam is CAT.
(B) The exam is not CAT.
(C) The exam is XAT.
(D) The exam is not XAT.

(a) AB (b) CD
(c) BA (d) BC

19. Mr. Condoleeni is either an engineer or a doctor.
(A) Mr. Condoleeni is an engineer.
(B) Mr. Condoleeni is not a doctor.
(C) Mr. Condoleeni is not an engineer.
(D) Mr. Condoleeni is a doctor.

(a) AB (b) AD
(c) DA (d) BC

20. Every inhabitant of the planet is either male or female. Given M is an inhabitant of the planet.
(A) M is male.
(B) M is female.
(C) M is not male
(D) M is not female.

(a) AB (b) CD
(c) AC (d) BC

21. Either Shravan is sick; or he is stoned.
(A) Shravan is sick.
(B) Shravan is not sick.
(C) Shravan is stoned.
(D) Shravan is not stoned.

(a) AB (b) DA
(c) AC (d) CD

22. Whenever Shyam hears of an exam, he loses sleep.
(A) Shyam heard of an exam.
(B) Shyam did not hear of the exam
(C) Shyam lost sleep.
(D) Shyam did not lose sleep.

(a) CA (b) BD
(c) DB (d) AD

23. Either the bus is late; or it has turned turtle.
(A) The bus is late.
(B) The bus is not late.
(C) The bus has turned turtle.
(D) The bus has not turned turtle.

(a) AB (b) DB
(c) CA (d) BC

24. When I see a horror movie I have a bad dream.
(A) I saw a horror movie.
(B) I did not see a horror movie.
(C) I did not have a bad dream.
(D) I had a bad dream.

(a) CB (b) AD
(c) BC (d) AC

25. Either Veronica is indisposed or she is sad.
 (A) Veronica is not indisposed.
 (B) Veronica is not sad.
 (C) Veronica is indisposed.
 (D) Veronica is sad.
 (a) AB (b) AD
 (c) BA (d) DA

26. Ravan gets a mild flu whenever he eats ice creams.
 (A) Ravan gets a mild flu.
 (B) Ravan does not eat ice creams.
 (C) Ravan does not get a mild flu.
 (D) Ravan eats ice creams.
 (a) AB (b) DC
 (c) AC (d) DA

27. Either they have no confidence in the management or they are irritable.
 (A) They are irritable.
 (B) They are not irritable.
 (C) They have confidence in the management.
 (D) They have no confidence in the management.
 (a) BA (b) CB
 (c) DA (d) BD

28. Whenever Vijay reads late into the night, his grandfather reprimands him.
 (A) His grandfather does not reprimand Vijay.
 (B) Vijay reads late into the night.
 (C) Vijay reads early in the morning.
 (D) Vijay's grandfather reprimands him in the morning.
 (a) CD (b) BD
 (c) AB (d) None of these

29. All irresponsible bosses shout if their workers do not fall in line.
 (A) All irresponsible bosses do not shout.
 (B) Workers fall in line.
 (C) Workers do not fall in line.
 (D) All irresponsible bosses shout.
 (a) AB (b) BA
 (c) CA (d) All of these

30. Either Aamir is angry, or he shows mock anger.
 (A) Aamir shows mock anger.
 (B) Aamir is angry.
 (C) Aamir does not show mock anger.
 (D) Aamir is not angry.
 (a) Only CB (b) Only DA
 (c) Only BA (d) CB and DA

ANSWER KEY

1. (c)	2. (d)	3. (c)	4. (a)
5. (a)	6. (a)	7. (c)	8. (b)
9. (b)	10. (d)	11. (b)	12. (d)
13. (c)	14. (d)	15. (c)	16. (b)
17. (a)	18. (d)	19. (a)	20. (d)
21. (b)	22. (c)	23. (d)	24. (a)
25. Both (b) and (d)	26. (d)	27. (d)	
28. (d)	29. (b)	30. (d)	

CHAPTER 13

Binary Logic

Chapter Launchpad

Scan this QR code for an introductory video on Binary Logic

These question types are called binary logic questions simply because each question contains two logic streams that have to be matched, in order to get to the correct answer. Mainly, there are two types of questions as below:

BINARY LOGIC QUESTION—PATTERNS

Type (I)

In this question type, three persons speak two statements each–one of which is true, the other is false.

The two logic streams to be considered are:

1. The logic of the Statements, i.e., the logic of what is said within the statements.
2. The logic of the Basic Conditions, i.e., the logic of the fact that if one sentence is taken as true, the other will be false automatically.

The process of solving these questions is best illustrated through an example.

Gauri Islands is the name of an island. The inhabitants of this island always answer any question with two sentences. One of which is always true and the other always false.

Milly, Silly and Dilly are the three daughters of the chief whip of this island. Out of them, two are minor and one is of a marriageable age. You have been caught as an intruder on the island and you have two options given by the Chief Whip: identify his daughter who is of marriageable age. If you do so, you can have the privilege of marrying her and becoming the new Chief Whip in the future. On the other hand, if you cannot, you will be executed. Only Silly has dentures in her teeth. On questioning the three daughters, these are the answers you get:

Milly: "I am shorter than Silly. The girl of marriageable age has dentures in her teeth."

Silly: "I am shorter than Milly. Dilly is the one who is of a marriageable age."

Dilly: The girl of marriageable age is amongst the three of us. I am of a marriageable age."

Who is the girl of marriageable age?

(a) Milly (b) Dilly
(c) Silly (d) Can't say

In the above question, you should see that, the first statement of Dilly has to be correct (By logic of the statement–if you evaluate what the statement is saying, it is clear that it has to be true. It can be easily understood that the girl of marriageable age is amongst the three of the girls.)

In this case, if this statement is true, then Dilly's second statement is automatically false. Further, since Dilly's second statement is false, Silly's second statement will also be false. (By evaluating the sentence logic–as both these statements are saying the same thing.) Hence, Silly's first statement will be true (Basic Condition logic) and hence further, Milly's first statement will be false (It is saying the opposite of Silly's true first statement–Statement Logic). Therefore, Milly's second statement has to be true. Hence, Silly has to be the one of marriageable age.

Type (II)

In these type of questions, we have two types of people: those who always speak the truth, and those who always lie. These questions are also classified as Binary Logic questions since they are solved on the basis of two logical streams that run parallel to each other, viz: Basic Condition Logic (BCL) and Logic of the Statements (LoS).

The Basic Condition Logic flows from the fact that if a person always speaks the truth, then whatever statement he says must be true. However, in some cases, a clash might arise between the Basic Condition Logic and the Statement Logic, if it can be seen that the statement is obviously false.

The best way to understand this question type is by looking at an example:

You meet three inhabitants–Rohit, Mohit and Sohit–standing together. You ask Rohit "Are you a type X or type Y?" He mumbles something, which you cannot catch, so you ask Mohit, "What did Rohit say?" Mohit replies "Rohit said that he is type Y." You look at Sohit and he says, "Do not believe Mohit, he is lying."

Which of the following is true?

1. Rohit is a type X
2. Mohit is a type Y

3. Sohit is a type Y
4. All of these

By BCL, Sohit could be Type X or Type Y:

If Sohit is Type Y, his statement must be false. That means Mohit is not lying. Hence, Mohit should be Type X and hence his statement must be true, i.e., Rohit must have said that he is Type Y.

However, if you look at Rohit, he could not have made this statement in either case.

If we assume that Rohit is Type X, he would only speak the truth and he would then say that he is Type X, not that he is Type Y.

On the other hand, if we were to assume that Rohit is a Type Y, he would only speak false. But then he could not have said that he is Type Y, since that statement would be true.

EXERCISE

TYPE (I)

Directions: *On an island 'Mola-Moola', the inhabitants always answer any question with two sentences–one of which is always true and the other always false.*

Read the description below very carefully and choose the correct answer for the questions that follow:

High Yield Questions

Scan this QR code to access video explanations of the following questions:
Type 1: Questions 1-6
Type 2: Questions 1-4

The commissioner of the island discovers that smuggling is rampant there. You have been hired as a private detective in order to determine the identity of the culprits and also to know more about the next heist on the basis of a plane. You question three suspects as to when the plane is expected and what it looks like. This is what they have to say:

Subhash: It arrives at 11:00 p.m. The colour of the plane is only red.

Rubhash: It arrives at 11:00 p.m. The colour of the plane is only yellow.

Bibhash: I know at what time the plane arrives. Rubhash is lying about the time of arrival.

1. At what time does the plane arrive?
   (a) 6 p.m. (b) 11 p.m.
   (c) Can't say (d) Won't arrive
2. What is the colour of the plane?
   (a) Can't say (b) Red
   (c) Yellow (d) Both red and yellow

Suddenly, a murder takes place on the island. It is imperative that you locate the murderer. On further investigation, you find that the murderer has to be a person who has been to the Chief Whip's house within the last five days (today is Friday). By careful questioning, you narrow the possibilities down to three people. This is what they have to say.

Rani: "I went to the Chief Whip's house. It was before Monday."

Vani: "Rani did not go to the Chief Whip's house. I have not gone to the Chief Whip's house in the last five days either".

Siwani: "Rani did not go to the Chief Whip's house. I am not the murderer."

3. Who is the murderer?
   (a) Siwani (b) Rani
   (c) Vani (d) Can't say

In the village of Rampur, all inhabitants always answer any question with two sentences, one of which is always true, the other is always false.

While visiting the village, Gauri meets three inhabitants– Rajesh, Mahesh and Ramesh, near the village square. One of them is wearing a suit. Knowing that they were there to resolve a dispute over the ownership of some land, you ask them–"Who got the land?" They answer as follows:

Rajesh: "I got the land. Ramesh is wearing the suit."

Mahesh: "I am wearing the suit. I got the land."

Ramesh: "I got the land. I am not wearing the suit."

4. Who is wearing the suit?
   (a) Rajesh (b) Mahesh
   (c) Ramesh (d) None of these
5. Who got the land?
   (a) Rajesh (b) Can't say
   (c) Ramesh (d) Mahesh

On waking up the next morning, you find that your brand new watch has been stolen. The suspects are the same trio you met the previous day. You question them (knowing that only one of them is guilty). And they reply as follows:

Rajesh: "Mahesh did not do it. I did not do it."

Mahesh: "I did not do it. Ramesh did not do it."

Ramesh: "I did not do it. I do not know who did it."

6. Who stole the watch?
   (a) Can't say (b) Ramesh
   (c) Mahesh (d) Rajesh

In a small island called Neverneverland, the people always answer any question with two sentences–one of which is always right and the other is false.

Perhaps due to this peculiar habit, there's been a high rate of suicides on the island. As a doctor, you have to identify potentially suicidal people and counsel them. You know that all people who are suicidal feel that life is futile. On questioning three inhabitants, these are the answers you get:

Anuj: "Himansu is suicidal. I am not suicidal."

Himansu: "I do not want to die. Akshay does not want to die."

Akshay: "Life is futile. I am suicidal."

7. Who among the three is suicidal?
(a) Anuj and Himansu
(b) Himansu
(c) Himansu and Akshay
(d) Akshay

8. Which of them is lying about another person's tendencies?
(a) Akshay
(b) Himansu
(c) Anuj and Himansu
(d) None of them is lying about another person's tendencies

Going around the village, you come across three people. One of them is a dentist, one a barrister and one a professor. You want to know who is who.

Peter says, "I am not a professor. Shina is not a professor."

Matt says, "Peter is not a barrister. Shina is a professor."

Shina says, "Peter is not a dentist. I am not a professor."

9. Which of the following is true?
(a) Shina is the professor
(b) Peter is the dentist
(c) Matt is the barrister.
(d) None of these

Further, you come across three women, one of whom is an excellent singer. You start questioning them, when you notice that Minaxi is wearing a flower in her hair.

Madhuri says, "I am not the singer. The singer wears a flower in her hair."

Minaxi says, "I am the singer. The singer is amongst us."

Jaya says, "Madhuri is the singer. Minaxi is not the singer."

10. Who is the singer?
(a) Madhuri (b) Minaxi
(c) Jaya (d) None of these

You want to expand your horizons and decide to go to the village of "Where is Who", which is further inside. You come to the border of "Kya Kya" and see a fork. One leads left and the other right. There are no other roads. You ask the inhabitants:

Maroof says, "I do not speak to strangers. I am new to these parts."

Nafish says, "Take the road to the right. I am married to Ayesha."

Ayesha says, "I am not Nafish's wife. Maroof is not new to these parts."

11. Which of the following is true?
(a) The road to the right leads to "Where is Who"
(b) The road to the left leads to "Where is Who"
(c) Nafish is married to Ayesha
(d) None of these

On moving further, you come across another small village of Patina, whose inhabitants answer all questions with two sentences–one of which is true and the other always false.

I asked Shahrukh, Amitabh and Abhishek, "Did it snow last night?" and I got the following replies:

Shahrukh: Yes, it snowed last night. Moreover, Amitabh fell sick last night.

Amitabh: Yes, it snowed last night. I never lie.

Abhishek: No, it did not snow last night. Shahrukh got married yesterday.

12. Which of the following statements is true?
(a) It did not snow last night
(b) Amitabh fell sick last night
(c) Shahrukh got married yesterday
(d) None of these

Rophas Khopas is a small land locked country in the Vindhyanchal forest range, with a distinct dress, culture, food habits, national language, national dance, a national bird, and a national animal. The inhabitants speak in two sentences–one of which is true and the other false.

I asked Shiva, Monu and Vijay, the three important citizens of Rophas Khopas, "What is the national language of Rophas Khopas?" and I got the following replies:

Shiva: "French is our national language. Hundred percent of our citizens are literate."

Monu: Latin is our national language. We have a very poor literacy rate in the country.

Vijay: We have a very poor literacy rate in the country. Our national language is Bhasha Khopas.

13. The national language of Rophas Khopas is
(a) French (b) Latin
(c) Bhasha Khopas (d) Can't be ascertained

14. With reference to question 13 above, the rate of literacy in Rophas Khopas is
(a) Very poor (b) Good
(c) 100% (d) Can't be ascertained

I asked Shiva, Monu and Vijay, "What is your national dress?" and I got the following replies:

Shiva: Our national dress is Pathani suit. People wear the national dress on very special occasions only.

Monu: Our national dress is Sari. People wear the national dress on very special occasions only.

Vijay: Our national dress is Suit Boot. But no one is ever permitted to wear the national dress.

15. The national dress of Rophas Khopas is

(a) Pathani suit (b) Sari
(c) Suit Boot (d) Can't be ascertained

I asked Shiva, Monu and Vijay, "What is your national food?" and I got the following replies:

Shiva: Our national food is *sabudana khichdi*. Most of our people are hale and hearty.

Monu: Our people are not hale and hearty at all. Our national food is *makki roti*.

Vijay: Most of our people are hale and hearty. Our national food is *rice kheer*.

16. The national food of Rophas Khopas is:

(a) sabudana khichdi (b) makki roti
(c) rice kheer (d) can't be ascertained

17. With reference to Question 16 above, in Rophas Khopas:

(a) People are not hale and hearty
(b) Some people are hale and hearty
(c) Most people are hale and hearty
(d) Can't be ascertained

I asked Shiva, Monu and Vijay, "What is your national bird?" and got the following replies:

Shiva: Our national animal is cackatoo. We are a peace loving country.

Monu. Our national animal is sparrow. We are a peace loving country.

Vijay: Our national bird is owl. But, we worship the sparrow.

18. The national bird of Rophas Khopas is

(a) Sparrow (b) Cackatoo
(c) Owl (d) Can't be ascertained

I asked Shiva, Monu and Vijay, "What is your national animal?" and I got following replies:

Shiva: Our national animal is kangaroo. We have thick growth of vegetation all over.

Monu: Our national animal is donkey. We have thick growth of vegetation all over.

Vijay: Ours is a mountainous country with almost no vegetation. Our national animal is koala.

19. The national animal of Rophas Khopas is

(a) Kangaroo (b) Donkey
(c) Koala (d) Can't be ascertained

I asked Shiva, Monu and Vijay, "What is your national dance?" and got the following replies:

Shiva: Samba is our national dance. We do not like or appreciate cricket.

Monu: Salsa is our national dance. We are great lovers of aggressive cricket.

Vijay: Disco is our national dance. We are great lovers of aggressive cricket.

20. The national dance of Rophas Khopas is

(a) Samba (b) Salsa
(c) Disco (d) Can't be ascertained

21. With reference to Question 20 above, people of Rophas Khopas:

(a) Do not like or appreciate cricket
(b) Like and appreciate cricket
(c) Are great lovers of aggressive cricket
(d) Can't be ascertained.

In the parliament of the Ravindra Rami, all members have a peculiar habit. Of any two sentences they speak, one is false and the other is true. You record the statements of three sitting members: Rozor, Sam, and Michael.

Rozor: The President claims he is the President. I am the President.

Sam: I am the President. Rozor is the President.

Michael: I am the President. Sam knows who is the President.

Answer the following questions based on these recorded statements.

22. The real President can be determined from

(a) Sam's and Rozor's statements alone
(b) Sam's and Michael's statements alone
(c) Michael's and Rozor's statements alone
(d) None of the above

23. If Rozor's first statement is false, which of the following cannot be President?

(a) Sam
(b) Rozor
(c) Michael
(d) Rozor's first statement cannot be false

24. Who is the President?

(a) Sam
(b) Rozor
(c) Michael
(d) Can't be determined

25. Whose first statement is true?

(a) Sam and Michael
(b) Michael and Rozor
(c) Sam and Rozor
(d) Can't be determined

26. Whose first statement is false?

(a) Sam (b) Rozor
(c) Michael (d) Sam and Michael

You move on. Next, you are asked to solve the mystery of who murdered Manmohan, the most influential resident of the village. You question three suspects:

Ali says, "It was me who killed Manmohan. It was Saif."
Saif says, "It was me who killed Manmohan. It was Ramu."
Ramu says, "It was not me who killed Manmohan. It was not Ali."

27. Who murdered Manmohan?
(a) Ali
(b) Saif
(c) Ramu
(d) Such a situation is not possible

28. While Balbir had his back turned, a dog ran into his butcher shop, snatched a piece of meat off the counter and ran out. Balbir was mad when he realised what had happened. He asked three other shopkeepers, who had seen the dog, to describe it. The shopkeepers really didn't want to help Balbir. So each of them made a statement which contained one truth and one lie.
(i) Shopkeeper number 1 said: "The dog had black hair and a long tail."
(ii) Shopkeeper number 2 said: "The dog had a short tail and wore a collar."
(iii) Shopkeeper number 3 said: "The dog had white hair and no collar."
Based on the above statements, which of the following could be a correct description?
(a) The dog had white hair, short tail and no collar.
(b) The dog had white hair, long tail and a collar.
(c) The dog had black hair, long tail and a collar.
(d) The dog had black hair, long tail and no collar.

29. Three tribes live on a remote island Rokas Phokas. The Greenies always tell the truth. The Fishmongers never tell the truth. The Wishy-Washies alternate telling the truth and lying with their statements alternating true and false or false and true.
The world renowned explorer, the Sammy, landed on the island and questionsed the natives, Tarun, Dipesh and Harish.

Explorer:
Tarun, to which tribe do you belong?
Tarun:
I'm a Greenie.
Explorer:
Dipesh, to which tribe do you belong?
Dipesh:
I'm a Fishmonger.
Explorer:
Was Tarun telling the truth?
Dipesh:
Yes.
Explorer:
Harish, to which tribe do you belong?
Harish:
I'm a Greenie.
Explorer:
To which tribe does Tarun belong?
Harish:
Tarun's a Wishy-Washie.
Which person is the Fishmonger?

(a) Dipesh (b) Harish
(c) Tarun (d) Cannot be determined

TYPE (II)

Directions for Questions 1 to 4: *The following questions are based on an island called Gutar Goo on which there are only two kinds of inhabitants:*
Type X: People who always speak the truth; and
Type Y: People who always lie.

1. You go to the island and see a group of three people–Arun, Bakshi and Calvin. You ask Arun, "How many type X's are there amongst you?" Unfortunately, Arun's reply is drowned by some noise and you ask Bakshi, "What did Arun say?" Bakshi says, "Arun said that there is one type X among us." However, Calvin immediately says, " Don't believe Bakshi, he is lying."
Which of the following is true?
(a) Bakshi is a type X
(b) Arun is a type Y
(c) Calvin is a type X
(d) None of these

2. You are very intrigued. You decide to find out more. You question two other persons–Manoj and Hemant. Manoj says, "At least one of us is a type Y."
Which of the following is true?
(a) Manoj is type X (b) Hemant is a type X
(c) Both (a) and (b) (d) None of these

3. You are further intrigued and decide to continue further on into the island of Gutar Goo. Coming across a group of three persons–Raju, Golu, and Suyash–you hear them make two statements:
Raju: "All of us are type Y's".
Golu: "Exactly one of us is a type X."
Which of the following is true?
(a) Raju is type Y
(b) Golu is a type X
(c) Suyash is a type Y
(d) All of these

4. By now you have had just a bit too much of the island–however, on the insistence of your friend Bakshi, you continue further. You meet two persons–Suyash and Divyansh. Suyash says, "I am a type Y. But Divyansh isn't."
Who is type X?
(a) Suyash (b) Divyansh
(c) Indeterminate (d) None of these

Directions for Questions 5 to 10: *Read the following paragraph and answer the questions that follow.*

There are two types of inhabitants in Tatabalery–A type and B type. The A type of inhabitants always speak the truth and the B type of inhabitants always lie.

5. Rocky says, "I always lie." Which type of an inhabitant is he?
   (a) A
   (b) B
   (c) Either A or B
   (d) The given statement is infeasible
6. Peter says, "According to Rocky, I always speak the truth." Which of the following is a correct conclusion?
   (a) Peter has to be of type A
   (b) Peter has to be of type B
   (c) Rocky has to be of type A
   (d) Rocky has to be of type B
7. Booker says. "Shane and I are of the same type." Which of the following is a correct conclusion?
   (a) Booker and Shane are necessarily of the same type
   (b) Shane has to be of type A
   (c) Booker and Shane cannot be of the same type
   (d) The given statement is infeasible
8. Ramu says "Basu and I are of different types." Which of the following is a correct conclusion?
   (a) Ramu and Basu are of Type B and Type A respectively
   (b) Ramu and Basu cannot be of the same type
   (c) Basu has to be of Type B
   (d) Shyam has to be of Type B
9. Shane says, "Booker and I are of different types." Which of the following is a correct conclusion?
   (a) Shane and Booker are of Type B and Type A respectively
   (b) Shane and Booker cannot be of the same type
   (c) Booker has to be of Type B
   (d) None of these
10. Booker says, "At least one person among Shane and I always lies." What types are Booker and Shane respectively?
   (a) B, A
   (b) B, B
   (c) A, B
   (d) It is not possible to deduce

Directions for Questions 11 to 13: *Refer to the passage below and answer questions given below it.*

The inhabitants of the Island of Dreams have very bright and interesting lives. Just as we earthlings have continuity in our daily lives, the inhabitants of the Island of Dreams have continuity in both their waking lives, as well as their dreams. As a result, the inhabitants of the Island of Dreams have great difficulty in knowing whether they are awake or asleep at a given time. However, the inhabitants can be classified into two broad types–Awakers and Asleepers.

An Awaker is characterised by the fact that everything they believe while they are awake is true, and everything they believe while they are asleep is false. An Asleeper on the other hand, has the characteristic that everything he believes while asleep is true, and everything he believes while awake is false.

11. The Island has a President, a Prime Minister and an Entertainment Minister. At one point, the Entertainment Minister believed that his bosses were of different types. Twelve hours later, he changed his state (from sleeping to waking or from waking to sleeping), and he then believed that the President was an Awaker and the Prime Minister was an Asleeper. What type is the President?
   (a) Awaker
   (b) Asleeper
   (c) Could be either of the two types
   (d) Data inconsistent
12. With reference to Question 11, what type is the Prime Minister?
   (a) Awaker
   (b) Asleeper
   (c) Could be either of the two types
   (d) Data inconsistent
13. At one time, an inhabitant believed that he was both asleep and awake, what was he really?
   (a) Awaker
   (b) Asleeper
   (c) Could be either of the two types
   (d) Data inconsistent

Directions for Questions 14 to 16: *On the Island of Who Went Where, there are only two kinds of people.* ***Type No*** *are those who, when they ask a question, must always get a 'No' for an answer and* ***Type Yes*** *are those who must always get a 'Yes' for an answer to every question they ask. Based on this, answer questions 14 to 16.*

14. Victor and Trish are married. Victor asks you: "Are both of us of the type No?" You can conclude that
   (a) It is impossible for him to have asked such a question.
   (b) Victor is a No
   (c) Trish is a No
   (d) His type cannot be identified
15. Jay, Ajay and Vijay all approach you. Jay asks "Are at least two of us of the type No?" You can infer that
   (a) Jay is a No
   (b) Jay is a Yes
   (c) None of them is No
   (d) Can't be determined

16. Abhay, Lokesh, and Rituraj approach you. Abhay asks, "Is it true that neither Lokesh nor Rituraj can be Yes?" You can infer that
    (a) Both Lokesh and Rituraj are Nos.
    (b) Abhay is a No
    (c) Abhay is a Yes
    (d) None of these
17. In the town of Rokas Phokas, all the married people lie all the time. All the single people tell the truth all the time.

    Tennis is a popular pastime in Rokas Phokas. One day three women and three men decided to play. There were two couples and two single people among them.

    If you asked Chandar whether Bandar is married to Tender, he would say, "Haan."

    If you asked Pammi if she is married to Chandar, she would say, "Haan."

    If you asked Jimmy if he is married to Rashmi, he would say, "Nahin."

    If you knew enough about the local language to know whether "Haan" means "Yes" and "Nahin" means "No" or visa versa, you could figure out who is married to whom.

    Can you figure it out who is married to Chandar?
    (a) Tendar **(b)** Rashmi
    (c) Pammi **(d)** None of these
18. A, B and C each make four statements about each other. But only one of them made four true statements.

    A said:
    1. B owes me $10.
    2. C owes me $5.
    3. All of C's statements are true.
    4. All of B's statements are false.

    B said:
    1. I owe no money to A
    2. C owes me $7
    3. I am Scandinavian
    4. All A's statements are false.

    C said:
    1. I owe no money to anyone.
    2. B is Italian.
    3. I always tell the truth.
    4. Two of B's statements are true and two are false.

    Find which statements are true and which are false for all three.
    (a) B–All statements true, A's and C's Statements are false.
    (b) B–All statements false, A–All statements true and C's Statements are false.
    (c) B–All statements true, A's and C's Statements are also true.
    (d) None of these
19. My next door neighbour lies a lot. In fact, he only tells the truth on one day a week! One day he told me, "I lie on Mondays and on Tuesdays."
    The next day he said, "Today is either Thursday, Saturday or Sunday."
    The next day he said, "I lie on Wednesdays and Fridays."
    On which day of the week does my neighbour tell the truth?
    (a) Monday
    (b) Tuesday
    (c) Wednesday
    (d) None of these

ANSWER KEY

TYPE (I)

1. (b)	2. (a)	3. (b)	4. (b)
5. (a)	6. (c)	7. (a)	8. (d)
9. (a)	10. (c)	11. (a)	12. (c)
13. (a)	14. (a)	15. (c)	16. (b)
17. (c)	18. (d)	19. (c)	20. (a)
21. (c)	22. (a)	23. (d)	24. (a)
25. (c)	26. (c)	27. (d)	28. (b)
29. (b)			

TYPE (II)

1. (c)	2. (a)	3. (d)	4. (c)
5. (d)	6. (c)	7. (b)	8. (c)
9. (c)	10. (c)	11. (b)	12. (a)
13. (d)	14. (b)	15. (d)	16. (d)
17. (d)	18. (b)	19. (b)	

PART **II**

Reasoning Question Types from Other MBA Exams

SECTION 2
Abstract/Visual Reasoning

Scan this QR code to access a video on this section's chapters and the strategy to tackle them

CHAPTER 1

Analogy

INTRODUCTION

Abstract reasoning (also referred to as visual reasoning or non-verbal reasoning) is an essential component of many management competitive exams. It tests a candidate's ability to understand and interpret visual information without relying on language or numerical data. One of the critical topics within non-verbal reasoning is analogy, which requires the identification of relationships between shapes, patterns, figures, or symbols. The ability to recognize these relationships is crucial for solving analogy-based questions effectively.

In non-verbal analogy questions, two figures or patterns are provided in the form of a pair that share a specific relationship. You are then required to apply the same logic to another pair by choosing the correct option from the given choices. These questions test your ability to recognize similarities, differences, and transformations between objects.

Analogies help assess your ability to:

- **Identify Relationships:** You must be able to spot how two figures are connected through changes in shape, size, orientation, shading, or pattern.
- **Recognize Patterns:** Candidates are tested on their ability to recognize repeating trends or operations (like rotation, flipping, etc.) in the given figures.
- **Apply Logical Thinking:** You need to apply the same type of transformation or relationship from one pair to another, often requiring quick mental rotations, mirroring, or comparison.

Types of Non-Verbal Analogy Questions

1. **Shape Analogies:** In this type, two shapes or figures are provided, and you need to identify the same relationship in another set. For instance, a triangle might be converted into a square in the first pair, and similarly, a square might need to be converted into a pentagon in the correct answer.
2. **Rotation and Movement Based Analogies:** These involve figures that are rotated or parts of the figure would have moved from one location to another. Candidates are required to recognize the type of movement (clockwise, anti-clockwise, flipped, etc.) and apply it to the given options.
3. **Size and Number Analogies:** In some questions, the size of the figure or the number of elements within it might be increased or decreased.
4. **Shading or Color Analogies:** The analogy might involve changes in shading, coloring, or pattern within the figures. For instance, a fully shaded figure might become half-shaded, and the same operation needs to be applied to another figure.
5. **Geometric or Symmetry Analogies:** Analogies based on Geometry or symmetry might exhibit some specific geometrical properties (angles/sides etc) or some form of symmetry.

Strategies to Solve Non-Verbal Analogy Questions

Some of the key strategies to solve Analogy questions, include:

Step 1: Identify the relationship by looking for patterns in the first pair of figures. Focus on repetitive or identifiable patterns within the figures. Recognizing symmetry, identical shapes, movement or transformations can help identify the correct answer quickly.

Step 2: Check through the options: **Compare the options** to identify the pair in the options that exhibits the same relationship as the original pair. Also use the strategy of **option elimination** to eliminate obviously wrong options.

Example 1: Find out missing figure (?) of the problem from the given answer figures.

Problem figures

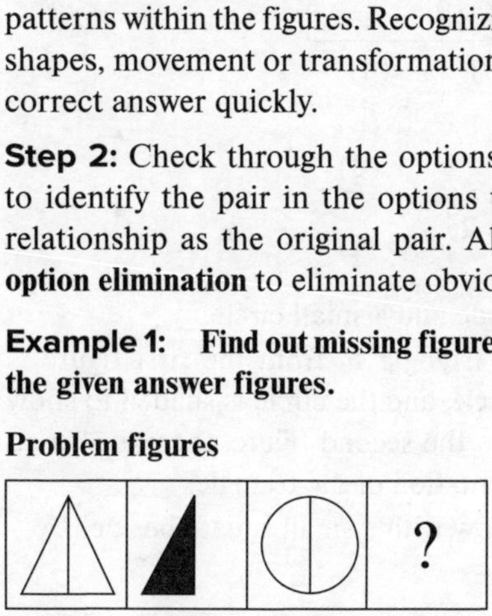

(A) (B) (C) (D)

Solution figures:

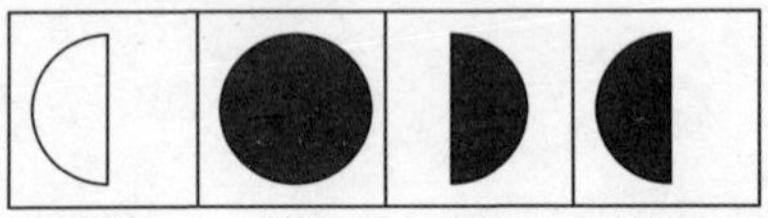

(1) (2) (3) (4)

(a) 1 (b) 2
(c) 3 (d) 4

Solution to Example 1:

Observing the sequence:

1. **First figure:** A triangle divided into two equal halves, one shaded and one unshaded.
2. **Second figure:** Remove the right portion of the figure 1 and shade the remaining part.
3. **Third figure:** A circle divided into two equal halves, one shaded and one unshaded.

Pattern Recognition:

- 2nd figure is the left half of 1st but in the shaded form. Similarly, 4th figure is the left half of 3rd but in the shaded form.

Fourth Figure Prediction:

Option (d) should come in place of?.

Example 2:

(A) (B) (C) (D)

(1) (2) (3) (4)

(a) 1 (b) 2
(c) 3 (d) 4

Solution to Example 2:

Detailed Explanation:

- **First figure**: A triangle and a small circle.
- **Second figure**: The **triangle** 1st from the first figure is placed inside the **circle**, and the circle is shaded to show a pie-like division. In the second figure, there is also an inversion of the orientation of the triangle.
- **Third figure**: An arrow with a small square beside it.

Identified Pattern:

- The second figure is formed by taking the first shape from the first figure (the triangle) and embedding it within the second shape (the circle), with a portion of the circle shaded. Also, the first shape is inverted in the second figure.
- Applying the same logic, the third figure (the arrow) should be embedded into the small square to form the fourth figure.

Correct Answer:

Option (d) is correct because it shows the **downward arrow embedded inside a square**, following the pattern observed from the earlier figures.

Example 3: Problem figures:

(A) (B) (C) (D)

Answer Figures:

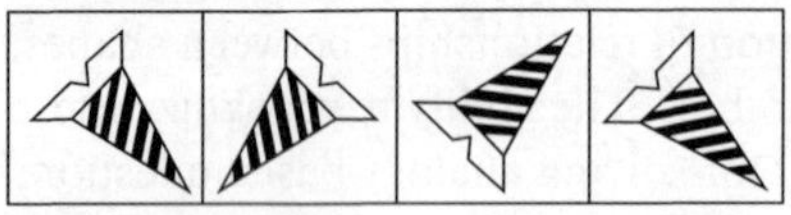

(1) (2) (3) (4)

(a) 1 (b) 2
(c) 3 (d) 4

Solution to Example 3: 2nd figure is the mirror image of the 1st figure. Using this analogy we get that the 5th figure is the mirror image of the 3rd figure. Option (d) is correct.

Example 4: Problem figures:

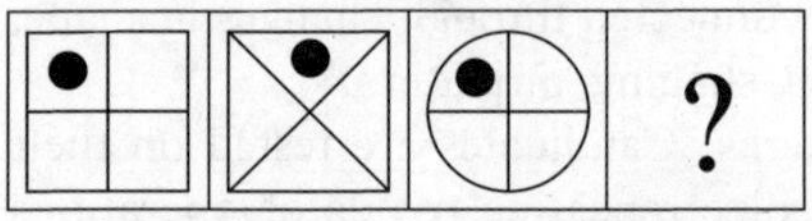

(A) (B) (C) (D)

Answer Figures:

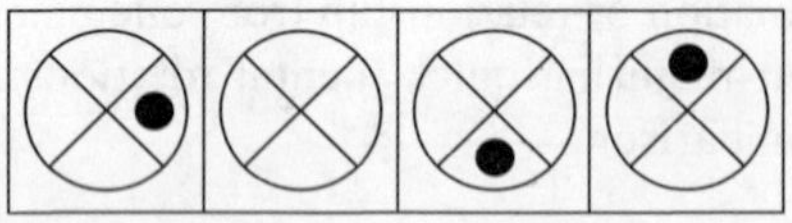

(1) (2) (3) (4)

(a) 1 (b) 2
(c) 3 (d) 4

Solution to Example 4: 2nd figure is the 45 degree clockwise rotation of the 1st figure. Using this analogy we get that option (d) is correct.

EXERCISE

Directions for Questions 1 to 5: *In the questions given below which one of the answer figures should come after the problem figures given, if the sequence were continued?*

1. Problem Figures:

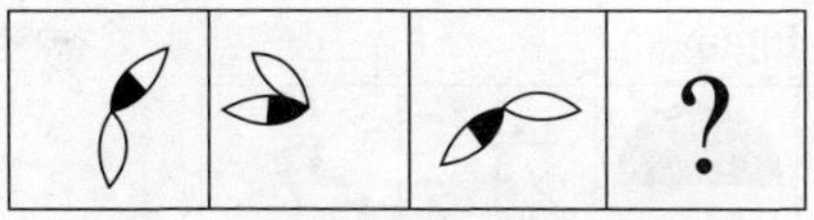

(A) (B) (C) (D)

Answer Figures:

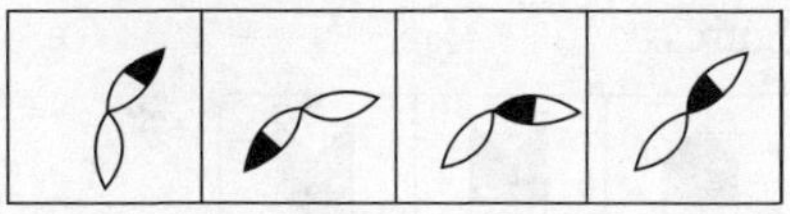

(1) (2) (3) (4)

(a) 1 (b) 2
(c) 3 (d) 4

2. Problem Figures:

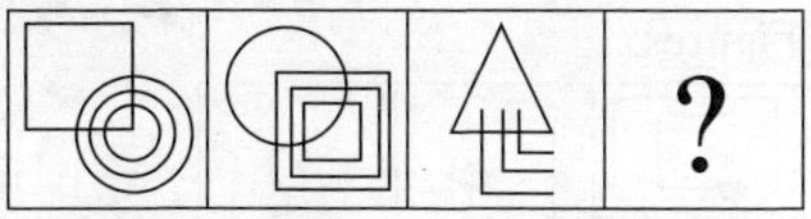

(A) (B) (C) (D)

Answer Figures:

(1) (2) (3) (4)

(a) 1 (b) 2
(c) 3 (d) 4

3. Problem Figures:

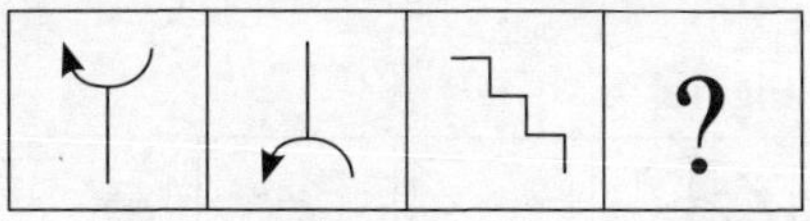

(A) (B) (C) (D)

Answer Figures:

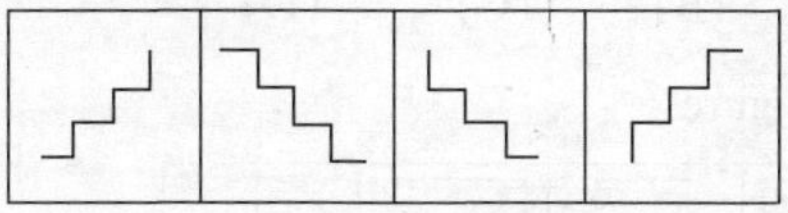

(1) (2) (3) (4)

(a) 1 (b) 2
(c) 3 (d) 4

4. Problem Figures:

(A) (B) (C) (D)

Answer Figures:

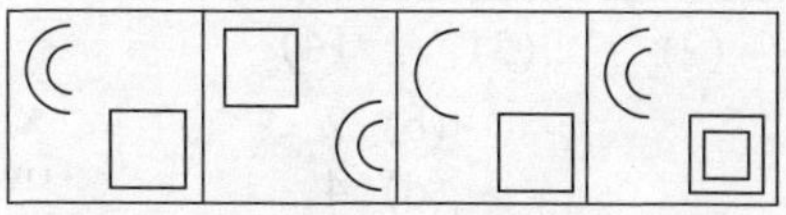

(1) (2) (3) (4)

(a) 1 (b) 2
(c) 3 (d) 4

5. Problem Figures:

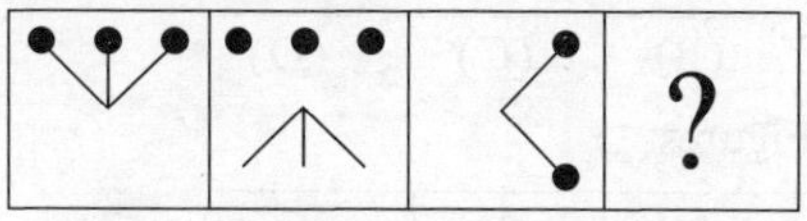

(A) (B) (C) (D)

Answer Figures:

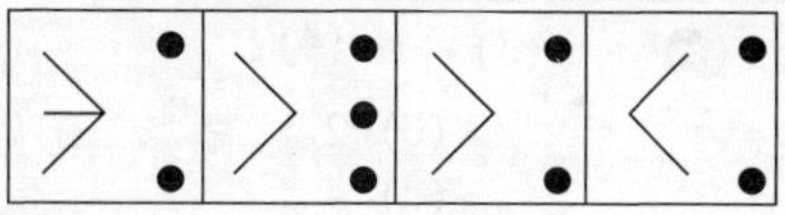

(1) (2) (3) (4)

(a) 1 (b) 2
(c) 3 (d) 4

Directions for Questions 6 to 15: *Select a suitable figure from the Answer Figures that would replace the question mark (?).*

6. Problem Figures:

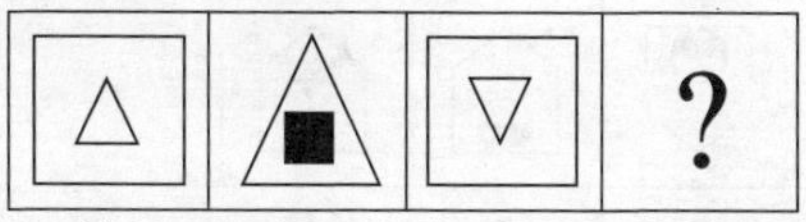

(A) (B) (C) (D)

Answer Figures:

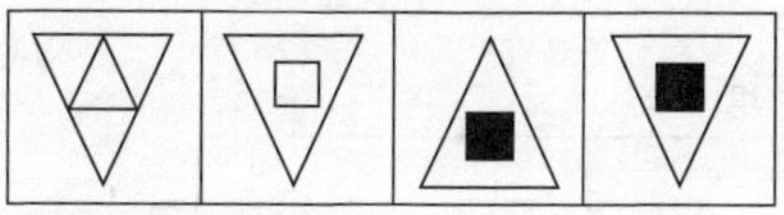

(1) (2) (3) (4)

(a) 1 (b) 2
(c) 3 (d) 4

7. Problem Figures:

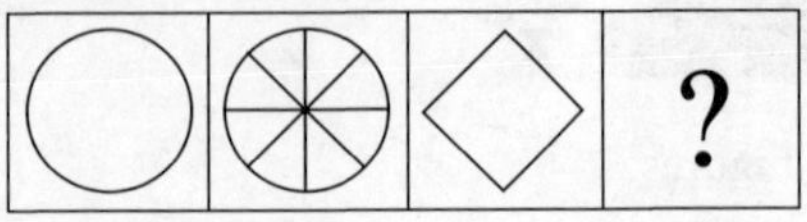

(A) (B) (C) (D)

Answer Figures:

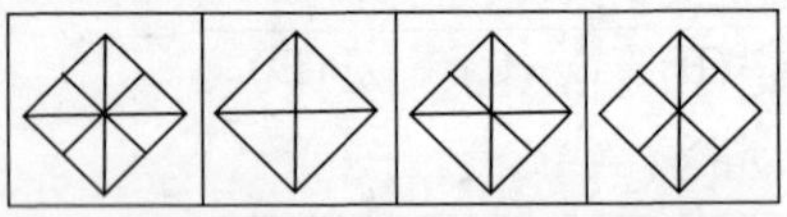

(1) (2) (3) (4)

(a) 1 (b) 2
(c) 3 (d) 4

8. Problem Figures:

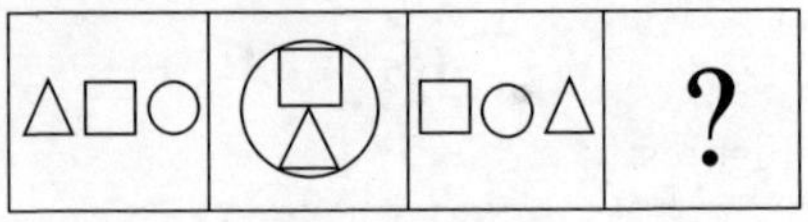

(A) (B) (C) (D)

Answer Figures:

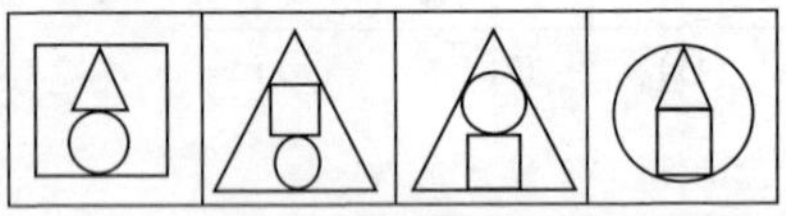

(1) (2) (3) (4)

(a) 1 (b) 2
(c) 3 (d) 4

9. Problem Figures:

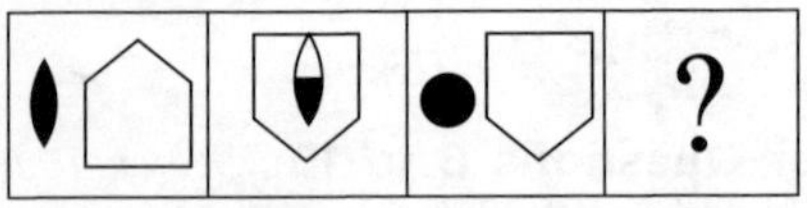

(A) (B) (C) (D)

Answer Figures:

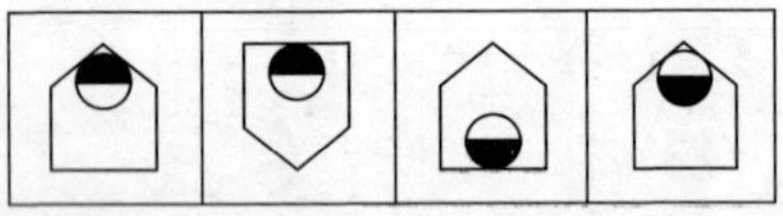

(1) (2) (3) (4)

(a) 1 (b) 2
(c) 3 (d) 4

10. Problem Figures:

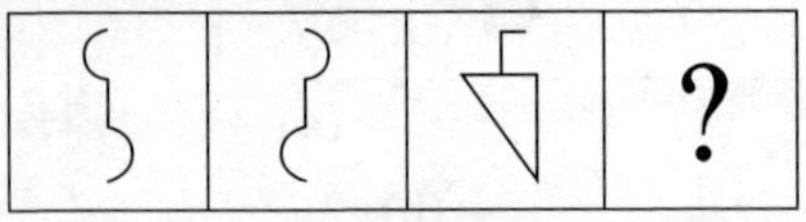

(A) (B) (C) (D)

Answer Figures:

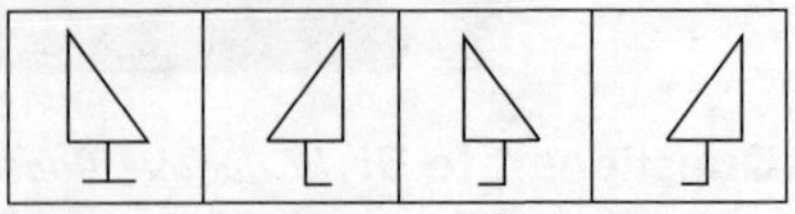

(1) (2) (3) (4)

(a) 1 (b) 2
(c) 3 (d) 4

11. Problem Figures:

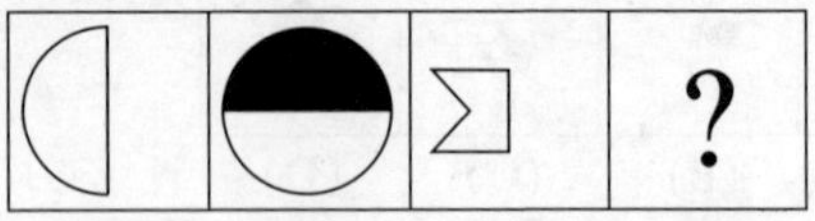

(A) (B) (C) (D)

Answer Figures:

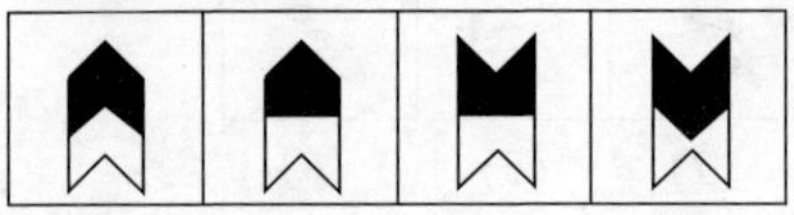

(1) (2) (3) (4)

(a) 1 (b) 2
(c) 3 (d) 4

12. Problem Figures:

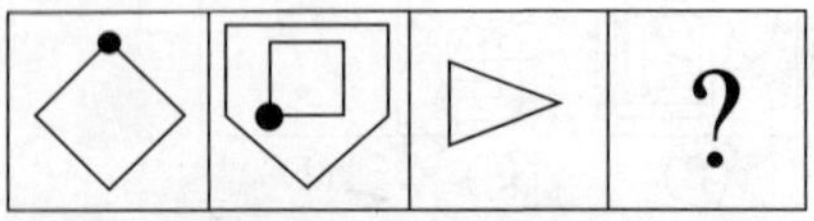

(A) (B) (C) (D)

Answer Figures:

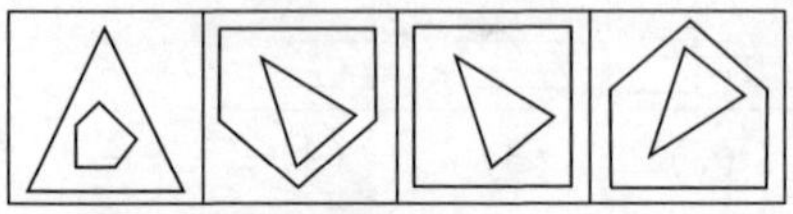

(1) (2) (3) (4)

(a) 1 (b) 2
(c) 3 (d) 4

13. Problem Figures:

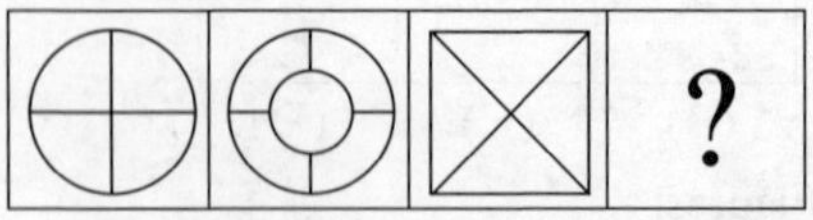

(A) (B) (C) (D)

Answer Figures:

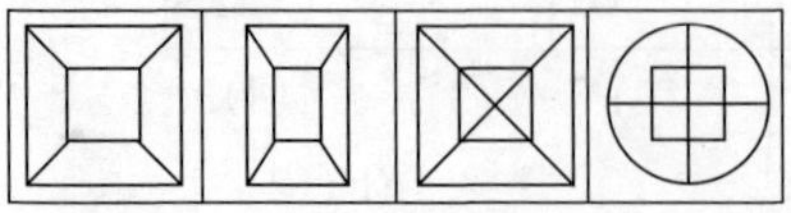

(1) (2) (3) (4)

(a) 1 (b) 2
(c) 3 (d) 4

14. Problem Figures:

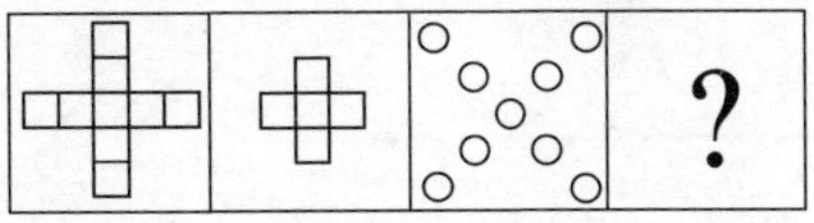

(A) (B) (C) (D)

Answer Figures:

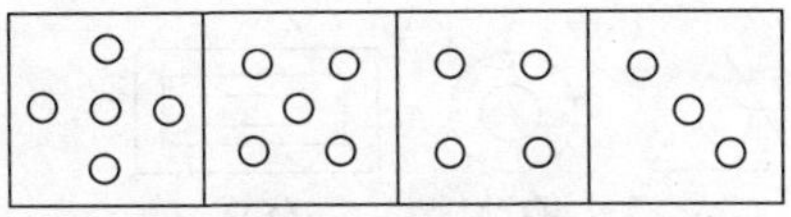

(1) (2) (3) (4)

(a) 1 (b) 2
(c) 3 (d) 4

15. Problem Figures:

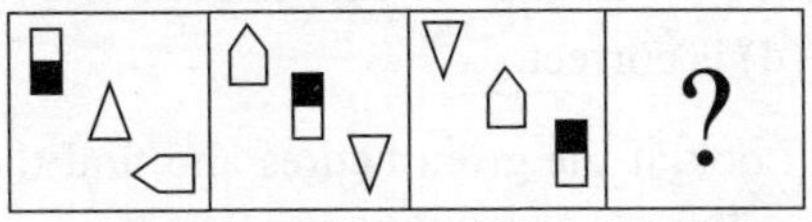

(A) (B) (C) (D)

Answer Figures:

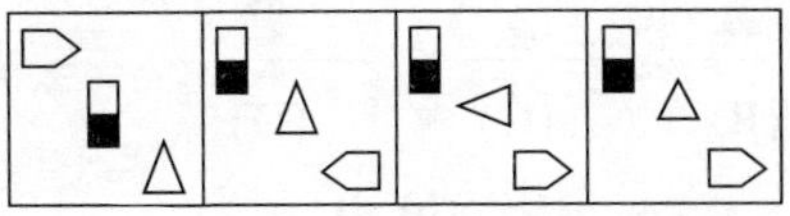

(1) (2) (3) (4)

(a) 1 (b) 2
(c) 3 (d) 4

High Yield Questions

Scan this QR code to access video explanations of questions 1, 12 and 15

ANSWER KEY

1. (c)	2. (d)	3. (d)	4. (b)
1. (c)	2. (a)	3. (a)	4. (b)
5. (c)	6. (d)	7. (a)	8. (c)
9. (d)	10. (d)	11. (c)	12. (c)
13. (a)	14. (b)	15. (d)	

SOLUTIONS AND SHORTCUTS

Solutions for Questions 1 to 5:

1. The half-shaded leaf rotates 135° anticlockwise, and the unshaded leaf rotates 135° clockwise. The shaded portion of the half-shaded leaf starts from the point where two leaves meet. Option (c) is correct.
2. The upper element is converted into an element like the lower elements, and each one of the lower elements is converted into a single element similar to the upper element. Option (a) is correct.
3. The figure gets vertically inverted. Option (a) is correct.
4. Each upper element is replaced by an element similar to the lower element(s), and each lower element is replaced by an element similar to the upper element(s). Option (b) is correct.
5. Except for the dots, the remaining part of the figure rotates 180° and shifts to the opposite side of the square boundary. Option (c) is correct.

Solutions for Questions 6 to 15:

6. Inner part of figure A is the outer part of figure B and outer part of figure A is the inner part of figure B but in a shaded part. So, figure D must have inverted triangle as the outer part and inner part is a shaded square. Hence, option (d) is correct.
7. To get figure B we divide figure A in eight parts. Similarly, if figure C will be divided into eight parts then we get figure D. Hence, option (a) is correct.
8. In figure A we have three shapes and figure B is same as the when we insert first two shapes into the 3rd shape of figure A. (1st shape at bottom and 2nd at top) So, option (c) is correct.
9. In figure A, if we invert pentagon and insert the other shape inside it with removing the shading of the top half. Applying the same analogy, we see that option (d) should be in place of figure D.
10. Figure (B) is the water image of figure A. So, figure D is the water image of figure C. Hence, option (d) is correct.
11. Rotate 90 degrees, replicate the same figure below the original and shade the upper part. Option (c) is correct.
12. Rotate the diagram by 225 degrees clockwise and place it in a shape with one more side. Hence, option (c) is correct.
13. Outer and inner shapes are same and division of shape is only for outer shape. Hence, option (a) is correct.
14. The four parts at the outer ends of the figure are removed without any other change in shape and size. Hence, option (b) is correct.
15. The three figures are shifting according to a pattern. Option (d) matches the required positions and orientations of all three figures.

CHAPTER 2

Odd Man Out

INTRODUCTION

The “Odd Man Out” chapter in non-verbal reasoning is a crucial topic for competitive exams. This type of question assesses your ability to identify patterns and detect anomalies within a set of figures. In each question, a group of figures is presented, where all but one share a common characteristic or pattern. Your task is to identify the figure that deviates from the rest based on shape, size, pattern, shading, symmetry, or other visual elements.

These questions test your logical thinking and attention to detail, as you need to discern subtle differences between the figures.

Odd Man Out Questions can be based on one of the following structures:

- **Geometrical shapes** (where you identify the odd man out based on sides/angles or overall geometry);
- **Shading and Coloring** (where the shape with a different pattern of shading/coloring has to be identified);
- **Symmetry** (All figures except one will exhibit some kind of symmetry or the lack of it); **Number of Elements** (All figures except one will have the same number of elements)
- **Rotation or Orientation** (All figures except one will have the same orientation or rotation pattern)
- **Size Differences** (All figures except one will have the same size or proportion pattern)

While solving odd man out questions, you have to focus on identifying common attributes amongst the set of figures and then spot the difference based on the attribute identified - also use the strategy of reducing the number of options in play, by eliminating obviously wrong options.

Example 1: Look at the given figures and find the odd one out. Choose the correct option.

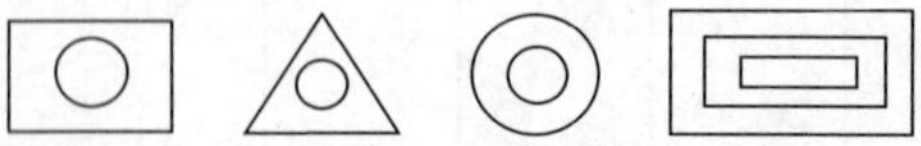

(A) (B) (C) (D)

(a) A **(b)** B
(c) C **(d)** D

Solution to Example 1: All the options have two shapes except option (d) which has three shapes in it. Hence, option (d) is correct.

Example 2: Look at the given figures and find the odd one out. Choose the correct option.

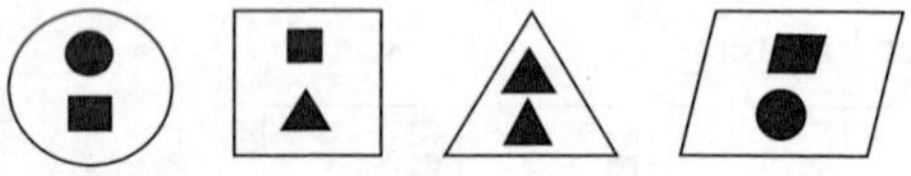

(A) (B) (C) (D)

(a) A **(b)** B
(c) C **(d)** D

Solution to Example 2: Figures A, B, D have different shapes in it but figure C has same shapes in it. So, option (c) is the odd one out.

Example 3: Look at the given figures and find the odd one out. Choose the correct option.

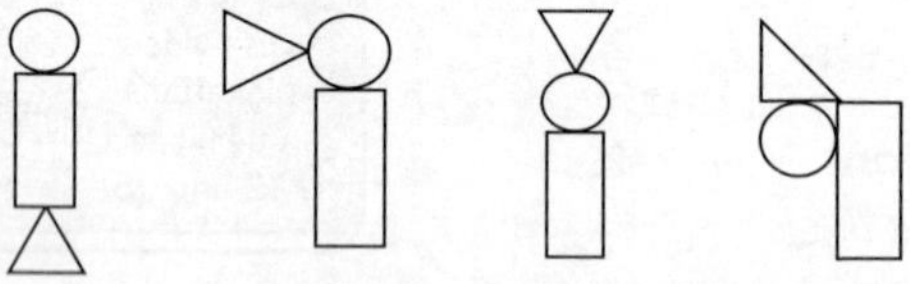

(A) (B) (C) (D)

(a) A **(b)** B
(c) C **(d)** D

Solution to Example 3: Figures A, B, C each shape touch exactly one shape. But in figure D each shape touches rest of the two shapes. So, Figure D is different from rest of the shapes. So, option (d) is the correct option.

EXERCISE

Directions for Questions 1 to 3:

1. Of the following 4 figures, 3 are alike in some manner and one differs from these in that manner. Select the odd figure.

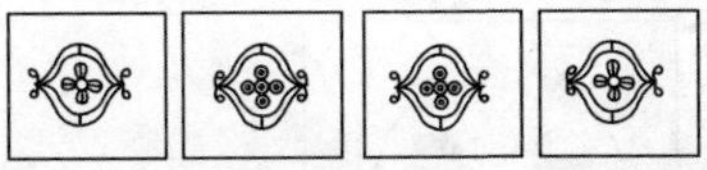

(a)  (b) 

(c)  (d) 

2. Of the following 4 figures, 3 are alike in some manner and one differs from these in that manner. Select the odd figure.

(a)  (b) 

(c)  (d) 

3. Find the odd one out of following:

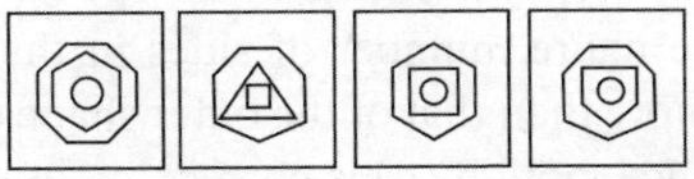

(A) (B) (C) (D)

(a) D (b) C
(c) B (d) A

Directions for Questions 4 to 15: *Look at the given figures and find the odd one out. Choose the correct option.*

4. 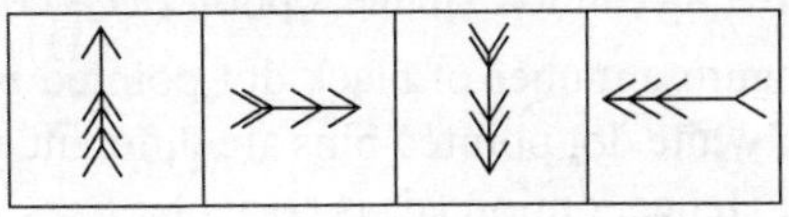

(A) (B) (C) (D)

(a) A (b) B
(c) C (d) D

5. 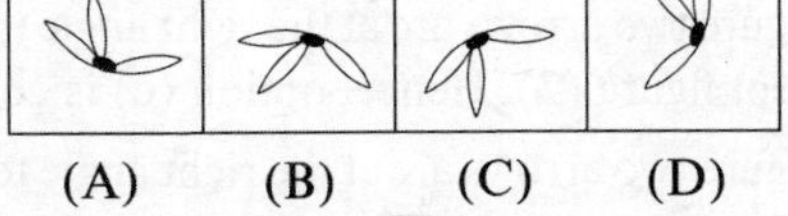

(A) (B) (C) (D)

(a) A (b) B
(c) C (d) D

6. 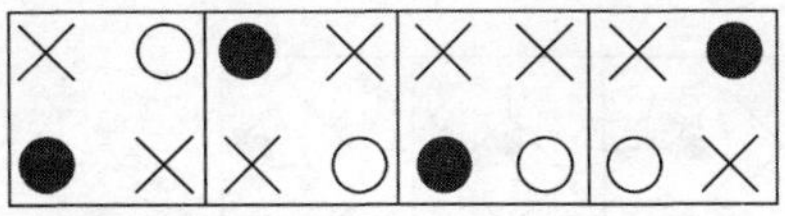

(A) (B) (C) (D)

(a) A (b) B
(c) C (d) D

7. 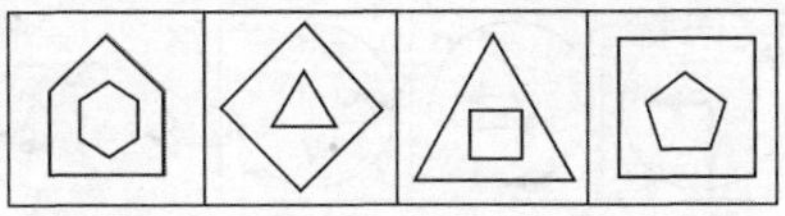

(A) (B) (C) (D)

(a) A (b) B
(c) C (d) D

8. 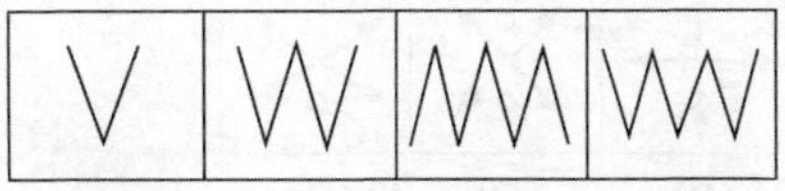

(A) (B) (C) (D)

(a) A (b) B
(c) C (d) D

9. 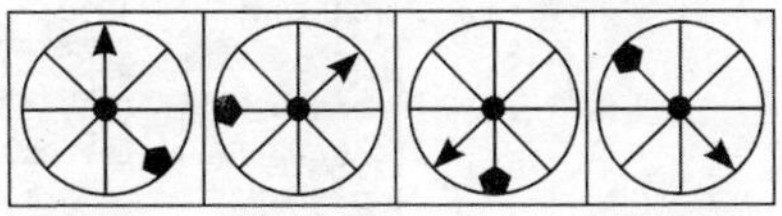

(A) (B) (C) (D)

(a) A (b) B
(c) C (d) D

10. 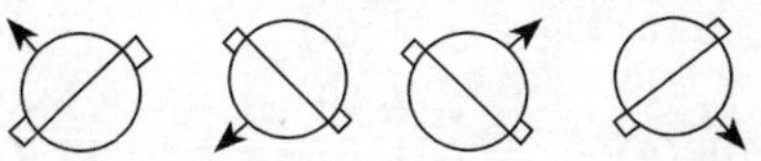

(A) (B) (C) (D)

(a) A (b) B
(c) C (d) D

11. 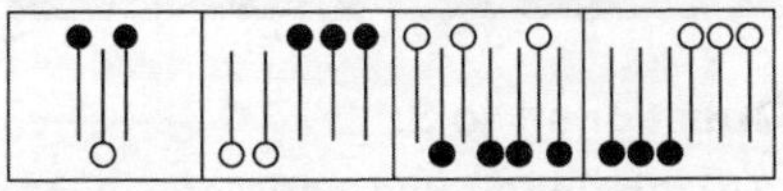

(A) (B) (C) (D)

(a) A (b) B
(c) C (d) D

12.

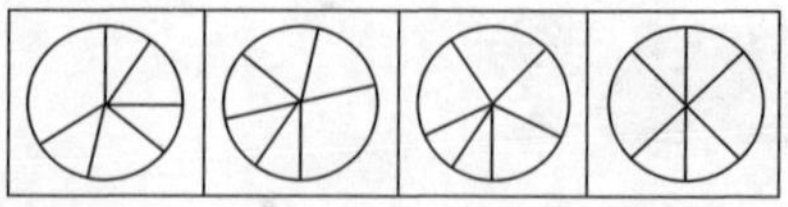

(A) (B) (C) (D)

(a) A (b) B
(c) C (d) D

13.

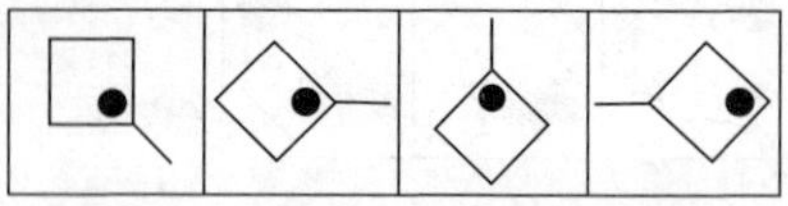

(A) (B) (C) (D)

(a) A (b) B
(c) C (d) D

14.

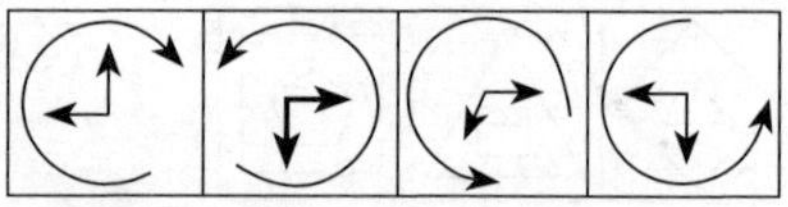

(A) (B) (C) (D)

(a) A (b) B
(c) C (d) D

15.

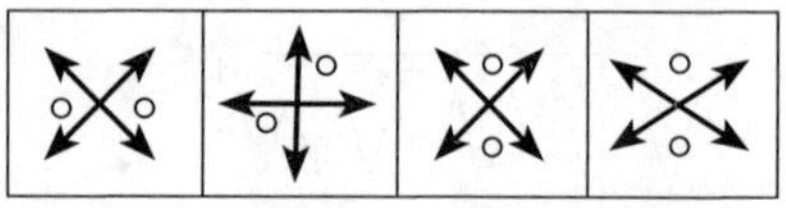

(A) (B) (C) (D)

(a) A
(b) B
(c) C
(d) D

High Yield Questions

Scan this QR code to access video explanations of questions 2, 3 and 5

ANSWER KEY

1. (a)	2. (a)	3. (c)	4. (d)
5. (a)	6. (c)	7. (b)	8. (c)
9. (d)	10. (a)	11. (d)	12. (d)
13. (d)	14. (c)	15. (d)	

SOLUTIONS AND SHORTCUTS

Solutions for Questions 1 to 3:

1. In figure (a), the encircled ends are in opposite directions, which is not aligning with the other figures.

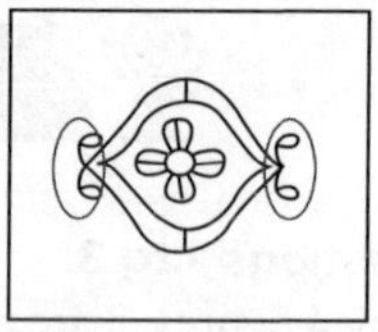

2. Except Figure (a), all other figures have their eyeballs in the same direction.

3. Counting number of sides from outer to inner:
   A: 8, 6, 0 **B: 7, 3, 4**
   C: 6, 4, 0 D: 7, 5, 0
   E: 5, 3, 0
   Option (b) is odd since the number of edges in the innermost figure is 4.

Solutions for Questions 4 to 15:

4. There are four arrowheads in both figures (B) and (D). We can differentiate the figure (D) from all, as there are minimum two arrowheads in the bottom of the arrow. Hence, option (d) is correct.
5. Except figure (1), rest can be converted to each other by rotation. Hence, option (a) is correct.
6. Except figure (3), rest of the figures have two crosses appearing at diagonally opposite ends. Hence, option (c) is correct.
7. In each of the figure, number of sides in the inner shape is one more than that of the outer shape except figure (2). Hence, option (b) is correct.
8. Each of the figures is opening upward except figure (3), which is opening downward. Hence, option (c) is correct.
9. In every figure the arrow and dot lies on different diameter except figure 4. Option (d) is correct.
10. Figures (B), (C) and (D) can be rotated into each other, while figure (A) cannot. Hence, option (a) is correct.
11. In every figure, number of black dot pointed pins & number of white dot pointed pins are different except figure (4). Hence, option (d) is correct.
12. In every figure circle is divided into asymmetrical sectors except figure (4). Hence, option (d) is correct.
13. In each figure, the dot and line appear at the same corner except figure (4). Hence, option (d) is correct.
14. In every figure two arrows are at the right angle to each other except figure (3). Hence, option (c) is correct.
15. In every figure two arrows are at the right angle to each other except figure (4). Hence, option (d) is correct.

CHAPTER 3 Embedded Figures

INTRODUCTION

Embedded Figures challenge the test taker's ability to recognize hidden shapes within complex images. These questions test visual pattern recognition, spatial intelligence, and attention to detail. In an embedded figures problem, a smaller figure is hidden within a larger design, and the task is to locate this figure within the bigger one.

These types of questions require high visual perception and the ability to detect patterns and symmetries. The embedded figure might be intentionally camouflaged by the complexity of the larger figure to test your concentration. The hidden figure doesn't change in terms of its size or shape but may be rotated, mirrored, or hidden at different angles within the bigger design. This requires candidates to mentally rotate and flip shapes to match them with the given smaller figure.

Strategies to Solve Embedded Figures Questions

Embedded figures are often based on Geometric Shapes & Objects and Letters. Some of the key strategies involved in solving embedded figures questions are:

Breaking down the image into its component parts and then looking for that component part in the options – for instance, the problem figure could have a half shaded circle as a part of it, so when you are looking for the correct options, you try to look for options that contain a similar sized half shaded circle. It is also a good idea to check the figure in a rotated or inverted fashion – as that is quite common in these kinds of questions. It is also a good strategy to focus your visualisation only to the critical matching components in the figures – and avoid distracting elements in the answer figures.

Example 1: Find out the alternative figure which contains figure (X) as its part.

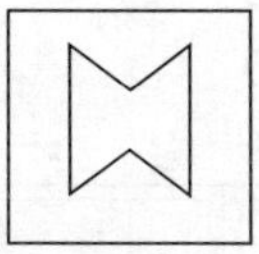

(X)

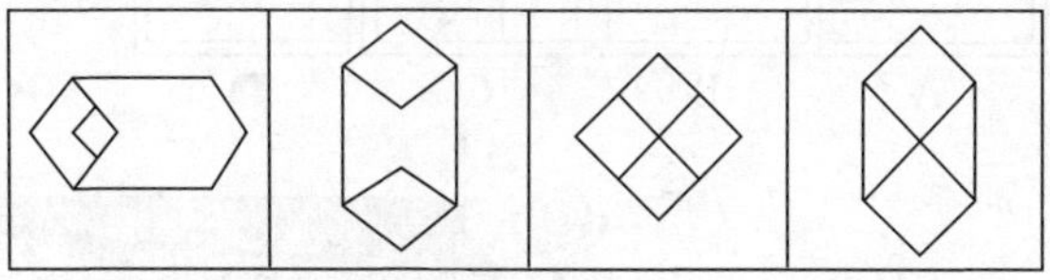

(1) (2) (3) (4)

(a) 1 (b) 2
(c) 3 (d) 4

Solution to Example 1: After analysing the problem figure, it is clear that (X) is a part of the figure 2. Hence, option (b) is correct.

Example 2: Select the option in which the given figure is embedded.

(X)

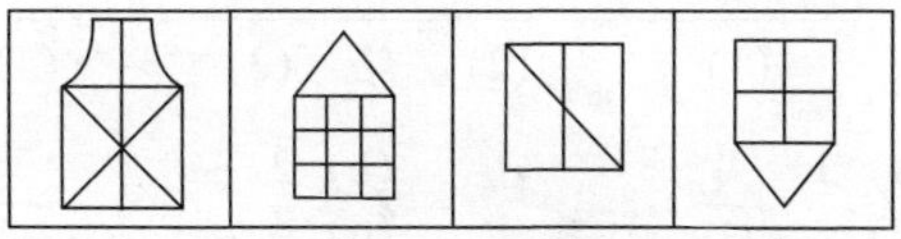

A B C D

(a) A (b) B
(c) C (d) D

Solution to Example 2: Look for individual sib-components of the original figure. For instance, the triangle at the top right is only contained in figures (A) and (D). After analysing the remaining components, it is clear that problem figure is embedded in figure A.

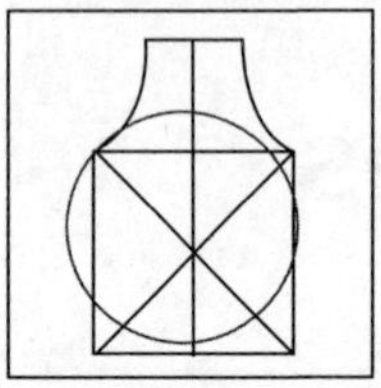

Hence, option (a) is correct.

Example 3: Select the option in which the given figure is embedded.

(X)

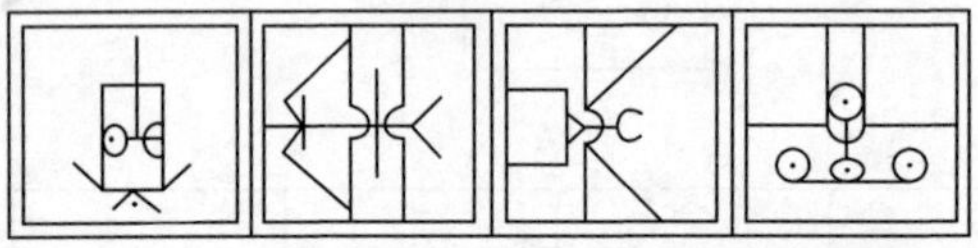

A B C D

(a) A (b) B
(c) C (d) D

Solution to Example 3: The original figure has a vertical axis line, and a semi circle opening upwards and a 3/4th circle opening downwards. Options (A) and (D) both exhibit this shape - however the crucial difference in the original figure that helps us eliminate option (A) is that the axis line continues a little further after the semicircle ends. After analysing the problem figure with these points, it is clear that the problem figure is embedded in figure D.

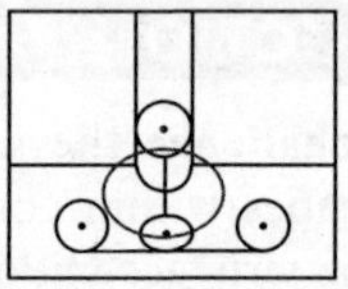

Therefore, the correct answer is **option (d)**.

EXERCISE

Directions for Questions 1 to 15: *In the question, among the answer figures, which figure can be formed from the cut-pieces given below in the question figure.*

1. Select the option in which the given figure is embedded.

(X)

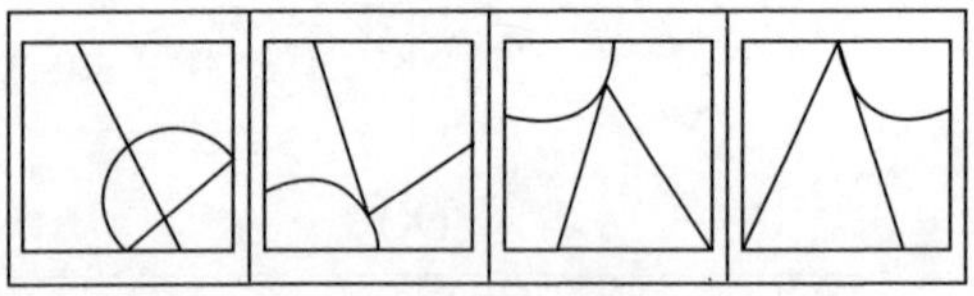

(1) (2) (3) (4)

(a) 1 (b) 2
(c) 3 (d) 4

2. Select the option in which the given figure is embedded.

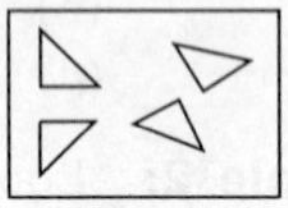

(X)

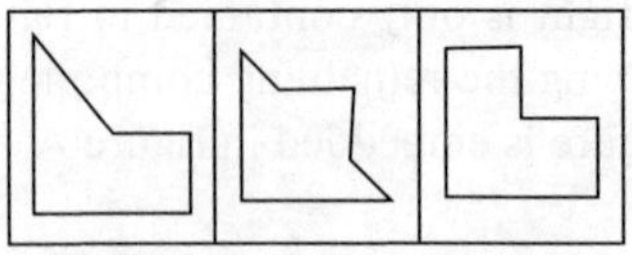

(1) (2) (3)

(a) 1 (b) 2
(c) 3 (d) None of these

3. Select the option in which the given figure is embedded.

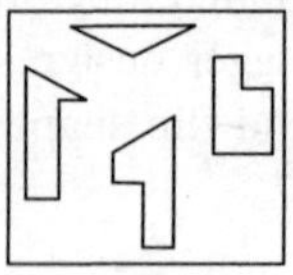

(X)

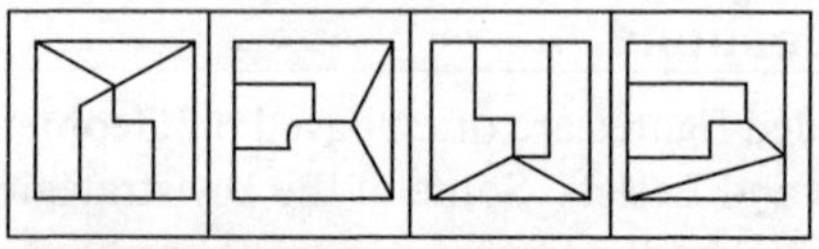

(1) (2) (3) (4)

(a) 1 (b) 2
(c) 3 (d) 4

4. Select the option in which the given figure is embedded.

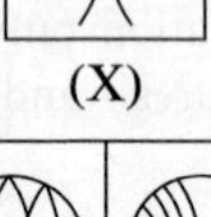

(X)

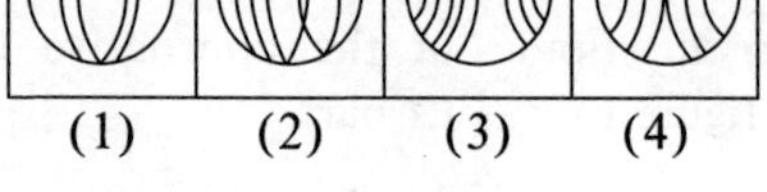

(1) (2) (3) (4)

(a) 1 (b) 2
(c) 3 (d) 4

5. Select the option in which the given figure is embedded.

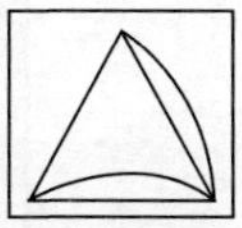

(X)

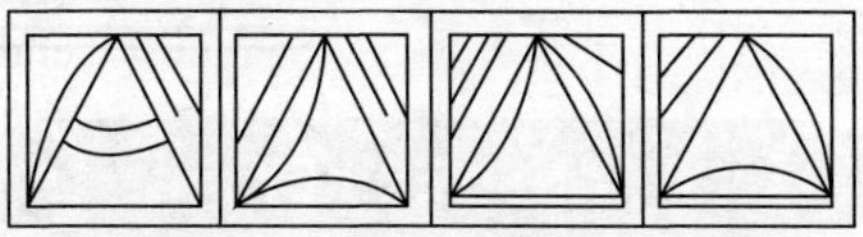

(1) (2) (3) (4)

(a) 1 (b) 2
(c) 3 (d) 4

6. Select the option in which the given figure is embedded.

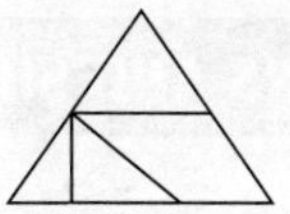

(X)

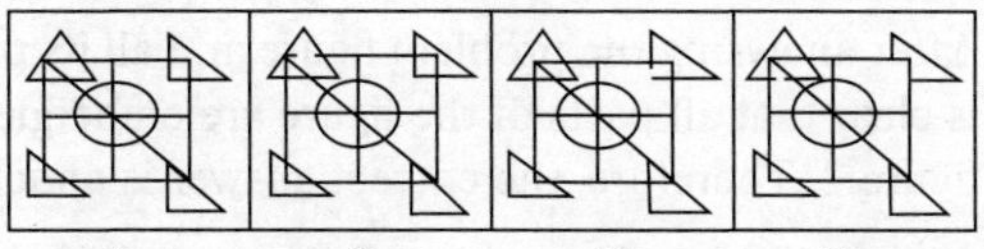

A B C D

(a) A (b) B
(c) C (d) D

7. Select the option in which the given figure is embedded.

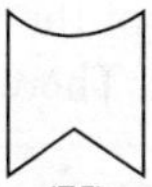

(X)

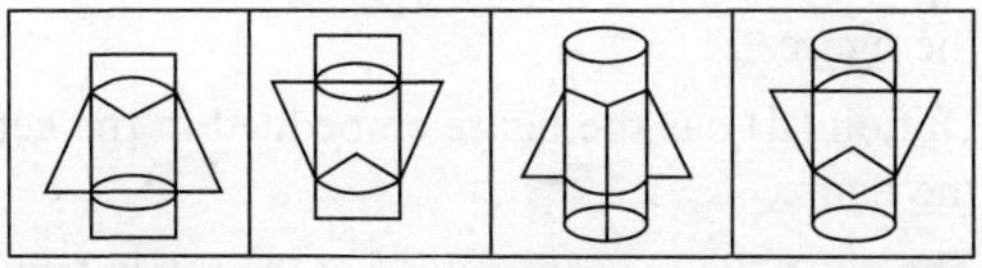

A B C D

(a) A (b) B
(c) C (d) D

8. Select the option in which the given figure is embedded.

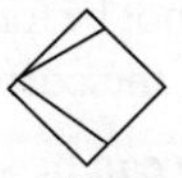

(X)

A B C

(a) A
(b) B
(c) C
(d) None of these

9. Select the option in which the given figure is embedded.

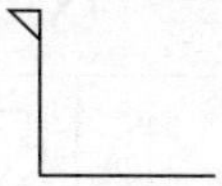

(X)

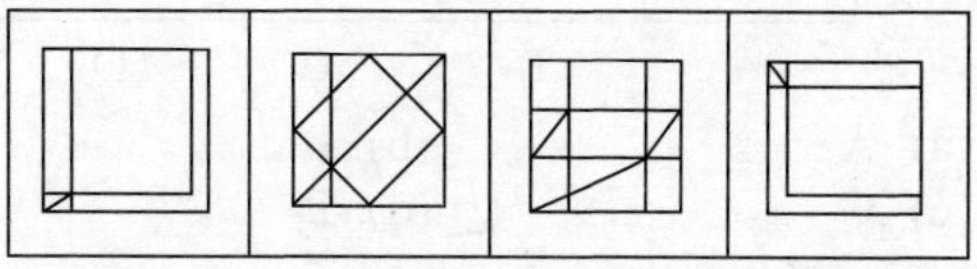

A B C D

(a) A (b) B
(c) C (d) D

10. Select the option in which the given figure is embedded.

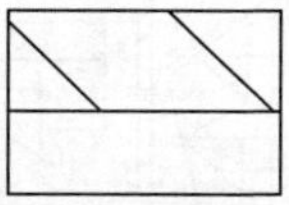

(X)

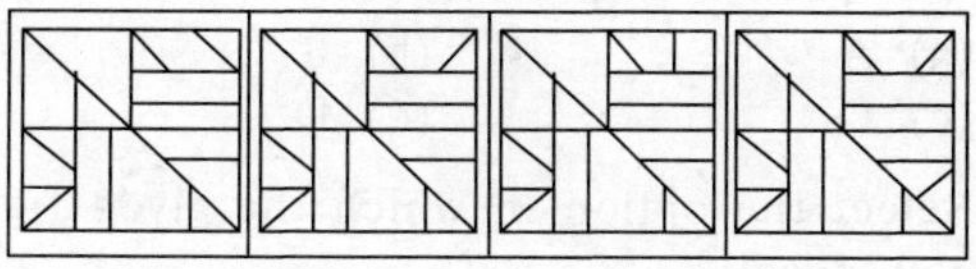

A B C D

(a) A (b) B
(c) C (d) D

11. Select the option that is not embedded in the given figure (X).

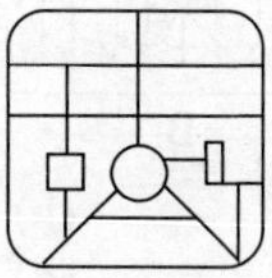

(X)

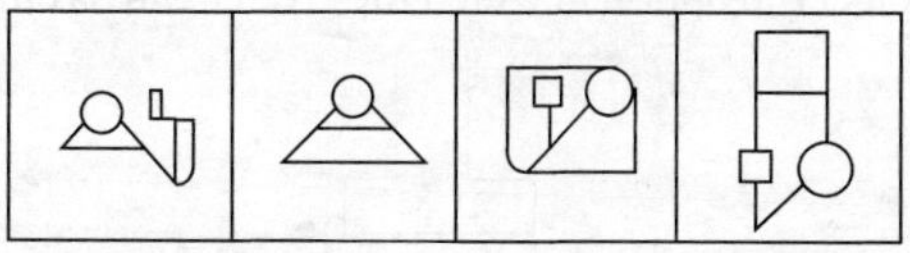

A B C D

(a) A (b) B
(c) C (d) D

12. Select the option that is embedded in the given figure (X).

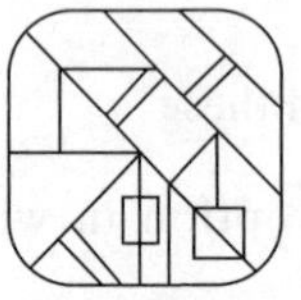

(X)

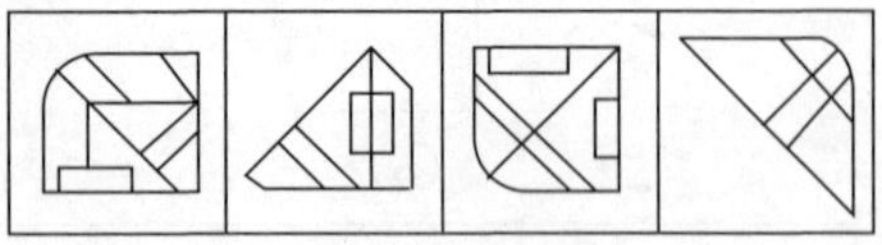

A B C D

(a) A (b) B
(c) C (d) D

13. Select the option in which the given figure is embedded.

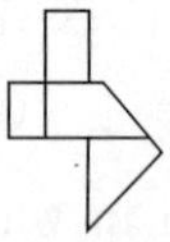

(X)

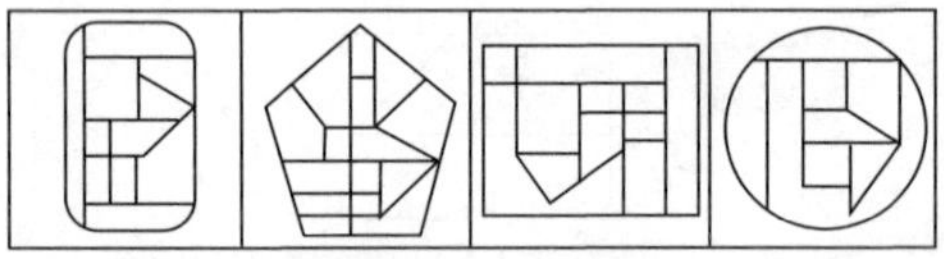

A B C D

(a) A (b) B
(c) C (d) D

14. Select the option in which the given figure is embedded.

(X)

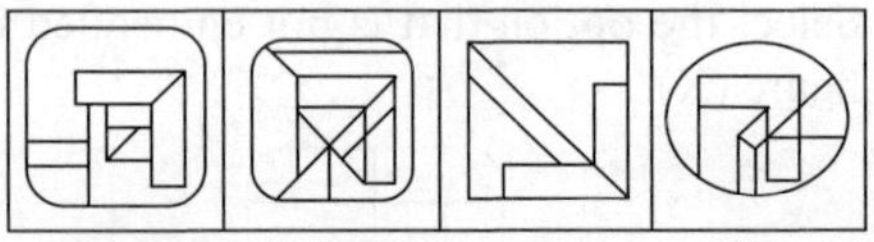

A B C D

(a) A (b) B
(c) C (d) D

15. Select the option in which the given figure is embedded.

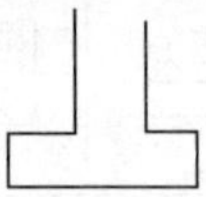

(X)

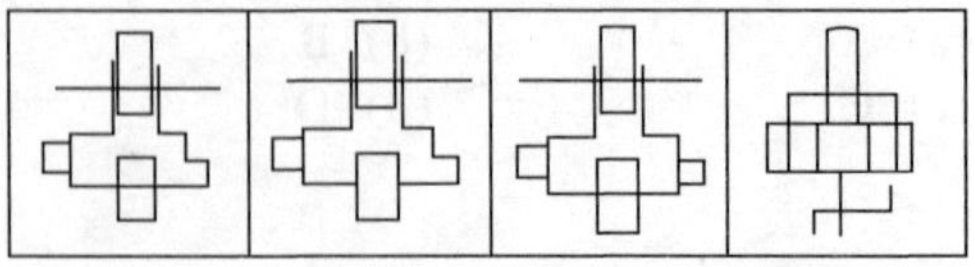

A B C D

(a) A
(b) B
(c) C
(d) D

High Yield Questions

Scan this QR code to access video explanations of questions 1, 12 and 13

ANSWER KEY

1. (b)	2. (d)	3. (c)	4. (d)
5. (d)	6. (a)	7. (b)	8. (d)
9. (a)	10. (a)	11. (c)	12. (b)
13. (b)	14. (b)	15. (c)	

SOLUTIONS AND SHORTCUTS

Solutions for Questions 1 to 15:

1. After analysing the problem figure and all its parts, it is clear that all parts of the figure are embedded into figure 2. Therefore, the correct answer is **option (b).**
2. After analysing the problem figure and all its parts, it is clear that all parts of the figure cannot be seen in any of the options. Therefore, the correct answer is **option (d).**
3. After analysing the problem figure and all its parts, it is clear that all parts of the figure can be seen to be embedded in figure 3. Therefore, the correct answer is **option (c).**
4. Option (d) has the figure embedded in the center of the figure.
5. Option (d) has the figure embedded in the center of the figure.
6. The given figure is embedded at the top left corner of figure A. Hence, option (a) is correct.
7. The given figure is embedded in the central part of the figure given in option (b). Therefore, the correct answer is **option (b).**
8. After analysing the problem figure, it is clear that problem figure cannot be formed from any of the given options. Therefore, the correct answer is **option (d).**
9. The problem figure can be seen in an inverted fashion in the figure given in option (a), with it's triangle at the bottom left of the figure. Therefore, the correct answer is **option (a).**
10. After analysing the problem figure, it is clear that problem figure can be seen in figure A (Top right corner). Therefore, the correct answer is **option (a).**

11. Option (c) is not embedded in figure (X). Hence, option (c) is correct.
12. Option (b) is embedded in figure (X). Hence, option (b) is correct.
13. After analysing the problem figure, it is clear that problem figure is embedded towards the center of figure B

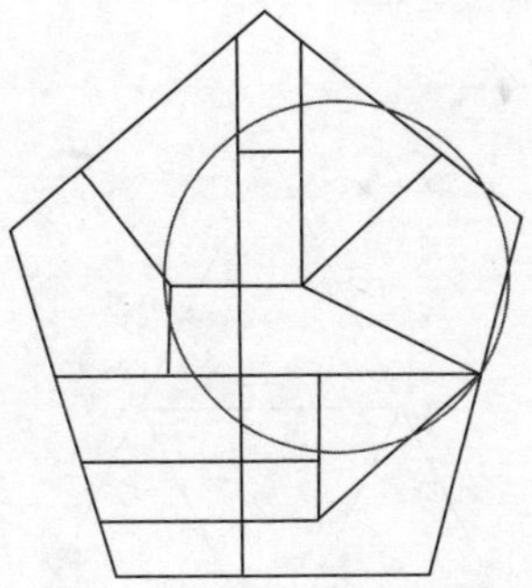

Hence, the correct answer is **option (b)**.

14. The problem figure can be seen at the center of the figure in option (b). Therefore, the correct answer is **option (b)**.
15. The correct answer is **option (c)**.

CHAPTER 4 Counting of Figures

INTRODUCTION

Problems based on counting of figures are designed to test a candidate's ability to count and analyse geometric shapes like triangles, squares, rectangles, circles, and various polygons. These problems can range from simple to highly complex, requiring strong spatial reasoning and attention to detail.

Key Concepts

The simplest problems involve counting basic geometric shapes such as triangles, squares, rectangles, and circles. More complex problems however The ability to recognize these shapes, either individually or embedded or overlapping in a larger structure, is fundamental to solving these problems.

A good strategy to use while solving questions based on counting figures (especially in complex situations with embedded and overlapping figures) is to identify the various sizes in which the figures appear and count them one size at a time.

In these questions, you might be asked to count **(a) Triangles; (b) Squares and Rectangles; (c) Circles.** In each of these cases, try to identify the various sizes in which each of the to be counted shape appears. For instance, in a 4 × 4 grid, count all squares, including 1 × 1, 2 × 2, 3 × 3, and 4 × 4 squares. Each size of square is formed by different combinations of intersecting lines.

Sometimes, you would also come across questions having Mixed Diagrams with Various Shapes:

A single figure may contain a mixture of triangles, squares, circles, and polygons. These problems require you to identify and count all the individual figures, including any shapes formed by intersections or combinations of the basic figures. Of course a good strategy in such cases, is to identify all the shapes separately and count each shape one by one. It might also help to use symmetry - if the figure has it. In such cases, you can count one part and multiply by the number of symmetrical sections.

Example: A large circle contains two intersecting triangles and a square in the center. Count all distinct shapes, including those formed by the intersections of the triangles and the square.

Example 1: How many triangle are there in the given figure?

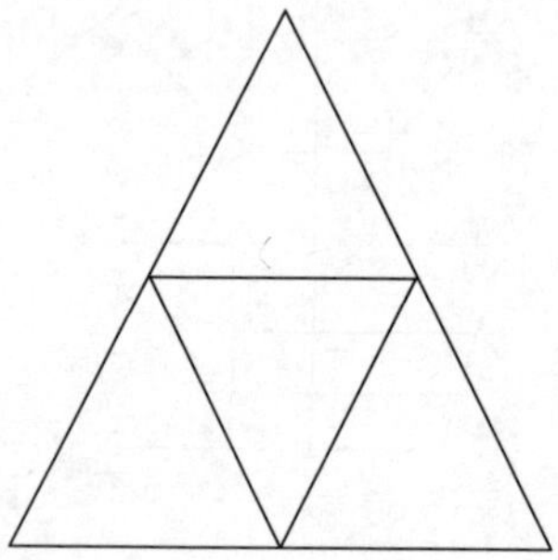

Solution to Example 1: Small triangles: You can see 4 of them, 3 at the bottom level and 1 at the top.

Plus you would also need to add the entire outer triangle to your count. Thus, there are a total of 4 + 1 = 5 triangles in the figure.

Example 2: How many triangles are there in the given figure?

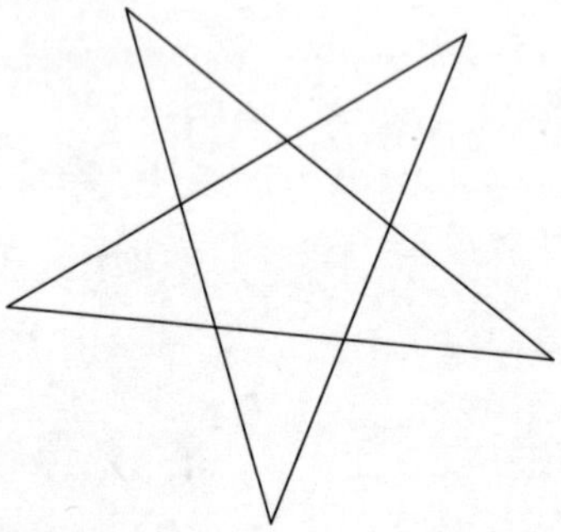

Solution to Example 2:

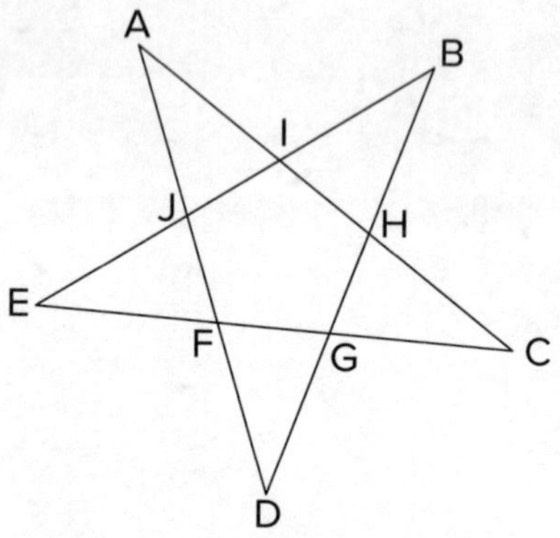

Triangles: First count the 5 outer triangles: AJI, BIH, CGH, DGF, JEF.

Next look for larger triangles using only one of the vertices, we can see that there are none like that. Next we see if we can make triangles using two of the vertices from amongst A, B, C, D, E, F, G, H, I, J: With AC-F; With AD-H; With BD-J; With BE-G; With CE-I. With DE, there are none and we do not need to check with DA, DB or DC as those will lead to double counting. Hence, the correct answer is 5+5=10.

Example 3: How many triangles are there in the given figure?

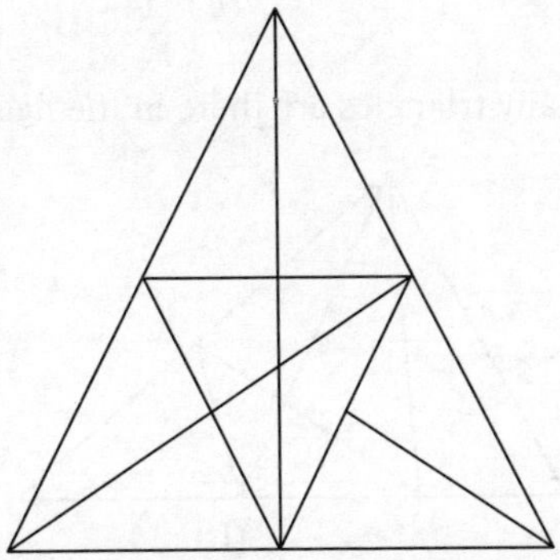

Solution to Example 3: We can start off by naming the various points in the original figure as shown:

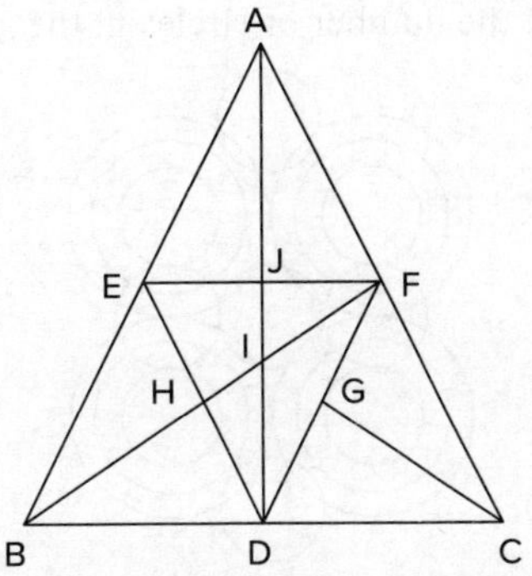

You need to do such counts systematically. It is a good idea to fix a point as a vertex and try to see all triangles with that point before moving your fixed vertex to the next point.

With A fixed: AEJ, AFJ, AEF, ABD, ABC, ADC, ABI, AIF, ABF, AED, AFD (11)

With B fixed (we no longer go back to A): BED, BHD, BDH, BEF, BDF, BDI, BCF (7)

With C fixed (avoiding using A and B) CFD, CGF, CGD (3)

With D fixed (avoiding using A, B, C): DEF, DFJ, DEJ, DIH, DIF, DHF (6)

With E fixed (avoiding A, B, C, D): EHF (1)

With F fixed (avoiding A, B, C, D, E): FJI (1)

Total: 11 + 7 + 3 + 6 + 1 + 1 = 29

EXERCISE

1. How many triangles are there in the given figure?

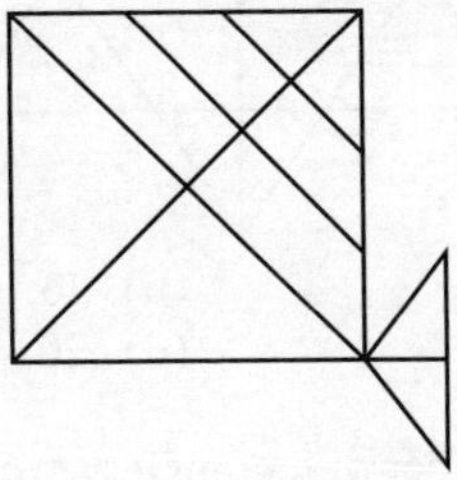

(a) 18 (b) 16
(c) 15 (d) 17

2. How many triangles are there in the given figure?

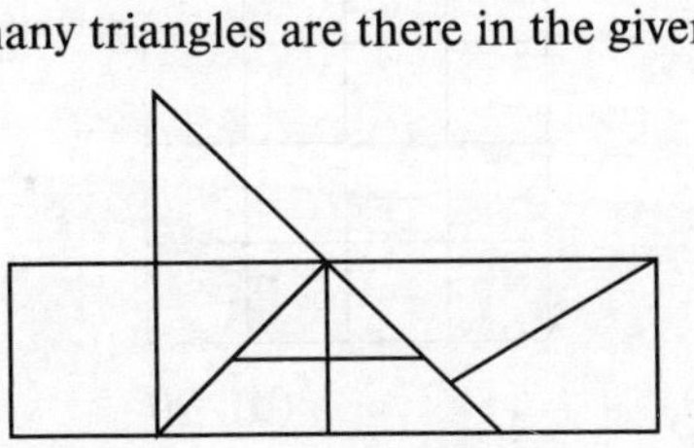

(a) 11 (b) 13
(c) 10 (d) 12

3. How many triangles are there in the following figure?

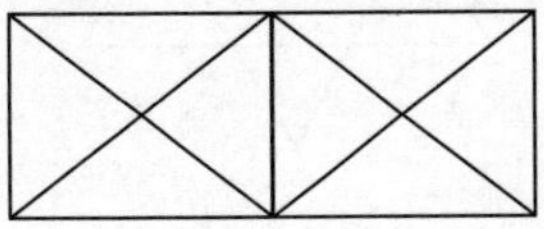

(a) 20
(b) 18
(c) 22
(d) 16

4. Count the number of blocks in the following figure.

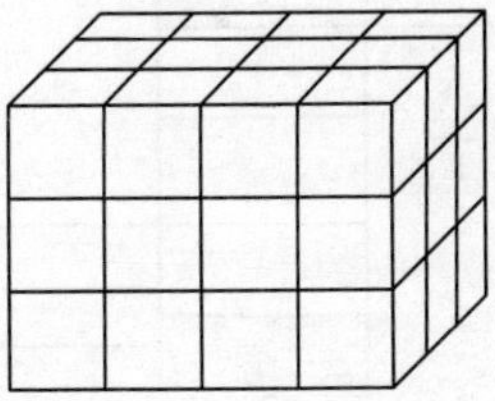

(a) 32
(b) 34
(c) 36
(d) 38

5. Find out the number of circles in the given figure.

(a) 14 (b) 16
(c) 17 (d) 18

6. How many standard pentagons are there in the given figure?

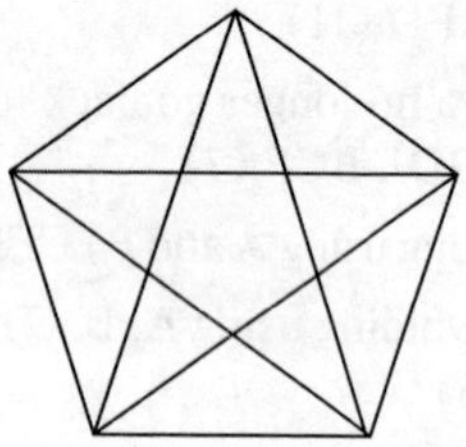

(a) 4 (b) 2
(c) 6 (d) 3

7. How many triangles are there in the given figure?

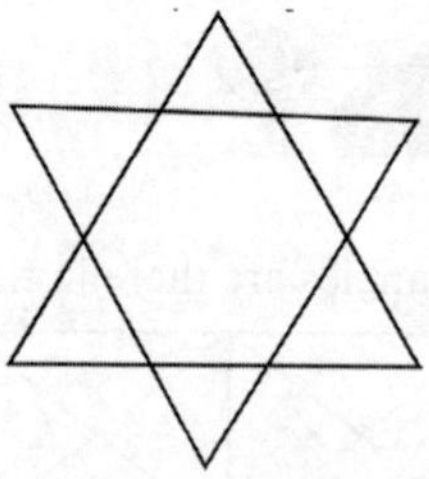

(a) 7 (b) 11
(c) 8 (d) 9

8. How many rectangles are there in the given figure?

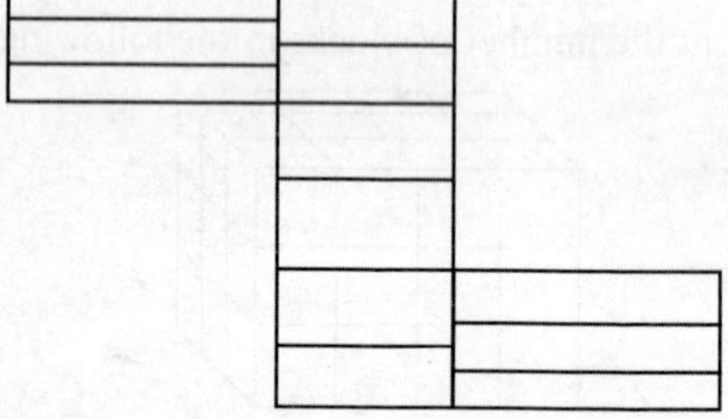

(a) 30 (b) 32
(c) 33 (d) 34

9. How many squares are there in the following figure?

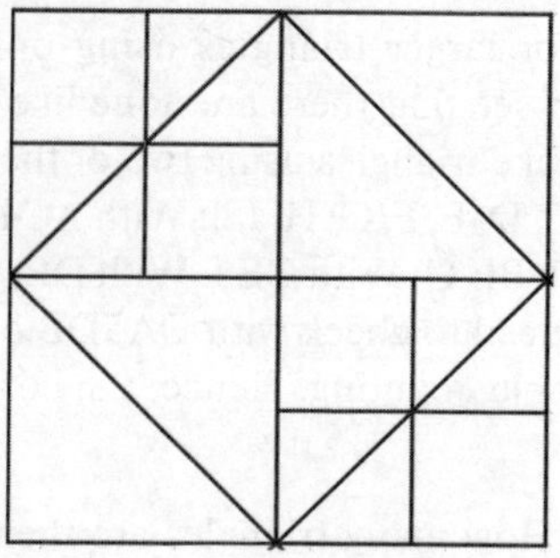

(a) 12 (b) 16
(c) 13 (d) 14

10. How many triangles are there in the figure?

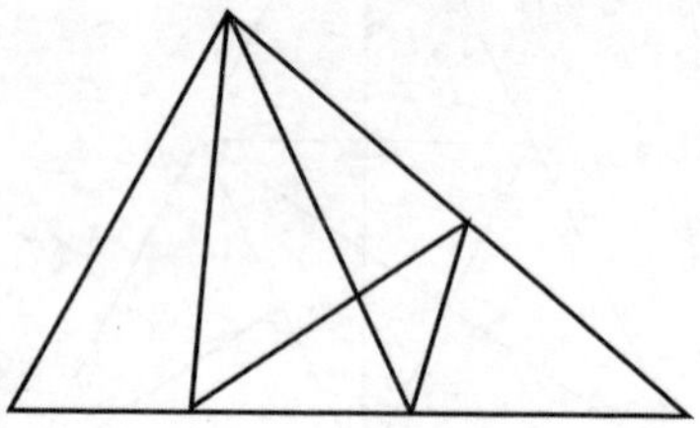

(a) 13 (b) 14
(c) 15 (d) 16

11. How many triangles are there in the given figure?

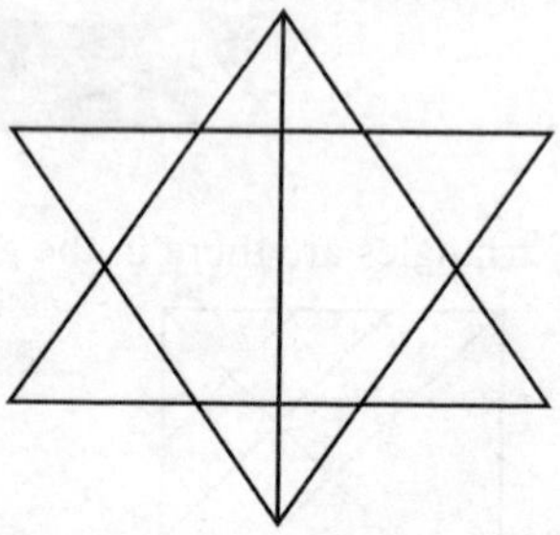

(a) 18 (b) 16
(c) 14 (d) 20

12. Find the number of rectangles (excluding squares) in the given diagram.

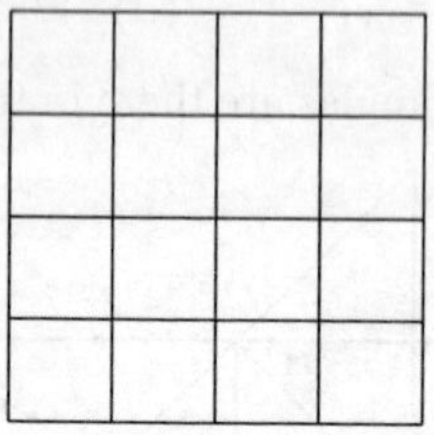

(a) 80 (b) 70
(c) 60 (d) 50

13. Find the number of squares in the given diagram.

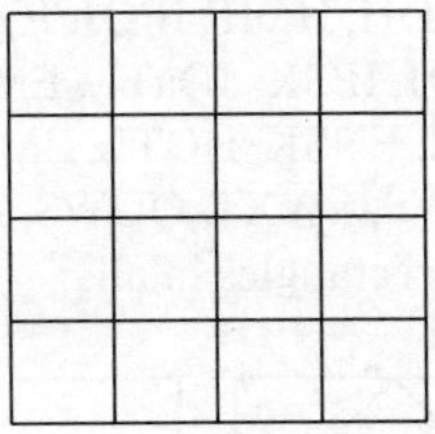

(a) 30
(b) 20
(c) 10
(d) 25

14. How many triangles are there in the given figure?

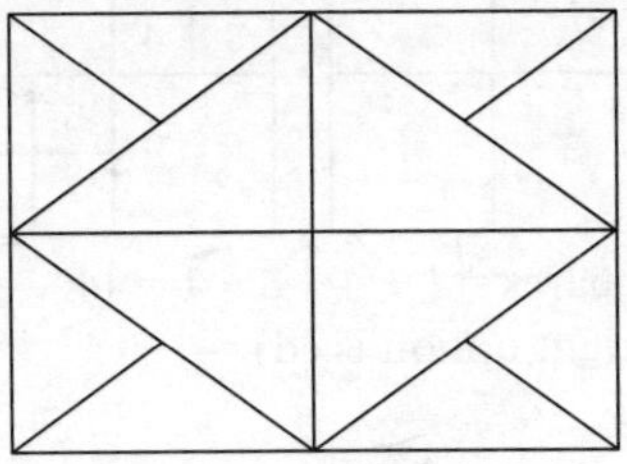

(a) 30
(b) 20
(c) 10
(d) 25

15. How many circles are there in the given figure?

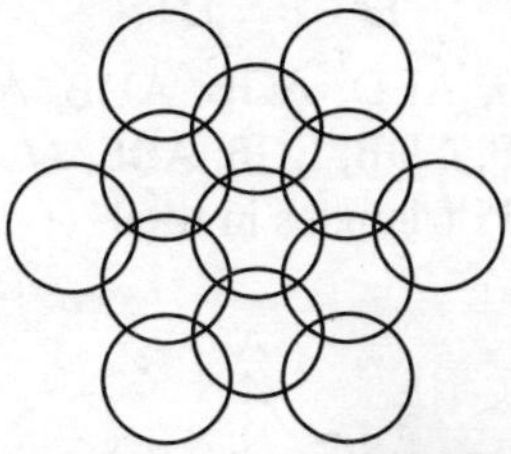

(a) 13
(b) 12
(c) 10
(d) 15

High Yield Questions

Scan this QR code to access video explanations of questions 6, 12, 13 and 14

ANSWER KEY

1. (d)	2. (c)	3. (b)	4. (c)
5. (c)	6. (b)	7. (c)	8. (c)
9. (d)	10. (c)	11. (b)	12. (b)
13. (a)	14. (b)	15. (a)	

SOLUTIONS AND SHORTCUTS

1.

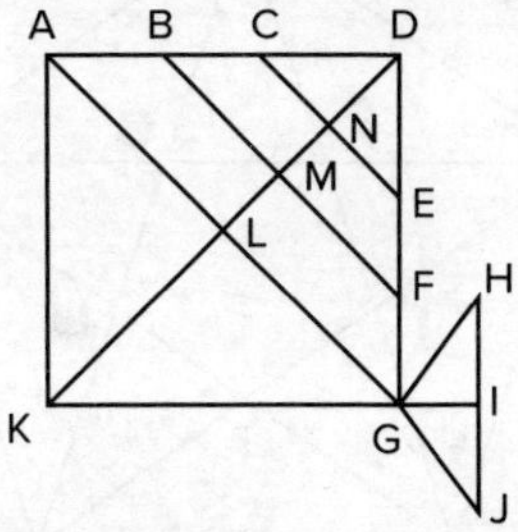

GHJ, GHI, GJI, AKG, AKL, GKL, AGD, ALD, LDG, BMD, DMF, BDF, DCE, CND, NDE, AKD, KDG (17 triangles)

2.

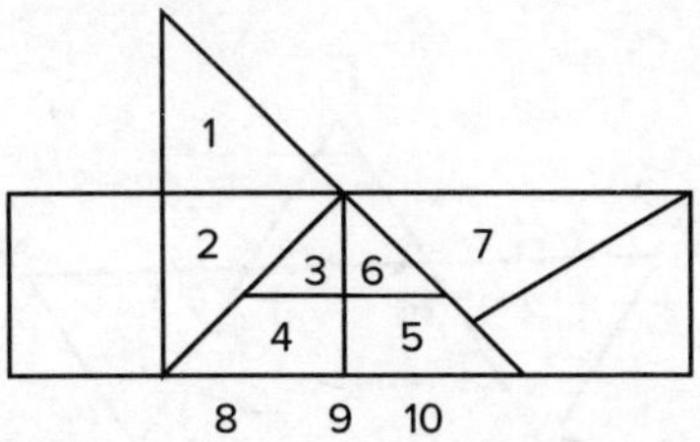

The number of triangles in the figure is 10.
So, option (c) is correct.

3.

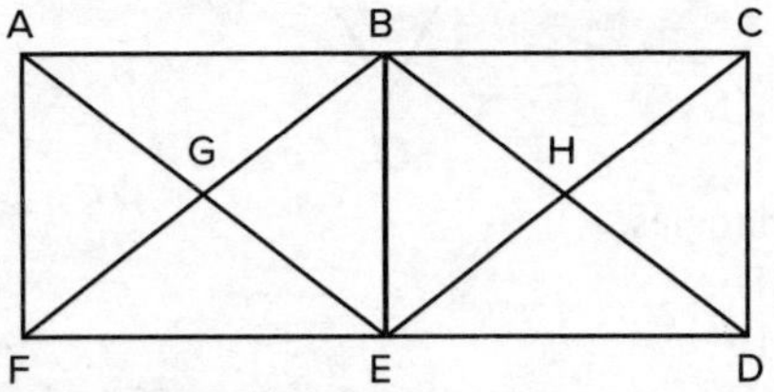

The triangles formed are:

AGB	DHC	FEB	EBD
AGF	DHE	AFE	FBD
FGE	EHB	EBC	AEC
EGB	FAB	BCD	
BHC	EAB	EDC	

Therefore, answer is option (b).

4. From the figure, In a cube there are 3 layers of blocks.
1st layer 12 block
2nd layer 12 blocks
3rd layer 12 blocks
Finally we get 12 + 12 + 12 = 36 blocks. So the answer is 36.

5. Initially we have 4 sets of 3 inner circles, counting to 12.
Then we have 5 small circles between them.
On counting the circles given, the correct option is 17.

6.

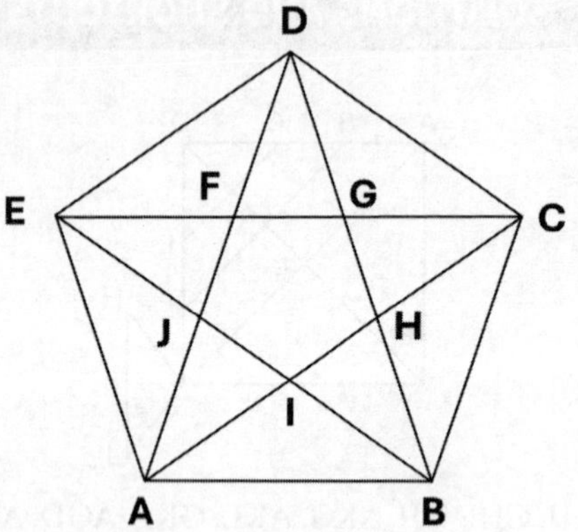

Only two pentagons: ABCDE, FGHIJ
Therefore, the answer is (b).

7.

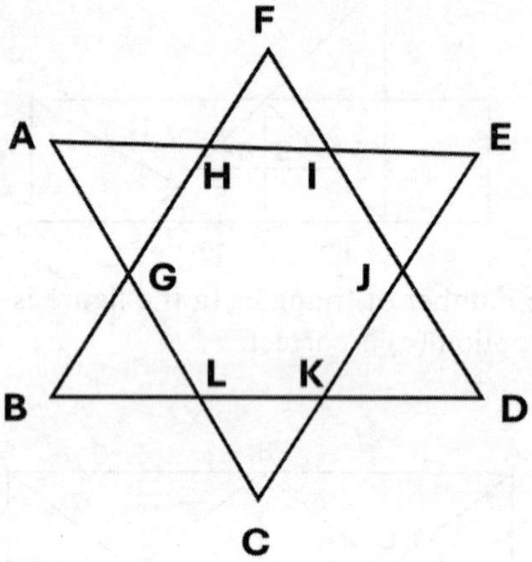

8 triangles:
AGH
BGL
CLK
DKJ
EJI
FHI
FBD
ACE

8.

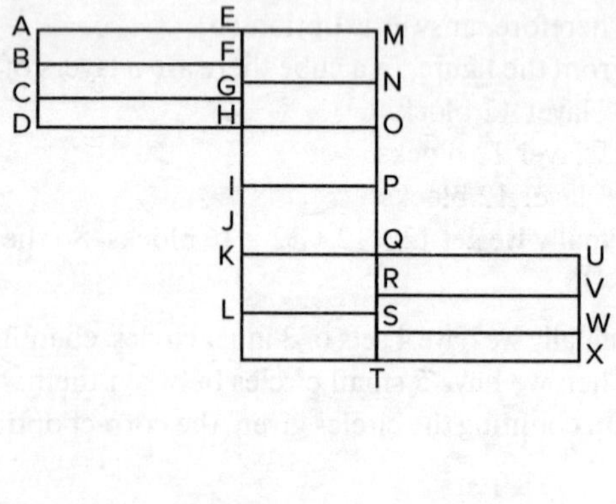

AEHD, AEFB, BFGC, CGHD AEGC, BFHD, EMNG, GNOH, HOIP, IPQJ, JQSK, KSTL, EMOH, GNPI, HOQJ, IPSK, JQaTL, EMPI, GNQJ, HOSK, IPTL, EMQJ, FNSK, HOTL, EMSK, GNTL, EMTL, QUVR, RVWS, SWXT, QUWS, RVXT, QUXTThus, there are 33 rectangles in all.

9.

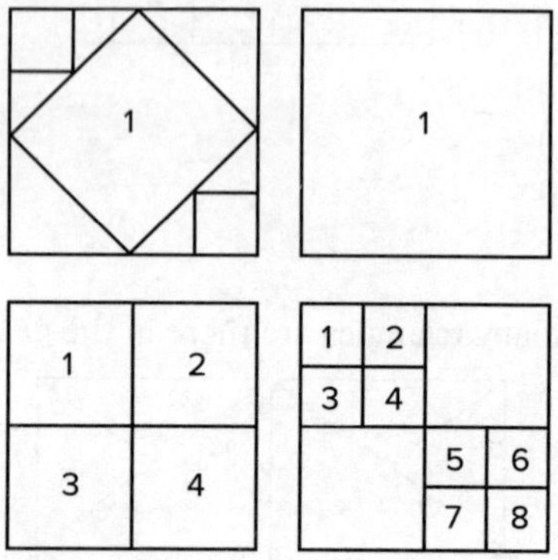

No of squares = 1 + 4 + 8 + 1 = 14
So, the right option is (d).

10.

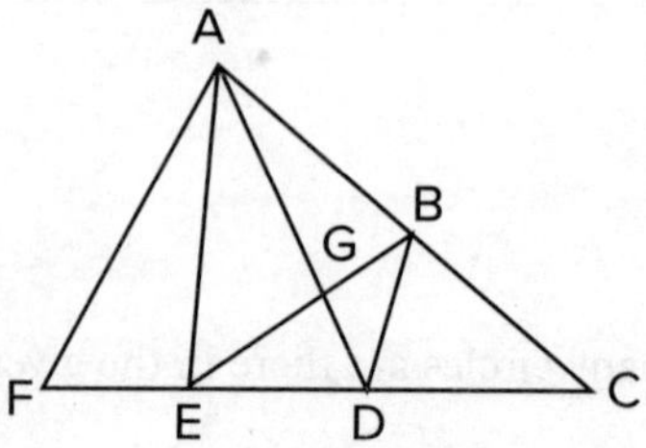

AFE, AEG, AED, AGB, ADB, ADC, AFD, AFC, GED, GDB, CDB, ECB, ABE, ACE, DBE
There are 15 triangles in total.

11.

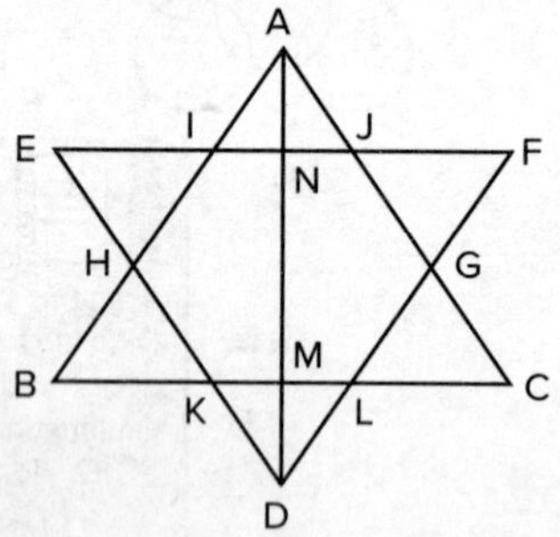

ABC, DEF, LKD, IAJ, HIE, JFG, AIN, ANJ, DMK, DML, ABM, AMC, DNF, DNE, BHK, LCG
Hence, the correct answer is option (b).

12. There is a short cut to count the number of rectangles: It is (1 + 2 + 3 + 4)(1 + 2 + 3 + 4) = 100 – the logic used is that there are 4 vertical and 4 horizontal divisions in the figure – hence in both brackets we add the natural numbers from 1 to 4. (Note: This always gives the exact total for number of rectangles. {You can check by trying a figure with 3 vertical and 4 horizontal divisions, would have (1 + 2 + 3)(1 + 2 + 3 + 4) = 60 rectangles. In general if there are m divisions vertically and n divisions horizontally, the number of rectangles can be counted with: $(1 + 2 + 3 + ... + m) \times (1 + 2 + 3... + n)$

Now, let's find the number of squares:

If there are m divisions vertically and n divisions horizontally, the number of squares is given as $m \times n + (m - 1) \times (n - 1) + (m - 2) \times (n - 2)...$ till either the m or n series reduces to 1. In this case, since there are 4 divisions each, we get: 4 × 4 + 3 × 3 + 2 × 2 + 1 × 1 = 30 squares in the figure.

Rectangles, which are not squares = 100 – 30 = 70.

13. The number of squares can be counted as 1 (Largest square) + 4 (3 by 3 squares) + 9 (2 by 2 squares) + 16 (1 by 1 squares) = 30.
14. There are 12 triangles at the corner of the figure and 8 in the center. Total triangles are 12+8=20. Hence, option (b) is correct.
15. Count the circles row wise - you can see 2 + 1 + 2 + 3 + 2 + 1 + 2 = 13.

CHAPTER 5

Completion of Figures

INTRODUCTION

This chapter tests your ability to recognize patterns, shapes, and logical arrangements within incomplete figures. The goal is to identify the missing portion of a figure from a set of options so that the figure is completed according to the pattern or design.

In such questions, part of a geometrical figure, design, or arrangement is missing, and the challenge is to mentally visualize how the figure should look when complete. This requires strong spatial awareness and the ability to understand symmetry, rotation, and other visual cues.

Types of Completion of Figures Questions

Geometrical Figures (questions will involve common shapes such as triangles, circles, squares or polygons) ; **Pattern Completion** (The figure may display a repeated pattern, and your task is to find the missing segment that continues the pattern logically and symmetrically.) ; **Symmetry-Based Completion** In these questions, figures are partially symmetrical. The missing part must complete the symmetry (vertically, diagonally or horizontally). **Complex Designs:** Some figures may include intricate designs, lines, or shapes. You must identify the part that maintains the flow or design of the figure.

Key elements in finding the solutions to these questions include, identifying shapes, sizes, visualising symmetry, visualising the whole from the part and also checking continuity of the design element in the figure. Besides option elimination is a crucial element of solving such questions.

Example 1: Identify the missing part of the given figure and select it from given answer figures.

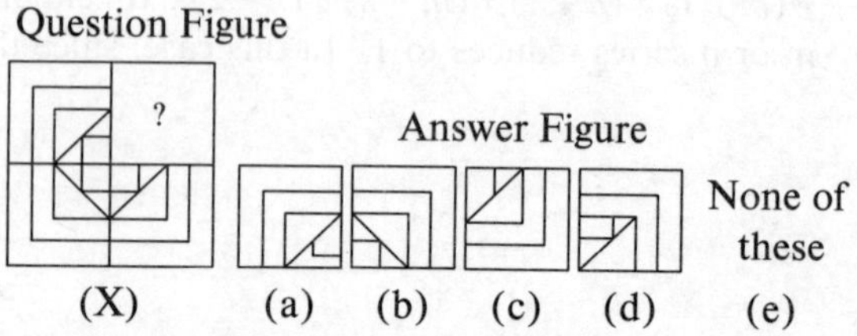

Solution to Example 1: In the figure, bottom right is the mirror image of bottom left. Using that pattern we get that option (b) is correct.

Example 2: Identify the missing part of the given figure and select it from the given answer figures.

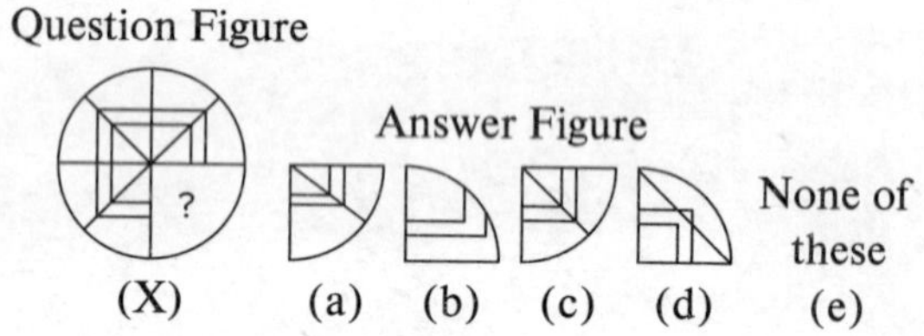

Solution to Example 2: In the figure, top right is the mirror image of top left. Using that pattern we get that option (c) is correct.

Example 3: Identify the figure that completes the pattern.

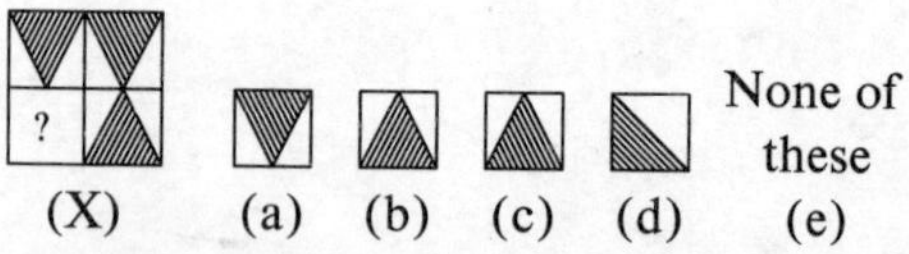

Solution to Example 3: Top right and bottom right are water image of each other. Using similar pattern we can say that top left and bottom left are also water image of each other.

Hence, option (c) is correct.

EXERCISE

1. Rotation is NOT allowed.
Select the option in which the given figure is embedded.

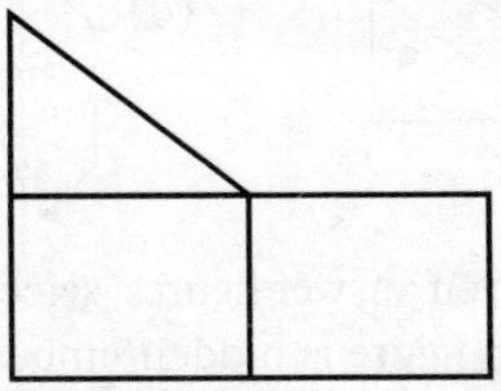

(X)

(a) 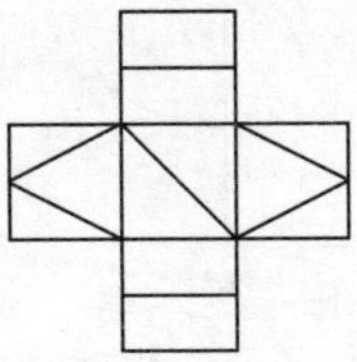

(b) 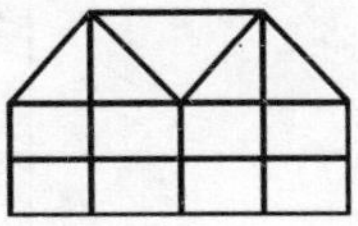

(c) 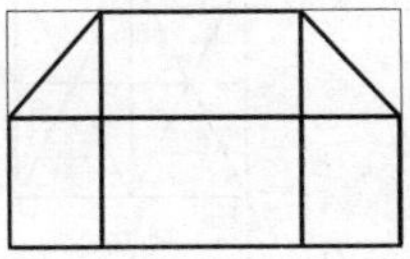

(d) 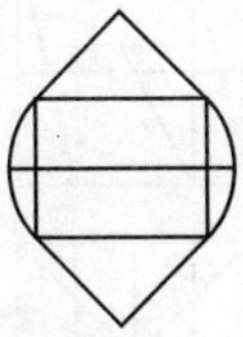

2. Select the option that is embedded in the given figure. Rotation is NOT allowed.

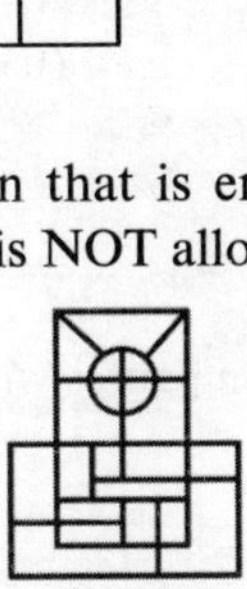

(X)

(a) 

(b) 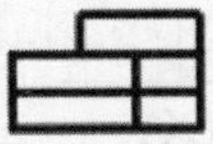

(c) 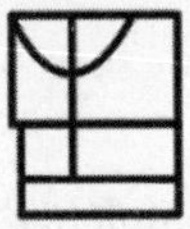

(d) 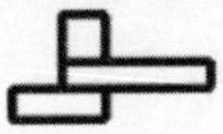

3. Select the option which shows missing part of figure.

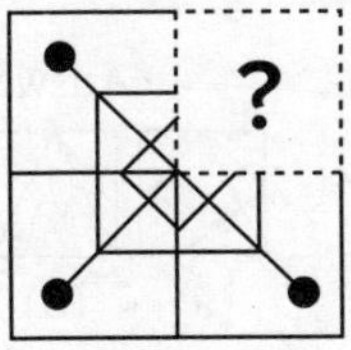

(X)

(a) 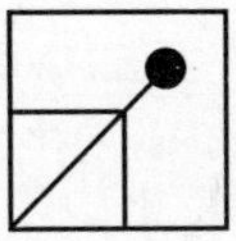

(b) 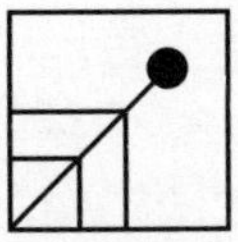

(c) 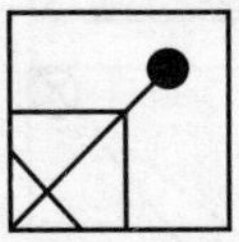

(d) 

4. Select the option in which the following figure is embedded.

(X)

(a) 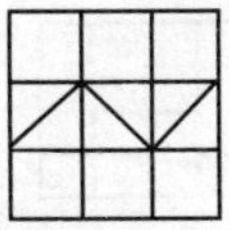

(b) 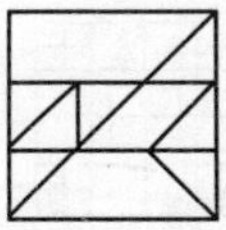

(c) 

(d) 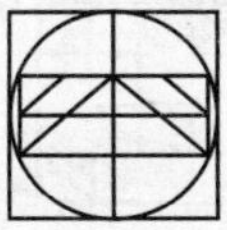

5. Select the figure from the options that can replace the question mark and complete pattern.

(X)

(a) 

(b) 

(c) 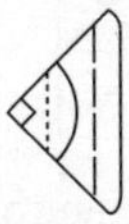

(d) 

6. Which answer figure will complete the pattern in the following question figure?

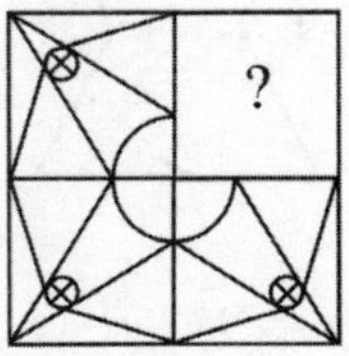

(X)

(a) 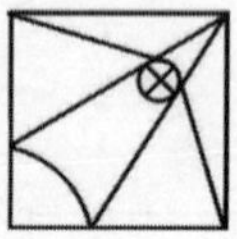 (b) 

(c)  (d) 

7. Select the option figure in which the given figure is embedded.

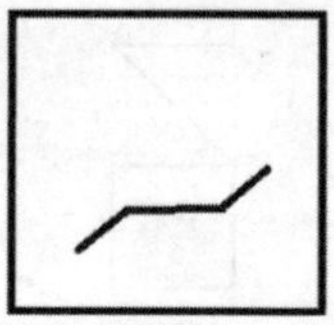

(X)

(a) 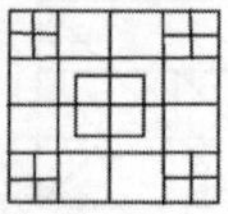 (b) 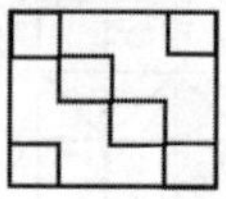

(c) 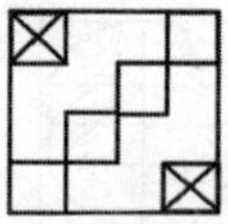 (d) 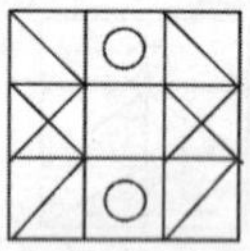

8. Select the option in which the given figure is embedded.

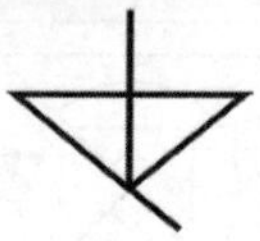

(X)

(a) 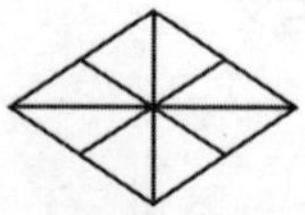 (b) 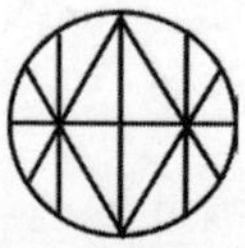

(c)  (d) 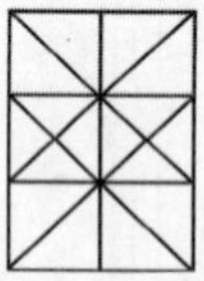

9. Select the option in which the given figure is hidden.

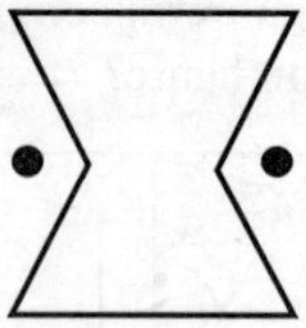

(X)

(a) 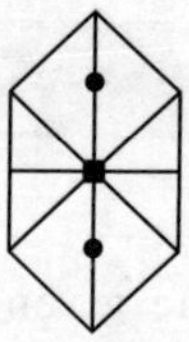 (b) 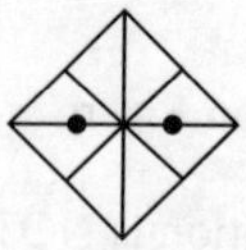

(c)  (d) 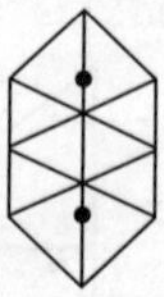

10. From the given answer figures, select the one in which the question figure is hidden/embedded.

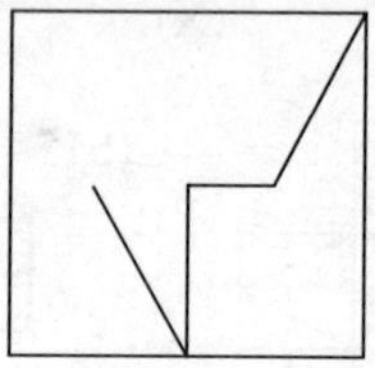

(X)

(a) 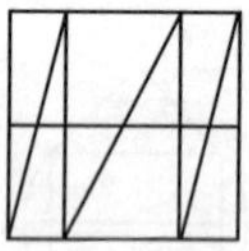 (b) 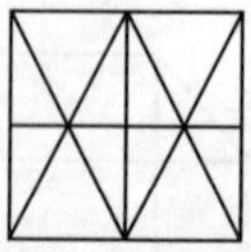

(c)  (d) 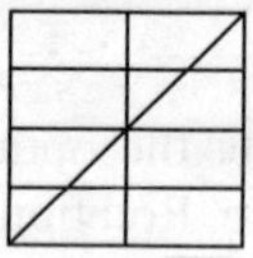

11. Which of the given figures will complete the pattern?

Question Figure

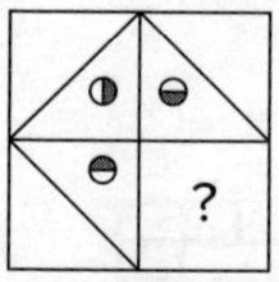

(X)

Answer Figure

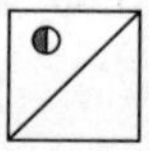   

(a) (b) (c) (d)

(a) a
(b) b
(c) c
(d) d

12. Which of the given figures will complete the pattern?

Question Figure

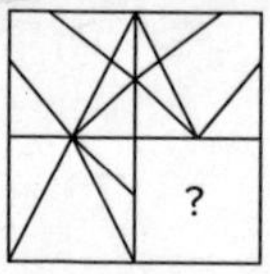

(X)

Answer Figure

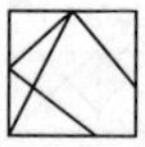 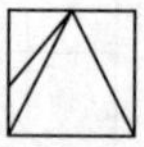  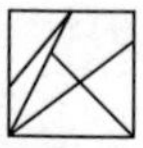

(a) (b) (c) (d)

(a) a
(b) b
(c) c
(d) d

13. Which of the given figures will complete the pattern?

Question Figure

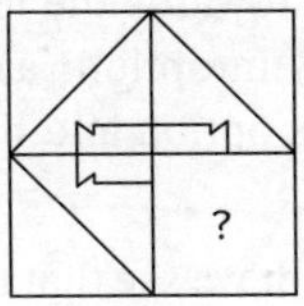

Answer Figure

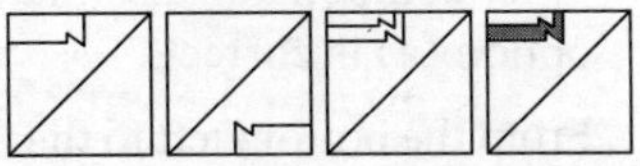

(X) (a) (b) (c) (d)

(a) a (b) b
(c) c (d) d

14. Which of the given figures will complete the pattern?

Question Figure

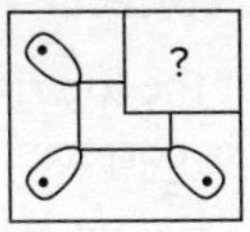

Answer Figure

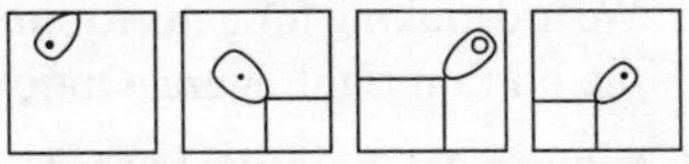

(X) (a) (b) (c) (d)

(a) a
(b) b
(c) c
(d) d

15. Which of the given figures will complete the pattern?

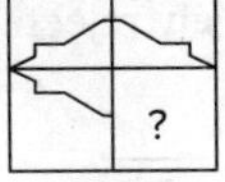

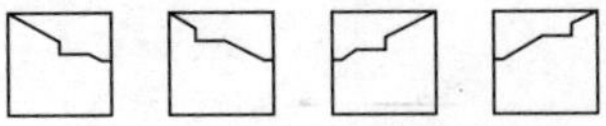

(X) (a) (b) (c) (d)

(a) a
(b) b
(c) c
(d) d

16. Which of the given figures will complete the pattern?

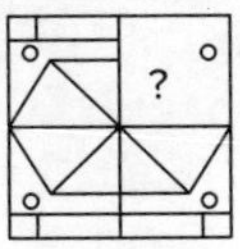

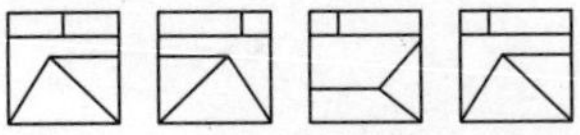

(X) (a) (b) (c) (d)

(a) a
(b) b
(c) c
(d) d

High Yield Questions

Scan this QR code to access video explanations of questions 7, 10 and 11

ANSWER KEY

1. (b)	2. (d)	3. (c)	4. (a)
5. (a)	6. (a)	7. (d)	8. (d)
9. (d)	10. (b)	11. (a)	12. (a)
13. (a)	14. (d)	15. (d)	16. (b)

SOLUTIONS AND SHORTCUTS

1. The given figure is embedded in option (B), as highlighted in thick grey.

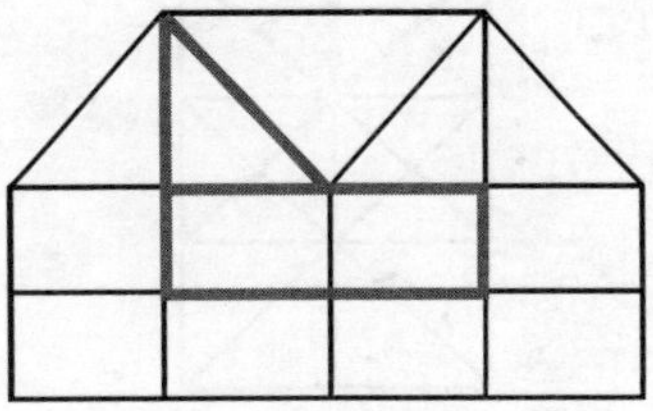

2.

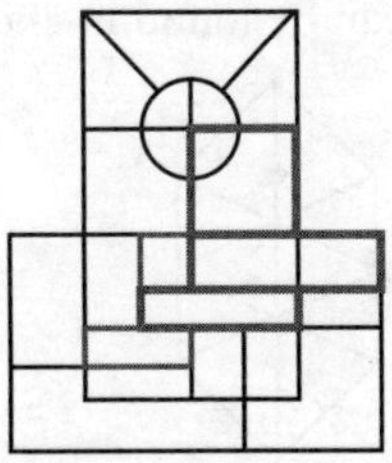

This highlighted part is the only part which is embedded in the figure rest are not.

3.

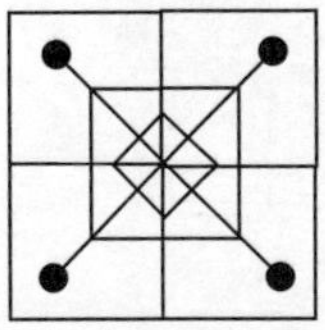

So, (c) is the correct option.

4.

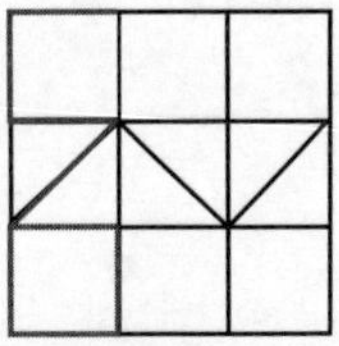

5. The correct completion part is:

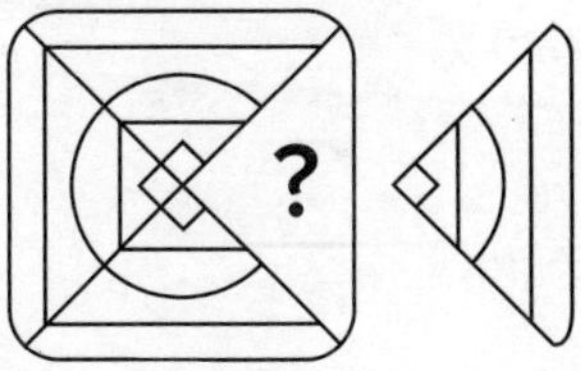

6. From the options Choice (a) completes the figure given.
7. The shape can be embedded only in option (d).

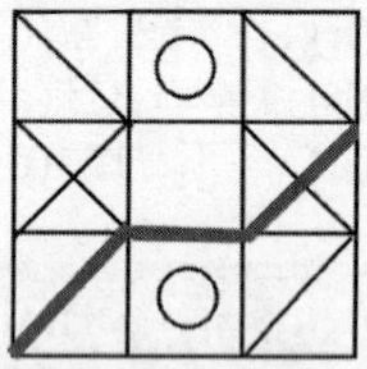

8. The shape can be embedded only in option (d)

9. The given image can be found in choice (d),

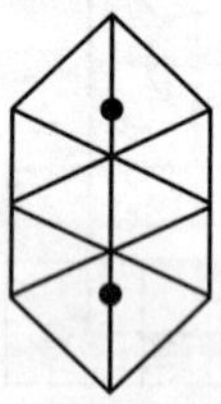

Hence, the correct answer is option (d).

10. The question figure can be seen to be hidden in the figure for option (b). Hence, the correct answer is option (b).
11. The shaded portion of the circle has to shift to the opposite side when we move from top left to bottom right - which means it should be towards the left of the vertical line. This is seen only in option (a). All other components also match this option and hence option (a) is correct.
12. From the bottom left to the top right we see that there is an increase of 1 in the number of lines inside the square. A similar increase would mean either 4 or 5 lines in the bottom right. None of the options has 5 lines- and hence the figure we are looking for has to have 3 lines inside the square. Option (d) is eliminated basis this thought. Looking at the other components and their shift, we see option (a) as correct.
13. We are looking for a mirror image of the top right for the bottom right figure. Option (a) is correct.
14. A black dot, pointing towards the right is what we are looking for, and we see it in option (d).
15. Options (a) and (b) are easily eliminated due to the orientation of the lines. We choose option (d) - while rejecting option (c) because we are also looking for a mirror image of the top right figure in the bottom right blank. Option (d) is correct.
16. Option (b) closes the hexagon in the middle of the figure - the other options can be easily rejected.

CHAPTER 6 Series

INTRODUCTION

The "Series of Diagrams" is a critical component within the abstract reasoning section and evaluates a candidate's ability to discern logical patterns, relationships, and sequences in a set of figures.

In diagram series questions, a sequence of figures is presented, and candidates are tasked with identifying the next figure in the series or determining the missing one. These figures typically consist of geometric shapes, lines, dots, or symbols, exhibiting various transformations such as

(i) Position changes (elements within the diagram may change positions – like a small shape inside a diagram could be moving in clockwise or counter clockwise fashion),
Example: A triangle inside a square might be moving clockwise from one corner to the next in consecutive figures.

(ii) Rotations (figures may rotate by specific angles like 45, 90, 135, 180 degrees etc)
Example: A triangle pointing rightwards in one figure rotates 90° clockwise in each subsequent figure.

(iii) Changes in the count of elements (the number of elements inside the figure may progressively increase or decrease).
Example: The first figure has one square, the second has two squares, the third has three, and so forth.

(iv) Reflection or Symmetry: Figures may flip along a horizontal or vertical axis,
Example: A shape with a dot on the top reflects to place the dot on the bottom side in the subsequent figure.

A lot of questions on series might involve a mix of more than one of these patterns – hence recognising these and understanding them will help you identify the correct answer to series questions.

Types of Diagram Series Questions

Candidates may encounter two primary types of questions:

- **Predicting the Next Diagram**: Based on the observed pattern, candidates must select the figure that logically follows in the sequence.
- **Identifying the Missing Diagram**: A diagram within the series is missing, and candidates must determine which figure completes the sequence.

Example 1: Directions: Each of the following questions consists of four/ five figures as the problem figure followed by four/five figures marked (a), (b), (c), (d), and (e) as the answer figures. Select the correct answer figure which will continue the series as established by the problem

Problem Figures

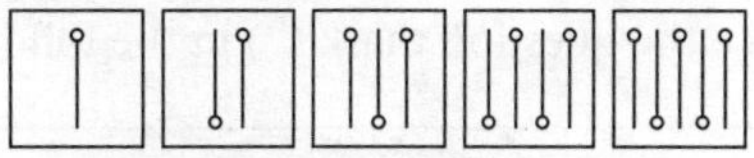

Answer Figures

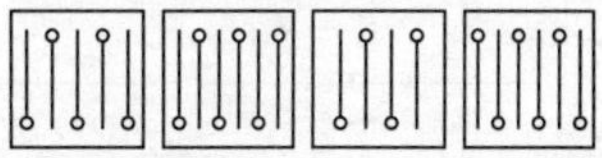

(a) (b) (c) (d)

A. (a) **B.** (b)
C. (c) **D.** (d)

Solution to Example 1: In every step one new line with circle in opposite direction to the left most line of the previous figure is introduced on the left side. So, in the answer figure we will have 6 lines and in the 6th the circle must be at bottom, rest of the part remains same, as the fifth figure of the question. Hence, option (b) is correct.

Example 2

Problem Figures

Answer Figures

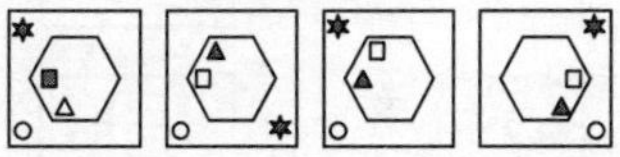

(a) (b) (c) (d)

A. (a) B. (b)
C. (c) D. (d)

Solution to Example 2: Star is rotating in clockwise direction so only options (a) and (c) can be correct. Square and triangles are changing shades alternatively. So triangle should be in dark shade which is true only for option c. Hence, option (c) is correct.

Example 3:

Problem Figure

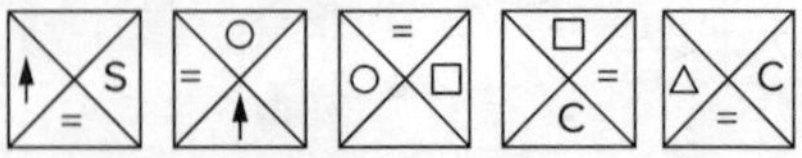

Answer Figure

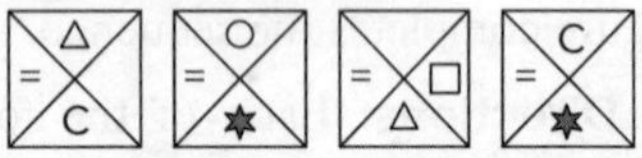

(a) (b) (c) (d)

A. (a)
B. (b)
C. (c)
D. (d)

Solution to Example 3: Only "=" is in all the blocks of question figure. It is also rotating in a clockwise fashion and can be predicted to be in the middle left of the answer figure - however all options have it there, so we will need to consider the other shapes. The 'C' shape has already appeared twice and will not be present in the answer figure - thus eliminating options (a) and (d). The triangle shape has appeared only once and should appear a second time at the bottom quadrant of the square - this is seen only in option (c) and hence is the correct answer.

EXERCISE

1. Select the figure from among the given options that can replace the question mark (?) in the following series.

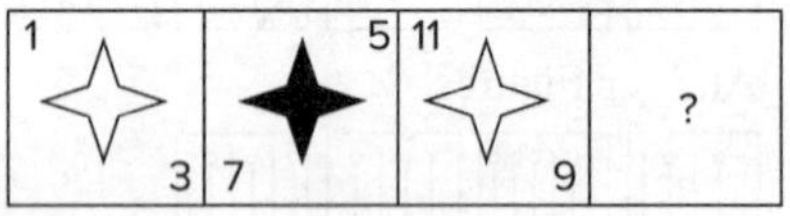

(a) 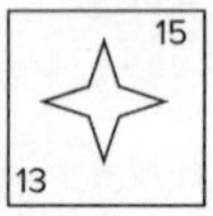 (b) 

(c)  (d) 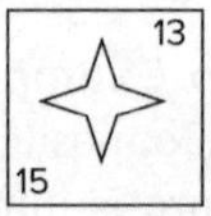

2. Select the figure from among the given options that can replace the question mark (?) in the following series.

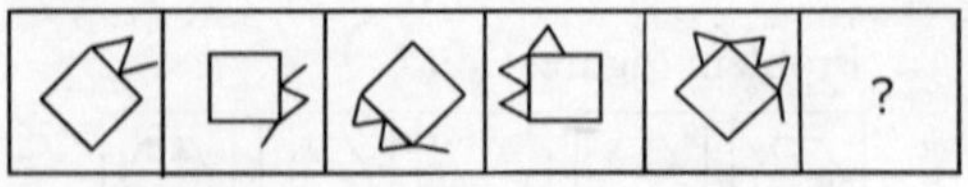

(a) 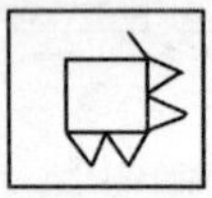 (b) 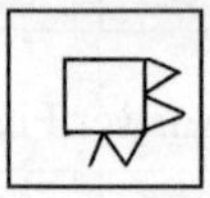

(c) 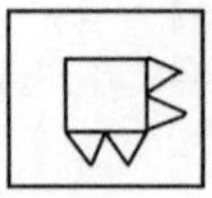 (d) 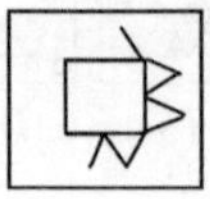

3. Select the figure from among the given options that can replace the question mark (?) in the following series.

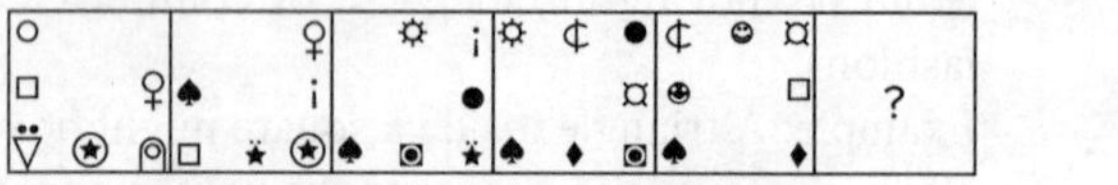

(a)  (b) 

(c)  (d) 

4. Select the figure from among the given options that can replace the question mark (?) in the following series:

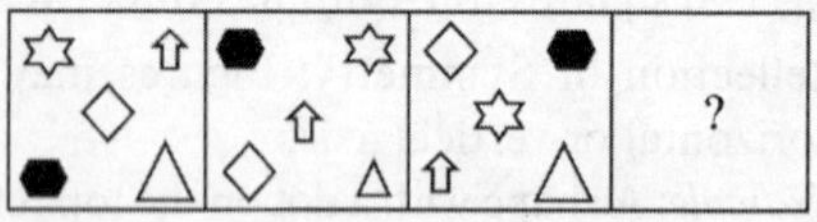

(a)  (b) 

(c)  (d) 

5. Identify the next figure in series

(a) 

(b) 

(c) 

(d) 

6. Select the option that will correctly fit in the blank space in the given figure series.

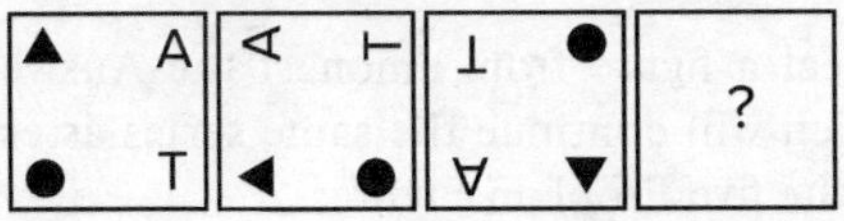

(a) 

(b) 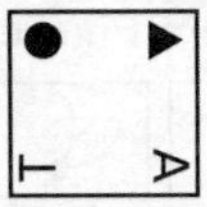

(c) 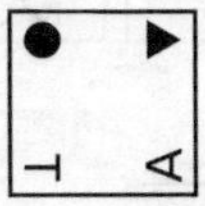

(d) 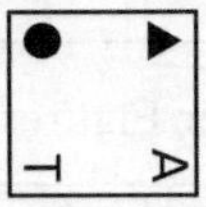

7. Select the figure that can replace the question mark (?) in the following series.

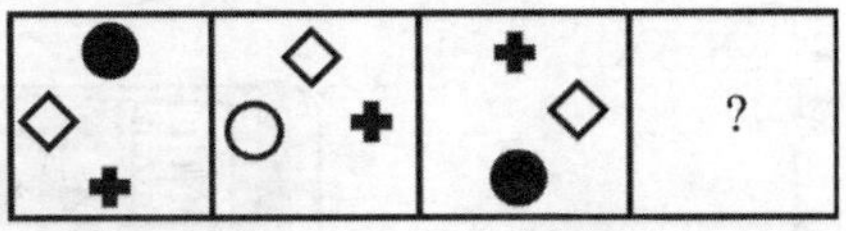

(a) 

(b) 

(c) 

(d) 

8. Select the figure that will come next in the following figure series.

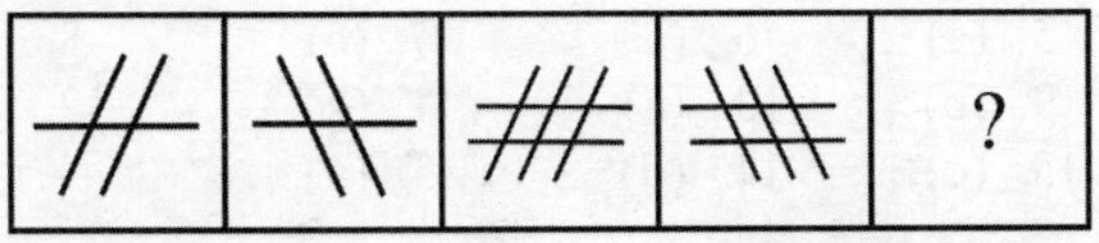

(a) 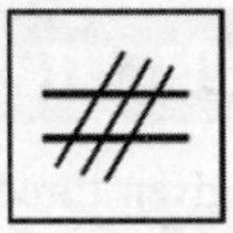

(b) 

(c) 

(d) 

9. Which answer figure completes the pattern in question figure?

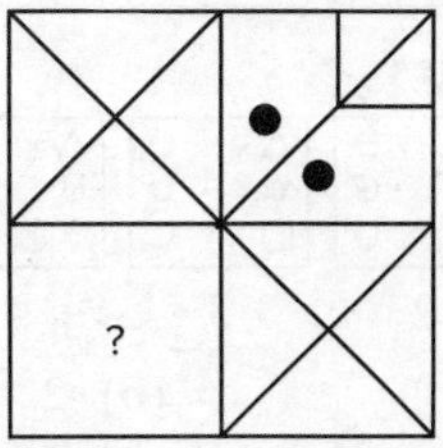

(a) 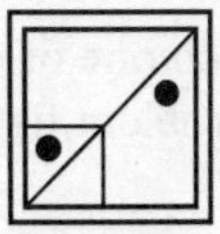

(b) 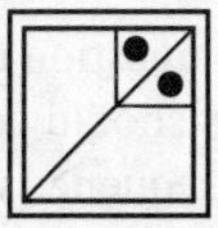

(c) 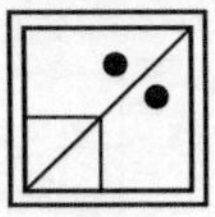

(d) 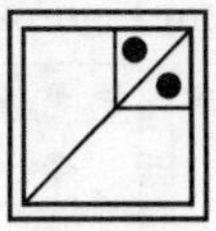

10. Which answer figure will complete the pattern in the question figure?

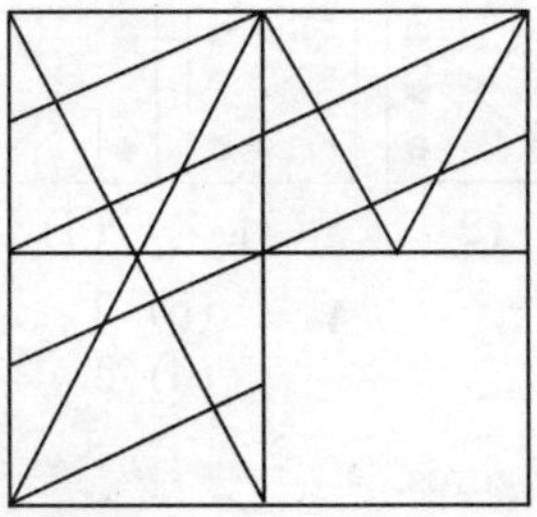

(a) 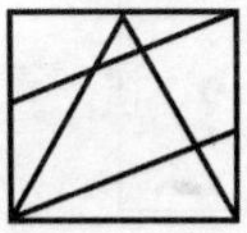

(b) 

(c) 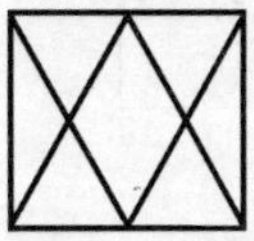

(d) 

11. In the question given below which one of the answer figures should come after the problem figures given, if the sequence were continued?

Problem Figures

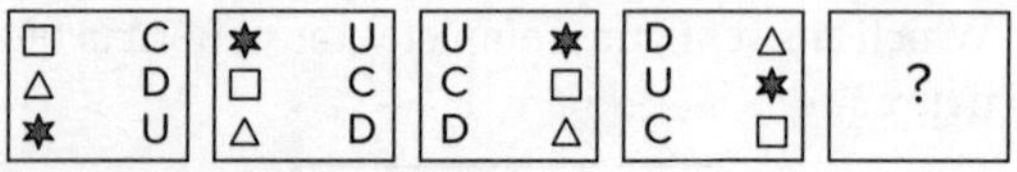

Answer Figures

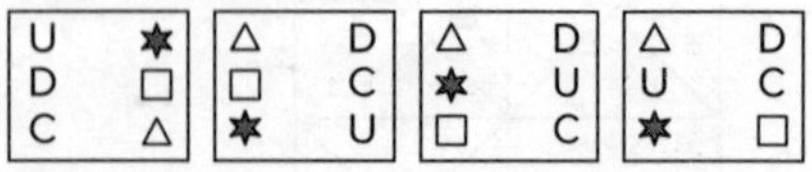

1 2 3 4

(a) 1 (b) 2
(c) 3 (d) 4

12. In the question given below which one of the answer figures should come after the problem figures given, if the sequence were continued?

Problem Figures

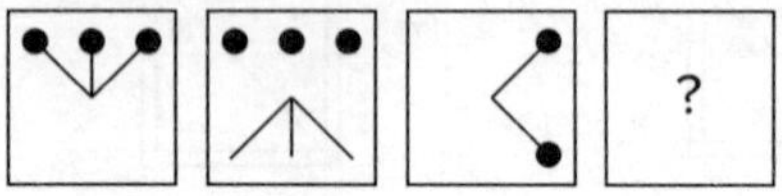

(A) (B) (C) (D)

Answer Figures

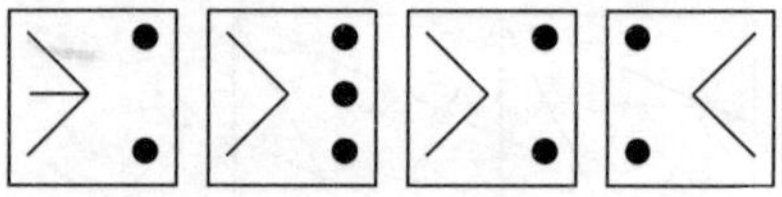

(1) (2) (3) (4)

(a) 1 (b) 2
(c) 3 (d) 4

13. Problem Figures:

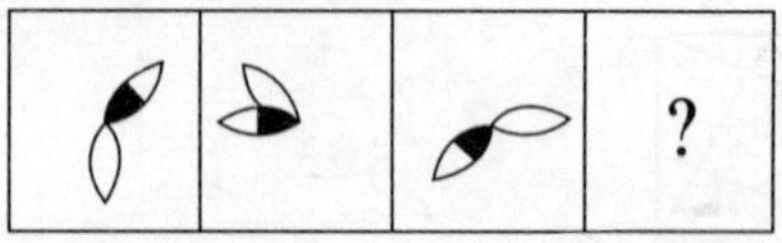

(A) (B) (C) (D)

Answer Figures:

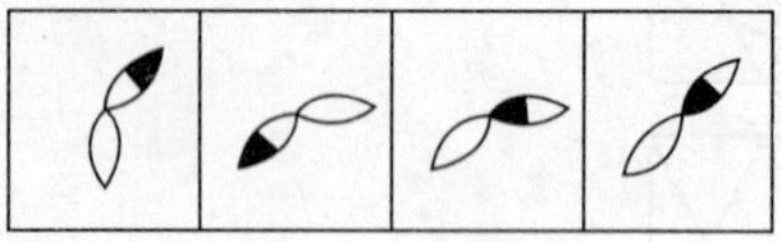

1 2 3 4

(a) 1 (b) 2
(c) 3 (d) 4

14. Select a figure from amongst the Answer Figures which will continue the same series as established by the five Problem Figures.

Problem Figures

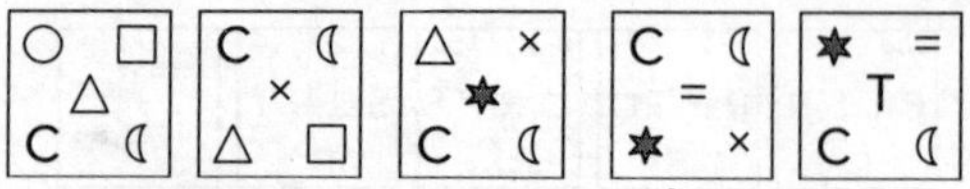

Answer Figures

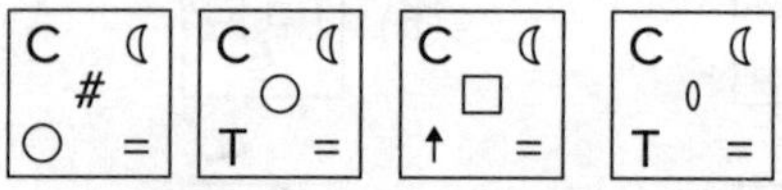

1 2 3 4

(a) 1
(b) 2
(c) 3
(d) 4

15. Select a figure from amongst the Answer Figures which will continue the same series as established by the five Problem Figures.

Problem Figures

Answer Figures

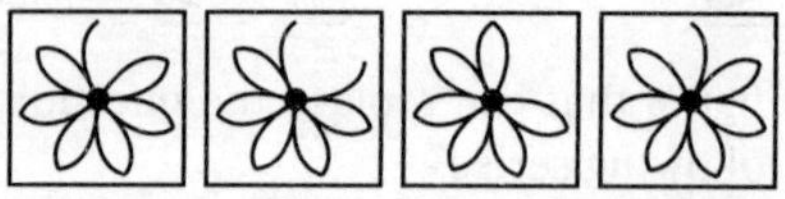

1 2 3 4

(a) 1
(b) 2
(c) 3
(d) 4

High Yield Questions

Scan this QR code to access video explanations of questions 1, 12 and 15

ANSWER KEY

1. (c)	2. (d)	3. (c)	4. (a)
5. (a)	6. (d)	7. (c)	8. (d)
9. (c)	10. (a)	11. (c)	12. (c)
13. (c)	14. (d)	15. (a)	

SOLUTIONS AND SHORTCUTS

1. From observing the pattern in given three figures, it can be clearly seen that:

(i) Stars are alternatively shaded.

(ii) Values are on main diagonal and antidiagonal alternatively.

From these two observations, '?' place will have shaded star and entries on antidiagonal.

Sequence is of odd numbers, next two odd numbers are 13 and 15.

In first two, smaller number is at top and in third smaller number is at bottom. So, to complete the pattern, smaller number (13) should be at bottom.

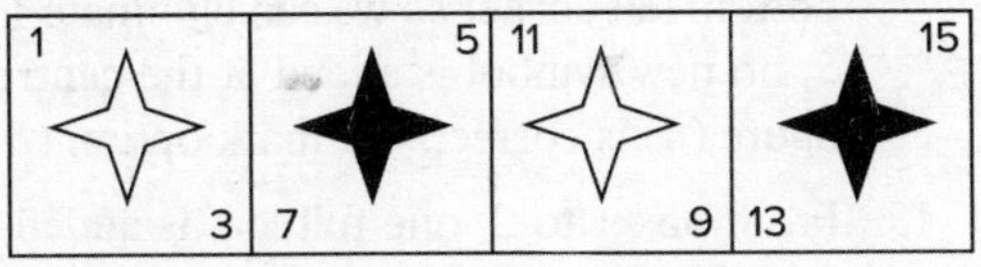

Thus option (c) is correct.

2. To transform a rhombus into a square, we follow this pattern each time:
   Rotate clockwise by 45 degrees.
   Flip the figure upside down.
   Draw a single line to the first point in the direction of rotation.

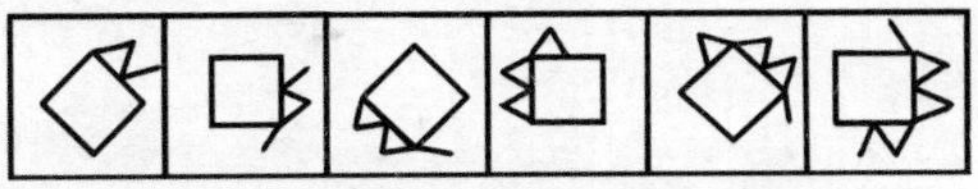

Applying these steps to the last given figure results in option (d) being correct.

3. Observe that the icons are moving in a pattern.

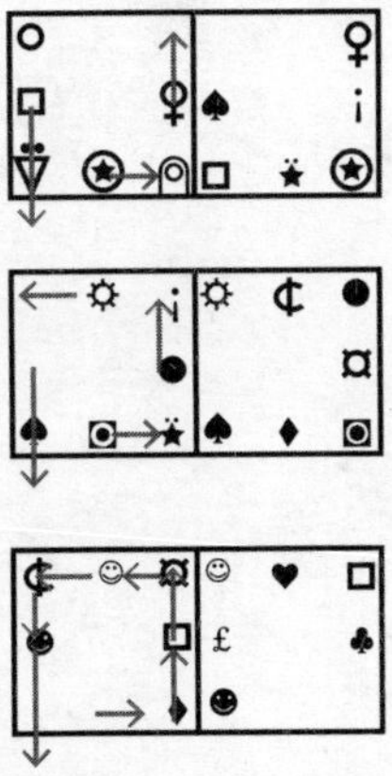

♦ is replaced by ♠
¤ is replaced by ♥
₵ is replaced by £

4. Observe that the icons are moving in a pattern, each icon on the left side of the square is moving clockwise.

And the triangle in the bottom right corner is just increasing and decreasing its size alternatively.

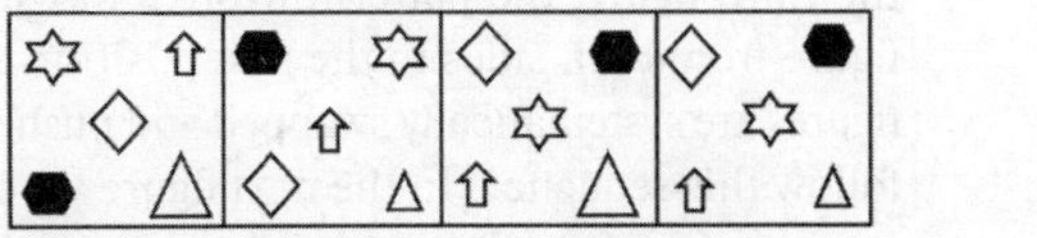

Using this pattern option (a) fits the best.

5. We can follow letters, letters follow a consistent pattern, the 2nd from right letter goes down and down letter comes at last in every consecutive cycle.
   The arrow in top left corner is changing with 90 and 180 degrees turn alternatively.

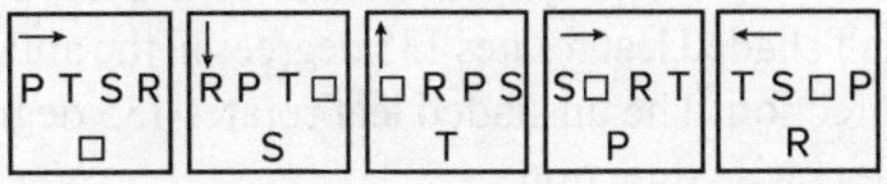

6. From the above series of diagrams, the option (d) fits the puzzle and finishes the series.

7. Pattern observed:
   + moves anticlockwise.
   Rhombus moves clockwise. Solid and empty alternatively.
   Circle moves clockwise. Solid and empty alternatively.

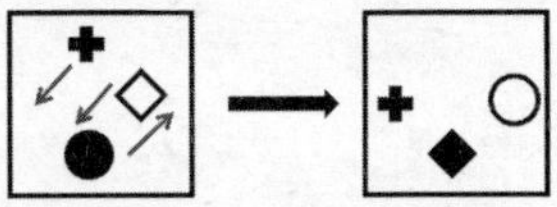

So, the complete series becomes:

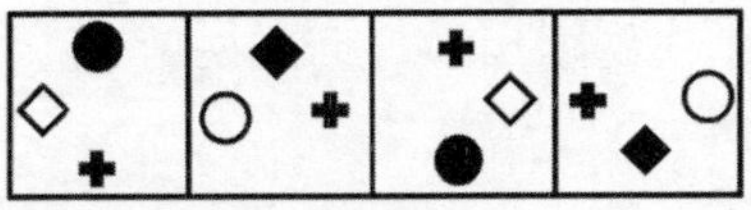

So, option (c) is correct.

8. Pattern observed-
   1. Vertical line in 1st block is on left and in 2nd block it is on right side and similarly pattern follows.
   2. The no. Of line inc. by 1 in both horizontal and vertical direction

   By the observation, the right answer is **(d)**.

9. 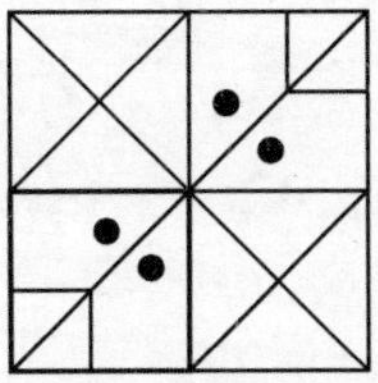

10. It can be observed that the upper sides of the left and right are the same. So, the lower sides should be the same.

11. In the second box, the last figure from both sides becomes the first figure, and the other figures are

pushed down. In the third box, the figures on the left and right exchange positions. After the exchange in the third figure, the pattern involves moving the last figure from both sides to the first position again. The figures are systematically swapped and pushed down to follow this sequence. In the next figure we can expect a swapping of the left and right sides - the correct option is (c).

12. In the figure from box 1 to 2, the dots retain their position and the lines rotate by 180 degrees and shifts to the opposite side of the square boundary. Based on this pattern, the correct option is (c).

13. In the given sequence, from box 1 to box 2, the half-shaded leaf rotates 135 degrees in the anti-clockwise direction. The unshaded leaf rotates 135 degrees in the clockwise direction.
    Thus, for the fourth figure, we rotate the shaded leaf anti-clockwise by 135 degrees and the unshaded leaf clockwise by 135 degrees. Also, the shaded portion of the half-shaded leaf always starts from the point where the two leaves meet. The correct option is C, as it continues the rotation pattern of both leaves correctly.

14. In each of the answer figures the C and the semicircle are in the same place so we have no need to trace their pattern. If we observer the pattern of the first five figures, we see that each time a new diagram is added in the center position and the new diagram shifts to bottom left and top right positions alternatively, in the following figure. Following this pattern T should be at bottom left corner so we can eliminate 1 & 3. In 2 and 5, no new symbol is added at the centre position. So figure (4) is correct. We mark option (d).

15. From box 1 to 2, one full leaf is added to the figure, from box 2 to 3, 1.5 leaves are added to the figure, from box 3 to 4, 1 leaf is added and from box 4 to 5, 1.5 leaves are added - the problem figure E has 5.5 leaves. For the next figure in the series, we should look for an addition of 1 leaf to make it 6.5 leaves. So, option (a) is correct.

CHAPTER 7

Mirror Image and Water Image

INTRODUCTION

In abstract reasoning **Mirror Image** and **Water Image** questions are very commonly asked. These problems test spatial reasoning, symmetry, and perception of reflections, commonly seen in both 2D and 3D shapes. The key difference between the two is that in a **Mirror Image**, the object or figure is Reflected of an object or figure along a vertical axis (left-right inversion), while in a **Water Image** – the Reflection of an object or figure is along a horizontal axis (top-bottom inversion).

Thus in a **mirror image** – the following changes occur:

(i) The **left side** becomes the **right side**.

(ii) The **right side** becomes the **left side**.

(iii) The **vertical orientation** (top and bottom) remains unchanged.

In a **Water Image,** the following changes occur:

(i) The **top side** becomes the **bottom side**.

(ii) The **bottom side** becomes the **top side**.

(iii) The **horizontal orientation** (left and right) remains unchanged.

Example: Letter A: Will appear same in a mirror image, while it will flip vertically in a water image, with it's bottom going on top and top going to bottom.

Letter C, will appear opposite in orientation with it's opening towards the left side in a mirror image. The water image of C will look exactly like the original.

Example 1: Which of the given answer figures will be the correct mirror image of the question figure?

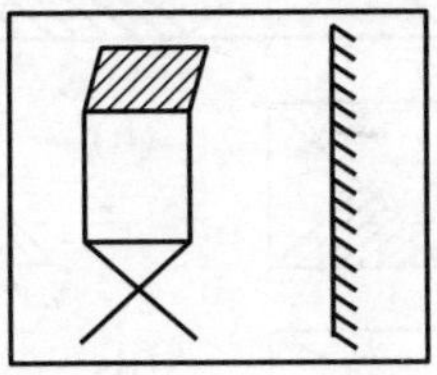

(a) 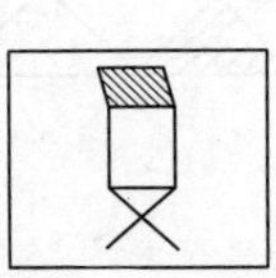

(b) 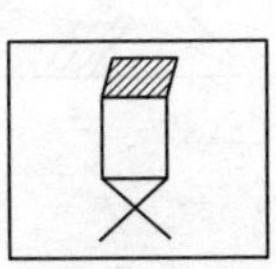

(c) 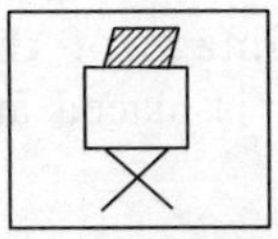

(d) 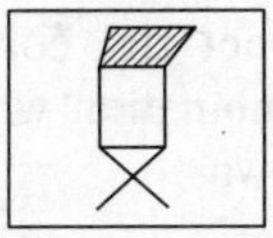

Solution to Example 1: In a mirror image, the left becomes right and the right becomes left. The tilted quadrilateral at the top will be slanting towards the left, while not changing anything else in the figure.

Hence, option (a) is correct.

Example 2: Which of the given answer figures will be the correct water image of the question figure?

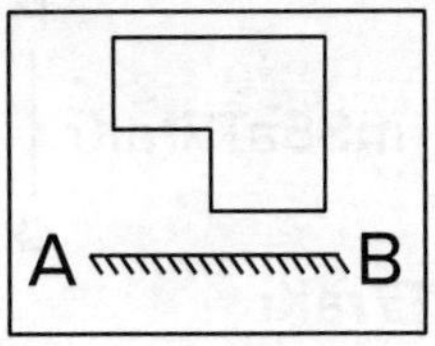

(a) 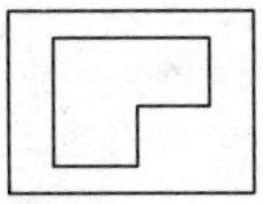

(b) 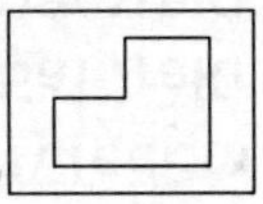

(c) 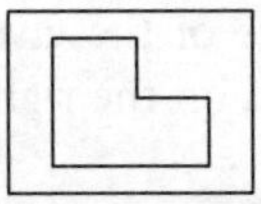

(d) 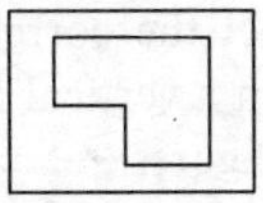

Solution to Example 2: The bottom will go to the top in a water image. Option (b) shows that.

Hence, option (b) is correct.

Example 3: Which of the given answer figures will be the correct mirror image of the question figure?

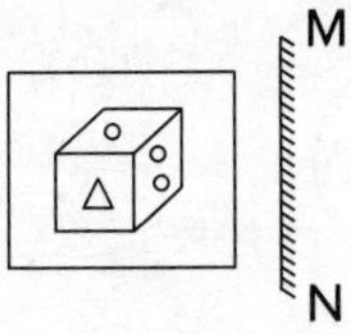

(a) 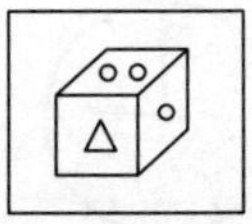

(b) 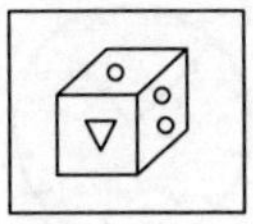

(c) 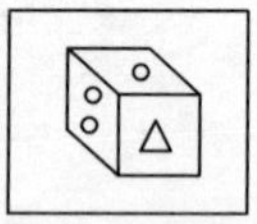 (d) 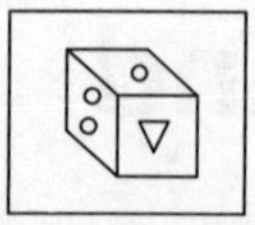

Solution to Example 3: In a mirror image, the left becomes right and the right becomes left. Thus, the central dot on top and the triangle in the front side will remain as they are - and we can easily eliminate options (a),(b) and (d) basis this thought. The two dots on the right, should flip towards the left - hence, the correct answer is option (c).

EXERCISE

1. Select the correct mirror image of the given combination when the mirror is placed at MN as shown

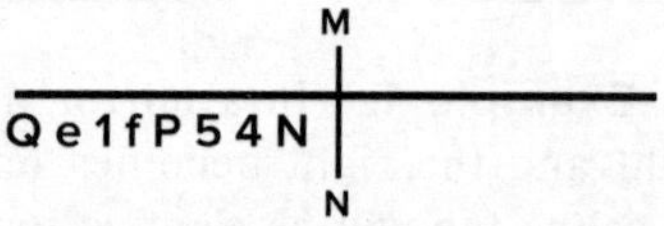

(a) 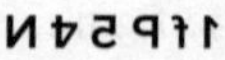 (b) 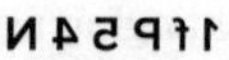

(c)  (d) 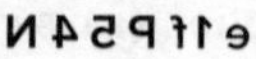

2. Select the correct mirror image of the given combination when the mirror is placed at 'PQ' as shown below.

(a) mS5aT7raKr

(b) 

(c) 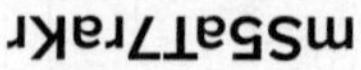

(d) 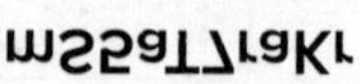

3. Select the correct mirror image of the given figure when a vertical mirror is placed on the right side of the figure.

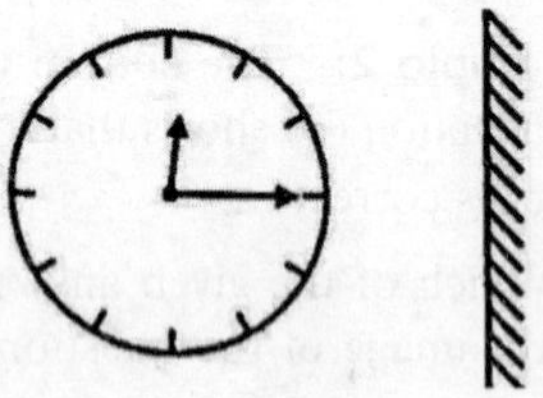

(a) 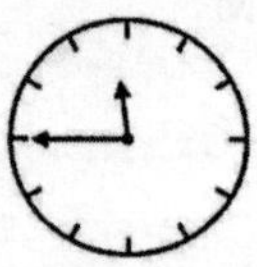 (b) 

(c)  (d) 

4. Which of the option figures is the exact mirror image of the given figure when the mirror is held at the right side?

RST2PK9LOX

(a)  (b) 

(c)  (d) 

5. If the mirror is placed on the right side of the diagram given below, then select the right mirror image to be made.

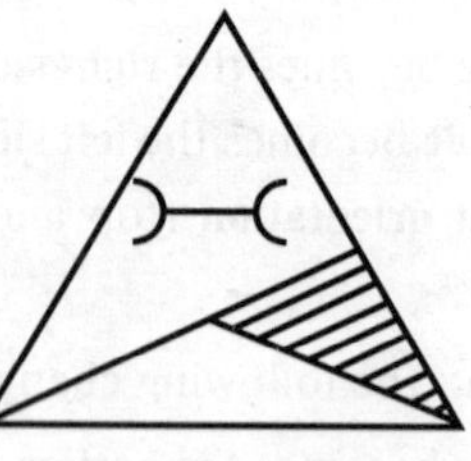

(a) 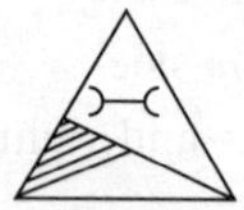 (b) 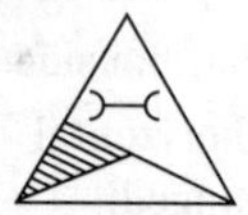

(c) 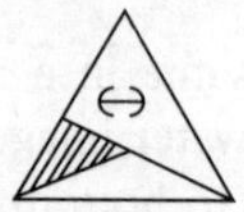 (d) 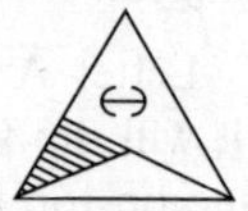

6. Select the correct mirror image of the given figure when the mirror is placed to the right of the figure.

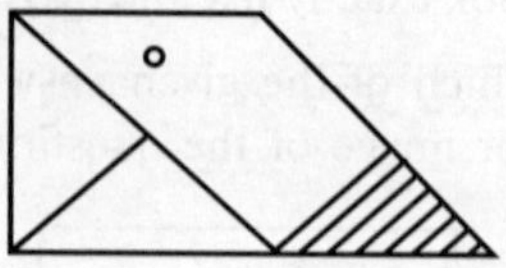

(a) 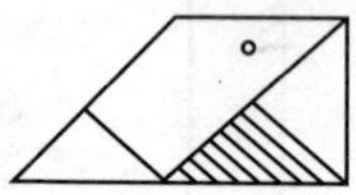 (b) 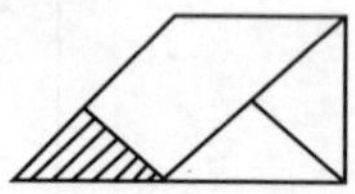

(c) 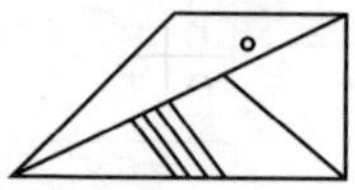 (d) 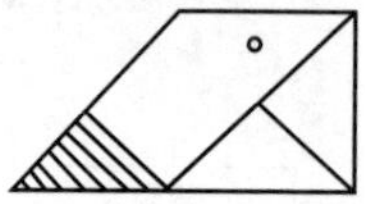

7. If a mirror is placed on the line MN, then which of the answer figures is the right image of the given figure?

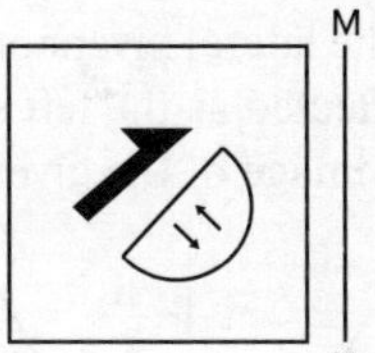

(a)  (b) 

(c)  (d) 

8. If mirror is placed on line AB , then which of the answer figure is the right image of the given figure.

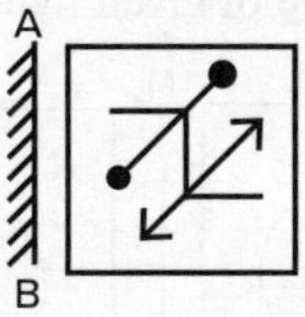

(a) 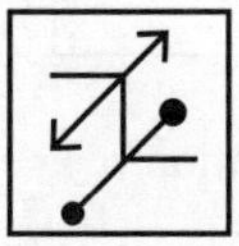 (b) 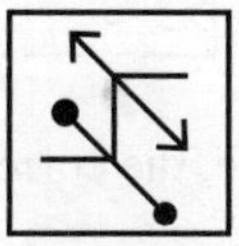

(c) 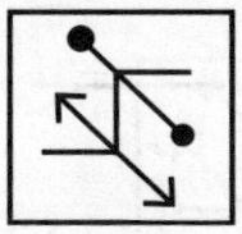 (d) 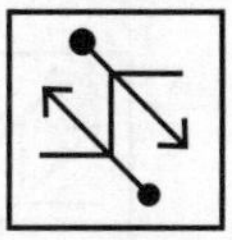

9. A word is represented by only one set of numbers as given in any one of the alternatives. The set of numbers given in the alternatives are represented by two classes of alphabets as shown in the given two matrices. The columns and rows of MATRIX-I are numbered from 0 to 4 and that of MATRIX-II are numbered from 5 to 9. A letter from these matrices can be represented first by it's row and next by its column, for example 'F' can be represented by 03, 34, etc. and 'A' can be represented by 31, 43, etc. Similarly, you have to identify the set for the word "RATES".

Matrix-I

	0	1	2	3	4
0	A	G	R	F	E
1	F	E	A	G	R
2	G	R	F	E	A
3	E	A	G	R	F
4	R	F	E	A	G

Matrix-II

	5	6	7	8	9
5	T	P	U	S	O
6	S	O	T	P	U
7	P	U	S	O	T
8	O	T	P	U	S
9	U	S	O	T	P

(a) 33, 00, 98, 30, 88 (b) 14, 43, 55, 11, 68
(c) 21, 24, 86, 42, 56 (d) 02, 12, 68, 04, 96

Directions for Questions 10 to 15: *In each of the following questions, choose the correct water image of the figure (X) from amongst the four alternatives (1), (2), (3), (4) given along with it.*

10. 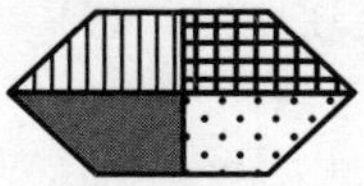

(X)

 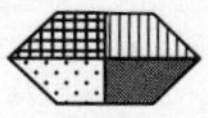  

(1) (2) (3) (4)

(a) 1 (b) 2
(c) 3 (d) 4

11. 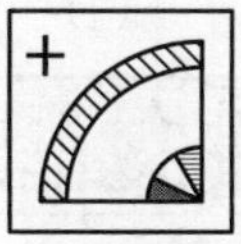

(X)

 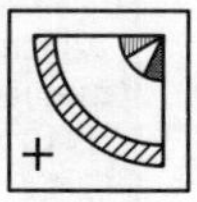 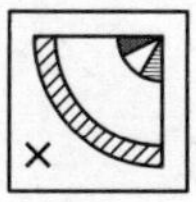 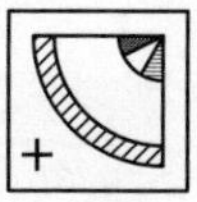

(1) (2) (3) (4)

(a) 1 (b) 2
(c) 3 (d) 4

12. 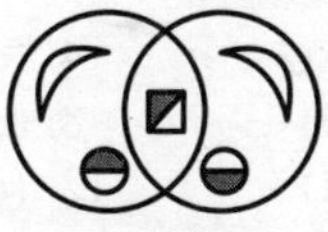

(X)

(1) (2) (3) (4)

(a) 1 (b) 2
(c) 3 (d) 4

13. 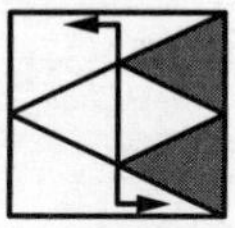

(X)

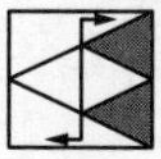 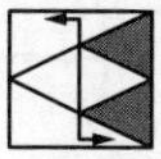 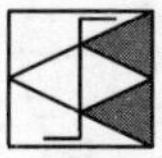 

(1) (2) (3) (4)

(a) 1 (b) 2
(c) 3 (d) 4

14. 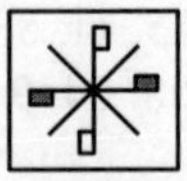

(X)

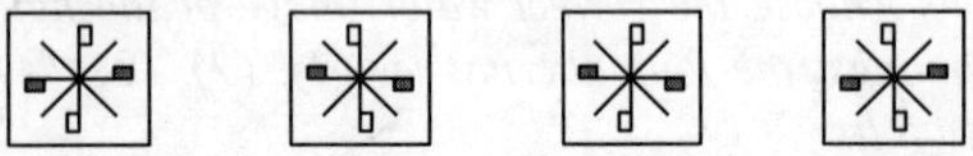

(1) (2) (3) (4)

(a) 1 (b) 2
(c) 3 (d) 4

15. 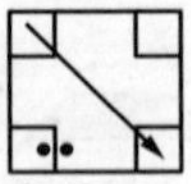

(X)

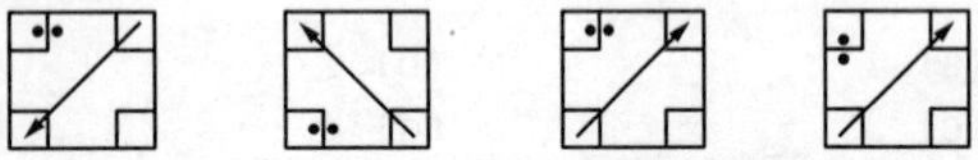

(1) (2) (3) (4)

(a) 1
(b) 2
(c) 3
(d) 4

High Yield Questions

Scan this QR code to access video explanations of questions 8, 10 and 15

ANSWER KEY

1. (b)	2. (b)	3. (a)	4. (d)
5. (b)	6. (d)	7. (d)	8. (c)
9. (d)	10. (a)	11. (d)	12. (d)
13. (a)	14. (b)	15. (c)	

SOLUTIONS AND SHORTCUTS

1. 

2. 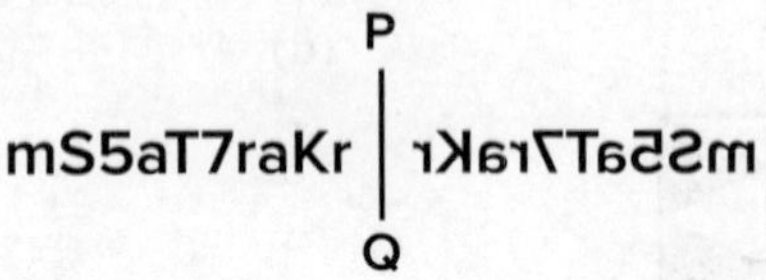

3. 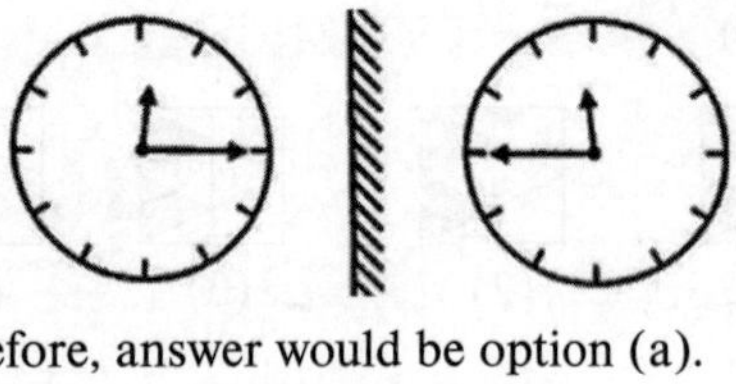

Therefore, answer would be option (a).

4. Option (d) is the correct mirror image.

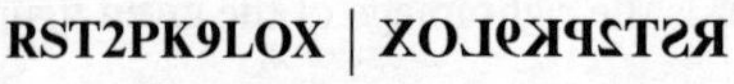

5. According to the lateral inversion rule, the left side of an object is reflected as the left side or vice versa. So, the mirror image of the given image is

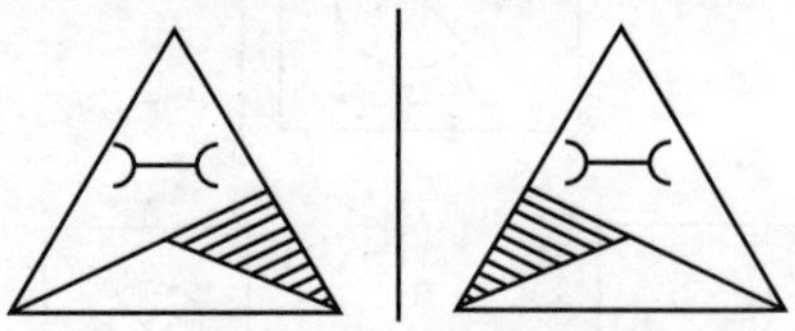

Hence, the correct answer is option (b).

6. Place mirror to right of the given figure. We get,

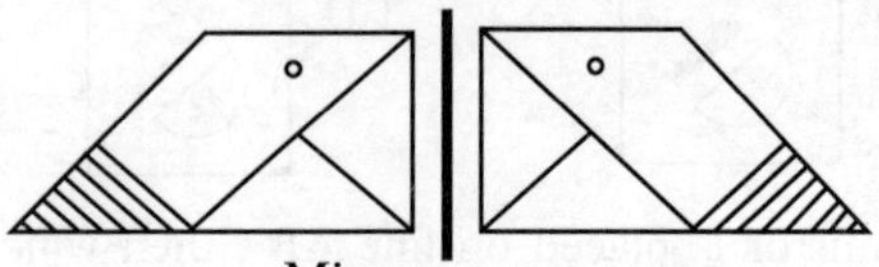

Mirror

7. The mirror image of given figure is,

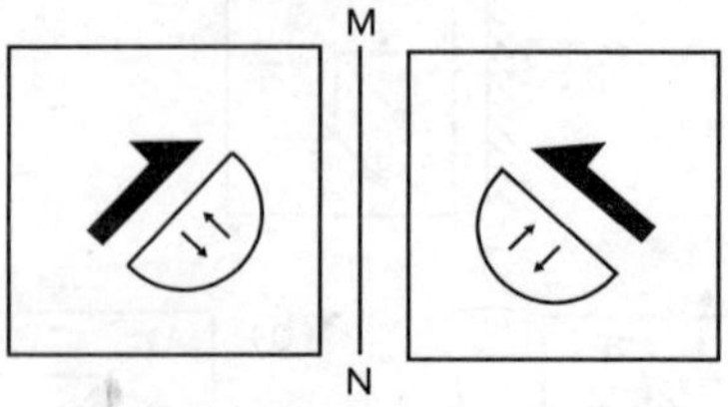

Hence, the correct answer is option (d).

8. 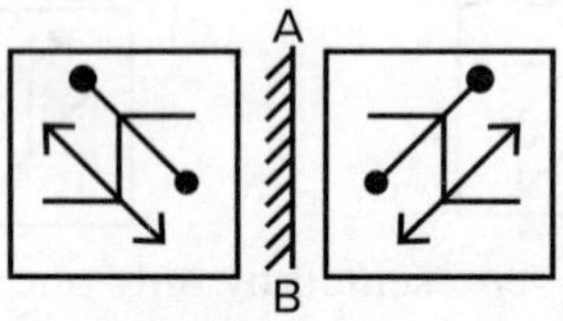

9. As per the given matrix, the correct numbers for the letters of "RATES" are 02, 12, 68, 04, 96. Hence, option (d) is correct.

Matrix-I

	0	1	2	3	4
0	A	G	R	F	E
1	F	E	A	G	R
2	G	R	F	E	A
3	E	A	G	R	F
4	R	F	E	A	G

Matrix-II

	5	6	7	8	9
5	T	P	U	S	O
6	S	O	T	P	U
7	P	U	S	O	T
8	O	T	P	U	S
9	U	S	O	T	P

10. There is a flip around the horizontal axis in the case of a water image - top inverts and goes to bottom and bottom inverts and goes to the top. Looking through the options, we see the fully shaded part going upwards only in (1) and (4). 4 is rejected because the

dotted part remains where it was. Hence, Option (a) is correct.

11. There is a flip around the horizontal axis in the case of a water image - top inverts and goes to bottom and bottom inverts and goes to the top. Based on this, we expect the + sign in the top left corner to come down to the bottom left in the mirror image. Only (2) and (4) show that. We reject 2, since the full black shaded part of the slice should be on top, which is not seen at it's correct position in (2). Only option (4) inverts all components correctly. Hence, option (d) is correct.

12. There is a flip around the horizontal axis in the case of a water image - top inverts and goes to bottom and bottom inverts and goes to the top. In this case, we see all the elements flipping and inverting in option (d). Note: Option (c) looks correct too, but the reason it can be rejected is because the inversion of the small square in the middle is not correct. Hence, option (d) is correct.

13. Based on the mirror image logic of flipping around the horizontal axis, we can see that the central two arrow line's correct orientation in the mirror image should be what we see in (1) and (3). We are also looking for the fully shaded triangle to be in the top half of the figure. Hence, option (a) is correct.

14. There is a flip around the horizontal axis in the case of a water image - top inverts and goes to bottom and bottom inverts and goes to the top. Based on the flipping of the horizontal line, the correct orientation is seen in (2) and (3). The correct flip of the vertical line is only seen in (2).
Hence, option (b) is correct.

15. There is a flip around the horizontal axis in the case of a water image - top inverts and goes to bottom and bottom inverts and goes to the top. Based on this, the arrow has to be pointing towards the top right in the correct mirror image. Moreover, the two dots should be placed in the same horizontal orientation in the top left corner of the figure. Only (3) shows both these elements in their correct positions and orientations. Hence, option (c) is correct.

CHAPTER 8 Paper Folding and Cutting

INTRODUCTION

Paper folding questions are an integral part of the Abstract reasoning. These questions assess your ability to visualize spatial relationships. These questions require you to imagine how a paper, after being folded and cut, will appear when unfolded. Success in this section hinges on your spatial reasoning skills and attention to detail. You would also need to use the visualisation that you learnt in solving mirror images and water images in the previous chapter- when a cut paper is unfolded.

These questions will first show you how a paper is folded once or multiple times- and then a cut is made on the folded paper. When you start unfolding the paper, a vertical axis unfolding acts like a mirror image creation - taking the cut on the left to the right or right to left as the case may be (as it's mirror image- meaning the orientation of the cut will flip with left becoming right and right becoming left in the unfolded part of the paper). When, the paper is unfolded around a horizontal axis, it acts like a water image creation - taking the cut on the top to the bottom or bottom to the top as the case may be (as it's water image- meaning the orientation of the cut will flip with top becoming the bottom and the bottom becoming the top in the unfolded part of the paper).

Example 1: A piece of paper is folded and cut as shown below. How will it appear after unfolding?

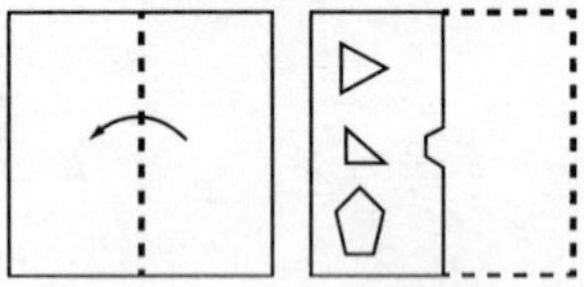

(i) (ii)

(a) 

(b) 

(c) 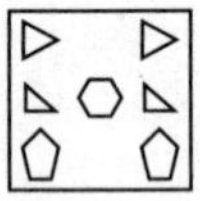

(d) 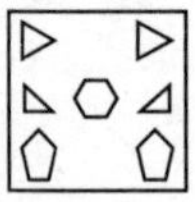

Solution to Example 1: Since there is a vertical axis folding and unfolding of the paper - we are looking for the right side of the paper exhibiting the mirror image of the left side once it is unfolded. We can see that option (b) is correct as it correctly replicates the 'mirror image of all the components on the left side of the figure to the right.

Example 2: A piece of paper is folded and cut as shown below. How will it appear after unfolding?

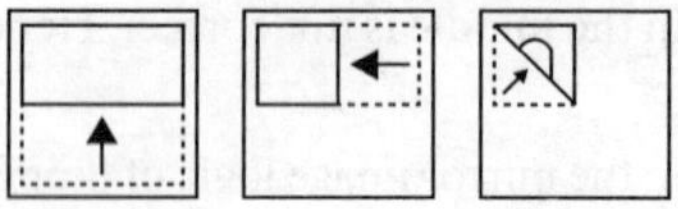

(a) 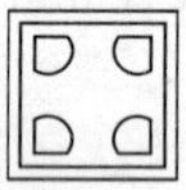

(b) 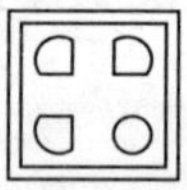

(c) 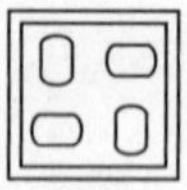

(d) 

Solution to Example 2: In this case, there is 3 level folding - first on the horizontal axis, then the vertical and finally a diagonal before the cut is made. When we reopen, the diagonally cut paper - we get:

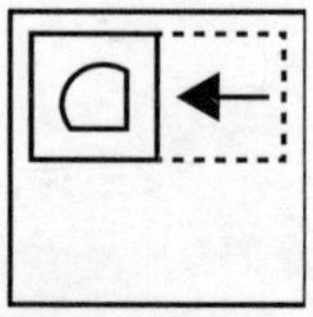

This shape is visible in the top left of the figure only for options (b) and (d). Also, once the other unfolding are done, the same shape will appear 4 times with mirror image and water image orientation. Option (d) shows us the required correct answer.

Example 3: A piece of paper is folded and cut as shown below. How will it appear after unfolding?

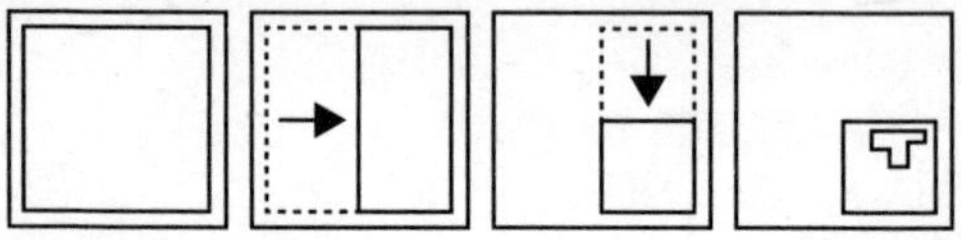

(a)  (b) 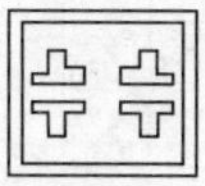

(c)  (d) 

Solution to Example 3: Look for the mirror image of the right bottom quadrant in the top right quadrant of the figure. This is visible only in (a), (c) and (d). Then, look for the mirror image of the right side of the paper on the left – This is visible only for (c). Hence, option (c) is correct.

Example 4: A piece of paper is folded and cut as shown below. How will it appear after unfolding?

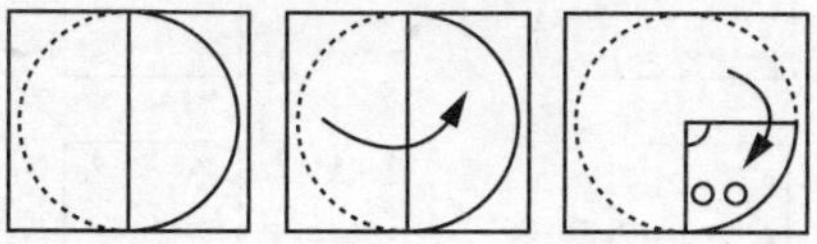

(a) 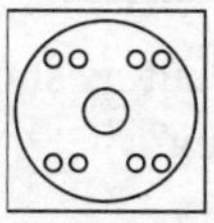 (b) 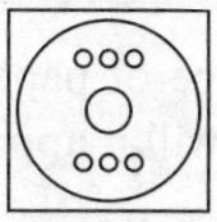

(c) 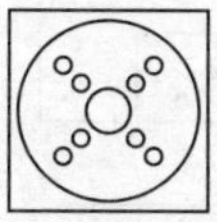 (d) 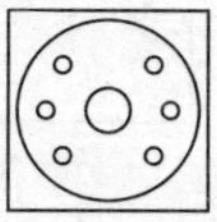

Solution to Example 4: The paper is folded twice, first along the vertical axis, next along the horizontal axis. When we unfold along the horizontal, we will see two blank circles appear on the top right of the paper, also the quarter circle in the middle will become a semi-circle. When we unfold along the vertical line, we will see a mirror image of the right on the left (the central circle will also get completed). Option (a) is correct.

Example 5: A piece of paper is folded and cut as shown below. How will it appear after unfolding?

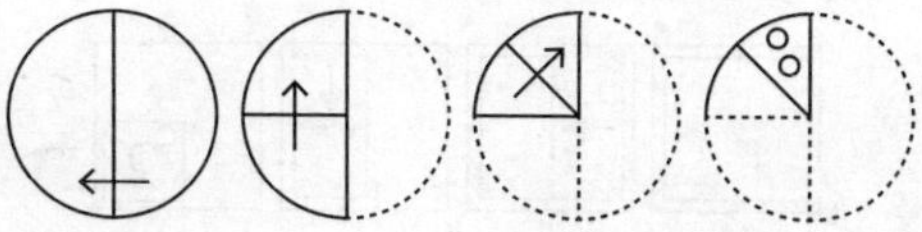

(a) 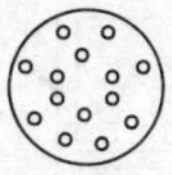 (b) 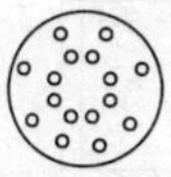

(c) 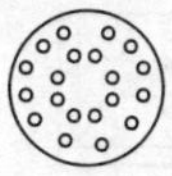 (d) 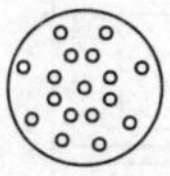

Solution to Example 5: The paper is folded thrice – vertically, horizontally and diagonally. Folding back along the diagonal will create a mirror image of the two circles along the diagonal. Folding back along the horizontal will then create a semi circular paper with 8 circles to the left of the vertical axis. When we unfold the paper finally along the vertical, it will show 16 circles. Option (b) is the only one which matches all these requirements. Hence, option (b) is correct.

EXERCISE

1. The sequence of folding a piece of paper and the way the folded paper has been cut is shown in the following figures.
   How would this paper look when unfolded?

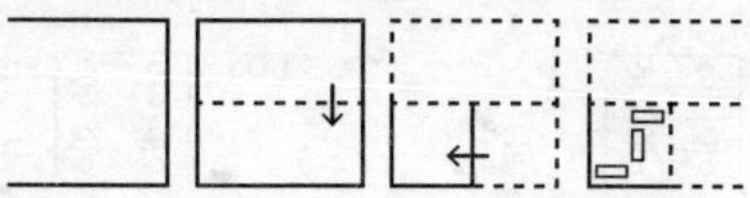

(a) 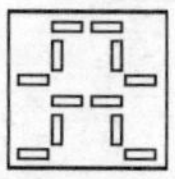 (b) 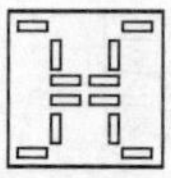

(c) 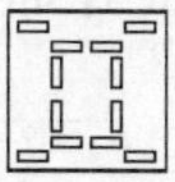 (d) 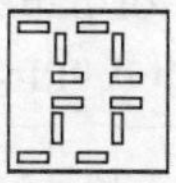

2. The sequence of folding a piece of paper and the way the folded paper has been cut is show in the following figures

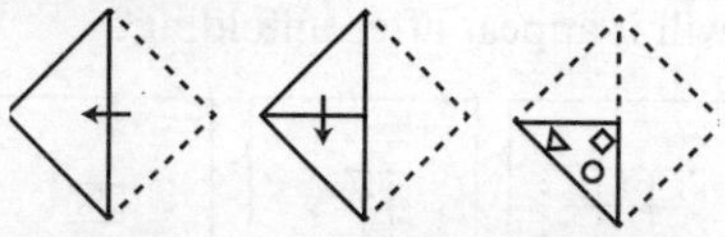

How would this look when unfolded?

(a)  (b) 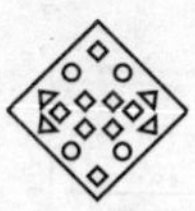

(c) 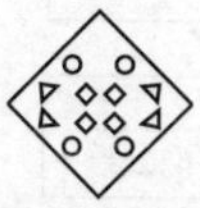 (d) 

3. A piece of paper is folded and punched as shown below in the question figures. From the given figure indicate how will it appear when opened?

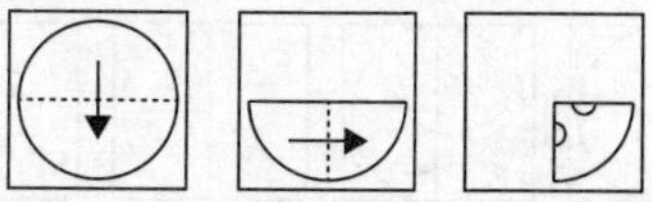

(a) 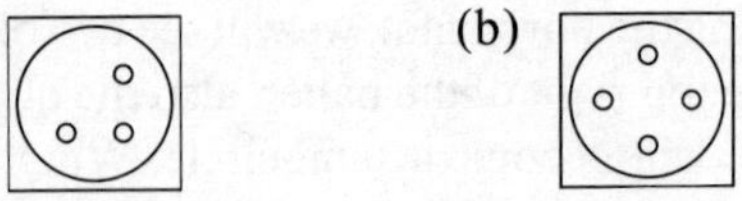

(c) 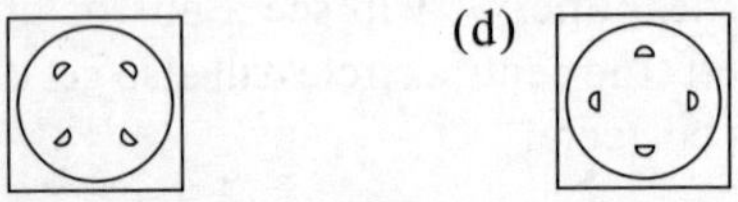 (d)

4. A piece of paper is folded and cut as shown below. How will it appear after unfolding?

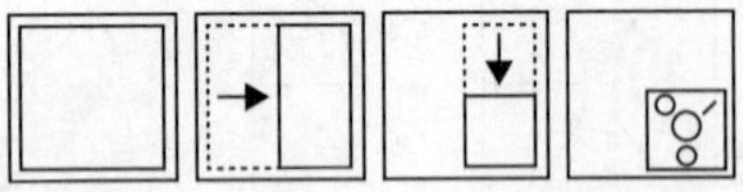

(a) 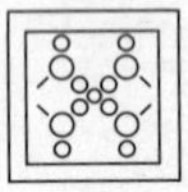 (b) 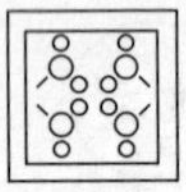

(c) 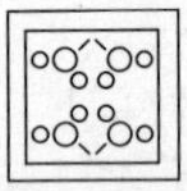 (d) 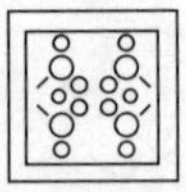

5. A piece of paper is folded and cut as shown below. How will it appear after unfolding?

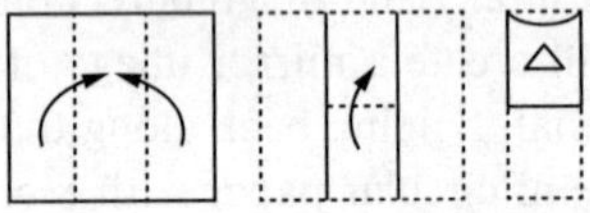

(a) 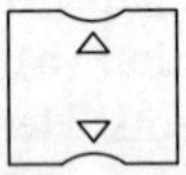 (b) 

(c)  (d) 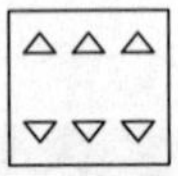

6. A piece of paper is folded and cut as shown below. How will it appear after unfolding?

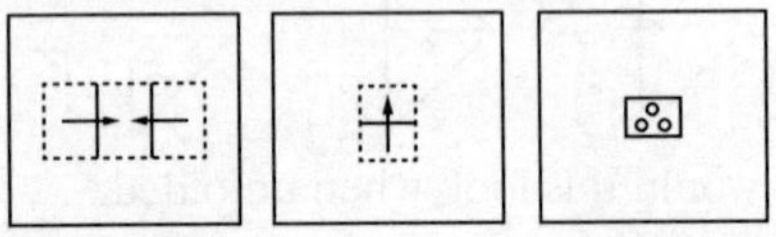

(a) 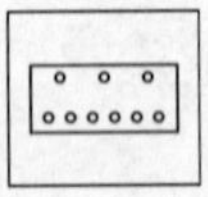 (b) 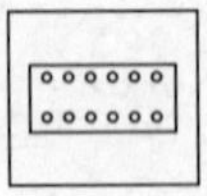

(c) 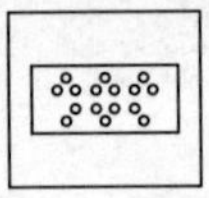 (d) 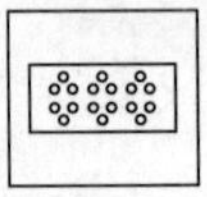

7. A piece of paper is folded and cut as shown below. How will it appear after unfolding?

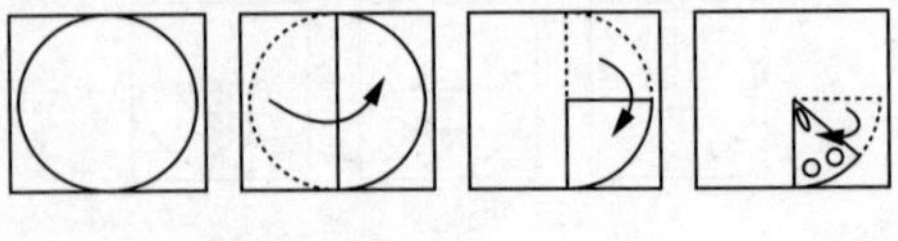

(a)  (b) 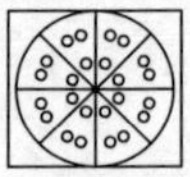

(c)  (d) 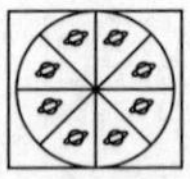

8. A piece of paper is folded and cut as shown below. How will it appear after unfolding?

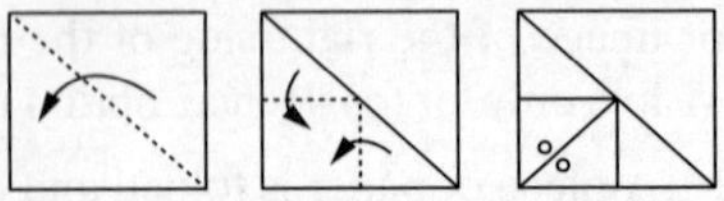

(a) 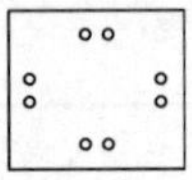 (b) 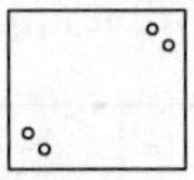

(c) 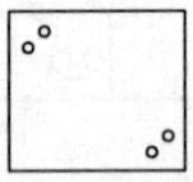 (d) 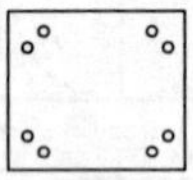

9. A piece of paper is folded and cut as shown below. How will it appear after unfolding?

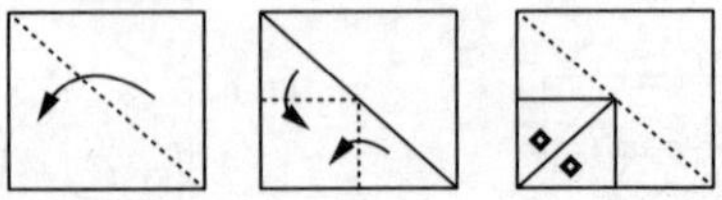

(a)  (b) 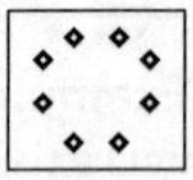

(c) 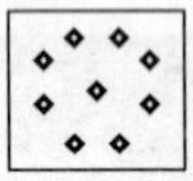 (d) 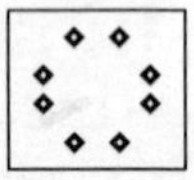

10. A piece of paper is folded and cut as shown below. How will it appear after unfolding?

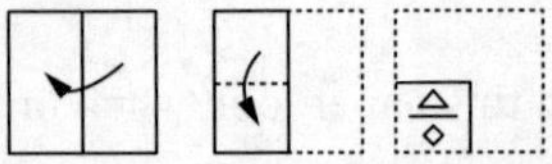

(a) 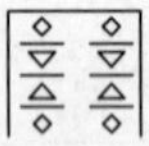 (b) 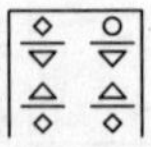

(c) 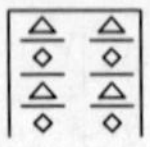 (d) 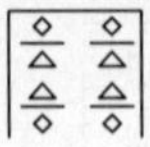

11. A piece of paper is folded and cut as shown below. How will it appear after unfolding?

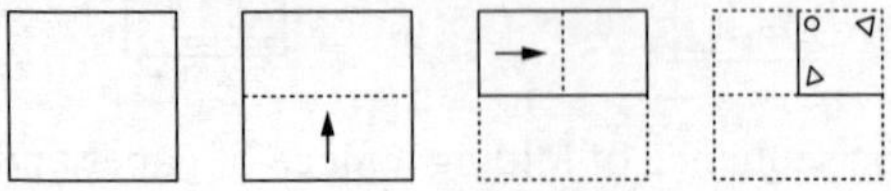

(a) 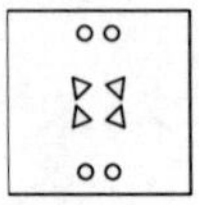 (b) 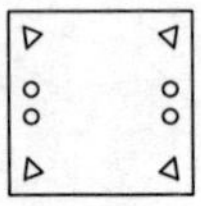

(c)  (d) 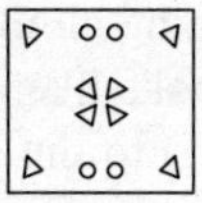

12. 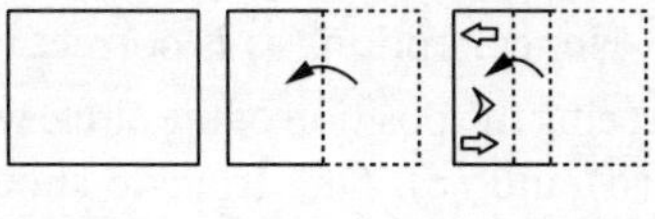

(a) 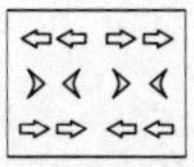 (b) 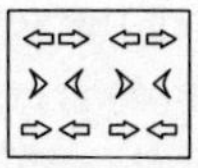

(c) 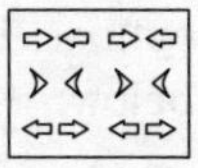 (d) 

13. A piece of paper is folded and cut as shown below. How will it appear after unfolding?

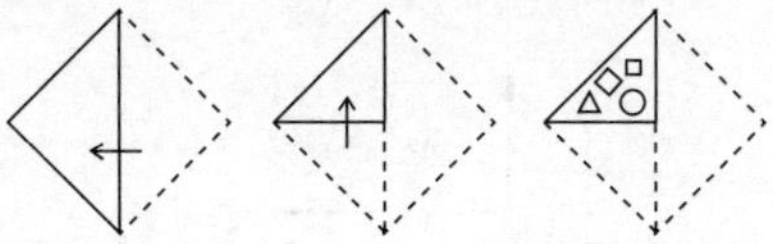

(a)  (b) 

(c)  (d) 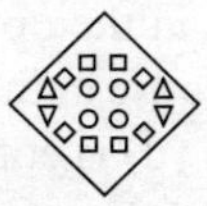

14. A piece of paper is folded and cut as shown below. How will it appear after unfolding?

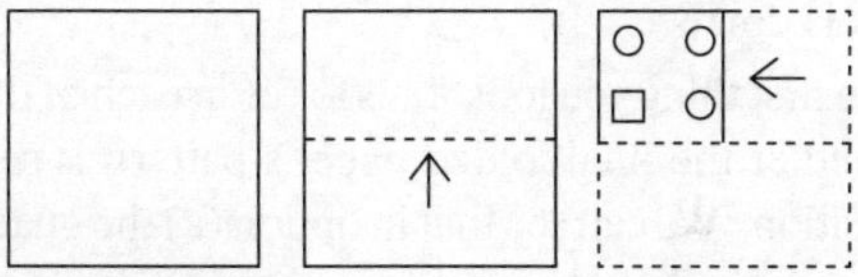

(a) 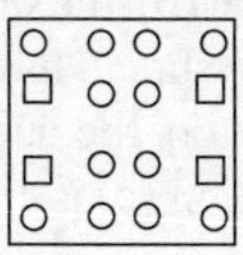 (b) 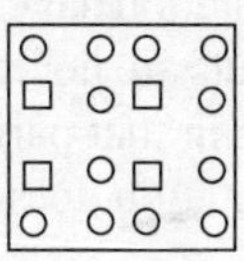

(c) 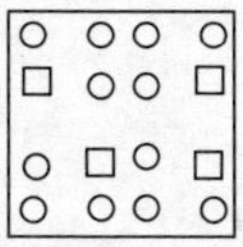 (d) 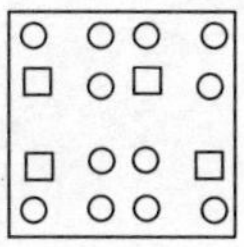

15. A piece of paper is folded and cut as shown below. How will it appear after unfolding?

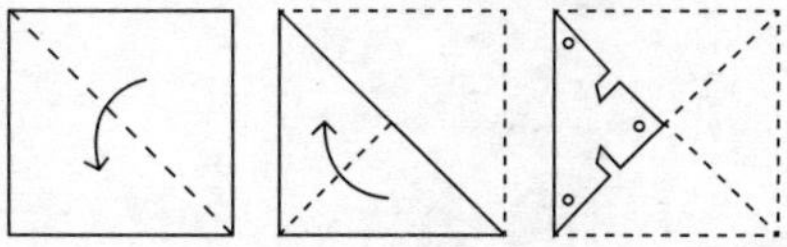

(a) 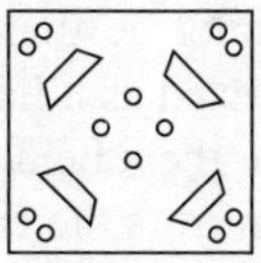 (b) 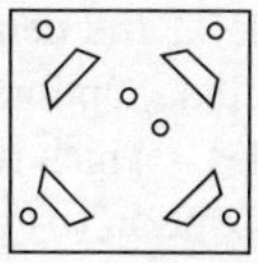

(c) 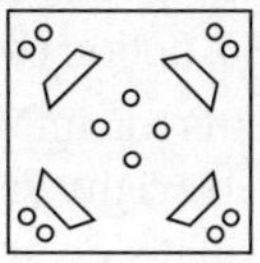 (d) 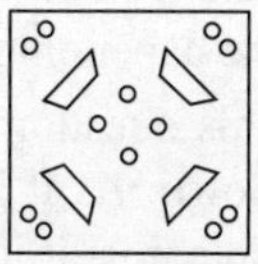

High Yield Questions

Scan this QR code to access video explanations of questions 12, 14 and 15

ANSWER KEY

1. (b)	2. (c)	3. (b)	4. (b)
5. (c)	6. (d)	7. (c)	8. (d)
9. (b)	10. (a)	11. (d)	12. (b)
13. (d)	14. (a)	15. (c)	

SOLUTIONS AND SHORTCUTS

1. 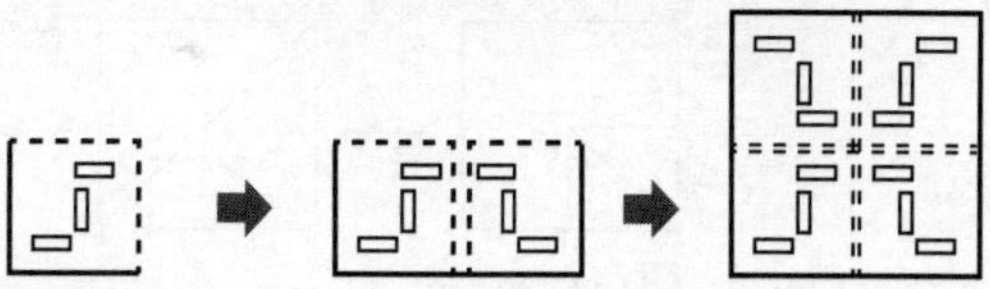

2. There are 4 square cuts in the center, then there are 4 circles in the bottom, the triangle should have correct orientation.
   Option (a): The orientation of the triangles is incorrect.
   Option (b): The orientation of the triangles is correct but there are additional squares.
   Option (c): The orientation and the number of cuts, both are correct.
   Option (d): The orientation of the triangles is incorrect.
3. When you unfold along the vertical, you get one full circle along the vertical and two semi circles. Then unfolding along the horizontal axis, will complete the two semi circles as full circles and also create a mirror image of one more circle towards the top. Thus, we are looking for 4 symmetrically placed circles. Option (b) is correct.
4. The final paper, will not change the bottom right quadrant – so, we can reject option (c). Option (a) has an extra

circle at the center, which cannot be there- hence is rejected. Option (d) is also rejected as it has two extra circles - which have no logic for them being there. It is only option (b) that correctly mirrors the bottom right quadrant on the top right and also mirrors, the right side of the paper onto the left side. So, option (b) is correct.

5. In this question first take the mirror image from up to down. As it is double folded (right & left both), so take mirror image on both right side and left side. Option (c) is correct.
6. When we first unfold along the horizontal, we will see 6 blank circles in one of the three vertical parts of the paper. When we open the left and right verticals, we will see another 6 on the right side and a similar set of 6 on the left side of the middle vertical. Only option (d) is correct.
7. In this question, we need to take mirror image three times. First take mirror image at 45 degree anti clock-wise (along the diagonal). This will create a bottom right quarter circle that has 4 small circles and the oval shaped cut will appear twice in this quarter of the circle. This will then get replicated on the upper right quarter circle (8 circles and 4 ovals). Which will then get replicated across the vertical diameter towards the left of it. The final figure will have 16 circles and 8 ovals placed symmetrically. Option (c) shows us this figure and hence, option (c) is correct.
8. 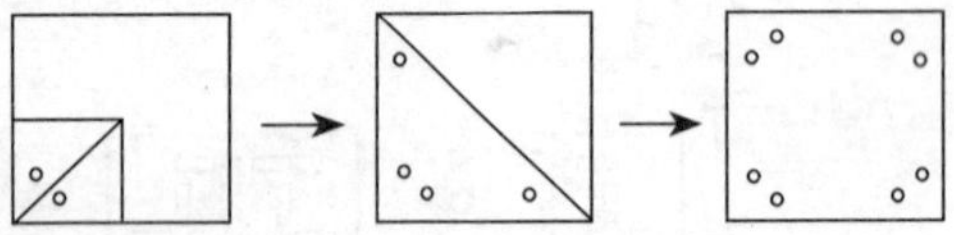

   Option (d) is correct.
9. There will be 4 square cuts to the left of the diagonal diameter and 4 to the right (as a mirror image to the left side. Also, the original 2 cuts seen in the question, will remain in their places as shown. Option (b) shows us the unfolded paper correctly.
10. Unfolding along the horizontal, will create a picture that looks like a mirror image of itself (from top to bottom) to the left of the imaginary central line that will divide the box into two equal halves. This will be mirrored on the right when we unfold along the vertical. Hence, option (a) is correct.
11. Just by seeing the position of the circle we can eliminate option (b) and (c). One triangle should be at every corner of the square so option (a) can be eliminated. Option (d) is correct.
12. The left-side portion is divided in two parts so we first complete that part and check the options. The left side portion should be like as shown below:

    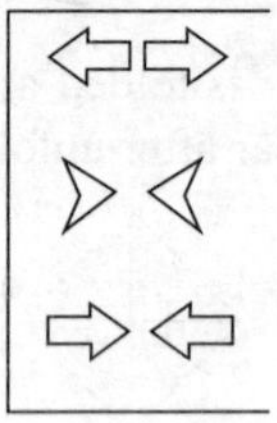

    Only option (b) is correct. No need to solve further
13. From the position of circle option (b) can be eliminated. From the position of triangle option (c) can be eliminated. Squares can never in the place as shown in the option (a). All the circles, triangles and squares are in the correct places in option (d). Hence, option (d) is correct.
14. First take the mirror image from left to right then from up to down. (You can eliminate the options by focusing on the position of the squares only). Option (a) is correct.
15. The first thing you look for is to see in each of the options, whether the final folded paper's pattern is seen in that position. We can see that in option (a) the quadrilateral's orientation has changed, in option (b), the small circular cutouts are not replicated - there should have been 3 of them in that part. In option (d) too, the quadrilateral's orientation does not match. Option (c) is correct.

PART III

Reasoning Archives

Previous Years' Solved Questions from CAT

SLOT 1 CAT 2025

High Yield Questions

Scan this QR code to access video explanations for select questions from CAT 2025

Directions for Questions 1 to 4: A round table has seven chairs around it. The chairs are numbered 1 through 7 in a clockwise direction. Four friends, Aslam, Bashir, Chhavi, and Davies, sit on four of the chairs. In the starting position, Aslam and Chhavi are sitting next to each other, while for Bashir as well as Davies, there are empty chairs on either side of the chairs that are sitting on.

The friends take turns moving either clockwise or counterclockwise from their chair. The friend who has to move in a turn occupies the first empty chair in whichever direction (s)he chooses to move. Aslam moves first (Turn 1), followed by Bashir, Chhavi, and Davies (Turns 2, 3, and 4, respectively). Then Aslam moves again followed by Bashir, and Chhavi (Turns 5, 6, and 7, respectively).

The following information is known:

(i) The four friends occupy adjacent chairs only at the end of Turn 2 and Turn 6.

(ii) Davies occupies Chair 2 after Turn 1 and Chair 4 after Turn 5, and Chhavi occupies Chair 7 after Turn 2.

1. What is the number of the chair initially occupied by Bashir?

2. Who sits on the chair numbered 4 at the end of Turn 3?
(a) Bashir
(b) Chhavi
(c) Davies
(d) No one

3. Which of the chairs are occupied at the end of Turn 6?
(a) Chairs numbered 1, 2, 3, and 4
(b) Chairs numbered 4, 5, 6, and 7
(c) Chairs numbered 2, 3, 4, and 5
(d) Chairs numbered 1, 2, 6, and 7

4. Which of the following BEST describes the friends sitting on chairs adjacent to the one occupied by Bashir at the end of Turn 7?
(a) Chhavi only
(b) Chhavi and Davies
(c) Aslam and Chhavi
(d) Davies only

Directions for Questions 5 to 8: Alia, Badal, Clive, Dilshan, and Ehsaan played a game in which each asks a unique question to all the others and they respond by tapping their feet, either once or twice or thrice. One tap means "Yes", two taps mean "No", and three taps mean "Maybe". A total of 40 taps were heard across the five questions. Each question received at least one "Yes", one "No", and one "Maybe."

The following information is known:

(i) Alia tapped a total of 6 times and received 9 taps to her question. She responded "Yes" to the questions asked by both Clive and Dilshan.

(ii) Dilshan and Ehsaan tapped a total of 11 and 9 times respectively. Dilshan responded "No" to Badal.

(iii) Badal, Dilshan, and Ehsaan received equal number of taps to their respective questions.

(iv) No one responded "Yes" more than twice.

(v) No one's answer to Alia's question matched the answer that Alia gave to that person's question. This was also true for Ehsaan.

(vi) Clive tapped more times in total than Badal.

5. How many taps did Clive receive for his question?

6. Which two people tapped an equal number of times in total?
(a) Dilshan and Clive
(b) Badal and Dilshan
(c) Clive and Ehsaan
(d) Alia and Badal

7. What was Clive's response to Ehsaan's question?
(a) Maybe
(b) Cannot be determined
(c) No
(d) Yes

8. How many "Yes" responses were received across all the questions?

Directions for Questions 9 to 13: A train travels from Station A to Station E, passing through stations B, C, and D, in that order. The train has a seating capacity of 200. A ticket may be booked from any station to any other station ahead on the route, but not to any earlier station.

A ticket from one station to another reserves one seat on every intermediate segment of the route. For example, a ticket from B to E reserves a seat in the intermediate segments B - C, C - D, and D - E.

The occupancy factor for a segment is the total number of seats reserved in the segment as a percentage of the seating capacity. The total number of seats reserved for any segment cannot exceed 200.

The following information is known:

(i) Segment C - D had an occupancy factor of 95%. Only segment B - C had a higher occupancy factor.

(ii) Exactly 40 tickets were booked from B to C and 30 tickets were booked from B to E.

(iii) Among the seats reserved on segment D - E, exactly four-sevenths were from stations before C.

(iv) The number of tickets booked from A to C was equal to that booked from A to E, and it was higher than that from B to E.

(v) No tickets were booked from A to B, from B to D and from D to E.

(vi) The number of tickets booked for any segment was a multiple of 10.

9. What was the occupancy factor for segment D - E?
(a) 35% (b) 84%
(c) 77% (d) 70%

10. How many tickets were booked from Station A to Station E?

11. How many tickets were booked from Station C?

12. What is the difference between the number of tickets booked to Station C and the number of tickets booked to Station D?

13. How many tickets were booked to travel in exactly one segment?

ANSWER KEY

1. 4	2. (d)	3. (b)	4. (d)
5. 7	6. (d)	7. (c)	8. 6
9. (d)	10. 50	11. 80	12. 40
13. 60			

SOLUTIONS AND SHORTCUTS

Solutions for Questions 1 to 4:

Figure 1

From turn 1 to 4

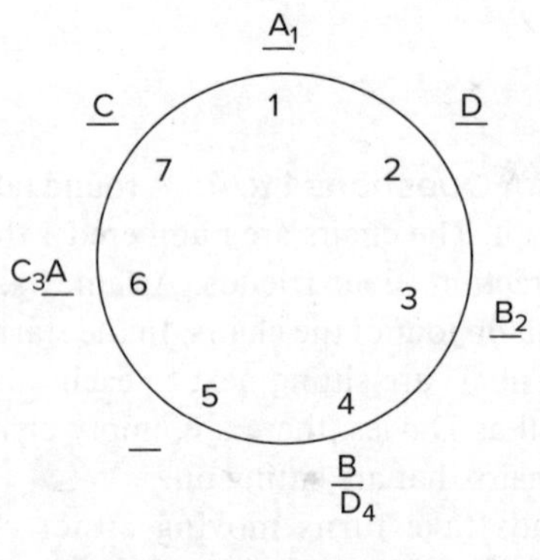

Deduction 1: In the first 2 turns only A and B are moving. Hence, the chair 7 for C (after turn 2) and chair 2 for D (after turn 1) are in fact their starting positions. Also, since A is next to C and D has an empty chair on both sides, it means that A must be in chair 6 and B would be in chair 4 to start with.

Deduction 2: We are given that the four friends are in adjacent chairs after turn 2. This can only occur if in turn 1 A moves clockwise from chair 6 to chair 1 (skipping chair 7 where C would be sitting). Also, in turn 2, B needs to necessarily move counter clockwise to chair 3. Subsequently, since D has to be in chair 4 after turn 5 (given), he must have moved in turn 4 from chair 2 to chair 4 (clockwise, skipping chair 3 as B would be sitting there after turn 2).

The movements of deductions 1 and 2 are visible in the figure 1, depicting original positions (A,B,C,D) followed by the movements after turn 1 (A_1); turn 2 (B_2); turn 3 (C_3) and turn 4 (D_4). In figure 2, we have depicted turns 5 and 6 with A,B,C and D representing their positions after turn 4.

Figure 2

From turn 4 to 6

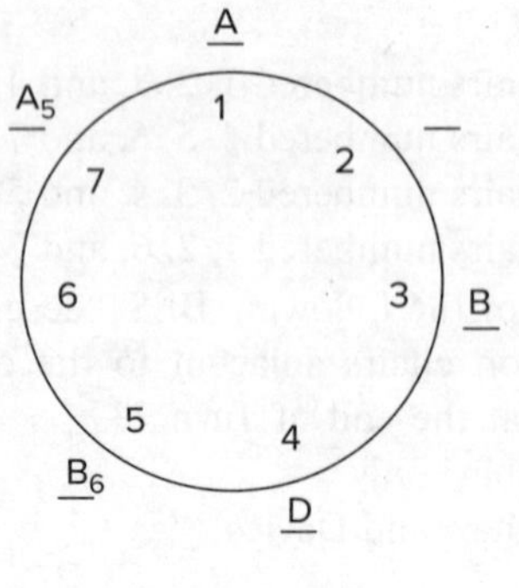

Deduction 3: With the position after turn 4 being A in chair 1, B in chair 3, D in chair 4 and C in chair 6 - if we want to get them into adjacent chairs after turn 6, the only way to do so is for turn 5 being A's counter clockwise movement to chair 7 and turn 6 being B's clockwise movement to Chair 5. After turn 6, D is in 4, B is in chair 5; C in chair 6 and A in chair 7.

In turn 7, C can move either clockwise to chair 1 (first empty chair) or counter clockwise to chair 3 - we cannot make out where C ends after turn 7.

The answers can be found out basis these deductions.

1. 4
2. It's empty. Hence, option (d) is correct.
3. Chairs 4,5,6,7 (as seen from deduction 3). Option (b) is correct.
4. Bashir is in chair 5. Chair 6 is empty and Davies is in chair 4. Hence, only Davies is adjacent to Bashir at the end of turn 7. Option (d) is correct.

Solutions for Questions 5 to 8: We can make a matrix with number of taps for each person vis-à-vis the question posed by the others. The completed matrix can be built using the deductions explained below (deduction numbers for filling the matrix expressed in # inside the table). Note: We start off with an assumed value of N for the sum of responses each of B,D and E got for their questions.

Answered by → / Question of ↓	A	B	C	D	E	Total taps
A	xxxxxx	1 #4	2 #4	3 (#2)	3 #4	9
B	2 #1	xxxxxx		2 (given)		N=8 #5
C	1 (given)	2/2/1	xxxxxx	3 (#2)	1/1/2	7 #5
D	1 (given)	2/1/2		xxxxxx		N=8 #5
E	2 #1	1/2/2	2/1/1	3 (#2)	xxxxxx	N=8 #5
Totals	6 (given)	6 #3	8 #3	11 (given)	9 (given)	40

Deduction 1: For the answers given by A, we can deduce that the two missing answers will both be 2 taps each (as the sum of the column is 6, and we already have two 1s in the column - and we are not allowed more than 2 1s in any column).

Deduction 2: The sum of taps given by D is 11 - and he has 2 taps for B's question. Hence, he must have 3 taps each for the questions of A,C and E.

Deduction 3: The sum of B's responses + C's responses = 40 - 6 - 11 - 9 =14. Also, B<C (given in clue 6). Thus, B = 6, C = 8. Note: B =5, C = 9 is not possible since a column sum of 5 would need us to use three 1s, which is not allowed as per clue 4).

Deduction 4: The only pattern that works for B's column is two 2s and two 1s.

B's response to A's question cannot be the same as A's response to B's question (which is 2 as per deduction 1). Hence, B's response to A's question has to be 1 tap. Consequently, E's response to A's question can only be 3 (it cannot be 2 as it cannot be the same as A's response to E's question. It cannot be 1 as then the sum of 9 will not be possible for the responses A got). At this point with B, D, E as 1, 3, 3 C will necessarily have a response of 2 for A's question to complete the sum of 9 in that row.

Deduction 5: The value of N can either be 7 (in which case, the sum of the responses C's question got would be 10) or 8 (in which case, the sum of the responses C's question got would be 7). Looking at C's row at this stage, we can see the value of the total for the row can reach a maximum of 9 (as B's response to C's question can only be 1 or 2). Hence, the value of N = 8 and the sum of taps B's question got was 7.

Deduction 6: This leaves us with a multiple possibility situation for the values of B's responses to C, D and E's question as also for E's response to C's question (all connected to each other). There are 3 possibilities for these, that you can see in the table.

Let us consider the cases one by one, to see if we can eliminate some of them.

If we use the 2, 1, 2 pattern from B's responses to C, D, E - then it also means that E's response to C's question will necessarily become 1, and also C's response to E's question will also become 1. in which case there is a contradiction of clue 5, which tells us that no one's answer to E's question matched E's answer to that person's question. i.e. C's response to E = 1 = E's response to C is not allowed. Hence, we reject this case.

The third case is also rejected, as the 1, 2, 2 pattern from B's responses to C, D, E -also means that C's response to E's question will necessarily become 1 and E's response to C will necessarily be 2. E's response to B's question cannot be 2 in this case - and hence has to be 1 or 3. If we use 1 here, we will need to use 3 for E's response to D's question, which will make it the same as D's response to E's question - in which case there is a contradiction of clue 5. The only case that exists is as shown in the final table.

When we put B's responses as 2,2,1 to C,D,E - C's response to E becomes 2, E's response to C becomes 1.

At this stage the remaining cells can be filled with E's response to D : Either 1 or 2 (as it cannot be 3- D's response to E). If we use 1 here, the total of E's column of responses cannot reach 9. Hence, this has to be filled as 2, which leads us to E's response to B being 3 taps, C's response to B being 1 tap and C's response to D being 3 taps.

Final table:

Answered by → Question of ↓	A	B	C	D	E	Total taps
A	xxxxxx	1	2	3	3	9
B	2	xxxxxx	1	2	3	8
C	1	2	xxxxxx	3	1	7
D	1	2	3	xxxxxx	2	8
E	2	1	2	3	xxxxxx	8
Totals	6	6	8	11	9	40

The answers can be read off from here:

5. 7
6. Option (d) is correct.
7. No. Option (c) is correct.
8. 6 (as counted from the final table).

Solutions for Questions 9 to 13: We construct a table for the given segments to map the journey for the train as follows: (Note the occupancy of the train from B to C has to be greater than 190, and can only be 200 - as it is a multiple of 10). The logic for filling the table is explained in the deductions and are marked with a # sign inside the table.

Segments covered → Tickets for ↓	A to B	B to C	C to D	D to E
A to B	0 (given)	xxxxxx	xxxxxx	xxxxxx
A to C	50 #2	50 #2	xxxxxx	xxxxxx
A to D	30 #4	30 #4	30 #4	xxxxxx
A to E	50 #2	50 #2	50 #2	50 #2
B to C	xxxxxx	40 (given)	xxxxxx	Xxxxxx
B to D	xxxxxx	0 (given)	0 (given)	xxxxxx
B to E	xxxxxx	30 (given)	30 (given)	30 (given)
C to D	xxxxxx	xxxxxx	20 #5	Xxxxxx
C to E	xxxxxx	xxxxxx	60 #3	60 #3
D to E	xxxxxx	xxxxxx	xxxxxx	0 (given)
Occupancy		200	190	140 #2

Deduction 1: We first need to understand that in the table, all the valid values in any row would be equal to each other - since they will be filled in with the number of tickets bought for that journey. For instance, if N tickets are purchased from A to D, then in the table, for the A to D row, each of the segments (viz: A to B; B to C and C to D) will get filled with N each.

Deduction 2: The occupancy for D to E has to be a multiple of 7 (&10). Hence, it can be either 70 or 140. For D to E occupancy being 70, an interpretation of clue 3 tells us that 4/7th of that (viz 40) needs to be from stations A and B (stations before C). This gives us A to E tickets as 10, which are lower than the B to E tickets (30 - given). This is a contradiction of the clue 4. Hence, we can reject 70 as a value for this number. Consequently, this number can only be 140 & A to E tickets + B to E tickets will be 4/7 × 140. Since, B to E is 30, we get A to E tickets as 50 and can fill the entire cells of the A to E row with 50 each. This is also equal to the A to C tickets.

Deduction 3: C to E tickets will be 140 - 30-50=60.

Deduction 4: A to D tickets will be 200 - 50-50-40-30=30.

Deduction 5: C to D tickets will be 190-60-30-50-30= 20

The answers can be read off the table:

9. 140 out of 200 = 70%. Option (d) is correct.
10. 50
11. 20 +60=80.
12. To station C (50 + 40). To Station D (30+0+20). Difference = 40.
13. 0+40+20+0=60

SLOT 2

CAT 2025

Directions for Questions 1 to 5: The two most populous cities and the non-urban region (NUR) of each of three states, Whimshire, Fogglia, and Humbleset, are assigned Pollution Measures (PMs). These nine PMs are all distinct multiples of 10, ranging from 10 to 90. The six cities in increasing order of their PMs are: Blusterburg, Noodleton, Splutterville, Quackford, Mumpypore, Zingaloo.

The Pollution Index (PI) of a state is a weighted average of the PMs of its NUR and cities, with a weight of 50% for the NUR, and 25% each for its two cities.

There is only one pair of an NUR and a city (considering all cities and all NURs) where the PM of the NUR is greater than that of the city. That NUR and the city both belong to Humbleset.

The PIs of all three states are *distinct integers*, with Humbleset and Fogglia having the highest and the lowest PI respectively.

1. What is the PI of Whimshire?

2. What is the PI of Fogglia?

3. What is the PI of Humbleset?

4. Which pair of cities definitely belong to the same state?

(a) Mumpypore, Zingaloo
(b) Splutterville, Quackford
(c) Noodleton, Quackford
(d) Blusterburg, Mumpypore

5. For how many of the cities and NURs is it possible to identify their PM and the state they belong to?

Directions for Questions 6 to 10: Ananya Raga, Bhaskar Tala, Charu Veena, and Devendra Sur are four musicians. Each of them started and completed their training as students under each of three Gurus – Pandit Meghnath, Ustad Samiran, and Acharya Raghunath between 2013 and 2024, including both the years. Each Guru trains any student for consecutive years only, for a span of 2, 3, or 4 years, with each Guru having a different span. During some of these years, a student may not have trained under these Gurus; however, they never trained under multiple Gurus in the same year.

In none of these years, any of these Gurus trained more than two of these students at the same time. When two students train under the same Guru at the same time, they are referred to as Gurubhai, irrespective of their gender.

The following additional facts are known:

(i) Ustad Samiran never trained more than one of these students in the same year.

(ii) Acharya Raghunath did not train any of these students during 2015-2018, as well as during 2021-24.

(iii) Ananya and Devendra were never Gurubhai; neither were Bhaskar and Charu. All other pairs of musicians were Gurubhai for exactly 2 years.

(iv) In 2013, Ananya and Bhaskar started their trainings under Pandit Meghnath and under Ustad Samiran, respectively.

6. In which of the following years were Ananya and Bhaskar Gurubhai?

(a) 2018 (b) 2014
(c) 2021 (d) 2020

7. In which year did Charu begin her training under Pandit Meghnath?

(a) 2021 (b) 2017
(c) 2015 (d) 2016

8. In which of the following years were Bhaskar and Devendra Gurubhai?

(a) 2015 (b) 2018
(c) 2022 (d) 2020

9. Which of the following statements is TRUE?

(a) Ananya was training under Ustad Samiran in 2015.
(b) Charu was training under Ustad Samiran in 2018.
(c) Ananya was training under Ustad Samiran in 2018.
(d) Charu was training under Ustad Samiran in 2019.

10. In how many of the years between 2013-24, were only two of these four musicians training under these three Gurus?

Directions for Questions 11 to 14: There are six spherical balls, B1, B2, B3, B4, B5, and B6, and four circular hoops H1, H2, H3, and H4.

Each ball was tested on each hoop once, by attempting to pass the ball through the hoop. If the diameter of a ball is not larger than the diameter of the hoop, the ball passes through the hoop and makes a "ping". Any ball having a diameter larger than that of the hoop gets stuck on that hoop and does not make a ping.

The following additional information is known:

(i) B1 and B6 each made a ping on H4, but B5 did not.
(ii) B4 made a ping on H3, but B1 did not.
(iii) All balls, except B3, made pings on H1.
(iv) None of the balls, except B2, made a ping on H2.

11. What was the total number of pings made by B1, B2, and B3?

12. Which of the following statements about the relative sizes of the balls is NOT NECESSARILY true?
(a) B1 < B6 < B3
(b) B1 < B5 < B3
(c) B2 < B1 < B5
(d) B4 < B5 < B3

13. Which of the following statements about the relative sizes of the hoops is true?
(a) H1 < H4 < H3 < H2
(b) H2 < H4 < H3 < H1
(c) H1 < H3 < H4 < H2
(d) H2 < H3 < H4 < H1

14. What BEST can be said about the total number of pings from all the tests undertaken?
(a) At least 9
(b) 12 or 13 or 14
(c) 13 or 14
(d) 12 or 13

ANSWER KEY

1. 45	2. 35	3. 50	4. (c)
5. 9	6. (d)	7. (c)	8. (c)
9. (d)	10. 4	11. 6 pings	12. (a)
13. (d)	14. (d)		

SOLUTIONS AND SHORTCUTS

Solutions for Questions 1 to 5: The starting table which will get formed for this question set will look as shown (all names in abbreviations using their first letters only):

	W	F	H	WEIGHTAGE FOR PI CALCULATION
City	City 1	City 3	City 5	0.25
City	City 2	City 4	City 6	0.25
NUR	NUR 1	NUR 2	NUR 3	0.5
PI		Minimum	Maximum	

We also know from the basic conditions that the PMs of each of the nine cities/regions have to be assigned from amongst 10/20/30/40/50/60/70/80 & 90. The key in this question is to understand the statement

'There is only one pair of an NUR and a city (considering all cities and all NURs) where the PM of the NUR is greater than that of the city. That NUR and the city both belong to Humbleset.'

Deduction 1: This means that of the three NURs only one of them has a PM greater than any one of the 6 cities (and only one of them). Also, this NUR and the city where the PM is lower than that of the NUR are in H. This can only happen if we allocate PMs 10 and 20 amongst the NURs of W and F in some order and the PM of 40 to the NUR of H. Further, the second city of H would have a PM that is less than 40 (and can only be 30).

Deduction 2: Also, we are given that the PMs of B < N < S < Q < M < Z. With 10,20 and 40 allocated, we can distribute 30,50,60,70,80 and 90 only as B (30) < N (50) < S(60) < Q (70) < M(80) < Z(90). B with a PM of 30 can be either of city 5 or 6. Also, the other city in H, can only be N, Q or Z (since the sum of the cities of H has to be a multiple of 4 (else, the PI of the state would become a non-integer). For instance, if we try to fit in say M (80) with B(30), under the H column, the value of the PI for H would become (30 + 80) × 0.25 + 40 × 0.5 = 47.5 (not allowed).

Further, since the PI for H has to be the largest we can see that if we allocate anything less than 90 for the second city of H, this condition would not be satisfied.

For instance, if H has 30,70 & 40 (NUR) – its PI would be (30 + 70) × 0.25 + 40 × 0.5 = 45.

Deduction 3: In this case, we will need to allocate 50, 90 to either W or F- giving us a PI of (50 + 90) × 0.25 + (10 or 20) × 0.5 = 35 + 5 or 35 + 10. But it is given to us that the PI of each state is a distinct integer. Hence, this can only be 35+5=40 (with PMs of 50,90 and 10 for the NUR).

Then, for the last state, we will use 60, 80 & 20 for the NUR giving us a PI of (60 + 80) × 0.25 + (20) × 0.5 = 45, which is the same as the PI of H. Hence, this allocation is rejected. Based on these deductions, we know that the PMs for H are: 30, 90 and 40(NUR) giving us a PM of (30 + 90) × 0.25 + (40) × 0.5 = 50. For the other two states, the allocation would necessarily be 50, 70 &10 for F and 60, 80 & 20 for W giving respective PIs of 35 for F and 45 for W.

The final table would look as follows:

	W	F	H	WEIGHTAGE FOR PI CALCULATION
City	80 M	70 Q	30 B	0.25
City	60 S	50 N	90 Z	0.25
NUR	20	10	40	0.5
PI	45	35 (Minimum)	50 (Maximum)	

The answers can be read off the table:

1. 45
2. 35
3. 50
4. Option (c)
5. We can identify the PMs and the states for all 9. Hence, the correct answer is 9.

Solutions for Questions 6 to 10: We can make a table for the trainees and the Gurus from 2013 to 2024 as follows. The logic of filling the table is given through deductions 1 to 5 explained below:

	2013	2014	2015	2016	2017	2018	2019	2020	2021	2022	2023	2024
Meghnath	A	A	A-C	A-C	C	C	D	D	D-B	D-B	B	B
Samiran	B	B	B	D	D	D	C	C	C	A	A	A
Raghunath	C-D	C-D	XXX	XXX	XXX	XXX	A-B	A-B	XXX	XXX	XXX	XXX

Deduction 1: Raghunath has to train groups of 2 in 2013-14 and 2019-20 as he has to train all the four musicians and he has to accommodate each of them in the years available in his row. Further, it is clear that Raghunath must be training an individual musician for 2 years consecutively.

Deduction 2: The sets of Gurubhais were: A-B; A-C;B-D and C-D. Since Raghunath has to have two trainees in 2013 and 2014, they can only be the Gurubhai pair of C-D. Consequently, he must be training the Gurubhai pair of A-B in 2019 and 2020.

Deduction 3: Samiran and Meghnath must be training for any of 3 years or 4 years in some order. Given that Samiran only trained one student a year, it means that we cannot allocate the 4 year training to Samiran. Thus, Samiran must be training his trainees for 3 years each – and also he would have had 1 trainee for each year from 2013 to 2024 (without any breaks). Meghnath must be training his trainees for 4 years each. Thus, we can extend B for 3 years from 2013 to 2015 with Samiran and A to 4 years from 2013 to 2016.

Deduction 4: At this stage, we have accounted for the Gurubhai pairs of C-D and A-B. There are two more Gurubhai pairs to be accounted for – viz:A-C and B-D and according to the question, both these pairs were together for 2 years each. They can only go under Meghnath (as Samiran only trains 1 student at a time). The only 2 years where A-C can overlap each other are 2015 and 2016. Thus, we can conclude that Meghnath must have trained C between the years 2015-2018 and the A-C Gurubhai overlap must have occurred in 2015 and 2016.

Deduction 5: The years 2016-17-18 under Samiran must be for D (as we cannot repeat B and also since A and C are already being trained in 2016 under Meghnath). Then, between 2019 and 2021 C would be Samiran's trainee and between 2022 to 24 A would be his trainee.

Deduction 6: We are left to place 4 years each of B and D under Meghnath between 2019 to 2024, with 2 years of overlap as Gurubhais for them. This can only be done, if we allocate years 2019 to 2022 to D and years 2021 to 2024 for B (Since B is already training under Raghunath in 2019, he cannot train under Meghnath in the same year. Therefore, D must be Meghnath's trainee from 2019.).

The answers can be read off this table:

6. Option (d) is correct.
7. Option (c) is correct.
8. Option (c) is correct.
9. Option (d) is correct.
10. There are 4 such years – 2017, 2018, 2023 and 2024. Hence, the correct answer is 4.

Solutions for Questions 11 to 14: The information given to us can be tabulised as shown:

Hoop→	Hoop 1	Hoop 2	Hoop 3	Hoop 4
Pings from	B1,B2,B4,B5,B6	B2	B4	B1,B6
No Pings from	B3	B1,B3,B4,B5,B6	B1	B5
Unknown			B2,B3,B5,B6	B2,B3,B4

The following deductions can be made from the given information:

Deduction 1: From H1, we can see that B3 is the largest ball and from H2, we can see that B2 is the smallest ball. Thus, we have to place B1, B4, B5 and B6 in the inequality:

B2 < ?? < ?? < ?? < ?? < B3

From Hoop 4 we can see that B1 & B6 are both smaller than B5. Also from Hoop 3, we can see that B1 is larger than B4. Thus, B5 is the largest amongst B1, B6, B4 and B5. We have no information to conclude about the relative sizes of B1 and B6. Thus, the following possibilities emerge:

Possibility 1: B2 < B4 < B1 < B6 < B5 < B3
Possibility 2: B2 < B4 < B6 < B1 < B5 < B3
Possibility 3: B2 < B6 < B4 < B1 < B5 < B3

11. B1 makes a ping on H1 and H4 while it does not make a ping on H2 and H3 (given). B2 will ping each of the hoops (H1 and H2 given) and H3 and H4 can be worked out – since B2 is the smallest ball. B3 on the other hand is not pinging H1 and H2 (given) and will also not ping H3 and H4 (as it is the largest ball and there is at least one ball not pinging H3 and H4. Thus, B1, B2, B3 will make a total of 6 pings.
12. Option (a) is not necessarily true and is hence the answer.
13. It can be seen that all balls pass through H1 (except the largest ball B3). Hence, H1 is the largest hoop. Similarly, we can see that H2 is the smallest hoop (since only the smallest ball B2 passes through it). Further, between H3 and H4, we can see that the ball B1 passes through H4 but not through H3. Thus, we conclude that H3 < H4. Hence, H2 < H3 < H4 < H1. Option (d) is correct.
14. There are exactly 5 pings on H1 and 1 ping on H2. On H3, the number of pings can be 2 or 3, depending on which possibility for ball sizes we go through with (amongst possibilities 1, 2, 3). For hoop 4 though, we can make out that there are exactly 4 pings in any of the possibilities. Hence, the total pings are 5 + 1 + 2 or 3 + 4 = 12 or 13. Hence, option (d) is correct.

SLOT 3

CAT 2025

Directions for Questions 1 to 5: Aurevia, Brelosia, Cyrenia and Zerathania are four countries with their currencies being Aurels, Brins, Crowns, and Zentars, respectively. The currencies have different exchange values. Crown's currency exchange rate with Zentars = 0.5, i.e., 1 Crown is worth 0.5 Zentars.

Three travelers, Jano, Kira, and Lian set out from Zerathania visiting exactly two of the countries. Each country is visited by exactly two travelers. Each traveler has a unique Flight Cost, which represents the total cost of airfare in traveling to both the countries and back to Zerathania. The Flight Cost of Jano was 4000 Zentars, while that of the other two travelers were 5000 and 6000 Zentars, not necessarily in that order.

When visiting a country, a traveler spent either 1000, 2000 or 3000 in the country's local currency. Each traveler had different spends (in the country's local currency) in the two countries he/she visited. Across all the visits, there were exactly two spends of 1000 and exactly one spend of 3000 (in the country's local currency).

The total "Travel Cost" for a traveler is the sum of his/her Flight Cost and the money spent in the countries visited.

The citizens of the four countries with knowledge of these travels made a few observations, with spends measured in their respective local currencies:

(i) Aurevia citizen: Jano and Kira visited our country, and their Travel Costs were 3500 and 8000, respectively.

(ii) Brelosia citizen: Kira and Lian visited our country, spending 2000 and 3000, respectively. Kira's Travel Cost was 4000.

(iii) Cyrenia citizen: Lian visited our country and her Travel Cost was 36000.

1. What is the sum of Travel Costs for all travelers in Zentars?

2. How many Zentars did Lian spend in the two countries he visited?

3. What was Jano's total spend in the two countries he visited, in Aurels?

4. One Brin is equivalent to how many Crowns?

(a) 8 (b) 4
(c) 0.125 (d) 0. 5

5. Which of the following statements is NOT true about money spent in the local currency?

(a) Jano spent 2000 in Cyrenia
(b) Lian spent 2000 in Cyrenia
(c) Jano spent 2000 in Aurevia
(d) Kira spent 1000 in Aurevia

Directions for Questions 6 to 9: Seven children, Aarav, Bina, Chirag, Diya, Eshan, Farhan, and Gaurav, are sitting in a circle facing inside (not necessarily in the same order) and playing a game of 'Passing the Buck'.

The game is played over 10 rounds. In each round, the child holding the Buck must pass it directly to a child sitting in one of the following positions:

- Immediately to the left;
- Immediate to the right;
- Second to the left; or
- Second to the right.

The game starts with Bina passing the Buck and ends with Chirag receiving the Buck. The table below provides some information about the pass types and the child receiving the Buck. Some information is missing and labelled as '?'.

Round	Position	Name
1	Immediately to the left	Aarav
2	Second to the right	?
3	Immediately to the right	Diya
4	?	?
5	?	Aarav
6	Second to the left	?
7	Immediately to the left	Gaurav
8	Immediately to the left	?
9	?	Farhan
10	?	Chirag

6. Who is sitting immediately to the right of Bina?

(a) Farhan (b) Aarav
(c) Chirag (d) Eshan

7. Who is sitting third to the left of Eshan?
   (a) Gaurav (b) Divya
   (c) Aarav (d) Chirag
8. For which of the following pass types can the total number of occurrences be uniquely determined?
   (a) Immediately to the right
   (b) Second to the right
   (c) Second to the left
   (d) Immediately to the left
9. For which of the following children is it possible to determine how many times they received the Buck?
   (a) Gaurav (b) Farhan
   (c) Bina (d) Eshan

ANSWER KEY

1. 41000 2. 13000 3. 1500 4. (a)
5. (c) 6. (d) 7. (d) 8. (a)
9. (a)

SOLUTIONS AND SHORTCUTS

Solutions for Questions 1 to 5: Let us denote the currencies and the countries as A, B, C and Z respectively and the people as J (Jano), K (Kira) and L (Lian).

We can make the following deductions based on the basic conditions of the problem:

The currency exchange rate between Z & C: 1C = 0.5Z (given). We are not aware of the rates of A and B against Z. Also, given, flight cost in Z: J = 4000 Z; K & L 5000Z and 6000Z (not necessarily respectively).

Deduction 1: Since each traveler visited exactly 2 countries and each country was visited by exactly 2 travelers, we deduce that there are 6 traveler - country combinations and it can be deduced that someone visited A & B; Someone else visited A & C & the third person visited countries B & C, respectively.

Deduction 2: Each person spent a different amount in the local currency of the countries visited. Also, given that we have three instances of 1000 spent & one instance of 3000 spent locally, it means that there must be two instances of 2000 spent locally. Also, the local currency spends for the three people would be 1000, 2000; 1000, 2000 & 2000, 3000.

Deduction 3: Since the A and B citizen report that Kira visited their country, it means K visited A & B. Further, J must have visited A and C; which can only mean that L visited the countries B & C.

Deduction 4: From Clue 2, we see that L spent 3000 in B. Hence, he must have spent 2000 in C. Likewise, since K spent 2000 in B, the spending for K in A would be 1000.

Deduction 5: K's travel costs are given to us as 8000A as well as 4000B. Thus, we can deduce 1B=2A.

The table would look as follows (local currency spends in brackets):

Country Visited	Kira	Jano	Lian	Currency rates
A	K (1000A)	J (1000A/2000A)		
B	K (2000B)		L (3000B)	
C		J (2000C/1000C)	L (2000C)	1C=0.5Z
Total local non travel spend	5000A = 2500B			
Travel costs (flight+ local)	8000A = 4000B	3500A	36000C	Hence, 1B=2A
Flight costs	Initially 5000Z/6000Z After deduction 6: 6000Z	4000Z	Initially 6000/5000Z= 12000C/10000C After deduction 6: 5000Z=10000C	
After deduction 7		1000A in A & 2000C in C		

Deduction 6: The total travel cost for Lian is given as 36000C. This is comprised of (local spends at B and C + flight costs) = 3000B + 2000C + 12000C/10000C = 36000C. The possibilities that emerge are: 3000B = 22000C or 3000B = 24000C giving us 1B = 7.33C or 1B = 8C. At this point the options in question 4 help us resolve this multiple possibility situation - as only the figure of 1B = 8C is there in the options for the question. Thus, we have the relationship: 1B = 8C. Also, since a C = 0.5Z and since we also know that 1B = 2A we get the relationship: 1B = 8C = 2A = 4Z. We can calculate the answers once we have this deduction.

Deduction 7: From Jano's column in the table: We know that flight costs 4000Z = 2000A. This means her local costs would be 1500A. Hence, she must have spent 1000A in country A and 2000C in country C.

1. Total Spending in Z = Kira (8000A = 16000Z) + Jano (3500A = 7000Z) + Lian (36000C = 18000Z) = 41000Z. The correct answer is 41000.
2. Lian spent 3000B = 12000Z and 2000C = 1000Z in the two countries he went to. Hence, 13000Z. The correct answer is 13000.
3. In Aurel's Jano's local spending would be 1500.
4. Option (a) is correct.
5. Option (c) is correct.

Solutions for Questions 6 to 9:

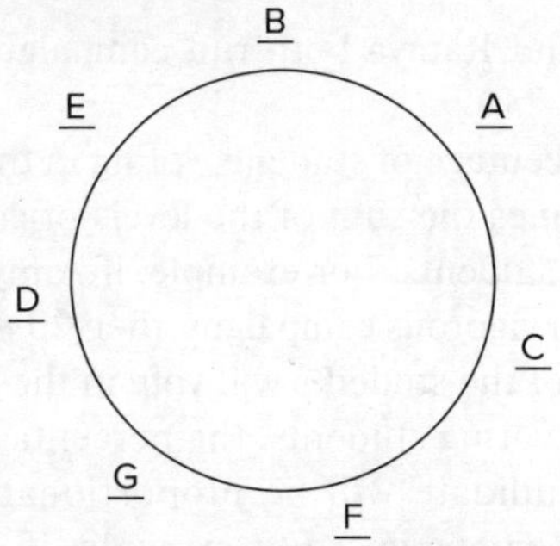

From Clues 1,2 and 3 – We can position Bina, Aarav and Diya in the positions shown in the diagram. At this stage, we cannot make out how to exactly position the movement back from Diya to Aarav (as to whether these are 1/2 left or 2 + 2 right). However, when we see the clues 6 and 7, we can get that Gaurav must be sitting 3 places to the left of Aarav (and hence is to the immediate right of Diya).

Thus, the 8th round pass from Gaurav immediately to the left would be to Diya – and she would have the buck. With this position fixed, the 9th and 10th round passing of the buck, can only be 2 right from Diya to Farhan (who will have the buck at the end of round 9) and 1 right from Farhan to Chirag, where the buck will finally rest at the end of round 10.

These placements only leave us one position for Eshan (to the left of Diya)

The answers are:

6. Eshan is to the immediate right of Bina. Hence, option (d) is correct.
7. Chirag is third to the left of Eshan. Option (d) is correct.
8. The 4th and fifth passes can have instances of immediately to the left, 2nd to the left and 2nd to the right. It is not possible to determine how many of these three were actually used. However, the pass type 'Immediately to the right' has a defined number of occurrences and hence, the correct answer is option (a).
9. The 4th pass can go to anyone of Eshan, Bina or Gaurav (and we cannot determine it exactly). Hence, for these three people, we cannot determine the number of times they receive the buck. However, there is no such complication for Gaurav – and hence we can determine exactly how many times he receives the buck. Hence, option (a) is correct.

SLOT 1 CAT 2024

High Yield Questions

Scan this QR code to access video explanations for select questions from CAT 2024

Directions for Questions 1 to 5: The game of QUIET is played between two teams. Six teams, numbered 1, 2, 3, 4, 5, and 6, play in a QUIET tournament. These teams are divided equally into two groups. In the tournament, each team plays every other team in the same group only once, and each team in the other group exactly twice. The tournament has several rounds, each of which consists of a few games. Every team plays exactly one game in each round.

The following additional facts are known about the schedule of games in the tournament:

(i) Each team played against a team from the other group in Round 8.

(ii) In Round 4 and Round 7, the match-ups, that is the pair of teams playing against each other, were identical. In Round 5 and Round 8, the match-ups were identical.

(iii) Team 4 played Team 6 in both Round 1 and Round 2.

(iv) Team 1 played Team 5 ONLY once and that was in Round 2.

(v) Team 3 played Team 4 in Round 3. Team 1 played Team 6 in Round 6.

(vi) In Round 8, Team 3 played Team 6, while Team 2 played Team 5.

1. How many rounds were there in the tournament?

2. What is the number of the team that played Team 1 in Round 5?

3. Which team among the teams numbered 2, 3, 4, and 5 was not part of the same group?

(a) 2 (b) 5
(c) 4 (d) 3

4. What is the number of the team that played against Team 1 in Round 7?

5. What is the number of the team that played against Team 6 in Round 3?

Directions for Questions 6 to 10: Two students, Amiya and Ramya, are the only candidates in an election for the position of class representative. Students will vote based on the intensity level of Amiya's and Ramya's campaigns and the type of campaigns they run. Each campaign is said to have a level of 1 if it is a staid campaign and a level of 2 if it is a vigorous campaign. Campaigns can be of two types, they can either focus on issues, or on attacking the other candidate.

If Amiya and Ramya both run campaigns focusing on issues, then:

- The percentage of students voting in the election will be 20 times the sum of the levels of campaigning of the two students. For example, if Amiya and Ramya both run vigorous campaigns, then $20 \times (2 + 2)\%$, that is, 80% of the students will vote in the election.
- Among voting students, the percentage of votes for each candidate will be proportional to the levels of their campaigns. For example, if Amiya runs a staid (i.e., level 1) campaign while Ramya runs a vigorous (i.e., level 2) campaign, then Amiya will receive $1/3$ of the votes cast, and Ramya will receive the other $2/3$.

The above-mentioned percentages change as follows if at least one of them runs a campaign attacking their opponent:

- If Amiya runs a campaign attacking Ramya and Ramya runs a campaign focusing on issues,then 10% of the students who would have otherwise voted for Amiya will vote for Ramya, and another 10% who would have otherwise voted for Amiya, will not vote at all.
- If Ramya runs a campaign attacking Amiya and Amiya runs a campaign focusing on issues, then 20% of the students who would have otherwise voted for Ramya will vote for Amiya, and another 5% who would have otherwise voted for Ramya, will not vote at all.
- If both run campaigns attacking each other, then 10% of the students who would have otherwise voted for them had they run campaigns focusing on issues, will not vote at all.

6. If both of them run staid campaigns attacking the other, then what percentage of students will vote in the election?

(a) 40% (b) 64%
(c) 60% (d) 36%

7. What is the minimum percentage of students who will vote in the election?
(a) 36% (b) 40%
(c) 38% (d) 32%

8. If Amiya runs a campaign focusing on issues, then what is the maximum percentage of votes that she can get?
(a) 40% (b) 44%
(c) 48% (d) 36%

9. If Ramya runs a campaign attacking Amiya, then what is the minimum percentage of votes that she is guaranteed to get?
(a) 15% (b) 30%
(c) 12% (d) 18%

10. What is the maximum possible voting margin with which one of the candidates can win?
(a) 26% (b) 20%
(c) 28% (d) 29%

ANSWER KEY

1. 8	2. 4	3. (b)	4. 3
5. 5	6. (d)	7. (a)	8. (c)
9. (a)	10. (d)		

SOLUTIONS AND SHORTCUTS

Solutions for Questions 1 to 5:

Deduction 1: There will be 3 teams in each group and each team will play 1 match against teams within the group and 2 matches each with teams from the other group. This means that any particular team will play 2 intra group matches and 6 inter group matches. Hence, every team plays 8 matches and consequently 8 rounds. We can also understand from clue 3 that teams 4 and 6 are in opposite groups. Let us think of this as two groups then – group A with team 4 and group B with team 6. From clue 4 we get that 1 and 5 are in the same group. They will either go together into group A or B.

Deduction 2: Also, since clue 2 tells us that the matches in round 4 and 7; and the matches in rounds 5 and 8 are identical, it means that these are all inter-group matches. Also, clue 8 tells us 3 played 6 in round 8, which means that 3 and 6 are in opposite groups. This also means that teams 1 and 5 can only be placed together if we add them to the group with Team 6. Thus, the groups would be:

Group A: Teams 4, 2, 3; **Group B:** Teams 6, 1, 5.

Deduction 3: The matches in round 4 and 7; and the matches in rounds 5 and 8 will be inter group matches. Thus, the matches in the tournament will look as shown in the table:

INTERGROUP MATCHES

1-3	3-5	3-6	2-1	2-5	2-6	4-1	4-5	4-6
1-3	3-5	3-6	2-1	2-5	2-6	4-1	4-5	4-6

INTRAGROUP MATCHES

Group A	2-3	2-4	3-4
Group B	1-5	1-6	5-6

With the direct information provided to us, we can start off a 8 round individual matches identification exercise. The initial table is as shown (Note: we have completed round 2 and round 8 using the left out teams and also replicated round 8's matches in round 5.

Round 1	4-6		
Round 2	4-6	1-5	2-3
Round 3	3-4		
Round 4			
Round 5	3-6	2-5	1-4
Round 6	1-6		
Round 7			
Round 8	3-6	2-5	1-4

If we delete these already placed matches from our list of all matches our residual matches look as shown:

Residual Matches:

INTERGROUP MATCHES

1-3	~~3-5~~	~~3-6~~	2-1	~~2-5~~	2-6	~~4-1~~	4-5	~~4-6~~
1-3	~~3-5~~	3-6	2-1	~~2-5~~	2-6	~~4-1~~	4-5	~~4-6~~

INTRAGROUP MATCHES

Group A	~~2-3~~	2-4	~~3-4~~
Group B	~~1-5~~	~~1-6~~	5-6

Deduction 4: The round 4 and 7 matches can only fit in if we use 4-5, since 4 has to be playing these rounds. The other two matches can be identified as 1-3 and 2-6 for these rounds. A this stage Rounds 2, 4, 5, 7 and 8 are complete in all respects. Rounds 1,3 and 6 have 2 matches each to place. Matches left to place are: two 3 vs 5 matches; two 1 vs 2 matches and 1 each of 2 vs 4 and 5 vs 6 matches.

Deduction 5: 3 is already playing 4 in round 3. Hence, the 3 vs 5 matches have to go to round 1 and 6. Likewise, 1 is already playing 6 in round 6 (given). Hence, the 1 vs 2 matches have to be placed in rounds 1 and 3. 5 vs 6 slots into round 3 and 2 vs 4 slots into round 6. The final solution table is as shown:

Round 1	4-6	3-5	1-2
Round 2	4-6	1-5	2-3
Round 3	3-4	1-2	5-6
Round 4	4-5 # 4	1-3 # 4	2-6 # 4
Round 5	3-6	2-5	1-4
Round 6	1-6	3-5	2-4
Round 7	4-5 # 4	1-3 # 4	2-6 # 4
Round 8	3-6	2-5	1-4

The answers are:

1. 8
2. 4
3. Team 5 was in the other group to teams 2, 3, 4. Hence, option (b) is correct.
4. 3
5. 5

Solutions for Questions 6 to 10:

6. Since both of them run staid campaigns, the total voters would have been 20 × (1 + 1) = 40%. They would each get 20% vote share. However, both would lose 10% of their votes since the campaigns are attacking each other. Thus, the total voters would be 90% of 40% = 36%. Option (d) is correct.
7. The minimum percentage of voters will happen in the adverse events of staid campaigns attacking each other. The previous answer helps us reason out that this value will be 36% again. Option (a) is correct.
8. In the event that Amiya runs a campaign focusing on issues, and both of them run vigorous campaigns (level 2), Amiya's vote percentage will be maximised if Ramya attacks Amiya in her campaign and hence loses out 20% of her vote share to Amiya.
   A level 2 campaign by both would mean 20 × (2 + 2) = 80% voters with a 1:1 split between them, thus giving an initial vote share of 40 to each. Then Ramya loses 20% of her vote share to Amiya (= 8%). Hence, Amiya's maximum vote share is 40 + 8 = 48%. Option (c) is correct.
9. Her minimum percentage would occur in the following situation:
   Ramya Level 1 campaign attacking Amiya; Amiya Level 1 campaign focusing on issues.
   Total vote percentage = 20 × (1 + 1) = 40%. Votes shared in the ratio 1:1. Hence, Ramya has 20% voters out of which she will lose 25% (20% will switch to Amiya - since Ramya was attacking her; 5% will not vote at all). Hence, Ramya's guaranteed vote is 20% - 25% of 20% = 15%.
   Ramya Level 1 campaign attacking Amiya; Amiya Level 2 campaign focusing on issues.
   Total vote percentage = 20 × (1 + 2) = 60%. Votes shared in the ratio 1:2. Hence, Ramya has 20% voters out of which she will lose 25% (20% will switch to Amiya - since Ramya was attacking her; 5% will not vote at all). Hence, Ramya's guaranteed vote is 20% - 25% of 20% = 15%.
   Thus, in either of these situations, Ramya has a guaranteed 15% vote share. Hence option (a) is correct.
10. Ramya Level 1 campaign attacking Amiya; Amiya Level 2 campaign focusing on issues.
   Total vote percentage = 20 × (1 + 2) = 60%. Votes shared in the ratio 1:2. Hence, Ramya has 20% voters out of which she will lose 25% (20% will switch to Amiya - since Ramya was attacking her; 5% will not vote at all). Hence, Ramya's vote is 20% - 25% of 20% = 15%. Amiya's vote = 40% + 4% (20% of Ramya's voters who switched) = 44%.
   Winning margin is 29%. Option (d) is correct.

SLOT 2

CAT 2024

Directions for Questions 1 to 5: Eight gymnastics players numbered 1 through 8 underwent a training camp where they were coached by three coaches – Xena, Yuki, and Zara. Each coach trained at least two players.Yuki trained only even numbered players, while Zara trained only odd numbered players.After the camp, the coaches evaluated the players and gave integer ratings to the respective players trained by them on a scale of 1 to 7, with 1 being the lowest rating and 7 the highest.

The following additional information is known:

(i) Xena trained more players than Yuki.

(ii) Player-1 and Player-4 were trained by the same coach, while the coaches who trained Player-2, Player-3 and Player-5 were all different.

(iii) Player-5 and Player-7 were trained by the same coach and got the same rating. All other players got a unique rating.

(iv) The average of the ratings of all the players was 4.

(v) Player-2 got the highest rating.

(vi) The average of the ratings of the players trained by Yuki was twice that of the players trained by Xena and two more than that of the players trained by Zara.

(vii) Player-4's rating was double of Player-8's and less than Player-5's.

1. What best can be concluded about the number of players coached by Zara?

(a) Exactly 2 (b) Either 2 or 3

(c) Either 2 or 3 or 4 (d) Exactly 3

2. What was the rating of Player-7?

3. What was the rating of Player-6?

4. For how many players the ratings can be determined with certainty?

5. Who all were the players trained by Xena?

(a) Player-1, Player-3, Player-4

(b) Player-1, Player-3, Player-4, Player-6

(c) Player-1, Player-3, Player-4, Player-8

(d) Player-1, Player-4, Player-6, Player-8

Directions for Questions 6 to 10: The numbers 1, 2, 3, 4, 5, 6, 7, 8, 9, and 10 are placed in ten slots of the following grid based on the conditions below:

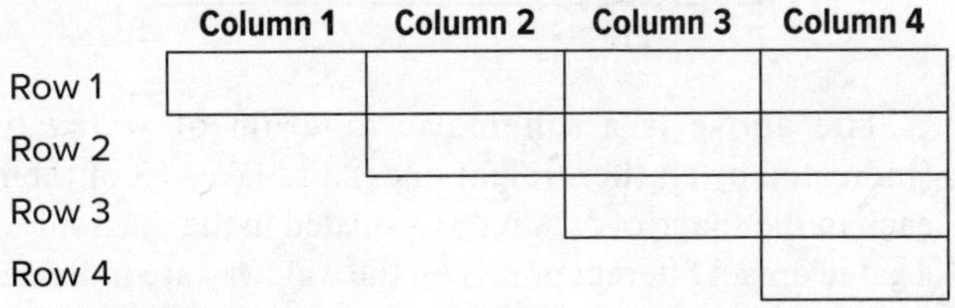

(i) Numbers in any row appear in an increasing order from left to right.

(ii) Numbers in any column appear in a decreasing order from top to bottom.

(iii) 1 is placed either in the same row or in the same column as 10.

(iv) Neither 2 nor 3 is placed in the same row or in the same column as 10.

(v) Neither 7 nor 8 is placed in the same row or in the same column as 9.

(vi) 4 and 6 are placed in the same row.

6. What is the row number which has the least sum of numbers placed in that row?

7. Which of the following statements MUST be true?

I. 10 is placed in a slot in Row 1.

II. 1 is placed in a slot in Row 4.

(a) Neither I nor II (b) Both I and II

(c) Only II (d) Only I

8. Which of the following statements MUST be true?

I. 2 is placed in a slot in Column 2.

II. 3 is placed in a slot in Column 3.

(a) Only I (b) Both I and II

(c) Only II (d) Neither I nor II

9. For how many slots in the grid, placement of numbers CANNOT be determined with certainty?

10. What is the sum of the numbers placed in Column 4?

Directions for Questions 11 to 14:

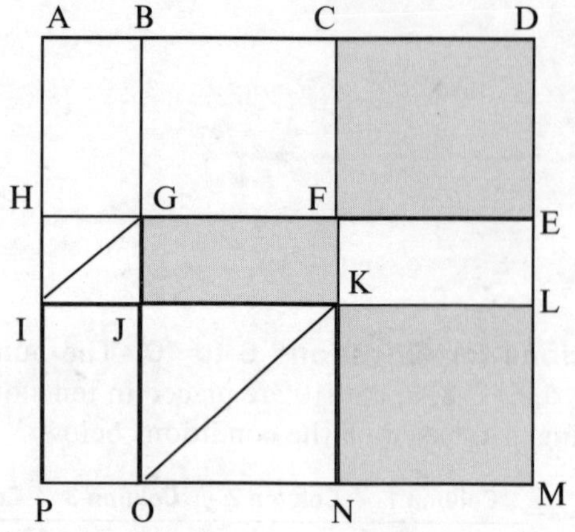

The above is a schematic diagram of walkways (indicated by all the straight-lines) and lakes (3 of them, each in the shape of rectangles - shaded in the diagram) of a gated area. Different points on the walkway are indicated by letters (A through P) with distances being OP = 150 m, ON = MN = 300 m, ML = 400 m, EL = 200 m, DE = 400 m.

The following additional information about the facilities in the area is known:

(i) The only entry/exit point is at C.
(ii) There are many residences within the gated area; all of them are located on the path AH and ML with four of them being at A, H, M, and L.
(iii) The post office is located at P and the bank is located at B.

11. One resident whose house is located at L, needs to visit the post office as well as the bank. What is the minimum distance (in m) he has to walk starting from his residence and returning to his residence after visiting both the post office and the bank?
(a) 3000 (b) 3200
(c) 2700 (d) 3000

12. One person enters the gated area and decides to walk as much as possible before leaving the area without walking along any path more than once and always walking next to one of the lakes. Note that he may cross a point multiple times. How much distance (in m) will he walk within the gated area?
(a) 2800 (b) 3200
(c) 3800 (d) 3000

13. One resident takes a walk within the gated area starting from A and returning to A without going through any point (other than A) more than once. What is the maximum distance (in m) she can walk in this way?

14. Visitors coming for morning walks are allowed to enter as long as they do not pass by any of the residences and do not cross any point (except C) more than once. What is the maximum distance (in m) that such a visitor can walk within the gated area?

ANSWER KEY

1. (a)	2. 4	3. 5	4. 6
5. (c)	6. 4	7. (b)	8. (d)
9. 2	10. 26	11. (b)	12. (c)
13. 5100	14. 3500		

SOLUTIONS AND SHORTCUTS

Solutions for Questions 1 to 5: The information can be put in the form of a table - using the following deductions to help us move ahead from the absolutely basic information.

Deduction 1: Everyone coached at least 2 players. This means that we can have a pattern of 3, 3, 2 or 4, 2, 2 for the 3 coaches in some order. However, once we get from Clue 1 that Xena trained more players than Yuki, it means that Yuki can only be 2, while Xena would have coached either 3 or 4 players.

Deduction 2: Player 1 and 4 having the same coach would mean that they have to be trained by Xena, since Yuki or Zara cannot coach 1 or 4 respectively.

Deduction 3: Player 2 has to be coached by Yuki - else, we would not be able to place players 2, 3, 5 under different coaches (as specified by clue 2).

	Xena (3 or 4)	Yuki (2)	Zara (2 or 3)
Other information		Only even numbered players	Only odd numbered players
Deductions 1 to 3	Player 1, Player 4	Player 2	

At this stage, we do not know who coached players 3, 5, 6, 7, 8. Just that 3 and 5 have to have different coaches. Also, 5 and 7 have to have the same coach (which could be either Zara or Xena). The following set of deductions takes us towards the solution:

Deduction 4: The average ratings of all players being 4 (clue 4) means that the sum of all 8 ratings is 32. Also, since apart from 5 and 7, all other got different ratings from 1 to 7, it means that the Sum of 1 to 7 + the repeated rating of 5 and 7 should be equal to 32. Since the sum of 1 to 7 is 28, this means that the only repeated rating is 4 - given to players 5 and 7. Also, we know player 2 got a rating of 7 (direct use of clue 5). Using clue 7, we can work out that the possibilities for Player 4's ratings could be 2, 4 or 6 (since it is double of the Player 8's rating). But out of these, 4 and 6 can be ruled out for Player 4's rating since his rating has to be less than Player 5's rating (which we have worked out as 4). Thus, Player 4's rating = 2; Player 8's rating = 1.

Deduction 5: We already know that the number of players coached by Xena, Yuki and Zara are either 3, 2, 3 or 4, 2, 2.

Using Clue 6, if we assume the average of Xena's trainees as x, then the average of Yuki's ratings is 2x, while the average of Zara's ratings for her students is 2x - 2.

For the 3, 2, 3 case, this works out to the sum of all ratings being 3x + 4x + 6x - 6 = 32 → 13x = 38, which is not possible. If we try the 4, 2, 2 case, we get that the sum of all the ratings is 4x + 4x + 4x - 4 = 32 → x = 3. This means that Xena's average rating for her students is 3, Yuki's average rating is 6 and Zara's average rating is 4. Thus, Xena must have coached 4 players, while Yuki and Zara would have coached 2 players each.

Deduction 6: Basis these averages, we can conclude that Players 5 and 7, with their ratings as 4 each can only be coached by Zara. Also, Player 3 must have been coached by Xena and Player 6 must have been coached by Yuki. Also, since Yuki's average for her two players is 6 and her trainee player 2 has a rating of 7, it can only mean that Player 6's rating must be 5.

Using these deductions, the table completes as (Ratings in brackets):

	Xena (4)	Yuki (2)	Zara (2)
	Player 1 (?), Player 4 (2)	Player 2 (7)	
Deductions 4,5,6	Player 8 (1), Player 3 (?)	Player 6 (5)	Player 5 (4), Player 7(4)
Ratings left to allocate (3) and (6)			

The answers can be read off this table:

1. Option (a) is correct.
2. 4
3. 5
4. 6 (we can determine the ratings of all players except players 1 and 3.)
5. Option (c) is correct.

Solutions for Questions 6 to 10: The rules for placement given to us are: Left to right increasing order; Top to bottom decreasing order.

Deduction 1: Based on this dual requirement, 10 has to be on the top right - i.e. column 4, row 1. (Deduction 1). This means that 2 and 3 cannot be in column 4 or in row 1. Thus, there are only 3 possible places for 2 and 3 to be placed - viz: Row 2 Column 2; Row 2 Column 3 or Row 3 Column 3. 1 could go to row 1 column 1 or row 4 column 4.

Deduction 2: The placement of 4, 6 in a single row, can be in rows 1, 2 or 3. We can rule out placing 4-6 in row 3, as we will then have to place 2, 3 in row 2 - columns 2 and 3, which would not obey the requirement of decreasing order in column 3 (as 3 would come above 4).

Deduction 3: Placing 4-6 in row 2. There are three possibilities for the same: Row 2 consists of 4-5-6; 4-6-?; or ?-4-6. We can easily discard 4-5-6 in row 2, as well as 4-6-?- as there will be no place left in the grid to place both 2 and 3. Checking for ?-4-6, we can see two possibilities as shown in the table. However, this possibility also gets rejected as it will end up with 7/8 in the same row as 9. Thus, we conclude that 4-6 have to be placed in the first row.

Possibility rejected:

Column 1	Column 2	Column 3	Column 4
			10 (#1)
Blank	3/2	4	6
Blank	Blank	2/3	
Blank	Blank	Blank	

Deduction 4: Placing 4-6 in row 1. There are three possibilities for the same: Row 2 consists of 4-5-6-10; 4-6-?-10; or 1-4-6-10. We can reject 1-4-6-10, since, 9, 8, 7 would have to go into the same column under 10, in this case. In the other two cases-1 will be in row 4, column 4. Once, we place 1 in row 4, column 4, we can easily discard the placement of 4-5-6-10 in row 1, since there will be no place to place 7, 8, 9 - while obeying the constraint of 2, 3 not being in the first row or the fourth column. Thus, we can work out the final arrangement of the grid as shown:

Final solution table:

Column 1	Column 2	Column 3	Column 4
4	6	9	10 (# 1)
Blank	3/2	5	8
Blank	Blank	2/3	7
Blank	Blank	Blank	1

The answers can be read off this table.

6. 4
7. Both I and II. Option (b) is correct.
8. Neither I nor II. Option (d) is correct.
9. We cannot determine the exact position of 2 and 3. Hence, the correct answer is 2.
10. 10 + 8 + 7 + 1 = 26.

Solutions for Questions 11 to 14:

11. For the shortest distance his path should be: L-K-O-P-I-G-B-G-F-K-L or L-K-O-P-I-G-B-C-F-K-L or L-K-O-P-I-G-B-G-J-K-L. In each of these cases, he is traversing through

the diagonals K-O and I-G, which can be worked out to be 500 and 250 meters long. The distance for each of these routes will be the same and can be worked out as: LK = 300; KO = 500; OP = 150; PI = 400; IG = 250; GB = 400; BG = 400; GF = 300; FK = 200; KL = 300. The total distance would be 3200. Option (b) is correct.

12. Since he is always going around lakes, we can trace a path like: C-D-E-F-G-J-K-L-M-N-K-F-C. In this route (or any other alternate longest route we create, he is going around all the sides of each of the lakes. The perimeters of the respective lakes CDEF, FGJK and LKNM are 1400,1000 and 1400 respectively. Hence, the total distance traveled would be 3800 meters. Option (c) is correct.

13. For this question, we have to chart out the most circuitous route possible, without crossing a point twice. The path: A-B-G-F-C-D-E-L-M-N-K-J-O-P-I-H-A would total 15 0 + 400 + 300 + 400 + 300 + 400 + 200 + 400 + 300 + 400 + 300 + 400 + 150 + 400 + 200 + 400 = 5100.

14. A path covering every possible point (except the residences) would be C-D-E-F-K-N-O-P-I-J-G-B-C. The distance covered would be 300 + 400 + 300 + 200 + 400 + 300 + 150 + 400 + 150 + 200 + 400 + 300 = 350.

SLOT 3 CAT 2024

Directions for Questions 1 to 5: The figure below shows a network with three parallel roads represented by horizontal lines R-A, R-B, and R-C and another three parallel roads represented by vertical lines V1, V2, and V3. The figure also shows the distance (in km) between two adjacent intersections. Six ATMs are placed at six of the nine road intersections. Each ATM has a distinct integer cash requirement (in Rs. Lakhs), and the numbers at the end of each line in the figure indicate the total cash requirements of all ATMs placed on the corresponding road. For example, the total cash requirement of the ATM(s) placed on road R-A is Rs. 22 Lakhs.

The following additional information is known.

(i) The ATMs with the minimum and maximum cash requirements of Rs. 7 Lakhs and Rs. 15 Lakhs are placed on the same road.

(ii) The road distance between the ATM with the second highest cash requirement and the ATM located at the intersection of R-C and V3 is 12 km.

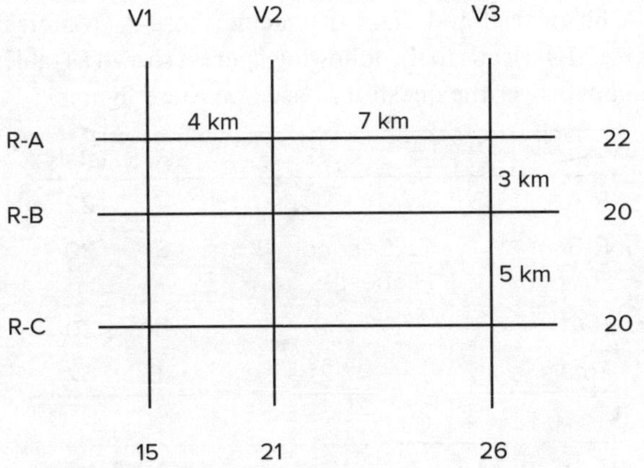

1. Which of the following statements is correct?
   (a) The ATM placed at the (R-C, V2) intersection has a cash requirement of Rs. 9 Lakhs.
   (b) There is no ATM placed at the (R-C, V2) intersection.
   (c) The ATM placed at the (R-C, V2) intersection has a cash requirement of Rs. 8 Lakhs.
   (d) The cash requirement of the ATM placed at the (R-C, V2) intersection cannot be uniquely determined.
2. How many ATMs have cash requirements of Rs. 10 Lakhs or more?
3. Which of the following two statements is/are DEFINITELY true?
   I. Statement A: Each of R-A, R-B, and R-C has two ATMs.
   II. Statement B: Each of V1, V2, and V3 has two ATMs.
   (a) Both Statement I and Statement II
   (b) Neither Statement I nor Statement II
   (c) Only Statement I
   (d) Only Statement II
4. What best can be said about the road distance (in km) between the ATMs having the second highest and the second lowest cash requirements?
   (a) 7 km
   (b) 5 km
   (c) 4 km
   (d) Either 4 km or 7 km
5. What is the number of ATMs whose locations and cash requirements can both be uniquely determined?

Directions for Questions 6 to 10: The air-conditioner (AC) in a large room can be operated either in REGULAR mode or in POWER mode to reduce the temperature.

If the AC operates in REGULAR mode, then it brings down the temperature inside the room (called inside temperature) at a constant rate to the set temperature in 1 hour. If it operates in POWER mode, then this is achieved in 30 minutes.

If the AC is switched off, then the inside temperature rises at a constant rate so as to reach the temperature outside at the time of switching off in 1 hour.

The temperature outside has been falling at a constant rate from 7 pm onward until 3 am on a particular night. The following graph shows the inside temperature between 11 pm (23:00) and 2 am (2:00) that night.

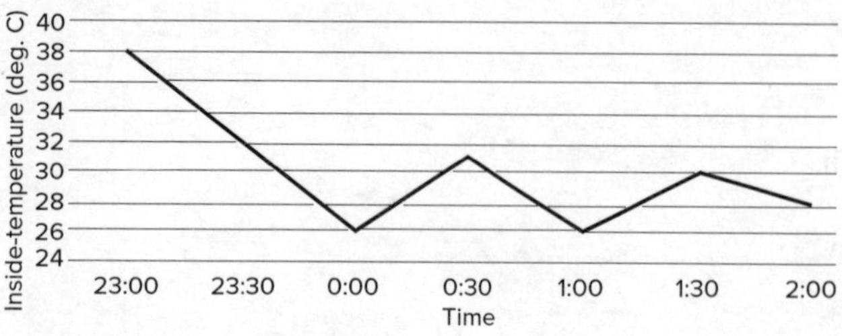

The following facts are known about the AC operation that night.

- The AC was turned on for the first time that night at 11 pm (23:00).
- The AC setting was changed (including turning it on/off, and/or setting different temperatures) only at the beginning of the hour or at 30 minutes after the hour.
- The AC was used in POWER mode for longer duration than in REGULAR mode during this 3-hour period.

6. How many times the AC must have been turned off between 11:01 pm and 1:59 am?
(a) 1
(b) 2
(c) cannot be determined
(d) 0

7. What was the temperature outside, in degree Celsius, at 1 am?

8. What was the temperature outside, in degree Celsius, at 9 pm?

9. What best can be concluded about the number of times the AC must have either been turned on or the AC temperature setting been altered between 11:01 pm and 1:59 am?
(a) More than 3 (b) Exactly 2
(c) Either 2 or 3 (d) Exactly 3

10. What was the maximum difference between temperature outside and inside temperature, in degree Celsius, between 11:01 pm and 1:59 am?

ANSWER KEY

1. (a) 2. 3 3. (c) 4. (d)
5. 3 6. (b) 7. 34 8. 42
9. (d) 10. 10

SOLUTIONS AND SHORTCUTS

Solutions for Questions 1 to 5: We can make the following deductions in order to place the 6 ATMs.

Deduction 1: The maximum value of cash in an ATM is 15 lakhs, minimum is 7 lakhs. The other four ATMs, have cash requirement between 8 to 14 lakhs with every ATM having a unique cash requirement. Also, the sum of cash requirements (overall) being 22 + 20 + 20 = 15 + 21 + 26 = 62, it means that the 4 ATMs whose cash requirements are not known must have a total cash requirement of 40 lakhs. Based on this, we try to think of what the value of the second highest ATM's cash requirement might be. It has to be less than 15. If we try to make it 14, we can see that 14 + 8 + 9 + 10 equal 41 lakhs - and there is no way to make the total of the 4 ATMs equal to 40. At 13, the possibility of 13,10,9,8 arises, while we also have the possibility of 12, 11, 9, 8 -lets think of these as possibilities 1 and 2.

Ruling out Possibility 1 - wherein the 6 ATMs contain 15, 13, 10, 9, 8 and 7 lakhs: It is given to us that the ATM with the second highest cash requirement is at the junction RB-V2. If we place 13 at this junction, the V2 column should contain an ATM with 8 lakhs. Also, it is given to us that the 15 lakh and 7 lakh ATMs are on the same road - considering the sums involved for each row and column, we can clearly make out that their placement is only possible in R-A. (R-B and R-C have a sum less than 22 and the same is the case of V1 and V2, while if we ty to place 15 and 7 in the V3 column, we need to add a 4 lakh ATM to this column, which is not there). Also, 15 lakh ATM would have to be placed at R-A V1 intersection and 7 lakh ATM at the R-A V3 intersection. We will then need to place a 9 lakh and a 8 lakh ATM in the V3 vertical - but with 13 lakhs at R-B V2 intersection and the R-B road only having a total of 20 lakhs, this is not possible. Hence, we reject this possibility and conclude that the 6 ATMs contain 15, 12, 11, 9, 8 and 7 lakhs respectively.

A bit of trial and error of placing these ATMs on the intersections leads to the following figures (shown as tables). We can answer the questions based on these figures.

	V1	V2	V3	Totals
R-A	15		7	22
R-B		12 (Second Highest)	8	20
R-C		9	11	20
Totals	15	21	26	62

	V1	V2	V3	Totals
R-A	7	--	15	22
R-B	8	12 (Second Highest)	--	20
R-C	--	9	11	20
Totals	15	21	26	62

1. Option (a) is correct.
2. 3
3. Only Statement A is true. Option (c) is correct.

4. The distance between the 12 lakh and the 8 lakh ATMs could be either 4 km or 7 km, depending on whether we place the 8 lakh ATM in the V1 or V3 vertical. Option (d) is correct.
5. We can only make out the exact location of the ATMs with 12 lakhs, 9 lakhs and 11 lakhs. There are two possibilities of placing the other three ATMs (15,8 and 7). Hence, the correct answer is 3.

Solutions for Questions 6 to 10: We can observe that the Air Conditioner was switched on for exactly 2 hours out of 3 between 11 AM and 2 AM. Since the AC was run on power mode for longer than it was run on Regular mode – this is only possible if we ran it on power mode for 90 minutes and regular mode for 30 minutes or on power mode for 120 minutes.

Note: This is interpreted from the given condition that the AC settings were changed only at the beginning of the hour or at 30 minutes after the hour.

From the falling and rising temperatures of the graph, we can make out that the AC was on between 11 to 12, off from 12 to 12:30, on again from 12:30 to 1, off from 1 to 1:30 and finally on from 1:30 to 2.

Further, we can also make out that when the AC was switched off at 0:00, the room temperature started rising and rose to 31 degrees in 30 minutes – since it is given that when the AC is off, the room temperature adjusts and becomes equal to the outside temperature at the time of switching off in 1 hour – it means that the room temperature was increasing to 36 degrees in one hour – and this must have been the outside temperature at 0:00. Also, since the outside temperature falls at a constant rate from 7 PM to 3 AM that day, it means that the temperature is falling by 2 degrees Celsius in every 1 hour – or 1 degree Celsius in every half an hour. We can thus make a table as shown.

Time	Inside Temperature	On/Off	Outside Temperature	Mode & Target Temperature
23:00	38	Switched On	38	Power 32
23:30	32	On (continues)	37	Power 26
00:00	26	Switched Off	36	NA
00:30	31	Switched On	35	Power 26
1:00	26	Switched Off	34	NA
1:30	30	Switched On	33	Power 28/regular 26
2:00	28		32	

The answers can be read off this table:

6. 2. Option (b) is correct.
7. 34
8. The temperature is falling steadily at 2 degree Celsius per hour. Hence, at 9 PM, the outside temperature must have been 38 + 4 = 42.
9. It was switched on twice – once at 0:30 and once at 1:30 and the temperature setting was changed from 32 to 26 at 23:30. Option (d) is hence, the correct answer.
10. At 0:00 the temperature difference is the maximum of 10. Hence, the correct answer is 10.

SLOT 1

CAT 2023

High Yield Questions

Scan this QR code to access video explanations for select questions from CAT 2023

Directions for Questions 1 to 5: *A visa processing office (VPO) accepts visa applications in four categories - US, UK, Schengen, and Others. The applications are scheduled for processing in twenty 15-minute slots starting at 9:00 am and ending at 2:00 pm. Ten applications are scheduled in each slot.*

There are ten counters in the office, four dedicated to US applications, and two each for UK applications, Schengen applications and Others applications. Applicants are called in for processing sequentially on a first-come-first-served basis whenever a counter gets freed for their category. The processing time for an application is the same within each category. But it may vary across the categories. Each US and UK application requires 10 minutes of processing time. Depending on the number of applications in a category and time required to process an application for that category, it is possible that an applicant for a slot may be processed later.

On a particular day, Ira, Vijay and Nandini were scheduled for Schengen visa processing in that order. They had a 9:15 am slot but entered the VPO at 9:20 am. When they entered the office, exactly six out of the ten counters were either processing applications, or had finished processing one and ready to start processing the next.

Mahira and Osman were scheduled in the 9:30 am slot on that day for visa processing inthe Others category.

The following additional information is known about that day.

(i) All slots were full.
(ii) The number of US applications was the same in all the slots. The same was true for the other three categories.
(iii) 50% of the applications were US applications.
(iv) All applicants except Ira, Vijay and Nandini arrived on time.
(v) Vijay was called to a counter at 9:25 am.

1. How many UK applications were scheduled on that day?

2. What is the maximum possible value of the total time (in minutes, nearest to its integer value) required to process all applications in the Others category on that day?

3. Which of the following is the closest to the time when Nandini's application process got over?

(a) 9:45 am (b) 9:37 am
(c) 9:35 am (d) 9:50 am

4. Which of the following statements is false?

(a) The application process of Mahira started after Nandini's.
(b) The application process of Osman was completed before Vijay's.
(c) The application process of Osman was completed before 9:45 am.
(d) The application process of Mahira was completed before Nandini's.

5. When did the application processing for all US applicants get over on that day?

(a) 2:05 pm (b) 2:00 pm
(c) 3:40 pm (d) 2:25 pm

Directions for Questions 6 to 10: Faculty members in a management school can belong to one of four departments - Finance and Accounting (F&A), Marketing and Strategy (M&S), Operations and Quants (O&Q) and Behaviour and Human Resources (B&H). The numbers of faculty members in F&A, M&S, O&Q and B&H departments are 9, 7, 5 and 3 respectively.

Prof. Pakrasi, Prof. Qureshi, Prof. Ramaswamy and Prof. Samuel are four members of the school's faculty who were candidates for the post of the Dean of the school. Only one of the candidates was from O&Q.

Every faculty member, including the four candidates, voted for the post. In each department, all the faculty members who were not candidates voted for the same candidate. The rules for the election are listed below:

(i) There cannot be more than two candidates from a single department.
(ii) A candidate cannot vote for himself/herself.
(iii) Faculty members cannot vote for a candidate from their own department.

After the election, it was observed that Prof. Pakrasi received 3 votes, Prof. Qureshi received 14 votes, Prof. Ramaswamy received 6 votes and Prof. Samuel received 1 vote. Prof. Pakrasi voted for Prof. Ramaswamy, Prof. Qureshi for Prof. Samuel, Prof. Ramaswamy for Prof. Qureshi and Prof. Samuel for Prof. Pakrasi.

6. Which two candidates can belong to the same department?
(a) Prof. Pakrasi and Prof. Samuel
(b) Prof. Pakrasi and Prof. Qureshi
(c) Prof. Ramaswamy and Prof. Samuel
(d) Prof. Qureshi and Prof. Ramaswamy

7. Which of the following can be the number of votes that Prof. Qureshi received from a single department?
(a) 6 (b) 7
(c) 8 (d) 9

8. If Prof. Samuel belongs to B&H, which of the following statements is/are true?
Statement A: Prof. Pakrasi belongs to M&S.
Statement B: Prof. Ramaswamy belongs to O&Q.
(a) Neither statement A nor statement B
(b) Only statement A
(c) Only statement B
(d) Both statements A and B

9. What best can be concluded about the candidate from O&Q?
(a) It was Prof. Ramaswamy.
(b) It was either Prof. Ramaswamy or Prof. Samuel.
(c) It was either Prof. Pakrasi or Prof. Qureshi.
(d) It was Prof. Samuel.

10. Which of the following statements is/are true?
Statement A: Non-candidates from M&S voted for Prof. Qureshi.
Statement B: Non-candidates from F&A voted for Prof. Qureshi.
(a) Neither statement A nor statement B
(b) Both statements A and B
(c) Only statement A
(d) Only statement B

ANSWER KEY

1. 0	2. 200	3. (a)	4. (a)
5. (a)	6. (b)	7. (d)	8. (d)
9. (b)	10. (d)		

SOLUTIONS AND SHORTCUTS

Solutions for Questions 1 to 5: The basic information collated through the clues tells us a few basic things:

The number of applicants in every slot was 10. Each slot had the same number of US visa applications – as well as the same number of Schengen visa applications, UK visa applications and Others Visa applications.

(i) US visa applications were 50% of the total applications, hence there were 5 US visa applications in each slot.
(ii) In the 9:15 slot, there were 3 Schengen visa applicants (Ira, Vijay and Nandini). This means that every slot had 3 Schengen visa applicants.
(iii) Also, the 9:30 slot had two applicants for Others visa. This means that every slot had 2 Others visa applicants.
(iv) Since there are a total of 10 applicants in each slot, these are distributed as US 5, UK 0, Schengen 3 and Others 2.
(v) It is also given to us that a US visa application takes 10 mins to process.

Thus,

	9:00 Slot	9:15 Slot	9.30 Slot	9:45 Slot	10:00 Slot
US (4 counters)	5	5	5	5	5
UK (2 counters)	0	0	0	0	0
Schengen (2 counters)	3	3	3	3	3
Others (2 counters)	2	2	2	2	2

We can also work out the processing of the US visa applications. Applicants 1 to 4 will get processed from 9 - 9:10, Applicant 5 will get processed from 9:10 - 9:20. Applicants 6 to 8 will get processed from 9:15 to 9:25; Applicant 9 will get processed from 9:20 - 9:30 and applicant 10 will get processed from 9:25 to 9:35.

Going forward, applicant 11 to 13 will get processed from 9:30 - 9:40. Applicant 14 will get processed from 9:35 to 9:45 and Applicant 15 will get processed from 9:40 to 9:50. We need to work out the Schengen visa and the Others Visa Processing times. The following thought process helps us do that:

Schengen Visas: Ira, Vijay and Nandini entered the VPO at 9:20. Vijay is only called in at 9:25, which means that one of the counters was not free at 9:20. It gets free only at 9:25. This can only happen if there is a 12.5 minute processing time for Schengen visas. Thus, Applicant 1 and 2 would get processed from 9 to 9:12.5. Applicant 3, will be processed from 9:12.5 to 9:25; Applicant 4 (Ira) will get processed from 9:20 to 9:32.5; Applicant 5 (Vijay) is processed from 9:25 to 9:37.5. Applicant 6 (Nandini) will go to the counter only at 9:32.5 (when Ira's application is finished processing) and finish at 9:45.

Others Visas: There are two Others applications in every slot. We need to work out the processing time for the others applications. The key to that is in the statement about Ira, Vijay and Nandini.

'When they entered the office, exactly six out of the ten counters were either processing applications, or had finished processing one and ready to start processing the next.'

We know that the two UK counters are free the whole day. We also know that all 4 USA counters and 2 Schengen counters were working at 9:20 (from our analysis above). This means that the two Others counters must have become free before 9:20. This means that the processing time for the Others visas is <5 minutes.

Based on these deductions and realizations we can answer the given questions:

1. 0. There were no UK applications on that day.
2. Given that the processing time for the Others visa is less than 5 minutes (It can be 4.999 minutes) and that there are a total of 20 slots with 2 applicants each. It means that the total time in minutes required to process all applications has to be a maximum of 40 × 5 = 200 minutes.
3. Nandini's application process would get over at 9:45. Option (a) is correct.
4. Mahira's application process starts promptly at 9:30, while Nandini's is definitely later. Hence, option (a) is incorrect.
5. It can be seen that all US visa applications for each slot are ending 5 minutes into the next slot. Thus, the last of the 5 applications of 1:45 would end at 2:05 PM. Option (a) is correct.

Solutions for Questions 6 to 10: We can make the following table to understand the given situation:

	Pakrasi	Qureshi	Ramaswamy	Samuel
Total votes	3	14	6	1
Other candidates' votes – 1 each	Samuel	Ramaswamy	Pakrasi	Qureshi
Balance votes	2	13	5	0
First set of deductions	3. Pakrasi's 2 votes must come from B&H voters. Thus B&H would have 1 candidate for dean.	1. Ramaswamy's total of 13 votes can only be if he gets 9 votes from F&A and 4 votes from O&Q. This means that F&A has no candidates for dean and O&Q has 1.	2. Ramaswamy can only get 5 votes from M&S, and this means that M&S had two candi- dates in the fray for Dean's post.	3. He has received no votes from the balance votes.
Second set of deductions There are 2 candidates from M&S, 1 from O&Q and 1 from B&H	Belongs to M&S or O&Q	Belongs to M&S Or B&H	Belongs to O&Q or B&H	Belongs to O&Q, M&S or B&H
After final set of deductions *	M&S	M&S	O&Q/B&H	B&H/O&Q

Final set of deductions *

As per the current status of the table after the second set of deductions, the 2 M&S candidates can be either (a) Pakrasi and Qureshi or (b) Pakrasi and Samuel or (c) Qureshi and Samuel. However, we can eliminate both (b) and (c) on the following logic.

Elimination of Pakrasi and Samuel as the pair from M&S: It is given to us that faculty members cannot vote for a candidate from their own department. However, we are given that Samuel has voted for Pakrasi. This means that both of them cannot be from the same department.

Elimination of Qureshi and Samuel as the pair from M&S: It is given to us that faculty members cannot vote for a candidate from their own department. However, we are given that Qureshi has voted for Samuel. This means that both of them cannot be from the same department.

After this, the answers can be read off from the table.

6. Option (b) is correct.
7. Qureshi receives 9 votes from the F&A department. Hence, option (d) is correct.
8. Both Statements A and B are true. Hence, option (d) is correct.
9. It was either Ramaswamy or Samuel. Option (b) is correct.
10. Only Statement B is correct. Option (d) is correct.

SLOT 2

CAT 2023

Directions for Questions 1 to 5: There are nine boxes arranged in a 3 × 3 array as shown in Tables 1 and 2. Each box contains three sacks. Each sack has a certain number of coins, between 1 and 9, both inclusive.

The average number of coins per sack in the boxes are all distinct integers. The total number of coins in each row is the same. The total number of coins in each column is also the same.

TABLE 1

	1st Column	2nd Column	3rd Column
1st row		9	6
2nd row	2		
3rd row	8		

TABLE 2

	1st Column	2nd Column	3rd Column
1st row	1**	2*	2*
2nd row	1**	0*	3*
3rd row	3*	2**	0**

Table 1 gives information regarding the median of the numbers of coins in the three sacks in a box for some of the boxes. In Table 2 each box has a number which represents the number of sacks in that box having more than 5 coins. That number is followed by a * if the sacks in that box satisfy exactly one among the following three conditions, and it is followed by ** if two or more of these conditions are satisfied.

(i) The minimum among the numbers of coins in the three sacks in the box is 1.

(ii) The median of the numbers of coins in the three sacks is 1.

(iii) The maximum among the numbers of coins in the three sacks in the box is 9.

1. What is the total number of coins in all the boxes in the 3rd row?

(a) 15 (b) 36
(c) 45 (d) 30

2. How many boxes have at least one sack containing 9 coins?

(a) 5 (b) 8
(c) 3 (d) 4

3. For how many boxes are the average and median of the numbers of coins contained in the three sacks in that box the same?

4. How many sacks have exactly one coin?

5. In how many boxes do all three sacks contain different numbers of coins?

Directions for Questions 6 to 10: Anjali, Bipasha, and Chitra visited an entertainment park that has four rides. Each ride lasts one hour and can accommodate one visitor at one point. All rides begin at 9 am and must be completed by 5 pm except for Ride-3, for which the last ride has to be completed by 1 pm. Ride gates open every 30 minutes, e.g. 10 am, 10:30 am, and so on. Whenever a ride gate opens, and there is no visitor inside, the first visitor waiting in the queue buys the ticket just before taking the ride. The ticket prices are Rs. 20, Rs. 50, Rs. 30 and Rs. 40 for Rides 1 to 4, respectively. Each of the three visitors took at least one ride and did not necessarily take all rides. None of them took the same ride more than once. The movement time from one ride to another is negligible, and a visitor leaves the ride immediately after the completion of the ride. No one takes a break inside the park unless mentioned explicitly.

The following information is also known:

(i) Chitra never waited in the queue and completed her visit by 11 am after spending Rs. 50 to pay for the ticket(s).

(ii) Anjali took Ride-1 at 11 am after waiting for 30 mins for Chitra to complete it. It was the only ride where Anjali waited.

(iii) Bipasha began her first of three rides at 11:30 am. All three visitors incurred the same amount of ticket expense by 12:15 pm.

(iv) The last ride taken by Anjali and Bipasha was the same, where Bipasha waited 30 mins for Anjali to complete her ride. Before standing in the queue for that ride, Bipasha took a 1-hour coffee break after completing her previous ride.

6. What was the total amount spent on tickets (in Rs.) by Bipasha?
(a) 110 (b) 100
(c) 120 (d) 90

7. Which were all the rides that Anjali completed by 2:00 pm?
(a) Ride-1 and Ride-3
(b) Ride-1, Ride-2, and Ride-3
(c) Ride-1, Ride-2, and Ride-4
(d) Ride-1 and Ride-4

8. Which ride was taken by all three visitors?
(a) Ride-3 (b) Ride-2
(c) Ride-1 (d) Ride-4

9. How many rides did Anjali and Chitra take in total?

10. What was the total amount spent on tickets (in Rs.) by Anjali?

Directions for Questions 11 to 15: Odsville has five firms - Alfloo, Bzygoo, Czechy, Drjbna and Elavalaki. Each of these firms was founded in some year and also closed down a few years later.

Each firm raised Rs. 1 crore in its first and last year of existence. The amount each firm raised every year increased until it reached a maximum, and then decreased until the firm closed down. No firm raised the same amount of money in two consecutive years. Each annual increase and decrease was either by Rs. 1 crore or by Rs. 2 crores.

The table below provides partial information about the five firms.

Firm	First year of existence	Last year of existence	Total amount raised (Rs.crores)
Alfloo	2009	2016	21
Bzygoo	2012	2015	
Czechy	2013		9
Drjbna	2011	2015	10
Elavalaki	2010		13

11. For which firm(s) can the amounts raised by them be concluded with certainty in each year?
(a) Only Drjbna
(b) Only Czechy
(c) Only Bzygoo and Czechy and Drjbna
(d) Only Czechy and Drjbna

12. What best can be concluded about the total amount of money raised in 2015?
(a) It is either Rs. 7 crores or Rs. 8 crores.
(b) It is exactly Rs. 8 crores.
(c) It is either Rs. 8 crores or Rs. 9 crores.
(d) It is either Rs. 7 crores or Rs. 8 crores or Rs. 9 crores.

13. What is the largest possible total amount of money (in Rs. crores) that could have been raised in 2013?

14. If Elavalaki raised Rs. 3 crores in 2013, then what is the smallest possible total amount of money (in Rs. crores) that could have been raised by all the companies in 2012?
(a) 12 (b) 11
(c) 10 (d) 9

15. If the total amount of money raised in 2014 is Rs. 12 crores, then which of the following is not possible?
(a) Alfloo raised the same amount of money as Drjbna in 2013.
(b) Bzygoo raised more money than Elavalaki in 2014.
(c) Bzygoo raised the same amount of money as Elavalaki in 2013.
(d) Alfloo raised the same amount of money as Bzygoo in 2014.

ANSWER KEY

1. (c)	2. (a)	3. 4	4. 9
5. 5	6. (a)	7. (b)	8. (c)
9. 6	10. 140	11. (d)	12. (a)
13. 17	14. (b)	15. (c)	

SOLUTIONS AND SHORTCUTS

Solutions for Questions 1 to 5: The given situation can be represented in a tabular form as shown. The numbers in parentheses in the table, refer to the deduction number that leads us to fill the numbers in the cell. However, before we head to the table, there are a couple of starting deductions:

Initial Deductions: The sum of the number of coins in each box has to be a multiple of 3 (as the average number of coins in per each in each box is a distinct integer) - this means that the 9 boxes have a total of 3, 6, 9, 12, 15, 18, 21, 24 and 27 =135 coins in total. Thus, every row and every column would have a total of 135/3 = 45 coins.

	Column 1	Column 2	Column 3	
Row 1	1, 1, 7 (Deduction 2) Average 3	3, 9, 9 (Deduction 1) Average 7	1, 6, 8 (Deduction 3) Average 5	45
Row 2	1, 2, 9 (Deduction 4) Average 4	1, 2, 3 (Deduction 5) Average 2	9, 9, 9 (Deduction 5) Average 9	45
Row 3	7, 8, 9 (Deduction 6) Average 8	1, 8, 9 (Deduction 6) Average 6	1, 1, 1 (Deduction 6) Average 1	45
Total	45	45	45	

Deduction 1: Row 1 column 2 has a median value of 9. Hence, it's 3rd number must be 9. Also, since this box has only 2 numbers above 5 and the sum of the box has to be a multiple of 3, we conclude that the first number in this box is 3.

Deduction 2: Row 1 Column 1. The two conditions it obeys has to be minimum coins 1 and median of the numbers of coins being 1. Thus, the number of coins in the three sacks in this box have to be 1, 1, 7. This is because, if we try to use the third condition there is an internal contradiction that occurs in row 1. (If we take 9 as maximum value being one of the conditions satisfied, then the sum of the three numbers in this box would have to be minimum 12, in such a case, the sum of the row 1 column 3 box has to be maximum 6, which is not possible, since that box has 2 numbers above 5.)

Deduction 3: Row 1 Column 3, we know the median is 6. Also, since row 1 column 1 and column 2 numbers add up to 9 + 21 = 30, this box would have a sum of 15. Hence, we cannot use 9 as the maximum value of this box. Thus, the single condition that must be satisfied in this box is that the minimum value is 1. The box contains sacks with 1, 6 and 8 coins.

Deduction 4: Row 2 Column 1, has to satisfy minimum 1 and maximum 9 condition. Thus, the numbers here are 1, 2, 9 and this box has an average of 4.

Deduction 5: From our initial deductions we know that there has to be a box where the average of the number of coins in the sacks is 9. This means that there is a 9, 9, 9 box. For this box all three numbers are above 5. Looking at Table 2 in the question there are only 2 boxes where all three numbers are above 5. The box in Row 3 column 1 and the box in row 2 column 3. We also see that the box in row 3 column 1 cannot have all three 9s since it's median is 8. Thus, Row 2 column 3 would have a (9, 9, 9) pattern. This then means that Row 2 column 2 has to total 6 and obey exactly one condition. This can be done only by using a 1, 2, 3 pattern for this box.

Deduction 6: The averages left to be allocated to the 3rd row are 1, 6 and 8. This means that Row 3 Column 3 has to have a 1, 1, 1 pattern. Row 3 Column 2 has to have a 7, 8, 9 pattern for an average of 8 (and obeying exactly 1 condition of maximum value being 9). For row 3 Column 2 (average 6 and total 18), we are given that there are two numbers above 5 and it also obeys 2 of the 3 conditions. This can only be if we use 1, 8, 9.

This completes the table and the answers can be read off the table.

1. Each row has 45 coins. Option (c) is correct.
2. 1 in the first row, 2 each in rows 2 and 3. Hence, a total of 5. Option (a) is correct.
3. This is exhibited by row 2 columns 2 and 3 and row 3 columns 1 and 3. Hence, 4.
4. 3 in the first row, 2 in the second row, 4 in the third row. Hence, 9.
5. Row 1 columns 3, rows 2 and 3 columns 1 and 2 each. Hence, 5.

Solutions for Questions 6 to 10: We need the following set of deductions to get us through to the answer.

Deduction 1: From Clues 1 and 2, we get that Chitra must have taken ride 1 from 10-11 and hence must have taken Ride 3 from 9 to 10 (as she has spent a total of 50 rupees and completed her visit by 11). Also, Anjali must have reached ride 1 at 10:30 and hence got the ride at 11 after waiting from 30 minutes. Further Anjali must have taken ride three either from 9:30 to 10:30 or from 12 -1 (since she has to spend a total of 50 rupees before 12:15) and she has not waited apart from for ride 1.

Deduction 2: Bipasha's first ride must have been the Ride 2 (as she has to spend 50 rupees before 12:15 and this can only be done by going for Ride 2 from 11:30 to 12:30. Further, it is given to us that nobody took a break except mentioned specifically. The clue 4 tells us that Bipasha waited for 30 minutes after a coffee break of 1 hour before her last ride. Since, Bipasha has taken 3 rides and started at 11:30, it means that she will take a total of 4 hours 30 minutes, if she had no waiting time in her second ride. In that case, her last ride would have to be from 3 to 4.

Deduction 3: Combining deductions 1 and 2 and from clue 4 talking about Anjali and Bipasha having the same last ride, it is obvious that the last ride for both of them is Ride 4. All conditions fit in only if we have Anjali take ride 4 at 2 PM to 3 PM, followed by Bipasha who must have taken that ride from 3 PM to 4 PM. This also means that since Anjali has not waited, she must have taken ride 2 during 1 to 2 PM. Also, Bipasha must have gone on ride 1 from 12:30 to 1:30 PM.

The final table looks as that shown and the answers can be read off it.

	Ride 1 (20)	Ride 2 (50)	Ride 3 (30) Closes at 1 PM	Ride 4 (40)
Anjali	Reached here at 10:30, Ride from 11 AM – 12 Noon	1 to 2 PM	12 Noon – 1 PM	2- 3 PM
Bipasha	12:30 to 1:30 PM	11:30 AM - 12:30 PM		3 to 4 PM
Chitra	10 to 11 AM		9 to 10 AM	

6. 20 + 50 + 40 = 110.
7. Option (b) is correct.
8. Ride 1. Option (c) is correct.
9. 4 + 2 = 6.
10. Anjali went on all 4 rides and hence spend 20 + 50 + 30 + 40 = 140.

Solutions for Questions 11 to 15: The given situation can be encapsulated on a table as shown:

TABLE 1

Year/Firm	2009	2010	2011	2012	2013	2014	2015	2016	2017?	Balance total
A	1	2	3	4/5	5/4	3	2	1		19
B	XXX	XXX	XXX	1	2/3	3/2	1	XXX	XXX	7
C					1	2	3	2	1	9
D	XXX	XXX	1	2	4	2	1	XXX	XXX	10
E – 5 year pattern	XXX	1	3	5	3	1	XXX	XXX	XXX	13
E- 6 year pattern	XXX	1	2	3/4	4/3	2	1	XXX	XXX	13

The following logics have led to table 1:

Row for B: B has a 4 year cycle from 2012 to 2015. In 2013 B's funding can be either 2 or 3 crores. In these cases, it's funding in 2014 would be 3 or 2 crores respectively. There is no other possibility for a 4 year cycle starting from 1 and ending at 1 with increments and decrements of + 1, + 2, - 1 and - 2 only.

Row for C: C's row can be completely worked out. It has a funding of 1 crore in first year of existence (2012) and 1 crore in last year of existence (Year unknown). The total funding being 9 crore, it means that the other years have to add up to 7 crores. Under the given conditions, it can only occur with a 3 year pattern of 2, 3, 2. Thus, C had a 5 year existence from 2013 to 2017 and it's funds raised were 1, 2, 3, 2, 1 = 9 crores.

Row for D: D's row can be completely worked out. It has a funding of 1 crore in first year of existence (2011) and 1 crore in last year of existence (Year 2015). The total funding being 10 crore, it means that the other 3 years have to add up to 8 crores. Under the given conditions, it can only occur with a 3 year pattern of 2, 4, 2. Thus, D had a 5 year existence from 2011 to 2015 and it's funds raised were 1, 2, 4, 2, 1 = 10 crores.

Row for A: A's first and last years are 2009 and 2016 and it got funding of 1 crore each during those years. Between 2010 to 2015, for 6 years, A raised a funding of 19 crore more. There are multiple ways this can occur. 2, 3, 4, 5, 3, 2 and 2, 3, 5, 4, 3, 2 are the two patterns that will satisfy the conditions.

Row for E: E's first year is 2010 and last year is unknown. It raises 1 crore in 2010 and 1 crore in it's last year while raising a total of 13 crores. Thus, in the intermediate years it raised 11 crores. Patterns possible are:

(i) 3 intermediate years with 3, 5, 3 - giving a 5 year pattern from 2010 to 2014 as 1, 3, 5, 3, 1

(ii) 4 intermediate years with 2, 3, 4, 2 - giving a 6 year pattern from 2010 to 2015 as 1, 2, 3, 4, 2, 1.

(iii) 4 intermediate years with 2, 4, 3, 2 - giving a 6 year pattern from 2010 to 2015 as 1, 2, 4, 3, 2, 1.

The answers can be read off the table.

11. We are certain only about C and D. Option (d) is correct.
12. It will be either 7 or 8 crores depending on whether E shuts down in 2014 or 2015. Hence, option (a) is correct.
13. The maximum would be got if A raises 4, B raises 3 and E raises 4. The total in such a case becomes 5 + 3 + 1 + 4 + 4 = 17.
14. 4 (A) + 1 (B) + 2 (D) + 4 (E) = 11.
15. 12 would occur in 2014 only for 3 (A) + 3 (B) + 2 (C) + 2 (D) + 2 (E) = 12. Option (c) can be seen to be false in this case, as B would raise 2 crore in 2013, while E would raise either 3 or 4 crore in 2013. Hence, option (c) is the correct answer.

SLOT 3

CAT 2023

Directions for Questions 1 to 5: There are only three female students - Amala, Koli and Rini - and only three male students - Biman, Mathew and Shyamal - in a course. The course has two evaluation components, a project and a test. The aggregate score in the course is a weighted average of the two components, with the weights being positive and adding to 1.

The projects are done in groups of two, with each group consisting of a female and a male student. Both the group members obtain the same score in the project.

The following additional facts are known about the scores in the project and the test.

(i) The minimum, maximum and the average of both project and test scores were identical - 40, 80 and 60, respectively.

(ii) The test scores of the students were all multiples of 10; four of them were distinct and the remaining two were equal to the average test scores.

(iii) Amala's score in the project was double that of Koli in the same, but Koli scored 20 more than Amala in the test. Yet Amala had the highest aggregate score.

(iv) Shyamal scored the second highest in the test. He scored two more than Koli, but two less than Amala in the aggregate.

(v) Biman scored the second lowest in the test and the lowest in the aggregate.

(vi) Mathew scored more than Rini in the project, but less than her in the test.

1. What was Rini's score in the project?

2. What was the weight of the test component?

(a) 0.75 (b) 0.50
(c) 0.60 (d) 0.40

3. What was the maximum aggregate score obtained by the students?

(a) 66 (b) 68
(c) 80 (d) 62

4. What was Mathew's score in the test?

5. Which of the following pairs of students were part of the same project team?

(i) Amala and Biman
(ii) Koli and Mathew

(a) Neither (i) nor (ii)
(b) Both (i) and (ii)
(c) Only (i)
(d) Only (ii)

Directions for Questions 6 to 10: A, B, C, D, E and F are the six police stations in an area, which are connected by streets as shown below. Four teams - Team 1, Team 2, Team 3 and Team 4 - patrol these streets continuously between 09:00 hrs. and 12:00 hrs. each day.

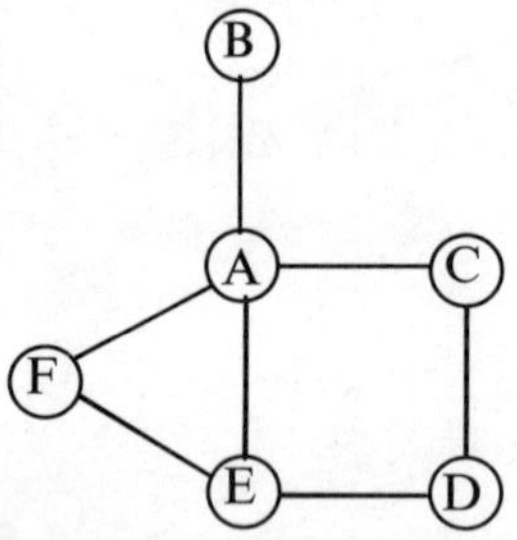

The teams need 30 minutes to cross a street connecting one police station to another. All four teams start from Station A at 09:00 hrs. and must return to Station A by 12:00 hrs. They can also pass via Station A at any point on their journeys. The following facts are known:

(i) None of the streets has more than one team traveling along it in any direction at any point in time.

(ii) Teams 2 and 3 are the only ones in stations E and D respectively at 10:00 hrs.

(iii) Teams 1 and 3 are the only ones in station E at 10:30 hrs.

(iv) Teams 1 and 4 are the only ones in stations B and E respectively at 11:30 hrs.

(v) Team 1 and Team 4 are the only teams that patrol the street connecting stations A and E.

(vi) Team 4 never passes through Stations B, D or F.

6. Which one among the following stations is visited the largest number of times?

(a) Station D (b) Station C
(c) Station F (d) Station E

7. How many times do the teams pass through Station B in a day?
8. Which team patrols the street connecting Stations D and E at 10:15 hrs?
   (a) Team 2 (b) Team 1
   (c) Team 4 (d) Team 3
9. How many times does Team 4 pass through Station E in a day?
10. How many teams pass through Station C in a day?
   (a) 2 (b) 1
   (c) 3 (d) 4

ANSWER KEY

1. 60	2. (c)	3. (b)	4. 40
5. (a)	6. (d)	7. 2	8. (d)
9. 2	10. (a)		

SOLUTIONS AND SHORTCUTS

Solutions for Questions 1 to 5: The following tables can be made with respect to the scores in the project and the test:

TABLE 1: SCORE IN PROJECT

Score	Female Student	Male Student
80	Amala (Deduction 1)	Matthew (Deduction 2)
60	Rini (Deduction 1)	Shyamal (Deduction 5)
40	Koli (Deduction 1)	Biman (Deduction 5)

TABLE 2: SCORE IN TEST

Score	Student Name
80 (Deduction 3)	Koli (Deduction 4)
70 (Deduction 3)	Shyamal (Clue 4)
60 (Deduction 3)	Amala (Deduction 4)
60 (Deduction 3)	Rini (Deduction 6)
50 (Deduction 3)	Biman (Clue 5)
40 (Deduction 3)	Matthew (Deduction 6)

Deductions for the project table:

Deduction 1: Clue 3 can be interpreted as Koli scores 40 and Amala scores 80. Hence, Rini scores 60 marks in her project.

Deduction 2: Clue 6 can be interpreted as Matthew scored 80 marks in the project and hence is Amala's partner.

Deduction 3: From the clues 1 and 2, we can work out that the scores for the test for the six students would be 40, 50, 60, 60, 70, 80.

Deduction 4: Koli and Amala would score either **Case 1: 60, 40** in the test or **Case 2: 80, 60** –(since Koli scored 20 marks more than Amala in the test).

Note: We know from Clue 4 that in terms of aggregate scores: The values for Amala, Shyamal and Koli are x, x-2 and x-4 respectively. Also from the options for the second question in the set, we know the possible weights for the project and test scores as: (0.25, 0.75) Option (a); (0.40, 0.60) Option (b); (0.60, 0.40) Option (c); (0.50, 0.50) Option (d)

Checking Case 1 (Test Scores: Koli 60, Amala 40): If we check Case 1 by corelating it to the weights provided for the project and test scores from the second question in the set we get the following calculations:

Option 1: Amala's score $0.25 \times 80 + 0.75 \times 40 = 50$; Koli's score $0.25 \times 40 + 0.75 \times 60 = 55$ (rejected)

Option 2: Amala's score $0.40 \times 80 + 0.60 \times 40 = 56$; Koli's score $0.40 \times 40 + 0.60 \times 60 = 52$;

(Possible). In this case, Shyamal's score needs to be exactly 54. We also know Shyamal has scored 70 in the test. So $0.40 \times (40 \text{ or } 60) + 0.60 \times 70$ is his total score. It can be seen that in no case does he end up with a score of 54. Hence, we reject this possibility too.

Option 3: Amala's score: $0.60 \times 80 + 0.40 \times 40 = 64$; Koli's score: $0.60 \times 40 + 0.40 \times 60 = 48$ (rejected)

Option 4: Amala's score: $0.5 \times 80 + 0.5 \times 40 = 60$; Koli's score: $0.5 \times 40 + 0.5 \times 60 = 50$ (rejected)

Thus, we reject this case. Hence, Koli scored 80 in the test and Amala scored 60.

Deduction 5: We also know that the difference in aggregate scores for Amala and Koli would be 4 only for weights of 0.4 (project) and 0.6 (test). In that case, Amala's aggregate $= 0.40 \times 80 + 0.60 \times 60 = 68$; Koli's aggregate $= 0.40 \times 40 + 0.60 \times 80 = 64$ and Shyamal's aggregate needs to be 66. This can only occur if he scores 60 in the project and hence must be Rini's partner. ($0.40 \times 60 + 0.60 \times 70 = 66$). Consequently, Biman will be Koli's partner

Deduction 6: We are left to split 40 and 60 test scores between Matthew and Rini and according to Clue 6, Rini > Matthew. Hence, Matthew scored 40 in the test and Rini scored 60.

The answers can be read off the table:

1. 60.
2. Checking option (c) we see that Amala's aggregate $= 0.40 \times 80 + 0.60 \times 60 = 68$; Koli's aggregate $= 0.40 \times 40 + 0.60 \times 80 = 64$. This is the only possibility where Amala scores 4 more than Koli. Hence, option (c) is correct.
3. Amala's aggregate of 68 is the maximum. Option (b) is correct.
4. Matthew scored 40.
5. Neither Amala Biman, nor Koli Matthew were a pair of the same project team. Hence, option (a) is correct.

Solutions for Questions 6 to 10: The following set of deductions helps us create the routes followed by each:

Deduction 1: Team 3 is at D at 10:00 (Clue 2) and at E at 10:30 (Clue 3). Hence, Team 3 follows the route A-C-D-E from 9 to 10:30.

Deduction 2: Team 2 is at E at 10:00 (Clue 2). Hence, it follows the route A-F-E from 9 to 10.

Deduction 3: Team 4 only travels the routes AE or AC (as it does not pass through stations B,D or F). Also, it is at E at 11:30, hence it must have followed the route A-E-A-C-A-E-A from 9 to 12.

Deduction 4: Team 1 is at E at 10:30 and at B at 11:30 (Clues 3 and 4). The only way this is possible is if Team 1 follows the route A-B-A-E-A-B-A from 9 to 12.

Thus, we can create the following tables for the movement of the four teams:

	9 to 9:30	9:30 to 10	10 to 10:30	10:30 to 11	11 to 11:30	11:30 to 12
Team 1	A-B	B-A	A-E	E-A	A-B	B-A
Team 2	A-F	F-E	?	?	?	?
Team 3	A-C	C-D	D-E	?	?	?
Team 4	A-E	E-A	A-C	C-A	A-E	E-A

Note: We cannot find out where teams 2 and 3 went once they reached E (both teams could have completed their circuit or reversed direction and gone back the route they came). Thus, Team 2 could have taken A-F-E-F-A (and reached back to A at 11 and then made a further two way trip to or C to reach A at 12). Alternately, it could have gone on in the route A-F-E-D-C-A (reaching A at 11:30). Likewise there would be two possibilities for Team 3 too - however, there is no information to ascertain the direction they took after 10 and 10:30 respectively.

Note: The problem states that the teams have to return to A 12:00 hours, which means that they can return to A before 12 too. Hence, we cannot determine the remaining chart of team 2 and 3's movements.

The answers can be read off the deductions we have made till now.

6. It can be seen that, E is visited by each of the teams and also twice by team 4. Hence, E is the most visited station. Option (d) is correct.
7. Only team 1 goes through station B – and it does so twice. The correct answer is 2.
8. Team 3. Option (d) is correct.
9. 2
10. Teams 3 and 4. Hence, 2. Option (a) is correct.

SLOT 1

CAT 2022

Directions for Questions 1 to 5: The management of a university hockey team was evaluating performance of four women players - Amla, Bimla, Harita and Sarita, for their possible selection in the university team for next year. For this purpose, the management was looking at the number of goals scored by them in the past 8 matches, numbered 1 through 8. The four players together had scored a total of 12 goals in these matches. In the 8 matches, each of them had scored at least one goal. No two players had scored the same total number of goals.

The following facts are known about the goals scored by these four players only. All the questions refer only to the goals scored by these four players.

(i) Only one goal was scored in every even numbered match.
(ii) Harita scored more goals than Bimla.
(iii) The highest goal scorer scored goals in exactly 3 matches including Match 4 and Match 8.
(iv) Bimla scored a goal in Match 1 and one each in three other consecutive matches.
(v) An equal number of goals were scored in Match 3 and Match 7, which was different from the number of goals scored in either Match 1 or Match 5.
(vi) The match in which the highest number of goals was scored is unique and it was not Match 5.

1. How many goals were scored in Match 7?
(a) 3 (b) Cannot be determined
(c) 2 (d) 1

2. Which of the following is the correct sequence of goals scored in matches 1, 3, 5 and 7?
(a) 3, 1, 2, 1 (b) 4, 1, 2, 1
(c) 5, 1, 0, 1 (d) 3, 2, 1, 2

3. Which of the following statement(s) is/are true?
Statement-1: Amla and Sarita never scored goals in the same match.
Statement-2: Harita and Sarita never scored goals in the same match.
(a) Statement-1 only
(b) Both the statements
(c) None of the statements
(d) Statement-2 only

4. Which of the following statement(s) is/are false?
Statement-1: In every match at least one player scored a goal.
Statement-2: No two players scored goals in the same number of matches.
(a) None of the statements
(b) Statement-1 only
(c) Statement-2 only
(d) Both the statements

5. If Harita scored goals in one more match as compared to Sarita, which of the following statement(s) is/are necessarily true?
Statement-1: Amla scored goals in consecutive matches.
Statement-2: Sarita scored goals in consecutive matches.
(a) None of the statements
(b) Statement-1 only
(c) Both the statements
(d) Statement-2 only

Directions for Questions 6 to 10:

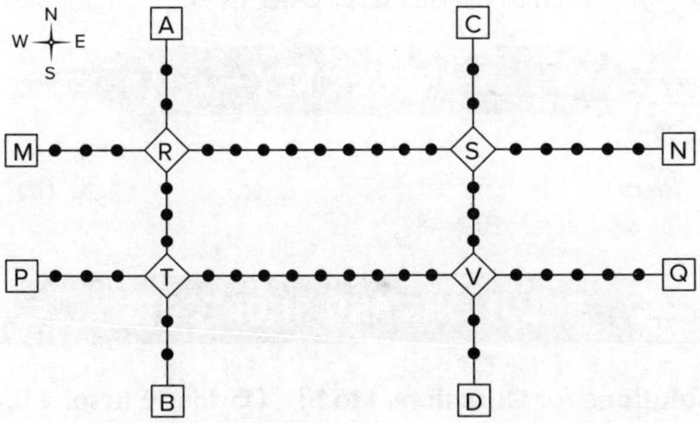

Given above is the schematic map of the metro lines in a city with rectangles denoting terminal stations (e.g. A), diamonds denoting junction stations (e.g. R) and small filled-up circles denoting other stations. Each train runs either in east-west or north-south direction, but not both. All trains stop for 2 minutes at each of the junction stations on the way and for 1 minute at each of the other stations. It takes 2 minutes to reach the next station for trains going in east-west direction and 3 minutes to reach the next station for trains going in north-south direction. From each terminal station, the first train starts at 6 am; the last trains leave the terminal stations at midnight. Otherwise, during the service hours, there are metro service every 15 minutes in the north-south lines and every 10 minutes in the east-west lines. A train must rest for at least 15 minutes after completing a trip at the terminal station, before it can undertake the next trip in the reverse direction.

(All questions are related to this metro service only. Assume that if someone reaches a station exactly at the time a train is supposed to leave, (s)he can catch that train.)

6. If Hari is ready to board a train at 8:05 am from station M, then when is the earliest that he can reach station N?
   (a) 9:01 am (b) 9:13 am
   (c) 9:06 am (d) 9:11 am
7. If Priya is ready to board a train at 10:25 am from station T, then when is the earliest that she can reach station S?
   (a) 11:22 am (b) 11:28 am
   (c) 11:12 am (d) 11:07 am
8. Haripriya is expected to reach station S late. What is the latest time by which she must be ready to board at station S if she must reach station B before 1 am via station R?
   (a) 11:35 pm (b) 11:39 pm
   (c) 11:43 pm (d) 11:49 am
9. What is the minimum number of trains that are required to provide the service on the AB line (considering both north and south directions)?
10. What is the minimum number of trains that are required to provide service in this city?

ANSWER KEY

1. (d)	2. (b)	3. (b)	4. (a)
5. (a)	6. (d)	7. (c)	8. (b)
9. 8	10. 48		

SOLUTIONS AND SHORTCUTS

Solutions for Questions 1 to 5: Obviously, to solve this question, we are going to create a table of goals for every match, segregated by the player name. The following set of deductions lead us to the answers:

Deduction 1: The total number of goals scored by the four players would be either 1, 2, 4, 5 or 1, 2, 3, 6 (these are the only possible values wherein everyone scores a different number of goals and the total comes to 12). To decide between these two possibilities, we can use clues 2 and 4 together. Clue 4 tells us that Bimla scored in 4 matches (at least). Hence, she would have a minimum of 4 goals, while at the same time, Harita has scored more goals than her (clue 2). This can only mean that the number of goals scored by the four girls is 1, 2, 4 (Bimla), 5 (Harita).

Deduction 2: From Clue 3, we have that Harita's 5 goals have to be in matches 4, 8 (1 goal each) and 3 goals in one more match, whose number we cannot work out unless we interpret the clues 5 and 6.

Deduction 3: The number of goals in the even matches are 1 each, which means that the matches 2, 4, 6, 8 account for exactly 4 goals. The odd numbered matches account for 8 goals, which are shared with the pattern that Match 3 = Match 7 and Matches 1 and 5 have different number of goals, which are different from each other. If we add the interpretation of clue 6 to this, we can make out that the highest number of goals scored would be in Match 1. We also have to adjust 3 goals for Harita in one match. The only way to distribute 8 goals in 4 odd numbered matches such that all these conditions are met is Match 1 = 4 goals; Match 3 = 1 goal; Match 5 = 2 goals; Match 7 = 1 goal.

Deduction 4: Bimla has scored one goal in match 1 (given) and not scored a goal in matches 4 and 8 (since the goals in those matches are scored by Harita- the highest scorer). This means that her 3 consecutive goals in 3 consecutive matches can only be fit into matches 5-6-7. Inserting all these deductions into the table for the 8 matches, we will get the following solution table. Note that, we are not able to determine between Amla and Sarita, as to who scored 1 goal and who scored 2. We are also not able to determine who scored the single remaining goal of match 5 as well as who amongst Amla and Sarita scored the single goals in matches 2 and 3.

Solution Table:

	Match 1	Match 2	Match 3	Match 4	Match 5	Match 6	Match 7	Match 8	Total
Amla	0			0		0	0	0	1/2
Bimla	1	0	0	0	1	1	1	0	4
Harita	3	0	0	1	0	0	0	1	5
Sarita	0			0		0	0	0	2/1
Total	4	1	1	1	2	1	1	1	12

We can answer the questions asked based on our reading of the table:

1. There was 1 goal scored in Match 7. Option (d) is the correct answer.
2. 4, 1, 2, 1 is the correct sequence. Option (b) is the correct answer.
3. Both the statements are true. Option (b) is the correct answer.
4. It can be seen that the first statement is true. The second statement is also true, since Bimla scored in 4 matches, Harita in 3, while Amla/Sarita would have scored in 1/2 matches in some order. Hence, both the statements are true. Option (a) is the correct answer.
5. In this case, Sarita would have scored in 2 matches, which means that she scored 1 goal each in any two of matches 2, 3 and 5. Statement 1 is clearly false, while statement 2 is a possibility but cannot be seen as necessarily true. Hence, Option (a) is the correct answer.

Solutions for Questions 6 to 10: From the information given, We deduce that A, B, C, D, M, N, P and Q are terminal stations and R, S, T and V are junction stations. Before we solve the questions in the set, we need to collect and organise the following information:

1. In the east west direction, inter-station time = 2 minutes, stoppage at other stations 1 minute, stoppage at junction station = 2 minutes. Thus a train leaving M for N at 6 am, will take have a travel time of 40 minutes (19 intermediate stations before reaching the terminal station N- so a total of 20 stations to traverse). Also, it's stoppage time would be: 17 × 1 + 2 × 2 = 21 minutes. Thus, the train leaving M at 6 am would reach N at 7:01 am and be ready to commence the return journey at 7:16 am. Also, note that the metro service would have trains departing M and N; P and Q respectively every 10 minutes.
2. In the North South direction, inter-station time = 3 minutes, stoppage at other stations 1 minute, stoppage at junction station = 2 minutes. Thus a train leaving A for B at 6 am, will take have a travel time of 30 minutes (9 intermediate stations before reaching the terminal station B- so a total of 10 stations to traverse). Also, its stoppage time would be: 7 × 1 + 2 × 2 = 11 minutes. Thus, the train leaving A at 6 am would reach B at 6:41 am (and vice versa) and be ready to commence the return journey at 6:56 am. Also, note that the metro service would have trains departing A and B; C and D respectively every 15 minutes.

   Lets now look at each question individually:

6. Although Hari is ready to board at 8:05 am, he can catch the train earliest at 8:10 am on the East-West Corridor to go from M to N.
   Commuting time = 20 × 2 = 40 mins
   Stoppage time = 17 × 1 min + 2 × 2 mins = 21 mins
   Total time = 40 + 21 = 61 mins.
   Therefore the earliest he can reach N is 9:11 am. Hence, option (d) is the correct answer.
7. Priya can go to S from T either via R or Via V. Both the routes involve the same number of stations in the South-North direction and the same number of stations in the East-West direction. This means that the in-train travel time for both the routes would be same. Hence, the preference would be for taking the route that would have the least waiting time.
   The train from P would come at 10:31 but the train from B would come at 10:26. So we can choose the T-R-S route as we get a headstart of 5 mins. The train would leave T at 10:28 and would reach R at 10:43 am. The train from M would reach R at 10:41 and be ready to leave at 10:43 am. Hence there would be no waiting time at R. This means that the total waiting time on this route is not increased at R. Further, it would take 29 mins to reach S from R. Therefore, Priya would be at S by 11:12 am. Hence, Option (c) is the correct answer.
8. To reach B at 1:00 am, Haripriya needs to catch the last North South train at R (this train would leave R at 12:13 am). So, she has to reach R before 12:13 am. The commute time from S to R is 29 minutes, which means that she has to catch a train at S for R at 11:44 or earlier (as per availability). The train just before 11:44 arrives at S at 11:37 pm and would depart from S towards r at 11:39 pm. So, Haripriya should be ready at S latest by 11:39 pm Hence, Option (b) is the correct answer.
9. We have already worked out that the total commuting time from terminal A to B (or B to A) = 41 mins (Includes wait time & travel time). So, the train that leaves A for B, would be ready for the return journey at 6:56 am.
   A train leaves station B every 15 mins. So, from 6 am to 6:45 am we would have 4 new trains and then at 7 am onwards the train which arrived from A would be ready for departure from B. Similarly, 4 trains would be required from A. Hence the answer is 8.
10. As deduced in the previous question, we would have 8 trains on the A-B route. Similarly, we would have 8 trains on the C-D route. Similarly, for the M-N and P-Q route, we would have 16 trains each. Hence, the answer is 48.

SLOT 2

CAT 2022

Directions for Questions 1 to 5: A specialty supermarket sells 320 products. Each of these products was either a cosmetic product or a nutrition product. Each of these products was also either a foreign product or a domestic product. Each of these products had at least one of two approvals – FDA or EU.

The following facts are also known:

(i) There were equal numbers of domestic and foreign products.

(ii) Half of the domestic products were FDA-approved cosmetic products.

(iii) None of the foreign products had both the approvals, while 60 domestic products had both the approvals.

(iv) There were 140 nutrition products, half of them were foreign products.

(v) There were 200 FDA-approved products. 70 of them were foreign products and 120 of them were cosmetic products.

1. How many foreign products were FDA-approved cosmetic products?

2. How many cosmetic products did not have FDA approval?

(a) Cannot be determined
(b) 50
(c) 10
(d) 60

3. Which among the following options best represents the number of domestic cosmetic products that had both the approvals?

(a) At least 10 and at most 60
(b) At least 20 and at most 50
(c) At least 10 and at most 80
(d) At least 20 and at most 70

4. If 70 cosmetic products did not have EU approval, then how many nutrition products had both the approvals?

(a) 10 (b) 30
(c) 50 (d) 20

5. If 50 nutrition products did not have EU approval, then how many domestic cosmetic products did not have EU approval?

Directions for Questions 6 to 10: Every day a widget supplier supplies widgets from the warehouse (W) to four locations – Ahmednagar (A), Bikrampore (B), Chitrachak (C), and Deccan Park (D). The daily demand for widgets in each location is uncertain and independent of each other. Demands and corresponding probability values (in parenthesis) are given against each location (A, B, C, and D) in the figure below. For example, there is a 40% chance that the demand in Ahmednagar will be 50 units and a 60% chance that the demand will be 70 units. The lines in the figure connecting the locations and warehouses represent two-way roads connecting those places with the distances (in km) shown beside the line. The distances in both the directions along a road are equal. For example, the road from Ahmednagar to Bikrampore and the road from Bikrampore to Ahmednagar are both 6 km long.

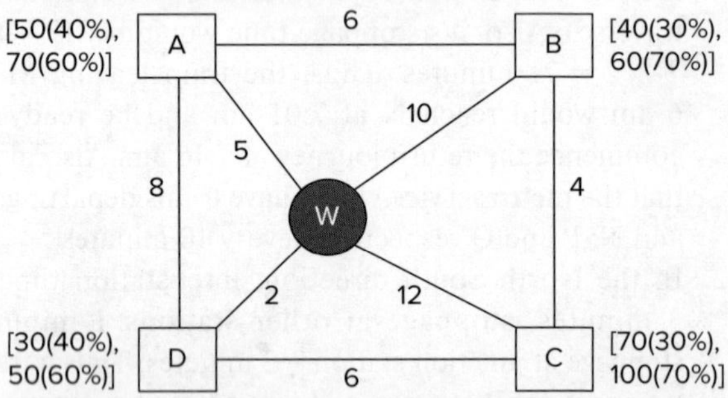

Every day the supplier gets the information about the demand values of the four locations and creates the travel route that starts from the warehouse and ends at a location after visiting all the locations exactly once. While making the route plan, the supplier goes to the locations in decreasing order of demand. If there is a tie for the choice of the next location, the supplier will go to the location closest to the current location. Also, while creating the route, the supplier can either follow the direct path (if available) from one location to another or can take the path via the warehouse. If both paths are available (direct and via warehouse), the supplier will choose the path with minimum distance.

6. If the last location visited is Ahmednagar, then what is the total distance covered in the route (in km)?
7. If the total number of widgets delivered in a day is 250 units, then what is the total distance covered in the route (in km)?
8. What is the chance that the total number of widgets delivered in a day is 260 units and the route ends at Bikrampore?
   (a) 10.80% (b) 33.33%
   (c) 7.56% (d) 17.64%
9. If the first location visited from the warehouse is Ahmednagar, then what is the chance that the total distance covered in the route is 40 km?
   (a) 3.24% (b) 30%
   (c) 5.4% (d) 18%
10. If Ahmednagar is not the first location to be visited in a route and the total route distance is 29 km, then which of the following is a possible number of widgets delivered on that day?
    (a) 210 (b) 200
    (c) 250 (d) 220

ANSWER KEY

1. 40	2. (d)	3. (a)	4. (a)
5. 50	6. Question Cancelled		7. 38 kms
8. (c)	9. (d)	10. (a)	

SOLUTIONS AND SHORTCUTS

Solutions for Questions 1 to 5: We can make a table to represent the given information, but while doing so, one needs to understand the exact data structure being used for this question. There are 2 × 2 = 4 categories of products viz: Foreign Cosmetic, Foreign Nutrition; Domestic Cosmetic and Domestic Nutrition. Further each foreign product has either an FDA approval or a EU approval but not both. On the other hand for domestic products, approvals are in 3 categories: a) Those approved only by FDA; b) Those approved by both FDA and EU; c) Those approved only by EU.

Note: For domestic products, if there is a number of products mentioned as approved by FDA, it would be the sum of (a) and (b) mentioned above.

Deduction 1: Total foreign products 160, Total domestic Products 160 (given clue 1). Total Nutrition products 140, hence total Cosmetic products = 320 - 140 = 180. Nutrition foreign products = 70 (clue 4), hence nutrition domestic Products = 140 - 70 = 70. Cosmetic foreign products = 160 - 70 = 90. Domestic Cosmetic Products = 180 - 90 = 90.

Deduction 2: From clue 2 and 6, we can make out that the total FDA-approved cosmetic products in domestic = 80, while Only FDA-approved foreign cosmetic products would be 120 - 80 = 40. Thus, only EU approved cosmetic foreign products would be 90 - 40 = 50. Also, foreign nutrition FDA approved products = Total FDA-approved foreign products - otal FDA-approved cosmetic foreign products = 70 - 40 = 30. Consequently, Nutrition, foreign only EU approved products = total nutrition foreign products (70)- nutrition foreign only FDA-approved products (30) = 40.

Deduction 3: The value of d + e (in the solution table) = omestic FDA-approved nutrition products, can be worked out from clue 5, which tells us that there were a total of 200 FDA-approved products. Out of this, we already know that the foreign FDA-approved products are 40 + 30 = 70. Also, Cosmetic domestic FDA-approved products = 80 (from clue 2). Thus, domestic FDA-approved nutrition products (d + e in the solution table) = 200 - 70 - 80 = 50. With this understanding we can make the solution table to capture the information. Note that in the table, what is variable is the relative values of a, b, d and e. Note also that the value of b + e in the solution table has to be 60 (from clue 3).

Solution table:

	Foreign (160)				Domestic (160)				
	Approvals	Only FDA	Only EU	Both	Approvals	Only FDA	FDA & EU	Only EU	
Cosmetic (180)	Cosmetic Foreign = 90	40	50	0	Cosmetic Domestic = 90	a	b	c =10	a + b = 80. Hence, c = 10.
Nutrition (140)	Nutrition Foreign = 70	30	40	0	Nutrition Domestic = 70	d	e	f =20	d + e = 50. Hence, f = 20 b + e = 60

We can interpret the answers to the questions, based on the table and the variables in the table.

1. 40. Can be directly read off from the solution table.
2. This would be the sum of only EU approved foreign cosmetic products (50) and only EU approved domestic cosmetic products (10). Hence, the answer is 50 + 10 = 60. Option (d) is correct.
3. From the solution table, this question is asking us the range of values for 'b'. Since, b + e = 60, if we maximise the value of e, b would be minimised. The value of e can be maximised at 50. (since that is the value of d + e). In this case, the value of b = 10 (minimum value of b). The value of b can be maximised at 60, if we take e as 0. Hence, the value of b varies from a minimum of 10 to a maximum of 60. Option (a) is correct.
4. This question tells us the value of a = 30 (Since the cosmetic products that did not have EU approval would be those that had only FDA approval = 40 + a = 70 → a = 30.). a = 30, gives us b = 50 and that in turn gives us the value of e as 10. This represents the nutrition products with both the approvals. Note: There are no foreign nutrition products with both approvals. Hence, option (a) is correct.
5. d + 30 = 50 (Nutrition products with only FDA approval, which means these are the nutrition products that did not have EU approval as referred to in the question). The value of d = 20. Hence, e = 30. Hence, b = 30. Hence, a = 50 (number of domestic cosmetic products with only FDA approval – hence, they did not have EU approval). The correct answer is 50.

Solutions for Questions 6 to 10:

6. This question was discarded by CAT as it was an incorrect question. In this question, it is not possible for the last location to be Ahmednagar at all, because of the fact that if Ahmednagar was indeed the last location, demand there should be 50. Also, demand at Deccan Park should also be 50. Chitrachak demand would be 100 or 70, and the demand at Bikrampore would be necessarily 60 and the starting route would be W-C-B. After this, the supply algortihm would necessarily route to Ahmednagar next (as it would be closer to B than D is.) Hence, in this case, the question stating that Ahmednagar is the last location is not correct. CAT discarded the question from evaluation as it accepted its error.
7. We can have a maximum of 280 widgets and a minimum of 190 widgets. The only possible way to achieve 250 widgets is to get a drop of 30 widgets (from the maximum) across the 4 locations. The drop values available are: 20 each in Ahmednagar, Bikrampore and Chitrachak, while in Deccan Park demand has a variance of 30 from the maximum. The only way to have a total demand of 250, is if Ahmednagar had a demand of 70 widgets, Bikampore had 60, Chitrachak had 70 and Deccan Park had 50. According to the conditions given to use, the route we would follow is W-A-W-C-B-W-D. Hence the total distance traveled is 38 kms.
8. If we end at Bikrampore, then the demand at that location is 40 (least demand). Hence the demand at Ahmednagar, Chitrachak and Deccan Park would be 70, 100 and 50 respectively. Chance of this happening would be $0.6 \times 0.3 \times 0.7 \times 0.6 = 7.56\%$. Hence Option (c) is the correct answer.
9. One can only start off from Ahmednagar if the demand at both A and C are 70 widgets each. The route for the above scenario would be W-A-W-C. This completes 22 kms. We have 18 kms left and that could be possible only if we got to Deccan park from Chitrachak and then to Bikrampore. For this to be possible, Deccan park has to have a demand of 50 widgets and Bikrampore would have 40 widgets. Hence the chance for this happen would be $0.6 \times 0.3 = 0.18 \rightarrow 18\%$. Hence Option (d) is the correct answer.
10. If Ahmednagar is not the first location where we are starting from, then the starting location is definitely Chitrachak. Thus, the first segment of the travel would be W-C a distance of 12 kms. This leaves us a further distance of 17 kms to be covered while visiting the other three locations. This is only possible, if we visit C-B-A-W-D. For this to be the priority of travel, we would need to have demands of 60 at B (necessary); 50 at A (necessary). At the same time, demand at C can be either 100 or 70 widgets, while the demand at D can be either 30 or 50 widgets. Possible values of the total demand can be thought of as: 100/70 + 60 + 50 + 50/30 = 260/240/230/210. Amongst the options given, only option (a) gives us a value amongst these.
Hence, Option (a) is the correct answer.

SLOT 3

CAT 2022

Directions for Questions 1 to 5: All the first-year students in the computer science (CS) department in a university take both the courses (i) AI and (ii) ML. Students from other departments (non-CS students) can also take one of these two courses, but not both. Students who fail in a course get an F grade; others pass and are awarded A or B or C grades depending on their performance. The following are some additional facts about the number of students who took these two courses this year and the grades they obtained.

(i) The numbers of non-CS students who took AI and ML were in the ratio 2 : 5.
(ii) The number of non-CS students who took either AI or ML was equal to the number of CS students.
(iii) The numbers of non-CS students who failed in the two courses were the same and their total is equal to the number of CS students who got a C grade in ML.
(iv) In both the courses, 50% of the students who passed got a B grade. But, while the numbers of students who got A and C grades were the same for AI, they were in the ratio 3 : 2 for ML.
(v) No CS student failed in AI, while no non-CS student got an A grade in AI.
(vi) The numbers of CS students who got A, B and C grades respectively in AI were in the ratio 3 : 5 : 2, while in ML the ratio was 4 : 5 : 2.
(vii) The ratio of the total number of non-CS students failing in one of the two courses to the number of CS students failing in one of the two courses was 3 : 1.
(viii) 30 students failed in ML

1. How many students took AI?
(a) 60 (b) 270
(c) 90 (d) 210

2. How many CS students failed in ML?

3. How many non-CS students got A grade in ML?

4. How many students got A grade in AI?
(a) 42 (b) 99
(c) 84 (d) 63

5. How many non-CS students got B grade in ML?
(a) 165 (b) 90
(c) 25 (d) 75

Directions for Questions 6 to 10: Pulak, Qasim, Ritesh, and Suresh participated in a tournament comprising eight rounds. In each round, they formed two pairs, with each of them being in exactly one pair. The only restriction in the pairing was that the pairs would change in successive rounds. For example, if Pulak formed a pair with Qasim in the first round, then he would have to form a pair with Ritesh or Suresh in the second round. He would be free to pair with Qasim again in the third round. In each round, each pair decided whether to play the game in that round or not. If they decided not to play, then no money was exchanged between them. If they decided to play, they had to bet either ₹1 or ₹2 in that round. For example, if they chose to bet ₹2, then the player winning the game got ₹2 from the one losing the game.

At the beginning of the tournament, the players had ₹10 each. The following table shows partial information about the amounts that the players had at the end of each of the eight rounds. It shows every time a player had ₹10 at the end of a round, as well as every time, at the end of a round, a player had either the minimum or the maximum amount that he would have had across the eight rounds. For example, Suresh had ₹10 at the end of Rounds 1, 3, and 8 and not after any of the other rounds. The maximum amount that he had at the end of any round was ₹13 (at the end of Round 5), and the minimum amount he had at the end of any round was ₹8 (at the end of Round 2). At the end of all other rounds, he must have had either ₹9, ₹11, or ₹12.

It was also known that Pulak and Qasim had the same amount of money with them at the end of Round 4.

	Pulak	Qasim	Ritesh	Suresh
Round 1		₹8	₹10	₹10
Round 2	₹13	₹10		₹8
Round 3				₹10
Round 4				
Round 5	₹10	₹10		₹13
Round 6				
Round 7		₹12	₹4	
Round 8	₹13			₹10

6. What BEST can be said about the amount of money that Ritesh had with him at the end of Round 8?
   (a) Exactly ₹6 (b) ₹4 or ₹5
   (c) Exactly ₹5 (d) ₹5 or ₹6
7. What BEST can be said about the amount of money that Pulak had with him at the end of Round 6?
   (a) Exactly ₹12 (b) ₹11 or ₹12
   (c) Exactly ₹11 (d) ₹12 or ₹13
8. How much money (in ₹) did Ritesh have at the end of Round 4?
9. How many games were played with a bet of ₹2?
10. Which of the following pairings was made in Round 5?
    (a) Pulak and Ritesh (b) Pulak and Qasim
    (c) Pulak and Suresh (d) Qasim and Suresh

ANSWER KEY

1. (b)	2. 12	3. 27	4. (d)
5. (d)	6. (a)	7. (a)	8. 6
9. 6	10. (c)		

SOLUTIONS AND SHORTCUTS

Solutions for Questions 1 to 5: We can make a starting table with the key structures that come out of the clues, which will look as shown in the starting solution table. Note, the following reactions in order to get to the starting solution table. Number of F grades in Non-CS AI = Number of F grades in Non-CS ML = 3a (from clue 3). Number of F grades in CS ML = 1/3rd of (3a + 3a) = 2a (from clue 7). Also, the number of CS students who got a C grade in ML = 6a (from clue 3). Then from Clue 6, we get CS students ML grades as 12a, 15a and 6a respectively. The number of A, B, C grades for CS students in AI can be assumed to be 3y, 5y and 2y respectively. Further, if we assume the Non-CS AI students to be 2x, then Non-CS ML students would be 5x. Then, the CS students would be 2x + 5x = 7x and all these 7x students would have taken each of AI and ML courses.

Starting Solution Table:

CS (7x)									Non- CS							
AI (7x)				ML (7x)					AI (2x)				ML (5x)			
A	B	C	F	A	B	C	F	Grades	A	B	C	F	A	B	C	F
3y	5y	2y	0	12a	15a	6a	2a		0			3a				3a

From this point, the following set of deductions helps us get to the final solution table.

Deduction 1: From clue 8, we get directly, that the value of 2a + 3a = 30 → a = 6. Hence, 12a = 72, 15a = 90, 6a = 36; 2a = 12 and 3a = 18.

Deduction 2: At this point, we also know that the total CS students (7x) = 72 + 90 + 36 + 12 = 210. Hence, 3y + 5y + 2y = 10y = 210 → y = 21. Hence, 3y = 63, 5y = 105, 2y = 42. Also, we realise the value of x = 30 and hence, the total students in Non-CS AI = 60 and Non-CS ML = 150.

Deduction 3: We know that the total B grades are equal to 50% of the total students who passed for each of the courses. We can also see that for AI, in CS students, the 50% ratio is exactly maintained for the B grade students. As the number of A grade Non-CS students are 0 (given) it means that the number of B and C grade students in Non-CS AI would be equal to each other and would equal half of 60-18 each. Hence, these numbers would be 21 each.

Deduction 4: For ML, we can work out the A, B, C grades for Non-CS students with the following thought structure. Total Passed students in ML Non-CS = 150 – 18 = 132. Total Passed students in ML for Both CS and Non-CS= 132 + 198 = 330. Thus, total B grades in ML = 50% of 330 = 165. As B grades in ML for CS students is 90, we get that the B grades for Non-CS ML students would be 165 – 90 = 75.

Deduction 5: We now pay attention to working out the final values in the table (A and C grades for Non-CS students, in ML.) Let these numbers be a and c respectively. We have: a + c = 150 – 75 – 18 = 57. Also from clue 4 (last part), we get the equation. $\frac{72 + a}{36 + c} = \frac{3}{2}$ Solving these two equations, we get a = 27 and c = 30. With these 5 deductions, we get the final solution table as shown.

Final Solution Table:

CS (210)									Non- CS							
AI (210)				ML (210)					AI (60)				ML (150)			
A	B	C	F	A	B	C	F	Grades	A	B	C	F	A	B	C	F
63	105	42	0	72	90	36	12		0	21	21	18	27	75	30	18

We can now move on to answer the questions given:

1. 210 + 60 = 270. Option (b) is the correct answer.
2. 12
3. 27
4. 63 + 0 = 63. Option (d) is the correct answer.
5. 75. Option (d) is the correct answer.

Solutions for Questions 6 to 10: From the information given in the initial paragraph, we can deduce the complete information up to round 2. Also, a critical thought to start the problem, is what values are possible at the end of each round for each person. The problem has already told us that the values possible are 9/11 or 12 for Suresh. Likewise, the possible values for Pulak are 11/12 (since his maximum is 13 and minimum is 10). Likewise, for Qasim, the values possible are 9 or 11 only since, his minimum is 8 and maximum value is 12. Thus, if Pulak and Qasim have the same amounts at the end of round 4, it could only be 11 each. For Ritesh, the possible values are 5/6/7/8 or 9, since his minimum value is 4 and maximum value is 10. Also, at the end of each round, the total money among the four people would always be ₹40. From this point, the following set of deductions helps us complete the table.

Deduction 1: Round 1: PQ would be one pair and RS the other. P would have won 2 rupees from Q and the stake between RS would be 0.

Deduction 2: Round 2: Q's value has gone up by 2, S's value has gone down by 2. At the same time P's value has gone up by 1 and R's value has gone down by 1. This means that, the pairings were QS (Q wins 2) and PR (P wins 1).

Deduction 3: Rounds 3 to 5: Round 3: Qasim cannot be involved in the ₹2 bet against Suresh because he doesn't have the necessary values for that. (Since he would lose the ₹2 bet and come down to 8, which isn't a possible value for him). He cannot maintain his value at 10 also, since in that case, it would have been indicated in the question's table. Hence, he either lost ₹1 or won ₹1.

So if he loses ₹1, someone would gain ₹1 which is not possible for any of Pulak or Ritesh.

Hence, he wins a ₹1 bet and has 11 at the end of round 3. We need to work out who lost this bet to Qasim. It has to be either P or R. If we make P lose this bet to Q, then P would have 12, Q 11, R 7 and S would have 10 with him. To meet the requirement of 11 in round 4, P would then have to lose a 1 rupee bet in round 4, while Q would have no bet in round 4. The no bet cannot be against Suresh, hence the no bet would be between Q and R. This would give us an 11, 11, 7, 11 structure for round 4. From this point, to get to the 10, 10, 7, 13 structure after round 5 is not possible. Hence, in round 3, R would lose this bet to Q and the numbers at the end of round 3 would be 11, 11, 8, 10. The pairings for round 3 would be PS (2, won by S) and QR (1, won by Q).

Deduction 4: Rounds 4 and 5: After deducing the final values after round 3, it becomes simply visible that in round 4, the pairings would be PQ (0) and RS. The RS bet needs to be worked out. It can be easily done if we look at the movement from round 4 to 5. In round 5, both P and Q have lost ₹1 each. Hence, R and S should gain ₹1 each in round 5. This means that R should be 6 and S 12 after round 4. This can only occur if the RS bet for round 4 is a ₹2 bet won by S. At this stage, we cannot work out the pairings for round 5.

Deduction 5: Round 6: Qasim had ₹11 at the end of Round 6. This is because, he cannot get to 12 (it would have been marked as 12 in the original table of the question, since 12 is his highest value). Also, he cannot remain at 10 (again because it would have been given to us, it his value of round 6 was 10). Also, if we take Qasim's round 6 value to be 9, he cannot reach 12 in round 7. Further, in this round Qasim would not be paired with Pulak because for Qasim to gain ₹1, Pulak would have to lose which is not possible (as 9 is not possible for Pulak). Ritesh can have ₹5 or ₹6 at the end of this round.

Deduction 6: Rounds 8 and 7: Qasim would have ₹11 at the end of round 8 as he cannot go to ₹9. Hence Ritesh would have ₹6 at the end of this round (to complete the total of 40). Since, Ritesh is gaining ₹2 in this round, He could only be paired with Suresh, who loses 2 to him. Thus, Suresh would have 12 at the end of round 7 and Pulak would also have 12 at the end of round 7. The stake between PQ in round 8 would be 1, won by P.

Also, since, Ritesh & Suresh are paired together in Round 8, each of them would have to be paired with Pulak & Qasim in round 7. We also know that Qasim would have won ₹1 in this round to go from 11 to 12. This he can gain only from Ritesh. Hence, Ritesh would have had ₹5 at the end of round 6. The other pairing for round 7 would be PS. The stake coud be 0, 1 or 2. A 1 stake won by P is not possible (since, P would go from 11 to 12 in such a case, while S would have to come down from 13 to 12 - for this to happen, S should have had 13 at the end of round 6 - which being his highest value is not possible). Likewise, a 1 stake won be S is also not possible. So also, a 2 stake won by P is not possible and also a 2 stake won by S is also not possible. Hence, in round 7, the PS stake is 0. Because of this deduction, we can determine the pairs for Rounds 4, 5, & 6.

Deduction 7: In round 6, the pairs would be PR (2, won by P) and QS (1, won by Q). Round 5's pairings would be PS (1, won by S) and QR (1, won by R).

The final solution table would look as shown.

	Pulak	Qasim	Ritesh	Suresh	Pairs
Round 1	12	₹8	₹10	₹10	PQ (2), RS (0)
Round 2	₹13	₹10	9	₹8	QS (2); PR (1)
Round 3	11	11	8	₹10	PS (2); QR (1)
Round 4	11	11	6	12	PQ (0); RS (2)
Round 5	₹10	₹10	7	₹13	PS (1); QR (1).
Round 6	12	11	5	12	PR (2); QS (1)
Round 7	12	₹12	₹4	12	QR (1); PS (0)
Round 8	₹13	11	6	₹10	RS (2); PQ (1)
Amount to be used	11/12	9/11	5/6/7/8/9	9/11/12	

Using the table, we can answer the questions given:

6. Option (a) is the correct answer.
7. Option (a) is the correct answer.
8. 6
9. 6
10. Option (c) is the correct answer.